* * * * * * * * * * *

American Literature,
American Culture

* * * * * * * * * *

* * * * * * * * *

American Literature, American Culture

* * * * * * * * *

GORDON HUTNER

University of Wisconsin, Madison

New York • Oxford
OXFORD UNIVERSITY PRESS
1999

Oxford University Press

Oxford   New York
Athens   Auckland   Bangkok   Bogotá   Buenos Aires   Calcutta
Cape Town   Chennai   Dar es Salaam   Delhi   Florence   Hong Kong   Istanbul
Karachi   Kuala Lumpur   Madrid   Melbourne   Mexico City   Mumbai
Nairobi   Paris   São Paulo   Singapore   Taipei   Tokyo   Toronto   Warsaw

and associated companies in
Berlin   Ibadan

Copyright © 1999 by Gordon Hutner

Published by Oxford University Press, Inc.,
198 Madison Avenue, New York, New York 10016
http://www.oup-usa.org

Oxford is a registered trademark of Oxford University Press

Library of Congress Cataloging-in-Publication Data
American literature, American culture / [compiled by] Gordon Hutner.
      p.   cm.
   ISBN 0-19-508521-3 (alk. paper)
     1. American literature—History and criticism—Theory, etc.
  2. National characteristics, American, in literature.   3. Literature
and society—United States.   4. United States—Civilization.
   5. Criticism—United States.   I. Hutner, Gordon.
PS25.A45   1999
810.9—dc21   97-31644
                                                   CIP

9 8 7 6 5 4 3 2

Printed in the United States of America
on acid-free paper

CONTENTS

★ ★ ★ ★ ★ ★

★ ★ ★ ★ ★ ★

******

PREFACE

******

This anthology represents a project of several years' development. The original idea for the collection came ten years ago when American literary criticism was becoming more self-conscious about its origins as well as its social and political goals. I thought it would be useful to gather the essays that I saw as contributing to this tradition of critical discussion, one that had been somewhat neglected since the 1960s. My hope was to create a book that gave students of contemporary debates in literary criticism fuller resources in the background of those controversies, just as I supposed that these historical examples of literary criticism as cultural critique might also prove interesting to new scholars of the subject.

Throughout the planning, my aim was to bring together a good many of the key documents in American cultural criticism and other pertinent contributions so that students could have in one book a sampling of the rich argument and luminous analysis that literature in the United States has stimulated. Many great essays and writers and traditions, however, have been omitted. Sometimes, the rationale was that these works were otherwise widely available. Sometimes, I had to make the kinds of choices and compromises that bedevil any editor. Indeed, the essays omitted from the present volume might constitute a table of contents just as attractive as this one. Nevertheless, the essays here show the changing history as well as the chronic concerns that have formed the dynamic, unfolding deliberation among critics and authors about the way literary values signify the state of American society.

The reader of this volume can trace several general debates regarding the literary formulation of issues like American nationhood and exceptionalism, the racial divide, gender politics, and class consciousness, as well as the substance and shadow of American culture—from antebellum romance fiction to late-capitalist postmodernism. Occasionally, I have tried to focus explicitly on well-known issues, like the possibilities of the Great American Novel or the cultural capital invested in Nathaniel Hawthorne's reputation, though such groupings are meant to be provocative rather than prescriptive ways of reading this material. I am confident that students, even beyond the book's intentions, will be able to discern connections and continuities as well as disjunctions and discontinuities among the essays.

Several critics and editors have helped me through the challenges of assembling this collection, especially in discriminating among the wealth of possible alternative selections. I am especially grateful to a learned predecessor, Richard Ruland, whose two-volume collection, *The Native Muse* and *This Storied Land,* has proven very instructive. It is a pleasure also to thank Henry Louis Gates Jr. and Morris Dickstein for their early help in sustaining the book's viability. They made valuable comments about the volume's organization and offered excellent advice. William Cain and Priscilla Wald made smart suggestions, precise refinements, and indisputable improvements. Ross Posnock also offered erudite counsel. I would like to acknowledge the generosity and guidance of Sargent Bush, Jeffrey Rubin-Dorsky, and Jonathan Veitch; they kept me from several misjudgments and mistakes of fact. My keenest appreciation is for Dale Bauer, my favorite colleague of all, who took time from her own work and collaborated in every phase.

I would also like to thank the graduate students of English 810 for their good sense and enthusiasm, particularly Tom Allen, Glen Van Der Ploeg, Amy Kort, Keiko Nitta, Warren Oberman, and Sarah Beth Grant. They tested this book in the classroom and helped me to see several deficiencies in an earlier version. Joan Parks deserves my thanks for shouldering so much of the permissions correspondence. I would also like to express gratitude to my former editors, Elizabeth Maguire and T. Susan Chang, for their interest in and support for the project. Tony English, an editor's editor, gave me the benefit of his acumen and experience; without his encouragement, it would have been impossible to see the book through its last stages.

★ ★ ★ ★ ★ ★ ★ ★ ★ ★ ★

American Literature,
American Culture

★ ★ ★ ★ ★ ★ ★ ★ ★ ★ ★

PART I

★★★★★★★★

FORMATIONS

★★★★★★★★

The early history of American literary criticism focuses its farthest-ranging questions on the cultural importance of the nation's literary record. Indeed, the original aims and purposes of literary criticism have preoccupied writers and scholars alike. Those first critics established a tradition of reading American writing as cultural critique. They asked what meaning should American literary expression make: did the meaning of our writers' works also help readers to make sense of ourselves as a nation? Did the meaning these books make also signify to the rest of the world something about the complicated experiment in democracy taking place within our changing borders?

The critical debates characterizing the early years of the republic through the post–Civil War era were focused on determining the salient attributes of a national literature, especially whether and how that literature was the expression of a people. Other countries with a demonstrable connection through the generations to an ancient past—France, England, Spain—had seemingly incontestable views of which people constituted their nation. So their literatures could readily be understood as expressing a cultural spirit or "genius," even though these countries, not to mention Italy and Germany, were far from being unitary societies. Through much of the first half of the nineteenth century, American literary culture, like these others, argued over what language or dialect—English or American—its literature would be written in, which was also a battle about how national identity was constituted. Was there an American language, and was that properly the language of literature in the United States? The "genius" of other literatures could also be known through the folklore and historical materials that a people recognize as its own, but what if a nation were inventing itself as a new entity? What if its people were from the outset so heterogenous and diversified that there were all too few generally agreed-upon exemplars or determinants of a life of ideas and expression—a culture—for that literature to embody?

Few countries have felt this chronic pressure to justify themselves; few have worried as anxiously about the legitimacy, coherence, and achievement of their nation's literary heritage as America has, insofar as that literature was supposed to express something true and profound about the United States. Yet it would be willfully naive to disregard this question of what constitutes American literature. The search for the answer has not only animated some of the most powerful imaginative writing in the United States but has also inspired a brilliant criticism.

That criticism has generally been more concerned with issues of identity and community and less with issues of form. Yet American critics' contributions to aesthetics have been real and sustained, especially through the tradition of poet-critics—Poe, Emerson, and Whitman through T. S. Eliot, Laura Riding, Langston Hughes, John Crowe Ransom, and Amiri Baraka—a criticism that continues today in the politically engaged theorizing of such Language Poets as Charles Bernstein and Susan Howe. As forceful as this tradition has been, another, no less vital and in many respects more in need of collocation, is the legacy of American literary criticism as an appraisal of a society coming into being.

Where does American literary criticism begin? The reviews of the first literary works? When does it make sense to divide British America from a U.S. tradition, and what is gained or lost by doing so? Should that separation be made immediately following the Declaration of Independence? Should the prehistory of American writing be the literature written in anticipation of independence, as if the function of the critic were to discern the energies of a new nation in the making? Or should the history of American writing begin with the recorded reactions of the indigenous peoples who the colonists invaded? From the early years of the republic, the discussion of literature in the United States has always involved a series of arguments over the character of American life. Debates about authors, movements, aesthetic values, poems, novels, histories, and plays have sooner or later staged this alternative set of concerns: what has been the promise of America, and what have been the consequences of this social and political experiment in creating a nation beyond tribal affiliations? What would the literature of such an amalgam look like, and what would it represent?

The critics represented here were sometimes quite influential during their careers, sometimes well-regarded authors in their own right. While the reputations of some have endured, others are now forgotten. Even so, they espouse views that still enliven the disputes about the cultural implications of literary endeavors. The selections include position statements about the mission of American writers: for some, the author's business included the broad cultural responsibility of representing the genius of democracy. For others, it was only to create good art, but the defining attributes of this evaluation were open to broad, sometimes bitter debate. Was an American artist someone who fashioned literary works out of existing European conventions, or was an American artist someone who worked with indigenous materials? Was good art that which drew from native materials but transmuted them into reconizable forms of European literatures?

What emotions should American art inspire? Was this art to be nationalist in its basic premises, or did it aim to please and instruct its readers, no matter what its subject? Were some subjects and genres inherently compromised, like sentimental novels about young girls who read romances? And were others, like epic poems in heroic couplets, significant by definition? What did it mean that, even during the War of 1812, Americans' love for Walter Scott's poetry made him the most popular author of the day?

The self-consciousness with which these questions were met might be suggested in the grim assessment that Sydney Smith, an English critic and clergyman, offered in the *Edinburgh Review* (1820). It now reads as a diatribe, but perhaps we ought to reconsider those famous lines as if they had been written with the intention of helping to modulate the claims being advanced for the achievements of this new culture:

> In the four quarters of the globe, who reads an American book? or goes to an American play? or looks at an American picture or statue? What does the world yet owe to American physicians or surgeons? What new substances have their chemists discovered? or what old ones have they analyzed? What new constellations have been discovered by the telescopes of Americans?—what have they done in mathematics? Who drinks out of American glasses? or eats from American plates? or wears American coats or gowns? or sleeps in American blankets—Finally, under which old tyrannical governments of Europe is every sixth man a Slave, whom his fellow-creatures may buy and sell and torture?
>
> When these questions are fairly and favourably to be answered, their laudatory epithets may be allowed: But, till that can be done, we would seriously advise them to keep clear of superlatives.

Smith's point is to caution advocates for America—especially English ones—that they should not overestimate this young democracy's exertions. His emphasis lies in the not-so-gentle reminder that, after four decades of nationhood, the United States had not advanced very far, even if his catalogue strikes us as relentlessly Eurocentric in its observation of what contributions make a culture substantive and serious: glasses, plates, coats, and gowns are placed on equal footing with literature, sculpture, medicine, astronomy, and abolition. If, as Henry James wrote sixty years later, it takes a great deal of history to produce a little literature, the United States by these criteria did not, in 1820, have much history.

Of course, America did have a rich history; it had 300 years and more of a past it did not know how to gauge. As William Tudor, founding editor of the *North American Review,* wrote in 1815 of the just way of assessing the period of settlement:

> From the close of the 16th to the middle of the 18th century many most interesting events and circumstances have concurred with time in casting a shade of obscurity resembling that of antiquity over the transactions of the period; while by the great revolutions that have since happened, the connexion between those days and our own is interrupted, and they are so disconnected with the present era that no passionate feeling is blended with their consideration; they are now exclusively the domain of history and poetry.

Instead, America tended to divide its self-scrutiny into two opposing sets of predicates—English and not-English anymore—colonial and postcolonial principles. On the one hand, America could still aspire to be English and internalize English standards and folkways as its own. On the other, America could understand itself as something that was once English but was now something else. In the ensuing dialogue between these parties, the definition of American culture was forged.

Literature would be one of the primary sites for this negotiation. As James Fenimore Cooper argued in 1828—in the context of urging copyright protection—U.S. literature should make "a subject of the highest interest to the rest of the civilized world." It will be felt, says Cooper, "with a force, a directness, and a common sense . . . that has never been known before." There were obstacles like the "poverty of native materials," but more important was the economic hindrance to fostering American authors: "The fact, that an American publisher can get an English work without money, must, for a few years longer (unless legislative protection shall be extended to their own author) have a tendency to repress a national literature. No man will pay a writer for an epic, a tragedy, a sonnet, a history, or a romance, when he can get a work of equal merit for nothing." Thus Cooper articulated American writers' fear that American publishers' pirating of English editions enabled them to flood the market with British books and thereby create profit margins against which American authors could not compete. Such cirumstances made it difficult to establish an American voice and an American following.

Yet some American writers, like Washington Irving, did find appreciative audiences. Moreover, Americans loved adventure tales, whether they took form as urban horror stories, like Maria Monk's *Awful Disclosures* or James Seaver's edition of Mary Jemison's captivity narrative. Also published in these years were such popular accounts of nation making as Robert Montgomery Bird's *Nick of the Woods* (1837) and Daniel Thompson's *The Green Mountain Boys* (1839), along with the more familiar efforts like Hawthorne's *Twice-Told Tales* (1837) and Longfellow's *Voices of the Night* (1839).

Varied as these books were, they appealed to readers for the way they illuminated aspirations and anxieties about the kind of people Americans were and the kind of polis the United States was becoming. There was no want of suggestions concerning the very subject matter of this new American literature. Conceding that a "national literature" need not be confined to local topics, Rufus Griswold could still enumerate the themes to which American writers had recourse:

> The perilous adventures of the Northmen; the noble heroism of Columbus; the rise and fall of the Peruvian and Mexican empires; the colonization of New-England by the Puritans; the witchraft delusion; the persecution of the Quakers and the Baptists; the rise and fall of the French dominion in the Canadas; the overthrow of the great confederacy of the Five nations; the settlement of New York, Pennsylvania, Maryland and Virginia, by people of the most varied and picturesque characters; the beautiful and poetic mythology of the aborigines, and the revolution, resulting in our independence and equal liberty, which forms a barrier between the traditionary past and the familiar present.

The injunctions that writers should fill new works with "a certain mysterious 'American spirit,' very difficult to describe and exceedingly hard to imagine," were often received skeptically: "It is a pity," says the *Knickerbocker*, "that some one of these gentlemen should not produce a work which would serve to show what this 'singular' American literature really is." American criticism might then be said to have been born out of this conflict between the internalizing of Old World expectations and the play of New World freedom. The defining of a national spirit, the imagining of a nation as an entity both dynamic and achieved, might be the first step to be taken in this argument. As soon as one critic might suggest that this book or that was "American," it is up to another to ask whose sense of American, what attributes stipulated, and what obscured.

The entries in the first section include some of the best-known pieces of nineteenth-century criticism: Emerson's "American Scholar," Fuller's "American Literature," Melville's "Hawthorne and His Mosses," Whitman's "Democratic Vistas," and Clemens' "Fenimore Cooper's Literary Offenses." Other documents are less familiar, like Simms's and Parker's, but they also address the central, vitalizing issues of what typifies a national literature and how its audience is constructed. At the same time, this discussion continues in arguments less apparent: the debates over female novelists and, following Frederick Douglass, the cultural identity of African Americans. After the Civil War, these discussions would be more and more crucial to American literary historiography, but they ensued during the antebellum years in ways that, in retrospect, seem to predict controversies to come.

St. Jean de Crèvecoeur

What Is an American?

From Letters from an American Farmer

I wish I could be acquainted with the feelings and thoughts which must agitate the heart and present themselves to the mind of an enlightened Englishman, when he first lands on this continent. He must greatly rejoice that he lived at a time to see this fair country discovered and settled; he must necessarily feel a share of national pride, when he views the chain of settlements which embellishes these extended shores. When he says to himself, this is the work of my countrymen, who, when convulsed by factions, afflicted by a variety of miseries and wants, restless and impatient, took refuge here. They brought along with them their national genius, to which they principally owe what liberty they enjoy, and what substance they possess. Here he sees the industry of his native country displayed in a new manner, and traces in their works the embrios of all the arts, sciences, and ingenuity which flourish in Europe. Here he beholds fair cities, substantial villages, extensive fields, an immense country filled with decent houses, good roads, orchards, meadows, and bridges, where an hundred years ago all was wild, woody and uncultivated! What a train of pleasing ideas this fair spectacle must suggest; it is a prospect which must inspire a good citizen with the most heartfelt pleasure. The difficulty consists in the manner of viewing so extensive a scene. He is arrived on a new continent; a modern society offers itself to his contemplation, different from what he had hitherto seen. It is not composed, as in Europe, of great lords who possess every thing, and of a herd of people who have nothing. Here are no aristocratical families, no courts, no kings, no bishops, no ecclesiastical dominion, no invisible power giving to a few a very visible one; no great manufacturers employing thousands, no great refinements of luxury. The rich and the poor are not so far removed from each other as they are in Europe. Some few towns excepted, we are all tillers of the earth, from Nova Scotia to West Florida. We are a people of cultivators, scattered over an immense territory, communicating with each other by means of good roads and navigable rivers, united by the silken bands of mild government, all respecting the laws, without dreading their power, because they are equitable. We are all animated with the spirit of an industry which is unfettered and inrestrained, because each person works for himself. If he travels through our rural districts he views not the hostile castle, and the haughty mansion, contrasted with the clay-built hut and miserable cabbin, where cattle and men help to keep each other warm and dwell in meanness, smoke, and indigence. A pleasing uniformity of decent competence appears throughout our habitations. The meanest of our log-houses is a dry and comfortable habitation. Lawyer or merchant are the fairest titles our towns afford; that of a farmer is the only appellation of the rural inhabitants of our country. It must take some time ere he can reconcile himself to our dictionary, which is but short in words of dignity, and names of honour. There, on a Sunday, he sees a congregation of respectable farmers and their wives, all clad in neat homespun, well mounted, or riding in their own humble waggons. There is not among them an esquire, saving the unlettered magistrate. There he sees a parson as simple as his flock, a farmer who does not riot on the labour of others. We have no princes, for whom we toil, starve, and bleed: we are the most perfect society now existing in the world. Here man is free as he ought to be; nor is this pleasing equality so transitory as many others are. Many ages will not see the shores of our great lakes replenished with inland nations, nor the unknown bounds of North America entirely peopled. Who can tell how far it extends? Who can tell the millions of men whom it will feed and contain? for no European foot has as yet travelled half the extent of this mighty continent!

The next wish of this traveller will be to know whence came all these people? they are a mixture of English, Scotch, Irish, French, Dutch, Germans, and Swedes. From this promiscuous breed, that race now called Americans have arisen. The eastern provinces must indeed be excepted, as being the unmixed descendents of Englishmen. I have heard many wish that they had been more intermixed also: for my part, I am no wisher, and think it much better as it has happened. They exhibit a most conspicuous figure in this great and variegated picture; they too enter for a great share in the pleasing perspective displayed in these thirteen provinces. I know it is fashionable to reflect on them, but I respect them for what they have done; for the accuracy and wisdom with which they have settled their territory; for the decency of their manners; for their early love of letters; their ancient college, the first in this hemisphere; for their industry; which to me who am but a farmer, is the criterion of everything. There never was a people, situated as they are, who with so ungrateful a soil have done more in so short a time. Do you think that the monarchical ingredients which are more prevalent in other governments, have purged them from all foul stains? Their histories assert the contrary.

In this great American asylum, the poor of Europe have by some means met together, and in consequence of various causes; to what purpose should they ask one another what countrymen they are? Alas, two thirds of them had no country. Can a wretch who wanders about, who works and starves, whose life is a continual scene of sore affliction or pinching penury; can that man call England or any other kingdom his country? A country that had no bread for him, whose fields procured him no harvest, who met with nothing but the frowns of the rich, the severity of the laws, with jails and punishments; who owned not a single foot of the extensive surface of this planet? No! urged by a variety of motives, here they come. Every thing has tended to regenerate them; new laws, a new mode of living, a new social system; here they are become men: in Europe they were as so many useless plants, wanting vegetative mould, and refreshing showers; they withered, and were mowed down by want, hunger, and war; but now by the power of transplantation, like all other plants they have taken root and flourished! Formerly they were not numbered in any civil lists of their country, except in those of the poor; here they rank as citizens. By what invisible power has the surprising metamorphosis been performed? By that of the laws and that of their industry. The laws, the indulgent laws, protect them as they arrive, stamping on them the symbol of adoption; they receive ample rewards for their labours; these accumulated rewards procure them lands; those lands confer on them the title of freemen, and to that title every benefit is affixed which men can possibly require. This is the great operation daily performed by our laws. From whence proceed these laws? From our government. Whence the government? It is derived from the original genius and strong desire of the people ratified and confirmed by the crown. This is the great chain which links us all, this is the picture which every province exhibits, Nova Scotia excepted. There the crown has done all; either there were no people who had genius, or it was not much attended to: the consequence is, that the province is very thinly inhabited indeed; the power of the crown in conjunction with the musketos has prevented men from settling there. Yet some parts of it flourished once, and it contained a mild harmless set of people. But for the fault of a few leaders, the whole were banished. The greatest political error the crown ever committed in America, was to cut off men from a country which wanted nothing but men!

What attachment can a poor European emigrant have for a country where he had nothing? The knowledge of the language, the love of a few kindred as poor as himself, were the only cords that tied him: his country is now that which gives him land, bread, protection, and consequence: *Ubi panis ibi patria,* is the motto of all emigrants. What then is the

American, this new man? He is either an European, or the descendant of an European, hence that strange mixture of blood, which you will find in no other country. I could point out to you a family whose grandfather was an Englishmen, whose wife was Dutch, whose son married a French woman, and whose present four sons have now four wives of different nations. *He* is an American, who leaving behind him all his ancient prjudices and manners, receives new ones from the new mode of life he has embraced, the new government he obeys, and the new rank he holds. He becomes an American by being received in the broad lap of our great *Alma Mater.* Here individuals of all nations are melted into a new race of men, whose labours and posterity will one day cause great changes in the world. Americans are the western pilgrims, who are carrying along with them that great mass of arts, sciences, vigour, and industry which began long since in the east; they will finish the great circle. The Americans were once scattered all over Europe; here they are incorporated into one of the finest systems of population which has ever appeared, and which will hereafter become distinct by the power of the different climates they inhabit. The American ought therefore to love this country much better than that wherein either he or his forefathers were born. Here the rewards of his industry follow with equal steps the progress of his labour; his labour is founded on the basis of nature, *self-interest;* can it want a stronger allurement? Wives and children, who before in vain demanded of him a morsel of bread, now, fat and frolicsome, gladly help their father to clear those fields whence exuberant crops are to arise to feed and to clothe them all; without any part being claimed, either by a despotic prince, a rich abbot, or a mighty lord. Here religion demands but little of him; a small voluntary salary to the minister, and gratitude to God; can he refuse these? The American is a new man, who acts upon new principles; he must therefore entertain new ideas, and form new opinions. From involuntary idleness, servile dependence, penury, and useless labour, he has passed to toils of a very different nature, rewarded by ample subsistence.—This is an American.

British America is divided into many provinces, forming a large association, scattered along a coast 1500 miles extent and about 200 wide. This society I would fain examine, at least such as it appears in the middle provinces; if it does not afford that variety of tinges and gradations which may be observed in Europe, we have colours peculiar to ourselves. For instance, it is natural to conceive that those who live near the sea, must be very different from those who live in the woods; the intermediate space will afford a separate and distinct class.

Men are like plants; the goodness and flavour of the fruit proceeds from the peculiar soil and exposition in which they grow. We are nothing but what we derive from the air we breathe, the climate we inhabit, the government we obey, the system of religion we profess, and the nature of our employment. Here you will find but few crimes; these have acquired as yet no root among us. I wish I were able to trace all my ideas; if my ignorance prevents me from describing them properly, I hope I shall be able to delineate a few of the outlines, which are all I propose.

Those who live near the sea, feed more on fish than on flesh, and often encounter that boisterous element. This renders them more bold and enterprising; this leads them to neglect the confined occupations of the land. They see and converse with a variety of people; their intercourse with mankind becomes extensive. The sea inspires them with a love of traffic, a desire of transporting produce from one place to another; and leads them to a variety of resources which supply the place of labour. Those who inhabit the middle settlements, by far the most numerous, must be very different; the simple cultivation of the earth purifies them, but the indulgences of the government, the soft remonstrances of religion, the rank of independent freeholders, most necessarily inspire them with sentiments, very little known in Europe among people of the same class. What do I say? Europe has no such class of men; the early knowledge they acquire, the early bargains they make, give them a great degree of sagacity. As freemen they will be litigious; pride and obstinacy are often the cause of law suits; the nature of our laws and governments may be another. As citizens it is easy to imagine, that they will carefully read the newspapers, enter into every political disquisition, freely blame or censure governors and others. As farmers they will be careful and anxious to get as much as they can, because what they get is their own. As northern men they will love the chearful cup. As Christians, religion curbs them not in their opinions; the general indulgence leaves every one to think for themselves in spiritual matters; the laws inspect our actions, our thoughts are left to God. Industry, good living, selfishness, litigiousness, country politics, the pride of freemen, religious indifference, are their characteristics. If you recede still farther from the sea, you will come into more modern settlements; they exhibit the same strong lineaments, in a ruder appearance. Religion seems to have still less influence, and their manners are less improved.

Now we arrive near the great woods, near the last inhabited districts; there men seem to be placed still farther beyond the reach of government, which in some measure leaves them to themselves. How can it pervade every corner; as they were driven there by misfortunes, necessity of beginnings, desire of acquiring large tracts of land, idleness, frequent want of economy, ancient debts; the re-union of such people does not afford a very pleasing spectacle. When discord, want of unity and friendship; when either drunkenness or idleness prevail in such remote districts; contention, inactivity, and wretchedness must ensue. There are not the same remedies to these evils as in a long established community. The few magistrates they have, are in general little better than the rest; they are often in a perfect state of war; that of man against man, sometimes decided by blows, sometimes by means of the law; that of man against every wild inhabitant of these venerable woods, of which they are come to dispossess them. There men appear to be no better than carnivorous animals of a superior rank, living on the flesh of wild animals when they can catch them, and when they are not able, they subsist on grain. He who would wish to see America in its proper light, and have a true idea of its feeble beginnings and barbarous rudiments, must visit our extended line of frontiers where the last settlers dwell, and where he may see the first labours of settlement, the mode of clearing the earth, in all their different appearances; where men are wholly left dependent on their native tempers, and on the spur of uncertain industry, which often fails when not sanctified by the efficacy of a few moral rules. There, remote from the power of example, and check of shame, many families exhibit the most hideous parts of our society. They are a kind of forlorn hope, preceding by ten or twelve years the most respectable army of veterans which come after them. In that space, prosperity will polish some, vice and the law will drive off the rest, who uniting again with others like themselves will recede still farther; making room for more industrious people, who will finish their improvements, convert the loghouse into a convenient habitation, and rejoicing that the first heavy labours are finished, will change in a few years that hitherto barbarous country into a fine fertile, well regulated district. Such is our progress, such is the march of the Europeans toward the interior parts of this continent. In all societies there are off-casts; this impure part serves as our precursors or pioneers; my father himself was one of that class, but he came upon honest principles, and was therefore one of the few who held fast; by good conduct and temperance, he transmitted to me his fair inheritance, when not above one in fourteen of his contemporaries had the same good fortune.

Forty years ago this smiling country was thus inhabited; it is now purged, a general decency of manners prevails throughout, and such has been the fate of our best countries.

Exclusive of those general characteristics, each province has its own, founded on the government, climate, mode of husbandry, customs, and peculiarity of circumstances. Europeans submit insensibly to these great powers, and become, in the course of a few generations, not only Americans in general, but either Pennsylvanians, Virginians, or provincials under some other name. Whoever traverses the continent must easily observe those strong differences, which will grow more evident in time. The inhabitants of Canada, Massachuset, the middle provinces, the southern ones will be as different as their climates; their only points of unity will be those of religion and language. . . .

There is no wonder that this country has so many charms, and presents to Europeans so many temptations to remain in it. A traveller in Europe becomes a stranger as soon as he quits his own kingdom; but it is otherwise here. We know, properly speaking, no strangers; this is every person's country; the variety of our soils, situations, climates, governments, and produce, hath something which must please every body. No sooner does an European arrive, no matter of what condition, than his eyes are opened upon the fair prospect; he hears his language spoke, he retraces many of his own country manners, he perpetually hears the names of families and towns with which he is acquainted; he sees happiness and prosperity in all places disseminated; he meets with hospitality, kindness, and plenty every where; he beholds hardly any poor, he seldom hears of punishments and executions; and he wonders at the elegance of our towns, those miracles of industry and freedom. He cannot admire enough our rural districts, our convenient roads, good taverns, and our many accommodations; he involuntarily loves a country where every thing is so lovely. When in England, he was a mere Englishman; here he stands on a larger portion of the globe, not less than its fourth part, and may see the productions of the north, in iron and naval stores; the provisions of Ireland, the grain of Egypt, the indigo, the rice of China. He does not find, as in Europe, a crouded society, where every place is overstocked; he does not feel that perpetual collision of parties, that difficulty of beginning, that contention which oversets so many. There is room for every body in America; has he any particular talent, or industry? he exerts it in order to procure a livelihood, and it succeeds. Is he a merchant? the avenues of trade are infinite; is he eminent in any respect? he will be employed and respected. Does he love a country life? pleasant farms present themselves; he may purchase what he wants, and thereby become an American farmer. Is he a labourer, sober and industrious? he need not go many miles, nor receive many informations before he will be hired, well fed at the table of his employer, and paid four or five times more than he can get in Europe. Does he want uncultivated lands? thousands of acres present themselves, which he may purchase cheap. Whatever be his talents or inclinations, if they are moderate, he may satisfy them. I do not mean that every one who comes will grow rich in a little time; no, but he may procure an easy, decent maintenance, by his industry. Instead of starving he will be fed, instead of being idle he will have employment; and these are riches enough for such men as come over here. The rich stay in Europe, it is only the middling and the poor that emigrate. Would you wish to travel in independent idleness, from north to south, you will find easy access, and the most chearful reception at every house; society without ostentation, good cheer without pride, and every decent diversion which the country affords with little expence. It is no wonder that the European who has lived here a few years is desirous to remain; Europe with all its pomp, is not to be compared to this continent for men of middle stations, or labourers.

An European, when he first arrives, seems limited in his intentions, as well as in his views; but he very suddenly alters his scale; two hundred miles formerly appeared a very great distance, it is not but a trifle; he no sooner breathes our air than he forms schemes, and embarks in designs he never would have thought of in his own country. There the plenitude of society confines many useful ideas and often extinguishes the most laudable schemes which here ripen into maturity. Thus Europeans become Americans.

But how is this accomplished in that croud of low, indigent people, who flock here every year from all parts of Europe? I will tell you; they no sooner arrive than they immediately feel the good effects of that plenty of provisions we possess: they fare on our best food, and are kindly entertained; their talents, character, and peculiar industry are immediately inquired into; they find countrymen every where disseminated, let them come from whatever part of Europe. Let me select one as an epitome of the rest; he is hired, he goes to work, and works moderately; instead of being employed by a haughty person, he finds himself with his equal, placed at the substantial table of the farmer, or else at an inferior one as good; his wages are high, his bed is not like that bed of sorrow on which he used to lie: if he behaves with propriety, and is faithful, he is caressed, and becomes as it were a member of the family. He begins to feel the effects of a sort of resurrection; hitherto he had not lived, but simply vegetated; he now feels himself a man, because he is treated as such; the laws of his own country had overlooked him in his insignificancy; the laws of this cover him with their mantle. Judge what an alteration there must arise in the mind and thoughts of this man; he begins to forget his former servitude and dependence, his heart involuntarily swells and glows; this first swell inspires him with those new thoughts which constitute an American. What love can he entertain for a country where his existence was a burthen to him; if he is a generous good man, the love of this new adoptive parent will sink deep into his heart. He looks around, and sees many a prosperous person, who but a few years before was as poor as himself. This encourages him much, he begins to form some little scheme, the first, alas, he ever formed in his life. If he is wise he thus spends two or three years, in which time he acquires knowledge, the use of tools, the modes of working the lands, felling trees, &c. This prepares the foundation of a good name, the most useful acquisition he can make. He is encouraged, he has gained friends; he is advised and directed, he feels bold, he purchases some land; he gives all the money he has brought over, as well as what he has earned, and trusts to the God of harvests for the discharge of the rest. His good name procures him credit. He is now possessed of the deed, conveying to him and his posterity the fee simple and absolute property of two hundred acres of land, situated on such a river. What an epocha in this man's life! He is a freeholder, from perhaps a German boor—he is now an American, a Pennsylvanian, an English subject. He is naturalized, his name is enrolled with those of the other citizens of the province. Instead of being a vagrant, he has a place of residence; he is called the inhabitant of such a county, or of such a district, and for the first time in his life counts for something; for hitherto he has been a cypher. I only repeat what I have heard many say, and no wonder their hearts should glow, and be agitated with a multitude of feelings, not easy to describe. From nothing to start into being; from a servant to the rank of a master; from being the slave of some despotic prince, to become a free man, invested with lands, to which every municipal blessing is annexed! What a change indeed! It is in consequence of that change that he becomes an American. This great metamorphosis has a double effect, it extinguishes all his European prejudices, he forgets that mechanism of subordination, that servility of disposition which poverty had taught him; and sometimes he is apt to forget too much, often passing from one extreme to the other. If he is a good man, he forms schemes of future prosperity, he proposes to educate his children better than he has been educated himself; he thinks of future modes of conduct, feels an ardor to labour he never felt before. Pride steps in and leads him to every thing that the laws do not forbid: he respects them; with a heart-felt gratitude he looks toward the east, toward that insular government from whose wisdom all his new felicity is derived, and under whose wings and protection he now lives. These reflections constitute him the good man and the good subject. Ye poor Europeans, ye, who sweat, and work for the great—ye, who are obliged to give so many sheaves to the church, so many to your lords, so many to your government, and have hardly any left for yourselves—ye, who are held in less estimation than favourite hunters or useless lap dogs—ye, who only breathe the air of nature, because it cannot be withheld from you; it is here that ye can conceive the possibility of those feelings I have been describing; it is here the laws of naturalization invite every one to partake of our great labours and felicity, to till unrented, untaxed lands! Many, corrupted beyond the power of amendment, have brought with them all their vices, and disregarding the advantages held to them, have gone on in their former career of iniquity, until they have been overtaken and punished by our laws. It is not every emigrant who succeeds; no, it is only the sober, the honest, and industrious: happy those to whom this transition has served as a powerful spur to labour, to prosperity, and to the good establishment of children, born in the days of their poverty; and who had no other portion to expect but the rags of their parents, had it not been for their happy emigration. Others again, have been led astray by this enchanting scene; their new pride, instead of leading them to the fields, has kept them in idleness; the idea of possessing lands is all that satisfies them—though surrounded with fertility, they have mouldered away their time in inactivity, misinformed husbandry, and ineffectual endeavours. How much wiser, in general, the honest Germans than almost all other Europeans; they hire themselves to some of their wealthy landsmen, and in that apprenticeship learn every thing that is necessary. They attentively consider the prosperous industry of others, which imprints in their minds a strong desire of possessing the same advantages. This forcible idea never quits them, they launch forth, and by dint of sobriety, rigid parsimony, and the most persevering industry, they commonly succeed. Their astonishment at their first arrival from Germany is very great—it is to them a dream; the contrast must be powerful indeed; they observe their countrymen flourishing in every place; they travel through whole counties where not a word of English is spoken; and in the names and the language of the people, they retrace Germany. They have been an useful acquisition to this continent, and to Pennsylvania in particular; to them it owes some share of its prosperity: to their mechanical knowledge and patience, it owes the finest mills in all America, the best teams of horses, and many other advantages. The recollection of their former poverty and slavery never quits them as long as they live. . . .

After a foreigner from any part of Europe is arrived, and become a citizen; let him devoutly listen to the voice of our great parent, which says to him, "Welcome to my shores, distressed European; bless the hour in which thou didst see my verdant fields, my fair navigable rivers, and my green mountains!—If thou wilt work, I have bread for thee; if thou wilt be honest, sober, and industrious, I have greater rewards to confer on thee—ease and independence. I will give thee fields to feed and cloath thee; a comfortable fire-side to sit by, and tell thy children by what means thou has prospered; and a decent bed to repose on. I shall endow thee beside with the immunities of a freeman. If thou wilt carefully educate thy children, teach them gratitude to God, and reverence to that government, that philanthropic government, which has collected here so many men and made them happy. I will also provide for thy progeny; and to every good man this ought to be the most holy, the most powerful, the most earnest wish he can possibly form, as well as the most consolatory prospect when he dies. Go thou and work and till; thou shalt prosper, provided thou be just, grateful and industrious." . . .   [1782]

Charles Brockden Brown

To The Public

Preface to *Edgar Huntly*

The flattering reception that has been given, by the public, to Arthur Mervyn, has prompted the writer to solicit a continuance of the same favour, and to offer to the world a new performance.

America has opened new views to the naturalist and politician, but has seldome furnished themes to the moral painter. That new springs of action, and new motives to curiosity should operate; that the field of investigation, opened to us by our own country, should differ essentially from those which exist in Europe, may be readily conceived. The sources of amusement to the fancy and instruction to the heart, that are peculiar to ourselves, are equally numerous and inexhaustible. It is the purpose of this work to profit by some of these sources; to exhibit a series of adventures, growing out of the condition of our country, and connected with one of the most common and most wonderful diseases or affections of the human frame.

One merit the writer may at least claim; that of calling forth the passions and engaging the sympathy of the reader, by means hitherto unemployed by preceding authors. Puerile superstition and exploded manners; Gothic castles and chimeras, are the materials usually employed for this end. The incidents of Indian hostility, and the perils of the western wilderness, are far more suitable; and, for a native of America to overlook these, would admit of no apology. These, therefore, are, in part, the ingredients of this tale, and these he has been ambitious of depicting in vivid and faithful colours. The success of his efforts must be estimated by the liberal and candid reader.   [1799]

William Tudor

Excerpt from *North American Review*

It has been said that one reason why we have not produced more good poems was owing to the want of subjects and though

> The poet's eye in a fine phrensy rolling,
> Glances from Heaven to earth, from earth to Heaven,

and makes the universe his domain, yet that the appropriate themes of other countries had been exhausted by their own poets and that none existed in ours. Thinking this opinion to be unfounded, the attempt to prove the latter part of it to be so may furnish a theme for this discourse during the few moments that I can presume to solicit your attention.

The early history of illustrious nations has been the source of the great master pieces of poetry: the fabulous ages of Greece are the foundation of the Iliad and Odyssey, and the same period gave Virgil his hero for the Æneid. Many modern epicks have taken the heroes of the earlier periods and revolutions of modern times. The American Revolution may some centuries hence become a fit and fruitful subject for an heroick poem; when ages will have consecrated its principles and all remembrance of party feuds and passions shall have been obliterated—when the inferiour actors and events will have been levelled by time, and a few memorable actions and immortal names shall remain the only monuments to engage and concentrate the admiration of a remote posterity.

From the close of the 16th to the middle of the 18th century many most interesting events took place on this continent and circumstances have concurred with time in casting a shade of obscurity resembling that of antiquity over the transactions of that period; while, by the great revolutions which have since happened, the connexion between those days and our own is interrupted, and they are so disconnected with the present era that no passionate feeling is blended with their consideration; they are now exclusively the domain of history and poetry. All the communities then standing have passed away or exist under new relations. The remarkable Confederacy of Indian tribes under the name of the five nations is extinct. The foundations of the French Empire in America have been torn up, the possessions that were once French are now held by the British, and the English colonies have become an independent nation. All these changes have insulated this portion of history and divested it of the irritation attendant on recent political affairs.

The region in which these occurrences took place abounds with grand and beautiful scenery, possessing some peculiar features. The numerous waterfalls, the enchanting beauty of Lake George and its pellucid flood, of Lake Champlain, and the lesser lakes, afford many objects of the most picturesque character; while the inland seas from Superiour to Ontario, and that astounding cataract whose roar would hardly be increased by the united murmurs of all the cascades of Europe, are calculated to inspire vast and sublime conceptions. The effects too of our climate composed of a Siberian winter and an Italian summer furnish peculiar and new objects for description. The circumstances of remote regions are here blended, and strikingly opposite appearances witnessed in the same spot, at different seasons of the year—In our winters, we have the sun at the same altitude as in Italy, shining on an unlimited surface of snow which can only be found in the higher latitudes of Europe where the sun in the winter rises little above the horizon. The dazzling brilliance of a winter's day, and a moon-light night when the utmost splendour of the sky is reflected from a surface of spotless white attended with the most excessive cold, is peculiar to the northern part of the United States. What too can surpass the celestial purity and transparency of the atmosphere in a fine autumnal day when our vision and our thoughts seem carried 'to the third heaven;' the gorgeous magnificence of their close, when the sun sinks from our view surrounded with varried masses of clouds, fringed with gold and purple, and reflecting in evanescent tints all the hues of the rainbow.[1]

---

[1] There is no climate in the world that presents more remarkable contrasts than that of the middle and northern parts of the United States. Boston, for instance, is in the same latitude with Rome, the cold in winter is occasionally as intense and the snow as deep as at Stockholm and St. Petersburg; but the sun hardly gleams on them in the winter months, while here his rays are shed from the same altitude as in Italy, and interrupts during the day that severity of cold, induced by the prevalence of the winds in the western quarter, coming to us over a continent of such vast extent covered with dense forests which shadow the earth and prevent the sun from warming and drying its surface. Our climate affords some of the worst and some of the finest weather that can be felt in any part of the world. The spring generally is the most capricious and disagreeable, the autumn the mellowest and most serene. Persons who are in the habit of remarking the appearance of the atmosphere cannot fail of admiring the extreme beauty of the sky at most seasons of the year. To witness the same effects, it is necessary in Europe to get into the same latitudes. The climate of England, modified by an insular situation, and the wide spread

   A most remarkable feature in the landscape at this same season, and which those who
see it for the first time must behold with astonishment, is the singular appearance of the
woods; where all the hues of the most lively flowers, the vivid colours of tulips, are given
to the trees of the forest, and nature appears in a moment of capricious gayety to have at-
tired the groves in the gaudiest and most fantastick livery. Nothing comparable to this effect can be seen in any part of Europe.[2]

cultivation of its surface is peculiarly temperate, but constantly vapoury and humid. France and Germany, colder and warmer than England, are still more temperate than the United States; it is necessary
to cross the Alps to find the same bright and beautiful atmosphere that surrounds us. In England it is
seldom that any distant object can be seen distinctly, and there is always such a degree of haziness in the
air that even neighbouring objects are never so clearly defined as they are under a purer sky; the artists
of the Continent commonly reproach the artists of England with carrying this imitation of nature in
their own country into their representations of the scenery of others, and in their engravings (the remark
was made particularly in criticising that magnificent work, Stuart's Antiquities of Athens,) giving the
misty, indistinct outline which they were accustomed to and which is not without its beauties but
which was entirely foreign to the appearance of objects in Greece. This same effect of great distinctness,
which is common to the south of Europe, may very often be seen here, especially in the summer. Any
person may judge of this in a clear day by regarding elevated buildings, looking from the sun and observing with what sharpness and distinctness their edges and angles are marked and how bold the relief
and distant the sky recedes. The most careless eye can hardly fail to be struck with the beauty of an
evening sky, after sunset, and the appearance of the western horizon when the darkness has encroached
on the eastern. On a summer or autumnal evening, when there are no clouds, as the twilight is advancing, the purity, transparency, brilliancy and harmonious subsiding and blending of the warmer tints
from where the sun has set, to the fine *chiaro oscuro* of the opposite point, where the shadows of night are
approaching, will afford a few minutes of delightful contemplation to the lover of nature. In contending
for this splendour of our atmosphere which has sometimes been denied it I am well aware of all its disadvantages and would gladly take a little less brilliance and a little more comfort; but, as we are fully
sensible, and are habitually repining at its inconveniences, it is well to know what compensation may be
derived from its beauties. To the poet and the artist it is replete with picturesque effect.

[2]This singular and beautiful appearance of the forests is peculiar to this country. It arises partly from the
greater variety of trees and perhaps from the early occurrence of frosts when the leaves are still vigorous
and filled with juices and which may be decomposed by the cold so as to produce these vivid colours;
when they might merely fade and be partially changed if their fall was not produced prematurely. The
forests in Europe in their autumnal dress have many shades of brown and yellow intemixed, but there is
nothing equal to the effect produced here. To select two of our forest trees for instance, the white walnut
and the maple, these trees attaining the height of forty feet and upwards and the whole foliage of the
former of the brightest yellow and the latter the deepest scarlet. No artist has hitherto ventured to give
this appearance in its full effect. There are many features in our forest scenery that are highly beautiful
from their variety and strong contrasts. Europeans who have a knowledge and love of botany always admire them. Most of our trees and plants have been transplanted into the nurseries of Europe, and are
much in request for all their ornamental plantations. It is not only the aspect of our forests, but the general aspect of our country, which have both been too much neglected by the American poets, who have
written their descriptions more from the study of the classick poets of ancient and modern Europe than
from meditating on the scenes familiar to them.—A painter who only makes pictures from copying the
ideas and style of the great masters, without animating his manner by a study of nature, may produce
correct but always cold and dry performances. Descriptive poetry, which borrows the fashion of other
countries, however classick its allusions, will be languid and spiritless, it will possess no raciness and
can never be rendered interesting. The general pysiognomy of the United States is different from that
of every country in Europe, its buildings, its cultivation, its natural and artificial objects have many peculiar features. There is no species of cultivation in Europe, not even the vine, except when cultivated
on espaliers or pendant between trees, which is seldom seen, that can compare with a field of Indian
corn, next to the sugar cane the richest in appearance of all plants. The care and labour which is bestowed on this grain in the Eastern States, the neatness and beauty of its appearance, form a strong

Many other beauties of inanimate nature might be enumerated, and these just mentioned are only cited as being in a degree peculiar. These extensive and variegated forests afford shelter to a variety of animals, beautiful in form and curious in their habits, such among others, are the beaver and the deer; and to birds of most exquisite plumage. The graceful shape and various species of some of the diminutive quadrupeds, the very abundance of some of these animals, and of certain kinds of birds, which almost darken the air in their flight, serve to enrich and animate the scenery. Prominent among objects of this class, is the king of birds, Joye's own imperial Eagle, the sacred emblem of our country: 'Formed by nature for braving the severest cold, feeding equally on the produce of the sea and of the land, possessing powers of flight capable of outstripping even the tempests themselves; unawed by any but man; and from the etherial heights to which he soars, looking abroad at one glance to an immeasurable expanse of forests, fields, lakes and ocean deep below him, he appears indifferent to the little localities of change of seasons; as in a few minutes he can pass from summer to winter, from the lower to the higher regions of the atmosphere, the adobe of eternal cold, and from thence descend at will to the torrid and arctick zones of the earth.'[3] In the same territories are found those enormous bones of animals now extinct that have generated so many fables among the savages and speculations among philosophers; and those extensive fortifications so buried in obscurity that even tradition is silent respecting them;—objects which lead to that musing on former times most propitious to poetry.

Such are some of the subordinate subjects that would be fruitful of allusion and fertile in description to the poet. The human actors on this theatre are still more striking and their history replete with interest and romantick adventure. The English and French were founding extensive empires here and their contiguous possessions produced a century of conflicts which terminated at last in the exclusive power of the former. European affairs were more than once affected by the disputes of these two nations in the regions of Canada, and the decision of the most important contests on the Old Continent has been produced by the issue of operations in the remote wilds of North America. The period also was one of great interest in European annals; France and England were rivals in glory, both in arts and arms.

Between these powers were interposed the Aborigines, who became the allies of these nations and the most efficient part of their force. Before speaking more particularly of them, it will be necessary to deprecate the prejudices naturally entertained on the subject from what we now see. The degenerate, miserable remains of the Indian nations which have dwindled into insignificance and lingered among us as the tide of civilization has flowed, mere floating deformities on its surface, poor, squalid and enervated with intoxicating liquors, should no more be taken for the representatives of their ancestors who first met the Europeans on the edge of their boundless forests, severe and untamed as the regions they tenanted, than the Greek slaves who now tremble at the frown of a petty Turkish tyrant can be considered the likeness of their immortal progenitors, of those immoveable bands, before whom at Platœa, Thermopylæ and Marathon, the whole Persian empire broke and subsided like the

---

contrast with the too careless and neglected appearance of other fields. This is the most splendid of all the gifts of Ceres, and it is difficult to say whether it is most pleasing to the eye in its growing state or at the period of harvest, when the ripened, luxuriant ears are discovered through their faded covering. It would extend this note too far to notice all the objects that may be cited as peculiar in some degree to our scenery.

[3] Wilson's Ornithology.

waves of the sea against the rocks they defended. To form an idea of what they once were, to see them in the energy and originality of their primitive condition, we must now journey a thousand miles. They possessed so many traits in common with some of the nations of antiquity that they perhaps exhibit the counterpart of what the Greeks were in the heroick ages, and particularly the Spartans during the vigour of their institutions. Their origin has been the source of many theories and conjectures, few of which are more reasonable than the suggestion of Spenser in his Fairy Queen that they are the descendants of the man whom Prometheus animated by stealing fire from Heaven. Whether this race of men could like the Greeks have gradually acquired civilization, or whether they are a distinct species incapable of being tamed, may be uncertain: sudden civilization at least has been shewn to be impossible; they diminish and waste before its progress like snow before the vernal influence. The sublime allegorical painting of Guido,[4] in which Apollo encircled by the hours is chasing night and her shadows over the surface of the globe might almost represent the extinction of our savage precursors before the dawn of science and cultivation. The history of these people then is not less interesting since in a short period they will exist no where else, and even in the next century the Indian warriour and hunter will perhaps only be found on the shores of the Pacifick ocean.

The virtues and vices of the original inhabitants of America have been generally exaggerated by their enemies or admirers. It would be as foolish to vindicate the one as to deny the other; both grew out of their condition: the influence of civilized society destroyed the former and nourished the latter. Their virtues were hospitality, reverence to age, unalterable constancy in friendship, and undaunted fortitude in every species of enterprise and suffering. They lived in a state of proud savage equality and had no esteem for any merit except that which was derived from superiority in the arts of hunting, war, and eloquence. These were their general characteristicks, but the difference between Indian was almost as great as among European nations, and the inferiority of some to others was quite as remarkable as that which exists between civilized people.

Among those who were distinguished, few are more eminent than the confederated tribes which were first known to us under the name of the Five Nations. These nations resided originally in the district where now stands Montreal. The Algonquins lived more in the interiour. The former were peaceable in their habits and subsisted by cultivating the earth; the latter were warlike and depended on hunting; the two nations were friendly and exchanged their corn and venison. At a certain period, when game was scarce, the Algonquins requested the Five Nations to send them some of their young men to assist in the increased toil of procuring food. These becoming very expert huntsmen, were murdered by the Algonquin employers out of jealousy and apprehension. When complaint was made of this treacherous cruelty, they only blamed the murderers and made some slight presents to the injured people, fearless of the resentment of a nation who subsisted by the effeminate employment, as they esteemed it, of agriculture. The Five Nations determined on revenge, which being discovered by the Algonquins, they resolved to reduce them to absolute obedience by force. In pursuing this scheme, they chased them from their place of living and obliged them to seek shelter in the region between the Hudson and Lakes Erie and Ontario. The Confederacy, goaded by the injustice of their enemies to relinquish their peaceable employments, gradually acquired a knowledge of war and courage to face them; and, though the latter aided by the French had the great advantage of the previous use of fire arms, the Five Nations eventually triumphed and, with the

[4]In the Rospigliosi Palace at Rome.

exception of a small number that were driven to the vicinity of Quebec, finally extinguished the Algonquins, one of the most warlike, numerous and politick tribes of North America. Having once acquired the habits and knowledge of war, they extended their dominion with restless ambition till they had either formed alliances with, or reduced to submission, most of the nations between the St. Lawrence, the sea coast, and the Ohio. The Dutch formed a treaty with them in 1609. The English made their first treaty of alliance with them in 1664, which was continued from time to time and never violated. They had also particular treaties with Massachusetts, New-York, Pennsylvania, Maryland and Virginia.

From this slight sketch of their history, it may be imagined that these nations must have held an important part in all the contests between the French and English. Indeed, the affairs of the former were more than once brought to the very brink of destruction by them. At a very critical moment, the English withdrew from the contest by the most positive orders of the Sovereign, which were artfully obtained by the French Ministry, from the bigoted subservience of the Stuarts to the Court of Rome, while, under pretence of religion, the Jesuit Missionaries were promoting the designs of France in that vast scheme of Colossal aggrandizement which, with one foot at New Orleans and the other at Quebec, would have bestrode the Empire of North America.

The actions of these people in war had a strong character of wildness and romance; their preparations for it and celebrations of triumph were highly picturesque. The solemn councils of their Sachems, the war-dance which preceded their expeditions, like the Pyrrhick Dance of antiquity, was full of terrifick expression. Many of their achievements were performed by a few or sometimes only one or two individuals. These were savage in their character and not admitted now in the practice of war among civilized nations and yet such actions may be rendered highly interesting in poetry. What was the nocturnal excursion of Diomed and Ulysses in the 10th book of the Iliad, in which they slew Rhesus, king of the Thracians, with many of his officers in their sleep, and brought away his beautiful horses? what was the enterprise of Nisus and Euryalus in the 9th book of the Æneid, in which they murdered so many in their sleep, and in which Euryalus, by taking from one of them his splendid helmet and belt was afterwards discovered by the moon gleaming on its polished surface, and the death of both occasioned by this spoil? These episodes are two of the finest in those immortal Epicks, yet it is only to the genius of Homer and Virgil that they are indebted for more than may be found in several Indian adventures.

Many of their friendships were as strong as that of the two followers of Æneas: their affection generally for those of their own nation was of the most powerful kind; a proof of this may be found in the speech of a Sachem of the Mohawks to an officer who was hurrying them to undertake an expedition, just after they had returned from holding a Council at Albany, where they had lost by sickness some of their finest young men: 'You seem,' said he 'to think that we are brutes, that we have no sense of the loss of our dearest relations, and some of them the bravest men we had in our nation; you must allow us time to bewail our misfortunes'—They were guilty of ferocious cruelty towards their enemies. Alas! cruelty is not peculiar to savages. They condemned to torture the foes who would have tortured them.—How many Christian nations are free from the reproach at every period of their history of having tortured their own subjects for mere matters of opinion? In war they laid waste the dwellings and cornfields of their enemies and murdered the defenceless.—Is there nothing in the conduct of nations pretending to the highest civilization that will, under this head, interfere with their exclusive claim to barbarism?

That they were not merely hunters and warriors, but sagacious in the management of affairs and capable of deep laid schemes of policy, there are many historical anecdotes to prove. One must suffice on this occasion. The most accomplished statesman of the Italian school could hardly surpass the following perfidious and subtle policy of an Indian Chieftain. In the year 1687, Adario, a very distinguished Sachem of the Hurons, finding that his nation had become suspected by the French on account of the intercourse they had held with the English, determined to recover their good graces by some signal action against the Five Nations, their common foe. For this purpose he left Michilimackinack with an hundred men and called on his way at the fort of Cadaraqui for intelligence. The French, after many attempts, had just succeeded in obtaining from a part of the Five Nations that they would send Ambassadours to Montreal to form a treaty of peace. The French commander informed the Huron Chief of this state of affairs, that the deputies were then on their way, and begged him to return home and attempt no enterprise that might interrupt these favourable prospects.

Surprised at this intelligence, the wily savage was under the greatest concern for his nation, least they should be sacrificed to the French interests if the latter could make peace with the Confederacy. Dissembling his feelings, he left the fort, not to return home as the Commander supposed, but to proceed to a spot where he knew the Ambassadours must pass, to await them. After a short time they made their appearance, guarded by forty young warriors. They were surprised, and all their guards either killed or made prisoners. When these latter were all secured, Adario told them that he had been informed by the Governour of Canada that fifty of their warriors were to pass that way about this period and that he had formed this ambush to intercept them. The deputies, astonished at this perfidy of the French, related the purpose of their journey to Adario; on hearing which he affected the utmost fury and rage at the atrocity which the French government had caused him to commit and swore he would be revenged. Then looking steadfastly on the prisoners, one of whom was Decanesora, a famous Chief of the Oneidas, he said, go, by brethren, I loose your bonds and send you home again, though our nations be at war; I shall never rest easy till the Five Nations have taken their revenge of the French for this treachery.

The Deputies were persuaded by his conduct and told him that he and his nation might make peace with them when they pleased. Adario, who had lost but one man in the affair, took one of theirs as usual to supply his place; then giving them a supply of arms and ammunition, dismissed them. These Chiefs were from the Oneida and Onondagua tribes which had received the Jesuit Missionaries, were the best disposed towards the French, and now returned home most deeply incensed.

Our circumstance remained to complete the effect; Adario, on his return, gave up his prisoner to the French officer commanding, who being ignorant of these circumstances, to nourish the hatred between the Five Nations and the Hurons, ordered him to be shot. The Huron Chief called an Indian of the former people to witness this execution of his countryman and the cruelty of the French from which even he was not able to save his own prisoner, and then bid him make his escape and relate what he had seen. The fugitive arrived at the very time when the French had sent to disown Adario in the action he had committed; but this additional circumstance exasperated them so highly that they would listen to no representations. Their thoughts were all bent on revenge. A short time after they made a descent on the island of Montreal, took all the Forts in their way, destroyed, with indiscriminate havock, men, women and children, and reduced the French power in Canada to the very verge of ruin.

As the government of these people was a republick, the practice of eloquence was of the highest importance, since the art of persuasion was a principal source of influence and power. None of the Indian Nations carried the science of speaking to greater perfection, of which there are many proofs on record. The general characteristicks of their style are well known. We have received their speeches under every disadvantage, since they come to us through the medium of ignorant interpreters who were incapable of transfusing the spirit and ornament of one language into the idiom of another when they thoroughly understood neither. The solemnity of their councils, the dignity and animation of their manner, their style of address, "Sachems and Warriours,' were all suited to command attention and respect. Colden thus describes one of their orators: 'Decanesora had for many years the greatest reputation among the Five Nations for speaking and was generally employed as their speaker in their negotiations with both French and English: he was grown old when I saw him and heard him speak, he had great fluency and a graceful elocution, that would have pleased in any part of the world. His person was tall and well made, and his features to my thinking resembled much the busto's of Cicero.'[5]

The speeches given by Homer to the characters in the Iliad and Odyssey, form some of the finest passages in those poems. The speeches of these Indians only want similar embellishment to excite admiration. A few fragments of one may serve as a specimen. It was delivered under the following circumstances. James the second, at the solicitation of the French Court, having given orders to the Colonies not to interfere, the French were

---

[5]There were many metaphors which were transmitted down among the Indians by the women whose business it was to retain and repeat them from one generation to another. The following remarks on the language and oratory of the Five Nations are taken from Colden's history.

'The people of the Five Nations are much given to speech-making, ever the natural consequence of a perfect Republican government; where no single person has a power to compel, the arts of persuasion alone must prevail. As their best speakers distinguish themselves in their public councils and treaties with other nations, and thereby gain the esteem and applause of their countrymen, (the only superiority which any one of them has over the others) it is probable they apply themselves to this art by some kind of study and exercise in a great measure. It is impossible for me to judge how far they excel, as I am ignorant of their language; but the speakers whom I have heard had all a great fluency of words and much more grace in their manner than any man could expect among a people entirely ignorant of all the liberal arts and sciences.

'I am informed that they are very nice in the turn of their expressions, and that few of themselves are so far masters of their language as never to offend the ears of their *Indian* auditory by an unpolite expression. They have, it seems, a certain *urbanitas* or *atticism* in their language, of which the common ears are ever sensible, though only their great speakers attain to it. They are so much given to speech-making that their common compliments to any person they respect at meeting and parting are made in harangues.

'They have some kind of elegance in varying and compounding their words, to which not many of themselves attain, and this principally distinguishes their best speakers. I have endeavoured to get some account of this, as a thing that might be acceptable to the curious; but, as I have not met with any one person who understands their language and also knows any thing of grammar or of the learned languages, I have not been able to attain the least satisfaction. Their present minister tells me that their verbs are varied, but in a manner so different from the *Greek* or *Latin* that he cannot discover by what rule it was done and even suspects that every verb has a peculiar mode. They have but few radical words, but they compound their words without end; by this their language becomes sufficiently copious and leaves room for a good deal of art to please a delicate ear. Sometimes one word among them includes an entire definition of the thing; for example they call *wine*, *Oneharadesehoengtseragherie*, as much as to say, *a liquor made of the juice of the grape*. The words expressing things lately come to their knowledge are all compounds; they have no labeals in their language, nor can they perfectly pronounce a word wherein there is a labeal; and when one endeavours to teach them to pronounce words, they tell one, they think it ridiculous that they must shut their lips to speak. Their language abounds with gutterals and strong aspirations; these make it very sonorous and bold; and their speeches abound with metaphors, after the manner of the Eastern nations, as will best appear by the speeches that I have copied.'

determined to bring the Five Nations to their own terms. For this purpose the governor of Canada proceeded with a strong force in 1684 to Lake Ontario. The Indian Chiefs had meanwhile been persuaded by the Jesuits to send a deputation to meet him having been promised that they should be cordially received and kindly treated. The French army however became so much weakened by sickness, so many of the soldiers had died, that all the formidable preparations were rendered useless and their Commander was unable to prosecute his designs by force. This situation of the French was well understood by the Indians. When they met, after many ceremonies the conference was opened with due form, the parties being drawn up in a circle of which the French officers formed one half and the Savages the other. The Governor delivered a most arrogant, menacing speech, to impress them with fear of the tremendous power of France. Garangula, the Indian speaker on this occasion, was much surprised at the difference of its tone from what he had been led to expect by the Jesuits and immediately returned an answer of which the following are extracts. The Indians called the Governor of Canada, Onondio; it was their custom to give a surname as a mark of houour to the Governor of each of the Provinces, which was never changed.

'ONONDIO

'I honor you, and the warriors that are with me all likewise honor you. Your interpreter has finished your speech, I now begin mine. My words hasten to reach your ears, pray listen to them.

'Onondio, you must have believed when you left Quebec that the sun had burnt up all the Forests which render our country inaccessible to the French, or that the Lakes had overflowed their banks and surrounded our Castles so that it was impossible for us to get out of them. Yes, Onondio, you must surely have dreamt this, and curiosity to see so great a wonder has brought you so far. Now you are undeceived, since I and the warriors here present are come to assure you that the Senekas, Cayugas, Onondagas, Oneidas and Mohawks are yet alive. I thank you, in their name, for bringing back into their country that Calumet which your predecessor received from their hands. I congratulate you for your good fortune in having left under ground that murdering hatchet which has been so often dyed with the blood of the French. Listen, Onondio, I am not asleep, I have my eyes open, and that sun which enlightens me discovers to me a great Captain at the head of a Company of soldiers who speaks as if he were dreaming. He says that he only came to the Lake to smoke on the great Calumet with the Onondagas. But Garangula asserts that he sees the contrary, that it was to have destroyed them if sickness had not weakened the arms of the French.

'I see Onondio raving in a camp of sick men whose lives the great Spirit has saved by inflicting this sickness on them. Hear, Onondio, our women had taken their clubs, our children and old men had carried their bows and arrows into the heart of your camp if our warriors had not disarmed them and kept them back when your messenger Oquesse came to our castles. Enough, I say no more on this subject.

'We may go where we please, and carry with us whom we please, and buy and sell what we please. If your allies be your slaves, use them as such, command them to receive no other but your people. This belt confirms my words.

'What I say is the voice of all the five nations; hear what they answer, open your ears to what they speak: The Senakas, Cayugas, Onondagas, Oneidas and Mohawks say, that when they buried the hatchet at Cadaraqui, in the presence of your predecessor, in the centre of the Fort, they planted the tree of peace in the same place to be there carefully preserved, that in place of being a retreat for soldiers, it might become a rendezvous for merchants; that in place of arms and ammunitions of war, beavers and merchandize should only enter there.

'Hearken Onondio, take care for the future, that so great a number of soldiers as appear there do not choak the Tree of Peace planted in so small a fort. It would be a great misfortune if after it had so easily taken root, you should stop its growth and prevent its covering your country and ours with its branches. I assure you in the name of the Five Nations that our warriors shall dance to the Calumet of peace under its leaves, and shall remain quiet on their matts, and shall never dig up the hatchet, till their brethren Onondio, or Corlaer, shall either jointly or separately endeavour to attack the country which the Great Spirit has given to our ancestors. This belt confirms my words, and this other the authority given to me by the Five Nations.'—Then addressing himself to the French Interpreter, he said—'Take courage, Oquesse, you have spirit, speak, explain my words, omit nothing, tell all that your brethren and friends say to Onondio, your Governor, by the mouth of Garangula, who loves you and desires you to accept this present of beaver and take part with him in his feast to which he invites you. This present of beaver is sent to Onondio on the part of the Five Nations.'

This speech may be compared with the celebrated message of the Scythians to Alexander in Quintius Curtius, and it affords materials which, if they were drest in the style of the great Roman Historians, would vie with any that they have transmitted to us; indeed, its figurative language, pungent sarcasm, and lofty tone can hardly be surpassed.

Perilous and romantick adventures,[6] figurative and eloquent harangues, strong contrasts

---

[6]The early history of our country furnishes many characters, adventures and incidents of the strongest interest. Prominent among the former is Capt. John Smith whose common and familiar name is the only thing pertaining to his history which is not elevated and heroick. His life is now very rare and the book commands a high price, but a very able abstract of it may be found in Dr. Belknap's American Biography. And there is hardly a marvellous tale on the shelves of any circulating library that can surpass the real adventures of this extraordinary man. From his very infancy to his death, which happened in the middle period of life, his whole career is a series of daring and romantick achievements in many different parts of the world. His reputation appears without stain, and he is a genuine hero of romance, being equally distinguished for the gallantry of love and war. He gave to the northern Cape of Massachusetts bay the name of a Turkish lady who interested herself in his fate, when a prisoner of the Turks; but *Cape Tragabizanda,* afterwards got the name of Cape Ann, which it will no doubt retain, though the other out of regard to Smith might be used in poetry. His name is best known in this country, from his encounters with the father of Pocahontas and the devoted affection of that interesting Indian princess towards him. The character of Standish among the Plymouth colonists; of the Sachem of Mount Hope, and the wars which ended his destruction: the singular and heroick character of Madame de la Tour of whom some account may be found in Hubbard's history recently published by the Historical Society from an ancient Ms.: the religious fanaticism and intrigues of Mrs. Hutchinson and her supporter in Sir Henry Vane, which caused as much trouble and commotion in the colony of Massachusetts as the Mystical doctrines of Madame Guyon occasioned in Paris and to the Court of Louis 14th. These and many others are interesting materials. The incident mentioned by President Stiles is very striking, of Dixwell one of the regicides suddenly emerging from his concealment, and by his presence animating an infant settlement when suddenly assailed from the Indians to repel the savages, and then returning unnoticed to his retreat; which made many of the people who knew nothing of his concealment regard him as a mysterious being, a good angel sent for their deliverance. If remarkable characters and actions are to be found in our history, the scenes where they lived or occurred must be interesting from association of ideas. There are many such, though they have been too much neglected. We have all felt the interest excited by Scott for the scenery he describes in the Lady of the Lake. Its natural beauty is doubtless great—yet, give a bard of equal genius, the spot described in the last volume of the Historical collections as the one chosen by Gosnold in his first voyage—on one of the Elizabeth Islands there is a small lake in which there is a rocky islet where is still to be seen the foundations of the first dwelling erected on these shores by Europeans. The remarkable security of this situation, its natural beauty, the interest attending this attempt

and important interests, are as frequent in this portion of history as the theatre on which these actions were performed is abundant in grand and beautiful scenery. There are many inferiour circumstances that might contribute appropriate materials for poetry. The armorial bearings of the Indians, their Hieroglyphick writings, and some of their superstitions may be made subservient to poetical effect. For instance, there is in Lake Champlain a high rock against which the waves dash with vehemence and the spray is thrown to a great height. The Savages believed that an ancient Indian resided under this rock, who had power over the winds; to propitiate him they always threw over a pipe, or made some other oblation in passing. A man of distinction among the early Dutch inhabitants of New York, by the name of Corlaer, who was held in such high veneration by the Indians that they treated with him as the Governor of that Province and ever after called the Governor by his name, while on his way to visit the Governor of Canada, ridiculed this Indian Eolus. He was drowned directly afterwards by the upsetting of his canoe, which the Indians always attributed to his disrespect for the old man who had the control of the winds. This at least is not more extravagant than Homer's account of the present made by the monarch of Eolia to Ulysses of an assortment of winds secured in bags which being untied by his sailors, a tempest was created that drove them on the coast of the Lestrigons.

There is an ingenious device of Epick poetry that might be here used with great effect. This is the prophetick narration, a prophecy after the facts have occurred. Such is the celebrated Ode of Gray, in which the last of the Bards predicts the misfortunes of Edward's posterity; such are the adventures of Ulysses in the 11th book of the Odyssey, and of Æneas in the 6th book of the Æneid, in which those heroes are told among the shades the future fortunes of their race. The poet might introduce the expedient as his fancy suggested. It may be supposed that a French and English Officer and an American colonist should accompany an Indian Sachem deputed by his tribe to consult some Indian sorcerer or divinity; the scene may be in one of those islands of Lake Superiour which some of their traditions represent as the abode of the blest, on shores perhaps untrodden by the foot of man, lone, distant and obscure as those Cimmerian climes in which lay the opening to Tartarus. In seeking for a knowledge of destiny, what wonderful events would be unfolded.

The prescient expounder of fate would declare to the Chieftain of the Five Nations, the alliances, contests, triumphs and utter extinction of his race; that they should disappear with the animals they hunted and the forests that sheltered both—they should vanish before the spirit of civvilization, like the mist of the Lakes before the morning sun, and leave

to colonize a country which has since played such an important part in the world, make this secluded spot more interesting than the Highland Lake; the time will come when this spot will be visited with as much interest, as the traveller at Rome goes to the Fountain of Egeria.

It would be encroaching too far to dwell longer on these topicks. No prejudice is more common, none more unfounded, none will more certainly be hereafter destroyed, than the one which supposes the early history of our country to be deficient in interest. To a person totally unacquainted with it, the mere mention of the leading circumstances on which it is founded would prove on very slight reflection that it was indeed impossible it should be so. Even saints and miracles may be incorporated in it if such be the taste of the poet. In the 'Lettres edifiantes' published at Paris in 1807, there are the letters of Father Charlevoix and the other Jesuits in Canada relating all the minute circumstances of the deaths of some holy Indian Virgins, who died in the odour of sancticy, and at whose tombs miracles were performed duly attested and sworn to by divers honourable men. Those who wish to investigate this department, may consult, *Smith's Life, Belknap's Biography, Hubbard's history, Colden's history of the Five Nations, La Hontan's Travels, and the histories of Virginia and Massachusetts. Charlevoix Nouvelle France. Lafitau's Mœurs des Sauvages, Adair's American Indians.*

no trace of their existence, but in the records of the white men. To the Englishman he would foretell the civil war, the death of Charles on the scaffold, the fanatical austerity of the times, the usurpation of Cromwell, and, at his decease, the restoration of Royalty and the licentious gayety that ensued—the final expulsion of the Stuarts and extinction of that family—the lustre of arts and arms during the reign of Anne; with the subsequent increasing splendour and grandeur of his nation till their empire should extend over both the Indies. To the American Colonist would be foretold the American Revolution, the fame of its heroes and statesmen—he would announce to him the first of these, the man who should be first in war, first in peace, and first in the hearts of his countrymen; the successful issue of the glorious contest for Independence would be predicted and he would be shewn the future greatness, happiness and glory of his country. To the Frenchman he would narrate the conquests, the splendour of the arts and of literature, the bigotry, disasters and miseries of the reign of Louis 14th—the profligacy and corruption of the regency, the loss of their possessions on this continent, and in the last conflict the death of the victorious and vanquished Generals under the walls of Quebec. The constant increase of luxury and refinement to the era of the Revolution. In revealing that Revolution, he would describe the contagious enthusiasm of hope which would intoxicate all nations at its dawn; the crimes, the horrours and wonderful events that would accompany its progress; and the foul, gloomy despotism that would attend its close.—The King, his family, and his nobles perishing on the scaffold, or withering in exile; religion prohibited, its altars profaned, its ministers proscribed.—France covered with the dust of her ruined palaces and drenched with the blood of her citizens. He would foretell the rapid rise, energetick progress, and portentous grandeur of the great usurper; his ambition, wars, and victories; the ravages committed, the remote regions invaded, the kingdoms overthrown, while

> at his heels
> Lash'd in like hounds, should famine, sword and fire,
> Crouch for employment,

he would predict at the hour of deepest gloom, the reaction of publick feeling, the overwhelming wave of retributive conquest pursuing him back from every country of Europe to his own capital, his abdication, the return of the—but no, plain prose and sober reason are confounded by these events, they must be left to the madness of verse, and the inspiration of the poet.

This is a cursory sketch of some of the scenes and events that would be fruitful in poetry. When we recollect what delightful performances have been composed by one modern poet out of the obscure quarrels of Border Banditti in barbarous ages, how another in thoughts that breathe and words that burn has immortalized the pirates of the Archipelago, much may surely be expected from this region when it shall be explored with the torch of imagination. The materials are rude, yet talent only is wanting to mould and animate them. The same block of marble which in the hands of an artisan might only have formed a step for the meanest feet to trample on, under the touch of genius unfolded the Belvidere Apollo, glowing with divine beauty and immortal youth, the destroyer of the Python, the companion of the Muses, the majestick God of Eloquence and Poetry.

[1815]

James Kirk Paulding

National Literature

It has been often observed by such as have attempted to account for the scarcity of romantic fiction among our native writers, that the history of the country affords few materials for such works, and offers little in its traditionary lore to warm the heart or elevate the imagination. The remark has been so often repeated that it is now pretty generally received with perfect docility, as an incontrovertible truth, though it seems to me without the shadow of a foundation.

Wherever there are men, there will be materials for romantic adventure. In the misfortunes that befall them; in the sufferings and vicissitudes which are everywhere the lot of human beings in the struggles to counteract fortune, and in the conflicts of the passions, in every situation of life, he who studies nature and draws his pictures from her rich and inexhaustible sources of variety, will always find enough of those characters and incidents which give relish to works of fancy. The aid of superstition, the agency of ghosts, fairies, goblins, and all that antiquated machinery which till lately was confined to the nursery, is not necessary to excite our wonder or interest our feelings; although it is not the least of incongruities, that in an age which boasts of having by its scientific discoveries dissipated almost all the materials of superstition, some of the most popular fictions should be founded upon a superstition which is now become entirely ridiculous, even among the ignorant.

The best and most perfect works of imagination appear to me to be those which are founded upon a combination of such characters as every generation of men exhibits, and such events as have often taken place in the world, and will again. Such works are only fictions, because the tissue of events which they record never perhaps happened in precisely the same train, and to the same number of persons, as are exhibited and associated in the relation. Real life is fraught with adventures, to which the wildest fictions scarcely afford a parallel; and it has this special advantage over its rival, that these events, however extraordinary, can always be traced to motives, actions and passions, arising out of circumstances no way unnatural, and partaking of no impossible or supernatural agency. . . .

That these materials have as yet been little more than partially interwoven into the few fictions which this country has given birth to, is not owing to their being inapplicable to that purpose, but to another cause entirely. We have been misled by bad models, or the suffrages of docile critics, who have bowed to the influence of rank and fashion, and given testimony in favor of works which their better judgment must have condemned. We have cherished a habit of looking to other nations for examples of every kind, and debased the genius of this new world by making it the ape and the tributary of that of the old. We have imitated where we might often have excelled; we have overlooked our own rich resources, and sponged upon the exhausted treasury of our impoverished neighbors; we were born rich, and yet have all our lives subsisted by borrowing. Hence it has continually occurred, that those who might have gone before had they chosen a new path, have been content to come last, merely by following the old track. Many a genius that could and would have attained an equal height, in some new and unexplored region of fancy, has dwindled into insignificance and contempt by stooping to track some inferior spirit, to whom fashion had assigned a temporary elevation. They ought to be told, that though fashion may give a momentary popularity to works that neither appeal to national attachments, domestic habits, or those feelings which are the same yesterday, today, and forever, and everywhere, still it is not by imitation that they can hope to equal any thing great. . . .

By freeing himself from a habit of servile imitation; by daring to think and feel, and express his feelings; by dwelling on scenes and events connected with our pride and our affections; by indulging in those little peculiarities of thought, feeling, and expression which belong to every nation; by borrowing from nature, and not from those who disfigure or burlesque her—he may and will in time destroy the ascendancy of foreign taste and opinions, and elevate his own in the place of them. These causes lead to the final establishment of a national literature, and give that air and character of originality which it is sure to acquire, unless it is debased and expatriated by a habit of servile imitation. . . . This country is not destined to be always behind in the race of literary glory. The time will assuredly come, when that same freedom of thought and action which has given such a spur to our genius in other respects, will achieve similar wonders in literature. It is then that our early specimens will be sought after with avidity, and that those who led the way in the rugged discouraging path will be honored, as we begin to honor the adventurous spirits who first sought, explored, and cleared this western wilderness.   [1820, 1835]

Edgar Allan Poe

....

Marginalia

Much has been said, of late, about the necessity of maintaining a proper *nationality* in American Letters; but what this nationality *is,* or what is to be gained by it, has never been distinctly understood. That an American should confine himself to American themes, or even prefer them, is rather a political than a literary idea—and at best is a questionable point. We would do well to bear in mind that "distance lends enchantment to the view." *Ceteris paribus,* a foreign theme is, in a strictly literary sense, to be preferred. After all, the world at large is the only legitimate stage for the autorial *histrio.*

But of the need of *that* nationality which defends our own literature, sustains our own men of letters, upholds our own dignity, and depends upon our own resources, there cannot be the shadow of a doubt. Yet here is the very point at which we are most supine. We complain of our want of an International Copyright, on the ground that this want justifies our publishers in inundating us with British opinion in British books; and yet when these very publishers, at their own obvious risk, and even obvious loss, do publish an American book, we turn up our noses at it with supreme contempt (this is the general thing) until it (the American book) has been dubbed "readable" by some illiterate Cockney critic. Is it too much to say that, with us, the opinion of Washington Irving—of Prescott—of Bryant—is a mere nullity in comparison with that of any anonymous sub-sub-editor of the "Spectator," the "Athenæum," or the "London Punch"? It is *not* saying too much, to say this. It is a solemn—an absolutely awful act. Every publisher in the country will admit it to be a fact. There is not a more disgusting spectacle under the sun than our subserviency to British criticism. It is disgusting, first, because it is trucking, servile, pusillanimous—secondly, because of its gross irrationality. We *know* the British to bear us little but ill will—we know that, in no case, do they utter unbiassed opinions of American books—we know that in a few instances in which our writers have been treated with com-

mon decency in England, these writers have either openly paid homage to English institutions, or have had lurking at the bottom of their hearts a secret principle at war with
Democracy: we *know* all this, and yet, day after day, submit our necks to the degrading
yoke of the crudest opinion that emanates from the fatherland. Now if we *must* have nationality, let it be a nationality that will throw off this yoke.   [1845]

William Gilmore Simms

Americanism in Literature[1]

This is the right title. It indicates the becoming object of our aim. Americanism in our
Literature is scarcely implied by the usual phraseology. American Literature seems to be a
thing, certainly,—but it is not the thing exactly. To put Americanism in our letters, is to
do a something much more important. The phrase has a peculiar signification which is
worth our consideration. By a liberal extension of the courtesies of criticism, we are already in possession of a due amount of American authorship; but of such as is individual,
and properly peculiar to ourselves, we cannot be said to enjoy much. Our writers are numerous—quite as many, perhaps, in proportion to our years, our circumstances and necessities, as might be looked for among any people. But, with very few exceptions, their
writings might as well be European. They are European. The writers think after European
models, draw their stimulus and provocation from European books, fashion themselves to
European tastes, and look chiefly to the awards of European criticism. This is to denation-
alize the American mind. This is to enslave the national heart—to place ourselves at the
mercy of the foreigner, and to yield all that is individual, in our character and hope, to the
paralyzing influence of his will, and frequently hostile purposes.

There is a season, perhaps, when such a condition of dependence is natural enough in
the history of every youthful nation. It is in the national infancy that such must be the
case. The early labours of a newly established people, in all the intellectual arts, must necessarily be imitative. They advance, by regular steps, from the necessary to the intellectual—from the satisfaction of vulgar cravings, to a desire for the gratification of moral and
spiritual tastes;—and, in this progress, they can only advance through the assistance of
other nations. This condition is inevitable in the history of a people wanting in homoge-
neousness at first, and but recently segregated from their several patriarchal trees. Time
must be allowed to such a people—time to combine—to exchange thoughts and sympathies—and to learn the difficult, but absolutely necessary duty, of working together, as a
community, in harmonious and mutually relying action. Generations must pass away, and

[1]*Americanism in Literature: An Oration before the Phi Kappa and Demosthenean Societies of the University
of Georgia, at Athens, August 8, 1844. By Alexander B. Meek, of Alabama, Charleston: Burges & James.
1844.* Originally published in the *Southern and Western Magazine*, I (January, 1845), 1–14.

other generations take their places, before they shall utterly lose the impressions made upon their plastic infancy by arbitrary models—before they shall begin to look around them, and within themselves, for those characteristics which are peculiar to their condition, and which distinguish the country of their present fortunes. It is idle to say, as has been urged by the British Reviewers in their reply to Mr. Jefferson, that the Anglo-Americans were of full age at the very birth of their country. This is scarcely true, even in physical respects. They did not represent the intellect of the nation which they left, though they did its moral and its temperament. They represented neither its tastes, nor its acquisitions, nor its luxuries. The eminence upon which the superior characteristics of the British nation stood, had never been reached by the footsteps of the Pilgrims. They were in possession of the Anglo-Norman genius, no doubt—upon this it will be the duty of the Americans to insist;—but its great attainments—its cherished acquisitions—its tastes, its refinements, its polish, were not theirs. In all these essentials, the founders of the Anglo-American States were in their infancy. And so they were kept for a century, by the novel necessities, the trying hardships, the perilous wars which followed upon their new condition. The conquest of a savage empire—the conflict with barbarian enemies,— kept them back from the natural acquisitions, which were due to their origin and genius. Great Britain herself is fairly chargeable, by her tyrannous exactions and the bloody wars with which she sought us out in the new homes so perilously won in the wilderness, with having withstood our people in their progress to the attainment of those objects the lack of which she this day makes our reproach.

But these excuses can be urged no longer, nor is it necessary that they should. Europe must cease to taunt us because of our prolonged servility to the imperious genius of the Old World. We must set ourselves free from the tyranny of this genius, and the time has come when we must do so. We have our own national mission to perform—a mission commensurate to the extent of our country,—its resources and possessions,—and the numerous nations, foreign and inferior, all about us, over whom we are required to extend our sway and guardianship. We are now equal to this sway and guardianship. The inferior necessities of our condition have been overcome. The national mind is now free to rise to the consideration of its superior wants and more elevated aims; and individuals, here and there, are starting out from the ranks of the multitude, ready and able to lead out, from the bondage of foreign guidance, the genius which, hitherto, because of its timidity, knew nothing of its own resources for flight and conquest.

If the time for this movement has not yet arrived, it is certainly very near at hand. This conviction grows out of the fact that we now daily taunt ourselves with our protracted servility to the European. We feel that we are still too humbly imitative, wanting in the courage to strike out boldly, hewing out from our own forests the paths which should lead us to their treasures, and from the giant masses around us the characteristic forms and aspects of native art. This reproach has been hitherto but too much deserved, qualified only by a reference to the circumstances in our condition at which we have been able to glance only for a moment. We have done little that may properly be called our own; and this failure, due to influences which still, in some degree, continue, is one which nothing but a high and stimulating sense of nationality will enable us to remedy. It is so easy, speaking the English language, to draw our inspiration from the mother country, and to seek our audience in her halls and temples, that, but for the passionate appeals of patriotic censure, it may be yet long years before we throw off the patient servility of our dependence. With a daily influx of thousands from foreign shores, seeking to share our political securities and the blessings of the generous skies and rich soil which we possess, Europe sends us her thoughts, her fashions, and her tastes. These have their influence in keeping us in bondage, and we shall require all the activity of our native mind to resist the influence which she thus exercises upon our national institutions and education. Besides, our very wealth of territory, and the ease with which we live, are obstacles in the way of our improvement. The temptations of our vast interior keep our society in a constant state of transition. The social disruptions occasioned by the wandering habits of the citizen, result invariably in moral loss to the whole. Standards of judgment fluctuate, sensibilities become blunted, principles impaired, with increasing insecurity at each additional remove; and this obstacle in the way of our literary progress must continue, until the great interior shall react, because of its own overflow, upon the Atlantic cities.

There is nothing really to distress us in this survey, unless,—either because of a supineness of character which is not our reproach in merely every-day pursuits, or because of an intrinsic deficiency of the higher intellectual resources,—we continue to yield ourselves to our European teachers. Our literature, so far, has been English in its character. We have briefly striven to show why. Glad are we that we can make some exceptions to this admission—that we can point, here and there throughout the country, to some individuals, and say, here stands a true scion of young America,—this is a plant of our own raising—true to the spirit of the country,—to its genuine heart—a man to represent and speak for the nature which we acknowledge, and of which time shall make us proud. In these instances we find our hope. It is thus that we feel ourselves encouraged to say to our people, and to the workers in the mind of Europe, that we too are making a beginning in a purely individual progress—evolving, however slowly, a national aim and idea, out of the fulness and overflow of the national heart. We are rejoiced to behold symptoms of this independent intellectual working, simultaneously, in remote regions of the country; and flatter ourselves with the vision of a generous growth in art and letters, of which tokens begin to make themselves felt from the Aroostook to the Rio Brave. This evidence needs but sympathy and encouragement to grow powerful, and to challenge a living rank among the great spirits of other lands and periods. As yet, perhaps, the shows are faint and feeble. Few of the hurrying multitude have leisure to behold them,—our progress declaring itself, as it now does, rather by its anxieties and cravings,—its discontents with itself, and its feverish impatience at the advance of other communities—than by its own proper performances. But such a condition of the popular mind is the precursor of performance. The wish to do, is the forerunner of the way. Let us only take something for granted. Let the nation but yield a day's faith to its own genius, and that day will suffice for triumph. We do not yet believe in ourselves,—unless in the meaner respects which prove our capacity for acquisition only in concerns the inferior—in the mechanical arts,—in pursuits regarded as simply useful,—in selfish desires, and such as are necessary to our physical condition merely. This scepticism is the great barrier to be overcome. Our development depends upon our faith in what we are, and in our independence of foreign judgment. A resolute will, a bold aim, and a spirit that courageously looks within for its encouragements and standards,—these are our securities for intellectual independence. To these acquisitions our labours must be addressed. To the want of these, and the necessity for them, the attention of our people must be drawn. The popular mind scarcely yet seems to perceive that there is a vast and vital difference between the *self-speaking* among our people, and that numerous herd, which, though born, living and walking in our midst, speak never *for* our hearts, and seldom *from* their own—whose thoughts, no less than language, are wholly English, and who, in all general characteristics—so far as the native progress and development are effected—might as well have been born, dwelling and dilating in Middlesex or London. It is but to see these things as we should—to understand the world-wide difference between writing *for,* and writing *from* one's people. This difference is the whole,—but *what* a difference! To write *from* a people, is to *write* a people—to make them live—to endow them with a life and a name—to preserve them with a history forever. Whether the poet shall frame his song according to custom, or according to the peculiar nature and the need of those for whom it is made, is, in other words, to ask whether he shall be a poet at all or not. It was by properly understanding this difference in ancient days that he grew into the stature of the poet, and won his reputation; and it was through the proper comprehension of this *difference* and this *duty,* on the part of the Poet, that the genius and the history of the great nations have survived all the political disasters which have bowed their pillars in the dust.

Up to the present day—the signs whereof encourage us with better hopes—the question might properly have been asked, how should objects, such as these, be to us of any consideration?—we who live not for the morrow but the day—whose plans are conceived for temporary not eternal refuge—who hurry forward as if we had no children, and who rear them as if we loved them not! Such is the profligacy of every people who show themselves indifferent to the developments of native art. It is by the exhibition of the constructive faculty that the intellectual nature of a people is distinguished. In proportion to the possession and exercise of this faculty, which embodies all the elements of the imagination, will be the moral rank of the nation. We have been very heedless of this matter. Our people have taken too little interest in the productions of the American mind, considered purely as American, whether in art or letters. In all that relates to the higher aims of the social and spiritual nature, England, and what she is pleased to give us, sufficiently satisfies our moral cravings. Yet we have an idea of independence in some respects which tends to show how wretchedly limited has been our ambition. Parties are formed among us to compel the manufacture of our own pots and kettles, our woollens and window glass; parties ready to revolutionize the country, and make all chaos again, if these things be not of our own making:—made too,—such is the peculiar excellence of the jest, at our own heavy cost and pecuniary injury;—but never a work is said, whether by good sense or patriotism, touching the grievous imposition upon us of foreign opinion and foreign laws, foreign tastes and foreign appetites, taught us through the medium of a foreign, and perhaps hostile and insulting teacher. These, say these profound haberdashers in the wares of patriotism, are really matters of slight concern. Thoughts are common, say the paper manufacturers, and though we insist upon supplying the paper from domestic mills, upon which such thoughts are to be printed, yet these are quite as properly brought from abroad, as conceived and put in proper utterance at home. The European may as well do our thinking. The matter is not worth the struggle. English literature is good enough for us for many hundred years to come.[2] So, for that matter, are English woollens.

But this will not suffice. The question is one which concerns equally our duties and our pride. Are we to aim and arrive at all the essentials of nationality—to rise into first rank and position as a people—to lift our heads, unabashed, among the great communities of

[2]This language was actually employed by one of the American reviews of highest rank. Yet these reviews, themselves are anticipated by foreign criticism, as, in most cases, they expend their analysis, upon foreign publications. I have heard an American author speak with wholesale scorn of all American art, and an American painter, of superior distinction, declare that he never allowed himself to read an American book. Neither of these unfortunate persons seemed to perceive, that, in thus disparaging the native genius, they were effectually sealing their own condemnation.

Europe—plant ourselves on the perfect eminence of a proud national will, and show our-selves not degenerate from the powerful and noble stocks from which we take our origin? This is a question not to be answered by the selfishness of the individual nature, unless it be in that generous sort of selfishness which is moved only by the highest promptings of ambi-tion. It is an argument addressed to all that is hopeful and proud in the hearts of an ardent and growing people. It is not addressed to the tradesman but to the man. We take it for granted, that we are not—in the scornful language of the European press,—a mere nation of shop-keepers[3]—that we have qualities of soul and genius, which if not yet developed in our moral constitution, are struggling to make themselves heard and felt;—that we have a pride of character,—growing stronger (as we trust) with the progress of each succeeding day,—which makes us anxious to realize for ourselves that position of independence, in all other departments, which we have secured by arms and in politics. Mere political secu-rity—the fact that we drink freely of the air around us, and at our own choosing partake of the fruits of the earth—is not enough,—constitutes but a small portion of the triumphs, and the objects of a rational nature. Nay, even political security is temporary, always inferior if not wholly uncertain, unless it be firmly based upon the certain and constant vigilance of the intellectual moral. A nation, properly to boast itself and to take and maintain its posi-tion with other States, must prove itself in possession of self-evolving attributes. Its charac-ter must be as individual as that of the noblest citizen that dwells within its limits. It must do its own thinking as well as its own fighting, for, as truly as all history has shown that the people who rely for their defence in battle upon foreign mercenaries inevitably become their prey, so the nation falls a victim to that genius of another, to which she passively defers. She must make, and not borrow or beg, her laws. Her institutions must grow out of her own condition and necessities, and not be arbitrarily framed upon those of others countries. Her poets and artists, to feel her wants, her hopes, her triumphs, must be born of the soil, and ar-dently devoted to its claims. To live, in fact, and secure the freedom of her children, a nation must live through them, in them, and by them,—by the strength of their arms, the purity of their morals, the vigour of their industry, and the wisdom of their minds. These are the essentials of a great nation, and no one of these qualities is perfectly available without the co-operation of the rest. And, as we adapt our warfare to the peculiarities of the country, and our industry to our climate, our resources and our soil, so the operations of the national mind must be suited to our characteristics. The genius of our people is required to declare it-self after a fashion of its own—must be influenced by its skies, and by those natural objects which familiarly address themselves to the senses from boyhood, and colour the fancies, and urge the thoughts, and shape the growing affections of the child to a something kindred with the things which he beholds. His whole soul must be imbued with sympathies caught from surrounding aspects within his infant horizon. The heart must be moulded to an in-tense appreciation of our woods and streams, our dense forests and deep swamps, our vast immeasurable mountains, our voluminous and tumbling waters. It must receive its higher moral tone from the exigencies of society, its traditions and its histories. Tutored at the knee of the grand-dame, the boy must grasp, as subjects of familiar and frequent consideration, the broken chronicles of senility, and shape them, as he grows older, into coherence and ef-fect. He must learn to dwell often upon the narratives of the brave fathers who first broke

---

[3]This language, originally applied by Napoleon to the English nation, at the very time when his highest ambition was to transfer to France a portion of that commerce upon which the great distinction and power of the rival country was built up,—has been transferred, by the latter, in a sense still more scornful, to our own. It is, perhaps, no bad sign of our successful progress as a nation, that our national enemy shows herself more angry with us than ever.

ground in the wilderness, who fought or treated with the red men, and who, finally, girded themselves up for the great conflict with the imperious mother who had sent them forth. These histories, making vivid impressions upon the pliant fancies of childhood, are the source of those vigorous shoots, of thought and imagination, which make a nation proud of its sons in turn, and which save her from becoming a by-word and reproach to other nations. In this, and from such impressions, the simplest records of a domestic history, expand into the most ravishing treasures of romance. But upon this subject let us hearken to the writer of the eloquent discourse before us.

> Literature, in its essence, is a spiritual immortality; no more than religion a creation of man; but, like the human soul, while enduring the mystery of its incarnation, is subject to the action of the elements, is the slave of circumstance. In the sense in which we would now view it, it is the expression of the spiritual part of our nature, in its intellectual action, whether taking form in philosophy, history, poetry, eloquence, or some other branch of thought. The sum of all this, in any nation, is what constitutes her literature, and it is always modified and coloured by the peculiarities about it. As the river, sliding under the sunset, imbibes for the time, the hues of the heavens, so the stream of literature receives, from the people through which it passes, not only the images and shadows of their condition, but the very force and direction of its current. Every literature, Greek or Roman, Arabic or English, French, Persian or German, acquired its qualities and impression from the circumstances of the time and people. The philosophic eye can readily detect the key, cause and secret of each, and expose the seminal principle from which they grew into their particular shape and fashion. The same scrutinizing analysis will enable us to determine the influences among ourselves, which are to operate in the formation of our literature; as well as to decide whether it will comport with those high spiritual requisitions which I have already avowed, should be demanded from it. Let us then attempt to see how Americanism will develop itself in Literature."[sic] pp. 11, 12.

There is something equally thoughtful and fanciful in the passage which follows. It betrays a mind as sensible to the picturesque, as it is searching and speculative. The writer proceeds to illustrate his proposition by glimpses of the physical material which our own country affords for the uses of the native poet.

> The physical atributes of our country are all partial to the loftiest manifestations of mind. Nature here presents her loveliest, sublimest aspects. For vastness of extent, grandeur of scenery, genial diversities of climate, and all that can munister to the comforts and tastes of man, this heritage of ours is without a parallel. In its mountains of stone and iron, its gigantic and far-reaching rivers, its inland seas, its forests of all woods, its picturesque and undulating prairies, in all its properties and proportions, it might well be considered, in comparison with the eastern hemisphere, the work of a more perfect and beneficent artist. To the eyes of the Genoese mariner, the wildest dreams of Diodorus and Plato were more than realized. Seneca sang,—

—— Venient annis
Sæcula series, quibus oceanus
Vincula rerum laxet, et ingens
Pateat tellus, Typhisque novos
Detegat orbes:

Yet, not even in the mirror of his prophetic fancy were these more than Elysian fields glossed with all their beauty and sublimity. Even the bilious British satirist, who could see no good in all our institutions, was compelled to confess that here

——Nature showed
The last ascending footsteps of the God!

Well nigh all this vast expanse of fruitfulness and beauty, too, has been subject to the control of civilized man. Our country has extended her jurisdiction over the fairest and most fertile regions. The rich bounty is poured into her lap, and breathes its influence upon her population. Their capacities are not pent and thwarted by the narrow limits which restrict the citizens of other countries. No speclative theorist, a Malthus, Stultz or Liceto, has cause here to apprehend the dangers of over-population. Room, bountiful room, is all about us, for humanity to breathe freely in, and to go on expanding in a long future. Do these things afford no promise of intellectual improvement? Are they no incitements to a lofty and expanded literature? Do they furnish no *matériel* for active, generous, elevated thought? Is there no voice coming out from all this fragrance and beauty and sublimity, appealing to the heart and fancy of man, for sympathy, utterance, embodiment? Why, it was once said, that the sky of Attica would make a Bœotian a poet; and we have seen even 'the red old hills of Georgia' draw inspiring melody from the heart of patriotic genius. Physical causes have always operated in the formation and fashioning of literature. In all the higher productions of mind, ancient and modern, we can easily recognize the influence of the climate and natural objects among which they were developed. The sunsets of Italy coloured the songs of Tasso and Petrarch; the vine-embowered fields of beautiful France are visible in all the pictures of Rousseau and La Martine; you may hear the solemn rustling of the Hartz forest, and the shrill horn of the wild huntsman throughout the creations of Schiller and Goethe; the sweet streamlets and sunny lakes of England smile upon you from the graceful verses of Spenser and Wordsworth; and the mist-robed hills of Scotland loom out in magnificence through the pages of Ossian, and the loftier visions of Marmion and Waverly.

Our country, then, must receive much of the character of her literature from her physical properties. If our minds are only original; if they be not base copyists, and servile echoes of foreign masters; if we can assert an intellectual as well as political independence; if we dare to think for ourselves, and faithfully picture forth, in our own styles of utterance, the impressions our minds shall receive from this great, fresh continent of beauty and sublimity; we can render to the world the most vigorous and picturesque literature it has ever beheld. Never had imagination nobler stimulants; never did nature look more encouragingly upon her geniune children. In poetry, romance, history and eloquence, what glorious objects, sights and sounds, for illustration and ornament! I have stood, down in Florida, beneath the overarching groves of magnolia, orange and myrtle, blending their fair flowers and voluptuous fragrance, and opening long vistas between their slender shafts, to where the green waters of the Mexican Gulf lapsed upon the silver-sanded beach, flinging up their light spray into the crimson beams of the declining sun, and I have thought that, for poetic beauty, for delicate inspiration, the scene was as sweet as ever wooed the eyes of a Grecian minstrel on the slopes of Parnassus, or around the fountains of Castaly.

Again: I have stood upon a lofty summit of the Alleghanies, among the splintered crags and vast gorges, where the eagle and the thunder make their home; and looked down upon an empire spread out in the long distance below. Far as the eye could reach, the broad forests swept away over territories of unexampled productiveness and beauty. At intervals, through the wide champaign, the domes and steeples of some fair town, which had sprung up with magical suddenness among the trees, would come out to the eye, giving evidence of the presence of a busy, thriving population. Winding away through the centre too, like a great artery of life to the scene, I could behold a noble branch of the Ohio, bearing upon its bosom the already active commerce of the region, and linking that spot with a thousand others, similar in their condition and character. As I thus stood, and thought of all that was being enacted in this glorious lannd of ours, and saw, in imagination, the stately centuries as they passed across the scene, diffusing wealth, prosperity and refinement, I could not but believe that it presented a nobler theatre, with sublimer accompaniment and inspirations, than ever rose upon the eye of a gazer from the summits of the Alps or the Appenines.

Such are some of the physical aspects of our country, and such the influence they are destined to have upon our national mind. Very evidently they constitute noble sources of inspiration, illustration and description. For all that part of literature which is drawn from the phases of nature, from the varying moods and phenomena of the outward world, the elements and the seasons, they will be more valuable than all the beauties of the Troad or Campania Felix. Rightly used, they would bring a freshness and spirit into the domain of high thought, which would revive it like a spring-time return, and we might take up, in a better hope, the exultation of Virgil,—

> Jam ultima ætas Cumali carmidis venit,
> Magnus ordo sæclorum nascitur abintegro,
> Et jam virgo redit Saturnia regna redeunt! pp. 12–17.

This is a long extract, but we have no apologies to make for it. Its pictures will interest, its grace, glow and eloquence, delight the reader, until he forgets its length. No one can question the fact that the scenery of a country has always entered largely into the inspiration of the native genius. The heart of the poet is apt to dwell frequently and fondly upon the regions on which the eyes of his youth first opened, with a rare acuteness of delight, even though these were wholly wanting in natural beauty and grossly barren of all the accessories of art. What then must be the effect upon the young genius where the scenery is beautiful or imposing in itself—distinguished by sweetness, grace and loveliness, or stirring deeper and sublimer sentiments by its wild and awe-compelling attributes. That our scenery has not yet found its painter on canvas or in fiction, is due to other than its own deficiencies. It must be our care to prove that it is not because the genius itself is not among us.

One remark may be offered here. In all probability, the merely descriptive poet will be among the latest productions of our land. Britain herself has not produced many poets of this order, nor do they rank, with the single exception of Thomson, among the very noble of her train. Bloomfield was a driveller, and the rank of Somerville is low. The genius of the Anglo-Saxon would seem to be too earnest, too intensely moral in its objects, for the consideration of still life except as subordinate to the action. He puts it in his story, as the painter upon his canvas, as a sort of back-ground, and he usually hurries from this sort of painting to that which better tasks his more exacting powers. In this characteristic the genius of the American is naturally like,—with this difference, that the circumstances of his career tends still more to increase his love of action and his disregard of mere adjuncts and dependencies. He has an aim, and, eager in its attainment, he pauses not to see how lovely is the lake and valley—how vast the mountain—how wild the gorge, how impetuous the foaming rush of the unbridled waters. If he sees or feels, it is but for an instant,—and he is driven forward, even as the cataract beneath his gaze, by a power of which he is himself unconscious, and in a direction, the goal of which he is not permitted to behold. Our orator has already, adequately and sufficiently, instanced the various charms of scenery which our country possesses. These will make themselves felt in due season, when the national mind is permitted to pause in its career of conflict—for such is the nature of its progress now—for a survey of its conquests and itself. We pass, with him, to other considerations of still more importance, as essential to Americanism in our Letters. The extract which we make is brief:

These pleasant anticipations are also justified in part, by the excellent and diversified character of the population of our country. Herein will reside one of the strong modifying influences of Americanism upon literature. Though our population is composed principally of the several varieties of the Anglo-Saxon stock, yet every other race of Europe, and some from the other continents, have contributed to swell the motley and singular combination. Coming from every quarter of the globe, they have brought with them their diverse manners, feelings, sentiments, and modes of thought, and fused them in the great American alembic. The stern, clear-headed, faith-abiding Puritan, the frank, chivalrous, imaginative Huguenot, the patient, deep-thoughted, contemplative German,—pilgrims from every clime, creed, and literature—are to be found in contact and intercourse here. They interact upon each other to fashion all the manifestations of society, in thought or deed. The contrasts and coincidences, they present under our institutions, afford new and graceful themes for the poet, the novelist and the philosopher; and the historian will have to give us pictures of life and humanity here, such as are found not elsewhere. I need but allude, in this connection, to the existence of three distinct races of men upon our continent, with their strongly marked peculiarities of condition, colour and history. The immense rapidity with which our numbers are increasing—well nigh doubling in every fifteen years!—will produce an unexampled demand for knowledge, and act as a powerful impetus to its elevation. Already has the great and fluctuating intermixture of our population had an influence upon the English language. In no part of the world is our mother tongue spoken with such general purity of pronunciation as in our country. The constant tide of internal emigration tends to rectify the provincialisms into which stationary communities so frequently fall. Otherwise is it even in England. The whole kingdom is broken up into dialects as numerous as her counties; and the respective inhabitants are almost as unintelligible to each other, as if they spoke languages radically distinct. Is it Utopian to expect the proudest results, when one common language shall be employed by the many millions who are to occupy this almost illimitable republic?—But it is in the strong, industrious and wholesome character of our population, that the best hope for our national mind depends. Their habits of life will generate a *muscularity* of intellect, becoming their position and destiny. No effeminacy of thought or feeling will be tolerated among a people, composed of the choicest varieties of every race, stimulating each other to mental exertion, and accumulating wealth and power with almost miraculous rapidity and extent. Such a people, if they should have no powerful impediments, are better fitted than any other to render the world an intellectual illumination, and to bring round in reality the poetic vision of the golden age. pp. 17–19

But the most imposing considerations arrayed by our author in this discussion, as indicative of the future resources of Americanism in our Literature, are to be found in those passages in which he considers the influence of our political institutions upon the mind of the country. It would afford us great pleasure did our limits suffice to give these passages, but we must content ourselves with a bare glance at their prominent suggestions. Mr. Meek justly draws our attention to the fact, that, of all the ancient tyrannies, but very few of them have contributed to the advancement of letters. He exhibits the baldness in literature of Chaldea, Babylon, Assyria and Phœnicia, and hurriedly compares their performances with the more glorious showings of the free states of the past. And he argues justly that this result is in the very nature of things;—that, as liberty of opinion is favourable to thought anf provocative of discussion, so almost must it favour the general development of intellect in all departments. The deduction is absolutely inevitable. Tyranny, on the other hand, always trembling for its sceptre, and jealous of every antagonist influence, watched with sleepless solicitude to impose every fetter upon the free speech of orator and poet. It would seem almost impertinent to insist upon these points, were it not that there really exists among thinking men a considerable difference of opinion upon them, and this difference of opinion is the natural fruit of a too hasty glance only at the surfaces. The friends of aristocracy, lingering fondly over those bright but unfrequent pages in literary history, as associated with a despotism, which are adorned by the works of genius, hurriedly conclude that they are the issues of that despotism itself. They point with confidence to such periods as those of Augustus Cæsar and Leo the Tenth. The courtly sway of the one, and the magnificent ambition of the other, are sufficient to delude the imagination, and hurry the reason aside from a consideration of the true analysis. They overlook the important fact that, in all these cases, it has so happened that men of literary tastes were themselves the despots. It was not that the despotism was itself favourable to such persons, but that the despotism, wielded by a particular hand, was not unwilling to smile with indulgence upon the obsequious poet, and the flattering painter. It so happened that an absolute tyrant was yet possessed of some of the higher sensibilities of the intellectual nature, and had almost as strong a passion for letters and the arts, as for political dominion. Thus feeling, he rendered the one passion in some degree subservient to the other. If it could be shown that his tastes were transmitted with his robes, to his successor, there might be some reason in the faith which we are required to have in the benignant literary influences of such a government; but the sufficient fact that, in the histories of despotism, these brief and beautiful periods shine out alone, and rest like green spots, at remote stages, through a long and lamentable wilderness, would seem to conclude the question.

It was the wealth and taste of the despot that made him a patron, and not because he held the reins of government with a rigorous or easy hand. The peculiar sort of rule in Rome and Italy had no part in making the poet or historian; and, for the patronage itself, accorded by the despot, let the reader turn to the histories of denied and defrauded genius, and see what a scorned and wretched beggar it has ever been in the courts of Aristocracy. Let him look to the history of Tasso for example—let him turn to that curious book of Benvenuto Cellini,—if he would see what sort of countenance is that which mere power is apt to bestow upon the labours of the man of letters or of art. Great wealth,—that of private persons—has done for them much more in every nation. Spenser owed much more to Sydney, and Shakspeare to Southhampton, than either of them ever owed to Elizabeth. We need not multiply examples. The man of genius, in all departments, has achieved his triumphs rather in despite and defiance of despotism than because of its benign and genial atmosphere. The true patron of letters is the lover of them, and where are these persons likely to be more numerous, than in regions where the great body of the people are lifted by the political institutions of the country into a responsibility which tasks the intellect, and requires a certain amount of knowledge in every department. The despotism is apt to absorb in itself all the taste and intellect where it governs. Democracy naturally diffuses them. At first, the diffusion would seem to lessen the amount of the whole,—to subtract from its spirit—reduce its volume, and, by too minute division of its parts, to render it feeble and inert for active purposes. But the constant attrition of rival minds in a country where the great body of the people are forced into consideration, strengthens and informs, with a peculiar and quickening vigour, each several share of that capacity with which the genius of the nation was at first endowed. The genius of the nation does not the less act together, because it acts through many rather than through one; and, by insensible transitions, the whole multitude rise to the same elevated platform, upon which, at the beginning, we may have beheld but one leading mind, and that, possibly, borrowed from a rival nation. It is a wondrous impulse to the individual, to his hope, his exertions and his final success, to be taught that there is nothing in his way, in the nature of the society in which he lives;—that he is not to be denied because of his birth or poverty, because of his wealth or his family;—that he stands fair with his comrades, on the same great arena,—with no social if no natural impediments,—and that the prize is always certain for the fleetest in the race.

This must be the natural influence of the democratic principle upon the minds of a people by whose political institutions its supremacy is recognized. Let no man deceive himself by a glance confined only to the actual condition of things around him. No doubt that, in the beginning of a democracy, in that first wild transition state, which follows upon the overthrow of favourite and long acknowledged authorities, art and literature, alarmed at the coil and clamour, will shroud themselves in their cells, venturing abroad only in those dim hours of dusk and twilight, in which a comparative silence promises comparative security. But this is also the history of nearly all of the arts of peace. Commerce and trade, mechanical and mercantile adventure, show themselves nearly equally timid. True, they are the first to recover from their panic, but this is solely because they belong to the more servile and earthly necessities of our nature. They are followed by the gradual steps of art and science, and these in turn by the lovelier and gentler offspring of united grace and muse. It is the error of persons of taste that, shrinking themselves from the uproar of this transition period, they regard its effects as likely to continue, as being not temporary only, and as destined to perpetuate the commotion which, in our notion, is nothing more than that natural outbreak of elements in the moral, which, in the natural world, almost always harbingers a clear sky and pure, salubrious and settled weather. Such, when the time comes,—when the first rude necessities of a new condition are pacified, and the machine begins to turn evenly and smoothly upon its axis,—such will be the working of democracy. This is not less our faith than our hope. The natural conclusions of reason led us directly to this confidence, even if the history of the past did not afford us sufficient guaranties for the future.

Our orator next instances, with effect, the wholesome influences in our government of the "let alone" principle. This, by the way, is an important matter to be understood. Democracy goes into society, with scarcely any farther desire than that men should be protected from one another—left free to the pursuit of happiness, each in the form and manner most agreeable to himself, so long as he does not trespass upon a solitary right of his neighbour. This is the principle. We do not tolerate any interference of government with those employments of its citizens which violate none of the rights of others, and which do not offend against the sense of a Christian country. To protect or to disparage that occupation of the individual or the community, which, in itself, is regarded as legitimate, is a power which, according to our construction of the social contract in America, is wholly unwarranted by our laws. Something is due certainly to the necessities of the whole; but, for the "general welfare" principle, we insist that the "general necessity and exigency" is the true standard by which we impose restraints, or hold out encouragements. Mr. Meek properly insists upon the value of this "let alone" practice, on the part of government, as vastly promotive of the interests of literature; and particularly dwells upon the advantages, in this regard, which grow out of our system of confederated sovereignties. The very inequalities of things in moral respects, in employments, in climate, soil and circumstance, which we find in these severalties, is at once calculated to provoke the mind in each to exertion, and to endow it with originality. There is none of that even tenor of aspect, in the genius of the country, which somewhat monotonously distinguishes an empire the whole energies of which spring from centralization. A natural rivalry and emulation are the consequence of a form of political independence, which, in all domestic subjects, leaves us utterly free to our own pursuits. We watch the progress of our neighbour, and strive rather to surpass than to follow. There is none of that servile, blind adhesion to a superior, which, in Europe, invariably brings the popular intellect, even in the most remote dependencies of the nation, to the beaten tracks which conduct them to the centre. The very divergencies of our paths are favourable to the boldness, the freedom and the flights of the national intellect. We make our own paths—we trace our out own progress—and, just in due degree as we turn aside from the dictation of those great cities, which, among us, are more immediately allied with the marts of Europe, so do we discover marks of the most certain freshness and originality, though coupled with rudeness and irregularity—a harshness which offends and a wilderness which, we are encouraged to believe, it is not beyond the power of time and training to subdue to equable and noble exercises. To any one who looks into the character of our people,—who passes below the surface, and sees in what way the great popular heart beats in the several States of the confederacy,—with what calm, consistent resolve in some—with what impatient heat in others—how cold but how clear in this region,—how fiery, but how clouded in that;—there will be ample promise for the future, not only in the value of the material, but in its exquisite and rich variety. And, even on the surface, how these varieties speak out for themselves, so that it shall not be difficult for a shrewd observer of men to distinguish at a glance, and to declare from what quarter of America the stranger comes,—whether from the banks of the Charles or the Hudson, the Savannah or the Mississippi.

Our orator justly reminds us, while treating of this part of his subject, that, by our compact, the interests of education and literature are left entirely in the control of the States. This vital matter is in our own hands, and nothing but our lachesse or our wilfulness, can possibly lose us the power of moulding the temper of our people in due compliance with our peculiar circumstances, whether moral or physical. We may make our literature what we please if we do not neglect the interests of education. We should confer upon it all the becoming characteristics of our section—our social sympathies, our political temper, and those moral hues and forms which the intellectual nature so happily imbibes from the aspects which surround us in the natural world. The airy structures of our imagination, born of a like sky and atmosphere with that of Greece, should not shrink from comparison with those of Dodona and Hymettus. Our Olympus rises at our will, and the divine spirits which we summon to make sacred its high abodes, clothed in a political freedom superior to that of Athens, with less danger of having their supremacy disputed and their rites disturbed, should surely bring to their altars a priesthood no less great and glorious.   [1845]

Margaret Fuller

American Literature

From *Papers on Literature and Art*

ITS POSITION IN THE PRESENT TIME, AND PROSPECTS FOR THE FUTURE

Some thinkers may object to this essay, that we are about to write of that which has as yet no existence.

For it does not follow because many books are written by persons born in America that there exists an American literature. Books which imitate or represent the thoughts and life of Europe do not constitute an American literature. Before such can exist, an original idea must animate this nation and fresh currents of life must call into life fresh thoughts along its shores.

We have no sympathy with national vanity. We are not anxious to prove that there is as yet much American literature. Of those who think and write among us in the methods and of the thoughts of Europe, we are not impatient; if their minds are still best adapted to such food and such action. If their books express life of mind and character in graceful forms, they are good and we like them. We consider them as colonists and useful school-masters to our people in a transition state; which lasts rather longer than is occupied in passing bodily the ocean which separates the New from the Old World.

We have been accused of an undue attachment to foreign continental literature, and it is true that in childhood we had well nigh "forgotten our English" while constantly reading in other languages. Still what we loved in the literature of continental Europe was the range and force of ideal manifestation in forms of national and individual greatness. A model was before us in the great Latins of simple masculine minds seizing upon life with unbroken power. The stamp both of nationality and individuality was very strong upon them; their lives and thoughts stood out in clear and bold relief. The English character has the iron force of the Latins, but not the frankness and expansion. Like their fruits, they need a summer sky to give them more sweetness and a richer flavor. This does not apply to Shakespeare, who has all the fine side of English genius, with the rich coloring and more fluent life of the Catholic countries. Other poets of England also are expansive more or less, and soar freely to seek the blue sky, but take it as a whole, there is in English literature, as in English character, a reminiscence of walls and ceilings, a tendency to the arbitrary and conventional that repels a mind trained in admiration of the antique spirit. It is only in later days that we are learning to prize the peculiar greatness which a thousand times outweighs this fault, and which has enabled English genius to go forth from its insular position and conquer such vast dominion in the realms both of matter and of mind.

Yet there is often between child and parent a reaction from excessive influence having been exerted, and such a one we have experienced in behalf of our country against England. We use her language and receive in torrents the influence of her thought, yet it is in many respects uncongenial and injurious to our constitution. What suits Great Britain, with her insular position and consequent need to concentrate and intensify her life, her limited monarchy and spirit of trade, does not suit a mixed race continually enriched with new blood from other stocks the most unlike that of our first descent, with ample field and verge enough to range in and leave every impulse free, and abundant opportunity to develop a genius wide and full as our rivers, flowery, luxuriant, and impassioned as our vast prairies, rooted in strength as the rocks on which the Puritan fathers landed.

That such a genius is to rise and work in this hemisphere we are confident; equally so that scarce the first faint streaks of that day's dawn are yet visible. It is sad for those that foresee, to know they may not live to share its glories, yet it is sweet, too, to know that every act and word uttered in the light of that foresight may tend to hasten or ennoble its fulfillment.

That day will not rise till the fusion of races among us is more complete. It will not rise till this nation shall attain sufficient moral and intellectual dignity to prize moral and intellectual no less highly than political freedom, not till the physical resources of the country being explored, all its regions studded with towns, broken by the plow, netted together by railways and telegraph lines, talent shall be left at leisure to turn its energies upon the higher department of man's existence. Nor then shall it be seen till from the leisurely and yearning soul of that riper time national ideas shall take birth, ideas craving to be clothed in a thousand fresh and original forms.

Without such ideas all attempts to construct a national literature must end in abortions like the monster of Frankenstein, things with forms and the instincts of forms, but soulless and therefore revolting. We cannot have expression till there is something to be expressed.

The symptoms of such a birth may be seen in a longing felt here and there for the sustenance of such ideas. At present it shows itself, where felt, in sympathy with the prevalent tone of society by attempts at external action, such as are classed under the head of social reform. But it needs to go deeper before we can have poets, needs to penetrate beneath the springs of action, to stir and remake the soil as by the action of fire.

Another symptom is the need felt by individuals of being even sternly sincere. This is the one great means by which alone progress can be essentially furthered. Truth is the nursing mother of genius. No man can be absolutely true to himself, eschewing cant, compromise, servile imitation, and complaisance, without becoming original, for there is in every creature a fountain of life which, if not choked back by stones and other dead rubbish, will create a fresh atmosphere and bring to life fresh beauty. And it is the same with the nation as with the individual man.

The best work we do for the future is by such truth. By use of that in whatever way, we harrow the soil and lay it open to the sun and air. The winds from all quarters of the globe bring seed enough, and there is nothing wanting but preparation of the soil and freedom in the atmosphere, for ripening of a new and golden harvest.

We are sad that we cannot be present at the gathering-in of this harvest. And yet we are joyous too, when we think that though our name may not be writ on the pillar of our country's fame, we can really do far more towards rearing it than those who come at a later period and to a seemingly fairer task. *Now,* the humblest effort, made in a noble spirit and with religious hope, cannot fail to be even infinitely useful. Whether we introduce some noble model from another time and clime to encourage aspiration in our own, or cheer into blossom the simplest wood-flower that ever rose from the earth, moved by the genuine impulse to grow, independent of the lures of money or celebrity; whether we speak boldly when fear or doubt keep others silent, or refuse to swell the popular cry upon an unworthy occasion, the spirit of truth, purely worshiped, shall turn our acts and forbearances alike to profit, informing them with oracles which the latest time shall bless.

Under present circumstances the amount of talent and labor given to writing ought to surprise us. Literature is in this dim and struggling state, and its pecuniary results exceedingly pitiful. From many well-known causes it is impossible for ninety-nine out of the hundred who wish to use the pen to ransom by its use the time they need. This state of things will have to be changed in some way. No man of genius writes for money; but it is essential to the free use of his powers that he should be able to disembarrass his life from care and perplexity. This is very difficult here; and the state of things gets worse and worse, as less and less is offered in pecuniary meed for works demanding great devotion of time and labor (to say nothing of the ether engaged) and the publisher, obliged to regard the transaction as a matter of business, demands of the author to give him only what will find an immediate market, for he cannot afford to take anything else. This will not do! When an immortal poet was secure only of a few copyists to circulate his works, there were princes and nobles to patronize literature and the arts. Here is only the public, and the public must learn how to cherish the nobler and rarer plants, and to plant the aloe, able to wait a hundred years for its bloom, or its garden will contain presently nothing but potatoes and potherbs. We shall have in the course of the next two or three years a convention of authors to inquire into the causes of this state of things and propose measures for its remedy. Some have already been thought of that look promising, but we shall not announce them till the time be ripe; that date is not distant, for the difficulties increase from day to day in consequence of the system of cheap publication on a great scale.

The ranks that led the way in the first half century of this republic were far better situated than we, in this respect. The country was not so deluged with the dingy page reprinted from Europe, and patriotic vanity was on the alert to answer the question, "Who reads an American book?" And many were the books written as worthy to be read as any out of the first class in England. They were, most of them, except in their subject matter, English books.

The list is large, and in making some cursory comments we do not wish to be understood as designating *all* who are worthy of notice, but only those who present themselves to our minds with some special claims. In history there has been nothing done to which the world at large has not been eager to award the full meed of its deserts. Mr. Prescott for instance has been greeted with as much warmth abroad as here. We are not disposed to undervalue his industry and power of clear and elegant arrangement. The richness and freshness of his materials is such that a sense of enchantment must be felt in their contemplation. We must regret, however, that they should have been first presented to the public by one who possesses nothing of the higher powers of the historian, great leading views or discernment as to the motives of action and the spirit of an era. Considering the splendor of the materials, the books are wonderfully tame, and everyone must feel that having once passed through them and got the sketch in the mind, there is nothing else to which it will recur. The absence of thought as to that great picture of Mexican life, with its heroisms, its terrible but deeply significant superstitions, its admirable civic refinement, seems to be quite unbroken.

Mr. Bancroft is a far more vivid writer; he has great resources and great command of them, and leading thoughts by whose aid he groups his facts. But we cannot speak fully of his historical works, which we have only read and referred to here and there.

In the department of ethics and philosophy we may inscribe two names as likely to live and be blessed and honored in the later time. These are the names of Channing and of Emerson.

Dr. Channing had several leading thoughts which corresponded with the wants of his time, and have made him in it a father of thought. His leading idea of the "dignity of human nature" is one of vast results, and the peculiar form in which he advocated it had a great work to do in this new world. The spiritual beauty of his writings is very great; they are all distinguished for sweetness, elevation, candor, and a severe devotion to truth. On great questions he took middle ground and sought a panoramic view; he wished also to stand high, yet never forgot what was above more than what was around and beneath him. He was not well acquainted with man on the impulsive and passionate side of his nature, so that his view of character was sometimes narrow, but it was always noble. He exercised an expansive and purifying power on the atmosphere, and stands a godfather at the baptism of this country.

The Sage of Concord has a very different mind, in everything except that he has the same disinterestedness and dignity of purpose, the same purity of spirit. He is a profound thinker. He is a man of ideas, and deals with causes rather than effects. His ideas are illustrated from a wide range of literary culture and refined observation, and embodied in a style whose melody and subtle fragrance enchant those who stand stupefied before the thought themselves, because their utmost depths do not enable them to sound his shallows. His influence does not yet extend over a wide space; he is too far beyond his place and his time to be felt at once or in full, but it searches deep, and yearly widens its circles. He is a harbinger of the better day. His beautiful elocution has been a great aid to him in opening the way for the reception of his written word.

In that large department of literature which includes descriptive sketches, whether of character or scenery, we are already rich. Irving, a genial and fair nature, just what he ought to be and would have been at any time of the world, has drawn the scenes amid which his youth was spent in their primitive lineaments, with all the charms of his graceful jocund humor. He has his niche and need never be deposed; it is not one that another could occupy.

The first enthusiasm about Cooper having subsided, we remember more his faults than his merits. His ready resentment and way of showing it in cases which it is the wont of gentlemen to pass by in silence or meet with a good-humored smile have caused unpleasant associations with his name, and his fellow-citizens, in danger of being tormented by suits for libel if they spoke freely of him, have ceased to spaek of him at all. But neither these causes, nor the baldness of his plots, shallowness of thought, and poverty in the presentation of character, should make us forget the grandeur and originality of his sea-sketches, nor the redemption from oblivion of our forest-scenery, and the noble romance of the hunter-pioneer's life. Already, but for him, this fine page of life's romance would be almost forgotten. He has done much to redeem these irrevocable beauties from the corrosive acid of a semi-civilized invasion.*

Miss Sedgwick and others have portrayed with skill and feeling scenes and personages from the revolutionary time. Such have a permanent value in proportion as their subject if fleeting. The same charm attends the spirited delineations of Mrs. Kirkland, and that amusing book, *A New Purchase.* The features of Hoosier, Sucker, and Wolverine life are worth fixing; they are peculiar to the soil and indicate its hidden treasures; they have also that charm which simple life lived for its own sake always has, even in rude and all but brutal forms.

What shall we say of the poets? The list is scanty; amazingly so, for there is nothing in the causes that paralyze other kinds of literature that could affect lyrical and narrative poetry. Men's hearts beat, hope, and suffer always, and they must crave such means to vent them; yet of the myriad leaves garnished with smooth, stereotyped rhymes that issue yearly from our press, you will not find, one time in a million, a little piece written from any such impulse or with the least sincerity or sweetness of tone. They are written for the press in the spirit of imitation or vanity, the paltriest offspring of the human brain, for the heart disclaims, as the ear is shut against them. This is the kind of verse which is

---

* Since writing the above we have read some excellent remarks by Mr. W. G. Simms on the writings of Cooper. We think the reasons are given for the powerful interest excited by Hawkeye and the Pilot, with great discrimination and force.

"They both think and feel, with a highly individual nature, that has been taught, by constant contemplation, in scenes of solitude. The vast unbroken ranges of forest to its one lonely occupant press upon the mind with the same sort of solemnity which one feels condemned to a life of partial isolation upon the ocean. Both are permitted that degree of commerce with their fellow beings, which suffices to maintain in strength the sweet and sacred sources of their humanity. . . . The very isolation to which, in the most successful of his stories, Mr. Cooper subjects his favorite personages, is, alone, a proof of his strength and genius. While the ordinary writer, the man of mere talent, is compelled to look around him among masses for his material, he contents himself with one man, and flings him upon the wilderness. The picture, then, which follows, must be one of intense individuality. Out of this one man's nature, his moods and fortunes, he spins his story. The agencies and dependencies are few. With self-reliance which is only found in true genius, he goes forward into the wilderness, whether of land or ocean; and the vicissitudes of either region, acting upon the natural resources of one man's mind, furnish the whole material of his work-shop. This mode of performance is highly dramatic, and thus it is that his scout, his trapper, his hunter, his pilot, all live to our eyes and thoughts, the perfect ideals of moral individuality."—*Views and Reviews* by W. G. Simms.

cherished by the magazines as a correspondent to the tawdry pictures of smiling milliners' dolls in the frontispiece. Like these they are only a fashion, a fashion based on no reality of love or beauty. The inducement to write them consists in a little money, or more frequently the charm of seeing an anonymous name printed at the top in capitals.

We must here in passing advert also to the style of story current in the magazines, flimsy beyond any texture that was ever spun or even dreamed of by the mind of man in any other age and country. They are said to be "written for the seamstresses," but we believe that every-way injured class could relish and digest better fare even at the end of long days of exhausting labor. There are exceptions to this censure; stories by Mrs. Child have been published in the magazines, and now and then good ones by Mrs. Stephens and others; but take them generally, they are calculated to do a positive injury to the public mind, acting as an opiate, and of an adulterated kind too.

But to return to the poets. At their head Mr. Bryant stands alone. His range is not great, nor his genius fertile. But his poetry is purely the language of his inmost nature, and the simple lovely garb in which his thoughts are arranged, a direct gift from the Muse. He has written nothing that is not excellent, and the atmosphere of his verse refreshes and composes the mind, like leaving the highway to enter some green lovely fragrant wood.

Halleck and Willis are poets of society. Though the former has written so little, yet that little is full of fire—elegant, witty, delicate in sentiment. It is an honor to the country that these occasional sparks struck off from the flint of commercial life should have kindled so much flame as they have. It is always a consolation to see one of them sparkle amid the rubbish of daily life. One of his poems has been published within the last year, written in fact long ago but new to most of us, and it enlivened the literary thoroughfare as a green wreath might some dusty, musty hall of legislation.

Willis has not the same terseness or condensed electricity. But he has grace, spirit, at times a winning pensiveness, and a lively though almost wholly sensuous delight in the beautiful.

Dana has written so little that he would hardly be seen in a more thickly garnished galaxy. But the masculine strength of feeling, the solemn tenderness and refined thought displayed in such pieces as the "Dying Raven" and the "Husband and Wife's Grave" have left a deep impression on the popular mind.

Longfellow is artificial and imitative. He borrows incessantly, and mixes what he borrows, so that it does not appear to the best advantage. He is very faulty in using broken or mixed metaphors. The ethical part of his writing has a hollow, secondhand sound. He has, however, elegance, a love of the beautiful, and a fancy for what is large and manly, if not a full sympathy with it. His verse breathes at times much sweetness; and if not allowed to supersede what is better, may promote a taste for good poetry. Though imitative, he is not mechanical.

We cannot say as much for Lowell, who, we must declare it, though to the grief of some friends and the disgust of more, is absolutely wanting in the true spirit and tone of poesy. His interest in the moral questions of the day has supplied the want of vitality in himself; his great facility at versification has enabled him to fill the ear with a copious stream of pleasant sound. But his verse is stereotyped; his thought sounds no depth; and posterity will not remember him.

R. W. Emerson, in melody, in subtle beauty of thought and expression, takes the highest rank upon this list. But his poems are mostly philosophical, which is not the truest kind of poetry. They want the simple force of nature and passion, and while they charm the ear and interest the mind, fail to wake far-off echoes in the heart. The imagery wears a symbolical air, and serves rather as illustration than to delight us by fresh and glowing forms of life.

We must here mention one whom the country has not yet learned to honor, perhaps never may, for he wants artistic skill to give complete form to his inspiration. This is William Ellery Channing, nephew and namesake of Dr. C., a volume of whose poems, published three or four years ago in Boston, remains unknown except to a few friends, nor if known would they probably excite sympathy, as those which have been published in the periodicals have failed to do so. Yet some of the purest tones of the lyre are his, the finest inspirations as to the feelings and passions of men, deep spiritual insight, and an entire originality in the use of his means. The frequently unfinished and obscure state of his poems, a passion for forcing words out of their usual meaning into one which they may appropriately bear, but which comes upon the reader with an unpleasing and puzzling surprise, may repel at first glance from many of these poems, but do not mar the following sublime description of the beings we want to rule, to redeem, to recreate this nation, and under whose reign alone can there be an American literature, for then only could we have life worth recording. The simple grandeur of this poem as a whole must be felt by every-one, while each line and thought will be found worthy of earnest contemplation and satis-faction after the most earnest life and thought.

> Hearts of Eternity! hearts of the deep!
> Proclaim from land to sea your mighty fate;
> How that for you no living comes too late;
> How ye cannot in Theban labyrinth creep;
> How ye great harvests from small surface reap;
> Shout, excellent band, in grand primeval strain,
> Like midnight winds that foam along the main,
> And do all things rather than pause to weep.
> A human heart knows naught of littleness,
> Suspects no man, compares with no man's ways,
> Hath in one hour most glorious length of days,
> A recompense, a joy, a loveliness;
> Like eaglet keen, shoots into azure far,
> And always dwelling nigh is the remotest star.

A series of poems called "Man in the Republic," by Cornelius Mathews, deserves a higher meed of sympathy than it has received. The thoughts and views are strong and noble, the exhibition of them imposing. In plastic power this writer is deficient. His prose works sin in exuberance, and need consolidating and chastening. We find fine things, but not so arranged as to be seen in the right places and by the best light. In his poems Mr. Mathews is unpardonably rough and rugged; the poetic substance finds no musical medium in which to flow. Yet there *is* poetic substance which makes full chords, if not a harmony. He holds a worthy sense of the vocation of the poet, and worthily expresses it thus:

> To strike or bear, to conquer or to yield
> Teach thou! O topmost crown of duty, teach,
> What fancy whispers to the listening ear,
> At hours when tongue nor taint of care impeach
> The fruitful calm of greatly silent hearts;
> When all the stars for happy thought are set,
> And, in the secret chambers of the soul,
> All blessed powers of joyful truth are met;
> Though calm and garlandless thou mayst appear,
> The world shall know thee for its crowned seer.

A considerable portion of the hope and energy of this country still turns towards, the drama, that greatest achievement when wrought to perfection of human power. For ourselves, we believe the day of the regular drama to be past; and though we recognize the need of some kind of spectacle and dramatic representation to be absolutely coincident with an animated state of the public mind, we have thought that the opera, ballet, pantomime, and briefer, more elastic forms, like the *vaudeville* of the French theater or the *proverb* of the social party, would take the place of elaborate tragedy and comedy.

But those who find the theaters of this city well filled all the year round by an audience willing to sit out the heroisms of Rolla, and the sentimentalism and stale morality of such a piece as we were doomed to listen to while the Keans were here (*Town and Country* was its name), still think there is room for the regular drama, if genius should engage in its creation. Accordingly there have been in this country, as well as in England, many attempts to produce dramas suitable for action no less than for the closet. The actor Murdoch, about to devote himself with enthusiasm and hope to prop up a falling profession, is to bring out a series of plays written not merely *for* him, but because his devotion is likely to furnish fit occasion for their appearance. The first of these, *Witchcraft, a Tragedy,* brought out successfully upon the boards at Philadelphia, we have read, and it is a work of strong and majestic lineaments; a fine originality is shown in the conception by which the love of a son for a mother is made a sufficient *motiv* (as the Germans call the ruling impulse of a work) in the production of tragic interest; no less original is the attempt, and delightful the success, in making an aged woman a satisfactory heroine to the piece through the greatness of her soul, and the magnetic influence it exerts on all around her, till the ignorant and superstitious fancy that the sky darkens and the winds wait upon her as she walks on the lonely hillside near her hut to commune with the past and seek instruction from Heaven. The working of her character on the other agents of the piece is depicted with force and nobleness. The deep love of her son for her; the little tender, simple ways in which he shows it, having preserved the purity and poetic spirit of childhood by never having been weaned from his first love, a mother's love; the anguish of his soul when he too becomes infected with distrust, and cannot discriminate the natural magnetism of a strong nature from the spells and lures of sorcery; the final triumph of his faith; all offered the highest scope to genius and the power of moral perception in the actor. There are highly poetic intimations of those lowering days with their veiled skies, brassy light, and sadly whispering winds, very common in Massachusetts, so ominous and brooding seen from any point, but from the idea of witchcraft, invested with an awful significance. We do not know, however, that this could bring it beyond what it has appeared to our own sane mind, as if the air was thick with spirits in an equivocal and surely sad condition, whether of purgatory or downfall; and the air was vocal with all manner of dark intimations. We are glad to see this mood of nature so fitly characterized.

The sweetness and naïveté with which the young girl is made to describe the effects of love upon her, as supposing them to proceed from a spell, are also original, and there is no other way in which this revelation could have been induced that would not have injured the beauty of the character and position. Her visionary sense of her lover as an ideal figure is of a high order of poetry, and these facts have very seldom been brought out from the cloisters of the mind into the light of open day.

The play is very deficient as regards rhythm; indeed we might say there is no apparent reason why the lines should begin with capital letters. The minor personages are mere caricatures, very coarsely drawn; all the power is concentrated on the main characters and their emotions. So did not Shakespeare, does not ever the genuine dramatist, whose mind teems with "the fullness of forms." As Raphael in his most crowded groups can put in no misplaced or imperfect foot or hand, neither neglect to invest the least important figure of his backgrounds with every characteristic trait, nor spare the invention of the most beautiful *coiffure* and accessories for the humblest handmaid of his Madonnas, so doth the great artist always clothe the whole picture with full and breathing life, for it appears so before his mental eye. But minds not perfectly artistic, yet of strong conceptions, subordinate the rest to one or two leading figures, and the imperfectly represented life of the others incloses them as in a frame.

In originality of conception and resting the main interest upon force of character in a woman, this drama naturally leads us to revert to a work in the department of narrative fiction, which on similar grounds comes to us as a harbinger of the new era. This book is *Margaret, or the Real and Ideal,* a work which has appeared within the past year; and, considering its originality and genuineness, has excited admiration and sympathy amazingly soon. Even some leading reviews of what Byron used to speak of as the "garrison" class (a class the most opposite imaginable to that of Garrison abolitionists) have discussed its pretensions and done homage to its merits. It is a work of great power and richness, a genuine disclosure of the life of mind and the history of character. Its descriptions of scenery and the common people, in the place and time it takes up, impart to it the highest value as a representative of transient existence which had a great deal of meaning. The beautiful simplicity of action upon and within the mind of Margaret, Heaven lying so clearly about her in the infancy of the hut of drunkards, the woods, the village, and their ignorant, simply human denizens; her unconscious growth to the stature of womanhood, the flow of life impelled by her, the spiritual intimations of her dreams; the prophecies of music in the character of Chilion; the naïve discussion of the leading reform movements of the day in their rudimental forms; the archness, the humor, the profound religious faith, make of this book an aviary from which doves shall go forth to discover and report of all the green spots of promise in the land. Of books like this, as good and still better, our new literature shall be full; and though one swallow does not make a summer, yet we greet in this one "Yankee novel" the sufficient earnest of riches that only need the skill of competent miners to be made current for the benefit of man.

Meanwhile the most important part of our literature, while the work of diffusion is still going on, lies in the journals which monthly, weekly, daily send their messages to every corner of this great land, and form at present the only efficient instrument for the general education of the people.

Among these, the magazines take the lowest rank. Their object is principally to cater for the amusement of vacant hours, and as there is not a great deal of wit and light talent in this country, they do not even this to much advantage. More wit, grace, and elegant trifling embellish the annals of literature in one day of France than in a year of America.

The reviews are more able. If they cannot compare on equal terms with those of France, England, and Germany, where if genius be rare, at least a vast amount of talent and culture is brought to bear upon all the departments of knowledge, they are yet very creditable to a new country where so large a portion of manly ability must be bent on making laws, making speeches, making railroads and canals. They are, however, much injured by a partisan spirit and the fear of censure from their own public. This last is always slow death to a journal; its natural and only safe position is to *lead;* if instead it bows to the will of the multitude, it will find the ostracism of democracy far more dangerous than the worst censure of a tyranny could be. It is not half so dangerous to a man to be immured in a dungeon alone with God and his own clear conscience as to walk the streets fearing the scrutiny of a thousand eyes, ready to veil with anxious care whatever may not suit the many-headed monster in its momentary mood. Gentleness is dignified but caution is debasing; only a noble fearlessness can give wings to the mind, with which to soar beyond the common ken and learn what may be of use to the crowd below. Writers have nothing to do but to love truth fervently, seek justice according to their ability, and then express what is in the mind; they have nothing to do with consequences, God will take care of those. The want of such noble courage, such faith in the power of truth and good desire, paralyzes mind greatly in this country. Publishers are afraid; authors are afraid; and if a worthy resistance is not made by religious souls, there is danger that all the light will soon be put under bushels, lest some wind should waft from it a spark that may kindle dangerous fire.

For want of such faith, and the catholic spirit that flows from it, we have no great leading review. The *North American* was once the best. While under the care of Edward Everett, himself a host in extensive knowledge, grace and adroitness in applying it, and the power of enforcing grave meanings by a light and flexible satire that tickled while it wounded, it boasted more force, more life, a finer scope of power. But now though still exhibiting ability and information upon special points, it is entirely deficient in great leadings and the *vivida vis,* but ambles and jogs at an old gentlemanly pace along a beaten path that leads to no important goal.

Several other journals have more life, energy, and directness than this, but there is none which occupies a truly great and commanding position, a beacon-light to all who sail that way. In order to do this, a journal must know how to cast aside all local and temporary considerations when new convictions command, and allow free range in its columns to all kinds of ability and all ways of viewing subjects. That would give it a life rich, bold, various.

The life of intellect is becoming more and more determined to the weekly and daily papers, whose light leaves fly so rapidly and profusely over the land. Speculations are afloat as to the influence of the electric telegraph upon their destiny, and it seems obvious that it should raise their character by taking from them in some measure the office of gathering and dispersing the news, and requiring of them rather to arrange and interpret it.

This mode of communication is susceptible of great excellence in the way of condensed essay, narrative, criticism, and is the natural receptacle for the lyrics of the day. That so few good ones deck the poet's corner, is because the indifference or unfitness of editors as to choosing and refusing makes this place at present undesirable to the poet. It might be otherwise.

The means which this organ affords of diffusing knowledge and sowing the seeds of thought where they may hardly fail of an infinite harvest, cannot be too highly prized by the discerning and benevolent. Minds of the first class are generally indisposed to this kind of writing; what must be done on the spur of the occasion and cast into the world so incomplete, as the hurried offspring of a day or hour's labor must generally be, cannot satisfy their judgment or do justice to their powers. But he who looks to the benefit of others and sees with what rapidity and ease instruction and thought are assimilated by men, when they come thus as it were on the wings of the wind, may be content, as an unhonored servant to the grand purposes of Destiny, to work in such a way at the Pantheon which the ages shall complete, on which his name may not be inscribed but which will breathe the life of his soul.

The confidnece in uprightness of intent and the safety of truth is still more needed here than in the more elaborate kinds of writing, as meanings cannot be fully explained nor expressions revised. Newspaper-writing is next door to conversation, and should be conducted on the same principles. It has this advantage: we address not our neighbor, who forces us to remember his limitations and prejudices, but the ideal presence of human nature as we feel it ought to be and trust it will be. We address America rather than Americans.

A worthy account of the vocation and duties of the journalist is given by Cornelius Mathews. Editors generally could not do better than every New Year's Day to read and insert the following verses.

> As shakes the canvas of a thousand ships,
>   Struck by a heavy land-breeze, far at sea,
> Ruffle the thousand broad sheets of the land,
>   Filled with the people's breath of potency.
>
> A thousand images the hour will take,
>   From him who strikes, who rules, who speaks, who sings,
> Many within the hour their grave to make,
>   Many to live, far in the heart of things.
>
> A dark-dyed spirit he, who coins the time,
>   To virtue's wrong, in base disloyal lies,
> Who makes the morning's breath, the evening's tide,
>   The utterer of his blighting forgeries.
>
> How beautiful who scatters, wide and free,
>   The gold-bright seeds of loved and loving truth!
> By whose perpetual hand, each day supplied,
>   Leaps to new life the empire's heart of youth.
>
> To know the instant and to speak it true,
>   Its passing lights of joy, its dark, sad cloud,
> To fix upon the unnumbered gazer's view,
>   Is to thy ready hand's broad strength allowed.
>
> There is an inwrought life in every hour,
>   Fit to be chronicled at large and told.
> 'Tis thine to pluck to light its secret power,
>   And on the air its many-colored heart unfold.
>
> The angel that in sand-dropped minutes lives,
>   Demands a message cautious as the ages,
> Who stuns, with dusk-red words of hate his ear,
>   That mighty power to boundless wrath enrages.

This feeling of the dignity of his office, honor and power in fulfilling it, are not common in the journalist, but where they exist, a mark has been left fully correspondent to the weight of the instrument. The few editors of this country who with mental ability and resource have combined strength of purpose and fairness of conduct, who have never merged the man and the gentleman in the partisan, who have been willing to have all sides fully heard while their convictions were clear on one, who have disdained groundless assaults or angry replies, and have valued what was sincere, characteristic, and free too much to bend to popular errors they felt able to correct, have been so highly prized that it is wonderful that more do not learn the use of this great opportunity. It will be learned yet; the resources of this organ of thought and instruction begin to be understood, and shall yet be brought out and used worthily.

We see we have omitted honored names in this essay. We have not spoken of Brown, as a novelist by far our first in point of genius and instruction as to the soul of things. Yet his works have fallen almost out of print. It is their dark deep gloom that prevents their being popular, for their very beauties are grave and sad. But we see that *Ormond* is being republished at this moment. The picture of Roman character, of the life and resources of a single noble creature, of Constantia alone, should make that book an object of reverence. All these novels should be republished; if not favorites, they should at least not be lost sight of, for there will always be some who find in such powers of mental analysis the only response to their desires.

We have not spoken of Hawthorne, the best writer of the day, in a similar range with Irving, only touching many more points and discerning far more deeply. But we have omitted many things in this slight sketch, for the subject even in this stage lies as a volume in our mind, and cannot be unrolled in completeness unless time and space were more abundant. Our object was to show that although by a thousand signs the existence is foreshown of those forces which are to animate an American literature, that faith, those hopes are not yet alive which shall usher it into a homogeneous or fully organized state of being. The future is glorious with certainties for those who do their duty in the present, and larklike, seeking the sun, challenge its eagles to an earthward flight, where their nests may be built in our mountains, and their young raise their cry of triumph unchecked by dullness in the echoes, . . .   [1846]

Ralph Waldo Emerson

The American Scholar

An Oration

MR. PRESIDENT, AND GENTLEMEN,

I greet you on the re-commencement of our literary year. Our anniversary is one of hope, and, perhaps, not enough of labor. We do not meet for games of strength or skill, for the recitation of histories, tragedies and odes, like the ancient Greeks; for parliaments of love and poesy, like the Troubadours; nor for the advancement of science, like our contemporaries in the British and European capitals. Thus far, our holiday has been simply a friendly sign of the survival of the love of letters amongst a people too busy to give to letters any more. As such, it is precious as the sign of an indestructible instinct. Perhaps the time is already come, when it ought to be, and will be something else; when the sluggard intellect of this continent will look from under its iron lids and fill the postponed expectation of the world with something better than the exertions of mechanical skill. Our day of dependence, our long apprenticeship to the learning of other lands, draws to a close. The millions that around us are rushing into life, cannot always be fed on the sere remains of foreign harvests. Events, actions arise, that must be sung, that will sing themselves. Who can doubt that poetry will revive and lead in a new age, as the star in the constellation Harp which now flames in our zenith, astronomers announce, shall one day be the pole-star for a thousand years?

Delivered Before the Phi Beta Kappa Society, at Cambridge, August 31, 1837.

In the light of this hope, I accept the topic which not only usage, but the nature of our association, seem to prescribe to this day,—the AMERICAN SCHOLAR. Year by year, we come up hither to read one more chapter of his biography. Let us inquire what light new days and events have thrown on his character, his duties and his hopes.

It is one of those fables, which out of an unknown antiquity, convey an unlooked-for wisdom, that the gods, in the beginning, divided Man into men, that he might be more helpful to himself; just as the hand was divided into fingers, the better to answer its end.

The old fable covers a doctrine ever new and sublime; that there is One Man,—present to all particular men only partially, or through one faculty; and that you must take the whole society to find the whole man. Man is not a farmer, or a professor, or an engineer, but he is all. Man is priest, and scholar, and statesman, and producer, and soldier. In the *divided* or social state, these functions are parcelled out to individuals, each of whom aims to do his stint of the joint work, whilst each other performs his. The fable implies that the individual to possess himself, must sometimes return from his own labor to embrace all the other laborers. But unfortunately, this original unit, this fountain of power, has been so distributed to multitudes, has been so minutely subdivided and peddled out, that it is spilled into drops, and cannot be gathered. The state of society is one in which the members have suffered amputation from the trunk, and strut about so many walking monsters, a good finger, a neck, a stomach, an elbow, but never a man.

Man is thus metamorphosed into a thing, into many things. The planter, who is Man sent out into the field to gather food, is seldom cheered by any idea of the true dignity of his ministry. He sees his bushel and his cart, and nothing beyond, and sinks into the farmer, instead of Man on the farm. The tradesman scarcely ever gives an ideal worth to his work, but is ridden by the routine of his craft, and the soul is subject to dollars. The priest becomes a form; the attorney, a statute-book; the mechanic, a machine; the sailor, a rope of a ship.

In this distribution of functions, the scholar is the delegated intellect. In the right state, he is, *Man Thinking.* In the degenerate state, when the victim of society, he tends to become a mere thinker, or, still worse, the parrot of other men's thinking.

In this view of him, as Man Thinking, the whole theory of his office is contained. Him nature solicits, with all her placid, all her monitory pictures. Him the past instructs. Him the future invites. Is not, indeed, every man a student, and do not all things exist for the student's behoof? And, finally, is not the true scholar the only true master? But, as the old oracle said, "All things have two handles. Beware of the wrong one." In life, too often, the scholar errs with mankind and forfeits his privilege. Let us see him in his school, and consider him in reference to the main influences he receives.

I. The first in time and the first in importance of the influences upon the mind is that of nature. Every day, the sun; and, after sunset, night and her stars. Ever the winds blow; ever the grass grows. Every day, men and women, conversing, beholding and beholden. The scholar must needs stand wistful and admiring before this great spectacle. He must settle its value in his mind. What is nature to him? There is never a beginning, there is never an end to the inexplicable continuity of this web of God, but always circular power returning into itself. Therein it resembles his own spirit, whose beginning, whose ending he never can find—so entire, so boundless. Far, too, as her splendors shine, system on system shooting like rays, upward, downward, without centre, without circumference,—in the mass and in the particle nature hastens to render account of herself to the mind. Classification begins. To the young mind, every thing is individual, stands by itself. By and by, it finds how to join two things, and see in them one nature; then three, then three thousand; and so, tyrannized over by its own unifying instinct, it goes on tying things together, diminishing anomalies, discovering roots running under ground, whereby contrary and remote things cohere, and flower out from one stem. It presently learns, that, since the dawn of history, there has been a constant accumulation and classifying of facts. But what is classification but the perceiving that these objects are not chaotic, and are not foreign, but have a law which is also a law of the human mind? The astronomer discovers that geometry, a pure abstraction of the human mind, is the measure of planetary motion. The chemist finds proportions and intelligible method throughout matter: and science is nothing but the finding of analogy, identity in the most remote parts. The ambitious soul sits down before each refractory fact; one after another, reduces all strange constitutions, all new powers, to their class and their law, and goes on forever to animate the last fibre of organization, the outskirts of nature, by insight.

Thus to him, to this school-boy under the bending dome of day, is suggested, that he and it proceed from one root; one is leaf and one is flower; relation, sympathy, stirring in every vein. And what is that Root? Is not that the soul of his soul?—A thought too bold—a dream too wild. Yet when this spiritual light shall have revealed the law of more earthly natures,—when he has learned to worship the soul, and to see that the natural philosophy that now is, is only the first gropings of its gigantic hand, he shall look forward to an ever expanding knowledge as to a becoming creator. He shall see that nature is the opposite of the soul, answering to it part for part. One is seal, and one is print. Its beauty is the beauty of his own mind. Its laws are the laws of his own mind. Nature then becomes to him the measure of his attainments. So much of nature as he is ignorant of, so much of his own mind does he not yet possess. And, in fine, the ancient precept, "Know thyself," and the modern precept, "Study nature," become at last one maxim.

II. The next great influence into the spirit of the scholar, is, the mind of the Past,—in whatever form, whether of literature, of art, of institutions, that mind is inscribed. Books are the best type of the influence of the past, and perhaps we shall get at the truth—learn the amount of this influence more conveniently—by considering their value alone.

The theory of books is noble. The scholar of the first age received into him the world around; brooded thereon; gave it the new arrangement of his own mind, and uttered it again. It came into him—life; it went out from him—truth. It came to him—short-lived actions; it went out from him—immortal thoughts. It came to him—business; it went from him—poetry. It was—dead fact; now, it is quick thought. It can stand, and it can go. It now endures, it now flies, it now inspires. Precisely in proportion to the depth of mind from which it issued, so high does it soar, so long does it sing.

Or, I might say, it depends on how far the process had gone, of transmuting life into truth. In proportion to the completeness of the distillation, so will the purity and imperishableness of the product be. But none is quite perfect. As no air-pump can by any means make a perfect vacuum, so neither can any artist entirely exclude the conventional, the local, the perishable from his book, or write a book of pure thought that shall be as efficient, in all respects, to a remote posterity, as to contemporaries, or rather to the second age. Each age, it is found, must write its own books; or rather, each generation for the next succeeding. The books of an older period will not fit this.

Yet hence arises a grave mischief. The sacredness which attaches to the act of creation,—the act of thought,—is instantly transferred to the record. The poet chanting, was felt to be a divine man. Henceforth the chant is divine also. The writer was a just and wise spirit. Henceforward it is settled, the book is perfect; as love of the hero corrupts into worship of his statue. Instantly, the book becomes noxious. The guide is a tyrant. We sought a brother, and lo, a governor. The sluggish and perverted mind of the multitude, always slow to open to the incursions of Reason, having once so opened, having once received this book, stands upon it, and makes an outcry, if it is disparaged. Colleges are built on it. Books are written on it by thinkers, not by Man Thinking; by men of talent, that is, who start wrong, who set out from accepted dogmas, not from their own sight of principles. Meek young men grow up in libraries, believing it their duty to accept the views which Cicero, which Locke, which Bacon have given, forgetful that Cicero, Locke and Bacon were only young men in libraries when they wrote these books.

Hence, instead of Man Thinking, we have the bookworm. Hence, the book-learned class, who value books, as such; not as related to nature and the human constitution, but as making a sort of Third Estate with the world and the soul. Hence, the restorers of readings, the emendators, the bibliomaniacs of all degrees.

This is bad; this is worse than it seems. Books are the best of things, well used; abused, among the worst. What is the right use? What is the one end which all means go to effect? They are for nothing but to inspire. I had better never see a book than to be warped by its attraction clean out of my own orbit, and made a satellite instead of a system. The one thing in the world of value, is, the active soul,—the soul, free, sovereign, active. This every man is entitled to; this every man contains within him, although in almost all men, obstructed, and as yet unborn. The soul active sees absolute truth; and utters truth, or creates. In this action, it is genius; not the privilege of here and there a favorite, but the sound estate of every man. In its essence, it is progressive. The book, the college, the school of art, the institution of any kind, stop with some past utterance of genius. This is good, say they,—let us hold by this. They pin me down. They look backward and not forward. But genius always looks forward. The eyes of man are set in his forehead, not in his hindhead. Man hopes. Genius creates. To create,—to create,—is the proof of a divine presence. Whatever talents may be, if the man create not, the pure efflux of the Deity is not his:—cinders and smoke, there may be, but not yet flame. There are creative manners, there are creative actions, and creative words; manners, actions, words, that is, indicative of no custom or authority, but springing spontaneous from the mind's own sense of good and fair.

On the other part, instead of being its own seer, let it receive always from another mind its truth, though it were in torrents of light, without periods of solitude, inquest and self-recovery, and a fatal disservice is done. Genius is always sufficiently the enemy of genius by over-influence. The literature of every nation bear me witness. The English dramatic poets have Shakspearized now for two hundred years.

Undoubtedly there is a right way of reading,—so it be sternly subordinated. Man Thinking must not be subdued by his instruments. Books are for the scholar's idle times. When he can read God directly, the hour is too precious to be wasted in other men's transcripts of their readings. But when the intervals of darkness come, as come they must,—when the soul seeth not, when the sun is hid, and the stars withdraw their shining,—we repair to the lamps which were kindled by their ray to guide our steps to the East again, where the dawn is. We hear that we may speak. The Arabian proverb says, "A fig tree looking on a fig tree, becometh fruitful."

It is remarkable, the character of the pleasure we derive from the best books. They impress us ever with the conviction that one nature wrote and the same reads. We read the verses of one of the great English poets, of Chaucer, of Marvell, of Dryden, with the most modern joy,—with a pleasure, I mean, which is in great part caused by the abstraction of all *time* from their verses. There is some awe mixed with the joy of our surprise, when this poet, who lived in some past world, two or three hundred years ago, says that which lies close to my own soul, that which I also had wellnigh thought and said. But for the evidence thence afforded to the philosophical doctrine of the identity of all minds, we should suppose some preestablished harmony, some foresight of souls that were to be, and some preparation of stores for their future wants, like the fact observed in insects, who lay up food before death for the young grub they shall never see.

I would not be hurried by any love of system, by any exaggeration of instincts, to underrate the Book. We all know, that as the human body can be nourished on any food, though it were boiled grass and the broth of shoes, so the human mind can be fed by any knowledge. And great and heroic men have existed, who had almost no other information than by the printed page. I only would say, that it needs a strong head to bear that diet. One must be an inventor to read well. As the proverb says, "He that would bring home the wealth of the Indies, must carry out the wealth of the Indies." There is then creative reading, as well as creative writing. When the mind is braced by labor and invention, the page of whatever book we read becomes luminous with manifold allusion. Every sentence is doubly significant, and the sense of our author is as broad as the world. We then see, what is always true, that as the seer's hour of vision is short and rare among heavy days and months, so is its record, perchance, the least part of his volume. The discerning will read in his Plato or Shakspeare, only that least part,—only the authentic utterances of the oracle,—and all the rest he rejects, were it never so many times Plato's and Shakspeare's.

Of course, there is a portion of reading quite indispensable to a wise man. History and exact science he must learn by laborious reading. Colleges, in like manner, have their indispensable office,—to teach elements. But they can only highly serve us, when they aim not to drill, but to create; when they gather from far every ray of various genius to their hospitable halls, and, by the concentrated fires, set the hearts of their youth on flame. Thought and knowledge are natures in which apparatus and pretension avail nothing. Gowns, and pecuniary foundations, though of towns of gold, can never countervail the least sentence or syllable of wit. Forget this, and our American colleges will recede in their public importance whilst they grow richer every year.

III. There goes in the world a notion that the scholar should be a recluse, a valetudinarian,—as unfit for any handiwork or public labor, as a penknife for an axe. The so-called "practical men" sneer at speculative men, as if, because they speculate or *see*, they could do nothing. I have heard it said that the clergy,—who are always more universally than any other class, the scholars of their day,—are addressed as women: that the rough, spontaneous conversation of men they do not hear, but only a mincing and diluted speech. They are often virtually disfranchised; and, indeed, there are advocates for their celibacy. As far as this is true of the studious classes, it is not just and wise. Action is with the scholar subordinate, but it is essential. Without it, he is not yet man. Without it, thought can never ripen into truth. Whilst the world hangs before the eye as a cloud of beauty, we cannot even see its beauty. Inaction is cowardice, but there can be no scholar without the heroic mind. The preamble of thought, the transition through which it passes from the unconscious to the conscious, is action. Only so much do I know, as I have lived. Instantly we know whose words are loaded with life, and whose not.

The world,—this shadow of the soul, or *other me,* lies wide around. Its attractions are the keys which unlock my thoughts and make me acquainted with myself. I run eagerly into this resounding tumult. I grasp the hands of those next me, and take my place in the ring to suffer and to work, taught by an instinct that so shall the dumb abyss be vocal with speech. I pierce its order; I dissipate its fear; I dispose of it within the circuit of my expanding life. So much only of life as I know by experience, so much of the wilderness have I vanquished and planted, or so far have I extended my being, my dominion. I do not see how any man can afford, for the sake of his nerves and his nap, to spare any action in which he can partake. It is pearls and rubies to his discourse. Drudgery, calamity, exasperation, want, are instructers in eloquence and wisdom. The true scholar grudges every opportunity of action past by, as a loss of power.

It is the raw material out of which the intellect moulds her splendid products. A strange process too, this, by which experience is converted into thought, as a mulberry leaf is converted into satin. The manufacture goes forward at all hours.

The actions and events of our childhood and youth are now matters of calmest observation. They lie like fair pictures in the air. Not so with our recent actions,—with the business which we now have in hand. On this we are quite unable to speculate. Our affections as yet circulate through it. We no more feel or know it, than we feel the feet, or the hand, or the brain of our body. The new deed is yet a part of life,—remains for a time immersed in our unconscious life. In some contemplative hour, it detaches itself from the life like a ripe fruit, to become a thought of the mind. Instantly, it is raised, transfigured; the corruptible has put on incorruption. Always now it is an object of beauty, however base its origin and neighborhood. Observe, too, the impossibility of antedating this act. In its grub state, it cannot fly, it cannot shine,—it is a dull grub. But suddenly, without observation, the selfsame thing unfurls beautiful wings, and is an angel of wisdom. So is there no fact, no event, in our private history, which shall not, sooner or later, lose its adhesive inert form, and astonish us by soaring from our body into the empyrean. Cradle and infancy, school and playground, the fear of boys, and dogs, and ferules, the love of little maids and berries, and many another fact that once filled the whole sky, are gone already; friend and relative, profession and party, town and country, nation and world, must also soar and sing.

Of course, he who has put forth his total strength in fit actions, has the richest return of wisdom. I will not shut myself out of this globe of action and transplant an oak into a flower pot, there to hunger and pine; nor trust the revenue of some single faculty, and exhaust one vein of thought, much like those Savoyards, who, getting their livelihood by carving shepherds, shepherdesses, and smoking Dutchmen, for all Europe, went out one day to the mountain to find stock, and discovered that they had whittled up the last of their pine trees. Authors we have in numbers, who have written out their vein, and who, moved by a commendable prudence, sail for Greece or Palestine, follow the trapper into the prairie, or ramble round Algiers to replenish their merchantable stock.

If it were only for a vocabulary the scholar would be covetous of action. Life is our dictionary. Years are well spent in country labors; in town—in the insight into trades and manufactures; in frank intercourse with many men and women; in science; in art; to the one end of mastering in all their facts a language, by which to illustrate and embody our perceptions. I learn immediately from any speaker how much he has already lived, through the poverty or the splendor of his speech. Life lies behind us as the quarry from whence we get tiles and copestones for the masonry of to-day. This is the way to learn grammar. Colleges and books only copy the language which the field and the work-yard made.

But the final value of action, like that of books, and better than books, is, that it is a resource. That great principle of Undulation in nature, that shows itself in the inspiring and expiring of the breath; in desire and satiety; in the ebb and flow of the sea, in day and night, in heat and cold, and as yet more deeply ingrained in every atom and every fluid, is known to us under the name of Polarity,—these "fits of easy transmission and reflection," as Newton called them, are the law of nature because they are the law of spirit.

The mind now thinks; now acts; and each fit reproduces the other. When the artist has exhausted his materials, when the fancy no longer paints, when thoughts are no longer apprehended, and books are a weariness,—he has always the resource *to live*. Character is higher than intellect. Thinking is the function. Living is the functionary. The stream retreats to its source. A great soul will be strong to live, as well as strong to think. Does he lack organ or medium to impart his truths? He can still fall back on this elemental force of living them. This is a total act. Thinking is a partial act. Let the grandeur of justice shine in his affairs. Let the beauty of affection cheer his lowly roof. Those "far from fame" who dwell and act with him, will feel the force of his constitution in the doings and passages of the day better than it can be measured by any public and designed display. Time shall teach him that the scholar loses no hour which the man lives. Herein he unfolds the sacred germ of his instinct, screened from influence. What is lost in seemliness is gained in strength. Not out of those on whom systems of education have exhausted their culture, comes the helpful giant to destroy the old or to build the new, but out of unhandselled savage nature, out of terrible Druids and Berserkirs, come at last Alfred and Shakespeare.

I hear therefore with joy whatever is beginning to be said of the dignity and necessity of labor to every citizen. There is virtue yet in the hoe and the spade, for learned as well as for unlearned hands. And labor is every where welcome; always we are invited to work; only be this limitation observed, that a man shall not for the sake of wider activity sacrifice any opinion to the popular judgments and modes of action.

I have now spoken of the education of the scholar by nature, by books, and by action. It remains to say somewhat of his duties.

They are such as become Man Thinking. They may all be comprised in self-trust. The office of the scholar is to cheer, to raise, and to guide men by showing them facts amidst appearances. He plies the slow, unhonored and upaid task of observation. Flamsteed and Herschel, in their glazed observatories, may catalogue the stars with the praise of all men, and, the results being splendid and useful, honor is sure. But he, in his private observatory, cataloguing obscure and nebulous stars of the human mind, which as yet no man has thought of as such,—watching days and months, sometimes, for a few facts; correcting still his old records;—must relinquish display and immediate fame. In the long period of his preparation, he must betray often an ignorance and shiftlessness in popular arts, incurring the disdain of the able who shoulder him aside. Long he must stammer in his speech; often forego the living for the dead. Worse yet, he must accept—how often! poverty and solitude. For the ease and pleasure of treading the old road, accepting the fashions, the education, the religion of society, he takes the cross of making his own, and, of course, the self-accusation, the faint heart, the frequent uncertainty and loss of time which are the nettles and tangling vines in the way of the self-relying and self-directed; and the state of virtual hostility in which he seems to stand to society, and especially to educated society. For all this loss and scorn, what offset? He is to find consolation in exercising the highest functions of human nature. He is one who raises himself from private considerations, and breathes and lives on public and illustrious thoughts. He is the world's eye. He is the world's heart. He is to resist the vulgar prosperity that retrogrades ever to barbarism, by preserving and communicating heroic sentiments, noble biographies, melodious verse, and the conclusions of history. Whatsoever oracles the human heart in all emergencies, in all solemn hours has uttered as its commentary on the world of actions,—these he shall receive and impart. And whatsoever new verdict Reason from her inviolable seat pronounces on the passing men and events of to-day,—this he shall hear and promulgate.

These being his functions, it becomes him to feel all confidence in himself, and to defer never to the popular cry. He and he only knows the world. The world of any moment is the merest appearance. Some great decorum, some fetish of a government, some ephemeral trade, or war, or man, is cried up by half mankind and cried down by the other half, as if all depended on this particular up or down. The odds are that the whole question is not worth the poorest thought which the scholar has lost in listening to the controversy. Let him not quit his belief that a popgun is a popgun, though the ancient and honorable of the earth affirm it to be the crack of doom. In silence, in steadiness, in severe abstraction, let him hold by himself; add observation to observation, patient of neglect, patient of reproach; and bide his own time,—happy enough if he can satisfy himself alone that this day he has seen something truly. Success treads on every right step. For the instinct is sure that prompts him to tell his brother what he thinks. He then learns that in going down into the secrets of his own mind, he has descended into the secrets of all minds. He learns that he who has mastered any law in his private thoughts, is master to that extent of all men whose language he speaks, and of all into whose language his own can be translated. The poet in utter solitude remembering his spontaneous thoughts and recording them, is found to have recorded that which men in crowded cities find true for them also. The orator distrusts at first the fitness of his frank confessions,—his want of knowledge of the persons he addresses,—until he finds that he is the complement of his hearers;—that they drink his words because he fulfils for them their own nature; the deeper he dives into his privatest secretest presentiment,—to his wonder he finds, this is the most acceptable, most public, and universally true. The people delight in it; the better part of every man feels, This is my music: this is myself.

In self-trust, all the virtues are comprehended. Free should the scholar be,—free and brave. Free even to the definition of freedom, "without any hindrance that does not arise out of his own constitution." Brave; for fear is a thing which a scholar by his very function puts behind him. Fear always springs from ignorance. It is a shame to him if his tranquillity, amid dangerous times, arise from the presumption that like children and women, his is a protected class; or if he seek a temporary peace by the diversion of his thoughts from politics or vexed questions, hiding his head like an ostrich in the flowering bushes, peeping into microscopes, and turning rhymes, as a boy whistles to keep his courage up. So is the danger a danger still: so is the fear worse. Manlike let him turn and face it. Let him look into its eye and search its nature, inspect its origin,—see the whelping of this lion,—which lies no great way back; he will then find in himself a perfect comprehension of its nature and extent; he will have made his hands meet on the other side, and can henceforth defy it, and pass on superior. The world is his who can see through its pretension. What deafness, what stone-blind custom, what overgrown error you behold, is there only by sufferance,—by your sufferance. See it to be a lie, and you have already dealt it its mortal blow.

Yes, we are the cowed,—we the trustless. It is a mischievous notion that we are come late into nature; that the world was finished a long time ago. As the world was plastic and fluid in the hands of God, so it is ever to so much of his attributes as we bring to it. To ignorance and sin, it is flint. They adapt themselves to it as they may; but in proportion as a man has anything in him divine, the firmament flows before him, and takes his signet and form. Not he is great who can alter matter, but he who can alter my state of mind. They are the kings of the world who give the color of their present thought to all nature and all art, and persuade men by the cheerful serenity of their carrying the matter, that this thing which they do, is the apple which the ages have desired to pluck, now at last ripe, and inviting nations to the harvest. The great man makes the great thing. Wherever Macdonald sits, there is the head of the table. Linnæus makes botany the most alluring of studies and wins it from the farmer and the herb-woman. Davy, chemistry: and Cuvier, fossils. The day is always his, who works in it with serenity and great aims. The unstable estimates of men crowd to him whose mind is filled with a truth, as the heaped waves of the Atlantic follow the moon.

For this self-trust, the reason is deeper than can be fathomed,—darker than can be enlightened. I might not carry with me the feeling of my audience in stating my own belief. But I have already shown the ground of my hope, in adverting to the doctrine that man is one. I believe man has been wronged: he has wronged himself. He has almost lost the light that can lead him back to his prerogatives. Men are become of no account. Men in history, men in the world of to-day are bugs, are spawn, and are called "the mass" and "the herd." In a century, in a millenium, one or two men; that is to say—one or two approximations to the right state of every man. All the rest behold in the hero or the poet their own green and crude being—ripened; yes, and are content to be less, so *that* may attain to its full stature. What a testimony—full of grandeur, full of pity, is borne to the demands of his own nature, by the poor clansman, the poor partisan, who rejoices in the glory of his chief. The poor and the low find some amends to their immense moral capacity, for their acquiescence in a political and social inferiority. They are content to be brushed like flies from the path of a great person, so that justice shall be done by him to that common nature which it is the dearest desire of all to see enlarged and glorified. They sun themselves in the great man's light, and feel it to be their own element. They cast the dignity of man from their downtrod selves upon the shoulders of a hero, and will perish to add one drop of blood to make that great heart beat, those giant sinews combat and conquer. He lives for us, and we live in him.

Men such as they are, very naturally seek money or power; and power because it is as good as money,—the "spoils," so called, "of office." And why not? for they aspire to the highest, and this, in their sleep-walking, they dream is highest. Wake them, and they shall quit the false good and leap to the true, and leave governments to clerks and desks. This revolution is to be wrought by the gradual domestication of the idea of Culture. The main enterprise of the world for splendor, for extent, is the upbuilding of a man. Here are the materials strown along the ground. The private life of one man shall be a more illustrious monarchy,—more formidable to its enemy, more sweet and serene in its influence to its friend, than any kingdom in history. For a man, rightly viewed, comprehendeth the particular natures of all men. Each philosopher, each bard, each actor, has only done for me, as by a delegate, what one day I can do for myself. The books which once we valued more than the apple of the eye, we have quite exhausted. What is that but saying that we have come up with the point of view which the universal mind took through the eyes of that one scribe; we have been that man, and have passed on. First, one; then, another; we drain all cisterns, and waxing greater by all these supplies, we crave a better and more abundant food. The man has never lived that can feed us ever. The human mind cannot be enshrined in a person who shall set a barrier on any one side to this unbounded, unboundable empire. It is one central fire which flaming now out of the lips of Etna, lightens the capes of Sicily; and now out of the throat of Vesuvius, illuminates the towers and vineyards of Naples. It is one light which beams out of a thousand stars. It is one soul which animates all men.

But I have dwelt perhaps tediously upon this abstraction of the Scholar. I ought not to delay longer to add what I have to say, of nearer reference to the time and to this country.

Historically, there is thought to be a difference in the ideas which predominate over successive epochs, and there are data for marking the genius of the Classic, of the Romantic, and now of the Reflective or Philosophical age. With the views I have intimated of the oneness or the identity of the mind through all individuals, I do not much dwell on these differences. In fact, I believe each individual passes through all three. The boy is a Greek; the youth, romantic; the adult, reflective. I deny not, however, that a revolution in the leading idea may be distinctly enough traced.

Our age is bewailed as the age of Introversion. Must that needs be evil? We, it seems, are critical. We are embarrassed with second thoughts. We cannot enjoy any thing for hankering to know whereof the pleasure consists. We are lined with eyes. We see with our feet. The time is infected with Hamlet's unhappiness,—

> Sicklied o'er with the pale cast of thought.

Is it so bad then? Sight is the last thing to be pitied. Would we be blind? Do we fear lest we should outsee nature and God, and drink truth dry? I look upon the discontent of the literary class as a mere announcement of the fact that they find themselves not in the state of mind of their fathers, and regret the coming state as untried; as a boy dreads the water before he has learned that he can swim. If there is any period one would desire to be born in,— is it not the age of Revolution; when the old and the new stand side by side, and admit of being compared; when the energies of all men are searched by fear and by hope; when the historic glories of the old, can be compensated by the rich possibilities of the new era? This time, like all times, is a very good one, if we but know what to do with it.

I read with joy some of the auspicious signs of the coming days as they glimmer already through poetry and art, through philosophy and science, through church and state.

One of these signs is the fact that the same movement which effected the elevation of what was called the lowest class in the state, assumed in literature a very marked and as benign an aspect. Instead of the sublime and beautiful, the near, the low, the common, was explored and poetized. That which had been negligently trodden under foot by those who were harnessing and provisioning themselves for long journeys into far countries, is suddenly found to be richer than all foreign parts. The literature of the poor, the feelings of the child, the philosophy of the street, the meaning of household life, are the topics of the time. It is a great stride. It is a sign—is it not? of new vigor, when the extremities are made active, when currents of warm life run into the hands and the feet. I ask not for the great, the remote, the romantic; what is doing in Italy or Arabia; what is Greek art, or Provencal Minstrelsy; I embrace the common, I explore and sit at the feet of the familiar, the low. Give me insight into to-day, and you may have the antique and future worlds. What would we really know the meaning of? The meal in the firkin; the milk in the pan; the ballad in the street; the news of the boat; the glance of the eye; the form and the gait of the body;—show me the ultimate reason of these matters;—show me the sublime presence of the highest spiritual cause lurking, as always it does lurk, in these suburbs and extremities of nature; let me see every trifle bristling with the polarity that ranges it instantly on an eternal law; and the shop, the plough, and the leger, referred to the like cause by which light undulates and poets sing;—and the world lies no longer a dull miscellany and lumber room, but has form and order; there is no trifle; there is no puzzle; but one design unites and animates the farthest pinnacle and the lowest trench.

This idea has inspired the genius of Goldsmith, Burns, Cowper, and, in a newer time, of Goethe, Wordworth, and Carlyle. This idea they have differently followed and with various success. In contrast with their writing, the style of Pope, of Johnson, of Gibbon, looks cold and pedantic. This writing is blood-warm. Man is surprised to find that things near are not less beautiful and wondrous than things remote. The near explains the far. The drop is a small ocean. A man is related to all nature. This perception of the worth of the vulgar, is fruitful in discoveries. Goethe, in this very thing the most modern of the moderns, has shown us, as none ever did, the genius of the ancients.

There is one man of genius who has done much for this philosophy of life, whose literary value has never yet been rightly estimated;—I mean Emanuel Swedenborg. The most imaginative of men, yet writing with the precision of a mathematician, he endeavored to engraft a purely philosophical Ethics on the popular Christianity of his time. Such an attempt, of course, must have difficulty which no genius could surmount. But he saw and showed the connexion between nature and the affections of the soul. He pierced the emblematic or spiritual character of the visible, audible, tangible world. Especially did his shade-loving muse hover over and interpret the lower parts of nature; he showed the mysterious bond that allies moral evil to the foul material forms, and has given in epical parables a theory of insanity, of beasts, of unclean and fearful things.

Another sign of our times, also marked by an analogous political movement is, the new importance given to the single person. Every thing that tends to insulate the individual,—to surround him with barriers of natural respect, so that each man shall feel the world is his, and man shall treat with man as a sovereign state with a sovereign state;—tends to true union as well as greatness. "I learned," said the melancholy Pestalozzi, "that no man in God's wide earth is either willing or able to help any other man." Help must come from the bosom alone. The scholar is that man who must take up into himself all the ability of the time, all the contributions of the past, all the hopes of the future. He must be an university of knowledges. If there be one lesson more than another which should pierce his ear, it is, The world is nothing, the man is all; in yourself is the law of all nature, and you know not yet how a globule of sap ascends; in yourself slumbers the whole of Reason; it is for you to know all, it is for you to dare all. Mr. President and Gentlemen, this confidence in the unsearched might of man, belongs by all motives, by all prophecy, by all preparation, to the American Scholar. We have listened too long to the courtly muses of Europe. The spirit of the American freeman is already suspected to be timid, imitative, tame. Public and private avarice make the air we breathe thick and fat. The scholar is decent, indolent, complaisant. See already the tragic consequence. The mind of this country taught to aim at low objects, eats upon itself. There is no work for any but the decorous and the complaisant. Young men of the fairest promise, who begin life upon our shores, inflated by the mountain winds, shined upon by all the stars of God, find the earth below not in unison with these,—but are hindered from action by the disgust which the principles on which business is managed inspire, and turn drudges, or die of disgust,—some of them suicides. What is the remedy? They did not yet see, and thousands of young men as hopeful now crowding to the barriers for the career, do not yet see, that if the single man plant himself indomitably on his instincts, and there abide, the huge world will come round to him. Patience—patience;—with the shades of all the good and great for company; and for solace, the perspective of your own infinte life; and for work, the study and the communication of principles, the making those instincts prevalent, the conversion of the world. Is it not the chief disgrace in the world, not to be an unit;—not to be reckoned one character;—not to yield that peculiar fruit which each man was created to bear, but to be reckoned in the gross, in the hundred, or the thousand, of the party, the section, to which we belong; and our opinion predicted geographically, as the north, or the south. Not so, brothers and friends,—please God, ours shall not be so. We will walk on our own feet; we will work with our own hands; we will speak our own minds. The study of letters shall be no longer a name for pity, for doubt, and for sensual indulgence. The dread of man and the love of man shall be a wall of defence and a wreath of joy around all. A nation of men will for the first time exist, because each believes himself inspired by the Divine Soul which also inspires all men.   [1837]

Cornelius Mathews

Nationality in Literature

> Behold, now, this vast city: a city of refuge, the mansion-house of liberty, encompassed and surrounded with God's protection; the shop of war hath not there more anvils and hammers waking, to fashion out the plates, and instruments of armed justice in defence of beleaguered truth, than there be pens and heads there sitting by their studious lamps, musing, searching, revolving new notions and ideas, wherewith to present, as with their homage and their fealty, the approaching reformation; others, as fast reading, trying all things, assenting to the force of reason and convincement. What could a man require more—from a nation so pliant and so prone to seek after knowledge? What wants there to such a towardly and pregnant soil, but wise and faithful laborers, to make a knowing people, a nation of prophets, of sages, and of worthies?
>
> *Milton's Areopagitica*

We are a nation of readers, thirty millions strong; but what are our books, and who are our writers?

There are many persons who have not yet tasted of death, who were living when Edmund Burke, on the floor of the British Parliament, described America as having been, within the life-time of the then Lord Bathurst, "a little speck, scarce visible in the mass of the national interest; a small seminal principle, rather than a formed body." That infant people, then "but in the gristle, and not yet hardened into the bone of manhood,"—struggling with the vicissitudes of life in a new country, and subduing the wilderness and the savage tribes who peopled it,—thirteen feeble colonies, "growing by the neglect of their parent state,—have, within the threescore years and ten which have since elapsed, achieved their National Independence, through the fiery ordeal of a long and bloody war,—erected new institutions of government, a new civil polity and social condition,—become the first political power in the Western hemisphere, and the second commercial power in the world,—and is beginning to exert an influence upon human affairs, which, if wisely directed, seems likely to change the destinies of our race, through all future time, and over the entire surface of the globe. Our Republic occupies a land, suited to the grand part which seems to be alloted to it on the great stage of time. Its shores washed by two oceans,—its interior penetrated by noble rivers, and dotted over with vast lakes and inland seas,—its mountains rich with the most useful and valuable minerals,—its fertile soil teeming with all the productions of the temperate zone, and thickly studded with broad prairies and nobly-timbered forests,—a domain equal in extent to the whole of Southern and Western Europe, adequate to the government of fifty independent states, and the maintenance of the hundreds of millions, who are advancing from the future to occupy it,—present elements of growth, of strength, and of greatness, which give assurance of the most splendid career to be traced in the annals of the human race.

The writer of the article "America," in the ENCYCLOPAEDIA BRITANNICA, (a foreign writer, and a foreign work of high authority,) after stating the then (in 1830) population of the United States, and the ratio of its increase to be such as to double itself every twenty-five years; and, after making a proper allowance for the diminished ratio of increase after it has reached a specified limit, makes an estimate of the population of the country at several remote periods of time. In 1880, he computes it at eighty-four millions; in 1905, at one hundred and sixty-eight millions; in 1966, at six hundred and seventy-two millions; in 2002, at one billion three hundred and forty-four millions; and in 2030, at two billions six hundred and eighty-eight millions; thus, in less than two centuries,— less than the period which has elapsed since the weary feet of the Pilgrims first pressed the rock at Plymouth,—the population of the United States will be about three times as great as the whole population now on the face of the globe. And the same writer, in the same authoritative work, remarking, that "History shows that wealth, power, science, and literature, all follow in the train of numbers, general intelligence and freedom," expresses the opinion, that "The same causes which transferred the sceptre of civilization from the banks of the Euphrates and the Nile to Western Europe, must, in the course of no long period, carry it from the lattter to the plains of the Mississippi and the Amazon."

Although based on sober calculation, and, apparently, a strict induction from well-ascertained data, these stupendous results almost exceed our power of belief. As, in contemplating the immense distances and vast magnitude of the planets, the almost inconceivable speed and complexity, yet harmony, of their motions, and the brilliancy of the myriad lights, which, from their high and distant orbs, flame upon us out of our cold, northern, midnight sky, our minds are overpowered by the greatness of the works of the All-Creating hand,—so these visions of the rising glory of our country overwhelm us with their brightness. Cold, indeed, must be the heart, which does not feel a quickened throb; sluggish the blood, which does not course with a fiercer current through the veins; dead the faith, which does not rise into rapture, in contemplating the destiny which seems to await the land of our birth, and in which those who bear our name and inherit our blood are to share, after we have done our appointed work, and passed away.

And yet this great country that is—this greater country that is to be; this nation of churches and school-houses, as well as canals and railroads—"pliant and prone to seek after knowledge," has no native literature, but is, in letters, in a state of colonial and provincial dependency upon the old world.

It is not difficult to point out the causes which have retarded the literary growth of this country. The settlers of a new country have neither the leisure to enjoy, nor the wealth to procure the means of enjoying the delights of literature. An inhospitable climate, a rude wilderness, savage enemies, privation and sickness, all had to be borne or overcome by the founders of the American States. And as if these were not sufficient to crush those who here planted the seeds of our civilization and freedom, the despotic hand of the parent government was laid heavily upon them. They gave what time they could to religious worship, to the instruction of the young, in the necessary rudiments of knowledge—to brief household endearments; to the government and order of the settlements; to necessary repose, and the rest was painfully devoted to toil. The forest had to be cleared, the crop sown and harvested—the hut, the dwelling, and the log-fort reared and defended from the fierce onslaught of savage foes, and the despotic authority of England to be watched and resisted. It can excite no surprise that letters were not cultivated under such adverse circumstances. Again, the loyalty of the colonists to the parent government operated in the same direction. They resisted exaction and oppression as infractions of the British Constitution, but they loved their country, and submitted cheerfully to the exercise of legitimate authority over themselves and their property. They were Englishmen, and English literature was the common heritage of Englishmen wherever their lot might be cast. Speaking the English tongue, deeply imbued with English tastes and prejudices, reared in the admiration of English writers, and acknowledging nothing as superior to English models, nothing is more natural than that whatever was attempted in composition in this country, should be a close imitation of, and bear a marked resemblance to, the literature of the old country.

And when the colonies finally asserted their independence, it was only against the political power of the mother-country. They retained her language, her letters, and the fame of her great writers, as their birth-right as Englishmen, or the descendants of Englishmen;

their young career in letters was commenced under all the influences of old habits, old associations, and old prejudices in favor of English models, and the mind of the country has not yet cast off this old literary domination.

This intellectual servitude produced the same effects upon the writings of this country, which was produced upon the literature of Germany by the despotic influence of the writers of France over those of Germany. Abounding in institutions of learning, in profound scholars, in all the elements of a national literature, Germany had no rank in letters, and was merely a French province. Her writers servilely imitated the writers of France, and, as is usually the case with mere imitators, imitated the worst of the French writers, and the worst parts of their worst writings. It was not till Goethe came, that Germany was delivered from this degrading intellectual bondage. Sir James Mackintosh, in his review of Madame De Stael's "De l'Allemagne," in the Edinburgh Review, says, that

> Till the middle of the eighteenth century, Germany was, in one important respect, singular among the great nations of Christendom. She had attained a high rank in Europe by discoveries and inventions, by science, by abstract speculation as well as positive knowledge, by the genius of the art of war, and above all, by the theological revolution, which unfettered the understanding in one part of Europe, and loosened its chains in the other; but she was without a national literature. The country of Guttenberg, of Copernicus, of Luther, of Kepler, and of Leibnitz, had no writer in her own language whose name was known in the neighboring nations. German captains and statesmen, philosophers and scholars, were celebrated, but German writers were unknown. Germany had, therefore, no exclusive mental possession; for poetry and eloquence may, and in some measure *must be, national.* A great revolution, however, at length began, which in the course of half a century terminated in bestowing on Germany a literature, perhaps *the most characteristic possessed by any European nation.* It had the important peculiarity of being the first which had its birth in an enlightened age.

Overmastered by the literature of England, we have consented to remain in a state of pupilage, instead of aspiring to be masters in the vocation of letters. "The parents have eaten sour grapes, and the children's teeth are set on edge." We have gone on from generation to generation, imitating old English authors, and working by old critical rules. "The imitation of our own antiquities," says Sir James Mackintosh, "may be as artificial as the copy of a foreign literature." In every department of literary composition, we have come to consider that which is but one mode of writing to be *the* mode, and the only permissible one. Instead of regarding the drama as comprehending an unlimited range of passion and of modes of manifestation, Shakespeare's plays are received by us as bounding the horizon of dramatic composition. So Milton is accepted as the only standard of sublimity, and Addison as the perfect measure of ease and grace. We are to make the metals, torn from the virgin soil of a new country, flow into these old moulds, and harden into these antique forms. We must take these shapes, or not be at all.

If Shakespeare or Milton had grown up in such a state of vassalage to a previous age, or to old writers, the boon of the Paradise Lost, of Lear, Macbeth and Hamlet, had been denied to the world. We shall emulate these examples of intellectual power and literary success in vain, unless we also emulate that intellectual intrepidity which dares to search for and walk in new paths, and which enabled Milton and Shakespeare to reach the highest eminences of English literature.

Something will be gained for the cause of an indigenous literature by a clear development of the idea and the necessity of nationality. First and foremost, nationality involves the idea of home writers. Secondly, the choice of a due proportion of home themes, affording opportunity for descriptions of our scenery, for the illustration of passing events, and the preservation of what tradition has rescued from the past, and for the exhibition of the manners of the people, and the circumstances which give form and pressure to the time and the spirit of the country; and all these penetrated and vivified by an intense and enlightened patriotism. The literature of a country should, as from a faithful mirror, reflect the physical, moral and intellectual aspects of the nation. Other nations and later ages should look to the writers of the land for the lineaments of its people, and to trace the influence of institutions, of civil and religious polity, upon the condition, the manners and the happiness of individuals, and upon the strength, the power and the permanency of the state. The Scriptures represent man as speaking "out of the abundance of the heart." The literature of a people should be its written thought, uttered "out of the abundance of its heart," and exhibiting its interior as well as exterior life. Madame De Stael's great work on the influence of literature upon society, was written, says that Aristarchus of modern criticism, Jeffrey, "to show that all the peculiarities in the literature of different ages and countries may be explained by a reference to the condition of society, and the political and religious institutions of each; and at the same time to point out in what way the progress of letters has, in its turn, modified and affected the government and religion of those nations among whom they have flourished." In the execution of her task, that distinguished authoress took a survey of literature and philosophy from Homer to the tenth year of the French revolution, and after characterising the literature of Greece and of Rome, and briefly sketching the dark ages, "she enters upon a more detailed examination of the peculiarities of all the different aspects of national taste and genius that characterise the literature of Italy, Spain, England, Germany and France, entering, as to each, into a pretty minute exposition of its general merits and defects; and not only of the circumstances in the situation of the country that have produced those characteristics, but even of the authors and productions in which they are chiefly exemplified." And as the result of her profound and elaborate investigation, she concludes, that the form of government, the laws, the private manners and pursuits, and the religion of a people, are reflected by, and characterize their literature; and that these circumstances, in their turn, react upon the form of the government, the spirit of the laws, and the temper and condition of the people.

What cultivated mind fails to distinguish between the literature of Greece and that of Rome; of Italy and that of Spain; of Germany and that of France and England? Undoubtedly, there are many things common to them all; but these are strongly marked and characteristic differences, which constitute the individuality of each. The dissimilarity of Homer and Virgil; of Camoens, Dante, and Milton; of Goethe, Racine, and Shakespeare, is not more sharply cut and strongly defined, than that between the general literature of the countries to which they respectively belonged. Referring to Madame De Stael's brilliant observations on the Greek Drama, and the prodigious effects produced by the representation of the Greek Tragedies, Jeffrey says: "A great part of the effect of these representations must have depended on *the exclusive nationality of their subjects, and the extreme nationality of their auditors.*" And the same eminent critic expresses the opinion, that Shakespeare could not have written his great dramas,—could not have been Shakespeare,—if he had been born in any other country than England. Indeed, Shakespeare, notwithstanding his infinite variety, and those "touches of nature which make the whole world kin," is a thorough Briton, and his writings are surcharged with the spirit of nationality. Could Milton have written the Iliad, or Homer the Paradise Lost? Could Goethe have wrought the Heart of Mid-Lothian, or Scott the Tragedy of Faust? Are not those works instinct with the characteristics of the country and age in which they were produced? What but a heroic age could have produced a Homer? What but Puritanical times a Milton? What age, but an age of unbelief; what country, except one given over for the time to irreligious opinions and social profligacy, could have produced the character of Mephistophiles?

What Lord Bacon, in his Advancement of Learning, says of laws, is equally true, in its spirit, of literature: "For there are," says Bacon, "in nature certain fountains of justice, whence all civil laws are derived, but as streams; and like as waters do take tinctures and tastes from the soils through which they run, so do civil laws vary according to the regions and governments where they are planted, though they proceed from the same fountains." And Montesquieu,—who of all writers had most profoundly studied the causes which influence national character, and the manifestation of that character in the laws and institutions of a country,—in his celebrated work on the Spirit of Laws, has an analogous passage, which forcibly illustrates the view we are inculcating:

> "Law in general," says he, (in Book I. chap. 3,) "is human reason, inasmuch as it governs all the inhabitants of the earth; the political and civil laws of each nation ought to be the only particular cases in which this human reason is applied. They should be adapted in such a manner to the people for whom they are framed, *as to render it very unlikely for those of one nation to be proper for another.* * * * * They should be adapted to the climate of each country, to the quality of the soil, to its situation and extent, to the manner of living of the natives, whether husbandmen, huntsmen, or shepherds; they should have a relation to the degree of liberty which the constitution will bear; to the religion of the inhabitants; to their inclinations, riches, numbers, commerce, manners, customs. These relations form what I call the Spirit of laws."

Do not these relations just as essentially enter into, and characterize, the spirit of a national literature?

It will thus be seen that our view of nationality is conceived in no narrow spirit. Illiberality and exclusiveness have no part in our creed. We would burn no books, banish no authors, shut our hearts against no appeal which speaks to them in the voice of nature. We would not narrow, but enlarge, the horizon of letters; we would not restrict the empire of thought, but annex our noble domain to it. A writer in the last Oct. number of the North American Review, says, that "an intense national self-consciousness, though the shallow may name it patriotism, is the worst foe to the true and generous unfolding of national genius." Against the opinion of this learned Theban, we set the high authorities we have already cited; we set the fact, that Greece, Rome and England, the nations which have possessed the most intense self-consciousness, whose writers have been most penetrated by the sense of nationality, and with whose people patriotism has risen almost into a religious sentiment,—have excelled all the other states of the world in their literature, no less than in their physical prowess. And this intense nationality, instead of narrowing the domain of their great writers, has made their chief works the peerless gifts and priceless treasures of the whole intellectual world. We would ask, especially, under what reigns was the national spirit of England, pervading alike the cot, the castle, and the palace, raised to a loftier tone, than during the reign of Elizabeth, and the period of the Commonwealth, under Cromwell,—a period to which the noblest names of English literature, Bacon, Shakspeare, and Milton, belong? We incline to the opinion that Homer must have possessed a burning, intense national self-consciousness; and that Burns was not less deficient in the same sentiment. And Scott, fired with the generous ardor of patriotism, ("an intense national self-consciousness,") rises into Homeric strains, in his "Lay of the Last Minstrel:"

> Breathes there a man, with soul so dead,
> Who never to himself hath said,
> This is my own, my native land!
> Whose heart hath ne'er within him burned,
> As home his footsteps he hath turn'd

From wandering on a foreign strand?
If such there breathe, go, mark him well;
For him no minstrel raptures swell;
High though his titles, proud his name,
Boundless his wealth, as wish can claim—
Despite those titles, power and pelf,
The wretch, concentrated all in self,
Living, shall forfeit all renown,
And doubly dying, shall go down
To the vile dust from whence he sprung,
Unwept, unhonored, and unsung.

The writer of the article on "Scotch Nationality," in the last number of the North British Review, states, that on lately passing through the Liddisdale district, where Scott collected many of the materials for his Border Minstrelsy, he was assured,

> That the old border traditions of Liddisdale are rapidly disappearing before the romantic fictions of Scott himself; and the glens and streams formerly remembered for the scene of some actual moss-trooping foray, are now associated with the "Lay of the Last Minstrel," or the adventures of Dandie Dinmount and Meg Merrilies. All who have visited Loch Katrine,—and who has not? know that it is the same there, and that the boatmen on the lake, instead of chanting a Highland legend, show you the scene of the stag hunt—the place where died the 'gallant grey,' and the path by which Fitz James climbed into sight of the lake; while the beautiful islet that once rejoiced in a hard Gaelic name, is now known only as "Ellen's Isle." These are the witcheries of genius, but it is a genius *national in its essence, and heightening and spreading its nationality;* it comprehends all clases; it makes itself felt by the most unimpressible; it affords a common ground for the most worldly and the most imaginative—for the utilitarian politician, and the poet in his finest frenzy. Harry Dundas and Robert Burns might meet there, and feel for once alike.

These memorials which the mighty "Wizard of the North" has left of himself in highland and lowland, and in the hearts of the highest no less than of the humblest of Scotchmen, are prouder monuments of his genius than that which art or the pride of his countrymen have reared to his memory in the metropolis of the land which gave him birth, and which enjoys an immortality in his world-wide renown.

Schlegel, in his Lectures on the History of Literature, says of Shakespeare,

> *The feeling by which he seems to have been most connected with ordinary men, is that of nationality.* He has represented the heroic and glorious period of English history, during the conquests in France, in a series of dramatic pieces, which possess all the simplicity and liveliness of the ancient chronicles, but approach in their ruling spirit of patriotism and glory to the most dignified and effected productions of the epic muse.

And the same eminent critic in another place says, that *"a single work, such as the Cid, is of more real value to a nation, than a whole library of books, however abounding in wit or intellect, which are destitute of the spirit of nationality."*

Our apology for thus accumulating authorities in support of a proposition which is nearly or quite self-evident, is that it has been denied in a quarter of respectability. We find a warrant for its truth in every drop of blood which bounds through our veins; in every pulsation of life that throbs at our heart; in every glimpse of the sky which beams upon our native land. Nationality in literature is only one of the many forms of patriotism. The instinct which prompts the eagle to shelter its young on the high cliffs, or the lions to guard their whelps in the wide forest, or human kind to love and cherish their offspring, is not more universal, and is scarcely more powerful, than the sentiment of love for country, and pride in whatever enhances her greatness or perpetuates her renown. The "spot where we were born"—where the ashes of our progenitors repose, and where our ashes and those of our offspring to the remotest posterity will mingle with the ashes of the forefathers; earth, river and skies; institutions of government and civil polity; neighborhood, kindred, household ties and household joys; the desire of honorable station and name, and of a worthy posterity; victorious fields, great works of art, and proud achievements in letters—all enter into the form a part of the sentiment of patriotism. More than towering battlements, more than serried ranks of steel, more than the most destructive enginery of war, does this sentiment of love for, and pride in country—an intense sense of nationality—guard the soil and preserve the sacred independence of nations.

The North American reviewer before referred to, says, that "the advocates of nationality seem to think that American authors ought to limit themselves to American subjects, and hear none but American criticism." This is erroneous. They have nowhere intimated such an opinion. We say that Shakespeare, Milton, Dante, Goethe and Racine, were all writers who wrote in a truly national spirit, and yet they did not limit themselves to subjects belonging exclusively to their own country or times. As we are men, whatever is common to humanity, falls fairly within the range of the American author; but as we are Americans, whatever is peculiar to our country and characteristic of our countrymen, is especially deserving of his regard. Is there any lack of home themes that our authors should lack home thoughts? Is there not the same variety in the play of human passions in the new world as in the old—in the present as in the past ages—under free as under despotic institutions? We would set no limits to the subjects on which our authors should write. We would leave to them the whole range of nature and humanity. We would wish them to strike every key in the grand scale of human passion. But we would have them true to their country. If there is anything peculiar in our institutions and condition, we would have some native bard to sing, some native historian to record it. We would have those who are born upon our soil; who have faith in republican governments; who cherish noble hopes and aspirations for our country; whose hearts beat in unison with our countrymen, to manifest their faith, their hopes, their sympathies, in some suitable manner. What we complain of is, the unnational spirit of our writers; that they slavishly adhere to old and foreign models; that alike in their subjects, and in their method of handling them, they are British, or German, or something else than American. We are not ungrateful for what some of our writers have done; but we ask, if the American people were suddenly destroyed by some great convulsion of nature, what fitting memorial of our national existence would be left, to instruct and delight, centuries hence, the nations which are yet in the womb of time?

The American writer who seems most deeply to have felt the want of, and who has most ably and earnestly, as well as earliest, insisted upon, nationality in our literature, is Mr. Cornelius Mathews. In an address before one of the Literary Societies of the New-York University, on "Home Writers, Home Writings, and Home Criticism," he thus alludes to some of the characteristics of a literature suited to the wants of the country:

> I, therefore, in behalf of this young America of ours, insist on nationality and true Americanism in the books this country furnishes to itself and to the world; nationality in its purest, highest broadest sense. Not such as is declaimed in taverns, ranted off in Congress, or made the occasion of boasting and self-laudation on public anniversaries. It need not (though it may) speak of the Revolution, nor Washington, nor the Declaration of Independence, nor Plymouth Rock, nor Bunker Hill, nor Bunker Hill Monument. And yet it may be instinct with the life of the country, full of a hearty, spontaneous, genuine home feeling; relishing of

the soil and of the spirit of the people. * * * The writings of a great country should sound of the great voices of nature, of which she is full. The march of a great people in literature should be majestic and assured as the action of their institutions is calm and secure.

It poorly comports with our lofty assertion of national superiority, or with even an ordinary and just sense of self-respect, to be dependent for the intellectual aliment of the people, for those things which most adorn and ennoble a nation, and which are the highest boast and pride of civilized states, upon foreign writers, who write upon impulses not imparted by us, who primarily, if not exclusively, aim to please a different reading community, to whose standards of opinion, feeling and taste, they subject their productions, and who often, in obedience to the influences which surround them, write in a spirit not only alien, but positively hostile to our people, our institutions and national character.

Having thus attempted to develope the idea of nationality, we shall, in another number, state some of the higher uses of a national literature, and point out the American writers and writings most deeply imbued with a national spirit.   [1847]

Theodore Parker

The American Scholar

Men of a superior culture get it at the cost of the whole community, and therefore at first owe for their education. They must pay back an equivalent or else remain debtors to mankind, debtors for ever; that is, beggars or thieves, such being the only class that are thus perpetually in debt and a burden to the race.

It is true that every man, the rudest Prussian boor as well as von Humboldt, is indebted to mankind for his culture, to their past history and their existing institutions, to their daily toil. Taking the whole culture into the account, the debt bears about the same ratio to the receipt in all men. I speak not of genius, the inborn faculty which costs mankind nothing, only of the education thereof, which the man obtains. The Irishman who can only handle his spade, wear his garments, talk his wild brogue, and bid his beads, has four or five hundred generations of ancestors behind him, and is as long descended and from as old a stock as the accomplished patrician scholar at Oxford and Berlin. The Irishman depends on them all, and on the present generation, for his culture. But he has obtained his development with no special outlay and cost of the human race. In getting that rude culture he has appropriated nothing to himself which is taken from another man's share. He has paid as he went along, so he owes nothing in particular for his education; and mankind has no claim on him as for value received. But the Oxford graduate has been a long time at school and college, not earning but learning; living therefore at the cost of mankind, with an obligation and an implied promise to pay back when he comes of age and takes possession of his educated faculties. He therefore has not only the general debt which he shares with all men, but an obligation quite special and peculiar for his support while at study.

This rule is general, and applies to the class of educated men, with some apparent exceptions, and a very few real ones. Some men are born of poor but strong-bodied parents, and endowed with great abilities; they inherit nothing except their share of the general civilization of mankind, and the onward impulse which that has given. These men devote themselves to study; and having behind them an ancestry of broad-shouldered, hard-handed, stalwart, temperate men, and deep-bosomed, red-armed, and industrious mothers, they are able to do the work of two or three men at the time. Such men work while they study; they teach while they learn; they hew their own way through the wood by superior strength and skill born in their bones, with an axe themselves have chipped out from the stone, or forged of metal, or paid for with the result of their first hewings. They are specially indebted to nobody for their culture. They pay as they go, owing the academic ferryman nothing for setting them over into the elysium of the scholar.

Only few men ever make this heroic and crucial experiment. None but poor men's sons essay the trial. Nothing but poverty has whips sharp enough to sting indolent men, even of genius, to such exertion of the manly part. But even this proud race often runs into another debt; they run up long scores with the body, which must one day be paid "with aching head and squeamish heart-burnings." The credit on account of the hardy fathers is not without limit. It is soon exhausted; especially in a land where the atmosphere, the institutions, and the youth of the people all excite to premature and excessive prodigality of effort. The body takes a mortgage on the spendthrift spirit, demands certain regular periodic payments, and will one day foreclose for breach of condition, impede the spirit's action in the premises, putting a very disagreeable keeper there, and finally expel the prodigal mortgagor. So it often happens that a man who in his youth scorned a pecuniary debt to mankind and would receive no favor, even to buy culture with, has yet unconsciously and against his will, contracted debts which trouble him in manhood, and impede his action all his life; with swollen feet and blear eyes famous Griesbach pays for the austere heroism of his penurious and needy youth. The rosy bud of genius on the poor man's tree, too often opens into a lean and ghastly flower. Could not Burns tell us this?

With the rare exceptions just hinted at, any man of a superior culture owes for it when obtained. Sometimes the debt is obvious; a farmer with small means and a large family sends the most hopeful of his sons to college. Look at the cost of the boy's culture. His hands are kept from work that his mind may be free. He fares on daintier food, wears more and more costly garments. Other members of the family must feed and clothe him, earn his tuition-fees, buy his books, pay for his fuel and room-rent. For this the father rises earlier than of old, yoking the oxen a great while before day of a winter's morning, and toils till long after dark of a winter's night, enduring cold and hardship. For this the mother stints her frugal fare, her humble dress; for this the brothers must forego [sic] sleep and pastime, must toil harder, late and early both; for this the sisters must seek new modes of profitable work, must wear their old finery long after it is finery no more. The spare wealth of the family, stinted to spare it, is spent on this one youth. From the father to the daughters, all lay their bones to extraordinary work for him; the whole family is pinched in body that this one youth may go brave and full. Even the family horse pays his tax to raise the education fee.

Men see the hopeful scholar, graceful and accomplished, receiving his academic honors, but they see not the hard-featured father standing unheeded in the aisle, nor the older sister in an obscure corner of the gallery, who had toiled in the factory for the favored brother, tending his vineyard, her own not kept; who had perhaps learned the letters of Greek to hear him recite the grammar at home. Father and sister know not a word of the language in which his diploma is writ and delivered. At what cost of the family tree is this one flower produced? How many leaves, possible blossoms, yea, possible branches, have been absorbed to create this one flower, which shall perpetuate the kind, after being beautiful and fragrant in its own season? Yet, while these leaves are growing for the blossom's sake, and the life of the tree is directed thither with special and urgent emphasis, the difference between branch and blossom, leaf and petal, is getting more and more. By and by the two cannot comprehend each other; the acorn has forgotten the leaf which reared it, and thinks itself of another kin. Grotius, who speaks a host of languages, talking with the learned of all countries and of every age, has forgot his mother tongue, and speech is at end with her that bore him. The son, accomplished with many a science, many an art, ceases to understand the simple consciousness of his father and mother. They are proud of him, that he has outgrown them; he ashamed of them when they visit him amid his scholarly company. To them he is a philosopher, they only clowns in his eyes. He learns to neglect, perhaps to despise them, and forgets his obligation and his debt. Yet by their rudeness is it that he is refined. His science and literary skill are purchased by their ignorance and uncouthness of manner and of speech. Had the educational cost been equally divided all had still continued on a level; he had known no Latin, but the whole family might have spoken good English. For all the difference which education made betwixt him and his kinsfolk he is a debtor.

In New England you sometimes see extremes of social condition brought together. The blue-frocked father, well advanced, but hale as an October morning, jostles into Boston in a milk-cart, his red-cheeked grand-daughter beside him, also coming for some useful daily work, while the youngest son, cultured at the cost of that grand-daughter's sire and by that father's toil, is already a famous man; perhaps also a proud one, eloquent at the bar, or powerful in the pulpit, or mighty in the senate. The family was not rich enough to educate all the children after this costly sort; one becomes famous, the rest are neglected, obscure, and perhaps ignorant; the cultivated son has little sympathy with them. So the men that built up the cathedrals of Strasbourg and Milan slept in mean hutches of mud and straw, dirty, cold, and wet; the finished tower looks proudly down upon the lowly thatch, all heedless of the cost at which itself arose. It is plain that this man owes for his education, it is plain whom he owes. But all men of a superior culture, though born to wealth, get their education in the same way, only there is this additional mischief to complicate the matter; the burden of self-denial is not borne by the man's own family, but by other fathers and mothers, other brothers and sisters. They also pay the cost of his culture, bear the burden for no special end, and have no personal or family joy in the success; they do not even know the scholar they help to train. They who hewed the topstone of society are far away when it is hoisted up with shouting. Most of the youths now-a-days trained at Harvard College are the sons of rich men, yet they also, not less, are educated at the public charge; beneficiaries not of the "Hopkins' Fund," but of the whole community. Society is not yet rich enough to afford so generous a culture to all who ask, who deserve, or who would pay for it a hundred-fold. The accomplished man who sits in his well-endowed scholarship at Oxford, or rejoices to be "Master of Trinity," though he have the estate of the Westminsters and Sutherlands behind him, is still the beneficiary of the public and owes for his schooling.

In the general way, among the industrious classes of New England, a boy earns his living after he is twelve years old. If he gets the superior education of the scholar solely by the pecuniary aid of his father or others, when he is twenty-five and enters on his profession,—law, medicine, or divinity, politics, school-keeping, or trade, he has not earned his Latin grammar; has rendered no appreciable service to mankind; others have worked that he might study, and taught that he might learn. He has not paid the first cent towards his own schooling; he is indebted for it to the whole community. The ox-driver in the fields, the paver in the city streets, the laborer on the railroad, the lumberer in the woods, the girl in the factory, each has a claim on him. If he despises these persons or cuts himself off from sympathy with them, if he refuses to perform his function for them after they have done their possible to fit him for it, he is not only the perpetual and ungrateful debtor, but is more guilty than the poor man's son who forgets the family that sent him to college; for that family consciously and willingly made the sacrifice, and got some satisfaction for it in the visible success of their scheme, nay, are sometimes proud of the pride which scorns them, while with the mass of men thus slighted there is no return for their sacrifice. They did their part, faithfully did it; their beneficiary forgets his function.

The democratic party in New England does not much favor the higher seminaries of education. There has long been a suspicion against them in the mass of the community, and among the friends of the public education of the people a serious distrust. This is the philosophy of that discontent: public money spent on the higher seminaries is so much taken from the humbler schools, so much taken from the colleges of all for the college of the few; men educated at such cost have not adequately repaid the public for the sacrifice made on their account; men of superior education have not been eminently the friends of mankind, they do not eminently represent truth, justice, philanthropy, and piety; they do not point men to lofty human life and go thitherward in advance of mankind; their superior education has narrowed their sympathies, instead of widening; they use their opportunities against mankind, and not in its behalf; think, write, legislate, and live not for the interest of mankind, but only for a class; instead of eminent wisdom, justice, piety, they have eminent cunning, selfishness and want of faith. These charges are matters of allegation, judge you if they be not also matters of fact.

Now, there is a common feeling amongst men that the scholar is their debtor, and in virtue of this that they have a right to various services from him. No honest man asks the aid of a farmer or a blacksmith without intending to repay him in money; no assembly of mechanics would ask another to come two hundred miles and give them a month's work, or a day's work. Yet they will ask a scholar to do so. What gratuitous services are demanded of the physician, of the minister, of the man of science and letters in general! No poor man in Boston but thinks he has a good claim on any doctor; no culprit in danger of liberty or life but will ask the services of a lawyer wholly without recompense to plead his cause. The poorest and most neglected class of men look on every good clergyman as their missionary and minister and friend; the better educated and more powerful he is, the juster and greater do they feel their claim on him. A pirate in gaol may command the services of any Christian minister in the land. Most of the high achievements in science, letters, and art, have had no apparent pay. The pay came beforehand; in general and from God, in the greater ability, "the vision and the faculty divine," but in particular also and from men, in the opportunity afforded them by others for the use and culture thereof. Divinely and humanly they are well paid. Men feel that they have this right to the services of the scholar, in part because they dimly know that his superior education is purchased at the general cost. Hence, too, they are proud of the few able and accomplished men, feeling that all have a certain property therein, as having contributed their mite to the accumulation, by their divine nature related to the men of genius, by their human toil partners in the acquirements of the scholar. This feeling is not confined to men who intellectually can appreciate intellectual excellence. The little parish in the mountains, and the great parish in the city, are alike proud of the able-headed and accomplished scholar who ministers to them; though neither the poor clowns of the village nor the wealthy clowns of the metropolis could enter into his consciousness and understand his favorite pursuits or loftiest thought. Both would think it insulting to pay such a man in full proportion to his work or their receipt. Nobody offers a salary to the House of Lords; their lordship is their pay, and they must give back, in the form of justice and sound government, an equivalent for all they take in high social rank. They must pay for their nobility by being noble lords.

How shall the scholar pay for his education? He is to give a service for the service received. Thus the miller and the farmer pay one another, each paying with service in his own kind. The scholar cannot pay back bread for bread, and cloth for cloth. He must pay in the scholar's kind, not the woodman's or the weaver's. He is to represent the higher modes of human consciousness; his culture and opportunities of position fit him for that. So he is not merely to go through the routine of his profession as minister, doctor, lawyer, merchant, school-master, politician, or maker of almanacs, and for his own advantage; he is also able to represent truth, justice, beauty, philanthropy, and religion, the highest facts of human experience; he must be common, but not vulgar, and, as a star, must dwell apart from the vulgarity of the selfish and low. He may win money without doing this, get fame and power, and thereby seem to pay mankind for their advance to him, while he rides upon their neck; but as he has not paid back the scholar's cost, and in the scholar's way, he is a debtor still, and owes for his past culture and present condition.

Such is the position of the scholar everywhere, and such his consequent obligation. But in America there are some circumstances which make the position and the duty still more important. Beside the natural aristocracy of genius, talent, and educated skill, in most countries there is also a conventional and permanent nobility based on royal or patrician descent and immoveable aristocracy. Its members monopolize the high places of society, and if not strong by nature are so by position. Those men check the natural power of the class of scholars. The descendant of some famous chief of old time takes rank before the Bacons, the Shakespeares, and the Miltons of new families,—born yesterday, to-day gladdened and gladdening with the joy of their genius,—usurps their place, and for a time "shoves away the worthy bidden guest" from the honors of the public board. Here there is no such class: a man born at all is well born; with a great nature, nobly born; the career opens to all that can run, to all men that wish to try; our aristocracy is movable, and the scholar has scope and verge enough.

   Germany has the largest class of scholars; men of talent, sometimes of genius, of great working power, exceedingly well furnished for their work, with a knowledge of the past and the present. On the whole, they seem to have a greater power of thought than the scholars of any other land. They live in a country where intellectual worth is rated at its highest value. As England is the paradise of the patrician and the millionaire, so is Germany for the man of thought; Goethe and Schiller and the Humboldts took precedence of the mere conventional aristocracy. The empire of money is for England, that of mind is for Germany. But there the scholar is positively hindered in his function by the power of the government, which allows freedom of thought, and by education tends to promote it, yet not its correlative freedom of speech, and still less the consequent of that, freedom of act. Revelations of new thought are indeed looked for, and encouraged in certain forms, but the corresponding revolution of old things is forbidden. An idea must remain an idea; the government will not allow it to become a deed, an institution, an idea organized in men. The children of the mind must be exposed to die, or if left alive their feet are cramped so that they cannot go alone; useless, joyless, and unwed, they remain in their father's house. The government seeks to establish national unity of action by the sacrifice of individual variety of action, personal freedom; every man must be a soldier and a Christian, wearing the livery of the government on the body and in the soul, and going through the spiritual

exercises of the church as through the manual exercise of the camp. In a nation so enlightened, personal freedom cannot be wholly sacrificed, so thought is left free, but speech restricted by censorship, speech with the human mouth or the iron lips of the press. Now, as
of old, is there a controversy between the temporal and the spiritual powers about the in-
vestiture of the children of the soul.

Then, on the other side, the scholar is negatively impeded by the comparative ignorance of the people, by their consequent lack of administrative power and self-help, and
their distrust of themselves. There a great illumination has gone on in the upper heavens
of the learned, meteors coruscating into extraordinary glory; it has hardly dawned on the
low valleys of the common people. If it shines there at all, it is but as the Northern Aurora, with a little crackling noise, lending a feeble and uncertain light, not enough to
walk with, and no warmth at all; a light which disturbs the dip and alters the variation of
the old historical compass, bewilders the eye, hides the stars, and yet is not bright enough
to walk by without stumbling. There is a learned class, very learned and very large, with
whom the scholar thinks, and for whom he writes, most uncouthly, in the language only
of the schools; and if not kept in awe by the government, they are contented that a
thought should remain always a thought; while in their own heart they disdain all authority but that of truth, justice, and love, they leave the people subject to no rule but the
priest, the magistrate, and old custom, which usurp the place of reason, conscience, and
affections. There is a very enlightened pulpit, and a very dull audience. In America, it is
said, for every dough-faced representative there is a dough-faced constituency; but in Germany there is not an intelligent people for each intelligent scholar. So on condition a great
thought be true and revolutionary, it is hard to get it made a thing. Ideas go into a nun-
nery, not a family. Phidias must keep his awful Jove only in his head; there is no marble to
carve it on. Eichhorn and Strauss, and Kant and Hegel, with all their pother among the
learned, have kept no boor from the communion-table, nor made him discontented with
the despotism of the state. They wrote for scholars, perhaps for gentlemen, for the enlightened, not for the great mass of the people, in whom they had no confidence. There is
no class of hucksters of thought who retail philosophy to the million. The million have as
yet no appetite for it. So the German scholar is hindered from his function on either land
by the power of the government, or the ignorance of the people. He talks to scholars and
not men; his great ideas are often as idle as shells in a lady's cabinet.

In America all is quite different. There are no royal or patrician patrons, no plebeian
clients in literature, no immoveable aristocracy to withstand or even retard the new genius, talent, or skill of the scholar. There is no class organized, accredited, and confided in,
to resist a new idea; only the unorganized inertia of mankind retards the circulation of
thought and the march of men. Our historical men do not found historical families; our
famous names of to-day are all new names in the state. American aristocracy is bottomed
on money which no unnatural laws make steadfast and immoveable. To exclude a scholar
from the company of rich men is not to exclude him from an audience that will welcome
and appreciate.

Then the government does not interfere to prohibit the free exercise of thought. Speaking is free, preaching is free, printing free. No administration in America could put down
a newspaper or suppress the discussion of an unwelcome theme. The attempt would be
folly and madness. There is no "tonnage and poundage" on thought. It is seldom that law-
less violence usurps the place of despotic government. The chief opponent of the new philosophy is the old philosophy. The old has only the advantage of a few years, the advantage
of possession of the ground. It has no weapons of defense which the new has not for attack.
What hinders the growth of the new democracy of to-day?—only the old democracy of

yesterday, once green, and then full-blown, but now going to seed. Everywhere else walled gardens have been built for it to go quietly to seed in, and men appointed, in God's name or the state's, to exterminate as a weed every new plant of democratic thought which may spring up and suck the soil or keep off the sun, so that the old may quietly occupy the ground and undisturbed continue to decay and contaminate the air. Here it has nothing but its own stalk to hold up its head, and is armed with only such spines as it has grown out of its own substance.

Here the only power which continually impedes the progress of mankind, and is conservative in the bad sense, is wealth, which represents life lived, not now a living, and labor accumulated, not now a doing. Thus the obstacle to free trade is not the notion that our meat must be home-grown and our coat home-spun, but the money invested in manufactures. Slavery is sustained by no prestige of antiquity, no abstract fondness for a patriarchal institution, no special zeal for "Christianity" which the churches often tell us demands it, but solely because the Americans have invested some twelve hundred millions of dollars in the bodies and souls of their countrymen, and fear they shall lose their capital. Whitney's gin for separating the cotton from its blue seed, making its culture and the labor of the slave profitable, did more to perpetuate slavery than all the "Compromises of the Constitution." The last argument in its favor is always this: "It brings money, and we would not lose our investment." Weapon a man with iron, he will stand and fight; with gold, he will shrink and run. The class of capitalists are always cowardly; here they are the only cowardly class that has much political or social influence. Here gold is the imperial metal, nothing but wealth is consecrated for life; the tonsure gets covered up or grown over; vows of celibacy are no more binding than dicers' oaths; allegiance to the state is as transferable as a cent, and may be alienated by going over the border; church-communion may be changed or neglected; as men will, they sign off from church and state; only the dollar holds its own continually, and is the same under all administrations, "safe from the bar, the pulpit, and the throne." Obstinate money continues in office spite of the proscriptive policy of Polk and Taylor; the laws may change, South Carolina move out of the nation, the Constitution be broken, the Union dissolved, still money holds its own. That is the only peculiar weapon which the old has wherewith to repel the new.

Here, too, the scholar has as much freedom as he will take; himself alone stands in his own light, nothing else between him and the infinite majesty of truth. He is free to think, to speak, to print his word and organize his thought. No class of men monopolize public attention or high place. He comes up to the Genius of America, and she asks: "What would you have, my little man?" "More liberty," lisps he. "Just as much as you can carry," is the answer. "Pay for it and take it, as much as you like, there it is." "But it is guarded!" "Only by gilded flies in the day-time; they look like hornets, but can only buzz, not bite with their beak, nor sting with their tail. At night it is defended by daws and beetles, noisy, but harmless. Here is marble, my son, not classic and famous as yet, but good as the parian stone; quarry as much as you will, enough for a nymph or a temple. Say your wisest and do your best thing, nobody will hurt you!"

Not much more is the scholar impeded by the ignorance of the people, not at all in respect to the substance of his thought. There is no danger that he will shoot over the heads of the people by thinking too high for the multitude. We have many authors below the market, scarce one above it. The people are continually looking for something better than our authors give. No American author has yet been too high for the comprehension of the people, and compelled to leave his writings "to posterity, after some centuries shall have passed by." If he has thought with the thinkers, and has something to say, and can speak it in plain speech, he is sure to be widely understood. There is no learned class to whom he may talk Latin or Sanscrit, and who will understand him if he write as ill as Immanuel Kant; there is not a large class to buy costly editions of ancient classics, however beautiful, or magnificent works on India, Egypt, Mexico—the class of scholars is too poor for that, the rich men have not the taste for such beauty; but there is an intelligent class of men who will hear a man if he has what is worth listening to and says it plain. It will be understood and appreciated, and soon reduced to practice. Let him think as much in advance of men as he will, as far removed from the popular opinion as he may, if he arrives at a great truth he is sure of an audience, not an audience of fellow-scholars, as in Germany, but of fellow-men; not of the children of distinguished or rich men, rather of the young parents of such, an audience of earnest, practical people, who if his thought be a truth will soon make it a thing. They will appreciate the substance of his thought, though not the artistic form which clothes it.

This peculiar relation of the man of genius to the people comes from American institutions. Here the greatest man stands nearest to the people, and without a mediator speaks to them face to face. This is a new thing: in the classic nations oratory was for the people, so was the drama and the ballad; that was all their literature. But this came to the people only in cities; the tongue travels slow and addresses only the ear, while swiftly hurries on the printed word and speaks at once to a million eyes. Thucydides and Tacitus wrote for a few; Virgil sang the labors of the shepherd in old Ascræan verse, but only to the wealthy wits of Rome. "I hate the impious crowd, and stave them off," was the scholar's maxim then. All writing was for the few. The best English literature of the sixteenth and seventeenth and eighteenth centuries is amenable to the same criticism, except the dramatic and the religious. It is so with all the permanent literature of Europe of that time. The same must be said even of much of the religious literature of the scholars then. The writings of Taylor, of Barrow and South, of Bossuet, Massillon, and Bourdaloue, clergymen though they were, speaking with a religious and therefore a universal aim, always presuppose a narrow audience of men of nice culture. So they drew their figures from the schoolmen from the Greek anthology, from heathen classics and the Christian Fathers. Their illustrations were embellishments to the scholar, but only palpable darkness to the people. This fact of writing for a few nice judges was of great advantage to the form of the literature thus produced, but a disadvantage to the substance thereof; a misfortune to the scholar himself, for it belittled his sympathies and kept him within a narrow range. Even the religious literature of the men just named betrays a lack of freedom, a thinking for the learned and not for mankind; it has breathed the air of the cloister, not the sky, and is tainted with academic and monastic diseases. So the best of it is over-sentimental, timid, and does not point to hardy, manly life. Only Luther and Latimer preached to the million hearts of their contemporaries. The dramatic literature, on the other hand, was for box, pit, and gallery; hence the width of poetry in its great masters, hence many of its faults of form; and hence the wild and wanton luxuriance of beauty which flowers out all over the marvellous field of art where Shakespeare walked and sung. In the pulpit excellence was painted as a priest, or monk, or nun, loving nothing but God; on the stage as a soldier, magistrate, a gentleman or simpleman, a wife and mother, loving also child and friend. Only the literature of the player and the singer of ballads was for the people.

Here all is changed, everything that is written is for the hands of the million. In three months Mr. Macaulay has more readers in America than Thucydides and Tacitus in twelve centuries. Literature, which was once the sacrament of the few, only a shew-bread to the people, is now the daily meat of the multitude. The best works get reprinted with great speed, the highest poetry is soon in all the newspapers. Authors know this and write accordingly. It is only scientific works which ask for a special public. But even science, the proudest of the day, must come down from the clouds of the academy, lay off its scholastic garb, and appear before the eyes of the multitude in common work-day clothes. To large and mainly unlearned audiences Agassiz and Walker set forth the highest teachings of physics and metaphysics, not sparing difficult things, but putting them in plain speech. Emerson takes his majestic intuitions of truth and justice, which transcend the experience of the ages, and expounds them to the mechanics' apprentices, to the factory girls at Lowell and Chicopee, and to the merchants' clerks at Boston. The more original the speaker, and the more profound, the better is he relished; the beauty of the form is not appreciated, but the original substance welcomed into new life over the bench, the loom, and even the desk of the counting-house. Of a deep man the people ask clearness also, thinking he does not see a thing wholly till he sees it plain.

From this new relation of the scholar to the people, and the direct intimacy of his intercourse with men, there comes a new modification of his duty; he is to represent the higher facts of human consciousness to the people, and express them in the speech of the people; to think with the sage and saint, but talk with common men. It is easy to discourse with scholars, and in the old academic carriage drive through the broad gateway of the cultivated class; but here the man of genius is to take the new thought on his shoulders and climb up the stiff, steep hill, and find his way where the wild asses quench their thirst, and the untamed eagle builds his nest. Hence our American scholar must cultivate the dialectics of speech as well as thought. Power of speech without thought, a long tongue in an empty head, calls the people together once or twice, but soon its only echo is from an audience of empty pews. Thought without power of speech finds little welcome here, there are not scholars enough to keep it in countenance. This popularity of intelligence gives a great advantage to the man of letters, who is also a man. He can occupy the whole space between the extremes of mankind, can be at once philosopher in his thought and people in his speech, deliver his world without an interpreter to mediate, and, like King Mithridates in the story, talk with the fourscore nations of his camp each in his own tongue.

Further still, there are some peculiarities of the American mind in which we differ from our English brothers. They are more inclined to the matter of fact, and appeal to history; we to the matter of ideas, and having no national history but of a revolution, may appeal at once to human nature. So while they are more historical, fond of names and precedents, enamored of limited facts and coy towards abstract and universal ideas, with the maxim, "Stand by the fixed," we are more metaphysical, ideal; do not think a thing right because actual, nor impossible because it has never been. The Americans are more metaphysical than the English, have departed more from the old sensational philosophy, have welcomed more warmly the transcendental philosophy of Germany and France. The Declaration of Independence, and all the State Constitutions of the North, begin with a universal and abstract idea. Even preaching is abstract and of ideas. Calvinism bears metaphysical fruit in New England.

This fact modifies still more the function of the duty of the scholar. It determines him to ideas, to facts for the ideas they cover, not so much to the past as the future, to the past only that he may guide the present and construct the future. He is to take his run in the past to acquire the momentum of history, his stand in the present, and leap into the future.

In this manner the position and duty of the scholar in America are modified and made peculiar; and thus is the mode determined for him in which to pay for his education in the manner most profitable to the public that has been at the cost of his training.

There is a test by which we measure the force of a horse or a steam-engine; the raising of so many pounds through so many feet in a given time. The test of the scholar's power is his ability to raise men in their development.

In America there are three chief modes of acting upon the public, omitting others of small account. The first is the power which comes of national wealth; the next, that of political station; the third, power of spiritual wealth, so to say, eminent wisdom, justice, love, piety, the power of sentiments and ideas, and the faculty of communicating them to other men, and organizing them therein. For the sake of shortness, let each mode of power be symbolized by its instrument, and we have the power of the purse, of the office, and of the pen.

The purse represents the favorite mode of power with us. This is natural in our present stage of national existence and human development; it is likely to continue for a long time. In all civilized countries which have outgrown the period when the sword was the favorite emblem, the purse represents the favorite mode of power with the mass of men; but here it is so with the men of superior education. This power is not wholly personal, but extra-personal, and the man's centre of gravity lies out of himself, less or more, somewhere between the man and his last cent, the distance being greater or less as the man is less or greater than the estate. This is wielded chiefly by men of little education, except the practical culture which they have gained in the process of accumulation. Their riches they get purposely, their training by the way, and accidentally. It is a singular misfortune of the country that while the majority of the people are better cultivated and more enlightened than any other population in the world, the greater part of the wealth of the nation is owned by men of less education and consequently of less enlightenment than the rich men of any leading nation in Europe. In England and France the wealth of this generation is chiefly inherited, and has generally fallen to men carefully trained, with minds disciplined by academic culture. Here wealth is new, and mainly in the hands of men who have scrambled for it adroitly and with vigor. They have energy, vigor, forecast, and a certain generosity, but as a class are narrow, vulgar, and conceited. Nine-tenths of the property of the people is owned by one-tenth of the persons; and these capitalists are men of little culture, little moral elevation. This is an accident of our position unavoidable, perhaps transient; but it is certainly a misfortune that the great estates of the country, and the social and political power of such wealth, should be mainly in the hands of such men. The melancholy result appears in many a disastrous shape, in the tone of the pulpit, of the press, and of the national politics; much of the vulgarity of the nation is to be ascribed to this fact, that wealth belongs to men who know nothing better.

The office represents the next most popular mode of power. This also is extra-personal, the man's center of gravity is out of himself, somewhere between him and the lowest man in the state; the distance depending on the proportion of manhood in him and the multitude, if the office is much greater than the man, then the officer's center of gravity is further removed from his person. This is sought for by the ablest and best educated men in the land. But there is a large class of educated persons who do not aspire to it from lack of ability, for in our form of government it commonly takes some saliency of character to win the high places of office and use respectably this mode of power, while it demands no great or lofty talents to accumulate the largest fortune in America. It is true the whirlwind of an election, by the pressure of votes, may now and then take a very heavy body up to a great height. Yet it does not keep him from growing giddy and ridiculous while there, and after a few years lets him fall again into complete insignificance, whence no Hercules can ever lift him up. A corrupt administration may do the same, but with the same result. This consideration keeps many educated men from the political arena; others are unwilling to endure the unsavory atmosphere of politics, and take part in a scramble so vulgar; but still a large portion of the educated and scholarly talent of the nation goes to that work.

The power of the pen is wholly personal. It is the appropriate instrument of the scholar, but it is least of all desired and sought for. The rich man sends his sons to trade, to make too much of inheritance yet more by fresh acquisitions of superfluity. He does not send them to literature, art, or science. You find the scholar slipping in to other modes of action, not the merchants and politicians migrating into this. He longs to act by the gravity of his money or station, not draw merely by his head. The office carries the day before the pen; the purse takes precedence of both. Educated men do not so much seek places that demand great powers as those which bring much gold. Self-denial for money or office is common, for scholarship rare and unpopular. To act by money, not mind, is the ill-concealed ambition of many a well-bred man; the desire of this colors his day-dream, which is less of wisdom and more of wealth, or of political station; so a first-rate clergy-man desires to be razed to a second-rate politician, and some "tall admiral" of a politician consents to be cut down and turned into a mere sloop of trade. The representative in Congress becomes a president of an insurance office or a bank or the agent of a cotton-mill; the judge deserts his station on the bench and presides over a railroad; the governor or senator wants a place in the post-office; the historian longs for a "chance in the custom-house." The pen stoops to the office, that to the purse. The scholar would rather make a fortune by a balsam of wild cherry than write Hamlet or Paradise Lost for nothing; rather than help mankind by making a Paradise Regained. The well-endowed minister thinks how much more money he might have made had he speculated in stocks and not theology, and mourns that the kingdom of heaven does not pay in this present life fourfold. The professor of Greek is sorry he was not a surveyor and superintendent of a railroad, he should have so much more money; that is what he has learned from Plato and Diogenes. We estimate the skill of an artist like that of a pedler, not by the pictures he has made, but by the money. There is a mercantile way of determining literary merit, not by the author's books, but by his balance with the publisher. No church is yet called after a man who is merely rich, something in the New Testament might hinder that; but the ministers estimate their brother minister by the greatness of his position, not of his character; not by his piety and goodness, not even by his reason and understanding, the culture he has attained thereby, and the use he makes thereof, but by the wealth of his church and the largeness of his salary; so that he is not thought the fortunate and great minister who has a large outgo of spiritual riches, rebukes the sins of the nation and turns many to righteousness, but he who has a large material income, ministers, though poorly, to rich men, and is richly paid for that function. The well-paid clergymen of a city tell the professor of theology that he must teach "such doctrines as the merchants approve" or they will not give money to the college, and he, it, and the "cause of the Lord," will all come to the ground at the same time and in kindred confusion. So blind money would put out the heavenly eyes of science, and lead her also to his own ditch. It must not be forgotten that there are men in the midst of us,—rich, respectable, and highly honored with social rank and political power, who practically and in strict conformity with their theory honor Judas, who made money by his treachery, far more than Jesus who laid down his life for men whose money is deemed better than manhood. It must indeed be so. Any outrage that is profitable to the controlling portion of society is sure to be welcome to the leaders of the state, and is soon pronounced divine by the leaders of the church.

It would seem as if the pen ought to represent the favorite mode of power at a college; but even there the waters of Pactolus are thought fairer than the Castalian, Heliconian spring, or "Siloa's brook that flowed fast by the oracle of God." The college is named after the men of wealth, not genius. How few professorships in America bear the names of men of science or letters, and not of mere rich men! Which is thought the greatest benefactor of a college, he who endows it with money or with mind? Even there it is the pure, not the pen, that is the symbol of honor, and the University is "up for California," not Parnassus.

Even in politics the purse turns the scale. Let a party wrestle never so hard, it cannot throw the dollar. Money controls and commands talent, not talent money. The successful shopkeeper frowns on and browbeats the accomplished politician, who has too much justice for the wharf and the board of brokers; he notices that the rich men avert their eye, or keep their beaver down, trembles and is sad, fearing that his daughter will never find a fitting spouse. The purse buys up able men of superior education, corrupts and keeps them as its retained attorneys, in congress or the church, not as counsel but advocate, bribed to make the worse appear the better reason, and so help money to control the state and wield its power against the interest of mankind. This is perfectly well known; but no politician or minister, bribed to silence or to speech, ever loses his respectability because he is bought by respectable men,—if he get his pay. In all countries but this the office is before the purse; here the state is chiefly an accessory of the exchange, and our politics only mercantile. This appears sometimes against our will, in symbols not meant to tell the tale. Thus in the House of Representatives in Massachusetts, a codfish stares the speaker in the face—not a very intellectual looking fish. When it was put there it was a symbol of the riches of the state, and so of the Commonwealth. With singular and unconscious satire it tells the legislature to have an eye "to the main chance," and, but for its fidelity to its highest instincts and its obstinate silence, might be a symbol good enough for the place.

Now, after the office and the purse have taken their votaries from the educated class, the ablest men are certainly not left behind. Three roads open before our young Hercules as he leaves college, having respectively as finger-post the pen, the office, and the purse. Few follow the road of letters. This need not be much complained of; nay, it might be rejoiced in, if the purse and the office in their modes of power did represent the higher consciousness of mankind. But no one contends it is so.

Still there are men who devote themselves to some literary callings which have no connection with political office, and which are not pursued for the sake of great wealth. Such men produce the greater part of the permanent literature of the country. They are eminently scholars, permanent scholars who act by their scholar-craft, not by the state-craft of the politician, or the purse-craft of the capitalist. How are these men paying their debt and performing their function? The answer must be found in the science and the literature of the land.

American science is something of which we may well be proud. Mr. Liebig, in Germany, has found it necessary to defend himself from the charge of following science for the loaves and fishes thereof; and he declares that he espoused chemistry not for her wealthy dower, not even for the services her possible children might render to mankind, but solely for her own sweet sake. Amongst the English race, on both sides of the ocean, science is loved rather for the fruit than the blossom; its service to the body is thought of more value than its service to the mind. A man's respectability would be in danger in America, if he loved any science better than the money or fame it might bring. It is characteristic of us that a scholar should write for reputation and gold. Here, as elsewhere, the unprofitable parts of science fall to the lot of poor men. When the rich man's son has the natural calling that way public opinion would dissuade him from the study of nature. The greatest scientific attainments do not give a man so high social consideration as a political office or a successful speculation, unless it be the science which makes money. Scientific schools we call after merely rich men, not men of wealthy minds. It is true we name streets and squares, towns and counties, after Franklin, but it is because he keeps the lightning from factories, churches, and barns; tells us not "to give too much for the whistle," and teaches "the way to make money plenty in every man's pocket." We should not name them after Cuvier and Laplace.

Notwithstanding this, the scientific scholars of America, both the home-born and the adopted sons, have manfully paid for their culture, and done honor to the land. This is true of men in all departments of science,—from that which searches the deeps of the sky to that which explores the shallows of the sea. Individuals, states, and the nation, have all done themselves honor by the scientific researches and discoveries that have been made. The outlay of money and of genius for things which only pay the head and not the mouth of man is beautiful and a little surprising in such a utilitarian land as this. Time would fail me to attend to particular cases.

Look at the literature of America. Reserving the exceptional portion thereof to be examined in a moment, let us study the instantial portion of it, American literature as a whole. This may be distributed into two main divisions: First comes the permanent literature, consisting of books not designed merely for a single and transient occasion, but elaborately wrought for a general purpose. This is literature proper. Next follows the transient literature, which is brought out for a particular occasion, and designed to serve a special purpose. Let us look at each.

The permanent literature of America is poor and meager; it does not bear the mark of manly hands, of original, creative minds. Most of it is rather milk for babes than meat for men, though much of it is neither fresh meat nor new milk, but the old dish often served up before. In respect to its form, this portion of our literature is an imitation. That is natural enough, considering the youth of the country. Every nation, like every man, even one born to genius, begins by imitation. Raphael, with servile pencil, followed his masters in his youth; but at length his artistic eye attracted new-born angels from the calm stillness of their upper heaven, and with liberal, free hand, with masterly and original touch, the painter of the newness amazed the world.

The early Christian literature is an imitation of the Hebrew or the classic type; even after centuries had passed by, Sidonius, though a bishop of the church, and destined to become a saint, uses the old heathen imagery, referring to Triptolemus as a model for Christian work, and talks about Triton and Galatea to the Christian Queen of the Goths. Saint Ambrose is a notorious imitator of pagan Cicero. The Christians were all anointed with Jewish nard; and the sour grapes they ate in sacrament have set on edge their children's teeth till now. The modern nations of Europe began their literature by the driest copies of Livy and Virgil. The Germans have the most original literature of the last hundred years. But till the middle of the past century their permanent literature was chiefly in Latin and French, with as little originality as our own. The real poetic life of the nation found vent in other forms. It is natural, therefore, and according to the course of history, that we should begin in this way. The best political institutions of England are cherished here, so her best literature; and it is not surprising that we are content with this rich inheritance of artistic toil. In many things we are independent, but in much that relates to the higher works of man we are still colonies of England. This appears not only in the vulgar fondness for English fashions, manners, and the like, which is chiefly an affectation, but in the servile style with which we copy the great or little models of English literature. Sometimes this is done consciously, oftener without knowing it.

But the substance of our permanent literature is as faulty as its form. It does not bear marks of a new, free, vigorous mind at work, looking at things from the American point of view, and, though it put its thought in antique forms, yet thinking originally and for itself. It represents the average thought of respectable men, directed to some particular subject, and their average morality. It represents nothing more; how could it, while the ablest men have gone off to politics or trade? It is such literature as almost anybody might get up if you would give him a little time to make the preliminary studies. There is little in it that is national, little individual and of the writer's own mind; it is ground out in the public literary mill. It has no noble sentiments, no great ideas; nothing which makes you burn, nothing which makes you much worse or much better. You may feed on this literature all your days, and whatsoever you may gain in girth, you shall not take in thought enough to add half an inch to your stature.

Out of every hundred American literary works printed since the century began, about eighty will be of his character. Compare the four most conspicuous periodicals of America with the four great Quarterlies of England, and you see how inferior our literature is to theirs—in all things, in form and in substance too. The European has the freedom of a well-bred man—it appears in the movement of his thought, his use of words, in the easy grace of his sentences, and the general manner of his work; the American has the stiffness and limitations of a big, raw boy, in the presence of his schoolmaster. They are proud of being English, and so have a certain lofty nationality which appears in their thought and the form thereof, even in the freedom to use and invent new words. Our authors of this class seem ashamed that they are Americans, and accordingly are timid, ungraceful, and weak. They dare not be original when they could. Hence this sort of literature is dull. A man of the average mind and conscience, heart and soul, studies a particular subject a short time—for this is the land of brief processes—and writes a book thereof, or thereon; a critic of the same average makes his special study of the book, not its theme, "reviews" the work; is as ready and able to pass judgment on Bowditch's translation of Laplace in ten days after its appearance as ten years, and distributes praise and blame, not according to the author's knowledge, but the critic's ignorant caprice; and then average men read the book and the critique with no immoderate joy or unmeasured grief. They learn some new facts, no new ideas, and get no lofty impulse. The book was written without inspiration, without philosophy, and is read with small profit. Yet it is curious to observe the praise which such men receive, how soon they are raised to the House of Lords in English literature. I have known three American Sir Walter Scotts, half a dozen Addisons, one or two Macaulays, a historian that was Hume and Gibbon both in one, several Burnses, and Miltons by the quantity, not "mute," the more is the pity, but "inglorious" enough; nay, even vainglorious at the praise which some penny-a-liner or dollar-a-pager foolishly gave their cheap extemporary stuff. In sacred literature it is the same; in a single winter at Boston we had two American Saint Johns in full blast for several months. Though no Felix trembles, there are now extant in the United States not less than six American Saint Pauls, in no manner of peril except the most dangerous, of idle praise.

A living, natural, and full-grown literature contains two elements. One is of mankind in general; that is human and universal. The other is of the tribe in special, and of the writer in particular. This is national and even personal; you see the idiosyncrasy of the nation and the individual author in the work. The universal human substance accepts the author's form, and the public wine of mankind runs into the private bottle of the author. Thus the Hebrew literature of the Old Testament is fresh and original in substance and in form; the two elements are plain enough, the universal and the particular. The staple of the Psalms of David is human, of mankind, it is trust in God; but the twist, the die, the texture, the pattern, all that is Hebrew—of the tribe, and personal—of David, shepherd, warrior, poet, king. You see the pastoral hill-sides of Judæa in his holy hymns; nay, "Uriah's beauteous wife" now and then sidles into his sweetest psalm. The Old Testament books smell of Palestine, of its air and its soil. The Rose of Sharon has Hebrew earth about its roots. The geography of the Holy Land, its fauna and its flora both, even its wind and sky, its early and its latter rain, all appear in the literature of historian and bard. It is so in the Iliad. You see how the sea looked from Homer's point of view, and know how he felt the west wind, cold and raw. The human element has an Ionian form and a Homeric hue. The ballads of the people in Scotland and England are national in the same way; the staple of human life is wrought into the Scottish form. Before the Germans had any permanent national literature of this character their fertile mind found vent in legends, popular stories, now the admiration of the learned. These had at home the German dress, but as the stories traveled into other lands, they kept their human flesh and blood, but took a different garb, and acquired a different complexion from every country which they visited; and, like the streams of their native Swabia, took the color of the soil they traveled through.

The permanent and instantial literature of America is not national in this sense. It has little that is American; it might as well be written by some bookwright in Leipsic or London, and then imported. The individuality of the nation is not there, except in the cheap, gaudy binding of the work. The nationality of America is only stamped on the lids and vulgarly blazoned on the back.

Is the book a history?—it is written with no such freedom as you should expect of a writer looking at the breadth of the world from the lofty stand-point of America. There is no new philosophy of history in it. You would not think it was written in a democracy that keeps the peace without armies or a national gaol. Mr. Macaulay writes the history of England as none but a North Briton could do. Astonishingly well-read, equipped with literary skill at least equal to the masterly art of Voltaire, mapping out his subject like an engineer, and adorning it like a painter, you yet see, all along, that the author is a Scotchman and a Whig. Nobody else could have written so. It is of Mr. Macaulay. But our American writer thinks about matters just as everybody else does; that is, he does not think at all, but only writes what he reads, and then, like the good-natured bear in the nursery story, "thinks he has been thinking." It is no such thing, he has been writing the common opinion of common men, to get the applause of men as common as himself.

Is the book of poetry?—the substance is chiefly old, the form old, the allusions are old. It is poetry of society, not of nature. You meet in it the same everlasting mythology, the same geography, botany, zoology, the same symbols; a new figure of speech suggested by the sight of nature, not the reading of books, you could no more find than a fresh shad in the Dead Sea. You take at random eight or ten "American poets" of this stamp, you see at once what was the favorite author with each new bard; you often see what particular work of Shelley, or Tennyson, or Milton, or George Herbert, or, if the man has culture enough, of Goethe or Uhland, Jean Paul or Schiller, suggested the "American original." His inspiration comes from literature, not from the great universe of nature or of human life. You see that this writer has read Percy's Reliques, and the German Wunderhorn; but you would not know that he wrote in a republic—in a land full of new life, with great rivers and tall mountains, with maple and oak trees that turn red in the autumn; amongst a people who hold town-meetings, have free schools for everybody, read newspapers voraciously, who have lightning rods on their steeples, ride in railroads, are daguerreotyped by the sun, and who talk by lightning from Halifax to New Orleans; who listen to the whippoorwill and the bobolink, who believe in slavery and the Declaration of Independence, in the devil and the five points of Calvinism. You would not know where our poet lived, or that he lived anywhere. Reading the Iliad you doubt that Homer was born blind; but our bard seems to have been deaf also, and for expressing what was national in his time might likewise have been dumb.

Is it a volume of sermons?—they might have been written at Edinburgh, Madrid, or Constantinople, as well as in New England; as well preached to the "Homo Sapiens" of

Linnæus or the man in the moon, as to the special audience that heard or heard them not, but only paid for having the things preached. There is nothing individual about them; the author seems as impersonal as Spinoza's conception of God. The sermons are like an almanac calculated for the meridian of no place in particular, for no time in special. There is no allusion to anything American. The author never mentions a river this side of the Jordan; knows no mountain but Lebanon, Zion, and Carmel, and would think it profane to talk of the Alleghanies and the Mississippi, of Monadnoc and the Androscoggin. He mentions Babylon and Jerusalem, not New York and Baltimore; you would never dream that he lived in a church without a bishop, and a state without a king, in a democratic nation that held three million slaves, with ministers chosen by the people. He is surrounded, clouded over, and hid by the traditions of the "ages of faith" behind him. He never thanks God for the dew and snow, only for "the early and the latter rain" of a classic sacred land; a temperance man, he blesses God for the wine because the great Psalmist did so thousands of years ago. He speaks of the olive and the fig-tree which he never saw, not of the apple-tree and the peach before his eyes all day long, their fruit the joy of his children's heart. If you guessed at his time and place, you would think he lived, not under General Taylor, but under King Ahab, or Jeroboam; that his audience rode on camels or in chariots, not in steam-cars; that they fought with bows and arrows against the children of Moab; that their favorite sin was the worship of some graven image, and that they made their children pass through the fire unto Moloch, not through the counting-house unto Mammon. You would not know whether the preacher was married or a bachelor, rich or poor, saint or sinner; you would probably conclude he was not much of a saint, nor even much of a sinner.

The authors of this portion of our literature seem ashamed of America. One day she will take her revenge. They are the parasites of letters, and live on what other men have made classic. They would study the Holy Land, Greece, Etruria, Egypt, Nineveh, spots made famous by great and holy men, and let the native races of America fade out, taking no pains to study the monuments which so swiftly pass away from our own continent. It is curious that most of the accounts of the Indians of North America come from men not natives here, from French and Germans; and characteristic that we should send an expedition to the Dead Sea, while wide tracts of this continent lie all untouched by the white man's foot; and, also, that while we make such generous and noble efforts to christianize and bless the red, yellow, and black heathens at the world's end, we should leave the American Indian and Negro to die in savage darkness, the South making it penal to teach a black man to write or read.

Yet, there is one portion of our permanent literature, if literature it may be called, which is wholly indigenous and original. The lives of the early martyrs and confessors are purely Christian, so are the legends of saints and other pious men; there was nothing like this in the Hebrew or heathen literature, cause and occasion were alike wanting for it. So we have one series of literary productions that could be written by none but Americans, and only here; I mean the Lives of Fugitive Slaves. But as these are not the work of the men of superior culture they hardly help to pay the scholar's debt. Yet all the original romance of Americans is in them, not in the white man's novel.

Next is the transient literature, composed chiefly of speeches, orations, state papers, political and other occasional pamphlets, business reports, articles in the journals, and other productions designed to serve some present purpose. These are commonly the work of educated men, though not of such as make literature a profession. Taking this department as a whole, it differs much from the permanent literature; here is freshness of thought and newness of form. If American books are mainly an imitation of old models, it would be difficult to find the prototype of some American speeches. They "would have made Quintilian stare and gasp." Take the state papers of the American government during the administration of Mr. Polk, the speeches made in Congress at the same time, the state papers of the several states—you have a much better and more favorable idea of the vigor and originality of the American mind than you would get from all the bound books printed in that period. The diplomatic writing of American politicians compare favorably with those of any nation in the world. In eloquence no modern nation is before us, perhaps none is our equal. Here you see the inborn strength and manly vigor of the American mind. You meet same spirit which fells the forest, girdles the land with railroads, annexes Texas, and covets Cuba, Nicaragua, all the world. You see that the authors of this literature are workers also. Others have read of wild beasts; here are the men that have seen the wolf.

A portion of this literature represents the past, and has the vices already named. It comes from human history and not human nature; as you read it, you think if the inertia and the cowardliness of mankind; nothing is progressive, nothing noble, generous, or just, only respectable. The past is preferred before the present; money is put before men, a vested right before a natural right. Such literature appears in all countries. The ally of despotism, and the foe of mankind, it is yet a legitimate exponent of a large class of men. The leading journals of America, political and commercial, or literary, are poor and feeble; our reviews of books afford matter for grave consideration. You would often suppose them written by the same hand which manufactures the advertisements of the grand caravan, or some patent medicine; or, when unfavorable, by some of the men who write defamatory articles on the eve of an election.

But a large part of this transient literature is very different in its character. Its authors have broken with the traditions of the past; they have new ideas, and plans for putting them in execution; they are full of hope, are national to the extreme, bragging and defiant. They put the majority before institutions, the rights of the majority before the privilege of a few; they represent the onward tendency and material prophecy of the nation. The new activity of the American mind here expresses its purpose and its prayer. Here is strength, hope, confidence, even audacity; all is American. But the great idea of the absolute right does not appear, all is more national than human; and in what concerns the nation, it is not justice, the point where all interests are balanced, and the welfare of each harmonizes with that of all, which is sought; but the "greatest good of the greatest number," that is, only a privilege had at the cost of the smaller number. Here is little respect for universal humanity; little for the eternal laws of God, which override all the traditions and contrivances of men; more reverence for a statute or constitution, which is indeed the fundamental law of the political state, but is often only an attempt to compromise between the fleeting passions of the day and the immutable morality of God.

Amid all the public documents of the nation and the several states, in the speeches and writings of favorite men, who represent and so control the public mind, for fifty years there is little that "stirs the feelings infinite" within you; much to make us more American, not more manly. There is more head than heart; native intellect enough, culture that is competent, but little conscience or real religion. How many newspapers, how many politicians in the land go at all beyond the Whig idea of protecting the property now accumulated, or the Democratic idea of insuring the greatest material good of the greatest number? Where are we to look for the representative of justice, of the unalienable rights of all the people and all the nations? In the triple host of article-makers, speech-makers, lay and clerical, and makers of laws, you find but few who can be trusted to stand up for the unalienable rights of men; who will never write, speak, nor vote in the interests of a party, but always in the interest of mankind, and will represent the justice of God in the forum of the world.

This literature, like the other, fails of the high end of writing and of speech; with more vigor, more freedom, more breadth of vision, and an intense nationality, the authors thereof are just as far from representing the higher consciousness of mankind, just as vulgar as the tame and well-licked writers of the permanent literature. Here are the men who have cut their own way through the woods, men with more than the average intelligence, daring, and strength; but with less than the average justice which is honesty in the abstract, less than the average honesty which is justice concentrated upon small particulars.

Examine both these portions of American literature, the permanent and the fleeting— you see their educated authors are no higher than the rest of men. They are the slaves of public opinion as much as the gossip in her little village. It may not be the public opinion of a coterie of crones, but of a great party; that makes little odds, they are worshippers of the same rank, idolaters of the same wealth; the gossiping granny shows her littleness the size of life, while their deformity is magnified by the solar microscope of high office. Many a popular man exhibits his pigmy soul to the multitude of a whole continent, idly mistaking it for greatness. They are swayed by vulgar passions, seek vulgar ends, address vulgar motives, use vulgar means; they may command by their strength, they cannot refine by their beauty or instruct by their guidance, and still less inspire by any eminence of manhood which they were born to or have won. They build on the surface-sand for to-day, not on the rock of ages for ever. With so little conscience, they heed not the solemn voice of history, and respect no more the prophetic instincts of mankind.

To most men, the approbation of their fellows is one of the most desirable things. This approbation appears in the various forms of admiration, respect, esteem, confidence, veneration, and love. The great man obtains this after a time, and in its highest forms, without seeking it, simply by faithfulness to his nature. He gets it by rising and doing his work, in the course of nature, as easily and as irresistibly as the sun gathers to the clouds the evaporation of land and sea, and, like the sun, to shed it down in blessings on mankind. Little men seek this, consciously or not knowing it, by stooping, cringing, flattering the pride, the passion or the prejudice of others. So they get the approbation of men, but never of man. Sometimes this is sought for by the attainment of some accidental quality, which low-minded men hold in more honor than the genius of sage or poet or the brave manhood of some great hero of the soul. In England, though money is power, it is patrician birth which is nobility, and valued most; and there, accordingly, birth takes precedence of all—of genius, and even of gold. Men seek the companionship or the patronage of titled lords, and social rank depends upon nobility of blood. The few bishops in the upper house do more to give conventional respectability to the clerical profession there than all the solid intellect of Hooker, Barrow, and of South, the varied and exact learning of philosophic Cudworth, the eloquence and affluent piety of Taylor, and Butler's vast and manly mind. In America, social rank depends substantially on wealth, an accident as much as noble birth, but movable. Here gold takes precedence of all,—of genius, and even of noble birth.

> Though your sire
> Had royal blood within him, and though you
> Possess the intellect of angels too,
> 'Tis all in vain; the world will ne'er inquire
> On such a score;—Why should it take the pains?
> 'Tis easier to weigh purses, sure, than brains.

Wealth is sought, not merely as a means of power, but of nobility. When obtained, it has the power of nobility; so poor men of superior intellect and education, powerful by nature, not by position, fear to disturb the opinion of wealthy men, to instruct their ignorance or rebuke their sin. Hence the aristocracy of wealth, illiterate and vulgar, goes unrebuked, and debases the natural aristocracy of mind and culture which bows down to it. The artist prostitutes his pencil and his skill, and takes his law of beauty from the fat clown, whose barns and pigs and wife he paints for daily bread. The preacher does the same; and though the stench of the rum-shop infests the pulpit, and death hews down the leaders of his flock, the preacher must cry, "Peace, peace," or else be still, for rum is power! But this power of wealth has its antagonistic force, the power of numbers. Much depends on the dollar. Nine-tenths of the property is owned by one-tenth of all these men—but much also on the votes of the million. The few are strong by money, the many by their votes. Each is worshipped by its votaries, and its approbation sought. He that can get the men controls the money too. So while one portion of educated men bows to the rich, and consecrates their passion and their prejudice, another portion bows, equally prostrate, to the passions of the multitude of men. The many and the rich have each a public opinion of their own, and both are tyrants. Here the tyranny of public opinion is not absolutely greater than in England, Germany, or France, but is far greater in comparison with other modes of oppression. It seems inherent in a republic; it is not in a republic of noble men. But here this sirocco blows flat to the ground full many an aspiring blade. Wealth can establish banks or factories; votes can lift the meanest man into the highest political place, can dignify any passion with the name and force of human law; so it is thought by the worshippers of both, seeking the approbation of the two, that public opinion can make truth of lies, and right even out of foulest wrong. Politicians begin to say, there is no law of God above the ephemeral laws of men.

There are few American works of literature which appeal to what is best in men; few that one could wish should go abroad and live. America has grown beyond hope in population, the free and bond, in riches, in land, in public material prosperity; but in a literature that represents the higher elements of manliness far less than wise men thought. They looked for the fresh new child; it is born with wrinkles, and dreadfully like his grandmother, only looking older and more effete. Our muse does not come down from an American Parnassus, with a new heaven in her eye, men not daring to look on the face of anointed beauty, coming to tell of noble thought, to kindle godlike feelings with her celestial spark, and stir mankind to noble deeds. She finds Parnassus steep and high, and hard to climb; the air austere and cold, the light severe, too stern for her effeminate nerves. So she has a little dwelling in the flat and close pent town, hard by the public street; breathers its Bœotian breath; walks with the money-lenders at high change; has her account at the bank, her pew in the most fashionable church and least austere; she gets approving nods in the street, flattery in the penny prints, sweetmeats and sparkling wine in the proper places. What were the inspirations of all God's truth to her? He "taunts the lofty land with little men."

There still remains the exceptional literature; some of it is only fugitive, some meant for permanent duration. Here is a new and different spirit; a respect for human nature above human history, for man above all the accidents of man, for God above all the alleged accidents of God; a veneration for the eternal laws which he only makes and man but finds; a law before all statutes, above all constitutions, and holier than all the writings of human hands. Here you find most fully the sentiments and ideas of America, not such as rule the nation now, but which, unconsciously to the people, have caused the noble deeds of our history, and now prophesy a splendid future for this young giant here. These sentiments and ideas are brought to consciousness in this literature. Here a precedent is not a limitation; a fact of history does not eclipse an idea of nature; an investment is not thought more sacred than a right. Here is more hope than memory; little deference to wealth and rank, but a constant aspiration for truth, justice, love, and piety; little fear of the public opinion of the many or the few, rather a scorn thereof, almost a defiance of it. It appears in books, in pamphlets, in journals, and in sermons, sorely scant in quantity as yet. New and fresh, it is often greatly deficient in form; rough, rude, and uncouth, it yet has in it a soul that will live. Its authors are often men of a wide and fine culture, though mainly tending to underrate the past achievements of mankind. They have little reverence for great names. They value the Greek and Hebrew mind for no more than it is worth. With them a wrong is no more respected because well descended, and supported by all the riches, all the votes; a right, not less a right because unjustly kept out of its own. These men are American all through; so intensely national that they do not fear to tell the nation of the wrong it does.

The form of this literature is American. It is indigenous to our soil, and could come up in no other land. It is unlike the classic literature of any other nation. It is American as the Bible is Hebrew, and the Odyssey is Greek. It is wild and fantastic, like all fresh original literature at first. You see in it the image of republican institutions—the free school, free state, free church; it reflects the countenance of free men. So the letters of old France, of modern England, of Italy and Spain, reflect the monarchic, oligarchic, and ecclesiastic institutions of those lands. Here appears the civilization of the nineteenth century, the treasures of human toil for many a thousand years. More than that, you see the result of a fresh contact with nature, and original intuitions of divine things. Acknowledging inspiration of old, these writers of the newness believe in it now not less, not miraculous, but normal. Here is humanity that overleaps the bounds of class and of nation, and sees a brother in the beggar, pirate, slave, one family of men variously dressed in cuticles of white or yellow, black or red. Here, too, is a new loveliness, somewhat akin to the savage beauty of our own wild woods, seen in their glorious splendor an hour before autumnal suns go down and leave a trail of glory lingering in the sky. Here, too, is a piety somewhat heedless of scriptures, liturgies, and forms and creeds; it finds its law written in nature, its glorious everlasting gospel in the soul of man; careless of circumcision and baptismal rites, it finds the world a temple, and rejoices everywhere to hold communion with the Infinite Father of us all, and keep a sacrament in daily life, conscious of immortality, and feeding continually on angels' bread.

The writers of this new literature are full of faults; yet they are often strong, though more by their direction than by native force of mind; more by their intuitions of the first good, first perfect, and first fair, than through their historical knowledge or dialectic power. Their ship sails swift, not because it is sharper built, or carries broader sails than oher craft, but because it steers where the current of the ocean coincides with the current of the sky, and so is borne along by nature's wind and nature's wave. Uninvited, its ideas steal into parlor and pulpit, its kingdom coming within men and without observation. The shoemaker feels it as he toils in his narrow shop; it cheers the maiden weaving in the mill, whose wheels the Merrimac is made to turn; the young man at college bids it welcome to his ingenuous soul. So at the breath of spring new life starts up in every plant; the sloping hills are green with corn, and sunny banks are blue and fragrant with the wealth of violets, which only slept till the enchanter came. The sentiments of this literature burn in the bosom of holy-hearted girls, of matrons, and of men. Ever and anon its great ideas are heard even in Congress, and in the speech of old and young, which comes tingling into most unwilling ears.

This literature has a work to do, and is about its work. Let the old man crow loud as he may, the young one will crow another strain; for it is written of God that our march is continually onward, and age shall advance over age for ever and for ever.

Already America has a few fair specimens from this new field to show. Is the work history? The author writes from the stand-point of American democracy,—I mean philanthropy, the celestial democracy, not the satanic; writes with a sense of justice and in the interest of men; writes to tell a nation's purpose in its deeds, and so reveal the universal law of God, which overrules the affairs of states as of a single man. You wonder that history was not before so writ that its facts told the nation's ideas, and its labors were lessons, and so its hard-won life became philosophy.

Is it poetry the man writes? It is not poetry like the old. The poet has seen nature with his own eyes, heard her with his own mortal, bodily ears, and felt her presence, not vicariously through Milton, Uhland, Ariosto, but personally, her heart against his heart. He sings of what he knows, sees, feels, not merely of what he reads in others' song. Common things are not therefore unclean. In plain New England life he finds his poetry, as magnets iron in the balcksmith's dust, and as the bee finds dew-bright cups of honey in the common woods and common weeds. It is not for him to rave of Parnassus, while he knows it not, for the soul of song has a seat upon Monadnoc, Wachusett, or Katahdin, quite as high. So Scottish Burns was overtaken by the muse of poetry, who met him on his own bleak hills, and showed him beauty in the daisy and the thistle and the tiny mouse, till to his eye the hills ran o'er with loveliness, and Caledonia became a classic land.

Is it religion the author treats of? It is not worship by fear, but through absolute faith, a never-ending love; for it is not worship of a howling and imperfect God,—grim, jealous, and revengeful, loving but a few, and them not well; but of the Infinite Father of all mankind, whose universal providence will sure achieve the highest good of all that are.

These men are few; in no land are they numerous, or were or will be. There were few Hebrew prophets, but a tribe of priests; there are but few mightly bards that hover o'er the world; but here and there a sage, looking deep and living high, who feels the heart of things, and utter oracles which pass for proverbs, psalms and prayers, and stimulate a world of men. They draw the nations, as conjoining moon and sun draw waters shoreward from the ocean springs; and as electrifying heat they elevate the life of men. Under their influence you cannot be as before. They stimulate the sound, and intoxicate the silly; but in the heart of noble youths their idea becomes a fact, and their prayer a daily life.

Scholars of such a stamp are few and rare, not without great faults. For every one of them there will be many imitators, as for each lion a hundred lion-flies, thinking their buzz as valiant as his roar, and wondering the forest does not quake thereat, and while they feed on him fancy they suck the breasts of heaven.

Such is the scholars' position in America; such their duty, and such the way in which they pay the debt they owe. Will men of superior culture not all act by scholar-craft and by the pen? It were a pity if they did. If a man work nobly, the office is as worthy, and the purse as blessed in its work. The pen is power, the office is power, the purse is power; and if the purse and office be nobly held, then in a high mode the cultivated man pays for his bringing up, and honors with wide sympathies the mass of men who give him chance to ride and rule. If not; if these be meanly held, for self and not for man, then the scholar is a debtor and a traitor too.

The scholar never had so fair a chance before; here is the noblest opportunity for one that wields the pen; it is mightier than the sword, the office, or the purse. All things concede at last to beauty, justice, truth and love, and these he is to represent. He has what freedom he will pay for and take. Let him talk never so heroic, he will find fit audience, nor will it long be few. Men will rise up and welcome his quickening words as vernal grass at the first rains of spring. A great nation which cannot live by bread alone asks for the bread of life; while the state is young a single great and noble man can deeply influence the nation's mind. There are great wrongs which demand redress; the present men who represent the office and the purse will not end these wrongs. They linger for the pen, with magic touch, to abolish and destroy this ancient serpentbrood. Shall it be only rude men and unlettered who confront the dragons of our time which prowl about the folds by day and night, while the scholar, the appointed guardian of mankind, but "sports with Amaryllis in the shade, or with the tangles of Neæra's hair?" The nation asks of her scholar better things than ancient letters ever brought; asks his wonders for the million, not the few alone. Great sentiments burn now in half-unconscious hearts, and great ideas kindle their glories round the heads of men. Unconscious electricity, truth and right, flashes out of the earth, out of the air. It is for the scholar to attract this ground-lightning and this lightning of the sky, condense it into useful thunder to destroy the wrong, then spread it forth a beauteous and a cheering light, shedding sweet influence and kindling life anew. A few great men of other times tell us what may be now.

Nothing will be done without toil—talent is only power of work, and genius greater power for higher forms of work—nothing without self-denial; nothing great and good save by putting your idea before yourself, and counting it dearer than your flesh and blood. Let it hide you, not your obesity conceal the truth God gave you to reveal. The quality of intellectual work is more than the quantity. Out of the cloudy world Homer has drawn a spark that lasts three thousand years. "One, but a lion," should be the scholar's maxim; let him do many things for daily need; one great thing for the eternal beauty of his art. A single poem of Dante, a book for the bosom, loves through the ages, surrounding its author with the glory of genius in the night of time. One sermon on the mount, compact of truths brought down from God, all molten by such pious trust in him, will still men's hearts by myriads, while words dilute with other words are a shame to the speaker, and a dishonor to men who have ears to hear.

It is a great charity to give beauty to mankind, part of the scholar's function. How we honor such as create mere sensuous loveliness! Mozart carves it on the unseen air; Phidias sculptures it out from the marble stone; Raphael fixes ideal angels, maidens, matrons, men, and his triple God upon the canvas; and the lofty Angelo, with more than Amphionic skill, bids the hills rise into a temple which constrains the crowd to pray. Look, see how grateful man repays there architects of beauty with never-ending fame! Such as create a more than sensuous loveliness, the Homers, Miltons, Shakespeares, who sing of man in never-dying and creative song—see what honors we have in store for such, what honor given for what service paid! But there is a beauty higher than that of art, above philosophy and merely intellectual grace; I mean the loveliness of noble life; that is a beauty in the sight of man and God. This is a new country, the great ideas of a noble man are easily spread abroad; soon they will appear in the life of the people, and be a blessing in our future history to ages yet unborn. A few great souls can correct the licentiousness of the American press, which is now but the type of covetousness and low ambition; correct the mean economy of the state, and amend the vulgarity of the American church, now the poor prostitute of every wealthy sin.

Oh, ingenuous young maid or man, if such you are,—if not, then let me dream you such,—seek you this beauty, complete perfection of a man, and having this go hold the purse, the office, or the pen, as suits you best; but out of that life, writing, voting, acting, living in all forms, you shall pay men back for your culture, and in the scholar's noble kind, and represent the higher facts of human thought. Will men still say, "This wrong is consecrated; it has stood for ages, and shall stand for ever!" Tell them, "No. A wrong, though old as sin, is not now sacred, nor shall it stand!" Will they say, "This right can never be; that excellence is lovely, but impossible!" Show them the fact, who will not hear the speech; the deed goes where the word fails, and life enchants where rhetoric cannot persuade.

Past ages offer their instruction, much warning, and a little guidance, many a wreck along the shore of time, a beacon here and there. Far off in the dim distance, present as possibilities, not actual as yet, future generations with broad and wishful eyes look at the son of genius, talent, educated skill, and seem to say "A word for us, it will not be forgot!" Truth and Beauty, God's twin daughters, eternal both yet ever young, wait there to offer each faithful man a budding branch,—in their hands budding, in his to blossom and mature its fruit,—wherewith he sows the field of time, gladdening the millions yet to come.

[1849]

Nathaniel Hawthorne

Preface to *The House of the Seven Gables*

When a writer calls his work a Romance, it need hardly be observed that he wishes to claim a certain latitude, both as to its fashion and material, which he would not have felt himself entitled to assume, had he professed to be writing a Novel. The latter form of composition is presumed to aim at a very minute fidelity, not merely to the possible, but to the probable and ordinary course of man's experience. The former—while, as a work of art, it must rigidly subject itself to laws, and while it sins unpardonably, so far as it may swerve aside from the truth of the human heart—has fairly a right to present that truth under circumstances, to a great extent, of the writer's own choosing or creation. If he think fit, also, he may so manage his atmospherical medium as to bring out or mellow the lights and deepen and enrich the shadows of the picture. He will be wise, no doubt, to make a very moderate use of the privileges here stated, and, especially, to mingle the Marvellous rather as a slight, delicate, and evanescent flavor, than as any portion of the actual substance of the dish offered to the Public. He can hardly be said, however, to commit a literary crime, even if he disregard this caution.

In the present work, the Author has proposed to himself (but with what success, fortunately, it is not for him to judge) to keep undeviatingly within his immunities. The point of view in which this Tale comes under the Romantic definition, lies in the attempt to connect a by-gone time with the very Present that is flitting away from us. It is a Legend, prolonging itself, from an epoch now gray in the distance, down into our own broad daylight, and bringing along with it some of its legendary mist, which the Reader, according to his pleasure, may either disregard, or allow it to float almost imperceptibly about the characters and events, for the sake of a picturesque effect. The narrative, it may be, is woven of so humble a texture as to require this advantage, and, at the same time, to render it the more difficult of attainment.

Many writers lay very great stress upon some definite moral purpose, at which they profess to aim their works. Not to be deficient, in this particular, the Author has provided himself with a moral;—the truth, namely, that the wrong-doing of one generation lives into the successive ones, and, divesting itself of every temporary advantage, becomes a pure and uncontrollable mischief;—and he would feel it a singular gratification, if this Romance might effectually convince mankind (or, indeed, any one man) of the folly of tumbling down an avalanche of ill-gotten gold, or real estate, on the heads of an unfortunate posterity, thereby to maim and crush them, until the accumulated mass shall be scattered abroad in its original atoms. In good faith, however, he is not sufficiently imaginative to flatter himself with the slightest hope of this kind. When romances do really teach anything, or produce any effective operation, it is usually through a far more subtle process than the ostensible one. The Author has considered it hardly worth his while, therefore, relentlessly to impale the story with its moral, as with an iron rod—or rather, as by sticking a pin through a butterfly—thus at once depriving it of life, and causing it to stiffen in an ungainly and unnatural attitude. A high truth, indeed, fairly, finely, and skilfully wrought out, brightening at every step, and crowning the final development of a work of fiction, may add an artistic glory, but is never any truer, and seldom any more evident, at the last page than at the first.

The Reader may perhaps choose to assign an actual locality to the imaginary events of this narrative. If permitted by the historical connection, (which, though slight, was essential to his plan,) the Author would very willingly have avoided anything of this nature. Not to speak of other objections, it exposes the Romance to an inflexible and exceedingly dangerous species of criticism, by bringing his fancy-pictures almost into positive contact with the realities of the moment. It has been no part of his object, however, to describe local manners, nor in any way to meddle with the characteristics of a community for whom he cherishes a proper respect and a natural regard. He trusts not to be considered as unpardonably offending, by laying out a street that infringes upon nobody's private rights, and appropriating a lot of land which had no visible owner, and building a house, of materials long in use for constructing castles in the air. The personages of the Tale—though they give themselves out to be of ancient stability and considerable prominence—are really of the Author's own making, or, at all events, of his own mixing; their virtues can shed no lustre, nor their defects redound, in the remotest degree, to the discredit of the venerable town of which they profess to be inhabitants. He would be glad, therefore, if—especially in the quarter to which he alludes—the book may be read strictly as a Romance, having a great deal more to do with the clouds overhead, than with any portion of the actual soil of the County of Essex.

LENOX, *January 27, 1851.*

Nathaniel Hawthorne

Preface to *Blithedale Romance*

In the 'Blithedale' of this volume, many readers will probably suspect a faint and not very faithful shadowing of BROOK FARM, in Roxbury, which (now a little more than ten years ago) was occupied and cultivated by a company of socialists. The Author does not wish to deny, that he had this Community in his mind, and that (having had the good fortune, for a time, to be personally connected with it) he has occasionally availed himself of his actual reminiscences, in the hope of giving a more lifelike tint to the fancy-sketch in the following pages. He begs it to be understood, however, that he has considered the Institution itself as not less fairly the subject of fictitious handling, than the imaginary personages whom he has introduced there. His whole treatment of the affair is altogether incidental to the main purpose of the Romance; nor does he put forward the slightest pretensions to illustrate a theory, or elicit a conclusion, favorable or otherwise, in respect to Socialism.

In short, his present concern with the Socialist Community is merely to establish a theatre, a little removed from the highway of ordinary travel, where the creatures of his brain may play their phantasmagorical antics, without exposing them to too close a comparison with the actual events of real lives. In the old countries, with which Fiction has long been conversant, a certain conventional privilege seems to be awarded to the romancer; his work is not put exactly side by side with nature; and he is allowed a license with regard to every-day Probability, in view of the improved effects which he is bound to produce thereby. Among ourselves, on the contrary, there is as yet no such Faery Land, so like the real world, that, in a suitable remoteness, one cannot well tell the difference, but with an atmosphere of strange enchantment, beheld through which the inhabitants have a propriety of their own. This atmosphere is what the American romancer needs. In its absence, the beings of imagination are compelled to show themselves in the same category as actually living mortals; a necessity that generally renders the paint and pasteboard of their composition but too painfully discernible. With the idea of partially obviating this difficulty, (the sense of which has always pressed very heavily upon him,) the Author has ventured to make free with his old, and affectionately remembered home, at BROOK FARM, as being, certainly, the most romantic episode of his own life—essentially a day-dream, and yet a fact—and thus offering an available foothold between fiction and reality. Furthermore, the scene was in good keeping with the personages whom he desired to introduce.

These characters, he feels it right to say, are entirely fictitious. It would, indeed, (considering how few amiable qualities he distributes among his imaginary progeny,) be a most grievous wrong to his former excellent associates, were the Author to allow it to be supposed that he has been sketching any of their likenesses. Had he attempted it, they would at least have recognized the touches of a friendly pencil. But he has done nothing of the kind. The self-concentrated Philanthropist; the high-spirited Woman, bruising herself against the narrow limitations of her sex; the weakly Maiden, whose tremulous nerves endow her with Sibylline attributes; the Minor Poet, beginning life with strenuous aspirations, which die out with his youthful fervor—all these might have been looked for, at BROOK FARM, but, by some accident, never made their appearance there.

The Author cannot close his reference to this subject, without expressing a most earnest wish that some one of the many cultivated and philosophic minds, which took an interest in that enterprise, might now give the world its history. Ripley, with whom rests the honorable paternity of the Institution, Dana, Dwight, Channing, Burton, Parker, for instance—with others, whom he dares not name, because they veil themselves from the public eye—among these is the ability to convey both the outward narrative and the inner truth and spirit of the whole affair, together with the lessons which those years of thought and toil must have elaborated, for the behoof of future experimentalists. Even the brilliant Howadji might find as rich a theme in his youthful reminiscenses of BROOK FARM, and a more novel one—close at hand as it lies—than those which he has since made so distant a pilgrimage to seek, in Syria, and along the current of the Nile.

CONCORD (MASS.), *May, 1852.*

Nathaniel Hawthorne

Preface to *The Marble Faun*

It is now seven or eight years (so many, at all events, that I cannot precisely remember the epoch) since the Author of this Romance last appeared before the Public. It had grown to be a custom with him, to introduce each of his humble publications with a familiar kind of Preface, addressed nominally to the Public at large, but really to a character with whom he felt entitled to use far greater freedom. He meant it for that one congenial friend—more comprehensive of his purposes, more appreciative of his success, more indulgent of his short-comings, and, in all respects, closer and kinder than a brother—that all-sympathizing critic, in short, whom an author never actually meets, but to whom he implicitly makes his appeal, whenever he is conscious of having done his best.

The antique fashion of Prefaces recognized this genial personage as the 'Kind Reader," the 'Gentle Reader,' the 'Beloved,' the 'Indulgent,' or, at coldest, the 'Honoured Reader,' to whom the prim old author was wont to make his preliminary explanations and apologies, with the certainty that they would be favourably received. I never personally encountered, nor corresponded through the Post, with this Representative Essence of all delightful and desirable qualities which a Reader can possess. But, fortunately for myself, I never therefore concluded him to be merely a mythic character. I had always a sturdy faith in his actual existence, and wrote for him, year after year, during which the great Eye of the Public (as well it might) almost utterly overlooked my small productions.

Unquestionably, this Gentle, Kind, Benevolent, Indulgent, and most Beloved and Honoured Reader, did once exist for me, and (in spite of the infinite chances against a letter's reaching its destination, without a definite address) duly received the scrolls which I flung upon whatever wind was blowing, in the faith that they would find him out. But, is he extant now? In these many years, since he last heard from me, may he not have deemed his earthly task accomplished, and have withdrawn to the Paradise of Gentle Readers, wherever it may be, to the enjoyments of which his kindly charity, on my behalf, must surely have entitled him? I have a sad foreboding that this may be the truth. The Gentle Reader, in the case of any individual author, is apt to be extremely short-lived; he seldom outlasts a literary fashion, and, except in very rare instances, closes his weary eyes before the writer has half done with him. If I find him at all, it will probably be under some mossy grave-stone, inscribed with a half-obliterated name, which I shall never recognize.

Therefore, I have little heart or confidence (especially, writing, as I do, in a foreign land, and after a long, long absence from my own) to presume upon the existence of that friend of friends, that unseen brother of the soul, whose apprehensive sympathy has so often encouraged me to be egotistical in my Prefaces, careless though unkindly eyes should skim over what was never meant for them. I stand upon ceremony, now, and, after stating a few particulars about the work which is here offered to the Public, must make my most reverential bow, and retire behind the curtain.

This Romance was sketched out during a residence of considerable length in Italy, and has been re-written and prepared for the press, in England. The author proposed to himself merely to write a fanciful story, evolving a thoughtful moral, and did not purpose attempting a portraiture of Italian manners and character. He has lived too long abroad, not to be aware that a foreigner seldom acquires that knowledge of a country, at once flexible and profound, which may justify him in endeavouring to idealize its traits.

Italy, as the site of his Romance, was chiefly valuable to him as affording a sort of poetic or fairy precinct, where actualities would not be so terribly insisted upon, as they are, and must needs be, in America. No author, without a trial, can conceive of the difficulty of writing a Romance about a country where there is no shadow, no antiquity, no mystery, no picturesque and gloomy wrong, nor anything but a common-place prosperity, in broad and simple daylight, as is happily the case with my dear native land. It will be very long, I trust, before romance-writers may find congenial and easily handled themes either in the annals of our stalwart Republic, or in any characteristic and probable events of our individual lives. Romance and poetry, like ivy, lichens, and wall-flowers, need Ruin to make them grow.

In re-writing these volumes, the Author was somewhat surprised to see the extent to which he had introduced descriptions of various Italian objects, antique, pictorial, and statuesque. Yet these things fill the mind, everywhere in Italy, and especially in Rome, and cannot easily be kept from flowing out upon the page, when one writes freely, and with self-enjoyment. And, again, while reproducing the book, on the broad and dreary sands of Redcar, with the gray German Ocean tumbling in upon me, and the northern blast always howling in my ears, the complete change of scene made these Italian reminiscences shine out so vividly, that I could not find in my heart to cancel them.

An act of justice remains to be performed towards two men of genius, with whose productions the Author has allowed himself to use a quite unwarrantable freedom. Having imagined a sculptor, in this Romance, it was necessary to provide him with such works in marble as should be in keeping with the artistic ability which he was supposed to possess. With this view, the Author laid felonious hands upon a certain bust of Milton and a statue of a Pearl-Diver, which he found in the studio of Mr. PAUL AKERS, and secretly conveyed them to the premises of his imaginary friend, in the Via Frezza. Not content even with these spoils, he committed a further robbery upon a magnificent statue of Cleopatra, the production of Mr. WILLIAM W. STORY, an artist whom his country and the world will not long fail to appreciate. He had thoughts of appropriating, likewise, a certain door of bronze, by Mr. RANDOLPH ROGERS, representing the history of Columbus in a series of admirable bas-reliefs, but was deterred by an unwillingness to meddle with public property. Were he capable of stealing from a lady, he would certainly have made free with Miss HOSMER's noble statue of Zenobia.

He now wishes to restore the above-mentioned beautiful pieces of sculpture to thier proper owners, with many thanks, and the avowal of his sincere admiration. What he has said of them, in the Romance, does not partake of the fiction in which they are imbedded, but expresses his genuine opinion, which, he has little doubt, will be found in accordance with that of the Public. It is perhaps unnecessary to say, that, while stealing their designs, the Author has not taken a similar liberty with the personal characters of either of these gifted Sculptors; his own Man of Marble being entirely imaginary.

LEAMINGTON, *October 15th, 1859.*

Herman Melville

Hawthorne and His Mosses

By a Virginian Spending July in Vermont

A papered chamber in a fine old farm-house—a mile from any other dwelling, and dipped to the eaves in foliage—surrounded by mountains, old woods, and Indian ponds,—this, surely, is the place to write of Hawthorne. Some charm is in this northern air, for love and duty seem both impelling to the task. A man of a deep and noble nature has seized me in this seclusion. His wild, witch voice rings through me; or, in softer cadences, I seem to hear it in the songs of the hill-side birds, that sing in the larch trees at my window.

Would that all excellent books were foundlings, without father or mother, that so it might be, we could glorify them, without including their ostensible authors. Nor would any true man take exception to this;—least of all, he who writes,—"When the Artist rises high enough to achieve the Beautiful, the symbol by which he makes it perceptible to mortal senses becomes of little value in his eyes, while his spirit possesses itself in the enjoyment of the reality."

But more than this. I know not what would be the right name to put on the title-page of an excellent book, but this I feel, that the names of all fine authors are fictitious ones, far more so than that of Junius,—simply standing, as they do, for the mystical, ever-eluding Spirit of all Beauty, which ubiquitously possesses men of genius. Purely imaginative as this fancy may appear, it nevertheless seems to receive some warranty from the fact, that on a personal interview no great author has ever come up to the idea of his reader. But that dust of which our bodies are composed, how can it fitly express the nobler intelligences among us? With reverence be it spoken, that not even in the case of one deemed more than man, not even in our Saviour, did his visible frame betoken anything of the augustness of the nature within. Else, how could those Jewish eyewitnesses fail to see heaven in his glance.

It is curious, how a man may travel along a country road, and yet miss the grandest, or sweetest of prospects, by reason of an intervening hedge, so like all other hedges, as in no way to hint of the wide landscape beyond. So has it been with me concerning the enchanting landscape in the soul of this Hawthorne, this most excellent Man of Mosses. His "Old Manse" has been written now four years, but I never read it till a day or two since. I had seen it in the book-stores—heard of it often—even had it recommended to me by a tasteful friend, as a rare, quiet book, perhaps too deserving of popularity to be popular. But there are so many books called "excellent", and so much unpopular merit, that amid the thick stir of other things, the hint of my tasteful friend was disregarded; and for four years the Mosses on the old Manse never refreshed me with their perennial green. It may be, however, that all this while, the book, like wine, was only improving in flavor and body. At any rate, it so chanced that this long procrastination eventuated in a happy result. At breakfast the other day, a mountain girl, a cousin of mine, who for the last two weeks has every morning helped me to strawberries and raspberries,—which, like the roses and pearls in the fairy-tale, seemed to fall into the saucer from those strawberry-beds her cheeks,—this delightful creature, this charming Cherry says to me—"I see you spend your mornings in the hay-mow; and yesterday I found there 'Dwight's Travels in New England'. Now I have something far better than that,—something more congenial to our summer on these hills. Take these raspberries, and then I will give you some moss."— "Moss!" said I.—"Yes, and you must take it to the barn with you, and good-bye to 'Dwight'".

With that she left me, and soon returned with a volume, verdantly bound, and garnished with a curious frontispiece in green,—nothing less, than a fragment of real moss cunningly pressed to a fly-leaf.—"Why this," said I spilling my raspberries, "this is the 'Mosses from an Old Manse'". "Yes" said cousin Cherry "yes, it is that flowery Hawthorne."—"Hawthorne and Mosses" said I "no more: it is morning: it is July in the country: and I am off for the barn".

Stretched on that new mown clover, the hill-side breeze blowing over me through the wide barn door, and soothed by the hum of the bees in the meadows around, how magically stole over me this Mossy Man! and how amply, how bountifully, did he redeem that delicious promise to his guests in the old Manse, of whom it is written—"Others could give them pleasure, or amusement, or instruction—these could be picked up anywhere— but it was for me to give them rest. Rest, in a life of trouble! What better could be done for weary and world-worn spirits? what better could be done for anybody, who came within our magic circle, than to throw the spell of a magic spirit over him?"—So all that day, half-buried in the new clover, I watched this Hawthorne's "Assyrian dawn, and Paphian sunset and moonrise, from the summit of our Eastern Hill."

The soft ravishments of the man spun me round about in a web of dreams, and when the book was closed, when the spell was over, this wizard "dismissed me with but misty reminiscences, as if I had been dreaming of him".

What a mild moonlight of contemplative humor bathes that Old Manse!—the rich and rare distilment of a spicy and slowly-oozing heart. No rollicking rudeness, no gross fun fed on fat dinners, and bred in the lees of wine,—but a humor so spiritually gentle, so high, so deep, and yet so richly relishable, that it were hardly inappropriate in an angel. It is the very religion of mirth; for nothing so human but it may be advanced to that. The orchard of the Old Manse seems the visible type of the fine mind that has described it. Those twisted, and contorted old trees, "that stretch out their crooked branches, and take such hold of the imagination, that we remember them as humorists, and odd-fellows." And then, as surrounded by these grotesque forms, and hushed in the noon-day repose of this Hawthorne's spell, how aptly might the still fall of his ruddy thoughts into your soul be symbolized by "the thump of a great apple, in the stillest afternoon, falling without a breath of wind, from the mere necessity of perfect ripeness"! For no less ripe than ruddy are the apples of the thoughts and fancies in this sweet Man of Mosses.

"Buds and Bird-voices"—What a delicious thing is that!—"Will the world ever be so decayed, that Spring may not renew its greenness?"—And the "Fire-Worship". Was ever the hearth so glorified into an alter before? The mere title of that piece is better than any common work in fifty folio volumes. How exquisite is this:—"Nor did it lessen the charm of his soft, familiar courtesy and helpfulness, that the mighty spirit, were opportunity offered him, would run riot through the peaceful house, wrap its inmates in his terrible embrace, and leave nothing of them save their whitened bones. This possibility of mad destruction only made his domestic kindness the more beautiful and touching. It was so sweet of him, being endowed with such power, to dwell, day after day, and one long, lonesome night after another, on the dusky hearth, only now and then betraying his wild nature, by thrusting his red tongue out of the chimney-top! True, he had done much mischief in the world, and was pretty certain to do more, but his warm heart atoned for all. He was kindly to the race of man."

But he has still other apples, not quite so ruddy, though full as ripe;—apples, that have been left to wither on the tree, after the pleasant autumn gathering is past. The sketch of "The Old Apple Dealer" is conceived in the subtlest spirit of sadness; he whose "subdued and nerveless boyhood prefigured his abortive prime, which, likewise, contained within itself the prophecy and image of his lean and torpid age". Such touches as are in this piece can not proceed from any common heart. They argue such a depth of tenderness, such a boundless sympathy with all forms of being, such an omnipresent love, that we must needs say, that this Hawthorne is here almost alone in his generation,—at least, in the artistic manifestation of these things. Still more. Such touches as these,—and many, very many similar ones, all through his chapters—furnish clews, whereby we enter a little way into the intricate, profound heart where they originated. And we see, that suffering, some time or other and in some shape or other,—this only can enable any man to depict it in others. All over him, Hawthorne's melancholy rests like an Indian Summer, which though bathing a whole country in one softness, still reveals the distinctive hue of every towering hill, and each far-winding vale.

But it is the least part of genius that attracts admiration. Where Hawthorne is known, he seems to be deemed a pleasant writer, with a pleasant style,—a sequestered, harmless man, from whom any deep and weighty thing would hardly be anticipated:—a man who means no meanings. But there is no man, in whom humor and love, like mountain peaks, soar to such a rapt height, as to receive the irradiations of the upper skies;—there is no man in whom humor and love are developed in that high form called genius; no such man can exist without also possessing, as the indispensable complement of these, a great, deep intellect, which drops down into the universe like a plummet. Or, love and humor are only the eyes, through which such an intellect views this world. The great beauty in such a mind is but the product of its strength. What, to all readers, can be more charming than the piece entitled "Monsieur du Miroir"; and to a reader at all capable of fully fathoming it, what, at the same time, can possess more mystical depth of meaning?—Yes, there he sits, and looks at me,—this "shape of mystery", this "identical Monsieur du Miroir".— "Methinks I should tremble now, were his wizard power of gliding through all impediments in search of me, to place him suddenly before my eyes".

How profound, nay appalling, is the moral evolved by the "Earth's Holocaust"; where—beginning with the hollow follies and affectations of the world,—all vanities and empty theories and forms, are, one after another, and by an admirabley graduated, growing comprehensiveness, thrown into the allegorical fire, till, at length, nothing is left but the all-engendering heart of man; which remaining still unconsumed, the great conflagration is nought.

Of a piece with this, is the "Intelligence Office", a wondrous symbolizing of the secret workings in men's souls. There are other sketches, still more charged with ponderous import.

"The Christmas Banquet", and "The Bosom Serpent" would be fine subjects for a curious and elaborate analysis, touching the conjectural part of the mind that produced them. For spite of all the Indian-summer sunlight on the hither side of Hawthorne's soul, the other side—like the dark half of the physical sphere—is shrouded in a blackness, ten times black. But this darkness but gives more effect to the ever-moving dawn, that forever advances through it, and circumnavigates his world. Whether Hawthorne has simply availed himself of this mystical blackness as a means to the wondrous effects he makes it to produce in his lights and shades; or whether there really lurks in him, perhaps unknown to himself, a touch of Puritanic gloom,—this, I cannot altogether tell. Certain it is, however, that this great power of blackness in him derives its force from its appeals to that Calvinistic sense of Innate Depravity and Original Sin, from whose visitations, in some shape or other, no deeply thinking mind is always and wholly free. For, in certain moods, no man can weigh this world, without throwing in something, somehow like Original Sin, to strike the uneven balance. At all events, perhaps no writer has ever wielded this terrific thought with greater terror than this same harmless Hawthorne. Still more: this black conceit pervades him, through and through. You may be witched by his sunlight,—transported by the bright gildings in the skies he builds over you;—but there is the blackness of darkness beyond; and even his bright gildings but fringe, and play upon the edges of thunder-clouds.—In one word, the world is mistaken in this Nathaniel Hawthorne, He himself must often have smiled at its absurd misconception of him. He is immeasurably deeper than the plummet of the mere critic. For it is not the brain that can test such a man; it is only the heart. You cannot come to know greatness by inspecting it; there is no glimpse to be caught of it, except by intuition; you need not ring it, you but touch it, and you find it is gold.

Now it is that blackness in Hawthorne, of which I have spoken, that so fixes and fascinates me. It may be, nevertheless, that it is too largely developed in him. Perhaps he does not give us a ray of his light for every shade of his dark. But however this may be, this blackness it is that furnishes the infinite obscure of his back-ground,—that back-ground, against which Shakespeare plays his grandest conceits, the things that have made for Shakespeare his loftiest, but most circumscribed renown, as the profoundest of thinkers. For by philosophers Shakespeare is not adored as the great man of tragedy and comedy.— "Off with his head! so much for Buckingham!" this sort of rant, interlined by another hand, brings down the house,—those mistaken souls, who dream of Shakespeare as a mere man of Richard-the-Third humps, and Macbeth daggers. But it is those deep far-away things in him; those occasional flashings-forth of the intuitive Truth in him; those short, quick probings at the very axis of reality;—these are the things that make Shakespeare, Shakespeare. Through the mouths of the dark characters of Hamlet, Timon, Lear, and Iago, he craftily says, or sometimes insinuates the things, which we feel to be so terrifically true, that it were all but madness for any good man, in his own proper character, to utter, or even hint of them. Tormented into desperation, Lear the frantic King tears off the mask, and speaks the sane madness of vital truth. But, as I before said, it is the least part of genius that attracts admiration. And so, much of the blind, unbridled admiration that has been heaped upon Shakespeare, has been lavished upon the least part of him. And few of his endless commentators and critics seem to have remembered, or even perceived, that the immediate products of a great mind are not so great, as that undeveloped, (and sometimes undevelopable) yet dimly-discernable greatness, to which these immediate products are but the infallible indices. In Shakespeare's tomb lies infinitely more than Shakespeare ever wrote. And if I magnify Shakespeare, it is not so much for what he did do, as for what he did not do, or refrained from doing. For in this world of lies, Truth is forced to fly like a scared white doe in the woodlands; and only by cunning glimpses will she reveal herself, as in Shakespeare and other masters of the great Art of Telling the Truth,—even though it be covertly, and by snatches.

But if this view of the all-popular Shakespeare be seldom taken by his readers, and if very few who extol him, have ever read him deeply, or, perhaps, only have seen him on the tricky stage, (which alone made, and is still making him his mere mob renown)—if few men have time, or patience, or palate, for the spiritual truth as it is in that great genius;— it is, then, no matter of surprise that in a contemporaneous age, Nathaniel Hawthorne is a man, as yet, almost utterly mistaken among men. Here and there, in some quiet arm-chair in the noisy town, or some deep nook among the noiseless mountains, he may be appreciated for something of what he is. But unlike Shakespeare, who was forced to the contrary course by circumstances, Hawthorne (either from simple disinclination, or else from inaptitude) refrains from all the popularizing noise and show of broad farce, and blood-be-smeared tragedy; content with the still, rich utterances of a great intellect in repose, and which sends few thoughts into circulation, except they be arterialized at his large warm lungs, and expanded in his honest heart.

Nor need you fix upon that blackness in him, if it suit you not. Nor, indeed, will all readers discern it, for it is, mostly, insinuated to those who may best understand it, and account for it; it is not obtruded upon every one alike.

Some may start to read of Shakespeare and Hawthorne on the same page. They may say, that if an illustration were needed, a lesser light might have sufficed to elucidate this Hawthorne, this small man of yesterday. But I am not, willingly, one of those, who, as touching Shakespeare at least, exemplify the maxim of Rochefoucault, that "we exalt the reputation of some, in order to depress that of others";—who, to teach all noble-souled aspirants that there is no hope for them, pronounce Shakespeare absolutely unapproachable. But Shakespeare has been approached. There are minds that have gone as far as Shakespeare into the universe. And hardly a mortal man, who, at some time or other, has not felt as great thoughts in him as any you will find in Hamlet. We must not inferentially malign mankind for the sake of any one man, whoever he may be. This to too cheap a purchase of contentment for conscious mediocrity to make. Besides, this absolute and unconditional adoration of Shakespeare has grown to be a part of our Anglo Saxon superstitions. The Thirty Nine articles are now Forty. Intolerance has come to exist in this matter. You must believe in Shakespeare's unapproachability, or quit the country. But what sort of a belief is this for an American, a man who is bound to carry republican progressiveness into Literature, as well as into Life? Believe me, my friends, that Shakespeares are this day being born on the banks of the Ohio. And the day will come, when you shall say who reads a book by an Englishman that is a modern? The great mistake seems to be, that even with those Americans who look forward to the coming of a great literary genius among us, they somehow fancy he will come in the costume of Queen Elizabeth's day,—be a writer of dramas founded upon old English history, or the tales of Boccaccio. Whereas, great geniuses are parts of the times; they themselves are the times; and possess a correspondent coloring. It is of a piece with the Jews, who while their Shiloh was meekly walking in their streets, were still praying for his magnificent coming; looking for him in a chariot, who was already among them on an ass. Nor must we forget, that, in his own lifetime, Shakespeare was not Shakespeare, but only Master William Shakespeare of the shrewd, thriving, business firm of Condell, Shakespeare & Co., proprietors of the Globe Theatre in London; and by a courtly author, of the name of Greene, was hooted at, as an "upstart crow" beautified "with other birds' feathers". For, mark it well, imitation is often the first charge brought against real originality. Why this is so, there is not space to set forth here. You must have plenty of sea-room to tell the Truth in; especially, when it seems to have an aspect of newness, as America did in 1492, though it was then just as old, and perhaps older than Asia, only those sagacious philosophers, the common sailors, had never seen it before; swearing it was all water and moonshine there.

Now, I do not say that Nathaniel of Salem is a greater than William of Avon, or as great. But the difference between the two men is by no means immeasurable. Not a very great deal more, and Nathaniel were verily William.

This, too, I mean, that if Shakespeare has not been equalled, he is sure to be surpassed, and surpassed by an American born now or yet to be born. For it will never do for us who in most other things out-do as well as out-brag the world, it will not do for us to fold our hands and say, In the highest department advance there is none. Nor will it at all do to say, that the world is getting grey and grizzled now, and has lost that fresh charm which she wore of old, and by virtue of which the great poets of past times made themselves what we esteem them to be. Not so. The world is as young today, as when it was created;

and this Vermont morning dew is as wet to my feet, as Eden's dew to Adam's. Nor has Nature been all over ransacked by our progenitors, so that no new charms and mysteries remain for this latter generation to find. Far from it. The trillionth part has not yet been said; and all that has been said, but multiplies the avenues to what remains to be said. It is not so much paucity, as superabundance of material that seems to incapacitate modern authors.

Let America then prize and cherish her writers; yea, let her glorify them. They are not so many in number, as to exhaust her good-will. And while she has good kith and kin of her own, to take to her bosom, let her not lavish her embraces upon the household of an alien. For believe it or not England, after all, is, in many things, an alien to us. China has more bowels of real love for us than she. But even were there no Hawthorne, no Emerson, no Whittier, no Irving, no Bryant, no Dana, no Cooper, no Willis (not the author of the "Dashes", but the author of the "Belfry Pigeon")—were there none of these, and others of like calibre among us, nevertheless, let America first praise mediocrity even, in her own children, before she praises (for everywhere, merit demands acknowledgment from every one) the best excellence in the children of any other land. Let her own authors, I say, have the priority of appreciation. I was much pleased with a hot-headed Carolina cousin of mine, who once said,—"If there were no other American to stand by, in Literature,—why, then, I would stand by Pop Emmons and his 'Fredoniad,' and till a better epic came along, swear it was not very far behind the Iliad." Take away the words, and in spirit he was sound.

Not that American genius needs patronage in order to expand. For that explosive sort of stuff will expand though screwed up in a vice, and burst it, though it were triple steel. It is for the nation's sake, and not for her authors' sake, that I would have America be heedful of the increasing greatness among her writers. For how great the shame, if other nations should be before her, in crowning her heroes of the pen. But this is almost the case now. American authors have received more just and discriminating praise (however loftily and ridiculously given, in certain cases) even from some Englishmen, than from their own countrymen. There are hardly five critics in America; and several of them are asleep. As for patronage, it is the American author who now patronizes his country, and not his country him. And if at times some among them appeal to the people for more recognition, it is not always with selfish motives, but patriotic ones.

It is true, that but few of them as yet have evinced that decided originality which merits great praise. But that graceful writer, who perhaps of all Americans has received the most plaudits from his own country for his productions,—that very popular and amiable writer, however good, and self-reliant in many things, perhaps owes his chief reputation to the self-acknowledged imitation of a foreign model, and to the studied avoidance of all topics but smooth ones. But it is better to fail in originality, than to succeed in imitation. He who has never failed somewhere, that man can not be great. Failure is the true test of greatness. And if it be said, that continual success is a proof that a man wisely knows his powers,—it is only to be added, that, in that case, he knows them to be small. Let us believe it, then, once for all, that there is no hope for us in these smooth pleasing writers that know their powers. Without malice, but to speak the plain fact, they but furnish an appendix to Goldsmith, and other English authors. And we want no American Goldsmiths; nay, we want no American Miltons. It were the vilest thing you could say of a true American author, that he were an American Tompkins. Call him an American, and have done; for you can not say a nobler thing of him.—But it is not meant that all American writers should studiously cleave to nationality in their writings; only this, no American writer should write like an Englishman, or a Frenchman; let him write like a man, for then he will be sure to write like an American. Let us away with this Bostonian leaven of literary flunkeyism towards England. If either must play the flunkey in this thing, let England do it, not us. And the time is not far off when circumstances may force her to it. While we are rapidly preparing for that political supremacy among the nations, which prophetically awaits us at the close of the present century; in a literary point of view, we are deplorably unprepared for it; and we seem studious to remain so. Hitherto, reasons might have existed why this should be; but no good reason exists now. And all that is requisite to amendment in this matter, is simply this: that, while freely acknowledging all excellence, everywhere, we should refrain from unduly lauding foreign writers and, at the same time, duly recognize the meritorious writers that are our own;—those writers, who breathe that unshackled, democratic spirit of Christianity in all things, which now takes the practical lead in this world, though at the same time led by ourselves—us Americans. Let us boldly contemn all imitation, though it comes to us graceful and fragrant as the morning; and foster all originality, though, at first, it be crabbed and ugly as our own pine knots. And if any of our authors fail, or seem to fail, then, in the words of my enthusiastic Carolina cousin, let us clap him on the shoulder, and back him against all Europe for his second round. The truth is, that in our point of view, this matter of a national literature has come to such a pass with us, that in some sense we must turn bullies, else the day is lost, or superiority so far beyond us, that we can hardly say it will ever be ours.

And now, my countrymen, as an excellent author, of your own flesh and blood,—an unimitating, and, perhaps, in his way, an inimitable man—whom better can I commend to you, in the first place, than Nathaniel Hawthrone. He is one of the new, and far better generation of your writers. The smell of your beeches and hemlocks is upon him; your own broad prairies are in his soul; and if you travel away inland into his deep and noble nature, you will hear the far roar of his Niagara. Give not over to future generations the glad duty of acknowledging him for what he is. Take that joy to your self, in your own generation; and so shall he feel those grateful impulses in him, that may possibly prompt him to the full flower of some still greater achievement in your eyes. And by confessing him, you thereby confess others; you brace the whole brotherhood. For genius, all over the world, stand hand in hand, and one shock of recognition runs the whole circle round.

In treating of Hawthorne, or rather of Hawthorne in his writings (for I never saw the man; and in the chances of a quiet plantation life, remote from his haunts, perhaps never shall) in treating of his works, I say, I have thus far omitted all mention of his "Twice Told Tales", and "Scarlet Letter". Both are excellent; but full of such manifold, strange and diffusive beauties, that time would all but fail me, to point the half of them out. But there are things in those two books, which, had they been written in England a century ago, Nathaniel Hawthorne had utterly displaced many of the bright names we now revere on authority. But I am content to leave Hawthorne to himself, and to the infallible finding of posterity; and however great may be the praise I have bestowed upon him, I feel, that in so doing, I have more served and honored myself, than him. For, at bottom, great excellence is praise enough to itself; but the feeling of a sincere and appreciative love and admiration towards it, this is relieved by utterance; and warm, honest praise ever leaves a pleasant flavor in the mouth; and it is an honorable thing to confess to what is honorable in others.

But I cannot leave my subject yet. No man can read a fine author, and relish him to his very bones, while he reads, without subsequently fancying to himself some ideal image of the man and his mind. And if you rightly look for it, you will almost always find that the author himself has somewhere furnished you with his own picture.—For poets (whether in prose or verse), being painters of Nature, are like their brethren of the pencil, the true portrait-painters, who, in the multitude of likenesses to be sketched, do not invariably omit their own; and in all high instances, they paint them without any vanity, though, at times, with a lurking something, that would take several pages to properly define.

I submit it, then, to those best acquainted with the man personally, whether the following is not Nathaniel Hawthorne;—and to himself, whether something involved in it does not express the temper of his mind,—that lasting temper of all true, candid men—a seeker, not a finder yet:—

> A man now entered, in neglected attire, with the aspect of a thinker, but somewhat too rough-hewn and brawny for a scholar. His face was full of sturdy vigor, with some finer and keener attribute beneath; though harsh at first, it was tempered with the glow of a large, warm heart, which had force enough to heat his powerful intellect through and through. He advanced to the Intelligencer, and looked at him with a glance of such stern sincerity, that perhaps few secrets were beyond its scope.
> "I seek for Truth", said he.

Twenty four hours have elapsed since writing the foregoing. I have just returned from the hay mow, charged more and more with love and admiration of Hawthorne. For I have just been gleaning through the Mosses, picking up many things here and there that had previously escaped me. And I found that but to glean after this man, is better than to be in at the harvest of others. To be frank (though, perhaps, rather foolish) notwithstanding what I wrote yesterday of these Mosses, I had not then culled them all; but had, nevertheless, been sufficiently sensible of the subtle essense, in them, as to write as I did. To what infinite heights of loving wonder and admiration I may yet be borne, when by repeatedly banquetting on these Mosses, I shall have thoroughly incorporated their whole stuff into my being,—that, I can not tell. But already I feel that this Hawthorne has dropped germinous seeds into my soul. He expands and deepens down, the more I contemplate him; and further, and further, shoots his strong New-England roots into the hot soil of my Southern soul.

By careful reference to the "Table of Contents", I now find, that I have gone through all the sketches; but that when I yesterday wrote, I had not at all read two particular pieces, to which I now desire to call special attention,—"A Select Party", and "Young Goodman Brown". Here, be it said to all those whom this poor fugitive scrawl of mine may tempt to the perusal of the "Mosses," that they must on no account suffer themselves to be trifled with, disappointed, or deceived by the triviality of many of the titles to these Sketches. For in more than one instance, the title utterly belies the piece. It is as if rustic demijohns containing the very best and costliest of Falernian and Tokay, were labelled "Cider", "Perry," and "Elderberry wine". The truth seems to be, that like many other geniuses, this Man of Mosses takes great delight in hoodwinking the world,—at least, with respect to himself. Personally, I doubt not, that he rather prefers to be generally esteemed but a so-so sort of author; being willing to reserve the thorough and acute appreciation of what he is, to that party most qualified to judge—that is, to himself. Besides, at the bottom of their natures, men like Hawthorne, in many things, deem the plaudits of the public such strong presumptive evidence of mediocrity in the object of them, that it would in some degree render them doubtful of their own powers, did they hear much and vociferous braying concerning them in the public pastures. True, I have been braying myself (if you please to be witty enough, to have it so) but then I claim to be the first that has so brayed in this particular matter; and therefore, while pleading guilty to the charge still claim all the merit due to originality.

But with whatever motive, playful or profound, Nathaniel Hawthorne has chosen to entitle his pieces in the manner he has, it is certain, that some of them are directly calculated to deceive—egregiously deceive, the superficial skimmer of pages. To be downright and

candid once more, let me cheerfully say, that two of these titles did dolefully dupe no less an
eagle-eyes reader than myself; and that, too, after I had been impressed with a sense of the
great depth and breadth of this American man. "Who in the name of thunder" (as the coun-
try-people say in this neighborhood) "who in the name of thunder", would anticipate any
marvel in a piece entitled "Young Goodman Brown"? You would of course suppose that it
was a simple little tale, intended as a supplement to "Goody Two Shoes". Whereas, it is
deep as Dante; nor can you finish it, without addressing the author in his own words—"It is
yours to penetrate, in every bosom, the deep mystery of sin". And with Young Goodman,
too, in allegorical pursuit of his Puritan wife, you cry out in your anguish,—

> "Faith!" shouted Goodman Brown, in a voice of agony and desperation; and the echoes of
> the forest mocked him, crying—"Faith! Faith!" as if bewildered wretches were seeking her
> all through the wilderness.

Now this same piece, entitled "Young Goodman Brown", is one of the two that I had
not all read yesterday; and I allude to it now, because it is, in itself, such a strong positive
illustration of that blackness in Hawthorne, which I had assumed from the mere occasional shadows of it, as revealed in several of the other sketches. But had I previously pe-
rused "Young Goodman Brown", I should have been at no pains to draw the conclusion,
which I came to, at a time, when I was ignorant that the book contained one such direct
and unqualified manifestation of it.

The other piece of the two referred to, is entitled "A Select Party", which, in my
first simplicity upon originally taking hold of the book, I fancied must treat of some
pumpkin-pie party in Old Salem, or some chowder party on Cape Cod. Whereas, by all the
gods of Peedee! it is the sweetest and sublimest thing that has been written since Spencer
wrote. Nay, there is nothing in Spencer that surpasses it, perhaps, nothing that equals it.
And the test is this: read any canto in "The Faery Queen", and then read "A Select Party",
and decide which pleases you the most,—that is, if you are qualified to judge. Do not be
frightened at this; for when Spencer was alive, he was thought of very much as Hawthorne
is now,—was generally accounted just such a "gentle" harmless man. It may be, that to
common eyes, the sublimity of Hawthorne seems lost in his sweetness,—as perhaps in this
same "Select Party" of his; for whom, he has builded so august a dome of sunset clouds, and
served them on richer plate, than Belshazzar's when he banquetted his lords in Babylon.

But my chief business now, is to point out a particular page in this piece, having reference to an honored guest, who under the name of "The Master Genius" but in the guise of
"a young man of poor attire, with no insignia of rank or acknowledged eminence", is introduced to the Man of Fancy, who is the giver of the feast. Now the page having reference
to this "Master Genius", so happily expresses much of what I yesterday wrote, touching
the coming of the literary Shiloh of America, that I cannot but be charmed by the coincidence; especially, when it shows such a parity of ideas, at least in this one point, between a
man like Hawthorne and a man like me.

And here, let me throw out another conceit of mine touching this American Shiloh, or
"Master Genius", as Hawthorne calls him. May it not be, that this commanding mind has
not been, is not, and never will be, individually developed in any one man? And would it,
indeed, appear so unreasonable to suppose, that this great fullness and overflowing may
be, or may be destined to be, shared by a plurality of men of genius? Surely, to take the
very greatest example on record, Shakespeare cannot be regarded as in himself the concre-
tion of all the genius of his time; nor as so immeasurably beyond Marlow, Webster, Ford,
Beaumont, Jonson, that those great men can be said to share none of his power? For one, I
conceive that there were dramatists in Elizabeth's day, between whom and Shakespeare
the distance was by no means great. Let anyone, hitheto little acquainted with those ne-

glected old authors, for the first time read them thoroughly, or even read Charles Lamb's Specimens of them, and he will be amazed at the wondrous ability of those Anaks of men, and shocked at this renewed example of the fact, that Fortune has more to do with fame than merit,—though, without merit, lasting fame there can be none.

Nevertheless, it would argue too illy of my country were this maxim to hold good concerning Nathaniel Hawthorne, a man, who already, in some few minds, has shed "such a light, as never illuminates the earth, save when a great heart burns as the household fire of a grand intellect."

The words are his,—in the "Select Party"; and they are a magnificent setting to a coincident sentiment of my own, but ramblingly expressed yesterday, in reference to himself. Gainsay it who will, as I now write, I am Posterity speaking by proxy—and after times will make it more than good, when I declare—that the American, who up to the present day, has evinced, in Literature, the largest brain with the largest heart, that man is Nathaniel Hawthorne. Moreover, that whatever Nathaniel Hawthorne may hereafter write, "The Mosses from an Old Manse" will be ultimately accounted his masterpiece. For there is a sure, though a secret sign in some works which prove the culmination of the powers (only the developable ones, however) that produced them. But I am by no means desirous of the glory of a prophet. I pray Heaven that Hawthorne may *yet* prove me an impostor in this prediction. Especially, as I somehow cling to the strange fancy, that, in all men, hiddenly reside certain wondrous, occult properties—as in some plants and minerals—which by some happy but very rare accident (as bronze was discovered by the melting of the iron and brass in the burning of Corinth) may chance to be called forth here on earth; not entirely waiting for their better discovery in the more congenial, blessed atmosphere of heaven.

Once more—for it is hard to be finite upon an infinite subject, and all subjects are infinite. By some people, this entire scrawl of mine may be esteemed altogether unnecessary, inasmuch, "as years ago" (they may say) "we found out the rich and rare stuff in this Hawthorne, whom you now parade forth, as if only *yourself* were the discoverer of this Portuguese diamond in our Literature".—But even granting all this; and adding to it, the assumption that the books of Hawthorne have sold by the five-thousand,—what does that signify?—They should be sold by the hundred-thousand; and read by the million; and admired by every one who is capable of admiration.   [1850]

Frederick Douglass

The Meaning of July Fourth for the Negro

Speech at Rochester, New York, July 5, 1852

Mr. President, Friends and Fellow Citizens:
He who could address this audience without a quailing sensation, has stronger nerves than I have. I do not remember ever to have appeared as a speaker before any assembly more shrinkingly, nor with greater distrust of my ability, than I do this day. A feeling has crept

over me quite unfavorable to the exercise of my limited powers of speech. The task before me is one which requires much previous thought and study for its proper performance. I know that apologies of this sort are generally considered flat and unmeaning. I trust, however, that mine will not be so considered. Should I seem at ease, my appearance would much misrepresent me. The little experience I have had in addressing public meetings, in country school houses, avails me nothing on the present occasion.

The papers and placards say that I am to deliver a Fourth of July Oration. This certainly sounds large, and out of the common way, for me. It is true that I have often had the privilege to speak in this beautiful Hall, and to address many who now honor me with their presence. But neither their familiar faces, not the perfect gage I think I have of Corinthian Hall seems to free me from embarrassment.

The fact is, ladies and gentlemen, the distance between this platform and the slave plantation, from which I escaped, is considerable—and the difficulties to be overcome in getting from the latter to the former are by no means slight. That I am here to-day is, to me, a matter of astonishment as well as of gratitude. You will not, therefore, be surprised, if in what I have to say I evince no elaborate preparation, nor grace my speech with any high sounding exordium. With little experience and with less learning, I have been able to throw my thoughts hastily and imperfectly together; and trusting to your patient and generous indulgence, I will proceed to lay them before you.

This, for the purpose of this celebration, is the Fourth of July. It is the birthday of your National Independence, and of your political freedom. This, to you, is what the Passover was to the emancipated people of God. It carries your minds back to the day, and to the act of your great deliverance; and to the signs, and to the wonders, associated with that act, and that day. This celebration also marks the beginning of another year of your national life; and reminds you that the Republic of America is now 76 years old. I am glad, fellow-citizens, that your nation is so young. Seventy-six years, though a good old age for a man, is but a mere speck in the life of a nation. Three score years and ten is the allotted time for individual men; but nations number their years by thousands. According to this fact, you are, even now, only in the beginning of your national career, still lingering in the period of childhood. I repeat, I am glad this is so. There is hope in the thought, and hope is much needed, under the dark clouds which lower above the horizon. The eye of the reformer is met with angry flashes, portending disastrous times; but his heart may well beat lighter at the thought that America is young, and that she is still in the impressible stage of her existence. May he not hope that high lessons of wisdom, of justice and of truth, will yet give direction to her destiny? Were the nation older, the patriot's heart might be sadder, and the reformer's brow heavier. Its future might be shrouded in gloom, and the hope of its prophets go out in sorrow. There is consolation in the thought that America is young.—Great streams are not easily turned from channels, worn deep in the course of ages. They may sometimes rise in quiet and stately majesty, and inundate the land, refreshing and fertilizing the earth with their mysterious properties. They may also rise in wrath and fury, and bear away, on their angry waves, the accumulated wealth of years of toil and hardship. They, however, gradually flow back to the same old channel, and flow on as serenely as ever. But, while the river may not be turned aside, it may dry up, and leave nothing behind but the withered branch, and the unsightly rock, to howl in the abyss-sweeping wind, the sad tale of departed glory. As with rivers so with nations.

Fellow-citizens, I shall not presume to dwell at length on the associations that cluster about this day. The simple story of it is, that, 76 years ago, the people of this country were British subjects. The style and title of your "sovereign people" (in which you now glory) was not then born. You were under the British Crown. Your fathers esteemed the English

Government as the home government; and England as the fatherland. This home government, you know, although a considerable distance from your home, did, in the exercise of its parental prerogatives, impose upon its colonial children, such restraints, burdens and limitations, as, in its mature judgment, it deemed wise, right and proper.

But your fathers, who had not adopted the fashionable idea of this day, of the infallibility of government, and the absolute character of its acts, presumed to differ from the home government in respect to the wisdom and the justice of some of those burdens and restraints. They went so far in their excitement as to pronounce the measures of government unjust, unreasonable, and oppressive, and altogether such as ought not to be quietly submitted to: I scarcely need say, fellow-citizens, that my opinion of those measures fully accords with that of your fathers. Such a declaration of agreement on my part would not be worth much to anybody. It would certainly prove nothing as to what part I might have taken had I lived during the great controversy of 1776. To say now that America was right, and England wrong, is exceedingly easy. Everybody can say it; the dastard, not less than the noble brave, can flippantly discant on the tyranny of England towards the American Colonies. It is fashionable to do so; but there was a time when, to pronouce against England, and in favor of the cause of the colonies, tried men's souls. They who did so were accounted in their day plotters of mischief, agitators and rebels, dangerous men. To side with the right against the wrong, with the weak against the strong, and with the oppressed against the oppressor! here lies the merit, and the one which, of all others, seems unfashionable in our day. The cause of liberty may be stabbed by the men who glory in the deeds of your fathers. But, to proceed.

Feeling themselves harshly and unjustly treated, by the home government, your fathers, like men of honesty, and men of spirit, earnestly sought redress. They petitioned and remonstrated; they did so in a decorous, respectful, and loyal manner. Their conduct was wholly unexceptionable. This, however, did not answer the purpose. They saw themselves treated with sovereign indifference, coldness and scorn. Yet they persevered. They were not the men to look back.

As the sheet anchor takes a firmer hold, when the ship is tossed by the storm, so did the cause of your fathers grow stronger as it breasted the chilling blasts of kingly displeasure. The greatest and best of British statesmen admitted its justice, and the loftiest eloquence of the British Senate came to its support. But, with that blindness which seems to be the unvarying characteristic of tyrants, since Pharaoh and his hosts were drowned in the Red Sea, the British Government persisted in the exactions complained of.

The madness of this course, we believe, is admitted now, even by England; but we fear the lesson is wholly lost on our present rulers.

Oppression makes a wise man mad. Your fathers were wise men, and if they did not go mad, they became restive under this treatment. They felt themselves the victims of grievous wrongs, wholly incurable in their colonial capacity. With brave men there is always a remedy for oppression. Just here, the idea of a total separation of the colonies from the crown was born! It was a startling idea, much more so than we, at this distance of time, regard it. The timid and the prudent (as has been intimated) of that day were, of course, shocked and alarmed by it.

Such people lived then, had lived before, and will, probably, ever have a place on this planet; and their course, in respect to any great change (no matter how great the good to be attained, or the wrong to be redressed by it), may be calculated with as much precision as can be the curse of the stars. They hate all changes, but silver, gold and copper change! Of this sort of change they are always strongly in favor.

These people were called Tories in the days of your fathers; and the appellation, probably, conveyed the same idea that is meant by a more modern, though a somewhat less euphonious term, which we often find in our papers, applied to some of our old politicians.

Their opposition to the then dangerous thought was earnest and powerful; but, amid all their terror and affrighted vociferations against it, the alarming and revolutionary idea moved on, and the country with it.

On the 2d of July, 1776, the old Continental Congress, to the dismay of the lovers of ease, and the worhshipers of property, clothed that dreadful idea with all the authority of national sanction. They did so in the form of a resolution; and as we seldom hit upon resolutions, drawn up in our day, whose transparency is at all equal to this, it may refresh your minds and help my story if I read it.

> Resolved, That these united colonies are, and of right, ought to be free and Independent States; that they are absolved from all allegiance to the British Crown; and that all political connection between them and the State of Great Britain is and ought to be, dissolved.

Citizens, your fathers made good that resolution. They succeeded; and to-day you reap the fruits of their success. The freedom gained is yours; and you, therefore, may properly celebrate this anniversary. The 4th of July is the first great fact in your nation's history— the very ringbolt in the chain of your yet undeveloped destiny.

Pride and patriotism, not less than gratitude, prompt you to celebrate and to hold it in perpetual remembrance. I have said that the Declaration of Independence is the ringbolt to the chain of your nation's destiny; so, indeed, I regard it. The principles contained in that instrument are saving principles. Stand by those principles, be true to them on all occasions, in all places, against all foes, and at whatever cost.

From the round top of your ship of state, dark and threatening clouds may be seen. Heavy billows, like mountains in the distance, disclose to the leeward huge forms of flinty rocks! That bolt drawn, that chain broken, and all is lost. Cling to this day—cling to it, and to its principles, with the grasp of a storm-tossed mariner to a spar at midnight.

The coming into being of a nation, in any circumstances, is an interesting event. But, besides general considerations, there were peculiar circumstances which make the advent of this republic an event of special attractiveness.

The whole scene, as I look back to it, was simple, dignified and sublime. The population of the country, at the time, stood at the insignificant number of three millions. The country was poor in the munitions of war. The population was weak and scattered, and the country a wilderness unsubdued. There were then no means of concert and combination, such as exist now. Neither steam nor lightning had then been reduced to order and discipline. From the Potomac to the Delaware was a journey of many days. Under these, and innumerable other disadvantages, your fathers declared for liberty and independence and triumphed.

Fellow Citizens, I am not wanting in respect for the fathers of this republic. The signers of the Declaration of Independence were brave men. They were great men, too—great enough to give frame to a great age. It does not often happen to a nation to raise, at one time, such a number of truly great men. The point from which I am compelled to view them is not, certainly, the most favorable; and yet I cannot contemplate their great deeds with less than admiration. They were statesmen, patriots and heroes, and for the good they did, and the principles they contended for, I will unite with you to honor their memory.

They loved their country better than their own private interests; and, though this is not the highest form of human excellence, all will concede that it is a rare virtue, and that when it is exhibited it ought to command respect. He who will, intelligently, lay down his life for his country is a man whom it is not in human nature to despise. Your fathers staked their lives, their fortunes, and their sacred honor, on the cause of their country. In their admiration of liberty, they lost sight of all other interests.

They were peace men; but they preferred revolution to peaceful submission to bondage. They were quiet men; but they did not shrink from agitating against oppression. They showed forbearance; but that they knew its limits. They believed in order; but not in the order of tyranny. With them, nothing was "settled" that was not right. With them, justice, liberty and humanity were "final"; not slavery and oppression. You may well cherish the memory of such men. They were great in their day and generation. Their solid manhood stands out the more as we contrast it with these degenerate times.

How circumspect, exact and proportionate were all their movements! How unlike the politicians of an hour! Their statesmanship looked beyond the passing moment, and stretched away in strength into the distant future. They seized upon eternal principles, and set a glorious example in their defence. Mark them!

Fully appreciating the hardships to be encountered, firmly believing in the right of their cause, honorably inviting the scrutiny of an on-looking world, reverently appealing to heaven to attest their sincerity, soundly comprehending the solemn responsibility they were about to assume, wisely measuring the terrible odds against them, your fathers, the fathers of this republic, did, most deliberately, under the inspiration of a glorious patriotism, and with a sublime faith in the great principles of justice and freedom, lay deep, the corner-stone of the national super-structure, which has risen and still rises in grandeur around you.

Of this fundamental work, this day is the anniversary. Our eyes are met with demonstrations of joyous enthusiasm. Banners and pennants wave exultingly on the breeze. The din of buisness, too, is hushed. Even mammon seems to have quitted his grasp on this day. The ear-piercing fife and the stirring drum unite their accents with the ascending peal of a thousand church bells. Prayers are made, hymns are sung, and sermons are preached in honor of this day; while the quick martial tramp of a great and multitudinous nation, echoed back by all the hills, valleys and mountains of a vast continent, bespeak the occasion one of thrilling and universal interest—a nation's jubilee.

Friends and citizens, I need not enter further into the causes which led to this anniversary. Many of you understand them better than I do. You could instruct me in regard to them. That is a branch of knowledge in which you feel, perhaps, a much deeper interest than your speaker. The causes which led to the separation of the colonies from the British crown have never lacked for a tongue. They have all been taught in your common schools, narrated at your firesides, unfolded from your pulpits, and thundered from your legislative halls, and are as familiar to you as household words. They form the staple of your national poetry and eloquence.

I remember, also, that, as a people, Americans are remarkably familiar with all facts which make in their own favor. This is esteemed by some as a national trait—perhaps a national weakness. It is a fact, that whatever makes for the wealth or for the reputation of Americans and can be had cheap! will be found by Americans. I shall not be charged with slandering Americans if I say I think the American side of any question may be safely left in American hands.

I leave, therefore, the great deed of your fathers to other gentlemen whose claim to have been regularly descended will be less likely to be disputed than mine!

My business, if I have any here to-day, is with the present. The accepted time with God and His cause is the ever-living now.

Trust no future, however pleasant,
  Let the dead past bury its dead;
Act, act in the living present,
  Heart within, and God overhead.

We have to do with the past only as we can make it useful to the present and to the future. To all inspiring motives, to noble deeds which can be gained from the past, we are welcome. But now is the time, the important time. Your fathers have lived, died, and have done their work, and have done much of it well. You live and must die, and you must do your work. You have no right to enjoy a child's share in the labor of your fathers, unless your children are to be blest by your labors. You have no right to wear out and waste the hard-earned fame of your fathers to cover your indolence. Sydney Smith tells us that men seldom eulogize the wisdom and virtues of their fathers, but to excuse some folly or wickedness of their own. This truth is not a doubtful one. There are illustrations of it near and remote, ancient and modern. It was fashionable, hundreds of years ago, for the children of Jacob to boast, we have "Abraham to our father," when they had long lost Abraham's faith and spirit. That people contented themselves under the shadow of Abraham's great name, while they repudiated the deeds which made his name great. Need I remind you that a similar thing is being done all over this country to-day? Need I tell you that the Jews are not the only people who built the tombs of the prophets, and garnished the sepulchers of the righteous? Washington could not die till he had broken the chains of his slaves. Yet his monument is built up by the price of human blood, and the traders in the bodies and souls of men shout—"We have Washington to *our father.*"—Alas! that it should be so; yet so it is.

The evil that men do, lives after them,
The good is oft interred with their bones.

Fellow-citizens, pardon me, allow me to ask, why am I called upon to speak here to-day? What have I, or those I represent, to do with your national independence? Are the great principles of political freedom and of natural justice, embodied in that Declaration of Independence, extended to us? and am I, therefore, called upon to bring our humble offering to the national altar, and to confess the benefits and express devout gratitude for the blessings resulting from your independence to us?

Would to God, both for your sakes and ours, that an affirmative answer could be truthfully returned to these questions! Then would my task be light, and my burden easy and delightful. For *who* is there so cold, that a nation's sympathy could not warm him? Who so obdurate and dead to the claims of gratitude, that would not thankfully acknowledge such priceless benefits? Who so stolid and selfish, that would not give his voice to swell the hallelujahs of a nation's jubilee, when the chains of servitude had been torn from his limbs? I am not that man. In a case like that, the dumb might eloquently speak, and the "lame man leap as an hart."

But such is not the state of the case. I say it with a sad sense of the disparity between us. I am not included within the pale of this glorious anniversary! Your high independence only reveals the immeasurable distance between us. The blessings in which you, this day, rejoice, are not enjoyed in common.—The rich inheritance of justice, liberty, prosperity and independence, bequeathed by your fathers, is shared by you, not by me. The sunlight that brought light and healing to you, has brought stripes and death to me. This Fourth July is *yours,* not *mine. You* may rejoice, *I* must mourn. To drag a man in fetters into the grand illuminated temple of liberty, and call upon him to join you in joyous anthems, were inhuman mockery and sacrilegious irony. Do you mean, citizens, to mock me, by asking me to speak to-day? If so, there is a parallel to your conduct. And let me warn you that it is dangerous to copy the example of a nation whose crimes, towering up to heaven, were thrown down by the breath of the Almighty, burying that nation in irrevocable ruin! I can to-day take up the plaintive lament of a peeled and woe-smitten people!

"By the rivers of Babylon, there we sat down. Yea! we wept when we remembered Zion. We hanged our harps upon the willows in the midst thereof. For there, they that carried us away captive, required of us a song; and they who wasted us required of us mirth, saying, Sing us one of the songs of Zion. How can we sing the Lord's song in a strange land? If I forget thee, O Jerusalem, let my right hand forget her cunning. If I do not remember thee, let my tongue cleave to the roof of my mouth."

Fellow-citizens, above your national, tumultuous joy, I hear the mournful wail of millions! whose chains, heavy and grievous yesterday, are, to-day, rendered more intolerable by the jubilee shouts that reach them. If I do forget, if I do not faithfully remember those bleeding children of sorrow this day, "may my right hand forget her cunning, and may my tongue cleave to the roof of my mouth!" To forget them, to pass lightly over their wrongs, and to chime in with the popular theme, would be treason most scandalous and shocking, and would make me a reproach before God and the world. My subject, then, fellow-citizens, is American slavery. I shall see this day and its popular characteristics from the slave's point of view. Standing there identified with the American bondman, making his wrongs mine, I do not hesitate to declare, with all my soul, that the character and conduct of this nation never looked blacker to me than on this 4th of July! Whether we turn to the declarations of the past, or to the professions of the present, the conduct of the nation seems equally hideous and revolting. America is false to the past, false to the present, and solemnly binds herself to be false to the future. Standing with God and the crushed and bleeding slave on this occasion, I will, in the name of humanity which is outraged, in the name of liberty which is fettered, in the name of the constitution and the Bible which are disregarded and trampled upon, dare to call in question and to denounce, with all the emphasis I can command, everything that serves to perpetuate slavery—the great sin and shame of America! "I will not equivocate; I will not excuse"; I will use the severest language I can command; and yet not one world shall escape me that any man, whose judgment is not blinded by prejudice, or who is not at heart a slaveholder, shall not confess to be right and just.

But I fancy I hear some one of my audience say, "It is just in this circumstance that you and your brother abolitionists fail to make a favorable impression on the public mind. Would you argue more, and denounce less; would you persuade more, and rebuke less; your cause would be much more likely to succeed." But, I submit, where all is plain there is nothing to be argued. What point in the anti-slavery creed would you have me argue? On what branch of the subject do the people of this country need light? Must I undertake to prove that the slave is a man? That point is conceded already. Nobody doubts it. The slaveholders themselves acknowledge it in the enactment of laws for their government. They acknowledge it when they punish disobedience on the part of the slave. There are seventy-two crimes in the State of Virginia which, if committed by a black man (no matter how ignorant he be), subject him to the punishment of death; while only two of the same crimes will subject a white man to the like punishment. What is this but the acknowledgment that the slave is a moral, intellectual, and responsible being? The manhood of the slave is conceded. It is admitted in the fact that Southern statute books are covered with enactments forbidding, under severe fines and penalties, the teaching of the slave to read or to write. When you can point to any such laws in reference to the beasts of the field, then I may consent to argue the manhood of the slave. When the dogs in your streets, when the fowls of the air, when the cattle on your hills, when the fish of the sea, and the reptiles that crawl, shall be unable to distinguish the slave for a brute, *then* will I argue with you that the slave is a man!

For the present, it is enough to affirm the equal manhood of the Negro race. Is it not astonishing that, while we are ploughing, planting, and reaping, using all kinds of mechanical tools, erecting houses, constructing bridges, building ships, working in metals of brass, iron, copper, silver and gold; that, while we are reading, writing and ciphering, acting as clerks, merchants and secretaries, having among us lawyers, doctors, ministers, poets, authors, editors, orators and teachers; that, while we are engaged in all manner of enterprises common to other men, digging gold in California, capturing the whale in the Pacific, feeding sheep and cattle on the hill-side, living, moving, acting, thinking, planning, living in families as husbands, wives and children, and, above all, confessing and worshipping the Christian's God, and looking hopefully for life and immortality beyond the grave, we are called upon to prove that we are men!

Would you have me argue that man is entitled to liberty? that he is the rightful owner of his own body? You have already declared it. Must I argue the wrongfulness of slavery? Is that a question for Republicans? Is it to be settled by the rules of logic and argumentation, as a matter beset with great difficulty, involving a doubtful application of the principle of justice, hard to be understood? How should I look to-day, in the presence of Americans, dividing, and subdividing a discourse, to show that men have a natural right to freedom? speaking of it relatively and positively, negatively and affirmatively. To do so, would be to make myself ridiculous, and to offer an insult to your understanding.—There is not a man beneath the canopy of heaven that does not know that slavery is wrong *for him.*

What, am I to argue that it is wrong to make men brutes, to rob them of their liberty, to work them without wages, to keep them ignorant of their relations to their fellow men, to beat them with sticks, to flay their flesh with the lash, to load their limbs with irons, to hunt them with dogs, to sell them at auction, to sunder their families, to knock out their teeth, to burn their flesh, to starve them into obedience and submission to their masters? Must I argue that a system thus marked with blood, and stained with pollution, is *wrong?* No! I will not. I have better employment for my time and strength than such arguments would imply.

What, then, remains to be argued? Is it that slavery is not divine; that God did not establish it; that our doctors of divinity are mistaken? There is blasphemy in the thought. That which is inhuman, cannot be divine! *Who* can reason on such a proposition? They that can, may; I cannot. The time for such argument is passed.

At a time like this, scorching irony, not convincing argument, is needed. O! had I the ability, and could reach the nation's ear, I would, to-day, pour out a fiery stream of biting ridicule, blasting reproach, withering sarcasm, and stern rebuke. For it is not light that is needed, but fire; it is not the gentle shower, but thunder. We need the storm, the whirlwind, and the earthquake. The feeling of the nation must be quickened; the conscience of the nation must be roused; the propriety of the nation must be startled; the hypocrisy of the nation must be exposed; and its crimes against God and man must be proclaimed and denounced.

What, to the American slave, is your 4th of July? I answer; a day that reveals to him, more than all other days in the year, the gross injustice and cruelty to which he is the constant victim. To him, your celebration is a sham; your boasted liberty, an unholy license; your national greatness, swelling vanity; your sounds of rejoicing are empty and heartless; your denunciation of tyrants, brass fronted impudence; your shouts of liberty and equality, hollow mockery; your prayers and hymns, your sermons and thanksgivings, with all your religious parade and solemnity, are, to Him, mere bombast, fraud, deception, impiety, and hypocrisy—a thin veil to cover up crimes which would disgrace a nation of savages. There is not a nation on the earth guilty of practices more shocking and bloody than are the people of the United States, at this very hour.

Go where you may, search where you will, roam through all the monarchies and despotisms of the Old World, travel through South America, search out every abuse, and when you have found the last, lay your facts by the side of the everyday practices of this nation, and you will say with me, that, for revolting barbarity and shameless hypocrisy, America reigns without a rival.

Take the American slave-trade, which we are told by the papers, is especially prosperous just now. Ex-Senator Benton tells us that the price of men was never higher than now. He mentions the fact to show that slavery is in no danger. This trade is one of the peculiarities of American institutions. It is carried on in all the large towns and cities in onehalf of this confederacy; and millions are pocketed every year by dealers in this horrid traffic. In several states this trade is a chief source of wealth. It is called (in contradistinction to the foreign slave-trade) *"the internal slave-trade."* It is, probably, called so, too, in order to divert from it the horror with which the foreign slave-trade is contemplated. That trade has long since been denounced by this government as piracy. It has been denounced with burning words from the high places of the nation as an execrable traffic. To arrest it, to put an end to it, this nation keeps a squadron, at immense cost, on the coast of Africa. Everywhere, in this country, it is safe to speak of this foreign slave-trade as a most inhuman traffic, opposed alike to the laws of God and of man. The duty to extirpate and destroy it, is admitted even by our doctors of divinity. In order to put an end to it, some of these last have consented that their colored brethren (nominally free) should leave this country, and establish themselves on the western coast of Africa! It is, however, a notable fact that, while so much execration is poured out by Americans upon all those engaged in the foreign slave-trade, the men engaged in the slave-trade between the states pass without condemnation, and their business is deemed honorable.

Behold the practical operation of this internal slave-trade, the American slave-trade, sustained by American politics and American religion. Here you will see men and women reared like swine for the market. You know what is a swine-drover? I will show you a man-drover. They inhabit all our Southern States. They perambulate the country, and crowd the highways of the nation, with droves of human stock. You will see one of these human flesh jobbers, armed with pistol, whip, and bowie-knife, driving a company of a hundred men, women, and children, from the Potomac to the slave market at New Orleans. These wretched people are to be sold singly, or in lots, to suit purchasers. They are food for the cotton-field and the deadly sugar-mill. Mark the sad procession, as it moves wearily along, and the inhuman wretch who drives them. Hear his savage yells and his blood-curdling oaths, as he hurries on his affrighted captives! There, see the old man with locks thinned and gray. Cast one glance, if you please, upon that young mother, whose shoulders are bare to the scorching sun, her briny tears falling on the brow of the babe in her arms. See, too, that girl of thirteen, weeping, *yes!* weeping, as she thinks of the mother from whom she has been torn! The drove moves tardily. Heat and sorrow have nearly consumed their strength; suddenly you hear a quick snap, like the discharge of a rifle; the fetters clank, and the chain rattles simultaneously; your ears are saluted with a scream, that seems to have torn its way to the centre of your soul! The crack you heard was the sound of the slave-whip; the scream you heard was from the woman you saw with the babe. Her speed had faltered under the weight of her child and her chains! that gash on her shoulder tells her to move on. Follow this drove to New Orleans. Attend the auction; see men examined like horses; see the forms of women rudely and brutally exposed to the shocking gaze of American slave-buyers. See this drove sold and separated forever; and never forget the deep, sad sobs that arose from that scattered multitude. Tell me, citizens, where, under the sun, you can witness a spectacle more fiendish and shocking. Yet this is but a glance at the American slave-trade, as it exists, at this moment, in the ruling part of the United States.

I was born amid such sights and scenes. To me the American slave-trade is a terrible reality. When a child, my soul was often pierced with a sense of its horrors. I lived on Philpot Street, Fell's Point, Baltimore, and have watched from the wharves the slave ships in the Basin, anchored from the shore, with their cargoes of human flesh, waiting for favorable winds to waft them down the Chesapeake. There was, at that time, a grand slave mart kept at the head of Pratt Street, by Austin Woldfolk. His agents were sent into every town and county in Maryland, announcing their arrival, through the papers, and on flaming *"hand-bills,"* headed cash for Negroes. These men were generally well dressed men, and very captivating in their manners; ever ready to drink, to treat, and to gamble. The fate of many a slave has depended upon the turn of a single card; and many a child has been snatched from the arms of its mother by bargains arranged in a state of brutal drunkenness.

The flesh-mongers gather up their victims by dozens, and drive them, chained, to the general depot at Baltimore. When a sufficient number has been collected here, a ship is chartered for the purpose of conveying the forlorn crew to Mobile or to New Orleans. From the slave prison to the ship, they are usually driven in the darkness of night; for since the antislavery agitation, a certain caution is observed.

In the deep, still darkness of midnight, I have been often aroused by the dead, heavy footsteps, and the piteous cries of the chained gangs that passed our door. The anguish of my boyish heart was intense; and I was often consoled, when speaking to my mistress in the morning, to hear her say that the custom was very wicked; that she hated to hear the rattle of the chains and the heart-rending cries. I was glad to find one who sympathized with me in my horror.

Fellow-citizens, this murderous traffic is, to-day, in active operation in this boasted republic. In the solitude of my spirit I see clouds of dust raised on the highways of the South; I see the bleeding footsteps; I hear the doleful wail of fettered humanity on the way to the slave-markets, where the victims are to be sold like *horses, sheep,* and *swine,* knocked off to the highest bidder. There I see the tenderest ties ruthlessly broken, to gratify the lust, caprice and rapacity of the buyers and sellers of men. My soul sickens at the sight.

> Is this the land your Fathers loved,
>   The freedom which they toiled to win?
> Is this the earth whereon they moved?
>   Are these the graves they slumber in?

But a still more inhuman, disgraceful, and scandalous state of things remains to be presented. By an act of the American Congress, not yet two years old, slavery has been nationalized in its most horrible and revolting form. By that act, Mason and Dixon's line has been obliterated; New York has become as Virginia; and the power to hold, hunt, and sell men, women and children, as slaves, remains no longer a mere state institution, but is now an institution of the whole United States. The power is co-extensive with the star-spangled banner, and American Christianity. Where these go, may also go the merciless slave-hunter. Where these are, man is not sacred. He is a bird for the sportsman's gun. By that most foul and fiendish of all human decrees, the liberty and person of every man are put in peril. Your broad republican domain is hunting ground for *men*. *Not* for thieves and robbers, enemies of society, merely, but for men guilty of no crime. Your law-makers have commanded all good citizens to engage in this hellish sport. Your President, your Secretary of State, your *lords, nobles,* and ecclesiastics enforce, as a duty you owe to your free and glorious country, and to your God, that you do this accursed thing. Not fewer than forty Americans have, within the past two years, been hunted down and, without a moment's warning, hurried away in chains, and consigned to slavery and excruciating torture. Some of these have had wives and children, dependent on them for bread; but of this, no account was made. The right of the hunter to his prey stand superior to the right of marriage, and to *all* rights in this republic, the rights of God included! For black men there is neither law nor justice, humanity nor religion. The Fugitive Slave *Law* makes mercy to them a crime; and bribes the judge who tries them. An American judge gets ten dollars for every victim he consigns to slavery, and five, when he fails to do so. The oath of any two villains is sufficient, under this hell-black enactment, to send the most pious and exemplary black man into the remorseless jaws of slavery! His own testimony is nothing. He can bring no witnesses for himself. The minister of American justice is bound by the law to hear but *one* side; and *that* side is the side of the oppressor. Let this damning fact be perpetually told. Let it be thundered around the world that in tyrant-killing, king-hating, people-loving, democratic, Christian America the seats of justice are filled with judges who hold their offices under an open and palpable *bribe,* and are bound, in deciding the case of a man's liberty, *to hear only his accusers!*

In glaring violation of justice, in shameless disregard of the forms of administering law, in cunning arrangement to entrap the defenceless, and in diabolical intent this Fugitive Slave Law stands alone in the annals of tyrannical legislation. I doubt if there be another nation on the globe having the brass and the baseness to put such a law on the statute-book. If any man in this assembly thinks differently from me in this matter, and feels able to disprove my statement, I will gladly confront him at any suitable time and place he may select.

I take this law to be one of the grossest infringements of Christian Liberty, and, if the churches and ministers of our country were not stupidly blind, or most wickedly indifferent, they, too, would so regard it.

At the very moment that they are thanking God for the enjoyment of civil and religious liberty, and for the right to worship God according to the dictates of their own consciences, they are utterly silent in respect to a law which robs religion of its chief significance and makes it utterly worthless to a world lying in wickedness. Did this law concern the *"mint, anise, and cummin"*—abridge the right to sing psalms, to partake of the sacrament, or to engage in any of the ceremonies of religion, it would be smitten by the thunder of a thousand pulpits. A general shout would go up from the church demanding *repeal, repeal, instant repeal!*—And it would go hard with that politician who presumed to solicit the votes of the people without inscribing this motto on his banner. Further, if this demand were not complied with, another Scotland would be added to the history of religious liberty, and the stern old covenanters would be thrown into the shade. A John Knox would be seen at every church door and heard from every pulpit, and Fillmore would have no more quarter than was shown by Knox to the beautiful, but treacherous, Queen Mary of Scotland. The fact that the church of our country (with fractional exceptions) does not esteem "the Fugitive

Slave Law" as a declaration of war against religious liberty, implies that that church regards religion simply as a form of worship, an empty ceremony, and *not* a vital principle, requiring active benevolence, justice, love, and good will towards man. It esteems sacrifice above mercy; psalm-singing above right doing; solemn meetings above practical righteousness. A worship that can be conducted by persons who refuse to give shelter to the houseless, to give bread to the hungry, clothing to the naked, and who enjoin obedience to a law forbidding these acts of mercy in a curse, not a blessing to mankind. The Bible addresses all such persons as "scribes, pharisees, hypocrites, who pay tithe of *mint, anise,* and *cummin,* and have omitted the weightier matters of the law, judgment, mercy, and faith."

But the church of this country is not only indifferent to the wrongs of the slave, it actually takes sides with the oppressors. It has made itself the bulwark of American slavery, and the shield of American slave-hunters. Many of its most eloquent Divines, who stand as the very lights of the church, have shamelessly given the sanction of religion and the Bible to the whole slave system. They have taught that man may, properly, be a slave; that the relation of master and slave is ordained of God; that to send back an escaped bondman to his master is clearly the duty of all the followers of the Lord Jesus Christ; and this horrible blasphemy is palmed off upon the world for Christianity.

For my part, I would say, welcome infidelity! welcome atheism! welcome anything! in preference to the gospel, *as preached by those Divines!* They convert the very name of religion into an engine of tyranny and barbarous cruelty, and serve to confirm more infidels, in this age, than all the infidel writings of Thomas Paine, Voltaire, and Bolingbroke put together have done! These ministers make religion a cold and flinty-hearted thing, having neither principles of right action nor bowels of compassion. They strip the love of God of its beauty and leave the throne of religion a huge, horrible, repulsive form. It is a religion for oppressors, tyrants, man-stealers, and *thugs.* It is not that *"pure and undefiled religion"* which is from above, and which is *"first pure, then peaceable, easy to be entreated,* full of mercy and good fruits, *without partiality, and without hypocrisy."* But a religion which favors the rich against the poor; which exalts the proud above the humble; which divides mankind into two classes, tyrants and slaves; which says to the man in chains, *stay there;* and to the oppressor, *oppress on;* it is a religion which may be professed and enjoyed by all the robbers and enslavers of mankind; it makes God a respecter of persons, denies his fatherhood of the race, and tramples in the dust the great truth of the brotherhood of man. All this we affirm to be true of the popular church, and the popular worship of our land and nation— a religion, a church, and a worship which, on the authority of inspired wisdom, we pronounce to be an abomination in the sight of God. In the language of Isaiah, the American church might be well addressed, "Bring no more vain oblations; incense is an abomination unto me: the new moons and Sabbaths, the calling of assemblies, I cannot away with; it is iniquity, even the solemn meeting. Your new moons, and your appointed feasts my soul hateth. They are a trouble to me; I am weary to bear them; and when ye spread forth your hands I will hide mine eyes from you. Yea! when ye make many prayers, I will not hear. Your hands are full of blood; cease to do evil, learn to do well; seek judgment; relieve the oppressed; judge for the fatherless; plead for the widow."

The American church is guilty, when viewed in connection with what it is doing to uphold slavery; but it is superlatively guilty when viewed in its connection with its ability to abolish slavery.

The sin of which it is guilty is one of omission as well as of commission. Albert Barnes but uttered what the common sense of every man at all observant of the actual state of the case will receive as truth, when he declared that "There is no power out of the church that could sustain slavery an hour, if it were not sustained in it."

Let the religious press, the pulpit, the Sunday School, the conference meeting, the great ecclesiastical, missionary, Bible and tract associations of the land array their immense powers against slavery, and slave-holding; and the whole system of crime and blood would be scattered to the winds, and that they do not do this involves them in the most awful responsibility of which the mind can conceive.

In prosecuting the anti-slavery enterprise, we have been asked to spare the church, to spare the ministry; but *how*, we ask, could such a thing be done? We are met on the threshold of our efforts for the redemption of the slave, by the church and ministry of the country, in battle arrayed against us; and we are compelled to fight or flee. From *what* quarter, I beg to know, has proceeded a fire so deadly upon our ranks, during the last two years, as from the Northern pulpit? As the champions of oppressors, the chosen men of American theology have appeared—men honored for their so-called piety, and their real learning. The Lords of Buffalo, the Springs of New York, the Lathrops of Auburn, the Coxes and Spencers of Brooklyn, the Gannets and Sharps of Boston, the Deweys of Washington, and other great religious lights of the land have, in utter denial of the authority of *Him* by whom they professed to be called to the ministry, deliberately taught us, against the example of the Hebrews, and against the remonstrance of the Apostles, *that we ought to obey man's law before the law of God.*

My spirit wearies of such blasphemy; and how such men can be supported, as the "standing types and representative of Jesus Christ," is a mystery which I leave others to penetrate. In speaking of the American church, however, let it be distinctly understood that I mean the *great mass* of the religious organizations of our land. There are exceptions, and I thank God that there are. Noble men may be found, scattered all over these Northern States, of whom Henry Ward Beecher, of Brooklyn; Samuel J. May, of Syracuse; and my esteemed friend (Rev. R. R. Raymond) on the platform, are shining examples; and let me say further, that, upon these men lies the duty to inspire our ranks with high religious faith and zeal, and to cheer us on in the great mission of the slave's redemption from his chains.

One is struck with the difference between the attitude of the American church towards the anti-slavery movement, and that occupied by the churches in England towards a similar movement in that country. There, the church, true to its mission of ameliorating, elevating and improving the condition of mankind, came forward promptly, bound up the wounds of the West Indian slave, and restored him to his liberty. There, the question of emancipation was a high religious question. It was demanded in the name of humanity, and according to the law of the living God. The Sharps, the Clarksons, the Wilberforces, the Buxtons, the Burchells, and the Knibbs were alike famous for their piety and for their philanthropy. The anti-slavery movement *there* was not an anti-church movement, for the reason that the church took its full share in prosecuting that movement: and the anti-slavery movement in this country will cease to be an anti-church movement, when the church of this country shall assume a favorable instead of a hostile position towards that movement.

Americans! your republican politics, not less than your republican religion, are flagrantly inconsistent. You boast of your love of liberty, your superior civilization, and your pure Christianity, while the whole political power of the nation (as embodied in the two great political parties) is solemnly pledged to support and perpetuate the enslavement of three millions of your countrymen. You hurl your anathemas at the crowned headed tyrants of Russia and Austria and pride yourselves on your Democratic institutions, while you yourselves consent to be the mere *tools* and *body-guards* of the tyrants of Virginia and Carolina. You invite to your shores fugitives of oppression from abroad, honor them with banquets, greet them with ovations, cheer them, toast them, salute them, protect them, and pour out your money to them like water; but the fugitives from your own land you advertise, hunt, arrest, shoot, and kill. You glory in your refinement and your universal education; yet you maintain a system as barbarous and dreadful as ever stained the character of a nation—a system begun in avarice, supported in pride, and perpetuated in cruelty. You shed tears over fallen Hungary, and make the sad story of her wrongs the theme of your poets, statesmen, and orators, till your gallant sons are ready to fly to arms to vindicate her cause against the oppressor; but, in regard to the ten thousand wrongs of the American slave, you would enforce the strictest silence, and would hail him as an enemy of the nation who dares to make those wrongs the subject of public discourse! You are all on fire at the mention of liberty for France or for Ireland; but are as cold as an iceberg at the thought of liberty for the enslaved of America. You discourse eloquently on the dignity of labor; yet, you sustain a system which, in its very essence, casts a stigma upon labor. You can bare your bosom to the storm of British artillery to throw off a three-penny tax on tea; and yet wring the last hard earned farthing from the grasp of the black laborers of your country. You profess to believe "that, of one blood, God made all nations of men to dwell on the face of all the earth," and hath commanded all men, everywhere, to love one another; yet you notoriously hate (and glory in your hatred) all men whose skins are not colored like your own. You declare before the world, and are understood by the world to declare that you *"hold these truths to be self-evident, that all men are created equal; and are endowed by their Creator with certain inalienable rights; and that among these are, life, liberty, and the pursuit of happiness;*["] and yet, you hold securely, in a bondage which, according to your own Thomas Jefferson, *"is worse than ages of that which your fathers rose in rebellion to oppose,"* *a seventh part* of the inhabitants of your country.

Fellow-citizens, I will not enlarge further on your national inconsistencies. The existence of slavery in this country brands your republicanism as a sham, your humanity as a base pretense, and your Christianity as a lie. It destroys your moral power abroad; it corrupts your politicians at home. It saps the foundation of religion; it makes your name a hissing and a bye-word to a mocking earth. It is the antagonistic force in your government, the only thing that seriously disturbs and endangers your *Union.* It fetters your progress; it is the enemy of improvement; the deadly foe of education; it fosters pride; it breeds insolence; it promotes vice; it shelters crime; it is a curse to the earth that supports it; and yet you cling to it as if it were the sheet anchor of all your hopes. Oh! be warned! be warned! a horrible reptile is coiled up in your nation's bosom; the venomous creature is nursing at the tender breast of your youthful republic; *for the love of God, tear away,* and fling from you the hideous monster, and *let the weight of twenty millions crush and destroy it forever!*

But it is answered in reply to all this, that precisely what I have now denounced is, in fact, guaranteed and sanctioned by the Constitution of the United States; that, the right to hold, and to hunt slaves is a part of that Constitution framed by the illustrious Fathers of this Republic.

Then, I dare to affirm, notwithstanding all I have said before, your father stooped, basely stooped

> To palter with us in a double sense:
> And keep the word of promise to the ear,
> But break it to the heart.

And instead of being the honest men I have before declared them to be, they were the veriest impostors that ever practised on mankind. This is the inevitable conclusion, and from it there is no escape; but I differ from those who charge this baseness on the framers of the Constitution of the United States. It is a slander upon their memory, at least, so I believe. There is not time now to argue the constitutional question at length; nor have I the ability to discuss it as it ought to be discussed. The subject has been handled with masterly power by Lysander Spooner, Esq., by William Goodell, by Samuel E. Sewall, Esq., and last, though not least, by Gerrit Smith, Esq. These gentlemen have, as I think, fully and clearly vindicated the Constitution from any design to support slavery for an hour.

Fellow-citizens! there is no matter in respect to which the people of the North have allowed themselves to be so ruinously imposed upon as that of the pro-slavery character of the Constitution. In that instrument I hold there is neither warrant, license, nor sanction of the hateful thing; but interpreted, as it ought to be interpreted, the Constitution is a glorious liberty document. Read its preamble, consider its purposes. Is slavery among them? Is it at the gateway? or is it in the temple? it is neither. While I do not intend to argue this question on the present occasion, let me ask, if it be not somewhat singular that, if the Constitution were intended to be, by its framers and adopters, a slaveholding instrument, why neither slavery, slaveholding, nor slave can anywhere be found in it. What would be thought of an instrument, drawn up, legally drawn up, for the purpose of entitling the city of Rochester to a tract of land, in which no mention of land was made? Now, there are certain rules of interpretation for the proper understanding of all legal instruments. These rules are well established. They are plain, commonsense rules, such as you and I, and all of us, can understand and apply, without having passed years in the study of law. I scout the idea that the question of the constitutionality, or unconstitutionality of slavery, is not a question for the people. I hold that every American citizen has a right to form an opinion of the constitution, and to propagate that opinion, and to use all honorable means to make his opinion the prevailing one. Without this right, the liberty of an American citizen would be as insecure as that of a Frenchman. Ex-Vice-President Dallas tells us that the constitution is an object to which no American mind can be too attentive, and no American heart too devoted. He further says, the Constitution, in its words, is plain and intelligible, and is meant for the home-bred, unsophisticated understandings of our fellow-citizens. Senator Berrien tells us that the Constitution is the fundamental law, that which controls all others. The charter of our liberties, which every citizen has a personal interest in understanding thoroughly. The testimony of Senator Breese, Lewis Cass, and many others that might be named, who are everywhere esteemed as sound lawyers, so regard the constitution. I take it, therefore, that it is not presumption in a private citizen to form an opinion of that instrument.

Now, take the Constitution according to its plain reading, and I defy the presentation of a single pro-slavery clause in it. On the other hand, it will be found to contain principles and purposes, entirely hostile to the existence of slavery.

I have detained my audience entirely too long already. At some future period I will gladly avail myself of an opportunity to give this subject a full and fair discussion.

Allow me to say, in conclusion, notwithstanding the dark picture I have this day presented, of the state of the nation, I do not despair of this country. There are forces in operation which must inevitably work the downfall of slavery. "The arm of the Lord is not shortened," and the doom of slavery is certain. I, therefore, leave off where I began, with hope. While drawing encouragement from "the Declaration of Independence," the great principles it contains, and the genius of American Institutions, my spirit is also cheered by the obvious tendencies of the age. Nations do not now stand in the same relation to each other that they did ages ago. No nation can now shut itself up from the surrounding world and trot round in the same old path of its fathers without interference. The time was when such could be done. Long established customs of hurtful character could formerly fence themselves in, and do their evil work with social impunity. Knowledge was then confined and enjoyed by the privileged few, and the multitude walked on in mental darkness. But a change has now come over the affairs of mankind. Walled cities and empires have become unfashionable. The arm of commerce has borne away the gates of the strong city. Intelligence is penetrating the darkest corners of the globe. It makes its pathway over and under the sea, as well as on the earth. Wind, steam, and lightning are its chartered agents. Oceans no longer divide, but link nations together. From Boston to London is now a holiday excursion. Space is comparatively annihilated.—Thoughts expressed on one side of the Atlantic are distinctly heard on the other.

The far off and almost fabulous Pacific rolls in grandeur at our feet. The Celestial Empire, the mystery of ages, is being solved. The fiat of the Almighty, "Let there be Light," has not yet spent its force. No abuse, no outrage whether in taste, sport or avarice, can now hide itself from the all-pervading light. The iron shoe, and crippled foot of China must be seen in contrast with nature. Africa must rise and put on her yet unwoven garment. "Ethiopia shall stretch out her hand unto God." In the fervent aspirations of William Lloyd Garrison, I say, and let every heart join in saying it:

God speed the year of jubilee
   The wide world o'er!
When from their galling chains set free,
Th' oppress'd shall vilely bend the knee,
And wear the yoke of tyranny
   Like brutes no more.
That year will come, and freedom's reign,
To man his plundered rights again
   Restore.

God speed the day when human blood
   Shall cease to flow!
In every clime be understood,
The claims of human brotherhood,
And each return for evil, good,
   Not blow for blow;
That day will come all feuds to end,
And change into a faithful friend
   Each foe.

God speed the hour, the glorious hour,
   When none on earth
Shall exercise a lordly power,
Nor in a tyrant's presence cower;
But to all manhood's stature tower,
   By equal birth!
That hour will come, to each, to all,
And from his prison-house, to thrall
   Go forth.

Until that year, day, hour, arrive,
With head, and heart, and hand I'll strive,
To break the rod, and rend the gyve,
The spoiler of his prey deprive—
So witness Heaven!
And never from my chosen post,
Whate'er the peril or the cost,
Be driven.   [1852]

Mary E. Bryan

How Should Women Write?

The idea of women writing books! There were no prophets in the days of King John to predict an event so far removed from probability. The women of the household sat by their distaffs, or toiled in the fields, or busied themselves in roasting and brewing for their guzzling lords. If ever a poetic vision or a half-defined thought floated through their minds, they sang it out to their busy wheels, or murmured it in rude sentences to lull the babies upon their bosoms, or silently wove it into their lives to manifest itself in patient love and gentleness. And it was all as it should have been; there was need for nothing more. Physical labor was then all that was required of woman; and to "act well her part," meant but to perform the domestic duties which were given her. Life was less complex then than now—the intellectual part of man's twofold nature being but unequally developed, while the absence of labor-saving implements demanded a greater amount of manual toil from men as well as from women.

It is different now. Modern ingenuity and Protean appliances of machinery have lessened the necessity of actual physical labor; and, in the constant progress of the human race, new fields have been opened, and new social needs and requirements are calling for workers in other and higher departments.

There is a cry now for intellectual food through the length and breadth of the land. The old oracles of the past, the mummied literary remains of a dead age, will not satisfy a generation that is pressing so vigorously forward. They want books imbued with the strong vitality and energy of the present. And as it is a moving, hurrying, changing time, with new influences and opinions constantly rising like stars above the horizon, men want books to keep pace with their progress—nay, to go before and guide them, as the pillar of fire and cloud did the Israelites in the desert. So they want books for every year, for every month—mirrors to "catch the manners living as they rise," lenses to concentrate the rays of the new stars that dawn upon them.

There is a call for workers; and woman, true to her mission as the helpmeet for man, steps forward to take her part in the intellectual labor, as she did when only manual toil was required at her hands. The pen has become the mighty instrument of reform and rebuke; the press is the teacher and the preacher of the world; and it is not only the privilege, but the duty of woman to aid in extending this influence of letters, and in supplying the intellectual demands of society, when she has been endowed with the power. Let her assure herself that she has been called to the task, and then grasp her pen firmly, with the stimulating consciousness that she is performing the work assigned to her.

Thus is apparent what has been gradually admitted, that it is woman's duty to write—but how and what? This is yet a mooted question. Men, after much demur and hesitation, have given women liberty to write; but they cannot yet consent to allow them full freedom. They may flutter out of the cage, but it must be with clipped wings; they may hop about the smooth-shaven lawn, but must, on no account, fly. With metaphysics they have nothing to do; it is too deep a sea for their lead to sound; nor must they grapple with those great social and moral problems with which every strong soul is now wrestling. They must not go beyond the surface of life, lest they should stir the impure sediment that lurks beneath. They may whiten the outside of the sepulchre, but must not soil their kidded hands by essaying to cleanse the inside of its rottenness and dead men's bones.

Nature, indeed, is given them to fustianize over, and religion allowed them as their chief capital—the orthodox religion, that says its prayers out of a prayer-book, and goes to church on Sabbaths; but on no account the higher, truer religion, that, despising cant and hypocrisy, and scorning forms and conventionalisms, seeks to cure, not to cloak, the plague-spots of society—the self-forgetting, self-abnegating religion that shrinks not from following in the steps of Christ, that curls not its lip at the touch of poverty and shame, nor fears to call crime by its right name, though it wear a gilded mask, nor to cry out earnestly and bravely, "Away with it! away with it!" No! not such religion as this. It is *unfeminine;* women have no business with it whatever, though they may ring changes as often as they please upon the "crowns of gold," the "jasper walls," and "seraph harps."

Having prescribed these bounds to the female pen, men are the first to condemn her efforts as tame and commonplace, because they lack earnestness and strength.

If she writes of birds, of flowers, sunshine, and *id omne genus,* as did Amelia Welby, noses are elevated superbly, and the effusions are said to smack of bread and butter.

If love, religion, and domestic obligations are her theme, as with Mrs. Hentz, "namby-pamby" is the word contemptuously applied to her productions. If, like Mrs. Southworth, she reproduces Mrs. Radcliffe in her possibility—scorning romances, her nonsensical clap-trap is said to be "beneath criticism;" and if . . . she gossips harmlessly of fashions and fashionables, of the opera and . . . of watering-places, lectures, and a railroad trip, she is *"pish"*-ed aside as silly and childish; while those who seek to go beyond the boundary-line are put down with the stigma of *"strong-minded."* Fanny Fern, who, though actuated by no fixed purpose, was yet more earnest than the majority of her sisterhood, heard the word hissed in her ears whenever she essayed to strike a blow at the root of social sin and inconsistency, and had whatever there was of noble and philanthropic impulse in her nature annihilated by the epithets of "bold" and "indelicate," which were hurled at her like poisoned arrows.

It will not do. Such dallying with surface-bubbles, as we find in much of our periodical literature, might have sufficed for another age, but not for this. We want a deeper troubling of the waters, that we may go down into the pool and be healed. It is an earnest age we live in. Life means more than it did in other days; it is an intense reality, crowded thick with eager, questioning thoughts and passionate resolves; with burning aspirations and agonized doubts. There are active influences at work, all tending to one grand object— moral, social, and physical advancement. The pen is the compass-needle that points to this pole. Shall woman dream on violet banks, while this great work of reformation is needing her talents and her energies? Shall she prate prettily of moonlight, music, love, and flowers, while the world of stern, staring, pressing realities of wrong and woe, of shame and toil, surrounds her? Shall she stifle the voice in her soul for fear of being sneered at as *strong-minded,* and shall her great heart throb and heave as did the mountain of Æsop, only to bring forth such insignificant mice—such productions—more paltry in purpose than in style and conception—which she gives to the world as the offspring of her brain?

It will not long be so. Women are already forming higher standards for themselves, learning that genius has no sex, and that, so the truth be told, it matters not whether the pen is wielded by a masculine or a female hand. The active, earnest, fearless spirit of the age, which sends the blood thrilling through the veins of women, will flow out through their pens, and give color to the pictures they delineate, to the principles they affirm. Literature must embody the prominent feeling of the age on which it is engrafted. It is only an isolated, excepted spirit, like Keats's, which can close its eyes to outward influences, and, amid the roar of gathering political storms, and the distant thunderings of the French Revolution, lie down among the sweet, wild English flowers, and dream out its dream of the old Greek beauty.

How should a woman write? I answer, as men, as all should write to whom the power of expression has been given—*honestly and without fear.* Let them write what they feel and think, even if there be errors in the thought and the feeling—better that than the lifeless inanities of which literature, and especially periodical literature, furnishes so many deplorable samples.

Our opinions on ethical and social questions change continually as the mind develops, and the light of knowledge shines more broadly through the far-off opening in the labyrinth of inquiry through which we wander seeking for truth. Thus, even when writers are most honest, their opinions, written at different times, often appear contradictory. This the discerning reader will readily understand. He will know that in ascending the ladder, upon whose top the angels stand, the prospect widens and changes continually as newer heights are won. Emerson, indeed, tells us that "a foolish consistency is the hobgoblin of little minds. With consistency, a great soul has simply nothing to do. Speak what you think now in hard words; and to-morrow, speak what to-morrow thinks in hard words again, though it contradict everything you said to-day."

This is strong—perhaps too unqualified, but even inconsistency is better than the dull, donkey-like obstinacy which refuses to move from one position, though the wooing spirit of inquiry beckon it onward, and winged speculation tempt it to scale the clouds.

Still, there should be in writing, as in acting, a fixed and distant purpose to which everything should tend. If this be to elevate and refine the human race, the purpose will gradually and unconsciously work out its own accomplishment. Not, indeed, through didactic homilies only; every image of beauty or sublimity crystallized in words, every philosophic truth, and every thought that has a tendency to expand the mind or enlarge the range of spiritual vision, will aid in advancing this purpose, will be as oil to the lamp we carry to light the footsteps of others.

As to the subjects that should be written upon, they are many and varied; there is no exhausting them while nature teems with beauty—while men live, and act, and love, and suffer—while the murmurs of the great ocean of the *Infinite* come to us in times when the soul is stillest, like music that is played too far off for us to catch the tune. Broad fields of thought lie before us, traversed, indeed, by many feet, but each season brings fresh fruits to gather and new flowers to crop.

Genius, like light, shines upon all things—upon the muck-heap as upon the gilded cupola.

As to the wrong and wretchedness which the novelist lays bare—it will not be denied that such really exists in this sin-beleaguered world. Wherefore shrink and cover our eyes when these social ulcers are probed? Better earnestly endeavor to eradicate the evil, than seek to conceal or ignore its existence. Be sure this will not prevent it eating deeper and deeper into the heart.

Genius, when true and earnest, will not be circumscribed. No power shall say to it: "Thus far shalt thou go, and no farther." Its province is in part, to daguerreotype the shifting influences, feelings, and tendencies at work in the age in which it exists—and sin, and grief, and suffering, as well as hope, and love, and joy, and star-eyed aspiration, pass across its pages as phantoms across the charmed mirror of the magician. Genius thrills along "the electric chain wherewith we are darkly bound," from the highest to the lowest link of the social ligature; for true genius is Christ-like; *it scorns nothing;* calls nothing that God made common or unclean, because of its great yearning over mankind, its longing to lift them up from the sordid things of sense in which they grovel to its own higher and purer intellectual or spiritual atmosphere. The noblest woman of us all, Mrs. Elizabeth Browning, whom I hold to have written, in "Aurora Leigh," the greatest book of this century,— the greatest, not from the wealth of its imagery, or the vigor of its thoughts, but because of the moral grandeur of its purpose,—Mrs. Browning, I say, has not shrunk from going down, with her purity encircling her, like the halo around the Saviour's head, to the abodes of shame and degradation for material to aid in elucidating the serious truths she seeks to impress for sorrowful examples of the evils for which she endeavors to find some remedy. She is led to this through that love which is inseparable from the higher order of genius. That noblest form of genius which generates the truest poetry—the poetry of feeling rather than of imagination—warm with human life, but uncolored by voluptuous passion—is strongly connected with love. Not the sentiment which dances through the world to the music of marriage-bells; but that divine, self-ignoring, universal love of which the inspired apostle wrote so burningly, when, caught up in the fiery chariot of the Holy Ghost, he looked down upon the selfish considerations of common humanity: the love (or charity) "which beareth all things, endureth all things, which suffereth long and is kind,"—the love which, looking to heaven, stretches its arms to enfold the whole human brotherhood.

This is the love which, hand in hand with genius, is yet to work out the redemption of society. I have faith to believe it; and sometimes, when the tide of hope and enthusiasm is high, I have thought that woman, with the patience and the long-suffering of her love, the purity of her intellect, her instinctive sympathy and her soul of poetry, might be God's chosen instrument in this work of gradual reformation, this reconciling of the harsh contrasts in society that jar so upon our sense of harmony, this righting of the grievous wrongs and evils over which we weep and pray, this final uniting of men into one common brotherhood by the bonds of sympathy and affection.

It may be but a Utopian dream; but the faith is better than hopelessness; it is elevating and cheering to believe it. It is well to aspire, though the aspiration be unfulfilled. It is better to look up at the stars, though they dazzle, than down at the vermin beneath our feet.   [1860]

Walt Whitman
....
Democratic Vistas

. . . I say that democracy can never prove itself beyond cavil, until it founds and luxuriantly grows its own forms of art, poems, schools, theology, displacing all that exists, or that has been produced anywhere in the past, under opposite influences. It is curious to me that while so many voices, pens, minds, in the press, lecture rooms, in our Congress, etc., are discussing intellectual topics, pecuniary dangers, legislative problems, the suffrage, tariff and labor questions, and the various business and benevolent needs of America, with propositions, remedies, often worth deep attention, there is one need, a hiatus the profoundest, that no eye seems to perceive, no voice to state. Our fundamental want today in the United States, with closest, amplest reference to present conditions, and to the future, is of a class, and the clear idea of a class, of native authors, literatuses, far different, far higher in grade, than any yet known, sacerdotal, modern, fit to cope with our occasions, lands, permeating the whole mass of American mentality, taste, belief, breathing into it a new breath of life, giving it decision, affecting politics far more than the popular superficial suffrage, with results inside and underneath the elections of Presidents or Congresses—radiating, begetting appropriate teachers, schools, manners, and, as its grandest result, accomplishing (what neither the schools nor the churches and their clergy have hitherto accomplish'd, and without which this nation will no more stand, permanently, soundly, than a house will stand without a sub-stratum), a religious and moral character beneath the political and productive and intellectual bases of the States. For know you not, dear, earnest reader, that the people of our land may all read and write, and may all possess the right to vote—and yet the main things may be entirely lacking?—(and this to suggest them).

View'd, today, from a point of view sufficiently over-arching, the problem of humanity all over the civilized world is social and religious, and is to be finally met and treated by literature. The priest departs, the divine literatus comes. Never was anything more wanted than, today, and here in the States, the poet of the modern is wanted, or the great literatus of the modern. At all times, perhaps, the central point in any nation, and that whence it is itself really sway'd the most, and whence it sways others, is its national literature, especially its archetypal poems. Above all previous lands, a great original literature is surely to become the justification and reliance (in some respects the sole reliance of American democracy).

Few are aware how the great literature penetrates all, gives hue to all, shapes aggregates and individuals, and, after subtle ways, with irresistible power, constructs, sustains, demolishes at will. Why tower, in reminiscence, above all the nations of the earth, two special lands, petty in themselves, yet inexpressibly gigantic, beautiful, columnar? Immortal Judah lives, and Greece immortal lives, in a couple of poems.

Nearer than this. It is not generally realized, but it is true, as the genius of Greece, and all the sociology, personality, politics, and religion of those wonderful states, resided in their literature or æsthetics, that what was afterwards the main support of European chivalry, the feudal, ecclesiastical, dynastic world over there—forming its osseous structure, holding it together for hundreds, thousands of years, preserving its flesh and bloom, giving it form, decision, rounding it out, and so saturating it in the conscious and unconscious blood, breed, belief, and intuitions of men, that it still prevails powerful to this day, in defiance of the mighty changes of time—was its literature, permeating to the very marrow, especially that major part, its enhancing songs, ballads, and poems.[1]

To the ostent of the senses and eyes, I know, the influences which stamp the world's history are wars, uprisings or downfalls of dynasties, changeful movement of trade, important inventions, navigation, military or civil governments, advent of powerful personalities, conquerors, etc. These of course play their part; yet, it may be, a single new thought, imagination, abstract principle, even literary style, fit for the time, put in shape by some

---

[1] See, for hereditaments, specimens, Walter Scott's Border Minstrelsy, Percy's collection, Ellis's early English Metrical Romances, the European continental poems of Walter of Aquitania, and the Nibelungen, of pagan stock, but monkish-feudal redaction; the history of the Troubadours, by Fauriel; even the far-back cumbrous old Hindu epics, as indicating the Asian eggs out of which European chivalry was hatch'd; Ticknor's chapters on the Cid, and on the Spanish poems and poets of Calderon's time. Then always, and, of course, as the superbest poetic culmination-expression of feudalism, the Shaksperean dramas, in the attitudes, dialogue, characters, etc., of the princes, lords, and gentlemen, the pervading atmosphere, the implied and express'd standard of manners, the high port and proud stomach, the regal embroidery of style, etc.

great literatus, and projected among mankind, may duly cause changes, growths, re-
movals, greater than the longest and bloodiest war, or the most stupendous merely political dynastic, or commercial overturn.

In short, as though it may not be realized, it is strictly true, that a few first-class poets,
philosophs, and authors have substantially settled and given status to the entire religion,
education, law, sociology, etc., of the hitherto civilized world, by tingeing and often creating the atmospheres out of which they have arisen, such also must stamp, and more than
ever stamp, the interior and real democratic construction of this American continent,
today, and days to come. Remember also this fact of difference, that, while through the
antique and through the mediæval ages, highest thoughts and ideals realized themselves,
and their expression made its way by other arts, as much as, or even more than by, technical literature (not open to the mass of persons, or even to the majority of eminent persons),
such literature in our day and for current purposes is not only more eligible than all the
other arts put together, but has become the only general means of morally influencing the
world. Painting, sculpture, and the dramatic theatre, it would seem no longer play an indispensable or even important part in the workings and mediumship of intellect, utility,
or even high æsthetics. Architecture remains, doubtless with capacities, and a real future.
Then music, the combiner, nothing more spiritual, nothing more sensuous, a god, yet
completely human, advances, prevails, holds highest place; supplying in certain wants
and quarters what nothing else could supply. Yet in the civilization of today it is undeniable that, over all the arts, literature dominates, serves beyond all—shapes the character of
church and school—or, in any rate, is capable of doing so. Including the literature of science, its scope is indeed unparallel'd.

Before proceeding further, it were perhaps well to discriminate on certain points. Literature tills its crops in many fields, and some may flourish, while others lag. What I say
in these Vistas has its main bearing on imaginative literature, especially poetry, the stock
of all. In the department of science, and the specialty of journalism, there appear, in these
States, promises, perhaps fulfillments, of highest earnestness, reality and life. These, of
course, are modern. But in the region of imaginative, spinal and essential attributes,
something equivalent to creation is, for our age and lands, imperatively demanded. For
not only is it not enough that the new blood, new frame of democracy shall be vivified and
held together merely by political means, superficial suffrage, legislation, etc., but it is
clear to me that, unless it goes deeper, gets at least as firm and as warm a hold in men's
hearts, emotions and belief, as, in their days, feudalism or ecclesiasticism, and inaugurates
its own perennial sources, welling from the center forever, its strength will be defective,
its growth doubtful, and its main charm wanting. I suggest, therefore, the possibility,
should some two or three really original American poets (perhaps artists or lecturers) arise,
mounting the horizon like planets, stars of the first magnitude, that, from their eminence,
fusing contributions, races, far localities, etc., together, they would give more compaction
and more moral identity (the quality to-day most needed) to these States, than all its Constitutions, legislative and judicial ties, and all its hitherto political, warlike, or materialistic experiences. As, for instance, there could hardly happen anything that would more
serve the States, with all their variety of origins, their diverse climes, cities, standards,
etc., than possessing an aggregate of heroes, characters, exploits, sufferings, prosperity or
misfortune, glory or disgrace, common to all, typical of it all—no less, but even greater
would it be to possess the aggregation of a cluster of mighty poets, artists, teachers, fit for
us, national expressers, comprehending and effusing for the men and women of the States,
what is universal, native, common to all, inland and seaboard, northern and southern. The
historians say of ancient Greece, with her ever-jealous autonomies, cities and states, that

the only positive unity she ever own'd or receiv'd, was the sad unity of a common subjection, at the last, to foreign conquerors. Subjection, aggregation of that sort, is impossible to America; but the fear of conflicting and irreconcilable interiors, and the lack of a common skeleton, knitting all close, continually haunts me. Or, if it does not, nothing is plainer than the need, a long period to come, of a fusion of the States into the only reliable identity, the moral and artistic one. For, I say, the true nationality of the States, the genuine union, when we come to a mortal crisis, is, and is to be, after all, neither the written law, nor (as is generally supposed) either self-interest, or common pecuniary or material object—but the fervid and tremendous IDEA, melting everything else with resistless heat, and solving all lesser and definite distinctions in vast, indefinite, spiritual, emotional power.

It may be claim'd (and I admit the weight of the claim) that common and general worldly prosperity, and a populace well-to-do, and with all life's material comforts, is the main thing, and is enough. It may be argued that our republic is, in performance, really enacting today the grandest arts, poems, etc., by beating up the wilderness into fertile farms, and in her railroads, ships, machinery, etc. And it may be ask'd, Are these not better, indeed, for America, than any utterances even of greatest rhapsode, artist, or literatus?

I too hail those achievements with pride and joy: then answer that the soul of man will not with such only—nay, not with such at all—be finally satisfied; but needs what, (standing on these and on all things, as the feet stand on the ground), is addressed to the loftiest, to itself alone.

Out of such considerations, such truths, arises for treatment in these Vistas the important question of character, of an American stock-personality, with literatures and arts for outlets and return-expressions, and, of course, to correspond, within outlines common to all. To these, the main affair, the thinkers of the United States, in general so acute, have either given feeblest attention, or have remain'd, and remain, in a state of somnolence.

For my part, I would alarm and caution even the political and business reader, and to the utmost extent, against the prevailing delusion that the establishment of free political institutions, and plentiful intellectual smartness, with general good order, physical plenty, industry, etc. (desirable and precious advantages as they all are), do, of themselves, determine and yield to our experiment of democracy the fruitage of success. With such advantages at present fully, or almost fully, possess'd—the Union just issued, victorious, from the struggle with the only foes it need ever fear (namely, those within itself, the interior ones), and with unprecedented materialistic advancement—society, in these States, is canker'd, crude, superstitious and rotten. Political, or law-made society is, and private, or voluntary society, is also. In any vigor, the element of the moral conscience, the most important, the verteber to State or man, seems to me either entirely lacking, or seriously enfeebled or ungrown.

I say we had best look our times and lands searchingly in the face, like a physician diagnosing some deep disease. Never was there, perhaps, more hollowness at heart than at present, and here in the United States. Genuine belief seems to have left us. The underlying principles of the States are not honestly believ'd in (for all this hectic glow, and these melodramatic screamings), nor is humanity itself believ'd in. What penetrating eye does not everywhere see through the mask? The spectacle is appalling. We live in an atmosphere of hypocrisy throughout. The men believe not in the women, nor the women in the men. A scornful superciliousness rules in literature. The aim of all the _littérateurs_ is to find something to make fun of. A lot of churches, sects, etc., the most dismal phantasms I know, usurp the name of religion. Conversation is a mass of badinage. From deceit in the spirit, the mother of all false deeds, the offspring is already incalculable. An acute and candid person, in the revenue department in Washington, who is led by the course of his employment to regularly visit the cities, north, south, and west, to investigate frauds, has talked much with me about his discoveries. The depravity of the business classes of our country is not less than has been supposed, but infinitely greater. The official services of America, national, state, and municipal, in all their branches and departments, except the judiciary, are saturated in corruption, bribery, falsehood, maladministration; and the judiciary is tainted. The great cities reek with respectable as much as non-respectable robbery and scoundrelism. In fashionable life, flippancy, tepid amours, weak infidelism, small aims, or no aims at all, only to kill time. In business (this all-devouring modern word, business), the one sole object is, by any means, pecuniary gain. The magician's serpent in the fable ate up all the other serpents; and moneymaking is our magician's serpent, remaining today sole master of the field. The best class we show, is but a mob of fashionably dress'd speculators and vulgarians. True, indeed, behind this fantastic farce, enacted on the visible stage of society, solid things and stupendous labors are to be discover'd, existing crudely and going on in the background, to advance and tell themselves in time. Yet the truths are none the less terrible. I say that our New World democracy, however great a success in uplifting the masses out of their sloughs, in materialistic development, products, and in a certain highly deceptive superficial popular intellectuality, is, so far, an almost complete failure in its social aspects, and in really grand religious, moral, literary, and æsthetic results. In vain do we march with unprecedented strides to empire so colossal, outvying the antique, beyond Alexander's, beyond the proudest sway of Rome. In vain have we annex'd Texas, California, Alaska, and reach north for Canada and south for Cuba. It is as if we were somehow being endow'd with a vast and more and more thoroughly appointed body and then left with little or no soul.

Let me illustrate further, as I write, with current observation, localities, etc. The subject is important, and will bear repetition. After an absence, I am now again (September, 1870) in New York City and Brooklyn, on a few weeks' vacation. The splendor, picturesqueness, and oceanic amplitude and rush of these great cities, the unsurpassed situation, rivers and bay, sparkling sea-tides, costly and lofty new buildings, façades of marble and iron, of original grandeur and elegance of design, with the masses of gay color, the preponderance of white and blue, the flags flying, the endless ships, the tumultuous streets, Broadway, the heavy, low, musical roar, hardly ever intermitted, even at night; the jobbers' houses, the rich shops, the wharves, the great Central Park, and the Brooklyn Park of hills (as I wander among them this beautiful fall weather, musing, watching, absorbing)—the assemblages of the citizens in their groups, conversations, trades, evening amusements, or along the by-quarters—these, I say, and the like of these, completely satisfy my senses of power, fullness, motion, etc., and give me, through such senses and appetites, and through my æsthetic conscience, a continued exaltation and absolute fulfillment. Always and more and more, as I cross the East and North rivers, the ferries, or with the pilots in their pilot-houses, or pass an hour in Wall Street, or the Gold Exchange, I realize (if we must admit such partialisms) that not Nature alone is great in her fields of freedom and the open air, in her storms, the shows of night and day, the mountains, forests, sea—but in the artificial, the work of man too is equally great—in this profusion of teeming humanity—in these ingenuities, streets, goods, houses, ships—these hurrying, feverish, electric crowds of men, their complicated business genius (not least among the geniuses), and all this mighty, many-threaded wealth and industry concentrated here.

But sternly discarding, shutting our eyes to the glow and grandeur of the general superficial effect, coming down to what is of the only real importance, Personalities, and examining minutely, we question, we ask, Are there, indeed, *men* here worthy the name? Are there athletes? Are there perfect women, to match the generous material luxuriance? Is there a pervading atmosphere of beautiful manners? Are there crops of fine youths, and majestic old persons? Are there arts worthy freedom and a rich people? Is there a great moral and religious civilization—the only justification of a great material one? Confess that to severe eyes, using the moral microscope upon humanity, a sort of dry and flat Sahara appears, these cities, crowded with petty grotesques, malformations, phantoms, playing meaningless antics. Confess that everywhere, in shop, street, church, theatre, barroom, official chair, are pervading flippancy and vulgarity, low cunning, infidelity—everywhere the youth puny, impudent, foppish, prematurely ripe—everywhere an abnormal libidinousness, unhealthy forms, male, female, painted, padded, dyed, chignon'd, muddy complexions, bad blood, the capacity for good motherhood deceasing or deceas'd, shallow notions of beauty, with a range of manners, or rather lack of manners (considering the advantages enjoy'd), probably the meanest to be seen in the world.[2]

Of all this, and these lamentable conditions, to breathe into them the breath recuperative of sane and heroic life, I say a new-founded literature, not merely to copy and reflect existing surfaces, or pander to what is called taste—not only to amuse, pass away time, celebrate the beautiful, the refined, the past, or exhibit technical, rhythmic, or grammatical dexterity—but a literature underlying life, religious, consistent with science, handling the elements and forces with competent power, teaching and training men—and, as perhaps the most precious of its results, achieving the entire redemption of woman out of these incredible holds and webs of silliness, millinery, and every kind of dyspeptic depletion—and thus insuring to the States a strong and sweet Female Race, a race of perfect Mothers—is what is needed.

And now, in the full conception of these facts and points, and all that they infer, pro and con—with yet unshaken faith in the elements of the American masses, the composites, of both sexes, and even consider'd as individuals—and ever recognizing in them the broadest bases of the best literary and æsthetic appreciation—I proceed with my speculations, Vistas. . . .

What, however, do we more definitely mean by New World literature? Are we not doing well enough here already? Are not the United States this day busily using, working, more printer's type, more presses, than any other country? uttering and absorbing more publications than any other? Do not our publishers fatten quicker and deeper? (helping themselves, under shelter of a delusive and sneaking law, or rather absence of law, to most of their forage, poetical, pictorial, historical, romantic, even comic, without money and without price—and fiercely resisting the timidest proposal to pay for it). Many will come under this delusion—but my purpose is to dispel it. I say that a nation may hold and circulate rivers and oceans of very readable print, journals, magazines, novels, library books, "poetry," etc.—such as the States today possess and circulate—of

---

[2] Of these rapidly sketch'd hiatuses, the two which seem to be most serious are, for one, the condition, absence, or perhaps the singular abeyance, of moral conscientious fiber all through American society; and, for another, the appaling depletion of women in their powers of sane athletic maternity, their crowning attribute, and ever making the woman, in loftiest spheres, superior to the man.

I have sometimes thought, indeed, that the sole avenue and means of a reconstructed sociology depended, primarily, on a new birth, elevation, expansion, invigoration of woman, affording, for races to come (as the conditions that antedate birth are indispensable), a perfect motherhood. Great, great, indeed, far greater than they know, is the sphere of women. But doubtless the question of such new sociology all goes together, includes many varied and complex influences and premises, and the man as well as the woman, and the woman as well as the man.

unquestionable aid and value—hundreds of new volumes annually composed and brought out here, respectable enough, indeed unsurpass'd in smartness and erudition—with further hundreds, or rather millions (as by free forage or theft aforementioned), also thrown into the market—and yet, all the while, the said nation, land, strictly speaking, may possess no literature at all.

Repeating our inquiry, what, then, do we mean by real literature? especially the democratic literature of the future? Hard questions to meet. The clues are inferential, and turn us to the past. At best, we can only offer suggestions, comparisons, circuits.

It must still be reiterated, as, for the purpose of these memoranda, the deep lesson of history and time, that all else in the contributions of a nation or age, through its politics, materials, heroic personalities, military *éclat,* etc., remains crude, and defers, in any close and thoroughgoing estimate, until vitalized by national, original archetypes in literature. They only put the nation in form, finally tell anything—prove, complete anything—perpetuate anything. Without doubt, some of the richest and most powerful and populous communities of the antique world, and some of the grandest personalities and events, have, to after and present times, left themselves entirely unbequeath'd. Doubtless, greater than any that have come down to us, were among those lands, heroisms, persons, that have not come down to us at all, even by name, date, or location. Others have arrived safely, as from voyages over wide, century-stretching seas. The little ships, the miracles that have buoy'd them, and by incredible chances safely convey'd them (or the best of them, their meaning and essence) over long wastes, darkness, lethargy, ignorance, etc., have been a few inscriptions—a few immortal compositions, small in size, yet compassing what measureless values of reminiscence, contemporary portraitures, manners, idioms, and beliefs, with deepest inference, hint, and thought, to tie and touch forever the old, new body, and the old, new soul! These! and still these! bearing the freight so dear— dearer than pride—dearer than love. All the best experience of humanity, folded, saved, freighted to us here. Some of these tiny ships we call Old and New Testament, Homer, Eschylus, Plato, Juvenal, etc. Precious minims! I think, if we were forced to choose, rather than have you, and the likes of you, and what belongs to, and has grown of you, blotted out and gone, we could better afford, appalling as that would be, to lose all actual ships, this day fasten'd by wharf, or floating on wave, and see them, with all their cargoes, scuttled and sent to the bottom.

Gathered by geniuses of city, race or age, and put by them in highest of art's forms, namely, the literary form, the peculiar combinations and the outshows of that city, age, or race, its particular modes of the universal attributes and passions, its faiths, heroes, lovers and gods, wars, traditions, struggles, crimes, emotions, joys (or the subtle spirit of these), having been pass'd on to us to illumine our own selfhood, and its experiences—what they supply, indispensable and highest, if taken away, nothing else in all the world's boundless storehouses could make up to us, or ever again return.

For us, along the great highways of time, those monuments stand—those forms of majesty and beauty. For us those beacons burn through all the nights. Unknown Egyptians, graving hieroglyphs; Hindus, with hymn and apothegm and endless epic; Hebrew prophet, with spirituality, as in flashes of lightning, conscience like red-hot iron, plaintive songs and screams of vengeance for tyrannies and enslavement; Christ, with bent head, brooding love and peace, like a dove; Greek, creating eternal shapes of physical and æsthetic proportion; Roman, lord of satire, the sword, and the codex;—of the figures, some far off and veil'd, others nearer and visible; Dante, stalking with lean form, nothing but fiber, not a grain of superfluous flesh; Angelo, and the great painters, architects, musicians; rich Shakspere, luxuriant as the sun, artist and singer of feudalism in its sunset, with all the gorgeous colors, owner thereof, and using them at will; and so to such as Ger-man Kant and Hegel, where they, though near us, leaping over the ages, sit again, impas-sive, imperturbable, like the Egyptian gods. Of these, and the like of these, is it too much, indeed, to return to our favorite figure, and view them as orbs and systems of orbs, mov-ing in free paths in the spaces of that other heaven, the kosmic intellect, the soul?

Ye powerful and resplendent ones! ye were, in your atmospheres, grown not for America, but rather for her foes, the feudal and the old—while our genius is democratic and modern. Yet could ye, indeed, but breathe your breath of life into our New World's nostrils—not to enslave us, as now, but, for our needs, to breed a spirit like your own—perhaps (dare we to say it?) to dominate, even destroy, what you yourselves have left! On your plane, and no less, but even higher and wider, must we mete and measure for today and here. I demand races of orbic bards, with unconditional, uncompromising sway. Come forth, sweet democratic despots of the west!

By points like these we, in reflection, token what we mean by any land's or people's genuine literature. And thus compared and tested, judging amid the influence of loftiest products only, what do our current copious fields of print, covering in manifold forms, the United States, better, for an analogy, present, than, as in certain regions of the sea, those spreading, undulating masses of squid, through which the whale swimming, with head half out, feeds?

Not but that doubtless our current so-called literature (like an endless supply of small coin) performs a certain service, and maybe too, the service needed for the time, (the preparation-service, as children learn to spell). Everybody reads, and truly nearly every-body writes, either books, or for the magazines or journals. The matter has magnitude, too, after a sort. But is it really advancing? or, has it advanced for a long while? There is something impressive about the huge editions of the dailies and weeklies, the mountain-stacks of white paper piled in the press-vaults, and the proud, crashing, ten-cylinder presses, which I can stand and watch any time by the half hour. Then (though the States in the field of imagination present not a single first-class work, not a single great litera-tus), the main objects, to amuse, to titillate, to pass away time, to circulate the news, and rumors of news, to rhyme, and read rhyme, are yet attain'd, and on a scale of infinity. Today, in books, in the rivalry of writers, especially novelists, success (so-called) is for him or her who strikes the mean flat average, the sensational appetite for stimulus, incident, persiflage, etc., and depicts, to the common caliber, sensual, exterior life. To such, or the luckiest of them, as we see, the audiences are limitless and profitable; but they cease presently. While this day, or any day, to workmen portraying interior or spiritual life, the audiences were limited, and often laggard—but they last forever.

Compared with the past, our modern science soars, and our journals serve—but ideal and even ordinary romantic literature, does not, I think, substantially advance. Behold the prolific brood of the contemporary novel, magazine tale, theatre play, etc. The same endless thread of tangled and superlative love story, inherited, apparently from the Amadises and Palmerins of the 13th, 14th, and 15th centuries over there in Europe. The costumes and associations brought down to date, the seasoning hotter and more varied, the dragons and ogres left out—but the *thing,* I should say, has not advanced—is just as sensational, just as strain'd—remains about the same, nor more, nor less.

What is the reason our time, our lands, that we see no fresh local courage, sanity, of our own—the Mississippi, stalwart Western men, real mental and physical facts, Southerners, etc., in the body of our literature? especially the poetic part of it. But always, instead, a parcel of dandies and ennuyees, dapper little gentlemen from abroad, who flood us with their thin sentiment of parlors, parasols, piano songs, tinkling rhymes, the five-hundredth importation—or whimpering and crying about something, chasing one aborted conceit after another, and forever occupied in dyspeptic amours with dyspeptic women. While, current and novel, the grandest events and revolutions, and stormiest passions of history, are crossing today with unparalleled rapidity and magnificence over the stages of our own and all the continents, offering new materials, opening new vistas, with largest needs, inviting the daring launching forth of conceptions in literature, inspired by them, soaring in highest regions, serving art in its highest (which is only the other name for serving God, and serving humanity), where is the man of letters, where is the book, with any nobler aim than to follow in the old track, repeat what has been said before—and, as its utmost triumph, sell well, and be erudite or elegant?

Mark the roads, the processes, through which these States have arrived, standing easy, henceforth ever-equal, ever-compact, in their range today. European adventures? the most antique? Asiatic or African? old history—miracles—romances? Rather, our own unquestion'd facts. They hasten, incredible, blazing bright as fire. From the deeds and days of Columbus down to the present, and including the present—and especially the late Secession War—when I con them, I feel, every leaf, like stopping to see if I have not made a mistake, and fall'n on the splendid figments of some dream. But it is no dream. We stand, live, move, in the huge flow of our age's materialism—in its spirituality. We have founded for us the most positive of lands. The founders have pass'd to other spheres—but what are these terrible duties they have left us?

Their policies the United States have, in my opinion, with all their faults, already substantially establish'd, for good, on their own native, sound, long-vista'd principles, never to be overturn'd, offering a sure basis for all the rest. With that, their future religious forms, sociology, literature, teachers, schools, costumes, etc., are of course to make a compact whole, uniform, on tallying principles. For how can we remain, divided, contradicting ourselves this way?[3] I say we can only attain harmony and stability by consulting ensemble and the ethic purports, and faithfully building upon them. For the New World, indeed, after two grand stages of preparation-strata, I perceive that now a third stage, being ready for (and without which the other two were useless), with unmistakable signs appears. The First stage was the planning and putting on record the political foundation rights of immense masses of people—indeed all people—in the organization or republican National, State, and municipal governments, all constructed with reference to each, and each to all. This is the American programme, not for classes, but for universal man, and is embodied in the compacts of the Declaration of Independence, and, as it began and has now grown, with its amendments, the Federal Constitution—and in the State governments, with all their interiors, and with general suffrage; those having the sense not only of what is in themselves, but that their certain several things started, planted, hundreds of others in the same direction duly arise and follow. The Second stage relates to material prosperity, wealth, produce, laborsaving machines, iron, cotton, local, State, and continental railways, intercommunication and trade with all lands, steamships, mining, general employment, organization of great cities, cheap appliances for comfort, numberless technical schools, books, newspapers, a currency for money circulation, etc. The Third

---

[3] Note, today, an instructive, curious spectacle and conflict. Science (twin, in its fields, of Democracy in its)—Science, testing absolutely all thoughts, all works, has already burst well upon the world—a sun, mounting, most illuminating, most glorious—surely never again to set. But against it, deeply entrench'd, holding possession, yet remains (not only through the churches and schools, but by imaginative literature, and unregenerate poetry), the fossil theology of the mythic-materialistic, superstitious, untaught and credulous, fable-loving, primitive ages of humanity.

stage, rising out of the previous ones, to make them and all illustrious, I, now, for one, promulge, announcing a native expression-spirit, getting into form, adult, and through mentality, for these States, self-contain'd, different from others, more expansive, more rich and free, to be evidenced by original authors and poets to come, by American personalities, plenty of them, male and female, traversing the States, none excepted—and by native superber tableaux and growths of language, songs, operas, orations, lectures, architecture—and by a sublime and serious Religious Democracy sternly taking command, dissolving the old, sloughing off surfaces, and from its own interior and vital principles, reconstructing, democratizing society.

For America, type of progress, and of essential faith in man, above all his errors and wickedness—few suspect how deep, how deep it really strikes. The world evidently supposes, and we have evidently supposed so too, that the States are merely to achieve the equal franchise, an elective government—to inaugurate the respectability of labor, and become a nation of practical operatives, law-abiding, orderly, and well-off. Yes, those are indeed parts of the task of America; but they not only do not exhaust the progressive conception, but rather arise, teeming with it, as the mediums of deeper, higher progress. Daughter of a physical revolution—mother of the true revolutions, which are of the interior life, and of the arts. For so long as the spirit is not changed, any change of appearance is of no avail.

The old men, I remember as a boy, were always talking of American independence. What is independence? Freedom from all laws or bonds except those of one's own being, control'd by the universal ones. To lands, to man, to woman, what is there at last to each, but the inherent soul, nativity, idiosyncrasy, free, highest poised, soaring its own flight, following out itself?

At present, these States, in their theology and social standards (of greater importance than their political institutions) are entirely held possession of by foreign lands. We see the sons and daughters of the New World, ignorant of its genius, not yet inaugurating the native, the universal, and the near still importing the distant, the partial, and the dead. We see London, Paris, Italy—not original, superb, as where they belong—but secondhand here, where they do not belong. We see the shreds of Hebrews, romans, Greeks; but where, on her own soil, do we see, in any faithful, highest, proud expression, America herself? I sometimes question whether she has a corner in her own house.

Not but that in one sense, and a very grand one, good theology, good art, or good literature, has certain features shared in common. The combination fraternizes, ties the races—is, in many particulars, under laws applicable indifferently to all, irrespective of climate or date, and, from whatever source, appeals to emotions, pride, love, spirituality, common to human-kind. Nevertheless, they touch a man closest (perhaps only actually touch him), even in these, in their expression through autochthonic lights and shades, flavors, fondnesses, aversions, specific incidents, illustrations, out of his own nationality, geography, surroundings, antecedents, etc. The spirit and the form are one, and depend far more on association, identity, and place, than is supposed. Subtly interwoven with the materiality and personality of a land, a race—Teuton, Turk, Californian, or what not—there is always something—I can hardly tell what it is—history but describes the results of it—it is the same as the untellable look of some human faces. Nature, too, in his stolid forms, is full of it—but to most it is there a secret. This something is rooted in the invisible roots, the profoundest meanings of that place, race, or nationality; and to absorb and again effuse it, uttering words and products as from its midst, and carrying it into highest regions, is the work, or a main part of the work, of any country's true author, poet, historian, lecturer, and perhaps even priest and philosoph. Here, and here only, are the foundations for our really valuable and permanent verse, drama, etc.

But at present (judged by any higher scale than that which finds the chief ends of existence to be to feverishly make money during one half of it, and by some "amusement," or perhaps foreign travel, flippantly kill time, the other half), and considered with reference to purposes of patriotism, health, a noble personality, religion, and the democratic adjustments, all these swarms of poems, literary magazines, dramatic plays, resultant so far from American intellect, and the formation of our best ideas, are useless and a mockery. They strengthen and nourish no one, express nothing characteristic, give decision and purpose to no one, and suffice only the lowest level of vacant minds.

Of what is called the drama, or dramatic presentation in the United States, as now put forth at the theatres, I should say it deserves to be treated with the same gravity, and on a par with the questions of ornamental confectionery at public dinners, or the arrangement of curtains and hangings in a ballroom—nor more, nor less. Of the other, I will not insult the reader's intelligence (once really entering into the atmosphere of these Vistas), by supposing it necessary to show, in detail, why the copious dribble, either of our little or well-known rhymesters, does not fulfill, in any respect, the needs and august occasions of this land. America demands a poetry that is bold, modern, and all-surrounding and kosmical, as she is herself. It must in no respect ignore science or the modern, but inspire itself with science and the modern. It must bend its vision toward the future, more than the past. Like America, it must extricate itself from even the greatest models of the past, and, while courteous to them, must have entire faith in itself, and the products of its own democratic spirit only. Like her, it must place in the van, and hold up at all hazards, the banner of the divine pride of man in himself (the radical foundation of the new religion). Long enough have the People been listening to poems in which common humanity, deferential, bends low, humiliated, acknowledging superiors. But America listens to no such poems. Erect, inflated, and full self-esteeming be the chant; and then America will listen with pleased ears.

Nor may the genuine gold, the gems, when brought to light at last, be probably usher'd forth from any of the quarters currently counted on. Today, doubtless, the infant genius of American poetic expression (eluding those highly refined imported and gilt-edged themes, and sentimental and butterfly flights, pleasant to orthodox publishers—causing tender spasms in the coteries, and warranted not to chafe the sensitive cuticle of the most exquisitely artificial gossamer delicacy), lies sleeping far away, happily unrecognized and uninjur'd by the coteries, the art-writers, the talkers and critics of the saloons, or the lecturers in the colleges—lies sleeping, aside, unrecking itself, in some western idiom, or native Michigan or Tennessee repartee, or stump speech—or in Kentucky or Georgia, or the Carolinas—or in some slang or local song or allusion of the Manhattan, Boston, Philadelphia, or Baltimore mechanic—or up in the Maine woods—or off in the hut of the California miner, or crossing the Rocky Mountains, or along the Pacific railroad—or on the breasts of the young farmers of the northwest, or Canada, or boatmen of the lakes. Rude and coarse nursing beds, these; but only from such beginnings and stocks, indigenous here, may haply arrive, be grafted, and sprout in time, flowers of genuine American aroma, and fruits truly and fully our own.

I say it were a standing disgrace to these States—I say it were a disgrace to any nation, distinguish'd above others by the variety and vastness of its territories, its materials, its inventive activity, and the splendid practicality of its people, not to rise and soar above others, also in its original styles in literature and art, and its own supply of intellectual and æsthetic masterpieces, archetypal, and consistent with itself. I know not a land except ours that has not, to some extent, however small, made its title clear. The Scotch have their born ballads, subtly expressing their past and present, and expressing character. The

Irish have theirs. England, Italy, France, Spain, theirs. What has America? With exhaust-less mines of the richest ore of epic, lyric, tale, tune, picture, etc., in the Four Years' War; with, indeed, I sometimes think, the richest masses of material ever afforded a nation, more variegated, and on a larger scale—the first sign of proportionate, native, imaginative Soul, and first-class works to match, is (I cannot too often repeat), so far wanting.

Long ere the second centennial arrives, there will be some forty to fifty great States, among them Canada and Cuba. When the present century closes, our population will be sixty or seventy millions. The Pacific will be ours, and the Atlantic mainly ours. There will be daily electric communication with every part of the globe. What an age! What a land! Where, elsewhere, one so great? The individuality of one nation must then, as al-ways, lead the world. Can there be any doubt who the leader ought to be? Bear in mind, though, that nothing less than the mightiest original non-subordinated SOUL has ever really, gloriously led, or ever can lead. (This Soul—its other name, in these Vistas, is LITERATURE.)

In fond fancy leaping those hundred years ahead let us survey America's works, poems, philosophies, fulfilling prophecies, and giving form and decision to best ideals. Much that is now undream'd of, we might then perhaps see establish'd, luxuriantly cropping forth, richness, vigor of letters and of artistic expression; in whose products character will be a main requirement, and not merely erudition or elegance.

Intense and loving comradeship, the personal and passionate attachment of man to man—which, hard to define, underlies the lessons and ideals of the profound saviors of every land and age, and which seems to promise, when thoroughly develop'd, cultivated, and recognized in manners and literature, the most substantial hope and safety of the fu-ture of these States, will then be fully express'd.[4]

A strong-fibered joyousness and faith, and the sense of health *al fresco,* may well enter into the preparation of future noble American authorship. Part of the test of a great lit-eratus shall be the absence in him of the idea of the covert, the lurid, the maleficent, the devil, the grim estimates inherited from the Puritans, hell, natural depravity, and the like. The great literatus will be known, among the rest, by his cheerful simplicity, his adher-ence to natural standards, his limitless faith in God, his reverence, and by the absence in him of doubt, ennui, burlesque, persiflage, or any strained and temporary fashion.

Nor must I fail, again and yet again, to clinch, reiterate more plainly still (O that in-deed such survey as we fancy may show in time this part completed also!) the lofty aim, surely the proudest and the purest, in whose service the future literatus, of whatever field, may gladly labor. As we have intimated, offsetting the material civilization of our race, our nationality, its wealth, territories, factories, population, products, trade, and military and naval strength, and breathing breath of life into all these, and more, must be its moral

---

[4] It is to the development, identification, and general prevalence of that fervid comradeship (the adhe-sive love, at least rivaling the amative love hitherto possessing imaginative literature, if not going be-yond it), that I look for the counterbalance and offset of our materialistic and vulgar American democ-racy, and for the spiritualization thereof. Many will say it is a dream, and will not follow my inferences; but I confidently expect a time when there will be seen, running like a half-hid warp through all the myriad audible and visible worldly interests of America, threads of manly friendship, fond and loving, pure and sweet, strong and life-long, carried to degrees hitherto unknown—not only giving tone to in-dividual character, and making it unprecedently emotional, muscular, heroic, and refined, but having the deepest relations to general politics. I say democracy infers such loving comradeship, as its most in-evitable twin or counterpart, without which it will be incomplete, in vain, and incapable of perpetuat-ing itself.

civilization—the formulation, expression, aidancy whereof, is the very highest height of literature. The climax of this loftiest range of civilization, rising above all the gorgeous shows and results of wealth, intellect, power, and art, as such—above even theology and religious fervor—is to be its development, from the eternal bases, and the fit expression, of absolute Conscience, moral soundness, Justice. Even in religious fervor there is a touch of animal heat. But moral conscientiousness, crystalline, without flaw, not Godlike only, entirely human, awes and enchants forever. Great is emotional love, even in the order of the rational universe. But, if we must make gradations, I am clear there is something greater. Power, love, veneration, products, genius, æsthetics, tried by subtlest comparisons, analyses, and in serenest moods, somewhere fail, somehow become vain. Then noiseless, with flowing steps, the lord, the sun, the last ideal comes. By the names right, justice, truth, we suggest, but do not describe it. To the world of men it remains a dream, an idea as they call it. But no dream is it to the wise—but the proudest, almost only solid lasting thing of all. Its analogy in the material universe is what holds together this world, and every object upon it, and carries its dynamics on forever sure and safe. Its lack, and the persistent shirking of it, as in life, sociology, literature, politics, business, and even sermonizing these times, or any times, still leaves the abysm, the mortal flaw and smutch, mocking civilization today, with all its unquestion'd triumphs, and all the civilization so far known.[5]

Present literature, while magnificently fulfilling certain popular demands, with plenteous knowledge and verbal smartness, is profoundly sophisticated, insane, and its very joy is morbid. It needs tally and express Nature, and the spirit of Nature, and to know and obey the standards. I say the question of Nature, largely considered, involves the questions of the æsthetic, the emotional, and the religious—and involves happiness. A fitly born and bred race, growing up in right conditions of outdoor as much as indoor harmony, activity and development, would probably, from and in those conditions, find it enough merely *to live*—and would, in their relations to the sky, air, water, trees, etc., and to the countless common shows, and in the fact of life itself, discover and achieve happiness—with Being suffused night and day by wholesome extasy, surpassing all the pleasures that wealth, amusement, and even gratified intellect, erudition, or the sense of art, can give.

In the prophetic literature of these States (the reader of my speculations will miss their principal stress unless he allows well for the point that a new Literature, perhaps a new Metaphysics, certainly a new Poetry, are to be, in my opinion, the only sure and worthy supports and expressions of the American Democracy), Nature, true Nature, and the true

---

[5] I am reminded as I write that out of this very conscience, or idea of conscience, of intense moral right, and in its name and strain'd construction, the worst fanaticisms, wars, persecutions, murders, etc., have yet, in all lands, in the past, been broach'd and have come to their devilish fruition. Much is to be said, but I may say here, and in response, that side by side with the unflagging stimulation of the elements of religion and conscience must henceforth move with equal sway, science, absolute reason, and the general proportionate development of the whole man. These scientific facts, deductions, are divine too—precious counted parts of moral civilization, and, with physical health, indispensable to it, to prevent fanaticism. For abstract religion, I perceive, is easily led astray, ever credulous, and is capable of devouring, remorseless like fire and flame. Conscience, too, isolated from all else, and from the emotional nature, may but attain the beauty and purity of glacial, snowy ice. We want, for these States, for the general character, a cheerful, religious fervor, endued with the ever-present modifications of the human emotions, friendship, benevolence, with a fair field for scientific inquiry, the right of individual judgment, and always the cooling influences of material Nature.

idea of Nature, long absent, must, above all, become fully restored, enlarged, and must furnish the pervading atmosphere to poems, and the test of all high literary and æsthetic compositions. I do not mean the smooth walks, trimm'd hedges, poseys and nightingales of the English poets, but the whole orb, with its geologic history, the kosmos, carrying fire and snow, that rolls through the illimitable areas, light as a feather, though weighing billions of tons. Furthermore, as by what we now partially call Nature is intended, at most, only what is entertainable by the physical conscience, the sense of matter, and of good animal health—on these it must be distinctly accumulated, incorporated, that man, comprehending these, has, in towering superaddition, the moral and spiritual consciences, indicating his destination beyond the ostensible, the mortal.

To the heights of such estimate of Nature indeed ascending, we proceed to make observations for our Vistas, breathing rarest air. What is I believe called Idealism seems to me to suggest (guarding against extravagance, and ever modified even by its opposite) the course of inquiry and desert of favor for our New World metaphysics, their foundation of and in literature, giving hue to all.[6]

The elevating and etherealizing ideas of the unknown and of unreality must be brought forward with authority, as they are the legitimate heirs of the known, and of reality, and at least as great as their parents. Fearless of scoffing, and of the ostent, let us take our stand, our

[6] The culmination and fruit of literary artistic expression, and its final fields of pleasure for the human soul, are in metaphysics, including the mysteries of the spiritual world, the soul itself, and the question of the immortal continuation of our identity. In all ages, the mind of man has brought up here—and always will. Here, at least, of whatever race or era, we stand on common ground. Applause, too, is unanimous, antique or modern. These authors who work well in this field—though their reward, instead of a handsome percentage, or royalty, may be but simply the laurel crown of the victors in the great Olympic games—will be dearest to humanity, and their works, however æsthetically defective, will be treasur'd forever. The altitude of literature and poetry has always been religion—and always will be. The Indian Vedas, the Nackas of Zoroaster, the Talmud of the Jews, the Old Testament, the Gospel of Christ and His disciples, Plato's works, the Koran of Mohammed, the Edda of Snorro, and so on toward our own day, to Swedenborg, and to the invaluable contributions of Leibnitz, Kant, and Hegel—these, with such poems only in which (while singing well of persons and events, of the passions of man, and the shows of the material universe), the religious tone, the consciousness of mystery, the recognition of the future, of the unknown, of Deity over and under all, and of the divine purpose, are never absent, but indirectly give tone to all—exhibit literature's real heights and elevations, towering up like the great mountains of the earth.

Standing on this ground—the last, the highest, only permanent ground—and sternly criticizing, from it, all works, either of the literary, or any art, we have peremptorily to dismiss every pretensive production, however fine its æsthetic or intellectual points, which violates or ignores, or even does not celebrate, the central divine idea of All, suffusing universe, of eternal trains of purpose, in the development, by however slow degrees, of the physical, moral, and spiritual kosmos. I say he has studied, meditated to no profit, whatever may be his mere erudition, who has not absorb'd this simple consciousness and faith. It is not entirely new—but it is for Democracy to elaborate it, and look to build upon and expand from it, with uncompromising reliance. Above the doors of teaching the inscription is to appear, Though little or nothing can be absolutely known, perceived, except from a point of view which is evanescent, yet we know at least one permanency, that Time and Space, in the will of God, furnish successive chains, completions of material births and beginnings, solve all discrepancies, fears and doubts, and eventually fulfill happiness—and that the prophecy of those births, namely spiritual results, throws the true arch over all teaching, all science. The local considerations of sin, disease, deformity, ignorance, death, etc., and their measurement by the superficial mind, and ordinary legislation and theology, are to be met by science, boldly accepting, promulging this faith, and planting the seeds of superber laws—of the explication of the physical universe through the spiritual—and clearing the way for a religion, sweet and unimpugnable alike to little child or great savant.

ground, and never desert it, to confront the growing excess and arrogance of realism. To the cry, now victorious—the cry of sense, science, flesh, incomes, farms, merchandise, logic, intellect, demonstrations, solid perpetuities, buildings of brick and iron, or even the facts of the shows of trees, earth, rocks, etc., fear not, my brethren, my sisters, to sound out with equally determin'd voice, that conviction brooding within the recesses of every envision'd soul—illusions! apparitions! figments all! True, we must not condemn the show, neither absolutely deny it, for the indispensability of its meanings; but how clearly we see that, migrate in soul to what we can already conceive of superior and spiritual points of view, and palpable as it seems under present relations, it all and several might, nay certainly would, fall apart and vanish.

I hail with joy the oceanic, variegated, intense practical energy, the demand for facts, even the business materialism of the current age, our States. But woe to the age and land in which these things, movements, stopping at themselves, do not tend to ideas. As fuel to flame, and flame to the heavens, so much wealth, science, materialism—even this democracy of which we make so much—unerringly feed the highest mind, the soul. Infinitude the flight; fathomless the mystery. Man, so diminutive, dilates beyond the sensible universe, competes with, outcopes space and time, meditating even one great idea. Thus, and thus only, does a human being, his spirit, ascend above, and justify, objective Nature, which, probably nothing in itself, is incredibly and divinely serviceable, indispensable, real, here. And as the purport of objective Nature is doubtless folded, hidden, somewhere here—as somewhere here is what this globe and its manifold forms, and the light of day, and night's darkness, and life itself, with all its experiences, are for—it is here the great literature, especially verse, must get its inspiration and throbbing blood. Then may we attain to a poetry worthy the immortal soul of man, and which, while absorbing materials, and, in their own sense, the shows of Nature, will, above all, have, both directly and indirectly, a freeing, fluidizing, expanding, religious character, exulting with science, fructifying the moral elements, and stimulating aspirations, and meditations on the unknown.

The process, so far, is indirect and peculiar, and though it may be suggested, cannot be defined. Observing, rapport, and with intuition, the shows and forms presented by Nature, the sensuous luxuriance, the beautiful in living men and women, the actual play of passions, in history and life—and, above all, from those developments either in Nature or human personality in which power (dearest of all to the sense of the artist) transacts itself—out of these, and seizing what is in them, the poet, the æsthetic worker in any field, by the divine magic of his genius, projects them, their analogies, by curious removes, indirections, in literature and art. (No useless attempt to repeat the material creation, by daguerrotyping the exact likeness by mortal mental means.) This is the image-making faculty, coping with material creation, and rivaling, almost triumphing over it. This alone, when all the other parts of a specimen of literature or art are ready and waiting, can breathe into it the breath of life, and endow it with identity. . . .

Our lands, embracing so much (embracing indeed the whole, rejecting none), hold in their breast that flame also, capable of consuming themselves, consuming us all. Short as the span of our national life has been, already have death and downfall crowded close upon us—and will again crowd close, no doubt, even if warded off. Ages to come may never know, but I know, how narrowly during the late Secession War—and more than once, and more than twice or thrice—our Nationality (wherein bound up, as in a ship in a storm, depended, and yet depend, all our best life, all hope, all value), just grazed, just by a hair escaped destruction. Alas! to think of them! the agony and bloody sweat of certain of those hours! those cruel, sharp, suspended crises!

Even today, amid these whirls, incredible flippancy, and blind fury of parties, infidelity, entire lack of first-class captains and leaders, added to the plentiful meanness and vulgarity of the ostensible masses—that problem, the labor question, beginning to open like a yawning gulf, rapidly widening every year—what prospect have we? We sail a dangerous sea of seething currents, cross and undercurrents, vortices—all so dark, untried—and whither shall we turn? It seems as if the Almighty had spread before this nation charts of imperial destinies, dazzling as the sun, yet with many a deep intestine difficulty, and human aggregate of cankerous imperfection—saying, lo! the roads, the only plans of development, long and varied with all terrible balks and ebullitions. You said in your soul, I will be empire of empires, overshadowing all else, past and present, putting the history of Old-World dynasties, conquests behind me, as of no account—making a new history, a history of democracy, making old history a dwarf—I alone inaugurating largeness, culminating time. If these, O lands of America, are indeed the prizes, the determination of your soul, be it so. But behold the cost, and already specimens of the cost. Thought you greatness was to ripen for you like a pear? If you would have greatness, know that you must conquer it through ages, centuries—must pay for it with a proportionate price. For you too, as for all lands, the struggle, the traitor, the wily person in office, scrofulous wealth, the surfeit of prosperity, the demonism of greed, the hell of passion, the decay of faith, the long postponement, the fossil-like lethargy, the ceaseless need of revolutions, prophets, thunderstorms, deaths, births, new projections and invigorations of ideas and men.

Yet I have dream'd, merged in that hidden-tangled problem of our fate, whose long unraveling stretches mysteriously through time—dream'd out, portray'd, hinted already—a little or a larger band—a band of brave and true, unprecedented yet—arm'd and equipt at every point—the members separated, it may be, by different dates and States, or south, or north, or east, or west—Pacific, Atlantic, Southern, Canadian—a year, a century here, and other centuries there—but always one, compact in soul, conscience-conserving, God-inculcating, inspired achievers, not only in literature, the greatest art, but achievers in all art—a new, undying order, dynasty, from age to age transmitted—a band, a class, at least as fit to cope with current years, our dangers, needs, as those who, for their times, so long, so well, in armor or in cowl, upheld and made illustrious, that far-back feudal, priestly world. To offset chivalry, indeed, those vanish'd countless knights, old altars, abbeys, priests, ages and strings of ages, a knightlier and more sacred cause today demands, and shall supply, in a New World, to larger, grander work, more than the counterpart and tally of them.

Arrived now, definitely, at an apex for these Vistas, I confess that the promulgation and belief in such a class or institution—a new and greater literatus order—its possibility (nay certainty), underlies these entire speculations—and that the rest, the other parts, as superstructures, are all founded upon it. It really seems to me the condition, not only of our future national and democratic development, but of our perpetuation. In the highly artificial and materialistic bases of modern civilization, with the corresponding arrangements and methods of living, the force-infusion of intellect alone, the depraving influences of riches just as much as poverty, the absence of all high ideals in character—with the long series of tendencies, shapings, which few are strong enough to resist, and which now seem, with steam-engine speed, to be everywhere turning out the generations of humanity like uniform iron castings—all of which, as compared with the feudal ages, we can yet do nothing better than accept, make the best of, and even welcome, upon the whole, for their oceanic practical grandeur, and their restless wholesale kneading of the masses— I say of all this tremendous and dominant play of solely materialistic bearings upon current life in the United States, with the results as already seen, accumulating, and reaching

far into the future, that they must either be confronted and met by at least an equally subtle and tremendous force-infusion for purposes of spiritualization, for the pure conscience,
for genuine æsthetics, and for absolute and primal manliness and womanliness—or else
our modern civilization, with all its improvements, is in vain, and we are on the road to a
destiny, a status, equivalent, in its real world, to that of the fabled damned.

Prospecting thus the coming unsped days, and that new order in them—marking the
endless train of exercise, development, unwind, in nation as in man, which life is for—we
see, fore-indicated, amid these prospects and hopes, new law-forces of spoken and written
language—not merely the pedagogue-forms, correct, regular, familiar with precedents,
made for matters of outside propriety, fine words, thoughts definitely told out—but a language fann'd by the breath of Nature, which leaps overhead, cares mostly for impetus and
effects, and for what it plants and invigorates to grow—tallies life and character, and sel-
domer tells a thing than suggests or necessitates it. In fact, a new theory of literary composition for imaginative works of the very first class, and especially for highest poems, is
the sole course open to these States. Books are to be call'd for, and supplied, on the assumption that the process of reading is not a half-sleep, but, in highest sense, an exercise,
a gymnast's struggle; that the reader is to do something for himself, must be on the alert,
must himself or herself construct indeed the poem, argument, history, metaphysical
essay—the text furnishing the hints, the clue, the start or framework. Not the book needs
so much to be the complete thing, but the reader of the book does. That were to make a
nation of supple and athletic minds, well-train'd, intuitive, used to depend on themselves,
and not on a few coteries of writers.

Investigating here, we see, not that it is a little thing we have, in having the be-
queath'd libraries, countless shelves of volumes, records, etc.; yet how serious the danger,
depending entirely on them, of the bloodless vein, the nerveless arm, the false application,
at second or third hand. We see that the real interest of this people of ours in the theology,
history, poetry, politics, and personal models of the past (the British islands, for instance,
and indeed all the past), is not necessarily to mold ourselves or our literature upon them,
but to attain fuller, more definite comparisons, warnings, and the insight to ourselves, our
own present, and our own far grander, different, future history), religion, social customs,
etc. We see that almost everything that has been written, sung, or stated, of old, with reference to humanity under the feudal and oriental institutes, religions, and for other lands,
needs to be rewritten, resung, restated, in terms consistent with the institution of these
States, and to come in range and obedient uniformity with them.

We see, as in the universes of the material kosmos, after meteorological, vegetable, and
animal cycles, man at last arises, born through them, to prove them, concentrate them, to
turn upon them with wonder and love—to command them, adorn them, and carry them
upward into superior realms—so, out of the series of the preceding social and political
universes, now arise these States. We see that while many were supposing things established and completed, really the grandest things always remain; and discover that the
work of the New World is not ended, but only fairly begun.

We see our land, America, her literature, æsthetics, etc., as, substantially, the getting
in form, or effusement and statement, of deepest basic elements and loftiest final meanings, of history and man—and the portrayal (under the eternal laws and conditions of
beauty) of our own physiognomy, the subjective tie and expression of the objective, as
from our own combination, continuation, and points of view—and the deposit and record
of the national mentality, character, appeals, heroism, wars, and even liberties—where
these, and all, culminate in native literary and artistic formulation, to be perpetuated; and
not having which native, first-class formulation, she will flounder about, and her other,

however imposing, eminent greatness, prove merely a passing gleam; but truly having which, she will understand herself, live nobly, nobly contribute, emanate, and, swinging, poised safely on herself, illumin'd and illuming, become a full-form'd world, and divine Mother not only of material but spiritual worlds, in ceaseless succession through time—the main thing being the average, the bodily, the concrete, the democratic, the popular, on which all the superstructures of the future are to permanently rest.   [1871]

Henry James

From "Hawthorne"

. . . I have said that Hawthorne was an observer of small things, and indeed he appears to have thought nothing too trivial to be suggestive. His Note-Books give us the measure of his perception of common and casual things, and of his habit of converting them into *memoranda*. These Note-Books, by the way—this seems as good a place as any other to say it—are a very singular series of volumes; I doubt whether there is anything exactly corresponding to them in the whole body of literature. They were published—in six volumes, issued at intervals—some years after Hawthorne's death, and no person attempting to write an account of the romancer could afford to regret that they should have been given to the world. There is a point of view from which this may be regretted; but the attitude of the biographer is to desire as many documents as possible. I am thankful, then, as a biographer, for the Note-Books, but I am obliged to confess that, though I have just re-read them carefully, I am still at a loss to perceive how they came to be written—what was Hawthorne's purpose in carrying on for so many years this minute and often trivial chronicle. For a person desiring information about him at any cost, it is valuable; it sheds a vivid light upon his character, his habits, the nature of his mind. But we find ourselves wondering what was its value to Hawthorne himself. It is in a very partial degree a register of impressions, and in a still smaller sense a record of emotions. Outward objects play much the larger part in it; opinions, convictions, ideas pure and simple, are almost absent. He rarely takes his Note-Book into his confidence or commits to its pages any reflections that might be adapted for publicity; the simplest way to describe the tone of these extremely objective journals is to say that they read like a series of very pleasant, though rather dullish and decidedly formal, letters, addressed to himself by a man who, having suspicions that they might be opened in the post, should have determined to insert nothing compromising. They contain much that is too futile for things intended for publicity; whereas, on the other hand, as a receptacle of private impressions and opinions, they are curiously cold and empty. They widen, as I have said, our glimpse of Hawthorne's mind (I do not say that they elevate our estimate of it), but they do so by what they fail to contain, as much as by what we find in them. Our business for the moment, however, is not with the light that they throw upon his intellect, but with the information they offer about his habits and his social circumstances.

I know not at what age he began to keep a diary; the first entries in the American volumes are of the summer of 1835. There is a phrase in the preface to his novel of *Transformation,* which must have lingered in the minds of many Americans who have tried to write novels and to lay the scene of them in the western world. "No author, without a trial, can conceive of the difficulty of writing a romance about a country where there is no shadow, no antiquity, no mystery, no picturesque and gloomy wrong, nor anything but a commonplace prosperity, in broad and simple daylight, as is happily the case with my dear native land." The perusal of Hawthorne's American Note-Books operates as a practical commentary upon this somewhat ominous test. It does so at least to my own mind; it would be too much perhaps to say that the effect would be the same for the usual English reader. An American reads between the lines—he completes the suggestions—he constructs a picture. I think I am not guilty of any gross injustice in saying that the picture he constructs from Hawthorne's American diaries, though by no means without charms of its own, is not, on the whole, an interesting one. It is characterised by an extraordinary blankness—a curious paleness of colour and paucity of detail. Hawthorne, as I have said, has a large and healthy appetite for detail, and one is therefore the more struck with the lightness of the diet to which his observation was condemned. For myself, as I turn the pages of his journals, I seem to see the image of the crude and simple society in which he lived. I use these epithets, of course, not invidiously, but descriptively; if one desire to enter as closely as possible into Hawthorne's situation, one must endeavour to reproduce his circumstances. We are struck with the large number of elements that were absent from them, and the coldness, the thinness, the blankness, to repeat my epithet, present themselves so vividly that our foremost feeling is that of compassion for a romancer looking for subjects in such a field. It takes so many things, as Hawthorne must have felt later in life, when he made the acquaintance of the denser, richer, warmer European spectacle—it takes such an accumulation of history and custom, such a complexity of manners and types, to form a fund of suggestion for a novelist. If Hawthorne had been a young Englishman, or a young Frenchman of the same degree of genius, the same cast of mind, the same habits, his consciousness of the world around him would have been a very different affair; however obscure, however reserved, his own personal life, his sense of the life of his fellow-mortals would have been almost infinitely more various. The negative side of the spectacle on which Hawthorne looked out, in his contemplative saunterings and reveries, might, indeed, with a little ingenuity, be made almost ludicrous; one might enumerate the items of high civilization, as it exists in other countries, which are absent from the texture of American life, until it should become a wonder to know what was left. No State, in the European sense of the word, and indeed barely a specific national name. No sovereign, no court, no personal loyalty, no aristocracy, no church, no clergy, no army, no diplomatic service, no country gentlemen, no palaces, no castles, nor manors, nor old country-houses, nor parsonages, nor thatched cottages nor ivied ruins; no cathedrals, nor abbeys, nor little Norman churches; no great Universities nor public schools—no Oxford, nor Eton, nor Harrow; no literature, no novels, no museums, no pictures, no political society, no sporting class—no Epsom nor Ascot! Some such list as that might be drawn up of the absent things in American life—especially in the American life of forty years ago, the effect of which, upon an English or a French imagination, would probably as a general thing be appalling. The natural remark, in the almost lurid light of such an indictment, would be that if these things are left out, everything is left out. The American knows that a good deal remains; what it is that remains—that is his secret, his joke, as one may say. It would be cruel, in this terrible denudation, to deny him the consolation of his national gift, that "American humour" of which of late years we have heard so much.

But in helping us to measure what remains, our author's Diaries, as I have already intimated, would give comfort rather to persons who might have taken the alarm from the brief sketch I have just attempted of what I have called the negative side of the American social situation, than to those reminding themselves of its fine compensations. Hawthorne's entries are to a great degree accounts of walks in the country, drives in stage-coaches, people he met in taverns. The minuteness of the things that attract his attention and that he deems worthy of being commemorated is frequently extreme, and from this fact we get the impression of a general vacancy in the field of vision. "Sunday evening, going by the jail, the setting sun kindled up the windows most cheerfully; as if there were a bright, comfortable light within its darksome stone wall." "I went yesterday with Monsieur S—— to pick raspberries. He fell through an old log-bridge, thrown over a hollow; looking back, only his head and shoulders appeared through the rotten logs and among the bushes.—A shower coming on, the rapid running of a little barefooted boy, coming up unheard, and dashing swiftly past us, and showing us the soles of his naked feet as he ran adown the path and up the opposite side." In another place he devotes a page to a description of a dog whom he saw running round after its tail; in still another he remarks, in a paragraph by itself—"The aromatic odor of peat-smoke, in the sunny autumnal air is very pleasant." The reader says to himself that when a man turned thirty gives a place in his mind—and his inkstand—to such trifles as these, it is because nothing else of superior importance demands admission. Everything in the Notes indicates a simple, democratic, thinly-composed society; there is no evidence of the writer finding himself in any variety or intimacy of relations with any one or with anything. We find a good deal of warrant for believing that if we add that statement of Mr. Lathrop's about his meals being left at the door of his room, to rural rambles of which an impression of the temporary phases of the local apple-crop were the usual, and an encounter with an organ-grinder, or an eccentric dog, the rarer, outcome, we construct a rough image of our author's daily life during the several years that preceded his marriage. He appears to have read a good deal, and that he must have been familiar with the sources of good English we see from his charming, expressive, slightly self-conscious, cultivated, but not too cultivated, style. Yet neither in these early volumes of his Note-Books, nor in the later, is there any mention of his reading. There are no literary judgments or impressions—there is almost no allusion to works or to authors. The allusions to individuals of any kind are indeed much less numerous than one might have expected; there is little psychology, little description of manners. We are told by Mr. Lathrop that there existed at Salem during the early part of Hawthorne's life "a strong circle of wealthy families," which "maintained rigorously the distinctions of class," and whose "entertainments were splendid, their manners magnificent." This is a rather pictorial way of saying that there were a number of people in the place—the commercial and professional aristocracy, as it were—who lived in high comfort and respectability, and who, in their small provincial way, doubtless had pretensions to be exclusive. Into this delectable company Mr. Lathrop intimates that his hero was free to penetrate. It is easy to believe it, and it would be difficult to perceive why the privilege should have been denied to a young man of genius and culture, who was very good-looking (Hawthorne must have been in these days, judging by his appearance later in life, a strikingly handsome fellow), and whose American pedigree was virtually as long as the longest they could show. But in fact Hawthorne appears to have ignored the good society of his native place almost completely; no echo of its conversation is to be found in his tales or his journals. Such an echo would possibly not have been especially melodious, and if we regret the shyness and stiffness, the reserve, the timidity, the suspicion, or whatever it was, that kept him from knowing what there was to be known, it is not because we have any very definite assurance that his gains would have been great. Still, since a beautiful writer was growing up in Salem, it is a pity that he should not have given himself a chance to commemorate some of the types that flourished in the richest soil of the place. Like almost all people who possess in a strong degree the story-telling faculty, Hawthorne had a democratic strain in his composition and a relish for the commoner stuff of human nature. Thoroughly American in all ways, he was in none more so than in the vagueness of his sense of social distinctions and his readiness to forget them if a moral or intellectual sensation were to be gained by it. He liked to fraternise with plain people, to take them on their own terms, and put himself if possible into their shoes. His Note-Books, and even his tales, are full of evidence of this easy and natural feeling about all his unconventional fellow-mortals—this imaginative interest and contemplative curiosity—and it sometimes takes the most charming and graceful forms. Commingled as it is with his own subtlety and delicacy, his complete exemption from vulgarity, it is one of the points in his character which his reader comes most to appreciate—that reader I mean for whom he is not as for some few, a dusky and malarious genius.

But even if he had had, personally, as many pretensions as he had few, he must in the nature of things have been more or less of a consenting democrat, for democracy was the very key-stone of the simple social structure in which he played his part. The air of his journals and his tales alike are full of the genuine democratic feeling. This feeling has by no means passed out of New England life; it still flourishes in perfection in the great stock of the people, especially in rural communities; but it is probable that at the present hour a writer of Hawthorne's general fastidiousness would not express it quite so artlessly. "A shrewd gentlewoman, who kept a tavern in the town," he says, in *Chippings with a Chisel,* "was anxious to obtain two or three gravestones for the deceased members of her family, and to pay for these solemn commodities by taking the sculptor to board." This image of a gentlewoman keeping a tavern and looking out for boarders, seems, from the point of view to which I allude, not at all incongruous. It will be observed that the lady in question was shrewd; it was probable that she was substantially educated, and of reputable life, and it is certain that she was energetic. These qualities would make it natural to Hawthorne to speak of her as a gentlewoman; the natural tendency in societies where the sense of equality prevails, being to take for granted the high level rather than the low. Perhaps the most striking example of the democratic sentiment in all our author's tales, however, is the figure of Uncle Venner, in *The House of the Seven Gables.* Uncle Venner is a poor old man in a brimless hat and patched trousers, who picks up a precarious subsistence by rendering, for a compensation, in the houses and gardens of the good people of Salem, those services that are known in New England as "chores." He carries parcels, splits fire-wood, digs potatoes, collects refuse for the maintenance of his pigs, and looks forward with philosophic equanimity to the time when he shall end his days in the almshouse. But in spite of the very modest place that he occupies in the social scale, he is received on a footing of familiarity in the household of the far-descended Miss Pyncheon; and when this ancient lady and her companions take the air in the garden of a summer evening, he steps into the estimable circle and mingles the smoke of his pipe with their refined conversation. This obviously is rather imaginative—Uncle Venner is a creation with a purpose. He is an original, a natural moralist, a philosopher; and Hawthorne, who knew perfectly what he was about in introducing him—Hawthorne always knew per-

fectly what he was about—wished to give in his person an example of humorous resignation and of a life reduced to the simplest and homeliest elements, as opposed to the fantastic pretensions of the antiquated heroine of the story. He wished to strike a certain exclusively human and personal note. He knew that for this purpose he was taking a licence;
but the point is that he felt he was not indulging in any extravagant violation of reality.
Giving in a letter, about 1830, an account of a little journey he was making in Connecticut, he says, of the end of a seventeen miles' stage, that "in the evening, however, I went
to a Bible-class with a very polite and agreeable gentleman, whom I afterwards discovered
to be a strolling tailor of very questionable habits."

Hawthorne appears on various occasions to have absented himself from Salem, and to
have wandered somewhat through the New England States. But the only one of these
episodes of which there is a considerable account in the Note-Books is a visit that he paid
in the summer of 1837 to his old college-mate, Horatio Bridge, who was living upon his
father's property in Maine, in company with an eccentric young Frenchman, a teacher of
his native tongue, who was looking for pupils among the northern forests. I have said that
there was less psychology in Hawthorne's Journals than might have been looked for; but
there is nevertheless a certain amount of it, and nowhere more than in a number of pages
relating to this remarkable "Monsieur S." (Hawthorne, intimate as he apparently became
with him, always calls him "Monsieur," just as throughout all his Diaries he invariably
speaks of all his friends, even the most familiar, as "Mr." He confers the prefix upon the
unconventional Thoreau, his fellow-woodsman at Concord, and upon the emancipated
brethren at Brook Farm.) These pages are completely occupied with Monsieur S., who was
evidently a man of character, with the full complement of his national vivacity. There is an
elaborate effort to analyse the poor young Frenchman's disposition, something conscientious and painstaking, respectful, explicit, almost solemn. These passages are very curious
as a reminder of the absence of the off-hand element in the manner in which many Americans, and many New Englanders especially, make up their minds about people whom they
meet. This, in turn, is a reminder of something that may be called the importance of
the individual in the American world; which is a result of the newness and youthfulness of
society and of the absence of keen competition. The individual counts for more, as it were,
and, thanks to the absence of a variety of social types and of settled heads under which he
may be easily and conveniently pigeon-holed, he is to a certain extent a wonder and a
mystery. An Englishman, a Frenchman—a Frenchman above all—judges quickly, easily,
from his own social standpoint, and makes an end of it. He has not that rather chilly and
isolated sense of moral responsibility which is apt to visit a New Englander in such
processes; and he has the advantage that his standards are fixed by the general consent of
the society in which he lives. A Frenchman, in this respect, is particularly happy and comfortable, happy and comfortable to a degree which I think is hardly to be over-estimated;
his standards being the most definite in the world, the most easily and promptly appealed
to, and the most identical with what happens to be the practice of the French genius itself. The Englishman is not quite so well off, but he is better off than his poor interroga-
tive and tentative cousin beyond the seas. He is blessed with a healthy mistrust of analysis, and hair-splitting is the occupation he most despises. There is always a little of the Dr.
Johnson in him, and Dr. Johnson would have had wofully little patience with that tendency to weigh moonbeams which in Hawthorne was almost as much a quality of race as
of genius; albeit that Hawthorne has paid to Boswell's hero (in the chapter on "Lichfield
and Uttoxeter," in his volume on England), a tribute of the finest appreciation. American
intellectual standards are vague, and Hawthorne's countrymen are apt to hold the scales
with a rather uncertain hand and a somewhat agitated conscience.   [1879]

William Dean Howells

From *Criticism and Fiction*

XXI

It is no doubt such work as Mr. James's that an English essayist (Mr. E. Hughes) has chiefly in mind, in a study of the differences of the English and American novel. He defines the English novel as working from within outwardly, and the American novel as working from without inwardly. The definition is very surprisingly accurate; and the critic's discovery of this fundamental difference is carried into particulars with a distinctness which is as unfailing as the courtesy he has in recognizing the present superiority of American work. He seems to think, however, that the English principle is the better, though why he should think so he does not make so clear. It appears a belated and rather voluntary effect of patriotism, disappointing in a philosopher of his degree; but it does not keep him from very explicit justice to the best characteristics of our fiction. "The American novelist is distinguished for the intellectual grip which he has of his characters. . . . He penetrates below the crust, and he recognizes no necessity of the crust to anticipate what is beneath. . . . He utterly discards heroics; he often even discards anything like a plot. . . . His story proper is often no more than a natural predicament. . . . It is no stage view we have of his characters, but one behind the scenes. . . . We are brought into contact with no strained virtues, illumined by strained lights upon strained heights of situation. . . . Whenever he appeals to the emotions it would seem to be with an appeal to the intellect too. . . . because he weaves his story of the finer, less self-evident though common threads of human nature, seldom calling into play the grosser and more powerful strain. . . . Everywhere in his pages we come across acquaintances undistinguished. . . . The characters in an American novel are never unapproachable to the reader. . . . The naturalness, with the every-day atmosphere which surrounds it, is one great charm of the American novel. . . . It is throughout examinative, discursory, even more—quizzical. Its characters are undergoing, at the hands of the author, calm, interested observation. . . . He is never caught identifying himself with them; he must preserve impartiality at all costs . . . but . . . the touch of nature is always felt, the feeling of kinship always follows. . . . The strength of the American novel is its optimistic faith. . . . If out of this persistent hopefulness it can evolve for men a new order of trustfulness, a tenet that between man and man there should be less suspicion, more confidence, since human nature sanctions it, its mission will have been more than an aesthetic, it will have been a moral one."

Not all of this will be found true of Mr. James, but all that relates to artistic methods and characteristics will, and the rest is true of American novels generally. For the most part in their range and tendency they are admirable. I will not say they are all good, or that any of them is wholly good; but I find in nearly every one of them a disposition to regard our life without the literary glasses so long thought desirable, and to see character, not as it is in other fiction, but as it abounds outside of all fiction. This disposition sometimes goes with poor enough performance, but in some of our novels it goes with performance that is excellent; and at any rate it is for the present more valuable than evenness of performance. It is what relates American fiction to the only living movement in imaginative literature, and distinguishes by a superior freshness and authenticity any group of American novels from a similarly accidental group of English novels, giving them the same good right to be as the like number of recent Russian novels, French novels, Spanish novels, Italian novels, Norwegian novels.

It is the difference of the American novelist's ideals from those of the Engligh novelist that give him his advantage, and seems to promise him the future. The love of the passionate and the heroic, as the Englishman has it, is such a crude and unwholesome thing, so deaf and blind to all the most delicate and important facts of art and life, so insensible to the subtle values in either that its presence or absence makes the whole difference, and enables one who is not obsessed by it to thank Heaven that he is not as that other man is.

There can be little question that many refinements of thought and spirit which every American is sensible of in the fiction of this continent, are necessarily lost upon our good kin beyond seas, whose thumb-fingered apprehension requires something gross and palpable for its assurance of reality. This is not their fault, and I am not sure that it is wholly their misfortune: they are made so as not to miss what they do not find, and they are simply content without those subtleties of life and character which it gives us so keen a pleasure to have noted in literature. If they perceive them at all it is as something vague and diaphanous, something that filmily wavers before their sense and teases them, much as the beings of an invisible world might mock one of our material frame by intimations of their presence. It is with reason, therefore, on the part of an Englishman, that Mr. Henley complains of our fiction as a shadow-land, though we find more and more in it the faithful report of our life, its motives and emotions, and all the comparatively etherealized passions and ideals that influence it.

In fact, the American who chooses to enjoy his birthright to the full, lives in a world wholly different from the Englishman's, and speaks (too often through his nose) another language: he breathes a rarefied and nimble air full of shining possibilities and radiant promises which the fog-and-soot-clogged lungs of those less-favored islanders struggle in vain to fill themselves with. But he ought to be modest in his advantage, and patient with the coughing and sputtering of his cousin who complains of finding himself in an exhausted receiver on plunging into one of our novels. To be quite just to the poor fellow, I have had some such experience as that myself in the atmosphere of some of our more attenuated romances.

Yet every now and then I read a book with perfect comfort and much exhilaration, whose scenes the average Englishman would gasp in. Nothing happens; that is, nobody murders or debauches anybody else; there is no arson or pillage of any sort; there is not a ghost, or a ravening beast, or a hairbreadth escape, or a shipwreck, or a monster of self-sacrifice, of a lady five thousand years old in the whole course of the story; "no promenade, no band of music, nossing!" as Mr. Du Maurier's Frenchman said of the meet for a fox-hunt. Yet it is all alive with the keenest interest for those who enjoy the study of individual traits and general conditions as they make themselves known to American experience.

These conditions have been so favorable hitherto (though they are becoming always less so) that they easily account for the optimistic faith of our novel which Mr. Hughes notices. It used to be one of the disadvantages of the practice of romance in America, which Hawthorne more or less whimsically lamented, that there were so few shadows and inequalities in our broad level of prosperity; and it is one of the reflections suggested by Dostoïevsky's novel, The Crime and the Punishment, that whoever struck a note so profoundly tragic in American fiction would do a false and mistaken thing—as false and as mistaken in its way as dealing in American fiction with certain nudities which the Latin peoples seem to find edifying. Whatever their deserts, very few American novelists have been led out to be shot, or finally exiled to the rigors of a winter at Duluth; and in a land where journeymen carpenters and plumbers strike for four dollars a day the sum of hunger and cold is comparatively small, and the wrong from class to class has been almost inappreciable, though all this is changing for the worse. Our novelists, therefore, concern themselves with the more smiling aspects of life, which are the more American, and seek the universal in the individual rather than the social interests. It is worth while, even at the risk of being called commonplace, to be true to our well-to-do actualities; the very passions themselves seem to be softened and modified by conditions which formerly at least could not be said to wrong any one, to cramp endeavor, or to cross lawful desire. Sin and suffering and shame there must always be in the world, I suppose, but I believe that in this new world of ours it is still mainly from one to another one, and oftener still from one to one's self. We have death too in America, and a great deal of disagreeable and painful disease, which the multiplicity of our patent medicines does not seem to cure; but this is tragedy that comes in the very nature of things, and is not peculiarly American, as the large, cheerful average of health and success and happy life is. It will not do to boast, but it is well to be true to the facts, and to see that, apart from these purely mortal troubles, the race here has enjoyed conditions in which most of the ills that have darkened its annals might be averted by honest work and unselfish behavior. . . .

XXIV

One of the great newspapers the other day invited the prominent American authors to speak their minds upon a point in the theory and practice of fiction which had already vexed some of them. It was the question of how much or how little the American novel ought to deal with certain facts of life which are not usually talked of before young people, and especially young ladies. Of course the question was not decided, and I forget just how far the balance inclined in favor of a larger freedom in the matter. But it certainly inclined that way; one or two writers of the sex which is somehow supposed to have purity in its keeping (as if purity were a thing that did not practically concern the other sex, preoccupied with serious affairs) gave it a rather vigorous tilt to that side. In view of this fact it would not be the part of prudence to make an effort to dress the balance; and indeed I do not know that I was going to make any such effort. But there are some things to say, around and about the subject, which I should like to have some one else say, and which I may myself possibly be safe in suggesting.

One of the first of these is the fact, generally lost sight of by those who censure the Anglo-Saxon novel for its prudishness that it is really not such a prude after all; and that if it is sometimes apparently anxious to avoid those experiences of life not spoken of before young people, this may be an appearance only. Sometimes a novel which has this shuffling air, this effect of truckling to propriety, might defend itself, if it could speak for itself, by saying that such experiences happened not to come within its scheme and that, so far from maiming or mutilating itself in ignoring them, it was all the more faithfully representative of the tone of modern life in dealing with love that was chaste, and with passion so honest that it could be openly spoken of before the tenderest society bud at dinner. It might say that the guilty intrigue, the betrayal, the extreme flirtation even, was the exceptional thing in life, and unless the scheme of the story necessarily involved it, that it would be bad art to lug it in, and as bad taste as to introduce such topics in a mixed company. It could say very justly that the novel in our civilization now always addresses a mixed company, and that the vast majority of the company are ladies, and that very many, if not most, of these ladies are young girls. If the novel were written for men and for married women alone, as in continental Europe, it might be altogether different. But the simple fact is that it is not written for them alone among us, and it is a question of writing, under cover of our universal acceptance, things for young girls to read which you would be put out-of-doors for saying to them, or of frankly giving notice of your intention, and so cutting yourself off from the pleasure—and it is a very high and sweet one—of appealing to these vivid, responsive intelligences, which are none the less brilliant and admirable because they are innocent.

One day a novelist who liked, after the manner of other men, to repine at his hard fate, complained to his friend, a critic, that he was tired of the restriction he had put upon himself in this regard; for it is a mistake, as can be readily shown, to suppose that others impose it. "See how free those French fellows are!" he rebelled. "Shall we always be shut up to our tradition of decency?"

"Do you think it's much worse than being shut up to their tradition of indecency?" said his friend.

Then that novelist began to reflect, and he remembered how sick the invariable motive of the French novel made him. He perceived finally that, convention for convention, ours was not only more tolerable, but on the whole was truer to life, not only to its complexion, but also to its texture. No one will pretend that there is not vicious love beneath the surface of our society; if he did, the fetid explosions of the divorce trials would refute him; but if he pretended that it was in any just sense characteristic of our society, he could be still more easily refuted. Yet it exists, and it is unquestionably the material of tragedy, the stuff from which intense effects are wrought. The question, after owning this fact, is whether these intense effects are not rather cheap effects. I incline to think they are, and I will try to say why I think so, if I may do so without offence. The material itself, the mere mention of it, has an instant fascination; it arrests, it detains, till the last word is said, and while there is anything to be hinted. This is what makes a love intrigue of some sort all but essential to the popularity of any fiction. Without such an intrigue the intellectual equipment of the author must be of the highest, and then he will succeed only with the highest class of readers. But any author who will deal with a guilty love intrigue holds all readers in his hand, the highest with the lowest, as long as he hints the slightest hope of the smallest potential naughtiness. He need not at all be a great author; he may be a very shabby wretch, if he has but the courage or the trick of that sort of thing. The critics will call him "virile" and "passionate;" decent people will be ashamed to have been limed by him; but the low average will only ask another chance of flocking into his net. If he happens to be an able writer, his really fine and costly work will be unheeded, and the lure to the appetite will be chiefly remembered. There may be other qualities which make reputations for other men, but in his case they will count for nothing. He pays this penalty for his success in that kind; and every one pays some such penalty who deals with some such material. It attaches in like manner to the triumphs of the writers who now almost form a school among us, and who maybe said to have established themselves in an easy popularity simply by the study of erotic shivers and fervors. They may find their account in the popularity, or they may not; there is no question of the popularity.

But I do not mean to imply that their ease covers the whole ground. So far as it goes, though, it ought to stop the mouths of those who complain that fiction is enslaved to propriety among us. It appears that of a certain kind of impropriety it is free to give us all it will, and more. But this is not what serious men and women writing fiction mean when they rebel against the limitations of their art in our civilization. They have no desire to deal with nakedness, as painters and sculptors freely do in the worship of beauty; or with certain facts of life, as the stage does, in the service of sensation. But they ask why, when the conventions of the plastic and histrionic arts liberate their followers to the portrayal of almost any phase of the physical or of the emotional nature, an American novelist may not write a story on the lines of Anna Karenina or Madame Bovary. Sappho they put aside, and from Zola's work they avert their eyes. They do not condemn him or Daudet, necessarily, or accuse their motives; they leave them out of the question; they do not want to do that kind of thing. But they do sometimes wish to do another kind, to touch one of the most serious and sorrowful problems of life in the spirit of Tolstoï and Flaubert, and they ask why they may not. At one time, they remind us, the Anglo-Saxon novelist did deal with such problems—De Foe in his spirit, Richardson in his, Goldsmith in his. At what moment did our fiction lose this privilege? In what fatal hour did the Young Girl arise and seal the lips of Fiction, with a touch of her finger, to some of the most vital interests of life?

Whether I wished to oppose them in their aspiration for greater freedom, or whether I wished to encourage them, I should begin to answer them by saying that the Young Girl had never done anything of the kind. The manners of the novel have been improving with those of its readers; that is all. Gentlemen no longer swear or fall drunk under the table, or abduct young ladies and shut them up in lonely country-houses, or so habitually set about the ruin of their neighbors' wives, as they once did. Generally, people now call a spade an agricultural implement; they have not grown decent without having also grown a little squeamish, but they have grown comparatively decent; there is no doubt about that. They require of a novelist whom they respect unquestionable proof of his seriousness, if he proposes to deal with certain phases of life; they require a sort of scientific decorum. He can no longer expect to be received on the ground of entertainment only; he assumes a higher function, something like that of a physician or a priest, and they expect him to be bound by laws as sacred as those of such professions; they hold him solemnly pledged not to betray them or abuse their confidence. If he will accept the conditions, they give him their confidence, and he may then treat to his greater honor, and not at all to his disadvantage, of such experiences, such relations of men and women as George Eliot treats in Adam Bede, in Daniel Deronda, in Romola, in almost all her books; such as Hawthorne treats in the Scarlet Letter; such as Dickens treats in David Copperfield; such as Thackeray treats in Pendennis, and glances at in every one of his fictions; such as most of the masters of English fiction have at some time treated more or less openly. It is quite false or quite mistaken to suppose that our novels have left untouched these most important realities of life. They have only not made them their stock in trade; they have kept a true perspective in regard to them; they have relegated them in their pictures of life to the space and place they occupy in life itself, as we know it in England and America. They have kept a correct proportion, knowing perfectly well that unless the novel is to be a map, with everything scrupulously laid down in it, a faithful record of life in far the greater extent could be made to the exclusion of guilty love and all its circumstances and consequences.

I justify them in this view not only because I hate what is cheap and meretricious, and hold in peculiar loathing the cant of the critics who require "passion" as something in itself admirable and desirable in a novel, but because I prize fidelity in the historian of feeling and character. Most of these critics who demand "passion" would seem to have no conception of any passion but one. Yet there are several other passions: the passion of grief, the passion of avarice, the passion of pity, the passion of ambition, the passion of hate, the passion of envy, the passion of devotion, the passion of friendship; and all these have a greater part in the drama of life than the passion of love, and infinitely greater than the passion of guilty love. Wittingly or unwittingly, English fiction and American fiction have recognized this truth, not fully, not in the measure it merits, but in greater degree than most other fiction.   [1891]

Mark Twain

....

Fenimore Cooper's Literary Offences

The Pathfinder and *The Deerslayer* stand at the head of Cooper's novels as artistic creations. There are other of his works which contain parts as perfect as are to be found in these, and scenes even more thrilling. Not one can be compared with either of them as a finished whole. The defects in both of these tales are comparatively slight. They were pure works of art.

Prof. Lounsbury

The five tales reveal an extraordinary fulness of invention.
. . . One of the very greatest characters in fiction, "Natty Bumppo." . . .
The craft of the woodsman, the tricks of the trapper, all the delicate art of the forest, were familiar to Cooper from his youth up.

Prof. Brander Matthews.

Cooper is the greatest artist in the domain of romantic fiction yet produced by America.

Wilkie Collins

It seems to me that it was far from right for the Professor of English Literature in Yale, the Professor of English Literature in Columbia, and Wilkie Collins, to deliver opinions on Cooper's literature without having read some of it. It would have been much more decorous to keep silent and let persons talk who have read Cooper.

Cooper's art has some defects. In one place in *Deerslayer,* and in the restricted space of two-thirds of a page, Cooper has scored 114 offences against literary art out of a possible 115. It breaks the record.

There are nineteen rules governing literary art in the domain of romantic fiction—some say twenty-two. In *Deerslayer* Cooper violated eighteen of them. These eighteen require:

1. That a tale shall accomplish something and arrive somewhere. But the *Deerslayer* tale accomplishes nothing and arrives in the air.

2. They require that the episodes of a tale shall be necessary parts of the tale, and shall help to develop it. But as the *Deerslayer* tale is not a tale, and accomplishes nothing and arrives nowhere, the episodes have no rightful place in the work, since there was nothing for them to develop.

3. They require that the personages in a tale shall be alive, except in the case of corpses, and that always the reader shall be able to tell the corpses from the others. But this detail has often been overlooked in the *Deerslayer* tale.

4. They require that the personages in a tale, both dead and alive, shall exhibit a sufficient excuse for being there. But this detail also has been overlooked in the *Deerslayer* tale.

5. They require that when the personages of a tale deal in conversation, the talk shall sound like human talk, and be talk such as human beings would be likely to talk in the given circumstances, and have a discoverable meaning, also a discoverable purpose, and a show of relevancy, and remain in the neighborhood of the subject in hand, and be interesting to the reader, and help out the tale, and stop when the people cannot think of anything more to say. But this requirement has been ignored from the beginning of the *Deerslayer* tale to the end of it.

6. They require that when the author describes the character of a personage in his tale, the conduct and conversation of that personage shall justify said description. But this law gets little or no attention in the *Deerslayer* tale, as "Natty Bumppo's" case will amply prove.

7. They require that when a personage talks like an illustrated, gilt-edged, tree-calf, hand-tooled, seven-dollar Friendship's Offering in the beginning of a paragraph, he shall not talk like a negro minstrel in the end of it. But this rule is flung down and danced upon in the *Deerslayer* tale.

8. They require that crass stupidities shall not be played upon the reader as "the craft of the woodsman, the delicate art of the forest," by either the author or the people in the tale. But this rule is persistently violated in the *Deerslayer* tale.

9. They require that the personages of a tale shall confine themselves to possibilities and let miracles alone; or, if they venture a miracle, the author must so plausibly set it forth as to make it look possible and reasonable. But these rules are not respected in the *Deerslayer* tale.

10. They require that the author shall make the reader feel a deep interest in the personages of his tale and in their fate; and that he shall make the reader love the good people in the tale and hate the bad ones. But the reader of the *Deerslayer* tale dislikes the good people in it, is indifferent to the others, and wishes they would all get drowned together.

11. They require that the characters in a tale shall be so clearly defined that the reader can tell beforehand what each will do in a given emergency. But in the *Deerslayer* tale this rule is vacated.

In addition to these large rules there are some little ones. These require that the author shall

12. *Say* what he is proposing to say, not merely come near it.

13. Use the right word, not its second cousin.

14. Eschew surplusage.

15. Not omit necessary details.

16. Avoid slovenliness of form.

17. Use good grammar.

18. Employ a simple and straightforward style.

Even these seven are coldly and persistently violated in the *Deerslayer* tale.

Cooper's gift in the way of invention was not a rich endowment; but such as it was he liked to work it, he was pleased with the effects, and indeed he did some quite sweet things with it. In his little box of stage properties he kept six or eight cunning devices, tricks, artifices for his savages and woodsmen to deceive and circumvent each other with, and he was never so happy as when he was working these innocent things and seeing them go. A favorite one was to make a mocassined person tread in the tracks of the moccasined enemy, and thus hide his own trail. Cooper wore out barrels and barrels of moccasins in working that trick. Another stage-property that he pulled out of his box pretty frequently was his broken twig. He prized his broken twig above all the rest of his effects, and worked it the hardest. It is a restful chapter in any book of his when somebody doesn't step on a dry twig and alarm all the reds and whites for two hundred yards around. Every time a Cooper person is in peril, and absolute silence is worth four dollars a minute, he is sure to step on a dry twig. There may be a hundred handier things to step on, but that wouldn't satisfy Cooper. Cooper requires him to turn out and find a dry twig; and if he can't do it, go and borrow one. In fact the Leather Stocking Series ought to have been called the Broken Twig Series.

I am sorry there is not room to put in a few dozen instances of the delicate art of the forest, as practiced by Natty Bumppo and some of the other Cooperian experts. Perhaps we may venture two or three samples. Cooper was a sailor—a naval officer; yet he gravely tells us how a vessel, driving toward a lee shore in a gale, is steered for a particular spot by her skipper because he knows of an *undertow* there which will hold her back against the gale and save her. For just pure woodcraft, or sailorcraft, or whatever it is, isn't that neat? For several years Cooper was daily in the society of artillery, and he ought to have noticed that when a cannon ball strikes the ground it either buries itself or skips a hundred feet or so; skips again a hundred feet or so—and so on, till it finally gets tired and rolls. Now in one place he loses some "females"—as he always calls women—in the edge of a wood near a plain at night in a fog, on purpose to give Bumppo a chance to show off the delicate art of the forest before the reader. These mislaid people are hunting for a fort. They hear a cannon-blast, and a cannon-ball presently comes rolling into the wood and stops at their feet. To the females this suggests nothing. The case is very different with the admirable Bumppo. I wish I may never know peace again if he doesn't strike out promptly and *follow the track* of that cannon-ball across the plain through the dense fog and find that fort. Isn't it a daisy? If Cooper had any real knowledge of Nature's ways of doing things, he had a most delicate art in concealing the fact. For instance: one of his acute Indian experts, Chingachgook (pronounced Chicago, I think), has lost the trail of a person he is tracking through the forest. Apparently that trail is hopelessly lost. Neither you nor I could ever have guessed out the way to find it. It was very different with Chicago. Chicago was not stumped for long. He turned a running stream out of its course, and there, in the slush in its old bed, were that person's moccasin-tracks. The current did not wash them away, as it would have done in all other like cases—no, even the eternal laws of Nature have to vacate when Cooper wants to put up a delicate job of woodcraft on the reader.

We must be a little wary when Brander Matthews tells us that Cooper's books "reveal an extraordinary fulness of invention." As a rule, I am quite willing to accept Brander Matthews's literary judgments and applaud his lucid and graceful phrasing of them; but that particular statement needs to be taken with a few tons of salt. Bless your heart, Cooper hadn't any more invention than a horse; and I don't mean a high-class horse, either; I mean a clothes-horse. It would be very difficult to find a really clever "situation" in Cooper's books; and still more difficult to find one of any kind which he has failed to render absurd by his handling of it. Look at the episodes of "the caves;" and at the celebrated scuffle between Magua and those others on the table-land a few days later; and at Hurry Harry's queer water-transit from the castle to the ark; and at Deerslayer's half hour with his first corpse; and at the quarrel between Hurry Harry and Deerslayer later; and at—but choose for yourself; you can't go amiss.

If Cooper had been an observer, his inventive faculty would have worked better, not more interestingly, but more rationally, more plausibly. Cooper's proudest creations in the way of "situations" suffer noticeably from the absence of the observer's protecting gift. Cooper's eye was splendidly inaccurate. Cooper seldom saw anything correctly. He saw nearly all things as through a glass eye, darkly. Of course a man who cannot see the commonest little everyday matters accurately is working at a disadvantage when he is constructing a "situation." In the *Deerslayer* tale Cooper has a stream which is fifty feet wide, where it flows out of a lake; it presently narrows to twenty as it meanders along for no given reason, and yet, when a stream acts like that it ought to be required to explain itself. Fourteen pages later the width of the brook's outlet from the lake has suddenly shrunk thirty feet, and become "the narrowest part of the stream." This shrinkage is not accounted for. The stream had bends in it, a sure indication that it has alluvial banks, and cuts them; yet these bends are only thirty and fifty feet long. If Cooper had been a nice and punctilious observer he would have noticed that the bends were oftener nine hundred feet long than short of it.

Cooper made the exit of that stream fifty feet wide in the first place, for no particular reason; in the second place, he narrowed it to less than twenty to accommodate some Indians. He bends a "sapling" to the form of an arch over this narrow passage, and conceals six Indians in its foliage. They are "laying" for a settler's scow or ark which is coming up the stream on its way to the lake; it is being hauled against the stiff current by a rope whose stationary end is anchored in the lake; its rate of progress cannot be more than a mile an hour. Cooper describes the ark, but pretty obscurely. In the matter of dimensions "it was little more than a modern canal boat." Let us guess, then, that it was about 140 feet long. It was of "greater breadth than common." Let us guess, then, that it was about sixteen feet wide. This leviathan had been prowling down bends which were but a third as long as itself, and scraping between banks where it had only two feet of space to spare on each side. We cannot too much admire this miracle. A low-roofed log dwelling occupies "two-thirds of the ark's length"—a dwelling ninety feet long and sixteen feet wide, let us say—a kind of vestibule train. The dwelling has two rooms—each forty-five feet long and sixteen feet wide, let us guess. One of them is the bed-room of the Hutter girls, Judith and Hetty; the other is the parlor, in the day time, at night it is papa's bed chamber. The ark is arriving at the stream's exit, now, whose width has been reduced to less than twenty feet to accommodate the Indians—say to eighteen. There is a foot to spare on each side of the boat. Did the Indians notice that there was going to be a tight squeeze there? Did they notice that they could make money by climbing down out of that arched sapling and just stepping aboard when the ark scraped by? No; other Indians would have noticed these things, but Cooper's Indians never notice anything. Cooper thinks they are marvellous creatures for noticing, but he was almost always in error about his Indians. There was seldom a sane one among them.

The ark is 140 feet long; the dwelling is 90 feet long. The idea of the Indians is to drop softly and secretly from the arched sapling to the dwelling as the ark creeps along under it at the rate of a mile an hour, and butcher the family. It will take the ark a minute and a half to pass under. It will take the 90-foot dwelling a minute to pass under. Now, then, what did the six Indians do? It would take you thirty years to guess, and even then you would have to give it up, I believe. Therefore, I will tell you what the Indians did. Their chief, a person of quite extraordinary intellect for a Cooper Indian, warily watched the canal boat as it squeezed along under him, and when he had got his calculations fined down to exactly the right shade, as he judged, he let go and dropped. And *missed the house!* That is actually what he did. He missed the house, and landed in the stern of the scow. It was not much of a fall, yet it knocked him silly. He lay there unconscious. If the house had been 97 feet long, he would have made the trip. The fault was Cooper's, not his. The error lay in the construction of the house. Cooper was no architect.

There still remained in the roost five Indians. The boat has passed under and is now out of their reach. Let me explain what the five did—you would not be able to reason it out for yourself. No. 1 jumped for the boat, but fell in the water astern of it. Then No. 2 jumped for the boat, but fell in the water still further astern of it. Then No. 3 jumped for the boat, and fell a good way astern of it. Then No. 4 jumped for the boat, and fell in the water *away* astern. Then even No. 5 made a jump for the boat—for he was a Cooper Indian. In the matter of intellect, the difference between a Cooper Indian and the Indian that stands in front of the cigar shop is not spacious. The scow episode is really a sublime burst of invention; but it does not thrill, because the inaccuracy of the details throws a sort of air of fictitiousness and general improbability over it. This comes of Cooper's inadequacy as an observer.

The reader will find some examples of Cooper's high talent for inaccurate observation in the account of the shooting match in *The Pathfinder*. "A common wrought nail was driven lightly into the target, its head having been first touched with paint." The color of the paint is not stated—an important omission, but Cooper deals freely in important omissions. No, after all, it was not an important omission; for this nail is *a hundred yards* from the marksman and could not be seen by them at that distance no matter what its color might be. How far can the best eyes see a common house fly? A hundred yards? It is quite impossible. Very well, eyes that cannot see a house fly that is a hundred yards away cannot see an ordinary nail head at that distance, for the size of the two objects is the same. It takes a keen eye to see a fly or a nail head at fifty yards—one hundred and fifty feet. Can the reader do it?

The nail was lightly driven, its head painted, and game called. Then the Cooper miracles began. The bullet of the first marksman chipped an edge of the nail head; the next man's bullet drove the nail a little way into the target—and removed all the paint. Haven't the miracles gone far enough now? Not to suit Cooper; for the purpose of this whole scheme is to show off his prodigy, Deerslayer-Hawkeye-Long-Rifle-Leather-Stocking-Pathfinder-Bumppo before the ladies.

> "Be all ready to clench it, boys!" cried out Pathfinder, stepping into his friend's tracks the instant they were vacant. "Never mind a new nail; I can see that, though the paint is gone, and what I can see, I can hit at a hundred yards, though it were only a mosquitoe's eye. Be ready to clench!"
>
> The rifle cracked, the bullet sped its way and the head of the nail was buried in the wood, covered by the piece of flattened lead.

There, you see, is a man who could hunt flies with a rifle, and command a ducal salary in a Wild West show to-day, if we had him back with us.

The recorded feat is certainly surprising, just as it stands; but it is not surprising enough for Cooper. Cooper adds a touch. He has made Pathfinder do this miracle with another man's rifle, and not only that, but Pathfinder did not have even the advantage of loading it himself. He had everything against him, and yet he made that impossible shot, and not only made it, but did it with absolute confidence, saying, "Be ready to clench." Now a person like that would have undertaken that same feat with a brickbat, and with Cooper to help he would have achieved it, too.

Pathfinder showed off handsomely that day before the ladies. His very first feat was a thing which no Wild West show can touch. He was standing with the group of marksmen, observing—a hundred yards from the target, mind: one Jasper raised his rifle and drove the centre of the bull's-eye. Then the quartermaster fired. The target exhibited no result this time. There was a laugh. "It's a dead miss," said Major Lundie. Pathfinder waited an impressive moment or two, then said in that calm, indifferent, know-it-all way of his, "No, Major—he has covered Jasper's bullet, as will be seen if any one will take the trouble to examine the target."

Wasn't it remarkable! How *could* he see that little pellet fly through the air and enter that distant bullet-hole? Yet that is what he did; for nothing is impossible to a Cooper person. Did any of those people have any deep-seated doubts about this thing? No; for that would imply sanity, and these were all Cooper people.

> The respect for Pathfinder's skill and for his *quickness and accuracy of sight* (the italics are mine) was so profound and general, that the instant he made this declaration the spectators began to distrust their own opinions, and a dozen rushed to the target in order to ascertain the fact. There, sure enough, it was found that the quartermaster's bullet had gone through the hole made by Jasper's, and that, too, so accurately as to require a minute examination to be certain of the circumstance, which, however, was soon clearly established by discovering one bullet over the other in the stump against which the target was placed.

They made a "minute" examination; but never mind, how could they know that there were two bullets in that hole without digging the latest one out? for neither probe nor eyesight could prove the presence of any more than one bullet. Did they dig? No; as we shall see. It is the Pathfinder's turn now; he steps out before the ladies, takes aim, and fires.

But alas! here is a disappointment; an incredible, an unimaginable disappointment— for the target's aspect is unchanged; there is nothing there but that same old bullet hole!

> "If one dared to hint at such a thing," cried Major Duncan, "I should say that the Pathfinder has also missed the target."

As nobody had missed it yet, the "also" was not necessary; but never mind about that, for the Pathfinder is going to speak.

> "No, no, Major," said he, confidently, "that *would* be a risky declaration. I didn't load the piece, and can't say what was in it, but if it was lead, you will find the bullet driving down those of the Quartermaster and Jasper, else is not my name Pathfinder."
>
> A shout from the target announced the truth of this assertion.

Is the miracle sufficient as it stands? Not for Cooper. The Pathfinder speaks again, as he "now slowly advances towards the stage occupied by the females":

> That's not all, boys, that's not all; if you find the target touched at all, I'll own to a miss. The Quartermaster cut the wood, but you'll find no wood cut by that last messenger.

The miracle is at last complete. He knew—doubtless *saw*—at the distance of a hundred yards—that his bullet had passed into the hole *without fraying the edges*. There were now three bullets in that one hole—three bullets imbedded processionally in the body of the stump back of the target. Everybody knew this—somehow or other—and yet nobody had dug any of them out to make sure. Cooper is not a close observer, but he is interesting. He is certainly always that, no matter what happens. And he is more interesting when he is not noticing what he is about than when he is. This is a considerable merit.

The conversations in the Cooper books have a curious sound in our modern ears. To believe that such talk really ever came out of people's mouths would be to believe that there was a time when time was of no value to a person who thought he had something to say; when it was the custom to spread a two-minute remark out to ten; when a man's mouth was a rolling-mill, and busied itself all day long in turning four-foot pigs of thought into thirty-foot bars of conversational railroad iron by attenuation; when subjects were seldom faithfully stuck to, but the talk wandered all around and arrived nowhere; when conversations consisted mainly of irrelevances, with here and there a relevancy, a relevancy with an embarrassed look, as not being able to explain how it got there.

Cooper was certainly not a master in the construction of dialogue. Inaccurate observation defeated him here as it defeated him in so many other enterprises of his. He even failed to notice that the man who talks corrupt English six days in the week must and will talk it on the seventh, and can't help himself. In the *Deerslayer* story he lets Deerslayer talk the showiest kind of book talk sometimes, and at other times the basest of base dialects. For instance, when some one asks him if he has a sweetheart, and if so, where she abides, this is his majestic answer:

> She's in the forest—hanging from the boughs of the trees, in a soft rain—in the dew on the open grass—the clouds that float about in the blue heavens—the birds that sing in the woods—the sweet springs where I slake my thirst—and in all the other glorious gifts that come from God's Providence!

And he preceded that, a little before, with this:

> It consarns me as all things that touches a fri'nd consarns a fri'nd.

And this is another of his remarks:

> "If I was Injin born, now, I might tell of this, or carry in the scalp and boast of the expl'ite afore the whole tribe; or if my inimy had only been a bear"—and so on.

We cannot imagine such a thing as a veteran Scotch Commander-in-Chief comporting himself in the field like a windy melodramatic actor, but Cooper could. On one occasion Alice and Cora were being chased by the French through a fog in the neighborhood of their father's fort:

> "*Point de quartier aux coquins!*" cried an eager pursuer, who seemed to direct the operations of the enemy.
> "Stand firm and be ready, my gallant 60ths!" suddenly exclaimed a voice above them; "wait to see the enemy; fire low, and sweep the glacis."
> "Father! father!" exclaimed a piercing cry from out the mist; "it is I! Alice! thy own Elsie! spare, O! save your daughters!"
> "Hold!" shouted the former speaker, in the awful tones of parental agony, the sound reaching even to the woods, and rolling back in solemn echo. "'Tis she! God has restored me my children! Throw open the sally-port; to the field, 60ths, to the field; pull not a trigger, lest ye kill my lambs! Drive off these dogs of France with your steel."

Cooper's word-sense was singularly dull. When a person has a poor ear for music he will flat and sharp right along without knowing it. He keeps near the tune, but it is *not* the tune. When a person has a poor ear for words, the result is a literary flatting and sharping; you perceive what he is intending to say, but you also perceive that he doesn't *say* it. This is Cooper. He was not a word-musician. His ear was satisfied with the *approximate* word. I will furnish some circumstantial evidence in support of this charge. My instances are gathered from half a dozen pages of the tale called *Deerslayer.* He uses "verbal," for "oral"; "precision," for "facility"; "phenomena," for "marvels"; "necessary," for "predetermined"; "unsophisticated," for "primitive"; "preparation," for "expectancy"; "rebuked," for "subdued"; "dependent on," for "resulting from"; "fact," for "condition"; "fact," for "conjecture"; "precaution," for "caution"; "explain," for "determine"; "mortified," for "disappointed"; "meretricious," for "factitious"; "materially," for "considerably"; "decreasing," for "deepening"; "increasing," for "disappearing"; "embedded," for "enclosed"; "treacherous," for "hostile"; "stood," for "stooped"; "softened," for "replaced"; "rejoined," for "remarked"; "situation," for "condition"; "different," for "differing"; "insensible," for "unsentient"; "brevity," for "celerity"; "distrusted," for "suspicious"; "mental imbecility," for "imbecility"; "eyes," for "sight"; "counteracting," for "opposing"; "funeral obsequies," for "obsequies."

There have been daring people in the world who claimed that Cooper could write English, but they are all dead now—all dead but Lounsbury. I don't remember that Lounsbury makes the claim in so many words, still he makes it, for he says that *Deerslayer* is a "pure work of art." Pure, in that connection, means faultless—faultless in all details—and language is a detail. If Mr. Lounsbury had only compared Cooper's English with the English which he writes himself—but it is plain that he didn't; and so it is likely that he imagines until this day that Cooper's is as clean and compact as his own. Now I feel sure, deep down in my heart, that Cooper wrote about the poorest English that exists in our language, and that the English of *Deerslayer* is the very worst that even Cooper ever wrote.

I may be mistaken, but it does seem to me that *Deerslayer* is not a work of art in any sense; it does seem to me that it is destitute of every detail that goes to the making of a work of art; in truth, it seems to me that *Deerslayer* is just simply a literary *delirium tremens*.

A work of art? It has no invention; it has no order, system, sequence, or result; it has no lifelikeness, no thrill, no stir, no seeming of reality; its characters are confusedly drawn, and by their acts and words they prove that they are not the sort of people the author claims that they are; its humor is pathetic; its pathos is funny; its conversations are—oh! indescribable; its love-scenes odious; its English a crime against the language.

Counting these out, what is left is Art. I think we must all admit that.   [1895]

William De Forest

The Great American Novel

A FRIEND of ours, a fairly clever person, and by no means lacking in common sense on common subjects, has the craze in his head that he will some day write a great American novel.

"If I can do it," he says, "I shall perform a national service, and be hailed as a national benefactor. It will be acknowledged that I have broken another of the bonds which make us spiritually colonists and provincials. Who does not like to have his portrait taken? If I ever can give expression to the idea which is in my brain, the American people will say, 'That is my picture,' and will lavish heart and pocket in remuneration. It is a feat worthy of vast labor and suffering."

During eight or ten years he has struggled for his prize. He has published two or three experiments which have been more or less well spoken of by the critics, and rather more than less neglected by the purchasing public. Now and then, collared by the material necessities of life, or by some national enthusiasm even stronger than his own, he has turned aside into other pursuits, has fought at the front, has aided in the work of reconstruction, has written articles and other things which he calls trivialities. But at every leisure moment he returns to his idea of producing "the Great American Novel."

Will he produce it? Will any one of this generation produce it? It is very doubtful, for the obstacles are immense. To write a great American poem is at present impossible, for the reason that the nation has not yet lived a great poem. It cost unknown centuries of Greek faiths and fightings to produce the "Iliad." It cost all the Roman kings and all the Roman republic to produce the "Æneid." The "Divina Commedia" is the result of a thousand years of the Papal Church. Europe had to live politically through the crusades and the feudal system before it could earn the "Gierusalemme Liberata" and the "Orlando Furioso." "Paradise Lost" is the summary of all gnosticism and Protestantism. We may be confident that the Great American Poem will not be written, no matter what genius attempts it, until democracy, the idea of our day and nation and race, has agonized and conquered through centuries, and made its work secure.

But the Great American Novel—the picture of the ordinary emotions and manners of American existence—the American "Newcomes" or "Misérables" will, we suppose, be possible earlier. "Is it time?" the benighted people in the earthen jars of commonplace life are asking. And with no intention of being disagreeable, but rather with sympathetic sorrow, we answer, "Wait." At least we fear that such ought to be our answer. This task of painting the American soul within the framework of a novel has seldom been attempted, and has never been accomplished further than very partially—in the production of a few outlines. Washington Irving was too cautious to make the trial; he went back to fictions of Knickerbockers and Rip Van Winkles and Ichabod Cranes; these he did well, and we may thank him for not attempting more and failing in the attempt. With the same consciousness of incapacity Cooper shirked the experiment; he devoted himself to Indians, of whom he knew next to nothing, and to back-woodsmen and sailors, whom he idealized; or where he attempted civilized groups, he produced something less natural than the wax figures of Barnum's old museum. If all Americans were like the heroes and heroines of Cooper, Carlyle might well enough call us "eighteen millions of bores." As for a tableau of American society, as for anything resembling the tableaux of English society by Thackeray and Trollope, or the tableaux of French society by Balzac and George Sand, we had better not trouble ourselves with looking for it in Cooper.

There come to us from the deserts of the past certain voices which "syllable men's names"—names that seem to sound like "Paulding," "Brown," "Kennedy"—and we catch nothing further. These are ghosts, and they wrote about ghosts, and the ghosts have vanished utterly. Another of these shadowy mediums, still living, if we are not misinformed, is W. Gilmore Simms, of whom the best and worst thing to be said is this—that he is nearly as good as Cooper, and deserves fame nearly as much.

Thus do we arrive, without frequent stoppage, at our own times. Hawthorne, the greatest of American imaginations, staggered under the load of the American novel. In "The Scarlet Letter," "The House of the Seven Gables," and "The Blithedale Romance" we have three delightful romances, full of acute spiritual analysis, of the light of other worlds, but also characterized by only a vague consciousness of this life, and by graspings that catch little but the subjective of humanity. Such personages as Hawthorne creates belong to the wide realm of art rather than to our nationality. They are as probably natives of the furthest mountains of Cathay or of the moon as of the United States of America. They are what Yankees might come to be who should shut themselves up for life to meditate in old manses. They have no sympathy with this eager and laborious people, which takes so many newspapers, builds so many railroads, does the most business on a given capital, wages the biggest war in proportion to its population, believes in the physically impossible and does some of it. Hawthorne's characters cannot talk? Certainly not in the style of this western world; rather in the language of men who never expressed themselves but on paper, and on paper in dreams. There is a curious lack of natural dialogue in Hawthorne's books, and with this, of course, a lack of almost all other signs of the dramatic faculty. Besides, his company is so limited. New Englanders they profess to be: to be sure, they are of the queerest; men and women of the oddest, shyest, most recluse nature, and often creatures purely ideal; but they never profess to be other than New Englanders. The profoundest reverence for this great man need prevent no one from saying that he has not written "the Great American Novel."

The nearest approach to the desired phenomenon is "Uncle Tom's Cabin." There were very noticeable faults in that story; there was a very faulty plot; there was (if idealism be a fault) a black man painted whiter than the angels, and a girl such as girls are to be, perhaps, but are not yet; there was a little village twaddle. But there was also a national breadth to the picture, truthful outlining of character, natural speaking, and plenty of strong feeling. Though comeliness of form was lacking, the material of the work was in many respects admirable. Such Northerneers as Mrs. Stowe painted we have seen; and we have seen such Southerners, no matter what the people south of Mason and Dixon's line may protest; we have seen such negroes, barring, of course, the impeccable Uncle Tom— uncle of no extant nephews, so far as we know. It was a picture of American life, drawn with a few strong and passionate strokes, not filled in thoroughly, but still a portrait. It seemed, then, when that book was published, easy to have more American novels. But in "Dred" it became clear that the soul which a throb of emotion had enabled to grasp this whole people was losing its hold on the vast subject which had so stirred us. Then, stricken with timidity, the author shrank into her native shell of New England. Only certain recluse spirits, who dwell between the Dan and Beersheba of Yankeedom, can care much for Doctor Hopkins as he goes through his exercises in "The Minister's Wooing," while the attempt to sketch Aaron Burr as a contrast to the clerical hero shows most conclusively happy ignorance of the style of heartless men of the world. "The Pearl of Orr's Island" is far better. It is an exquisite little story, a thoroughly finished bit of work, but how small! There, microscope in hand over the niceties of Orr's Island, we wait for another cameo of New England life. But what special interest have Southerners and Westerners and even New Yorkers in Yankee cameos?

There was another dainty and by no means feeble story about a still farther northeastern realm of rocks and sand and fog. A brother of James Russell Lowell, a poet in soul, though he writes in prose, went to Newfoundland in search of the ideal, and wrote "The New Priest of Conception Bay." A few choice, critical souls praised it, we believe, and we believe the purchasing public hardly noticed it. It should not have been let die, and its author should have been called on for more novels. True, large, and kindly portraits of rustic souls were in it, and, as we judge of such things, the best landscape pictures ever done by any American, unless we except Thoreau. Story there was almost none, and no more passion than in a Fra Angelico. What can be hoped for such books in presence of a popular taste which accepts Headley as a Tacitus, and J. S. C. Abbott as a Livy, and Dr. Holland as a Virgil? One is tempted, even as Congressmen often are, to fall back upon "lore," and cry "O tempora? O mores!" We mention this book partly to call attention to the fact that its author, like so many of his competitors, evaded the trial of sketching American life and fled abroad for his subjects.

We shall always be grateful to Oliver Wendell Holmes for "The Autocrat of the Breakfast Table," and hardly less grateful for "The Professor." Lighter, brighter, keener, defter prose has rarely been written in America. It would not be unworthy of a Parisian; it would not be scorned by Taine or Veuillot or Henri de Rochefort. He has also created a personage or two whom we shall not forget. A truer American than "the young man called John" never breathed. We would let him vote anywhere on the mere credit of his ideas. If men and angels should swear to us that he was born abroad, we would not believe them. He is one of us, and was from conception. If he lives, he reads the *Ledger* and John S. C. Abbott, and does not read "The New Priest of Conception Bay." Heaven prosper him and give him more wisdom! There is true picturing of intelligent and unintelligent Eastern Americans in "The Autocrat" and "The Professor." But when the author undertakes a novel, he enters upon a field where passion is needed, to say nothing of his lack of what the poor despised phrenologer calls "constructiveness," and in that he is lacking. We have carefully watched his efforts, not in hardness of spirit, but with sympathy; we know how much easier it is to look on than to run. We acknowledge that "Elsie Venner" and "The Guardian Angel" are interesting books. They show us faithfully the exterior of commonplace New England life, and they travesty the solemnities of New England's spiritual life with an amusing manual dexterity. But the artist is hampered by his scientific theories and by his lack of fervent emotional sympathy. His characters do not go; they do not drag him along; they do not drag us. We seem to see that they disappoint their creator; that they do not move as he thought they would when he devised them; that they do not fulfil the double purpose of living for themselves and for him. From time to time he stops and rubs one up, seeking to galvanize it into life and action. We have little doubt that he was far better satisfied with "the Guardian Angel," for instance, when he commenced it than when he wrote the closing lines.

Moreover, these two tales are not American novels; they are only New England novels; they are localisms. We shall not be suspected of desiring to belittle New England, of denying its moral strength, keen intellect, and wide influence. But Dr. Holmes has not sketched that Yankeehood which goes abroad and leavens the character of the Republic. The Yankeehood which he exhibits is that which stays in corners, speechless and impotent—a community of old maids, toothless doctors, small-souled lawyers, village poets, and shelved professors; the coterie of an antique borough, amusing, queer, and of no account. We do not say that he should have put a Wendell Phillips or an Emerson on the canvas; we only say that he has given no prominence to those moral characteristics of New England which produce such movers of the national heart and teachers of the national intellect. He has scarcely alluded to the kind of society which made these men what they are, unless we allow an exception in favor of the suggestiveness of Byles Gridley. Thus his stories are not only provincial in scene and in the form of the dialogue, but provincial to the very depths of the spirit which animates them.

Of "Waiting for the Verdict" we have little to add beyond what we have already said. While acknowledging anew the breadth of the plan, we must reiterate our abhorrence of the execution. In reading it we remember with wicked sympathy the expression of a bachelor friend, "I hate poor people's children," and we are tempted to add, "and poor people." We do not believe that "the poor and lowly of God's creatures" are his chosen; we hold that, if he has any preference, it must be for the wisest, sweetest, and noblest. It is dreadful to have low, tattered, piebald, and stupid people so rubbed into one. Remembering Mr. Dolls, we feel a desire to burn a rag under the noses of Mrs. Davis's characters. The mild sermonizing twaddle of the "Hills of the Shatemuc" was better than this pertinacious exhibition of moral dwarfs, bearded women, Siamese twins, and headless calves. Bad taste in the selection of minor features and a rushing of adjectives to the head spoil a book which, in its table of contents, gives grand promise of an American novel.

There are other experiments. There are novels by Mr. Mitchell, and Mr. Bayard Taylor, and Mr. Beecher, and many more, but none is better than those already mentioned and few are nearly as good. Is there in the whole catalogue a "Newcomes," a "Vanity Fair," a "Misérables," or even a "Little Dorrit" or a "Small House at Allington"? Is there, in other words, a single tale which paints American life so broadly, truly, and sympathetically that every American of feeling and culture is forced to acknowledge the picture as a likeness of something which he knows. Throwing out "Uncle Tom's Cabin," we must answer, Not one!

And why not? There are several reasons, some material, some spiritual, some pertaining to the artists, some to the subject. It is not necessary to dwell upon the fact that, as we produce few books of any kind, we must consequently produce a duly small proportion of good ones. Another cause of barrenness is not less obvious; but it has been upheld by selfishness, shortsightedness, and national prejudice; it has been so strenuously defended that argument is pardonable. For lack of an international copyright the American author is undersold in his own market by the stolen brain-labor of other countries. The ordinary reader, wanting a book and not caring what, providing it will amuse him, steps into a bookstore and finds "Little Dorrit" alongside of "Elsie Venner." He is pretty sure that both are good, but he sees that the former costs a dollar and three-quarters, and the latter two dollars. He buys the cheaper because it is the cheaper. "Little Dorrit" is stolen and sold without any profit to Dickens; and "Elsie Venner" remains unsold, to the loss of Holmes. Nine readers out of ten do this; each one is glad of the twenty-five cents saved; then he wonders "why we don't have an American literature." Depend upon it that, if "Little Dorrit" were the dearest, more "Elsie Venners" would be sold, and Dr. Holmes would give more time to planning and perfecting novels. The American reader must have his book cheap. He will pay high for his coat, his sofa, his piano, his portrait; but the furniture and clothing and adornment of his mind must be cheap, even if nasty. To charge the English price for a good novel might provoke an indignation meeting, if not a riot. When the "young man called John" buys a book for two dollars, he wants very nearly the worth of his "stamps" in paper and binding. The intellectual or moral value of his purchase is a trifle in his estimation, and he does not mean to pay much for it. In short, the American author has first a small sale, and second a small profit on his sale. His business does not keep him, and so he works carelessly at it, or he quits it. His first book is marked by inexperience; his second is produced in haste to meet a board-bill; and he stops disgusted before he has learned his trade. If he could make a living, and if in addition he saw a chance, the merest chance, of doing as well as a grocery merchant, he would go on and perhaps be our glory; who knows?

We do not say that he would do miraculously well, even under favoring pecuniary circumstances. The child of a community which is given to estimating the claims of books by their cheapness, his culture is not of the highest. Clever, but not trained, he knows better what to write than what not to write. Just consider the educational advantages of an English writer of by no means the highest rank, Miss Thackeray, the author of "The Village on the Cliff." Surrounded from infancy by such men as the creator of "Vanity Fair," the creator of "David Copperfield," and their compeers, she may be said to have inherited the precious knowledge of what not to write. You can see it in her books; there is no great power, but there is nothing threadbare, nothing sophomorical; there is a careful, intelligent workmanship, like that of an old hand. The power of an author is frequently, if not generally, no more than the expression of the community which produced him. Have we as yet the literary culture to educate Thackerays and Balzacs? Ah! we only buy them— cheap.

So much for the artist; now for the sitter. Ask a portrait-painter if he can make a good likeness of a baby, and he will tell you that the features are not sufficiently marked nor the expression sufficiently personal. Is there not the same difficulty in limning this continental infant of American society, who is changing every year not only in physical attributes, but in the characteristics of his soul? Fifteen years ago it was morality to return fugitive slaves to their owners—and now? Five years ago everybody swore to pay the national debt in specie—and now? Our aristocracy flies through the phases of Knickerbocker, codfish, shoddy, and petroleum. Where are the "high-toned gentlemen" whom North and South gloried in a quarter of a century since? Where are the Congressmen who could write "The Federalist?" Where is everything that was? Can a society which is changing so rapidly be painted except in the daily newspaper? Has any one photographed fireworks or the shooting-stars? And then there is such variety and even such antagonism in the component parts of this cataract. When you have made your picture of petrified New England village life, left aground like a boulder near the banks of the Merrimac, does the Mississippian or the Minnesotian or the Pennsylvanian recognize it as American society? We are a nation of provinces, and each province claims to be the court.

When Mr. Anthony Trollope commences a novel, he is perplexed by no such kaleidoscopic transformations and no such conflicting claims of sections. Hundreds of years ago English aristocracy assumed the spiritual nature which it holds with little change to the present day. It had made its code of honor; it had established its relations with the mass of the nation; it had become the model for all proper Englishmen. At this time it is a unit of social expression throughout the kingdom. A large class of people go up to London at the same season, go into the country at the same season, lead very nearly the same lives, have the same ideas and tastes. There you have something fixed to paint; there you have the novelist's sitter; there you have his purchaser. All successful English romances are written with reference to this class; they may attack it, they may defend it, they always paint it. Wealthy, it pays high prices for books; anxious to be amused, it buys them freely. For such a sitter who would not, if possible, learn to paint well? Thus also, in France, only that the subject is always in your studio, for the studio is Paris. If George Sand writes a provincial novel, she does it not for the people of the province described but for the Parisians, who occasionally like a novelty. But the French author need not know more than that one city to have his subject and his public, in divided Germany there have been few good novels. In distracted Italy there has been, perhaps, but one—"I Promessai Sposi"—and that historical, the result of half a lifetime, the task of a great poet. Even Manzoni found it a mighty labor to depict the life of a nation of provinces.

Well, what are our immediate chances for a "great American novel"? We fear that the wonder will not soon be wrought unless more talent can be enlisted in the work, and we are sure that this sufficient talent can hardly be otained without the encouragement of a international copyright. And, even then, is it time?   [1867]

Thomas S. Perry
....
American Novels

We have often wondered that the people who raise the outcry for the "Great American Novel" did not see that, so far from being of any assistance to our fellow-countryman who is trying to win fame by writing fiction, they have rather stood in his way by setting up before him a false aim for his art, and by giving the critical reader a defective standard by which to judge his work. Whenever this so-longed-for novel does appear, we may be sure that our first impression will not be that it is American. It may be American, without a doubt, but it will not be ostentatiously so; that will not be its chief merit. If it is written in this country and about this country, there will be of course a flavor of the soil, which is to be desired, but the epicure does not want his coffee muddy. There is an American nature, but then there is human nature underlying it, and to that the novel must be true before anything else. That is what is of importance; it is that alone which makes the novel great, which causes it to be read in all times and in all countries. If the author so far forgets this, his first duty, as to imagine that the simple rehearsal of the barrenest external phenomena of life and nature in this country can be of any real interest to the reader, he makes as great a mistake as would an actor who should fancy that nothing more was needed for representing Hamlet than to dress in black, wear a light wig, and to powder his cheeks to look pale. It is the bane of realism, as of all *isms,* to forget that it represents only one important side of truth, and to content itself, as complacently as an advocate, with seeing its own rules obeyed, and, generally, with the narrowest construction of the law. By insisting above all things on the novel being American, we mistake the means for the end; we have a perfect right to demand accuracy in the writer,—in spite of Mrs. Spofford we cannot read about castles in New England,—but we should not regard it as anything but the merest machinery, the least part of a novel; it is a *sine qua non,* to be sure, but so in man is the spinal marrow; we think no more of a friend on account of his having a spinal marrow. So long as we over-estimate the value of this formal accuracy, it will be possible for any one to prove to his own satisfaction and to ours that such and such a novel is the best. "See here," he will say, "So-and-so makes the Connecticut River two hundred and fifty miles long, while 'Civis Americanus' gives it its proper length; and then 'Geographicus' says on page 343, just before the Boston horsecar conductor declares his love to the Nova Scotia servant of the selectman, that Vermont has thirty-five inhabitants to the square mile; he was thinking of New Hampshire; he's no novelist." No one fancies a novel that can be proved to be better than another, like a manual of geometry. Nor do we care for one that loses its value at every census. It may be well that novels should be of temporary interest, but they should at least outlast the year's almanac.

It might not be amiss to pause for a moment to consider the origin of this expression, "The great American novel." Critics would differ about the great English novel or the great French novel; why should America have one? Nevertheless, novelists have striven for this prize, genial critics have imperilled their reputations by rashly awarding it to various writers, who have as rapidly faded into oblivion, and we are as far from unanimity about it as we ever were. We imagine that it is a term that has come down to us from the time, a generation or two ago, when, America having an army and navy, consideration in the eyes of Europe for its material strength and future importance, the absence of a fully developed literature was keenly felt. Literature, too, was considered a branch of manufactures and not a thing of growth. We were to have an American Byron; possibly with good Presidents and a proper tariff, an American Shakespeare; and then the public, detecting the great differences between the society of Europe and that of this country, cried aloud for the novel that should do for us what Fielding had already, and Thackeray has since, done for England. That this should be done is indeed desirable; but our hopes will be vain unless our writers, with keener vision than the public, see the uselessness of a mere outside resemblance to their models.

That a novel is not good by simply being un-American, one can see by recalling a by no means unreadable story—"Miss Van Kortland"—that appeared about four or five years ago. The effect of reading to excess the modern English novel was here clearly seen. There was the general air of English country life barely disguised by American names. Congress was made exactly like Parliament. It was an English bottom sailing under American colors. Of the elaborate Americanism of "Lady Judith," we need not speak. The reader could not help being reminded of the Yankees in Punch's caricatures, who would be arrested as suspicious characters in the backwoods of Maine, nor could their apt use of "old hoss" save them. Such hybrids we may trust will be soon forgotten; but in vastly the greater number of the American novels of the present day we find perhaps equally damaging faults, although of a different kind. Let us take, for example, Mr. De Forest's novels. In his writings we find a great deal that is American, but not so much that goes to the making of a really great novel. His stories have certain undeniable merits, and if the great American novel needed only to be American, he would easily bear off the palm. "Miss Ravenel's Conversion," "Overland," "Kate Beaumont," are three novels that could have been written in no other country; but such geographical criticism wholly leaves their real value out of the question, as if Charles Reade were to be exalted for having written the "great Australian novel," "Never too Late to Mend," or De Foe for his "great Juan Fernandez novel." In the true novel the scene, the incidents, are subordinated to the sufferings, actions, and qualities of the characters. They are for the time living beings, and our greatest sympathy is necessarily given to those who deserve it from some internal reason, not from the number of miles they may have travelled, or the number of times they may have been shot at in the dark. Such incidents lend an interest, it is true, but it is not of the highest kind. The geology, the botany, the ethnography, may be accurate to date, the reader may be in perpetual shivers from the urgency of the dangers that threaten every one in the novel, but the real story lies beneath the hats and bonnets of those concerned, not in the distant cataracts that wet them, nor the bullets that sear them. It would seem as if the author had contented himself too readily with but one side, and that not the most valuable, of the novelist's work. He should retain the skill that he now possesses and use it, not as a thing of lasting value in itself, but as an aid to the representation of what is more genuine art. We should be sorry, however, if we did not do justice to the vividness with which he has drawn many of his side-characters, especially in his latest novels and in many of his less ambitious magazine sketches. As a simple narrator he is deserving of much praise; he can draw admirably the less important personages, so that one only notices more sharply his smaller degree of success when he undertakes to represent that more difficult character, a man under the influence of some all-controlling passion. What he can see he can write down for our reading, and this is certainly a rare gift, but his eye is stronger than his imagination. It is when he comes to this more delicate part of his work that the reader is disappointed, and all the more, as we have said, from his skill elsewhere.

Of the society novel this is the more common form. One takes the manly A and represents some possible complications of his "heart-agony," and that of the lovely C, from the persecution of flinty-hearted parents, loss of money, jealousy, etc. One would be averse to saying that his own country cannot supply as good material for such novels as any other. There are here pretty women and good men. In spite of our race for wealth, our early marriages, our bolting our meals and consequent dyspepsia, the devious course of what is strangely called the tender passion may still be observed by those who watch their kind. Lovers languish and rejoice, hearts threaten to break and then grow indifferent, as truly here as in any German village, where the full moon shines every night of the year. But can any one name a good American love-story? With the exception of "Esmond" it might be hard to find one in the language; but let us consider America alone. What are the American novels of society, in which we might suppose love-making would have full sway?

Those of Mrs. Stowe suggest themselves at once. We cannot believe that her great popularity is due entirely to her wonderful success with "Uncle Tom's Cabin." To her youngest readers that book must be already a thing of the past; but we fancy that it is because she has succeeded in catching certain traits of American life that she is so widely read. Besides, with all her faults, she is a humorist, and is often entertaining enough; but what could be more ignoble than her last two novels of society, "Pink and White Tyranny," and "My Wife and I"? It is profound criticism to call Thackeray a cynic; perhaps Mrs. Stowe is one in disguise, but no man would dare show his head in a drawingroom after describing such a character as the heroine of the last of these novels. One would have to be disappointed in love a great many times before young ladies made upon him such an impression of furbelowed, curled, food-despising, thin-voiced flirts as one finds here. The men are the infant heroes of Mrs. Sherwood's tales grown up. As for the manners of these people, their giggling, their love-making, it is what one imagines to be the romance of a "calico and neck-tie ball." For example, we find in Chapter XXX of "My Wife and I":—

"'O, you know!—this inextricable puzzle,—what does ail a certain person? Now he didn't come at all last night, and when I asked Jim Fellows where his friend was (one must pass the compliment of inquiring, you know), he said, "Henderson had grown dumpy lately," and he couldn't get him out anywhere.'

"'Well, Eva, I'm sure I can't throw any light on the subject. I know no more than you.'

"'Now, Ida, let me tell you, this afternoon when we stopped in the park, I went into that great rustic arbor on the top of the hill there, and just as we came in on one side, I saw him in all haste hurrying out on the other, as if he were afraid to meet me.'

"'How very odd.'

"'Odd! well, I should think it was; but what was worse, he went and stationed himself on a bench under a tree where he could hear and see us, and there my lord sat—perhaps he thought I didn't see him, but I did.'

"'Lillie and Belle Forester and Wat Jerrold were with me, and we were having such a laugh! I don't know when I have had such a frolic, and how silly it was of him to sit there glowering like an owl in an ivy-bush, when he might have come out and joined us, and had a good time! I'm quite out of patience with the creature, it's so vexatious to have him act so!'"

Further on we find:

(*Enter* ALICE *with empressement.*)

"'Girls, what do you think? Wat Sydney come back and going to give a great croquet party out at Clairmont, and of course we are all invited with notes in the most resplendent style, with crest and coat of arms, and everything—perfectly *"mag."* There's to be a steamboat, with a band of music, to take the guests up, and no end of splendid doings: *marquées* and tents and illuminations and fireworks, and to return by moonlight after all's over; isn't it lovely? I do think Wat Sydney's perfectly splendid, and its all on your account, Eva, I know it is,'" etc., etc.

And so they artlessly prattle on. This is by no means an extract, which, taken away from its context, seems unduly ridiculous; far from it, it is a very good specimen of the whole tone of the book. Be these the manners of good society? Is there nothing nobler in life than a horse-car flirtation? Is it necessary that society novels should be like fashion-plates, with the same jaunty ease and simpering gentility that mark those illustrations of the happy life of the rich and great? If the people are tawdrily dressed, if their talk is empty enough to shame the silliest school-girl that ever chattered until she gasped for breath, if their manners are either rude or pompously haughty, how can one take a genuine interest in the story? Let their manners be as bad as possible, their clothes and grammar in tatters, provided they have one trait, one quality, be it one that makes or mars human beings, and then we can read the story. To be interested in characters in fiction, as with human beings in life, our sympathy must be aroused; for beings who simply giggle and pout, indifference is kindness.

Most American writers are afraid of their heroes and heroines. They give them homes by the side of imaginary rivers, in impossible cities. They are as shy of fairly introducing their characters as if we were all strangers at a watering-place hotel, and were very nervous about tainting our tender gentility. That this is the result of attempting to represent in this country, with its changing, uncertain classes, what in England is clear enough from its fixed social laws, is highly probable. But a novel to be good may well let good society alone. The best that Mrs. Stowe has done leaves the dancing master out entirely. For the English novel the task is greatly simplified by the fact that every man in that country is much more closely connected with the whole social system than is the case with us. In their novels we are introduced to distinct characters, say to a barrister, an officer, a young lord. Besides, whatever personal characteristics may belong to each of these persons, they all stand in a certain definite relation to society at large. Each carries a certain atmosphere with him. With us when we read about a lawyer in one of our stories, nothing more is told us than if we were informed that he always wore Roman scarfs, perhaps not so much. We have all sorts of lawyers; no one man is a representative of the class. Occasionally we find that a good word is given to an omniscient professor who sits by a lamp and dabbles in Sanskrit, botany, methaphysics, chemistry, anatomy, zoölogy, etc., etc. He generally wears a long beard, has acquired patience by his severe studies, and is especially remarkable for the unexpected way in which he makes an offer of marriage after nourishing an untold and unsuspected love for a long time, while he pretended to be looking out words in the dictionary. Occasionally, we say, this representative of the quiet ideal appears in fiction, but he is an uncertain and artificial creation. In spite of the young girl's rapture over hops at West Point, an officer is not always an entrancing lover in fiction. There is, possibly, a vague Bohemian glamour around the artist, but even that is by no means certain. Since in general this deficiency exists, the task of the writer is rendered more difficult. Our democracy certainly equalizes us: it enlists us, as it were, into a vast army, but a peaceful, unheroic army, and to make any fictitious person interesting the author is put to the greater task of distinctly drawing his character as a man; he gets no aid from his surroundings. One would say that the natural tendency of the American novelist would be toward romance; that the very uniformity of our social life would offer nothing tempting to the writer, unless, indeed, to the satirist, who should turn to ridicule the shallowness, greedy pretence, and emptiness which he might see about him. In spite of the contumely that is thrown upon the frivolities of fashion in "Pink and White Tyranny" and in "My Wife and I," it may be said that it is not given to every one to be a satirist. No satire is keener than that which tells the truth. One is only tender about his favorite vice. To call a selfish man a murderer, or a pirate, would be as idle as to write odes in praise of an honest bank clerk. And so in these stories Mrs. Stowe has overshot her mark by caricaturing what only needed to be shown in real dulness to appear worthless. To her, and to many others, American society seems frivolous, but it is only exalted when a writer wastes his powder by attacking it as he would a dangerously false religion.

While the American writer finds these difficulties in the way of the "novel of society," it may be just that those tales should be considered that take up man from some other point of view than that which controls the respectable matron who is making out a list of invitations for her daughter's party. There are the dry-humored Yankees, the Yankee-despising, self-praising Westerners, and the lordly Southrons, who hate both. What has been done with such characters as these?

In hardly any book do we get more of the Yankee than in the novel "Margaret," by Sylvester Judd. It is a story of life in New England nearly a hundred years ago, and, although it stands in about the same relation to most novels that Burton's "Anatomy of Melancholy" does to ordinary manuals of anatomy, it has a certain interest of its own. This is, to be sure, hardly great enough to beguile the reader, to the reading of the book, which is written in defiance of every rule of literary composition; but yet, in spite of a crabbed style, as rough as a corduroy road, of tedious and impossible converstions, of great delays in the telling of the story, the reader can readily see a sincerity in the writer that is often much less evident in the works of much cleverer writers. As an example of its artistic crudeness we quote the following conversation:—

"Another day Mr. Evelyn came to the Pond. Margaret watched his approach with composure, and returned his greeting without confusion. 'You have been at the Head,' said she, 'and I must take you to other places to-day. First the Maples.'

"'This is a fine mineralogical region,' said he, as they entered the spot. 'I wish I had a hammer.'

"'I will get one,' said she. 'Let me go for it.'

"'You are not in health, you told me, and you do not look very strong. I must go by all means. I will be back in a trice. You will have quite as much walking as you can master before the day is through.'

"'I fear I shall be more tired wandering than in going.'

"'See this,' said he, exposing a hollow stone filled with rare crystals, which he found and broke during her absence.

"'I thank you, I thank you,' she replied. 'The master has given me an inkling of geology, but I never imagined such beauty was hidden here.'

"'With definite forms and brilliant texture these gems vegetate in the centre of this rough rusty stone.'

"'Incomparable mystery! New anagogies! I begin to be in love with what I understand not.'

"'Humanity is like that.'

"'What is humanity?'

"'It is only another name for the world that you asked me about.'

"'I am perplexed by the duplicity of words. He is humane who helps the needy.'

"'That is one form of humanity. I use the term as expressing all men collectively viewed in their better light. Much depends upon this light phase, or aspect, what subjectively to us is by the Germans called stand-point. Indian's Head, in one position, resembles a human face; in another, quite as much a fish's tail. Man, like this stone, is geodic,—such stones, you know, are called geodes.'

"'Have you the skill to discover them?'

"'It is more difficult to break then find them. Yet if I could crack any man as I do this stone, I should open to crystals.'

"'Any man?'

"'All men.'

"'Passing wonderful! I would run a thousand miles for the hammer! I have been straining after the stars, how much there is in the stone! Most divine earth, henceforth I will worship thee! Geodic Androids! What will the master say?'

"'I see traces of more gems in these large rocks. Let me rap here, and lo! a beryl; there is an agate, younder is a growth of garnets.'"

"'Let me cease to be astonished, and only learn to love.'

"'An important lesson, and one not too well learned.'

"'Under this tree I will erect a temple to the god of rocks. Was there any such? Certes, I remember none.'

"'The god of rocks is God.'

"'You sport enigmas. Let us to Diana's Walk.'"

We will not follow them. Their talk flows on as easily and naturally as in the extract given above, closely resembling the conversations in the chapters in the phrase-book for advanced pupils. But with all these obvious faults, and an almost impossible plot, the writer shows a genuine love of nature, and an appreciation of character that is really poetical. It is a book that is good in spite of itself, but yet it is barely readable. Its merits are those that are hardly evident enough to tempt the ordinary reader, who, naturally enough, wishes the way made easy before him. He takes a novel as he takes a walk, for amusement; he does not care for ruggedness,—that wearies him, everyday life gives him that,—any more than he does for an afternoon stroll through the thickets of the untrodden forest.

In Dr. Holmes's novels,—if we can call them novels,—in spite of his way of treating his characters like pathological or anatomical specimens, and in Mr. Henry Ward Beecher's "Norwood," we find the humorous Yankee admirably given. But, while "Elsie Venner" is in its way a well-constructed romance, and Hiram in "Norwood" is an amusingly and accurately drawn character, neither novel deserves the highest praise. They are both very clever attempts by men who are not novelists. Sam Lawson, in Mrs. Stowe's "Old Town Stories," is an extremely amusing person. This lady has certainly, to a remarkable extent, the power of detecting the humorous side of what she sees and of representing it. The Yankee in her writings is an admirable copy of an original that can be found in almost every New England village,—a man, namely, of greater or less worthlessness, but with a wisdom, or rather shrewdness, that makes him far superior to the ordinary people around him. It is part of the novelist's work to introduce just such characters. They are, so to speak, picturesque, and yet true to nature. Of the immense superiority of a story that contains one personage that is really a human being, it would be needless to speak. Most novels leave as shadowy an impression of the genuineness of their heroes and heroines upon the minds of their readers, as does the pictured Quaker of the advertisements of the soundness of his religious views. But the introduction of a character that is only of dramatic importance, that is to say, who is more truly drawn as a representative of a class than as a human being, does not of itself make a good novel. The reader is more easily satisfied with a superficial sketch in the former case than he would be in the latter. A man may be well drawn as a village loafer, he may give us the very impression that the genuine idler makes upon us, and to do this is no light task; it is one for which a writer deserves high praise, and this no one would deny to Mrs. Stowe. But there is beyond this a feeling in the reader's mind that he has a right to expect a solution of more difficult characters, a representation not only of one or two persons, but also of some probable and well-connected incidents. In the better sort of novels we get some human beings, but we also demand a story, a plot that shall be probable and interesting. One character, no matter if very lifelike, in an awkwardly constructed story is as out of place as would be a poet on a desert island. But still it cannot be denied that it is the drawing of a character which is the most difficult part of the novelist's task, and if he succeeds he has thereby the surest hold upon his readers. If he fails in this, he fails indeed, for even the most imaginative are cold to the dangers that threaten even the most carefully dressed puppets. But a well-drawn character, one which we fell to be an accurate representation of what a human being might be, one who seems to us not merely what we fancy fellow-travellers, for instance, are, but who is a consistent creation, moved by passion, with feelings of his own, and his own special temptations, who may differ entirely from ourselves, but yet of the truth of whose delineation every one can instinctively be sure, is a rare person in fiction. For creating him there are no infallible rules, any more than there are for painting a good portrait in oils. It all depends upon the writer's brains. But if he is successful, if he creates a character with whom we can feel any sympathy, although the feeling may not be one of admiration, we are sure that the writer has done something of which he may well be proud.

The story that is to be told is another thing for which no definite *a priori* rules can be given. Great tragedies can be utterly spoiled and the humblest incidents can be exalted by the attitude which the writer's mind takes toward them. To argue from analogy is often unsafe, because the argument generally begins where the analogy ceases; but a Bierstadt can choose for himself in the whole wide world the most wonderful spot to paint, with mountains, rivers, likes, and forests—such as poets are said to dream of—before him, but his canvas, when he has done his best, leaves us as cold as if we had been looking at a new drop-curtain in the theatre; while Millet can paint a little rustic scene, a woman driving sheep into their pen, a dim road in a dark wood, that we can never forget. It is not what the writer selects that moves us, but his way of treating it. A vulgar mind can degrade "King Lear," and a poet can throw a charm over the tritest line in the copy-book.

We need not go far for illustrations of what we have been saying; it is only necessary to recall some of the fantastic stories for which Southern novelists often betray a fondness. For example, there is one which is both described and criticised by its title, "Heart-Hungry." We need not go into a special examination of that novel, however, for the same thing may be said of the whole class, that they deal with the most tremendous manifestations of the power of love and jealousy, which combine to poison young lives and leads to the most heinous crimes. The books are, so to speak, thunder-storms in print, and seem to be written to make the way easy for some future Taine in a history of American literature to illustrate his remarks on the influence of hot climates upon the tastes of writers. But there is already good authority against tearing a passion to tatters. It has been widely acknowledged, and for a long time, that bombast is not the most effective means that a writer can use.

Of novels that fail from their dulness, whether caused by their photographic accuracy, or by the sluggish imagination of the author, we are sure that no examples need be given, especially in a land of circulating-libraries. All that we have tried to do is to set before our readers some of the more obvious faults of some of our popular writers. To do this it is by no means necessary to discuss at length all the American novels of recent years. They are, naturally, of different degrees of merit, from these weird visions of the Southern novelist to the innocently prattling stories for which Harper's Magazine is famous. The great novel is yet unwritten. We hope that he who shall attempt to write it will see the simplicity, the singleness of the problem that lies before him. The surer he is of this, the better will be his work. The less conscious he is of trying to be American, the more truly will he succeed in being so. Self-consciousness does not make a strong character, and so it is with this quality of the novelist. Lay the scene on the limitless prairie or in limited Fifth Avenue, but let the story rise above its geographical boundaries; let the characters be treated as human beings, not simply as inhabitants of such or such a place, with nothing to distinguish them from the beasts that perish, except certain peculiarities of dress and language. They must dwell somewhere, but they must be something besides citizens. Fantastic creatures dwelling in pure ether are not what the reader demands, but beings true, not to fashion, but to those higher laws and passions that alone are real, that exist above all the petty, accidental caprice of time and place. The real novelist, he who is to write the "great

American novel," must be a poet; he must look at life, not as the statistician, not as the census-taker, nor yet as the newspaper reporter, but with an eye that sees, through temporary disguises, the animating principles, good or bad, that direct human existence; these he must set before us, to be sure, under probable conditions, but yet without mistaking the conditions for the principles. He must idealize. The idealizing novelist will be the real novelist. All truth does not lie in facts.   [1872]

Robert Herrick

The American Novel

One hears much of the romantic quality of American life, which when analyzed is found to consist for the most part of our dazzling performances in conquering wealth and the frequently bizarre conduct of the successful rich. The feeling, still widespread, that opportunities for similar individual achievements exist more abundantly here than elsewhere continues this romantic note even in the face of sobering economic facts. In harmony with the rest of the world, American literature is less flamboyantly romantic than it was a scant decade ago, but it vaunts at all times a robust optimism that verges upon the romantic. We are also told that ours is a fertile soil artistically, ripe for a creative period of self-expression. How does it happen then, one is likely to ask, that the most significant imaginative work of the day still comes to us from the other side of the ocean—the best plays from Austria and Germany, the best novels from the much worked English field? Why is it that Wells, Bennett, and Galsworthy—not to mention half a dozen others almost as distinguished as these three—are writing in England at the present time, while in America one would have to strain patriotism to the point of absurdity to name any novelist of similar performance? In answering this pertinent question we shall have to consider incidentally the quality of our imaginative life to-day and thus continue the theme of my paper in the January number of this magazine.

We have had a literature in America—not an American literature, to be sure,—but a good sort of literature in America. The best of it came from the New England group of writers—the purest, the most authentic expression we have yet had. When Emerson, Hawthorne, Longfellow, and Lowell were writing, New England may have been but one province of a greater country, but it was intellectually a dominant and fairly homogeneous province. Mr. Howells has garnered admirably the last sheaves from that soil. Puritan America found its ultimate expression in "Silas Lapham," "A Modern Instance," and "The Hazard of New Fortunes." Mrs. Freeman and others have gleaned faithfully the last stalks. Some of their disciples are still trying to revive the cold ashes on the hearth.

Meanwhile, following the more robust inspiration of Bret Harte and Mark Twain, a large number of writers have risen to take possession of local fields—Cable in the South, Miss Murfree in the mountain districts of Tennessee, Owen Wister and many others in the varied localities of the great West, to name but a few of these fruitful writers. Already that period of local literature is passing, and the reason for its swift passing is obvious. It was in no sense national, and was largely sentimental in its appeal—pretty and pictuesque. The people, the country as a whole, was never reflected therein. It offered nothing, so to speak, to go on: it opened no new vistas for the younger generation. There is, of course, nothing incompatible with greatness in the use of purely local material. Hauptmann in his "Weavers" has shown that a great modern labor play can be written with a Silesian background of the Forties. More recently, Gustav Frenssen has written an important German novel with a Hamburg lad as the hero and a narrow North German background. It is the spirt always that counts. The spirit of our American local literature has been generally, to be quite frank, merely provincial—always seeking the picturesque, the sensational, the so-called romantic. And those are the elements of any civilization that are most surely discarded, swept aside in the flow of national life. Wister's cowboys were already romantic memories when he drew them. Social settlements, railroads, and hook-worm commissions are eradicating the picturesque conditions that provided Miss Murfree and Mr. John Fox with their material. The Panama Canal will abolish the last vestiges of Cable's New Orleans, as general prosperity has already effaced the sentimental South of Mr. Thomas Nelson Page and Mr. Hopkinson Smith. The swift current of our national life has swept into all these backwater places and stripped them of the peculiar aspects that charmed the story-tellers.

While these local fields were still being enthusiastically worked, we had our romantic historical revival of the Nineties. Janice Merediths and Richard Carvels were circulated by the ton, not to mention the purely imitative output of machine-made American historical novels. They were our recognition of the pseudo-romantic wave started by Stevenson. The preceding generation of school children got their history from the story books. Then suddenly as we turned into the new century, the demand for this sort of imaginative solace stopped. Authors who had sold hundreds of thousands of these candied products could not sell fifty thousand. Why was this? The distressed publishers have never been able to account satisfactorily for the sudden cessation in the demand for such books and have been seeking hither and yon for "a new line of goods" that shall have the same popular appeal. What happened to the American reading public? Had they become sufficiently educated to go direct to the history books for their history, and to "foreign-made literature" for imaginative realization? It would surely seem so, if we consider the steady increase in the number and the sales of so-called serious books, and the broadening demand for the novels and plays and poems of contemporary European writers.

To understand the situation intelligently, we must first realize a great social phenomenon that has appeared, one might almost say, since the time of the New England writers,—and that is journalism. I mean not merely daily and weekly and monthly journalism, but journalistic drama and journalistic books. In short, the thing done for the immediate moment, whatever form it may take,—that is what I mean by journalism. It is not my affair to account for the tidal wave of journalism that has swept around the earth in our day and reached its height in this country, nor to judge it socially or æsthetically. For the moment it seems to have crowded serious literature quite out of public attention—I mean the ordered, leisurely, imaginative product. And this other sort of thing, which I call perforce literature, if it is to emerge once more, must absorb journalism and transcend it. I am not interested in the moral or æsthetic or educational value of journalism. I see merely the facts as they apply to that other sort of product in which I am fervently interested: I see that journalism because it pays tremendously well has drawn into its ranks the more vital writers of our day; that it has insensibly affected the form as well as the content of literature; lastly that it has fed a huge reading public with the raw meat of imagination, on which it gorges until it has no appetite for more refined dishes. To be quite specific, why should we read picaresque novels when we can follow the McNamara case day by day? What detective story can compete with Burns and the San Francisco "grafters," or with the snaky involutions and pollutions of the Lorimer scandal? Is "Robert Elsmere" any more profoundly human and ethical than Judge Lindsey's story of his struggle to save the souls of Denver children? The point can be indefinitely illustrated by a thousand instances drawn from our newspapers and magazines. And these journalistic "stories" are true—or supposed to be—and the persons described are real people—or pretend to be. How, then, can literature contend in interest with these revelations of the actual social life going on around us?

For one thing, it can feebly reproduce them, as has been the case with our commercial fiction, for example, in the "big business" stories, conveniently shaped to the requirements of the magazines. Especially in the short story—a product that our magazines have made almost their own—incidents and types familiar to us through the newspaper are reproduced again and again. The short story of commerce and the magazined novel have done more, I believe, to debauch our literary situation than any other one thing. They enervate both writers and readers.

But all who think on such matters know that neither journalism nor commercialized fiction is an adequate medium for interpreting life deeply—for realizing ourselves and our country. We know that these are not literature and never can become such by any perversion of terms. Life is a flowing stream, and to mirror that stream with its multiform drama we must have some large, organic form—something epic in size and in purpose. Every race has had its epics, in prose or verse,—its famous deeds, its heroes and its villains, its own perculiar themes. Ours cannot be the exception. In the modern socialized world these epics must take the form of prose fiction. The large, loose form of the novel, so thoroughly developed yet not exhausted in the last two hundred years, resembles the stream of life in its volume, and is the only literary form known to us that is adequate to the task of interpreting and realizing the complex life of our day. To say that it is dead, that the play, or the newspaper, or the magazine, has come to take its place, is as absurd as to hold that men will no longer rear families and build homes for them because they have taken to flats. And as a matter of easily verifiable of fact, the novel has never shown more vitality, developed in more promising spontaneity, than during the last decade, when all the noise has been about the play.

We as a people have not had our due share in this renaissance of the prose epic. Since that boom in the fiction market, to which I have referred, when quarter-million sales of favorite novels were not uncommon, there have been comparatively few successful novels from the publishers' exact viewpoint. Nor has there been much consideration given to the American novel by that minority of the reading public that is supposed to be superior to the publishers' viewpoint. For the moment, we seem to have a distaste for our own fiction product and are going abroad for imaginative wares. Witness the success with us, among the intelligent, and one suspects among the less intelligent also, of De Morgan, Locke, Galsworthy, Wells, and more recently of Arnold Bennett and Leonard Merrick,—not to mention such journalistic stuff as "The Rosary" and "The Broad Highway," both being "English-made." Is it possible that we have outgrown the American novel such as we have had, that we realize it does not truly represent us, does not satisfy our aspirations for self-realization? Do we feel the artificiality and the thinness of the pictures it gives us of American life? It seems so. It world be hardly gracious for me to enter into personalities and to examine in detail the work of contemporary craftsmen. I prefer to give four general reasons for the inferiority that I find in the American novel, four ways in which it is inadequate and not to be considered in the same class with the best foreign work of the day.

And I am thinking only of the more representative and serious novels, not of that machine-made product which the weekly and monthly magazines provide by the million words. For that is a commercial, not an artistic product, and has nothing to do with the question, although in passing I may point out that America without the aid of protection leads the world in this sort of manufacture—machine-made fiction. I am concerned with the sincere efforts for vital self-expression in the novel form, not with commerce.

In the first place, our novels are weakly sentimental. As a people we have always been excessively sentimental beneath our practical surface. Among the great mass, sentimentality is one of our blind spots, and "the mass" here does not imply poverty or ignorance. "The Rosary," which might justly be described as the most syrupy concoction of current years, found its immense market among American women. But we are no longer as sentimental as the novelists think us to be: at least, our more intelligent readers are fast losing the vice. The tone of public discussion, the note of the newspaper world, no longer has the sickly sentimentality that has characterized it largely since the Civil War. Our charities no longer dare to put forward the sentimental plea. The vice conditions of our cities are not only being exposed with sensational candor, but are being met with unsentimental efforts at reform. When we consider the verdict of the press and of the people upon the McNamara case, we cannot be accused of the maudlin, sentimental squint that has often made our criminal procedure a farce. But with all the evidence of a growing appetite for healthy fact, sentimentalism persists in our novels. We sentimentalize in them success and business warfare; above all we sentimentalize our women—both the amorous relation of the sexes and the home. One of the benefits we may expect from the present woman movement is that American women will rise in resentment and kick over the false pedestal of chivalrous sentimentality on which (in our novels) American men have posed them inanely for so long.

But sentimentalism dies hard. It is an insidious disease inherited through romance from the miasmatic mysticism of the Middle Ages. It has proved peculiarly corrupting to art in all forms, because it is the easy means of gaining an immediate popular appeal. Therefore sentimentalism should be fought hard wherever it makes an appearance. Until we as a people are able and willing to look all the facts of our civilization in the face and recognize the unpleasant as well as the "pleasant," until we demand in our literature the same strong tonic of clear-sighted truth that we get from science, we shall remain morally flabby—soft. What can we expect of a young man or woman who accepts the prevailing type of serialized novel in our magazines as a true or desirable picture of life? As a people, we are far more mature than our novelists assume: we have a clearer vision and a sterner temper. Publishers say that our novels are no longer read by adult persons. The commercial product, at any rate, is manifestly designed for the consumption of the young person. That is a great pity, for a virile literature must represent both a man's world and a woman's world—with the interests and the values of maturity.

Again, our novels are weak religiously. For the most part, they avoid altogether the religious side of life, perhaps as unfit for the tired reader in his hour of relaxation; and at the best they represent a conventionally or negatively religious social world. In a few cases, survivals of the New England tradition, they iterate the old Puritan themes of sin, self-sacrifice, and regeneration. The Puritan tradition is dead, however: for good or for bad it no longer expresses the spiritual life of the people. Yet there is abundant religious feeling in America. We have always had a strain of transcendental mysticism, cropping out in the least expected spots, developing latterly into Christian Science and other healing cults. The ancient creed of Catholicism still has a vital hold, especially in the cities, and the older Protestant creeds have some influence in the smaller towns. It is perhaps not surprising that these formal religions have not shown their influence on our literature. For as a people, our attitude towards the whole subject of religion has fundamentally changed. We demand increasingly an effective religion—a religion that shall have its *point d'appui* on this terrestial abode. Moreover, American life is becoming peculiarly paganized, yet without renouncing a vital religious interest. It is not a sensual or self-indulgent paganism, but a vital, active, effective paganism, with a popular creed that might read like this:— "Life is good! I desire to make it better. For me life is here and now, and what I can do to make it better must be done here and now, and done not by prayer and fasting but by strong deeds." All our interest in social betterment, which is literally immense, is permeated with this spirit, at once scientific, pagan, and mystic. But very little of this spirit gets into our novels. A lot of it gets into the novels of Mr. Wells and Mr. Galsworthy. In these writers are felt always the stirrings of a new social and religious world. Even when—as in "Ann Veronica"—the medium is one of gentle ridicule or irony, the new spirit is found just the same. As for Mr. Galsworthy, his work is saturated with social and religious speculation of the kind I am describing: his characters move always in an atmosphere of awakened social consciousness that is the special contribution of the creator. Our novelists still cling to the old individualistic string,—the story of the triumphant industrial pirate and his adventures with the stock market and incidentally womankind. Socialism, for instance, which in many of its protean manifestations is surely religious, is scarcely tolerated in the American novel. Our imaginative writers in ignoring it display the same ignorance of its meaning as have our two ex-Presidents in their published utterances.

In the third place, there is our prudery in the sex realm. This attitude was perfectly expressed recently in a little essay by one of "The Outlook" pundits, in which he said with a good deal of moral unction that Americans would not tolerate in their literature the treatment of "certain subjects." Ours had been always a "pure literature" he boasted, and seemed to imply that our social life was peculiarly free from certain forms of vice due to a lax attitude on the sex question. Our literature has certainly been an emasculated literature, if that is what he means by "pure." As a matter of statistical fact, of which we are becoming painfully aware, American civilization is by no means as free from sexual vice as the editor of "The Outlook" would have us assume, even among the superior classes that make the typical American home. The vice reports of New York and Chicago have wakened us to the meaning of our increased public expenditure for asylums for the blind and feebleminded, which even the newer western States are forced to maintain. All this would seem to indicate that as a people we must squarely face sex questions, and there is much evidence of our will to do so. Of course, the recognition of sex problems in novels is another matter, and it is not my intention to debate at length that threadbare topic of the proper treatment of sex in literature. The only arguments that are of importance on either side are specific instances of sex relations described by novelists, and this is not the place for such an extended discussion. It is obvious to me that a literature which persistently ignores any subject of considerable human interest is an imperfect and superficial literature. That is exactly what we have tried to do in America, what the editor of "The Outlook" prides himself on our novelists having done successfully in regard to sex—with the result that our more intelligent people read with apparent interest and profit English and German books that deal with the subject from the modern point of view. That amiable generation of Americans who preferred to look the other way when any perplexing or "dangerous" topic was broached and preserved an unspotted optimism by strenuously refusing to use their intelligence on "certain subjects," is fast disappearing, fortunately. Our magazines are still hypocritical, for magazine editors are a timid race. But our press is frank enough and hopelessly vulgar about all sorts of sex matters. What we need is the same honest, unwavering, unsqueamish treatment of this eternal human subject as of any other.

Nobody denies that sex is of profound importance in life. Probably more than half of the larger issues of living are affected in one way or another by the sex impulse—at least are colored by it. One can't persistently ignore half life, or give a sentimentally false interpretation to its phenomena with any hope of creating a human literature of enduring significance. It is easy to be misunderstood in this delicate ground, for we have somehow tied up four-fifths of our morality in sex prohibitions, and any statement in opposition to the conventional beliefs about sex at once arouses suspicion of gross immorality. No serious writer believes in encouraging "boudoir literature," which is unhealthy, nor in the deliberate exploitation of sex "problems" for the sensation that may be found in them. But he should not be forced by a prudish and fearful public opinion, which is not the opinion of the public, into dodging the sex side of life when it comes inevitably into the picture as I believe it must. There is, of course, the "young person." But the young man, if he reads at all, should read what his elders do, and as for the young woman, she will get less harm from "Madame Bovary" than from perusing one of our sentimental boy-and-girl serial stories. Unless she were neurotic and degenerate, she would get from Flaubert's masterpiece a truthful picture of sex relations that should give her a profound horror of emotional indulgence. From the American book she might get an entirely false conception of the healthy relations of the sexes, from which some day she must awake, possibly with a rude shock of experience. And in either case, man or woman, the young person must face the facts of life, no matter how much we sterilize the reading. All we need is more honesty in this matter, and that it seems to me we are fast learning, to the advantage of our novels and also of our essential morality.

Lastly, for a democratic people, as we call ourselves, we have a singularly unreal and aristocratic literature. The preoccupation of our popular novelists with the lives and the possessions of the rich, who perforce are our aristocrats, is something amazing. Even that much read novel "The House of Mirth," which came near being the woman's epic of our day, betrays this unbalanced absorption in the lives of the privileged, with little or no shading of the commoner experience. American women must be held responsible for this aristocratic taste. They are still by far the chief reading public, and they prefer books about rich and luxurious people. Their favorite epic still remains the old barbaric one of the triumphant male who conquers the riches and the powers of this earth, only to lay them at the feet of his loved one, chivalrously surrounding her with all the glories of his conquest, and rewarded by her with faithfulness and love. Another less childish epic is already emerging into sight—that of woman making her struggle for life and accomplishment, conquering in an honorably equal strife with her male comrades. Why does not some woman write that epic for us? The fact that our novels are written largely by women and for the entertainment of women, is in itself a weakening element in our literature. It would be idle to champion a male literature as opposed to a feminine one, but our literature should represent both sexes and interest both sexes. The man's conception of life ought to interest women, and what the woman feels about it ought to interest men—if true and not merely sentimental.

To return for a moment to the aristocratic aspect of our novels, wealth has been the great American fact for the past generation—the making, the conquest, the control, the disposal of money. The figures that have fascinated the imagination of our people have been the forceful men who have taken, often ruthlessly, what they wanted out of life, who have directed the economic energies of the race. The capitalist has been both our buccaneer and our epic hero. So we had for a time a great many business novels that described commercial struggles and money conquests. But this rich material of the pioneer days of capitalism was largely wasted: it never gave us one great epic figure, enduring, illustrative for all time of our predatory period. The future American will have to go to the magazine biographies of Gould, Rockefeller, Harriman, or Morgan to get the epic, not to our novels. The pity of it! For it was the one big theme of the past twenty years—the story of the money-maker, his inner meaning and his self-explanation. We are already passing out of that period of towering industrial creators: we have come to the era of luxury and trustee-ship—the family life of wealth in the second and third generations. And what we get of them in our novels is a profusion of motors, country houses,—Palm Beach and Fifth Avenue. We do not get the stories of the little people, and they make up the living of most of our ninety millions. As I have said in my previous articles, our writers belong to the old stocks; perhaps they too have been easily prosperous. The little people—not necessarily the submerged elements of society—have got themselves abundantly into modern English novels. It is often said that the experiences of the ordinary citizen are tame and his soul commonplace. The test of real imagination is the power to find the significant beneath the commonplace. At any rate, a literature to be truly national must concern itself with more than the prosperous classes—especially in a democratic society!

On these four grounds, then, among others, I find the American novel to-day lacking in importance, not really representative of our richest and most significant life. I find it thin and impermanent—and not a little shoddy. Naturally, in dealing with such a subject in this broad and generalized fashion, I am aware that I have ignored certain instances of genuine worth—signs, let us hope, of a fuller, richer development for our imaginative literature. It is a matter of private judgment with all of us as to how far I may be correct in estimating the trend of the current, as to how significant the scattered instances of serious effort to create less superficially may be. Unfortunately in America it must always be an affair of private judgment. For we have no criticism of literature worth the name. Criticism along with much else has been handed over to the daily newspaper. Our few journals professedly devoted to literary criticism have slight vogue and practically no weight in the utterance of their opinions. We have had no critic of recognized reputation since Lowell and seem in no haste to produce one. Our literary criticism remains a haphazard affair of personal taste, enormously laudatory, cocksure, and ignorant of all but the season's grist of books. Just how far this state of things may be another ground for our inadequate creative performance it would be hard to say. Under the circumstances, the wisest course for the imaginative writer to pursue is to ignore all so-called criticism and do his best in his own way, untroubled by journalistic chatter.

Thus far I have been oliged to dwell rather insistently upon the negative side of the situation; and before concluding, it would be well to glance at the other side and try to see what there is of hope for us in gettting a more vital, a more representative presentation of ourselves as a people in the imaginative record. There is, of course, much to be said on this side. Our reading public has expanded enormously of recent years, in spite of the motor car, and has become more discriminating and more intelligent as well as better educated. If it were not true that we are gaining in intelligence and discrimination, it would be depressing for us to go on pouring out of our colleges each year tens of thousands of young men and women, who presumably have made some acquaintence with ideas and formed some standards of judgment. The fact that the reading public tends to split up into many different circles, each one demanding its own kind of imaginative food, is another healthy sign of progress, although it has undoubtedly cut down the huge sales of a few popular books. The demand for the works of the more advanced foreign authors, which is now quite considerable in this country, is also an encouraging sign, because an appetite for mature and virile literature once formed cannot be satisfied with froth and frivol. To-day in all our book stores are found the plays and novels of writers that a few years ago had to be imported specially from Europe. More broadly suggestive than these signs is the evidence of general improvement in the intellectual grasp of our people: they are thinking on tough political and economic problems, trying to realize themselves in this twentieth-century life, and the longer they do that the more insistently will they demand that life as they perceive it be portrayed in the fiction offered them. If it cannot be said that in general the tone of our amusements has become more elevated, it is certainly possible to satisfy occasionally a more exacting taste at our theatres than ever before. Nothing moves by itself in modern society. Every interest helps in some way every other interest. To make a literature intelligent and virile, there must first be an intelligent and open-minded public, and somehow one feels that we are getting that faster than we are getting the literature. For we await the writer or writers keen enough to perceive the opportunity, powerful enough to interest the public in what it has been unwilling to heed, and of course endowed with sufficient insight to comprehend our big new world.

The material in that world is crying for expression—as rich human material as the creative artist has ever had. In place of the narrow individualistic epic of the "captain of industry," we have the social struggle. That struggle is already expressing itself confusedly in our political life, and from it must emerge picturesque and powerful types suggestive to the novelist. Hitherto our novels have scarcely dabbled in politics because for the most part we as a people have merely dabbled in politics. We are beginning now to understand that modern social life must be largely political, that each and all, including women, must take a hand in politics if we are to make our destiny something nearer the ideal than our fathers have made theirs. Already our political life is putting upon the screen certain enticing figures for artistic interpretation—not great heroes, perhaps, but Americans spotted with the weaknesses of our civilization and terribly human. Their types should not be lost in the ephemeral columns of the newspapers. As our less favored classes become more expressive, we may hope to hear from them and have imaginative pictures of those who have lived all their lives in the treadmill of American industrialism. Certain magazine studies of men and women in factory life are the harbingers of a more epic treatment of the labor subject. Our literature will not continue to ignore for another twenty years the daily lives and spiritual experiences of four-fifths of the people, nor of all those of stranger blood whom fate has placed in our social system. In this way, I foresee our novels coming to include the larger interests which occupy the thoughts of many of us. It will not be necessarily a "problem" or "thesis" literature: the imaginative writer ought never to make a propaganda of his social beliefs. But he should represent men and women as they are in the struggle of modern life, actuated by the serious ideas and ideals of their time, not solely as sentimental puppets preoccupied with getting married.

This leads me to another class of great themes that awaits the modern writer—women, the emergence and the transformation of women. We sentimentalize a good deal as a people over the position of American women, but in our literature, at any rate, we treat them conventionally. Yet everyone knows that the status of women in the world has changed, and what is even more significant to my thinking, the self-consciousness of women is changing rapidly. They are thinking differently about themselves from what their mothers ever thought. The suffrage agitation is comparatively unimportant or rather merely one prominent straw on the stream that marks the current. Of much more immediate significance is the way in which women are being absorbed in the economic machine of our industrialism, as breadwinners, as competitors of men, and in the freer strata of society as independent creators. All this must change profoundly the inner life of the sex and the attitude of men and women towards each other. The emancipation of women that the suffrage agitators harp upon is coming all the time, not so much through obtaining the vote as through their growing ability to compete with men in the conditions of modern civilization, and to make a strong, independent life in cooperation with men, apart from a merely sex or sentimental relationship. Nothing is more thrilling in our life to-day than the struggles of women to win this superior sort of freedom, to become the real equals of men. Why, then, do not our novelists, especially our women novelists, celebrate this epic of their sex? They should give us these newer women, with their changing attitude towards life and especially towards the sex relation and the family. They should not leave this topic, most vital to them of all, to the funny paper and the ridicule of the obtuse male—not even to Mr. Wells. Again, the magazine writers have discovered the riches of this field. Miss Jane Addams's series of papers entitled "An Ancient Evil and a New Conscience," is an example—it offers vivid glimpses of many human women stories. No one can stand in our city streets mornings and evenings and watch the hurrying throng of working women without feeling that a wealth of imaginative material lies here close at hand, if we only knew the daily experiences, the life stories of these women units in the struggle. Thus far the school-teacher and the woman stenographer who marries her employer are the only permanent types of the industrial woman that our novelists have availed themselves of.

Nothing has yet been said about the technique of the modern American novel. The style and the special form that his material takes in the hands of the artist are, of course, of absorbing importance to the creator, and should be his constant preoccupation. But they must be always secondary to the quality of his vision. As a matter of fact, our writers are skillful rather than original or distinguished workmen in the novelist's art. The improvement in form in our ordinary magazine fiction has been marked of late years. The standard of technical accomplishment is being pushed up all the time. But however interesting and important style and form and facility may be to the writer, they are negligible in comparison with the matters I have tried to discuss—theme and spirit and ideas. I have no fear but that we shall always produce clever and graceful writers. It is more essential that they should have the seeing eye and the comprehending soul than the practised pen.

If our stories are for the most part superficial and sentimental and ephemeral fancies, we as audience must all take our share of the blame, because with our national impatience, our eagerness to be amused at any cost, we demand sensation and entertainment from all our art. The "tired business man" argument that has encouraged musical comedy may be sufficient to justify a fatuous stage, but it does not create a strong and enduring literature. We must become strongminded enough to find interest—the keenest interest—in ideas, in the use of our minds apart from any utilitarian purpose, Recreation should not mean sodden sensuality nor mere distraction. The "tired business man" should take a lesson from modern psychology and learn that rest comes as much from change of mental occupation as from mere vacuity of mind. Preaching on such matters, however, never made a convert. It must remain to the imaginative writer to make his epic tale of life so true, so vivid that it will complete in interest with the newspaper and the magazine. If he is able to reflect but a small part of our life accurately and convincingly, he will not fail of an audience.

For, as has been said before, we have the richest background in a purely human way that the story-teller ever had offered him. It abounds with new notes of character, of situation, of theme, of human drama. It is religious and pagan, selfish and generous, adventurous and mean, sordid and splendid,—at one and the same time. Our novels should reveal all that. They should reflect not merely the lives of the successful, the predatory, the indulgent, but also the lives of the small, the struggling, the obscure. They should give us not simply the sensual atmosphere of prodigal spenders, but the strong religious impulses moving in new ways to sanctify our lives. I say our novels—not *the* American novel, which is a figment of the newspaper critic's imagination. The newspaper critic seems distressed because he cannot find one book that displays all these powers and riches. He complacently discovers *the* American novel each season—the one that most nearly pleased him of the last consignment. Every year a number of these discoveries are proclaimed to be *the* American novel—the epic masterpiece of our civilization. But they quickly fall back into the ranks.

The truth is that we are not yet ready for the masterpiece, if we ever shall be,—if, indeed, one epic, no matter how splendid, will ever serve for the complete record. Before that appears we must have developed a truly national spirit: our society must have a greater solidarity. We must be clearer about what we want to do, what we think about momentous matters, where we stand as a people. We must lose that excessive consciousness of our individualism that characterizes us now, and become more conscious of our nationalism. When in spirit and in purpose we are truly national, we shall doubtless create a national literature. The local and the individual will be merged in the broader type of the nation. Then we may speak of the American novel.   [1914]

Edith Wharton

....

The Great American Novel

What exactly is meant by that term of "American novel" on which American advertisers and reviewers lay an equal and ever-increasing stress—a stress unparalleled in the literary language of other countries?

To European critics the term "great English" or "great French" novel signifies merely a great novel written by an English or a French novelist; and the greatest French or English novel would be the greatest novel yet produced in one or the other of these literatures. It might be, like "La Chartreuse de Parme" (assuredly one of the greatest of French novels), a tale of eighteenth-century Italian life; or, as in the case of "Lord Jim" or "Nostromo" or "Kim," its scene might be set on the farther side of the globe; it would none the less be considered typical of the national genius that went to its making, as, for example, "La Tentation de Saint Antoine" and "Salammbô" of Flaubert are so considered, though the one is situated in Egypt in the sixth century of the Christian era and the other in Carthage, B.C. 150, or as "The Wrecker" or "The Ebb-tide" must be regarded, though the life described in them has so largely an exotic setting. In the opinion of European critics only one condition is needful to make a novel typical of the country of its origin: that its writer should possess, in sufficient richness, the characteristics of his race. "John Inglesant" is not considered less typically English than "Lorna Doone" because it ranges through a cosmopolitan world reaching from the Tiber to the Thames while the other tale concerns the intensely local lives of a handful of peasants in the west of England.

Wharton, Edith. "The Great American Novel," *The Yale Review,* 16 (1927), pp. 646–656.

It would appear that in the opinion of recent American reviewers the American novelist must submit to much narrower social and geographical limitations before he can pretend to have produced *the* (or *the greatest,* or even simply *an*) American novel; indeed the restrictions imposed appear to differ only in kind from those to which a paternal administration subjects drinkers of wine, wearers of short skirts, and upholders of the evolutionary hypothesis. The range allotted is so narrow that the feat of producing the "greatest" American novel, if ever accomplished, will rank the author with the music-hall artist who is locked and corded into a trunk, and then expected to get out of it in full view of his audience.

First of all, the novelist's scene must be laid in the United States, and his story deal exclusively with citizens of those States; furthermore, if his work is really to deserve the epithet "American," it must tell of persons so limited in education and opportunity that they live cut off from all the varied sources of culture which used to be considered the common heritage of English-speaking people. The great American novel must always be about Main Street, geographically, socially, and intellectually.

In an address made not long ago Mr. Kipling cited the curious fate of certain famous books which, surviving the conditions that produced them, have become to later generations something utterly different from what their authors designed, or their original readers believed, them to be. The classic examples are "The Merchant of Venice," a rough-and-tumble Jew-baiting farce to Shakespeare's contemporaries, and "Don Quixote," composed by Cervantes, and accepted by his public, as a gently humorous parody of the picaresque novel of the day; but Mr. Kipling found a still more striking instance in "Gulliver's Travels," fiercest and most brutal of social satires when it was written, and now one of the favorites of the nursery.

Some such fate, in a much shorter interval, has befallen Mr. Sinclair Lewis's "Main Street," that pioneering work which with a swing of the pen hacked away the sentimental vegetation from the American small town, and revealed Main Street as it is, with all its bareness in the midst of plenty. The novel was really epoch-making; but the epoch it made turned into something entirely different from what its author purposed. Mr. Lewis opened the eyes of the millions of dwellers in all the American Main Streets to the inner destitution of their lives, but by so doing apparently created in them not the desire to destroy Main Street but only to read more and more and ever more about it. The dwellers in Main Street proved themselves to be like the old ladies who send for the doctor every day for the pleasure of talking over their symptoms. They do not want to be cured; they want to be noticed.

It must not be regarded as diminishing Mr. Lewis's achievement to remind his readers that he was not the first discoverer of Main Street. Over thirty years ago, Robert Grant situated "Unleavened Bread" in the same thoroughfare; and so, a little later, did Frank Norris his "McTeague," and Graham Phillips his "Susan Lenox"—and they were all, as it happens, not only "great American novels," but great novels. But they came before their time, their bitter taste frightened a public long nurtured on ice-cream soda and marshmallows, and a quick growth of oblivion was trained over the dreary nakedness of the scene they had exposed. It was necessary that a later pioneer should arise and clear this vegetation away again, and if Mr. Lewis had done no more than demolish the tottering stage-fictions of a lavender-scented New England, a chivalrous South, and a bronco-busting West he would have rendered a great service to American fiction. This having been accomplished, however, it is permissible to wonder whether, as a theme, Main Street—in a literary sense—has not received as much notice as its width and length will carry, or even more. The difficulty is that it is now established as a canon, a first principle in the laws of American fiction; and thence it will be difficult to dislodge it.

The term is of course used to typify something much more extended, geographically, than Mr. Lewis's famous thoroughfare. "Main Street" has come to signify the common mean of American life anywhere in its million cities and towns, its countless villages and immeasurable wildernesses. It stands for everything which does not rise above a very low average in culture, situation, or intrinsic human interest; and also for every style of depicting this dead level of existence, from the photographic to the pornographic—sometimes inclusively.

The novelist's—any novelist's—proper field, created by his particular way of apprehending life, is limited only by the bounds of his natural, his instinctive interests. The writer who sees life in terms of South Sea cannibals, as Herman Melville did, will waste his time (as, incidentally, Melville did) if he tries to depict it as found in drawing-rooms and conservatories; though this by no means implies that the cannibal is intrinsically a richer and more available subject than the inhabitant of drawing-rooms. No subject is foreign to the artist in which there is something corresponding to a something within himself. The famous theory of the "atomes crochus" is as true of affinities between novelist and subject as of those between one human being and another. To the creator the only needful preliminary to successful expression is to have in him the root of the matter to be expressed.

Nevertheless, there remains—there must always remain—the question of the amount and quality of material to be extracted from a given subject. Other things being equal, nothing can alter the fact that a "great argument" will give a greater result than the perpetual chronicling of small beer. And the conditions of modern life in America, so far from being productive of great arguments, seem almost purposely contrived to eliminate them.

America has indeed deliberately dedicated herself to other ideals. What she has chosen—and realized—is a dead level of prosperity and security. Main Street abounds in the unnecessary, but lacks the one thing needful. Inheriting an old social organization which provided for nicely shaded degrees of culture and conduct, modern America has simplifed and Taylorized it out of existence, forgetting that in such matters the process is necessarily one of impoverishment. As she has reduced the English language to a mere instrument of utility (for example, by such simplifications as the substituting of "a wood," or, mysteriously, "a woods," for the innumerable shadings of coppice, copse, spinney, covert, brake, holt, grove, etc.), so she has reduced relations between human beings to a dead level of vapid benevolence, and the whole of life to a small house with modern plumbing and heating, a garage, a motor, a telephone, and a lawn undivided from one's neighbor's.

Great as many be the material advantage of these diffused conveniences, the safe and uniform life resulting from them offers to the artist's imagination a surface as flat and monotonous as our own prairies. If it be argued that the greatest novelists, both French and English, have drawn some of their richest effects from the study of narrow lives and parochial problems, the answer is that Balzac's provincial France, Jane Austen's provincial England, if limited in their external contacts compared to a Main Street linked to the universe by telephone, motor and wireless, nevertheless made up for what they lacked in surface by the depth of the soil in which they grew. This indeed is still true of the dense old European order, all compounded of differences and *nuances,* all interwoven with intensities and reticences, with passions and privacies, inconceivable to the millions brought up in a safe, shallow, and shadowless world. It is because we have chose to be what Emerson called "mixed of middle clay" that we offer, in spite of all that patriotism may protest to the contrary, so meagre a material to the imagination. It is not because we are middle-class but because we are middling that our story is so soon told.

Another reason is to be found precisely in that universal facility of communication, the lack of which might seem to have made the life of Balzac's narrow towns all the narrower. In fact, that life was not only fed from the deep roots of the past, the long confused inheritance of feudalism, burgherdom, diocesan and monastic influences, the activities of the guilds, the dogged labors of the peasants, and the fervors of an ornate religion; it had, besides, the concentrated flavor which comes of long isolation. Bad roads, slow communications, dangers from flood and foe, all these factors, for generations, for centuries, combined to make of each little town a hot-bed for its own idiosyncrasies. Even in the English novels of Trollope's day, a day so much airier and more sanitated, the weight of a long past, and the comparative isolation of each social group, helped to differentiate the dull people, and to give a special color to each of their humdrum backgrounds. Only when mediocrity has achieved universal diffusion does it become completely unpaintable.

Nothing is less easy to standardize then the curve of an artist's secret affinities; (but literary criticism in modern America is a perpetual incentive to standardization). The public (as everywhere and always) likes best what it has had before; the magazine editor encourages the young writer to repeat his effects; and the critic urges him to confine himself to the protrayal of life in the American small town—or in New York or Chicago as viewed from the small-town angle.

Still more insistent is the demand of reviewers that the novelist shall deal only with what the wife of one of our late Presidents touchingly described as "just folks." The idea that genuineness is to be found only in the rudimentary, and that whatever is complex is unauthentic, is a favorite axiom of the modern American critic. To students of natural history such a theory is somewhat disconcerting. The tendency of all growth, animal, human, social, is towards an ever-increasing complexity. The mere existence of art as a constant form of human expression, the recurring need of it shown by its reappearance in every age of history, proves man's inherent inability to live by bread alone. Traditional society, with its old-established distinctions of class, its pass-words, exclusions, delicate shades of language and behavior, is one of man's oldest works of art, the least conscious and the most instinctive; yet the modern American novelist is told that the social and educated being is an unreality unworthy of his attention, and that only the man with the dinner-pail is human, and hence available for his purpose.

Mr. Van Wyck Brooks makes much of Howells's resonant but empty reply to Henry James's complaint that there was little material for the novelist in a rudimentary social order: "There is the whole of human nature!" But what does "human nature" thus denuded consist in, and how much of it is left when it is separated from the web of custom, manners, culture it has elaborately spun about itself? Only that hollow unreality, "Man," an evocation of the eighteenth-century demagogues who were the first inventors of "standardization." As to real men, unequal, unmanageable, and unlike each other, they are all bound up with the effects of climate, soil, laws, religion, wealth—and, above all, leisure. Leisure, itself the creation of wealth, is incessantly engaged in transmuting wealth into beauty by secreting the surplus energy which flowers in great architecture, great painting, and great literature. Only in the atmosphere thus engendered floats that impalpable dust of ideas which is the real culture. A colony of ants or bees will never create a Parthenon.

It is a curious, and deeply suggestive, fact that America's acute literary nationalism has developed in inverse ratio to the growth of modern travelling facilities, and in exact proportion to the very recent Americanism of the majority of our modern literary leaders.

Like all Anglo-Saxons, the old-time Americans came of a wandering, an exploring stock; unlike the Latins, we have never been sedentary except when it was too difficult to get about. Old New York and old New England (owing to this difficulty) sat chiefly at home, and, as Henry James somewhere has it, brightened their leisure by turning the pages of a volume of Flaxman Outlines in a bare parlor looking out on a snowy landscape; but in those steamless and wireless days Poe was letting his fiery fancy range over all heaven and earth, Melville was situating his tales in the tropics, and Hawthorne coloring his with the prismatic hues of a largely imaginary historic past. Our early novelists were, in fact, instinctively choosing those scenes and situations which offered the freest range to their invention, without fear of being repudiated as un-American if they wandered beyond the twelve-mile limit.

America's sedentary days are long since past. The whole world has become a vast escalator, and Ford motors and Gillette razors have bound together the uttermost parts of the earth. The universal infiltration of our American plumbing, dentistry, and vocabulary has reduced the globe to a playing-field for our people; and Americans have been the first to profit by the new facilities of communication which are so largely of their invention and promotion. We have, in fact, internationalized the earth, to the deep detriment of its picturesqueness, and of many far more important things; but the deed is done, the consequences are in operation, and it is at the very moment when America is pouring out her annual millions over the old world that American reviewers and publishers are asking for a portrayal of American life which shall represent us as tethered to the village pump.

It seems as though it would not only be truer to fact but would offer far more lights and shades, more contrasts and juxtapositions, to the novelist, if he depicted the modern American as a sort of missionary-drummer selling his wares and inculcating his beliefs from China to Peru, with all the unexpected (and, to the missionaries, mostly unperceived) reactions produced in the societies thus edified. It is not intended to suggest that the wandering or the expatriate American is the only fit theme for fiction, but that he is peculiarly typical of modern America—of its intense social acquisitiveness and insatiable appetite for new facts and new sights. The germ of European contacts is disseminated among thousands who have never crossed the Atlantic, just as other thousands who have done so remain blissfully immune from it; and to enjoin the modern novelist to depict only New Thermopylae in its pristine purity is singularly to limit his field.

It is doubtful if a novelist of one race can ever really penetrate into the soul of another, and hitherto the attempts to depict foreign character from the inside have resulted in producing figures very much like the Englishman of the French farce, or the Frenchman of "Punch." Even Meredith, James, and Trollope never completely achieved the trick, and their own racial characteristics peep disconcertingly through the ill-fitting disguise. But there is another way of "catching the likeness" of the foreigner, and that is as his idiosyncrasies are reflected in the minds of the novelist's characters who are of the latter's own kin. This is the special field which the nomadic habits of modern life have thrown wide open to the American novelist. Thirty years ago, in attempting this kind of reflected portraiture, he was hampered by the narrowness of the reflecting surface. The travelling American of that day was almost always a mild dilettante en route for the Coliseum or the Château of Chillon; and his contacts with the indigenous were brief and superficial. Now innumerable links of business, pleasure, study, and sport join together the various races of the world. The very novelists who still hug the Main Street supersitition settle down in the Quartier Latin or on the Riviera to write their tales of the little suburban house at number one million and ten Volstead Avenue. And the exploring is no longer one-sided. The same motives which sent more and more Americans abroad now draw an annually increasing number of foreigners to America. This perpetual interchange of ideas and influences is resulting, on both sides of the globe, in the creation of a new world, ephemeral, shifting, but infinitely curious to study and interesting to note, and as yet hardly heeded by the novelist. It is useless, at least for the story-teller, to deplore what the new order of things has wiped out, vain to shudder at what it is creating; there it is, whether for better or worse, and the American novelist, whose compatriots have helped, above all others, to bring it into being, can best use his opportunity by plunging both hands into the motley welter. As the Merry Person says in the Prologue to "Faust": "Wherever you seize it, there it is interesting"—if not in itself, at any rate as a subject for fiction, as a new opening into that "full life of men" which is the proper theme of the novelist's discourse.

The "great American novel" continues to be announced every year; in good years there are generally several of them. But as a rule they turn out to be (at best) only the great American novels of the year. Moreover, the proof of their greatness (according to their advertisers) is usually based on the number of copies sold; and this kind of glory does not keep a book long afloat.

Of really great novels we have hitherto produced fewer than the future traveller from New Zealand will be led to infer from a careful study of our literary statistics; but we have perhaps half a score to our credit, which is something; and another, and the greatest, may come at any moment.

When it does, it will probably turn out to be very different from what the critics counsel, the publishers hope, or the public is accustomed to. Its scene may be laid in an American small town or in a European capital; it may deal with the present or the past, with great events or trivial happenings; but in the latter case it will certainly contrive to relate them to something greater than themselves. The ability to do this is indeed one of the surest signs of the great novelist; and another is that he usually elaborates his work in quietness, and that when it appears there is every chance that it will catch us all napping, that the first year's sales will be disappointingly small, and that event those defatigable mythomaniacs, the writers for the jackets, may for once not be ready with their superlatives.

PART II

* * * * * * * *

MODERN AMERICAN
CRITICISM, 1900–1945

* * * * * * * *

In talking about books—their excellence or mediocrity—American cultural critics could assume an audience that read poetry and fiction avidly and that considered these pursuits significant as both instruction and entertainment. Magazines, literary clubs, poetry journals, and other formal institutions, including author societies and, later, book clubs, were extremely popular ways of participating in what may have been an unprecedentedly literate reading public. By the 1920s, book talk had become so customary that newspapers were developing Sunday review sections. The need for informed opinion about which new books were valuable and which were not had never been so pronounced.

As in the other arts, a class of connoisseurs emerged to meet this need, critics who might be said to replace genteel magazine editors and the clergy in prescribing reading tastes. This cadre of experts included professors as well as intellectuals—that recently designated group of thinkers who wrote on social, literary, political, and cultural matters for opinion and belles-lettres magazines. Both sorts of publications provided venues where critics could express their views about what kinds of writing should be regarded as important and what kinds faddish. Some of these magazines, like *The Nation* (1865) and the *New Republic* (1914), still perform this office of guiding citizens through the social and political ramifications of recent books. Others, once influential, like *The Dial* (1880–1929) or *The Seven Arts* (1916–1917), no longer exist, having served their mission of bringing together, for awhile, some like-minded critics who could make a more forceful collective statement about society, its ideas and their expression, than they could individually.

In introducing literary modernism, these critics followed the tradition of William Dean Howells insofar as they monitored avant-garde writing for the enlightened middle class. One may say that this is the very achievement of Edmund Wilson's first book, *Axel's Castle* (1931), a series of essays that make accessible the complex techniques of some major examples of the new writing—Stein, Proust, Eliot, and Yeats. Wilson went on to write a number of important cultural analyses, blending his talents as a journalist with his capacities as a man of letters. While the memory of his particular accomplishments has faded, he is still recalled, both inside and outside academe, as one of America's enduring "public intellectuals," a critic whose cultural percipience wins a following among people who make their living beyond the university. Yet even while Wilson and such highbrow critics as Ezra Pound and T. S. Eliot were delivering the news about European modernism, other critics, like Randolph Bourne and Van Wyck Brooks, were mediating the changes within U.S. culture, especially in their interpretations of American writers old and new.

For observers on all sides of the political spectrum, Theodore Dreiser proved to be a test case, perhaps even more so than the new evaluations of Henry James or the recent re-

vival of Melville. Critics who sponsored him, like H. L. Mencken, spoke for his democratic virtues—especially his subject matter; critics who opposed his rude "force," like
Stuart Sherman, saw him as the embodiment of the new chaos, the writer who not only
scorned the genteel tradition but whose relentless critique of idealism made the dream of
progress we associate with Victorianism seem impossible as a cultural value. While
Dreiser's modernity had none of the unsettling stylistic difficulties—the disjunctions of
time and the disarrangements of space—that we find in Joyce or Proust or Freud or Picasso or Stravinsky, his aggressive insistence on the primacy of the material world, including the sexual appetite, and his disbelief in such ordering principles as religion or law
made his novels controversial up through the twenties.

The new humanists, like Irving Babbitt and Paul Elmer More, were battling modernists to define cultural possibilities for the "American Century," a conflict much like the
wars of ideas in the previous century over the need to ascertain the merit and character of
a national literature, one that is also akin to contemporary debates about multicultural-
ism, since the argument was over whose critical values would prevail. In the first quarter
of the twentieth century, the stakes were extraordinary. Not only was the face of America
changing amid the new immigration and not only was the new consumer economy being
put into place, but Western culture was undergoing its greatest challenge in the Great
War that raged across Europe. The criticism of literature became one of the primary ways
that citizens could gauge the vitality of a national spirit and thus preserve a sense of the
nation's destiny, even as readers were learning what it meant, in Pound's phrase, to "make
it new."

Eventually, the book critics—whether they were intellectuals or dilettantes—lost their
purchase on the national attention, as fiction and poetry became less favored pastimes and
movies, radio, and, finally, TV surpassed them as popular entertainments. Except for the
newspapers and an ever-diminishing number of magazines, by the 1950s there were fewer
and fewer paying jobs for critics, who then turned to the academy for their living. Actually, it was soon after the Great War that the professional study of American literature first
thrived: initially, through the publication of the *Cambridge History of American Literature*
and then in the formation of a new organization—the American Literature Group (now
called the American Literature Section) within the Modern Language Association, which
professors like Norman Foerster, Clarence Gohdes, and Ernest Leisy had formed to certify
and uphold scholarly standards. That enterprise took shape through the Group's supervi-
sion of publication projects, the regulation of dissertations, and the creation of a journal,
American Literature.

Until this time, the professional study of American letters had been dominated by a vision of history deriving from a New England–based account of the nation's past. From
this perspective, first Moses Coit Tyler and then Barrett Wendell of Harvard wrote influential textbooks that were supposed to record the history of American writing and develop a canon of prestigious forebears. Indeed, much of the intellectual energy in these
textbooks was spent adjudicating who might sit in a pantheon of American greats (and
who was to be considered second-rate). These judgments have sometimes changed with
the years, but the extent to which more recent Americanists have argued about who belongs and who doesn't recalls these initiating impulses. In fact, one of the primary sources
of critical attention that the scholars of the first half of the century paid was to the importance of establishing reliable biographies and then, later, reliable texts, a devotion that
preceded both New Criticism and ideological critique.

For a few years, in the 1920s and 1930s, there existed two real, animating conversations about American letters. The first ensued among critics who, following in the tradi-

tion of Van Wyck Brooks, sought to discover a "usable past" or who, like Ludwig Lewisohn, applied psychoanalytic concepts to the history of U.S. writing. In this first group were also journalist-critics, like V. F. Calverton, Granville Hicks, and Maxwell Geismar, who read American literature through a Marxist framework. No matter what their orientation, such studies were routinely reviewed in magazines and sometimes given pride of place in the newspaper supplements, intended as they were for an audience of potential book buyers. One extremely influential set of literary critics was the group often referred to as the New York or *Partisan Review* intellectuals, in recognition of the bimonthly periodical that followed their arguments about the relation between radical politics and European modernism.

A second discussion occurred among academics, largely through articles but also through books. This conversation was restricted to scholarly concerns: historical and folklore antecedents for plots, dialectology, and biographical studies. These arguments took place away from public view, in professional journals and conferences, since they reflected the enthusiasm of specialists, that new class of researchers invented by the modern university. Generally, the professors and the critics took little notice of each other, though occasionally the two discussions would coincide, as in the rehabilitation of Whitman or the revaluation of Henry James.

The academy made a much more vivid impact on the study of American literature through the somewhat circuitous route of the New Criticism. This mode of reading was developed under the leadership of the poet-critic John Crowe Ransom, who first exerted an influence on American criticism through a manifesto he edited, *I'll Take My Stand* (1930), the introduction of which appears in this volume. One can search a long time in the history of critical opinion in the 1930s to find anyone who took seriously the ideas of the twelve Southerners who contributed to this book, but in retrospect it has acquired an aura as the work that signaled the political—for some, reactionary—character of the critical movement that later dominated English departments in the 1950s and 1960s. Students who are even to this day exhorted to "press the text" and to search for ambiguities might be surprised to learn that they are doing so, according to some contemporary critics, as part of an anti-industrial, pro-sectionalist agenda for 1930s America. That "agrarian" program feared the tumult that modernity promised, especially changes in an economic power structure supporting the planter class in the south. Loosely put, the New Criticism, with its resistance to the propounding of social issues and its aggressive emphasis on formal issues, has been seen to endorse the politics of nostalgia and racist elitism.

The New Critics was Ransom's term for the contemporaries he admired, like the linguist William Empson, the scholar-critic Yvor Winters, and, most important of all, the poet-critic T. S. Eliot (arguably the most influential figure in any history of literary studies in the first half of the twentieth century), who all insisted on reading the literary work, not something else, and responding, in the tradition of Immanuel Kant, to its aesthetic qualities. Unlike the U.S. dons of American literature, they cared less for sources or biography than they did for the rhetorical anlysis of language. For their followers, that insistence sometimes meant the exclusion of history, but this was a misjudgment of the New Critics' original corrective stress on textual reading. The New Critics, led by Ransom's protégés—the scholar-teacher Cleanth Brooks and the novelist-poet, critic, and historian Robert Penn Warren—made sure to propagate their theories in college textbooks, such as *Understanding Poetry* and *Understanding Fiction,* both of which became standard. These books were successful because they accomplished what no previous textbooks could: they disseminated a methodology to be used throughout the country—first at Louisiana State, Yale, and Kenyon College, and then everywhere else. With students learning to concentrate on "literary language"—image clusters, paradoxes, tensions—the professors, now free of cumbersome histories (in an era before large-scale paperbacking), could teach an agreed-upon curriculum, one that valued reading skills and strategies of interpretation rather than the literary impressionism of their predecessors.

The New Criticism was the victim of its success: what began as a democratizing of critical skills became, inadvertently, monolithic. In its first phase, it reinvigorated the discussion of artistic merit and profundity, making that conversation seem like more than a simple matter of taste. For what vitalizes this era, and what makes it seem such a golden age of criticism, is that society did care a great deal about what its writers and critics had to say. In the first half of the twentieth century, especially once the New Criticism established itself, literature was valued widely enough that a class of critics arose, in priestly fashion, to meet the need of interpreting it—eventually via the colleges—to a readership willing to appreciate both the power and complexity of literary art. Usurping the power that during the genteel tradition was often invested in the clergy or the amateur, cultural critics participated in a discussion on several fronts: literature, politics, economics, and social justice. Inevitably, the audience dwindled, and the middlebrow public turned toward entertainments, drawing on the ever-increasing appeal of mass culture, whose main point was often to resist the criticial spirit.

In the midst of the battle over the rights to determine the qualities of U.S. culture, race became a central feature of these debates. For mainstream critics—intellectuals, journalists, and academics alike—the discussion of U.S. culture was inevitably an argument about the relation of American letters to those of Europe, especially of England. American literature was understood to be about Americans of European extraction, especially of Northern and Western European heritages—unsurprisingly so, since the vast majority of the critics of American culture shared this background. Important works, especially anthologies of African-American writing such as those edited by Alain Locke and Sterling Brown, saw print and won notice, but for mainstream critics, American racial identity was just as surely being challenged by the children of the recently arrived immigrants of Eastern and Southern European extraction. Part of the rise of American literary studies in the academy may be said to derive from the urgency of codifying a heritage and transmitting it to these new Americans, or so it seemed in the 1910s and 1920s, when the combination of immigration and the Great War ruptured the U.S. Victorian ideal of harmony and American lit, as a college subject, was given a boost.

While this racial drama was being played out, a more enduring one in U.S. history was continuing to unfold: after years of post-Reconstruction suppression, African-American culture began to reach an ever larger public. Presided over by the magisterial example and instruction of W. E. B. Du Bois, African-American artists in every endeavor established a coherent and recognizable culture beyond, but also including, that of the folk. That such practitioners had always existed was less important than the sense that a "New Negro" had come of age. The writers and artists who argued the case for "cultural equality" spoke both to black people and to white, in such works as Locke's *The New Negro,* Jean Toomer's *Cane,* Langston Hughes' poetry, Nella Larsen's novels, and Zora Neale Hurston's fiction and folklore. By the time Richard Wright scored critical and commercial successes with *Native Son* (1940) and then *Black Boy* (1945), racial identity had entered into the discussion of U.S. culture in ways that Charles Chesnutt, and Pauline Hopkins, and James Weldon Johnson, half a century before, had found impossible. It would be years before critics developed a vocabulary for treating the work of African-American writers, though the early efforts of J. Saunders Redding, Melvin Tolson, and Sterling Brown were estimable beginnings.

W. E. B. Du Bois

The Sorrow Songs

From *The Souls of Black Folk*

> I walk through the churchyard
>   To lay this body down;
> I know moon-rise, I know star-rise;
> I walk in the moonlight, I walk in the starlight;
> I'll lie in the grave and stretch out my arms,
> I'll go to judgment in the evening of the day,
> And my soul and thy soul shall meet that day,
>   When I lay this body down.

Negro Song.

They that walked in darkness sang songs in the olden days—Sorrow Songs—for they were weary at heart. And so before each thought that I have written in this book I have set a phrase, a haunting echo of these weird old songs in which the soul of the black slave spoke to men. Ever since I was a child these songs have stirred me strangely. They came out of the South unknown to me, one by one, and yet at once I knew them as of me and of mine. Then in after years when I came to Nashville I saw the great temple builded of these songs towering over the pale city. To me Jubilee Hall seemed ever made of the songs themselves, and its bricks were red with the blood and dust of toil. Out of them rose for me morning, noon, and night, bursts of wonderful melody, full of the voices of my brothers and sisters, full of the voices of the past.

Little of beauty has America given the world save the rude, grandeur God himself stamped on her bosom; the human spirit in this new world has expressed itself in vigor and ingenuity rather than in beauty. And so by fateful chance the Negro folk-song—the rhythmic cry of the slave—stands today not simply as the sole American music, but as the most beautiful expression of human experience born this side [of] the seas. It has been neglected, it has been, and is, half despised, and above all it has been persistently mistaken and misunderstood; but notwithstanding, it still remains as the singular spiritual heritage of the nation and the greatest gift of the Negro people.

Away back in the thirties the melody of these slave songs stirred the nation, but the songs were soon half forgotten. Some, like "Near the lake where drooped the willow," passed into current airs and their source was forgotten; others were caricatured on the "minstrel" stage and their memory died away. Then in war-time came the singular Port Royal experiment after the capture of Hilton Head, and perhaps for the first time the North met the Southern slave face to face and heart to heart with no third witness. The Sea Islands of the Carolinas, where they met, were filled with a black folk of primitive type, touched and moulded less by the world about them than any others outside the Black Belt. Their appearance was uncouth, their language funny, but their hearts were human and their singing stirred men with a mighty power. Thomas Wentworth Higginson hastened to tell of these songs, and Miss McKim and others urged upon the world their rare beauty. But the world listened only half credulously until the Fisk Jubilee Singers sang the slave songs so deeply into the world's heart that it can never wholly forget them again.

There was once a blacksmith's son born at Cadiz, New York, who in the changes of time taught school in Ohio and helped defend Cincinnati from Kirby Smith. Then he fought at Chancellorsville and Gettysburg, and finally served in the Freedman's Bureau at Nashville. Here he formed a Sunday-school class of black children in 1866, and sang with them and taught them to sing. And then they taught him to sing, and when once the glory of the Jubilee songs passed into the soul of George L. White, he knew his life-work was to let those Negroes sing to the world as they had sung to him. So in 1871 the pilgrimage of the Fisk Jubilee Singers began. North to Cincinnati they rode,—four half-clothed black boys and five girl-women,—led by a man with a cause and a purpose. They stopped at Wilberforce, the oldest of Negro schools, where a black bishop blessed them. Then they went, fighting cold and starvation, shut out of hotels, and cheerfully sneered at, ever northward; and ever the magic of their song kept thrilling hearts, until a burst of applause in the Congregational Council at Oberlin revealed them to the world. They came to New York and Henry Ward Beecher dared to welcome them, even though the metropolitan dailies sneered at his "Nigger Minstrels." So their songs conquered till they sang across the land and across the sea, before Queen and Kaiser, in Scotland and Ireland, Holland and Switzerland. Seven years they sang, and brought back a hundred and fifty thousand dollars to found Fisk University.

Since their day they have been imitated—sometimes well, by the singers of Hampton and Atlanta, sometimes ill, by straggling quartettes. Caricature has sought again to spoil the quaint beauty of the music, and has filled the air with many debased melodies which vulgar ears scarce know from the real. But the true Negro folk-song still lives in the hearts of those who have heard them truly sung and in the hearts of the Negro people.

What are these songs, and what do they mean? I know little of music and can say nothing in technical phrase, but I know something of men, and knowing them, I know that these songs are the articulate message of the slave to the world. They tell us in these eager days that life was joyous to the black slave, careless and happy. I can easily believe this of some, of many. But not all the past South, though it rose from the dead, can gainsay the heart-touching witness of these songs. They are the music of an unhappy people, of the children of disappointment; they tell of death and suffering and unvoiced longing toward a truer world, of misty wanderings and hidden ways.

The songs are indeed the siftings of centuries; the music is far more ancient than the words, and in it we can trace here and there signs of development. My grandfather's grandmother was seized by an evil Dutch trader two centuries ago; and coming to the valleys of the Hudson and Housatonic, black, little, and lithe, she shivered and shrank in the harsh north winds, looked longingly at the hills, and often crooned a heathen melody to the child between her knees, thus:

The child sang it to his children and they to their children's children, and so two hundred years it has travelled down to us and we sing it to our children, knowing as little as our fathers what its words may mean, but knowing well the meaning of its music.

This was primitive African music; it may be seen in larger form in the strange chant which heralds "The Coming of John":

> You may bury me in the East,
> You may bury me in the West,
> But I'll hear the trumpet sound in that morning,

—the voice of exile.

Ten master songs, more or less, one may pluck from this forest of melody—songs of undoubted Negro origin and wide popular currency, and songs peculiarly characteristic of the slave. One of these I have just mentioned. Another whose strains begin this book is "Nobody knows the trouble I've seen." When, struck with a sudden poverty, the United States refused to fulfil its promises of land to the freedmen, a brigadier-general went down to the Sea Islands to carry the news. An old woman on the outskirts of the throng began singing this song; all the mass joined with her, swaying. And the soldier wept.

This third song is the cradle-song of death which all men know—"Swing low, sweet chariot,"—whose bars begin the life story of "Alexander Crummell." Then there is the song of many waters, "Roll, Jordan, roll," a mighty chorus with minor cadences. There were many songs of the fugitive like that which opens "The Wings of Atalanta," and the more familiar "Been a-listening." The seventh is the song of the End and the Beginning—"My Lord, what a mourning! when the stars begin to fall"; a strain of this is placed before "The Dawn of Freedom." The song of groping—"My way's cloudy"—begins "The Meaning of Progress"; the ninth is the song of this chapter—"Wrestlin' Jacob, the day is abreaking,"—a paean of hopeful strife. The last master song is the song of songs—"Steal away,"—sprung from "The Faith of the Fathers."

There are many others of the Negro folk-songs as striking and characteristic as these, as, for instance, the three strains in the third, eighth, and ninth chapters; and others I am sure could easily make a selection on more scientific principles. There are, too, songs that seem to me a step removed from the more primitive types: there is the maze-like medley, "Bright sparkles," one phrase of which heads "The Black Belt"; The Easter carol, "Dust, dust and ashes"; the dirge, "My mother's took her flight and gone home"; and that burst of melody hovering over "The Passing of the First-Born"—"I hope my mother will be there in that beautiful world on high."

These represent a third step in the development of the slave song, of which "You may bury me in the East" is the first, and songs like "March on" and "Steal away" are the second. The first is African music, the second Afro-American, while the third is a blending of Negro music with the music heard in the foster land. The result is still distinctively Negro and the method of blending original, but the elements are both Negro and Caucasian. One might go further and find a fourth step in this development, where the songs of white America have been distinctively influenced by the slave songs or have incorporated whole phrases of Negro melody, as "Swanee River" and "Old Black Joe." Side by side, too, with the growth has gone the debasements and imitations—the Negro "minstrel" songs, many of the "gospel" hymns, and some of the contemporary "coon" songs,—a mass of music in which the novice may easily lose himself and never find the real Negro melodies.

In these songs, I have said, the slave spoke to the world. Such a message is naturally veiled and half articulate. Words and music have lost each other and new and cant phrases of a dimly understood theology have displaced the older sentiment. Once in a while we catch a strange word of an unknown tongue, as the "Mighty Myo," which figures as a river of death; more often slight words or mere doggerel are joined to music of singular sweetness. Purely secular songs are few in number, partly because many of them were turned into hymns by a change of words, partly because the frolics were seldom heard by the stranger, and the music less often caught. Of nearly all the songs, however, the music is distinctly sorrowful. The ten master songs I have mentioned tell in word and music of trouble and exile, of strife and hiding; they grope toward some unseen power and sigh for rest in the End.

The words that are left to us are not without interest, and, cleared of evident dross, they conceal much of real poetry and meaning beneath conventional theology and unmeaning rhapsody. Like all primitive folk, the slave stood near to Nature's heart. Life was a "rough and rolling sea" like the brown Atlantic of the Sea Islands; the "Wilderness" was the home of God, and the "lonesome valley" led to the way of life. "Winter'll soon be over," was the picture of life and death to a tropical imagination. The sudden wild thunderstorms of the South awed and impressed the Negroes,—at times the rumbling seemed to them "mournful," at time imperious:

> My Lord calls me,
> He calls me by the thunder,
> The trumpet sounds it in my soul.

The monotonous toil and exposure is painted in many words. One sees the ploughmen in the hot, moist furrow, singing:

> Dere's no rain to wet you,
> Dere's no sun to burn you,
> Oh, push along, believer,
> I want to go home.

The bowed and bent old man cries, with thrice-repeated wail:

> O Lord, keep me from sinking down,

and he rebukes the devil of doubt who can whisper:

> Jesus is dead and God's gone away.

Yet the soul-hunger is there, the restlessness of the savage, the wail of the wanderer, and the plaint is put in one little phrase:

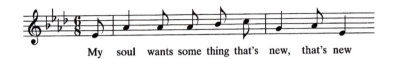

My   soul   wants some thing that's   new,   that's new

Over the inner thoughts of the slaves and their relations one with another the shadow of fear ever hung, so that we get but glimpses here and there, and also with them, eloquent omissions and silences. Mother and child are sung, but seldom father; fugitive and weary wanderer call for pity and affection, but there is little of wooing and wedding; the rocks and the mountains are well known, but home is unknown. Strange blending of love and helplessness sings through the refrain:

> Yonder's my ole mudder,
> Been waggin' at de hill so long;
> 'Bout time she cross over,
> Git home bime-by.

Elsewhere comes the cry of the "motherless" and the "Farewell, farewell, my only child."

Love-songs are scarce and fall into two categories—the frivolous and light, and the sad. Of deep successful love there is ominous silence, and in one of the oldest of these songs there is a depth of history and meaning:

Poor Ro-sy, poor— gal; Poor Ro-sy, poor— gal. Ro-sy break my poor heart. Heav'n shall-a-be my home.

A black woman said of the song, "It can't be sung without a full heart and a troubled sperrit." The same voice sings here that sings in the German folk-song:

> Jetz Geh i' an's brunele, trink' aber net.

Of death the Negro showed little fear, but talked of it familiarly and even fondly as simply a crossing of the waters, perhaps—who knows?—back to his ancient forests again. Later days transfigured his fatalism, and amid the dust and dirt the toiler sang:

> Dust, dust and ashes, fly over my grave,
> But the Lord shall bear my spirit home.

The things evidently borrowed from the surrounding world undergo characteristic change when they enter the mouth of the slave. Especially is this true of Bible phrases. "Weep, O captive daughter of Zion," is quaintly turned into "Zion, weep-a-low," and the wheels of Ezekiel are turned every way in the mystic dreaming of the slave, till he says:

> There's a little wheel a-turnin' in-a-my heart.

As in olden time, the words of these hymns were improvised by some leading minstrel of the religious band. The circumstances of the gathering, however, the rhythm of the songs, and the limitations of allowable thought, confined the poetry for the most part to single or double lines, and they seldom were expanded to quatrains or longer tales, although there are some few examples of sustained efforts, chiefly paraphrases of the Bible. Three short series of verses have always attracted me,—the one that heads this chapter, of one line of which Thomas Wentworth Higginson has fittingly said, "Never, it seems to me, since man first lived and suffered was his infinite longing for peace uttered more plaintively." The second and third are descriptions of the Last Judgment,—the one a late improvisation, with some traces of outside influence:

> Oh, the stars in the elements are falling,
> And the moon drips away into blood,
> And the ransomed of the Lord are returning unto God,
> Blessed be the name of the Lord.

And the other earlier and homelier picture from the low coast lands:

> Michael, haul the boat ashore,
> Then you'll hear the horn they blow,

Then you'll hear the trumpet sound,
Trumpet sound the world around,
Trumpet sound for rich and poor,
Trumpet sound the Jubilee,
Trumpet sound for you and me.

Through all the sorrow of the Sorrow Songs there breathes a hope—a faith in the ultimate justice of things. The minor cadences of despair change often to triumph and calm confidence. Sometimes it is faith in life, sometimes a faith in death, sometimes assurance of boundless justice in some fair world beyond. But whichever it is, the meaning is always clear: that sometime, somewhere, men will judge men by their souls and not by their skins. Is such a hope justified? Do the Sorrow Songs sing true?

The silently growing assumption of this age is that the probation of races is past, and that the backward races of to-day are of proven inefficiency and not worth the saving. Such an assumption is the arrogance of peoples irreverent toward Time and ignorant of the deeds of men. A thousand years ago such an assumption, easily possible, would have made it difficult for the Teuton to prove his right to life. Two thousand years ago such dogmatism, readily welcome, would have scouted the idea of blond races ever leading civilization. So wofully unorganized is sociological knowledge that the meaning of progress, the meaning of "swift" and "slow" in human doing, and the limits of human perfectability, are veiled, unanswered sphinxes on the shores of science. Why should Æschylus have sung two thousand years before Shakespeare was born? Why has civilization flourished in Europe, and flickered, flamed, and died in Africa? So long as the world stands meekly dumb before such questions, shall this nation proclaim its ignorance and unhallowed prejudices by denying freedom of opportunity to those who brought the Sorrow Songs to the Seats of the Mighty?

Your country? How came it yours? Before the Pilgrims landed we were here. Here we have brought our three gifts and mingled them with yours: a gift of story and song—soft, stirring melody in an ill-harmonized and unmelodious land; the gift of sweat and brawn to beat back the wilderness, conquer the soil, and lay the foundations of this vast economic empire two hundred years earlier than your weak hands could have done it; the third, a gift of the Spirit. Around us the history of the land has centred for thrice a hundred years; out of the nation's heart we have called all that was best to throttle and subdue all that was worst; fire and blood, prayer and sacrifice, have billowed over this people, and they have found peace only in the altars of the God of Right. Nor has our gift of the Spirit been merely passive. Actively we have woven ourselves with the very warp and woof of this nation,—we fought their battles, shared their sorrow, mingled our blood with theirs, and generation after generation have pleaded with a headstrong, careless people to despise not Justice, Mercy, and Truth, lest the nation be smitten with a curse. Our song, our toil, our cheer, and warning have been given to this nation in blood-brotherhood. Are not these gifts worth the giving? Is not this work and striving? Would America have been America without her Negro people?

Even so is the hope that sang in the songs of my fathers well sung. If somewhere in this whirl and chaos of things there dwells Eternal Good, pitiful yet masterful, then anon in His good time America shall rend the Veil and the prisoned shall go free. Free, free as the sunshine trickling down the morning into these high windows of mine, free as yonder fresh young voices welling up to me from the caverns of brick and mortar below— swelling with song, instinct with life, tremulous treble and darkening bass. My children, my little children, are singing to the sunshine, and thus they sing:

Let us cheer the wea - ry trav - el - ler.____

Cheer the wea - ry trav-el-ler. Let us cheer the wea - ry

trav - el - ler A - long the heav-en - ly way.

And the traveller girds himself, and sets his face toward the Morning, and goes his way.

THE AFTER-THOUGHT

Hear my cry, O God the Reader; vouchsafe that this my book fall not still-born into the world-wilderness. Let there spring, Gentle One, from out its leaves vigor of thought and thoughtful deed to reap the harvest wonderful. (Let the ears of a guilty people tingle with truth, and seventy millions sign for the righteousness which exalteth nations, in this drear day when human brotherhood is mockery and a snare.) Thus in Thy good time may infinite reason turn the tangle straight, and these crooked marks on a fragile leaf be not indeed.   [1903]

Gertrude Atherton

Why Is American Literature Bourgeois?

American literature after its first natural imitation of Old-World standards showed for a time a disposition to take its cue from the Declaration of Independence. In reading the state papers of the great men of the first era of the Republic—Hamilton, Madison, Jefferson, and the rest—one sees plainly the influence of the "Spectator"; and even Hawthorne and Poe, to say nothing of the Boston groups, and Washington Irving, might never have breathed the free air of a young republic. Cooper was American in nothing but choice of subject. But when Mark Twain and Bret Harte appeared, then indeed we had produced two authors who could have been born and nourished nowhere else on the planet.

Mark Twain, in particular, was so intensely individual, so rampantly—one may say without disrespect—American, that it must have seemed, to those watching what was then the lawn rather than the field of literature in the United States, that the new force was destined to redirect the whole course of American letters. He might indeed have been apprehended as a mighty hose or hydraulic pump, washing the very earth out of the carefully trimmed beds on the lawn. As one looks back to-day, it seems almost incredible that his uncommon and instantly popular methods, his quite unconscious disdain of petty conventions, his convincing expression of the best as well as the most salient of our national characteristics, did not immediately found a school. Even the facts that the true greatness of his intellect was not appreciated, and that he let Cupid severely alone, are not a sufficient explanation of the riddle of his standing apart to-day. Neither does his originality explain it: other original writers have founded their schools. At least his triumphs might have encouraged the young to be as free and individual as himself, even if more slenderly equipped as to creative power: it is not the imitators, of course, who count in the final summing up of literary achievement, almost sure as they are to win temporary success by adhering to the footprints of some leader whom the critic knows it is safe to praise. If Twain ever had so much as an imitator—barring mere humorists—I never heard of him. Harte had many, but they are forgotten. But that is not the point. What is truly remarkable is the fact that the brilliant success of these two men did not remind others that originality is the final and supreme touch which secures an artist a permanent position on the heights, which commands forever the attention of the intelligent masses below.

As a rule, originality has a hard fight, for those who write of writers are, necessarily, unoriginal, and, therefore, no matter how conscientious, timid about endorsing a bold deviation from long established standards. But Twain and Harte had no struggle for recognition, from the public at least. No one remembers today what their critics wrote; all the world knows of their success. Undoubtedly, there were reasons for this, quite aside from their worth, and it would be unfair not to state them: Twain published his first books by subscription, and was already a personality; Harte published in his own magazine, "The Overland Monthly." Both from the start were independent of editors and reviewers. But if this explains their skilful avoidance of the average great author's weary bystanding at the public portals, it by no means explains their failure to encourage others.

American literature to-day, taking it as a whole, taking no account of its strangely few exceptions, is the most timid, the most anæmic, the most lacking in individualities, the most bourgeois, that any country has ever known. There is not a breath of American independence, impatience, energy, contempt of ancient convention in it. It might, indeed, be the product of a great village censored by the village gossip. How utterly unrepresentative it is may be seen by holding it up to contrast with the general trend and conduct of American affairs, political, financial, commercial, with all that is typical of what has come to be recognized as the genius of the American race. Compare it with the bold defiance of the weak and scattered colonies who rose against a mighty nation; with the group of men who literally evolved another nation out of their own brains; with the fierce love of liberty and determination to realize their unique independence which has characterized this country for a century and a quarter. Compare it even with the enterprise of the four men, who, with a few thousand dollars in their pockets, projected and carried to triumphant conclusion the great Central Pacific Railway. These four men have been accused of all the crimes, and perhaps they were guilty of them; but the fact remains that they were men of a magnificent audacity, and that they conferred an inestimable blessing on the United States. Compare our literary intelligence with the boldness and dynamic energy of the American race in general, and of thousands in particular, who in the last thirty years alone have made the progress of this country phenomenal in the history of nations. To-day, we are more feared, hated, and admired than any country on the two hemispheres—with the possible exception of England. We are a synonym in Europe*—which knows little of our literature and cares less—for cleverness of a new order; for all that is unique, startling, unexpected; for dangerous and unfathomed power; for a personality so original that we are thought of as a mass rather than as individuals of varying mental and social degree. Above all, we are envied because of our personal liberty, our divorce courts, our notorious attitude of standing on our own feet and bidding the rest of the world like us or let us alone.

Up to a certain point they understand us; and they have not derived their enlightenment from our fiction. European women sneer at American women, but envy them. The women of the upper and professional classes of the Old World may be more deeply educated, more elaborately accomplished than ours, more intellectual, through their life-long association with men of affairs, through dwelling in an atmosphere where cleverness and intellect are the final seals of distinction; but the dash of the American woman, born of the spirit of independence, too often puts them out of court. Full of knowledge, as distinct from mere information, they sit dumb and discontented before the rush of the American tongue—when unaccented—and, no doubt, long for the time when Europe shall be quite Americanized.

It would seem almost superfluous to wonder what would be a European's reply if one asked him what parallel he found between those of our men whom he regards as typical—such men as Roosevelt, Piermont Morgan, Yerkes, Cleveland, or even Croker—between our imminent financial supremacy, our devouring commercial inroads, our gigantic trusts violating many laws, our colossal strikes, our utter contempt for the survival of the monarchical superstition in the Old World—and our literature. Where *is* the parallel? And where shall we seek the cause of this temporary misrepresentation of the most original and audacious country the world has ever known? I use the word temporary with aforethought, for phenomena have appeared recently which would have been quite impossible a few years ago. The public would seem to be disentangling itself from leading strings, rebellion is in the air, much that provoked loud protest a few years ago is now accepted as a matter of course, and there are signs everywhere that, in the course of another

---

*Geographically, Europe may include England, but to the modern habit of thought, at least, it is "England and Europe."

generation, we shall have discarded our Puritanism, and have grown into a broad tolerant, and no less virtuous race. But habit is hard to kill, and we may count upon a persistence of the present order of things for some time to come, and in spite of the occasional success achieved without the sanction of the American literary powers.

In the late eighties, when I began to indulge in coherent dreams of the literary career, I cut from some weekly newspaper, or magazine, a picture of Mr. Howells's study, pasted it on cardboard, enthroned it upon my desk. At this time he was the controlling force in American letters—James was a sort of wayward younger brother; and although Mr. Howells's novels dealt too much with the small side of daily life to appeal to my temperament and demands, I read them dutifully, with becoming humility; for California—when you are there—seems a planet away from the great centres, which loom, with their famous ones, high in the glowing fancy. I had made no study of literary conditions at that time—enthusiastic young writers who are equally sincere never do; but I caught the Howells fever and was even a little awed. Alas! my first book, written on that very desk, written in the very shadow of Mr. Howells's study, was perhaps the wildest contribution which has been made to American fiction. I shall not mention its name, and I sincerely hope it is forgotten. But it convinced me that I should waste time did I indulge in the hope of becoming a member of the Howells school. Its four years of wandering before it reached a doubtful haven, the universal disapproval it provoked, the frank statements that I was not wanted, and had best leave the field at once, before my battered remains were removed to potter's field, the widely copied paraphrase of a line of George Eliot: "If this is originality give us 'the millionth book in superfluous herds,'" failed to transplant me into the straight and narrow way; for the one good reason that with this track nothing in me claimed affinity. Even had I been so poor-spirited as to make the attempt, certain literary phenomena would have called a halt, bidding me meditate upon the fallibility of the powers. In the first place, several novels, notably "The Story of a Country Town," hailed as little less than great, were even by this time quite forgotten, and their authors already mute. In the second place, my book being a tale of metempsychosis had been refused, many times with manifest annoyance, on the ground that the public would not for a moment consider such a preposterous subject; yet, shortly after its appearance, the market was flooded with the "reincarnation novel"; and even my own nameless attempt sold some ten thousand copies on the strength of its theme. These other books, so quickly does the human mind readjust itself, were treated by the reviewers as a matter of course, and even my own effusion was no longer held up to anathema.

Nevertheless, the main current of Realism—or would it not be better to call it Littleism?—flowed placidly on. There was nothing in the reincarnation outburst, including my own performance, or in other outbursts, such as are always bubbling on the surface of letters, to deflect its course or dispute its empire. Its first serious blow came at the close of the war with Spain, when an apparently insatiable demand arose for history and romance, fighting men and picturesque women, incident, adventure, a total repudiation of the little and the obvious. This new drove of literary sheep has been almost invariably without style, distinction; it has been more lacking in the deep personal note than the work of the Littleists, it has been full of exaggeration; it has even been ungrammatical. Nevertheless, it has done a good work in rousing the public to demand in their literature that which is not familiar to them from their uprising to their chaste retiring. The right medium will be reached, but the time is not yet; for the average new writer comes apologetically to the field, stiff with the old superstitions: the influential newspapers of the better class will

praise nothing which the big magazines and their publishing-houses have not approved—
and approval is dear to the heart of the young aspirant to literary honors; reverence for the
critic is planted in his soul. The big magazines and their houses will publish nothing that
does not conform to the standard which has weathered other upheavals; and the authors
who have defied the powers and won an honorable position independent of any temporary
demand, are so few in number that they rather terrify than encourage the youthful aspirant: their fight has been too long and arduous, and that other way lies sure, if not very
brilliant, success.

It is safe to say that it is the ambition of every new writer to "get into the magazines."
Perhaps the grim necessity of daily bread demands immediate recognition, but I fancy it
is more in the nature of an obsession. The magazines are taken in every well-conducted
household, so carefully has the public been educated, and the aspiring young mind is
trained by this eminently correct fiction—which it reads long before novels are permitted.
It is natural, therefore, that those who have the creative gift in an attenuated form should
not only admire but emulate. And although it may be difficult to "get into the magazines," it is still more difficult to get out. Indeed, if we may judge by the results, that has
never been attempted. So great has the power of the magazines been that they have convinced half the world they stand for the true aristocracy of letters, that he who ignores
their canons must withdraw, and forever dwell, beyond the pale. The newspapers have
taken their cue from them; it saves thinking; and there is, beyond all question, a certain
public which will not recognize the existence of an author who has not been bred in one of
the magazines or launched by one of the associate publishing-houses. To be a pariah is not
a pleasant thing in this world, particularly if there was a moment when you dwelt with
the elect. It is safe and pleasant to be consistently approved; moreover, it is profitable. Not
recklessly so perhaps, but it is agreeable to look forward to a nice little income for a reasonable number of years. All this begets timidity; and timidity is a leech at the throat of
originality.

Let us examine the canons which govern the "aristocracy of American letters." Originality, except in the mildest form, we have seen is proscribed. "What never has been done
never can be done" may be said to be the motto of American literature. If this statement
be thought to stand in need of corroboration let the reader invest not only in the best of
current novels, but in two bound volumes of any one of the big magazines and examine
the fiction. In two such volumes that I have under my table at the present moment there
are a number of stories which are still fresh in my mind. One, by a popular magazine
writer of long standing, is about a girl who went from San Francisco to Chicago in a Pull-
man car and returned. That is all that happened. Another is about a married woman who
flirted platonically with an author, and upon his death received her effusive, but presumably virtuous, epistles from the hand of his wife. Another is an interminable "study" of a
dressmaker. One by Gelett Burgess is quite unworthy of him; it contains not an echo of
his eerie talent. Not one, possibly with the exception of Burgess's story, is redeemed by a
single grace of phrase, a fine thought, careful or distinguished writing. Indeed, I have
more than once found the most serious grammatical offences in these magazine stories.
The majority, however, are guiltless in this respect, cleverly written, if without individuality. There are perhaps four or five regular contributors to the magazines who write with
distinction, and conform admirably to all the canons of the short story. But each year they
manifest more plainly that they have relinquished all intention of attempting to rise
above the high-water mark of mediocrity—the pink-and-blue signal of the magazine.
They are something to be grateful for, however; and are as salient a credit to these periodi-

cals as the beautiful illustrations, typography, and paper, which make a sumptuous whole of which any country might be proud.

The second canon is firm adherence to the most curious convention that has ever been insisted upon in any country: that this world is not as it is, but as it ought to be. The sole taboo is not sex by any means; many another tendency of the human mind, many another exposition of life, must be forever ignored and denounced. Whether or not this convention originated with certain men, powerful in shaping American literature, who had seen nothing of the world, or whether there was a deliberate concerted attempt on the part of the literary powers to make American literature "refined," aristocratic, undemocratic, a rarified thing in the third stratum above mortals, it would be hard to say. The result, however, it may be observed here, is not aristocratic, but distinctly middle-class. It is the expression of that *bourgeoisie* which is afraid of doing the wrong thing, not of the indifferent aristocrat; of that element which dares not use slang, shrinks from audacity, rarely utters a bold sentiment and as rarely feels one. It is as correct as Sunday clothes and as innocuous as sterilized milk, but it is not aristocratic. The natural result of its success is, that American writers feel no necessity to see the world. Too much knowledge, indeed, would upset the prescribed poise, and they spend their years comfortably describing the little life about them, adding nothing whatever to the knowledge of mankind. Their utmost range is after dialect—*i.e.,* illiterate phrases—and local color. They mildly interest people who are used to them and can get nothing else.

A third canon, which is indeed but a part of the second, is that fiction to be literature—American literature—must be anæmic. Vigor, vitality, richness, vividness, audacity of thought or phrase, any quality in short which is distinctively American, must be weeded out, bleached out, of the ambitious author, would he receive recognition as an American of letters. Here again, if they are trying to be aristocratic they are making a curious blunder. The qualities I have enumerated as anathema distinguish the aristocracies of all nations, and, as your true democrat is an aristocrat, therein lies the close relationship between the high civilization of the Old World and the superb Americanism which laughs at ancient forms and superstitions, goes its own gait with apologies to no one. Our literature fairly represents the bourgeois spirit of Europe, but it does not represent the United States in anything but matter of a sort.

A fourth canon, still to subdivide the second, is what might be called the fetish of the body. Magazine editors, their confederate publishers, their writers and readers, deify the body, grovel in the dust before it. It never has done and can do no wrong; at all events it must be protected at every hazard and cost. Let the brain rot. The brain is invisible and insignificant. Let the mind close its doors to the best of literatures, to the immensity of life, but let it keep its physical frame-work even as a little child. That the body was materialized for no other purpose in the world but for reproduction, and as a more tangible expression for the mind, and that the mind is given us that we may put into it all the knowledge that can be found in this world, has never occurred to any of these teachers.

A fifth canon is that sleep must not be disturbed nor even the nerves titillated. Some years ago there was an institution in New York known as "Uncut Leaves." Before its assemblages authors read stories, articles, and poems, designed for the magazines. The tickets sold at a high price, the gatherings were attended by the demi-fashionable. At one time they were almost as notable as Bagby's Monday Mornings. A young author who had not made her *début* in the magazines, but had attracted considerable attention, was, with rare audacity, invited to read—but with prudent reservation she was asked to submit the

MS. first. The story the writer selected was impeccable in its morals, but it was extremely, though briefly, tragic, and its climax was rather terrible. It was submitted, and re-turned—kindly and politely—with the excuse that there "might be sensitive ladies pres-ent whose nerves would be distressingly affected." The obvious reply, that that women whose nerves were in a delicate condition had better stay at home, may or may not have been made.

It is this curious shrinking from the larger life that is most characteristic of what at present stands for American literature. It is quite true that the magazines and the pub-lishing-houses may retort that they are money-making institutions, and that the great body of the people are commonplace, narrow, and prudish; also that the great majority of readers are women. This is quite true. It is also true that the genius of any race is deter-mined by the thousand active exceptions, not by the million vegetables—what Clarence King calls "the vulgar fractions in the census"; also by the men, not by the women. But if no educating force is applied to the million, how are they to advance? If their literature—which, being sheep, they meekly accept—tells them only of their own life and kind, if not a hint from the real great world ever reaches them, how are they to deepen and augment their spots? If American middle-class human nature is like other middle-class nature, commonplace and narrow, they owe a large percentage of the infliction to the levelling in-fluence of the literary powers, for there are natural promptings in their blood to help them—other assistance being equal—to quicker understandings.

As for the authors these powers have educated and encouraged, their writing conveys the impression of having flowed forth in snug studies, between a well-filled stomach and an ear cocked to catch the prattle of the nursery. There is not one of these arbitrary cre-ations of the leading publishing-houses and their magazines who reads as if he had ever suffered a pang, ever descended even in chaste thought to the vast underworld where the greatest writers of the earth have found their inspirations, ever travelled except in a subli-mated Cook fashion, ever—alas never!—heard of Dickens's advice to a young author. They are all good family men, who eat well, rarely drink, are too dull to be bored with their own wives, but who have reached a certain perfection of literary phrase and construc-tion which would be a credit to any country. As well-drilled brains, finished, acute, and polished, they are above reproach. But there is not an ego among them. Each could do the other's work and never be detected.

It is almost an unpardonable lapse into the obvious to remark that such a school will never produce even one great writer. To be great, it is above all things necessary to develop your ego, your power, and there is only one way to do it: by divorcing yourself from all that is smug, that is easy, that is comfortable, that is orthodox and conventional, by seeing life from its peaks to its chasms. No writer with a real gift and with a real ambition has any business with a home, children, the unintermittent comforts of life which stultify and stifle. If a man has the gift to write, to create,—the greatest of all gifts—what more does he want? To insist upon the right to lounge amidst the commonplace comforts, and the mild distractions of "society," is not only ungrateful but fatal. Art, the most jealous of all mistresses, is always prompt to desert him of the divided allegiance, and leave him to fin-ish his career with the husks, with the shell from which the soul has gone. Even the writer who has no inclination to deal with the great passions—which the fastidious American calls "temperament"!—should study unceasingly the great map of life. He has no right to ask people to buy his books if he cannot tell them something they did not know before. To be great, you must know as much as one can learn in one life, and by experience, even if you never intend to use one-third of your knowledge. He of the slender equipment is always running about looking for copy, for local color, but his eyes are closed to the great things. I do not mean to intimate that any one of our prosperous family authors would in any condition be great; had they had greatness in them they would have broken loose long ago, and snapped their fingers at the powers—Henry James is a case in point—but they might be improved.

I should never venture to admonish women in any such fashion, for very few women know how to use their liberty, above all how to take life impersonally, to regard all life as a spectacle, to disassociate the mind from the body. Where one develops the strength of brain and ego triumphantly to override every convention and always remain high and dry, always the spectator, whom no circumstance can affect, the great number, indubitably, are the miserable victims of their own personalities; which in their turn are the victims of tradition. It is more than probable that the next fifty years will see the highly civilized woman as truly emancipated as man—as a very few women have been in the past; those who have genius needing nothing else to encourage and advise them. But there is no such excuse for men of genius or of talent. They should be content with their art, gratefully demanding nothing more, developing their ego in that service and absolutely indifferent whether the world approves of them as citizens or not. A writer who is singled out to create—to be useful to the race—owes all to that gift, nothing to his trifling self. Who cares to-day that Poe was a drunkard, Coleridge an opium-eater, that Byron had forty mistresses and Georges Sand forty lovers? Not that excess is necessary, not by any means; many of the greatest men in literature have been sane, and careful of themselves; the temperaments that demand artificial stimulation pay a bitter price, and, what is worse, limit their contribution to art. Alcohol, stimulant of any sort—even strong coffee—in nine cases out of ten, and particularly in the case of women, who have active nerves enough, scatter the brain, weakening its coherence and logic long before actual decay sets in; or pitches it a note too high, so that the effect is bizarre rather than original.

There is only one way in which man or woman can develop real strength, and that is to fight unceasingly and to stand absolutely alone.   [1904]

George Santayana

The Genteel Tradition in American Philosophy

Ladies and Gentlemen: The privilege of addressing you to-day is very welcome to me, not merely for the honor of it, which is great, nor for the pleasures of travel, which are many, when it is California that one is visiting for the first time, but also because there is something I have long wanted to say which this occasion seems particularly favorable for saying. America is still a young country, and this part of it is especially so; and it would have been nothing extraordinary if, in this young country, material preoccupations had altogether absorbed people's minds, and they had been too much engrossed in living to reflect upon life, or to have any philosophy. The opposite, however, is the case. Not only have you already found time to philosophize in California, as your society proves, but the eastern colonists from the very beginning were a sophisticated race. As much as in clearing the land and fighting the Indians they were occupied, as they expressed it, in wrestling with the Lord. The country was new, but the race was tried, chastened, and full of solemn memories. It was an old wine in new bottles; and America did not have to wait for its present universities, with their departments of academic philosophy, in order to possess a living philosophy,—to have a distinct vision of the universe and definite convictions about human destiny.

Now this situation is a singular and remarkable one, and has many consequences, not all of which are equally fortunate. America is a young country with an old mentality: it has enjoyed the advantages of a child carefully brought up, and thoroughly indoctrinated; it has been a wise child. But a wise child, an old head on young shoulders, always has a comic and an unpromising side. The wisdom is a little thin and verbal, not aware of its full meaning and grounds; and physical and emotional growth may be stunted by it, or even deranged. Or when the child is too vigorous for that, he will develop a fresh mentality of his own, out of his observations and actual instincts; and this fresh mentality will interfere with the traditional mentality, and tend to reduce it to something perfunctory, conventional, and perhaps secretly despised. A philosophy is not genuine unless it inspires and expresses the life of those who cherish it. I do not think the hereditary philosophy of America has done much to atrophy the natural activities of the inhabitants; the wise child has not missed the joys of youth or of manhood; but what has happened is that the hereditary philosophy has grown stale, and that the academic philosophy afterwards developed has caught the stale odor from it. America is not simply, as I said a moment ago, a young country with an old mentality: it is a country with two mentalities, one a survival of the beliefs and standards of the fathers, the other an expression of the instincts, practice, and discoveries of the younger generations. In all the higher things of the mind—in religion, in literature, in the moral emotions—it is the hereditary spirit that still prevails, so much so that Mr. Bernard Shaw finds that America is a hundred years behind the times. The truth is that that one-half of the American mind, that not occupied intensely in practical affairs, has remained, I will not say high-and-dry, but slightly becalmed; it has floated gently in the backwater, while, alongside, in invention and industry and social organization the other half of the mind was leaping down a sort of Niagara Rapids. This division may be found symbolized in American architecture: a neat reproduction of the colonial mansion—with some modern comforts introduced surreptitiously—stands beside the sky-scraper. The American Will inhabits the sky-scraper; the American Intellect inhabits the colonial mansion. The one is the sphere of the American man; the other, at least predominantly, of the American woman. The one is all aggressive enterprise; the other is all genteel tradition.

Now, with your permission, I should like to analyze more fully how this interesting situation has arisen, how it is qualified, and whither it tends. And in the first place we should remember what, precisely, that philosophy was which the first settlers brought with them into the country. In strictness there was more than one; but we may confine our attention to what I will call Calvinism, since it is on this that the current academic philosophy has been grafted. I do not mean exactly the Calvinism of Calvin, or even of Jonathan Edwards; for in their systems there was much that was not pure philosophy, but rather faith in the externals and history of revelation. Jewish and Christian revelation was interpreted by these men, however, in the spirit of a particular philosophy, which might have arisen under any sky, and been associated with any other religion as well as with Protestant Christianity. In fact, the philosophical principle of Calvinism appears also in the Koran, in Spinoza, and in Cardinal Newman; and persons with no very distinctive Christian belief, like Carlyle or like Professor Royce, may be nevertheless, philosophically, perfect Calvinists. Calvinism, taken in this sense, is an expression of the agonized conscience. It is a view of the world which an agonized conscience readily embraces, if it takes itself seriously, as, being agonized, of course it must. Calvinism, essentially, asserts three things: that sin exists, that sin is punished, and that it is beautiful that sin should exist to be punished. The heart of the Calvinist is therefore divided between tragic concern at his own miserable condition, and tragic exultation about the universe at large. He oscillates between a profound abasement and a paradoxical elation of the spirit. To be a Calvinist philosophically is to feel a fierce pleasure in the existence of misery, especially of one's own, in that this misery seems to manifest the fact that the Absolute is irresponsible or infinite or holy. Human nature, it feels, is totally depraved: to have the instincts and motives that we necessarily have is a great scandal, and we must suffer for it; but that scandal is requisite, since otherwise the serious importance of being as we ought to be would not have been vindicated.

To those of us who have not an agonized conscience this system may seem fantastic and even unintelligible; yet it is logically and intently thought out from its emotional premises. It can take permanent possession of a deep mind here and there, and under certain conditions it can become epidemic. Imagine, for instance, a small nation with an intense vitality, but on the verge of ruin, ecstatic and distressful, having a strict and minute code of laws, that paint life in sharp and violent chiaroscuro, all pure righteousness and black abominations, and exaggerating the consequences of both perhaps to infinity. Such a people were the Jews after the exile, and again the early Protestants. If such a people is philosophical at all, it will not improbably be Calvinistic. Even in the early American communities many of these conditions were fulfilled. The nation was small and isolated; it lived under pressure and constant trial; it was acquainted with but a small range of goods and evils. Vigilance over conduct and an absolute demand for personal integrity were not merely traditional things, but things that practical sages, like Franklin and Washington, recommended to their countrymen, because they were virtues that justified themselves visibly by their fruits. But soon these happy results themselves helped to relax the pressure of external circumstances, and indirectly the pressure of the agonized conscience within. The nation became numerous; it ceased to be either ecstatic or distressful; the high social morality which on the whole it preserved took another color; people remained honest and helpful out of good sense and good will rather than out of scrupulous adherence to any fixed principles. They retained their instinct for order, and often created order with surprising quickness; but the sanctity of law, to be obeyed for its own sake, began to escape them; it seemed too unpractical a notion, and not quite serious. In fact, the second and native-born American mentality began to take shape. The sense of sin totally evaporated. Nature, in the words of Emerson, was all beauty and commodity; and while operating on it laboriously, and drawing quick returns, the American began to drink in inspiration from it aesthetically. At the same time, in so broad a continent, he had elbow-room. His neighbors helped more than they hindered him; he wished their number to increase. Good-will became the great American virtue; and a passion arose for counting heads, and square miles, and cubic feet, and minutes saved—as if there had been anything to save them for. How strange to the American now that saying of Jonathan Edwards, that men are naturally God's enemies! Yet that is an axiom to any intelligent Calvinist, though the words he uses may be different. If you told the modern American that he is totally depraved, he would think you were joking, as he himself usually is. He is convinced that he always has been, and always will be, victorious and blameless.

Calvinism thus lost its basis in American life. Some emotional natures, indeed, reverted in their religious revivals or private searchings of heart to the sources of the tradition; for any of the radical points of view in philosophy may cease to be prevalent, but none can cease to be possible. Other natures, more sensitive to the moral and literary influences of the world, preferred to abandon part of their philosophy, hoping thus to reduce the distance which should separate the remainder from real life.

Meantime, if anybody arose with a special sensibility or a technical genius, he was in great straits; not being fed sufficiently by the world, he was driven in upon his own resources. The three American writers whose personal endowment was perhaps the finest—Poe, Hawthorne, and Emerson—had all a certain starved and abstract quality. They could not retail the genteel tradition; they were too keen, too perceptive, and too independent for that. But life offered them little digestible material, nor were they naturally voracious. They were fastidious, and under the circumstances they were starved. Emerson, to be sure, fed on books. There was a great catholicity in his reading; and he showed a fine tact in his comments, and in his way of appropriating what he read. But he read transcendentally, not historically, to learn what he himself felt, not what others might have felt before him. And to feed on books, for a philosopher or a poet, is still to starve. Books can help him to acquire form, or to avoid pitfalls; they cannot supply him with substance, if he is to have any. Therefore the genius of Poe and Hawthorne, and even of Emerson, was employed on a sort of inner play, or digestion of vacancy. It was a refined labor, but it was in danger of being morbid, or tinkling, or self-indulgent. It was a play of intramental rhymes. Their mind was like an old musicbox, full of tender echoes and quaint fancies. These fancies expressed their personal genius sincerely, as dreams may; but they were arbitrary fancies in comparison with what a real observer would have said in the premises. Their manner, in a word, was subjective. In their own persons they escaped the mediocrity of the genteel tradition, but they supplied nothing to supplant it in other minds.

The churches, likewise, although they modified their spirit, had no philosophy to offer save a selection or a new emphasis on parts of what Calvinism contained. The theology of Calvin, we must remember, had much in it besides philosophical Calvinism. A Christian tenderness, and a hope of grace for the individual, came to mitigate its sardonic optimism; and it was these evangelical elements that the Calvinistic churches now emphasized, seldom and with blushes referring to hell-fire or infant damnation. Yet philosophic Calvinism, with a theory of life that would perfectly justify hell-fire and and infant damnation if they happened to exist, still dominates the traditional metaphysics. It is an ingredient, and the decisive ingredient, in what calls itself idealism. But in order to see just what part Calvinism plays in current idealism, it will be necessary to distinguish the other chief element in that complex system, namely, transcendentalism.

Transcendentalism is the philosophy which the romantic era produced in Germany, and independently, I believe, in America also. Transcendentalism proper, like romanticism, is not any particular set of dogmas about what things exist; it is not a system of the universe regarded as a fact, or as a collection of facts. It is a method, a point of view, from which any world, no matter what it might contain, could be approached by a self-conscious observer. Transcendentalism is a systematic subjectivism. It studies the perspectives of knowledge, as they radiate from the self; it is a plan of those avenues of inference by which our ideas of things must be reached, if they are to afford any systematic or distant vistas. In other words, transcendentalism is the critical logic of science. Knowledge, it says, has a station, as in a watch-tower; it is always seated here and now, in the self of the moment. The past and the future, things inferred and things conceived, lie around it, painted as upon a panorama. They cannot be lighted up save by some centrifugal ray of the mind.

This is hardly the occasion for developing or explaining this delicate insight; suffice it to say, lest you should think later that I disparage transcendentalism, that as a method I regard it as correct and, when once suggested, unforgettable. I regard it as the chief contribution made in modern times to speculation. But it is a method only, an attitude we may always assume if we like and that will always be legitimate. It is no answer, and involves no particular answer, to the question: What exists; in what order is what exists produced; what is to exist in the future? This question must be answered by observing the object, and tracing humbly the movement of the object. It cannot be answered at all by harping on the fact that this object, if discovered, must be discovered by somebody who has an interest in discovering it. Yet the Germans who first gained the full transcendental insight were romantic people; they were more or less frankly poets; they were colossal egotists, and wished to make not only their own knowledge but the whole universe center about themselves. And full as they were of their romantic isolation and romantic liberty, it occurred to them to imagine that all reality might be a transcendental self and a romantic dreamer like themselves; nay, that it might be just their own transcendental self and their own romantic dreams extended indefinitely. Transcendental logic, the method of discovery for the mind, was to become also the method of evolution in nature and history. Transcendental method, so abused, produced transcendental myth. A conscientious critique of knowledge was turned into a sham system of nature. We must therefore distinguish sharply the transcendental grammar of the intellect, which is significant and potentially correct, from the various transcendental systems of the universe, which are chimeras.

In both its parts, however, transcendentalism had much to recommend it to American philosophers, for the transcendental method appealed to the individualistic and revolutionary temper of their youth, while transcendental myths enabled them to find a new status for their inherited theology, and to give what parts of it they cared to preserve some semblance of philosophical backing. This last was the use to which the transcendental method was put by Kant himself, who first brought it into vogue, before the terrible weapon had got out of hand, and became the instrument of pure romanticism. Kant came, he himself said, to remove knowledge in order to make room for faith, which in his case meant faith in Calvinism. In other words, he applied the transcendental method to matters of fact, reducing them thereby to human ideas, in order to give to the Calvinistic postulates of conscience a metaphysical validity. For Kant had a genteel tradition of his own, which he wished to remove to a place of safety, feeling that the empirical world had become too hot for it; and this place of safety was the region of transcendental myth. I need hardly say how perfectly this expedient suited the needs of philosophers in America, and it is no accident if the influence of Kant soon became dominant here. To embrace this philosophy was regarded as a sign of profound metaphysical insight, although the most mediocre minds found no difficulty in embracing it. In truth it was a sign of having been brought up in the genteel tradition, of feeling it weak, and of wishing to save it.

But the transcendental method, in its way, was also sympathetic to the American mind. It embodied, in a radical form, the spirit of Protestantism as distinguished from its inherited doctrines; it was autonomous, undismayed, calmly revolutionary; it felt that Will was deeper than Intellect; it focused everything here and now, and asked all things to show their credentials at the bar of the young self, and to prove their value for this latest born moment. These things are truly American; they would be characteristic of any young society with a keen and discursive intelligence, and they are strikingly exemplified in the thought and in the person of Emerson. They constitute what he called self-trust. Self-trust, like other transcendental attitudes, may be expressed in metaphysical fables. The romantic spirit may imagine itself to be an absolute force, evoking and molding the plastic world to express its varying moods. But for a pioneer who is actually a worldbuilder this metaphysical illusion has a partial warrant in historical fact; far more warrant than it could boast of in the fixed and articulated society of Europe, among the moonstruck rebels and sulking poets of the romantic era. Emerson was a shrewd Yankee, by instinct on the winning side; he was a cheery, child-like soul, impervious to the evidence of evil, as of everything that it did not suit his transcendental individuality to appreciate or to notice. More, perhaps, than anybody that has ever lived, he practiced the transcendental method in all its purity. He had no system. He opened his eyes on the world every morning with a fresh sincerity, marking how things seemed to him then, or what they suggested to his spontaneous fancy. This fancy, for being spontaneous, was not always novel; it was guided by the habits and training of his mind, which were those of a preacher. Yet he never insisted on his notions so as to turn them into settled dogmas; he felt in his bones that they were myths. Sometimes, indeed, the bad example of other transcendentalists, less true than he to their method, or the pressing questions of unintelligent people, or the instinct we all have to think our ideas final, led him to the very verge of system-making; but he stopped short. Had he made a system out of his notion of compensation, or the over-soul, or spiritual laws, the result would have been as thin and forced as it is in other transcendental systems. But he coveted truth; and he returned to experience, to history, to poetry, to the natural science of his day, for new starting-points and hints toward fresh transcendental musing.

To covet truth is a very distinguished passion. Every philosopher says he is pursuing the truth, but this is seldom the case. As Mr. Bertrand Russell has observed, one reason why philosophers often fail to reach the truth is that often they do not desire to reach it. Those who are genuinely concerned in discovering what happens to be true are rather the men of science, the naturalists, the historians; and ordinarily they discover it, according to their lights. The truths they find are never complete, and are not always important, but they are integral parts of the truth, facts and circumstances that help to fill in the picture, and that no later interpretation can invalidate or afford to contradict. But professional philosophers are usually only scholastics: that is, they are absorbed in defending some vested illusion or some eloquent idea. Like lawyers or detectives, they study the case for which they are retained, to see how much evidence or semblance of evidence they can gather for the defense, and how much prejudice they can raise against the witnesses for the prosecution; for they know they are defending prisoners suspected by the world, and perhaps by their own good sense, of falsification. They do not covet truth, but victory and the dispelling of their own doubts. What they defend is some system, that is, some view about the totality of things, of which men are actually ignorant. No system would ever have been framed if people had been simply interested in knowing what is true, whatever it may be. What produces systems is the interest in maintaining against all comers that some favorite or inherited idea of ours is sufficient and right. A system may contain an account of many things which, in detail, are true enough; but as a system, covering infinite possibilities that neither our experience nor our logic can prejudge, it must be a work of imagination, and a piece of human soliloquy. It may be expressive of human experience, it may be poetical; but how should any one who really coveted truth suppose that it was true?

Emerson had no system; and his coveting truth had another exceptional consequence: he was detached, unworldly, contemplative. When he came out of the conventicle or the reform meeting, or out of the rapturous close atmosphere of the lecture-room, he heard nature whispering to him: "Why so hot, little sir?" No doubt the spirit or energy of the world is what is acting in us, as the sea is what rises in every little wave; but it passes through us, and cry out as we may, it will move on. Our privilege is to have perceived it as it moves. Our dignity is not in what we do, but in what we understand. The whole world is doing things. We are turning in that vortex; yet within us is silent observation, the speculative eye before which all passes, which bridges the distances and compares the combatants. On this side of his genius Emerson broke away from all conditions of age or country and represented nothing except intelligence itself.

There was another element in Emerson, curiously combined with transcendentalism, namely, his love and respect for Nature. Nature, for the transcendentalist, is precious because it is his own work, a mirror in which he looks at himself and says (like a poet relishing his own verses), "What a genius I am! Who would have thought there was such stuff in me?" And the philosophical egotist finds in his doctrine a ready explanation of whatever beauty and commodity nature actually has. No wonder, he says to himself, that nature is sympathetic, since I made it. And such a view, onesided and even fatuous as it may be, undoubtedly sharpens the vision of a poet and a moralist to all that is inspiriting and symbolic in the natural world. Emerson was particularly ingenious and clear-sighted in feeling the spiritual uses of fellowship with the elements. This is something in which all Teutonic poetry is rich and which forms, I think, the most genuine and spontaneous part of modern taste, and especially of American taste. Just as some people are naturally enthralled and refreshed by music, so others are by landscape. Music and landscape make up the spiritual resources of those who cannot or dare not express their unfulfilled ideals in words. Serious poetry, profound religion (Calvinism, for instance) are the joys of an unhappiness that confesses itself; but when a genteel tradition forbids people to confess that they are unhappy, serious poetry and profound religion are closed to them by that; and since human life, in its depths, cannot then express itself openly, imagination is driven for comfort into abstract arts, where human circumstances are lost sight of, and human problems dissolve in a purer medium. The pressure of care is thus relieved, without its quietus being found in intelligence. To understand oneself is the classic form of consolation; to elude oneself is the romantic. In the presence of music or landscape human experience eludes itself; and thus romanticism is the bond between transcendental and naturalistic sentiment.

Have there been, we may ask, any successful efforts to escape from the genteel tradition, and to express something worth expressing behind its back? This might well not have occurred as yet; but America is so precocious, it has been trained by the genteel tradition to be so wise for its years, that some indications of a truly native philosophy and poetry are already to be found. I might mention the humorists, of whom you here in California have had your share. The humorists, however, only half escape the genteel tradition; their humor would lose its savor if they had wholly escaped it. They point to what contradicts it in the facts; but not in order to abandon the genteel tradition, for they have nothing solid to put in its place. When they point out how ill many facts fit into it, they do not clearly conceive that this militates against the standard, but think it a funny perversity in the facts. Of course, did they earnestly respect the genteel tradition, such an incongruity would seem to them sad, rather than ludicrous. Perhaps the prevalence of humor in America, in and out of season, may be taken as one more evidence that the genteel tradition is present pervasively, but everywhere weak. Similarly in Italy, during the Renaissance, the Catholic tradition could not be banished from the intellect, since there was nothing articulate to take its place; yet its hold on the heart was singularly relaxed. The consequence was that humorists could regale themselves with the foibles of monks and of cardinals, with the credulity of fools, and the bogus miracles of the saints; not intending to deny the theory of the church, but caring for it so little at heart, that they could find it infinitely amusing that it should be contradicted in men's lives, and that no harm should come of it. So when Mark Twain says, "I was born of poor but dishonest parents," the humor depends on the parody of the genteel Anglo-Saxon convention that it is disreputable to be poor; but to hint at the hollowness of it would not be amusing if it did not remain at bottom one's habitual conviction.

The one American writer who has left the genteel tradition entirely behind is perhaps Walt Whitman. For this reason educated Americans find him rather an unpalatable person, who they sincerely protest ought not to be taken for a representative of their culture; and he certainly should not, because their culture is so genteel and traditional. But the foreigner may sometimes think otherwise, since he is looking for what may have arisen in America to express, not the polite and conventional American mind, but the spirit and the inarticulate principles that animate the community, on which its own genteel mentality seems to sit rather lightly. When the foreigner opens the pages of Walt Whitman, he thinks that he has come at last upon something representative and original. In Walt Whitman democracy is carried into psychology and morals. The various sights, moods, and emotions are given each one vote; they are declared to be all free and equal, and the innumerable common-place moments of life are suffered to speak like the others. Those moments formerly reputed great are not excluded, but they are made to march in the ranks with their companions,—plain foot-soldiers and servants of the hour. Nor does the refusal to discriminate stop there; we must carry our principle further down, to the animals, to inanimate nature, to the cosmos as a whole. Whitman became a pantheist; but his pantheism, unlike that of the Stoics and of Spinoza, was unintellectual, lazy, and self-indulgent; for he simply felt jovially that everything real was good enough, and that he was good enough himself. In him Bohemia rebelled against the genteel tradition; but the reconstruction that alone can justify revolution did not ensue. His attitude, in principle, was utterly disintegrating; his poetic genius fell back to the lowest level, perhaps, to which it is possible for poetic genius to fall. He reduced his imagination to a passive sensorium for the registering of impressions. No element of construction remained in it, and therefore no element of penetration. But his scope was wide; and his lazy, desultory apprehension was poetical. His work, for the very reason that it is so rudimentary, contains a beginning, or rather many beginnings, that might possibly grow into a noble moral imagination, a worthy filling for the human mind. An American in the nineteenth century who completely disregarded the genteel tradition could hardly have done more.

But there is another distinguished man, lately lost to this country, who has given some rude shocks to this tradition and who, as much as Whitman, may be regarded as representing the genuine, the long silent American mind—I mean William James. He and his brother Henry were as tightly swaddled in the genteel tradition as any infant geniuses could be, for they were born in Cambridge, and in a Swedenborgian household. Yet they burst those bands almost entirely. The ways in which the two brothers freed themselves, however, are interestingly different. Mr. Henry James has done it by adopting the point of view of the outer world, and by turning the genteel American tradition, as he turns everything else, into a subject-matter for analysis.

For him it is a curious habit of mind, intimately comprehended, to be compared with other habits of mind, also well known to him. Thus he has overcome the genteel tradition in the classic way, by understanding it. With William James too this infusion of worldly insight and European sympathies was a potent influence, especially in his earlier days; but the chief source of his liberty was another. It was his personal spontaneity, similar to that of Emerson, and his personal vitality, similar to that of nobody else. Convictions and ideas came to him, so to speak, from the subsoil. He had a prophetic sympathy with the dawning sentiments of the age, with the moods of the dumb majority. His scattered words caught fire in many parts of the world. His way of thinking and feeling represented the true America, and represented in a measure the whole ultramodern, radical world. Thus he eluded the genteel tradition in the romantic way, by continuing it into its opposite. The romantic mind, glorified in Hegel's dialectic (which is not dialectic at all, but a sort of tragi-comic history of experience), is always rendering its thoughts unrecognizable through the infusion of new insights, and through the insensible transformation of the moral feeling that accompanies them, till at last it has completely reversed its old judgments under cover of expanding them. Thus the genteel tradition was led a merry dance when it fell again into the hands of a genuine and vigorous romanticist, like William James. He restored their revolutionary force to its neutralized elements; by picking them out afresh, and emphasizing them separately, according to his personal predilections.

For one thing, William James kept his mind and heart wide open to all that might seem, to polite minds, odd, personal, or visionary in religion and philosophy. He gave a sincerely respectful hearing to sentimentalists, mystics, spiritualists, wizards, cranks, quacks, and imposters—for it is hard to draw the line, and James was not willing to draw it prematurely. He thought, with his usual modesty, that any of these might have something to teach him. The lame, the halt, the blind, and those speaking with tongues could come to him with the certainty of finding sympathy; and if they were not healed, at least they were comforted, that a famous professor should take them so seriously; and they began to feel that after all to have only one leg, or one hand, or one eye, or to have three, might be in itself no less beauteous than to have just two, like the stolid majority. Thus William James became the friend and helper of those groping, nervous, half-educated, spiritually disinherited, emotionally hungry individuals of which America is full. He became, at the same time, their spokesman and representative before the learned world; and he made it a chief part of his vocation to recast what the learned world has to offer, so that as far as possible it might serve the needs and interests of these people.

Yet the normal practical masculine American, too, had a friend in William James. There is a feeling abroad now, to which biology and Darwinism lend some color, that theory is simply an instrument for practice, and intelligence merely a help toward material survival. Bears, it is said, have fur and claws, but poor naked man is condemned to be intelligent, or he will perish. This feeling William James embodied in that theory of thought and of truth which he called pragmatism. Intelligence, he thought, is no miraculous, idle faculty, by which we mirror passively any or every thing that happens to be true, reduplicating the real world to no purpose. Intelligence has its roots and its issue in the context of events; it is one kind of practical adjustment, an experimental act, a form of vital tension. It does not essentially serve to picture other parts of reality, but to connect them. This view was not worked out by William James in its psychological and historical details; unfortunately he developed it chiefly in controversy against its opposite, which he called intellectualism, and which he hated with all the hatred of which his kind heart was capable. Intellectualism, as he conceived it, was pure pedantry; it impoverished and verbalized everything, and tied up nature in red tape. Ideas and rules that may have been occasionally useful, it put in the place of the full-blooded irrational movement of life which had called them into being; and these abstractions, so soon obsolete, it strove to fix and to worship forever. Thus all creeds and theories and all formal precepts sink in the estimation of the pragmatist to a local and temporary grammar of action; a grammar that must be changed slowly by time, and may be changed quickly by genius. To know things as a whole, or as they are eternally, if there is anything eternal in them, is not only beyond our powers, but would prove worthless, and perhaps even fatal to our lives. Ideas are not mirrors, they are weapons; their function is to prepare us to meet events, as future experience may unroll them. Those ideas that disappoint us are false ideas; those to which events are true are true themselves.

This may seem a very utilitarian view of the mind; and I confess I think it a partial one, since the logical force of beliefs and ideas, their truth or falsehood as assertions, has been overlooked altogether, or confused with the vital force of the material processes which these ideas express. It is an external view only, which marks the place and conditions of the mind in nature, but neglects its specific essence; as if a jewel were defined as a round hole in a ring. Nevertheless, the more materialistically we interpret the pragmatist theory of what the mind is, the more vitalistic our theory of nature will have to become. If the intellect is a device produced in organic bodies to expedite their processes, these organic bodies must have interests and a chosen direction in their life; otherwise their life could not be expedited, nor could anything be useful to it. In other words—and this is a third point at which the philosophy of William James has played havoc with the genteel tradition, while ostensibly defending it—nature must be conceived anthropomorphically and in psychological terms. Its purposes are not to be static harmonies, self-unfolding destinies, the logic of spirit, the spirit of logic, or any other formal method and abstract law; its purposes are to be concrete endeavors, finite efforts of souls living in an environment which they transform and by which they, too, are affected. A spirit, the divine spirit as much as the human, as this new animism conceives it, is a romantic adventurer. Its future is undetermined. Its scope, its duration, and the quality of its life, are all contingent. This spirit grows; it buds and sends forth feelers, sounding the depths around for such other centers of force or life as may exist there. It has a vital momentum, but no predetermined goal. It uses its past as a stepping-stone, or rather as a diving-board, but has an absolutely fresh will at each moment to plunge this way or that into the unknown. The universe is an experiment; it is unfinished. It has no ultimate or total nature, because it has no end. It embodies no formula or statable law; any formula is at best a poor abstraction, describing what, in some region and for sometime, may be the most striking characteristic of existence; the law is a description *a posteriori* of the habit things have chosen to acquire, and which they may possibly throw off altogether. What a day may bring forth is uncertain; uncertain even to God. Omniscience is impossible; time is real; what had been omniscience hitherto might discover something more to-day. "There shall be news," William James was fond of saying with rapture, quoting from the unpublished poem of an obscure friend, "there shall be news in heaven!" There is almost certainly, he thought, a God now; there may be several gods, who might exist together, or one after the other. We might, by our conspiring sympathies, help to make a new one. Much in us is doubtless immortal; we survive death for some time in a recognizable form; but what our career and transformations may be in the sequel, we cannot tell, although we may help to determine them by our daily choices. Observation must be continual if our ideas are to remain true. Eternal vigilance is the price of knowledge; perpetual hazard, perpetual experiment keep quick the edge of life.

This is, so far as I know, a new philosophical vista; it is a conception never before presented, although implied, perhaps, in various quarters, as in Norse and even Greek mythology. It is a vision radically empirical and radically romantic; and as William James himself used to say, the vision and not the arguments of a philosopher is the interesting and influential thing about him. William James, rather too generously, attributed this vision to M. Bergson, and regarded him in consequence as a philosopher of the first rank, whose thought was to be one of the turning-points in history. M. Bergson had killed intellectualism. It was his book on creative evolution, said James with humorous emphasis, that had come at last to *"écraser l'enfâme."* We may suspect, notwithstanding, that intellectualism, infamous and crushed, will survive the blow; and if the author of the Book of Ecclesiastes were now alive, and heard that there shall be news in heaven, he would doubtless say that there may possibly be news there, but that under the sun there is nothing new—not even radical empiricism or radical romanticism, which from the beginning of the world has been the philosophy of those who as yet had had little experience; for to the blinking little child it is not merely something in the world that is new daily, but everything is new all day.

I am not concerned with the rights and wrongs of that controversy; my point is only that William James, in this genial evolutionary view of the world, has given a rude shock to the genteel tradition. What! The world a gradual improvisation? Creation unpremeditated? God a sort of young poet or struggling artist? William James is an advocate of theism; pragmatism adds one of the evidences of religion; that is excellent. But is not the cool abstract piety of the genteel getting more than it asks for? This empirical naturalistic God is too crude and positive a force; he will work miracles, he will answer prayers, he may inhabit distinct places, and have distinct conditions under which alone he can operate; he is a neighboring being, whom we can act upon, and rely upon for specific aids, as upon a personal friend, or a physician, or an insurance company. How disconcerting! Is not this new theology a little like superstition? And yet how interesting, how exciting, if it should happen to be true! I am far from wishing to suggest that such a view seems to me more probable than conventional idealism or than Christian orthodoxy. All three are in the region of dramatic system-making and myth, to which probabilities are irrelevant. If one man says the moon is sister to the sun, and another that she is his daughter, the question is not which notion is more probable, but whether either of them is at all expressive. The so-called evidences are devised afterwards, when faith and imagination have prejudged the issue. The force of William James's new theology, or romantic cosmology, lies only in this: that it has broken the spell of the genteel tradition, and enticed faith in a new direction, which on second thoughts may prove no less alluring than the old. The important fact is not that the new fancy might possibly be true—who shall know that?—but that it has entered the heart of a leading American to conceive and to cherish it. The genteel tradition cannot be dislodged by these insurrections, there are circles to which it is still congenial, and where it will be preserved. But it has been challenged and (what is perhaps more insidious) it has been discovered. No one need be brow-beaten any longer into accepting it. No one need be afraid, for instance, that his fate is sealed because some young prig may call him a dualist; the pint would call the quart a dualist, if you tried to pour the quart into him. We need not be afraid of being less profound, for being direct and sincere. The intellectual world may be traversed in many directions; the whole has not been surveyed; there is a great career in it open to talent. That is a sort of knell, that tolls the passing of the genteel tradition. Something else is now in the field; something else can appeal to the imagination, and be a thousand times more idealistic than academic idealism, which is often simply a way of white-washing and adoring things as they are. The illegitimate monopoly which the genteel tradition had established over what ought to be assumed and what ought to be hoped for has been broken down by the first-born of the family, by the genius of the race. Henceforth there can hardly be the same peace and the same pleasure in hugging the old proprieties. Hegel will be to the next generation what Sir William Hamilton was to the last. Nothing will have been disproved, but everything will have been abandoned. An honest man has spoken, and the cant of the genteel tradition has become harder for young lips to repeat.

With this I have finished such a sketch as I am here able to offer you of the genteel tradition in American philosophy. The subject is complex, and calls for many an excursus and qualifying footnote; yet I think the main outlines are clear enough. The chief fountains of this tradition were Calvinism and transcendentalism. Both were living fountains; but to keep them alive they required, one an agonized conscience, and the other a radical subjective criticism of knowledge. When these rare metaphysical preoccupations disappeared—and the American atmosphere is not favorable to either of them—the two systems ceased to be inwardly understood; they subsisted as sacred mysteries only; and the combination of the two in some transcendental system of the universe (a contradiction in principle) was doubly artificial. Besides, it could hardly be held with a single mind. Natural science, history, the beliefs implied in labor and invention, could not be disregarded altogether; so that the transcendental philosopher was condemned to a double allegiance, and to not letting his left hand know the bluff that his right hand was putting up. Nevertheless, the difficulty in bringing practical inarticulate convictions to expression is very great, and the genteel tradition has subsisted in the academic mind, for want of anything equally academic to take its place.

The academic mind, however, has had its flanks turned. On the one side came the revolt of the Bohemian temperament, with its poetry of crude naturalism; on the other side came an impassioned empiricism, welcoming popular religious witnesses to the unseen, reducing science to an instrument of success in action, and declaring the universe to be wild and young, and not to be harnessed by the logic of any school.

This revolution, I should think, might well find an echo among you, who live in a thriving society, and in the presence of a virgin and prodigious world. When you transform nature to your uses, when you experiment with her forces, and reduce them to industrial agents, you cannot feel that nature was made by you or for you, for then these adjustments would have been preestablished. You must feel, rather, that you are an offshoot of her life; one brave little force among her immense forces. When you escape, as you love to do, to your forests and your Sierras, I am sure again that you do not feel you made them, or that they were made for you. They have grown, as you have grown, only more massively and more slowly. In their non-human beauty and peace they stir the sub-human depths and the super-human possibilities of your own spirit. It is no transcendental logic that they teach; and they gave no sign of any deliberate mortality seated in the world. It is rather the vanity and superficiality of all logic, the needlessness of argument, the finitude of morals, the strength of time, the fertility of matter, the variety, the unspeakable variety, of possible life. Everything is measurable and conditioned, indefinitely repeated, yet in repetition, twisted somewhat from its old form. Everywhere is beauty and nowhere permanence, everywhere an incipient harmony [and] nowhere an intention, nor a responsibility, nor a plan. It is the irresistible suasion of this daily spectacle, it is the daily discipline of contact with things, so different from the verbal discipline of the schools, that will, I trust, inspire the philosophy of your children. A Californian whom I had recently the pleasure of meeting observed that, if the philosophers had lived among your mountains their systems would have been different from what they are. Certainly, I should say, very different from what those systems are from which the European genteel tradition has handed down since Socrates; for these systems are egotistical; directly or indirectly they are anthropocentric, and inspired by the conceited notion that man, or human reason, or the human distinction between good and evil, is the center and pivot of the universe. That is what the mountains and the woods should make you at last ashamed to assert. From what, indeed, does the society of nature liberate you, that you find it so sweet? It is hardly (is it?) that you wish to forget your past or your friends, or that you have any secret contempt for your present ambitions. You respect these, you respect them perhaps too much; you are not suffered by the genteel tradition to criticize or to reform them at all radically. No; it is the yoke of this genteel tradition itself, your tyrant from the cradle to the grave, that these primeval solitudes lift from your shoulders. They suspend your forced sense of your own importance not merely as individuals, but even as men. They allow you, in one happy moment, at once to play and to worship, to take yourselves simply, humbly, for what you are, and to salute the wild, indifferent, noncensorious infinity of nature. You are admonished that what you can do avails little materially, and in the end nothing. At the same time, through wonder and pleasure, you are taught speculation. You learn what you are really fitted to do, and where lie your natural dignity and joy, namely, in representing many things, without being them, and in letting your imagination, through sympathy, celebrate and echo their life. Because the peculiarity of man is that his machinery for reaction on external things has involved an imaginative transcript of these things, which is preserved and suspended in his fancy; and the interest and beauty of this inward landscape, rather than any fortunes that may await his body in the outer world, constitute his proper happiness. By their mind, its scope, quality, and temper, we estimate men, for by the mind only do we exist as men, and are more than so many storage-batteries for material energy. Let us therefore be frankly human. Let us be content to live in the mind.

[1911]

Van Wyck Brooks

On Creating a Usable Past

There is a kind of anarchy that fosters growth and there is another anarchy that prevents growth, because it lays too great a strain upon the individual—and all our contemporary literature in America cries out of this latter kind of anarchy. Now, anarchy is never the sheer wantonness of mind that academic people so often think it; it results from the sudden unbottling of elements that have had no opportunity to develop freely in the open; it signifies, among other things, the lack of any sense of inherited resources. English and French writers, European writers in general, never quite separate themselves from the family tree that nourishes and sustains them and assures their growth. Would American writers have done so, plainly against their best interest, if they had had any choice in the matter? I doubt it, and that is why it seems to me significant that our professors continue to pour out a stream of historical works repeating the same points of view to such an astonishing degree that they have placed a sort of Talmudic seal upon the American tradition. I suspect that the past experience of our people is not so much without elements that might be made to contribute to some common understanding in the present, as that the interpreters of that past experience have put a gloss upon it which renders it sterile for the living mind.

I am aware, of course, that we have had no cumulative culture, and that consequently the professors who guard the past and the writers who voice the present inevitably have less in common in this country than anywhere in the Old World. The professors of American literature can, after all, offer very little to the creators of it. But there is a vendetta between the two generations, and the older generation seems to delight in cutting off the supplies of the younger. What actuates the old guard in our criticism and their energetic following in the university world is apparently no sort of desire to fertilize the present, but rather to shame the present with the example of the past. There is in their note an almost pathological vindictiveness when they compare the "poetasters of today" with certain august figures of the age of pioneering who have long since fallen into oblivion in the minds of men and women of the world. Almost pathological, I say, their vindictiveness appears to be; but why not actually so? I think it is; and therefore it seems to me important, as a preliminary step to the reinterpretation of our literature, that we should have the reinterpretation of our professors that now goes merrily forward.

For the spiritual past has no objective reality; it yields only what we are able to look for in it. And what people find in literature corresponds precisely with what they find in life. Now it is obvious that professors who accommodate themselves without effort to an academic world based like ours upon the exigencies of the commerical mind cannot see anything in the past that conflicts with a commerical philosophy. Thanks to his training and environment and the typically non-creative habit of his mind, the American professor by instinct interprets his whole field of learning with reference to the ideal not of the creative, but of the practical life. He does this very often by default, but not less conclusively for that. The teaching of literature stimulates the creative faculty but it also and far more effactually thwarts it, so that the professor turns against himself. He passively plays into the hands that underfeed his own imaginative life and permits the whole weight of his meticulous knowledge of the past to tip the beam against the living present. He gradually comes to fulfill himself in the vicarious world of the dead and returns to the actual world of struggling and miseducated mortals in the majestic raiment of borrowed immortalities. And he pours out upon that world his own contempt for the starveling poet in himself. That is why the histories of our literature so often end with a deprecating gesture at about the year 1890, why they stumble and hesitate when they discuss Whitman, why they disparage almost everything that comes out of the contemporary mind.

Now it is this that differentiates the accepted canon of American literature from those of the literatures of Europe and invalidates it. The European professor is relatively free from these inhibitions; he views the past through the spectacles of his own intellectual freedom; consequently the corpus of inherited experience which he lays before the practicing author is not only infinitely richer and more inspiring than ours, but also more usable. The European writer, whatever his personal education may be, has his racial past, in the first place, and then he has his racial past *made available* for him. The American writer, on the other hand, not only has the most meager of birthrights but is cheated out of that. For the professorial mind, as I have said, puts a gloss upon the past that renders it sterile for the living mind. Instead of reflecting the creative impulse in American history, it reafffirms the values established by the commerical tradition; it crowns everything that has passed the censorship of the commercial and moralistic mind. And it appears to be justified because on the whole, only those American writers who have passed that censorship have undergone a reasonably complete development and in this way entered what is often considered the purview of literary criticism.

What kind of literature it is that has passed that censorship and "succeeded" in this bustling commercial democracy of ours, we all know very well. It has been chiefly a literature of exploitation, the counterpart of our American life. From Irving and Longfellow and Cooper and Bryant, who exploited the legendary and scenic environment of our grandfathers through the local colorists, who dominated our fiction during the intermediate age and to whom the American people accounted for artistic righteousness their own provincial quaintnesses, down to such living authors, congenial to the academic mind, as Winston Churchill, who exploits one after another the "problems" of modern society, the literature that has been allowed to live in this country, that has been imaginatively nourished, has been not only a literature acceptable to the mind that is bent upon turning the tangible world to account but a literature produced by a cognate process. Emerson, Thoreau, Whitman—there you have the exceptions, the *successful* exceptions; but they have survived not because of what they still offer us, but because they were hybrids, with enough pioneer instinct to pay their way among their contemporaries.

There is nothing to resent in this; it has been a plain matter of historic destiny. And historically predestined also is the professorial mind of today. But so is the revolt of the younger generation against the professorial mind. Aside from any personal considerations, we have the clearest sort of evidence that exploitation is alien to the true method of literature, if only because it produces the most lamentable effect on the exploiter. Look at the local colorists! They have all come to a bad end, artistically speaking. Is it necessary to recall the later work of Bret Harte after he had squeezed the orange of California? Or the lachrymosity of Mr. James Lane Allen's ghost revisiting the Kentucky apple tree from which he shook down all the fruit a generation ago? That is the sort of spectacle you have to accept complacently if you take the word of the professors that the American tradition in literature is sound and true; and the public in general does accept it complacently, because it is not averse to lachrymosity and cares nothing about the ethics of personal growth. But the conscientious writer turns aside in disgust. Seeing nothing in the past but an oblivion of all things that have meaning to the creative mood, he decides to paddle his own course, even if it leads to shipwreck.

Unhappily, the spiritual welfare of this country depends altogether upon the fate of its creative minds. If they cannot grow and ripen, where are we going to get the new ideals, the finer attitudes, that we must get if we are ever to emerge from our existing travesty of a civilization? From this point of view our contemporary literature could hardly be in a graver state. We want bold ideas, and we have nuances. We want courage, and we have universal fear. We want individuality, and we have idiosyncrasy. We want vitality, and we have intellectualism. We want emblems of desire, and we have Niagaras of emotionality. We want expansion of soul, and we have an elephantiasis of the vocal organs. Why? Because we have no cultural economy, no abiding sense of spiritual values, no body of critical understanding? Of course; that is the burden of all our criticism. But these conditions result largely, I think, from another condition that is, in part at least, remediable. The present is a void, and the American writer floats in that void because the past that survives in the common mind of the present is a past without living value. But is this the only possible past? If we need another past so badly, is it inconceivable that we might discover one, that we might even invent one?

Discover, invent a usable past we certainly can, and that is what a vital criticism always does. The past that Carlyle put together for England would never have existed if Carlyle had been an American professor. And what about the past that Michelet, groping about in the depths of his own temperament, picked out for the France of his generation? We have had our historians, too, and they have held over the dark backward of time the divining-rods of their imagination and conjured out of it what they wanted and what their contemporaries wanted—Motley's great epic of the self-made man, for instance, which he called *The Rise of the Dutch Republic*. The past is an inexhaustible storehouse of apt attitudes and adaptable ideals; it opens of itself at the touch of desire; it yields up, now this treasure, now that, to anyone who comes to it armed with a capacity for personal choices. If, then, we cannot use the past our professors offer us, is there any reason why we should not create others of our own? The grey conventional mind casts its shadow backward. But why should not the creative mind dispel that shadow with shafts of light?

So far as our literature is concerned, the slightest acquaintance with other national points of view than our own is enough to show how many conceptions of it are not only possible but already exist as commonplaces in the mind of the world. Every people selects from the experience of every other people whatever contributes most vitally to its own development. The history of France that survives in the mind of Italy is totally different from the history of France that survives in the mind of England, and from this point of view there are just as many histories of America as there are nations to possess them. Go to England and you will discover that in English eyes "American literature" has become, while quite as complete an entity as it is with us, an altogether different one. You will find that an entire scheme of ideas and tendencies has survived there out of the American past to which the American academic point of view is wholly irrelevant. This, I say, is a commonplace to anyone whose mind has wandered even the shortest way from home, and to travel in one's imagination from country to country, from decade to decade, is to have this experience indefinitely multiplied. Englishmen will ask you why we Americans have so neglected Herman Melville that there is no biography of him. Russians will tell you that we never really understood the temperament of Jack London. And so on and so on, through all the ramifications of national psychology. By which I do not mean at all that we ought to cut our cloth to fit other people. I mean simply that we have every precedent for cutting it to fit ourselves. Presumably the orthodox interpreters of our literature imagine that they speak of the common reason of humankind. But evidently as regards modern literature that common reason is a very subtle and precarious thing, by no means in the possession of minds that consider it a moral duty to impose upon the world notions that have long since lost their sap. The world is far too rich to tolerate this. When Matthew Arnold once objected to Sainte-Beuve that he did not consider Lamartime an important writer, Sainte-Beuve replied, "Perhaps not, but he is important *for us*." Only by the exercise of a little pragmatism of that kind, I think, can the past experience of our people be placed at the service of the future.

What is important for us? What, out of all the multifarious achievements and impulses and desires of the American literary mind, ought we to elect to remember? The more personally we answer this question, it seems to me, the more likely we are to get a vital order out of the anarchy of the present. For the impersonal way of answering it has been at least in part responsible for this anarchy, by severing the warm artery that ought to lead from the present back into the past. To approach our literature from the point of view not of the successful fact but of the creative impulse, is to throw it into an entirely new focus. What emerges then is the desire, the aspiration, the struggle, the tentative endeavor, and the appalling obstacles our life has placed before them. Which immediately casts over the spiritual history of America a significance that, for us, it has never had before.

Now it is impossible to make this approach without having some poignant experience of the shortcomings, the needs, and the difficulties of our literary life as it is now conditioned. Its anarchy is merely a compound of these, all of which are to be explained not so much by the absence of a cultural past as by the presence of a practical one. In particular, as I have said, this anarchy results from the sudden unbottling of elements that have had no opportunity to develop freely in the open. Why not trace those elements back, analyzing them on the way, and showing how they first manifested themselves, and why, and what repelled them? How many of Theodore Dreiser's defects, for example, are due to an environment that failed to produce the naturalistic mind until the rest of the world had outgrown it and given birth to a more advanced set of needs? And there is Vachel Lindsay. If he runs to sound and color in excess and for their sake voids himself within, how much is that because the life of a Middle Western town sets upon those things an altogether scandalous premium? Well, there you have two of the notorious difficulties of contemporary authorship; and for all that our successful tradition may say, difficulties like those have been the death of our creative life in the past. The point for us is that they have never prevented the creative impulse from being born. Look back and you will see, drifting in and out of the books of history, appearing and vanishing in the memoirs of more aggressive and more acceptable minds, all manner of queer geniuses, wraith-like personalities that have left behind them sometimes a fragment or so that has meaning for us now, more often a mere eccentric name. The creative past of this country is a limbo of the non-elect, the fathers and grandfathers of the talent of today. If they had had a little of the sun and rain that fell so abundantly upon the Goliaths of nineteenth-century philistinism, how much better conditioned would their descendants be!

The real task for the American literary historian, then, is not to seek for masterpieces— the few masterpieces are all too obvious—but for tendencies. Why did Ambrose Bierce go wrong? Why did Stephen Crane fail to acclimatize the modern method in American fiction twenty years ago? What became of Herman Melville? How did it happen that a mind capable of writing *The Story of a Country Town* should have turned up thirty years later with a book like *Success Easier Than Failure*? If we were able to answer the hundred and one questions of this sort that present themselves to every curious mind, we might throw an entirely new face not only over the past but over the present and the future also. Knowing that others have desired the things we desire and have encountered the same obstacles, and that in some degree time has begun to face those obstacles down and make the way straight for us, would not the creative forces of this country lose a little of the hectic individualism that keeps them from uniting against their common enemies? And would this not bring about, for the first time, that sense of brotherhood in effort and in aspiration which is the best promise of a national culture?   [1918]

Irving Babbitt

The Critic and American Life

A frequent remark of the French about Americans is: "They're children"; which, interpreted, means that from the French point of view Americans are childishly uncritical. The remark is relevant only in so far as it refers to general critical intelligence. In dealing with the special problems of a commercial and industrial society, Americans have shown that they can be abundantly critical. Certain Americans, for example, have developed a critical keenness in estimating the value of stocks and bonds that is nothing short of uncanny.[1] The very persons, however, who are thus keen in some particular field are, when confronted with questions that call for general critical intelligence, often puerile. Yet in an age like the present, which is being subjected to a constant stream of propaganda in everything from the choice of religion to its cigarettes, general critical intelligence would seem desirable.

As a matter of fact, most persons aspire nowadays to be not critical but creative. We have not merely creative poets and novelists, but creative readers and listeners and dancers. Lately a form of creativeness has appeared that may in time swallow up all the others—creative salesmanship. The critic himself has caught the contagion and also aspires to be creative. He is supposed to become so when he receives from the creation of another, conceived as pure temperamental overflow, so vivid an impression that, when passed through his temperament, it issues forth as a new creation. What is eliminated in both critic and creator is any standard that is set above temperament, and that therefore might interfere with their eagerness to get themselves expressed.

This notion of criticism as self-expression is important for our present subject, for it has been adopted by the writer who is, according to the *Encyclopedia Britannica*,[2] "The greatest critical force in America"—Mr. H. L. Mencken. Creative self-expression, as practiced by himself and others, has, according to Mr. Mencken, led to a salutary stirring up of the stagnant pool of American letters: "Today for the first time in years there is strife in American criticism. . . . Heretics lay on boldly and the professors are forced to make some defense. Often going further they attempt counterattacks. Ears are bitten off, noses are bloodied. There are wallops both above and below the belt."

But it may be that criticism is something more than Mr. Mencken would have us believe, more in short than a squabble between Bohemians, each eager to capture the attention of the public for his brand of self-expression. To reduce criticism indeed to the satisfaction of a temperamental urge, to the uttering of one's gustos and disgustos (in

Irving Babbitt's "The Critic and American Life" (1932), published in *On Being Creative and Other Essays*, by Irving Babbitt, is reprinted with permission of the National Humanities Institute, Washington, D.C.

[1]This was written before the collapse of the great common stock bubble in the autumn of 1929. It then became evident that what the financial leaders of the "Boom" period lacked was not so much expertness in their own field as general critical intelligence—especially some working knowledge of the ways of Nemesis. There were, of course, honorable exceptions. The late Paul M. Warburg showed that he was one of them when he remarked, apropos of the so-called business cycle, that "it is a subject for psychologists rather than for economists." [What is involved] "is the answer to the question: How long—in industry, commerce and finance—does the memory of painful experiences prevent human greed and conceit from regaining control, etc."

[2]Thirteenth edition. In the fourteenth edition we are informed that Mr. Mencken is a satirist rather than a critic.

Mr. Mencken's case chiefly the latter) is to run counter to the very etymology of the word which implies discrimination and judgment. The best one would anticipate from a writer like Mr. Mencken, possessing an unusual verbal virtuosity and at the same time temperamentally irresponsible, is superior intellectual vaudeville. One must grant him, however, certain genuine critical virtues—for example, a power of shrewd observation within rather narrow limits. Yet the total effect of his writing is nearer to intellectual vaudeville than to serious criticism.

The serious critic is more concerned with achieving a correct scale of values and so seeing things proportionately than with self-expression. His essential virtue is poise. The specific benefit he confers is to act as a moderating influence on the opposite insanities between which mankind in the lump is constantly tending to oscillate—oscillations that Luther compares to the reelings of a drunken peasant on horseback. The critic's survey of any particular situation may very well seem satirical. The complaint that Mr. Mencken is too uniformly disgruntled in his survey of the American situation rather misses the point. Behind the pleas for more constructiveness it is usually easy to detect the voice of the booster. A critic who did not get beyond a correct diagnosis of existing evils might be very helpful. If Mr. Mencken has fallen short of being such a diagnostician, the failure is due not to his excess of severity but to his lack of discrimination.

The standards with reference to which men have discriminated in the past have been largely traditional. The outstanding fact of the present period, on the other hand, has been the weakening of traditional standards. An emergency has arisen not unlike that with which Socrates sought to cope in ancient Athens. Anyone who is untraditional and seeks at the same time to be discriminating must almost necessarily own Socrates as his master. As is well known, Socrates above all sought to be discriminating in his use of general terms. Before allowing one's imagination and finally one's conduct to be controlled by a general term, it would seem wise to submit it to a Socratic scrutiny.

It is, therefore, unfortunate that at a time like the present, which plainly calls for a Socrates, we should instead have got a Mencken. One may take as an example of Mr. Mencken's failure to discriminate adequately, his attitude towards the term that for several generations past has been governing the imagination of multitudes—democracy. His view of democracy is simply that of Rousseau turned upside down, and nothing, as has been remarked, resembles a hollow so much as a swelling. A distinction of which he has failed to recognize the importance is that between a direct or unlimited and a constitutional democracy. In the latter we probably have the best thing in the world. The former, on the other hand, as all thinkers of any penetration from Plato and Aristotle down have perceived, leads to the loss of liberty and finally to the rise of some form of despotism. The two conceptions of democracy involve not merely incompatible views of government but ultimately of human nature. The desire of the constitutional democrat for institutions that act as checks on the immediate will of the people implies a similar dualism in the individual—a higher self that acts restrictively on his ordinary and impulsive self. The partisan of unlimited democracy on the other hand is an idealist in the sense the term assumed in connection with the so-called romantic movement. His faith in the people is closely related to the doctrine of natural goodness proclaimed by the sentimentalists of the eighteenth century and itself marking an extreme recoil from the dogmas of total depravity. The doctrine of natural goodness favors the free temperamental expansion that I have already noticed in speaking of the creative critic.

It is of the utmost importance, however, if one is to understand Mr. Mencken, to discriminate between two types of temperamentalist—the soft and sentimental type, who cherishes various "ideals" and the hard, or Nietzschean type, who piques himself on being realistic. As a matter of fact, if one sees in the escape from traditional controls merely an opportunity to live temperamentally, it would seem advantageous to pass promptly from the idealistic to the Nietzschean phase, sparing oneself as many as possible of the intermediary disillusions. It is at all events undeniable that the rise of Menckenism has been marked by a certain collapse of romantic idealism in the political field and elsewhere. The numerous disillusions that have supervened upon the War have provided a favoring atmosphere.

The symptoms of Menckenism are familiar: a certain hardness and smartness and dispositon to rail at everything that, rightly or wrongly, is established and respected; a tendency to identify the real with what Mr. Mencken terms "the cold and clammy facts" and to assume that the only alternative to facing these facts is to fade away into sheer romantic unreality. These and similar traits are becoming so widely diffused that, whatever one's opinion of Mr. Mencken as a writer and thinker, one must grant him representativeness. He is a chief prophet at present of those who deem themselves emancipated but who are, according to Mr. Brownell, merely unbuttoned.

The crucial point in any case is one's attitude towards the principle of control. Those who stand for this principle in any form or degree are dismissed by the emancipated as reactionaries or, still graver reproach, as Puritans. Mr. Mencken would have us believe that the historical Puritan was not even sincere in his moral rigorism, but was given to "lamentable transactions with loose women and fiery jugs." This may serve as a sample of the assertions, picturesquely indiscriminate, by which a writer wins immediate notoriety at the expense of his permanent reputation. The facts about the Puritan happen to be complex and need to be dealt with very Socratically. It has been affirmed that the point of view of the Puritan was stoical rather than truly Christian, and the affirmation is not wholly false. The present discussion of the relationship between Puritanism and the rise of capitalism with its glorification of the acquisitive life also has its justification. It is likewise a fact that the Puritan was from the outset unduly concerned with reforming others as well as himself, and this trait relates him to the humanitarian meddler or "wowser" of the present day, who is Mr. Mencken's pet aversion.

Yet it remains true that awe and reverence and humility are Christian virtues and that there was some survival of these virtues in the Puritan. For a representative Puritan like Jonathan Edwards they were inseparable from the illumination of grace, from what he terms a "divine and supernatural light." In the passage from the love and fear of God of an Edwards to the love and service of man professed by the humanitarian, something has plainly dropped out, something that is very near the center. What has tended to disappear is the inner life with the special type of control it imposes. With the decline of this inner control there has been an increasing resort to outer control. Instead of the genine Puritan we then have the humanitarian legalist who passes innumerable laws for the control of people who refuse to control themselves. The activity of the uplifters is scarcely suggestive of any "divine and supernatural light." Here is a discrimination of the first importance that has been obscured by the muddy thinking of our half-baked intelligentsia. One is thus kept from perceiving the real problem, which is to retain the inner life, even though one refuses to accept the theological nightmare with which the Puritan associated it. More is involved in the failure to solve this problem than the Puritan tradition. It is the failure of our contemporary life in general. Yet, unless some relation is reached by a full and free exercise of the critical spirit, one remains a mere modernist and not a thoroughgoing and complete modern; for the modern spirit and the critical spirit are in their essence one.

What happens, when one sets out to deal with questions of this order without sufficient depth of reflection and critical maturity, may be seen in Mr. Sinclair Lewis's *Elmer*

Gantry. He has been lured from art into the writing of a wild diatribe which, considered even as such, is largely beside the mark. If the Protestant Church is at present threatened with bankruptcy, it is not because it has produced an occasional Elmer Gantry. The true reproach it has incurred is that, in its drift toward modernism, it has lost its grip not merely on certain dogmas, but simultaneously on the facts of human nature. It has failed above all to carry over in some modern and critical form the truth of a dogma that unfortunately receives much support from these facts—the dogma of original sin. At first sight Mr. Mencken would appear to have a conviction of evil—when, for example, he reduces democracy in its essential aspect to a "combat between jackals and jackasses"—that establishes at least one bond between him and the austere Christian.

The appearance, however, is deceptive. The Christian is conscious above all of the "old Adam" in himself; hence his humility. The effect of Mr. Mencken's writing, on the other hand, is to produce pride rather than humility, a pride ultimately based on flattery. The reader, especially the young and callow reader, identifies himself imaginatively with Mr. Mencken, and conceives of himself as a sort of morose and sardonic divinity surveying from some superior altitude an immeasurable expanse of "boobs." This attitude will not seem especially novel to anyone who has traced the modern movement. One is reminded in particular of Flaubert, who showed a diligence in collecting bourgeois imbecilities comparable to that displayed by Mr. Mencken in his *Americana.* Flaubert's discovery that one does not add to one's happiness in this way would no doubt be dismissed by Mr. Mencken as irrelevant, for he has told us that he does not believe in happiness. Another discovery of Flaubert's may seem to him more worthy of consideration. "By dint of railing at idiots," Flaubert reports, "one runs the risk of becoming idiotic oneself."

It may be that the only way to escape from the unduly complacent cynicism of Mr. Mencken and his school, is to reaffirm once more the truths of the inner life. In that case it would seem desirable to disengage, so far as possible, the principle of control on which the inner life finally depends from mere creeds and traditions and assert it as a psychological fact; a fact, moreover, that is neither "cold" nor "clammy." The coldness and clamminess of much so-called realism arises from its failure to give this fact due recognition. A chief task, indeed, of the Socratic critic would be to rescue the noble term "realist" from its present degradation. A view of reality that overlooks the element in man that moves in an opposite direction from mere temperament, the specifically human factor, in short, may prove to be singularly one-sided. Is the Puritan, John Milton, when he declares that "he who reigns within himself and rules passions, desires, and fears is more than a king," less real than Mr. Theodore Dreiser when he discourses in his peculiar dialect of "those rearranging chemisms upon which all the morality and immorality of the world is based"?

As a matter of fact, according to the degree and nature of the exercise of the principle of control, one may distinguish two main types of realism which may be denominated respectively religious and humanistic: as the principle of control falls into abeyance, a third type tends to emerge, which may be termed naturalistic realism. That the decline of the traditional controls have been followed by a lapse to the naturalistic level is indubitable. The characteristic evils of the present age arise from unrestraint and violation of the law of measure and not, as our modernists would have us believe, from the tyranny of taboos and traditional inhibitions. The facts cry to heaven. The delicate adjustment that is required between the craving for emancipation and the need of control has been pointed out once for all by Goethe, speaking not as a Puritan, but as a clear-eyed man of the world. Everything, he says, that liberates the spirit without a corresponding growth in self-mastery is pernicious. This one sentence would seem to cover the case of our "flaming youth" rather completely.

The movement in the midst of which we are still living was from its inception unsound in its dealing with the principle of control. It is vain to expect from the dregs of this movement what its "first sprightly running failed to give." Mr. Carl Sandburg speaks of the "marvelous rebellion of man at all signs reading *Keep off.*" An objection to this purely insurrectional attitude is that, as a result of its endless iteration during the past century and more, it has come to savor too strongly of what has been called the "humdrum of revolt." A more serious objection to the attitude is that it encourages an unrestricted and merely temperamental liberty which, paradoxically enough, at first sight affords the modern man no avenue of escape from the web that is being woven about him by the scientific determinist.

Realists of the current type are in point of fact intimately allied with the psychologists—glandular, behavioristic, and psychoanalytical—who, whatever their divergences among themselves, unite in their deterministic trend and therefore class fundamentally with both religious and humanistic realists. The proper method of procedure in defending the freedom of the will would seem to insist upon it as a fact of experience, a fact so primary that the position of the determinist involves an evasion of one of the immediate data of consciousness in favor of a metaphysical dream. What is genuinely experimental in naturalistic psychology should of course be received with respect; but the facts of which it takes account in its experiments are unimportant compared with the facts it either neglects or denies. Practically it is running into grotesque extremes of pseudo-science that make it a shining mark for the Socratic critic.

Here at all events is the issue on which all other issues finally hinge; for until the question of moral freedom—the question of whether man is a responsible agent or only the plaything of his impulses and impressions—is decided, nothing is decided; and to decide the question under existing circumstances calls for the keenest critical discrimination. Creation that is not sufficiently supported by such discrimination is likely to prove premature.

One may illustrate from Mr. Dreiser's *American Tragedy,* hailed in certain quarters as the "Mount Everest" of recent fiction. He has succeeded in producing in this work something genuinely harrowing; but one is harrowed to no purpose. One has in more than full measure the tragic qualm but without the final relief and enlargement of spirit that true tragedy succeeds somehow in giving, and that without recourse to explicit moralizing. It is hardly worth while to struggle through eight hundred and more very pedestrian pages to be left at the end with a feeling of sheer oppression. The explanation of this oppression is that Mr. Dreiser does not rise sufficiently above the level of "rearranging chemisms," in other words, of animal behavior. Tragedy may admit fate—Greek tragedy admits it—but not of the naturalistic variety. Confusion on this point may compromise in the long run the reputations of writers more eminent than Mr. Dreiser—for example, of Thomas Hardy. Fatalism of the naturalistic type is responsible in large measure for the atmosphere of futility and frustration that hangs heavily over so much contemporary writing. One finally comes to feel with a recent poet that "dust" is the common source from which

stream
The cricket's cry and Dante's dream.

Anyone who admits reality only in what derives from the dust, whether in a cricket or Dante, must, from the point of view of the religious or the humanistic realist, be prepared to make substantial sacrifices. In the first place, he must sacrifice the depth and subtlety that arise from the recognition in some form of the duality in man's nature. For the interest that may rise from the portrayal of the conflict between a law of the spirit and a law of the members, the inordinate interest in sex for its own sake promoted by most of the so-called realists is a rather shabby substitute. A merely naturalistic realism also involves the sacrifice of beauty in almost any sense of that elusive term. Closely related to this sacrifice is the sacrifice of delicacy, elevation, and distinction. The very word realism has come to connote the opposite of these qualities. When we learn, for example, that someone has written a realistic study of a great man, we are sure in advance that he has devoted his main effort to proving that "Plutarch lied." The more the great man is reduced to the level of commonplace or worse, the more we feel he has been "humanized."

Mr. Sherwood Anderson has argued ingeniously that, inasmuch as we ourselves are crude, our literature, if it is not to be unreal and fictitious, should be crude likewise. But the writer who hopes to achieve work of importance cannot afford to be too deeply immersed in the atmosphere of the special place and passing moment. Still less can he afford to make us feel, as writers like Mr. Anderson and Mr. Dreiser and Mr. Sinclair Lewis do, that, if there were any lack of vulgarity in what they are depicting, they would be capable of supplying the defect from their own abundance. More is involved here than the mere loss of distinction. We have come, indeed, to the supreme sacrifice that every writer must make who does not transcend a naturalistic realism. He must forgo the hope of the enduring appeal—the hope that every writer worthy of his salt cherishes in some degree. In the absence of humanistic or religious standards, he is prone to confound the real with the welter of the actual, and so to miss the "grandeur of generality."

Certain books in the current mode are so taken up with the evanescent surfaces of life that they will survive, if at all, not as literature but as sociological documents. The very language in which they are written will, in a generation or two, require a glossary. So far from imposing an orderly pattern on the raw material of experience, they rather emphasize the lack of pattern. The resulting effect, to borrow a phrase from the late Stephen Crane, who has had a marked influence on the recent movement, is that of a "cluttered incoherency." As an extreme example of this tendency one may cite *Manhattan Transfer,* by John Dos Passos. In the name of reality Mr. Dos Passos has perpetrated a literary nightmare. Such a work would seem to have slight value even as a sociological document; unless, indeed, one is prepared to admit that contemporary Manhattan is inhabited chiefly by epileptic Bohemians.

"It is as much a trade," says La Bruyère, "to make a book as it is to make a clock"; in short, literature is largely a matter of technique. The technique of *Manhattan Transfer* is as dubious as its underlying philosophy. Neither can be justified save on the assumption that the aim of art is to exaggerate the clutter and incoherency of the mundane spectacle instead of eliciting its deeper meaning. Technique counts for even more in poetry than in prose. It would be possible to base on technical grounds alone a valid protest against the present preposterous overestimate of Walt Whitman. Fundamental questions need, in these very untraditional days, to be critically elucidated with a view to right definition if the poet is not to lack technique or still worse, if he is not, like certain recent practitioners of free verse, to be hagridden by a false technique. It evidently concerns both the form and substance of poetry, whether one define it with Aristotle as the portrayal of representative human action, or whether one define it with Mr. Carl Sandburg as a "mystic, sensuous mathematics of fire, smokestacks, waffles, pansies, people, and purple sunsets."

There is no doubt much in America of today that suggests a jazzy impressionism. Still our naturalistic deliquescence has probably not gone so far as one might infer from poetry like that of Mr. Sandburg or fiction like that of Mr. Dos Passos. The public response to some of the realistic novels has been considerable: allowance must be made however for the *succès de scandale,* also for the skill attained by the modern publisher in the art of merchandising. The reputation of certain books one might mention may be regarded as a triumph of "creative" advertising. What has been created is a mirage of masterpieces where no masterpieces are. It is well also to remember in regard to some of the works that have been most discussed that, so far from being an authentic reflection of the American scene, they are rather a belated echo of certain European movements. For it is as certain that in our literary and artistic modes we follow Europe—usually at an interval of from five to forty years—as it is that we lead Europe in our bathtubs and sanitary plumbing. Anyone who resided in Paris in the nineties and later in America, will, as I can testify from personal experience, have the sense of having lived through the same literary fads twice. Mr. Dreiser reminds one of Zola and his school. The technique of Mr. Dos Passos recalls that of the Goncourts. Our experimenters in free verse have followed in the wake not merely of Walt Whitman but of the French symbolists, and so on.

We shall presently begin to hear of certain new developments in French literature and critical thought that point, though indecisively as yet, to a radical departure from what has been the main current since the eighteenth century and in some respects since the Renaissance. It is well that we should become familiar with the writers who reveal in different ways this latest trend—notably with Maritain, Maurras, Lasserre, Seillière, and Benda; for they give evidence of a quality of cerebration that is rare in our own literati. At the same time we should not adopt with our usual docility the total outlook of any of these writers: for no one of them has worked out a point of view exactly adapted to our requirements. In general, it is not fitting that a great nation at the very height of its power should go on indefinitely trailing after Europe. It is time for us to initiate something of our own. This does not mean that we should proceed forthwith to inbreed our own "originality." It means almost the exact opposite. The most original thing one could do nowadays would be to question the whole theory of originality as mere temperamental overflow and self-expression that has prevailed from the "geniuses" of the eighteenth century down to one of our youthful and very minor bards who aspires to "spill his bright illimitable soul."

A genuinely critical survey would make manifest that the unsatisfactoriness of our creative effort is due to a lack of the standards that culture alone can supply. Our cultural crudity and insignificance can be traced in turn to the inadequacy of our education, especially our higher education. Mr. Mencken's attack on the "professors" is therefore largely justified; for if the professors were performing their function properly Mr. Mencken himself would not be possible. One must add in common justice that the professors themselves, or at least some of them, are becoming aware that all is not well with existing conditions. One could not ask anything more perspicacious than the following paragraph from a recent report of Committee G to the American Association of University Professors:

American education has suffered from the domination, conscious or unconscious, direct or indirect, of political and sentimental, as well as educational, theories that are demonstrably false. If the views of some men are to prevail the intellectual life of the country is doomed; everybody except the sheer idiot is to go to college and pursue chiefly sociology, nature study, child study, and community service—and we shall have a society unique only in its mediocrity, ignorance, and vulgarity. It will not do to dismiss lightly even so extreme a view as this; it is too indicative. Such influences are very strong, their pressure is constant; and if education has largely failed in America, it has been due primarily to them.

In short, as a result of the encroachments of an equalitarian democracy, the standards of our higher education have suffered in two distinct particulars: first, as regards the quality of students; second, as regards the quality of the studies these students pursue. The first of these two evils is generally recognized. There is even some prospect of remedial measures. Certain institutions, Harvard, for example, without being as yet severely selective, are becoming more critical of the incompetent student. On the other hand, there seems to be less hope than ever of any righting of the second and more serious evil—the failure to distinguish qualitatively between studies. The main drift is still towards what one may term a blanket degree. (Darmouth, for example, has just merged its bachelor of arts and bachelor of science.) Yet rather than blur certain distinctions it would have been better, one might suppose, to use up all the letters of the alphabet devising new degrees to meet the real or supposed educational needs of the modern man. To bestow the A.B. degree indiscriminately on a student for whom education has meant primarily a specialization in chemistry and one for whom it has meant primarily an assimilation of the masterpieces of Greek literature is to empty it of any effective meaning. At the present rate, indeed, the time may come when the A.B. degree will not throw much more light on the cultural quality of its recipient than it would if, as has been suggested, it were bestowed on every American child at birth.

It goes without saying that those who have been lowering and confusing educational standards have been profuse in their professions of "service." A critical examination, not merely of American education, but of American life at the present time, will almost necessarily hinge on this term. The attitude of the Socratic critic toward it is not to be confounded with that of Mr. Mencken and the "hardboiled" contingent. "When a gang of real estate agents," says Mr. Mencken, "bond salesmen, and automobile dealers get together to sob for Service, it takes no Freudian to Surmise that someone is about to be swindled." But if one entertains doubts about this current American gospel, why waste one's ammunition on any such small fry? Other and more exalted personages than the members of the Rotary Club at Zenith have, in Mr. Mencken's elegant phrase, been "yipping for Service." If one is to deal with this idea of service Socratically, one needs to consider it in relation to the two figures who have rightly been taken to be most representative in our cultural background—Benjamin Franklin and Jonathan Edwards. Franklin's idea of service is already humanitarian. Edwards' idea is still traditionally Christian—service not of man but of God. What Franklin stood for is flourishing prodigiously at the present moment, so much so that he may perhaps be defined in his chief line of influence as the great superrotarian. What Edwards stood for is, on the other hand, largely obsolete or survives only in the form of habits, which, lacking doctrinal support, are steadily declining along with the whole Puritan culture.

Intermediary types are possible. One may in one's character reflect the Puritan background and at the same time in one's idea of service derive rather from Franklin. Precisely that combination is found in the most influential of our recent educational leaders—the late President Eliot. A legitimate admiration for his personal qualities should not interfere with the keenest critical scrutiny of his views about education, for the two things stand in no necessary connection. Practically this means to scrutinize the humanitarian ideal that he probably did more than any other man of his generation to promote. In this respect most of the heads of our institutions of learning have been and still are understudies of President Eliot.

In an address on the occasion of his ninetieth birthday President Eliot warned his hearers against introspection, lest it divert them from a whole-hearted devotion to service. Between this attitude and a religious or humanistic attitude there is a clash of first principles. Both humanism and religion require introspection as a prerequisite of the inner life and its appropriate activity. With the disappearance of this activity what is left is the outer activity of the utilitarian, and this leads straight to the one-sided cult of material efficiency and finally to the standardization that is, according to nearly all foreign critics and many of our own, a chief American danger. We cannot return to the introspection of the Puritan. We shudder at the theology an Edwards would impose as the condition of his "divine and supernatural light." Yet it does not follow, as I have already suggested, that we should reject the inner life along with this theology. One may recognize innumerable advantages in the gospel of service and yet harbor an uneasy suspicion withal that in the passage from the old religion to the modern humanitarian dispensation something vital has disappeared, something from which neither the outer working of the utilitarian nor again the expansive sympathy of the sentimentalist can offer an equivalent.

The problem of the inner life is very much bound up with two other problems that are now pressing for solution in our higher education and have as yet found none: the problem of the specialist and the problem of leisure. The man of leisure is engaged in an inner and specifically human form of activity, a form that is, according to Aristotle, needful if he is to compass the end of ends—his own happiness. The question is whether one should consent like the specialist to forego this activity and to live partially and as a mere instrument for the attainment of some outer end—even though this end be the progress of humanity. We are beginning to hear a great deal nowadays about the "menace" of leisure. It has been estimated that with the perfecting of mechanical devices the man of the future will be able to satisfy his material wants by working not more than four hours a day. It is vain to anticipate that the rank and file will use this release from outer activity intelligently unless the leaders, notably those in high academic station, show the way. The notion of true leisure is the ultimate source of the standards of any education that deserves to be called liberal. When even a few of our college and university presidents show that they are thinking to some purpose on the nature of leisure it will be time enough to talk of "America's coming of age."

As it is, our institutions of learning seem to be becoming more and more hotbeds of "idealism." Their failure, on the whole, to achieve standards as something quite distinct from ideals, on the one hand, and standardization, on the other, may prove a fact of sinister import for the future of American civilization. The warfare that is being waged at the present time by Mr. Sinclair Lewis and others against a standardized Philistinism continues in the main the protest that has been made for several generations past by the temperamentalists, hard or soft, against the mechanizing of life by the utilitarian. This protest has been, and is likely to continue to be, ineffectual. The fruitful opposite of the standardized Philistine is not the Bohemian, nor again the hard temperamentalist or superman, as Mr. Mencken conceives him, but the man of leisure. Leisure involves an inner effort with reference to standards that is opposed to the sheer expansion of temperament, as it is to every other form of sheer expansion.

Perhaps a reason why the standards of the humanist are less popular in this country than the ideals of the humanitarian is that these standards set bounds to the acquisitive life; whereas it seems possible to combine a perfect idealism with an orgy of unrestricted commercialism. It is well for us to try to realize how we appear to others in this matter. Our growing unpopularity abroad is due no doubt in part to envy of our material success, but it also arises from the proneness of the rest of the world to judge us, not by the way we feel about ourselves, but by our actual performance. If we are in our own eyes a nation of idealists, we are, according to a recent French critic, M. André Siegfried,[3] a "nation of Pharisees." The European, M. Siegfried would have us believe, still has a concern for the higher values of civilization, whereas the American is prepared to sacrifice these values ruthlessly to mass production and material efficiency.

[3]See his volume *Les États-Unis d'aujourd'hui* (1927), translated under the title *America Comes of Age.*

It is easy to detect under this assumption the latest form of a "certain condescension in foreigners." The breakdown of cultural standards is European as well as American. It is not clear that M. Siegfried himself has an adequate notion of the form of effort that can alone serve as a counterpoise to the one-sided activity of the utilitarian. At the same time his anatomy of our favorite ideal of service is not without interest. This ideal opposes no effective barrier to our expansiveness. An unchecked expansiveness on the national scale is always imperialistic. Among the ingredients of a possible American imperialism M. Siegfried enumerates the American's "great self-satisfaction, his rather brutal sense of his own interests, and *the consciousness, still more dangerous, of his 'duties' towards humanity.*" M. Siegfried admits however that our imperialism is likely to be of a new and subtle essence, not concerned primarily with territorial aggrandizement.

A proper discussion of M. Siegfried's position as well as of other issues I have been raising would transcend the limits of an essay. My end has been accomplished if I have justified in some measure that statement with which I started as to the importance of cultivating a general critical intelligence. James Russell Lowell's dictum that before having an American literature we must have an American criticism was never truer than it is today. The obvious reply to those who call for more creation and less criticism is that one needs to be critical above all in examining what now passes for creation. A scrutiny of this kind would, I have tried to show, extend beyond the bounds of literature to various aspects of our national life and would converge finally on our higher education.

We cannot afford to accept as substitute for this true criticism the self-expression of Mr. Mencken and his school, unless indeed we are to merit the comment that is, I am told, made on us by the South Americans: "They are not a very serious people!" To be sure, the reader may reflect that I am myself a critic, or a would-be critic. I can only express the hope that, in my magnifying of the critical function, I do not offer too close a parallel to the dancingmaster of Molière who averred, it will be remembered, that "all the mistakes of men, the fatal reverses that fill the world's annals, the shortcomings of statesmen, and the blunders of great captains arise from not knowing how to dance."

H. L. Mencken

The American Novel

It is an ancient platitude of historical criticism that great wars and their sequelae are inimical to the fine arts, and particularly to the arts of letters. The kernel of truth in it lies in the obvious fact that a people engaged in a bitter struggle for existence have no time for such concerns, which demand not only leisure but also a certain assured feeling of security, well-being and self-sufficiency—in brief, the thing often called aristocratic (or sometimes intellectual) detachment. No man ever wrote good poetry with his wife in parturition in the next room, or the police preparing to raid his house, or his shirt-tail afire. He needs to be comfortable to do it, and if not actually comfortable, then at all events safe. Wars tend to make life uncomfortable and unsafe—but not, it must be observed, inevitably and necessarily, not always and invariably. A bitter and demoralizing struggle goes with wars that are lost, and the same struggle goes with wars that are won only by dint of stupendous and ruinous effort, but it certainly does not go with wars that are won easily. These last do not palsy and asphyxiate the artist, as he is palsied and asphyxiated by cholera morbus, suits for damages or marriage. On the contrary, they pump him full of ozone, and he is never more alive and lively than following them.

I point to a few familiar examples. The Civil War, as everyone knows, bankrupted the South and made life a harsh and bitter struggle for its people, and especially for the gentler and more civilized minority of its people. In consequence, the South became as sterile artistically, after Lee's surrender, as Mexico or Portugal, and even today it lags far behind the North in beautiful letters, and even further behind in music, painting and architecture. But the war, though it went on for four years, strained the resources of the North very little, either in men or in money, and so its conclusion found the Northerners very rich and cocky, and full of a yearning to astonish the world, and that yearning, in a few decades, set up a new and extremely vigorous American literature, created an American architecture of a revolutionary character, and even laid the first courses of American schools of music and painting. Mark Twain, Walt Whitman, Henry James, and William Dean Howells, all of them draft dodgers in the war itself, were in a very real sense products of the war, for they emerged as phenomena of the great outburst of creative energy that followed it, and all of them, including even James, were as thoroughly American as Jay Gould, P. T. Barnum, or Jim Fisk. The stars of the national letters in the years before the war had been Americans only by geographical accident. About Emerson there hung a smell of Königsberg and Weimar; Irving was simply a New York Englishman; Poe was a citizen of No Man's Land; even Hawthorne and Cooper, despite their concern with American themes, showed not the slightest evidence of an American point of view. But Mark Twain, Howells, and Whitman belonged to the Republic as palpably as Niagara Falls or Tammany Hall belonged to it, and so did James, though the thought horrified him and we must look at him through his brother William to get the proof. Turn now to Europe. France, harshly used in the war of 1870–71, was sterile for a decade, but the wounds were not deep, and recovery was in full swing by 1880. Germany, injured scarcely at all, produced Nietzsche almost before the troops got home, and was presently offering an asylum and an inspiration to Ibsen, preparing the way for the reform and modernization of the theatre, and making contributions of the utmost value to practically all of the arts and sciences. Spain, after the Armada, gave the world Cervantes and then expired; England produced Shakespeare and founded a literature that is not surpassed in history.

What has thus happened over and over again in the past—and I might pile up examples for pages—may be in process of repetition today, and under our very noses. All Europe, plainly enough, is in a state of exhaustion and depression, and in no department of human activity is the fact more visible than in that of the arts. Not only are the defeated nations, Russia, Germany, and Austria, producing nothing save a few extravagant eccentricities; there is also a great lowness of spirit in the so-called victorious nations, for their victory was almost as ruinous as defeat. France, as after 1870, is running to a pretentious and artificial morbidity in letters, and marking time in music and painting; Italy is producing little save psychopathological absurdities by such mountebanks as D'Annunzio and Papini; even England shows all the signs of profound fatigue. The great English writers of the age before the war are passing. Meredith is gone; Hardy has put up his shutters; Kipling went to wreck in the war itself; Conrad is dead; Shaw, once so agile and diverting, becomes a seer and prophet. Nor is there any sign of sound progress among the younger men. Arnold Bennett, a star of brilliant promise in 1913, is today a smoking smudge. Wells has ceased to be an artist and become a prophet in the Sunday supplements. Masefield has got no further than he was on August 2, 1914. The rest of the novelists are simply chasing their own tails. The Georgian poets, having emerged gloriously during the war, now disappear behind their manners. Only a few women, led by May Sinclair, and a few iconoclastic young men, led by Aldous Huxley, are still indubitably alive.

It seems to me that, in the face of this dark depression across the water, the literary spectacle on this side takes on an aspect that is extremely reassuring, and even a bit exhilarating. For the first time in history, there begins to show itself the faint shadow of a hope that, if all goes well, leadership in the arts, and especially in all the art of letters, may eventually transfer itself from the eastern shore of the Atlantic to the western shore. Our literature, as I have more than once pointed out in the past, is still oppressed by various heavy handicaps, chiefly resident in the failure of the new aristocracy of money to function as an aristocracy of taste. The artist among us is still a sort of pariah, beset by public contempt on the one hand and by academic enmity on the other; he still lacks the public position that his brothers enjoy in older and more civilized countries. Nevertheless, it must be obvious to everyone that his condition tends to improve materially—that, in our own time, it has improved materially—that though his rewards remain meager, save in mere money, his freedom grows steadily greater. And it must be obvious, too, that he begins to show that that increasing freedom is not wholly wasted upon him—that he knows how to use it, and is disposed to do so with some gusto. What all the younger American writers have in common is a sort of new-found elasticity or goatishness, a somewhat exaggerated sense of aliveness, a glowing delight in the spectacle before them, a vigorous and naive self-consciousness. The schoolmaster critics belabor them for it, and call it a disrespect for tradition, and try to put it down by denouncing it as due to corrupt foreign influences. But it is really a proof of the rise of nationalism—perhaps of the first dawn of a genuine sense of nationality. No longer imitative and timorous, as most of their predecessors were, these youngsters are attempting a first-hand examination of the national scene, and making an effort to represent it in terms that are wholly American. They are the pioneers of a literature that, whatever its defects in the abstract, will at least be a faithful reflection of the national life, that will be more faithful, indeed, in its defects than in its merits. In England the novel subsides into formulae, the drama is submerged in artificialities, and even poetry, despite occasional revolts, moves toward scholarliness and emptiness. But in America, since the war, all three show the artless and super-abundant energy of little children. They lack, only too often, manner and urbanity; it is no wonder that they are often shocking to pedants. But there is the breath of life in them, and that life is far nearer its beginning than its end.

The causes of all this are not far to seek. The American Legion is right: we won the war. It cost us nothing in men; it brought us a huge profit in money; as Europe has gone down, we have gone up. Moreover, it produced a vast discharge of spiritual electricity, otherwise and more injuriously dissipated in the countries more harshly beset. The war was fought ignobly; its first and most obvious effect was to raise up a horde of cads, and set them in authority as spokesmen of the nation. But out of that swinishness there was bound to come reaction, and out of the reaction there was bound to flow a desire to re-examine the whole national pretension—to turn on the light, to reject old formulae, to think things out anew and in terms of reality. Suddenly the old houses of cards came tumbling down, and the professors inhabiting them ran about in their nightshirts, bawling for the police. The war, first and last, produced a great deal more than John Dos Passos' *Three Sol-*

diers. It also produced Lewis' *Babbitt,* and Cabell's *Jurgen,* and Fergusson's *Capitol Hill* and O'Neill's *The Emperor Jones.* And, producing them, it ended an epoch of sweetness and light.

II

The young American literatus of today, with publishers ready and eager to give him a hearing, can scarcely imagine the difficulties which beset his predecessor of twenty years ago; he is, indeed, far too little appreciative of the freedom he has, and far too prone to flee from hard work to the solace of the martyr's shroud. When I first began practice as a critic, in 1908, there was yet plenty of excuse for putting it on. It was a time of almost inconceivable complacency and conformity. Hamilton Wright Mabie was still alive and still taken seriously, and all the young pedagogues who aspired to the critical gown imitated him in his watchful stupidity. This camorra had delivered a violent wallop to Theodore Dreiser eight years before, and he was yet suffering from his bruises; it was not until 1911 that he printed *Jennie Gerhardt.* Miss Harriet Monroe and her gang of new poets were still dispersed and inarticulate; Miss Amy Lowell, as yet unaware of Imagism, was writing polite doggerel in the manner of a New England schoolmarm; the reigning dramatists of the nation were Augustus Thomas, David Belasco, and Clyde Fitch; Miss Cather was imitating Mrs. Wharton; Hergesheimer had six years to go before he'd come to *The Lay Anthony;* Cabell was known only as one who provided the text for illustrated gift-books; the American novelists most admired by most publishers, by most readers and by all practicing critics were Richard Harding Davis, Robert W. Chambers, and James Lane Allen. It is hard indeed, in retrospect, to picture those remote days just as they were. They seem almost fabulous. The chief critical organ of the Republic was actually the Literary Supplement of the *New York Times. The Dial* was down with diabetes in Chicago; *The Nation* was made dreadful by the gloomy humors of Paul Elmer More; *The Bookman* was even more saccharine and sophomoric than it is today. When the mild and pianissimo revolt of the middle 90's—a feeble echo of the English revolt—had spent itself, the Presbyterians marched in and took possession of the works. Most of the erstwhile revoltés boldly took the veil—notably Hamlin Garland. No novel that told the truth about life as Americans were living it, no poem that departed from the old patterns, no play that had the merest ghost of an idea in it had a chance. When, in 1908, Mrs. Mary Roberts Rinehart printed a conventional mystery story which yet managed to have a trace of sense in it, it caused a sensation. And when, two years later, Dr. William Lyon Phelps printed a book of criticism in which he actually ranked Mark Twain alongside Emerson and Hawthorne, there was as great a stirring beneath the college elms as if a naked fancy woman had run across the campus. If Hergesheimer had come into New York in 1908 with *Cytherea* under his arm, he would have worn out his pantaloons on publishers' benches without getting so much as a polite kick. If Eugene O'Neill had come to Broadway with *The Hairy Ape,* he would have been sent to Edward E. Rose to learn the elements of his trade. The devilish and advanced thing, in those days, was for the fat lady star to give a couple of matinées of Ibsen's *A Doll's House.*

A great many men and a few women addressed themselves to the dispersal of this fog. Some of them were imaginative writers who found it simply impossible to bring themselves within the prevailing rules; some were critics; others were young publishers. As I look back, I can't find any sign of concerted effort; it was, in the main, a case of each on his own. The more contumacious of the younger critics, true enough, tended to rally 'round Huneker, who, as a matter of fact, was very little interested in American letters, and the young novelists had a leader in Dreiser, who, I suspect, was quite unaware of most of them. However, it was probably Dreiser who chiefly gave form to the movement, despite the fact that for eleven long years he was silent. Not only was there a useful rallying-point in the idiotic suppression of *Sister Carrie;* there was also the encouraging fact of the man's massive immovability. Physically and mentally he loomed up like a sort of headland—a great crag of basalt that no conceivable assault seemed able to touch. His predecessor, Frank Norris, was of much softer stuff. Norris, had he lived longer, would have been wooed and ruined, I fear, by the Mabies, Boyntons, and other such Christian critics, as Garland had been wooed and ruined before him. Dreiser, fortunately for American letters, never had to face any such seduction. The critical schoolmarms, young and old, fell upon him with violence the moment he appeared above the horizon of his native steppe, and soon he was the storm center of a battle-royal that lasted nearly twenty years. The man himself was solid, granitic, without nerves. Very little cunning was in him and not much bellicose enterprise, but he showed a truly appalling tenacity. The pedagogues tried to scare him to death, they tried to stampede his partisans and they tried to put him into Coventry and get him forgotten, but they failed every time. The more he was reviled, sneered at, neglected, the more resolutely he stuck to his formula. That formula is now every serious American novelist's formula. They all try to write better than Dreiser, and not a few of them succeed, but they all follow him in his fundamental purpose—to make the novel true. Dreiser added something, and here following him is harder: he tried to make the novel poignant—to add sympathy, feeling, imagination to understanding. It will be a long while before that enterprise is better managed than he managed it in *Jennie Gerhardt.*

Today, it seems to me, the American imaginative writer, whether he be novelist, poet or dramatist, is quite as free as he deserves to be. He is free to depict the life about him precisely as he sees it, and to interpret it in any manner he pleases. The publishers of the land, once so fearful of novelty, are now so hospitable to it that they constantly fail to distinguish the novelty that has hard thought behind it from that which has only some Village mountebank's desire to stagger the wives of Rotarians. Our stage is perhaps the freest in the world—not only to sensations, but also to ideas. Our poets get into print regularly with stuff so bizarre and unearthly that only Christian Scientists can understand it. The extent of this new freedom, indeed, is so great that large numbers of persons appear to be unable to believe in it; they are constantly getting into sweats about the taboos and inhibitions that remain, for example, those nourished by comstockery. But the importance and puissance of comstockery, I believe, is quite as much over-estimated as the importance and puissance of the objurgations still hurled at sense and honesty by the provincial professors of American Idealism, the Genius of America, and other such phantasms. The Comstocks, true enough, still raid an occasional book, particularly when their funds are running low and there is need to inflame Christian men, but that their monkeyshines ever actually suppress a book of any consequence I very much doubt. The flood is too vast for them. Chasing a minnow with desperate passion, they let a whole school of whales go by. In any case, they confine their operations to the single field of sex, and it must be plain that it is not in the field of sex that the hottest battles against the old American manner have been fought and won. *Three Soldiers* was far more subversive of that manner than all the stories of sex ever written in America—and yet *Three Soldiers* came out with the imprint of one of the most respectable American publishers, and was scarcely challenged. *Babbitt* scored a victory that was still easier, and yet more significant, for its target was the double one of American business and American Christianity; it set the whole world to laughing at two things that are far more venerated in the United States than the bodily chastity of women. Nevertheless, *Babbitt* went down so easily that even the alfalfa *Gelehrten* joined in whooping for it, apparently on the theory that praising Lewis would make the young of the national species forget Dreiser. Victimized by their own craft, the *Gelehrten* thus made a foul attack upon their own principles, for if their principles did not stand against just such anarchistic and sacrilegious books, then they were without any sense whatever, as was and is, indeed, the case.

I shall not rehearse the steps in the advance from *Sister Carrie,* suppressed and proscribed, to *Babbitt,* swallowed and hailed. The important thing is that, despite the caterwauling of the Comstocks, and the pedagogues, a reasonable freedom for the serious artist now prevails—that publishers stand ready to print him, that critics exist who are competent to recognize him and willing to do battle for him, and that there is a large public eager to read him. What use is he making of opportunity? Certainly not the worst use possible, but also certainly not the best. He is free, but he is not yet, perhaps, worthy of freedom. He lets the popular magazine, the movie and the cheap-John publisher pull him too hard in one direction; he lets the vagaries of his politics pull him too hard in another. Back in 1908 I predicted the destruction of Upton Sinclair the artist by Upton Sinclair the visionary and reformer. Sinclair's bones now bleach upon the beach. Beside them repose those of many another man and woman of great promise—for example, Winston Churchill. Floyd Dell is on his way—one novel and two doses of Greenwich Village psychology. Hergesheimer writes novelettes for the *Saturday Evening Post.* Willa Cather has won the Pulitzer Prize—a transaction comparable to the election of Charles W. Eliot to the Elks. Masters turns to prose that somehow fails to come off. Dreiser, forgetting his trilogy, experiments rather futilely with the drama, the essay, free verse. Fuller renounces the novel for book reviewing. Tarkington is another Pulitzer prizeman, always on the verge of first-rate work but always falling short by an inch. Many of the White Hopes of ten or fifteen years ago perished in the war, as surely victims of its slaughter as Rupert Brooke or Otto Braun; it is, indeed, curious to note that practically every American author who moaned and sobbed for democracy between the years 1914 and 1919 is now extinct. The rest have gone down the chute of the movies.

But all this, after all, may signify little. The shock troops have been piled up in great masses, but the ground is cleared for those that follow. Well, then, what of the youngsters? Do they show any sign of seizing their chance? The answer is yes and no. On the one hand there is a group which, revolving 'round *The Bookman,* talks a great deal and accomplishes nothing. On the other hand there is a group which, revolving 'round *The Dial* and *The Little Review,* talks even more and does even less. But on the third hand, as it were, there is a group which says little and saws wood. There seems to be little in common between its members, no sign of a formal movement, with its blague and its bombast, but all of them have this in common: that they owe both their opportunity and their method to the revolution that followed *Sister Carrie.* Most of them are from the Middle West, but they are distinct from the Chicago crowd, now degenerated to posturing and worse. They are sophisticated, disillusioned, free from cant, and yet they have imagination. The raucous protests of the evangelists of American Idealism seem to have no more effect upon them than the advances of the Expressionists, Dadaists, and other such café-table prophets. Out of this dispersed and ill-defined group, I believe, something will come. Its members are those who are free from the two great delusions which, from the beginning, have always cursed American letters: the delusion that a work of art is primarily a moral document, that its purpose is to make men better Christians and more docile cannon-fodder, and the delusion that it is an exercise in logic, that its purpose is to prove something. These delusions, lingering beyond their time, are responsible for most of the disasters visible in the national literature today—the disasters of the radicals as well as those of the 100 per cent dunderheads. The writers of the future, I hope and believe, will carefully avoid both of them.

Alain Locke

The New Negro

In the last decade something beyond the watch and guard of statistics has happened in the life of the American Negro and the three norms who have traditionally presided over the Negro problem have a changeling in their laps. The Sociologist, the Philanthropist, the Race-leader are not unaware of the New Negro, but they are at a loss to account for him. He simply cannot be swathed in their formulæ. For the younger generation is vibrant with a new psychology; the new spirit is awake in the masses, and under the very eyes of the professional observers is transforming what has been a perennial problem into the progressive phases of contemporary Negro life.

Could such a metamorphosis have taken place as suddenly as it has appeared to? The answer is no; not because the New Negro is not here, but because the Old Negro had long become more of a myth than a man. The Old Negro, we must remember, was a creature of moral debate and historical controversy. His has been a stock figure perpetuated as an historical fiction partly in innocent sentimentalism, partly in deliberate reactionism. The Negro himself has contributed his share to this through a sort of protective social mimicry forced upon him by the adverse circumstances of dependence. So for generations in the mind of America, the Negro has been more of a formula than a human being—a something to be argued about, condemned or defended, to be "kept down," or "in his place," or "helped up," to be worried with or worried over, harassed or patronized, a social bogey or a social burden. The thinking Negro even has been induced to share this same general attitude, to focus his attention on controversial issues, to see himself in the distorted perspective of a social problem. His shadow, so to speak, has been more real to him than his personality. Through having had to appeal from the unjust stereotypes of his oppressors and traducers to those of his liberators, friends and benefactors he has had to subscribe to the traditional positions from which his case has been viewed. Little true social or self-understanding has or could come from such a situation.

But while the minds of most of us, black and white, have thus burrowed in the trenches of the Civil War and Reconstruction, the actual march of development has simply flanked these positions, necessitating a sudden reorientation of view. We have not been watching in the right direction; set North and South on a sectional axis, we have not noticed the East till the sun has us blinking.

Recall how suddenly the Negro spirituals revealed themselves; suppressed for generations under the stereotypes of Wesleyan hymn harmony, secretive, half-ashamed, until the
courage of being natural brought them out—and behold, there was folk-music. Similarly
the mind of the Negro seems suddenly to have slipped from under the tyranny of social
intimidation and to be shaking off the psychology of imitation and implied inferiority. By
shedding the old chrysalis of the Negro problem we are achieving something like a spiritual emancipation. Until recently, lacking self-understanding, we have been almost as
much of a problem to ourselves as we still are to others. But the decade that found us with
a problem has left us with only a task. The multitude perhaps feels as yet only a strange
relief and a new vague urge, but the thinking few know that in the reaction the vital inner
grip of prejudice has been broken.

With this renewed self-respect and self-dependence, the life of the Negro community
is bound to enter a new dynamic phase, the buoyancy from within compensating for
whatever pressure there may be of conditions from without. The migrant masses, shifting
from countryside to city, hurdle several generations of experience at a leap, but more important, the same thing happens spiritually in the life-attitudes and self-expression of the
Young Negro, in his poetry, his art, his education and his new outlook, with the additional advantage, of course, of the poise and greater certainty of knowing what it is all
about. From this comes the promise and warrant of a new leadership. As one of them has
discerningly put it:

> We have tomorrow
> Bright before us
> Like a flame,
>
> Yesterday, a night-gone thing
> A sun-down name.
>
> And dawn today
> Broad arch above the road we came.
> We march!

This is what, even more than any "most creditable record of fifty years of freedom," requires that the Negro of to-day be seen through other than the dusty spectacles of past
controversy. The day of "aunties," "uncles" and "mammies" is equally gone. Uncle Tom
and Sambo have passed on, and even the "Colonel" and "George" play barnstorm rôles
from which they escape with relief when the public spotlight is off. The popular melodrama has about played itself out, and it is time to scrap the fictions, garret the bogeys
and settle down to a realistic facing of facts.

First we must observe some of the changes which since the traditional lines of opinion
were drawn have rendered these quite obsolete. A main change has been, of course, that
shifting of the Negro population which has made the Negro problem no longer exclusively or even predominantly Southern. Why should our minds remain sectionalized,
when the problem itself no longer is? Then the trend of migration has not only been toward the North and the Central Midwest, but city-ward and to the great centers of industry—the problems of adjustment are new, practical, local and not peculiarly racial. Rather
they are an integral part of the large industrial and social problems of our presentday
democracy. And finally, with the Negro rapidly in process of class differentiation, if it ever
was warrantable to regard and treat the Negro *en masse* it is becoming with every day less
possible, more unjust and more ridiculous.

In the very process of being transplanted, the Negro is becoming transformed.

The tide of Negro migration, northward and city-ward, is not to be fully explained as a blind flood started by the demands of war industry coupled with the shutting off of foreign migration, or by the pressure of poor crops coupled with increased social terrorism in certain sections of the South and Southwest. Neither labor demand, the bollweevil nor the Ku Klux Klan is a basic factor, however contributory any or all of them may have been. The wash and rush of this human tide on the beach line of the northern city centers is to be explained primarily in terms of a new vision of opportunity, of social and economic freedom, of a spirit to seize, even in the face of an extortionate and heavy toll, a chance for the improvement of conditions. With each successive wave of it, the movement of the Negro becomes more and more a mass movement toward the larger and the more democratic chance—in the Negro's case a deliberate flight not only from countryside to city, but from medieval America to modern.

Take Harlem as an instance of this. Here in Manhattan is not merely the largest Negro community in the world, but the first concentration in history of so many diverse elements of Negro life. It has attracted the African, the West Indian, the Negro American; has brought together the Negro of the North and the Negro of the South; the man from the city and the man from the town and village; the peasant, the student, the business man, the professional man, artist, poet, musician, adventurer and worker, preacher and criminal, exploiter and social outcast. Each group has come with its own separate motives and for its own special ends, but their greatest experiment has been the finding of one another. Proscription and prejudice have thrown these dissimilar elements into a common area of contact and interaction. Within this area, race sympathy and unity have determined a further fusing of sentiment and experience. So what began in terms of segregation becomes more and more, as its elements mix and react, the laboratory of a great race-welding. Hitherto, it must be admitted that American Negroes have been a race more in name than in fact, or to be exact, more in sentiment than in experience. The chief bond between them has been that of a common condition rather than a common consciousness; a problem in common rather than a life in common. In Harlem, Negro life is seizing upon its first chances for group expression and self-determination. It is—or promises at least to be—a race capital. That is why our comparison is taken with those nascent centers of folk-expression and self-determination which are playing a creative part in the world to-day. Without pretense to their political significance, Harlem has the same rôle to play for the New Negro as Dublin has had for the New Ireland or Prague for the new Czechoslovakia.

Harlem, I grant you, isn't typical—but it is significant, it is prophetic. No sane observer, however sympathetic to the new trend, would contend that the great masses are articulate as yet, but they stir, they move, they are more than physically restless. The challenge of the new intellectuals among them is clear enough—the "race radicals" and realists who have broken with the old epoch of philanthropic guidance, sentimental appeal and protest. But are we after all only reading into the stirrings of a sleeping giant the dreams of an agitator? The answer is in the migrating peasant. It is the "man farthest down" who is most active in getting up. One of the most characteristic symptoms of this is the professional man, himself migrating to recapture his constituency after a vain effort to maintain in some Southern corner what for years back seemed an established living and clientele. The clergyman following his errant flock, the physician or lawyer trailing his clients, supply the true clues. In a real sense it is the rank and file who are leading, and the leaders who are following. A transformed and transforming psychology permeates the masses.

When the racial leaders of twenty years ago spoke of developing race-pride and stimulating race-consciousness, and of the desirability of race solidarity, they could not in any accurate degree have anticipated the abrupt feeling that has surged up and now pervades the awakened centers. Some of the recognized Negro leaders and a powerful section of white opinion identified with "race work" of the older order have indeed attempted to discount this feeling as a "passing phase," an attack of "race nerves" so to speak, an "aftermath of the war," and the like. It has not abated, however, if we are to gauge by the present tone and temper of the Negro press, or by the shift in popular support from the officially recognized and orthodox spokesmen to those of the independent, popular, and often radical type who are unmistakable symptoms of a new order. It is a social disservice to blunt the fact that the Negro of the Northern centers has reached a stage where tutelage, even of the most interested and well-intentioned sort, must give place to new relationships, where positive self-direction must be reckoned with in ever increasing measure. The American mind must reckon with a fundamentally changed Negro.

The Negro too, for his part, has idols of the tribe to smash. If on the one hand the white man has erred in making the Negro appear to be that which would excuse or extenuate his treatment of him, the Negro, in turn, has too often unnecessarily excused himself because of the way he has been treated. The intelligent Negro of to-day is resolved not to make discrimination an extenuation for his shortcomings in performance, individual or collective; he is trying to hold himself at par, neither inflated by sentimental allowances nor depreciated by current social discounts. For this he must know himself and be known for precisely what he is, and for that reason he welcomes the new scientific rather than the old sentimental interest. Sentimental interest in the Negro has ebbed. We used to lament this as the falling off of our friends; now we rejoice and pray to be delivered both from self-pity and condescension. The mind of each racial group has had a bitter weaning, apathy or hatred on one side matching disillusionment or resentment on the other; but they face each other to-day with the possibility at least of entirely new mutual attitudes.

It does not follow that if the Negro were better known, he would be better liked or better treated. But mutual understanding is basic for any subsequent coöperation and adjustment. The effort toward this will at least have the effect of remedying in large part what has been the most unsatisfactory feature of our present stage of race relationships in America, namely the fact that the more intelligent and representative elements of the two race groups have at so many points got quite out of vital touch with one another.

The fiction is that the life of the races is separate, and increasingly so. The fact is that they have touched too closely at the unfavorable and too lightly at the favorable levels.

While inter-racial councils have sprung up in the South, drawing on forward elements of both races, in the Northern cities manual laborers may brush elbows in their everyday work, but the community and business leaders have experienced no such interplay or far too little of it. These segments must achieve contact or the race situation in America becomes desperate. Fortunately this is happening. There is a growing realization that in social effort the co-operative basis must supplant long-distance philanthropy, and that the only safeguard for mass relations in the future must be provided in the carefully maintained contacts of the enlightened minorities of both race groups. In the intellectual realm a renewed and keen curiosity is replacing the recent apathy; the Negro is being carefully studied, not just talked about and discussed. In art and letters, instead of being wholly caricatured, he is being seriously portrayed and painted.

To all of this the New Negro is keenly responsive as an augury of a new democracy in American culture. He is contributing his share to the new social understanding. But the desire to be understood would never in itself have been sufficient to have opened so completely the protectively closed portals of the thinking Negro's mind. There is still too much possibility of being snubbed or patronized for that. It was rather the necessity for fuller, truer self-expression, the realization of the unwisdom of allowing social discrimination to segregate him mentally, and a counter-attitude to cramp and fetter his own living—and so the "spite-wall" that the intellectuals built over the "color-line" has happily been taken down. Much of this reopening of intellectual contacts has centered in New York and has been richly fruitful not merely in the enlarging of personal experience, but in the definite enrichment of American art and letters and in the clarifying of our common vision of the social tasks ahead.

The particular significance in the re-establishment of contact between the more advanced and representative classes is that it promises to offset some of the unfavorable reactions of the past, or at least to re-surface race contacts somewhat for the future. Subtly the conditions that are molding a New Negro are molding a new American attitude.

However, this new phase of things is delicate; it will call for less charity but more justice; less help, but infinitely closer understanding. This is indeed a critical stage of race relationships because of the likelihood, if the new temper is not understood, of engendering sharp group antagonism and a second crop of more calculated prejudice. In some quarters, it has already done so. Having weaned the Negro, public opinion cannot continue to paternalize. The Negro to-day is inevitably moving forward under the control largely of his own objectives. What are these objectives? Those of his outer life are happily already well and finally formulated, for they are none other than the ideals of American institutions and democracy. Those of his inner life are yet in process of formation, for the new psychology at present is more of a consensus of feeling than of opinion, of attitude rather than of program. Still some points seem to have crystallized.

Up to the present one may adequately describe the Negro's "inner objectives" as an attempt to repair a damaged group psychology and reshape a warped social perspective. Their realization has required a new mentality for the American Negro. And as it matures we begin to see its effects; at first, negative, iconoclastic, and then positive and constructive. In this new group psychology we note the lapse of sentimental appeal, then the development of a more positive self-respect and self-reliance; the repudiation of social dependence, and then the gradual recovery from hyper-sensitiveness and "touchy" nerves, the repudiation of the double standard of judgment with its special philanthropic allowances and then the sturdier desire for objective and scientific appraisal; and finally the rise from social disillusionment to race pride, from the sense of social debt to the responsibilities of social contribution, and offsetting the necessary working and commonsense acceptance of restricted conditions, the belief in ultimate esteem and recognition. Therefore the Negro to-day wishes to be known for what he is, even in his faults and shortcomings, and scorns a craven and precarious survival at the price of seeming to be what he is not. He resents being spoken of as a social ward or minor, even by his own, and to being regarded a chronic patient for the sociological clinic, the sick man of American Democracy. For the same reasons, he himself is through with those social nostrums and panaceas, the so-called "solutions" of his "problem," with which he and the country have been so liberally dosed in the past. Religion, freedom, education, money—in turn, he has ardently hoped for and peculiarly trusted these things; he still believes in them, but not in blind trust that they alone will solve his life-problem.

Each generation, however, will have its creed, and that of the present is the belief in the efficacy of collective effort, in race co-operation. This deep feeling of race is at present the mainspring of Negro life. It seems to be the outcome of the reaction to proscription and prejudice; an attempt, fairly successful on the whole, to convert a defensive into an offensive position, a handicap into an incentive. It is radical in tone, but not in purpose and only the most stupid forms of opposition, misunderstanding or persecution could make it otherwise. Of course, the thinking Negro has shifted a little toward the left with the world-trend, and there is an increasing group who affiliate with radical and liberal move-

ments. But fundamentally for the present the Negro is radical on race matters, conservative on others, in other words, a "forced radical," a social protestant rather than a genuine
radical. Yet under further pressure and injustice iconoclastic thought and motives will inevitably increase. Harlem's quixotic radicalisms call for their ounce of democracy to-day
lest to-morrow they be beyond cure.

The Negro mind reaches out as yet to nothing but American wants, American ideas.
But this forced attempt to build his Americanism on race values is a unique social experiment, and its ultimate success is impossible except through the fullest sharing of American culture and institutions. There should be no delusion about this. American nerves in
sections unstrung with race hysteria are often fed the opiate that the trend of Negro advance is wholly separatist, and that the effect of its operation will be to encyst the Negro
as a benign foreign body in the body politic. This cannot be—even if it were desirable.
The racialism of the Negro is no limitation or reservation with respect to American life; it
is only a constructive effort to build the obstructions in the stream of his progress into an
efficient dam of social energy and power. Democracy itself is obstructed and stagnated to
the extent that any of its channels are closed. Indeed they cannot be selectively closed. So
the choice is not between one way for the Negro and another way for the rest, but between
American institutions frustrated on the one hand and American ideals progressively fulfilled and realized on the other.

There is, of course, a warrantably comfortable feeling in being on the right side of the
country's professed ideals. We realize that we cannot be undone without America's undoing. It is within the gamut of this attitude that the thinking Negro faces America, but
with variations of mood that are if anything more significant than the attitude itself.
Sometimes we have it taken with the defiant ironic challenge of McKay:

> Mine is the future grinding down to-day
> Like a great landslip moving to the sea,
> Bearing its freight of débris far away
> Where the green hungry waters restlessly
> Heave mammoth pyramids, and break and roar
> Their eerie challenge to the crumbling shore.

Sometimes, perhaps more frequently as yet, it is taken in the fervent and almost filial appeal and counsel of Weldon Johnson's:

> O Southland, dear Southland!
> Then why do you still cling
> To an idle age and a musty page,
> To a dead and useless thing?

But between defiance and appeal, midway almost between cynicism and hope, the prevailing mind stands in the mood of the same author's *To America,* an attitude of sober query
and stoical challenge:

> How would you have us, as we are?
>   Or sinking 'neath the load we bear,
> Our eyes fixed forward on a star,
>   Or gazing empty at despair?
>
> Rising or falling? Men or things?
>   With dragging pace or footsteps fleet?
> Strong, willing sinews in your wings,
>   Or tightening chains about your feet?

More and more, however, an intelligent realization of the great discrepancy between the American social creed and the American social practice forces upon the Negro the taking of the moral advantage that is his. Only the steadying and sobering effect of a truly characteristic gentleness of spirit prevents the rapid rise of a definite cynicism and counter-hate and a defiant superiority feeling. Human as this reaction would be, the majority still deprecate its advent, and would gladly see it forestalled by the speedy amelioration of its causes. We wish our race pride to be a healthier, more positive achievement than a feeling based upon a realization of the shortcomings of others. But all paths toward the attainment of a sound social attitude have been difficult; only a relatively few enlightened minds have been able as the phrase puts it "to rise above" prejudice. The ordinary man has had until recently only a hard choice between the alternatives of supine and humiliating submission and stimulating but hurtful counter-prejudice. Fortunately from some inner, desperate resourcefulness has recently sprung up the simple expedient of fighting prejudice by mental passive resistance, in other words by trying to ignore it. For the few, this manna may perhaps be effective, but the masses cannot thrive upon it.

Fortunately there are constructive channels opening out into which the balked social feelings of the American Negro can flow freely.

Without them there would be much more pressure and danger than there is. These compensating interests are racial but in a new and enlarged way. One is the consciousness of acting as the advance-guard of the African peoples in their contact with Twentieth-Century civilization; the other, the sense of a mission of rehabilitating the race in world esteem from that loss of prestige for which the fate and conditions of slavery have so largely been responsible. Harlem, as we shall see, is the center of both these movements; she is the home of the Negro's "Zionism." The pulse of the Negro world has begun to beat in Harlem. A Negro newspaper carrying news material in English, French and Spanish, gathered from all quarters of America, the West Indies and Africa has maintained itself in Harlem for over five years. Two important magazines, both edited from New York, maintain their news and circulation consistently on a cosmopolitan scale. Under American auspices and backing, three pan-African congresses have been held abroad for the discussion of common interest, colonial questions and the future co-operative development of Africa. In terms of the race question as a world problem, the Negro mind has leapt, so to speak, upon the parapets of prejudice and extended its cramped horizons. In so doing it has linked up with the growing group consciousness of the dark-peoples and is gradually learning their common interests. As one of our writers has recently put it: "It is imperative that we understand the white world in its relations to the non-white world." As with the Jew, persecution is making the Negro international.

As a world phenomenon this wider race consciousness is a different thing from the much asserted rising tide of color. Its inevitable causes are not of our making. The consequences are not necessarily damaging to the best interests of civilization. Whether it actually brings into being new Armadas of conflict or argosies of cultural exchange and enlightenment can only be decided by the attitude of the dominant races in an era of critical change. With the American Negro, his new internationalism is primarily an effort to recapture contact with the scattered peoples of African derivation. Garveyism may be a transient, if spectacular, phenomenon, but the possible rôle of the American Negro in the future development of Africa is one of the most constructive and universally helpful missions that any modern people can lay claim to.

Constructive participation in such causes cannot help giving the Negro valuable group incentives, as well as increased prestige at home and abroad. Our greatest rehabilitation may possibly come through such channels, but for the present, more immediate hope rests in the revaluation by white and black alike of the Negro in terms of his artistic endowments and cultural contributions, past and prospective. It must be increasingly recognized that the Negro has already made very substantial contributions, not only in his folkart, music especially, which has always found appreciation, but in larger, though humbler and less acknowledged ways. For generations the Negro has been the peasant matrix of that section of America which has most undervalued him, and here he has contributed not only materially in labor and in social patience, but spiritually as well. The South has unconsciously absorbed the gift of his folk-temperament. In less than half a generation it will be easier to recognize this, but the fact remains that a leaven of humor, sentiment, imagination and tropic nonchalance has gone into the making of the South from a humble, unacknowledged source. A second crop of the Negro's gifts promises still more largely. He now becomes a conscious contributor and lays aside the status of a beneficiary and ward for that of a collaborator and participant in American civilization. The great social gain in this is the releasing of our talented group from the arid fields of controversy and debate to the productive fields of creative expression. The especially cultural recognition they win should in turn prove the key to that revaluation of the Negro which must precede or accompany any considerable further betterment of race relationships. But whatever the general effect, the present generation will have added the motives of selfexpression and spiritual development to the old and still unfinished task of making material headway and progress. No one who understandingly faces the situation with its substantial accomplishment or views the new scene with its still more abundant promise can be entirely without hope. And certainly, if in our lifetime the Negro should not be able to celebrate his full initiation into American democracy, he can at least, on the warrant of these things, celebrate the attainment of a significant and satisfying new phase of group development, and with it a spiritual Coming of Age.

Mike Gold

Proletarian Realism

Labor may lose all the battles, but it will win the class war. Labor has seemed to lose every battle, every strike and frameup for the past hundred years, and yet today there is a Soviet Russia, a nascent Soviet China, a great international labor movement. Labor is doggedly and surely winning its great war for the management of the world.

Every day this is evidenced, too, on the cultural front. It is difficult for the bourgeois intellectuals to understand or acknowledge this. One of their favorite superstitions is that culture is always the product of a few divinely ordained individuals, operating in a social vacuum.

We know and assert that culture is a social product; as bees who feed upon sumach or buckwheat produce honey of those flavors, so will the individuals living within a specific social environment give off an inevitably flavored culture.

"Proletarian Realism" by Mike Gold. International Publishers. Reprinted with permission of the Evelyn Singer Agency.

It could not be otherwise. Who could expect a Walt Whitman at the court of Louis the Fourteenth? Who, among the cacophonies and tensions of a modern industrial city, would ask a musician to originate bland gavottes and minuets?

But the intellectuals sneer at the idea of a proletarian literature. They will acknowledge the possibility of nationalist cultures; but they have not reached the understanding that the national idea is dying, and that the class ideologies are alone real in the world today.

I believe I was the first writer in America to herald the advent of a world proletarian literature as a concomitant to the rise of the world proletariat. This was in an article published in the *Liberator* in 1921, called, "Towards Proletarian Art." Mine was a rather mystic and intuitive approach; nothing had yet been published in English on this theme; the idea was not yet in the air, as it is today; I was feeling my way.

But the little path has since become a highroad. Despite the bourgeois ultra-leftism of Trotsky in his *Literature and Revolution,* where he predicts there will not be time enough to develop a proletarian literature, this greatest and most universal of literary schools is now sweeping across the world.

One would not want a better text for a survey of the new movement than this paragraph from the conservative *Japan Magazine* on the situation of Japan.

> It appears that the greatest demand for the year was the proletarian literature, due perhaps to the excitement over the arrest of so many youths and maidens for being guilty of dangerous thought. The result is that henceforth there will be a more clearly marked distinction between the writers of this school and authors in general.

In North China, there is the powerful Owl Society, with a string of newspapers, magazines, bookshops and publishing houses, all devoted to the spread of proletarian literature.

Thousands of books and articles on the theories of proletarian literature have been published in Soviet Russia, in Germany, Japan, China, France, England, and other countries. There is not a language in the world today in which a vigorous bold youth is not experimenting with the materials of proletarian literature. It is a world phenomenon; and it grows, changes, criticizes itself, expands without the blessing of all the official mandarins and play-actor iconoclasts and psalm-singing Humanists of the moribund bourgeois culture. It does not need them any longer; it will soon boot them into their final resting places in the museum.

No, the bourgeois intellectuals tell us, there can be no such thing as a proletarian literature. We answer briefly: There *is.* Then they say, it is mediocre; where is your Shakespeare? And we answer: Wait ten years more. He is on his way. We gave you a Lenin; we will give you a proletarian Shakespeare, too; if that is so important.

To us the culture of the world's millions is more important; the soil must be prepared; we know our tree is sound; we are sure of the fruit: we promise you a hundred Shakespeares.

We have only one magazine in America, the *New Masses,* dedicated to proletarian literature. And there is no publishing house of standing and intelligent direction to help clarify the issues. Nearest is the International Publishers perhaps, but this house devotes itself solely to a rather academic approach to economics and makes little attempt to influence either the popular mind or our intellectuals. It is as stodgy and unenterprising, in a Communist way, as the Yale University Press, and similar organizations.

If there were a live publishing house here, such as the *Cenit* of Madrid, for instance, it could issue a series of translations of proletarian novels, poetry, criticism that might astound some of our intellectuals. There would be a clarification, too, for some of our own adherents.

For proletarian literature is a living thing. It is not based on a set of fixed dogmas, any-more than is Communism or the science of biology.

Churches are built on dogma. The Catholic Church is the classic illustration of how the rule of dogma operates. Here is a great mass political and business movement that hypno-tizes its victims with a set of weird formulas of magic which must not be tested or exam-ined but must be swallowed with faith.

In Marxism or any other science there is no dogma; there are laws which have been dis-covered running through the phenomena of nature. These laws must not be taken on faith. They are the result of experiment and statistics, and they are meant to be tested daily. If they fail to work, they can be discarded; they are constantly being discarded.

The law of class struggle is a Marxian discovery that has been tested, and that works, and that gives one a major clue to the movements of man in the mass.

In proletarian literature, there are several laws which seem to be demonstrable. One of them is that all culture is the reflection of a specific class society. Another is, that bour-geois culture is in process of decay, just as bourgeois society is in a swift decline.

The class that will inherit the world will be the proletariat, and every indication points inevitably to the law that this proletarian society will, like its predecessors, create its own culture.

This we can be sure of; upon this we all agree. Proletarian literature will reflect the struggle of the workers in their fight for the world. It portrays the life of the workers; not as do the vulgar French populists and American jazzmaniacs, but with a clear revolution-ary point; otherwise it is meaningless, merely a new *frisson*.

1. Because the Workers are skilled machinists, sailors, farmers and weavers, the prole-tarian writer must describe their work with technical precision. The Workers will scorn any vague fumbling poetry, much as they would scorn a sloppy workman. Hemingway and others have had the intuition to incorporate this proletarian element into their work, but have used it for the *frisson,* the way some actors try to imitate gangsters of men. These writers build a machine, it functions, but it produces nothing; it has not been planned to produce anything; it is only an adult toy.

2. Proletarian realism deals with the *real conflicts* of men and women who work for a living. It has nothing to do with the sickly mental states of the idle Bohemians, their sub-tleties, their sentimentalities, their fine-spun affairs. The worst example and the best of what we do not want to do is the spectacle of Proust, master-masturbator of the bourgeois literature. We know the suffering of hungry, persecuted and heroic millions is enough of a theme for anyone, without inventing these precious silly little agonies.

3. Proletarian realism is never pointless. It does not believe in literature for its own sake, but in literature that is useful, has a social function. Every major writer has always done this in the past; but it is necessary to fight the battle constantly, for there are more intellectuals than ever who are trying to make literature a plaything. Every poem, every novel and drama, must have a social theme, or it is merely confectionery.

4. As few words as possible. We are not interested in the verbal acrobats—this is only another form for bourgeois idleness. The Workers live too close to reality to care about these literary show-offs, these verbalist heroes.

5. To have the courage of the proletarian experience. This was the chief point of my "mystic" essay in 1921; let us proletarians write with the courage of our own experience. I mean, if one is a tanner and writer, let one dare to write the drama of a tannery; or of a clothing shop, or of a ditch-digger's life, or of a hobo. Let the bourgeois writers tell us

about their spiritual drunkards and super-refined Parisian emigres; or about their spiritual marriages and divorces, etc., that is their world; we must write about our own mud-puddle; it will prove infinitely more important. This is being done by the proletarian realism.

6. Swift action, clear form, the direct line, cinema in words; this seems to be one of the principles of proletarian realism. It knows exactly what it believes and where it is going; this makes for its beautiful youthful clarity.

7. Away with drabness, the bourgeois notion that the Worker's life is sordid, the slummer's disgust and feeling of futility. There *is* horror and drabness in the Worker's life; and we will portray it; but we know this is not the last word; we know that this manure heap is the hope of the future; we know that not pessimism, but revolutionary elan will sweep this mess out of the world forever.

8. Away with all lies about human nature. We are scientists; we know what a man thinks and feels. Everyone is a mixture of motives; we do not have to lie about our hero in order to win our case. It is this honesty alone, frank as an unspoiled child's, that makes proletarian realism superior to the older literary schools.

9. No straining or melodrama or other effects; life itself is the supreme melodrama. Feel this intensely, and everything becomes poetry—the new poetry of materials, of the so-called "common man," the Worker molding his real world.   [1930]

John Crowe Ransom

Reconstructed but Unregenerate

Preface to *I'll Take My Stand!*

I

It is out of fashion in these days to look backward rather than forward. About the only American given to it is some unreconstructed Southerner, who persists in his regard for a certain terrain, a certain history, and a certain inherited way of living. He is punished as his crime deserves. He feels himself in the American scene as an anachronism, and knows he is felt by his neighbors as a reproach.

Of course he is a tolerably harmless reproach. He is like some quaint local character of eccentric but fixed principles who is thoroughly and almost pridefully accepted by the

Note—This article is made up largely from articles of the author's that have appeared in the *Sewanee Review* and *Harper's Magazine.*

Ransom, John Crowe, "Reconstructed but Unregenerate," *I'll Take My Stand: The South and the Agrarian Tradition.* Harper and Brothers, 1930.

village as a rare exhibit in the antique kind. His position is secure from the interference of the police, but it is of a rather ambiguous dignity.

I wish now that he were not so entirely taken for granted, and that as a reproach he might bear a barb and inflict a sting. I wish that the whole force of my own generation in the South would get behind his principles and make them an ideal which the nation at large would have to reckon with. But first I will describe him in the light of the position he seems now to occupy actually before the public.

His fierce devotion is to a lost cause—though it grieves me that his contemporaries are so sure it is lost. They are so far from fearing him and his example that they even in the excess of confidence offer him a little honor, a little petting. As a Southerner I have observed this indulgence and I try to be grateful. Obviously it does not constitute a danger to the Republic; distinctly it is not treasonable. They are good enough to attribute a sort of glamour to the Southern life as it is defined for them in a popular tradition. They like to use the South as the nearest available locus for the scenes of their sentimental songs, and sometimes they send their daughters to the Southern seminaries. Not too much, of course, is to be made of this last gesture, for they do not expose to this hazard their sons, who in our still very masculine order will have to discharge the functions of citizenship, and who must accordingly be sternly educated in the principles of progress at progressive institutions of learning. But it does not seem to make so much difference what principles of a general character the young women acquire, since they are not likely to be impaired by principles in their peculiar functions, such as virtue and the domestic duties. And so, at suitable seasons, and on the main-line trains, one may see them in some numbers, flying south or flying north like migratory birds; and one may wonder to what extent their philosophy of life will be affected by two or three years in the South. One must remember that probably their parents have already made this calculation and are prepared to answer, Not much.

The Southerner must know, and in fact he does very well know, that his antique conservatism does not exert a great influence against the American progressivist doctrine. The Southern idea today is down, and the progressive or American idea is up. But the historian and the philosopher, who take their views that are thought to be respectively longer and deeper than most, may very well reverse this order and find that the Southern idea rather than the American has in its favor the authority of example and the approval of theory. And some prophet may even find it possible to expect that it will yet rise again.

I will propose a thesis which seems to have about as much cogency as generalizations usually have: The South is unique on this continent for having founded and defended a culture which was according to the European principles of culture; and the European principles had better look to the South if they are to be perpetuated in this country.

II

The nearest of the European cultures which we could examine is that of England; and this is of course the right one in the case, quite aside from our convenience. England was actually the model employed by the South, in so far as Southern culture was not quite indigenous. And there is in the South even today an Anglophile sentiment quite anomalous in the American scene.

England differs from America doubtless in several respects, but most notably in the fact that England did her pioneering an indefinite number of centuries ago, did it well

enough, and has been living pretty tranquilly on her establishment ever since, with infre-
quent upheavals and replacements. The customs and institutions of England seem to the
American observer very fixed and ancient. There is no doubt that the English tradition expresses itself in many more or less intangible ways, but it expresses itself most importantly in a material establishment; and by this I mean the stable economic system by
which Englishmen are content to take their livelihood from the physical environment.
The chief concern of England's half-mythical pioneers, as with pioneers anywhere, was
with finding the way to make a living. Evidently they found it. But fortunately the methods they worked out proved transmissible, proved, in fact, the main reliance of the succeeding generations. The pioneers explored the soil, determined what concessions it
might reasonably be expected to make them, housed themselves, developed all their necessary trades, and arrived by painful experiment at a thousand satisfactory recipes by
which they might secure their material necessities. Their descendents have had the good
sense to consider that this establishment was good enough for them. They have elected to
live their comparatively easy and routine lives in accordance with the tradition which they
inherited, and they have consequently enjoyed a leisure, a security, and an intellectual
freedom that were never the portion of pioneers.

The pioneering life is not the normal life, whatever some Americans may suppose. It is
not, if we look for the meaning of European history. The lesson of each of the European
cultures now extant is in this—that European opinion does not make too much of the intense practical enterprises, but is at pains to define rather narrowly the practical effort
which is prerequisite to the reflective and asthetic life. Boys are very well pleased to employ their muscles almost exclusively, but men prefer to exercise their minds. It is the European intention to live materially along the inherited line of least resistance, in order to
put the surplus of energy into the free life of the mind. Thus is engendered that famous,
or infamous, European conservatism, which will appear stupid, necessarily, to men still
fascinated by materialistic projects, men in a state of arrested adolescence; for instance, to
some very large if indefinite fraction of the population of these United States.

I have in mind here the core of unadulterated Europeanism, with its self-sufficient,
backward-looking, intensely provincial communities. The human life of English provinces
long ago came to terms with nature, fixed its roots somewhere in the spaces between the
rocks and in the shade of the trees, founded its comfortable institutions, secured its modest prosperity—and then willed the whole in perpetuity to the generations which should
come after, in the ingenuous confidence that it would afford them all the essential human
satisfactions. For it is the character of a seasoned provincial life that it is realistic, or successfully adapted to its natural environment, and that as a consequence it is stable, or
hereditable. But it is the character of our urbanized, anti-provincial, progressive, and mobile American life that it is in a condition of eternal flux. Affections, and long memories,
attach to the ancient bowers of life in the provinces; but they will not attach to what is always changing. Americans, however, are peculiar in being somewhat averse to these affections for natural objects, and to these memories.

Memories of the past are attended with a certain pain called nostalgia. It is hardly a
technical term in our sociology or our psychiatry, but it might as well be. Nostalgia is a
kind of growing-pain, psychically speaking. It occurs to our sorrow when we have decided
that it is time for us, marching to some magnificent destiny, to abandon an old home, an
old provincial setting, or an old way of living to which we had become habituated. It is
the complaint of human nature in its vegetative aspect, when it is plucked up by the roots
from the place of its origin and transplanted in foreign soil, or even left dangling in the

air. And it must be nothing else but nostalgia, the instinctive objection to being transplanted, that chiefly prevents the deracination of human communities and their complete
geographical dispersion as the casualties of an insatiable wanderlust.

Deracination in our Western life is the strange discipline which individuals turn upon
themselves, enticed by the blandishments of such fine words as Progressive, Liberal, and
Forward-looking. The progressivist says in effect: Do not allow yourself to feel homesick;
form no such powerful attachments that you will feel a pain in cutting them loose; prepare your spirit to be always on the move. According to this gospel, there is no rest for the
weary, not even in heaven. The poet Browning expresses an ungrateful intention, the moment he shall enter into his reward, to "fight onward, there as here." The progressivist
H. G. Wells has outlined very neatly his scheme of progress, the only disheartening feature being that he has had to revise it a good many times, and that the state to which he
wants us to progress never has any finality or definition. Browning and Wells would have
made very good Americans, and I am sure they have got the most of their disciples on this
side of the Atlantic; they have not been good Europeans. But all the true progressivists intend to have a program so elastic that they can always propose new worlds to conquer. If
his Utopia were practicable really, and if the progressivists should secure it, he would then
have to defend it from further progress, which would mean his transformation from a progressivist into a conservative. Which is unthinkable.

The gospel of Progress is a curious development, which does not reflect great credit
on the supposed capacity of our species for formulating its own behavior. Evidently the
formula may involve its practitioners in self-torture and suicide just as readily as in the
enjoyment of life. In most societies man has adapted himself to environment with
plenty of intelligence to secure easily his material necessities from the graceful bounty
of nature. And then, ordinarily, he concludes a truce with nature, and he and nature
seem to live on terms of mutual respect and amity, and his loving arts, religions, and
philosophies come spontaneously into being: these are the blessings of peace. But the
latter-day societies have been seized—none quite so violently as our American one—
with the strange idea that the human destiny is not to secure an honorable peace with
nature, but to wage an unrelenting war on nature. Men, therefore, determine to conquer
nature to a degree which is quite beyond reason so far as specific human advantage is
concerned, and which enslaves them to toil and turnover. Man is boastfully declared to
be a natural scientist essentially, whose strength is capable of crushing and making over
to his own desires the brute materiality which is nature; but in his infinite contention
with this materiality he is really capitulating to it. His engines transform the face of
nature—a little—but when they have been perfected, he must invent new engines that
will perform even more heroically. And always the next engine of his invention, even
though it be that engine which is to invade the material atom and exploit the most
secret treasury of nature's wealth, will be a physical engine; and the man who uses it
will be engaged in substantially the same struggle as was the primitive Man with the
Hoe.

This is simply to say that Progress never defines its ultimate objective, but thrusts its
victims at once into an infinite series. Our vast industrial machine, with its laboratory
centers of experimentation, and its far-flung organs of mass production, is like a Prussian-
ized state which is organized strictly for war and can never consent to peace. Or, returning
to the original figure, our progressivists are the latest version of those pioneers who conquered the wilderness, except that they are pioneering on principle, or from force of habit,
and without any recollection of what pioneering was for.

III

Along with the gospel of Progress goes the gospel of Service. They work beautifully as a team.

Americans are still dreaming the materialistic dreams of their youth. The stuff these dreams were made on was the illusion of preëminent personal success over a material opposition. Their tone was belligerence, and the euphemism under which it masqueraded was ambition. But men are not lovely, and men are not happy, for being too ambitious. Let us distinguish two forms under which ambition drives men on their materialistic projects; a masculine and a feminine.

Ambitious men fight, first of all, against nature; they propose to put nature under their heel; this is the dream of scientists burrowing in their cells, and then of the industrial men who beg of their secret knowledge and go out to trouble the earth. But after a certain point this struggle is vain, and we only use ourselves up if we prolong it. Nature wears out man before man can wear out nature; only a city man, a laboratory man, a man cloistered from the normal contacts with the soil, will deny that. It seems wiser to be moderate in our expectations of nature, and respectful; and out of so simple a thing as respect for the physical earth and its teeming life comes a primary joy, which is an inexhaustible source of arts and religions and philosophies.

Ambitious men are belligerent also in the way they look narrowly and enviously upon one another; and I do not refer to such obvious disasters as wars and the rumors of wars. Ambition of the first form was primary and masculine, but there is a secondary form which is typically feminine, though the distribution between the sexes may not be without the usual exceptions. If it is Adam's curse to will perpetually to work his mastery upon nature, it is Eve's curse to prompt Adam every morning to keep up with the best people in the neighborhood in taking the measure of his success. There can never be stability and establishment in a community whose every lady member is sworn to see that her mate is not eclipsed in the competition for material advantages; that community will fume and ferment, and every constituent part will be in perpetual physical motion. The good life depends on leisure, but leisure depends on an establishment, and the establishment depends on a prevailing magnanimity which scorns personal advancement at the expense of the free activity of the mind.

The masculine form is hallowed by Americans, as I have said, under the name of Progress. The concept of Progress is the concept of man's increasing command, and eventually perfect command, over the forces of nature; a concept which enhances too readily our conceit, and brutalizes our life. I believe there is possible no deep sense of beauty, no heroism of conduct, and no sublimity of religion, which is not informed by the humble sense of man's precarious position in the universe. The feminine form is likewise hallowed among us under the name of Service. The term has many meanings, but we come finally to the one which is critical for the moderns; service means the function of Eve, it means the seducing of laggard men into fresh struggles with nature. It has special application to the apparently stagnant sections of mankind, it busies itself with the heathen Chinee, with the Roman Catholic Mexican, with the "lower" classes in our own society. Its motive is missionary. Its watchwords are such as Protestantism, Individualism, Democracy, and the point of its appeal is a discontent, generally labeled "divine."

Progress and Service are not European slogans, they are Americanisms. We alone have devoted our lives to ideals which are admirable within their proper limits, but which expose us to slavery when pursued without critical intelligence. Some Europeans are taken in by these ideals, but hardly the American communities on the whole. Herr Spengler, with a gesture of defeat, glorifies the modern American captain of industry when he compares his positive achievements with the futilities of modern poets and artists. Whereupon we may well wish to save Europe from even so formidable a European as Spengler, hoping that he may not convert Europe to his view. And it is hardly likely; Europe is founded on a principle of conservatism, and is deeply scornful of the American and pioneer doctrine of the strenuous life. In 1918 there was danger that Europe might ask to be Americanized, and American missionaries were quite prepared to answer the call. But since then there has been a revulsion in European opinion, and this particular missionary enterprise confronts now an almost solid barrier of hostility. Europe is not going to be Americanized through falling suddenly in love with strenuousness. It only remains to be seen whether Europe may not be Americanized after all through envy, and through being reminded ceaselessly of our superior prosperity. That is an event to be determined by the force of European magnanimity; Europe's problem, not ours.

IV

The Southern states were settled, of course, by miscellaneous strains. But evidently the one which determined the peculiar tradition of the South was the one which came out of Europe most convinced of the virtues of establishment, contrasting with those strains which seem for the most part to have dominated the other sections, and which came out of Europe feeling rebellious toward all establishments. There are a good many faults to be found with the old South, but hardly the fault of being intemperately addicted to work and to gross material prosperity. The South never conceded that the whole duty of man was to increase material production, or that the index to the degree of his culture was the volume of his material production. His business seemed to be rather to envelop both his work and his play with a leisure which permitted the activity of intelligence. On this assumption the South pioneered her way to a sufficiently comfortable and rural sort of establishment, considered that an establishment was something stable, and proceeded to enjoy the fruits thereof. The arts of the section, such as they were, were not immensely passionate, creative, and romantic; they were the eighteenth-century social arts of dress, conversation, manners, the table, the hunt, politics, oratory, the pulpit. These were arts of living and not arts of escape; they were also community arts, in which every class of society could participate after its kind. The South took life easy, which is itself a tolerably comprehensive art.

But so did other communities in 1850, I believe. And doubtless some others do so yet; in parts of New England, for example. If there are such communities, this is their token, that they are settled. Their citizens are comparatively satisfied with the life they have inherited, and are careful to look backward quite as much as they look forward. Before the Civil War there must have been many such communities this side of the frontier. The difference between the North and the South was that the South was constituted by such communities and made solid. But solid is only a comparative term here. The South as a culture had more solidity than another section, but there were plenty of gaps in it. The most we can say is that the Southern establishment was completed in a good many of the Southern communities, and that this establishment was an active formative influence on the spaces between, and on the frontier spaces outlying, which had not yet perfected their organization of the economic life.

The old Southern life was of course not so fine as some of the traditionalists like to believe. It did not offer serious competition against the glory that was Greece or the
grandeur that was Rome. It hardly began to match the finish of the English, or any other
important European civilization. It is quite enough to say that it was a way of life which
had been considered and authorized. The establishment had a sufficient economic base, it
was meant to be stable rather than provisional, it had got beyond the pioneering stage, it
provided leisure, and its benefits were already being enjoyed. It may as well be admitted
that Southern society was not an institution of very showy elegance, for the so-called aristocrats were mostly home-made and countrified. Aristocracy is not the word which defines
this social organization so well as squirearchy, which I borrow from a recent article by Mr.
William Frierson in the *Sewanee Review.* And even the squires, and the other classes, too,
did not define themselves very strictly. They were loosely graduated social orders, not
fixed as in Europe. Their relations were personal and friendly. It was a kindly society, yet a
realistic one; for it was a failure if it could not be said that people were for the most part in
their right places. Slavery was a feature monstrous enough in theory, but, more often than
not, humane in practice; and it is impossible to believe that its abolition alone could have
effected any great revolution in society.

The fullness of life as it was lived in the ante-bellum South by the different social orders can be estimated today only by the application of some difficult sociological technique. It is my thesis that all were committed to a form of leisure, and that their labor itself was leisurely. The only Southerners who went abroad to Washington and elsewhere,
and put themselves into the record, were those from the top of the pyramid. They held
their own with their American contemporaries. They were not intellectually as seasoned
as good Europeans, but then the Southern culture had had no very long time to grow, as
time is reckoned in these matters: it would have borne a better fruit eventually. They had
a certain amount of learning, which was not as formidable as it might have been: but at
least it was classical and humanistic learning, not highly scientific, and not wildly scattered about over a variety of special studies.

V

Then the North and the South fought, and the consequences were disastrous to both. The
Northern temper was one of jubilation and expansiveness, and now it was no longer
shackled by the weight of the conservative Southern tradition. Industrialism, the latest
form of pioneering and the worst, presently overtook the North, and in due time has now
produced our present American civilization. Poverty and pride overtook the South;
poverty to bring her institutions into disrepute and to sap continually at her courage; and
a false pride to inspire a distaste for the thought of fresh pioneering projects, and to doom
her to an increasing physical enfeeblement.

It is only too easy to define the malignant meaning of industrialism. It is the contemporary form of pioneering; yet since it never consents to define its goal, it is a pioneering
on principle, and with an accelerating speed. Industrialism is a program under which
men, using the latest scientific paraphernalia, sacrifice comfort, leisure, and the enjoyment
of life to win Pyrrhic victories from nature at points of no strategic importance. Ruskin
and Carlyle feared it nearly a hundred years ago, and now it may be said that their fears
have been realized partly in England, and with almost fatal completeness in America. Industrialism is an insidious spirit, full of false promises and generally fatal to establish-

ments since, when it once gets into them for a little renovation, it proposes never again to leave them in peace. Industrialism is rightfully a menial, of almost miraculous cunning but no intelligence; it needs to be strongly governed or it will destroy the economy of the household. Only a community of tough conservative habit can master it.

The South did not become industrialized; she did not repair the damage to her old establishment, either, and it was in part because she did not try hard enough. Hers is the case to cite when we would show how the good life depends on an adequate pioneering, and how the pioneering energy must be kept ready for call when the establishment needs overhauling. The Southern tradition came to look rather pitiable in its persistence when the twentieth century had arrived, for the establishment was quite depreciated. Unregenerate Southerners were trying to live the good life on a shabby equipment, and they were grotesque in their effort to make an art out of living when they were not decently making the living. In the country districts great numbers of those broken-down Southerners are still to be seen in patched blue-jeans, sitting on ancestral fences, shotguns across their laps and hound-dogs at their feet, surveying their unkempt acres while they comment shrewdly on the ways of God. It is their defect that they have driven a too easy, an unmanly bargain with nature, and that their æstheticism is based on insufficient labor.

But there is something heroic, and there may prove to be yet something very valuable to the Union, in their extreme attachment to a certain theory of life. They have kept up a faith which was on the point of perishing from this continent.

Of course it was only after the Civil War that the North and the South came to stand in polar opposition to each other. Immediately after Appomattox it was impossible for the South to resume even that give-and-take of ideas which had marked her ante-bellum relations with the North. She was offered such terms that acquiescence would have been abject. She retired within her borders in rage and held the minimum of commerce with the enemy. Persecution intensified her tradition, and made the South more solid and more Southern in the year 1875, or thereabouts, than ever before. When the oppression was left off, naturally her guard relaxed. But though the period of persecution had not been long, nevertheless the Southern tradition found itself then the less capable of uniting gracefully with the life of the Union; for that life in the meantime had been moving in the opposite direction. The American progressive principle was like a ball rolling down the hill with an increasing momentum, and by 1890 or 1900 it was clear to any intelligent Southerner that it was a principle of boundless aggression against nature which could hardly offer much to a society devoted to the arts of peace.

But to keep on living shabbily on an insufficient patrimony is to decline, both physically and spiritually. The South declined.

VI

And now the crisis in the South's decline has been reached.

Industrialism has arrived in the South. Already the local chambers of commerce exhibit the formidable data of Southern progress. A considerable party of Southern opinion, which might be called the New South party, is well pleased with the recent industrial accomplishments of the South and anxious for many more. Southerners of another school, who might be said to compose an Old South party, are apprehensive lest the section become completely and uncritically devoted to the industrial ideal precisely as the other sections of the Union are. But reconstruction is actually under way. Tied politically and economically to the Union, her borders wholly violable, the South now sees very well that she can restore her prosperity only within the competition of an industrial system.

After the war the Southern plantations were often broken up into small farms. These have yielded less and less of a living, and it [is] said that they will never yield a good living until once more they are integrated into large units. But these units will be industrial units, controlled by a board of directors or an executive rather than a squire, worked with machinery, and manned not by farmers living at home, but by "labor." Even so they will not, according to Mr. Henry Ford, support the population that wants to live on them. In the off seasons the laborers will have to work in factories, which henceforth are to be counted on as among the charming features of Southern landscape. The Southern problem is complicated, but at its center is the farmer's problem, and this problem is simply the most acute version of that general agrarian problem which inspires the despair of many thoughtful Americans today.

The agrarian discontent in America is deeply grounded in the love of the tiller for the soil, which is probably, it must be confessed, not peculiar to the Southern specimen, but one of the more ineradicable human attachments, be the tiller as progressive as he may. In proposing to wean men from this foolish attachment, industrialism sets itself against the most ancient and the most humane of all the modes of human livelihood. Do Mr. Hoover and the distinguished thinkers at Washington see how essential is the mutual hatred between the industrialists and the farmers, and how mortal is their conflict? The gentlemen at Washington are mostly preaching and legislating to secure the fabulous "blessings" of industrial progress; they are on the industrial side. The industrialists have a doctrine which is monstrous, but they are not monsters personally; they are forward-lookers with nice manners, and no American progressivist is against them. The farmers are boorish and inarticulate by comparison. Progressivism is against them in their fight, though their traditional status is still so strong that soft words are still spoken to them. All the solutions recommended for their difficulties are really enticements held out to them to become a little more coöperative, more mechanical, more mobile—in short, a little more industrialized. But the farmer who is not a mere laborer, even the farmer of the comparatively new places like Iowa and Nebraska, is necessarily among the more stable and less progressive elements of society. He refuses to mobilize himself and become a unit in the industrial army, because he does not approve of army life.

I will use some terms which are hardly in his vernacular. He identifies himself with a spot of ground, and this ground carries a good deal of meaning; it defines itself for him as nature. He would till it not too hurriedly and not too mechanically to observe in it the contingency and the infinitude of nature; and so his life acquires its philosophical and even its cosmic consciousness. A man can contemplate and explore, respect and love, an object as substantial as a farm or a native province. But he cannot contemplate nor explore, respect or love, a mere turnover, such as an assemblage of "natural resources," a pile of money, a volume of produce, a market, or a credit system. It is into precisely these intangibles that industrialism would translate the farmer's farm. It means the dehumanization of his life.

However that may be, the South at last, looking defensively about her in all directions upon an industrial world, fingers the weapons of industrialism. There is one powerful voice in the South which, tired of a long status of disrepute, would see the South made at once into a section second to none in wealth, as that is statistically reckoned, and in progressiveness, as that might be estimated by the rapidity of the industrial turnover. This desire offends those who would still like to regard the South as, in the old sense, a home; but its expression is loud and insistent. The urban South, with its heavy importation of regular American ways and regular American citizens, has nearly capitulated to these novelties. It is the village South and the rural South which supply the resistance, and it is lucky for them that they represent a vast quantity of inertia.

Will the Southern establishment, the most substantial exhibit on this continent of a society of the European and historic order, be completely crumbled by the powerful acid of the Great Progressive Principle? Will there be no more looking backward but only looking forward? Is our New World to be dedicated forever to the doctrine of newness?

It is in the interest of America as a whole, as well as in the interest of the South, that these questions press for an answer. I will enter here the most important items of the situation as well as I can; doubtless they will appear a little over-sharpened for the sake of exhibition.

1. The intention of Americans at large appears now to be what it was always in danger of becoming: an intention of being infinitely progressive. But this intention cannot permit of an established order of human existence, and of that leisure which conditions the life of intelligence and the arts.

2. The old South, if it must be defined in a word, practiced the contrary and European philosophy of establishment as the foundation of the life of the spirit. The ante-bellum Union possessed, to say the least, a wholesome variety of doctrine.

3. But the South was defeated by the Union on the battlefield with remarkable decisiveness, and the two consequences have been dire: the Southern tradition was physically impaired, and has ever since been unable to offer an attractive example of its philosophy in action; and the American progressive principle has developed into a pure industrialism without any check from a Southern minority whose voice ceased to make itself heard.

4. The further survival of the Southern tradition as a detached local remnant is now unlikely. It is agreed that the South must make contact again with the Union. And in adapting itself to the actual state of the Union, the Southern tradition will have to consent to a certain industrialization of its own.

5. The question at issue is whether the South will permit herself to be so industrialized as to lose entirely her historic identity, and to remove the last substantial barrier that has stood in the way of American progressivism; or will accept industrialism, but with a very bad grace, and will manage to maintain a good deal of her traditional philosophy.

VII

The hope which is inherent in the situation is evident from the terms in which it is stated. The South must be industrialized—but to a certain extent only, in moderation. The program which now engages the Southern leaders is to see how the South may handle this fire without being burnt badly. The South at last is to be physically reconstructed; but it will be fatal if the South should conceive it as her duty to be regenerated and get her spirit reborn with a totally different orientation toward life.

Fortunately, the Southern program does not have to be perfectly vague. There are at least two definite lines, along either of which an intelligent Southern policy may move in the right general direction; it may even move back and forth between them and still advance.

The first course would be for the Southern leaders to arouse the sectional feeling of the South to its highest pitch of excitement in defense of all the old ways that are threatened. It might seem ungrateful to the kind industrialists to accept their handsome services in such a churlish spirit. But if one thing is more certain than another, it is that these gentlemen will not pine away in their discouragement; they have an inextinguishable enthusiasm for their rôle. The attitude that needs artificial respiration is the attitude of resistance on the part of the natives to the salesmen of industrialism. It will be fiercest and most effective if industrialism is represented to the Southern people as—what it undoubtedly is for the most part—a foreign invasion of Southern soil, which is capable of doing more devastation than was wrought when Sherman marched to the sea. From this point of view it will be a great gain if the usually-peaceful invasion forgets itself now and then, is less peaceful, and commits indiscretions. The native and the invader will be sure to come to an occasional clash, and that will offer the chance to revive ancient and almost forgotten animosities. It will be in order to proclaim to Southerners that the carpet-baggers are again in their midst. And it will be well to seize upon and advertise certain Northern industrial communities as horrible examples of a way of life we detest—not failing to point out the human catastrophe which occurs when a Southern village or rural community becomes the cheap labor of a miserable factory system. It will be a little harder to impress the people with the fact that the new so-called industrial "slavery" fastens not only upon the poor, but upon the middle and better classes of society, too. To make this point it may be necessary to revive such an antiquity as the old Southern gentleman and his lady, and their scorn for the dollar-chasers.

Such a policy as this would show decidedly a sense of what the Germans call *Realpolitik*. It could be nasty and it could be effective.

Its net result might be to give to the South eventually a position in the Union analogous more or less to the position of Scotland under the British crown—a section with a very local and peculiar culture that would, nevertheless, be secure and respected. And Southern traditionalists may take courage from the fact that it was Scottish stubbornness which obtained this position for Scotland; it did not come gratuitously; it was the consequence of an intense sectionalism that fought for a good many years before its fight was won.

That is one policy. Though it is not the only one, it may be necessary to employ it, with discretion, and to bear in mind its Scottish analogue. But it is hardly handsome enough for the best Southerners. Its methods are too easily abused; it offers too much room for the professional demagogue; and one would only as a last resort like to have the South stake upon it her whole chance of survival. After all, the reconstruction may be undertaken with some imagination, and not necessarily under the formula of a literal restoration. It does not greatly matter to what extent the identical features of the old Southern establishment are restored; the important consideration is that there be an establishment for the sake of stability.

The other course may not be so easily practicable, but it is certainly more statesmanlike. That course is for the South to reënter the American political field with a determination and an address quite beyond anything she has exhibited during her half-hearted national life of the last half a century. And this means specifically that she may pool her own stakes with the stakes of other minority groups in the Union which are circumstanced similarly. There is an active American politics already, to start with, a very belligerent if somewhat uninformed Western agrarian party. Between this party and the South there is much community of interest; both desire to defend home, stability of life, the practice of leisure, and the natural enemy of both is the insidious industrial system. There are also, scattered here and there, numerous elements with the same general attitude which would have some power if united: the persons and even communities who are thoroughly tired of progressivism and its spurious benefits, and those who have recently acquired, or miraculously through the generations preserved, a European point of view—sociologists, educators, artists, religionists, and ancient New England townships. The combination of these elements with the Western farmers and the old-fashioned South would make a formidable bloc. The South is numerically much the most substantial of these three groups, but has done next to nothing to make the cause prevail by working inside the American political system.

The unifying effective bond between these geographically diverse elements of public opinion will be the clean-cut policy that the rural life of America must be defended, and the world made safe for the farmers. My friends are often quick to tell me that against the power of the industrial spirit no such hope can be entertained. But there are some protests in these days rising against the industrial ideal, even from the centers where its grip is the stoutest; and this would indicate that our human intelligence is beginning again to assert itself. Of course this is all the truer of the European countries, which have required less of the bitter schooling of experience. Thus Dean Inge declares himself in his Romanes Lecture on "The Idea of Progress":

> I believe that the dissatisfaction with things as they are is caused not only by the failure of nineteenth-century civilization, but partly also by its success. We no longer wish to progress on those lines if we could. Our apocalyptic dream is vanishing into thin air. It may be that the industrial revolution which began in the reign of George the Third has produced most of its fruits, and has had its day. We may have to look forward to such a change as is imagined by Anatole France at the end of his *Isle of the Penguins,* when, after an orgy of revolution and destruction, we shall slide back into the quiet rural life of the early modern period. If so, the authors of the revolution will have cut their own throats, for there can be no great manufacturing towns in such a society. Their disappearance will be no great loss. The race will have tried a great experiment, and will have rejected it as unsatisfying.

The South has an important part to play, if she will, in such a counter-revolution. But what pitiful service have the inept Southern politicians for many years been rendering to the cause! Their Southern loyalty at Washington has rarely had any more imaginative manifestation than to scramble vigorously for a Southern share in the federal pie. They will have to be miraculously enlightened.

I get quickly beyond my depth in sounding these political possibilities. I will utter one last fantastic thought.

No Southerner ever dreams of heaven, or pictures his Utopia on earth, without providing room for the Democratic party. Is it really possible that the Democratic party can be held to a principle, and that the principle can now be defined as agrarian, conservative, anti-industrial? It may not be impossible, after all. If it proves possible, then the South may yet be rewarded for a sentimental affection that has persisted in the face of many betrayals.

[1930]

Constance Rourke

From *American Humor*

An exhilarated and possessive consciousness of a new earth and even of the wide universe ran through this tall talk and the tall tales; they were striated by a naturalistic poetry. Inflation appeared with an air of wonder, which became mock wonder at times but maintained the poetic mode. The Crockett stories even distantly approached the realm of the epic, not merely because of the persistent effect of scale or because of their theme of wandering adventure, but because they embodied something of those interwoven destinies of gods and men which have made the great epical substance. The tales were brief and scattered; the bias was comic; a perverse and wayward spirit was abroad. The animistic might take the place of the god-like presence, appearing in the spirit which sent the squash vines chasing pigs or hoisted Brother Joe to the skies through the medium of shrinking leather. But half-gods had taken shape and walked the earth with a familiar look in the later Davy Crockett and Mike Fink; and around them faint shapes emerged of a similar large mold.

"I saw a little woman streaking it along through the woods like all wrath," said Crockett in one of the almanac stories. Sally Ann Thunder Ann Whirlwind Crockett wore a hornet's nest trimmed with wolves' tails for a bonnet and a dress of a whole bear's hide with the tail for a train; she could shoot a wild goose flying, wade the Mississippi without wetting her shift, and stamp on a litter of wild cats. Mike Fink had a huge daughter who could whistle with one corner of her mouth, eat with the other, and scream with the middle, and who had tamed a full-grown bear. Another figure appeared as an occasional companion of Crockett's, Ben Hardin, a well-known character in Kentucky who claimed that he had been a sailor on far seas and had consorted with mermaids. It was with Hardin in tow that Crockett performed some of his boldest exploits. The outlines of a supernatural hierarchy were sketched in these figures; and beyond them lay dim others belonging to local legend who might grow into a dynamic stature.

The whole history of these tales can never be traced, so transient were they, so quickly passed on and embellished, so rarely recorded. They belonged to that wide portion of the West known as the old Southwest, which spread from Kentucky and Tennessee in a broad encirclement through Georgia and the Gulf States to Texas and Arkansas, reaching beyond the Mississippi as the scout and huntsman and pioneer moved from his first base of the dark and bloody ground. The tales spread indeed over the entire country. The Crockett almanacs, widely circulated in the West, were reprinted in New England; and the stories which they contained were often caught up by other local almanacs and newspapers. Some of the almanac stories were clearly the work of sophisticated minds, but even when the hand of the skilled writer shows, a homely origin is usually plain. Many of them appear as direct transcriptions of tales current in the West. They were linked at times to make a consistent legend, but fragments were given place which sound like casual talk picked up first hand; and gross inconsistency in tone or handling was uncommon. The talk was that southern talk with a mellowed roughness which became the popular speech of the West.

Even on their own ground these tales took on finish, for they flourished not only among boatmen and backwoodsmen, but at the annual meetings of the bar in the West and Southwest, where the members, who often lived in remote isolation, joined in bouts of story-telling, as after long drouth. The strangest, most comic experiences, quiddities, oddities, tales, and bits of novel expression were treasured and matched one against another.

These fabulous stories underwent the many changes to which popular legends have always been subject, but they never coalesced into large forms. The more extravagant of the Crockett legends were unattached to the older body of the Crockett story; they slipped into oblivion as the almanacs were scattered and lost. They exist now only in fragments. On the brink of a coherent wide expression, reaching toward forms that might have partaken of the epical, the popular fancy turned aside—turned to a theme which had always been dominant in the native mind—that of the native character.

The true tall tale with its stress upon the supernatural was laid against others of a prosaic grounding. Out of this new cycle would stride a man who rose six feet without surplus flesh, pantherlike, with a mouth like a wolf-trap and red-brown hair sticking up like the quills of a porcupine, who shook rafters when he spoke and was bent on litigation; or a small stubby man in a calico vest with a cravat like a tablecloth, his head upheld by his shirt collar. Stories were told of such characters as Cave Burton, familiarly known as Blowing Cave, with observations on his Gargantuan feasts and the devices by which he was occasionally deprived of the spread banquet.

A scrupulous attention was devoted to well-known and accomplished liars. "Bolus was a natural liar, just as some horses are natural pacers, and some dogs natural setters. What he did in that walk, was from the irresistible promptings of instinct, and a disinterested love of art. His genius and his performances were free from the vulgar alloy of interest and temptation. Accordingly he did not labor a lie: he lied with a relish: he lied with a coming appetite, growing with what it fed on: he lied from the delight of invention and the charm of fictitious narrative. . . . The truth was too small for him. He adopted a fact occasionally to start with, but like a Sheffield razor and the crude ore, the workmanship, polish, and value were all his own. A Tibet shawl could as well be credited to the insensate goat that grew in the wool, as the author of a fact Bolus honored with his artistical skill could claim to be the inventor of the story. . . . He was fluent but choice of diction, a little sonorous in the structure of the sentences to give effect to a voice like an organ. His countenance was open and engaging, usually sedate in expression, but capable of any modification on the slightest notice. . . . Such a spendthrift never made a track even in the flush times of 1836. It took as much to support him as a first-class steamboat."

Scalawags, gamblers, ne'er-do-wells, small rapscallions, or mere corncrackers were drawn into a careless net of stories, against a background of pine barrens, sandy wastes, half-plowed fields, huts with leaky roofs. Their implements were rusty, their horses walleyed and spavined. They belonged to a rootless drift that had followed in the wake of the huntsman and scout, and they were not wholly different in kind. Sly instead of strong, they pursued uncharted ways, breaking from traditions, bent on triumph. Their adventures—of the rascally Simon Suggs, the worthless Sut Lovingood, the garrulous Major Jones, the characters in *Georgia Scenes* and *Flush Times on the Mississippi*—had to do with vast practical jokes, pranks played on ministers and camp-meetings and on settled respectable people generally, or on Yankees; their jokes on Yankees were perennial. These stories were as coarsegrained as poplar wood and equally light as timber. Grotesquerie and irreverence and upset made their center; caricature was drawn in the single line or phrase. "He drawed in the puckerin'-string ov that legil face of his'n," said Sut Lovingood of a sheriff. Another remarked of an ungenial adversary, "The feller looked as slunk in the face as a baked apple." "When he seed me," said Major Jones of Count Barraty, who had lectured on Greek art in a Georgia village, "he relaxed the austerity of his mustaches and walked out of the Square."

Within these tales character and custom in small sections of the Southwest were portrayed with such close and ready detail as to provide something of a record of the time and place. Dialect was differentiated with a fine gift for mimicry. Yet with all this steady seizure of the circumstantial these tales had little or nothing to do with a genuine actuality. They were rough fantasies cast into the habitual large outline. As in the tales of the deep backwoods, their odd local figures were generic, the events preposterous. These characters formed a regiment of small Tyll Eulenspiegels scattered over the West, upsetting remnants of the old order, hinting a new. This action and their triumph seemed the secret of the pleasure they induced—this, and their portraiture of new types in the new country.

Thin as much of their humor has worn, as mere upset is likely to be reduced to its barest outline by time, they were enormously popular in the quarter of a century during which most of them appeared, from 1835 to 1860. Longstreet's *Georgia Scenes* led the train; and scattered stories appeared in newspapers like the New Orleans *Picayune,* the St. Louis *Reveille,* the Louisville *Courier,* and in that prime sporting weekly and compendium of western humor, the New York *Spirit of the Times.* They were gathered in books and again widely circulated, adding a smutch of gross and homely color to the half-formed American portrait.

In the final and more poetic legends Crockett commanded the whole western world or even the universe. But in the early period of his vogue, in fact during his own lifetime, he appeared not as a half-god with a piece of sunrise in his pocket, but as a national figure. Like the Yankee he was drawn in a graphic stage portrait, under the name of Colonel Nimrod Wildfire in *The Lion of the West* and *The Kentuckian.* The author of the first play, Paulding, denied the identity, but the resemblances were many, and Wildfire was generally believed to be Crockett. The play was never a stable affair because it was always being altered by improvisation after the manner of western story-telling, and the original text has been lost; but there was no question as to its vogue. This early backwoodsman, leaping, crowing, neighing, boasting, dancing breakdowns and delivering rhapsodic monologues, traveled throughout the country and was enthusiastically received in the West; his reception in New York was uproarious. Other backwoodsmen of similar character soon appeared on the stage. For a brief time in fact the backwoodsman fairly matched the Yankee in the general view. He was appropriated; his eccentricities were considered not only western but American, and he was warmly applauded therefor.

This newest portrait of the American was taken to England, where it was scrutinized with care, and considered "pleasing . . . open-hearted . . . childish." Discussions as to western humor were soon under way. "The muses of these curious phenomena are found in the wilderness . . . in dreary solitudes where the mind has no useful employment, and in the uncertain and extraordinary circumstances of a society so fast and loose that it has not and never had any parallel in the history of mankind," said one critic. He added, "The humors of our own Anglo-Saxon flesh and blood transported to America, and often located in wildernesses, are like nothing among the family which has remained at home." Precise Miss Mitford collected western tales, declaring that her purpose was "to promote kindly feelings between the two nations." "I have grasped at the broadest caricature," she said, "so that it contained indications of local manners; and clutched the wildest sketch, so that it gave a bold outline of local scenery."

The backwoodsman had emerged as a full-bodied American figure, but a curious circumstance became clear. A Yankee infusion appeared in many of these drawings. Nimrod Wildfire was made the nephew of a Yankee. In *The Gamecock of the Wilderness* the hero was clad in a buckskin shirt with a rooster for a cap, and his antics and talk were western. "The devil might dance a reel in my pocket 'thout dangering' his shins 'ginst silver," he declared; and the inflation belonged to the backwoods. But his name was a composite of western strength and Yankee acumen, Samson Hardhead; and the double strain ran through the character. The part, moreover, belonged to a Yankee actor schooled in the Yankee fable, Dan Marble.

If the backwoodsman became Yankee, the Yankee of legend also absorbed the character of the backwoodsman. Sam Slick declared, "Many's the time I've danced 'possum up a gum tree' at a quiltin' frolic or huskin' party with a tumblerful of cider on my head and never spilt a drop." The song and the feat and the boasting belonged to the West, as did

Slick's leap over three horses standing side by side. He even confessed that he was "a ring-tailed roarer." A Sam Slick broadside in London contributed to folk-talk and back-talk between the two nations, and stressed the double character. "It isn't every day that you see a genuine Yankee Doodle, I calculate! Oh, no. Now look at me. I'm cast iron all over, and pieced with rock. . . . I'm half fire, half love, and a little touch of thunder-bolt! . . .

> So here I am, just down from South,
> In everything a meddler,
> Spruce and slick in everything
> Is Sam the Yankee peddler! . . .

"We Yankees are a tarnation cute race; we make our fortune with the right hand, and lose it with the left. . . . We Yankees don't do things like you Britishers; we are born in a hurry, educated at full-speed, our spirit is at high pressure, and our life resembles a shooting star, till death surprises us like an electric shock. . . . I am Sam Slick the Yankee peddler—I can ride on a flash of lightning and catch a thunderbolt in my fist. . . .

> Oh, here I come before you all,
> And reckon yourselves lucky,
> That I have brought the news along,
> From wonderful Kentucky.

> My mother from Virginny came,
> My father was no noodle,
> And 'twixt them both they brought me up
> A regular Yankee Doodle!

In the wake of Wildfire and Slick came Sam Patch, a spinner at Pawtucket with an aptitude for jumping, whose feats quickly passed into legend. He jumped over Niagara Falls but was unable to leap the Falls of the Genesee, and plunged through to the other side of the world and bobbed up in China—pure Yankee again though still jumping, and promising to take the shine off the sea serpent when he got back to Boston. He bobbed up in Paris. Plays were written around him, stories told, poems composed. An epidemic of jumping developed. Clerks called themselves Patch as they jumped counters, country lads as they leapt over rail fences; men traveled through village streets, jumping. Sam Patch became a symbol of quickness and power. Even today a small boy's red express wagon may bear the lineal name Dan Patch. "Some things can be done as well as others," said Sam Patch laconically. The character belonged to the backwoods, but the drawling tone and dry talk were Yankee.

"The leetle ends of the Yankee's coat-tails was soon standin' out toward sunset," concluded the story of a Yankee who pushed into the West with a pewter dollar. More and more frequently the Yankee was shown against the western background. The two figures seemed to join in a new national mythology, forming a striking composite, with a blank mask in common, a similar habit of sporting in public the faults with which they were charged, both speaking in copious monologues, both possessing a bent toward the self-conscious and theatrical, not merely because they appeared on stage but because of essential combinations in mythical character. Both were given to homely metaphor. "A bear sat in the crotch of a tree looking at them dogs calm as a pond in low water," said a backwoodsman in one of the tales. Both figures had produced a strain of homely poetry.

Even on more prosaic ground some fusion appeared, drawn from life. Swapping was an ardent pursuit in the West and Southwest as well as in New England. "I am perhaps a *lee-tle*—jist a *leetle*—of the best man at a horseswap that ever stole cracklin's out of his mammy's gourd," said a character in one of the southwestern stories. Those evasive dialogues by which the Yankee sought to learn everything and tell nothing and accomplish an expanded sociability were repeated by the backwoodsman. "What mout your name be?" asked an old Georgia cracker in *Georgia Scenes*. "It *might* be anything," answered the traveler, who knew his interlocutor's mode of conversation. "Well, what *is* it then?" "It is Hall, but it might as well have been anything else." "Pretty digging!" said the cracker; and when he was asked to give his own name, "To be sure I will," he replied. "Take it, take it, and welcome. Anything else you'd like to have?" "No," said the traveler, "there's nothing else about you worth having." "Oh, yes, there is, stranger!" said the cracker, raising his rifle, shedding the Yankee, and becoming the backwoodsman.

In the mixed portrayals it was always possible to see where the Yankee left off and the backwoodsman began. The low key of the Yankee was maintained against the rhapsody of the backwoodsman. Yankee humor was gradual in its approaches, pervasive rather than explicit in its quality, subtle in its range. Backwoods drawing was broad, with a distinct bias toward the grotesque, or the macabre. Backwoods profusion was set againgst Yankee spareness. The Yankee might compare himself or another with a weasel or a blacksnake, but he never was the weasel or the blacksnake as the backwoodsman was the alligator or the raccoon or the tornado. And the Yankee as a figure stood alone or apart, a red-white-and-blue apparition which was still the dominant national figure. The backwoodsman was likely to appear in pairs, leaping or boasting or telling stories in matches with the background of a crowd. Yet a basic tie remained between them, even beyond effects of talk and masquerade, a tie which had been fashioned by the common mind out of which they sprang. Neither invited the literal view or the prosaic touch. The fantasies surrounding them might often be crude and earthy, but they were fantasies. These odd and variegated creatures were firmly planted in the spacious realm of legend.

Zora Neale Hurston

Characteristics of Negro Expression

DRAMA

The Negro's universal mimicry is not so much a thing in itself as an evidence of something that permeates his entire self. And that thing is drama.

His very words are action words. His interpretation of the English language is in terms of pictures. One act described in terms of another. Hence the rich metaphor and simile.

The metaphor is of course very primitive. It is easier to illustrate than it is to explain because action came before speech. Let us make a parallel. Language is like money. In primitive communities actual goods, however bulky, are bartered for what one wants. This finally evolves into coin, the coin being not real wealth but a symbol of wealth. Still later even coin is abandoned for legal tender, and still later for cheques in certain usages.

Every phase of Negro life is highly dramatised. No matter how joyful or how sad the case there is sufficient poise for drama. Everything is acted out. Unconsciously for the most part of course. There is an impromptu ceremony always ready for every hour of life. No little moment passes unadorned.

Now the people with highly developed languages have words for detached ideas. That is legal tender. "That-which-we-squat-on" has become "chair." "Groan-causer" has evolved into "spear," and so on. Some individuals even conceive of the equivalent of cheque words, like "ideation" and "pleonastic." Perhaps we might say that *Paradise Lost* and *Sartor Resartus* are written in cheque words.

The primitive man exchanges descriptive words. His terms are all close fitting. Frequently the Negro, even with detached words in his vocabulary—not evolved in him but transplanted on his tongue by contact—must add action to it to make it do. So we have "chop-axe," "sitting-chair," "cook-pot" and the like because the speaker has in his mind the picture of the object in use. Action. Everything illustrated. So we can say the white man thinks in a written language and the Negro thinks in hieroglyphics.

A bit of Negro drama familiar to all is the frequent meeting of two opponents who threaten to do atrocious murder one upon the other.

Who has not observed a robust young Negro chap posing upon a street corner, possessed of nothing but his clothing, his strength and his youth? Does he bear himself like a pauper? No, Louis XIV could be no more insolent in his assurance. His eyes say plainly "Female, halt!" His posture exults "Ah, female, I am the eternal male, the giver of life. Behold in my hot flesh all the delights of this world. Salute me, I am strength." All this with a languid posture, there is no mistaking his meaning.

A Negro girl strolls past the corner lounger. Her whole body panging[1] and posing. A slight shoulder movement that calls attention to her bust, that is all of a dare. A hippy undulation below the waist that is a sheaf of promises tied with conscious power. She is acting out "I'm a darned sweet woman and you know it."

These little plays by strolling players are acted out daily in a dozen streets in a thousand cities, and no one ever mistakes the meaning.

WILL TO ADORN

The will to adorn is the second most notable characteristic in Negro expression. Perhaps his idea of ornament does not attempt to meet conventional standards, but it satisfies the soul of its creator.

In this respect the American Negro has done wonders to the English language. It has often been stated by etymologists that the Negro has introduced no African words to the language. This is true, but it is equally true that he has made over a great part of the tongue to his liking and has had his revision accepted by the ruling class. No one

[1]From "pang."

listening to a Southern white man talk could deny this. Not only has he softened and toned down strongly consonated words like "aren't" to "Aint" and the like, he has made new force words out of old feeble elements. Examples of this are "Ham-shanked," "battle-hammed," "double-teen," "bodaciously," "muffle-jawed."

But the Negro's greatest contribution to the language is: (1) the use of metaphor and simile; (2) the use of the double descriptive; (3) the use of verbal nouns.

1. Metaphor and Simile

One at a time, like lawyers going to heaven.
You sho is propaganda.
Sobbing hearted.
I'll beat you till: (*a*) rope like okra, (*b*) slack like lime, (*c*) smell like onions.
Fatal for naked.
Kyting along.
That's a lynch.

That's a rope.
Cloakers—deceivers.
Regular as pig-tracks.
Mule blood—black molasses.
Syndicating—gossiping.
Flambeaux—cheap café (lighted by flambeaux).
To put yo'self on de ladder.

2. The Double Descriptive

High-tall.
Little-tee-ninchy (tiny).
Low-down.
Top-superior.
Sham-polish.
Lady-people.
Kill-dead.

Hot-boiling.
Chop-axe.
Sitting-chairs.
De watch wall.
Speedy-hurry.
More great and more better.

3. Verbal Nouns

She features somebody I know.
Funeralize.
Sense me into it.
Puts the shamery on him.
'Taint everybody you kin confidence.
I wouldn't friend with her.

Jooking—playing piano or guitar as it is done in Jook-houses (houses of ill-fame).
Uglying away.
I wouldn't scorn my name all up on you.
Bookooing (beaucoup) around—showing off.

Nouns from Verbs

Won't stand a broke.
She won't take a listen.
He won't stand straightening.

That is such a complement.
That's a lynch.

The stark, trimmed phrases of the Occident seem too bare for the voluptuous child of the sun, hence the adornment. It arises out of the same impulse as the wearing of jewelry and the making of sculpture—the urge to adorn.

On the walls of the homes of the average Negro one always finds a glut of gaudy calendars, wall pockets and advertising lithographs. The sophisticated white man or Negro would tolerate none of these, even if they bore a likeness to the Mona Lisa. No commercial art for decoration. Nor the calendar nor the advertisement spoils the picture for this lowly man. He sees the beauty in spite of the declaration of the Portland Cement Works or the butcher's announcement. I saw in Mobile a room in which there was an over-stuffed mohair living-room suite, an imitiation mahogany bed and chifferobe, a console victrola. The walls were gaily papered with Sunday supplements of the *Mobile Register.* There were seven calendars and three wall pockets. One of them was decorated with a lace doily. The mantel-shelf was covered with a scarf of deep home-made lace, looped up with a huge bow of pink crêpe paper. Over the door was a huge lithograph showing the Treaty of Versailles being signed with a Waterman fountain pen.

It was grotesque, yes. But it indicated the desire for beauty. And decorating a decoration, as in the case of the doily on the gaudy wall pocket, did not seem out of place to the hostess. The feeling back of such an act is that there can never be enough of beauty, let alone too much. Perhaps she is right. We each have our standards of art, and thus are we all interested parties and so unfit to pass judgment upon the art concepts of others.

Whatever the Negro does of his own volition he embellishes. His religious service is for the greater part excellent prose poetry. Both prayers and sermons are tooled and polished until they are true works of art. The supplication is forgotton in the frenzy of creation. The prayer of the white man is considered humorous in its bleakness. The beauty of the Old Testament does not exceed that of a Negro prayer.

ANGULARITY

After adornment the next most striking manifestation of the Negro is Angularity. Everything that he touches becomes angular. In all African sculpture and doctrine of any sort we find the same thing.

Anyone watching Negro dancers will be struck by the same phenomenon. Every posture is another angle. Pleasing, yes. But an effect achieved by the very means which an European strives to avoid.

The pictures on the walls are hung at deep angles. Furniture is always set at an angle. I have instances of a piece of furniture in the *middle* of a wall being set with one nearer the wall than the other to avoid the simple straight line.

ASYMMETRY

Asymmetry is a definite feature of Negro art. I have no samples of true Negro painting unless we count the African shields, but the sculpture and carvings are full of this beauty and lack of symmetry.

It is present in the literature, both prose and verse. I offer an example of this quality in verse from Langston Hughes:

> I aint gonna mistreat ma good gal any more,
> I'm just gonna kill her next time she makes me sore.
>
> .   .   .   .
>
> I treats her kind but she don't do me right,
> She fights and quarrels most ever' night.
>
> .   .   .   .
>
> I can't have no woman's got such low-down ways
> Cause de blue gum woman ain't de style now'days.
>
> .   .   .   .
>
> I brought her from the South and she's goin on back,
> Else I'll use her head for a carpet track.

It is the lack of symmetry which makes Negro dancing so difficult for white dancers to learn. The abrupt and unexpected changes. The frequent change of key and time are evidences of this quality in music. (Note the St. Louis Blues.)

The Dancing of the justly famous Bo-Jangles and Snake Hips are excellent examples.

The presence of rhythm and lack of symmetry are paradoxical, but there they are. Both are present to a marked degree. There is always rhythm, but it is the rhythm of segments. Each unit has a rhythm of its own, but when the whole is assembled it is lacking in symmetry. But easily workable to a Negro who is accustomed to the break in going from one part to another, so that he adjusts himself to the new tempo.

DANCING

Negro dancing is dynamic suggestion. No matter how violent it may appear to the beholder, every posture gives the impression that the dancer will do much more. For example, the performer flexes one knee sharply, assumes a ferocious face mask, thrusts the upper part of the body forward with clenched fists, elbows taut as in hard running or grasping a thrusting blade. That is all. But the spectator himself adds the picture of ferocious assault, hears the drums and finds himself keeping time with the music and tensing himself for the struggle. It is compelling insinuation. That is the very reason the spectator is held so rapt. He is participating in the performance himself—carrying out the suggestions of the performer.

The difference in the two arts is: the white dancer attempts to express fully; the Negro is restrained, no art ever can express all the variations conceivable, the Negro must be considered the greater artist, his dancing is realistic suggestion, and that is about all a great artist can do.

NEGRO FOLKLORE

Negro folklore is not a thing of the past. It is still in the making. Its great variety shows the adaptability of the black man: nothing is too old or too new, domestic or foreign, high or low, for his use. God and the Devil are paired, and are treated no more reverently than Rockefeller and Ford. Both of these men are prominent in folklore, Ford being particularly strong, and they talk and act like good-natured stevedores or mill-hands. Ole Massa is sometimes a smart man and often a fool. The automobile is ranged alongside of the ox-cart. The angels and the apostles walk and talk like section hands. And through it all walks Jack, the greatest culture hero of the South; Jack beats them all—even the Devil, who is often smarter than God.

CULTURE HEROES

The Devil is next after Jack as a culture hero. He can out-smart everyone but Jack. God is absolutely no match for him. He is good-natured and full of humour. The sort of person one may count on to help out in any difficulty.

Peter the Apostle is the third in importance. One need not look far for the explanation. The Negro is not a Christian really. The primitive gods are not deities of too subtle inner reflection; they are hard-working bodies who serve their devotees just as laboriously as the suppliant serves them. Gods of physical violence, stopping at nothing to serve their follower. Now of all the apostles Peter is the most active. When the other ten fell back trembling in the garden, Peter wielded the blade on the posse. Peter first and foremost is all action. The gods of no peoples have been philosophic until the people themselves have approached that state.

The rabbit, the bear, the lion, the buzzard, the fox are culture heroes from the animal world. The rabbit is far in the lead of all the others and is blood brother to Jack. In short, the trickster-hero of West Africa has been transplanted to America.

John Henry is a culture hero in song, but no more so than Stacker Lee, Smokey Joe or Bad Lazarus. There are many, many Negroes who have never heard of any of the song heroes, but none who do not know John (Jack) and the rabbit.

Examples of Folklore and the Modern Culture Hero

WHY DE PORPOISE'S TAIL IS ON CROSSWISE

Now, I want to tell you 'bout de porpoise. God had done made de world and everything. He set de moon and de stars in de sky. He got de fishes of de sea, and de fowls of de air completed. He made de sun and hung it up. Then He made a nice gold track for it to run on. Then He said, "Now, Sun, I got everything made but Time. That's up to you. I want you to start out and go round de world on dis track just as fast as you kin make it. And de time it takes you to go and come, I'm going to call day and night." De Sun went zoonin' on cross de elements. Now, de porpoise was hanging round there and heard God what he tole de Sun, so he decided he'd take dat trip round de world hisself. He looked up and saw de Sun kytin' along, so he lit out too, him and dat Sun!

So de porpoise beat de Sun round De world by one hour and three minutes. So God said, "Aw now, this aint gointer do! I didn't mean for nothin to be faster than de Sun!" So God run dat porpoise for three days before he run him down and caught him, and took his tail off and put it on crossways to slow him up. Still he's de fastest thing in the water.

And dat's why de porpoise got his tail on crosswise.

ROCKEFELLER AND FORD

Once John D. Rockefeller and Henry Ford was woofing at each other. Rockefeller told Henry Ford he could build a solid gold road round the world. Henry Ford told him if he would he would look at it and see if he liked it, and if he did he would buy it and put one of his tin lizzies on it.

ORIGINALITY

It has been said so often that the Negro is lacking in originality that it has almost become a gospel. Outward signs seem to bear this out. But if one looks closely its falsity is immediately evident.

It is obvious that to get back to original sources is much too difficult for any group to claim very much as a certainty. What we really mean by originality is the modification of ideas. The most ardent admirer of the great Shakespeare cannot claim first source even for him. It is his treatment of the borrowed material.

So if we look at it squarely, the Negro is a very original being. While he lives and moves in the midst of a white civilization, everything that he touches is re-interpreted for his own use. He has modified the language, mode of food preparation, practice of medicine, and most certainly the religion of his new country, just as he adapted to suit himself the Sheik hair-cut made famous by Rudolph Valentino.

Everyone is familiar with the Negro's modification of the white's musical instruments, so that his interpretation has been adopted by the white man himself and then re-interpreted. In so many words, Paul Whiteman is giving an imitation of a Negro orchestra making use of white-invented musical instruments in a Negro way. Thus has arisen a new art in the civilised world, and thus has our so-called civilisation come. The exchange and re-exchange of ideas between groups.

IMITATION

The Negro, the world over, is famous as a mimic. But this in no way damages his standing as an original. Mimicry is an art in itself. If it is not, then all art must fall by the same blow that strikes it down. When sculpture, painting, acting, dancing, literature neither reflect nor suggest anything in nature or human experience we turn away with a dull wonder in our hearts at why the thing was done. Moreover, the contention that the Negro imitates from a feeling of inferiority is incorrect. He mimics for the love of it. The group of Negroes who slavishly imitate is small. The average Negro glories in his ways. The highly educated Negro the same. The self-despisement lies in a middle class who scorns to do or be anything Negro. "That's just like a Nigger" is the most terrible rebuke one can lay upon this kind. He wears drab clothing, sits through a boresome church service, pretends to have no interest in the community, holds beauty contests, and otherwise apes all the mediocrities of the white brother. The truly cultured Negro scorns him, and the Negro "farthest down" is too busy "spreading his junk" in his own way to see or care. He likes his own things best. Even the group who are not Negroes but belong to the "Sixth race," buy such records as "Shake dat thing" and "Tight lak dat." They really enjoy hearing a good bible-beater preach, but wild horses could drag no such admission from them. Their ready-made expression is: "We done got away from all that now." Some refuse to countenance Negro music on the grounds that it is niggerism, and for that reason should be done away with. Roland Hayes was thoroughly denounced for singing spirituals until he was accepted by white audiences. Langston Hughes is not considered a poet by this group because he writes of the man in the ditch, who is more numerous and real among us than any other.

But, this group aside, let us say that the art of mimicry is better developed in the Negro than in other racial groups. He does it as the mocking-bird does it, for the love of it, and not because he wishes to be like the one imitated. I saw a group of small Negro boys imitating a cat defecating and the subsequent toilet of the cat. It was very realistic, and they enjoyed it as much as if they had been imitating a coronation ceremony. The dances are full of imitations of various animals. The buzzard lope, walking the dog, the pig's hind legs, holding the mule, elephant squat, pigeon's wing, falling off the log, seabord (imitation of an engine starting), and the like.

ABSENCE OF THE CONCEPT OF PRIVACY

It is said that Netroes keep nothing secret, that they have no reserve. This ought not to seem strange when one considers that we are an outdoor people accustomed to communal life. Add this to all-permeating drama and you have the explanation.

There is no privacy in an African village. Loves, fights, possessions are, to misquote Woodrow Wilson, "Open disagreements openly arrived at." The community is given the benefit of a good fight as well as a good wedding. An audience is a necessary part of any drama. We merely go with nature rather than against it.

Discord is more natural than accord. If we accept the doctrine of the survival of the fittest there are more fighting honors than there are honors for other achievements. Humanity places premiums on all things necessary to its well-being, and a valiant and good fighter is valuable in any community. So why hide the light under a bushel? Moreover, intimidation is a recognised part of warfare the world over, and threats certainly must be listed under that head. So that a great threatener must certainly be considered an aid to the fighting machine. So then if a man or a woman is a facile hurler of threats, why should he or she not show their wares to the community? Hence the holding of all quarrels and fights in the open. One relieves one's pent-up anger and at the same time earns laurels in intimidation. Besides, one does the community a service. There is nothing so exhilarating as watching well-matched opponents go into action. The entire world likes action, for that matter. Hence prize-fighters become millionaires.

Likewise love-making is a biological necessity the world over and an art among Negroes. So that a man or woman who is proficient sees no reason why the fact should not be moot. He swaggers. She struts hippily about. Songs are built on the power to charm beneath the bed-clothes. Here again we have individuals striving to excel in what the community considers an art. Then if all of his world is seeking a great lover, why should he not speak right out loud?

It is all in a view-point. Love-making and fighting in all their branches are high arts, other things are arts among other groups where they brag about their proficiency just as brazenly as we do about these things that others consider matters for conversation behind closed doors. At any rate, the white man is despised by Negroes as a very poor fighter individually, and a very poor lover. One Negro, speaking of white men, said, "White folks is alright when dey gits in de bank and on de law bench, but dey sho' kin lie about wimmen folks."

I pressed him to explain. "Well you see, white mens makes out they marries wimmen to look at they eyes, and they know they gets em for just what us gits em for. 'Nother thing, white mens say they goes clear round de world and wins all de wimmen folks way from they men folks. Dat's a lie too. They don't win nothing, they buys em. Now de way I figgers it, if a woman don't want me enough to be wid me, 'thout I got to pay her, she kin rock right on, but these here white men don't know what to do wid a woman when they gits her—dat's how come they gives they wimmen so much. They got to. Us wimmen works jus as hard as us does an come home an sleep wid us every night. They own wouldn't do it and its de mens fault. Dese white men done fooled theyself bout dese wimmen.

"Now me, I keeps me some wimmens all de time. Dat's whut dey wuz put here for—us mens to use. Dat's right now, Miss. Y'all wuz put here so us mens could have some pleasure. Course I don't run round like heap uh men folks. But if my ole lady go way from me and stay more't two weeks, I got to git me somebody, aint I?"

THE JOOK

Jook is the word for a Negro pleasure house. It may mean a bawdy house. It may mean the house set apart on public works where the men and women dance, drink and gamble. Often it is a combination of all these.

In past generations the music was furnished by "boxes," another word for guitars. One guitar was enough for a dance; to have two was considered excellent. Where two were playing one man played the lead and the other seconded him. The first player was "picking" and the second was "framming," that is, playing chords while the lead carried the melody by dexterous finger work. Sometimes a third player was added, and he played a tom-tom effect on the low strings. Believe it or not, this is excellent dance music.

Pianos soon came to take the place of the boxes, and now player-pianos and victrolas are in all of the Jooks.

Musically speaking, the Jook is the most important place in America. For in its smelly, shoddy confines has been born the secular music known as blues, and on blues has been founded jazz. The singing and playing in the true Negro style is called "jooking."

The songs grow by incremental repetition as they travel from mouth to mouth and from Jook to Jook for years before they reach outside ears. Hence the great variety of subject-matter in each song.

The Negro dances circulated over the world were also conceived inside the Jooks. They too make the round of Jooks and public works before going into the outside world.

In this respect it is interesting to mention the Black Bottom. I have read several false accounts of its origin and name. One writer claimed that it got its name from the black sticky mud on the bottom of the Mississippi river. Other equally absurd statements gummed the press. Now the dance really originated in the Jook section of Nashville, Tennessee, around Fourth Avenue. This is a tough neighborhood known as Black Bottom—hence the name.

The Charleston is perhaps forty years old, and was danced up and down the Atlantic seaboard from North Carolina to Key West, Florida.

The Negro social dance is slow and sensuous. The idea in the Jook is to gain sensation, and not so much exercise. So that just enough foot movement is added to keep the dancers on the floor. A tremendous sex stimulation is gained from this. But who is trying to avoid it? The man, the woman, the time and the place have met. Rather, little intimate names are indulged in to heap fire on fire.

These too have spread to all the world.

The Negro theatre, as built up by the Negro, is based on Jook situations, with women, gambling, fighting, drinking. Shows like "Dixie to Broadway" are only Negro in cast, and could just as well have come from pre-Soviet Russia.

Another interesting thing—Negro shows before being tampered with did not specialise in octoroon chorus girls. The girl who could hoist a Jook song from her belly and lam it against the front door of the theatre was the lead, even if she were as black as the hinges of hell. The question was "Can she jook?" She must also have a good belly wobble, and her hips must, to quote a popular work song, "Shake like jelly all over and be so broad, Lawd, Lawd, and be so broad." So that the bleached chorus is the result of a white demand and not the Negro's.

The woman in the Jook may be nappy headed and black, but if she is a good lover she gets there just the same. A favorite Jook song of the past has this to say:

Singer: It aint good looks dat takes you through dis world.

Audience: What is it, good mama?
Singer: Elgin[1] movements in your hips
        Twenty years guarantee.
And it always brought down the house too.

> Oh de white gal rides in a Cadillac,
> De yaller gal rides de same,
> Black gal rides in a rusty Ford
> But she gits dere just de same.

The sort of woman her men idealise is the type that is put forth in the theatre. The art-creating Negro prefers a not too thin woman who can shake like jelly all over as she dances and sings, and that is the type he put forth on the stage. She has been banished by the white producer and the Negro who takes his cue from the white.

Of course a black woman is never the wife of the upper class Negro in the North. This state of affairs does not obtain in the South, however. I have noted numerous cases where the wife was considerably darker than the husband. People of some substance too.

This scornful attitude towards black women receives mouth sanction by the mud-sills.

Even on the works and in the Jooks the black man sings disparagingly of black women. They say that she is evil. That she sleeps with her fist doubled up and ready for action. All over they are making a little drama of waking up a yaller[2] wife and a black one.

A man is lying beside his yaller wife and wakes her up. She says to him, "Darling, do you know what I was dreaming when you woke me up?" He says, "No honey, what was you dreaming?" She says, "I dreamt I had done cooked you up a big, fine dinner and we was setting down to eat out de same plate and I was setting on yo' lap jus huggin you and kissin you and you was so sweet."

Wake up a black woman, and before you kin git any sense into her she be done up and lammed you over the head four or five times. When you git her quite she'll say, "Nigger, know whut I was dreaming when you woke me up?"

You say, "No honey, what was you dreaming?" She says, "I dreamt you shook yo' rusty fist under my nose and I split yo' head open wid a axe."

But in spite of disparaging fictitious drama, in real life the black girl is drawing on his account at the commissary. Down in the Cypress Swamp as he swings his axe he chants:

> Dat ole black gal, she keep on grumblin,
> New pair shoes, new pair shoes,
> I'm goint to buy her shoes and stockings
> Slippers too, slippers too.

Then adds aside: "Blacker de berry, sweeter de juice."

To be sure the black gal is still in power, men are still cutting and shooting their way to her pillow. To the queen of the Jook!

Speaking of the influence of the Jook, I noted that Mae West in "Sex" had much more flavor of the turpentine quarters than she did of the white bawd. I know that the piece she played on the piano is a very old Jook composition. "Honey let yo' drawers hang low" had been played and sung in every Jook in the South for at least thirty-five years. It has always puzzled me why she thought it likely to be played in a Canadian bawdy house.

---

[1] Elegant (?).

[2] Yaller (yellow), light mulatto.

Speaking of the use of Negro material by white performers, it is astonishing that so many are trying it, and I have never seen one yet entirely realistic. They often have all the elements of the song, dance, or expression, but they are misplaced or distorted by the accent falling on the wrong element. Every one seems to think that the Negro is easily imitated when nothing is further from the truth. Without exception I wonder why the black-face comedians *are* black-face; it is a puzzle—good comedians, but darn poor niggers. Gershwin and the other "Negro" rhapsodists come under this same axe. Just about as Negro as caviar or Ann Pennington's athletic Black Bottom. When the Negroes who knew the Black Bottom in its cradle saw the Broadway version they asked each other, "Is you learnt dat *new* Black Bottom yet?" Proof that it was not *their* dance.

And God only knows what the world has suffered from the white damsels who try to sing Blues.

The Negroes themselves have sinned also in this respect. In spite of the goings up and down on the earth, from the original Fisk Jubilee Singers down to the present, there has been no genuine presentation of Negro songs to white audiences. The spirituals that have been sung around the world are Negroid to be sure, but so full of musicians' tricks that Negro congregations are highly entertained when they hear their old songs so changed. They never use the new style songs, and these are never heard unless perchance some daughter or son has been off to college and returns with one of the old songs with its face lifted, so to speak.

I am of the opinion that this trick style of delivery was originated by the Fisk Singers; Tuskegee and Hampton followed suit and have helped spread this misconception of Negro spirituals. This Glee Club style has gone on so long and become so fixed among concert singers that it is considered quite authentic. But I say again, that not one concert singer in the world is singing the songs as the Negro song-makers sing them.

If anyone wishes to prove the truth of this let him step into some unfashionable Negro church and hear for himself.

To those who want to institute the Negro theatre, let me say it is already established. It is lacking in wealth, so it is not seen in the high places. A creature with a white head and Negro feet struts the Metropolitan boards. The real Negro theatre is in the Jooks and the cabarets. Self-conscious individuals may turn away the eye and say, "Let us search elsewhere for our dramatic art." Let 'em search. They certainly won't find it. Butter Beans and Susie, Bo-Jangles and Snake Hips are the only performers of the real Negro school it has ever been my pleasure to behold in New York.

DIALECT

If we are to believe the majority of writers of Negro dialect and the burnt-cork artists, Negro speech is a weird thing, full of "ams" and "Ises." Fortunately we don't have to believe them. We may go directly to the Negro and let him speak for himself.

I know that I run the risk of being damned as an infidel for declaring that nowhere can be found the Negro who asks "am it?" nor yet his brother who announces "Ise uh gwinter." He exists only for a certain type of writers and performers.

Very few Negroes, educated or not, use a clear clipped "I." It verges more or less upon "Ah." I think the lip form is responsible for this to a great extent. By experiment the reader will find that a sharp "I" is very much easier with a thin taut lip than with a full soft lip. Like tightening violin strings.

If one listens closely one will note too that a word is slurred in one position in the sentence but clearly pronounced in another. This is particularly true of the pronouns. A pronoun as a subject is likely to be clearly enunciated, but slurred as an object. For example: "You better not let me ketch yuh."

There is a tendency in some localities to add the "h" to "it" and pronounce it "hit." Probably a vestige of old English. In some localities "if" is "ef."

In story telling "so" is universally the connective. It is used even as an introductory word, at the very beginning of a story. In religious expression "and" is used. The trend in stories is to state conclusions; in religion, to enumerate.

I am mentioning only the most general rules in dialect because there are so many quirks that belong only to certain localities that nothing less than a volume would be adequate.

[1934]

Kenneth Burke

Literature as Equipment for Living

Here I shall put down, as briefly as possible, a statement in behalf of what might be catalogued, with a fair degree of accuracy, as a *sociological* criticism of literature. Sociological criticism in itself is certainly not new. I shall here try to suggest what partially new elements or emphasis I think should be added to this old approach. And to make the "way in" as easy as possible. I shall begin with a discussion of proverbs.

1

Examine random specimens in *The Oxford Dictionary of English Proverbs.* You will note, I think, that there is no "pure" literature here. Everything is "medicine." Proverbs are designed for consolation or vengeance, for admonition or exhortation, for foretelling.

Or they name typical, recurrent situations. That is, people find a certain social relationship recurring so frequently that they must "have a word for it." The Eskimos have special names for many different kinds of snow (fifteen, if I remember rightly) because variations in the quality of snow greatly affect their living. Hence, they must "size up" snow much more accurately than we do. And the same is true of social phenomena. Social structures give rise to "type" situations, subtle subdivisions of relationships involved in competitive and cooperative acts. Many proverbs seek to chart, in more or less homey and picturesque ways, these "type" situations. I submit that such naming is done, not for the sheer glory of the thing, but because of its bearing upon human welfare. A different name for snow implies a different kind of hunt. Some names for snow imply that one should not hunt at all.

And similarly, the names for typical, recurrent social situations are not developed out of "disinterested curiosity," but because the names imply a command (what to expect, what to look out for).

To illustrate with a few representative examples:

Proverbs designed for consolation: "The sun does not shine on both sides of the hedge at once." "Think of ease, but work on." "Little troubles the eye, but far less the soul." "The worst luck now, the better another time." "The wind in one's face makes one wise." "He that hath lands hath quarrels." "He knows how to carry the dead cock home." "He is not poor that hath little, but he that desireth much."

For vengeance: "At length the fox is brought to the furrier." "Shod in the cradle, bare-foot in the stubble." "Sue a beggar and get a louse." "The higher the ape goes, the more he shows his tail." "The moon does not heed the barking of dogs." "He measures another's corn by his own bushel." "He shuns the man who knows him well." "Fools tie knots and wise men loose them."

Proverbs that have to do with foretelling: (The most obvious are those to do with the weather.) "Sow peas and beans in the wane of the moon, Who soweth them sooner, he soweth too soon." "When the wind's in the north, the skilful fisher goes not forth." "When the sloe tree is as white as a sheet, sow your barley whether it be dry or wet." "When the sun sets bright and clear, An easterly wind you need not fear. When the sun sets in a bank, A westerly wind we shall not want."

In short: "Keep your weather eye open": be realistic about sizing up today's weather, because your accuracy has bearing upon tomorrow's weather. And forecast not only the meteorological weather, but also the social weather: "When the moon's in the full, then wit's in the wane." "Straws show which way the wind blows." "When the fish is caught, the net is laid aside." "Remove an old tree, and it will wither to death." "The wolf may lose his teeth, but never his nature." "He that bites on every weed must needs light on poison." "Whether the pitcher strikes the stone, or the stone the pitcher, it is bad for the pitcher." "Eagles catch no flies." "The more laws, the more offenders."

In this foretelling category we might also include the recipes for wise living, some-times moral, sometimes technical: "First thrive, and then wive." "Think with the wise but talk with the vulgar." "When the fox preacheth, then beware your geese." "Venture a small fish to catch a great one." "Respect a man, he will do the more."

In the class of "typical, recurrent situations" we might put such proverbs and prover-bial expressions as: "Sweet appears sour when we pay." "The treason is loved but the trai-tor is hated." "The wine in the bottle does not quench thirst." "The sun is never the worse for shining on a dunghill." "The lion kicked by an ass." "The lion's share." "To catch one napping." "To smell a rat." "To cool one's heels."

By all means, I do not wish to suggest that this is the only way in which the proverbs could be classified. For instance, I have listed in the "foretelling" group the proverb, "When the fox preacheth, then beware your geese." But it could obviously be "taken over" for vindictive purposes. Or consider a proverb like, "Virtue flies from the heart of a merce-nary man." A poor man might obviously use it either to console himself for being poor (the implication being, "Because I am poor in money I am rich in virtue") or to strike at another (the implication being, "When he got money, what else could you expect of him but deterioration?"). In fact, we could even say that such symbolic vengeance would itself be an aspect of solace. And a proverb like "The sun is never the worse for shining on a dunghill" (which I have listed under "typical recurrent situations") might as well be put in the vindictive category.

The point of issue is not to find categories that "place" the proverbs once and for all. What I want is categories that suggest their active nature. Here there is no "realism for its own sake." There is realism for promise, admonition, solace, vengeance, foretelling, instruction, charting, all for the direct bearing that such acts have upon matters of welfare.

2

Step two: Why not extend such analysis of proverbs to encompass the whole field of literature? Could the most complex and sophisticated works of art legitimately be considered somewhat as "proverbs writ large"? Such leads, if held admissible, should help us to discover important facts about literary organization (thus satisfying the requirements of technical criticism). And the kind of observation from this perspective should apply beyond literature to life in general (thus helping to take literature out of its separate bin and give it a place in a general "sociological" picture).

The point of view might be phrased in this way: Proverbs are *strategies* for dealing with *situations.* In so far as situations are typical and recurrent in a given social structure, people develop names for them and strategies for handling them. Another name for strategies might be *attitudes.*

People have often commented on the fact that there are contrary *proverbs.* But I believe that the above approach to proverbs suggests a necessary modification of that comment. The apparent contradictions depend upon differences in *attitude,* involving a correspondingly different choice of *strategy.* Consider, for instance, the *apparently* opposite pair, "Repentance comes too late" and "Never too late to mend." The first is admonitory. It says in effect: "You'd better look out, or you'll get yourself too far into this business." The second is consolatory, saying in effect:"Buck up, old man, you can still pull out of this."

Some critics have quarreled with me about my selection of the word "strategy" as the name for this process. I have asked them to suggest an alternative term, so far without profit. The only one I can think of is "method." but if "strategy" errs in suggesting to some people an overly *conscious* procedure, "method" errs in suggesting an overly *"methodical"* one. Anyhow, let's look at the documents:

Concise Oxford Dictionary: "Strategy: Movement of an army or armies in a campaign, art of so moving or disposing troops or ships as to impose upon the enemy the place and time and conditions for fighting preferred by oneself" (from a Greek word that refers to the leading of an army).

New English Dictionary: "Strategy: The art of projecting and directing the larger military movements and operations of a campaign."

André Cheron, *Traité Complet d'Echecs: "On entend par stratégie les manoeuvres qui ont pour but la sortie et le bon arrangement des pièces."*

Looking at these definitions, I gain courage. For surely, the most highly alembicated and sophisticated work of art, arising in complex civilizations, could be considered as designed to organize and command the army of one's thoughts and images, and to so organize them that one "imposes upon the enemy the time and place and conditions for fighting preferred by oneself." One seeks to "direct the larger movements and operations" in one's campaign of living. One "maneuvers," and the maneuvering is an "art."

Are not the final results one's "strategy"? One tries, as far as possible, to develop a strategy whereby one "can't lose." One tries to change the rules of the game until they fit his own necessities. Does the artist encounter disaster? He will "make capital" of it. If one is a victim of competition, for instance, if one is elbowed out, if one is willy-nilly more jock-eyed against than jockeying, one can by the solace and vengeance of art convert this very "liability" into an "asset." One tries to fight on his own terms, developing a strategy for imposing the proper "time, place, and conditions."

But one must also, to develop a full strategy, be *realistic.* One must *size things up* properly. One cannot accurately know how things *will* be, what is promising and what is menacing, unless he accurately knows how things are. So the wise strategist will not be content with strategies of merely a self-gratifying sort. He will "keep his weather eye open." He will not too eagerly "read into" a scene an attitude that is irrelevant to it. He won't sit on the side of an active volcano and "see" it as a dormant plain.

Often, alas, he will. The great allurement in our present popular "inspirational literature," for instance, may be largely of this sort. It is a strategy for easy consolation. It "fills a need," since there is always a need for easy consolation—and in an era of confusion like our own the need is especially keen. So people are only too willing to "meet a man halfway" who will *play down* the realistic naming of our situation and *play up* such strategies as make solace cheap. However, I should propose a reservation here. We usually take it for granted that people who consume our current output of books on "How to Buy Friends and Bamboozle Oneself and Other People" are reading as *students* who will attempt applying the recipes given. Nothing of the sort. *The reading of a book on the attaining of success is in itself the symbolic attaining of that success.* It is *while they read* that these readers are "succeeding." I'll wager that, in by far the majority of cases, such readers made no serious attempt to apply the book's recipes. The lure of the book resides in the fact that the reader, while reading it, is then living in the aura of success. What he wants is *easy* success: and he gets it in symbolic form by the mere reading itself. To attempt applying such stuff in real life would be very difficult, full of many disillusioning difficulties.

Sometimes a different strategy may arise. The author may remain realistic, avoiding too easy a form of solace—yet he may get as far off the track in his own way. Forgetting that realism is an aspect for foretelling, he may take it as an end in itself. He is tempted to do this by two factors: (1) an *ill-digested* philosophy of science, leading him mistakenly to assume that "relentless" naturalistic "truthfulness" is a proper end in itself, and (2) a merely *competitive* desire to outstrip other writers by being "more realistic" than they. Works thus made "efficient" by tests of competition internal to the book trade are a kind of academicism not so named (the writer usually thinks of it as the *opposite* of academicism. Realism thus stepped up competitively might be distinguished from the proper sort by the name of "naturalism." As a way of "sizing things up," the naturalistic tradition tends to become as inaccurate as the "inspirational" strategy, though at the opposite extreme.

Anyhow, the main point is this: A work like *Madame Bovary* (or its homely American translation, *Babbitt*) is the strategic naming of a situation. It singles out a pattern of experience that is sufficiently often *mutandis mutatis,* for people to "need a word for it" and to adopt an attitude towards it. Each work of art is the addition of a word to an informal dictionary (or, in the case of purely derivative artists, the addition of a subsidiary meaning to a word already given by some originating artist). As for *Madame Bovary,* the French critic Jules de Gaultier proposed to add it to our formal dictionary by coining the world "Bovarysme" and writing a whole book to say what he meant by it.

Mencken's book on *The American Language,* I hate to say, is splendid. I console myself with the reminder that Mencken didn't write it. Many millions of people wrote it, and Mencken was merely the amanuensis who took it down from their dictation. He found a true "vehicle" (that is, a book that could be greater than the author who wrote it). He gets the royalties, but the job was done by a collectivity. As you read that book, you see a people who were up against a new set of typical recurrent situations, situations typical of their business, their politics, their criminal organizations, their sports. Either there were no words for these in standard English, or people didn't know them, or they didn't "sound right." So a new vocabulary arose, to "give us a word for it." I see no reason for believing that Americans are unusually fertile in word-coinage. American slang was not developed out of the fact that new typical situations had arisen and people needed names for them. They had to "size things up." They had to console and strike, to promise and admonish. They had to describe for purposes of forecasting. And "slang" was the result. It is, by this analysis, simple *proverbs not so named,* a kind of "folk criticism."

3

With what, then, would "sociological criticism" along these lines be concerned? It would seek to codify the various strategies which artists have developed with relation to the naming of situations. In a sense, much of it would even be "timeless," for many of the "typical, recurrent situations" are not peculiar to our own civilization at all. The situations and strategies framed in Aesop's Fables, for instance, apply to human relations now just as fully as they applied in ancient Greece. They are, like philosophy, sufficiently "generalized" to extend far beyond the particular combination of events named by them in any one instance. They name an "essence." Or, as Korzybski might say, they are on a "high level of abstraction." One doesn't usually think of them as "abstract," since they are usually so concrete in their stylistic expression. But they invariably aim to discern the "general behind the particular" (which would suggest that they are good Goethe).

The attempt to treat literature from the standpoint of situations and strategies suggests a variant of Spengler's notion of the "contemporaneous." By "contemporaneity" he meant corresponding stages of different cultures. For instance, if modern New York is much like decadent Rome, then we are "contemporaneous" with decadent Rome, or with some corresponding decadent city among the Mayas, etc. It is in this sense that situations are "timeless," "nonhistorical," "contemporaneous." A given human relationship may be at one time named in terms of foxes and lions, if there are foxes and lions about; or it may now be named in terms of salesmanship, advertising, the tactics of politicians, etc. But beneath the change in particulars, we may often discern the naming of the one situation.

So sociological criticism, as here understood, would seek to assemble and codify this lore. It might occasionally lead us to outrage good taste, as we sometimes found exemplified in some great sermon or tragedy or abstruse work of philosophy the same strategy as we found exemplified in a dirty joke. At this point, we'd put the sermon and the dirty joke together, thus "grouping by situation" and showing the range of possible particularizations. In his exceptionally discerning essay, "A Critic's Job of Work," R. P. Blackmur says, "I think on the whole his (Burke's) method could be applied with equal fruitfulness to Shakespeare, Dashiell Hammett, or Marie Corelli." When I got through wincing, I had to admit that Blackmur was right. This article is an attempt to say for the method what can be said. As a matter of fact, I'll go a step further and maintain: You can't properly put Marie Corelli and Shakespeare apart until you have first put them together. First genus, then differentia. The strategy in common is the genus. The *range* or *scale of spectrum* of particularizations is the differentia.

Anyhow, that's what I'm driving at. And that's why reviewers sometimes find in my work "intuitive" leaps that are dubious as "science." They are not "leaps" at all. They are classifications, groupings, made on the basis of some strategic element common to the items grouped. They are neither more nor less "intuitive" than *any* grouping or classification of social events. Apples can be grouped with bananas as fruit, and they can be grouped with tennis balls as round. I am simply proposing, in the social sphere, a method of classification with reference to *strategies.*

The method of these things to be said in its favor: It gives definite insight into the organization of literary works; and it automatically breaks down the barriers erected about literature as a specialized pursuit. People can classify novels by reference to three kinds, eight kinds, seventeen kinds. It doesn't matter. Students patiently copy down the professor's classification and pass examinations on it, because the range of possible academic classifications is endless. Sociological classification, as herein suggested, would derive its relevance from the fact that it should apply both to works of art and to social situations outside of art.

It would, I admit, violate current pieties, break down current categories, and thereby "outrage good taste." But "good taste" has become *inert.* The classifications I am proposing would be *active.* I think that what we need is active categories.

These categories will lie on the bias across the categories of modern specialization. The new alignment will outrage in particular those persons who take the division of faculties in our universities to be an exact replica of the way in which God himself divided up the universe. We have had the Philosophy of the Being; and we have had the Philosophy of the Becoming. In contemporary specialization, we have been getting the Philosophy of the Bin. Each of these mental localities has had its own peculiar way of life, its own values, even its own special idiom of seeing, thinking, and "proving." Among other things, a sociological approach should attempt to provide a reintegrative point of view, a broader empire of investigation encompassing the lot.

What would such sociological categories be like? They would consider works of art, I think as strategies for selecting enemies and allies, for socializing losses, for warding off evil eye, for purification, propitiation, and desanctification, consolation and vengeance, admonition and exhortation, implicit commands or instructions of one sort or another. Art forms like "tragedy" or "comedy" or "satire" would be treated as *equipments for living,* that size up situations in various ways and in keeping with correspondingly various attitudes. The typical ingredients of such forms would be sought. Their relation to typical situations would be stressed. Their comparative values would be considered, with the intention of formulating a "strategy of strategies," the "over-all" strategy obtained by inspection of the lot.   [1941]

J. Saunders Redding

The Forerunners

Excerpt from *To Make a Poet Black*

1

The literature of the Negro in America, motivated as it is by his very practical desire to adjust himself to the American environment, is "literature of necessity." Until recent years the Negro writer has not known what it is to write without this motivation, and even now, of the dozens of writers who have published in the last twenty years the work of but two seems wholly independent of this influence. At the very heart of this literature, then, lies the spore of a cankerous growth. This might be said to be the necessity of ends. But there is also a necessity of means. Negro writers have been obliged to have two faces. If they wished to succeed they have been obliged to satisfy two different (and opposed when not entirely opposite) audiences, the black and the white. This necessity of means, perhaps, has been even stronger than the necessity of ends, and as writers have increased, the necessity has grown almost to the point of desperation.

From Jupiter Hammon, the first Negro writer in America, to Countee Cullen and Langston Hughes, these two necessities can be traced with varying degrees of clarity—now one and now the other predominant—like threads through the whole cloth. With the very earliest writers the needs did not encompass more than personal self, but as consciousness of others awakened in later writers and as the simplicity of the Negro's primary position in America changed successively to the complexity of the times of abolition agitation, freedom, enfranchisement, and social self-determination, the artless personality of his literature dropped away and he became the sometimes frenzied propagandist of racial consciousness and advancement.

2

Jupiter Hammon was the first American Negro to see his name in print as a maker of verse. The date of his birth is uncertain, but the earliest reference to him is found in a letter dated May 19, 1730, when he was probably little more than ten years old. At this time he was the slave of Henry Lloyd of Queens Village, Long Island. The date of his death is likewise uncertain, but was very probably not earlier than 1806.

Hammon's first published work was "An Evening Thought: Salvation by Christ, with Penentential Cries" in 1760. His next work, "A Poetical Address to Phillis Wheatley," was published eighteen years later, but it is improbable that the intervening years were devoid of literary activity, especially considering that Hammon was something of a preacher among his people, a fact which plainly had a bearing upon his work. "An Essay on the Ten Virgins," of which no copy is extant, was printed in 1779. In 1782 he published "A Winter Piece" and "A Poem for Children with Thoughts on Death" and "An Evening's Improvement" to which was appended a rhymed dialogue entitled "The Kind Master and

Dutiful Servant." The last of his printed work, "An Address to Negroes in the State of New York," was issued in 1787 and reached three editions.

Hammon was an intelligent and privileged slave, respected by the master class for his skill with tools and by the slaves for his power as a preacher. His verse is rhymed prose, doggerel, in which the homely thoughts of a very religious and superstitious man are expressed in limping phrases. Now and then his lines have a lyric swing that seems to mark them as having been chanted spontaneously in the sermons he preached. Undoubtedly some lines from "An Evening Thought" have this lyric significance. The alternately rhyming lines lend themselves very easily and nicely to religious chanting.

> Salvation comes by Christ alone,
> The only son of God;
> Redemption now to every one,
> That love his holy word.
>
> Dear Jesus unto Thee we cry,
> Give us the preparation;
> Turn not away they tender eye;
> We seek thy true salvation.

Of the work of this kind, the piece addressed to Phillis Wheatley is the best. Hammon must have struck responsive chords in the breast of the young Massachusetts slave who already at this time had been acclaimed in England as an unusual poet. Both were extremely religious, and both preferred slavery in America to freedom in Africa. Each of the twenty-one quatrains of "The Address to Phillis Wheatley" has a marginal note of reference to the Bible.

> I
> O come you pious youth! Adore
>   The wisdom of they God,
> In bringing thee from distant shore
>   To learn his holy word.
>
> II
> Thou mightst been left behind,
>   Admidst a dark abode;
> God's tender mercy still combin'd,
>   Thou has the holy word.
>
> IV
> God's tender mercy brought thee here;
>   Tost o'er the raging main;
> In Christian faith thou hast a share,
>   Worth all the gold of Spain.
>
> IX
> Come you, Phillis, now aspire,
>   And seek the living God,
> So step by step thou mayest go higher,
>   Till perfect in the word.

Almost did Miss Wheatley express Hammon's exact thought in her lines "To the University of Cambridge."

'T was not long since I left my native shore,
The land of errors and Egyptian gloom;
Father of mercy! 't was thy gracious hand
Brought me in safety from those dark abodes.

On the whole, Hammon's untutored art offered but narrow scope for the fullest expression. His most substantial contribution to Negro literature prior to the Civil War is in prose, and whatever of literary merit he possessed must be looked for in his single prose piece, "An Address to the Negroes in the State of New York." This work reveals more of Hammon's workaday character than all his poetry together. The thoughts expressed in "An Address to Negroes" are not typical of the thoughts of slaves, especially those who were unfortunate enough to have had some education. With the notable exception of Phillis Wheatley, the slave writers were bitterly reproachful of bondage. Many slaves who could neither read nor write but who were nonetheless truly poetic burned themselves out in revolt. To the splendid folly of their deeds Hammon's equivocal statement is an outrage. A summation of his philosophy and a clearcut statement of his resignation to a life of servitude is found in his words:

"Respecting obedience to masters. Now whether it is right and lawful in the sight of God, for them to make slaves of us or not, I am certain that while we are slaves, it is our duty to obey our masters in all their lawful commands, and mind them. . . . As we depend upon our masters for what we eat and drink and wear, we cannot be happy unless we obey them."

Hammon's life was motivated by the compulsion of obedience to his earthly and his heavenly master. Perhaps the inevitability of his position tended to wilt his moral fiber. Perhaps the beneficence of his masters lightened the burden of his bondage. Though he was the first Negro slave to publish an adverse opinion on the institution of slavery, his opinion was robbed of its force by the words "though for my own part I do not wish to be free." Perhaps it was the very weakness of the statement that recommended it for publication. At the same time, however, his hedging was not without its wisdom. He says:

"Now I acknowledge that liberty is a great thing, and worth seeking for, if we can get it honestly; and by our good conduct prevail upon our masters to set us free: though for my own part I do not wish to be free, yet I should be glad if others, especially the young negroes, were to be free; for many of us who are grown up slaves, and have always had masters to take care of us, should hardly know how to take care of ourselves. . . . That liberty is a great thing we may know from our own feelings, and we may likewise judge so from the conduct of the white people in the late war. How much money has been spent and how many lives have been lost to defend their liberty! I must say that I have hoped that God would open their eyes, when they were so much engaged for liberty, to think of the state of the poor blacks, and to pity us."

As to literary values, there is not much to choose between Hammon's poetry and prose. Though he was not without the romantic gift of spontaneity, he lacked any knowledge of metrics and sought only to make rhymes. In prose the artlessness of his construction, the rambling sentences, the repetitions reveal, sometimes at the expense of thought, his not unattractive personality. When he is most lucid there is a force in the quaintness of his thought evocative of the highly personal flavor of early American letters.

3

Little more is known of the birth of Phillis Wheatley than of Jupiter Hammon. At the time of her purchase by John Wheatley in 1761 she was judged to be in her seventh or eighth year from "the circumstance of shedding her front teeth." She was a scrawny child, alert with the precocity so often associated with physical frailty. Mrs. Wheatley was quick to realize Phillis's unusual intelligence, but she could not possibly tell that this little slave girl, scarcely more than a useless luxury at first, was to become in England the best-known of contemporary American poets.

Phillis's life with the Wheatleys was in every way exceptional. Taught to read and write, nurtured and tutored with the greatest care, within a year and a half of her arrival from Africa she had acquired a sufficient command of the English language "to read any, the most difficult parts of the sacred writings." Two years later she had written her first poems.

There is no question but that Miss Wheatley considered herself a Negro poet: the question is to what degree she felt the full significance of such a designation. Certainly she was not a *slave* poet in any sense in which the term can be applied to many who followed her. She stood far outside the institution that was responsible for her. As for the question of degree, though she refers to herself time and again as an "Ethiop," she seems to make such reference with a distinct sense of abnegation and self-pity.

> Father of mercy! 'T was thy gracious hand
> Brought me in safety from those dark abodes.

This attitude on the part of Miss Wheatley was the result of the training and conduct of her life. Treated as one of the Wheatley family on terms of almost perfect equality, petted and made much of, she was sagacious enough to see that this was due in part at least to her exotic character and sensitive enough to feel that her color was really a bar to a more desirable, if less flattering, attention. At best this life was not too dear to Phillis. She recounts the joys of the life to come in the strains of one who looks upon this life as though it were a strange and bitter preparation for an eternity of bliss. The Wheatleys had adopted her, but she had adopted their terrific New England conscience. Her conception of the afterlife was different from that of most of the slaves as we find it expressed in songs and spirituals. No contemplation of physical luxuries of feastings, jeweled crowns, and snowy robes enticed her. Her heaven must be a place of the purest sublimation of spirit. Less than this would serve but to remind her of this dark bourne of flesh and blood.

But if the degree to which she felt herself a Negro poet was slight, the extent to which she was attached spiritually and emotionally to the slaves is even slighter. By 1761 slavery was an important, almost daily topic. The Boston home of the Wheatleys, intelligent and alive as it was, could not have been deaf to the discussions of restricting the slave trade, especially since by 1770 Massachusetts, Pennsylvania, and Virginia had each taken steps in that direction. Nothing so hard and definite as the abolition movement had been put forward, but when Miss Wheatley landed in England in 1773 freedom was a vital topic in pulpit and Parliament. Not once, however, did she express in either word or action a thought on the enslavement of her race; not once did she utter a straightforward word for the freedom of the Negro. When she did speak of freedom in a letter to the Earl of Dartmouth, it was:

> No more, America, in mournful strain,
> Of wrongs and grievances unredressed complain;
> No longer shall thou dread the iron chain
> Which wanton Tyranny with lawless hand,
> Had made, and with it meant t' enslave the land.

Toward the end of this poetic epistle she says the only thing that may be taken as an indictment of human slavery. Yet even in these lines the effect is vitiated.

> Should you, my lord, while you peruse my song,
> Wonder from whence my love of freedom sprung,
> Whence flow these wishes for the common good,
> By feeling hearts alone best understood,
> I, young in life, by seeming cruel fate
> Was snatched from Afric's fancied happy seat.

"Seeming cruel" and "fancied happy" give her away as not believing either in the cruelty of the fate that had dragged thousands of her race into bondage in America nor in the happiness of their former freedom in Africa. How different the spirit of her work, and how unracial (not to say unnatural) are the stimuli that release her wan creative energies. How different are these from the work of George Horton who twenty-five years later could cry out with bitterness, without cavil or fear:

> Alas! and am I born for this,
> To wear this slavish chain?

It is this negative, bloodless, unracial quality in Phillis Wheatley that makes her seem superficial, especially to members of her own race. Hers is a spirit-denying-the-flesh attitude that somehow cannot seem altogether real as the essential quality and core of one whose life should have made her sensitive to the very things she denies. In this sense none of her poetry is real. Compared to the Negro writers who followed her, Miss Wheatley's passions are tame, her skill the sedulous copy of established techniques, and her thoughts the hand-me-downs of her age. She is chilly. Part of her chill is due to the unmistakable influence of Pope's neoclassicism upon her. She followed the fashion in poetry. Overemphasis of religion was a common fault of the time. She indulged it in poetic epistles, eulogistic verse, verses written in praise of accomplishments. Her ready submission to established forms was a weakness of the period. First and last, she was the fragile product of three related forces—the age, the Wheatley household, and New England America. Her work lacks spontaneity because of the first, enthusiasm because of the second, and because of the third it lacks an unselfish purpose that drives to some ultimate goal of expression.

And yet she had poetic talent, was in fact a poet. No one who reads the following lines from "Thoughts on the Works of Providence" can deny it.

> Infinite love, where'r we turn our eyes,
> Appears: this ev'ry creatures want supplies;
> This most is heard in nature's constant voice;
> This makes the morn, and this the eve, rejoice:
> This bids the fostering rains and dews descend
> To nourish all, to serve one gen'ral end,
> The good of man: yet man ungrateful pays
> But little homage, and but little praise,
> To Him whose works arrayed in mercy shine,
> What songs should rise, how constant, how divine!

Judged in the light of the day in which she wrote, judged by that day's standards and accomplishments, she was an important poet. As a Negro poet she stands out remarkably, for her work lacks the characteristics of thought one would expect to find. She was the first Negro woman in American to write and publish poetry.

The story of her life following her return from England is soon told by the anonymous writer of the *Memoirs of Phillis Wheatley*. Her health, never sound, grew precarious. In 1778 she married a Negro doctor, lawyer, and groceryman named John Peters, by whom she had two children. Peters proved worthless, deserting her in her utmost need, when the older Wheatleys were dead and the younger ones scattered.

"In a filthy apartment, in an obscure part of the metropolis, lay the dying mother and child. The woman who had stood honored and respected by the wise and good in that country which was hers by adoption, or rather compulsion, who had graced the ancient halls of old England, and had rolled about in the splendid equipages of the proud nobles of Britain, was now numbering the last hours of her life in a state of the most abject misery, surrounded by all the emblems of squalid poverty. . . .

"The friends of Phillis who had visited her in her sickness, knew not of her death. . . . A grand-niece of Phillis's benefactress, passing up Court Street, met the funeral of an adult and a child: a by-stander informed her that they were bearing Phillis to that silent mansion."

4

What Hammon lacked in audacity and color and what Miss Wheatley failed to show in enthusiasm and racial kinship is more than supplied by George Moses Horton. If the former were motivated only by an aimless urge to write, finding as they went along, willy-nilly, ideas, emotions, and thoughts to give expression to, Horton started from an emotional basis. He first wanted to say something. Hammon and Miss Wheatley were negative; Horton was positive. He felt, albeit selfishly, the motivation derived from the Negro's position in America. He felt, too, something of the wonder and mystery, the tragic beauty, and the pathetic ugliness of life. Above all, he had the gift of laughter. He was the first "natural-born" poet of the Negro race in America.

Horton was born a slave in North Carolina about the year 1797. The exact date is uncertain. At a reception given him in Philadelphia in 1866, he was said to have remarked that his former master reckoned his age by looking into his mouth, judged the state of his health by whipping him, and determined the condition of his immortal soul by damning him to hell. Horton was an incorrigible actor and laugh-baiter, never missing an opportunity (at the cost of no matter what falsehood) to dramatize himself. When his first volume, *Hope of Liberty,* was published in 1829, Weston R. Gales, editor of the *Raleigh Register* and one of the men interested in helping Horton gain his freedom, judged him to be about thirty-two years old.

Though Horton very soon gave evidence of hating slavery, it does not seem that he was more than nominally restrained by his slave status. What Horton's occupations and wanderings were we do not know, but he gained somehow considerably more knowledge of the world than fell to the lot of most slaves. By the 1820's he had become known in Raleigh and was probably at that time working around the State University at Chapel Hill and writing for students the poems that made him something of a campus celebrity.

The poems of this period are not available, but they must have been light and more or less humorously concerned with love, the sort of jingles that would delight young college students. Certainly it is inconceivable that the provincial sons of the South, many of them slaveholders, would have paid the poet for poems in which he railed against slavery. Indeed it may be that at this time Horton's feelings about slavery had not crystallized into hatred. It seems fair to judge these earlier poems, then, by later work of the same kind.

Later Horton learned to hate. Perhaps his disappointment over his failure to purchase his freedom had something to do with it. As early as 1822 he had had elaborate dreams of migrating to the free colony of Liberia. Perhaps from the North there had drifted down to him some word of the sympathetic interest his scattered poems had created. At any rate, he was fully aware of the desirability of a life of freedom. Though only three poems on slavery appeared in *Hope of Liberty,* one is inclined to the belief that "some of the poems deleted in the interest of the author" were of this nature. Since the volume was manifestly published to obtain funds with which to purchase Horton's freedom, this seems all the more likely.

Though throughout the book he shows a consistently good and original nature, dwelling much on religion, nature, and love, now and then he expresses the dark bitterness with which his lot afflicted him. From the hopeful hymn that opens the volume,

> Creation fires my tongue!
> Nature, thy anthems raise;
> And spread the universal song
> Of thy Creator's praise!

he could come to the following lament, the meter of which was certainly inspired by the Methodist hymns with which he was familiar;

> Alas! and am I born for this,
> To wear this slavish chain?
> Deprived of all created bliss,
> Through hardship, toil, and pain?
>
> How long have I in bondage lain,
> And languished to be free!
> Alas! and must I still complain,
> Deprived of liberty?

The financial purpose of the book failed, and from 1829 on there is increasing evidence that Horton "played" his misfortunes, real or imaginary, "to the grandstand." It is not known who inspired the editor's hint in the preface to the Philadelphia edition of *Hope of Liberty* (1837) that Weston Gales had retained the money realized from the Raleigh printing, but an impartial judgment of Horton's later character makes one believe it was likely Horton himself. Naïvely selfish and stuffed with the vanity of a child, his conduct after his escape to Philadelphia and freedom toward the close of the civil struggle was said to have been unbearable. The free Negroes, of which at the time there were considerable numbers in Philadelphia, could not tolerate his demeanor, the childish strutting that had made him a character in the South. After a few weeks, they dropped him so completely that John Hawkins, who was a boy of thirteen in 1880, and whose parents knew Horton well, could not recall when or where the poet died.

Though Horton fully realized the bitterness of bondage, he tasted its gall only for himself. He seems to have thought that slavery was created for himself alone. In this he differs from Miss Wheatley in that she seemed never fully to appreciate her slave status. If she was not aroused by it for others, neither was she aroused by it for herself. Horton, wholly aware, satisfied himself with but one expressed thought for others:

> Love which can ransom every slave,
> And set the pris'ner free;
> Gild the dark horrors of the grave,
> And still the raging sea.

Even later when the *New York Tribune,* probably America's greatest paper at that time, began to publish antislavery sentiment and the editor, Horace Greeley, became interested in Horton, it was the same. The best that Horton could attain was a conceited plea for his own deliverance:

> Let me no longer be a slave,
>   But drop the fetters and be free.
>
> .   .   .   .   .   .
>
> Oh, listen all who never felt
>   For fettered genius heretofore,
> Let hearts of petrification melt,
>   And bid the gifted negro soar.

After 1837 various of Horton's poems appeared in northern periodicals of abolitionist leanings or declaration, like the *North Star,* Frederick Douglass's Rochester paper, the *Liberator,* and the *Lancaster* (Pa.) *Gazette.* In 1833, George Light published in Boston an edition of Horton's *Hope of Liberty* and bound it with the memoir and poems of Phillis Wheatley. The full title of this edition was, *Memoir and Poems of Phillis Wheatley, a Native African and Slave: Also, Poems by a Slave.* In 1865 there was printed at Raleigh the second and final volume of Horton's poems, *Naked Genius,* which seems to contain a great many earlier poems not published before.

Between 1829 and 1865 Horton seems not to have grown at all, though the later pieces in *Naked Genius* reveal a return of that good humor that helped the sale of his earlier poems to the university students. He never lost his naïve conceit. His poems are concerned with love and nature, heavenly grace and divine miracles. Remarkable among his characteristics is his imagery, generally as confused and wasteful and rich as a tropic sunset, but sometimes astonishingly fine and telling.

> 'T was like fair Helen's sweet return to Troy.

> At his command the water blushed
> And all was turned to wine.

Remarkable, too, are the turns of humor which deny the simplicity of his mind and character. It is unfortunate that so much of his Chapel Hill verse was lost, for in those days of his youth the humor must have been much more audacious and sparkling, though perhaps less sophistical. It may be that those early verses are an important loss to American humor. The finger-snapping flippancy of "Jeff Davis in a Tight Place" and "Creditor to His Proud Debtor" are not unworthy of a Holmes.

> My duck bill boots would look as bright,
> Had you in justice served me right;
> Like you, I then could step as light,
>   Before a flaunting maid.
> As nicely could I clear my throat,
> And to my tights my eyes devote;
> But I'd leave you bare, without the coat
>   For which you have not paid.
>
> Then boast and bear the crack,
> With the sheriff at your back,
> Huzzah for dandy Jack,
> My jolly fop, my Jo!

Beside the gray-mantled figures of Hammon and Phillis Wheatley, Horton appears dressed in motley. His humor, his audacious and homely wit, his lack of dignity give him important historical place as the forerunner of the minstrel poets, and this consideration outweighs whatever of intrinsic poetical value his poems possess.

Philip Rahv

The Cult of Experience in American Writing

Every attentive reader of Henry James remembers that highly dramatic scene in *The Ambassadors*—a scene singled out by its author as giving away the "whole case" of his novel—in which Lambert Strether, the elderly New England gentleman who had come to Paris on a mission of business and duty, proclaims his conversion to the doctrine of experience. Caught in the spell of Paris, the discovery of whose grace and form is marked for him by a kind of meaning and intensity that can be likened only to the raptures of a mystic vision, Strether feels moved to renounce publicly the morality of abstention he had brought with him from Woollett, Massachusetts. And that mellow Sunday afternoon, as he mingles with the charming guests assembled in the garden of the sculptor Gloriani, the spell of the world capital of civilization is so strong upon the sensitive old man that he trembles with happiness and zeal. It is then that he communicates to little Bilham his newly acquired piety toward life and the fruits thereof. The worst mistake one can make, he admonishes his youthful interlocutor, is not to live all one can—"Do what you like so long as you don't make my mistake . . . Live! . . . It doesn't so much matter what you do in particular, so long as you have your life. If you haven't had that, what *have* you had? . . . This place and these impressions . . . have had their abundant message for me, I have just dropped *that* into my mind. I see it now . . . and more than you'd believe or I can express . . . The right time is now yours. The right time is any *time* that one is still so lucky as to have . . . Live, Live!"

To an imaginative European, unfamiliar with the prohibitive American past and the long-standing national habit of playing hide-and-seek with experience, Strether's pronouncements in favor of sheer life may well seem so commonplace as scarcely to be worth the loving concentration of a major novelist. While the idea that one should "live" one's life came to James as a revelation, to the contemporary European writers this idea had long been a thoroughly assimilated and natural assumption. Experience served them as the concrete medium for the testing and creation of values, whereas in James's work it stands for something distilled or selected from the total process of living; it stands for romance, reality, civilization—a self-propelling autonomous "presence" inexhaustibly alluring in its own right. That is the "presence" which in the imagination of Hyacinth Robinson, the hero of *The Princess Casamassima,* takes on a form at once "vast, vague, and dazzling—an irradiation of light from objects undefined, mixed with the atmosphere of Paris and Venice."

"The Cult of Experience in American Writing" by Philip Rahv first appeared in *Partisan Review,* vol. 7, No. 6, 1940.

The significance of this positive approach to experience and identification of it with life's "treasures, felicities, splendors and successes" is that it represents a momentous break with the then dominant American morality of abstention. The roots of this morality are to be traced on the one hand to the religion of the Puritans and, on the other, to the inescapable need of a frontier society to master its world in sober practice before appropriating it as an object of enjoyment. Such is the historical content of that native "innocence" which in James's fiction is continually being ensnared in the web of European "experience." And James's tendency is to resolve this drama of entanglement by finally accepting what Europe offers on condition that it cleanse itself of its taint of evil through an alliance with New World virtue.

James's attitude toward experience is sometimes overlooked by readers excessively impressed (or depressed) by his oblique method and effects of remoteness and ambiguity. Actually, from the standpoint of the history of the national letters, the lesson he taught in *The Ambassadors,* as in many of his other works, must be understood as no less than a revolutionary appeal. It is a veritable declaration of the rights of man—not, to be sure, of the rights of the public, of the social man, but of the rights of the private man, of the rights of personality, whose openness to experience provides the sole effective guaranty of its development. Already in one of his earliest stories we find the observation that "in this country the people have rights but the person has none." And insofar as any artist can be said to have had a mission, his manifestly was to brace the American individual in his moral struggle to gain for his personal and subjective life that measure of freedom which, as a citizen of a prosperous and democratic community, he had long been enjoying in the sphere of material and political relations.

Strether's appeal, in curiously elaborated, varied, as well as ambivalent forms, pervades all of James's work; and for purposes of critical symbolization it might well be regarded as the compositional key to the whole modern movement in American writing. No literature, it might be said, takes on the qualities of a truly national body of expression unless it is possessed by a basic theme and unifying principle of its own. Thus the German creative mind has in the main been actuated by philosophical interests, the French by the highest ambitions of the intelligence unrestrained by system or dogma, the Russian by the passionately candid questioning and shaping of values. And since Whitman and James the American creative mind, seizing at last upon what had long been denied to it, has found the terms and objects of its activity in the urge toward and immersion in experience. It is this search for experience, conducted on diverse and often conflicting levels of consciousness, which has been the dominant, quintessential theme of the characteristic American literary productions—from *Leaves of Grass* to *Winesburg, Ohio* and beyond; and the more typically American the writer—a figure like Thomas Wolfe is a patent example—the more deeply does it engulf him.

It is through this preoccupation, it seems to me, that one can account, perhaps more adequately than through any other factor, for some of the peculiarities of American writing since the close of its classic period. A basis is thus provided for explaining the unique indifference of this literature to certain cultural aims implicit in the aesthetic rendering of experience—to ideas generally, to theories of value, to the wit of the speculative and problematical, and to that new-fashioned sense of irony which at once expresses and modulates the conflicts in modern belief. In his own way even a writer as intensely aware as James shares his indifference. He is the analyst of fine consciences, and fine minds too, but scarcely of minds capable of grasping and acting upon those ineluctable problems that enter so prominently and with such significant results into the literary art developed in Europe during the past hundred years. And the question is not whether James belonged among the "great thinkers"—very few novelists do—but whether he is "obsessed" by those universal problems, whether, in other words, his work is vitally associated with that prolonged crisis of the human spirit to which the concept of modernity is ultimately reducible. What James asks for, primarily, is the expansion of life beyond its primitive needs and elementary standards of moral and material utility; and of culture he conceives as the reward of this expansion and as its unfailing means of discrimination. Hence he searches for the whereabouts of "Life" and for the exact conditions of its enrichment. This is what makes for a fundamental difference between the inner movement of the American and that of the European novel, the novel of Tolstoy and Dostoevsky, Flaubert and Proust, Joyce, Mann, Lawrence, and Kafka, whose problem is invariably posed in terms of life's intrinsic worth and destiny.

The intellectual is the only character missing in the American novel. He may appear in it in his professional capacity—as artist, teacher, or scientist—but very rarely as a person who thinks with his entire being, that is to say, as a person who transforms ideas into actual dramatic motives instead of merely using them as ideological conventions or as theories so externally applied that they can be dispensed with at will. Everything is contained in the American novel except ideas. But what are ideas? At best judgments of reality and at worst substitutes for it. The American novelist's conversion to reality, however, has been so belated that he cannot but be baffled by judgments and vexed by substitutes. Thus his work exhibits a singular pattern consisting, on the one hand, of a disinclination to thought and, on the other, of an intense predilection for the real: and the real appears in it as a vast pheonomenology swept by waves of sensation and feeling. In this welter there is little room for the intellect, which in the unconscious belief of many imaginative Americans is naturally impervious, if not wholly inimical, to reality.

Consider the literary qualities of Ernest Hemingway, for example. There is nothing Hemingway dislikes more than experience of a make-believe, vague, or frigid nature, but in order to safeguard himself against the counterfeit he consistently avoids drawing upon the more abstract resources of the mind, he snubs the thinking man and mostly confines himself to the depiction of life on its physical levels. Of course, his rare mastery of the sensuous element largely compensates for whatever losses he may sustain in other spheres. Yet the fact remains that a good part of his writing leaves us with a sense of situations unresolved and with a picture of human beings tested by values much too simplified to do them justice. Cleanth Brooks and Robert Penn Warren have recently remarked on the interrelation between qualities of Hemingway's style and his bedazzlement by sheer experience. The following observation in particular tends to bear out the point of view expressed in this essay: "The short simple rhythms, the succession of coordinate clauses, the general lack of subordination—all suggest a dislocated and ununified world. The figures which live in this world live a sort of hand-to-mouth existence perceptually, and conceptually, they hardly live at all. Subordination implies some exercise of discrimination—the sifting of reality through the intellect. But Hemingway has a romantic anti-intellectualism which is to be associated with the premium which he places upon experience as such."*

But Hemingway is only a specific instance. Other writers, less gifted and not so self-sufficiently and incisively one-sided, have come to grief through this same creative psychology. Under its conditioning some of them have produced work so limited to the recording of the unmistakably and recurrently real that it can truly be said of them that their art ends exactly where it should properly begin.

---

*"The Killers," by Cleanth Brooks and Robert Penn Warren, in *American Prefaces,* spring 1942.

"How can one make the best of one's life?" André Malraux asks in one of is novels. "By converting as wide a range of experience as possible into conscious thought." It is precisely this reply which is alien to the typical American artist, who all too often is so absorbed in experience that he is satisfied to let it "write its own ticket"—to carry him, that is, to its own chance or casual destination.

In the first part of *Faust* Goethe removes his hero, a Gothic dreamer, from the cell of scholastic devotion in order to embroil him in the passions and high-flavored joys of "real life." But in the second part of the play this hero attains a broader stage of consciousness, reconciling the perilous freedom of his newly released personality with the enduring interests of the race, with high art, politics, and the constructive labor of curbing the chaotic forces in man and nature alike. This progress of Faust is foreshadowed in an early scene, when Mephisto promises to reveal to him "the little and then the great world [*Wir sehen die kleine, dann die grosse Welt*]." The little world is the world of the individual bemused by his personal experience, and his sufferings, guilt feelings, and isolation are to be understood as the penalty he pays for throwing off the traditional bonds that once linked him to God and his fellowmen. Beyond the little world, however, lies the broader world of man the inhabitant of his own history, who in truth is always losing his soul in order to gain it. Now the American drama of experience constitutes a kind of half-*Faust*, a play with the first part intact and the second part missing. And the Mephisto of this shortened version is the familiar demon of the Puritan morality play, not at all the Goethian philosopher-sceptic driven by the nihilistic spirit of the modern epoch. Nor is the plot of this half-*Faust* consistent within itself. For its protagonist, playing Gretchen as often as he plays Faust, is evidently unclear in his own mind as to the role he is cast in—that of the seducer or the seduced?

It may be that this confusion of roles is the inner source of the famous Jamesian ambiguity and ever-recurring theme of betrayal. James's heroines—his Isabel Archers and Milly Theales and Maggie Ververs—are they not somehow always being victimized by the "great world" even as they succeed in mastering it? Gretchen-like in their innocence, they nonetheless enact the Faustian role in their uninterrupted pursuit of experience and in the use of the truly Mephistophelean gold of their millionaire-fathers to buy up the brains and beauty and nobility of the civilization that enchants them. And the later heroes of American fiction—Hemingway's young man, for instance, who invariably appears in each of his novels, a young man posing his virility against the background of continents and nations so old that, like Tiresias, they have seen all and suffered all—in his own way he, too, responds to experience in the schizoid fashion of the Gretchen-Faust character. For what is his virility if not at once the measure of his innocence and the measure of his aggression? And what shall we make of Steinbeck's fable of Lennie, that mindless giant who literally kills and gets killed from sheer desire for those soft and lovely things of which fate has singularly deprived him? He combines an unspeakable innocence with an unspeakable aggression. Perhaps it is not too farfetched to say that in this grotesque creature Steinbeck has unconsciously created a symbolic parody of a figure such as Thomas Wolfe, who likewise crushed in his huge caresses the delicate objects of the art of life.

The disunity of American literature, its polar division into above and below or paleface and redskin writing, I have noted elsewhere. Whitman and James, who form a kind of fatal antipodes, have served as the standard examples of this dissociation. There is one sense, however, in which the contrast between these two archetypal Americans may be said to have been overdrawn. There is, after all, a common ground on which they finally, though perhaps briefly, meet—an essential Americanism subsuming them both that is best defined by their mutual affirmation of experience. True, what one affirmed the other was apt to negate; still it is not in their attitudes toward experience as such that the difference between them becomes crucial but rather in their contradictory conceptions of what constitutes experience. One sought its ideal manifestations in America, the other in Europe. Whitman, plunging with characteristic impetuosity into the turbulent, formless life of the frontier and the big cities, accepted experience in its total ungraded state, whereas James, insisting on a precise scrutiny of its origins and conditions, was endlessly discriminatory, thus carrying forward his ascetic inheritance into the very act of reaching out for the charms and felicities of the great European world. But the important thing to keep in mind here is that this plebeian and patrician are historically associated, each in his own incomparable way, in the radical enterprise of subverting the puritan code of stark utility in the conduct of life and in releasing the long compressed springs of experience in the national letters. In this sense, Whitman and James are the true initiators of the American line of modernity.

If a positive approach to experience is the touchstone of the modern, a negative approach is the touchstone of the classic in American writing. The literature of early America is a sacred rather than a profane literature. Immaculately spiritual at the top and local and anecdotal at the bottom, it is essentially, as the genteel literary historian Barrett Wendell accurately noted, a "record of the national inexperience" marked by "instinctive disregard of actual fact." For this reason it largely left untouched the two chief experiential media—the novel and the drama. Brockden Brown, Cooper, Hawthorne, and Melville were "romancers" and poets rather than novelists. They were incapable of apprehending the vitally new principle of realism by virtue of which the art of fiction in Europe was in their time rapidly evolving toward a hitherto inconceivable condition of objectivity and familiarity with existence. Not until James did a fiction writer appear in America who was able to sympathize with and hence to take advantage of the methods of George Eliot, Balzac, and Turgenev. Since the principle of realism presupposes a thoroughly secularized relationship between the ego and experience, Hawthorne and Melville could not possibly have apprehended it. Though not religious men themselves, they were nevertheless held in bondage by ancestral conscience and dogma, they were still living in the afterglow of a religious faith that drove the ego, on its external side, to aggrandize itself by accumulating practical sanctions while scourging and inhibiting its intimate side. In Hawthorne the absent or suppressed experience reappears in the shape of spectral beings whose function is to warn, repel, and fascinate. And the unutterable confusion that reigns in some of Melville's narratives (*Pierre, Mardi*) is primarily due to his inability either to come to terms with experience or else wholly and finally to reject it.

Despite the featureless innocence and moral enthusiastic air of the old American books, there is in some of them a peculiar virulence, a feeling of discord that does not easily fit in with the general tone of the classic age. In such worthies as Irving, Cooper, Bryant, Longfellow, Whittier, and Lowell there is scarcely anything more than meets the eye, but in Poe, Hawthorne, and Melville there is an incandescent symbolism, a meaning within meaning, the vitality of which is perhaps only now rightly appreciated. D. H. Lawrence was close to the truth when he spoke of what serpents they were, of the "inner diabolism of their underconsciousness." Hawthorne, "that blue-eyed darling," as well as Poe and Melville, insisted on a subversive vision of human nature at the same time as cultivated Americans were everywhere relishing the orations of Emerson who, as James put it, was helping them "to take a picturesque view of one's internal possibilities and to find in the landscape of the soul all sorts of fine sunrise and moonlight effects." Each of these three creative men displays a healthy resistance to the sentimentality and vague idealism of his contemporaries; and along with this resistance they display morbid qualities that, aside from any specific biographical factors, might perhaps be accounted for by the contradiction between the poverty of the experience provided by the society they lived in and the high development of their moral, intellectual, and affective natures—though in Poe's case there is no need to put any stress on his moral character. And the curious thing is that whatever faults their work shows are reversed in later American literature, the weaknesses of which are not to be traced to poverty of experience but to an inability to encompass it on a significant level.

The dilemma that confronted these early writers chiefly manifests itself in their frequent failure to integrate the inner and outer elements of their world so that they might stand witness for each other by way of the organic linkage of object and symbol, act and meaning. For that is the linkage of art without which its structure cannot stand. Lawrence thought that *Moby Dick* is profound *beyond* human feeling—which in a sense says as much against the book as for it. Its further defects are dispersion, a divided mind: its real and transcendental elements do not fully interpenetrate, the creative tension between them is more fortuitous than organic. In *The Scarlet Letter* as in a few of his shorter fictions, and to a lesser degree in *The Blithedale Romance,* Hawthorne was able to achieve an imaginative order that otherwise eluded him. A good deal of his writing, despite his gift for precise observation, consists of fantasy unsupported by the conviction of reality.

Many changes had to take place in America before its spiritual and material levels could fuse in a work of art in a more or less satisfactory manner. Whitman was already in the position to vivify his democratic ethos by an appeal to the physical features of the country, such as the grandeur and variety of its geography, and to the infinite detail of common lives and occupations. And James too, though sometimes forced to resort to makeshift situations, was on the whole successful in setting up a lively and significant exchange between the moral and empiric elements of his subject matter. Though he was, in a sense, implicity bound all his life by the morality of Hawthorne, James nonetheless perceived what the guilt-tossed psyche of the author of *The Marble Faun* prevented him from seeing—that it is not the man trusting himself to experience but the one fleeing from it who suffers the "beast in the jungle" to rend him.

The Transcendentalist movement is peculiar in that it expresses the native tradition of inexperience in its particulars and the revolutionary urge to experience in its generalities. (Perhaps that is what Van Wyck Brooks meant when, long before prostrating himself at his shrine, he wrote that Emerson was habitually abstract where he should be concrete, and vice versa.) On a purely theoretical plane, in ways curiously inverted and idealistic, the cult of experience is patently prefigured in Emerson's doctrine of the uniqueness and infinitude, as well as in Thoreau's equally steep estimate, of the private man. American culture was then unprepared for anything more drastic than an affirmation of experience in theory alone, and even the theory was modulated in a semiclerical fashion so as not to set it in too open an opposition to the dogmatic faith that, despite the decay of its theology, still prevailed in the ethical sphere. "The love which is preached nowadays," wrote Thoreau, "is an ocean of new milk for a man to swim in. I hear no surf nor surge, but the winds coo over it." No wonder, then, that Transcendentalism declared itself most clearly and dramatically in the form of the essay—a form in which one can preach without practicing.

Personal liberation from social taboos and conventions was the war cry of the group of writers that came to the fore in the second decade of the century. They employed a variety of means to formulate and press home this program. Dreiser's tough-minded though somewhat arid naturalism, Anderson's softer and spottier method articulating the protest of shut-in people, Lewis's satires of Main Street, Cabell's florid celebrations of pleasure, Edna Millay's emotional expansiveness, Mencken's worldly wisdom and assaults on the provincial pieties, the early Van Wyck Brooks's high-minded though bitter evocations of the inhibited past, his ideal of creative self-fulfillment—all these were weapons brought to bear by the party of rebellion in the struggle to gain free access to experience. And the secret of energy in that struggle seems to have been the longing for what was then called "sexual freedom"; for at the time Americans seeking emancipation were engaged in a truly elemental discovery of sex whose literary expression on some levels, as Randolph Bourne remarked, easily turned into "caricatures of desire." The novel, the poem, the play—all contributed to the development of a complete symptomatology of sexual frustration and release. In his *Memoirs,* written toward the end of his life, Sherwood Anderson recalled the writers of that period as "a little band of soldiers who were going to free life . . . from certain bonds." Not that they wanted to overplay sex, but they did want "to bring it back into real relation to the life we lived and saw others living. We wanted the flesh back in our literature, wanted directly in our literature the fact of men and women in bed together, babies being born. We wanted the terrible importance of the flesh in human relations also revealed again." In retrospect much of this writing seems but a naive inversion of the dear old American innocence, a turning inside out of inbred fear and reticence, but the qualities one likes in it are its positiveness of statement, its zeal and pathos of the limited view.

The concept of experience was then still an undifferentiated whole. But as the desire for personal liberation, even if only from the less compulsive social pressures, was partly gratified and the tone of the literary revival changed from eagerness to disdain, the sense of totality gradually wore itself out. Since the 1920s a process of atomization of experience has forced each of its spokesmen into a separate groove from which he can step out only at the risk of utterly disorienting himself. Thus, to cite some random examples, poetic technique became the special experience of Ezra Pound, language that of Gertrude Stein, the concrete object was appropriated by W. C. Williams, super-American phenomena by Sandburg and related nationalists, Kenneth Burke experienced ideas (which is by no means the same as thinking them), Archibald MacLeish experienced public attitudes, F. Scott Fitzgerald the glamor and sadness of the very rich, Hemingway death and virile sports, and so on and so forth. Finally Thomas Wolfe plunged into a chaotic recapitulation of the cult of experience as a whole, traversing it in all directions and ending nowhere.

Though the crisis of the 1930s arrested somewhat the progress of the experiential mode, it nevertheless managed to put its stamp on the entire social-revolutionary literature of the decade. A comparison of European and American left-wing writing of the same period will at once show that whereas Europeans like Malraux and Silone enter deeply into the meaning of political ideas and beliefs, Americans touch only superficially on such matters, as actually their interest is fixed almost exclusively on the class war as an experience which, to them at least, is new and exciting. They succeed in representing incidents of oppression and revolt, as well as sentimental conversions, but conversions of the heart and mind they merely sketch in on the surface or imply in a gratuitous fashion. (What does a radical novel like *The Grapes of Wrath* contain, from an ideological point of view, that agitational journalism cannot communicate with equal heat and facility? Surely its vogue cannot be explained by its radicalism. Its real attraction for the millions who read it lies elsewhere—perhaps in its vivid recreation of "a slice of life" so horridly unfamiliar that it can be made to yield an exotic interest.) The sympathy of these ostensibly political writers with the revolutionary cause is often genuine, yet their understanding of its inner movement, intricate problems, and doctrinal and strategic motives is so deficient as to call into question their competence to deal with political material. In the complete works of the so-called "proletarian school" you will not find a single viable portrait of a Marxist intellectual or of any character in the revolutionary drama who, conscious of his historical role, is not a mere automaton of spontaneous class force or impulse.

What really happened in the 1930s is that due to certain events the public aspects of experience appeared more meaningful than its private aspects, and literature responded accordingly. But the subject of political art is *history,* which stands in the same relation to experience as fiction to biography; and just as surely as failure to generalize the biographical element thwarts the aspirant to fiction, so the ambition of the literary Left to create a political art was thwarted by its failure to lift experience to the level of history. (For the benefit of those people who habitually pause to insist on what they call "strictly literary values," I might add that by "history" in this connection I do not mean "history books" or anything resembling what is known as the "historical novel" or drama. A political art would succeed in lifting experience to the level of history if its perception of life—any life—were organized around a perspective relating the artist's sense of the *society* of the dead to his sense of the *society* of the living and as yet unborn.)

Experience, in the sense of "felt life" rather than as life's total practice, is the main but by no means the total substance of literature. The part experience plays in the aesthetic sphere might well be compared to the part that the materialist conception of history assigns to economy. Experience, in the sense of this analogy, is the substructure of literature above which there rises a superstructure of values, ideas, and judgments—in a word, of the multiple forms of consciousness. But this base and summit are not stationary: they continually act and react upon each other.

It is precisely this superstructural level which is seldom reached by the typical American writer of the modern era. Most of the well-known reputations will bear out my point. Whether you approach a poet like Ezra Pound or novelists like Steinbeck and Faulkner, what is at once noticeable is the uneven, and at times quite distorted, development of the various elements that constitute literary talent. What is so exasperating about Pound's poetry, for example, is its peculiar combination of a finished technique (his special share in the distribution of experience) with amateurish and irresponsible ideas. It could be maintained that for sheer creative power Faulkner is hardly excelled by any living novelist, yet the diversity and wonderful intensity of the experience represented in his narratives cannot entirely make up for their lack of order, of a self-illuminating structure, and obscurity of value and meaning. One might naturally counter this criticism by stating that though Faulkner rarely or never sets forth values directly, they nonetheless exist in his work by implication. Yes, but implications incoherently expressed are no better than mystifications, and nowadays it is values that we can least afford to take on faith. Moreover, in a more striking manner perhaps than any of his contemporaries, Faulkner illustrates the tendency of the experiential mode, if pursued to its utmost extreme, to turn into its opposite through unconscious self-parody. In Faulkner the excess, the systematic inflation of the horrible is such a parody of experience. In Thomas Wolfe the same effect is produced by his swollen rhetoric and compulsion to repeat himself—and repetition is an obvious form of parody. This repetition compulsion has plagued a good many American writers. Its first and most conspicuous victim, of course, was Whitman, who occasionally slipped into unintentional parodies of himself.

Yet there is a positive side to the primacy of experience in late American literature. For this primacy has conferred certain benefits upon it, of which none is more bracing than its relative immunity from abstraction and otherworldliness. The stream of life, unimpeded by the rocks and sands of ideology, flows through it freely. If inept in coping with the general, it particularizes not at all badly; and the assumptions of sanctity that so many European artists seem to require as a kind of guaranty of their professional standing are not readily conceded in the lighter and clearer American atmosphere. "Whatever may have been the case in years gone by," Whitman wrote in 1888, "the true use for the imaginative faculty of modern times is to give ultimate vivification to facts, to science, and to common lives, endowing them with glows and glories and final illustriousness which belong to every real thing, and to real things only." As this statement was intended as a prophecy, it is worth noting that while the radiant endowments that Whitman speaks of—the "glows and glories and final illustriousness"—have not been granted, the desired and predicted vivification of facts, science, and common lives has in a measure been realized, though in the process Whitman's democratic faith has as often been belied as confirmed.

It is not the mere recoil from the inhibitions of puritan and neo-puritan times that instigated the American search for experience. Behind it is the extreme individualism of a country without a long past to brood on, whose bourgeois spirit had not worn itself out and been debased in a severe struggle against an old culture so tenacious as to retain the power on occasion to fascinate and render impotent even its predestined enemies. Moreover, in contrast to the derangements that have continually shaken Europe, life in the United States has been relatively fortunate and prosperous. It is possible to speak of American history as "successful" history. Within the limits of the capitalist order—until the present period the objective basis for a different social order simply did not exist here—the American people have been able to find definitive solutions for the great historical problems that faced them. Thus both the Revolutionary and the Civil wars were complete actions that virtually abolished the antagonisms which had initially caused the breakdown of national equilibrium. In Europe similar actions have usually led to festering compromises that in the end reproduced the same conflicts in other forms.

It is plain that until very recently there has really been no urgent need in America for high intellectual productivity. Indeed, the American intelligentsia developed very slowly as a semi-independent grouping; and what is equally important, for more than a century now and especially since 1865, it has been kept at a distance from the machinery of social and political power. What this means is that insofar as it has been deprived of certain opportunities, it has also been sheltered and pampered. There was no occasion or necessity for the intervention of the intellectuals—it was not mentality that society needed most in order to keep its affairs in order. On the whole the intellectuals were left free to cultivate private interests, and, once the moral and aesthetic ban on certain types of exertion had been removed, uninterruptedly to solicit individual experience. It is this lack of a sense of extremity and many-sided involvement which explains the peculiar shallowness of a good deal of American literary expression. If some conditions of insecurity have been known to retard and disarm the mind, so have some conditions of security. The question is not whether Americans have suffered less than Europeans, but of the quality of whatever suffering and happiness have fallen to their lot.

The consequence of all this has been that American literature has tended to make too much of private life, to impose on it, to scour it for meanings that it cannot always legitimately yield. Henry James was the first to make a cause, if not a fetish, of personal relations and the justice of his case, despite his vaunted divergence from the pioneer type, is that of a pioneer too, for while Americans generally were still engaged in "gathering in the preparations and necessities" he resolved to seek out "the amenities and consummations." Furthermore by exploiting in a fashion altogether his own the contingencies of private life that fell within his scope, he was able to dramatize the relation of the new world to the old, thus driving the wedge of historical consciousness into the very heart of the theme of experience. Later not a few attempts were made to combine experience with consciousness, to achieve the balance of thought and being characteristic of the great traditions of European art. But except for certain narratives of James and Melville, I know of very little American fiction which can unqualifiedly be said to have attained this end.

Since the decline of the regime of gentility many admirable works have been produced, but in the main it is the quality of felt life comprised in them that satisfies, not their quality of belief or interpretive range. In poetry there is evidence of more distinct gains, perhaps because the medium has reached that late stage in its evolution when its chance of survival depends on its capacity to absorb ideas. The modern poetic styles—metaphysical and symbolist—depend on a conjunction of feeling and idea. But, generally speaking, bare experience is still the *leitmotif* of the American writer, though the literary depression of recent years tends to show that this theme is virtually exhausted. At bottom it was the theme of the individual transplanted from an old culture taking inventory of himself and of his new surroundings. This inventory, this initial recognition and experiencing of oneself and one's surroundings, is all but complete now, and those who persist in going on with it are doing so out of mere routine and inertia.

The creative power of the cult of experience is almost spent, but what lies beyond is still unclear. One thing, however, is certain: whereas in the past, throughout the nineteenth and well into the twentieth century, the nature of American literary life was largely determined by national forces, now it is international forces that have begun to exert a dominant influence. And in the long run it is in the terms of this historic change that the future course of American writing will define itself.

R. P. Blackmur

The Economy of the American Writer

Preliminary Notes

Something like a century ago Alexis de Tocqueville in the second volume of his great work, *La Démocratie en Amérique,* made the following observations on The Trade of Literature:

> Democracy not only fuses a taste for letters among the trading classes, but introduces a trading spirit into literature.
>
> In aristocracies, readers are fastidious and few in number; in democracies, they are far more numerous and far less difficult to please. The consequence is, that among aristocratic nations no one can hope to succeed without immense exertions and that these exertions may bestow a great deal of fame, but can never earn much money; while among democratic na-

First published in the *Sewanee Review,* vol. 53, no. 2, Spring 1945. Copyright 1945, 1973 by the University of the South. Reprinted with the permission of the editor.

tions, a writer may flatter himself that he will obtain at a cheap rate a meager reputation and a large fortune. For this purpose he need not be admired, it is enough that he is liked.

The ever-increasing crowd of readers, and their continual craving for something new, insures the sale of books which nobody much esteems.

In democratic periods the public frequently treat authors as kings do their courtiers; they enrich and they despise them. What more is needed by the venal souls which are born in courts, or which are worthy to live there?

Democratic literature is always infested with a tribe of writers who look upon letters as a mere trade; and for some great authors who adorn it, you may reckon thousands of idea-mongers.

De Tocqueville was addressing himself to this country; but he used general terms, and I think they apply pretty generally elsewhere, if not in his time, at least in ours. The trade of writing is the chief positive obstacle, in our world, to the preservation and creation of the art of literature, and it is an obstacle all the harder to overcome because there is a greater and negative obstacle, which goes with it, in the absence, through all our societies, of any social, public, or quasi-public institution which consistently and continuously encourages the serious writer to do his best work. This is again, I think, the general situation and has to one degree or another always been so. It is only that to us who live in it, the situation seems worse today than it seems to have been in the past. The serious writer has had always to overcome the obstacle of the audience who wanted something less than he could provide and the obstacle of institutions which wanted commitments of him he could not make and which rejected the commitments he did make. What makes the serious writer think he is worse off today in both respects, is that his readers if he has any, and his institutions if he can find any, both seem to judge him by the standards of the market and neither by the standards of literature nor by those of the whole society. He has therefore rather less to fight either for or against than at previous times.

The causes for this unwelcome and I think morbidly disintegrative situation can be laid down in terms of this country's experience. Some of the causes are common to Western Europe, and to these I shall return. But let us begin with those which seem peculiar to this continent. Whether they are true causes is immaterial; they make up some part of the predispositions with which the American writer has gone to work in the past, and which still work harm—and occasionally strength—in the minds of young men and women at work today.

First, there is the fact that there has never been a dominant class in our society which has set a high value on the aesthetic mode of understanding or expressing human life. There have always been individuals and often categories or groups, but never a dominant class, nor, until possibly our own day, any dominant institutions.

This fact has two consequences. One is that without such a dominant class there was no existing prestige the power of which the new writer or new artist of any kind could borrow in order to attract an audience. He had either to make his own prestige by personal means—as an entertainer, like Mark Twain; or to do without prestige if he stopped being an entertainer, which is what happened to Herman Melville when he quit writing South Sea Romances and published *Moby Dick*. Besides the lack of a continuing fund of prestige, the absence of a dominant class with aesthetic values had a direct consequence upon the personality of the artist. He became, like the individuals, categories, or groups who alone took an interest in him, full of snobbery or preciousness with relation to his society and a victim to subjective, even introspective standards with relation to his work. This applies largely of course to writers whose names and works have disappeared, but it applies also, and with much greater damage, to the work of Hawthorne and Melville and Whitman even, for the great dross in Whitman, it seems to me, is far more due to a kind of inverted snobbery and subjectivism than it is to defect of inspiration.

Perhaps the absence of a dominant class that understood aesthetic value itself had causes in our nineteenth-century history, among which at least two worked directly upon the rôle of the artist. One is the fact that the United States was during that century a society expanding physically at a rate hitherto unknown. The other is the fact that while there was no cultural capital, no economic capital, and indeed for the most part no political capital in the country, the country did have a kind of *engineering* capital which had no fixed locus but which rather moved to that place or places where things most needed to get done.

The breaking of a continental wilderness and the expansion of population from five to a hundred millions within a century built up over what it used an enormous dispersed, unorganized reserve of human energy—intellectual and artistic as well as mechanical and economical. It did not begin to concentrate the intellectual energy till about 1900 and has not yet effectively concentrated the artistic energy; and until energy is concentrated—or organized in some way—it can have only a low degree of availability. Thus intellect and art in the United States tended to operate on a kind of average or low level of potential though in relatively great quantity. That is, the mass was great but the intensity was almost non-existent. Thus our society has been administered more by the forward drive of its inertia in the mass, which happened to be accelerating and therefore kept ahead of its problems, than it was administered by direct intelligence and imagination. Nineteenth-century Russia had a similar experience, except that its movement of mass did not accelerate.

It was natural in such a society to do without a cultural capital, and even more natural that the society should either ignore or indifferently reject attempts to provide it with one. Thus the efforts of Presidents Jefferson and J. Q. Adams to create a National Observatory and a National University failed. The intelligence trained by a common education was thought not only to be enough but also to be the most practicable and the only useful version of the ideal. Even the private universities and colleges—except insofar as they trained the clergy—operated at very low standards until 1875 at the earliest and have not yet, as a general rule, overcome the obstacle of the tradition of the all-sufficing average intelligence. There was, to repeat, no way to concentrate, organize, and make available for its best work the original talent that existed in the literary and artistic realms. The bigger movements of mass either obliterated or drove out the smaller movements of intensity.

That is, I think, why on the one hand the country has always been full of eager young talents forming into abortive and sterile groups, and why so many of those who, on the other hand, succeeded in keeping their talent alive into middle age either reduced their standards, fell silent, became eccentric, or went abroad. Their work had neither a centre where it could gain strength and by concentration penetrate the mass, nor was it congruous to any purpose of which the mass was conscious.

Gradually, as a result of increasing economic wealth and power, the number of men and women grew who felt personally, if only partially, committed to a life in which aesthetic values ruled, or in which, rather, it was felt that they ought to rule. Mass education and relative mass-prosperity gave them opportunity and time to multiply until, in the Census of 1940, some 11,806 persons reported themselves as professional authors, and some 44,000 additional reported as editors and reporters. These figures, of course, take no account of the thousands upon thousands who at one time or another would have liked to be authors, nor of the thousands more who write on the side or as a subordinate function of their profession—as scholars and scientists and military men and autobiographers; but say there might well be something over a hundred thousand in all who spend a major fraction of their effort in writing for publication. It is a small per cent of the population, but still, a hundred thousand writing persons make up something like an inert mass of their own in a society of a hundred and thirty millions, and of these the 11,806 may be thought of as the relatively intense concentration. They would not so long ago have been thought of as a small army, impossible to manage except by low and rigid standards, moving no more rapidly than the slowest man could march.

How slow that is may be roughly estimated as a generous average by dividing the total receipts of book publishers, or $130,000,000 by ten to reach $13,000,000 or the royalty paid the 11,000 professional authors. This gives an average income to the authors from the sale of books as about $1,181 a year. But this is too large, because the authors of non-literary works and autobiographies are necessarily included and would bulk large in the totals. The account may be clarified a little by particular examples. One of the most distinguished poets of my acquaintance, well and favorably known here and abroad, who devotes his entire time to writing, has never in thirty odd years of writing earned more than three thousand in a year, and has averaged about five hundred. One of the most distinguished novelists in this country, who has sold widely in England, and has been translated into French, German, and Russian—and who has not, I should add, any extravagant tastes or heavy burdens—was nevertheless only able to live a year or so ago with the aid of a $2,000 Guggenheim Fellowship, and subsequently applied for a job teaching freshman composition at Harvard. Of the three most distinguished painters I know, one has private means but has never sold more than enough to pay his overhead as a painter, one lived—or starved—on about six dollars a week, and the third told me that he had not paid an income tax for six years even though his children were grown and he could no longer claim a dependency for them.

What I want to point out as a result of these figures is, first, that the theory of a cultural market does not work. I do not know that a cultural capital is possible in our time—unless it be on the lines of Hollywood; we may not have the kind of culture which it is possible to capitalize; but I do know that the market system of open competition does not work at all from the point of view of our presumed over-all social aim: the fostering and evaluation of the serious arts and the discouragement and devaluation of, not the frivolous, but the plain bad arts. It may work well enough for the secondary or popular entertainment arts, but only at the expense of engulfing the serious arts in the new illiteracy of the nineteenth and twentieth centuries which has more than kept pace with the new literacy of the common schools.

The market system as it affects writers is very much like the market system as it affects society as a whole; it dissolves all but the lowest values and preserves only the cheapest values: those which can be satisfactorily translated into money; for it is only the cheapest sort of life, of thought, of art that can throw its values into the competition of the open market as the market developed in the nineteenth and early twentieth century without loss of the values themselves. In the market system the automatic adjustment of economic value under free competition is supposed to take care of all the human values which make economic value significant, and it is supposed to do so by natural law. As an illustration of what actually happens instead I suggest consideration of the transformation of the policy of THE SATURDAY EVENING POST from an editorial to an economic policy. That magazine no longer tries either to create or to buttress opinion or a special form of entertainment; it no longer attempts to get the best material within its standards on subjects which its editors believe important; instead, it runs a sort of Gallup Poll among its readers, and commissions contributions according to its findings.

But THE SATURDAY EVENING POST is only going one further step towards accepting the standards of the new illiteracy, than has been the general tendency of magazines ever since automatic universal education and the automatic free market began their double growth.

The table . . . presents circulation figures extracted from one or another of the directories of newspapers and periodicals. Those from 1904 to 1944 are taken from Ayer; earlier figures come from different but similar directories. Unfortunately figures are lacking on many of the most interesting magazines, either because they carried no advertising or because the publishers were unwilling to release figures or because the management of the directories overlooked them.

It will be observed that under the year is inserted the population of the United States in millions from the nearest census. This is to make possible more nearly actual comparisons between different circulations of the same or comparable magazines. Thus, to take the only magazine for which figures are supplied for the whole period from 1872 to 1944, HARPER'S MONTHLY had in 1872 a circulation of 130,000 against a population of 38,000,000, and a circulation of 105,276 in 1944 against 131,000,000 population. Would not this represent a reduction by three-fourths of potential circulation? The question becomes sharper if the figures for HARPER'S WEEKLY in 1872, or 160,000, are compared with that of its counterpart in 1944, LIFE with a circulation of 3,750,000. The ratio seems about right to suggest that the old HARPER'S MONTHLY readers now read LIFE, and that LIFE also got the additional stock of literates. If the figures for FORTUNE, TIME, ESQUIRE are added to those of LIFE it seems certain that the new Literacy is of a very different quality from that of the old.

On a somewhat higher editorial level, note that THE ATLANTIC MONTHLY was held to 25,000 through the editorship of Bliss Perry, but that when it reduced its standards to those of HARPER'S MONTHLY, it began to approach HARPER'S circulation. So, in more recent times THE AMERICAN MERCURY under Hazlitt was able to reach the circulation it now has, in tabloid form, under Eugene Lyons. Perhaps more striking is the 3,000 maximum paid circulation for a literary quarterly, 10,000 for a monthly, and 23,000 for a weekly. Against this is the relative high success of FOREIGN AFFAIRS with a maximum circulation in 1944 of 14,796 which on a comparative basis is half again as large as the 2,000 circulation in 1872 of THE NORTH AMERICAN REVIEW, a journal of much wider scope and greater influence—perhaps even in foreign affairs.

But the number of comparisons that can be set up is endless, and most of them are self-evident. LIFE and FORTUNE and ESQUIRE have apparently taken over art as well as literature. What the Comic Weeklies have taken over is not certain.

Worse than that, these figures suggest that De Tocqueville was exactly right in the first sentence in the passage quoted above. I repeat it. "Democracy not only infuses a taste for letters among the trading classes, but introduces a trading spirit into literature." Even in a society so populous as ours, there cannot possibly be, unless the creative ability of man should profoundly change, 11,806 professional authors, and if there were they could not possibly be read. A few hundred good authors of all kinds—a half dozen great authors of any kind—would be the greatest stroke of luck plausible. Yet the few hundred—and the half dozen, if they existed—must under present conditions compete in open market for a limited possibility of paid publication. It follows that most of them must, like the society which they express, lower their standards; or as an alternative earn their livings otherwise and devote only their spare time to their arts.

The alternative is clearly the desirable course, when it exists and can be seen, and when the writer can bring himself to accept it. For only the great and rare genius can accept the

Year	1872	1904	1921	1926	1934	1939	1944
U.S.population in millions	38	75	105	113	122	131	131
North American Review (Q)	2,000	30,000*	22,000				
Harper's Monthly	130,000	150,000	85,000	69,000	100,000	101,000	105,000
Scribner's Monthly	55,000	175,000	97,000	71,000			
Atlantic Monthly	35,000	25,000 (1910)	107,000	119,000	99,000	107,000	109,000
Nation	6,000 (1800)		28,000	30,000	37,000	38,000	33,000
New Republic				30,000	25,000	27,000	29,000
Dial			7,000	10,000			
Poetry					about 3,000 throughout		
Foreign Affairs				11,000			14,000
Fortune					75,000	138,000	177,000
Time					544,000	766,000	1,000,000
Life (160,000: Harper's Weekly)						1,891,000	3,745,000
Mercury					33,000	61,000	62,000
Saturday Review of Literature							23,000
Saturday Evening Post							3,393,000
Esquire							691,000
New Yorker							205,000
Virginia Quarterly						regulary about 3,000	
The American Scholar						regulary about 5,000	
Journal History Ideas							700
Comic Weeklies aggregate of three-fourths reporting							23,000,000

*Monthly.

conditions of the trade of writing and yet make great literature out of them. It has never seemed possible to educate either oneself or others of lesser talent to do so. It is the writers who have reacted to their failure to do so who have so far felt themselves no part of their culture as to write the poems no one can read and add the novels in which nobody exists and the plays in which no one can bring himself to action. Their reaction was false, but natural; almost the only possible reaction without great will and great ability and extraordinary luck.

I do not know how far these remarks may apply to the British Commonwealth or to the countries of Western Europe; I should expect that some fairly close parallel would apply. Certainly both the general production of literature and the general complaints of authors the world over suggest as much. But I am at least certain of this, that with the possible exception of Soviet Russia, and I am very doubtful there, there is no country in the world in which there is at this time, or likely to be in the future, either a dominant class or dominant institutions which assert a high aesthetic value against either the market system or its evident successor, the monopoly system. This is contrary to the most part of history—at least in those times when the arts greatly flourished.

I do not know that there is a cure, or if it is even the kind of an evil that can be cured; but I do know that it is an evil. I can only ask a few questions. Can contemporary artists deliberately ally themselves with existing institutions which show potential aesthetic bias—the universities and Foundations?—or (put the other way) can contemporary artists in any probable society permit themselves the pride, or the waste, as the case may be, of the total rôle of artist? Must not all serious artists rather grasp, both for their livelihood and for anchorage for their art, at any institutions, no matter how otherwise unlikely, that remove their values from the market? In this country writers and artists have for some years been penetrating the universities; but it is too soon to tell with what results. The risk in the experiment is that the universities are themselves increasingly becoming social and technical service stations—are increasingly, that is, attracted into the orbit of the market system. The hope in the experiment is that it is being tried, as every experiment in value must be tried, against the economy that makes it possible. Not good in itself, and with the clear possibility that it will help mostly only the middling good, the experiment might yet redeem in a few instances the paradox of a flourishing literary trade that has found no means to pay for its source in literary art. But the universities will need the courage as well as the judgment to see how vitally implicated are their own standards in the experiment. All's Alexandrian else.

PART III

****

POSTWAR ERA, 1945–1970

****

The years following the Second World War witnessed a dramatic change in the tradition of American cultural critique. Critics of American literature moved more thoroughly into the mainstream, surrendering their connection to the Emersonian tradition of oppositionalism—i.e., anti-institutional, anti-essential, and antifoundational convictions—that had animated the first half of the century. Some critics, like Leslie Fiedler, Alfred Kazin, Mary McCarthy, and James Baldwin, did preserve an antagonistic edge, demanding of American literature old and new something deeper and more radiant than the consolations of a corpse-cold "vital center." So had Arthur Schlesinger, Jr., described the consensus politics in the postwar era, which associated a middle course with the new peace and the new prosperity, a vision easily enough understood as (some would say confused with) a renewed commitment to democratic virtues.

By and large, critics of American literature fell into this new line, offering ingenious, spirited interpretations of liberal humanism to be found in *The Scarlet Letter, Moby-Dick,* and *Huckleberry Finn,* three of the era's favorite occasions for arguing the expansiveness or tragic limits of the American character. In this pursuit, many were self-consciously following the path of F. O. Matthiessen's *American Renaissance* (1941), a magisterial study of antebellum writing, a decade of profound and furious composition that gave us the major works of Hawthorne, Emerson, Melville, Whitman, and Thoreau. The studies generated by Matthiessen's tome were legion, and perhaps no other single book in its time was understood to define so decisively the course American scholarship was to take for the next twenty or thirty years. In the revisionist age that has followed, none has seemed more responsible for obstructing the recognition, perhaps even negating the presence, of the literature it excludes.

Yet as powerful as Matthiessen's example was, it was not the only influential one. Indeed, the "vital center" could not retain its illusion of vitality without summoning a critic capable of testing its pieties. That critic was to prove equally authoritative: Lionel Trilling, a professor of modern literature at Columbia. While Trilling wrote on a number of writers—British, American, and continental authors, novelists and poets alike—his most profound effect has been on the study of American fiction, which he reviewed regularly throughout his career. Trilling's success depended on negotiating his outsider status into that of the liberal critic par excellence. Told in the 1930s that he could expect no future at Columbia—for being a Marxist (a brief partisanship), a Freudian, and a Jew—Trilling defied and eventually overcame his university antagonists. Once secure in academe as the author of a critical study of Matthew Arnold, he also capitalized on his associations in the New York magazine world of literary politics and emerged as a distinguished man of letters. His essays in such collections as *The Liberal Imagination* (1950), *Opposing Self* (1956), and *Beyond Culture* (1965) often seemed to define the agenda of much of America's intellectual life in their time. Trilling's preeminence was achieved through the cogency of his style, a prose supple enough to meet the complexities of modernism and its relation to contemporary culture. Trilling's special appeal was that he could make such issues sensible to readers both inside and outside the universities.

At the same time, literary criticism was moving farther and farther into the academy through an English curriculum less and less concerned with historicism and politics. Especially prized were the tenets of New Criticism, which focused on the literary work as an aesthetic object. Perhaps because the 1930s were a time when many issues were understood as "political," ensuing decades tried to distance themselves from a discourse that seemed outdated, even wrong-headed. New Critical attention to the work itself, not its historical and cultural purposes and meanings, seemed a refreshing, even empowering alternative to the endless arguments about the class struggle that typified social criticism of the 1930s at its most elementary. "Politics" itself was to be distinguished as that which was practiced by those whom the reigning consensus could not contain.

There were notable exceptions to this antihistoricism, and they were scarcely marginal figures: Perry Miller, as much as any single scholar, designed the field of colonial studies, and he did so largely through his prodigious gifts as a historian, especially as they were evinced through such studies as *The New England Mind*. In fact, Miller was at the center of a powerful new movement in academe, although its range and effect would not be felt in English departments for decades to come. Harvard, in the years immediately following World War II, sponsored an incredible collection of scholar-teachers devoted to the study of ideas and arts in America. They included Miller and Matthiessen, as well as Kenneth Murdock and Leo Marx. Harvard's American Civilization program, along with similar ones at Minnesota and Pennsylvania in the 1940s and 1950s, spearheaded the American Studies movement, the new commitment to an inter- and multidisciplinary approach to U.S. culture. By 1949, the American Studies Association was formed for the purpose of organizing conferences, where scholars in several disciplines could address their shared interest in U.S. culture. They would pursue these concerns, as well as sustain relations with the international community of scholars of American society, in their new journal, *American Quarterly*.

Such aims were significant. While there had been passing interest in American studies nationally and internationally before the war, U.S. culture—as subject and commodity—gave rise to an urgency that many countries were newly cultivating, even eagerly importing, largely as a result of America's popularity after the war. Some now see this phenomenon as a form of cultural imperialism, with the United States—through the U.S. Information Agency and, sometimes, the CIA—dispensing the wisdom of Franklin and Emerson along with the temptations of Coca-Cola and Disney.

As important as such a backdrop is to the invention of American studies, more telling are its exciting critical accomplishments. Henry Nash Smith's *Virgin Land*, R. W. B. Lewis's *American Adam*, and Marx's *Machine in the Garden* perhaps stand out as the books that most forcefully contested the New Critical mandate found in such formalist classics as Richard Chase's *American Novel and Its Tradition*, Charles Feidelson's *Symbolism and American Literature*, and Roy Harvey Pearce's *The Continuity of American Poetry*, along with the myriad author studies that populated the critical landscape. Of course, some writers flourished, like James, Dickinson, Frost, and Faulkner, while others were neglected, especially minorities. It seems improbable, but even during an era when authors like Bellow, Mailer, and Roth were the subject of intense scrutiny among critics, the journal of record in the field, *American Literature*, did not publish an article on a Jewish writer until 1970.

The ascendancy of Americanist criticism came at the cost of imagining that there was some easy coherence to be assumed about our national literature, a conviction that pervaded every phase of mainstream scholarship and criticism. While there had been anthologies of American literature for a century, and while Cambridge and Oxford university presses had already brought out encyclopedias, one of the most influential books ever devoted to the subject, a book that was said, more or less, to codify the field, was published in 1948. Its stranglehold, however, was testimony not to the brilliance of its commentaries or the coherence with which they fit together but to the convenience that they provided. The *Literary History of the United States,* written by some very esteemed diverse hands and edited by Robert Spiller, was a compilation of overviews of the figures, periods, and genres of American writing. It has gone through numerous editions, but its popularity has had little to do with the uniformity of its parts or even its summary power. Instead, it became something of a bible for graduate students as they made their way through doctoral preliminaries, part of the rush to create Ph.Ds to meet the new postwar demand for professors. These professors-in-waiting needed credentials, and the *LHUS,* more than any single tool, helped them to gain command of facts and a broad acquaintance with U.S. writing.

The results were mixed. The profession yielded hundreds of monographs that were devoted to the works of one author, often elaborating one critical insight into the organizing principles of the writer's work. Other scholars offered a conception of American writing based on seven or eight or nine books, drawn from a period of fifty years or so. Many of these studies still have their interest and use, but, like all such commentary, they are limited by the questions they ask. Intended to meet the demand for explicating texts, neither mode of analysis promoted a vigorous historical or ideological or theoretical engagement.

One book, finally, did break through the logjam of author studies and helped to inaugurate a new era of American literary studies. Not as erudite as Laurence Holland's reading of Henry James, *The Expense of Vision* (1964), Frederick Crews's psychoanalytic study of Hawthorne, *The Sins of the Fathers* (1966), was virtually the first psychoanalytic study of American writing in some three decades. While Crews has since had second (and third) thoughts about the usefulness of this analysis—as any sensible critic might have in the thirty years since the book appeared—it so convincingly deployed Freudian concepts to interpret the literature, not the author, that its method suggested how a psychoanalytic reading might reach the deepest levels of an artist's meaning that American critics and scholars could no longer ignore what had come to be called "extratextual" meanings.

The lesson was that critics did not have to content themselves solely with aesthetic questions, nor did they have to say that content was important insofar as it shaped a work's form. While Northrop Frye's *Anatomy of Criticism* (1957) had emancipated critics of English literature from formalism, Americanists had been slower to digest the principles of archetypalism or the myth criticism that preceded and prepared for structuralism. When one considers that Crews's book appeared at roughly the same time as did the famous conference at Johns Hopkins heralding for a U.S. audience the revolution in the human sciences taking place in Europe—the "structuralist controversy"—one sees how hidebound the academic study of American writing had grown. It took Americanists more than a decade to catch up.

With a canon more or less in place and a methodological orthodoxy virtually cemented, the study of American writing risked a certain sluggishness. Were there exceptions? Of course—many valuable ones, including John Berryman's study of Stephen Crane, Daniel Hoffman's *Form and Fable in American Fiction,* Irving Howe's *Politics and the Novel,* Richard Poirier's *A World Elsewhere,* books much appreciated in their time. Yet consider, for example, that there was barely a syllable of Marxist critique of American literature from 1940 to 1980. (Some might explain this absence by recalling that it would have been risky for professors young and old to enlist this discourse during the years of McCarthyism. Others might say that some departments were riven with Marxists, so that whatever didn't get in print still made its way into the classroom.) Whatever else Marxism is and was, it has been the sharpest, most comprehensive criticism of capitalism, providing a system and vocabulary that critics of English literature had readily learned from and adapted.

Enlivening the legacy of American criticism, however, were several countertraditions that were beginning to achieve cogency and influence. While there had always been a vigorous African-American school of literary criticism as cultural critique, and while university presses had published early studies of African-American writing intermittently, institutionally speaking, it was often treated as a subset of Southern writing. Without a canon to guide graduate students and professors—and with only a few professional incentives to excite them—the study of African-American writing made slow progress, especially among white scholars, during this era. It was not until the ascendancy of the Black Arts Movement, which shared its political affinities with the Black nationalist movements of the mid-1960s, that the study of "black lit" captured the imaginations of young African-American writers and critics, like Houston Baker and, later, Barbara Christian and Henry Louis Gates, Jr. Thus, this cultural movement helped to stimulate a more robust recovery of writers as well as a more deeply theorized engagement with African-American cultural and linguistic traditions.

The era of multicultural criticism and identity politics had not yet arrived, even if a major study appeared here and there to suggest the foment to come, books like Americo Paredes's *With His Pistol in His Hand* (1958), a study of "corrido" culture. While it is altogether defensible to ascribe, as so many have done, the roots of the critical movements of the 1980s and 1990s to the protest movements of the 1960s, it was in the middle decades that the bibliographical work preparing for these countertraditions was sustained, thus setting the stage for the new pluralism in American literary studies that, for many observers, returns academic criticism to a radical paradigm of cultural criticism.

F. O. Matthiessen

The Responsibilities of the Critic

My deliberately grave title is in the tradition from Matthew Arnold, my first critical enthusiasm as an undergraduate thirty years ago. But at that very time a new critical movement was rising, the critical movement in which we are living today. T. S. Eliot's first important essay, 'Tradition and the Individual Talent,' was written in 1917, when he was twenty-nine; and I. A. Richards' first independent and most influential book, *The Principles of Literary Criticism,* came out in 1924, when he was in his early thirties. The talents and principles of those two then young men have been the most pervasive forces upon the criticism of the past quarter-century.

We know now what a revolution they instigated, if one may use such a violent word as revolution in the field of the arts, where all victories fortunately are bloodless, and where what was overthrown remains undestroyed and capable of being rediscovered at the next turn of the wheel of taste. When Eliot was growing up, the tastes and standards of Arnold were still prevailing; and Eliot found himself wholly dissatisfied with Arnold's preoccupation with the spirit of poetry rather than with its form. The form of Eliot's own first poems was deceptively radical, since he was really rejecting the easily flowing forms of the romantics and the Elizabethans for the more intricately weighted forms of the symbolists and the metaphysicals.

When Richards, as a psychologist who believed in the basic importance of the words with which men try to fathom their meanings, began to read Eliot's poems, he encountered the kind of language that proved most compelling to readers just after the First World War. The immense loosening of speech that had accompanied the rapid expansions in mass education and mass communication had reached the point where, if the artist was again to communicate the richness and denseness of real experience, he must use a language that compelled the reader to slow down, to be concerned once more with the trip rather than with the arrival. As the young English critic T. E. Hulme had been arguing, before he was killed in battle in 1915, poetry must always endeavor thus 'to arrest you . . . to make you continuously see a physical thing, to prevent you gliding through an abstract process.'

What resulted from the joint influence of Eliot and Richards was a criticism that aimed to give the closest possible attention to the text at hand, to both the structure and texture of the language. You are all familiar with the names of its practitioners who, if we confine ourselves to America alone, have already produced a more serious and exacting body of work than we had previously witnessed in this country. To be sure, Richards' most gifted follower was one of his own students at Cambridge, England. William Empson, in his precocious *Seven Types of Ambiguity* (1929), begun when he was still an undergraduate, pushed to its subtle extreme Richards' kind of linguistic analysis. Empson in turn has had a particular vogue here among the critics whom we now associate with the newly founded Kenyon School of Criticism, most notably with John Crowe Ransom, Robert Penn Warren, and Cleanth Brooks. Others whose names are linked with that school, Kenneth Burke, R. P. Blackmur, Allen Tate, Austin Warren, and Yvor Winters, however divergent their methods and emphases, reveal throughout their work how they have had to reckon with Eliot and Richards, whether in concord or belligerence.

The effect of this new movement upon the study of literature in our universities has been by now considerable. Although opposed by both the old guards of philologists and literary historians, most of the critics I have mentioned now hold academic appointments, which may or may not have been good for their work. But their work has thereby become instrumental in the revolt against concentrating exclusively on the past, and against concentrating on literary history instead of on literature. As a result both teachers and students are more capable of close analysis and lively appreciation than they were a generation ago.

But by now we have reached the stage where revolt has begotten its own set of conventions, to use the terms of one of Harvard's great former teachers, John Livingston Lowes. As we watch our own generation producing whole anthologies of criticism devoted to single contemporary authors and more and more detailed books of criticism of criticism, we should realize that we have come to the unnatural point where textual analysis seems to be an end in itself. The so-called little magazines have been essential and valiant outposts of revolt in our time when the magazines of wide circulation, in decline from their standards in the nineteenth century, have abandoned serious discussion of literature almost entirely.

But the little magazines seem now to be giving rise to the conventions and vocabulary of a new scholasticism and to be not always distinguishable from the philological journals which they abhor. The names of the authors may be modern, but the smell is old. The trouble is that the terms of the new criticism, its devices and strategies and semantic exercises, can become as pedantic as any other set of terms if they are not handled as the means to fresh discoveries but as counters in a stale game. In too many recent articles literature seems to be regarded merely as a puzzle to be solved.

This is not to underestimate the great and continuing service performed by the few quarterlies devoted to criticism, or by those even littler magazines that often last only long enough to introduce one or two new talents in poetry or fiction. The important experimental work of our time has again and again been able to secure its first publication only through their pages. This is one of the consequences of what F. R. Leavis, the editor of *Scrutiny,* has called the split between 'mass civilization' and 'minority culture.' But to recognize that phenomenon in our democracy should only be to combat it.

There is potentially a much greater audience in America for the art of literature than the blurb-writers, who often pass for reviewers in the Sunday supplements, would seem to suspect. The effectiveness of the critics in the little magazines in having by now prepared a wider public for, say, Joyce or Kafka or Eliot, amply testifies to that. But the dilemma for the serious critic in our dangerously split society is that, feeling isolated, he will become serious in the wrong sense, aloof and finally taking an inverted superiority in his isolation. At that point criticism becomes a kind of closed garden.

My views are based on the conviction that the land beyond the garden's walls is more fertile, and that the responsibilities of the critic lie in making renewed contact with that soil. William James used to insist that the first duty of any thinker is to know as much as possible about life in his own time. Such an exhortation may seem too general to be of much use, but it can be grasped more concretely if we envisage the particular responsibilities of the critic in a whole series of awarenesses. These awarenesses may encompass some of the breadth and comprehensiveness which James assumed to be the thinker's goal, and some of the feeling of being drenched with actual life, which he believed to be the thinker's best reward. Much of the ground that we will traverse was also implied to be within the critic's scope by the early work of Eliot and Richards, though some of it has been lost sight of by their followers.

The first awareness for the critic should be of the works of art of our own time. This applies even if he is not primarily a critic of modern literature. One of Eliot's observations which has proved most salutary is that of the inescapable interplay between past and present: that the past is not what is dead, but what is already living; and that the present is continually modifying the past, as the past conditions the present. If one avails himself of the full resources latent in that perception, one is aware that it is not possible to be a good critic of Goethe today without knowing Mann, or of Stendhal or Balzac without knowing Proust, or of Donne or Dryden without knowing Eliot.

The converse is equally true, if less necessary to be argued in the academy. But once outside, particularly in the rapid and rootless life of our cities, the tendency even for practitioners in the arts is to be immersed wholly in the immediate. This is not what James foresaw, since he took for granted the constant meeting-point between what was already known and what was still to be known. But today we can take no tradition for granted, we must keep repossessing the past for ourselves if we are not to lose it altogether. The value in this urgency is that what we manage to retain will really belong to us, and not on authority at second hand. The proper balance, even for the critic who considers his field to be the present, is to bring to the elucidation of that field as much of the art of the past as he can command.

A recently dead critic, Paul Rosenfeld, was a heartening example of this balance. Prolonging in this country the rich cultural life of his German-Jewish forebears, he moved naturally among the arts, and it would never have occurred to him that a critic of contemporary music would try to speak without having all the great composers of the past at his finger tips. But he regarded the work of the present, especially in America, as his particular province, and often said that if our younger composers were to have a sense of possessing any audience, someone must make it his function to listen to them all. In complete modesty and selflessness he took that task upon himself. As his friends knew, Paul Rosenfeld gave himself away to his generation, a very unusual act in our fiercely competitive world, where even our intellectual life seems so often to become poisoned by the habits of our business civilization.

I have cited Rosenfeld because his generous openness to all the arts and his devoted impressions of what he found now seem so foreign to the grimly thin-lipped disciples of a more rigorous analysis. Indeed, one of them, writing currently in *The Hudson Review,* has declared that the recent volume of tribute by Rosenfeld's contemporaries from the 'twenties and 'thirties praised him for a 'thoroughly degraded function.' Such total lack of comprehension is a devastating illustration of what Auden meant by saying that one of the worst symptoms of sterility in our present culture is that of 'intellectuals without love.'

No incapacity could be less fruitful in the presence of the arts. Its recent frequency may be another unhappy by-product of the sort of specialization that leaves the student knowing only his own field. Such self-enclosed knowledge may often mean that he really knows nothing at all. At least it is hard to conceive of a good critic of literature who does not have an alert curiosity about other fields and techniques. Anyone understands his own subject and discipline better if he is aware of some other subject and discipline. To what extent this awareness should lead to mastery will vary greatly with individual aptitude. It does not seem profitable to insist that any given critic should also be expert in linguistic theory or mathematical logic or Marx or Freud, but I can hardly think of a critic today being indifferent to the access of power his mind could gain from a close study of one or more of these.

This does not mean that the misapplication of theory from one field to another is not as big a pitfall as it always was, or that fads don't often outrun facts. But as one instance of valuable cross-fertilization between fields there is cultural anthropology. Utilizing the disciplines of history and sociology, it has proved a particularly stimulating ally to the study of literature in a period when literature itself, in the hands of Joyce and Mann, has been rediscovering the vitality of primitive myth. Through our renewed awareness of folk patterns we now realize that the fertility rites which solemnize the death and rebirth of the year are equally germane to our understanding of *The Waste Land* or *The Winter's Tale* or *The Peace* of Aristophanes or the *Bacchae* of Euripides.

Another awareness which our split society makes it hard for us to keep in the right proportion is that of the popular arts of our technological age. The consequences for all our lives of the mass media of communication become ever more insistent, so that we must either channel them to socially valuable ends or be engulfed by them. The first results of our new discoveries are often as discouraging as when Thoreau scorned the transatlantic cable on the grounds that the initial news that would 'leak through into the broad, flapping American ear' would be that the Princess Adelaide had the whooping cough.

The first results of television would appear to be that it has made conversation impossible in one of its few remaining American strongholds, the barroom, and is debauching the customers with entertainment that is a long throwback to the juvenile days of the penny arcade. But then one recalls how the radio, despite its intolerable deal of soap, has during the past twenty-five years built up a taste for the best symphony music among millions of listeners who would not otherwise have ever heard it. The chief art form of our age, the moving picture, is the compelling reminder of our immense potentialities and continual corruptions. Even now when, in its postwar doldrums, Hollywood seems again to have forgotten that standardization through mass production is more suitable for soup than for art, the great new Italian films are demonstrating the important access of social truth that the art of the film can gain by utilizing some of the solid techniques of the documentary.

I have mentioned these disparate examples of good and bad as a way of enforcing my conviction that we in the universities cannot afford to turn our backs upon them or upon the world from which they come. The proper place for the thinker, as William James conceived it, was at the central point where a battle is being fought. It is impossible for us to take that metaphor with the lightness that he could. Everywhere we turn in these few fateful years since the first atom bomb dropped on Hiroshima we seem menaced by such vast forces that we may well feel that we advance at our peril. But even greater peril would threaten us if those whose prime responsibility as critics is to keep open the life-giving communications between art and society should waver in their obligations to provide ever fresh thought for our own society.

In using metaphors of battle here and now, I am not thinking in an academic void. If we believe that freedom of thought and of speech are the distinguishing features of the culture of a true democracy, we must realize by what a thin margin they now survive in this country. Within the past year there have been the most serious violations of academic freedom, caused, ironically, by officials who are determined to prove that the United States is so much better than any other country that it is above criticism. We must recognize the full gravity of these casualties of the cold war, for they are a product of the very kind of blind suppression that their instigators declare exists only behind what they denounce as 'the iron curtain.'

The most flagrant recent case of national importance has nothing to do with the issue of communism, and thus furnishes a concrete demonstration of how, once official opinion embarks on the course of stamping out dangerous views, every shade of dissent becomes dangerous. Olivet College, as you all here know, was founded in the great pioneering period of our education, when Americans were expanding the frontiers of their thought as well as of their territory. Its recent career, particularly in the period between two world wars, added a notable chapter to our experiments with education by tutorial work and group discussion. When members of its faculty of such national distinction as a Pulitzer prize winner for biography and the candidate for vice-president on the Socialist ticket are dismissed, none of us can stand aloof or feel that we are not implicated.

If what I have just been saying seems an unwarranted digression from the responsibilities of the critic of the arts, I want to correct that impression. The series of awarenesses which I believe the critic must possess lead ineluctably from literature to life, and I do not see how the responsible intellectual in our time can avoid being concerned with politics. It is at this point that my divergence becomes most complete from the formalists who have followed in the wake of Eliot, as well as from Eliot himself, whose reverence for the institutions of monarchy and aristocracy seems virtually meaningless for life in America.

I would like to recall the atmosphere of the early nineteen-thirties, of the first years of the last depression, when the critical pendulum had swung to the opposite pole, from the formalists to the Marxists. I am not a Marxist myself but a Christian, and I have no desire to repeat the absurdities of the moment when literary men, quite oblivious theretofore of economics, were finding sudden salvation in a dogma that became more rigid the less they had assimilated it. But I believe the instinct of that moment was right, as our greatest recent cultural historian, Vernon Parrington's instinct was right, in insisting upon the primacy of economic factors in society. Most artists and students of literature remain amateurs in the field of economics, but that does not prevent them from utilizing some of the basic and elementary truths which economists have made available for our culture.

Emerson held that a principle is an eye to see with, and despite all the excesses and exaggerated claims of the Marxists of the 'thirties, I still believe that the principles of Marxism—so much under fire now—can have an immense value in helping us to see and comprehend our literature. Marx and Engels were revolutionary in many senses of that word. They were pioneers in grasping the fact that the industrial revolution had brought about—and would continue to bring about—revolutionary changes in the whole structure of society. By cutting through political assumptions to economic realities, they revolutionized the ways in which thinking men regarded the modern state. By their rigorous insistence upon the economic foundations underlying any cultural superstructure, they drove, and still drive, home the fact that unless the problems rising from the economic inequalities in our own modern industrialized society are better solved, we cannot continue to build democracy. Thus the principles of Marxism remain at the base of much of the best social and cultural thought of our century. No educated American can afford to be ignorant of them, or to be delinquent in realizing that there is much common ground between these principles and any healthily dynamic America.

This is not to say that Marxism gives what I consider an adequate view of the nature of man, or that it or any other economic theory can provide a substitute for the critic's essential painstaking discipline in the interplay between form and content in concrete works of art. But a concern with economics can surely quicken and enlarge the questions that a critic asks about the content of any new work of art with which he is faced, about the fullness to which it measures and reveals the forces that have produced both it and its author. Walt Whitman might have said, in *Democratic Vistas:* 'Man becomes free, not by realizing himself in opposition to society, but by realizing himself through society.' That sentence was actually written by Christopher Caudwell, a young English Marxist who was killed fighting for the Loyalists in Spain. His book *Illusion and Reality,* published in 1937, has recently been reissued, and is having a renewed vogue now with younger writers and students. Their enthusiasm for it, I gather, springs from the fact that Caudwell, despite the sweeping immaturity of many of his judgments, keeps asking the big questions about man in society that the school of close textual analysis has tended to ignore.

I do not mean for a moment to underestimate the value of that school. It has taught us in particular how to read poetry with an alertness and resilience of attention that were in danger of being altogether lost through the habits set up by an age of quick journalism. All I would suggest is that analysis itself can run to seed unless the analyzing mind is also absorbed in a wider context than the text before it.

Mention of Caudwell's name has brought me to the last of the awarenesses that I would urge upon the critic: that of the wide gap which still exists between America and Europe. Henry James discovered long ago his leading theme in the contrast between American innocence and European experience. Although the world that he contemplated has been altered beyond recognition, that theme is still peculiarly urgent when we are faced with the difference between a Europe which has undergone fascism and destructive war at first hand and an America which has come out of the war richer and more powerful than ever before. Stephen Spender has noticed the difference in reading Randall Jarrell's book of poems called *Losses*. For the American, as Spender observes, even when the losses are those of our own fliers, they are something that happens far away on distant continents, they are not yet immediately overhead and inescapable. Allen Tate has described the kind of false superiority that can be engendered by such special isolation:

> The American people fully armed
> With assurance policies, righteous and harmed,
> Battle the world of which they're not at all.

How do Americans become part of that greater world? Not by pretending to be something they are not, nor by being either proud or ashamed of their vast special fortune. It does no good, for example, to adopt the vocabulary of the Paris existentialists in order to emulate the crisis of occupation which we have not passed through. The ironic lines of Tate's 'Sonnet at Christmas' suggest a more mature way of meeting experience. None of us can escape what we are, but by recognizing our limitations, and comprehending them, we can transcend them by the span of that knowledge.

Here is the area where breadth of concern becomes most rewarding for the critic. By perceiving what his country is and is not in comparison with other countries, he can help contribute, in this time of fierce national tensions, to the international understanding without which civilization will not survive. He will also find that he has come to know his own country better.

The art of a country always becomes richer by being open to stimulus from outside, and criticism can find a particularly fertile field in observing the results of that interchange. For one fascinating instance, how much can we learn about both Europe and America from the high estimation that French writers are now giving to the novels of Faulkner. At a period when the French have felt a debilitation in their own tradition, they have turned to the new world for an access of vitality. But what has seemed to them most real in America is not our surface of optimism, but the terrible underlying violence that has possessed the imaginations of nearly all our naturalistic novelists. It may seem a strange paradox that America, spared so far the worst violences of fascism and war, has imagined violence in a way that impresses men who have experienced the savage brutality of both.

But as we look back at America through French eyes, we become more conscious of what the preponderantly genteel reviewers for our organs of mass circulation have done their best to obscure: that Faulkner is not a writer of meaningless sensationalism but one who has seized upon basic forces in our history, particularly upon the tensions resulting from our initial injustice to the Negro. Faulkner may often overwrite and use some of the cheap devices of melodrama, but we should not allow these to deflect us from the truth of his record. If we prefer a more smiling version of ourselves, we are liable to the peculiarly American dilemma of passing from innocence to corruption without ever having grasped maturity. By which I mean the maturity that comes from the knowledge of both good and evil.

In proposing an ever widening range of interests for the ideal critic, I have moved from his central responsibility to the text before him out to an awareness of some of the world-wide struggles of our age. We must come back to where we started, to the critic's primary function. He must judge the work of art as work of art. But knowing form and content to be inseparable, he will recognize his duty to both. Judgment of art is unavoidably both an aesthetic and a social act, and the critic's sense of social responsibility gives him a deeper thirst for meaning.

This is not a narrow question of the wrong right or right left politics. The *locus classicus* on this matter was furnished by Marx's judgment of Balzac, who as a monarchist and Catholic reactionary supported the very forces to which Marx was most opposed. Yet Marx could perceive that, no matter what this novelist's views, his vision of the deep corruption of French society by money made him the most searching historian of his time. Engels proceeded to evolve the principle inherent in this judgment:

> The father of tragedy, Aeschylus, and the father of comedy, Aristophanes, were both very clearly poets with a thesis . . . But I believe that the thesis must inhere in the situation and the action, without being explicitly formulated; and it is not the poet's duty to supply the reader in advance with the future historical solution of the conflict he describes.

A poet describes many other things besides conflict, yet without some sense of conflict there is no drama to engage us. The way in which the artist implies social judgments and entices the critic to meditate upon them may be elucidated by a pair of examples. Wallace Stevens' second book, *Ideas of Order,* appeared in 1935. Until then he had been known by his richly musical *Harmonium,* by what he himself had called 'the essential gaudiness of poetry.' The besetting weakness of criticism, when faced with a new writer, is to define his work too narrowly, and then to keep applying that definition like a label. Stevens had been bracketed as 'a dandy of poetry'; as an epicurean relisher of 'sea surfaces full of clouds,' as one who had found his role in discovering 'thirteen ways of looking at a blackbird,' as identical with his own Crispin in his relish of 'good, fat, guzzly fruit.'

He was, to be sure, all these enchanting things. But no one seemed to have been prepared for the fact that his imagination was so fecund and robust that it would compel him to launch forth, in his mid-fifties, upon the new territory indicated by his explicitly philosophical title. He was also making his own response to the vast disequilibrium that every sensitive mind had to feel at the pit of the depression. He had come to recognize that 'a violent order is disorder.' Or, as Horace Gregory put it more explicitly, Stevens' new poems were demonstrating that he was not merely a connoisseur of nuances, but—not unlike Henry James—a shrewdly trained observer of 'the decadence that follows upon the rapid acquisition of wealth and power.'

Stevens' kind of symbolist poetry never makes the explicit approach. So far as he has any political or social views, they would appear to be conservative. Yet in 'Sad Strains of a

Gay Waltz,' the second poem in *Ideas of Order,* he gave to a then young radical like myself a sudden clarification of the clouded time in which we are living. It is this kind of 'momentary stay against confusion,' as Robert Frost has said, that a poem is designed to give, and that becomes one of the measures of its authenticity.

In listening to almost any poem by Stevens, the first thing that strikes you is his pastmasterly command of rhetoric, a reminder that, unlike the poets of the imagist movement, he is still rooted in the older tradition that leads from Bridges back to Milton. In this poem his rhetoric is formed into three-lined unrhymed stanzas of a basically iambic pentameter pattern, but with many irregular line lengths which quicken but do not break that pattern. The conflict that constitutes his theme is between an age that is dying and a hazardous potential new birth. He adumbrates this by offsetting a character whom he calls Hoon, a lover of solitude like Thoreau, against the rising masses of men in a still formless society. But his controlling symbols are more oblique, they are 'waltzes' and 'shadows.' Music that has become played out seems to its listeners to be 'empty of shadows,' and by a very effective repetition of the phrase, 'Too many waltzes have ended,' Stevens sets up his counterpoise for a new, more dynamic music that will again be full of shadows:

> The truth is that there comes a time
> When we can mourn no more over music
> That is so much motionless sound.
>
> There comes a time when the waltz
> Is no longer a mode of desire, a mode
> Of revealing desire and is empty of shadows.
>
> Too many waltzes have ended. And then
> There's that mountain-minded Hoon,
> For whom desire was never that of the waltz,
>
> Who found all form and order in solitude,
> For whom the shapes were never the figures of men
> Now, for him, his forms have vanished.
>
> There is order in neither sea nor sun.
> The shapes have lost their glistening.
> There are these sudden mobs of men.
>
> These sudden clouds of faces and arms,
> An immense suppression, freed,
> These voices crying without knowing for what,
>
> Except to be happy, without knowing how,
> Imposing forms they cannot describe,
> Requiring order beyond their speech.
>
> Too many waltzes have ended. Yet the shapes
> For which the voices cry, these, too, may be
> Modes of desire, modes of revealing desire.
>
> Too many waltzes—The epic of disbelief
> Blares oftener and soon, will soon be constant,
> Some harmonious skeptic soon in a skeptical music

> Will unite these figures of men and their shapes
> Will glisten again with motion, the music
> Will be motion and full of shadows.

The extension of our sense of living by compelling us to contemplate a broader world is the chief gift that literature holds out to us. This sense is never limited to our own place or time. What makes the art of the past still so full of undiscovered wealth is that each age inevitably turns to the past for what it most wants, and thereby tends to remake the past in its own image. The cardinal example is Shakespeare. What the nineteenth century saw in Hamlet was what Coleridge saw, the figure of a transcendental philosopher absorbed in himself. What we see is a man inextricably involved with his own society, as may be suggested in brief by one of the scenes which nineteenth-century producers usually cut. This is the scene in the fourth act where Hamlet, on his way to England, encounters a Captain from Fortinbras' army. The Captain is bitter at what his orders are compelling him to do:

> Truly to speak, and with no addition,
> We go to gain a little patch of ground
> That hath in it no profit but the name.
> To pay five ducats, five, I would not farm it.

The effect of this speech upon Hamlet is to heighten his awareness of the difference between the Captain's situation and his own, of how he, Hamlet, has every reason for action and yet cannot bring himself to act:

> Examples gross as earth exhort me;
> Witness this army of such mass and charge
> Led by a delicate and tender prince,
> Whose spirit with divine ambition puff'd
> Makes mouths at the invisible event,
> Exposing what is mortal and unsure
> To all that fortune, death, and danger dare,
> Even for an egg-shell. Rightly to be great
> Is not to stir without great argument,
> But greatly to find quarrel in a straw
> When honor's at the stake. How stand I then,
> That have a father kill'd, a mother stain'd,
> Excitements of my reason and my blood,
> And let all sleep, while to my shame I see
> The imminent death of twenty thousand men,
> That for a fantasy and trick of fame
> Go to their graves like beds, fight for a plot
> Whereon the numbers cannot try the cause,
> Which is not tomb enough and continent
> To hide the slain?

As John Gielgud speaks these lines, we feel what Shakespeare meant his audience to feel, the necessity for Hamlet's revenge. But we also bring to the passage our own sense of vast insecurity, our need of being engaged in the public issues of our menaced time, and yet the need of making sure that the seeming issues are the true issues, that we are not betrayed into engagements that are merely 'th'imposthume of much wealth and peace.'

There is a basic distinction between bringing everything in your life to what you read and reading into a play of the past issues that are not there. All I am suggesting is the extent to which our awareness of ourselves as social beings is summoned by the greatest art. That is the root of my reason for believing that the good critic becomes fully equipped for his task by as wide a range of interests as he can master. The great temptation for the young writer at the present moment is to think that because the age is bad, the artist should escape from it and, as a superior being, become a law simply to himself. Some memorable romantic poetry has been written on that assumption, but not the great forms of drama or epic, nor the comparable great forms in prose. However, the critic should freely grant that the artist writes as he must. But for his own work the critic has to be both involved in his age and detached from it. This double quality of experiencing our own time to the full and yet being able to weigh it in relation to other times is what the critic must strive for, if he is to be able to discern and demand the works of art that we need most. The most mature function of the critic lies finally in that demand.   [1949]

Leslie Fiedler

Come Back to the Raft Ag'in, Huck Honey!

It is perhaps to be expected that the Negro and the homosexual should become stock literary themes, compulsive, almost mythic in their insistence, in a period when the reassertion of responsibility and of the inward meaning of failure has become again a primary concern of our literature. Their locus is, of course, discrepancy—in a culture which has no resources (no tradition of courtesy, no honored mode of cynicism) for dealing with a contradiction between principle and practice. It used once to be fashionable to think of puritanism as a force in our life encouraging hypocrisy; quite the contrary, its rigid emphasis upon the singleness of belief and action, its turning of the most prosaic areas of common life into arenas where one's state of grace is symbolically tested, confuse the outer and the inner and make among us, perhaps more strikingly than ever elsewhere, hypocrisy *visible*, visibly detestable, a cardinal sin. It is not without significance that the shrug of the shoulders (the acceptance of circumstance as a sufficient excuse, the vulgar sign of self-pardon before the inevitable lapse) seems in America an unfamiliar, an alien gesture.

And yet before the underground existence of crude homosexual love (the ultimate American epithets of contempt notoriously exploit the mechanics of such affairs), before the blatant ghettos in which the cast-off Negro conspicuously creates the gaudiness and stench that offend him, the white American must over and over make a choice between coming to uneasy terms with an institutionalized discrepancy, or formulating radically new ideologies. There are, to be sure, stop-gap devices, evasions of that final choice; not the least interesting is the special night club; the fag café, the black-and-tan joint, in which fairy or Negro exhibit their fairyness, their Negro-ness as if they were mere divertissements, gags thought up for the laughs and having no reality once the lights go out and the chairs are piled on the tables for the cleaning-women. In the earlier minstrel show, a negro performer was required to put on with grease paint and burnt cork the formalized mask of blackness.

The situations of the Negro and the homosexual in our society pose precisely opposite problems, or at least problems suggesting precisely opposite solutions: Our laws on homosexuality and the context of prejudice and feeling they objectify must apparently be changed to accord with a stubborn social fact, whereas it is the social fact, our overt behavior toward the Negro, that must be modified to accord with our laws and the, at least official, morality they objectify.

It is not, of course, quite so simple. There is another sense in which the fact of homosexual passion contradicts a national myth of masculine love, just as our real relationship with the Negro contradicts a myth of that relationship, and those two myths with their betrayals are, as we shall see, one.

The existence of overt homosexuality threatens to compromise an essential aspect of American sentimental life: the camaraderie of the locker-room and ball park, the good fellowship of the poker game and fishing trip, a kind of passionless passion, at once gross and delicate, homoerotic in the boy's sense, possessing an innocence above suspicion. To doubt for a moment this innocence, which can survive only as *assumed*, would destroy our stubborn belief in a relationship simple, utterly satisfying, yet immune to lust; physical as the handshake is physical, this side of copulation. The nineteenth-century myth of the Immaculate Young Girl has failed to survive in any *felt* way into our time; rather in the dirty jokes shared among men in the smoking-car, the barracks, or the dormitory there is a common male revenge against women for having flagrantly betrayed that myth, and under the revenge, there is the rather smug assumption of the chastity of the group as a masculine society. From what other source could that unexpected air of good clean fun which overhangs such sessions arise? It is this self-congratulatory buddy-buddiness, its astonishing naiveté, that breeds at once endless opportunities for inversion and the terrible reluctance to admit its existence, to surrender the last believed-in stronghold of love without passion.

It is, after all, what we know from a hundred other sources that is here verified: the regressiveness, in a technical sense, of American life, its implacable nostalgia for the infantile, at once wrongheaded and somehow admirable. The mythic America is boyhood—and who would dare be startled to realize that two (and the two most popular, the two most *absorbed,* I think) of the handful of great books in our native heritage are customarily to be found, illustrated, on the shelves of the Children's Library. I am referring of course to *Moby Dick* and *Huckleberry Finn,* splendidly counterpoised in their oceanic complexity and fluminal simplicity, but alike children's books, or more precisely, *boys'* books.

Among the most distinguished novelists of the American past, only Henry James escapes completely classification as a writer of juvenile classics; even Hawthorne, who did write sometimes for children, must in his most adult novels endure, though not as Mark Twain and Melville submit to, the child's perusal; a child's version of *The Scarlet Letter* would seem a rather far-fetched joke if it were not a part of our common experience. On a lower level of excellence, there are the Leatherstocking Tales of Cooper and Dana's *Two Years Before the Mast,* books read still, though almost unaccountably in Cooper's case, by boys. What do all these novels have in common?

As boys' books we would expect them shyly, guilelessly as it were, to proffer a chaste male love as the ultimate emotional experience—and this is spectacularly the case. In Dana, it is the narrator's melancholy love for the *kanaka,* Hope; in Cooper, the lifelong affection of Natty Bumpo and Chingachgook; in Melville, Ishmael's love for Queequeg; in Twain, Huck's feeling for Nigger Jim. At the focus of emotion, where we are accustomed to find in the world's great novels some heterosexual passion, be it Platonic love or adultery, seduction, rape or long-drawn-out flirtation, we come instead upon the fugitive slave and the no-account boy lying side by side on a raft borne by the endless river towards an impossible escape, or the pariah sailor waking in the tatooed arms of the brown harpooner on the verge of their impossible quest. "Aloha, aikane, aloha nui," Hope cries to the lover who prefers him above his fellow-whites; and Ishmael, in utter frankness, tells us: "Thus, then, in our heart's honeymoon, lay I and Queequeg—a cosy, loving pair." Physical it all is, certainly, yet of an ultimate innocence; there is between the lovers no sword but a childlike ignorance, as if the possibility of a fall to the carnal had not yet been discovered. Even in the *Vita Nuova* of Dante there is no vision of love less offensively, more unremittingly chaste; that it is not adult seems sometimes beside the point.

The tenderness of Huck's repeated loss and refinding of Jim, Ishmael's sensations as he wakes under the pressure of Queequeg's arm, the role of almost Edenic helpmate played for Bumpo by the Indian—these shape us from childhood: we have no sense of first discovering them, of having been once without them.

Of the infantile, the homoerotic aspects of these stories we are, though vaguely, aware, but it is only with an effort that we can wake to a consciousness of how, among us who at the level of adulthood find a difference in color sufficient provocation for distrust and hatred, they celebrate, all of them, the mutual love of *a white man and a colored.*

So buried at a level of acceptance which does not touch reason, so desperately repressed from overt recognition, so contrary to what is usually thought of as our ultimate level of taboo—the sense of that love can survive only in the obliquity of a symbol, persistent, archtypical, in short, as a myth: the boy's homoerotic crush, the love of the black fused at this level into a single thing.

I hope I have been using here a hopelessly abused word with some precision; by myth I mean a coherent pattern of beliefs and feelings, so widely shared at a level beneath consciousness that there exists no abstract vocabulary for representing it, and (this is perhaps another aspect of the same thing) so "sacred" that unexamined, irrational restraints inhibit any explicit analysis. Such a complex achieves a formula or pattern story, which serves both to embody it, and, at first at least, to conceal its full implications. Later the secret may be revealed, the myth (I use a single word for the formula and what is formulized) "analyzed" or "allegorically interpreted" according to the language of the day.

I find the situation we have been explicating genuinely mythic; certainly it has the concealed character of the true myth, eluding the wary pounce of Howells or of Mrs. Twain who excised from *Huckleberry Finn* the cussin' as unfit for children, but left, unperceived, a conventionally abhorrent doctrine of ideal love. Even the writers in whom we find it, attained it, in a sense, dreaming. The felt difference between *Huckleberry Finn* and Twain's other books must lie surely in the release from conscious restraint inherent in the author's assumption of the character of Huck; the passage in and out of darkness and river mist, the constant confusion of identities (Huck's ten or twelve names—the questions of who is the real uncle, who the true Tom), the sudden intrusions into alien violences without past or future, give the whole work for all its carefully observed detail, the texture of a dream. For *Moby Dick,* such a point need scarcely be made. Even Cooper, despite his insufferable gentlemanliness, his civilized tedium, cannot conceal from the kids who continue to read him the secret behind the overconscious, stilted prose: the childish impossible dream. D. H. Lawrence saw in him clearly the kid's Utopia: the absolute wilderness in which the stuffiness of home yields to the wigwam and "My Wife" to Chingachgook.

I do not recall ever having seen in the commentaries of the social anthropologist or psychologist an awareness of the role of this profound child's dream of love in our relation to the Negro. (I say Negro, though the beloved in the books we have mentioned is variously

Indian and Hawaiian, because the Negro has become more and more exclusively for us *the* colored man, the colored man par excellence.) Trapped in what has by now become a shackling cliché: the concept of the white man's sexual envy of the Negro male, they do not sufficiently note the complementary factor of physical attraction, the mythic love of white male and black. I am deliberately ignoring here an underlying Indo-European myth of great antiquity, the Manichæan notion of an absolute Black and White, hostile yet needing each other for completion, as I ignore more recent ideologies that have nourished the view that concerns us: the Shakespearian myth of good homosexual love opposed to an evil heterosexual attachment, the Rousseauistic concept of the Noble Savage; I have tried to stay within the limits of a single unified myth, re-enforced by disparate materials.

Ishmael and Queequeg, arm in arm, about to ship out, Huck and Jim swimming beside the raft in the peaceful flux of the Mississippi,—it is the motion of water which completes the syndrome, the American dream of isolation afloat. The Negro as homoerotic lover blends with the myth of running off to sea, of running the great river down to the sea. The immensity of water defines a loneliness that demands love, its strangeness symbolizes the disavowal of the conventional that makes possible all versions of love.

In *Two Years Before the Mast,* in *Moby Dick,* in *Huckleberry Finn* the water is there, is the very texture of the novel; the Leatherstocking Tales propose another symbol for the same meaning: the virgin forest. Notice the adjective—the virgin forest and the forever inviolable sea. It is well to remember, too, what surely must be more than a coincidence, that Cooper who could dream this myth invented the novel of the sea, wrote for the first time in history the sea-story proper. The rude pederasty of the forecastle and the Captain's cabin, celebrated in a thousand jokes, is the profanation of a dream. In a recent book of Gore Vidal's an incipient homosexual, not yet aware of the implications of his feelings, indulges in the apt reverie of running off to sea with his dearest friend. The buggery of sailors is taken for granted among us, yet it is thought of usually as an inversion forced on men by their isolation from women, though the opposite case may well be true, the isolation sought more or less consciously as an occasion for male encounters. There is a context in which the legend of the sea as escape and solace, the fixated sexuality of boys, the dark beloved are one.

In Melville and Twain at the center of our tradition, in the lesser writers at the periphery, the myth is at once formalized and perpetuated; Nigger Jim and Queequeg make concrete for us what was without them a vague pressure upon the threshold of our consciousness; the proper existence of the myth is in the realized character, who waits, as it were, only to be asked his secret. Think of Oedipus biding in silence from Sophocles to Freud.

Unwittingly we are possessed in childhood by the characters and their undiscriminated meaning, and it is difficult for us to dissociate them without a sense of disbelief. What! these household figures clues to our subtlest passions! The foreigner finds it easier to perceive the remoter significance; D. H. Lawrence saw in our classics a linked mythos of escape and immaculate male love; Lorca in *The Poet in New York* grasped instinctively the kinship of Harlem and Walt Whitman, the fairy as bard. Yet in every generation of our own writers the myth appears; in the Gothic reverie of Capote's *Other Voices, Other Rooms,* both elements of the syndrome are presented, though disjunctively: the boy moving between the love of a Negro maid-servant and his inverted cousin.

In the myth, one notes finally, it is always in the role of outcast, ragged woodsman, or despised sailor (Call me Ishmael!), or unregenerate boy (Huck before the prospect of being 'sivilized' cries, "I been here before!") that we turn to the love of a colored man. But how, we must surely ask, does the vision of the white American as pariah correspond with our long-held public status: the world's beloved, the success? It is perhaps only the artist's portrayal of *himself,* the notoriously alienated writer in America, at home with such images, child of the town drunk, the survivor. But no, Ishmael is all of us, our unconfessed universal fear objectified in the writer's status as in the sailor's: that compelling anxiety, which every foreigner notes, that we may not be loved, that we are loved for our possessions and not ourselves, that we are really—*alone!* It is that underlying terror which explains our almost furtive incredulity in the face of adulation or favor, what is called (once more the happy adjective) our "boyish modesty."

Our dark-skinned beloved will take us, we assure ourselves, when we have been cut off, or have cut ourselves off from all others, without rancor or the insult of forgiveness; he will fold us in his arms saying "Honey" or "Aikane!", he will comfort us, as if our offense against him were long ago remitted, were never truly *real.* And yet we cannot really forget our guilt ever; the stories that embody the myth dramatize almost compulsively the role of the colored man as victim: Dana's Hope is shown dying of the white man's syphilis; Queequeg is portrayed as racked by fever, a pointless episode except in the light of this necessity; Cooper's Indian smolders to a hopeless old age conscious of the imminent disappearance of his race; Jim is shown loaded down with chains, weakened by the hundred torments of Tom's notion of bullyness. The immense gulf of guilt must be underlined, just as is the disparity of color (Queequeg is not merely brown but monstrously tattooed, Chingachgook is horrid with paint, Jim is shown as the Sick A-rab dyed blue), so that the final reconciliation will seem more unbelievable, more tender. The myth makes no attempt to whitewash our outrage as a fact; it portrays it as meaningless in the face of love.

There would be something insufferable, I think, in that final vision of remission if it were not for the apparent presence of a motivating anxiety, the sense always of a last chance; behind the white American's nightmare that someday, no longer tourist, inheritor, or liberator, he will be rejected, refused—he dreams of his acceptance at the breast he has most utterly offended. It is a dream so sentimental, so outrageous, so desperate that it redeems our concept of boyhood from nostalgia to tragedy.

In each generation we *play* out the impossible mythos, and we live to see our children play it, the white boy and the black we can discover wrestling affectionately on any American street, along which they will walk in adulthood, eyes averted from each other, unwilling to touch. The dream recedes; the immaculate passion and the astonishing reconciliation become a memory, and less, a regret, at last the unrecognized motifs of a child's book. "It's too good to be true, Honey," Jim says to Huck. "It's too good to be true."   [1948]

Lionel Trilling
···
Reality in America

I. It is possible to say of V. L. Parrington that with his *Main Currents in American Thought* he has had an influence on our conception of American culture which is not equaled by that of any other writer of the last two decades. His ideas are now the accepted ones wherever the college course in American literature is given by a teacher who conceives himself to be opposed to the genteel and the academic and in alliance with the vigorous and the actual. And whenever the liberal historian of America finds occasion to take account of the national literature, as nowadays he feels it proper to do, it is Parrington who is his standard and guide. Parrington's ideas are the more firmly established because they do not have to be imposed—the teacher or the critic who presents them is likely to find that his task is merely to make articulate for his audience what it has always believed, for Parrington formulated in a classic way the suppositions about our culture which are held by the American middle class so far as that class is at all liberal in its social thought and so far as it begins to understand that literature has anything to do with society.

Parrington was not a great mind; he was not a precise thinker or, except when measured by the low eminences that were about him, an impressive one. Separate Parrington from his informing idea of the economic and social determination of thought and what is left is a simple intelligence, notable for its generosity and enthusiasm but certainly not for its accuracy or originality. Take him even with his idea and he is, once its direction is established, rather too predictable to be continuously interesting; and, indeed, what we dignify with the name of economic and social determinism amounts in his use of it to not much more than the demonstration that most writers incline to stick to their own social class. But his best virtue was real and important—he had what we like to think of as the saving salt of the American mind, the lively sense of the practical, workaday world, of the welter of ordinary undistinguished things and people, of the tangible, quirky, unrefined elements of life. He knew what so many literary historians do not know, that emotions and ideas are the sparks that fly when the mind meets difficulties.

Yet he had after all but a limited sense of what constitutes a difficulty. Whenever he was confronted with a work of art that was complex, personal and not literal, that was not, as it were, a public document, Parrington was at a loss. Difficulties that were complicated by personality or that were expressed in the language of successful art did not seem quite real to him and he was inclined to treat them as aberrations, which is one way of saying what everybody admits, that the weakest part of Parrington's talent was his aesthetic judgment. His admirers and disciples like to imply that his errors of aesthetic judgment are merely lapses of taste, but this is not so. Despite such mistakes as his notorious praise of Cabell, to whom in a remarkable passage he compares Melville, Parrington's taste was by no means bad. His errors are the errors of understanding which arise from his assumptions about the nature of reality.

Parrington does not often deal with abstract philosophical ideas, but whenever he approaches a work of art we are made aware of the metaphysics on which his aesthetics is based. There exists, he believes, a thing called *reality;* it is one and immutable, it is wholly external, it is irreducible. Men's minds may waver, but reality is always reliable, always the same, always easily to be known. And the artist's relation to reality he conceives as a simple one. Reality being fixed and given, the artist has but to let it pass through him, he is the lens in the first diagram of an elementary book on optics: Fig. 1, Reality; Fig. 2, Artist; Fig. 1′, Work of Art. Figs. 1 and 1′ are normally in virtual correspondence with each other. Sometimes the artist spoils this ideal relation by "turning away from" reality. This results in certain fantastic works, unreal and ultimately useless. It does not occur to Parrington that there is any other relation possible between the artist and reality than this passage of reality through the transparent artist; he meets evidence of imagination and creativeness with a settled hostility the expression of which suggests that he regards them as the natural enemies of democracy.

In this view of things, reality, although it is always reliable, is always rather sobersided, even grim. Parrington, a genial and enthusiastic man, can understand how the generosity of man's hopes and desires may leap beyond reality; he admires will in the degree that he suspects mind. To an excess of desire and energy which blinds a man to the limitations of reality he can indeed be very tender. This is one of the many meanings he gives to *romance* or *romanticism,* and in spite of himself it appeals to something in his own nature. The praise of Cabell is Parrington's response not only to Cabell's elegance—for Parrington loved elegance—but also to Cabell's insistence on the part which a beneficent self-deception may and even should play in the disappointing fact-bound life of man, particularly in the private and erotic part of his life.[1]

The second volume of *Main Currents* is called *The Romantic Revolution in America* and it is natural to expect that the word romantic should appear in it frequently. So it does, more frequently than one can count, and seldom with the same meaning, seldom with the sense that the word, although scandalously vague as it has been used by the literary historians, is still full of complicated but not wholly pointless ideas, that it involves many contrary but definable things; all too often Parrington uses the word romantic with the word romance close at hand, meaning a romance, in the sense that *Graustark* or *Treasure Island* is a romance, as though it signified chiefly a gay disregard of the limitations of everyday fact. Romance is refusing to heed the counsels of experience (p. iii); it is ebullience (p. iv); it is utopianism (p. iv); it is individualism (p. vi); it is self-deception (p. 59)—"romantic faith . . . in the beneficent processes of trade and industry" (as held, we inevitably ask, by the romantic Adam Smith?); it is the love of the picturesque (p. 49); it is the dislike of innovation (p. 50) but also the love of change (p. iv); it is the sentimental (p. 192); it is patriotism, and then it is cheap (p. 235). It may be used to denote what is not classical, but chiefly it means that which ignores reality (pp. ix, 136, 143, 147, and *passim*); it is not critical (pp. 225, 235), although in speaking of Cooper and Melville, Parrington admits that criticism can sometimes spring from romanticism.

Whenever a man with whose ideas he disagrees wins from Parrington a reluctant measure of respect, the word romantic is likely to appear. He does not admire Henry Clay, yet something in Clay is not to be despised—his romanticism, although Clay's romanticism is made equivalent with his inability to "come to grips with reality." Romanticism is thus, in most of its significations, the venial sin of *Main Currents;* like carnal passion in the *Inferno,* it evokes not blame but tender sorrow. But it can also be the great and saving virtue which Parrington recognizes. It is ascribed to the transcendental reformers he so much admires; it is said to mark two of his most cherished heroes, Jefferson and Emerson: "they were both romantics and their idealism was only a different expression of a common spirit." Parrington held, we may say, at least two different views of romanticism which suggest two different views of reality. Sometimes he speaks of reality in an honorific way, meaning the substantial stuff of life, the ineluctable facts with which the mind must cope, but sometimes he speaks of it pejoratively and means the world of established social forms; and he speaks of realism in two ways: sometimes as the power of dealing intelligently with fact, sometimes as a cold and conservative resistance to idealism.

Just as for Parrington there is a saving grace and a venial sin, there is also a deadly sin, and this is turning away from reality, not in the excess of generous feeling, but in what he believes to be a deficiency of feeling, as with Hawthorne, or out of what amounts to sinful pride, as with Henry James. He tells us that there was too much realism in Hawthorne to

---

[1] See, for example, how Parrington accounts for the "idealizing mind"—Melville's—by the discrepancy between "a wife in her morning kimono" and "the Helen of his dreams." Vol. II, p. 259.

allow him to give his faith to the transcendental reformers: "he was too much of a realist to change fashions in creeds"; "he remained cold to the revolutionary criticism that was eager to pull down the old temples to make room for nobler." It is this cold realism, keeping Hawthorne apart from his enthusiastic contemporaries, that alienates Parrington's sympathy—"Eager souls, mystics and revolutionaries, may propose to refashion the world in accordance with their dreams; but evil remains, and so long as it lurks in the secret places of the heart, utopia is only the shadow of a dream. And so while the Concord thinkers were proclaiming man to be the indubitable child of God, Hawthorne was critically examining the question of evil as it appeared in the light of his own experience. It was the central fascinating problem of his intellectual life, and in pursuit of a solution he probed curiously into the hidden, furtive recesses of the soul." Parrington's disapproval of the enterprise is unmistakable.

Now we might wonder whether Hawthorne's questioning of the naïve and often eccentric faiths of the transcendental reformers was not, on the face of it, a public service. But Parrington implies that it contributes nothing to democracy, and even that it stands in the way of the realization of democracy. If democracy depends wholly on a fighting faith, I suppose he is right. Yet society is after all something that exists at the moment as well as in the future, and if one man wants to probe curiously into the hidden furtive recesses of the contemporary soul, a broad democracy and especially one devoted to reality should allow him to do so without despising him. If what Hawthorne did was certainly nothing to build a party on, we ought perhaps to forgive him when we remember that he was only one man and that the future of mankind did not depend upon him alone. But this very fact serves only to irritate Parrington; he is put out by Hawthorne's loneliness and believes that part of Hawthorne's insufficiency as a writer comes from his failure to get around and meet people. Hawthorne could not, he tells us, establish contact with the "Yankee reality," and was scarcely aware of the "substantial world of Puritan reality that Samuel Sewall knew."

To turn from reality might mean to turn to romance, but Parrington tells us that Hawthorne was romantic "only in a narrow and very special sense." He was not interested in the world of, as it were, practical romance, in the Salem of the clipper ships; from this he turned away to create "a romance of ethics." This is not an illuminating phrase but it is a catching one, and it might be taken to mean that Hawthorne was in the tradition of, say, Shakespeare; but we quickly learn that, no, Hawthorne had entered a barren field, for although he himself lived in the present and had all the future to mold, he preferred to find many of his subjects in the past. We learn too that his romance of ethics is not admirable because it requires the hard, fine pressing of ideas, and we are told that "a romantic uninterested in adventure and afraid of sex is likely to become somewhat graveled for matter." In short, Hawthorne's mind was a thin one, and Parrington puts in evidence his use of allegory and symbol and the very severity and precision of his art to prove that he suffered from a sadly limited intellect, for so much fancy and so much art could scarcely be needed unless the writer were trying to exploit to the utmost the few poor ideas that he had.

Hawthorne, then, was "forever dealing with shadows, and he knew that he was dealing with shadows." Perhaps so, but shadows are also part of reality and one would not want a world without shadows, it would not even be a "real" world. But we must get beyond Parrington's metaphor. The fact is that Hawthorne was dealing beautifully with realities, with substantial things. The man who could raise those brilliant and serious doubts about the nature and possibility of moral perfection, the man who could keep himself aloof from the "Yankee reality" and who could dissent from the orthodoxies of dissent and tell us so much about the nature of moral zeal, is of course dealing exactly with reality.

Parrington's characteristic weakness as a historian is suggested by his title, for the culture of a nation is not truly figured in the image of the current. A culture is not a flow, nor even a confluence; the form of its existence is struggle, or at least debate—it is nothing if not a dialectic. And in any culture there are likely to be certain artists who contain a large part of the dialectic within themselves, their meaning and power lying in their contradictions; they contain within themselves, it may be said, the very essence of the culture, and the sign of this is that they do not submit to serve the ends of any one ideological group or tendency. It is a significant circumstance of American culture, and one which is susceptible of explanation, that an unusually large proportion of its notable writers of the nineteenth century were such repositories of the dialectic of their times—they contained both the yes and the no of their culture, and by that token they were prophetic of the future. Parrington said that he had not set up shop as a literary critic; but if a literary critic is simply a reader who has the ability to understand literature and to convey to others what he understands, it is not exactly a matter of free choice whether or not a cultural historian shall be a literary critic, nor is it open to him to let his virtuous political and social opinions do duty for percipience. To throw out Poe because he cannot be conveniently fitted into a theory of American culture, to speak of him as a biological sport and as a mind apart from the main current, to find his gloom to be merely personal and eccentric, "only the atrabilious wretchedness of a dipsomaniac," as Hawthorne's was "no more than the skeptical questioning of life by a nature that knew no fierce storms," to judge Melville's response to American life to be less noble than that of Bryant or of Greeley, to speak of Henry James as an escapist, as an artist similar to Whistler, a man characteristically afraid of stress—this is not merely to be mistaken in aesthetic judgment; rather it is to examine without attention and from the point of view of a limited and essentially arrogant conception of reality the documents which are in some respects the most suggestive testimony to what America was and is, and of course to get no answer from them.

Parrington lies twenty years behind us, and in the intervening time there has developed a body of opinion which is aware of his inadequacies and of the inadequacies of his coadjutors and disciples, who make up what might be called the literary academicism of liberalism. Yet Parrington still stands at the center of American thought about American culture because, as I say, he expresses the chronic American belief that there exists an opposition between reality and mind and that one must enlist oneself in the party of reality.

II. This belief in the incompatibility of mind and reality is exemplified by the doctrinaire indulgence which liberal intellectuals have always displayed toward Theodore Dreiser, an indulgence which becomes the worthier of remark when it is contrasted with the liberal severity toward Henry James. Dreiser and James: with that juxtaposition we are immediately at the dark and bloody crossroads where literature and politics meet. One does not go there gladly, but nowadays it is not exactly a matter of free choice whether one does or does not go. As for the particular juxtaposition itself, it is inevitable and it has at the present moment far more significance than the juxtaposition which once used to be made between James and Whitman. It is not hard to contrive factitious oppositions between James and Whitman, but the real difference between them is the difference between the moral mind, with its awareness of tragedy, irony, and multitudinous distinctions, and the transcendental mind, with its passionate sense of the oneness of multiplicity. James and Whitman are unlike not in quality but in kind, and in their very opposition they serve to complement each other. But the difference between James and Dreiser is not of kind, for both men addressed themselves to virtually the same social and moral fact. The difference here is one of quality, and perhaps nothing is more typical of American liberalism than the way it has responded to the respective qualities of the two men.

Few critics, I suppose, no matter what their political disposition, have ever been wholly blind to James's great gifts, or even to the grandiose moral intention of these gifts. And few critics have ever been wholly blind to Dreiser's great faults. But by liberal critics James is traditionally put to the ultimate question: of what use, of what actual political use, are his gifts and their intention? Granted that James was devoted to an extraordinary moral perceptiveness, granted too that moral perceptiveness has something to do with politics and the social life, of what possible practical value in our world of impending disaster can James's work be? And James's style, his characters, his subjects, and even his own social origin and the manner of his personal life are adduced to show that his work cannot endure the question. To James no quarter is given by American criticism in its political and liberal aspect. But in the same degree that liberal criticism is moved by political considerations to treat James with severity, it treats Dreiser with the most sympathetic indulgence. Dreiser's literary faults, it gives us to understand, are essentially social and political virtues. It was Parrington who established the formula for the liberal criticism of Dreiser by calling him a "peasant"; when Dreiser thinks stupidly, it is because he has the slow stubbornness of a peasant; when he writes badly, it is because he is impatient of the sterile literary gentility of the bourgeoisie. It is as if wit, and flexibility of mind, and perception, and knowledge were to be equated with aristocracy and political reaction, while dullness and stupidity must naturally suggest a virtuous democracy, as in the old plays.

The liberal judgment of Dreiser and James goes back of politics, goes back to the cultural assumptions that make politics. We are still haunted by a kind of political fear of the intellect which Tocqueville observed in us more than a century ago. American intellectuals, when they are being consciously American or political, are remarkably quick to suggest that an art which is marked by perception and knowledge, although all very well in its way, can never get us through gross dangers and difficulties. And their misgivings become the more intense when intellect works in art as it ideally should, when its processes are vivacious and interesting and brilliant. It is then that we like to confront it with the gross dangers and difficulties and to challenge it to save us at once from disaster. When intellect in art is awkward or dull we do not put it to the test of ultimate or immediate practicality. No liberal critic asks the question of Dreiser whether *his* moral preoccupations are going to be useful in confronting the disasters that threaten us. And it is a judgment on the proper nature of mind, rather than any actual political meaning that might be drawn from the works of the two men, which accounts for the unequal justice they have received from the progressive critics. If it could be conclusively demonstrated—by, say, documents in James's handwriting—that James explicitly intended his books to be understood as pleas for co-operatives, labor unions, better housing, and more equitable taxation, the American critic in his liberal and progressive character would still be worried by James because his work shows so many of the electric qualities of mind. And if something like the opposite were proved of Dreiser, it would be brushed aside—as his doctrinaire anti-Semitism has in fact been brushed aside—because his books have the awkwardness, the chaos, the heaviness which we associate with "reality." In the American metaphysic, reality is always material reality, hard, resistant, unformed, impenetrable, and unpleasant. And that mind is alone felt to be trustworthy which most resembles this reality by most nearly reproducing the sensations it affords.

In *The Rise of American Civilization,* Professor Beard uses a significant phrase when, in the course of an ironic account of James's career, he implies that we have the clue to the irrelevance of that career when we know that James was "a whole generation removed from the odors of the shop." Of a piece with this, and in itself even more significant, is the comment which Granville Hicks makes in *The Great Tradition* when he deals with James's stories about artists and remarks that such artists as James portrays, so concerned for their art and their integrity in art, do not really exist: "After all, who has ever known such artists? Where are the Hugh Verekers, the Mark Ambients, the Neil Paradays, the Overts, Limberts, Dencombes, Delavoys?" This question, as Mr. Hicks admits, had occurred to James himself, but what answer had James given to it? "If the life about us for the last thirty years refused warrant for these examples," he said in the preface to volume XII of the New York Edition, "then so much the worse for that life. . . . There are decencies that in the name of the general self-respect we must take for granted, there's a rudimentary intellectual honor to which we must, in the interest of civilization, at least pretend." And to this Mr. Hicks, shocked beyond argument, makes this reply, which would be astonishing had we not heard it before: "But this is the purest romanticism, this writing about what ought to be rather than what is!"

The "odors of the shop" are real, and to those who breathe them they guarantee a sense of vitality from which James is debarred. The idea of intellectual honor is not real, and to that chimera James was devoted. He betrayed the reality of what is in the interests of what ought to be. Dare we trust him? The question, we remember, is asked by men who themselves have elaborate transactions with what ought to be. Professor Beard spoke in the name of a growing, developing, and improving America. Mr. Hicks, when he wrote *The Great Tradition,* was in general sympathy with a nominally radical movement. But James's own transaction with what ought to be is suspect because it is carried on through what I have called the electrical qualities of mind, through a complex and rapid imagination and with a kind of authoritative immediacy. Mr. Hicks knows that Dreiser is "clumsy" and "stupid" and "bewildered" and "crude in his statement of materialistic monism"; he knows that Dreiser in his personal life—which is in point because James's personal life is always supposed to be so much in point—was not quite emancipated from "his boyhood longing for crass material success," showing "again and again a desire for the ostentatious luxury of the successful business man." But Dreiser is to be accepted and forgiven because his faults are the sad, lovable, honorable faults of reality itself, or of America itself—huge, inchoate, struggling toward expression, caught between the dream of raw power and the dream of morality.

"The liability in what Santayana called the genteel tradition was due to its being the product of mind apart from experience. Dreiser gave us the stuff of our common experience, not as it was hoped to be by any idealizing theorist, but as it actually was in its crudity." The author of this statement certainly cannot be accused of any lack of feeling for mind as Henry James represents it; nor can Mr. Matthiessen be thought of as a follower of Parrington—indeed, in the preface to *American Renaissance* he has framed one of the sharpest and most cogent criticisms of Parrington's method. Yet Mr. Matthiessen, writing in the *New York Times Book Review* about Dreiser's posthumous novel, *The Bulwark,* accepts the liberal cliché which opposes crude experience to mind and establishes Dreiser's value by implying that the mind which Dreiser's crude experience is presumed to confront and refute is the mind of gentility.

This implied amalgamation of mind with gentility is the rationale of the long indulgence of Dreiser, which is extended even to the style of his prose. Everyone is aware that Dreiser's prose style is full of roughness and ungainliness, and the critics who admire Dreiser tell us it does not matter. Of course it does not matter. No reader with a right sense of style would suppose that it does matter, and he might even find it a virtue. But it has been taken for granted that the ungainliness of Dreiser's style is the only possible objection to be made to it, and that whoever finds in it any fault at all wants a prettified genteel style (and is objecting to the ungainliness of reality itself). For instance, Edwin Berry Burgum, in a leaflet on Dreiser put out by the Book Find club, tells us that Dreiser was one of those who used—or, as Mr. Burgum says, utilized—"the diction of the Middle West, pretty much as it was spoken, rich in colloquialism and frank in the simplicity and directness of the pioneer tradition," and that this diction took the place of "the literary English, formal and bookish, of New England provincialism that was closer to the aristocratic spirit of the mother country than to the tang of everyday life in the new West." This is mere fantasy. Hawthorne, Thoreau, and Emerson were for the most part remarkably colloquial—they wrote, that is, much as they spoke; their prose was specifically American in quality, and, except for occasional lapses, quite direct and simple. It is Dreiser who lacks the sense of colloquial diction—that of the Middle West or any other. If we are to talk of bookishness, it is Dreiser who is bookish; he is precisely literary in the bad sense; he is full of flowers of rhetoric and shines with paste gems; at hundreds of points his diction is not only genteel but fancy. It is he who speaks of "a scene more distingué than this," or of a woman "artistic in form and feature," or of a man who, although "strong, reserved, aggressive, with an air of wealth and experience, was *soi-disant* and not particularly eager to stay at home." Colloquialism held no real charm for him and his natural tendency is always toward the "fine":

> . . . . Moralists come and go; religionists fulminate and declare the pronouncements of God as to this; but Aphrodite still reigns. Embowered in the festal depths of the spring, set above her altars of prophyry, chalcedony, ivory and gold, see her smile the smile that is at once the texture and essence of delight, the glory and despair of the world! Dream on, oh Buddha, asleep on your lotus leaf, of an undisturbed Nirvana! Sweat, oh Jesus, your last agonizing drops over an unregenerate world! In the forests of Pan still ring the cries of the worshippers of Aphrodite! From her altars the incense of adoration ever rises! And see, the new red grapes dripping where votive hands new-press them!

Charles Jackson, the novelist, telling us in the same leaflet that Dreiser's style does not matter, remarks on how much still comes to us when we have lost by translation the stylistic brilliance of Thomas Mann or the Russians or Balzac. He is in part right. And he is right too when he says that a certain kind of conscious, supervised artistry is not appropriate to the novel of large dimensions. Yet the fact is that the great novelists have usually written very good prose, and what comes through even a bad translation is exactly the power of mind that made the well-hung sentence of the original text. In literature style is so little the mere clothing of thought—need it be insisted on at this late date?—that we may say that from the earth of the novelist's prose spring his characters, his ideas, and even his story itself.[2]

---

[2] The latest defense of Dreiser's style, that in the chapter on Dreiser in the *Literary History of the United States,* is worth noting: "Forgetful of the integrity and power of Dreiser's whole work, many critics have been distracted into a condemnation of his style. He was, like Twain and Whitman, an organic artist; he wrote what he knew—what he was. His many colloquialisms were part of the coinage of his time, and his sentimental and romantic passages were written in the language of the educational system and the popular literature of his formative years. In his style, as in his material, he was a child of his time, of his class. Self-educated, a type or model of the artist of plebeian origin in America, his language, like his subject matter, is not marked by internal inconsistencies." No doubt Dreiser was an organic artist in the sense that he wrote what he knew and what he was, but so, I suppose, is every artist; the question for criticism comes down to *what* he knew and *what* he was. That he was a child of his time and class is also true, but this can be said of everyone without exception; the question for criticism is how he transcended the imposed limitations of his time and class. As for the defense made on the ground of his particular class, it can only be said that liberal thought has come to a strange pass when it assumes that a plebeian origin is accountable for a writer's faults through all his intellectual life.

To the extent that Dreiser's style is defensible, his thought is also defensible. That is, when he thinks like a novelist, he is worth following—when by means of his rough and ungainly but no doubt cumulatively effective style he creates rough, ungainly, but effective characters and events. But when he thinks like, as we say, a philosopher, he is likely to be not only foolish but vulgar. He thinks as the modern crowd thinks when it decides to think: religion and morality are nonsense, "religionists" and moralists are fakes, tradition is a fraud, what is man but matter and impulses, mysterious "chemisms," what value has life anyway? "What, cooking, eating, coition, job holding, growing, aging, losing, winning, in so changeful and passing a scene as this, important? Bunk! It is some form of titillating illusion with about as much import to the superior forces that bring it all about as the functions and gyrations of a fly. No more. And maybe less." Thus Dreiser at sixty. And yet there is for him always the vulgarly saving suspicion that maybe, when all is said and done, there is Something Behind It All. It is much to the point of his intellectual vulgarity that Dreiser's anti-Semitism was not merely a social prejudice but an idea, a way of dealing with difficulties.

No one, I suppose, has ever represented Dreiser as a masterly intellect. It is even commonplace to say that his ideas are inconsistent or inadequate. But once that admission has been made, his ideas are hustled out of sight while his "reality" and great brooding pity are spoken of. (His pity is to be questioned: pity is to be judged by kind, not amount, and Dreiser's pity—*Jennie Gerhardt* provides the only exception—is either destructive of its object or it is self-pity.) Why has no liberal critic ever brought Dreiser's ideas to the bar of political practicality, asking what use is to be made of Dreiser's dim, awkward speculation, of his self-justification, of his lust for "beauty" and "sex" and "living" and "life itself," and of the showy nihilism which always seems to him so grand a gesture in the direction of profundity? We live, understandably enough, with the sense of urgency; our clock, like Baudelaire's, has had the hands removed and bears the legend, "It is later than you think." But with us it is always a little too late for mind, yet never too late for honest stupidity; always a little too late for understanding, never too late for righteous, bewildered wrath; always too late for thought, never too late for naïve moralizing. We seem to like to condemn our finest but not our worst qualities by pitting them against the exigency of time.

But sometimes time is not quite so exigent as to justify all our own exigency, and in the case of Dreiser time has allowed his deficiencies to reach their logical, and fatal, conclusion. In *The Bulwark* Dreiser's characteristic ideas come full circle, and the simple, didactic life history of Solon Barnes, a Quaker business man, affirms a simple Christian faith, and a kind of practical mysticism, and the virtues of self-abnegation and self-restraint, and the belief in and submission to the hidden purposes of higher powers, those "superior forces that bring it all about"—once, in Dreiser's opinion, so brutally indifferent, now somehow benign. This is not the first occasion on which Dreiser has shown a tenderness toward religion and a responsiveness to mysticism. *Jennie Gerhardt* and the figure of the Reverend Duncan McMillan in *An American Tragedy* are forecasts of the avowals of *The Bulwark,* and Dreiser's lively interest in power of any sort led him to take account of the power implicit in the cruder forms of mystical performance. Yet these rifts in his nearly monolithic materialism cannot quite prepare us for the blank pietism of *The Bulwark,* not after we have remembered how salient in Dreiser's work has been the long surly rage against the "religionists" and the "moralists," the men who have presumed to believe that life can be given any law at all and who have dared to suppose that will or mind or faith can shape the savage and beautiful entity that Dreiser liked to call "life itself." Now for Dreiser the law may indeed be given, and it is wholly simple—the safe conduct of the personal life requires only that we follow the Inner Light according to the regimen of the Society of Friends, or according to some other godly rule. And now the smiling Aphrodite set above her altars of porphyry, chalcedony, ivory, and gold is quite forgotten, and we are told that the sad joy of cosmic acceptance goes hand in hand with sexual abstinence.

Dreiser's mood of "acceptance" in the last years of his life is not, as a personal experience, to be submitted to the tests of intellectual validity. It consists of a sensation of cosmic understanding, of an overarching sense of unity with the world in its apparent evil as well as in its obvious good. It is no more to be quarreled with, or reasoned with, than love itself—indeed, it is a kind of love, not so much of the world as of oneself in the world. Perhaps it is either the cessation of desire or the perfect balance of desires. It is what used often to be meant by "peace," and up through the nineteenth century a good many people understood its meaning. If it was Dreiser's own emotion at the end of his life, who would not be happy that he had achieved it? I am not even sure that our civilization would not be the better for more of us knowing and desiring this emotion of grave felicity. Yet granting the personal validity of the emotion, Dreiser's exposition of it fails, and is, moreover, offensive. Mr. Matthiessen has warned us of the attack that will be made on the doctrine of *The Bulwark* by "those who believe that any renewal of Christianity marks a new 'failure of nerve.'" But Dreiser's religious avowal is not a failure of nerve—it is a failure of mind and heart. We have only to set his book beside any work in which mind and heart are made to serve religion to know this at once. Ivan Karamazov's giving back his ticket of admission to the "harmony" of the universe suggests that *The Bulwark* is not morally adequate, for we dare not, as its hero does, blandly "accept" the suffering of others; and the Book of Job tells us that it does not include enough in its exploration of the problem of evil, and is not stern enough. I have said that Dreiser's religious affirmation was offensive; the offense lies in the vulgar ease of its formulation, as well as in the comfortable untroubled way in which Dreiser moved from nihilism to pietism.[3]

The Bulwark is the fruit of Dreiser's old age, but if we speak of it as a failure of thought and feeling, we cannot suppose that with age Dreiser weakened in mind and heart. The weakness was always there. And in a sense it is not Dreiser who failed but a whole way of dealing with ideas, a way in which we have all been in some degree involved. Our liberal, progressive culture tolerated Dreiser's vulgar materialism with its huge negation, its simple cry of "Bunk!," feeling that perhaps it was not quite intellectually adequate but certainly very *strong*, certainly very *real*. And now, almost as a natural consequence, it has been given, and is not unwilling to take, Dreiser's pietistic religion in all its inadequacy.

Dreiser, of course, was firmer than the intellectual culture that accepted him. He *meant* his ideas, at least so far as a man can mean ideas who is incapable of following them to their consequences. But we, when it came to his ideas, talked about his great brooding pity and shrugged the ideas off. We are still doing it. Robert Elias, the biographer of Dreiser, tells us that "it is part of the logic of [Dreiser's] life that he should have completed *The Bulwark* at the same time that he joined the Communists." Just what kind of logic this is we learn from Mr. Elias's further statement. "When he supported left-wing movements and finally, last year, joined the Communist Party, he did so not because he

---

[3] This ease and comfortableness seem to mark contemporary religious conversions. Religion nowadays has the appearance of what the ideal modern house has been called, "a machine for living," and seemingly one makes up one's mind to acquire and use it not with spiritual struggle but only with a growing sense of its practicability and convenience. Compare *The Seven Storey Mountain*, which Monsignor Sheen calls "a twentieth-century form of the *Confessions* of St. Augustine," with the old, the as it were original, *Confessions* of St. Augustine.

had examined the details of the party line and found them satisfactory, but because he agreed with a general program that represented a means for establishing his cherished goal of greater equality among men." Whether or not Dreiser was following the logic of his own life, he was certainly following the logic of the liberal criticism that accepted him so undiscriminatingly as one of the great, significant expressions of its spirit. This is the liberal criticism, in the direct line of Parrington, which establishes the social responsibility of the writer and then goes on to say that, apart from his duty of resembling reality as much as possible, he is not really responsible for anything, not even for his ideas. The scope of reality being what it is, ideas are held to be mere "details," and, what is more, to be details which, if attended to, have the effect of diminishing reality. But ideals are different from ideas; in the liberal criticism which descends from Parrington ideals consort happily with reality and they urge us to deal impatiently with ideas—a "cherished goal" forbids that we stop to consider how we reach it, or if we may not destroy it in trying to reach it the wrong way.

Ralph Ellison

Richard Wright's Blues

> *If anybody ask you*
> *who sing this song*
> *Say it was ole [Black Boy]*
> *done been here and gone.* [1]

As a writer, Richard Wright has outlined for himself a dual role: to discover and depict the meaning of Negro experience; and to reveal to both Negroes and whites those problems of a psychological and emotional nature which arise between them when they strive for mutual understanding.

Now, in *Black Boy,* he has used his own life to probe what qualities of will, imagination and intellect are required of a Southern Negro in order to possess the meaning of his life in the United States. Wright is an important writer, perhaps the most articulate Negro American, and what he has to say is highly perceptive. Imagine Bigger Thomas projecting his own life in lucid prose, guided, say, by the insights of Marx and Freud, and you have an idea of this autobiography.

Published at a time when any sharply critical approach to Negro life has been dropped as a wartime expendable, it should do much to redefine the problem of the Negro and American Democracy. Its power can be observed in the shrill manner with which some professional "friends of the Negro people" have attempted to strangle the work in a noose of newsprint.

[1]Signature formula used by blues singers at conclusion of song.

What in the tradition of literary autobiography is it like, this work described as a "great American autobiography"? As a non-white intellectual's statement of his relationship to Western culture, *Black Boy* recalls the conflicting pattern of identification and rejection found in Nehru's *Toward Freedom.* In its use of fictional techniques, its concern with criminality (sin) and the artistic sensibility, and in its author's judgment and rejection of the narrow world of his origin, it recalls Joyce's rejection of Dublin in *A Portrait of the Artist.* And as a psychological document of life under oppressive conditions, it recalls *The House of the Dead,* Dostoievsky's profound study of the humanity of Russian criminals.

Such works were perhaps Wright's literary guides, aiding him to endow his life's incidents with communicable significance; providing him with ways of seeing, feeling and describing his environment. These influences, however, were encountered only after these first years of Wright's life were past and were not part of the immediate folk culture into which he was born. In that culture the specific folk-art form which helped shape the writer's attitude toward his life and which embodied the impulse that contributes much to the quality and tone of his autobiography was the Negro blues. This would bear a word of explanation:

The blues is an impulse to keep the painful details and episodes of a brutal experience alive in one's aching consciousness, to finger its jagged grain, and to transcend it, not by the consolation of philosophy but by squeezing from it a near-tragic, near-comic lyricism. As a form, the blues is an autobiographical chronicle of personal catastrophe expressed lyrically. And certainly Wright's early childhood was crammed with catastrophic incidents. In a few short years his father deserted his mother, he knew intense hunger, he became a drunkard begging drinks from black stevedores in Memphis saloons; he had to flee Arkansas, where an uncle was lynched; he was forced to live with a fanatically religious grandmother in an atmosphere of constant bickering; he was lodged in an orphan asylum; he observed the suffering of his mother, who became a permanent invalid, while fighting off the blows of poverty-stricken relatives with whom he had to live; he was cheated, beaten and kicked off jobs by white employees who disliked his eagerness to learn a trade; and to these objective circumstances must be added the subjective fact that Wright, with his sensitivity, extreme shyness and intelligence, was a problem child who rejected his family and was by them rejected.

Thus along with the themes, equivalent descriptions of milieu and the perspectives to be found in Joyce, Nehru, Dostoievsky, George Moore and Rousseau, *Black Boy* is filled with blues-tempered echoes of railroad trains, the names of Southern towns and cities, estrangements, fights and flights, deaths and disappointments, charged with physical and spiritual hungers and pain. And like a blues sung by such an artist as Bessie Smith, its lyrical prose evokes the paradoxical, almost surreal image of a black boy singing lustily as he probes his own grievous wound.

In *Black Boy,* two worlds have fused, two cultures merged, two impulses of Western man become coalesced. By discussing some of its cultural sources I hope to answer those critics who would make of the book a miracle and of its author a mystery. And while making no attempt to probe the mystery of the artist (who Hemingway says is "forged in injustice as a sword is forged"), I do hold that basically the prerequisites to the writing of *Black Boy* were, on the one hand, the microscopic degree of cultural freedom which Wright found in the South's stony injustice, and, on the other, the existence of a personality agitated to a state of almost manic restlessness. There were, of course, other factors, chiefly ideological; but these came later.

Wright speaks of his journey north as

. . . taking a part of the South to transplant in alien soil, to see if it could grow differently, if it could drink of new and cool rains, bend in strange winds, respond to the warmth of other suns, and perhaps, to bloom. . . .

And just as Wright, the man, represents the blooming of the delinquent child of the autobiography, just so does *Black Boy* represent the flowering—cross-fertilized by pollen blown by the winds of strange cultures—of the humble blues lyric. There is, as in all acts of creation, a world of mystery in this, but there is also enough that is comprehensible for Americans to create the social atmosphere in which other black boys might freely bloom.

For certainly, in the historical sense, Wright is no exception. Born on a Mississippi plantation, he was subjected to all those blasting pressures which in a scant eighty years have sent the Negro people hurtling, without clearly defined trajectory, from slavery to emancipation, from log cabin to city tenement, from the white folks' fields and kitchens to factory assembly lines; and which, between two wars, have shattered the wholeness of its folk consciousness into a thousand writhing pieces.

Black Boy describes this process in the personal terms of *one* Negro childhood. Nevertheless, several critics have complained that it does not "explain" Richard Wright. Which, aside from the notion of art involved, serves to remind us that the prevailing mood of American criticism has so thoroughly excluded the Negro that it fails to recognize some of the most basic tenets of Western democratic thought when encountering them in a black skin. They forget that human life possesses an innate dignity and mankind an innate sense of nobility; that all men possess the tendency to dream and the compulsion to make their dreams reality; that the need to be ever dissatisfied and the urge ever to seek satisfaction is implicit in the human organism; and that all men are the victims and the beneficiaries of the goading, tormenting, commanding and informing activity of that imperious process known as the Mind—the Mind, as Valéry describes it, "armed with its inexhaustible questions."

Perhaps all this (in which lies the very essence of the human, and which Wright takes for granted) has been forgotten because the critics recognize neither Negro humanity nor the full extent to which the Southern community renders the fulfillment of human destiny impossible. And while it is true that *Black Boy* presents an almost unrelieved picture of a personality corrupted by brutal environment, it also presents those fresh, human responses brought to its world by the sensitive child:

> There was the *wonder* I felt when I first saw a brace of mountain like, spotted, black-and-white horses clopping down a dusty road . . . the *delight* I caught in seeing long straight rows of red and green vegetables stretching away in the sun . . . the faint, cool kiss of *sensuality* when dew came on to my cheeks . . . the vague *sense of the infinite* as I looked down upon the yellow, dreaming waters of the Mississippi . . . the echoes of *nostalgia* I heard in the crying strings of wild geese . . . the *love* I had for the mute regality of tall, moss-clad oaks . . . the hint of *cosmic cruelty* that I *felt* when I saw the curved timbers of a wooden shack that had been warped in the summer sun . . . and there was the *quiet terror* that suffused my senses when vast hazes of gold washed earthward from star-heavy skies on silent nights. . . .[2]

And a bit later, his reactions to religion:

> Many of the religious symbols appealed to my sensibilities and I responded to the dramatic vision of life held by the church, feeling that to live day by day with death as one's sole

[2]Italics mine.

thought was to be so compassionately sensitive toward all life as to view all men as slowly dying, and the trembling sense of fate that welled up, sweet and melancholy, from the hymns blended with the sense of fate that I had already caught from life.

There was also the influence of his mother—so closely linked to his hysteria and sense of suffering—who (though he only implies it here) taught him, in the words of the dedication prefacing *Native Son,* "to revere the fanciful and the imaginative." There were also those white men—the one who allowed Wright to use his library privileges and the other who advised him to leave the South, and still others whose offers of friendship he was too frightened to accept.

Wright assumed that the nucleus of plastic sensibility is a human heritage: the right and the opportunity to dilate, deepen and enrich sensibility—democracy. Thus the drama of *Black Boy* lies in its depiction of what occurs when Negro sensibility attempts to fulfill itself in the undemocratic South. Here it is not the individual that is the immediate focus, as in Joyce's *Stephen Hero,* but that upon which his sensibility was nourished.

Those critics who complain that Wright has omitted the development of his own sensibility hold that the work thus fails as art. Others, because it presents too little of what they consider attractive in Negro life, charge that it distorts reality. Both groups miss a very obvious point: That whatever else the environment contained, it had as little chance of prevailing against the overwhelming weight of the child's unpleasant experiences as Beethoven's Quartets would have of destroying the stench of a Nazi prison.

We come, then, to the question of art. The function, the psychology, of artistic selectivity is to eliminate from art form all those elements of experience which contain no compelling significance. Life is as the sea, art a ship in which man conquers life's crushing formlessness, reducing it to a course, a series of swells, tides and wind currents inscribed on a chart. Though drawn from the world, "the organized significance of art," writes Malraux, "is stronger than all the multiplicity of the world; . . . that significance alone enables man to conquer chaos and to master destiny."

Wright saw his destiny—that combination of forces before which man feels powerless—in terms of a quick and casual violence inflicted upon him by both family and community. His response was likewise violent, and it has been his need to give that violence significance which has shaped his writings.

What were the ways by which other Negroes confronted their destiny?

In the South of Wright's childhood there were three general ways: They could accept the role created for them by the whites and perpetually resolve the resulting conflicts through the hope and emotional catharsis of Negro religion; they could repress their dislike of Jim Crow social relations while striving for a middle way of respectability, becoming—consciously or unconsciously—the accomplices of the whites in oppressing their brothers; or they could reject the situation, adopt a criminal attitude, and carry on an unceasing psychological scrimmage with the whites, which often flared forth into physical violence.

Wright's attitude was nearest the last. Yet in it there was an all-important qualitative difference: it represented a groping for *individual* values, in a black community whose values were what the young Negro critic, Edward Bland, has defined as "pre-individual." And herein lay the setting for the extreme conflict set off, both within his family and in the community, by Wright's assertion of individuality. The clash was sharpest on the psychological level, for, to quote Bland:

In the pre-individualistic thinking of the Negro the stress is on the group. Instead of seeing in terms of the individual, the Negro sees in terms of "races," masses of peoples separated from other masses according to color. Hence, an act rarely bears intent against him as a Negro individual. He is singled out not as a person but as a specimen of an ostracized group. He knows that he never exists in his own right but only to the extent that others hope to make the race suffer vicariously through him.

This pre-individual state is induced artificially—like the regression to primitive states noted among cultured inmates of Nazi prisons. The primary technique in its enforcement is to impress the Negro child with the omniscience and omnipotence of the whites to the point that whites appear as a human as Jehovah, and as relentless as a Mississippi flood. Socially it is effected through an elaborate scheme of taboos supported by a ruthless physical violence, which strikes not only the offender but the entire black community. To wander from the paths of behavior laid down for the group is to become the agent of communal disaster.

In such a society the development of individuality depends upon a series of accidents, which often arise, as in Wright's case, from conditions within the Negro family. In Wright's life there was the accident that as a small child he could not distinguish between his fair-skinned grandmother and the white women of the town, thus developing skepticism as to their special status. To this was linked the accident of his having no close contacts with whites until after the child's normal formative period.

But these objective accidents not only link forward to these qualities of rebellion, criminality and intellectual questioning expressed in Wright's work today. They also link backward into the shadow of infancy where environment and consciousness are so darkly intertwined as to require the skill of a psychoanalyst to define their point of juncture. Nevertheless, at the age of four, Wright set the house afire and was beaten near to death by his frightened mother. This beating, followed soon after by his father's desertion of the family, seems to be the initial psychological motivation of his quest for a new identification. While delirious from this beating Wright was haunted "by huge wobbly white bags like the full udders of a cow, suspended from the ceiling above me [and] I was gripped by the fear that they were going to fall and drench me with some horrible liquid . . ."

It was as though the mother's milk had turned acid, and with it the whole pattern of life that had produced the ignorance, cruelty and fear that had fused with mother-love and exploded in the beating. It is significant that the bags were of the hostile color white, and the female symbol that of the cow, the most stupid (and, to the small child, the most frightening) of domestic animals. Here in dream symbolism is expressed an attitude worthy of an Orestes. And the significance of the crisis is increased by virtue of the historical fact that the lower-class Negro family is matriarchal; the child turns not to the father to compensate if he feels mother-rejection, but to the grandmother, or to an aunt—and Wright rejected both of these. Such rejection leaves the child open to psychological insecurity, distrust and all of those hostile environmental forces from which the family functions to protect it.

One of the Southern Negro family's methods of protecting the child is the severe beating—a homeopathic dose of the violence generated by black and white relationships. Such beatings as Wright's were administered for the child's own good; a good which the child resisted, thus giving family relationships an undercurrent of fear and hostility, which differs qualitatively from that found in patriarchal middle-class families, because here the severe beating is administered by the mother, leaving the child no parental sanctuary. He must ever embrace violence along with maternal tenderness, or else reject, in his helpless way, the mother.

The division between the Negro parents of Wright's mother's generation, whose sensibilities were often bound by their proximity to the slave experience, and their children, who historically and through the rapidity of American change stand emotionally and psychologically much farther away, is quite deep. Indeed, sometimes as deep as the cultural distance between Yeats' *Autobiographies* and a Bessie Smith blues. This is the historical background to those incidents of family strife in *Black Boy* which have caused reviewers to question Wright's judgment of Negro emotional relationships.

We have here a problem in the sociology of sensibility that is obscured by certain psychological attitudes brought to Negro life by whites.

The first is the attitude which compels whites to impute Negroes sentiments, attitudes and insights which, as a group living under certain definite social conditions, Negroes could not humanly possess. It is the identical mechanism which William Empson identifies in literature as "pastoral." It implies that since Negroes possess the richly human virtues credited to them, then their social position is advantageous and should not be bettered; and, continuing syllogistically, the white individual need feel no guilt over his participation in Netro oppression.

The second attitude is that which leads whites to misjudge Negro passion, looking upon it as they do, out of the turgidity of their own frustrated yearning for emotional warmth, their capacity for sensation having been constricted by the impersonal mechanized relationships typical of bourgeois society. The Negro is idealized into a symbol of sensation, of unhampered social and sexual relationships. And when *Black Boy* questions their illusion they are thwarted much in the manner of the occidental who, after observing the erotic character of a primitive dance, "shacks up" with a native woman—only to discover that far from possessing the hair-trigger sexual responses of a Stork Club "babe," she is relatively phlegmatic.

The point is not that American Negroes are primitives, but that as a group their social situation does not provide for the type of emotional relationships attributed them. For how could the South, recognized as a major part of the backward third of the nation, nurture in the black, most brutalized section of its population, those forms of human relationships achievable only in the most highly developed areas of civilization?

Champions of this "Aren't-Negroes-Wonderful?" school of thinking often bring Paul Robeson and Marian Anderson forward as examples of highly developed sensibility, but actually they are only its *promise.* Both received their development from an extensive personal contact with European culture, free from the influences which shape Southern Negro personality. In the United States, Wright, who is the only Negro literary artist of equal caliber, had to wait years and escape to another environment before discovering the moral and ideological equivalents of his childhood attitudes.

Man cannot express that which does not exist—either in the form of dreams, ideas or realities—in his environment. Neither his thoughts nor his feelings, his sensibility nor his intellect are fixed, innate qualities. They are processes which arise out of the interpenetration of human instinct with environment, through the process called experience; each changing and being changed by the other. Negroes cannot possess many of the sentiments attributed to them because the same changes in environment which, through experience, enlarge man's intellect (and thus his capacity for still greater change) also modify his feelings; which in turn increase his sensibility, i.e., his sensitivity, to refinements of impression and subtleties of emotion. The extent of these changes depends upon the quality of political and cultural freedom in the environment.

Intelligence tests have measured the quick rise in intellect which takes place in Southern Negroes after moving north, but little attention has been paid to the mutations effected in their sensibilities. However, the two go hand in hand. Intellectual complexity is accompanied by emotional complexity; refinement of thought, by refinement of feeling. The movement north affects more than the Negro's wage scale, it affects his entire psychosomatic structure.

The rapidity of Negro intellectual growth in the North is due partially to objective factors present in the environment, to influences of the industrial city and to a greater political freedom. But there are also changes within the "inner world." In the North energies are released and given *intellectual* channelization—energies which in most Negroes in the South have been forced to take either a *physical* form or, as with potentially intellectual types like Wright, to be expressed as nervous tension, anxiety and hysteria. Which is nothing mysterious. The human organism responds to environmental stimuli by converting them into either physical and/or intellectual energy. And what is called hysteria is suppressed intellectual energy expressed physically.

The "physical" character of their expression makes for much of the difficulty in understanding American Negroes. Negro music and dances are frenziedly erotic; Negro religious ceremonies violently ecstatic; Negro speech strongly rhythmical and weighted with image and gesture. But there is more in this sensuousness than the unrestraint and insensitivity found in primitive cultures; nor is it simply the relatively spontaneous and undifferentiated responses of a people living in close contact with the soil. For despite Jim Crow, Negro life does not exist in a vacuum, but in the seething vortex of those tensions generated by the most highly industrialized of Western nations. The welfare of the most humble black Mississippi sharecropper is affected less by the flow of the seasons and the rhythm of natural events than by the fluctuations of the stock market; even though, as Wright states of his father, the sharecropper's memories, actions and emotions are shaped by his immediate contact with nature and the crude social relations of the South.

All of this makes the American Negro far different from the "simple" specimen for which he is taken. And the "physical" quality offered as evidence of his primitive simplicity is actually the form of his complexity. The American Negro is a Western type whose social condition creates a state which is almost the reverse of the cataleptic trance: Instead of his consciousness being lucid to the reality around it while the body is rigid, here it is the body which is alert, reacting to pressures which the constricting forces of Jim Crow block off from the transforming, concept-creating activity of the brain. The "eroticism" of Negro expression springs from much the same conflict as that displayed in the violent gesturing of a man who attempts to express a complicated concept with a limited vocabulary; thwarted ideational energy is converted into unsatisfactory pantomime, and his words are burdened with meanings they cannot convey. Here lies the source of the basic ambiguity of *Native Son,* wherein in order to translate Bigger's complicated feelings into universal ideas, Wright had to force into Bigger's consciousness concepts and ideas which his intellect could not formulate. Between Wright's skill and knowledge and the potentials of Bigger's mute feelings lay a thousand years of conscious culture.

In the South the sensibilities of both blacks and whites are inhibited by the rigidly defined environment. For the Negro there is relative safety as long as the impulse toward individuality is suppressed. (Lynchings have occurred because Negroes painted their homes.) And it is the task of the Negro family to adjust the child to the Southern milieu; through it the currents, tensions and impulses generated within the human organism by the flux and flow of events are given their distribution. This also gives the group its distinctive character. Which, because of Negroes' suppressed minority position, is very much in the nature of an elaborate but limited defense mechanism. Its function is dual: to protect the Negro from whirling away from the undifferentiated mass of his people into the unknown, symbolized in its most abstract form by insanity, and most concretely by lynching; and to protect him from those unknown forces *within himself* which might urge him to reach out for that social and human equality which the white South says he cannot have. Rather than throw himself against the charged wires of his prison he annihilates the impulses within him.

The pre-individualistic black community discourages individuality out of self-defense. Having learned through experience that the whole group is punished for the actions of the single member, it has worked out efficient techniques of behavior control. For in many Southern communities everyone knows everyone else and is vulnerable to his opinions. In some communities everyone is "related" regardless of blood-ties. The regard shown by the group for its members, its general communal character and its cohesion are often mentioned. For by comparison with the coldly impersonal relationships of the urban industrial community, its relationships are personal and warm.

Black Boy, however, illustrates that this personal quality, shaped by outer violence and inner fear, is ambivalent. Personal warmth is accompanied by an equally personal coldness, kindliness by cruelty, regard by malice. And these opposites are as quickly set off against the member who gestures toward individuality as a lynch mob forms at the cry of rape. Negro leaders have often been exasperated by this phenomenon, and Booker T. Washington (who demanded far less of Negro humanity than Richard Wright) described the Negro community as a basket of crabs, wherein should one attempt to climb out, the others immediately pull him back.

The member who breaks away is apt to be more impressed by its negative than by its positive character. He becomes a stranger even to his relatives and he interprets gestures of protection as blows of oppression—from which there is no hiding place, because every area of Negro life is affected. Even parental love is given a qualitative balance akin to "sadism." And the extent of beatings and psychological maimings meted out by Southern Negro parents rivals those described by the nineteenth-century Russian writers as characterist of peasant life under the Czars. The horrible thing is that the cruelty is also an expression of concern, of love.

In discussing the inadequacies for democratic living typical of the education provided Negroes by the South, a Negro educator has coined the term *mis-education.* Within the ambit of the black family this takes the form of training the child away from curiosity and adventure, against reaching out for those activities lying beyond the borders of the black community. And when the child resists, the parent discourages him; first with the formula, "That there's for white folks. Colored can't have it," and finally with a beating.

It is not, then, the family and communal violence described by *Black Boy* that is unusual, but that Wright *recognized* and made no peace with its essential cruelty—even when, like a babe freshly emerged from the womb, he could not discern where his own personality ended and it began. Ordinarily both parent and child are protected against this cruelty—seeing it as love and finding subjective sanction for it in the spiritual authority of the Fifth Commandment, and on the secular level in the legal and extralegal structure of the Jim Crow system. The child who did not rebel, or who was unsuccessful in his rebellion, learned a masochistic submissiveness and a denial of the impulse toward Western culture when it stirred within him.

Why then have Southern whites, who claim to "know" the Negro, missed all this? Simply because they, too, are armored against the horror and the cruelty. Either they deny the Negro's humanity and feel no cause to measure his actions against civilized norms; or they protect themselves from their guilt in the Negro's condition and from their fear that their cooks might poison them, or that their nursemaids might strangle their infant charges, or that their field hands might do them violence, by attributing to them a superhuman capacity for love, kindliness and forgiveness. Nor does this in any way contradict their stereotyped conviction that all Negroes (meaning those with whom they have no contact) are given to the most animal behavior.

It is only when the individual, whether white or black, *rejects* the pattern that he awakens to the nightmare of his life. Perhaps much of the South's regressive character springs from the fact that many, jarred by some casual crisis into wakefulness, flee hysterically into the sleep of violence or the coma of apathy again. For the penalty of wakefulness is to encounter ever more violence and horror than the sensibilities can sustain unless translated into some form of social action. Perhaps the impassioned character so noticeable among those white Southern liberals so active in the Negro's cause is due to their sense of accumulated horror; their passion—like the violence in Faulkner's novels—is evidence of a profound spiritual vomiting.

This compulsion is even more active in Wright and the increasing number of Negroes who have said an irrevocable "no" to the Southern pattern. Wright learned that it is not enough merely to reject the white South, but that he had also to reject that part of the South which lay within. As a rebel he formulated that rejection negatively, because it was the negative face of the Negro community upon which he looked most often as a child. It is this he is contemplating when he writes:

> Whenever I thought of the essential bleakness of black life in America, I knew that Negroes had never been allowed to catch the full spirit of Western civilization, that they lived somehow in it but not of it. And when I brooded upon the cultural barrenness of black life, I wondered if clean, positive tenderness, love, honor, loyalty and the capacity to remember were native to man. I asked myself if these human qualities were not fostered, won, struggled and suffered for, preserved in ritual from one generation to another.

But far from implying that Negroes have no capacity for culture, as one critic interprets it, this is the strongest affirmation that they have. Wright is pointing out what should be obvious (especially to his Marxist critics) that Negro sensibility is socially and historically conditioned; that Western culture must be won, confronted like the animal in a Spanish bullfight, dominated by the red shawl of codified experience and brought heaving to its knees.

Wright knows perfectly well that Negro life is a by-product of Western civilization, and that in it, if only one possesses the humanity and humility to see, are to be discovered all those impulses, tendencies, life and cultural forms to be found elsewhere in Western society.

The problem arises because the special condition of Negroes in the United States, including the defensive character of Negro life itself (the "will toward organization" noted in the Western capitalist appears in the Negro as a will to camouflage, to dissimulate), so distorts these forms as to render their recognition as difficult as finding a wounded quail against the brown and yellow leaves of a Mississippi thicket—even the spilled blood blends with the background. Having himself been in the position of the quail—to expand the metaphor—Wright's wounds have told him both the question and the answer which every successful hunter must discover for himself: "Where would I hide if *I* were a wounded quail?" But perhaps that requires more sympathy with one's quarry than most hunters possess. Certainly it requires such a sensitivity to the shifting guises of humanity under pressure as to allow them to identify themselves with the human content, whatever its outer form; and even with those Southern Negroes to whom Paul Robeson's name is only a rolling sound in the fear-charged air.

Let us close with one final word about the blues: Their attraction lies in this, that they at once express both the agony of life and the possibility of conquering it through sheer toughness of spirit. They fall short of tragedy only in that they provide no solution, offer no scapegoat but the self. Nowhere in America today is there social or political action based upon the solid realities of Negro life depicted in *Black Boy;* perhaps that is why, with its refusal to offer solutions, it is like the blues. Yet in it thousands of Negroes will for the first time see their destiny in public print. Freed here of fear and the threat of violence, their lives have at last been organized, scaled down to possessable proportions. And in this lies Wright's most important achievement: He has converted the American Negro impulse toward self-annihilation and "going-under-ground" into a will to confront the world, to evaluate his experience honestly and throw his findings unashamedly into the guilty conscience of America.   [1945]

James Baldwin

Everybody's Protest Novel

In *Uncle Tom's Cabin,* that cornerstone of American social protest fiction, St. Clare, the kindly master, remarks to his coldly disapproving Yankee cousin, Miss Ophelia, that, so far as he is able to tell, the blacks have been turned over to the devil for the benefit of the whites in this world—however, he adds thoughtfully, it may turn out in the next. Miss Ophelia's reaction is, at least, vehemently right-minded: "This is perfectly horrible!" she exclaims. "You ought to be ashamed of yourselves!"

Miss Ophelia, as we may suppose, was speaking for the author; her exclamation is the moral, neatly framed, and incontestable like those improving mottoes sometimes found hanging on the walls of furnished rooms. And, like these mottoes, before which one invariably flinches, recognizing an insupportable, almost an indecent glibness, she and St. Clare are terribly in earnest. Neither of them questions the medieval morality from which their dialogue springs: black, white, the devil, the next world—posing its alternatives between heaven and the flames—were realities for them as, of course, they were for their creator. They spurned and were terrified of the darkness, striving mightily for the light; and considered from this aspect, Miss Ophelia's exclamation, like Mrs. Stowe's novel, achieves a bright, almost a lurid significance, like the light from a fire which consumes a witch. This is the more striking as one considers the novels of Negro oppression written in our own, more enlightened day, all of which say only: "This is perfectly horrible! You ought to be ashamed of yourselves!" (Let us ignore, for the moment, those novels of oppression written by Negroes, which add only a raging, near-paranoiac postscript to this statement and actually reinforce, as I hope to make clear later, the principles which activate the oppression they decry.)

Uncle Tom's Cabin is a very bad novel, having, in its self-righteous, virtuous sentimentality, much in common with *Little Women.* Sentimentality, the ostentatious parading of excessive and spurious emotion, is the mark of dishonesty, the inability to feel; the wet eyes of the sentimentalist betray his aversion to experience, his fear of life, his arid heart; and it is always, therefore, the signal of secret and violent inhumanity, the mask of cruelty; *Uncle Tom's Cabin*—like its multitudinous, hard-boiled descendants—is a catalogue of violence. This is explained by the nature of Mrs. Stowe's subject matter, her laudable determination to flinch from nothing in presenting the complete picture; an explanation which falters only if we pause to ask whether or not her picture is indeed complete; and what constriction or failure of perception forced her to so depend on the description of brutality—unmotivated, senseless—and to leave unanswered and unnoticed the only important question: what it was, after all, that moved her people to such deeds.

But this, let us say, was beyond Mrs. Stowe's powers; she was not so much a novelist as an impassioned pamphleteer; her book was not intended to do anything more than prove that slavery was wrong; was, in fact, perfectly horrible. This makes material for a pamphlet but it is hardly enough for a novel; and the only question left to ask is why we are bound still within the same constriction. How is it that we are so loath to make a further journey than that made by Mrs. Stowe, to discover and reveal something a little closer to the truth?

But that battered word, truth, having made its appearance here, confronts one immediately with a series of riddles and has, moreover, since so many gospels are preached, the unfortunate tendency to make one belligerent. Let us say, then, that truth, as used here, is meant to imply a devotion to the human being, his freedom and fulfillment; freedom which cannot be legislated, fulfillment which cannot be charted. This is the prime concern, the frame of reference; it is not to be confused with a devotion to Humanity which is too easily equated with a devotion to a Cause; and Causes, as we know, are notoriously blood-thirsty. We have, as it seems to me, in this most mechanical and interlocking of civilizations, attempted to lop this creature down to the status of a time-saving invention. He is not, after all, merely a member of a Society or a Group or a deplorable conundrum to be explained by Science. He is—and how old-fashioned the words sound!—something more than that, something resolutely indefinable, unpredictable. In overlooking, denying, evading his complexity—which is nothing more than the disquieting complexity of ourselves—we are diminished and we perish; only within this web of ambiguity, paradox, this hunger, danger, darkness, can we find at once ourselves and the power that will free us from ourselves. It is this power of revelation which is the business of the novelist, this journey toward a more vast reality which must take precedence over all other claims. What is today parroted as his Responsibility—which seems to mean that he must make formal declaration that he is involved in, and affected by, the lives of other people and to say something improving about this somewhat self-evident fact—is, when he believes it, his corruption and our loss; moreover, it is rooted in, interlocked with and intensifies this same mechanization. Both *Gentleman's Agreement* and *The Postman Always Rings Twice* exemplify this terror of the human being, the determination to cut him down to size. And in *Uncle Tom's Cabin* we may find foreshadowing of both: the formula created by the necessity to find a lie more palatable than the truth has been handed down and memorized and persists yet with a terrible power.

It is interesting to consider one more aspect of Mrs. Stowe's novel, the method she used to solve the problem of writing about a black man at all. Apart from her lively procession of field hands, house niggers, Chloe, Topsy, etc.—who are the stock, lovable figures presenting no problem—she has only three other Negroes in the book. These are the important ones and two of them may be dismissed immediately, since we have only the author's word that they are Negro and they are, in all other respects, as white as she can make them. The two are George and Eliza, a married couple with a wholly adorable child—whose quaintness, incidentally, and whose charm, rather put one in mind of a darky bootblack doing a buck and wing to the clatter of condescending coins. Eliza is a beautiful, pious hybrid, light enough to pass—the heroine of *quality* might, indeed, be her reincarnation—differing from the genteel mistress who was overseered her education only in the respect that she is a servant. George is darker, but makes up for it by being a mechanical genius, and is, moreover, sufficiently un-Negroid to pass through town, a fugitive from his master, disguised as a Spanish gentleman, attracting no attention whatever beyond admiration. They are a race apart from Topsy. It transpires by the end of the novel, through one of those energetic, last-minute convolutions of the plot, that Eliza has some connection with French gentility. The figure from whom the novel takes its name, Uncle Tom, who is a figure of controversy yet, is jet-black, wooly-haired, illiterate; and he is phenomenally forbearing. He has to be; he is black; only through this forbearance can he survive or triumph. (C*f*. Faulkner's preface to *The Sound and the Fury:* These others were not Compsons. They were black:—They endured.) His triumph is metaphysical, unearthly; since he is black, born without the light, it is only through humility, the incessant mortification of the flesh, that he can enter into communion with God or man. The virtuous rage of Mrs. Stowe is motivated by nothing so temporal as a concern for the relationship of men to one another—or, even, as she would have claimed, by a concern for their relationship to God—but merely by a panic of being hurled into the flames, of being caught in traffic with the devil. She embraced this merciless doctrine with all her heart, bargaining shamelessly before the throne of grace: God and salvation becoming her personal property, purchased with the coin of her virtue. Here, black equates with evil and white with grace; if, being mindful of the necessity of good works, she could not cast out the blacks—a wretched, huddled mass, apparently, claiming, like an obsession, her inner eye—she could not embrace them either without purifying them of sin. She must cover their intimidating nakedness, robe them in white, the garments of salvation; only thus could she herself be delivered from ever-present sin, only thus could she bury, as St. Paul demanded, "the carnal man, the man of the flesh." Tom, therefore, her only black man, has been robbed of his humanity and divested of his sex. It is the price for that darkness with which he has been branded.

Uncle Tom's Cabin, then, is activated by what might be called a theological terror, the terror of damnation; and the spirit that breathes in this book, hot, self-righteous, fearful, is not different from that spirit of medieval times which sought to exorcize evil by burning witches; and is not different from that terror which activates a lynch mob. One need not, indeed, search for examples so historic or so gaudy; this is a warfare waged daily in the heart, a warfare so vast, so relentless and so powerful that the interracial handshake or the interracial marriage can be as crucifying as the public hanging or the secret rape. This panic motivates our cruelty, this fear of the dark makes it impossible that our lives shall be other than superficial; this, interlocked with and feeding our glittering, mechanical, inescapable civilization which has put to death our freedom.

This, notwithstanding that the avowed aim of the American protest novel is to bring greater freedom to the oppressed. They are forgiven, on the strength of these good intentions, whatever violence they do to language, whatever excessive demands they make of credibility. It is, indeed, considered the sign of a frivolity so intense as to approach decadence to suggest that these books are both badly written and wildly improbable. One is told to put first things first, the good of society coming before the niceties of style or characterization. Even if this were incontestable—for what exactly is the "good" of society?—it argues an insuperable confusion, since literature and sociology are not one and the same; it is impossible to discuss them as if they were. Our passion for categorization, life neatly fitted into pegs, has led to an unforeseen, paradoxical distress; confusion, a breakdown of meaning. Those categories which were meant to define and control the world for us have boomeranged us into chaos; in which limbo we whirl, clutching the straws of our definitions. The "protest" novel, so far from being disturbing, is an accepted and comforting aspect of the American scene, ramifying that framework we believe to be so necessary.

Whatever unsettling questions are raised are evanescent, titillating; remote, for this has nothing to do with us, it is safely ensconced in the social arena, where, indeed, it has nothing to do with anyone, so that finally we receive a very definite thrill of virtue from the fact that we are reading such a book at all. This report from the pit reassures us of its reality and its darkness and of our own salvation; and "As long as such books are being published," an American liberal once said to me, "everything will be all right."

But unless one's ideal of society is a race of neatly analyzed, hard-working ciphers, one can hardly claim for the protest novels the lofty purpose they claim for themselves or share the present optimism concerning them. They emerge for what they are: a mirror of our confusion, dishonesty, panic, trapped and immobilized in the sunlit prison of the American dream. They are fantasies, connecting nowhere with reality, sentimental; in exactly the same sense that such movies as *The Best Years of Our Lives* or the works of Mr. James M. Cain are fantasies. Beneath the dazzling pyrotechnics of these current operas one may still discern, as the controlling force, the intense theological preoccupations of Mrs. Stowe, the sick vacuities of *The Rover Boys*. Finally, the aim of the protest novel becomes something very closely resembling the zeal of those alabaster missionaries to Africa to cover the nakedness of the natives, to hurry them into the pallid arms of Jesus and thence into slavery. The aim has now become to reduce all Americans to the compulsive, bloodless dimensions of a guy named Joe.

It is the peculiar triumph of society—and its loss—that it is able to convince those people to whom it has given inferior status of the reality of this decree; it has the force and the weapons to translate its dictum into fact, so that the allegedly inferior are actually made so, insofar as the societal realities are concerned. This is a more hidden phenomenon now than it was in the days of serfdom, but it is no less implacable. Now, as then, we find ourselves bound, first without, then within, by the nature of our categorization. And escape is not effected through a bitter railing against this trap; it is as though this very striving were the only motion needed to spring the trap upon us. We take our shape, it is true, within and against that cage of reality bequeathed us at our birth; and yet it is precisely through our dependence on this reality that we are most endlessly betrayed. Society is held together by our need; we bind it together with legend, myth, coercion, fearing that without it we will be hurled into the void, within which, like the earth before the Word was spoken, the foundations of society are hidden. From this void—ourselves—it is the function of society to protect us; but it is only this void, our unknown selves, demanding, forever, a new act of creation, which can save us—"from the evil that is in the world." With the same motion, at the same time, it is this toward which we endlessly struggle and from which, endlessly, we struggle to escape.

It must be remembered that the oppressed and the oppressor are bound together within the society; they accept the same criteria, they share the same beliefs, they both alike depend on the same reality. Within this cage it is romantic, more, meaningless, to speak of a "new" society as the desire of the oppressed, for that shivering dependence on the props of reality which he shares with the *Herrenvolk* makes a truly "new" society impossible to conceive. What is meant by a new society is one in which inequalities will disappear, in which vengeance will be exacted; either there will be no oppressed at all, or the oppressed and the oppressor will change places. But, finally, as it seems to me, what the rejected desire is, is an elevation of status, acceptance within the present community. Thus, the African, exile, pagan, hurried off the auction block and into the fields, fell on his knees before that God in Whom he must now believe; who had made him, but not in His image. This tableau, this impossibility, is the heritage of the Negro in America: *Wash me,* cried the slave to his Maker, *and I shall be whiter, whiter than snow!* For black is the color of evil; only the robes of the saved are white. It is this cry, implacable on the air and in the skull, that he must live with. Beneath the widely published catalogue of brutality—bringing to mind, somehow, an image, a memory of church-bells burdening the air—is this reality which, in the same nightmare notion, he both flees and rushes to embrace. In America, now, this country devoted to the death of the paradox—which may, therefore, be put to death by one—his lot is as ambiguous as a tableau by Kafka. To flee or not, to move or not, it is all the same; his doom is written on his forehead, it is carried in his heart. In *Native Son,* Bigger Thomas stands on a Chicago street corner watching airplanes flown by white men racing against the sun and "Goddamn" he says, the bitterness bubbling up like blood, remembering a million indignities, the terrible, rat-infested house, the humiliation of home-relief, the intense, aimless, ugly bickering, hating it; hatred smoulders through these pages like sulphur fire. All of Bigger's life is controlled, defined by his hatred and his fear. And later, his fear drives him to murder and his hatred to rape; he dies, having come, through this violence, we are told, for the first time, to a kind of life, having for the first time redeemed his manhood. Below the surface of this novel there lies, as it seems to me, a continuation, a complement of that monstrous legend it was written to destroy. Bigger is Uncle Tom's descendant, flesh of his flesh, so exactly opposite a portrait that, when the books are placed together, it seems that the contemporary Negro novelist and the dead New England woman are locked together in a deadly, timeless battle; the one uttering merciless exhortations, the other shouting curses. And, indeed, within this web of lust and fury, black and white can only thrust and counter-thrust, long for each other's slow, exquisite death; death by torture, acid, knives and burning; the thrust, the counter-thrust, the longing making the heavier that cloud which blinds and suffocates them both, so that they go down into the pit together. Thus has the cage betrayed us all, this moment, our life, turned to nothing through our terrible attempts to insure it. For Bigger's tragedy is not that he is cold or black or hungry, not even that he is American, black; but that he has accepted a theology that denies him life, that he admits the possibility of his being sub-human and feels constrained, therefore, to battle for his humanity according to those brutal criteria bequeathed him at his birth. But our humanity is our burden, our life; we need not battle for it; we need only to do what is infinitely more difficult—that is, accept it. The failure of the protest novel lies in its rejection of life, the human being, the denial of his beauty, dread, power, in its insistence that it is his categorization alone which is real and which cannot be transcended.   [1949]

T. S. Eliot

American Literature
and the American Language[1]

It is almost exactly forty-eight years ago that I made my first appearance on a public platform before a large audience. This was at the graduation exercises of the Class of 1905 of Smith Academy, an offshoot of this University; and my part in the ceremony was to

[1] An address delivered at Washington University, St. Louis, Missouri, on June 9th, 1953.

deliver the valedictory poem of the year. I was informed afterwards, by one of my teachers, that the poem itself was excellent, as such poems go, but that my delivery was very bad indeed. Since then I have made some progress in elocution, and I have been more often criticized for the content of my speeches than for my manner of delivery; but I knew that today I should experience something like the trepidation which I well remember feeling on that evening so long ago. When I sat down to prepare my notes for this address, I found myself distracted by so many memories of my early years, that I was tempted either to talk about nothing else, or to pass them all over in silence. The first alternative would have produced something too personal and autobiographic for the dignity of this occasion; the second would have meant the suppression of feelings which I do not wish to suppress. I shall therefore, before proceeding to my subject, say something to indicate what it means to me to be here in St. Louis and to be speaking at Washington University in the hundredth year since its foundation; and I trust that a preamble somewhat longer than usual will not be amiss.

It is the fact that this is the centennial year of the University that gives me the excuse, as well as the stronger urge, to allude to my own upbringing. The early history of this University which my grandfather served with tireless devotion until his death, is inextricably involved for me in family and personal history. I never knew my grandfather: he died a year before my birth. But I was brought up to be very much aware of him: so much so, that as a child I thought of him as still the head of the family—a ruler for whom *in absentia* my grandmother stood as viceregent. The standard of conduct was that which my grandfather had set; our moral judgments, our decisions between duty and self-indulgence, were taken as if, like Moses, he had brought down the tables of the Law, any deviation from which would be sinful. Not the least of these laws, which included injunctions still more than prohibitions, was the law of Public Service: it is no doubt owing to the impress of this law upon my infant mind that, like other members of my family, I have felt, ever since I passed beyond my early irresponsible years, an uncomfortable and very inconvenient obligation to serve upon committees. This original Law of Public Service operated especially in three areas: the Church, the City, and the University. The Church meant, for us, the Unitarian Church of the Messiah, then situated in Locust Street, a few blocks west of my father's house and my grandmother's house; the City was St. Louis—the utmost outskirts of which touched on Forest Park, terminus of the Olive Street streetcars, and to me, as a child, the beginning of the Wild West; the University was Washington University, then housed in a modest building in lower Washington Avenue. These were the symbols of Religion, the Community and Education: and I think it is a very good beginning for any child, to be taught that personal and selfish aims should be subordinated to the general good which they represent.

Unlike my father, my uncles, my brother, and several of my cousins, I was never enrolled as an undergraduate in Washington University, but was sent to another institution with which also there were family associations. But the earlier part—and I believe, the most important part—of my education is what I received in that preparatory department of the University which was named Smith Academy. My memories of Smith Academy are on the whole happy ones; and when, many years ago, I learned that the school had come to an end, I felt that a link with the past had been painfully broken. It was a good school. There one was taught, as is now increasingly rare everywhere, what I consider the essentials: Latin and Greek, together with Greek and Roman history, English and American history, elementary mathematics, French and German. Also English! I am happy to remember that in those days English composition was still called *Rhetoric*. Lest you infer that the curriculum was incredibly primitive, I will add that there was a laboratory, in which physical and chemical experiments were performed successfully by the more adroit. As I failed to pass my entrance examination in physics, you will not be surprised that I have forgotten the name of the master who taught it. But I remember other names of good teachers, my gratitude to whom I take this opportunity of recording: Mr. Jackson in Latin, Mr. Robinson in Greek, Mr. Rowe—though I was not one of his good pupils—in mathematics, Madam Jouvet-Kauffmann and Miss Chandler in French and German respectively. Mr. Hatch, who taught English, commended warmly my first poem, written as a class exercise, at the same time asking me suspiciously if I had had any help in writing it. Mr. Jeffries I think taught modern history; our ancient history was taught by the Greek and Latin masters. Well! so far as I am educated, I must pay my first tribute to Smith Academy; if I had not been well taught there, I should have been unable to profit elsewhere. And so far as I am badly educated, that is attributable to laziness and caprice. And before passing from the subject of Smith Academy, I wish to say that I remember it as a good school also because of the boys who were there with me: it seems to me that, for a school of small numbers, we were a well-mixed variety of local types.

Many other memories have invaded my mind, since I received the invitation to speak to you today; but I think these are enough to serve as a token of my thoughts and feelings. I am very well satisfied with having been born in St. Louis; in fact I think I was fortunate to have been born here, rather than in Boston, or New York, or London.

The title I have chosen for this address seems to indicate that I have two subjects. Why am I talking about both: 'American literature', and 'the American language'? First, because they are related, and second because they must be distinguished. It is profitable to clear our minds about the meaning of the term 'the American language' before proceeding to talk of American literature. As I have a reputation for affecting pedantic precision, a reputation I should not like to lose, I will add that I shall not ask 'what is literature?' However various may be people's notions as to what printed matter is literature and what is not, such differences of taste and judgment do not affect my problem.

My attention was recently called to this question of the differences between the English and the American language, on receiving a copy of a new American dictionary. It appeared to me an excellent dictionary of its size, and likely to be useful in England as well as in this country; and to those interested in the making of dictionaries and the problems arising in the definition of words, I commend also a pamphlet by one of the editors, Mr. David B. Guralnik, which struck me as very sound sense. But I was puzzled by the sub-title: it is called a dictionary 'of the American language'. Perhaps I am unconsciously bi-lingual, so that whichever language I hear or read seems to me my own; but certainly the vast majority of the words in this dictionary are words belonging to both America and England, and having the same meaning in both. And the definitions seemed to me to be written in English too. True, the spelling, where English and American usage differ, was the American spelling: but this presents no difficulty in England, where various editions of the work of Noah Webster (a famous lexicographer who I believe married my great-aunt) are in current use. And about spelling, I do not believe in hard and fast rules, and least of all in the hard and fast rules of champions of simplified spelling, such as the late Bernard Shaw. I hold that a word is something more than the noise it makes: it is also the way it looks on the page. I am averse to simplified spelling which destroys all traces of a word's origin and history. But I think, for example, that the English would do well to omit, from a word like 'labour', the superfluous U, which appears to be merely an etymological error. As to whether 'centre' should be spelt 'centre' or 'center', that seems to me a matter of indifference. There is much to be said for the American spelling 'catalog'; on the other hand I distrust simplifications of spelling that tend to alter pronounciation, as, for example, the shortening of 'programme' to 'program', which throws the stress onto the first syllable. And I think that the advocates of a systematic simplified spelling—such as those who recently introduced a Bill in Parliament—overlook the fact that in attempting to fix spelling phonetically, they are also attempting to fix pronunciation: and both pronunciation and spelling, in both England and America, must inevitably change from age to age under the pressure of usage and convenience.

Apart from the differences of spelling and pronunciation, the only other important difference which I discovered between this dictionary and the standard dictionaries in England, is that a number of words are included, which have not yet found their way into the latter. I was gratified, for instance, to find *grifter* and *shill,* two words which I first encountered in a fascinating book about one specialized area of the American vocabulary, called *The Big Con.* And about such words as *grifter* and *shill* I am willing to risk a prediction. Either they will disappear from the American vocabulary, to be replaced by newer shinier words with the same meaning, or, if they become permanently settled, as Dr. Guralnik expects, they will find their way into the English vocabulary as well, and eventually into a supplement to the great Oxford dictionary. They will first appear in the vocabulary of that very large section of British society whose speech is constantly enriched from the films, and will make their way through the tabloid press to *The Times,* in *The Times* proceeding from the levity of the fourth editorial article to the solemnity of the first editorial article; and so their dictionary status in Britain will be assured. Many new words, of course, are ephemeral; and as Dr. Guralnik, in the essay to which I have referred, ruefully admits, a lexicographer may make the mistake of admitting a word to his dictionary just as it is on the point of going out of fashion: a mistake not unlike that of buying shares in a company just before its compulsory liquidation. Words can even disappear, and come into currency again after a period of seclusion. When I was a small boy, in this city, I was reproved by my family for using the vulgar phrase 'O.K.'. Then there was a period during which it seemed to have expired; but at some subsequent date it came to life again, and twenty-odd years ago swept like a tidal wave over England, to establish itself in English speech. As for its respectability here, I hold the most convincing piece of evidence yet: it occurs in a cable I received from Professor Cardwell.

Apart from some differences of spelling, pronunciation and vocabulary, there are between English and American a number of differences of idiom, for the most part reciprocally intelligible; there are also a few dangerous idioms, the same phrases with totally different meanings—in some cases leading to awkward misunderstanding and embarrassment. The sum total of these differences, however, does not seem to me to go so far as to justify us in speaking of English and American as different languages; the differences are no greater than between English as spoken in England and as spoken in Ireland, and negligible compared to the difference between English and Lowland Scots. But we must carry the question further, and ask: is it probable that speech in England and speech in America are developing in such a way that we can predict the eventual division into two languages, so distinct that each country will provide one more foreign language for the school curriculum of the other?

Perhaps we can draw some conclusions from the transformations of languages in the past. The obvious examples, of course, are the decline of Latin and its transmutation into the several Romance languages; and the development from Sanskrit, through Pali, of the modern Indian languages Bengali, Mahratti and Gujarati. I make no pretence of being a philologist; but even to a person untrained in that science there is a striking parallel between the relation of Italian to Latin, and the relation of Pali to Sanskrit. It would at first sight seem within the bounds of possibility, that in the course of time American speech and writing might come to differ as much from present-day English, as Italian and Bengali differ from Latin and Sanskrit.

The question has, of course, no bearing on the literature of today; and far from presenting a pleasing prospect to a living author, it is one which he must shudder to contemplate. Even if we refrain from calling our works 'immortal', we all of us like to believe that what we write will go on being read for a very long time indeed. We cannot relish the thought that our poems and plays and novels will, at best, be preserved only in texts heavily annotated by learned scholars, who will dispute the meaning of many passages and will be completely in the dark as to how our beautiful lines should be pronounced. Most of us, we know, have a pretty good chance of oblivion anyway; but to those of us who succeed in dying in advance of our reputations, the assurance of a time when our writings will only be grappled with by two or three graduate students in Middle Anglo-American 42 B is very distasteful. As it would not have pleased a late Latin poet in Southern Gaul to be told by a soothsayer that his language, over which he took so much trouble, would in a few centuries be replaced by something more up-to-date.

We must also face the possibility, if we can draw any conclusions from the metamorphosis of Latin, of a long period of time during which everything written in our language will be arid, pedantic and imitative. It is, of course, a necessary condition for the continuance of a literature, that the language should be in constant change. If it is changing it is alive; and if it does not change, then new writers have no escape from imitating classics of their literature without hope of producing anything so good. But when a change occurs such as that which led to the supersession of Latin by French, Italian, Spanish and Portuguese, the new languages have to grow up from the roots of the old, that is, from the common speech of uneducated people, and for a long time will be crude and capable of expressing only a narrow range of simple thoughts and feelings. The old culture had to decline, before the new cultures could develop. And for the development of a new and crude language into a great language, how much is not due to the happy accident of a few writers of great genius, such as Dante or Shakespeare?

Is the parallel with Latin and Sanskrit, however, valid? Is such a transformation, for better or worse, of English into two distinct languages on the two sides of the Atlantic likely to take place? I think that the circumstances nowadays are very different. If such a transformation should occur, it will be due to social, political and economic changes very different from anything that is happening now, and on such a vast scale that we cannot even imagine them. There is, I suspect, behind the thinking of such students of language as Mr. Mencken (whose monumental book on the American language is a philologist's picnic) a mistaken assimilation of language to politics. Such prophets seem to be issuing a kind of linguistic Declaration of Independence, an act of emancipation of American from English. But these patriotic spirits may be overlooking the other side of the picture.

In October last occurred an event which, while not as spectacular as the descent of Col. Lindbergh at Le Bourget in 'The Spirit of St. Louis', is equally remarkable in its kind. For the first time, apparently, an American robin, well named *Turdus migratorius,* crossed the Atlantic under its own power, 'favoured' according to the report, by 'a period of strong westerly weather'. This enterprising bird was also intelligent, for it chose to alight on Lundy Island, off the coast of Devon, which happens to be a bird sanctuary. Of course even birds, nowadays, are not allowed to travel without undergoing official inquisition, so our robin was trapped, photographed, and released; and, I hope, provided with a ration book. It is interesting to speculate on the future of this pilgrim. Either he (or she, for the sex is not stated) will be followed by another of the opposite sex, in which event we may expect that England will soon be populated by American robins; or else our lone pioneer must make the best of it, and breed with the English thrush, who is not *migratorius* but *musicus*. In the latter event, the English must look out for a new species of thrush, with a faint red spot on the male breast in springtime; a species which, being a blend of *migratorius* and *musicus,* should become known as the troubador-bird, or organ-grinder.

Now, if the American robin can perform such feats, what cannot the American language do? Favoured by very strong westerly weather, of course. Unless you yourselves draw a linguistic iron curtain (and I think Hollywood, to say nothing of the proprietors of *Time, Life, The New Yorker* and other periodicals, would object to that) you cannot keep the American language out of England. However fast the American language moves, there will be always behind it the pattering of feet: the feet of the great British public eager for a new word or phrase. The feet may sometimes be a long way behind, but they are tireless. In the long run, I don't see how you can keep the American language to yourselves. Britain is of course eager also to export, though baffled by tariff walls; but it seems that at present the current language flows from west to east. The last war strengthened the flow in that direction; and people from Land's End to John o'Groats are nourished on American films, the speech of which they understand, I have been told, a good deal better than the American public understand that of British films. It may be, that this west-east current will be the stronger for a long time to come: but, whatever happens, I believe that there will always be a movement in one direction or the other. So that, against the influences towards the development of separate languages, there will always be other influences tending towards fusion.

It has seemed to me worth while to get this question of language out of the way before attempting to say what I mean by American Literature: as I believe that we are now justified in speaking of what has never, I think, been found before, two literatures in the same language.

When, however, I assert that the term 'American literature' has for me a clear and distinct meaning, I do not believe that this meaning is wholly definable; and I shall try to explain in what respect I think it is undesirable to try to define it. Like many other terms, the term 'American literature' has altered and developed its meaning in the course of time. It means something different for us today from what it could have meant a hundred years ago. It has much fuller meaning now than it could have had then. By this I do not mean that American literature of the nineteenth century is less deserving of the name than American literature of the twentieth. I mean that the phrase could not mean quite the same thing to the writers of a century ago that it means to us; that it is only in retrospect that their Americanness is fully visible. At the beginning, to speak of 'American literature' would have been only to establish a geographical distinction: Jonathan Edwards could hardly have understood what the term means today. Early American literature, without the achievements of later writers, would merely be literature written in English by men born or living in America. Washington Irving is less distinctively American than Fenimore Cooper. I suspect that the Leatherstocking novels, to a contemporary English reader, must have appeared to depict, not a new and different society, but the adventures of English pioneers in new and undeveloped country; just as I suppose they still have, for English boys, much the same fascination as good tales of adventure of early life in British dominions and colonies anywhere. (Cooper has suffered, like Walter Scott, from being read in early youth, and by many people never read again: it remained for D. H. Lawrence, who discovered Cooper later in life, to write probably the most brilliant of critical essays on him.) The English reader of the day, certainly, would hardly have recognized in Natty Bumppo, a new kind of man: it is only in retrospect that such differences are visible.

The literature of nineteenth century New England, however, is patently marked by something more than the several personalities of its authors; it has its own particular *civilized* landscape and the ethos of a local society of English origin with its own distinct traits. It remains representative of New England, rather than of America: and Longfellow, Whittier, Bryant, Emerson, Thoreau—and even the last of the pure New Englanders, Robert Frost—yield more of themselves, I believe, to people of New England origin than to others; they have, in addition to their qualities of wider appeal, a peculiar nostalgic charm for New Englanders settled elsewhere. And as for the writer who to me is the greatest among them, Nathaniel Hawthorne, it seems to me that there is something in Hawthorne that can best be appreciated by the reader with Calvinism in his bones and witch-hanging (*not* witch-hunting) on his conscience. So the landmarks I have chosen for the identification of American literature are not found in New England. I am aware that my choice may appear arbitrary; but in making such wide generalizations one must always take the risk. The three authors of my choice are Poe, Whitman, and Mark Twain.

I must hasten to explain what I do *not* mean. I do not imply that these writers are necessarily greater than others whom I have mentioned or could mention. Nor am I suggesting that these three men were individually 'more American' than the others. Nor am I suggesting that American literature today *derives* from these three. Nor am I assuming that from a study of these three writers one could arrive at a formula of Americanism in literature. What their common American characteristics may be, is something I should consider it folly to attempt to define; and in seeking for their common qualities, one might easily overlook the essence of each.

I wish to emphasize the point that I am not concerned, in making such a selection, with questions of *influence.* A comparison of Poe and Whitman is illuminating. Amongst American poets, it is undoubtedly Poe and Whitman who have enjoyed the highest reputation abroad, both in English-speaking lands and in countries where they are known in translation. What is remarkable about the posthumous history of Poe is the fact that his influence in France, on and through the intermediary of three great French poets, has been immense; and that his influence in America and in England has been negligible. I cannot think of any good poet, here or in England, who has been sensibly influenced by Poe—except perhaps Edward Lear. How is it that Poe can be chosen as a distinctively American author, when there is so little evidence that any American poet since Poe has written any differently than he would have written if Poe had never lived?

To Walt Whitman, on the other hand, a great influence on modern poetry has been attributed. I wonder if this has not been exaggerated. In this respect he reminds me of Gerard Manley Hopkins—a lesser poet than Whitman, but also a remarkable innovator in style. Whitman and Hopkins, I think, both found an idiom and a metric perfectly suited for what they had to say; and very doubtfully adaptable to what anyone else has to say. One reason why such writers as Whitman and Hopkins attract imitators, is that in their less inspired verse they tend—as a writer with a highly idiosyncratic idiom may be tempted to do—to imitate themselves; and it is a man's imitation of himself, rather than his best work, that is most catching and most easily imitated. A true disciple is impressed by what his master has to say, and *consequently* by his way of saying it; an imitator—I might say, a borrower—is impressed chiefly by the way the master said it. If he manages to mimic his master well enough, he may succeed even in disguising from himself the fact that he has nothing to say.

It is possible, on the other hand, that the influence of Mark Twain may prove to have been considerable. If so, it is for this reason: that Twain, at least in *Huckleberry Finn,* reveals himself to be one of those writers, of whom there are not a great many in any literature, who have discovered a new way of writing, valid not only for themselves but for others. I should place him, in this respect, even with Dryden and Swift, as one of those rare writers who have brought their language up to date, and in so doing, 'purified the dialect of the tribe'. In this respect I should put him above Hawthorne: though no finer a stylist, and in obvious ways a less profound explorer of the human soul. Superficially, Twain is equally local, strongly local. Yet the Salem of Hawthorne remains a town with a particular tradition, which could not be anywhere but where it is; whereas the Mississippi of Mark Twain is not only the river known to those who voyage on it or live beside it, but the universal river of human life—more universal, indeed, than the Congo of Joseph Conrad. For Twain's readers anywhere, the Mississippi is *the* river. There is in Twain, I think, a great unconscious depth, which gives *Huckleberry Finn* this symbolic value: a symbolism all the more powerful for being uncalculated and unconscious.

Here we arrive at two characteristics which I think must be found together, in any author whom I should single out as one of the landmarks of a national literature: the strong local flavour combined with unconscious universality. We must not suppose that the former can always be identified on superficial examination. What is identifiably local about Poe? Apart from *The Gold Bug* and a few other prose pieces, there is little in the work of Poe that appears to be based on the landscapes and the types of human being that he knew. His favourite settings are imaginary romantic places: a Paris or a Venice which he had never visited. It is very puzzling; but then Poe remains an enigma, a stumbling-block for the critic. Perhaps Poe's local quality is due simply to the fact that he never had the opportunity to travel, and that when he wrote about Europe, it was a Europe with which he had no direct acquaintance. A cosmopolitan experience might have done Poe more harm than good; for cosmopolitanism can be the enemy of universality—it may dissipate attention in superficial familiarity with the streets, the cafés and some of the local dialect of a number of foreign capitals; whereas universality can never come except through writing about what one knows thoroughly. Dostoevski is none the less universal, for having stopped in Russia. Perhaps all that one can say of Poe is that his was a type of imagination that created its own dream world; that anyone's dream world is conditioned by the world in which he lives; and that the real world behind Poe's fancy was the world of the Baltimore and Richmond and Philadelphia that he knew.

You will have noticed that the three authors on whom I am concentrating my attention are three of those who have enjoyed the greatest reputation abroad. It is possible for foreigners to be mistaken about contemporary writers: I know that the contemporary English estimate of the importance of some French writer, or the contemporary French estimate of the importance of some English writer, can be grotesque. But I think that when enough time has elapsed the continued appreciation of foreigners is likely to indicate that an author does combine the local with the universal. The foreigner may at first be attracted by the differences: an author is found interesting because he is so unlike anything in the foreigner's own literature. But a vogue due to novel differences will soon fade out; it will not survive unless the foreign reader recognizes, perhaps unconsciously, identity as well as difference. When we read a novel of Dostoevski, or see a play by Tchekhov, for the first time, I think that we are fascinated by the odd way in which Russians behave; later, we come to recognize that theirs is merely an odd way of expressing thoughts and feelings which we all share. And, though it is only too easy for a writer to be local without being universal, I doubt whether a poet or novelist can be universal without being local too. Who could be more Greek than Odysseus? Or more German than Faust? Or more Spanish than Don Quixote? Or more American than Huck Finn? Yet each one of them is a kind of archetype in the mythology of all men everywhere.

Having got to this point, let me now suggest that a national literature comes to consciousness at the stage at which any young writer must be aware of several generations of writers behind him, in his own country and language, and amongst these generations several writers generally acknowledged to be of the great. The importance of this background should provide him with models for imitation. The young writer, certainly, should not be consciously bending his talent to conform to any supposed American or other tradition. The writers of the past, especially of the immediate past, in one's own place and language may be valuable to the young writer simply as something definite to rebel against. He will recognize the common ancestry: but he needn't necessarily *like* his relatives. For models to imitate, or for styles from which to learn, he may often more profitably go to writers of another country and another language, or of a remoter age. Some of my strongest impulse to original development, in early years, has come from thinking: 'here is a man who has said something, long ago or in another language, which somehow corresponds to what I want to say now; let me see if I can't do what he has done, in my own language—in the language of my own place and time.'

Such considerations should put us all on guard against an attitude of narrow national pride in our literature. Especially against asking questions such as 'is this new writer truly American or not? Does his work conform to the standards of America, to our definitions of what constitutes Americanism in literature?' It is obvious that such a critical censorship could only stifle originality. The cry has so often been raised about new writers: 'This isn't English!' or 'this isn't French!' or whatever the language may be. Also, there is always the danger of overvaluing the local product just because it is local; and of unconsciously judging our own writers by less exacting standards than those we apply to writers of other nations. We are, in every country, always exposed to that danger. And to narrow your admission to subject matter or to style already accepted, would be to affirm that what is American has been settled once for all. A living literature is always in process of change; contemporaneous living literatures are always, through one or more authors, changing each other; and the literature written in America in future generations will, you may be sure, render obsolete any formulations of 'what is American' based on the work of writers up to and including those now writing.

From time to time there occurs some revolution, or sudden mutation of form and content in literature. Then, some way of writing which has been practised for a generation or more, is found by a few people to be out of date, and no longer to respond to contemporary modes of thought, feeling and speech. A new kind of writing appears, to be greeted at first with disdain and derision; we hear that the tradition has been flouted, and that chaos has come. After a time it appears that the new way of writing is not destructive but re-creative. It is not that we have repudiated the past, as the obstinate enemies—and also the stupidest supporters—of any new movement like to believe; but that we have enlarged our conception of the past; and that in the light of what is new we see the past in a new pattern. We might now consider such a revolution as that which has taken place in poetry, both in England and in America, during the last forty years.

In talking about such an event, one must mention names. So, in order to be quite fair, I explain that I choose names as typical illustrations, that the poets mentioned are not necessarily valued in the order in which their names will occur, and that they are not all necessarily superior to all of the poets who are not mentioned. Furthermore, in any such literary revolution there is an overlap: some of the poets who continue to write in what is usually called a 'more traditional' manner are first-rate in their kind, and by the verdict of history may prove to be more highly prized than many of the poets who have written in newer ways.

In the first decade of the century the situation was unusual. I cannot think of a single living poet, in either England or America, then at the height of his powers, whose work was capable of pointing the way to a young poet conscious of the desire for a new idiom. It was the tail-end of the Victorian era. Our sympathies, I think, went out to those who are known as the English poets of the nineties, who were all, with one exception, dead. The exception was W. B. Yeats, who was younger, more robust, and of more temperate habits than the poets of the Rhymers' Club with whom he had associated in his youth. And Yeats himself had not found his personal speech; he was a late developer; when he emerged as a great modern poet, about 1917, we had already reached a point such that he appeared not as a precursor but as an elder and venerated contemporary. What the poets of the nineties had bequeathed to us besides the new tone of a few poems by Ernest Dowson, John Davidson and Arthur Symons, was the assurance that there was something to be learned from the French poets of the Symbolist Movement—and most of them were dead, too.

I do not propose to define the change that came about; I am merely tracing its course. Such a transformation as we have experienced in this century cannot be altogether attributed to one group of poets, still less to one individual. As so often happens in the fields of science, when a new discovery is made, it has been preceded by a number of scattered investigators who have happened to be groping, each at first in ignorance of the efforts of the others, in the same direction. In retrospect, it is often impossible to attribute the discovery to the genius of one scientist alone. The *point de repère* usually and conveniently taken, as the starting-point of modern poetry, is the group denominated 'imagists' in London about 1910. I was not there. It was an Anglo-American group: literary history has not settled the question, and perhaps never will, whether imagism itself, or the name for it, was invented by the American Ezra Pound or the Englishman T. E. Hulme. The poets in the group seem to have been drawn together by a common attraction towards modern poetry in French, and a common interest in exploring the possibilities of development through study of the poetry of other ages and languages. If imagism became more quickly and widely known in America than in England, that was largely because of the zealous, though sometimes misguided activity of Amy Lowell, who assumed the role of Advertising Manager for a movement which, on the whole, is chiefly important because of the stimulus it gave to later developments.

I think it is just to say that the pioneers of twentieth century poetry were more conspicuously the Americans than the English, both in number and in quality. Why this should have been must remain a matter for conjecture. I do not believe that it is attributable to the fact that so many more Britons were killed in the first war: the most remarkable of the British poets killed in that war whose work has been published, is in my opinion Isaac Rosenberg, who was outside the movement. Perhaps the young Americans of that age were less oppressed by the weight of the Victorian tradition, more open to new influences and more ready for experiment. (So far as my observation goes, I should say in general, of contemporary verse, that the most dangerous tendency of American versifiers is towards eccentricity and formlessness, whereas that of English versifiers is rather towards conventionality and reversion to the Victorian type.) But, looking at my own generation, the names that come immediately to mind are those of Ezra Pound, W. C. Williams, Wallace Stevens—and you may take pride in one who is a St. Louisan by birth: Miss Marianne Moore. Even of a somewhat younger generation: Cummings, Hart Crane, Ransom, Tate. And I am choosing names only from among those whose work places them among the more radical experimenters: among poets of an intermediate type of technique the names of distinction are as numerous here as in England. And this is a new thing. In the nineteenth century, Poe and Whitman stand out as solitary international figures; in the last forty years, for the first time, there has been assembled a *body* of American poetry which has made its total impression in England and in Europe.

I am merely stating what seem to me cold facts. During the thirties the tide seemed to be turning the other way: the representative figure of that decade is W. H. Auden, though there are other British poets of the same generation whose best work will I believe prove equally permanent. Now, I do not know whether Auden is to be considered as an English or as an American poet: his career has been useful to me in providing me with an answer to the same question when asked about myself, for I can say: 'whichever Auden is, I suppose I must be the other'. Today there are several interesting younger poets in both countries, and England has acquired some valuable recruits from Wales. But my point in making this hurried review is simply this. In my time, there have been influences in both directions, and I think, to the mutual profit of literature on both sides of the Atlantic. But English and American poetry do not in consequence tend to become merged into one common international type, even though the poetry of today on one side of the ocean may show a closer kinship with poetry on the other side, than either does with that of an earlier generation. I do not think that a satisfactory statement of what constitutes the difference between an English and an American 'tradition' in poetry could be arrived at: because the moment you produce your definition, and the neater the definition is, the more surely some poet will turn up who doesn't fit into it at all, but who is nevertheless definitely either English or American. And the tradition itself, as I have said long ago, is altered by every new writer of genius. The difference will remain undefined, but it will remain; and this is I think as it should be: for it is because they are different that English poetry and American poetry can help each other, and contribute towards the endless renovation of both.

Henry Nash Smith

The Myth of the Garden and Turner's Frontier Hypothesis

By far the most influential piece of writing about the West produced during the nineteenth century was the essay on "The Significance of the Frontier in American History" read by Frederick Jackson Turner before the American Historical Association at Chicago in 1893. The "frontier hypothesis" which he advanced on that occasion revolutionized American historiography and eventually made itself felt in economics and sociology, in literary criticism, and even in politics.[1]

Reprinted by permission of the publishers from *Virgin Land: The American West as Symbol and Myth* by Henry Nash Smith, Cambridge, Mass.: The Belknap Press of Harvard University Press. Copyright 1950 by the President and Fellows of Harvard College, renewed 1978 by Henry Nash Smith.

[1] *References on the Significance of the Frontier in American History,* compiled by Everett E. Edwards (United States Department of Agriculture Library, Bibliographical Contributions, No. 25, 2nd ed. [April, 1939]. Mimeographed), lists 124 items bearing on the subject, ranging in date from Franklin's "Observations on the Peopling of Countries" (1751) to 1939. A passage from a radio address by Franklin D. Roosevelt in 1935 which Dr. Edwards quotes in his excellent Introduction illustrates the political application of Turner's ideas: "Today we can no longer escape into virgin territory. We must master our environment . . . We have been compelled by stark necessity to unlearn the too comfortable superstition that the American soil was mystically blessed with every kind of immunity to grave economic maladjustments . . ." (p.3).

Turner's central contention was that "the existence of an area of free land, its continuous recession, and the advance of American settlement westward explain American development."[2] This proposition does not sound novel now because it has been worked into the very fabric of our conception of our history, but in 1893 it was a polemic directed against the two dominant schools of historians: the group interpreting American history in terms of the slavery controversy, led by Hermann Edouard von Holst, and the group headed by Turner's former teacher, Herbert B. Adams of Johns Hopkins, who explained American institutions as the outgrowth of English, or rather ancient Teutonic germs planted in the New World. Turner maintained that the West, not the proslavery South or the antislavery North, was the most important among American sections, and that the novel attitudes and institutions produced by the frontier, especially through its encouragement of democracy, had been more significant than the imported European heritage in shaping American society.

To determine whether Turner's hypothesis is or is not a valid interpretation of American history forms no part of the intention of this book.[3] The problem here is to place his main ideas in the intellectual tradition that has been examined in earlier chapters. Whatever the merits or demerits of the frontier hypothesis in explaining actual events, the hypothesis itself developed out of the myth of the garden. Its insistence on the importance of the West, its affirmation of democracy, and its doctrine of geographical determinism derive from a still broader tradition of Western thought that would include Benton and Gilpin as well, but its emphasis on agricultural settlement places it clearly within the stream of agrarian theory that flows from eighteenth-century England and France through Jefferson to the men who elaborated the ideal of a society of yeoman farmers in the Northwest from which Turner sprang. Turner's immersion in this stream of intellectual influence had an unfortunate effect in committing him to certain archaic assumptions which hampered his approach to twentieth-century social problems. But one must not forget that the tradition was richer than these assumptions, and that it conferred on him the authority of one who speaks from the distilled experience of his people.[4] If the myth of the garden embodied certain erroneous judgments made by these people concerning the economic forces that had come to dominate American life, it was still true to their experience in the large, because it expressed beliefs and aspirations as well as statistics. This is not the only kind of historical truth, but it is a kind historians need never find contemptible.

[2]"The Significance of the Frontier in American History," in *The Early Writings of Frederick Jackson Turner, with a List of All His Works Compiled by Everett E. Edwards and an Introduction by Fulmer Mood* (Madison, Wisconsin, 1938), p. 186.

[3]A growing body of scholarship is being devoted to this challenging question. George W. Pierson has called attention to inconsistencies in Turner's doctrines and has inquired into the extent of their currency among historians at the present time: "The Frontier and Frontiersman of Turner's Essays: A Scrutiny of the Foundations of the Middle Western Tradition," *Pennsylvania Magazine of History and Biography,* LXIV, 449–478 (October, 1940); "The Frontier and American Institutions: A Criticism of the Turner Theory," *New England Quarterly,* XV, 224–255 (June, 1942); "American Historians and the Frontier Hypothesis in 1941," *Wisconsin Magazine of History,* XXVI, 36–60, 170–185 (September, December, 1942). I am indebted to Professor Pierson for many ideas, especially the remark he quotes from a colleague to the effect that Turner's frontiersman closely resembles the stock eighteenth-century picture of the small farmer of Britain (*Wisconsin Magazine of History,* XXVI, 183–184) and the suggestion that Turner's "poetic interpretations" revived "the grandest ideas that had gone to make up the American legend" (*idem*).

[4]James C. Malin points out that most of Turner's ideas were "in the air." He remarks that great thinkers are normally "the beneficiaries of the folk process and are probably seldom so much true creators as channels through which the folk process finds its fullest expression in explicit language . . ." "Space and History: Reflections on the Closed-Space Doctrines of Turner and Mackinder and the Challenge of Those Ideas by the Air Age," *Agricultural History,* XVIII, 67–68, April, 1944).

Turner's most important debt to his intellectual tradition is the ideas of savagery and civilization that he uses to define his central factor, the frontier. His frontier is explicitly "the meeting point between savagery and civilization."[5] For him as for his predecessors, the outer limit of agricultural settlement is the boundary of civilization, and in his thought as in that of so many earlier interpreters we must therefore begin by distinguishing two Wests, one beyond and one within this all-important line.

From the standpoint of economic theory the wilderness beyond the frontier, the realm of savagery, is a constantly receding area of free land. Mr. Fulmer Mood has demonstrated that Turner derived this technical expression from a treatise on economics by Francis A. Walker used as a text by one of his teachers at Johns Hopkins, Richard T. Ely. In Walker's analysis Turner found warrant for his belief that free land had operated as a safety valve for the East and even for Europe by offering every man an opportunity to acquire a farm and become an independent member of society. Free land thus tended to relieve poverty outside the West, and on the frontier itself it fostered economic equality. Both these tendencies made for an increase of democracy.[6] Earlier writers from the time of Franklin had noted that the West offered freedom and subsistence to all,[7] but Turner restated the idea in a more positive form suggested by his conviction that democracy, the rise of the common man, was one of the great movements of modern history.

In an oration delivered in 1883 when he was still an undergraduate he had declared: "Over all the world we hear mankind proclaiming its existence, demanding its rights. Kings begin to be but names, and the sons of genius, springing from the people, grasp the real sceptres. The reign of aristocracy is passing; that of humanity begins."[8] Although "humanity" is a broad term, for Turner it referred specifically to farmers. He conceived of democracy as a trait of agricultural communities. About this time, for example, he wrote in his Commonplace Book that historians had long occupied themselves with "noble warriors, & all the pomp and glory of the higher class—But of the other phase, of the common people, the lowly tillers of the soil, the great mass of humanity . . . history has hitherto said but little." And he fully accepted the theory of small landholdings that underlay the cult of the yeoman. He planned to develop the idea in an "Oration on Peasant Proprietors in U.S." (by which he meant small farmers tilling their own land).

> . . . the work of the Cobden Club on Land Tenure [he wrote] giving the systems of the various countries the paper on America—opens by showing how uninteresting is the subject being as it is purely peasant proprietorship— In this simplicity of our land system lies one of the greatest factors in our progress. Enlarge on the various systems & show the value of it here—point out the fact that if our lands in the west had not been opened to & filled with foreign emigrant it is not unlikely that they would have fallen into the hands of capitalists

---

[5]*Early Writings,* p. 187.

[6]Fulmer Mood, "The Development of Frederick Jackson Turner as a Historical Thinker," *Publications of the Colonial Society of Massachusetts,* XXXIV: *Transactions 1937–1942* (Boston, 1943), pp. 322–325.

[7]Turner copied into a Commonplace Book that he kept in 1886, during his first year of teaching, a quotation ascribed to Franklin: "The boundless woods of America which are sure to afford freedom and subsistence to any man who can bait a hook or pull a trigger" (Commonplace Book [II], p. [1]. Turner Papers, Henry E. Huntington Library). The idea occurs often in Franklin but I have not been able to find these words.

[8]"The Poet of the Future," delivered at the Junior Exhibition, University of Wisconsin, May 25, 1883, and reported in full in the Madison *University Press* (May 26, 1883), p. 4 (clipping in Turner Papers, Henry E. Huntington Library).

& hav been made great estates—e.g. Dalyrymple farm— Show effects of great estates in Italy—in Eng.[9]

In systems of land tenure, he felt, lay the key to the democratic upsurge that had reached a climax in the nineteenth century:

> It is not by Contrat Socials that a nation wins freedom & prosperity for its people—; it is by attention to minor details—like this—it is by evolution—
>
> Show place of F. R. [French Revolution]—ring in Shelleys Prometheus this was an awakening but now—in our own age is the real revolution going on which is to raise *man* from his low estate to his proper *dignity* (enlarge from previous oration)—in this grand conception it is not an anticlimax to urge the value—the essential necessity of such institutions as the peasant proprietors—a moving force, all the stronger that it works quietly in the great movement.[1]

This is the theoretical background of the proposition in the 1893 essay that "democracy [is] born of free land,"[2] as well as of the celebrated pronouncement made twenty years later: "American democracy was born of no theorist's dream; it was not carried in the Susan Constant to Virginia, nor in the Mayflower to Plymouth. It came stark and strong and full of life out of the American forest, and it gained new strength each time it touched a new frontier."[3]

But while economic theory still underlies this later statement, the change of terminology has introduced new and rich overtones. We have been transferred from the plane of the economist's abstractions to a plane of metaphor, and even of myth—for the American forest has become almost an enchanted wood, and the image of Antaeus has been invoked to suggest the power of the Western earth. Such intimations reach beyond logical theory. They remind us that the wilderness beyond the limits of civilization was not only an area of free land; it was also nature. The idea of nature suggested to Turner a poetic account of the influence of free land as a rebirth, a regeneration, a rejuvenation of man and society

---

[9]Commonplace Book [I], 1883, pp. [25–27]. Turner Papers, Henry E. Huntington Library.

[1]*Ibid.,* pp. [49–53].

[2]*Early Writings,* p. 221.

[3]"The West and American Ideals," an address delivered at the University of Washington, June 17, 1914, *Washington Historical Quarterly,* V, 245 (October, 1914. When Turner revised this address for inclusion in the volume of collected papers *The Frontier in American History* in 1920, he omitted the words "stark and strong and full of life" (New York, 1920, reprint ed., 1931, p. 293). Although Turner repudiated the "germ theory" of constitutional development in his 1893 essay (*Early Writings,* p. 188), he had accepted it for a time after he left Herbert B. Adams' seminar at Johns Hopkins. Reviewing the first two volumes of Theodore Roosevelt's *The Winning of the West* in the Chicago *Dial* in August of 1889 (X, 72), he remarked that "the old Germanic 'tun'" reappeared in the "forted village" of early Kentucky and Tennessee, the "folkmoot" in popular meetings of the settlers, and the "witenagemot" in representative assemblies like the Transylvania legislature. "These facts," he added, "carry the mind back to the warrior-legislatures in the Germanic forests, and forward to those constitutional conventions now at work in our own newly-made states in the Far West; and they make us proud of our English heritage." In an undergraduate address he had asserted that "The spirit of individual liberty slumbered in the depths of the German forest" from the time of the barbarian invasions of Rome until it burst forth in the American and French Revolutions (Madison *University Press* [May 26, 1883], p. 4). Turner's discovery of the American frontier as a force encouraging democracy may exhibit some imaginative persistence of this association between desirable political institutions and a forest.

constantly recurring where civilization came into contact with wilderness along the frontier.[4]

Rebirth and regeneration are categories of myth rather than of economic analysis, but ordinarily Turner kept his metaphors under control and used them to illustrate and vivify his logical propositions rather than as a structural principle or a means of cognition: that is, he used them rhetorically not poetically. The nonpoetic use of a vivid metaphor is illustrated in a speech he delivered in 1896:

> Americans had a safety valve for social danger, a bank account on which they might continually draw to meet losses. This was the vast unoccupied domain that stretched from the borders of the settled area to the Pacific Ocean. . . . No grave social problem could exist while the wilderness at the edge of civilizations [*sic*] opened wide its portals to all who were oppressed, to all who with strong arms and stout heart desired to hew out a home and a career for themselves. Here was an opportunity for social development continually to begin over again, wherever society gave signs of breaking into classes. Here was a magic fountain of youth in which America continually bathed and was rejuvenated.[5]

The figure of the magic fountain is merely a rhetorical ornament at the end of a paragraph having a rational structure and subject to criticism according to recognized canons. But sometimes, especially when the conception of nature as the source of occult powers is most vividly present, Turner's metaphors threaten to become themselves a means of cognition and to supplant discursive reasoning. This seems to happen, for example, in an essay he wrote for the *Atlantic* in 1903. After quoting a clearly animistic passage from Lowell's Harvard Commemoration Ode on how Nature had shaped Lincoln of untainted clay from the unexhausted West, "New birth of our new soil, the first American," Turner builds an elaborate figurative structure:

> Into this vast shaggy continent of ours poured the first feeble tide of European settlement. European men, institutions, and ideas were lodged in the American wilderness, and this great American West took them to her bosom, taught them a new way of looking upon the destiny of the common man, trained them in adaptation to the conditions of the New World, to the creation of new institutions to meet new needs; and ever as society on her

---

[4]A characteristic phrase is the reference to "this rebirth of American society" that has gone on, decade after decade, in the West (from an essay in the *Atlantic,* 1896, reprinted in *The Frontier in American History,* p. 205). In his undergraduate Commonplace Book Turner had jotted down, among notes for an oration, "See Emerson's preface to 'Nature' . . ." and had added part of a sentence: ". . . let us believe in the eternal genesis, the freshness & value of things present, act as though, just created, we stood looking a new world in the face and investigate for ourselves and act regardless of past ideas" (Commonplace Book [I], p. [3]). This is quite Emersonian; it might well be a paraphrase of the familiar first paragraph of Emerson's essay: "Why should not we also enjoy an original relation to the universe? Embosomed for a season in nature, whose floods of life stream around and through us, and invite us, by the powers they supply, to action proportioned to nature, why should we grope among the dry bones of the past, or put the living generation into masquerade out of its faded wardrobe?" (*Complete Works,* Volume I: *Nature, Addresses, and Lectures* [Boston, 1903], p. [3]). Turner said in 1919 that he had been impressed with Woodrow Wilson's emphasis on Walter Bagehot's idea of growth through "breaking the cake of custom" (Frederick Jackson Turner to William E. Dodd, Cambridge, Mass., October 7, 1919, copy in Turner Papers, Henry E. Huntington Library). The phrase appears in the *Atlantic* essay (*The Frontier in American History,* p. 205).

[5]Address at the dedication of a new high school building at Turner's home town of Portage, Wisconsin, January 1, 1896, reported in the Portage *Weekly Democrat,* January 3, 1896 (clipping in Turner Papers, Henry E. Huntington Library).

eastern border grew to resemble the Old World in its social forms and its industry, ever, as it began to lose faith in the ideal of democracy, she opened new provinces, and dowered new democracies in her most distant domains with her material treasures and with the ennobling influence that the fierce love of freedom, the strength that came from hewing out a home, making a school and a church, and creating a higher future for his family., furnished to the pioneer.[6]

It would be difficult to maintain that all these metaphors are merely ornamental. Is it wholly meaningless, for example, that the West, the region close to nature, is feminine, while the East, with its remoteness from nature and its propensity for aping Europe, is neuter?

In the passage just quoted, a beneficent power emanating from nature is shown creating an agrarian utopia in the West. The myth of the garden is constructed before our eyes. Turner is asserting as fact a state of affairs that on other occasions he recognized as merely an ideal to be striven for. Earlier in the same essay, for example, he had summarized Jefferson's "platform of political principles" and his "conception that democracy should have an agricultural basis."[7] The "should" easily becomes "did": Jefferson's agrarian ideal proves to be virtually identical with the frontier democracy that Turner believed he had discovered in the West. To imagine an ideal so vividly that it comes to seem actual is to follow the specific procedure of poetry.

The other member of the pair of ideas which defined the frontier for Turner was that of civilization. If the idea of nature in the West provided him with a rich and not always manageable store of metaphorical coloring, his use of the idea of civilization had the equally important consequence of committing him to the theory that all societies, including those of successive Wests, develop through the same series of progressively higher stages. Mr. Mood has traced this conception also to Ely and to Walker, and back of them to the German economic theorist Friedrich List.[8] But, as we have had occasion to notice earlier in this study, the idea had been imported into the United States from France soon after 1800 and by the 1820's had become one of the principal instruments for interpreting the agricultural West.

Turner's acceptance of this theory involved him in the difficulties that it had created for earlier observers of frontier society, such as Timothy Flint. For the theory of social stages was basically at odds with the conception of the Western farmer as a yeoman surrounded by utopian splendor. Instead, it implied that the Western farmer was a coarse and unrefined representative of a primitive stage of social evolution. Turner's adoption of these two contradictory theories makes it difficult for him to manage the question of whether frontier character and society, and frontier influence on the rest of the country, have been good or bad. As long as he is dealing with the origins of democracy in the West he evidently considers frontier influence good. A man who refers to "the familiar struggle of West against East, of democracy against privileged classes"[9] leaves no doubt concerning his own

---

[6]*The Frontier in American History,* pp. 255, 267.

[7]*Ibid.,* p. 250.

[8]*Publications of the Colonial Society of Massachusetts,* XXXIV, 304–307. Mr. Mood says that the idea of applying the theory of evolution to social phenomena was the "fundamental, unifying concept" of Turner's early writings (p. 304), but adds that the *a priori* idea of a sequence of social stages "can be asserted to be, as a universal rule . . . fallacious. . . . It is one component element in Turner's [1893] essay that will not now stand the test of inspection" (p. 307n.).

[9]*The Frontier in American History,* p. 121 (1908).

allegiance. This attitude was in fact inevitable as long as one maintained the doctrine that frontier society was shaped by the influence of free land, for free land was nature, and nature in this system of ideas is unqualifiedly benign. Indeed, it is itself the norm of value. There is no way to conceive possible bad effects flowing from the impact of nature on man and society.

But when Turner invokes the concept of civilization, the situation becomes more complex. His basic conviction was that the highest social values were to be found in the relatively primitive society just within the agricultural frontier. But the theory of social stages placed the highest values at the other end of the process, in urban industrial society, amid the manufacturing development and city life which Jefferson and later agrarian theorists had considered dangerous to social purity. Turner wavered between the two views. In the 1893 essay, to take a minute but perhaps significant bit of evidence, he referred to the evolution of each successive region of the West "into a higher stage"—in accord with the orthodox theory of civilization and progress. When he revised the essay for republication in 1899, he realized that such an assumption might lead him into inconsistency and substituted "a different industrial stage."[1]

But he could not always maintain the neutrality implied in this revision. For one thing, he strongly disapproved of the Western love of currency inflation, which he considered a consequence of the primitive state of frontier society. "The colonial and Revolutionary frontier," he asserted in the 1893 essay, "was the region whence emanated many of the worst forms of an evil currency," and he pointed out that each of the periods of lax financial integrity in American history had coincided with the rise of a new set of frontier communities. The Populist agitation for free coinage of silver was a case in point.

> Many a state that now declines any connection with the tenets of the Populists [he wrote] itself adhered to such ideas in an earlier stage of the development of the state. A primitive society can hardly be expected to show the intelligent appreciation of the complexity of business interests in a developed society.[2]

In his revision of the essay in 1899 Turner noted with satisfaction that Wisconsin had borne out his principles:

> Wisconsin, to take an illustration, in the days when it lacked varied agriculture and complex industrial life, was a stronghold of the granger and greenback movements; but it has undergone an industrial transformation, and in the last presidential contest Mr. Bryan carried but one county in the state.[3]

Here the evolution of society from agrarian simplicity toward greater complexity is assumed to bring about improvement.

Yet if Turner could affirm progress and civilization in this one respect, the general course of social evolution in the United States created a grave theoretical dilemma for him. He had based his highest value, democracy, on free land. But the westward advance of civilization across the continent had caused free land to disappear. What then was to become of democracy? The difficulty was the greater because in associating democracy with free land he had inevitably linked it also with the idea of nature as a source of spiritual values. All the overtones of his conception of democracy were therefore tinged

[1]*Early Writings,* pp. 199, 285.

[2]*Ibid.,* p. 222.

[3]*Ibid,,* p. 285.

with cultural primitivism, and tended to clash with the ideal of civilization. In itself this was not necessarily a disadvantage; the conception of civilization had been invoked to justify a number of dubious undertakings in the course of the nineteenth century, including European exploitation of native peoples all over the world. Furthermore, as we have had occasion to observe in studying the literary interpretation of the agricultural West, the theory of social progress through a uniform series of stages was poor equipment for any observer who wished to understand Western farmers. But Turner had accepted the idea of civilization as a general description of the society that had been expanding across the continent, and with the final disappearance of free land this idea was the only remaining principle with which he could undertake the analysis of contemporary American society.

Since democracy for him was related to the idea of nature and seemed to have no logical relation to civilization, the conclusion implied by his system was that post-frontier American society contained no force tending toward democracy. Fourierists earlier in the century, reaching a conclusion comparable to this, had maintained that civilization was but a transitory social stage, and that humanity must transcend it by advancing into the higher stage of "association." Henry George in Turner's own day had announced that progress brought poverty, that civilization embodied a radical contradiction and could be redeemed only by a revolutionary measure, the confiscation of the unearned increment in the value of natural resources. But Turner did not share the more or less revolutionary attitude that lay back of these proposals.[4] On the contrary, he conceived of social progress as taking place within the existing framework of society, that is, within civilization. Whatever solution might be found for social problems would have to be developed according to the basic principles already accepted by society. This meant that his problem was to find a basis for democracy in some aspect of civilization as he observed it about him in the United States. His determined effort in this direction showed that his mind and his standards of social ethics were subtler and broader than the conceptual system within which the frontier hypothesis had been developed, but he was the prisoner of the assumptions he had taken over from the agrarian tradition.[5] He turned to the rather unconvincing idea that the Midwestern state universities might be able to save democracy by producing trained leaders,[6] and later he placed science beside education as another force to which men might turn for aid in their modern perplexity. But these suggestions were not really satisfying to him, and he fell back at last on the faith he had confided to his Commonplace Book as an undergraduate—a faith neither in nature nor in civilization but simply in man, in the common people. In 1924, after reviewing the most urgent of the world's problems, Turner declared with eloquence and dignity:

> I prefer to believe that man is greater than the dangers that menace him; that education and science are powerful forces to change these tendencies and to produce a rational solution of the problems of life on the shrinking planet. I place my trust in the mind of man seeking solutions by intellectual toil rather than by drift and by habit, bold to find new ways of

[4]Frederick Jackson Turner to Merle E. Curti, San Marino, Cal., January 5, 1931. Copy in Turner Papers, Henry E. Huntington Library. Turner says he had not read George before writing the 1893 essay and that he had never accepted the single-tax idea.

[5]Professor Malin has emphasized the fact that in his later career Turner was "baffled by his contemporary world and had no satisfying answer to the closed-frontier formula in which he found himself involved" (*Essays on Historiography,* Lawrence, Kansas, 1946, p. 38).

[6]*The Frontier in American History,* p. 285 (1910).

adjustment, and strong in the leadership that spreads new ideas among the common people of the world; committed to peace on earth, and ready to use the means of preserving it.[7]

This statement is an admission that the notion of democracy born of free land, colored as it is by the primitivism, is not an adequate instrument for dealing with a world dominated by industry, urbanization, and international conflicts. The First World War had shaken Turner's agrarian code of values as it destroyed so many other intellectual constructions of the nineteenth century. He continued to struggle with the grievous problems of the modern world, but his original theoretical weapons were no longer useful.

Turner's predicament illustrates what has happened to the tradition within which he worked. From the time of Franklin down to the end of the frontier period almost a century and a half later, the West had been a constant reminder of the importance of agriculture in American society. It had nourished an agrarian philosophy and an agrarian myth that purported to set forth the character and destinies of the nation. The philosophy and the myth affirmed an admirable set of values, but they ceased very early to be useful in interpreting American society as a whole because they offered no intellectual apparatus for taking account of the industrial revolution. A system which revolved about a half-mystical conception of nature and held up as an ideal a rudimentary type of agriculture was powerless to confront issues arising from the advance of technology. Agrarian theory encouraged men to ignore the industrial revolution altogether, or to regard it as an unfortunate and anomalous violation of the natural order of things. In the restricted but important sphere of historical scholarship, for example, the agrarian emphasis of the frontier hypothesis has tended to divert attention from the problems created by industrialization for a half century during which the United States has become the most powerful industrial nation in the world.[8] An even more significant consequence of the agrarian tradition has been its effect on politics. The covert distrust of the city and of everything connected with industry that is implicit in the myth of the garden has impeded coöperation between farmers and factory workers in more than one crisis of our history, from the time of Jefferson to the present.

The agrarian tradition has also made it difficult for Americans to think of themselves as members of a world community because it has affirmed that the destiny of this country leads her away from Europe toward the agricultural interior of the continent. This tendency is quite evident in Turner.[9] Although he devoted much attention to the diplomatic issues arising out of westward expansion, the frontier hypothesis implied that it would be a last misfortune for American society to maintain close connections with Europe. The

---

[7]"Since the Foundation," an address delivered at Clark University, February 4, 1924, *Publications of the Clark University Library*, VII, No. 3, p. 29. After the words "dangers that menace him" Turner has indicated in his personal copy in the Henry E. Huntington Library (No. 222544) the addition of the following words: "that there are automatic adjustments in progress."

[8]Charles A. Beard makes this point in what seems to me a convincing manner in "The Frontier in American History," *New Republic*, XCVII, 359–362 (February 1, 1939). Professor Malin asserts vigorously that "among other things, the frontier hypothesis is an agricultural interpretation of American history which is being applied during an industrial urban age . . ." ("Mobility and History," *Agricultural History*, XVII, 177, October, 1943).

[9]Benjamin F. Wright has a similar comment in his review of *The Significance of Sections in American History, New England Quarterly*, VI, 631 (September, 1933). Professor Malin calls the fronter hypothesis "an isolationist interpretation in an international age" (*Agricultural History*, XVII, 177). "It seemed to confirm the Americans," he remarks elsewhere, "in their continental isolationism. Was not their United States a unique civilization; was it not superior to that of Europe and Asia?" (*ibid.*, XVIII, 67, April, 1944).

frontier which produced Anderw Jackson, wrote Turner with approval in 1903, was "free from the influence of European ideas and institutions. The men of the 'Western World' turned their backs upon the Atlantic Ocean, and with a grim energy and self-reliance began to build up a society free from the dominance of ancient forms."[1] It was only later, when he was trying to find a theoretical basis for democracy outside the frontier, that Turner criticized the American attitude of "contemptuous indifference" to the social legislation of European countries.[2]

But if interpretation of the West in terms of the idea of nature tended to cut the region off from the urban East and from Europe, the opposed idea of civilization had even greater disadvantages. It not only imposed on Westerners the stigma of social, ethical, and cultural inferiority, but prevented any recognition that the American adventure of settling the continent had brought about an irruption of novelty into history. For the theory of civilization implied that America in general, and the West *a fortiori,* were meaningless except in so far as they managed to reproduce the achievements of Europe. The capital difficulty of the American agrarian tradition is that it accepted the paired but contradictory ideas of nature and civilization as a general principle of historical and social interpretation. A new intellectual system was requisite before the West could be adequately dealt with in literature or its social development fully understood.

Perry Miller

Errand into the Wilderness

[The title of an election sermon preached in 1670 provided the fitting title for an exhibition of New England imprints at the John Carter Brown Library in Brown University, where I delivered this address on May 16, 1952. Only thereafter did I discover that the Reverend Samuel Danforth had also given me a title.

In his own language, Danforth was trying to do what I too am attempting: to make out some deeper configuration in the story than a mere modification, by obvious and natural necessity, of an imported European culture in adjustment to a frontier. He recognized, as

[1] *The Frontier in American History,* p. 253 (1903).

[2] *Ibid.,* p. 294 (1914). In the 1903 article Turner had emphasized the contrast between American democracy, which was "fundamentally the outcome of the experiences of the American people in dealing with the West," and the "modern efforts of Europe to create an artificial democratic order by legislation" (*ibid.,* p. 266). The implication is clearly that American democracy is the opposite of artificial, i.e., natural, and that this natural origin establishes its superiority.

do I, that a basic conditioning factor was the frontier—the wilderness. Even so, the achievement of a personality is not so much the presence of this or that environmental element—no matter how pressing, how terrifying—as the way in which a given personality responds. The real theme is so complex that any simplification does it injustice, though for the sake of communication simplifications are manufactured. Danforth made his simplification by stressing the "errand" more than the "wilderness." So I follow him, and in my context, as in his, "errand" is not a formal thesis but a metaphor.

A metaphor is a vastly different thing from Frederick Jackson Turner's "thesis" that democracy came out of the forest. Happily we no longer are obliged to believe this, although we are ready to recognize, thanks to Turner, that unless we acknowledge the existence of the forest the character of American history is obscure. A newer generation, confessing the importance of Turner's speculations, is concerned with an inherent cultural conflict, in relation to which the forest was, so to speak, as external as the Atlantic Ocean. This ostentatiously simple and monolithic America is in fact a congeries of inner tensions. It has been so from the beginning; it is more so now than at the beginning—as is proved by the frenetic insistence of many Americans that this statement is untrue. Confronted with so gigantic a riddle, the analyst becomes wary of generalizations, though incessantly he strives to comprehend.

In this address, then, I am not thinking, nor in any paper of this volume am I thinking, within the framework of interpretation—the "frontier hypothesis"—that Turner bequeathed us. Immense as is the debt that all seekers after national self-knowledge owe to Turner, we have to insist—at least I do—that he did as much to confuse as to clarify the deepest issue. He worked on the premise—which any Puritan logician (being in this regard a scholastic) could have corrected—that the subject matter of a liberal art determines the form, that the content of a discipline automatically supplies the angle of vision. I might even argue that, by remote implication, the struggle of a Protestant culture in America against its weakening hold on the Puritan insight into this law of the mind, namely, that form controls matter, constitutes one theme of the collection. From Turner's conception of the ruling and compulsive power of the frontier no further avenue could be projected to any cultural synthesis. Ideally, this volume might include a study of Turner as being himself an exemplification—I might more accurately say the foremost victim—of his fallacy, rather than the master of it. However, by now it has become rather the mode to point out the romantic prepossessions of Turner; I mention him not only to salute a great name but also, by calling attention to my dissent from him, to underscore my use of the two concepts, both "errand" and "wilderness," as figures of speech.]

It was a happy inspiration that led the staff of the John Carter Brown Library to choose as the title of its New England exhibition of 1952 a phrase from Samuel Danforth's election sermon, delivered on May 11, 1670: *A Brief Recognition of New England's Errand into the Wilderness.* It was of course an inspiration, if not of genius at least of talent, for Danforth to invent his title in the first place. But all the election sermons of this period—that is to say, the major expressions of the second generation, which, delivered on these forensic occasions, were in the fullest sense community expression—have interesting titles; a mere listing tells the story of what was happening to the minds and emotions of the New England people: John Higginson's *The Cause of God and His People in New-England* in 1663, William Stoughton's *New England's True Interest, Not to Lie* in 1668, Thomas Shepard's *Eye-Salve* in 1672, Urian Oakes's *New England Pleaded With* in 1673, and, climactically and most explicitly, Increase Mather's *A Discourse Concerning the Danger of Apostasy* in 1677.

All of these show by their title pages alone—and, as those who have looked into them know, infinitely more by their contents—a deep disquietude. They are troubled utterances, worried, fearful. Something has gone wrong. As in 1662 Wigglesworth already was saying in verse, God has a controversy with New England; He has cause to be angry and to punish it because of its innumerable defections. They say, unanimously, that New England was sent on an errand, and that it has failed.

To our ears these lamentations of the second generation sound strange indeed. We think of the founders as heroic men—of the towering stature of Bradford, Winthrop, and Thomas Hooker—who braved the ocean and the wilderness, who conquered both, and left to their children a goodly heritage. Why then this whimpering?

Some historians suggest that the second and third generations suffered a failure of nerve; they weren't the men their fathers had been, and they knew it. Where the founders could range over the vast body of theology and ecclesiastical polity and produce profound works like the treatises of John Cotton or the subtle psychological analyses of Hooker, or even such a gusty though wrongheaded book as Nathaniel Ward's *Simple Cobler,* let alone such lofty and righteaded pleas as Roger Williams' *Bloudy Tenent,* all these children could do was tell each other that they were on probation and that their chances of making good did not seem very promising.

Since Puritan intellectuals were thoroughly grounded in grammar and rhetoric, we may be certain that Danforth was fully aware of the ambiguity concealed in his world "errand." It already had taken on the double meaning which it still carries with us. Originally, as the word first took form in English, it meant exclusively a short journey on which an inferior is sent to convey a message or to perform a service for his superior. In that sense we today speak of an "errand boy"; or the husband says that while in town on his lunch hour, he must run an errand for his wife. But by the end of the Middle Ages, errand developed another connotation; it came to mean the actual business on which the actor goes, the purpose itself, the conscious intention in his mind. In this signification, the runner of the errand is working for himself, is his own boss; the wife, while the husband is away at the office, runs her own errands. Now in the 1660's the problem was this: which had New England originally been—an errand boy or a doer of errands? In which sense had it failed? Had it been despatched for a further purpose, or was it an end in itself? Or had it fallen short not only in one or the other, but in both of the meanings? If so, it was indeed a tragedy, in the primitive sense of a fall from a mighty designation.

If the children were in grave doubt about which had been the original errand—if, in fact, those of the founders who lived into the later period and who might have set their progeny to rights found themselves wondering and confused—there is little chance of our answering clearly. Of course, there is no problem about Plymouth Colony. That is the charm about Plymouth: its clarity. The Pilgrims, as we have learned to call them, were reluctant voyagers; they had never wanted to leave England, but had been obliged to depart because the authorities made life impossible for Separatists. They could, naturally, have stayed at home had they given up being Separatists, but that idea simply did not occur to them. Yet they did not go to Holland as though on an errand; neither can we extract the notion of a mission out of the reasons which, as Bradford tells us, persuaded them to leave Leyden for "Virginia." The war with Spain was about to be resumed, and the economic threat was ominous; their migration was not so much an errand as a shrewd forecast, a plan to get out while the getting was good, lest, should they stay, they would be "intrapped or surrounded by their enemies, so as they should neither be able to fight or flie." True, once the decision was taken, they congratulated themselves that they might become a means for propagating the gospel in remote parts of the world, and thus of serving as steppingstones to others in the performance of this great work; nevertheless, the substance of their decision was that they "thought it better to dislodge betimes to some place of better advantage and less danger, if any such could be found." The great hymn that Bradford, looking back in his old age, chanted about the landfall is one of the greatest passages, if not the very greatest, in all New England's literature; yet it does not resound with the sense of a mission accomplished—instead, it vibrates with the sorrow and exultation of suffering, the sheer endurance, the pain and the anguish, with the somberness of death faced unflinchingly:

> May not and ought not the children of these fathers rightly say: Our fathers were English-men which came over this great ocean, and were ready to perish in this wilderness; but they cried unto the Lord, and he heard their voyce, and looked on their adversitie . . . .

We are bound, I think, to see in Bradford's account the prototype of the vast majority of subsequent immigrants—of those Oscar Handlin calls "The Uprooted": they came for better advantage and for less danger, and to give their posterity the opportunity of success.

The Great Migration of 1630 is an entirely other story. True, among the reasons John Winthrop drew up in 1629 to persuade himself and his colleagues that they should com-mit themselves to the enterprise, the economic motive frankly figures. Wise men thought that England was overpopulated and that the poor would have a better chance in the new land. But Massachusetts Bay was not just an organization of immigrants seeking advan-tage and opportunity. It had a positive sense of mission—either it was sent on an errand or it had its own intention, but in either case the deed was deliberate. It was an act of will, perhaps of willfulness. These Puritans were not driven out of England (thousands of their fellows stayed and fought the Cavaliers)—they went of their own accord.

So, concerning them, we ask the question, why? If we are not altogether clear about precisely how we should phrase the answer, this is not because they themselves were reti-cent. They spoke as fully as they knew how, and none more magnificently or cogently than John Winthrop in the midst of the passage itself, when he delivered a lay sermon aboard the flagship *Arbella* and called it "A Modell of Christian Charity." It distinguishes the motives of this great enterprise from those of Bradford's forlorn retreat, and especially from those of the masses who later have come in quest of advancement. Hence, for the stu-dent of New England and of America, it is a fact demanding incessant brooding that John Winthrop selected as the "doctrine" of his discourse, and so as the basic proposition to which, it then seemed to him, the errand was committed, the thesis that God had dis-posed mankind in a hierarchy of social classes, so that "in all times some must be rich, some poor, some highe and eminent in power and dignitie; others mean and in subjec-cion." It is as though, preternaturally sensing what the promise of America might come to signify for the rank and file, Winthrop took the precaution to drive out of their heads any notion that in the wilderness the poor and the mean were ever so to improve themselves as to mount above the rich or the eminent in dignity. Were there any who had signed up under the mistaken impression that such was the purpose of their errand, Winthrop told them that, although other peoples, lesser breeds, might come for wealth or pelf, this mi-gration was specifically dedicated to an avowed end that had nothing to do with incomes. We have entered into an explicit covenant with God, "we have professed to enterprise these Accions vpon these and these ends"; we have drawn up indentures with the Almighty, wherefore if we succeed and do not let ourselves get diverted into making money, He will reward us. Whereas if we fail, if we "fall to embrace this present world and prosecute our carnall intencions, seeking greate things for our selves and our poster-ity, the Lord will surely breake out in wrathe against us be revenged of such a periured people and make us knowe the price of the breache of such a Covenant."

Well, what terms were agreed upon in this covenant? Winthrop could say precisely—
"It is by a mutuall consent through a specially overruleing providence, and a more than
ordinary approbation of the Churches of Christ to seeke out a place of Cohabitation and
Consorteshipp under a due forme of Government both civill and ecclesiasticall." If it
could be said thus concretely, why should there be any ambiguity? There was no doubt
whatsover about what Winthrop meant by a due form of ecclesiastical government: he
meant the pure Biblical polity set forth in full detail by the New Testament, that method
which later generations, in the days of increasing confusion, would settle down to calling
Congregational, but which for Winthrop was no denominational peculiarity but the very
essence of organized Christianity. What a due form of civil government meant, therefore,
became crystal clear: a political regime, possessing power, which would consider its main
function to be the erecting, protecting, and preserving of this form of polity. This due
form would have, at the very beginning of its list of responsibilities, the duty of suppressing heresy, of subduing or somehow getting rid of dissenters—of being, in short, deliberately, vigorously, and consistently intolerant.

Regarded in this light, the Massachusetts Bay Company came on an errand in the second and later sense of the word: it was, so to speak, on its own business. What it set out to
do was the sufficient reason for its setting out. About this Winthrop seems to be perfectly
certain, as he declares specifically what the due forms will be attempting: the end is to improve our lives to do more service to the Lord, to increase the body of Christ, and to preserve our posterity from the corruptions of this evil world, so that they in turn shall work
out their salvation under the purity and power of Biblical ordinances. Because the errand
was so definable in advance, certain conclusions about the method of conducting it were
equally evident: one, obviously, was that those sworn to the covenant should not be allowed to turn aside in a lust for mere physical rewards; but another was, in Winthrop's
simple but splendid words, "we must be knit together in this worke as one man, wee
must entertaine each other in brotherly affection." We must actually delight in each other,
"always having before our eyes our Commission and community in the worke, our community as members of the same body." This was to say, were the great purpose kept
steadily in mind, if all gazed only at it and strove only for it, then social solidarity (within
a scheme of fixed and unalterable class distinctions) would be an automatic consequence.
A society despatched upon an errand that is in its own reward would want no other rewards: it could go forth to possess a land without ever becoming possessed by it; social
gradations would remain eternally what God had originally appointed; there would be no
internal contention among groups or interests, and though there would be hard work for
everybody, prosperity would be bestowed not as a consequence of labor but as a sign of approval upon the mission itself. For once in the history of humanity (with all its sins), there
would be a society so dedicated to a holy cuase that success would prove innocent and triumph not raise up sinful pride or arrogant dissension.

Or, at least, this would come about if the people did not deal falsely with God, if they
would live up to the articles of their bond. If we do not perform these terms, Winthrop
warned, we may expect immediate manifestations of divine wrath; we shall perish out
of the land we are crossing the sea to possess. And here in the 1660's and 1670's, all the
jeremiads (of which Danforth's is one of the most poignant) are castigations of the people
for having defaulted on precisely these articles. They recite the long list of afflictions an
angry God had rained upon them, surely enough to prove how abysmally they had deserted the covenant: crop failures, epidemics, grasshoppers, caterpillars, torrid summers,
arctic winters, Indian wars, hurricanes, shipwrecks, accidents, and (most grievous of all)
unsatisfactory children. The solemn work of the election day, said Stoughton in 1668, is

"Foundation-work"—not, that is, to lay a new one, "but to continue, and strengthen, and beautifie, and build upon that which has been laid." It had been laid in the covenant before even a foot was set ashore, and thereon New England should rest. Hence the terms of survival, let alone of prosperity, remained what had first been propounded:

> If we should so frustrate and deceive the Lords Expectations, that his Covenant-interest in us, and the Workings of his Salvation be made to cease, then All were lost indeed; Ruine upon Ruine, Destruction upon Destruction would come, until one stone were not left upon another.

Since so much of the literature after 1660—in fact, just about all of it—dwells on this theme of declension and apostasy, would not the story of New England seem to be simply that of the failure of a mission? Winthrop's dread was realized: posterity had not found their salvation amid pure ordinances but had, despite the ordinances, yielded to the seductions of the good land. Hence distresses were being piled upon them, the slaughter of King Philip's War and now the attack of a profligate king upon the sacred charter. By about 1680, it did in truth seem that shortly no stone would be left upon another, that history would record of New England that the founders had been great men, but that their children and grandchildren progressively deteriorated.

This would certainly seem to be the impression conveyed by the assembled clergy and lay elders who, in 1679, met at Boston in a formal synod, under the leadership of Increase Mather, and there prepared a report on why the land suffered. The result of their deliberation, published under the title *The Necessity of Reformation,* was the first in what has proved to be a distressingly long succession of investigations into the civic health of Americans, and it is probably the most pessimistic. The land was afflicted, it said, because corruption had proceeded apace; assuredly, if the people did not quickly reform, the last blow would fall and nothing but desolation be left. Into what a moral quagmire this dedicated community had sunk, the synod did not leave to imagination; it published a long and detailed inventory of sins, crimes, misdemeanors, and nasty habits, which makes, to say the least, interesting reading.

We hear much talk nowadays about corruption, most of it couched in generalized terms. If we ask our current Jeremiahs to descend to particulars, they tell us that the republic is going on the rocks, or to the dogs, because the wives of politicians aspire to wear mink coats and their husbands take a moderate five per cent cut on certain deals to pay for the garments. The Puritans were devotees of logic, and the verb "methodize" ruled their thinking. When the synod went to work, it had before it a succession of sermons, such as that of Danforth and the other election-day or fast-day orators, as well as such works as Increase Mather's *A Brief History of the Warr With the Indians,* wherein the decimating conflict with Philip was presented as a revenge upon the people for their transgressions. When the synod felt obliged to enumerate the enormities of the land so that the people could recognize just how far short of their errand they had fallen, it did not, in the modern manner, assume that regeneration would be accomplished at the next election by turning the rascals out, but it digested this body of literature; it reduced the contents to method. The result is a staggering compendium of iniquity, organized into twelve headings.

First, there was a great and visible decay of godliness. Second, there were several manifestations of pride—contention in the churches, insubordination of inferiors toward superiors, particularly of those inferiors who had, unaccountably, acquired more wealth than their betters, and, astonishingly, a shocking extravagance in attire, especially on the part of these of the meaner sort, who persisted in dressing beyond their means. Third, there were heretics, especially Quakers and Anabaptists. Fourth, a notable increase in swearing and a spreading disposition to sleep at sermons (these two phenomena seemed basically connected). Fifth, the Sabbath was wantonly violated. Sixth, family government had decayed, and fathers no longer kept their sons and daughters from prowling at night. Seventh, instead of people being knit together as one man in mutual love, they were full of contention, so that lawsuits were on the increase and lawyers were thriving. Under the eighth head, the synod described the sins of sex and alcohol, thus producing some of the juiciest prose of the period: militia days had become orgies, taverns were crowded; women threw temptation in the way of befuddled men by wearing false locks and displaying naked necks and arms "or, which is more abominable, naked Breasts"; there were "mixed Dancings," along with light behavior and "Company-keeping" with vain persons, wherefore the bastardy rate was rising. In 1672, there was actually an attempt to supply Boston with a brothel (it was suppressed, but the synod was bearish about the future). Ninth, New Englanders were betraying a marked disposition to tell lies, especially when selling anything. In the tenth place, the business morality of even the most righteous left everything to be desired: the wealthy speculated in land and raised prices excessively; "Day-Labourers and Mechanicks are unreasonable in their demands." In the eleventh place, the people showed no disposition to reform, and in the twelfth, they seemed utterly destitute of civic spirit.

"The things here insisted on," said the synod, "have been oftentimes mentioned and inculcated by those whom the Lord has set as Watchmen to the house of Israel." Indeed they had been, and thereafter they continued to be even more inculcated. At the end of the century, the synod's report was serving as a kind of handbook for preachers: they would take some verse of Isaiah or Jeremiah, set up the doctrine that God avenges the iniquities of a chosen people, and then run down the twelve heads, merely bringing the list up to date by inserting the new and still more depraved practices an ingenious people kept on devising. I suppose that in the whole literature of the world, including the satirists of imperial Rome, there is hardly such another uninhibited and unrelenting documentation of a people's descent into corruption.

I have elsewhere endeavored to argue[1] that, while the social or economic historian may read this literature for its contents—and so construct from the expanding catalogue of denunciations a record of social progress—the cultural anthropologist will look slightly askance at these jeremiads; he will exercise a methodological caution about taking them at face value. If you read them all through, the total effect, curiously enough, is not at all depressing: you come to the paradoxical realization that they do not bespeak a despairing frame of mind. There is something of a ritualistic incantation about them; whatever they may signify in the realm of theology, in that of psychology they are purgations of soul; they do not discourage but actually encourage the community to persist in its heinous conduct. The exhortation to a reformation which never materializes serves as a token payment upon the obligation, and so liberates the debtors. Changes there had to be: adaptations to environment, expansion of the frontier, mansions constructed, commercial adventures undertaken. These activities were not specifically nominated in the bond Winthrop had framed. They were thrust upon the society by American experience; because they were not only works of necessity but of excitement, they proved irresistible—whether making money, haunting taverns, or committing fornication. Land speculation meant not only wealth but dispersion of the people, and what was to stop the march of settlement? The covenant doctrine preached on the *Arbella* had been formulated in England, where land was not to be had for the taking; its adherents had been utterly oblivious of what the

---

[1] See *The New England Mind: From Colony to Province* (1952), Chapter II.

fact of a frontier would do for an imported order, let alone for a European mentality. Hence I suggest that under the guise of this mounting wail of sinfulness, this incessant and never successful cry for repentance, the Puritans launched themselves upon the process of Americanization.

However, there are still more pertinent or more analytical things to be said of this body of expression. If you compare it with the great productions of the founders, you will be struck by the fact that the second and third generations had become oriented toward the social, and only the social, problem; herein they were deeply and profoundly different from their fathers. The finest creations of the founders—the disquisitions of Hooker, Shepard, and Cotton—were written in Europe, or else, if actually penned in the colonies, proceeded from a thoroughly European mentality, upon which the American scene made no impression whatsoever. The most striking example of this imperviousness is the poetry of Anne Bradstreet: she came to Massachusetts at the age of eighteen, already two years married to Simon Bradstreet; there, she says, "I found a new world and new manners, at which my heart rose" in rebellion, but soon convincing herself that it was the way of God, she submitted and joined the church. She bore Simon eight children, and loved him sincerely, as her most charming poem, addressed to him, reveals:

> If ever two were one, then surely we;
> If ever man were loved by wife, then thee.

After the house burned, she wrote a lament about how her pleasant things in ashes lay and how no more the merriment of guests would sound in the hall; but there is nothing in the poem to suggest that the house stood in North Andover or that the things so tragically consumed were doubly precious because they had been transported across the ocean and were utterly irreplaceable in the wilderness. In between rearing children and keeping house she wrote her poetry; her brother-in-law carried the manuscript to London, and there published it in 1650 under the ambitious title, *The Tenth Muse Lately Sprung Up in America.* But the title is the only thing about the volume which shows any sense of America, and that little merely in order to prove that the plantations had something in the way of European wit and learning, that they had not receded into barbarism. Anne's flowers are English flowers, the birds, English birds, and the landscape is Lincolnshire. So also with the productions of immigrant scholarship: such a learned and acute work as Hooker's *Survey of the Summe of Church Discipline,* which is specifically about the regime set up in America, is written entirely within the logical patterns, and out of the religious experience, of Europe; it makes no concession to new and peculiar circumstances.

The titles alone of productions in the next generation show how concentrated have become emotion and attention upon the interest of New England, and none is more revealing than Samuel Danforth's conception of an errand into the wilderness. Instead of being able to compose abstract treatises like those of Hooker upon the soul's preparation, humiliation, or exultation, or such a collection of wisdom and theology as John Cotton's *The Way of Life* or Shepard's *The Sound Believer,* these later saints must, over and over again, dwell upon the specific sins of New England, and the more they denounce, the more they must narrow their focus to the provincial problem. If they write upon anything else, it must be about the halfway covenant and its manifold consequences—a development enacted wholly in this country—or else upon their wars with the Indians. Their range is sadly constricted, but every effort, no matter how brief, is addressed to the persistent question: what is the meaning of this society in the wilderness? If it does not mean what Winthrop said it must mean, what under Heaven is it? Who, they are forever asking themselves, who are we?—and sometimes they are on the verge of saying, who the Devil are we, anyway?

This brings us back to the fundamental ambiguity concealed in the word "errand," that *double entente* of which I am certain Danforth was aware when he published the words that give point to the exhibition. While it was true that in 1630, the covenant philosophy of a special and peculiar bond lifted the migration out of the ordinary realm of nature, provided it with a definite mission which might in the secondary sense be called its errand, there was always present in Puritan thinking the suspicion that God's saints are at best inferiors, despatched by their Superior upon particular assignments. Anyone who has run errands for other people, particularly for people of great importance with many things on their minds, such as army commanders, knows how real is the peril that, by the time he returns with the report of a message delivered or a bridge blown up, the Superior may be interested in something else; the situation at headquarters may be entirely changed, and the gallant errand boy, or the husband who desperately remembered to buy the ribbon, may be told that he is too late. This tragic pattern appears again and again in modern warfare: an agent is dropped by parachute and, after immense hardships, comes back to find that, in the shifting tactical or strategic situations, his contribution is no longer of value. If he gets home in time and his service proves useful, he receives a medal; otherwise, no matter what prodigies he has performed, he may not even be thanked. He has been sent, as the devastating phrase has it, upon a fool's errand, than which there can be a no more shattering blow to self-esteem.

The Great Migration of 1630 felt insured against such treatment from on high by the covenant; nevertheless, the God of the covenant always remained an unpredictable Jehovah, a *Deus Absconditus.* When God promises to abide by stated terms, His word, of course, is to be trusted; but then, what is man that he dare accuse Omnipotence of tergiversation? But if any such apprehension was in Winthrop's mind as he spoke on the *Arbella,* or in the minds of other apologists for the enterprise, they kept it far back and allowed it no utterance. They could stifle the thought, not only because Winthrop and his colleagues believed fully in the covenant, but because they could see in the pattern of history that their errand was not a mere scouting expedition: it was an essential maneuver in the drama of Christendom. The Bay Company was not a battered remnant of suffering Separatists thrown up on a rocky shore; it was an organized task force of Christians, executing a flank attack on the corruptions of Christendom. These Puritans did not flee to America; they went in order to work out that complete reformation which was not yet accomplished in England and Europe, but which would quickly be accomplished if only the saints back there had a working model to guide them. It is impossible to say that any who sailed from Southampton really expected to lay his bones in the new world; were it to come about—as all in their heart of hearts anticipated—that the forces of righteousness should prevail against Laud and Wentworth, that England after all should turn toward reformation, where else would the distracted country look for leadership except to those who in New England had perfected the ideal polity and who would know how to administer it? This was the large unspoken assumption in the errand of 1630: if the conscious intention were realized, not only would a federated Jehovah bless the new land, but He would bring back these temporary colonials to govern England.

In this respect, therefore, we may say that the migration was running an errand in the earlier and more primitive sense of the word—performing a job not so much for Jehovah as for history, which was the wisdom of Jehovah expressed through time. Winthrop was aware of this aspect of the mission—fully conscious of it. "For wee must Consider that Wee shall be as a Citty upon a Hill, the eies of all people are uppon us." More was at stake than just one little colony. If we deal falsely with God, not only will He descend upon us in wrath, but even more terribly, He will make us "a story and a by-word through the world, wee shall open the mouthes of enemies to speake evill of the wayes of god and all professours for Gods sake." No less than John Milton was New England to justify God's ways to man, though not, like him, in the agony and confusion of defeat but in the confidence of approaching triumph. This errand was being run for the sake of Reformed Christianity; and while the first aim was indeed to realize in America the due form of government, both civil and ecclesiastical, the aim behind that aim was to vindicate the most rigorous ideal of the Reformation, so that ultimately all Europe would imitate New England. If we succeed, Winthrop told his audience, men will say of later plantations, "the lord make it like that of New England." There was an elementary prudence to be observed: Winthrop said that the prayer would arise from subsequent plantations, yet what was England itself but one of God's plantations? In America, he promised, we shall see, or may see, more of God's wisdom, power, and truth "then formerly wee have beene acquainted with." The situation was such that, for the moment, the model had no chance to be exhibited in England; Puritans could talk about it, theorize upon it, but they could not display it, could not prove that it would actually work. But if they had it set up in America—in a bare land, devoid of already established (and corrupt) institutions, empty of bishops and courtiers, where they could start *de novo,* and the eyes of the world were upon it—and if then it performed just as the saints had predicted of it, the Calvinist internationale would know exactly how to go about completing the already begun but temporarily stalled revolution in Europe.[2]

When we look upon the enterprise from this point of view, the psychology of the second and third generations becomes more comprehensible. We realize that the migration was not sent upon its errand in order to found the United States of America, nor even the New England conscience. Actually, it would not perform its errand even when the colonists did erect a due form of government in church and state: what was further required in order for this mission to be a success was that the eyes of the world be kept fixed upon it in rapt attention. If the rest of the world, or at least of Protestantism, looked elsewhere, or turned to another model, or simply got distracted and forgot about New England, if the new land was left with a polity nobody in the great world of Europe wanted—then every success in fulfilling the terms of the covenant would become a diabolical measure of failure. If the due form of government were not everywhere to be saluted, what would New England have upon its hands? How give it a name, this victory nobody could utilize? How provide an identity for something conceived under misapprehensions? How could a universal which turned out to be nothing but a provincial particular be called anything but a blunder or an abortion?

If an actor, playing the leading role in the greatest dramatic spectacle of the century, were to attire himself and put on his make-up, rehearse his lines, take a deep breath, and stride onto the stage, only to find the theater dark and empty, no spotlight working, and himself entirely alone, he would feel as did New England around 1650 or 1660. For in the 1640's, during the Civil Wars, the colonies, so to speak, lost their audience. First of all, there proved to be, deep in the Puritan movement, an irreconcilable split between the Presbyterian and Independent wings, wherefore no one system could be imposed upon England, and so the New England model was unserviceable. Secondly—most horrible to

[2]See the perceptive analysis of Alan Heimert (*The New England Quarterly,* XXVI, September 1953) of the ingredients that ultimately went into the Puritans' metaphor of the "wilderness," all the more striking a concoction because they attached no significance a priori to their wilderness destination. To begin with, it was simply a void.

relate—the Independents, who in polity were carrying New England's banner and were supposed, in the schedule of history, to lead England into imitation of the colonial order, betrayed the sacred cause by yielding to the heresy of toleration. They actually welcomed Roger Williams, whom the leaders of the model had kicked out of Massachusetts so that his nonsense about liberty of conscience would not spoil the administrations of charity.

In other words, New England did not lie, did not falter; it made good everything Winthrop demanded—wonderfully good—and then found that its lesson was rejected by those choice spirits for whom the exertion had been made. By casting out Williams, Anne Hutchinson, and the Antinomians, along with an assortment of Gortonists and Anabaptists, into that cesspool then becoming known as Rhode Island, Winthrop, Dudley, and the clerical leaders showed Oliver Cromwell how he should go about governing England. Instead, he developed the utterly absurd theory that so long as a man made a good soldier in the New Model Army, it did not matter whether he was a Calvinist, an Antinomian, an Arminian, an Anabaptist or even—horror of horrors—a Socinian! Year after year, as the circus tours this country, crowds howl with laughter, no matter how many times they have seen the stunt, at the bustle that walks by itself: the clown comes out dressed in a large skirt with a bustle behind; he turns sharply to the left, and the bustle continues blindly and obstinately straight ahead, on the original course. It is funny in a circus, but not in history. There is nothing but tragedy in the realization that one was in the main path of events, and now is sidetracked and disregarded. One is always able, of course, to stand firm on his first resolution, and to condemn the clown of history for taking the wrong turning: yet this is a desolating sort of stoicism, because it always carries with it the recognition that history will never come back to the predicted path, and that with one's own demise, righteousness must die out of the world.

The must humiliating element in the experience was the way the English brethren turned upon the colonials for precisely their greatest achievement. It must have seemed, for those who came with Winthrop in 1630 and who remembered the clarity and brilliance with which he set forth the conditions of their errand, that the world was turned upside down and inside out when, in June 1645, thirteen leading Independent divines—such men as Goodwin, Owen, Nye, Burroughs, formerly friends and allies of Hooker and Davenport, men who might easily have come to New England and helped extirpate heretics—wrote the General Court that the colony's law banishing Anabaptists was an embarrassment to the Independent cause in England. Opponents were declaring, said these worthies, "that persons of our way, principall and spirit cannot beare with Dissentors from them, but Doe correct, fine, imprison and banish them wherever they have power soe to Doe." There were indeed people in England who admired the severities of Massachusetts, but we assure you, said the Independents, these "are utterly your enemyes and Doe seeke your extirpation from the face of the earth: those who now in power are your friends are quite otherwise minded, and doe professe they are much offended with your proceedings." Thus early commenced that chronic weakness in the foreign policy of Americans, an inability to recognize who in truth constitute their best friends abroad.

We have lately accustomed ourselves to the fact that there does exist a mentality which will take advantage of the liberties allowed by society in order to conspire for the ultimate suppression of those same privileges. The government of Charles I and Archbishop Laud had not, where that danger was concerned, been liberal, but it had been conspicuously inefficient; hence, it did not liquidate the Puritans (although it made halfhearted efforts), nor did it herd them into prison camps. Instead, it generously, even lavishly, gave a group of them a charter to Massachusetts Bay, and obligingly left out the standard clause requiring that the document remain in London, that the grantees keep their office within reach of Whitehall. Winthrop's revolutionaries availed themselves of this liberty to get the charter overseas, and thus to set up a regime dedicated to the worship of God in the manner they desired—which meant allowing nobody else to worship any other way, especially adherents of Laud and King Charles. All this was perfectly logical and consistent. But what happened to the thought processes of their fellows in England made no sense whatsoever. Out of the New Model Army came the fantastic notion that a party struggling for power should proclaim that, once it captured the state, it would recognize the right of dissenters to disagree and to have their own worship, to hold their own opinions. Oliver Cromwell was so far gone in this idiocy as to become a dictator, in order to impose toleration by force! Amid this shambles, the errand of New England collapsed. There was nobody left at headquarters to whom reports could be sent.

Many a man has done a brave deed, been hailed as a public hero, had honors and ticker tape heaped upon him—and then had to live, day after day, in the ordinary routine, eating breakfast and brushing his teeth, in what seems protracted anticlimax. A couple may win their way to each other across insuperable obstacles, elope in a blaze of passion and glory—and then have to learn that life is a matter of buying the groceries and getting the laundry done. This sense of the meaning having gone out of life, that all adventures are over, that no great days and no heroism lie ahead, is particularly galling when it falls upon a son whose father once was the public hero or the great lover. He has to put up with the daily routine without ever having known at first hand the thrill of danger or the ecstasy of passion. True, he has his own hardships—clearing rocky pastures, hauling in the cod during a storm, fighting Indians in a swamp—but what are these compared with the magnificence of leading an exodus of saints to found a city on a hill, for the eyes of the world to behold? He might wage a stout fight against the Indians, and one out of ten of his fellows might perish in the struggle, but the world was no longer interested. He would be reduced to writing accounts of himself and scheming to get a publisher in London, in a desperate effort to tell a heedless world, "Look, I exist!"

His greatest difficulty would be not the stones, storms, and Indians, but the problem of his identity. In something of this sort, I should like to suggest, consists the anxiety and torment that inform productions of the late seventeenth and early eighteenth centuries—and should I say, some thereafter? It appears most clearly in *Magnalia Christi Americana,* the work of that soul most tortured by the problem, Cottom Mather: "I write the Wonders of the Christian Religion, flying from the Depravations of Europe, to the American Strand." Thus he proudly begins, and at once trips over the acknowledgment that the founders had not simply fled from depraved Europe but had intended to redeem it. And so the book is full of lamentations over the declension of the children, who appear, page after page, in contrast to their mighty progenitors, about as profligate a lot as ever squandered an inheritance.

And yet, the *Magnalia* is not an abject book; neither are the election sermons abject, nor is the inventory of sins offered by the synod of 1679. There is bewilderment, confusion, chagrin, but there is no surrender. A task has been assigned upon which the populace are in fact intensely engaged. But they are not sure any more for just whom they are working; they know they are moving, but they do not know where they are going. They seem still to be on an errand, but if they are no longer inferiors sent by the superior forces of the Reformation, to whom they should report, then their errand must be wholly of the second sort, something with a purpose and an intention sufficient unto itself. If so, what is it? If it be not the due form of government, civil and ecclesiastical, that they brought into being, how otherwise can it be described?

The literature of self-condemnation must be read for meanings far below the surface, for meanings of which, we may be so rash as to surmise, the authors were not fully conscious, but by which they were troubled and goaded. They looked in vain to history for an explanation of themselves; more and more it appeared that the meaning was not to be found in theology, even with the help of the covenantal dialectic. Thereupon, these citizens found that they had no other place to search but within themselves—even though, at first sight, that repository appeared to be nothing but a sink of iniquity. Their errand having failed in the first sense of the term, they were left with the second, and required to fill it with meaning by themselves and out of themselves. Having failed to rivet the eyes of the world upon their city on the hill, they were left alone with America.

Americo Paredes

The Hero's Progress

From *With His Pistol in His Hand*

THEME AND VARIATIONS

For more than half a century the Rio Grande people have remembered Gregorio Cortez, and in that time the figure of a folk hero has been shaped out of historical fact. It has been the vivid, dramatic narrative of the *corrido*—a well-established form—that has kept the image of Cortez fresh in the minds of Border people, but something needs to be said about the amorphous body of narrative that makes up the prose legend.

The stories that make up the Cortez legend are anecdotal for the most part, arising from the singing of the *corrido,* it would seem. Yet, though by-products of it, they have in their turn influenced the *corrido.* And because of their many variations they have been responsible for the growth of Gregorio Cortez as a folk hero. It is the legend that has developed the heroic figure, which the ballad keeps alive. . . .

In this chapter I mention other values of the legend, compare fact with fancy, and attempt to show how the latter grew out of the former. Because they are so closely intertwined, one cannot discuss the legend without making some references to the *corrido.* Such general remarks will be treated more fully in Part Two of this book, which attempts a critical study of *El Corrido de Gregorio Cortez* and considers its position in the balladry of the Lower Border.

Both ballad and legend apparently began in 1901, almost immediately after the capture of Cortez at Abrán de la Garza's sheep camp. In the half-century since then, nothing seems to have been added to the ballad, which on the contrary has lost much of its original detail. The legend, on the other hand, has grown considerably. This is due, no doubt, to its lack of precise form and to the way that it is usually passed from one person to another.

There is no standard version of the legend and it is never, as far as I know, told complete at one sitting. Each individual hears and learns the parts one at a time. A singing of the ballad may lead to the telling of part of the legend, or a part may be told in relation to some other ballad with a similar theme. Even a chance conversation, such as one on horses, may lead to the narration of some part of the legend—Román's horse trade or the speed, endurance, and faithfulness of the little sorrel mare.

It is up to the individual hearer to put the separate parts together, and to choose from among the versions those he prefers or those that seem the true ones to him. The legend as it appears in Chapter II is my own creation. I have put together those parts that seemed to me the farthest removed from fact and the most revealing of folk attitudes. But there are other variants, which may be considered now.

The most significant have to do with the reasons for the killing of Morris. I have heard at least six variants to this part of the legend, the one about the two sorrel horses and the sorrel mare being the best and the most detailed. Another leaves out the horse trade altogether. Román Cortez and Leonor, Gregorio's wife, are riding in a buggy when they meet the Major Sheriff and two of his deputies, who are looking for smugglers. The sheriff searches the buggy and to do so pulls Leonor down. Román objects and the sheriff shoots him. Then Gregorio appears and kills the sheriff and one of the deputies, while the other deputy runs away. Gregorio puts his wife and Román in the buggy, takes them to a safe place, and then rides the buggy for some distance. He comes to a friendly ranch and is given a horse, and from then on he keeps changing horses until he reaches the Border. When he gets to a ranch house, all he has to say is "I am Gregorio Cortez" and he is given a fresh horse.

This variant comes a little closer to fact in some respects. The sheriff actually was out looking for wrongdoers, and he had two deputies with him. The killing of the deputy was probably transferred from the Belmont incident, in which Glover and his deputy, Schnabel, were both killed. Leonor Cortez may very well have been mistreated after the shooting of Morris; here the result is made the cause. The surrey which Morris rode is given to the Cortezes. In the matter of the smuggling, so far from the border line, the Border narrator is applying local conditions to those of unknown parts of the country.

Another variant has Román and Gregorio working as field hands for an American. They do their work well, but the American demands even more than a man can do. He gets abusive and Román objects. The American shoots Román, and Gregorio shoots the American and then kills the sheriff who comes to arrest him. The story is sometimes told in a slightly different way. Cortez is working alone, and the American slaps his face, whereupon Cortez kills him. These versions diverge the most from actual events.

A fifth variant comes pretty close to fact. The sheriff comes to the Cortez house looking for some stolen cattle. Román and Gregorio have just finished butchering one of their own steers, and the hide is hanging on the fence. The hide happens to be of the same color as the stolen cattle; so the sheriff shoots Román as a rustler, after which Gregorio shoots the sheriff and his deputy. In still another variant, the sheriff is out looking for mule thieves. He stops Román on the road, questions him and shoots him. Gregorio runs out of the house and shoots the sheriff.

There are probably many more variants, since I have made no attempt to collect them all. These, however, are some of the most common ones. In all of them the point emphasized is that Cortez was peacefully pursuing his own business when the sheriff or another American showed up and committed some outrage. That actual facts coincide with this central point is not the question here; in all events the peaceful man minding his own business is essential to the concept of the Border hero.

There is much variation in oral accounts concerning Cortez's personal appearance, even among people who knew him well. Those who knew him describe him as oposite to themselves. Short men describe him as tall; tall men say he was short. Fair men call him dark, dark men call him fair. In height and complexion Cortez was somewhat in-between. Prison records put his height at five feet nine inches, neither short nor tall. His complexion appears to have been neutral, dark from a North European's point of view, light from a Mexican one. When captured and when released from Huntsville, Cortez was well sunburned. During his four-year sojourn in county jails he lost a great deal of his tan. All these things explain the variation in details given by people who actually knew Cortez. They are a commentary on the extreme elasticity of reminiscence and of oral report, even when based on direct observation.

More interesting still are the descriptions given of Cortez by people who have known him only in legend. If people who knew him tend to describe him as their opposite, those who did not know him describe him as being like themselves. A short, very dark man told me that Cortez had been just a little dark man, *chiquitito y prietito.* Ah, but what a man! All heart and testicles; that is to say, all kindness and courage.[1] A fair, blue-eyed Anglo-American who as a little boy once met Cortez, and who admired the man, remembers him as fair. In some parts of the Border where the ideal *norteño* type is the tall dark man with green or tawny eyes, Cortez is said to have been a tall dark man with *ojos borrados.* The variant according to which Gregorio is a field hand was given to me by laboring people. Thus it appears that as the story moves farther away from fact into legend, the narrator identifies himself personally with Cortez.

The way Cortez got out of prison also has its variants. Some do not mention President Lincoln's daughter, making his rescuer merely an American girl. The story is basically the same, having as its core the belief that the governor of Texas will give a prisoner to any pretty girl who asks for him at Christmas. One variant has Cortez released through the efforts of Sarita Kenedy, daughter of Mifflin Kenedy (founder of the Kenedy Ranch and partner of Richard King) and of his Border Mexican wife, Doña Petra Vela.

Sarita Kenedy, later Mrs. Sarah Spohn of Corpus Christi, must have been in her thirties when Cortez rode for the Border, and was middle-aged when Cortez regained his freedom. There is no evidence that she had anything to do in the Cortez case. However the Kenedys, perhaps because of their Mexican connections, did have a reputation as benefactors of Texas-Mexicans. It may very well be that Mrs. Spohn, known to this day to Border people as Sarita Kenedy, was one of the many who contributed to the defense or to the release of Cortez, and that for this reason the legend was attached to her name.

The least romantic variant has Cortez released through the personal intercession of Col. F. A. Chapa of San Antonio. Colonel Chapa is said to have been a member of Teddy Roosevelt's Rough Riders, as well as a leader of his people in San Antonio. When everything else failed and Cortez went to prison, Colonel Chapa talked to his friend the governor, and the governor pardoned Cortez for the sake of his friendship with Chapa. (All variants agree, by the way, that Cortez was imprisoned for one year only, and that he died a year after his release.) As has been said, Chapa worked hard in favor of Cortez. But from the pardon documents it is evident that Colquitt's personal feelings had little or nothing to do with the actual granting of the pardon.

One concludes that the variants of the Cortez legend reflect the Border Mexican's identification of himself with his hero. Attitudes and interests of different kinds are mirrored

[1]According to folk physiology the heart is the seat of man's kinder virtues. Courage and fighting spirit reside in the testicles. A typical ranchero belief, since steers and geldings do not fight for mates.

in different variants. The story about the horse trade is fittingly elaborate. Trading horses was a subject of supreme interest to all horseback people. In American frontier literature, for example, the horse trade has been a fertile subject for humor.

Smuggling was commonplace on the Border, as were efforts to stop it, especially by American authorities. One is not surprised to find in one variant of the Cortez story that the sheriff stops the Cortezes to search for smuggled goods. Another variant makes Cortez a day laborer insulted by his boss, reflecting the point of view of the laborer, whose numbers increased as the land ceased to be cattle country and was turned to citrus and truck farming, and still later to cotton.

Thus the laborer made of Cortez a laborer, the farmer a farmer, the vaquero a vaquero, the suspected smuggler a smuggling suspect—each applying his own situation, his own disagreeable contacts with the Anglo-American, as the reasons for Cortez's defending of his right. The short man saw Cortez as short, the dark man as dark; and the tall man saw him tall. The man that the *corrido* shows at bay saying, "So many mounted rangers, all against one Mexican" became in the legend a synthesis of the Border Mexican, who saw himself collectively in Cortez.

Before leaving the matter of variants, one might mention an Anglo-American one. In *The Mustangs* J. Frank Dobie records the end of Gregorio Cortez as told to him by R. R. Smith of Jourdanton. "Gregorio Cortez did not remain in the penitentiary at Huntsville for 'feefty year.' A governor pardoned him. He became a horse thief and was killed out near El Paso."[2]

That the Anglo-American variant should attribute to Cortez a criminal's end is not surprising. Surprising is the fact that another, much more convenient and much more opprobrious possibility should have been passed by. In April 1917, four years after Gregorio Cortez Lira was released from prison and less than one year after he is said to have died at Anson, a man by the name of Gregorio Cortez was convicted of the rape of his own daughter at Del Rio.

It took a great deal of investigation, and the lucky finding of a bill of particulars on the case, for me to establish the fact that these two were entirely different and unrelated men. Newspaper readers in 1917 could very justifiably have confused the two. But no such thing seems to have happened. In Anglo-American legend it is the Negro who is the rapist. The Mexican is the horse thief, and it is as a horse thief that the Smith-Dobie variant has Gregorio die.

FACT AND FANCY

The legend of Gregorio Cortez is made up of three kinds of ingredients: of straight fact, of fact exaggerated into fiction, and of pure folklore, found in easily recognizable motifs. Many of the more realistic parts of the story, though often invented in the case of other Border heroes, appear to have been true about Cortez. He was a good shot and a superb rider, a man of nerve, ingenuity, and endurance. Some of the things with which legend credits him appear to have been fact, such as his use of cattle to cover up his trail and his walking into town to escape pursuit in the brush. The broad outlines of the ideal border-conflict hero were actually present in Cortez, and they were incorporated into the legend as they were.

[2]Dobie, *The Mustangs,* p. 238.

Other parts of the legend are mere exaggerations of the kind that one often finds in and out of folkore. Cortez killed two sheriffs; legend has him kill dozens. He was actually chased by hundreds of men, and in one or two cases posses (or mobs, rather) of three hundred men were reported scouring the country for "accomplices." In legend Cortez fights off posses made up of three hundred men each. Cortez did leap into the San Antonio River with the little brown mare, though the leap was not so high and he had to blindfold her with a piece of his shirttail.

The story of his driving a herd of steers to water to get near a tank guarded by posse-men seems to be true, though somewhat exaggerated. Occasionally Cortez did meet lone officers or small groups of them, who were sufficiently impressed by what the newspapers said about him to go for additional help rather than tackle him alone. In the legend groups of twenty or thirty men are afraid to approach him. Blown-up facts of this kind make a good part of the legend, as is probably the case with the stories of every popular hero.

The purely folkloric elements in the legend of Cortez, motifs which can be compared to those found in other folklores, very often owe their presence to some little fact, perhaps unimportant in itself, that serves as a nucleus around which legend grows.

One of the purely legendary parts of the story has to do with the sharp horse trade that Román pulls on the owner of the little sorrel mare. It is one of the most detailed passages in the legend, and one of the most important to the structure of that particular version of it. The horse trade causes the deaths of the Major Sheriff and Román. It provides the mare with which Cortez reaches the Border, and the mare is the cause of Cortez's going to prison.

At first glance the episode seems to have been pure invention. Court records show, however, that the killings of Romaldo and Sheriff Morris did in fact arise out of a horse trade. Gregorio and not his brother had traded a mare for a horse, not a horse for a mare, to a man named Villarreal. It was about this trade that Morris came to see Gregorio Cortez the day Morris and Romaldo were shot. This incident provides the framework upon which the detailed story about Román and his sorrel horses and the little sorrel mare are woven.

The sorrel mare herself is a synthesis of four different mares which figured in the events. There was the mare, of unknown color, which Cortez traded to Villarreal. Cortez left home after the shooting of Morris on a sorrel mare that he owned. He rode her only about five miles, halfway to Kenedy, completing the journey on foot with his wounded brother. Of the two mares which Cortez did ride to the Border, one was a sorrel and the other—the fleetest and most enduring—was brown.

The little brown mare received a great deal of publicity in the English-language news-papers, but in the Border legend she is amalgamated with the other three. And since in Border tradition the sorrel mare is as much a convention as the honey-colored horse, the mare becomes a sorrel, as indeed two of the four mares she represents actually were.

The legend's insistence that Cortez went to prison not for the killings of Morris and Glover but for stealing the little sorrel mare also has an echo in fact. Throughout the court proceedings against him, the prosecution attempted to show Cortez as a horse thief and thus to prove that he was not, as the defense argued, acting in self-defense when he shot Morris. He was even taken to Pleasanton and hastily convicted of horse theft so the prosecution could refer to him in court as a convicted horse thief, though the Court of Criminal Appeals later threw out the horse-theft charge. And, as we have seen, the English-speaking legend has Cortez die a horse thief after all.

Román Cortez in the horse-trade episode is pictured as loud, foulmouthed, and a trick-ster. There is no factual evidence to support this legendary view of Gregorio Cortez's brother, but again one finds a clue for it in actual fact. Román, or Romaldo as was really his name, was hit in the mouth by Morris' bullet. The legend seems to have worked back from this bit of fact, taking it as punishment fitting some crime of Román's, and spinning out a whole character sketch to go with it. The changing of Romaldo's name to Román appears to be merely a corruption, perhaps occurring in the *corrido* for the sake of meter. Yet the father of the Cortezes actually was named Román and like his son Romaldo was known for his size and sterngth, again pointing to a basis in fact for a detail in the legend.

When Cortez was captured, many Texas-Mexicans believed he had surrendered. The belief received support from a statement made by Cortez soon after his capture. After the brown mare gave out at Cotulla, he had lost heart for a couple of hours and had thought of surrendering. The *corrido* maker (who seems to have gone to work immediately after Cortez's capture) explained the supposed surrender as the result of Cortez's concern over the killings of innocent people by the *rinches.*

It soon became known that Cortez had been handed over to the Rangers without his consent. The betrayal of the hero was a more established and a much more fitting theme for the *corrido* than the hero's surrender without a fight. But no change was made in the ballad. It may have been too late for the original author to make any changes. Or it may have been that the Border people found in the concept of the hero who gives himself up to save his people a novel but an extremely satisfying twist. The legend, however, did attempt to reconcile both views, the surrender and the betrayal. The result is an oddly Christ-like situation, in which Cortez recognizes his betrayer but willingly goes to his own betrayal in order that his people be saved.

Cortez's personal surrender to the governor seems to be a late addition to the legend. He will surrender only to the governor, and he comes all the way to Austin to do so. Cortez did come to Austin to see the governor, after his release from prison in 1913. Evidently the story about his personal surrender to the governor developed after his visit to Colquitt to thank the governor for the pardon. It seems that the older parts of the legend continued to develop while newer ones were being added.

A comparison of some of the folkloric elements in the Cortez legend with their connecting points of fact tells us something about the age and the method of development of the legend. It must have begun during Cortez's flight; and as his capture, trial, and imprisonment were noised about, the legend took them up, following Cortez all the way up to the time of his release and his death.

Under the influence of tradition, the facts were transformed into folklore, often by the blending of similar elements, as in the case of the four mares, or by an interweaving of conflicting ones, as with the surrender and the betrayal views about Cortez's capture. The Cortez legend shows evidence of continuous growth from the time that Cortez first attracted the notice of the Border folk until very recent times, a growth that has added not only to the number of events but to the complexity and the wealth of detail in the narrative.

In the legend the character of Cortez is more fully developed than it is in the *corrido,* but he shares interest with others, who represent folk-hero types too. This is especially true of Román and the little sorrel mare. Román plays a dual role. On the one hand he is the loudmouth; on the other he is the clever hero who gets what he wants through trickery. It is Román's loud mouth that gets him into trouble rather than the trick he plays on the owner of the sorrel mare. Fittingly enough, it is in the mouth that Morris shoots him.

In this character Román plays the part of the anti-hero. He is what men should not be: loud, boisterous, disrespectful, an eternal joker. Men should be quiet and hardworking, excellent vaqueros and good farmers. They should be respectful to their elders, peaceful in manner, and ready to defend their right. In other words, they should be like Gregorio Cortez, who is not only a projection of the Border Mexican's reaction to border conflict but a pattern of behavior as well.

In the horse-trading episode Román appears as another kind of hero, a favorite in the Mexican folk tale. He is the clever rogue of the Coyote type, who triumphs over his enemy not by force but by guile, taking advantage of his enemy's fancied superiority to trick him. The clever hero is common in Border tales. He is the smuggler who feigns deafness in court, the Texas-Mexican who pretends ignorance of the English language in order to get the best of the American who is trying to swindle him. He is also found in more universal tales, from Spanish and Indian tradition. The cry of the turtle about to be executed by the other animals, "Don't throw me in the water or I'll drown!" has come to stand for the rogue who gets what he wants by pretending not to want it.

The little sorrel mare is a character in her own right, partaking of the attributes of human folk heroes. As a heroine the mare has something in common with those human heroes who begin their careers in obscure or even despised status, men of hidden talents, which come out in an emergency. The mare begins the story in a despised status. Neither her owner nor Román thinks much of her. But Gregorio Cortez recognizes her worth, and she proves herself by outrunning many a better-regarded horse.

She is the youngest son who makes good after his elder brothers fail, the prince who comes disguised as a peasant, the little shepherd who fells the giant warrior with a stone. In short, she is Cinderella herself. The theme is a universal one, but the mare descends directly from the horses celebrated in the ballad form preceding the *corrido*, the sung *décima*, in which the sorry-looking mustang beats the blooded horse when the big stakes are down.

CORTEZ AS A FOLK HERO

Gregorio Cortez remains the chief figure of the legend, appearing in it in three different phases: before the killing of Morris, during the flight, and during his captivity. In each phase Cortez is given different characteristics, though the main outlines are maintained throughout: he continues to be the peaceful man driven to violence and finally brought to bay.

Before the killing of Morris, Cortez is the hero in disguise. His talent for violence, flight, and escape is for the most part unknown to his enemies, hidden as it is behind a peaceful disposition. He is the unknown and unproved hero.

There is just a slight hint of the supernatural in the fact that Cortez is the seventh son of a seventh son, thus destined for great things, and that he has premonitions about future events. Cortez is also, though incidentally, a workman hero, somewhat akin to the work heros of Anglo-American folklore. He can pick more cotton, plant more corn, and clear more land than any other man. He is a better vaquero and tracker than anybody else. Unlike John Henry and Paul Bunyan, however, Cortez is not a prodigy. His feats are due to industry rather than to superhuman powers. He is a hero who works rather than a worker hero. His excellence as a workman serves to emphasize his character as a peaceful man in his disguised period.

In the killing of Morris and in his subsequent flight, Cortez becomes the warrior hero. It is in this phase of the legend that he resembles most closely the hero of the *corridos*. He becomes the typical guerrilla, the border raider fighting and fleeing, and using warrior's tricks to throw the enemy off. He discourages a group of *rinches* who have "made him a corral" by talking to himself and pretending that he has a large body of men with him. This is a motif that is also found in popular literature. A boys' story about the American Revolution had an American soldier and a little drummer boy capture a whole troop of redcoats by shouting commands at each other, as if they were officers of a large contingent. The same trick is sometimes attributed to Davy Crockett. In the *romances* the beseiged garrison throws out its last crust of bread to the enemy, who raise the siege because they think the garrison is too well-provisioned to be starved out. In Chinese tales, the general of the besieged garrison throws open the gates, and the besiegers withdraw.

In some of his feats, the Cortez of the legend resembles folk heroes like Robin Hood. Like Robin he surprises his enemy and provisions himself from them, taking food, arms, and other necessaries and letting them go unharmed. In a way reminiscent of Robin Hood, Pancho Villa, and the Saxon King Alfred, Cortez comes into town in disguise while the chase after him is on, mingles with the townspeople and listens to the tales told about him. He sits among the crowd at the station and listens to them talk about the deeds of Gregorio Cortez, and no one knows that Cortez is sitting there with them.

The hero is recognized and aided by a pretty girl. Again one is reminded, among others, of Robin Hood, whose chief protector is the queen herself. In *Robin Hood's Chase* [Child 146][3] the king goes out hunting for Robin.

> But when that Robin Hood he did hear
>   The king had him in chase,
> Then said Little John, 'Tis time to be gone
>   And go to some other place.

The "other place" turns out to be Queen Katherine's palace. There Robin is safe from pursuit, while the king hunts him in the wood for three weeks.

In the part of the legend dealing with Cortez's captivity, some elements of the warrior-hero pattern remain. The hero escapes all major risks, but he is finally imprisoned by a trick of his enemies, who dare not fight him. And it is a woman, a woman of the enemy, who procures his release. The castle warden's daughter who steals the keys and the princess who intercedes with her father the emperor are represented by President Lincoln's daughter.

In the absence of an emperor, the President of the United States did just as well. Lincoln is chosen because his is the most familiar name, that of the good president. Before Franklin D. Roosevelt's name was added on the "good" side of the list, the most familiar presidential names were Lincoln, Wilson, and Teddy Roosevelt. Both Wilson and Teddy Roosevelt were disliked. Lincoln, the champion of liberty and the friend of Juárez, was admired.

The girl is not President Lincoln's daughter in all variants, but she is always a "Gringo girl," always a daughter of the enemy. The situation between Cortez and President Lincoln's daughter is especially close to that found in some British ballads. In *The Fair Flower of Northumberland* [Child 9] the English girl falls in love with the captive Scottish knight and sets him free, after which he abandons her. The Scottish knight had promised to marry the girl.

---

[3]A number in brackets after a British ballad indicates its position in Francis J. Child's *English and Scottish Popular Ballads,* Boston, 1904.

> If curteously you will set me free,
> I vow that I wil marrie thee,
> So soone as I come in faire Scotland.

He abandons her, telling her he has a wife and children, once she helps him escape.

Because the ballad comes from the English side of that border it shows the Scotsman as false. Had it been Scottish the knight would have promised nothing, in the manner of Cortez. Such is the case in a ballad of Scottish provenience, *James Hatley* [Child 244].

Young James Hatley is accused of stealing the king's jewels and is sentenced to be hanged. The identity of the court is not revealed, but it is one in which English lords have a great deal of influence. The English want to see Hatley hanged. The king's daughter steals into prison, talks to Hatley, and is convinced that he is innocent. She gets the king to spare his life and arranges a trial by combat with Hatley's accuser, Sir Fenwick, who seems to be an Englishman. Hatley wounds Fenwick three times and Fenwick confesses. The English lords still want Hatley to hang, but they do not get their wish. The ballad ends with the king's daughter's speech.

> Up and spake the king's daughter,
> "Come hame, James Hatley, and dine wi' me
> For I've made a vow, I'll keep it true,
> I'll never marry a man but thee."

These might have been the very words of President Lincoln's daughter, though the British ballad leads us to believe that James Hatley accepted the invitation, while Gregorio Cortez does not.

When Cortez leaves his pursuers looking for him in the brush and walks into town, travel-stained and weary and armed with his pistols, he wanders among the people at the station who are retelling the deeds he has done, and no one recognizes him. A short while later, after he has washed, changed clothes, and put his pistols inside a *morral,* he walks along the road toward the river, and everyone who meets him knows him, though no one will tell the *rinches.*

There is no inconsistency here, because when Cortez starts walking along the road to the river he has entered into a different phase of his legend and has become a hero of a different type. When he walks into town, armed but unrecognized, and listens to people tell of his exploits, he is still the pursued hero, the border raider or the Robin Hood. When he begins walking down the road he begins to walk toward captivity.

It is in this last phase that the legend of Gregorio Cortez most closely approaches myth. There are some pagan elements in this part, but it is the Christian influence that is the strongest. Cortez becomes the type of hero who sacrifices his liberty, and eventually his life, in the interests of his people. This motif is not common in Border tradition, which usually takes too personal, too individual a view to admit concepts of this sort. It appears as far as I know only in the legend and in the longer variations of *El Corrido de Gregorio Cortez.*

It has been mentioned that the combination of the surrender theme with that of the betrayal, both being believed true, has given the captivity of Cortez a strongly Christian tone. El Teco is openly called a Judas, and his fate is somewhat similar to Judas'. He does not hang himself, but neither does he enjoy his money, the thousand *pesos plata* or silver dollars that he receives for his treachery. Like Judas he is reviled, feels remorse, and finally dies. He is shown as acting like a friend to his victim, and if he does not kiss Cortez on the cheek he does put out his hand, a corresponding custom.

The necessity of making Cortez both surrender and be betrayed has led the folk to show Cortez as understanding that he is being betrayed but accepting the betrayal as part of the things he has to undergo, thus making the Christian parallel even closer than may have been originally intended. Twelve years later, when Huerta betrayed and murdered President Madero, a Greater Mexican *corrido* maker was to use the same situation. Madero is shown putting Huerta in control of the army, with the knowledge that Huerta will betray him.[4]

Finally taken, Cortez faces his accusers in court and talks them out of countenance, also like the pre-Christian figure of Socrates at his trial. Unlike Christ and Socrates, however, Cortez convinces his judges and they set him free, but his enemies pursue him still and find another excuse for putting him in prison. The legendary Texas custom which President Lincoln's daughter invokes to free Cortez also echoes the Jewish-Christian tradition. It was supposed to be a Jewish custom at the time of Christ to release a prisoner on the feast of Passover, and it was according to this custom that the insurrectionist Barrabas was released instead of Christ.

The legends that accompany many Border *corridos* have their own pattern, one that embraces the narrative of the *corrido* and goes beyond it. Knowing the *corrido* alone, one would hardly guess that the same people that produced it had the turn of mind that could create the legend too. The pattern of the legend is repeated in some details with each hero. The betrayed hero is often found; Cortina is said to have died by poison. The pattern may be so well established that it influences fact. Esther Martínez, who wrote to Governor Colquitt pleading for Cortez's release, sounds as if she believed that the governor gave girls a convict each for Christmas if they asked for them. The wording of her letter reflects tradition, while her action in writing the governor on the other hand reinforced the same traditional beliefs.

Louise Pound once said that most medieval ballads have aristocratic rather than peasant or rural origins because the heroes are kings, princes, and noblemen rather than farmers, tanners, weavers, and tinkers.[5] By the same token Greater Mexican Revolutionary *corridos* should be the product of the officers because their heroes are generals for the most part. There were no kings or princes within the ken of the Border folk, or they would have made the legendary Gregorio Cortez a prince and set him out in a corral or a cotton patch, in disguise of course.

It is significant that Cortez in fact is in disguise when his story begins. He is the warrior passing for a peaceful man. One sees the identification of the average folk member with something he admires as better than himself. The medieval peasant had his prince disguised as a peasant, or at least talking and acting like one. The inoffensive Border Mexican had his warrior hero, disguised—until the proper moment arrived—as an inoffensive man.

Coming half a century after the beginning of border conflict, Gregorio Cortez epitomized the ideal type of hero of the Rio Grande people, the man who defends his right with his pistol in his hand, and who either escapes at the end or goes down before superior odds—in a sense a victor even in defeat. He was an incarnation of a Border legend whose first model forty years before had been Juan Nepomuceno Cortina.

For one of the most striking things about Gregorio Cortez is the way the actual facts of his life conformed to pre-existing legend. In his free, careless youth, in the reasons for his

[4]*El Cuartelazo Felicista* in Vincente T. Mendoza, *El corrido mexicano,* Mexico, 1954, p. 30.

[5]Louise Pound, *Poetic Origins and the Ballad,* New York, 1921, pp 95ff.

going outside the law, in his betrayal, his imprisonment, and release, and even in the somewhat cloudy circumstances surrounding his death—the actual facts about Cortez's life (so far as we know them) follow the Border-hero tradition that was already well established before Cortez made his celebrated ride.

It was as if the Border people had dreamed Gregorio Cortez before producing him, and had sung his life and his deeds before he was born.

Edmund Wilson

Harriet Beecher Stowe

From *Patriotic Gore*

Let us begin with *Uncle Tom's Cabin.*

This novel by Harriet Beecher Stowe was one of the greatest successes of American publishing history as well as one of the most influential books—immediately influential, at any rate—that have ever appeared in the United States. A year after its publication on March 20, 1852, it had sold 305,000 copies in America and something like two million and a half copies in English and in translation all over the world. As for its influence, it is enough to remember the greeting of Lincoln to Mrs. Stowe when she was taken to call on him at the White House: "So this is the little lady who made this big war." Yet, in the period after the war, the novel's popularity steadily declined. Mrs. Stowe's royalty statements for the second half of 1887 showed a sale of only 12,225, and eventually *Uncle Tom* went out of print. Up to the time when it was reprinted, in 1948, in the Modern Library Series, it was actually unavailable except at secondhand.

What were the reasons for this eclipse? It is often assumed in the United States that *Uncle Tom* was a mere propaganda novel which disappeared when it had accomplished its purpose and did not, on its merits, deserve to live. Yet in continued to be read in Europe, and, up to the great Revolution, at any rate, it was a popular book in Russia. If we come to *Uncle Tom* for the first time today, we are likely to be surprised at not finding it what we imagined it and to conclude that the postwar neglect of it has been due to the strained situation between the North and the South. The Northerners, embarrassed by the memory of the war and not without feelings of guilt, did not care to be reminded of the issue which had given rise to so much bitterness. In the South, where before the war any public discussion of slavery had by general tacit agreement been banned, nothing afterwards was wanted less than Northern criticism of pre-war conditions. It was still possible at the beginning of this century for a South Carolina teacher to make his pupils hold up their right hands and swear that they would never read *Uncle Tom*. Both sides, after the terrible years of the war, were glad to disregard the famous novel. The characters did still remain by-words, but they were mostly kept alive by the dramatizations, in which Mrs. Stowe had had no hand and which had exploited its more obviously comic and its more melodramatic elements. These versions for the stage kept at first relatively close to the novel, but in the course of half a century they grotesquely departed from it. By the late seventies, *Uncle Tom's Cabin* was half a minstrel show and half a circus. The live bloodhounds that were supposed to pursue Eliza as she was crossing the ice with her baby—which did not occur in the novel—began to figure in 1879, and were typical of this phase of the play. The original characters were now sometimes doubled: you had two Topsys, two Lawyer Markses, two Uncle Toms. Topsy sang comic songs, and Uncle Tom was given minstrel interludes, in which he would do a shuffle and breakdown. In the meantime, on account of sectional feeling, the book could not be read in schools as the New England classics were, and it even disappeared from the home. It may be said that by the early nineteen-hundreds few young people had any at all clear idea of what *Uncle Tom's Cabin* contained. One could in fact grow up in the United States without ever having seen a copy.

To expose oneself in maturity to *Uncle Tom* may therefore prove a startling experience. It is a much more impressive work than one has ever been allowed to suspect. The first thing that strikes one about it is a certain eruptive force. This is partly explained by the author in a preface to a late edition, in which she tells of the oppressive silence that hung over the whole question of slavery before she published her book. "It was a general saying," she explains, "among conservative and sagacious people that this subject was a dangerous one to investigate, and that nobody could begin to read and think upon it without becoming practically insane; moreover, that it was a subject of such delicacy that no discussion of it could be held in the free states without impinging upon the sensibilities of the slave states, to whom alone the management of the matter belonged." The story came so suddenly to Mrs. Stowe and seemed so irresistibly to write itself that she felt as if some power beyond her had laid hold of her to deliver its message, and she said sometimes that the book had been written by God. This is actually a little the impression that the novel makes on the reader. Out of a background of undistinguished narrative, inelegantly and carelessly written, the characters leap into being with a vitality that is all the more striking for the ineptitude of the prose that presents them. These characters—like those of Dickens, at least in his early phase—express themselves a good deal better than the author expresses herself. The Shelbys and George Harris and Eliza and Aunt Chloe and Uncle Tom project themselves out of the void. They come before us arguing and struggling, like real people who cannot be quiet. We feel that the dams of discretion of which Mrs. Stowe has spoken have been burst by a passionate force that, compressed, has been mounting behind them, and which, liberated, has taken the form of a flock of lamenting and ranting, prattling and preaching characters, in a drama that demands to be played to the end.

Not, however, that it is merely a question of a troubled imagination and an inhibited emotional impulse finding vent in a waking fantasy. What is most unexpected is that, the farther one reads in *Uncle Tom,* the more one becomes aware that a critical mind is at work, which has the complex situation in a very firm grip and which, no matter how vehement the characters become, is controlling and coördinating their interrelations. Though there is much that is exciting in *Uncle Tom's Cabin,* it is never the crude melodrama of the decadent phase of the play; and though we find some old-fashioned moralizing and a couple of Dickensian deathbeds, there is a good deal less sentimentality than we may have been prepared for by our memories of the once celebrated stage apotheosis—if we are old enough to have seen it: "Little Eva in the Realms of Gold." We may even be surprised to discover that the novel is by no means an indictment drawn up by New England against the South.

Mrs. Stowe has, on the contrary, been careful to contrive her story in such a way that the Southern states and New England shall be shown as involved to an equal degree in the kidnapping into slavery of the Negroes and the subsequent maltreatment of them, and that the emphasis shall all be laid on the impracticability of slavery as a permanent institution. The author, if anything, leans over backwards in trying to make it plain that the New Englanders are as much to blame as the South and to exhibit the Southerners in a favorable light; for St. Clare and Miss Ophelia, intended as typical products of, respectively, Louisiana and Vermont, are, after all, first cousins; they are the children of two New England brothers, both of whom are described as "upright, energetic, noble-minded, with an iron will," but one of whom had "settled down in New England, to rule over rocks and stones, and to force an existence out of Nature," while the other had "settled in Louisiana, to rule over men and women, and force existence out of *them.*" The difference between the two cousins is, then, chiefly a difference of habitat: the result of the diverse effects of a society in which you have to do things for yourself and of a society in which everything is done for you. And as for Simon Legree—a plantation owner, not an overseer, as many people imagine him to be (due, no doubt, to some telescoping of episodes, in the later productions of the play, which would have made him an employee of St. Clare's)—Simon Legree is not a Southerner: he is a Yankee, and his harsh inhumanity as well as his morbid solitude are evidently regarded by Mrs. Stowe as characteristic of his native New England. Nor are these regional characterizations—though later, by the public, turned into *clichés*—of an easy or obvious kind. The contrasted types of the book, through their conflicts, precipitate real tragedy, and even, in some episodes, high comedy—the Sisyphean efforts, for example, of the visitor from Vermont, Miss Ophelia, to bring system into the St. Clare household, and her bafflement by the Negro-run kitchen, a place of confusion and mystery, out of which she is unable to understand how the magnificent meals are produced. There is, in fact, in *Uncle Tom,* as well as in its successor *Dred,* a whole drama of manners and morals and intellectual points of view which corresponds somewhat to the kind of thing that was then being done by Dickens, and was soon to be continued by Zola, for the relations of the social classes, and which anticipates such later studies of two sharply contrasting peoples uncomfortably involved with one another as the *John Bull's Other Island* of Bernard Shaw or E. M. Forster's *A Passage to India.*

But such a writer as Forster or Shaw is a well-balanced man of letters contriving a fable at his leisure. Mrs. Stowe's objectivity is taut, intent. She has nothing of the partisan mentality that was to become so inflamed in the fifties; and Lord Palmerston, who had read the book three times, was evidently quite sincere in complimenting her on the "statesmanship" of *Uncle Tom's Cabin.* She is national, never regional, but her consciousness that the national ideal is in danger gave her book a desperate candor that shook South and North alike, and a dramatic reverberation that, perpetuated by the run of the play, has outlasted the analysis of the novel. In what terms this ideal of the United States was conceived by Harriet Beecher Stowe appears very clearly from a passage in her autobiographical notes: "There was one of my father's books that proved a mine of wealth to me. It was a happy hour when he brought home and set up in his bookcase Cotton Mather's *Magnalia,* in a new edition of two volumes. What wonderful stories those! Stories, too, about my own country. Stories that made me feel the very ground I trod on to be consecrated by some special dealing of God's providence." And she tells of her emotions, in her childhood, on hearing the Declaration of Independence read: "I had never heard it before," wrote Mrs. Stowe, "and even now had but a vague idea of what was meant by some parts of it. Still I gathered enough from the recital of the abuses and injuries that had driven my nation to this course to feel myself swelling with indignation, and ready with all my little mind and strength to applaud the concluding passage, which Colonel Talmadge rendered with resounding majesty. I was as ready as any of them to pledge my life, fortune, and sacred honor for such a cause. The heroic element was strong in me, having come down by ordinary generation from a long line of Puritan ancestry, and just now it made me long to do something. I knew not what: to fight for my country, or to make some declaration on my own account." Her assumption, in writing *Uncle Tom,* is that every worthy person in the United States must desire to preserve the integrity of our unprecedented republic; and she tries to show how Negro slavery must disrupt and degrade this common ideal by tempting the North to the moral indifference, the half-deliberate ignorance, which encourages inhuman practices, and by weakening the character of the South through the luxury and the irresponsibility that the institution of slavery breeds. For Harriet Beecher Stowe, besides, the American Union had been founded under the auspices of the Christian God, and she could not accept institutions that did such violence to Christian teaching. One of the strongest things in the novel is the role played by Uncle Tom—another value that was debased in the play. The Quakers who shelter Eliza are, of course, presented as Christians; but not one of the other white groups that figure in *Uncle Tom's Cabin* is living in accordance with the principles of the religion they all profess. It is only the black Uncle Tom who has taken the white man's religion seriously and who—standing up bravely, in the final scene, for the dignity of his own soul but at the same time pardoning Simon Legree—attempts to live up to it literally. The sharp irony as well as the pathos is that the recompense he wins from the Christians, as he is gradually put through their mill, is to be separated from his family and exiled; tormented, imprisoned and done to death.

Another feature of the stage melodrama that is misleading in regard to the novel is the unity, or effect of unity, imposed on its locale and chronology. The play is made to center on New Orleans, and one sensational scene is made to follow another so fast that we do not have any idea of the actual passage of time. The two distinct strands of the story have, furthermore, to be tied up together in a way that they are not in the book. The novel has a quite different pattern, for in it the Negro characters—Uncle Tom and his family, on the one hand; George Harris and Eliza, on the other—are involved in a series of wanderings which progressively and excitingly reveal, like the visits of Chíchikov in Gogol's *Dead Souls,* the traits of a whole society. One of the main sources of interest, as in Gogol, is the variety of Southern households to which, one after the other, we are introduced; first, the bourgeois Kentuckian Shelbys, who are naturally decent and kindly, but also essentially conventional and very much attached to their comfort; then the homelier Ohio Quakers, with their kitchen-centered existence and their language based on the Bible; then the St. Clares, in their villa on Lake Ponchartrain—their wastefulness and laxness and charm, the whole family languishing with maladies that are real or imaginary, full of bad conscience, baffled affections and unfulfillable longings; then, finally—in the lowest circle—the nightmare plantation of Simon Legree, a prison and a place of torture, with its Negroes set to flog other Negroes and its tensions of venomous hatred between Simon Legree and his mistress—where, amidst the black moss and the broken stumps of the muddy and rank Red River, the intractable New England soul is delivered to its deepest damnation. The creator of this long sequence, with its interconnecting episodes of riverboat, tavern and slave market, was no contemptible novelist. Even Henry James, that expert professional, is obliged to pay her his tribute when he tells us, in *A Small Boy and Others,* of a performance of the play that had been for him in childhood a thrilling "aesthetic adventure," which had first, he says, awakened his critical sense, and admits that the novel constitutes a perhaps unique literary case of a book which has made its impression without the author's ever having concerned herself with literary problems at all, "as if," as he says, "a fish, a wonderful 'leaping' fish, had simply flown through the air." One hardly knows, in this connection to what other book of its period one can properly compare *Uncle Tom*. Turgenev's *A Sportsman's Sketches*, exactly contemporary with it, which is supposed to have had some effect in expediting the abolition of serfdom and which has sometimes been spoken of as "the Russian *Uncle Tom's Cabin*," belongs so much more to the level of sophisticated literary art that it is difficult today to realize how subversive its implications once were. The Brontës have something in common with Harriet Beecher Stowe, but even they belong more to *belles lettres*, and their subjects are not social problems but passionate feminine daydreams. *Uncle Tom* is more closely akin to some such early novel of Dickens as *Oliver Twist*, and Dickens, who admired the book, was correct in detecting his own influence.

Uncle Tom was an explosive that had been shot into the world by a whole combination of pressures, personal as well as historical. Harriet Beecher had been born in Litchfield, Connecticut, but she had gone to live in Cincinnati, Ohio, in 1832, when her father Lyman Beecher, a then famous Presbyterian preacher, had founded in that Western city Lane Theological Seminary. Four years later, when she was twenty-five, she married Calvin Ellis Stowe, the professor of Biblical literature at Lane, and, with widely spaced visits to New England, which were evidently blessed escapes, she remained eighteen years in Ohio. Cincinnati was then a pork-packing center, and the streets were obstructed with pigs; it was also a river-town, and the bar-rooms were full of bad characters. The situation across the state line was a constant source of disturbance. There were always desperate slaves fleeing from over the river, and some Ohioans wanted to help them while others wanted to hunt them down. Lyman Beecher was opposed to slavery but had not been converted to Abolition. On this subject, as in his theology, he tried to steer a politic course; but at the time of his absence one summer, the trustees of his new theological school provoked an Abolitionist movement by suppressing an Anti-Slavery Society and forbidding discussion of the subject "in any public room of the Seminary." A self-confident and brilliant student rallied and led a sedition of the whole student body, who left their buildings and encamped in a suburb, and eventually, in 1835, he carried away a large part of the seminary, students and faculty both, to Oberlin College, also in Ohio, which had just received an endowment for a theological department that was to be open to colored students. In the summer of 1836, a mob in Cincinnati wrecked the press of an Abolitionist paper, and this was followed by further riots, in the course of which Harriet Stowe, going into the kitchen one day, found her brother, Henry Ward Beecher, pouring melted lead into a mold. When she asked, "What on earth are you doing, Henry?" he answered, "Making bullets to kill men with." He faced the streets with two guns in his pockets. Both Harriet and Henry, as a result of this experience, seem secretly to have become Abolitionists. The Stowes a little later took into their household a colored girl who said she was free but who was presently claimed by her master; Calvin Stowe and Henry Beecher, armed with pistols, arranged her escape at night. This girl was the original of Eliza Harris. In the meantime, another of Harriet's brothers, Edward, now the head of Illinois College, had encouraged Elijah Lovejoy, one of the most zealous of the Abolitionists, who had been publishing a paper in St. Louis and was threatened by the pro-slavery element, to transfer his operations to Alton, Illinois. In the November of 1837, the year after the Cincinnati riots, Lovejoy was shot to death while defending his printing press, which had just been unloaded from a Mississippi steamboat, and it was reported—though this turned out to be false—that Edward Beecher had also been murdered.

In this period, the issue of slavery was becoming involved with church politics. An exacerbated controversy was going on between the Princeton Theological Seminary and the Yale Divinity School, with Princeton on the unyieldingly conservative and Yale on the relatively liberal side. Lyman Beecher, who had studied at Yale, had found in Cincinnati a bitter opponent, a certain Dr. Joshua Wilson, the pastor of the First Presbyterian Church, a Calvinist fanatic so uncompromising that he refused to have pictures in his house on the ground that they were graven images. Dr. Wilson had occupied unchallenged the position of leader of the Church in the West, and he seems to have been jealous of Beecher. He succeeded—taking his cue, it is said, from Princeton—in having Lyman Beecher tried for heresy in 1835, first before the Presbytery, then before the Synod, but in both cases his victim had been acquitted. Though rugged and open in manner, Lyman Beecher was a very astute politician. It is wonderful to find him declaring that he is sound on infant depravity by putting into solemn language his conviction that young children were badly behaved, exhibiting, as he says, "selfishness, self-will, malignant anger, envy and revenge," the evidence of "a depraved state of mind, voluntary and sinful in its character and qualities." (His denial that infant damnation had ever been an article of the Calvinist creed was evidently derived from Calvin's reservation in favor of children who belonged to the Elect.) When his son Henry Ward Beecher was about to be examined for ordination at Fort Wayne, Indiana—to which the old man rode seventy miles, arriving 'besplashed and bespattered," as another of his sons has written, "with smoking steed and his saddle-bags encrusted with mud"—the father admonished him as follows: "Preach little doctrine except what is of moldy orthodoxy; keep all your improved breeds, your short-horned Durhams, your Berkshires, etc., away off to pasture. They will get fatter and nobody will be scared. Take hold of the most practical subjects; popularize your sermons. I do not ask you to change yourself; but, for a time, while captious critics are lurking, adapt your mode so as to insure that you shall be rightly understood." Yet a split in the Church now took place. "The South," said Dr. Beecher in later years, "had generally stood neutral. They had opposed going to extremes in theology either way. Rice, of Virginia, was a noble fellow, and held all steady. It was Rice who said, after my trial, that I ought to be tried once in five years, to keep up the orthodoxy of the church. He was full of good humor, and did so much good. But they got scared about abolition. Rice got his head full of that thing, and others. John C. Calhoun was at the bottom of it. I know of his doing things— writing to ministers, and telling them to do this and that. The South finally took the Old School side. It was a cruel thing to do—it was a cursed thing, and 'twas slavery that did it."

At the General Assembly in Philadelphia in 1838, Dr. Wilson had Beecher and Calvin Stowe read out of the Presbyterian Church. That same day in Philadelphia, a new building called Liberty Hall, which had just been dedicated to Abolition and to which white Quaker women had been seen going arm in arm with Negro men, was burned down by a mob, with the firemen refusing to put out the blaze. Dr. Beecher set out in the autumn on a kind of marauding expedition and persuaded several students from other colleges to transfer to Lane Seminary. In Louisville, he ran into a man he knew who was keeping a store in the city, and he induced him to give up his business and study for the ministry at Lane. When Beecher got back to the seminary, he found that his son-in-law, Calvin Stowe, who was a periodic hypochondriac, had succumbed to discouragement and taken to his bed. "Wake up!" cried Dr. Beecher. "I've brought ye twelve students. Get up and wash, and eat bread, and prepare to have a good class."

The Stowes had by this time four children—the first two of which were twins—and Harriet began to write stories in order to bring in some money. In the summer of 1841, several incidents of violence occurred. A man who was hiding a slave that had run away from Kentucky went so far as to attack the owner when the latter attempted to search his house; and at about the same time a local farmer was murdered by Negroes who were stealing his berries, and in the city a white woman was raped. In September, there were race riots that lasted a week, with several persons killed and wounded. A farmer with a Dutch name, who was to turn up in *Uncle Tom's Cabin* as Old John Van Trompe, made an effort to rescue nine slaves, only one of whom succeeded in getting away; but for the loss of this slave he was sued by the owner. He was defended by Salmon P. Chase, at that time a young lawyer in Cincinnati, who had played a courageous part in the 1836 riots and who was later to defend Dr. Beecher when the relentless Old School Presbyterians tried to oust him from the presidency of his seminary in order to take it over themselves. In Beecher's case, Chase was successful, but he failed in his defense of the farmer. He took it up to the Supreme Court at his own expense, but he lost on every decision. His client was finally ruined by having to pay the costs as well as fines and damages. A third brother of Harriet's, Charles, who was also to have entered the ministry, had been shaken in his faith at college by a treatise of Jonathan Edwards's, in which Edwards appeared to be arguing that man was completely deprived of the power of moral choice and yet that God held him accountable. Though Charles's resourceful father found it possible to interpret Edwards in a less discouraging way, the boy abandoned religion and became what he called a fatalist. Eventually, however, to Lyman's great joy, he emerged from this state of mind and, like his brothers, went into the ministry; but in the meantime he had been working as a clerk in New Orleans and, returning to Cincinnati at the time when mob violence was running high, he brought stories of plantation life in Louisiana that were later to be used by Harriet for the episode of Simon Legree. During the winter of 1842–43, there was a typhoid epidemic in the Seminary, and everybody turned out to nurse the sick. In July, just as Harriet Stowe was on the point of having another baby, her brother George, also a minister, accidentally shot himself. She was an invalid for months after the birth of the child, nor did the baby seem likely to live, and yet the little girl did survive. The Stowes, with their growing family, had no other means than Calvin's meager salary, and their life became rather sordid. A letter of Harriet's to Calvin, written on June 16, 1845, when Calvin is away at a minister's convention, strikes the note of this dismal period:

"My dear Husband,—It is a dark, sloppy, rainy, muddy, disagreeable day, and I have been working hard (for me) all day in the kitchen, washing dishes, looking into closets, and seeing a great deal of that dark side of domestic life which a housekeeper may who will investigate too curiously into minutiæ in warm, damp weather, especially after a girl who keeps all clean on the *outside* of cup and platter, and is very apt to make good the rest of the text in the *inside* of things.

"I am sick of the smell of sour milk, and sour meat, and sour everything, and then the clothes *will* not dry, and no wet thing does, and everything smells moldy; and altogether I feel as if I never wanted to eat again.

"Your letter, which was neither sour nor moldy, formed a very agreeable contrast to all these things; the more so for being unexpected. I am much obliged to you for it. As to my health, it gives me very little solicitude, although it is bad enough and daily growing worse. I feel no life, no energy, no appetite, or rather a growing distaste for food; in fact, I am becoming quite ethereal. Upon reflection I perceive that it pleases my Father to keep me in the fire, for my whole situation is excessively harassing and painful. I suffer with sensible distress in the brain, as I have done more or less since my sickness last winter, a distress which some days takes from me all power of planning or executing anything; and you know that, except this poor head, my unfortunate household has no mainspring, for nobody feels any kind of responsibility to do a thing in time, place, or manner, except as I oversee it.

"Georgina is so excessively weak, nervous, cross, and fretful, night and day, that she takes all Anna's strength and time with her; and then the children are, like other little sons and daughters of Adam, full of all kinds of absurdity and folly.

"When the brain gives out, as mine often does, and one cannot think or remember anything, then what is to be done? All common fatigue, sickness, and exhaustion is nothing to this distress. Yet do I rejoice in my God, and know in whom I believe, and only pray that the fire may consume the dross; as to the gold, that is imperishable. No real evil can happen to me, so I fear nothing for the future, and only suffer in the present tense.

"God, the mighty God, is mine, of that I am sure, and I know He knows that though flesh and heart fail, I am all the while desiring and trying for his will alone. As to a journey, I need not ask a physician to see that it is needful to me as far as health is concerned, that is to say, all human appearances are that way, but I feel no particular choice about it. If God wills I go, He can easily find means. Money, I suppose, is as plenty with Him now as it always has been, and if He sees it is really best, He will doubtless help me."

It was a very hard summer for both of them. Calvin, who was supposed to be raising money for the Seminary, stayed away till the beginning of October. He detested this money-raising, for which he was entirely unfitted. "This work," he writes Harriet on June 30, "is beyond measure irksome and trying to me, and the long absence from you and the children almost insupportable. And after all, it is not going to result in any immediate pecuniary *affluence* I can assure you. At most it will just enable us to struggle through another year, and give us hope that we shall not be obliged through excessive poverty to quit our post." And in September: "I am so nervous that any attempt to preach on the subject of raising money brings on neuralgic pains that are intolerable and lay me aside for a week or two. . . . If I cannot live without begging money, I must die; the sooner the better." He is passing, besides, through a serious crisis. He fears that he is losing his faith, and he has been frightened by recent scandals created in the clerical world by certain "licentious hypocrites" into wondering whether it might not be possible for him, too, to disgrace his calling.

"I long to be with you once more," he writes in the letter first quoted. "I am a miserable creature without a wife, and having been blessed with such a wife as you are, it is the harder to be alone so much and so long, and in an employment so essentially disagreeable to me. Let me have a competent salary, let me be permitted to study and teach and lecture everyday, let me have my dear little children around me every evening, and let me sleep in my own bed with my own good wife every night, and Prince Albert himself is not so happy a man as I. Though I have, as you well know, a most enthusiastic admiration of fresh, youthful female beauty; yet it never comes anywhere near the kind of feeling I have for you. With you, every desire I have, mental and physical, is completely satisfied and filled up, and leaves me nothing more to ask for. My enjoyment with you is not weakened by time nor blunted by age, and every reunion after separation is just as much of a honeymoon as was the first month after the wedding. Is not your own experience and observation a proof of what I say? Does it not always *seem to be* just as I represent it? Just as it seems, so it is in reality. No man can love and respect his wife more than I do mine. Yet we are not as happy as we might be. I have many faults, and you have some failings, and Anna [the Stowes' maid and nurse], with all her good qualities, is rather aggravating sometimes—but the grace of God can mend all.

"I have thought much of our domestic happiness lately in connection with the melancholy licentiousness, recently detected, of several clergymen of high reputation in the east."

A bishop in Philadelphia, whom Calvin has admired as a writer for his effective refutation of the "historical argument against Christianity," "it now appears has long been addicted to intoxication, and while half boozled has caught young ladies who were so unfortunate to meet him alone, and pawed them over in the most disgusting manner, and actually attempted to do them physical violence. This has been going on for years until it could be borne no longer, and now it all comes out against him, to the dishonor of religion, his own unspeakable shame and anguish, and the distress unutterable of his wife and children." And: "Another distinguished high church episcopalian clergyman in Philadelphia, nearly 60 years old, is said to be in precisely the same predicament as his bishop. Bless the Lord, O my soul, that with all my strong relish for brandy and wine, and all my indescribable admiration and most overflowing delight in handsome young ladies, no offences of this kind have yet been written down against me in God's book. Next comes the most melancholy case of N. E. Johnson, lately editor of the N.Y. evangelists and recently pastor of the Meth. Church in Bloomfield, N.J. Though he has been admired as an evangelical, spiritual, revival preacher of great talent and concentrated piety, and married to an intelligent, amiable and pious woman who has borne him children, though associating without suspicion with the most pious men and the most accomplished and Christian women, it now appears that for 8 or 9 years past he has been in the habit of not only visiting the theaters . . . but also the brothels and bawdy houses of the city of N.Y. where he would get beastly drunk and revel and swelter with the vilest harlots. . . .

"Last in this dreadful catalogue, J. H. Fairchild, formerly pastor of the Orthodox church in South Boston, and lately of Exeter N.H. a man 55 years old, twice married, and whose daughters are mothers. Circumstances have recently occurred, which show that he has for years been licentious, that while elder he seduced one of his own kitchen girls, committed adultery with a member of his own church; and lately he has cut his throat and killed himself in the agony of his shame, while pastor of one of the most respectable churches in Exeter. . . .

"Now what shall we think of all these horrid disclosures? Is there anybody we can trust? Are all ministers brutes? I confess I feel almost ashamed to go into a pulpit or ask anyone to contribute a cent for ministerial education. . . ."

Harriet's answer is prompt and firm: she takes the situation seriously, and that she and Calvin were quite right in doing so was to be proved by the later justification of a "presentiment" she speaks of here, in connection with a visit from her younger brother, Henry Ward Beecher, who was eventually to become involved in a similar, if less sordid, scandal: ". . . Yesterday Henry came from Crawfordsville uncommonly depressed and sober and spoke in church meeting of unexpected falls among high places in the church and the need of prayer for Christians. He seemed so depressed that a horrible presentiment crept over me. I though of all my brothers and of you—and could it be, that the great Enemy has prevailed against any of you, and as I am gifted with a most horrible vivid imagination, in a moment I imagined—nay saw as in a vision all the distress and despair that would follow a fall on your part. I felt weak and sick—I took a book and lay down on the bed, but it pursued me like a nightmare—and something seemed to ask Is your husband any better *seeming* than so and so!—I looked in the glass and my face which since spring has been something of the palest was so haggard that it frightened me. The illusion lasted a whole forenoon and then evaporated like a poisonous mist—but God knows how I pity those heart wrung women—wives worse than widows, who are called to lament that the grave has *not* covered their husband—the father of their children! Good and merciful God—why are such agonies reserved for the children of men! I can conceive now of misery which in one night would change the hair to grey and shrivel the whole frame to premature decrepitude!—misery to which all other agony is as a mocking sound! What terrible temptations lie in the way of your sex—till now I never realised it—for tho I did love you with an almost *insane* love before I married you I never knew yet or felt the pulsation which showed me that I could be tempted in any way—there never was a moment when I felt anything by which you could have drawn me astray—for I loved you as I now love God—and I can conceive of no higher love—and as I have no passion—I have no jealousy,—the most beautiful woman in the world could not make me jealous so long as she only *dazzled the senses*—but still my dear, you must not wonder if I want to warn you not to look or *think* too freely on womankind. If your sex would guard the outworks of *thought,* you would never fall—and when so dizzying so astounding are the advantages which Satan takes it scarce is implying a doubt to say 'be cautious' . . ."

But Calvin's religious difficulties he confides to his father-in-law rather than to Harriet. "I wanted to tell you something of the state of my soul," he writes to Lyman Beecher on July 17. "Since I left Cleveland I have suffered a great deal of mental agony, partly no doubt from physical causes. I feel that my heart is not right in the sight of God, that I do not yet know Christ as I ought to know him. I have been exceedingly distressed with skeptical doubts as to the reality of experimental religion, and whether the whole Bible is not after all a humbug; or at least merely the most simple and touching development of the religious sensibilities natural to man, which the human mind has yet been able to produce and whether in this state of things I ought not to leave the ministry and all studies connected with it, and devote myself to education, which is always a good, let the truth of religion stand as it may. I think with excessive pain of the great amount of exaggeration and humbug that exists in the so-called benevolent movement of the day, and of the great amount of selfishness and sectarianism in religious movements. I pray, and it is speaking to a dead wall and not to God—I call upon Christ, and he is a dead man who was buried 18 centuries ago—I try to be spiritually-minded, and find in myself a most exquisite relish, and deadly longing for all kinds of sensual gratification—I think of the revival ministers who have lived long in licentiousness with good reputation, and then been detested,—and ask myself, who knows whether there be any real piety on earth? O wretched man that I am! Who shall deliver me? . . . You are near the close of a long life spent in spreading the Gospel. Is the vail rent, and can you see through it into the holy of holies? Oh happy man if you can, and God grant me the same privilege, even at the expense of my life, O happy day when I and my wife and children are all in the quiet grave!"

To Harriet he writes three days later: "Though I can cheerfully trust the final salvation of my soul to Christ; yet I cannot now trust him for the temporal wants of my family and the institution. A strange inconsistency! Like Melanchthon, I have an unshaken hope of being forgiven and getting to heaven at last but everything else distresses me to death almost." He reproaches her on the 29th for not writing to strengthen his faith, to support his "feeble and tottering steps." "*My soul is weary of my life,* and I feel it would be the greatest of mercies to take me out of this world . . . Still I have felt that I could have some hold on Christ through you, and I have longed for your letters to come that I might stay myself on those thrilling paragraphs with which they at first abounded—but there are lately no special religious views in them—no more than what I or any ordinary professor of religion might write. Perhaps it is because my letters have had so little of the spirit of Christ in them that they have chilled and discouraged you. Lean and barren they have been I do not doubt but I hope you will not allow my deathfulness to deprive you of life when you are capable of living and I am not." He did feel, however, that his paralyzing despair might prove to be merely a test, "a process of spiritual purification" through which the Lord was leading him; and by August 17, he seems to have emerged and recovered his faith: "My mind is now free," he writes from Portland, Maine, "and I can commune with my God and Saviour, but my nervous system has received such a shock that I am incapable of any serious exertion. My nerves in every part of my body feel sore, and there is danger of universal neuralgia unless I keep quiet . . . I had a grand sail the other day all around the harbor, and while some of the company were profane and rebellious enough to amuse themselves with catching fish which they did not want, and knew nothing what to do with them after they had got them, I left the boat and scrambled around on the rocks, and let the waves roar and dash all over me, and felt quite delighted." When he had spoken in the earlier letter of not being able to rely on Christ "for the temporal wants of my family and the institution," he meant that he was unsuccessful in raising funds for the Seminary; and Harriet—September 3—tries heartily to reassure him that he can perfectly rely both on God and her: "My love you do wrong to worry so much about temporal matters—you really *do wrong:* You treat your Saviour ungenerously and you ought not to do it—Every letter of yours contains such unbelieving doubts 'Who will take care of us and keep us out of debt?'—My love if you were *dead* this day—and I feeble as I am with five little children I would not doubt nor despond nor expect to starve—tho *if* I *did* expect to starve I could bear it very well since Heaven is eternal . . . It is all humbug—got up by Satan—this fussing about a temporal future—if you will put the affairs all into my hands and let me manage them my own way and not give a thought during winter only to be good and grow in grace *I'l engage* to bring things out right in spring . . .—Now do take me up on this—"

In Calvin's two last letters to Harriet—of September 29 and 30—as the end of their separation draws near, we get for the first time a glimpse of what their life together had been. He is not looking forward now to a reunion which will be "just as much of a honeymoon as was the first month after the wedding." With a sudden return to the practical and a dropping of his valetudinarian tone, he explains to her all her faults, though admitting certain faults on his own part. She is slack and forbearing, he tells her, while he is methodical and irritable. He likes to have morning prayers and meals on time; she doesn't care when they have them. He likes to have the things in the house assigned to their places and left there; but it "seems to be your special delight to keep everything . . . on the move." He likes to have his newspapers "properly folded"; but she and Ann have vexed him "beyond all endurance" by "dropping them sprawling on the floor, or wabbling them all up in one wabble, and squashing them on the table like an old hen with her guts and gizzard squashed out."

But the next day a pang of compunction compels him to write her again: "The last letter I wrote you does not satisfy me, because it does not do you justice on a point on which you have seldom had justice done you, I mean your earnest and successful endeavour for self-improvement. In all respects in which both nature and an exceedingly defective or one-sided education have made you imperfect, I recognise and admire in you an earnest and Christian-like purpose to amend. Nature and bad education have done me great injury, and I know by my own experience how hard it is to get the better of such defects; and you have succeeded on your part far better than I have on mine." He cannot, however, refrain from enlarging on her shortcomings further: "Naturally thoughtless of expense and inclined to purchase whatever strikes your eye, without much reflection on the proportion of expenditure to be devoted to such objects, this propensity was indulged and greatly increased by your relations with Kate [her sister Catharine]. It can be corrected only by a rigid habit of keeping strict written accounts of all available income, of all absolute wants, and of all actual expense. . . . But there is another matter which needs care. When your mind is on any particular point, it is your nature to feel and act as if that were the only thing in the world; and you drive at it and make every thing bend to it, to the manifest injury of other interests. For instance, when you are intent on raising flowers,

you are sure to visit them and inspect them very carefully every morning; but your
kitchen would go for two or three days without any inspection at all, you would be quite
ignorant of what there was in the house to be cooked, or the way in which the work was
done. Your oversight of the flowers would be systematic and regular; of the kitchen, at
haphazard, and now and then. You should be as regular in the kitchen as in the garden.—
Again, you seldom hesitate to make a promise, whether you have ability to perform it or
not, like your father and Kate, only not quite so bad; and promises so easily made are very
easily broken. On this point Kate has no conscience at all, your father very little; and you
have enough to keep you from making such promises, if you would only think beforehand
whether you could fulfill them or not. . . .

"Well, no more on this subject at present. I got your flower seeds and a pound of the
guano. An ounce of the guano is to be dissolved in a gallon of water and applied to the
plant once a week. This is the scientific direction so that a pound of guano will last a long
time. I hope you will be content this winter with keeping a very few choice plants—for
labor is a great article in our family; and we must adopt some plan to save labor and fuel.
By the way, there is one other thing I will mention, because it has often vexed and irritated me intolerably. I must clean the stable, wash the carriage, grease the wheels, black
my boots, etc. etc. but you scorn to sweep the carriage, you must always call your servant
to do it, and not stoop yourself to so menial an act. This makes me mad, for you are not
too good to do in your line what I am everyday obliged to do in mine. Now I believe I
have opened my whole budget, and in these two letters given you all my grievances. I
pray the Lord to strengthen me on my return to treat you with uniform tenderness, kindness, and love. I suffer amazingly every day I live. I hardly know what to make of it, unless
it be the Lord's penance of our sin. You have suffered a great deal, but I doubt whether you
have ever suffered as I have this summer.

"I will try to come home cheerful and confiding in God. By the good hand of God
upon me I expect to be in Pittsburg Wednesday night, and then in Cincinnati as soon as I
can get there—Probably I shall not write you again. Forgive me all the wrong I have ever
done you, and give me credit for sincere endeavours to do better. I cannot tell you what
admiration I have heard expressed of you wherever I have been, and not always in a way at
all calculated to sooth my vanity. Good bye.

"affectionately C.E.S."

Harriet succeeded, the following spring, in getting away to Brattleboro, Vermont,
where she took "the water cure" and remained for almost a year. But soon after she returned to the West, she found that she was pregnant again. And now Calvin, who, in Harriet's absence, had relapsed into hypochondria, decided that he, too, required a cure. He,
too, had recourse to Brattleboro and remained away fifteen months. The completeness,
during such absences, of Calvin's eclipse and the extent to which he unloaded on Harriet
all the responsibility for the family may be gauged from a letter of July 29, 1855, written
during another long absence: "I shall return as soon as possible after the meeting in N.
York in Sept.—and until then you must manage all household matters in your own
way—just as you would if I were dead, and you had never anything more to expect from
me. Indeed, to all practical purposes I am dead for the present and know not when I shall
live again. If I have the ability to do it, I will by and by write you a letter about household
matters the coming season." A series of cholera epidemics had been added, in the years of
their residence, to the other nerve-taxing elements of Cincinnati life; and while Harriet
was handling the household alone, this series reached a terrible climax. At the peak of the
new epidemic, a thousand people a week were dying. The city was filled with the fumes of
the soft coal that was burned as a disinfectant, and everything was black with soot. There

was general demoralization, and many people less austere than the Beechers and Stowes did their best to stay drunk all the time. Harriet wrote to her husband that he must not think of coming back. The Stowe children's pet dog died; then their old colored laundress died—the twins helped to make her a shroud. Then Harriet's most recent baby began to have convulsions, and in four days it, too, was dead. Harriet herself was attacked by cramps, and the doctor assumed she was dying; but her father, who had been away attending the Yale Commencement, was back now to give her support. The indomitable old preacher, now seventy, rubbed Harriet's hands, as he writes his wife, "with perseverance and vigor"; and he always remained by her side, spending the night "on a settee in the dining room, hot as an oven and thronged with mosquitoes, sleepless from their annoyance, and conscious of every noise and movement." He gave Harriet a dose of brandy, which made her at first delirious, but he seems to think it pulled her through. "The night of suspense passed safely, and she was better in the morning." "I am not sick," he adds, to reassure his wife, "—never was better in my life, though last week I had to diet and abstain from corn and succotash; but this week I have studied and worked like Jehu every day, trimming up the trees, hoeing in the garden till my face was bathed and my shirt soaked, and yet I have not felt so well for a year past—so much like being young again."

So one's picture of this phase of Harriet's life is not really one of unrelieved horror. Such clerical New England families had a heritage of hearty vitality as well as of moral fortitude that prevented them from becoming pathetic. Yet, in the first sixteen years of her marriage, poor Harriet was suffering from miseries that must have been as little avowed— such complaints as the one I have quoted are rare—as the ever-rankling anxieties of slavery. *Uncle Tom,* with its lowering threats and its harassing persecutions, its impotence of well-meaning people, its outbreaks of violence and its sudden bereavements, had been lived in the Beecher home, where the trials and tribulations, as they used to be called, of the small family world inside were involved with, were merged in, the travail of the nation to which it belonged. This obscure personal anguish of Harriet Stowe went to energize her famous novel which had so strong an impact on public affairs, as did also the courage and faith, the conviction that God, after all, was just. And finally a turn does come in the fortunes of Calvin and Harriet Stowe: God does at last provide; a door of escape is unlocked; He is now at last giving them something which will offset their doubt, their ordeal, their self-imposed obligations, their self-control under His difficult exactions; the world will at last yield them something for what they have done and are. In the autumn of 1849, Bowdoin College in Maine offers Calvin a professorship, and though he knows that the chair is the worst-paid in the college—a thousand dollars a year—he is only too glad to accept. The Seminary tries to keep him by offering him fifteen hundred, and, immediately after this, the Theological Seminary at Andover makes him an even better offer. But he is definitely committed to Bowdoin, and the next spring the Stowes move to Maine. When they arrive, it is still very cold, and the house they are going to live in is shabby and bare and forlorn, but they light up a fire and set to work. Harriet spreads a long table on which the family can eat and she can write, and she repaints the woodwork and repapers the walls, and this is the end of their long testing: they will never be so poor or so racked again.

At the end of the year 1850, the Fugitive Slave Bill became a law. Non-Southerners were now held responsible for Negroes who had fled from the South, and, as an inducement to the local officials who decided on the claims of ownership, a premium was put on returning them. When Harriet got a letter from a sister-in-law which said: "Hattie, if I could use a pen as you can, I would write something that will make this whole nation feel what an accursed thing slavery is," she read the letter to her children, then, crumpling it in her hand, stood up and said, "I will if I live." When her brother Henry Ward Beecher came to see her a little later, they talked about the odious law. He was now preaching Abolition from his pulpit in Plymouth Church, Brooklyn, and holding benevolent "auctions," in which he brought before his congregation slaves that had escaped from the South, and called for contributions in order to buy their freedom. He, too, urged Harriet to write a book. She had met, a short time before, at the house of her brother Edward, who now had a church in Boston, a Negro preacher who had once been a slave and both of whose arms had been crippled by flogging, but who had succeeded in escaping to Canada and getting himself an education there; and one Sunday, when she had just taken Communion, the death of Uncle Tom was revealed to her "almost as a tangible vision." Scarcely able to restrain her emotion, she went home and wrote it down; and now the rest of Uncle Tom's story "rushed upon her with a vividness and importunity that would not be denied." She poured it out late in the evenings, after the demands of the household had been dealt with. She does not seem to have planned the story in advance, yet the course that it was taking imposed itself as something uncontrollable, unalterable. The novel appeared first as a serial in an anti-slavery weekly which was published in Washington, and it ran to such length—it continued from June 8, 1851, to April 1, 1852—that the editor begged her to cut it short; but the story had taken possession of its readers as well as of Mrs. Stowe, and when the editor published a note suggesting that the public might have had enough, this elicited a violent protest, and Uncle Tom was spared none of the stages which were to lead him to the final scene which had come to Mrs. Stowe in church.

Dwight MacDonald

Masscult and Midcult

For about two centuries Western culture has in fact been two cultures: the traditional kind—let us call it High Culture—that is chronicled in the textbooks, and a novel kind that is manufactured for the market. This latter may be called Mass Culture, or better Masscult, since it really isn't culture at all. Masscult is a parody of High Culture. In the older forms, its artisans have long been at work. In the novel, the line stretches from the eighteenth-century "servant-girl romances" to Edna Ferber, Fannie Hurst and such current ephemera as Burdick, Drury, Michener, Ruark and Uris; in music, from Hearts and Flowers to Rock 'n Roll; in art, from the chromo to Norman Rockwell; in architecture, from Victorian Gothic to ranch-house moderne; in thought, from Martin Tupper's *Proverbial Philosophy* ("Marry not without means, for so shouldst thou tempt Providence; / But wait not for more than enough, for marriage is the DUTY of most men.") to Norman Vincent Peale. (Thinkers like H. G. Wells, Stuart Chase, and Max Lerner come under the head of Midcult rather than Masscult.) And the enormous output of such new media as the radio, television and the movies is almost entirely Masscult.

"Masscult and Midcult I and II" by Dwight MacDonald first appeared in *Partisan Review,* Vol. 27, No. 2, 1949, and Vol. 27, No. 4, 1960, respectively.

I

This is something new in history. It is not that so much bad art is being produced. Most High Culture has been undistinguished, since talent is always rare—one has only to walk through any great art museum or try to read some of the forgotten books from past centuries. Since only the best works still have currency, one thinks of the past in their terms, but they were really just a few plums in a pudding of mediocrity.

Masscult is bad in a new way: it doesn't even have the theoretical possibility of being good. Up to the eighteenth century, bad art was of the same nature as good art, produced for the same audience, accepting the same standards. The difference was simply one of individual talent. But Masscult is something else. It is not just unsucessful art. It is non-art. It is even anti-art.

> There is a novel of the masses but no Stendhal of the masses; a music for the masses but no Bach or Beethoven, whatever people say . . . [André Malraux observes in "Art, Popular Art and the Illusion of the Folk"—(*Partisan Review,* September–October, 1951).] It is odd that no word . . . designates the common character of what we call, separately, bad painting, bad architecture, bad music, etc. The word "painting" only designates a domain in which art is possible. . . . Perhaps we have only one word because bad painting has not existed for very long. There is no bad Gothic painting. Not that all Gothic painting is good. But the difference that separates Giotto from the most mediocre of his imitators is not of the same kind as that which separates Renoir from the caricaturists of *La Vie Parisienne.* . . . Giotto and the Gaddi are separated by talent, Degas and Bonnat by a schism, Renoir and "suggestive" painting by what? By the fact that this last, totally subjected to the spectator, is a form of advertising which aims at selling itself. If there exists only one word . . . it is because there was a time when the distinction between them had no point. Instruments played real music then, for there was no other.

But now we have pianos playing Rock 'n Roll and *les sanglots longs des violons* accompanying torch singers.

Masscult offers its customers neither an emotional catharsis nor an aesthetic experience, for these demand effort. The production line grinds out a uniform product whose humble aim is not even entertainment, for this too implies life and hence effort, but merely distraction. It may be stimulating or narcotic, but it must be easy to assimilate. It asks nothing of its audience, for it is "totally subjected to the spectator." And it gives nothing.*

Some of its producers are able enough. Norman Rockwell is technically skilled, as was Meissonier—though Degas was right when he summed up the cavalry charge in *Friedland, 1806:* "Everything is steel except the breastplates." O. Henry could tell a story better than many contributors to our Little Magazines. But a work of High Culture, however inept, is an expression of feelings, ideas, tastes, visions that are idiosyncratic and the audience similarly responds to them as individuals. Furthermore, both creator and audience accept certain standards. These may be more or less traditional; sometimes they are so

*"Distraction is bound to the present mode of production, to the rationalized and mechanized process of labor to which . . . the masses are subject. . . . People want to have fun. A fully concentrated and conscious experience of art is possible only to those whose lives do not put such a strain on them that in their spare time they want relief from both boredom and effort simultaneously. The whole sphere of cheap commercial entertainment reflects this dual desire."—T. W. Adorno: *On Popular Music.*

much less so as to be revolutionary, though Picasso, Joyce and Stravinsky knew and re-spected past achievements more than did their academic contemporaries; their works may be seen as a heroic breakthrough to earlier, sounder foundations that had been obscured by the fashionable gimcrackery of the academies. But Masscult is indifferent to standards. Nor is there any communication between individuals. Those who consume Masscult might as well be eating ice-cream sodas, while those who fabricate it are no more express-ing themselves than are the "stylists" who design the latest atrocity from Detroit.

The difference appears if we compare two famous writers of detective stories, Mr. Erle Stanley Gardner and Mr. Edgar Allen Poe. It is impossible to find any personal note in Mr. Gardner's enormous output—he has just celebrated his centenary, the hundredth novel under his own name (he also has knocked off several dozen under pseudonyms). His prose style varies between the incompetent and the nonexistent; for the most part, there is just no style, either good or bad. His books seem to have been manufactured rather than com-posed; they are assembled with the minimum expenditure of effort from identical parts that are shifted about just enough to allow the title to be changed from *The Case of the Cu-rious Bride* to *The Case of the Fugitive Nurse*. Mr. Gardner obviously has the production problem licked—he has rated his "native abilities" as Very Good as a lawyer, Good as a business analyst, and Zero as a writer, the last realistic estimate being the clue to his pro-duction-line fertility—and his popularity indicates he has the problem of distribution well in hand. He is marketing a standard product, just like Kleenex, that precisely be-cause it is not related to any other individual needs on the part of either the producer or the consumer appeals to the widest possible audience. The obsession of our fact-minded culture with the processes of the law is probably the lowest common denominator that has made Mr. Gardner's unromantic romances such dependable commodities.

Like Mr. Gardner, Mr. Poe was a money-writer. (That he didn't make any is irrelevant.) The difference, aside from the fact that he was a good writer, is that, even when he was turning out hack work, he had an extraordinary ability to use the journalistic forms of his day to express his own peculiar personality, and indeed, as Marie Bonaparte has shown in her fascinating study, to relieve his neurotic anxieties. (It is simply impossible to imagine Mr. Gardner afflicted with anything as individual as a neurosis.) The book review, the macabre-romantic tale, the magazine poem, all served his purposes, and he even invented a new one, the detective story, which satisfied the two chief and oddly disparate drives in his psychology—fascination with horror (*The Murders in the Rue Morgue*) and obsession with logical reasoning or, as he called it, "ratiocination" (*The Purloined Letter*). So that while his works are sometimes absurd, they are rarely dull.

It is important to understand that the difference between Mr. Poe and Mr. Gardner, or between High Culture and Masscult, is not mere popularity. From *Tom Jones* to the films of Chaplin, some very good things have been too popular; *The Education of Henry Adams* was the top nonfiction best seller of 1919. Nor is it that Poe's detective stories are harder to read than Gardner's, though I suppose they are for most people. The difference lies in the qualities of Masscult already noted: its impersonality and its lack of standards, and "total subjection to the spectator." The same writer, indeed the same book or even the same chapter, may contain elements of both Masscult and High Culture. In Balzac, for instance, the most acute psychological analysis and social observation is bewilderingly interlarded with the cheapest, flimsiest kind of melodrama. In Dickens, superb comedy alternates with bathetic sentimentality, great descriptive prose with the most vulgar kind of theatri-cality. All these elements were bound between the same covers, sold to the same mass au-dience, and, it may well be, considered equally good by their authors—at least I know of no evidence that either Dickens or Balzac was aware of when he was writing down and when he was writing up. Masscult is a subtler problem than is sometimes recognized. . . . that has made it remarkable. It is the work of a great array of highly paid and incompatible writers to distinguish this quality, separate it and obliterate it." This process is called "licking the book"—i.e., licking it into shape, as mother bears were once thought to lick their amorphous cubs into real bears; though here the process is reversed and the book is licked not into but out of shape. The other meaning of "licked" also applies; before a proper Hollywood film can be made, the work of art has to be defeated.

II

The question of Masscult is part of the larger question of the masses. The tendency of modern industrial society, whether in the USA or the USSR, is to transform the individual into the mass man. For the masses are in historical time what a crowd is in space: a large quantity of people unable to express their human qualities because they are related to each other neither as individuals nor as members of a community. In fact, they are not related *to each other* at all but only to some impersonal, abstract, crystallizing factor. In the case of crowds, this can be a football game, a bargain sale, a lynching; in the case of the masses, it can be a political party, a television program, a system of industrial production. The mass man is a solitary atom, uniform with the millions of other atoms that go to make up "the lonely crowd," as David Riesman well calls our society. A community, on the contrary, is a group of individuals linked to each other by concrete interests. Something like a family, each of whose members has his or her special place and function while at the same time sharing the group's economic aims (family budget), traditions (family history), sentiments (family quarrels, family jokes), and values ("That's the way we do it in *this* family!"). The scale must be small enough so that it "makes a difference" what each person does—this is the first condition for human, as against mass, existence. Paradoxically, the individual in a community is both more closely integrated into the group than is the mass man and at the same time is freer to develop his own special personality. Indeed, an individual can only be defined in relation to a community. A single person in nature is not an individual but an animal; Robinson Crusoe was saved by Friday. The totalitarian regimes, which have consciously tried to create the mass man, have systematically broken every communal link—family, church, trade union, local and regional loyalties, even down to ski and chess clubs—and have reforged them so as to bind each atomized individual directly to the center of power. . . .

IX

. . . the separation of Folk Art and High Culture in fairly watertight compartments corresponded to the sharp line once drawn between the common people and the aristocracy. The blurring of this line, however desirable politically, has had unfortunate results culturally. Folk Art had its own authentic quality, but Masscult is at best a vulgarized reflection of High Culture and at worst a cultural nightmare, a *Kulturkatzenjammer.* And while High Culture could formerly address itself only to the *cognoscenti,* now it must take the *ignoscenti* into account even when it turns its back on them. For Masscult is not merely a parallel formation to High Culture, as Folk Art was; it is a competitor. The problem is especially acute in this country because class lines are especially weak here. If there were a clearly defined cultural elite here, then the masses could have their *Kitsch* and the classes could have their High Culture, with everybody happy. But a significant part of our population is chronically confronted with a choice between looking at TV or old masters, between reading Tolstoy or a detective story; i.e., the pattern of their cultural lives is "open" to the point of being porous. For a lucky few, this openness of choice is stimulating. But for most, it is confusing and leads at best to that middlebrow compromise called Midcult.

The turning point in our culture was the Civil War, whose aftermath destroyed the New England tradition almost as completely as the October Revolution broke the continuity of Russian culture. (Certain disturbing similarities between present-day American and Soviet Russian culture and society may be partly due to these seismic breaks, much more drastic than anything in European history, including the French Revolution.) The New England culture was simply pushed aside by history, dwindling to provincial gentility, and there was no other to take its place; it was smothered by the growth of mass industry, by westward expansion, and above all by the massive immigration from non-English-speaking countries. The great metaphor of the period was the melting pot; the tragedy was that it melted so thoroughly. A pluralistic culture might have developed, enriched by the contributions of Poles, Italians, Serbs, Greeks, Jews, Finns, Croats, Germans, Swedes, Hungarians, and all the other peoples that came here from 1870 to 1910. It is with mixed feelings one reads Emma Lazarus' curiously condescending inscription on the Statue of Liberty:

> Give me your tired, your poor,
> Your huddled masses yearning to breathe free,
> The wretched refuse of your teeming shore,
> Send these, the homeless, tempest-tossed, to me:
> I lift my lamp beside the golden door.

For indeed these *were* the poor and tempest-tossed, the bottom-dogs of Europe, and for just this reason they were all too eager to give up their old-world languages and customs, which they regarded as marks of inferiority. Uprooted from their own traditions, offered the dirtiest jobs at the lowest pay, the masses from Europe were made to feel that their only hope of rising was to become "Americanized," which meant being assimilated at the lowest cultural (as well as economic) level. They were ready-made consumers of *Kitsch*. A half-century ago, when the issue was still in the balance, Randolph Bourne wrote:

> What we emphatically do not want is that these distinctive qualities should be washed out into a tasteless, colorless fluid of uniformity. Already we have far too much of this insipidity— masses of people who are half-breeds. . . . Our cities are filled with these half-breeds who retain their foreign names but have lost the foreign savor. This does not mean that . . . they have been really Americanized. It means that, letting slip from them whatever native culture they had, they have substituted for it only the most rudimentary American—the American culture of the cheap newspaper, the movies, the popular song, the ubiquitous automobile. . . .
>
> Just so surely as we tend to disintegrate these nuclei of nationalistic culture do we tend to create hordes of men and women without a spiritual country, cultural outlaws without taste, without standards but those of the mob. We sentence them to live on the most rudimentary planes of American life.*

---

*From "Trans-National America." Of course the immigrants were not all "huddled masses." Many, especially the Jews, were quite aware of the inferior quality of American cultural life. In *The Spirit of the Ghetto* (1902), Hutchins Hapgood quotes a Jewish immigrant: "In Russia, a few men, really cultivated and intellectual, give the tone and everybody follows them. But in America the public gives the tone and the literary man simply expresses the public. So that really intellectual Americans do not express as good ideas as less intellectual Russians. The Russians all imitate the best. The Americans imitate what the mass of the people want." A succinct definition of Masscult.

Bourne's fears were realized. The very nature of mass industry and of its offshoot, Masscult, made a pluralistic culture impossible. The melting pot produced merely "the taste-
less, colorless fluid of uniformity." This much can be said for the dominant Anglo-Saxon
Americans: they didn't ask the immigrants to accept anything they themselves were unwilling to accept. One recalls Matthew Josephson's vignette of Henry Clay Frick sitting
on a Renaissance chair under a Rembrandt reading the *Saturday Evening Post*. They were
preoccupied with building railroads, settling the West, expanding industry, perfecting
monopolies and other practical affairs. Pioneers, O Pioneers! And the tired pioneer preferred Harold Bell Wright to Henry James.

X

We are now in a more sophisticated period. The West has been won, the immigrants
melted down, the factories and railroads built to such effect that since 1929 the problem
has been consumption rather than production. The work week has shrunk, real wages
have risen, and never in history have so many people attained such a high standard of living as in this country since 1945. College enrollment is now well over four million, three
times what it was in 1929. Money, leisure and knowledge, the prerequisites for culture,
are more plentiful and more evenly distributed than ever before.

In these more advanced times, the danger to High Culture is not so much from Masscult as from a peculiar hybrid bred from the latter's unnatural intercourse with the former.
A whole middle culture has come into existence and it threatens to absorb both its
parents. This intermediate form—let us call it Midcult—has the essential qualities of
Masscult—the formula, the built-in reaction, the lack of any standard except popularity—but it decently covers them with a cultural figleaf. In Masscult the trick is plain—to
please the crowd by any means. But Midcult has it both ways: it pretends to respect the
standards of High Culture while in fact it waters them down and vulgarizes them.*

The enemy outside the walls is easy to distinguish. It is its ambituity that makes Midcult alarming. For it presents itself as part of High Culture. Not that coterie stuff, not those
snobbish inbred so-called intellectuals who are only talking to themselves. Rather the great
vital mainstream, wide and clear though perhaps not so deep. You, too, can wade in it for a
mere $16.70 pay nothing now just fill in the coupon and receive a full year six hard-cover
lavishly illustrated issues of *Horizon: A Magazine of the Arts*, "probably the most beautiful
magazine in the world . . . seeks to serve as guide to the long cultural advance of modern
man, to explore the many mansions of the philosopher, the painter, the historian, the architect, the sculptor, the satirist, the poet . . . to build bridges between the world of scholars and the world of intelligent readers. It's a good buy. Use the coupon *now*." *Horizon* has
some 160,000 subscribers, which is more than the combined circulations, after many years
of effort, of *Kenyon, Hudson, Sewanee, Partisan, Art News, Arts, American Scholar, Dissent, Commentary,* and half a dozen of our other leading cultural-critical magazines.

---

*It's not done, of course, as consciously as this suggests. The editors of the *Saturday Review* or *Harper's* or
the *Atlantic* would be honestly indignant at this description of their activities, as would John Steinbeck,
J. P. Marquand, Pearl Buck, Irwin Shaw, Herman Wouk, John Hersey and others of that remarkably
large group of Midcult novelists we have developed. One of the nice things about Zane Grey was that it
seems never to have occurred to him that his books had anything to do with literature.

Midcult is not, as might appear at first, a raising of the level of Masscult. It is rather a corruption of High Culture which has the enormous advantage over Masscult that while also in fact "totally subjected to the spectator," in Malraux's phrase, it is able to pass itself off as the real thing. Midcult is the Revised Standard Version of the Bible, put out several years ago under the aegis of the Yale Divinity School, that destroys our greatest monument of English prose, the King James Version, in order to make the text "clear and meaningful to people today," which is like taking apart Westminster Abbey to make Disneyland out of the fragments. Midcult is the Museum of Modern Art's film department paying tribute to Samuel Goldwyn because his movies are alleged to be (slightly) better than those of other Hollywood producers—though why they are called "producers" when their function is to prevent the production of art (cf., the fate in Hollywood of Griffith, Chaplin, von Stroheim, Eisenstein and Orson Welles) is a semantic puzzle. Midcult is the venerable and once venerated *Atlantic*—which in the last century printed Emerson, Lowell, Howells, James, and Mark Twain—putting on the cover of a recent issue a huge photograph of Dore Schary, who has lately transferred his high-minded sentimentality from Hollywood to Broadway and who is represented in the issue by a homily, "To A Young Actor," which synthesizes Jefferson, Polonius and Dr. Norman Vincent Peale, concluding: "Behave as citizens not only of your profession but of the full world in which you live. Be indignant with injustice, be gracious with success, be courageous with failure, be patient with opportunity, and be resolute with faith and honor." Midcult is the Book-of-the-Month Club, which since 1926 has been supplying its members with reading matter of which the best that can be said is that it could be worse, i.e., they get John Hersey instead of Gene Stratton Porter. Midcult is the transition from Rodgers and Hart to Rodgers and Hammerstein, from the gay tough lyrics of *Pal Joey,* a spontaneous expression of a real place called Broadway, to the folk-fakery of *Oklahoma!* and the orotund sentimentalities of *South Pacific.* * Midcult is or was, "Omnibus," subsidized by a great foundation to raise the level of television, which began its labors by announcing it would "be aimed straight at the average American audience, neither high-brow nor lowbrow, the audience that made the *Reader's Digest, Life,* the *Ladies' Home Journal,* the audience which is the solid backbone of any business as it is of America itself" and which then proved its good faith by programming Gertrude Stein and Jack Benny, Chekhov and football strategy, Beethoven and champion ice skaters. "Omnibus" failed. The level of television, however, was not raised, for some reason.

---

*An interesting Midcult document is the editorial the *New York Times* ran August 24, 1960, the day after the death of Oscar Hammerstein 2nd:

> . . . The theatre has lost a man who stood for all that is decent in life. . . . The concern for racial respect in *South Pacific,* the sympathy and respect for a difficult though aspiring monarch in *The King and I,* the indomitable faith that runs through *Carousel* were not clever bits of showmanship. They represented Mr. Hammerstein's faith in human beings and their destiny. . . .
>
> Since he was at heart a serious man, his lyrics were rarely clever. Instead of turning facetious phrases he made a studious attempt to write idiomatically in the popular tradition of the musical theatre, for he was a dedicated craftsman. But the style that was apparently so artless has brought glimpses of glory into our lives. "There's a bright, golden haze on the meadow," sings Curly in *Oklahoma!* and the gritty streets of a slatternly city look fresher. "June is bustin' out all over," sing Carrie and Nettie in *Carousel* and the harshness of our winter vanishes. . . . To us it is gratifying that he had the character to use his genius with faith and scruple.

The contrast of faith (good) with cleverness (bad) is typical of Midcult, as is the acceptance of liberalistic moralizing as a satisfactory substitute for talent. Indeed, talent makes the midbrow uneasy: "Since he was a serious man, his lyrics were rarely clever." The death of Mr. Hart did not stimulate the *Times* to editorial elegy.

XI

But perhaps the best way to define Midcult is to analyze certain typical products. The four I have chosen are Ernest Hemingway's *The Old Man and the Sea,* Thornton Wilder's *Our Town,* Archibald MacLeish's *J.B.* and Stephen Vincent Benét's *John Brown's Body.* They have all been Midcult successes: each has won the Pulitzer Prize, has been praised by critics who should know better, and has been popular not so much with the masses as with the educated classes. Technically, they are advanced enough to impress the midbrows without worrying them. In content, they are "central" and "universal," in that line of hollowly portentous art which the French call *pompier* after the glittering, golden beplumed helmets of their firemen. Mr. Wilder, the cleverest of the four, has actually managed to be at once ultra-simple and grandiose. "Now there are some things we all know, but we don't take 'm out and look at 'm very often," says his stage manager, sucking ruminatively on his pipe. "We all know that *something* is eternal. And it ain't houses and it ain't names, and it ain't earth, and it ain't even the stars. . . . Everybody knows in their bones that *something* is eternal, and that something has to do with human beings. All the greatest people ever lived have been telling us for five thousand years and yet you'd be surprised how people are always losing hold of it. There's something way down deep that's eternal about every human being." The last sentence is an eleven-world summary, in form and content, of Midcult. I agree with everything Mr. Wilder says but I will fight to the death against his right to say it in this way.

The Old Man and the Sea was (appropriately) first published in *Life* in 1952. It won the Pulitzer Prize in 1953 and it helped Hemingway win the Nobel Prize in 1954 (the judges cited its "style-forming mastery of the art of modern narration"). It is written in that fake-biblical prose Pearl Buck used in *The Good Earth,* a style which seems to have a malign fascination for midbrows—Miss Buck also got a Nobel Prize out of it. There are only two characters, who are not individualized because that would take away from the Universal Significance. In fact they are not even named, they are simply "the old man" and "the boy"—I think it was a slip to identify the fish as a marlin though, to be fair, it is usually referred to as "the great fish." The dialogue is at once quaint (democracy) and dignified (literature). "Sleep well, old man," quothes The Boy; or, alternatively, "Wake up, old man." It is also very poetic, as The Boy's speech: "I can remember the tail slapping and banging. . . . and the noise of you clubbing him like chopping a tree down and the sweet blood smell all over me." (Even the Old Man is startled by this cadenza. "Can you really remember that?" he asks.) In the celebrated baseball dialogues we have a fusion of Literature & Democracy:

> "The great DiMaggio is himself again. I think of Dick Sisler and those great drives in the old park. . . . The Yankees cannot lose."
> "But I fear the Indians of Cleveland."
> "Have faith in the Yankees, my son. Think of the great DiMaggio."

And this by the man who practically invented realistic dialogue.

It is depressing to compare this story with "The Undefeated," a bullfighting story Hemingway wrote in the 'twenties when, as he would say, he was knocking them out of the park. Both have the same theme: an old-timer, scorned as a has-been, gets one last chance; he loses (the fish is eaten by sharks, the bullfighter is gored) but his defeat is a moral victory, for he has shown that his will and courage are still intact. The contrast begins with the opening paragraphs:

Manuel Garcia climbed the stairs to Don Miguel Retana's office. He set down his suitcase and knocked on the door. There was no answer. Manuel, standing in the hallway, felt there was some one in the room. He felt it through the door.

He was an old man who fished alone in a skiff in the Gulf Stream and he had gone eighty-four days now without taking a fish. In the first forty days a boy had been with him. But after forty days without a fish the boy's parents had told him that the old man was now definitely and finaly *salao,* which is the worst form of unlucky, and the boy had gone at their orders in another boat which caught three good fish the first week. It made the boy sad to see the old man come in each day with his skiff empty and he always went down to help him carry either the coiled lines or the gaff and the harpoon and the sail that was furled around the mast. The sail was patched with flour sacks and, furled, it looked like the flag of permanent defeat.

The contrast continues—disciplined, businesslike understatement v. the drone of the pastiche parable, wordy and sentimental ("the flag of permanent defeat" fairly nudges us to sympathize). And all those "ands."

"Undefeated" is 57 pages long, as against *Old Man*'s 140, but not only does much more happen in it but also one feels that more has happened than is expressed, so to speak, while *Old Man* gives the opposite impression. "Undefeated" has four people in it, each with a name and each defined through his words and actions; *Old Man* has no people, just two Eternal, Universal types. Indeed, for three-fourths it has one only one, since The Boy doesn't go along on the fishing trip. Perhaps a Kafka could have made something out of it, but in Hemingway's realistic manner it is monotonous. "Then he began to pity the great fish"—that sort of thing. At times the author, rather desperate one imagines, has him talk to the fish and to the birds. He also talks to his hand: "How does it go, hand?" In "Undefeated," the emotion arises naturally out of the dialogue and action, but in *Old Man,* since there's little of either, the author has to spell it out. Sometimes he reports the fisherman's improbable musings: "He is a great fish and I must convince him, he thought. . . . Thank God, they are not as intelligent as we who kill them, although they are more noble and more able." Sometimes the author tips us off: "He was too simple to wonder when he had attained humility. But he knew he had attained it." (A humble man who knows he has attained humility seems to me a contradiction in terms.) This constant editorializing—an elementary sin against which I used to warn my Creative Writing class at Northwestern University—contrasts oddly with the stripped, no-comment method that made the young Hemingway famous. "I am a strange old man," the hero tells The Boy. Prove it, old man, don't say it. . . .

XIII

The special threat of Midcult is that it exploits the discoveries of the avant-garde. This is something new. Midcult's historical predecessor, Academicism, resembled it in being *Kitsch* for the elite, outwardly High Culture but really as much a manufactured article as the cheaper cultural goods produced for the masses. The difference is that Academicism was intransigently opposed to the avant-garde. It included painters like Bouguereau, Alma-Tadema, and Rosa Bonheur; critics like Edmund Gosse and Edmund Clarence Stedman; composers like Sir Edward Elgar; poets like Alfred Austin and Stephen Phillips;

writers like Rostand, Stevenson, Cabell, and Joseph Hergesheimer.* Academicism in its own dreary way was at least resisting Masscult. It had standards, the old ones, and it educated the *nouveaux riches,* some of whom became so well educated that they graduated to an appreciation of the avant-garde, realizing that it was carrying on the spirit of the tradition which the Academics were killing. It is possible to see Academicism as the growing pains of High Culture, the restrictive chrysalis from which something new might emerge. That it was always destroyed after a few decades carries out the simile—who looks at Alma-Tadema today, who reads Hergesheimer?

Midcult is a more dangerous opponent of High Culture because it incorporates so much of the avant-garde. The four works noticed above were more advanced and sophisticated, for their time, than were the novels of John Galsworthy. They are, so to speak, the products of lapsed avant-gardists who know how to use the modern idiom in the service of the banal. Their authors were all expatriates in the 'twenties—even Mr. Benét, who dates his Americanesque epic "Neuilly-sur-seine, 1928." That they are not conscious of any shifting of gears, that they still think of themselves as avant-gardists is just what makes their later works so attractive in a Midcult sense. "Toward the end of the 'twenties I began to lose pleasure in going to the theater," Mr. Wilder begins the preface to the 1957 edition of *Three Plays.* He explains that, while Joyce, Proust and Mann still compelled his belief, the theater didn't, and he continues: "I began to feel that the theater was not only inadequate, it was evasive; it did not wish to draw on its deeper potentialities. . . . It aimed to be *soothing.* The tragic had no heat; the comic had no bite; the social criticism failed to indict us with responsibility. I began to search for the point where the theater had run off the track, where it had . . . become a minor art and an inconsequential diversion." That point, he found, was "the box-set stage," with its realistic sets and props and its proscenium dividing the actors from the audience. He fixed that, all right, but the plays he mounted on his advanced stage were evasive, soothing, without tragic heat or comic bite and spectacularly without social criticism. *The Skin of Our Teeth,* for instance, is as vast in theme as *Our Town* is modest, dealing with the whole history of the human race, but its spirit and its dialogue are equally folksy, and its point, hammered home by the maid, Sabina, is identical: life goes on and, to lapse into the idiom of Sabina's opposite number in *Our Town,* there ain't a thing you can do about it. "This is where you came in," she says at the final curtain. "We have to go on for ages and ages yet. You go home. The end of this play isn't written yet. Mr. and Mrs. Antrobus! Their heads are full of plans and they're as confident as the first day they began." A soft impeachment—but Midcult specializes in soft impeachments. Its cakes are forever eaten, forever intact.

The Skin of Our Teeth was first produced in 1942, at the low point of the war; its message—the adaptability and tenacity of the human race through the most catastrophic events—was a welcome one and was well received. "I think it mostly comes alive under

---

*A typical Academic victory over the avant-garde was that by the "Beaux Arts" school of architecture, led by McKim, Mead & White, over the Chicago school, led by Louis Sullivan and including Frank Lloyd Wright, at the turn of the century. A stroll down Park Avenue illustrates the three styles. Academic: The Italian loggia of the Racquet & Tennis Club, the Corinthian extravagances of Whitney Warren's Grand Central Building. Avant-garde: the Seagram Building, by Mies van der Rohe and Philip Johnson, and the Lever Building, by Skidmore, Owings & Merrill. Midcult: the glass boxes—imitating as cheaply as possible the Lever and Seagram buildings—that are going up as fast as the old Academic-Renaissance apartment houses can be pulled down. One can hardly regret the destruction of the latter on either aesthetic or antiquarian grounds, but they did have a mild kind of "character" which their Midcult successors lack.

conditions of crisis," writes the author. "It has often been charged with being a bookish fantasia about history, full of rather bloodless schoolmasterish jokes. But to have seen it in Germany soon after the war, in the shattered churches and beerhalls that were serving as theaters, with audiences whose price of admission meant the loss of a meal . . . it was an experience that was not so cool. I am very proud that this year [1957] it has received a first and overwhelming reception in Warsaw. The play is deeply indebted to James Joyce's *Finnegans Wake.*" Personally, its bookish quality is one of the things I like about the play, and its jokes are often good; in fact, as entertainment *The Skin of Our Teeth* is excellent, full of charm and ingenuity; its only defect is that whenever it tries to be serious, which is quite often, it is pretentious and embarrassing. I quite believe the author's statement about its reception in postwar Germany—he enjoys a much greater reputation abroad than here—and I agree that the audiences responded to it because it seemed to speak to them of the historical cataclysm they had just been through. I find this fact, while not unexpected, depressing. The bow to *Finnegans Wake* is a graceful retrieve of a foul ball batted up in the *Saturday Review* fifteen years earlier by Messrs. Campbell and Robinson, the authors of *A Skeleton Key to Finnegans Wake.* They hinted at plagiarism, but I think one should rather admire the author's ability to transmute into Midcult such an impenetrably avant-garde work. There seems to be no limit to this kind of alchemy in reverse, given a certain amount of brass.

Alfred Kazin
The Jew as Modern American Writer

Emma Lazarus, who wrote these lines inscribed on the base of the Statue of Liberty ("Give me your tired, your poor . . . Your huddled masses, yearning to breathe free"), was the first Jew whom Ralph Waldo Emerson ever met. Emerson's daughter Ellen, an old Sunday-school teacher, noted how astonishing it was "to get at a real unconverted Jew (who had no objections to calling herself one, and talked freely about 'our Church' and 'we Jews'), and to hear how Old Testament sounds to her, and find she has been brought up to keep the Law, and the Feast of the Passover, and the day of Atonement. The interior view was more interesting than I could have imagined. She says her family are outlawed now, they no longer keep the Law, but Christian institutions don't interest her either."

Emma Lazarus had been sending Emerson her poems for years; he responded with uncertain praise, for they were excessively literary and understandably raised questions in the mind of so subtle a critic. But although she was not to become a consciously "Jewish" poet until the Russian pogroms aroused her, her being a Jew had certainly distinguished her in the literary world of Victorian America. She was that still exotic figure, that object of Christian curiosity, "the Jew"—and to descendants of the New England Puritans, straight out of their Bible.

"The Jew as Modern American Writer" by Alfred Kazin. Reprinted from *Commentary,* April 1966, by permission; all rights reserved.

Proust was to say that in every Jew "there is a prophet and a bounder." Emma Lazarus was still the "prophet" when she visited Concord. This was in 1876, when Jews in this country were getting known as "bounders." General Grant in a Civil War order had said "Jew" when he meant peddler, but impoverished farmers in the West now said "Jew" when they meant Wall Street financier. New England writers like James Russell Lowell and Henry Adams became obsessed with Jews and "the Jewish question" as soon as there were real Jews on the American scene. The "prophet" figure that literary New England had always known from books had become the "bounder"—and, worse, the ragged *shtetl* Jew whom Adams examined with such loathing from a Russian railway car and in New York when he heard him speaking "a weird guttural Yiddish." Henry James, returning to his native downtown streets, announced that "the denizens of the New York Ghetto, heaped as thick as the splinters on the table of a glass-blower, had each, like the fine glass particle, his or her individual share of the whole hard glitter of Israel." The Jew in New York was an instance of alienness, an object to be studied. James would have been astonished to think of a writer coming out of this milieu. And, to do him justice, not many immigrant Jews saw themselves as writers in English. Henry Adams' sometime protégé, Bernard Berenson, who had come here from Lithuania, was to find himself only as an art historian in Italy.

William Dean Howells, now a Socialist in New York, praised Abraham Cahan's *Yekl: A Tale of the New York Ghetto.* But Howells was predisposed to Russian literature, Cahan was a "Russian" realist in English, and Howells, like so many Westerners enjoying or soon to enjoy New York's "Europeanness," was also a democratic idealist, naturally friendly to all these new peoples in New York. His friend Mark Twain said that Jews were members of the human race; "that is the worst you can say about them." But this easy Western humor was still very far from the creative equality that Jewish and non-Jewish writers were some day to feel. Mark Twain, like Maxim Gorky in Russia, protested against pogroms and was friendly to Jews; but as late as 1910, when he died, there was no significant type of the Jewish writer in this country. The older German-Jewish stock had produced many important scholars and publicists; it was to produce an original in Gertrude Stein. But the positive, creative role of the Jew as modern American, and above all as a modern American writer, was in the first years of this century being prepared not in the universities, not even in journalism, but in the vaudeville theaters, music halls, and burlesque houses where the pent-up eagerness of penniless immigrant youngsters met the raw urban scene on its own terms. It was not George Jean Nathan, Robert Nathan, or Ludwig Lewisohn any more that it was Arthur Krock, David Lawrence, Adolph Ochs, or Walter Lippmann who established the Jew in the national consciousness as a distinctly American figure; it was the Marx Brothers, Eddie Cantor, Al Jolson, Fannie Brice, George Gershwin. Jewish clowns, minstrels, song-writers helped to fit the Jew to America, and America to the Jew, with an élan that made for future creativity in literature as well as for the mass products of the "entertainment industry."

Proust, with his artist's disengagement from both "prophet" and "bounder"; Henry Adams, with his frivolous hatred of the immigrant ("five hundred thousand Jews in New York eating kosher, and saved from the drowning they deserve"), had never conceived of the Jew as a representative national entertainer. But in the naturalness and ease with which the Jewish vaudevillian put on blackface, used stereotypes, and ground out popular songs, in the avidity with which the public welcomed him, was the Jew's share in the common experience, the Jew's averageness and typicality, that were to make possible the Jew-as-writer in this country. In Western Europe, Jewish "notables" had been a handful— as odd as the occasional prime minister of Italy or Britain; in Eastern Europe, where the

Jews were a mass, it was their very numbers that was so disturbing to anti-Semites in office, who even in Soviet Russia were to keep Jews down because the thought of too many Jews being allowed to exercise their talents at once could obviously be viewed as a threat to their own people. As Mikoyan was to say some years ago to a Jewish delegation, "We have our own cadres now." But in this country the very poverty and cultural rawness of the Jewish immigrant masses, the self-assertive egalitarianism of the general temper, and the naturalness with which different peoples could identify with each other in the unique halfway house that was New York (without New York it would no doubt all have been different, but without New York there would have been no immigrant epic, no America) gave individual performers the privilege of representing the popular mind. Never before had so numerous a mass of Jews been free citizens of the country in which they lived, and so close to the national life. And although many a genteel young literatus now analyzing Nathanael West and Saul Bellow shudders at his connection with Potash and Perlmutter, Eddie Cantor, and Fannie Brice, it is a fact that this "vulgar culture," proceeding merrily to the irreverent genius of the Marx Brothers (whose best movies were written by S. J. Perelman, the college chum and brother-in-law of Nathanael West), helped to found, as a natural habitat for the Jews in this country, the consciously grotesque style of parody that one finds in Perelman, West, Odets, Bellow, in many Broadway-Hollywood satirists, and even in an occasional literary critic, like Isaac Rosenfeld and Harold Rosenberg, impatient with the judicial tone that comes with the office. The Jewish writer, a late arrival in this country and admittedly of uncertain status, had to find his model in the majority culture, and although this had some depressing consequences in the mass, it was on the whole fortunate, for the sharply independent novelists, poets, and critics to come, that they were influenced more by the language of the street than by the stilted moralism that has always been a trap for the Jewish writer.

But of course the popular culture was invigorating and even liberating so long as it was one of many cultures operating simultaneously on the Jewish writer's mind. Ever since the legal emancipation of the Jews in Western Europe, there had been two principal cultures among the Jews—the orthodox, religious tradition, pursuing its own way often magnificently indifferent to the issues shaking European thought; and the newly secularistic culture of the "Jewish intellectuals," who found in the cause of "progressive humanity," in philosophic rationalism, in socialism, and cultural humanism, their sophisticated equivalent of Judaism. In Western Europe, for the most part, these two cultures no longer irritated each other. But among the Yiddish-speaking Jews of Eastern Europe, "enlightenment" did not appear until late in the 19th century; while in Western Europe the medieval ghettos were a barely tolerated memory, in Russia the Jewish Pale of Settlement, restricting most Jews to certain areas and restricting the intensity of their existence to the *shtetl* and its religious customs, remained a searing memory in the lives of immigrants and their children. The "dark" ages and the "modern" age, the ghetto and the revolutionary movement, persecution and free human development, were conjoined in the Jewish mind. The tension and ardor with which the two cultures of modern Jewry were related, in individual after individual, helps to explain the sudden flowering of painters among Russian Jews in the first years of this century, the extraordinary spiritual energy invested in the idea of socialism, the "twist" that Isaac Babel liked to give his Russian sentences, the general passion for "culture" and "cultural advancement," the revolutionary zeal with which former yeshiva boys turned political commissars spoke of the great new age of man.

Babel wrote of ex-seminarists riding away with the Red Cavalry from their "rotted" Bibles and Talmuds, Chagall's *rebbes* sprouted wings over the thatched roofs of Vitebsk and sang the joys of the flesh. The force of some immense personal transformation could be seen in the conscious energy of Trotsky's public role in the Russian Revolution. These revolutionaries, writers, scientists, painters were the "new men," the first mass secularists in the long religious history of the Jews, yet the zeal with which they engaged themselves to the "historic" task of desacralizing the European tradition often came from the profound history embedded in Judaism itself—it certainly did not come from the experience of Jews with other peoples in Eastern Europe. These "new men" had a vision of history that, as their critics were to tell them, was fanatically all of one piece, obstinately "Jewish" and "intellectual"—a vision in which some subtle purposiveness to history always managed to reassert itself in the face of repeated horrors. But what their critics could not recognize was that this obstinate quest for "meaning" was less a matter of conscious thought than a personal necessity, a requirement of survival, the historic circumstance that reasserted itself in case after case among the Jews, many of whom had good reason to believe that their lives were a triumph over every possible negation, and who, with the modesty of people for whom life itself is understandably the greatest good, found it easy to rejoice in the political and philosophical reasoning that assured them civic respect, civic peace, and the life of the mind.

"Excess of sorrow laughs," wrote Blake in *The Marriage of Heaven and Hell.* "Excess of joy weeps." For Jews in this country, who had triumphed over so much, remembered so much, were in such passionate relations with the two cultures—of religion and "modernity" that many believed in simultaneously—their conscious progress often became something legendary, a drama rooted in the existential fierceness of life lived and barely redeemed every single day. There was an intensity, a closeness to many conflicting emotions, that often seemed unaccountably excessive to other peoples. The need to explain himself to himself, to put his own house in order, was a basic drive behind many a Jewish writer. People to whom existence has often been a consciously fearful matter, who have lived at the crossroads between the cultures and on the threshold between life and death, naturally see existence as tension, issue, and drama, woven out of so many contradictions that only a work of art may appear to *hold* these conflicts, to compose them, to allow the human will some detachment. Surely never in history has a whole people had to endure such a purgation of emotions as took place at the Eichmann trial. It was this that led Harold Rosenberg to show the cruel dramatic necessity behind the trial—the need of the Jews to tell their story, to relive the unbearable, the inadmissible, the inexpressible. The Jew who has lived through the age of Hitler cannot even say, with Eliot, "After such knowledge, what forgiveness?" For he has to live with his knowledge if he is to live at all, and this "knowledge" enforces itself upon him as a fact both atrocious and dramatic, a mockery of the self-righteous Christianity that has always surrounded him, a parody of the Orthodox Judaism that has sought to justify the ways of God to man, a drama founded on the contrast between the victims and all those who remained spectators when the Jews were being slaughtered.

There are experiences so extreme that, after living them, one can do nothing with them *but* put them into words. There are experiences so terrible that one can finally do nothing with them but not forget them. This was already the case with many of the young Jewish writers just out of the city ghettos, who began to emerge in significant numbers only in the early 30's. Looking back on this emergence, one can see that it needed the peculiar crystallization of ancient experiences, and then the avidity with which young writers threw themselves on the American scene, to make possible that awareness of the Jew as a new force that one sees in such works of the 30's as Henry Roth's *Call It Sleep*, Michael Gold's *Jews Without Money*, Daniel Fuchs's *Summer in Williamsburg*, Albert Halper's *The Chute*, Odets' *Awake and Sing*, Meyer Levin's *The Old Bunch*, and even in West's *Miss*

Lonelyhearts, whose hero is not named a Jew but who is haunted by the indiscriminate pity that was to mark the heroes of Bernard Malamud and Edward Wallant. In the 20's there had been several extraordinarily sensitive writers, notably Paul Rosenfeld and Waldo Frank, out of the older, German-Jewish stock; but on the whole, it needed the turbulent mixing of the ghetto and the depression to make possible the wild flurry of strong new novels and plays in the 30's.

Yet the social realists of the 30's were often boxed in, mentally, by the poverty and hopelessness of their upbringing and the bitterness, deprivations, and anti-Semitism of depression America. The extraordinary brevity of so many literary careers in America is a social fact that any account of the Jewish writer in America must contend with as an omen for the future. Although the aborted career is common enough in American writing and was particularly marked among writers of the 30's—many were shipwrecked by the failure of their political hopes, and many crippled as artists by the excessive effort it took to bring out their non-selling books—it is also a fact that writers from the "minorities" have a harder time getting started, and tend, as a group, to fade out more easily, than those writers from the older stocks whose literary culture was less deliberately won and is less self-conscious. A historian of the Negro novel in this country says that most Negroes who have published one book have never published another—and one might well wonder what, until the sudden fame of James Baldwin, would have induced any Negro writer in this country to keep at it except the necessity of telling his own story. Thinking of the family situation portrayed in *Call It Sleep,* one can see why, having written *that* up, to the vast indifference of the public in the 30's, the author should have felt that he was through. The real drama behind most Jewish novels and plays, even when they are topical and revolutionary in feeling, is the contrast between the hysterical tenderness of the Oedipal relation and the "world"; in the beginning there was the Jewish mother and her son, but the son grew up, he went out into the world, he became a writer. That was the beginning of his career and usually the end of the novel. Jews don't believe in original sin, but they certainly believe in the original love that they once knew in the *shtetl,* in the kitchen, in the Jewish household—and after *that* knowledge, what forgiveness? In this, at least, the sentimental author of *Jews Without Money* parallels the master of childhood in *Call It Sleep.*

What saved Jewish writing in America from its innate provincialism, what enabled it to survive the moral wreckage of the 30's, was the coming of the "intellectuals"—writers like Delmore Schwartz, Saul Bellow, Lionel Trilling, Karl Shapiro, Harold Rosenberg, Isaac Rosenfeld, Lionel Abel, Clement Greenberg, Bernard Malamud, Irving Howe, Philip Rahv, Leslie Fiedler, Robert Warshow, Paul Goodman, Norman Mailer, Philip Roth, William Phillips. It was these writers, and younger writers in their tradition, who made possible intellectual reviews like *Partisan Review* and serious, objective, unparochial magazines like *Commentary*—a magazine which has emphasized general issues and regularly included so many writers who are not Jews. *Commentary,* founded in November 1945, was hospitable to this new maturity and sophistication among Jewish writers in America; it established itself on the American scene easily, and with great naturalness, exactly in those years immediately after the war when American Jews began to publish imaginative works and intellectual studies of distinction—*Dangling Man, The Victim, The Middle of the Journey, The Liberal Imagination, Death of a Salesman, The Naked and the Dead, The World Is a Wedding, The Lonely Crowd, The Natural, The Adventures of Augie March, The Mirror and the Lamp, The Tradition of the New.*

Even a gifted writer outside this group, Salinger, contemptuous of its ideologies, was an "intellectual" writing about "intellectuals. " Even a middlebrow sullenly critical of its preoccupations, Herman Wouk, did it the honor of "exposing" an intellectual in *The Caine*

Mutiny. Whether they were novelists or just intellectual pundits at large, what these writers all had in common was the ascendancy of "modern literature," which has been more destructive of bourgeois standards than Marxism, was naturally international-minded, and in a culture bored with middle-class rhetoric upheld the primacy of intelligence and the freedom of the imagination. The heroes of these "intellectuals" were always Marx, Freud, Trotsky, Eliot, Joyce, Valéry; the "intellectuals" believed in the "great enlighteners," because their greatest freedom was to be enlighteners of all culture themselves, to be the instructors and illuminati of the modern spirit. Unlike so many earlier writers, who had only their hard story to tell and then departed, the Jewish "intellectuals" who emerged in the 40's found shelter under the wide wings of the "modern movement," and so showed an intellectual spirit that Jews had not always managed in the great world.

Commentary has, more than any other "Jewish" magazine known to me, been a symbol of and a home for this intellectual spirit. I remember that as the first issues began to appear at the end of that pivotal year of 1945, I was vaguely surprised that it dealt with so many general issues in so subtly critical and detached a fashion, regularly gave a forum to non-Jewish writers as well as to Jewish ones. Like many Jewish intellectuals of my time and place, brought up to revere the universalism of the Socialist ideal and of modern culture, I had equated "Jewish" magazines with a certain insularity of tone, subject matter, writers' names —with mediocrity. To be a "Jewish writer"—I knew several, and knew of many more, who indefatigably managed this by not being any particular kind of writer at all—was somehow to regress, to strike attitudes, to thwart the natural complexities of truth. There were just too many imprecisions and suppressions in the parochially satisfied "Jewish" writer. It was enough to be a Jew *and* a writer. "Jewish" magazines were not where literature [was] most conformist—novelists like Saul Bellow and Norman Mailer dealt in the drama of concepts, had heroes who lived by concepts, and suffered for them. The world seemed suspended on concepts, and in the mass magazines as in the universities and publishing houses, a mass of indistinguishable sophisticates genuflected to the modern idols and talked the same textbook formulae about Joyce, James, Eliot, Faulkner, Picasso, Stravinsky. The Sunday book supplements were soon all as apocalyptic as a Jewish novelist after a divorce, and one could regularly read footnotes to the absurdity of the human condition, the death of tragedy, and the end of innocence by pseudo-serious minds who imitated Bellow, Mailer, Fiedler, Ginsberg, Goodman as humorlessly as teen-age girls copied hair styles from the magazines.

Definitely, it was now the thing to be Jewish. But in Western universities and small towns many a traditional novelist and professor of English felt out of it, and asked, with varying degrees of self-control, if there was no longer a good novel to be written about the frontier, about Main Street, about the good that was in marriage? Was it possible, these critics wondered aloud, that American life had become so deregionalized and lacking in local color that the big power units and the big cities had pre-empted the American scene, along with the supple Jewish intellectuals who were at home with them? Was it possible that Norman Mailer had become the representative American novelist?

It was certainly possible, and certainly the thought would not have astonished Mailer, just as the power of his example for other novelists did not astonish Saul Bellow. Whatever pain this ascendancy might cause to writers who felt out of it because they lived in Montana or in the wrong part of California, it was a fact that there were now Jewish novelists who, as writers, had mastered the complex resources of the modern novel, who wrote English lovingly, possessively, masterfully, for whom the language and the form, the intelligence of art, had become as natural a way of living as the Law had been to their grandfathers. Literature had indeed become their spiritual world, their essential personal salvation, in a world where all traditional markers were fast disappearing. But in the frothy turbulent "mix" of America in the 60's, with its glut, its power drives, its confusion of values, the Jewish writer found himself so much read, consulted, imitated, that he knew it would not be long before the reaction set in—and in fact the decorous plaint of the "Protestant minority" has been succeeded by crudely suggestive phrases about the "Jewish Establishment," the "O.K. writers and the Poor Goy," "The Jewish-Americah Push." Yet it is plainly a certain success that has been resented, not the Jew. And if the Jew has put his distinct mark on modern American writing, it is surely because, in a time when the old bourgeois certainties and humanist illusions have crumbled, the Jew is practiced in what James called "the imagination of disaster" and "does indeed see life as ferocious and sinister." The contemporary literary temper is saturnine, panicky, black in its humor but adroit in shifting the joke onto the shoulders of society. And the Jewish writer, with his natural interest in the social fact, has been particularly quick to show the lunacy and hollowness of so many present symbols of authority. Anxiety hangs like dry electricity in the atmosphere of modern American life, and the stimulus of this anxiety, with all its comic overtones, is the realized subject in the novels of Joseph Heller, Bruce Jay Friedman, Richard Stern, Jeremy Larner, the plays of Jack Gelber and Arthur Kopit. There is real madness to modern governments, modern war, modern moneymaking, advertising, science, and entertainment; this madness has been translated by many a Jewish writer into the country they live in, the time that offers them everything but hope. In a time of intoxicating prosperity, it has been natural for the Jewish writer to see how superficial society can be, how pretentious, atrocious, unstable—and comic. This, in a secular age when so many people believe in nothing but society's values, is the significance to literature of the Jewish writer's being a Jew.

Adrienne Rich

Vesuvius at Home: The Power of Emily Dickinson

I am traveling at the speed of time, along the Massachusetts Turnpike. For months, for years, for most of my life, I have been hovering like an insect against the screens of an existence which inhabited Amherst, Massachusetts, between 1830 and 1886. The methods, the exclusions, of Emily Dickinson's existence could not have been my own; yet more and more, as a woman poet finding my own methods, I have come to understand her necessities, could have been witness in her defense.

"Home is not where the heart is," she wrote in a letter, "but the house and the adjacent buildings." A statement of New England realism, a directive to be followed. Probably no poet ever lived so much and so purposefully in one house; even, in one room. Her niece

Reprinted from *On Lies, Secrets, and Silence: Selected Prose 1966–1978* by Adrienne Rich, by permission of the author and W.W. Norton & Company, Inc. Copyright 1979 by W.W. Norton & Company, Inc.

Martha told of visiting her in her corner bedroom on the second floor at 280 Main Street, Amherst, and of how Emily Dickinson made as if to lock the door with an imaginary key, turned, and said: "Matty: here's freedom."

I am traveling at the speed of time, in the direction of the house and buildings.

Western Massachusetts: the Connecticut Valley: a countryside still full of reverberations: scene of Indian uprisings, religious revivals, spiritual confrontations, the blazing-up of the lunatic fringe of the Puritan coal. How peaceful and how threatened it looks from Route 91, hills gently curled above the plain, the tobacco barns standing in fields sheltered with white gauze from the sun, and the sudden urban sprawl: ARCO, MacDonald's, shopping plazas. The country that broke the heart of Jonathan Edwards, that enclosed the genius of Emily Dickinson. It lies calmly in the light of May, cloudy skies breaking into warm sunshine, light-green spring softening the hills, dogwood and wild fruit-trees blossoming in the hollows.

From Northampton bypass there's a four-mile stretch of road to Amherst—Route 9— between fruit farms, steakhouses, supermarkets. The new University of Massachusetts rears its skyscrapers up from the plain against the Pelham Hills. There is new money here, real estate, motels. Amherst succeeds on Hadley almost without notice. Amherst is green, rich-looking, secure; we're suddenly in the center of town, the crossroads of the campus, old New England college buildings spread around two village greens, a scene I remember as almost exactly the same in the dim past of my undergraduate years when I used to come there for college weekends.

Left on Seelye Street, right on Main; driveway at the end of a yellow picket fence. I recognize the high hedge of cedars screening the house, because twenty-five years ago I walked there, even then drawn toward the spot, trying to peer over. I pull into the driveway behind a generous nineteenth-century brick mansion with wings and porches, old trees and green lawns. I ring at the back door—the door through which Dickinson's coffin was carried to the cemetery a block away.

For years I have been not so much envisioning Emily Dickinson as trying to visit, to enter her mind, through her poems and letters, and through my own intimations of what it could have meant to be one of the two mid–nineteenth-century American geniuses, and a woman, living in Amherst, Massachusetts. Of the other genius, Walt Whitman, Dickinson wrote that she had heard his poems were "disgraceful." She knew her own were unacceptable by her world's standards of poetic convention, and of what was appropriate, in particular, for a woman poet. Seven were published in her lifetime, all edited by other hands; more than a thousand were laid away in her bedroom chest, to be discovered after her death. When her sister discovered them, there were decades of struggle over the manuscripts, the manner of their presentation to the world, their suitability for publication, the poet's own final intentions. Narrowed-down by her early editors and anthologists, reduced to quaintness or spinsterish oddity by many of her commentators, sentimentalized, fallen-in-love with like some gnomic Garbo, still unread in the breadth and depth of her full range of work, she was, and is, a wonder to me when I try to imagine myself into that mind.

I have a notion that genius knows itself; that Dickinson chose her seclusion, knowing she was exceptional and knowing what she needed. It was, moreover, no hermetic retreat, but a seclusion which included a wide range of people, of reading and correspondence. Her sister Vinnie said, "Emily is always looking for the rewarding person." And she found, at various periods, both women and men: her sister-in-law Susan Gilbert, Amherst visitors and family friends such as Benjamin Newton, Charles Wadsworth, Samuel Bowles, editor of the Springfield *Republican,* and his wife; her friends Kate Anthon and

Helen Hunt Jackson, the distant but significant figures of Elizabeth Barrett, the Brontës, George Eliot. But she carefully selected her society and controlled the disposal of her time. Not only the "gentlewomen in plush" of Amherst were excluded; Emerson visited next door but she did not go to meet him; she did not travel or receive routine visits; she avoided strangers. Given her vocation, she was neither eccentric nor quaint; she was determined to survive, to use her powers, to practice necessary economies.

Suppose Jonathan Edwards had been born a woman; suppose William James, for that matter, had been born a woman? (The invalid seclusion of his sister Alice is suggestive.) Even from men, New England took its psychic toll; many of its geniuses seemed peculiar in one way or another, particularly along the lines of social intercourse. Hawthorne, until he married, took his meals in his bedroom, apart from the family. Thoreau insisted on the values both of solitude and of geographical restriction, boasting that "I have traveled much in Concord." Emily Dickinson—viewed by her bemused contemporary Thomas Higginson as "partially cracked," by the twentieth century as fey or pathological—has increasingly struck me as a practical woman, exercising her gift as she had to, making choices. I have come to imagine her as somehow too strong for her environment, a figure of powerful will, not at all frail or breathless, someone whose personal dimensions would be felt in a household. She was her father's favorite daughter though she professed being afraid of him. Her sister dedicated herself to the everyday domestic labors which would free Dickinson to write. (Dickinson herself baked the bread, made jellies and gingerbread, nursed her mother through a long illness, was a skilled horticulturalist who grew pomegranates, calla lilies, and other exotica in her New England greenhouse.)

Upstairs at last: I stand in the room which for Emily Dickinson was "freedom." The best bedroom in the house, a corner room, sunny, overlooking the main street of Amherst in front, the way to her brother Austin's house on the side. Here, at a small table with one drawer, she wrote most of her poems. Here she read Elizabeth Barrett's *Aurora Leigh,* a woman poet's narrative poem of a woman poet's life; also George Eliot; Emerson; Carlyle; Shakespeare; Charlotte and Emily Brontë. Here I become, again, an insect, vibrating at the frames of windows, clinging to panes of glass, trying to connect. The scent here is very powerful. Here in this white-curtained, high-ceilinged room, a red-haired woman with hazel eyes and a contralto voice wrote poems about volcanoes, deserts, eternity, suicide, physical passion, wild beasts, rape, power, madness, separation, the daemon, the grave. Here, with a darning needle, she bound these poems—heavily emended and often in variant versions— into booklets, secured with darning thread, to be found and read after her death. Here she knew "freedom," listening from above-stairs to a visitor's piano-playing, escaping from the pantry where she was mistress of the household bread and puddings, watching, you feel, watching ceaselessly, the life of sober Main Street below. From this room she glided downstairs, her hand on the polished bannister, to meet the complacent magazine editor, Thomas Higginson, unnerve him while claiming she herself was unnerved. "Your scholar," she signed herself in letters to him. But she was an independent scholar, used his criticism selectively, saw him rarely and always on *her* premises. It was a life deliberately organized on her terms. The terms she had been handed by society—Calvinist Protestantism, Romanticism, the nineteenth-century corseting of women's bodies, choices, and sexuality—could spell insanity to a woman genius. What this one had to do was retranslate her own unorthodox, subversive, sometimes volcanic propensities into a dialect called metaphor: her native language: "Tell all the Truth—but tell it Slant—." It is always what is under pressure in us, especially under pressure of concealment—that explodes in poetry.

The women and men in her life she equally converted into metaphor. The masculine pronoun in her poems can refer simultaneously to many aspects of the "masculine" in the patriarchal world—the god she engages in dialogue, again on *her* terms; her own creative powers, unsexing for a woman, the male power-figures in her immediate environment— the lawyer Edward Dickinson, her brother Austin, the preacher Wadsworth, the editor Bowles—it is far too limiting to trace that "He" to some specific lover, although that was the chief obsession of the legend-mongers for more than half a century. Obviously, Dickinson was attracted by and interested in men whose minds had something to offer her; she was, it is by now clear, equally attracted by and interested in women whose minds had something to offer. There are many poems to and about women, and some which exist in two versions with alternate sets of pronouns. Her latest biographer, Richard Sewall, rejecting an earlier Freudian biographer's theory that Dickinson was essentially a psychopathological case, the by-product of which happened to be poetry, creates a context in which the importance, and validity, of Dickinson's attachments to women may now, at last, be seen in full. She was always stirred by the existences of women like George Eliot or Elizabeth Barrett, who possessed strength of mind, articulateness, and energy. (She once characterized Elizabeth Fry and Florence Nightingale as "holy"—one suspects she merely meant, "great.")

But of course Dickinson's relationships with women were more than intellectual. They were deeply charged, and the sources both of passionate joy and pain. We are only beginning to be able to consider them in a social and historical context. The historian Carroll Smith-Rosenberg has shown that there was far less taboo on intense, even passionate and sensual, relationships between women in the American nineteenth-century "female world of love and ritual," as she terms it, than there was later in the twentieth century. Women expressed their attachments to other women both physically and verbally; a marriage did not dilute the strength of a female friendship, in which two women often shared the same bed during long visits, and wrote letters articulate with both physical and emotional longing. The nineteenth-century close woman friend, according to the many diaries and letters Smith-Rosenberg has studied, might be a far more important figure in a woman's life than the nineteenth-century husband. None of this was perceived or condemned as "lesbianism."[1] We will understand Emily Dickinson better, read her poetry more perceptively, when the Freudian imputation of scandal and aberrance in women's love for women has been supplanted by a more informed, less misogynistic attitude toward women's experiences with each other.

But who, if you read through the seventeen hundred and seventy-five poems—who— woman or man—could have passed through that imagination and not come out transmuted? Given the space created by her in that corner room, with its window-light, its potted plants and work-table, given that personality, capable of imposing its terms on a household, on a whole community, what single theory could hope to contain her, when she'd put it all together in that space?

"Matty: here's freedom," I hear her saying as I speed back to Boston along the turnpike, as I slip the ticket into the toll-collector's hand. I am thinking of a confined space in which the genius of the nineteenth-century female mind in America moved, inventing a language more varied, more compressed, more dense with implications, more complex of syntax, than any American poetic language to date; in the trail of that genius my mind has been moving, and with its language and images my mind still has to reckon, as the mind of a woman poet in America today.

---

[1]"The Female World of Love and Ritual: Relations between Women in Nineteenth-Century America," *Signs*, vol. 1, no. 1.

In 1971, a postage stamp was issued in honor of Dickinson; the portrait derives from the one existing daguerrotype of her, with straight, center-parted hair, eyes staring somewhere beyond the camera, hands poised around a nosegay of flowers, in correct nineteenth-century style. On the first-day-of-issue envelope sent me by a friend there is, besides the postage stamp, an engraving of the poet as popular fancy has preferred her, in a white lace ruff and with hair as bouffant as if she had just stepped from a Boston beauty-parlor. The poem chosen to represent her work to the American public is engraved, alongside a dew-gemmed rose, below the portrait:

> If I can stop one heart from breaking
> I shall not live in vain
> If I can ease one life the aching
> Or cool one pain
> Or help one fainting robin
> Unto his nest again
> I shall not live in vain.

Now, this is extremely strange. It is a fact that, in 1864, Emily Dickinson wrote this verse; and it is a verse which a hundred or more nineteenth-century versifiers could have written. In its undistinguished language, as in its conventional sentiment, it is remarkably untypical of the poet. Had she chosen to write many poems like this one we would have no "problem" of nonpublication, of editing, of estimating the poet at her true worth. Certainly the sentiment—a contented and unambiguous altruism—is one which even today might in some quarters be accepted as fitting from a female versifier—a kind of Girl Scout prayer. But we are talking about the woman who wrote:

> He fumbles at your Soul
> As Players at the Keys
> Before they drop full Music on—
> He stuns you by degrees—
> Prepares your brittle Nature
> For the Ethereal Blow
> By fainter Hammers—further heard—
> Than nearer—Then so slow
> Your breath has time to straighten—
> Your brain—to bubble Cool—
> Deals—One—imperial—Thunderbolt—
> That scalps your naked Soul—
>
> When Winds take Forests in their Paws—
> The Universe—is still—
>
> (#315)

Much energy has been invested in trying to identify a concrete, flesh-and-blood male lover whom Dickinson is supposed to have renounced, and to the loss of whom can be traced the secret of her seclusion and the vein of much of her poetry. But the real question, given that the art of poetry is an art of transformation, is how this woman's mind and imagination may have used the masculine element in the world at large, or those elements personified as masculine—including the men she knew; how her relationship to this reveals itself in her images and language. In a patriarchal culture, specifically the Judeo-Christian, quasi-Puritan culture of nineteenth-century New England in which Dickinson grew up, still inflamed with religious revivals, and where the sermon was still an active, if perishing, literary form, the equation of divinity with maleness was so fundamental that it is hardly surprising to find Dickinson, like many an early mystic, blurring erotic with religious experience and imagery. The poem I just read has intimations both of seduction and rape merged with the intense force of a religious experience. But are these metaphors for each other, or for something more intrinsic to Dickinson? Here is another:

> He put the Belt around my life—
> I heard the Buckle snap—
> And turned away, imperial,
> My Lifetime folding up—
> Deliberate, as a Duke would do
> A Kingdom's Title Deed—
> Henceforth, a Dedicated sort—
> A member of the Cloud.
>
> Yet not too far to come at call—
> And do the little Toils
> That make the Circuit of the Rest—
> And deal occasional smiles
> To lives that stoop to notice mine—
> And kindly ask it in—
> Whose invitation, know you not
> For Whom I must decline?
>
> (#273)

These two poems are about possession, and they seem to me a poet's poems—that is, they are about the poet's relationship to her own power, which is exteriorized in masculine form, much as masculine poets have invoked the female Muse. In writing at all—particularly an unorthodox and original poetry like Dickinson's—women have often felt in danger of losing their status as women. And this status has always been defined in terms of relationship to men—as daughter, sister, bride, wife, mother, mistress, Muse. Since the most powerful figures in partiarchal culture have been men, it seems natural that Dickinson would assign a masculine gender to that in herself which did not fit in with the conventional ideology of womanliness. To recognize and acknowledge our own interior power has always been a path mined with risks for women; to acknowledge that power and commit oneself to it as Emily Dickinson did was an immense decision.

Most of us, unfortunately, have been exposed in the schoolroom to Dickinson's "little-girl" poems, her kittenish tones, as in "I'm Nobody! Who are You?" (a poem whose underlying anger translates itself into archness) or

> I hope the Father in the skies
> Will lift his little girl—
> Old fashioned—naughty—everything—
> Over the stile of "Pearl."
>
> (#70)

or the poems about bees and robins. One critic—Richard Chase—has noted that in the nineteenth century "one of the careers open to women was perpetual childhood." A strain in Dickinson's letters and some—though by far a minority—of her poems was a self-diminutivization, almost as if to offset and deny—or even disguise—her actual dimensions as she must have experienced them. And this emphasis on her own "littleness," along with the deliberate strangeness of her tactics of seclusion, have been, until recently, accepted as the prevailing character of the poet: the fragile poetess in white, sending flowers and poems by messenger to unseen friends, letting down baskets of gingerbread to the neighborhood children from her bedroom window; writing, but somehow naively. John Crowe Ransom, arguing for the editing and standardization of Dickinson's punctuation and typography, calls her "a little home-keeping person" who, "while she had a proper notion of the final destiny of her poems . . . was not one of those poets who had advanced to that later stage of operations where manuscripts are prepared for the printer, and the poet's diction has to make concessions to the publisher's style-book." (In short, Emily Dickinson did not wholly know her trade, and Ransom believes a "publisher's style-book" to have the last word on poetic diction.) He goes on to print several of her poems, altered by him "with all possible forbearance." What might, in a male writer—a Thoreau, let us say, or a Christopher Smart or a William Blake—seem a legitimate strangeness, a unique intention, has been in one of our two major poets devalued into a kind of naiveté, girlish ignorance, feminine lack of professionalism, just as the poet herself has been made into a sentimental object. ("Most of us are half in love with this dead girl," confesses Archibald MacLeish. Dickinson was fifty-five when she died.)

It is true that more recent critics, including her most recent biographer, have gradually begun to approach the poet in terms of her greatness rather than her littleness, the decisiveness of her choices instead of the surface oddities of her life or the romantic crises of her legend. But unfortunately anthologists continue to plagiarize other anthologies, to reprint her in edited, even bowdlerized versions; the popular image of her and of her work lags behind the changing consciousness of scholars and specialists. There still does not exist a selection from her poems which depicts her in her fullest range. Dickinson's greatness cannot be measured in terms of twenty-five or fifty or even five hundred "perfect" lyrics; it has to be seen as the accumulation it is. Poets, even, are not always acquainted with the full dimensions of her work, or the sense one gets, reading in the one-volume complete edition (let alone the three-volume variorum edition) of a mind engaged in a lifetime's musing on essential problems of language, identity, separation, relationship, the integrity of the self; a mind capable of describing psychological states more accurately than any poet except Shakespeare. I have been surprised at how narrowly her work, still, is known by women who are writing poetry, how much her legend has gotten in the way of her being repossessed, as a source and a foremother.

I know that for me, reading her poems as a child and then as a young girl already seriously writing poetry, she was a problematic figure. I first read her in the selection heavily edited by her niece which appeared in 1937; a later and fuller edition appeared in 1945 when I was sixteen, and the complete, unbowdlerized edition by Johnson did not appear until fifteen years later. The publication of each of these editions was crucial to me in successive decades of my life. More than any other poet, Emily Dickinson seemed to tell me that the intense inner event, the personal and psychological, was inseparable from the universal; that there was a range for psychological poetry beyond mere self-expression. Yet the legend of the life was troubling, because it seemed to whisper that a woman who undertook such explorations must pay with renunciation, isolation, and incorporeality. With the publication of the *Complete Poems,* the legend seemed to recede into unimportance beside the unquestionable power and importance of the mind revealed there. But taking possession of Emily Dickinson is still no simple matter.

The 1945 edition, entitled *Bolts of Melody,* took its title from a poem which struck me at the age of sixteen and which still, thirty years later, arrests my imagination:

I would not paint—a picture—
I'd rather be the One
Its bright impossiblity
To dwell—delicious—on—
And wonder how the fingers feel
Whose rare—celestial—stir
Evokes so sweet a Torment—
Such sumptuous—Despair—

I would not talk, like Cornets—
I'd rather be the One
Raised softly to the Ceilings—
And out, and easy on—
Through Villages of Ether
Myself endured Balloon
By but a lip of Metal
The pier to my Pontoon—

Nor would I be a Poet—
It's finer—own the Ear—
Enamored—impotent—content—
The License to revere,
A privilege so awful
What would the Dower be,
Had I the Art to stun myself
With Bolts of Melody!

                                        (#505)

This poem is about choosing an orthodox "feminine" role: the receptive rather than the creative; viewer rather than painter, listener rather than musician; acted-upon rather than active. Yet even while ostensibly choosing this role she wonders "how the fingers feel/ whose rare-celestial—stir—/ Evokes so sweet a Torment—" and the "feminine" role is praised in a curious sequence of adjectives: "Enamored—*impotent*—content—." The strange paradox of this poem—its exquisite irony—is that it is about choosing not to be a poet, a poem which is gainsaid by no fewer than one thousand seven hundred and seventy-five poems made during the writer's life, including itself. Moreover, the images of the poem rise to a climax (like the Balloon she evokes) but the climax happens as she describes, not what it is to be the receiver, but the maker and receiver at once: "A Privilege so awful/ What would the Dower be/ Had I the Art to stun myself/ With Bolts of Melody!"—a climax which recalls the poem: "He fumbles at your Soul/ As Players at the Keys/ Before they drop full Music on—" And of course, in writing those lines she possesses herself of that privilege and that Dower. I have said that this is a poem of exquisite ironies. It is, indeed, though in a very different mode, related to Dickinson's "little-girl" strategy. The woman who feels herself to be the Vesuvius at home has need of a mask, at least, of innocuousness and of containment.

On my volcano grows the Grass
A meditative spot—
An acre for a Bird to choose
Would be the General thought—

> How red the Fire rocks below—
> How insecure the sod
> Did I disclose
> Would populate with awe my solitude.
>
> (#1677)

Power, even masked, can still be perceived as destructive.

> A still—Volcano—Life—
> That flickered in the night—
> When it was dark enough to do
> Without erasing sight—
>
> A quiet—Earthquake style—
> Too subtle to suspect
> By natures this side of Naples—
> The North cannot detect
>
> The Solemn—Torrid—Symbol—
> The lips that never lie—
> Whose hissing Corals part—and shut—
> And Cities—ooze away—
>
> (#601)

Dickinson's biographer and editor Thomas Johnson has said that she often felt herself possessed by a daemonic force, particularly in the years 1861 and 1862 when she was writing at the height of her drive. There are many poems besides "He put the Belt around my Life" which could be read as poems of possession by the daemon—poems which can also be, and have been, read, as poems of possession by the deity, or by a human lover. I suggest that a woman's poetry about her relationship to her daemon—her own active, creative power—has in patriarchal culture used the language of heterosexual love or patriarchal theology. Ted Hughes tells us that

> the eruption of [Dickinson's] imagination and poetry followed when she shifted her passion, with the energy of desperation, from [the] lost man onto his only possible substitute,—the Universe in its Divine aspect. . . . Thereafter, the marriage that had been denied in the real world, went forward in the spiritual . . . just as the Universe in its Divine aspect became the mirror-image of her "husband," so the whole religious dilemma of New England, at that most critical moment in history, became the mirror-image of her relationship to him, of her "marriage" in fact.[2]

This seems to me to miss the point on a grand scale. There are facts we need to look at. First, Emily Dickinson did not marry. And her nonmarrying was neither a pathological retreat as John Cody sees it, nor probably even a conscious decision; it was a fact in her life as in her contemporary Christina Rossetti's; both women had more primary needs. Second: unlike Rossetti, Dickinson did not become a religiously dedicated woman; she was heretical, heterodox, in her religious opinions, and stayed away from church and dogma. What, in fact, *did* she allow to "put the Belt around her Life"—what *did* wholly occupy her mature years and possess her? For "Whom" did she decline the invitations of other lives? The writing of poetry. Nearly two thousand poems. Three hundred and sixty-six

---

[2]Hughes, ed., *A Choice of Emily Dickinson's Verse* (London: Faber & Faber, 1968), p. 11.

poems in the year of her fullest power. What was it like to be writing poetry you knew (and I am sure she did know) was of a class by itself—to be fueled by the energy it took first to confront, then to condense that range of psychic experience into that language; then to copy out the poems and lay them in a trunk, or send a few here and there to friends or relatives as occasional verse or as gestures of confidence? I am sure she knew who she was, as she indicates in this poem:

> Myself was formed—a Carpenter—
> An unpretending time
> My Plane—and I, together wrought
> Before a Builder came—
>
> To measure our attainments
> Had we the Art of Boards
> Sufficiently developed—He'd hire us
> At Halves—
>
> My Tools took Human—Faces—
> The Bench, where we had toiled—
> Against the Man—persuaded—
> We—Temples build—I said—
>
> (#488)

This a poem of the great year 1862, the year in which she first sent a few poems to Thomas Higginson for criticism. Whether it antedates or postdates that occasion is unimportant; it is a poem of knowing one's measure, regardless of the judgments of others.

There are many poems which carry the weight of this knowledge. Here is another one:

> I'm ceded—I've stopped being Theirs—
> The name They dropped upon my face
> With water, in the country church
> Is finished using, now,
> And They can put it with my Dolls,
> My childhood, and the string of spools,
> I've finished threading—too—
>
> Baptized before, without the choice,
> But this time, consciously, of Grace—
> Unto supremest name—
> Called to my Full—The Crescent dropped—
> Existence's whole Arc, filled up,
> With one small Diadem.
>
> My second Rank—too small the first—
> Crowned—Crowing—on my Father's breast—
> A half unconscious Queen—
> But this time—Adequate—Erect—
> With Will to choose, or to reject—
> And I choose, just a Crown—
>
> (#508)

Now, this poem partakes of the imagery of being "twice-born" or, in Christian liturgy, "confirmed"—and if this poem had been written by Christina Rossetti I would be inclined to give more weight to a theological reading. But it was written by Emily Dickinson, who used the Christian metaphor for more than she let it use her. This is a poem of great pride—not pridefulness, but *self*-confirmation—and it is curious how little Dickinson's critics, perhaps misled by her diminutives, have recognized the will and pride in her poetry. It is a poem of movement from childhood to womanhood, of transcending the patriarchal condition of bearing her father's name and "crowing—on my Father's breast—." She is now a conscious Queen "Adequate—Erect/ With Will to Choose, or to reject—."

There is one poem which is the real "onlie begetter" of my thoughts here about Dickinson; a poem I have mused over, repeated to myself, taken into myself over many years. I think it is a poem about possession by the daemon, about the dangers and risks of such possession if you are a woman, about the knowledge that power in a woman can seem destructive, and that you cannot live without the daemon once it has possessed you. The archetype of the daemon as masculine is beginning to change, but it has been real for women up until now. But this woman poet perceives herself as a lethal weapon:

> My life had stood—a Loaded Gun—
> In Corners—till a Day
> The Owner passed—identified—
> And carried Me away—
>
> And now We roam in Sovereign Woods—
> And now We hunt the Doe—
> And every time I speak for Him—
> The Mountains straight reply—
>
> And do I smile, such cordial light
> Upon the Valley glow—
> It is as a Vesuvian face
> Had let its pleasure through—
>
> And when at Night—Our good Day done—
> I guard My Master's Head—
> 'Tis better than the Eider-Duck's
> Deep Pillow—to have shared—
>
> To foe of His—I'm deadly foe—
> None stir the second time—
> On whom I lay a Yellow Eye—
> Or an emphatic Thumb—
>
> Though I than He—may longer live
> He longer must—than I—
> For I have but the power to kill,
> Without—the power to die—

(#754)

Here the poet sees herself as split, not between anything so simple as "masculine" and "feminine" identity but between the hunter, admittedly masculine, but also a human person, an active, willing being, and the gun—an object, condemned to remain inactive until the hunter—the *owner*—takes possession of it. The gun contains an energy capable of rousing echoes in the mountains and lighting up the valleys; it is also deadly, "Vesuvian"; it is also its owner's defender against the "foe." It is the gun, furthermore, who *speaks for him*. If there is a female consciousness in this poem it is buried deeper than the images: it exists in the ambivalence toward power, which is extreme. Active willing and creation in women are forms of aggression, and aggression is both "the power to kill" and punishable by death. The union of gun with hunter embodies the danger of identifying and taking hold of her forces, not least that in so doing she risks defining herself—and being defined—as aggressive, as unwomanly ("and now we hunt the Doe"), and as potentially lethal. That which she experiences in herself as energy and potency can also be experienced as pure destruction. The final stanza, with its precarious balance of phrasing, seems a desperate attempt to resolve the ambivalence; but, I think, it is no resolution, only a further extension of ambivalence.

> Though I than He—may longer live
> He longer must—than I—
> For I have but the power to kill,
> Without—the power to die—

The poet experiences herself as loaded gun, imperious energy; yet without the Owner, the possessor, she is merely lethal. Should that possession abandon her—but the thought is unthinkable: "He longer *must* than I." The pronoun is masculine; the antecedent is what Keats called "The Genius of Poetry."

I do not pretend to have—I don't even wish to have—explained this poem, accounted for its every image; it will reverberate with new tones long after my words about it have ceased to matter. But I think that for us, at this time, it is a central poem in understanding Emily Dickinson, and ourselves, and the condition of the woman artist, particularly in the nineteenth century. It seems likely that the nineteenth-century woman poet, especially, felt the medium of poetry as dangerous, in ways that the woman novelist did not feel the medium of fiction to be. In writing even such a novel of elemental sexuality and anger as *Wuthering Heights,* Emily Brontë could at least theoretically separate herself from her characters; they were, after all, fictitious beings. Moreover, the novel is or can be a construct, planned and organized to deal with human experiences on one level at a time. Poetry is too much rooted in the unconscious; it presses too close against the barriers of repression; and the nineteenth-century woman had much to repress. It is interesting that Elizabeth Barrett tried to fuse poetry and fiction in writing *Aurora Leigh*—perhaps apprehending the need for fictional characters to carry the charge of her experience as a woman artist. But with the exception of *Aurora Leigh* and Christina Rossetti's "Goblin Market"— that extraordinary and little-known poem drenched in oral eroticism—Emily Dickinson's is the only poetry in English by a woman of that century which pierces so far beyond the ideology of the "feminine" and the conventions of womanly feeling. To write it at all, she had to be willing to enter chambers of the self in which

> Ourself behind ourself, concealed—
> Should startle most—

and to relinquish control there, to take those risks, she had to create a relationship to the outer world where she could feel in control.

It is an extremely painful and dangerous way to live—split between a publicly acceptable persona, and a part of yourself that you perceive as the essential, the creative and powerful self, yet also as possibly unacceptable, perhaps even monstrous.

> Much Madness is divinest Sense—
> To a discerning Eye—
> Much Sense—the starkest Madness—
> 'Tis the Majority

> In this, as All, prevail—
> Assent—and you are sane—
> Demur—you're straightway dangerous—
> And handled with a Chain—
>
> (#435)

For many women the stresses of this splitting have led, in a world so ready to asert our innate passivity and to deny our independence and creativity, to extreme consequences: the mental asylum, self-imposed silence, recurrent depression, suicide, and often severe loneliness.

Dickinson is *the* American poet whose work consisted of exploring states of psychic extremity. For a long time, as we have seen, this fact was obscured by the kinds of selections made from her work by timid if well-meaning editors. In fact, Dickinson was a great psychologist; and like every great psychologist, she began with the material she had at hand: herself. She had to possess the courage to enter, through language, states which most people deny or veil with silence.

> The first Day's Night had come—
> And grateful that a thing
> So terrible—had been endured—
> I told my Soul to sing—
>
> She said her Strings were snapt—
> Her Bow—to Atoms blown—
> And so to mend her—gave me work
> Until another Morn—
>
> And then—a Day as huge
> As Yesterdays in pairs,
> Unrolled its horror in my face—
> Until it blocked my eyes—
>
> My Brain—begun to laugh—
> I mumbled—like a fool—
> And tho' 'tis Years ago—that Day—
> My Brain keeps giggling—still.
>
> And Something's odd—within—
> That person that I was—
> And this One—do not feel the same—
> Could it be Madness—this?
>
> (#410)

Dickinson's letters acknowledge a period of peculiarly intense personal crisis; her biographers have variously ascribed it to the pangs of renunciation of an impossible love, or to psychic damage deriving from her mother's presumed depression and withdrawal after her birth. What concerns us here is the fact that she chose to probe the nature of this experience in language:

> The Soul has Bandaged moments—
> When too appalled to stir—
> She feels some ghastly Fright come up
> And stop to look at her—

> Salute her—with long fingers—
> Caress her freezing hair—
> Sip, Goblin, from the very lips
> The Lover—hovered—o'er—
> Unworthy, that a thought so mean
> Accost a Theme—so—fair—
>
> The soul has moments of Escape—
> When bursting all the doors—
> She dances like a Bomb, abroad,
> And swings upon the Hours. . . .
>
> The Soul's retaken moments—
> When, Felon led along,
> With shackles on the plumed feet,
> And staples, in the Song,
>
> The Horror welcomes her, again,
> These, are not brayed of Tongue—
>
> (#512)

In this poem, the word "Bomb" is dropped, almost carelessly, as a correlative for the soul's active, liberated states—it occurs in a context of apparent euphoria, but its implications are more than euphoric—they are explosive, destructive. The Horror from which in such moments the soul escapes has a masculine, "Goblin" form, and suggests the perverse and terrifying rape of a "Bandaged" and powerless self. In at least one poem, Dickinson depicts the actual process of suicide:

> He scanned it—staggered—
> Dropped the Loop
> To Past or Period—
> Caught helpless at a sense as if
> His mind were going blind—
>
> Groped up, to see if God was there—
> Groped backward at Himself—
> Caressed a Trigger absently
> And wandered out of Life.
>
> (#1062)

The precision of knowledge in this brief poem is such that we must assume that Dickinson had, at least in fantasy, drifted close to that state in which the "Loop" that binds us to "Past or Period" is "Dropped" and we grope randomly at what remains of abstract notions of sense, God, or self, before—almost absent-mindedly—reaching for a solution. But it's worth noting that this is a poem in which the suicidal experience has been distanced, refined, transformed through a devastating accuracy of language. It is not suicide that is studied here, but the dissociation of self and mind and world which precedes.

Dickinson was convinced that a life worth living could be found within the mind and against the grain of external circumstance: "Reverse cannot befall/ That fine prosperity/ Whose Sources are interior—" (#395). The horror, for her, was that which set "Staples in the Song"—the numbing and freezing of the interior, a state she describes over and over:

> There is a Languor of the Life
> More imminent than Pain—
> 'Tis Pain's Successor—When the Soul
> Has suffered all it can—
>
> A Drowsiness—diffuses—
> A Dimness like a Fog
> Envelopes Consciousness—
> As Mists—obliterate a Crag.
>
> The Surgeon—does not blanch—at pain—
> His Habit—is severe—
> But tell him that it ceased to feel—
> The creature lying there—
>
> And he will tell you—skill is late—
> A Mighter than He—
> Has ministered before Him—
> There's no Vitality.
>
> (#396)

I think the equation surgeon-artist is a fair one here; the artist can work with the materials of pain; she cuts to probe and heal; but she is powerless at the point where

> After great pain, a formal feeling comes—
> The Nerves sit ceremonious, like Tombs—
> The stiff Heart questions was it He, that bore,
> And Yesterday, or Centuries before?
>
> The Feet, mechanical, go round—
> Of Ground, or Air, or Ought—
> A Wooden way
> Regardless grown,
> A Quartz contentment, like a stone—
>
> This is the Hour of Lead
> Remembered, if outlived
> As Freezing persons, recollect the Snow—
> First—Chill—then Stupor—then the letting go—
>
> (#341)

For the poet, the terror is precisely in those periods of psychic death, when even the possibility of work is negated; her "occupation's gone." Yet she also describes the unavailing effort to numb emotion:

> Me from Myself—to banish—
> Had I Art—
> Impregnable my Fortress
> Unto All Heart—
>
> But since Myself—assault Me—
> How have I peace
> Except by subjugating
> Consciousness?

And since We're mutual Monarch
How this be
Except by Abdication—
Me—of Me?

(#642)

The possibility of abdicating oneself—of ceasing to be—remains.

Severer Service of myself
I—hastened to demand
To fill the awful Longitude
Your life had left behind—

I worried Nature with my Wheels
When Hers had ceased to run—
When she had put away Her Work
My own had just begun.

I strove to weary Brain and Bone—
To harass to fatigue
The glittering Retinue of nerves—
Vitality to clog

To some dull comfort Those obtain
Who put a Head away
They knew the Hair to—
And forget the color of the Day—

Affliction would not be appeased—
The Darkness braced as firm
As all my stratagem had been
The Midnight to confirm—

No Drug for Consciousness—can be—
Alternative to die
Is Nature's only Pharmacy
For Being's Malady—

(#786)

Yet consciousness—not simply the capacity to suffer, but the capacity to experience intensely at every instant—creates the death not a blotting-out but a final illumination:

This Consciousness that is aware
Of Neighbors and the Sun
Will be the one aware of Death
And that itself alone

Is traversing the interval
Experience between
And most profound experiment
Appointed unto Men—

How adequate unto itself
Its properties shall be
Itself unto itself and none
Shall make discovery.

> Adventure most unto itself
> The Soul condemned to be—
> Attended by a single Hound
> Its own identity.
>
> (#822)

The poet's relationship to her poetry has, it seems to me—and I am not speaking only of Emily Dickinson—a twofold nature. Poetic language—the poem on paper—is a concretization of the poetry of the world at large, the self, and the forces within the self; and those forces are rescued from formlessness, lucidified, and integrated in the act of writing poems. But there is a more ancient concept of the poet, which is that she is endowed to speak for those who do not have the gift of language, or to see for those who—for whatever reasons—are less conscious of what they are living through. It is as though the risks of the poet's existence can be put to some use beyond her own survival.

> The Province of the Saved
> Should be the Art—To save—
> Through Skill obtained in Themselves—
> The Science of the Grave
>
> No Man can understand
> But He that hath endured
> The Dissolution—in Himself—
> That Man—be qualified
>
> To qualify Despair
> To Those who failing new—
> Mistake Defeat for Death—Each time—
> Till acclimated—to—
>
> (#539)

The poetry of extreme states, the poetry of danger, can allow its readers to go further in our own awareness, take risks we might not have dared; it says, at least: "Someone has been here before."

> The Soul's distinct Connection
> With immortality
> Is best disclosed by Danger
> Or quick Calamity—
>
> As Lightning on a Landscape
> Exhibits Sheets of Place—
> Not yet suspected—but for Flash—
> And Click—and Suddenness.
>
> (#974)

> Crumbling is not an instant's Act
> A fundamental pause
> Dilapidation's processes
> Are organized Decays.
>
> 'Tis first a Cobweb on the Soul
> A cuticle of Dust
> A Borer in the Axis
> An Elemental Rust—

Ruin is formal—Devil's work
Consecutive and slow—
Fail in an instant—no man did
Slipping—is Crash's law.

(#997)

I felt a Cleaving in my Mind
As if my Brain had split—
I tried to match it—Seam by Seam—
But could not make them fit.

The thought behind, I strove to join
Unto the thought before—
But Sequence ravelled out of Sound
Like Balls—upon a Floor.

(#937)

There are many more Emily Dickinsons than I have tried to call up here. Wherever you take hold of her, she proliferates. I wish I had time here to explore her complex sense of Truth; to follow the thread we unravel when we look at the numerous and passionate poems she wrote to or about women; to probe her ambivalent feelings about fame, a subject pursued by many male poets before her; simply to examine the poems in which she is directly apprehending the natural world. No one since the seventeenth century had reflected more variously or more probingly upon death and dying. What I have tried to do here is follow through some of the origins and consequences of her choice to be, not only a poet but a woman who explored her own mind, without any of the guidelines of orthodoxy. To say "yes" to her powers was not simply a major act of nonconformity in the nineteenth century; even in our own time it has been assumed that Emily Dickinson, not patriarchal society, was "the problem." The more we come to recognize the unwritten and written laws and taboos underpinning patriarchy, the less problematical, surely, will seem the methods she chose.   [1975]

PART IV

* * * * * * * * *

CONTEMPORARIES,

1970–1998

* * * * * * * * *

The period we think of as the contemporary era of criticism—the past twenty-five years or so—has been characterized by paradigm shifts that, for many, were unanticipated, even incomprehensible. These changes in the values and functions of literary analysis have resulted in a divorce between the readers of literature and the readers of criticism. On the one hand, the academy has taken over the business of criticism and, from the outside, seems to have created an impenetrable jargon; certainly, it is more difficult to comprehend than criticism ever has been before. In defending against such claims, apologists for the newest criticism remind us that, in their day, New Critics like Cleanth Brooks and Robert Penn Warren were also charged with specialized writing. Now, the number of regular readers of criticism has dwindled to the point that there is really no market pressure to create a critical prose that general readers can understand.

Although no single factor explains the origin of this state of affairs, perhaps the most celebrated cause of the split lies in the advent of theory. What came to set academics notoriously apart, even from themselves, was an appetite for philosophical systems that yielded a set of critical questions that turned the humanistic tradition on its head. The movement toward abstraction goes back to some thinkers from earlier parts of the century, but the fashion began in earnest in the middle of the 1970s. Moribund as the New Criticism had become, sterile as many found methodologies like archetypalism and Freudian psychoanalysis to be, the way was open to discover a new paradigm for literary interpretation. Many ideas circulated, but none—not hermeneutics, phenomenology, semiotics, structuralism, narratology, nor reader response—awakened the imagination of any significant proportion of Americanist critics. Americanists proved skeptical of several of the new systems as systems, thereby recalling an earlier vein of pragmatism in their makeup. In addition, American literature critics and scholars still wished to preserve what their colleagues in English literature had already forsaken, a profound connection to what they loosely termed—in the cold-war rhetoric that was once so unquestioned—the national spirit or the democratic ethos or the liberal tradition or the American dream. Once literary and cultural theory made an impact on American criticism, such concepts would be deconstructed—interrogated, problematized, and reinscribed.

Replacing the vivifying relation to social values that literary critics had once found in the historicist tendencies in American studies was a new concern for the writing of women and blacks. This interest had begun to assert itself, after the advent of civil rights movement and, later, by the early 1970s, of the second wave of feminism. It was most explicitly expressed in the call, especially by leftist critics, to revise the "canon" of American literature, which had come to be understood as repressive. An egalitarian politics of revision was readily created, one that could accommodate the differences that these writers, genres, and linguistic strategies produced.

Unsettling to scholars from the 1950s and early 1960s was the implication that the canon had remained static or was perceived to be ossified. Hadn't that generation recouped the reputations of Dickinson, Wharton, Fitzgerald, and, to some extent, Frederick Douglass? Such questions missed the point, for many revisionists wanted nothing so much as to throw the question of canonicity into doubt, to uncover the ideological premises behind the operations of canonizing. Consider how American literature was rendered to students and scholars-in-training in books like *Eight American Authors* or *Sixteen Modern American Authors*. One supposes that merely being familiar with the critical history that these few writers represent was a legitimate background. This model of major figures had dominated the study of British literature, and American literature professors had assimilated, consciously or not, their colleagues' professional anxiety about the quantity of American writing worth critical attention—or so the argument has gone—for about a hundred years.

The radical commitment to canon reform, it is generally argued, was the academic legacy of the New Left's presence on college campuses, as well as the result of changing demographics of students and the professoriate. In the name of "relevance," several liberationist movements—on their own and sometimes as a coalition—did develop scholarly and critical aims, which included forming a countertradition to what passed as orthodoxy in the classroom. By the early 1970s, Black Studies and then women's studies had organized themselves as disciplines and academic departments or programs. There were also movements toward Jewish studies, Chicano studies, Native American studies, and, later, gay studies and Asian-American studies. Much of the work, drawing on the scholarship of a few predecessors, was archival and bibliographical, a summoning of materials and an accounting of assets, which in turn created the foundation for ideological and polemical arguments concerning the richness of materials and the urgency of the endeavor. The next phase was the vigorous reinterpretation as older writers, like W. E. B. Du Bois and Harriet Jacobs, were recovered and the complexities of their example addressed. In a further movement, these studies gave way to more rhetorical arguments about language and voice, as well as the social values underlying literary politics.

In the tradition of criticizing American culture, American literature studies rediscovered in these new movements something of the oppositional edge that had been lost with the passing of the public literary intellectual of the earlier part of the century. Feminism played a key role in effecting this new agonism. Developing out of the initial "images" method of critiquing male-inscribed visions of female identity, feminist criticism came to challenge the whole hierarchy of values and assumptions on the basis of which criticism had proceeded. It combatted the "great woman" theory, even as it revolutionized the way we read Anne Bradstreet or Emily Dickinson. One of the first books to make a substantial impact on American literary studies was Nina Baym's *Woman's Fiction* (1978), a historical study that read the works of such mid-nineteenth-century authors as Susan Warner and Fanny Fern with the care and incisiveness with which Baym had previously read Hawthorne's career. No one could read this important book without realizing that his or her previous training was in a significant way deficient. After this book was published, Baym's "Melodramas of Beset Manhood" threw the gender basis of critical methodology into high relief. It was as persuasive a case as heretofore had been waged. Other controversial studies, like Ann Douglas's *Feminization of American Culture,* which analyzed the process of creating cultural value according to gender-based premises, and Annette Kolodny's *Lay of the Land,* a study of the gendered poetics of early American visions of the landscape, activated a new generation of feminist criticism, one that looked beyond the representation of women and into the rhetorical and social processes by which cultural meanings were transacted.

A great many essays and books followed that elaborated on the implications of Baym's teachings, along with Douglas's and Kolodny's, and that also more radically developed insights of feminist criticism. One of the most influential of these books was Jane Tompkins's *Sensational Designs* (1985). Previously, Tompkins had embraced the reader-response school of criticism, but her key lesson here was to take that study out of psychological inquiry and to give it to a sociohistorical application. So she read Stowe, who had been consigned by earlier critics to the category of "domestic novelists," for the "cultural work" her writing performed. Tompkins's argument harkened back to one of the earliest modes of critical inquiry by asking how *Uncle Tom's Cabin* did what everyone of the time, including President Lincoln, understood it to do: incite the conscience of the republic. Tompkins took seriously an idea that the New Critics had seemed to bleach out of criticism: what "good" did good literature do to make it good, that is, what social good? For several generations of Americanists, this question had been dismissed as a dualism or was defused as something peripheral to the critic's job of work. Older anthologies of criticism used to contain a topic called "Moral Criticism" to distinguish it from the other approaches. Surely part of the political endeavor of contemporary criticism rehabilitates this conception of ethical engagement.

Tompkins's principle of a novel's cultural work—the negotiation of social concerns, the complicating of values, the dramatizing of large-scale bewilderment and anxieties—has been the most enduring lesson of *Sensational Designs*. Over the next ten years, critics learned from Tompkins, as well as from critics like Sacvan Bercovitch, that American authors have often been quite knowledgeable about the political specifics of their milieus and have returned to American texts to discover things that only a small group of keepers of the flame had previously known about these writers—Emerson's and Whitman's concern about native Americans. Hawthorne's interest in European politics and his lack of sympathy for American Negroes. Prior generations had thought that such beliefs were merely conventional, that such issues were peripheral to the interpreting of these authors at their profoundest. The new wisdom held that only through reading what these writers omit or repress—the textual unconscious—could their writing be seen for what it was: an ambivalent embroilment with hierarchies of power. Tompkins's work, like that of many other Americanists, resounds with the tenets of response-criticism of Mikhail Bakhtin and Wolfgang Iser, just as it also benefits from the lessons of Jacques Derrida, Roland Barthes, and Michel Foucault, French philosophers whose influence through the 1980s and 1990s has been exceptionally strong. These theorists disseminated values for reading that distrusted a rational understanding of how language communicates meaning, conventional relations between author's intentions and reader's reactions, and how meaning and ideology are commingled.

Such views helped Americanists, coinciding as they did with one of the most influential teachings of the contemporary era, one that gave critics and scholars a new literary history to write. That history was basically revisionist, drawing on democratic principles of inclusion. Its most forceful impetus, however, came in its conviction that the progress of American literature was far from the chronicle celebrating American society that an earlier scholarship had written. Instead of this "consensus" model of literary history and the relation of literature to society, Sacvan Bercovitch taught that this society did not empower our writers as much as make its "very terms of cultural restriction . . . a source of creative release: they serve to incite the imagination, to unleash the energies of reform, to encourage diversity and accommodate change—all this, while directing the rights of diversity into a rite of cultural assent." Bercovitch called this paradigm for a new literary history "dissensus," and it proved powerful over the next decade in persuading scholars of American literature that "America" was not an *e pluribus unum* but "a rhetorical battleground, a symbol that has been made to stand for diverse and sometimes mutually antagonistic outlooks." The corollary was that what looks like debate or rebellion in America really represents the political dynamic of containment that Herbert Marcuse called "repressive tolerance"—in this case, the belief that bourgeois individualist culture allows free speech only because it knows that ultimately some voices, like those of the disenfranchised, will rarely be heard. Thus, Bercovitch adjusted the study of American literary history by insisting that "all those concepts—history, literature, American, and transcendence—are now subjects of ideological debate." A collection of essays by diverse hands that he co-edited with Myra Jehlen, *Ideology and Classic American Literature* (1986) helped to secure this position.

The results of these changes are still to be gauged. Bercovitch's teachings coincided nicely with the principles of the New Historicism, one of the most exciting changes in methodology, which disrupts the historicist model of treating the text as supporting a historical context and instead reads text and context as interanimating. The new primacy placed on "dissensus" also helped to ready mainstream professors to assimilate into their study the work of minority writers. Indeed, the question so often heard with regard to the literature of the new pluralism is one that ignores the lessons of the past twenty-five years of criticism, a question that returns criticism to its Arnoldian focus: "Is it any good?," the detractors of the new pluralism want to know. Does this literature have the vitality and artistry of Whitman, the complexity of Melville, the coherence and sophistication of Henry James? We might ask what else it has to warrant its study. Then we would find that this literature gives pleasures different from those that Whitman, Melville, and James give, pleasures whose sources and meanings critics find it just as imperative to locate and to praise.

One result of the academicizing of criticism, however, is the end of the independent literary critic; that cultural office seems to have expired. At the same time, American literary critics have been developing a new sense of American literature and have been turning their attention to the very recent work of Chicano/a, Native American, and Asian-American writers, among others. Moreover, critics have expanded the idea of the literary; by reconfiguring the object of literary criticism and scholarship, they have widened their audience. Critics are now likely to write about the literature of North America, or the literature of the Americas and thus to see U.S. writing in its hemispheric context as well as in combination with other forms of cultural representation—sign-systems, such as movies, TV shows, advertisements, all the icons and artifacts of popular culture. Cultural studies has taken literature out of the realm of a special language and placed it in a context of other cultural productions, situating literature's power of definition and description within ever more various discursive forms, none of which is to be privileged over another.

Through such discourse analysis, the tradition of American cultural critique is sure to prosper. For even though the protest era did give impetus to changes in humanistic practice, it is still younger scholars who have sustained the intensity of the reforming spirit, students who came of age less than twenty years ago. These critics explore such issues as the cultural relevance of reading, access to literary study, and the reforming of institutions. In aspiring to reach a broader public than their predecessors did, these new scholar-critics are also giving a new currency to the spirit of American cultural criticism.

Nina Baym

Melodramas of Beset Manhood: How Theories of American Fiction Exclude Women Authors

This paper is about American literary criticism rather than American literature. It proceeds from the assumption that we never read American literature directly or freely, but always through the perspective allowed by theories. Theories account for the inclusion and exclusion of texts in anthologies, and theories account for the way we read them. My concern is with the fact that the theories controlling our reading of American literature have led to the exclusion of women authors from the canon.

Let me use my own practice as a case in point. In 1977 there was published a collection of essays on images of women in major British and American literature, to which I contributed.[1] The American field was divided chronologically among six critics, with four essays covering literature written prior to World War II. Taking seriously the charge that we were to focus only on the major figures, the four of us—working quite independently of each other—selected altogether only four women writers. Three of these were from the earliest period, a period which predates the novel: the poet Anne Bradstreet and the two diarists Mary Rowlandson and Sarah Kemble Knight. The fourth was Emily Dickinson. For the period between 1865 and 1940 no women were cited at all. The message that we—who were taking women as our subject—conveyed was clear: there have been almost no major women writers in America; the major novelists have all been men.

Now, when we wrote our essays we were not undertaking to reread all American literature and make our own decisions as to who the major authors were. That is the point: we accepted the going canon of major authors. As late as 1977, that canon did not include any women novelists. Yet, the critic who goes beyond what is accepted and tries to look at the totality of literary production in America quickly discovers that women authors have been active since the earliest days of settlement. Commercially and numerically they have probably dominated American literature since the middle of the nineteenth century. As long ago as 1854, Nathaniel Hawthorne complained to his publisher about the "damn'd mob of scribbling women" whose writings—he fondly imagined—were diverting the public from his own.

Names and figures help make this dominance clear. In the years between 1774 and 1799—from the calling of the First Continental Congress to the close of the eighteenth century—a total of thirty-eight original works of fiction were published in this country.[2] Nine of these, appearing pseudonymously or anonymously, have not yet been attributed to any author. The remaining twenty-nine are the work of eighteen individuals, of whom four are women. One of these women, Susannah Rowson, wrote six of them, or more than a fifth of the total. Her most popular work, *Charlotte* (also known as *Charlotte Temple*), was printed three times in the decade it was published, nineteen times between 1800 and 1810, and eighty times by the middle of the nineteenth century. A novel by a second of the four women, Hannah Foster, was called *The Coquette* and had thirty editions by mid-nineteenth century. *Uncle Tom's Cabin,* by a woman, is probably the all-time biggest seller

[1]Marlene Springer, ed., *What Manner of Woman: Essays on English and American Life and Literature* (New York: New York Univ. Press, 1977).

[2]See Lyle Wright, *American Fiction 1744–1850* (San Marino, Calif.: Huntington Library Press, 1969).

in American history. A woman, Mrs. E.D.E.N. Southworth, was probably the most widely read novelist in the nineteenth century. How is it possible for a critic or historian of American literature to leave these books, and these authors, out of the picture?

I see three partial explanations for the critical invisibility of the many active women authors in America. The first is simple bias. The critic does not like the idea of women as writers, does not believe that women can be writers, and hence does not see them even when they are right before his eyes. His theory or his standards may well be nonsexist but his practice is not. Certainly, an *a priori* resistance to recognizing women authors as serious writers has functioned powerfully in the mindset of a number of influential critics. One can amusingly demonstrate the inconsistencies between standard and practice in such critics, show how their minds slip out of gear when they are confronted with a woman author. But this is only a partial explanation.

A second possibility is that, in fact, women have not written the kind of work that we call "excellent," for reasons that are connected with their gender although separable from it. This is a serious possibility. For example, suppose we required a dense texture of classical allusion in all works that we called excellent. Then, the restriction of a formal classical education to men would have the effect of restricting authorship of excellent literature to men. Women would not have written excellent literature because social conditions hindered them. The reason, though gender-connected, would not be gender per se.

The point here is that the notion of the artist, or of excellence, has efficacy in a given time and reflects social realities. The idea of "good" literature is not only a personal preference, it is also a cultural preference. We can all think of species of women's literature that do not aim in any way to achieve literary excellence as society defines it: e.g., the "Harlequin Romances." Until recently, only a tiny proportion of literary women aspired to artistry and literary excellence in the terms defined by their own culture. There tended to be a sort of immediacy in the ambitions of literary women leading them to professionalism rather than artistry, by choice as well as by social pressure and opportunity. The gender-related restrictions were really operative, and the responsible critic cannot ignore them. But again, these restrictions are only partly explanatory.

There are, finally, I believe, gender-related restrictions that do not arise out of cultural realities contemporary with the writing woman, but out of later critical theories. These theories may follow naturally from cultural realities pertinent to their own time, but they impose their concerns anachronistically, after the fact, on an earlier period. If one accepts current theories of American literature, one accepts as a consequence—perhaps not deliberately but nevertheless inevitably—a literature that is essentially male. This is the partial explanation that I shall now develop.

Let us begin where the earliest theories of American literature begin, with the hypothesis that American literature is to be judged less by its form than its content. Traditionally, one ascertains literary excellence by comparing a writer's work with standards of performance that have been established by earlier authors, where formal mastery and innovation are paramount. But from its historical beginnings, American literary criticism has assumed that literature produced in this nation would have to be ground-breaking, equal to the challenge of the new nation, and completely original. Therefore, it could not be judged by referring it back to earlier achievements. The earliest American literary critics began to talk about the "most American" work rather than the "best" work because they knew no way to find out the best other than by comparing American to British writing. Such a criticism struck them as both unfair and unpatriotic. We had thrown off the political shackles of England; it would not do for us to be servile in our literature. Until a tradition of American literature developed its own inherent forms, the early critic looked for a standard of Americanness rather than a standard of excellence. Inevitably, perhaps, it came to seem that the quality of "Americanness," whatever it might be, *constituted* literary excellence for American authors. Beginning as a nationalistic enterprise, American literary criticism and theory has retained a nationalist orientation to this day.

Of course, the idea of Americanness is even more vulnerable to subjectivity than the idea of the best. When they speak of "most American," critics seldom mean the statistically most representative or most typical, the most read or the most sold. They have some qualitative essence in mind, and frequently their work develops as an explanation of this idea of "American" rather than a description and evaluation of selected authors. The predictable recurrence of the term "America" or "American" in works of literary criticism treating a dozen or fewer authors indicates that the critic has chosen his authors on the basis of their conformity to his idea of what is truly American. For examples: *American Renaissance, The Romance in America, Symbolism and American Literature, Form and Fable in American Fiction, The American Adam, The American Novel and its Tradition, The Place of Style in American Literature* (a subtitle), *The Poetics of American Fiction* (another subtitle). But an idea of what is American is no more than an idea, needing demonstration. The critic all too frequently ends up using his chosen authors as demonstrations of Americanness, arguing through them to his definition.

So Marius Bewley explains in *The Eccentric Design* that "for the American artist there was no social surface responsive to his touch. The scene was crude, even beyond successful satire," but later, in a concluding chapter titled "The Americanness of the American Novel," he agrees that "this 'tradition' as I have set it up here has no room for the so-called realists and naturalists."[3] F. O. Matthiessen, whose *American Renaissance* enshrines five authors, explains that "the one common denominator of my five writers, uniting even Hawthorne and Whitman, was their devotion to the possibilities of democracy."[4] The jointly written *Literary History of the United States* proclaims in its "address to the reader" that American literary history "will be a history of the books of the great and the near-great writers in a literature which is most revealing when studied as a by-product of American experience."[5] And Joel Porte announces confidently in *The Romance in America* that "students of American literature . . . have provided a solid theoretical basis for establishing that the rise and growth of fiction in this country is dominated by our authors' conscious adherence to a tradition of non-realistic romance sharply at variance with the broadly novelistic mainstream of English writing. When there has been disagreement among recent critics as to the contours of American fiction, it has usually disputed, not the existence *per se* of a romance tradition, but rather the question of which authors, themes, and stylistic strategies *deserve* to be placed with certainty at the heart of that tradition" (emphasis added).[6]

Before he is through, the critic has had to insist that some works in America are much more American than others, and he is as busy excluding certain writers as "un-American" as he is including others. Such a proceeding in the political arena would be extremely suspect, but in criticism it has been the method of choice. Its final result goes far beyond the conclusion that only a handful of American works are very good. *That* statement is one we

[3]Marius Bewley, *The Eccentric Design* (New York: Columbia Univ. Press, 1963), 15, 291.

[4]F. O. Matthiessen, *American Renaissance* (New York: Oxford Univ. Press, 1941), ix.

[5]Robert E. Spiller et al., eds., *Literary History of the United States* (New York: Macmillan, 1959), xix.

[6]Joel Porte, *The Romance in America* (Middletown, Conn.: Wesleyan Univ. Press, 1969), ix.

could agree with, since very good work is rare in any field. But it is odd indeed to argue that only a hundred of American works are really American.[7]

Despite the theoretical room for an infinite number of definitions of Americanness, critics have generally agreed on it—although the shifting canon suggests that agreement may be a matter of fad rather than fixed objective qualities.[8] First, America as a nation must be the ultimate subject of the work. The author must be writing about aspects of experience and character that are American only, setting Americans off from other people and the country from other nations. The author must be writing his story specifically to display these aspects, to meditate on them, and to derive from them some generalizations and conclusions about "the" American experience. To Matthiessen the topic is the possibilities of democracy; Sacvan Bercovitch (in *The Puritan Origins of the American Self*) finds it in American identity. Such content excludes, at one extreme, stories about universals, aspects of experience common to people in a variety of times and places—mutability, mortality, love, childhood, family, betrayal, loss. Innocence versus experience is an admissible theme *only* if innocence is the essence of the American character, for example.

But at the other extreme, the call for an overview of America means that detailed, circumstantial portrayals of some aspect of American life are also, peculiarly, inappropriate: stories of wealthy New Yorkers, Yugoslavian immigrants, southern rustics. Jay B. Hubbell rather ingratiatingly admits as much when he writes, "in both my teaching and my research I had a special interest in literature as a reflection of American life and thought. This circumstance may explain in part why I found it difficult to appreciate the merits of the expatriates and why I was slow in doing justice to some of the New Critics. I was repelled by the sordid subject matter found in some of the novels written by Dreiser, Dos Passos, Faulkner, and some others."[9] Richard Poirier writes that "the books which in my view constitute a distinctive American tradition . . . resist within their pages forces of environment that otherwise dominate the world" and he distinguishes this kind from "the fiction of Mrs. Wharton, Dreiser, or Howells."[10] The *Literary History of the United States* explains that "historically, [Edith Wharton] is likely to survive as the memorialist of a dying aristocracy" (1211). And so on. These exclusions abound in all the works which form the stable core of American literary criticism at this time.

Along with Matthiessen, the most influential exponent of this exclusive Americanness is Lionel Trilling, and his work has particular applicability because it concentrates on the novel form. Here is a famous passage from his 1940 essay, "Reality in America," in which Trilling is criticizing Vernon Parrington's selection of authors in *Main Currents in American Thought*:

> A culture is not a flow, nor even a confluence: the form of its existence is struggle—or at least debate—it is nothing if not a dialectic. And in any culture there are likely to be certain artists who contain a large part of the dialectic within themselves, their meaning and power lying in their contradictions; they contain within themselves, it may be said, the very essence of the culture. To throw out Poe because he cannot be conveniently fitted into a theory of American culture . . . to find his gloom to be merely personal and eccentric . . . as

[7]A good essay on this topic is William C. Spengemann's "What is American Literature?" *CentR*, 22 (1978), 119–38.

[8]See Jay B. Hubbell, *Who Are the Major American Authors?* (Durham, N. C.: Duke Univ. Press, 1972).

[9]Ibid., 335–36.

[10]Richard Poirier, *A World Elsewhere: The Place of Style in American Literature* (New York: Oxford Univ. Press, 1966), 5.

> Hawthorne's was . . . to judge Melville's response to American life to be less noble than that of Bryant or of Greeley, to speak of Henry James as an escapist . . . this is not merely to be mistaken in aesthetic judgment. Rather it is to examine without attention and from the point of view of a limited and essentially arrogant conception of reality the documents which are in some respects the most suggestive testimony to what America was and is, and of course to get no answer from them.[11]

Trilling's immediate purpose is to exclude Greeley and Bryant from the list of major authors and to include Poe, Melville, Hawthorne, and James. We probably share Trilling's aesthetic judgment. But note that he does not base his judgment on aesthetic grounds; indeed, he dismisses aesthetic judgment with the word "merely." He argues that Parrington has picked the wrong artists because he doesn't understand the culture. Culture is his real concern.

But what makes Trilling's notion of culture more valid than Parrington's? Trilling really has no argument; he resorts to such value-laden rhetoric as "a limited and essentially arrogant conception of reality" precisely because he cannot objectively establish his version of culture over Parrington's. For the moment, there are two significant conclusions to draw from this quotation. First, the disagreement is over the nature of our culture. Second, there is no disagreement over the value of literature—it is valued as a set of "documents" which provide "suggestive testimony to what America was and is."

One might think that an approach like this which is subjective, circular, and in some sense nonliterary or even antiliterary would not have had much effect. But clearly Trilling was simply carrying on a longstanding tradition of searching for cultural essence, and his essays gave the search a decided and influential direction toward the notion of cultural essence as some sort of tension. Trilling succeeded in getting rid of Bryant and Greeley, and his choice of authors is still dominant. They all turn out—and not by accident—to be white, middle-class, male, of Anglo-Saxon derivation or at least from an ancestry which had settled in this country before the big waves of immigration which began around the middle of the nineteenth century. In every case, however, the decision made by these men to become professional authors pushed them slightly to one side of the group to which they belonged. This slight alienation permitted them to belong, and yet not to belong, to the so-called "mainstream." These two aspects of their situation—their membership in the dominant middle-class white Anglo-Saxon group, and their modest alienation from it—defined their boundaries, enabling them to "contain within themselves" the "contradictions" that, in Trilling's view, constitute the "very essence of the culture." I will call the literature they produced, which Trilling assesses so highly, a "consensus criticism of the consensus."

This idea plainly excludes many groups but it might not seem necessarily to exclude women. In fact, nineteenth-century women authors were overwhelmingly white, middle-class, and anglo-Saxon in origin. Something more than what is overtly stated by Trilling (and others cited below) is added to exclude them. What critics have done is to assume, for reasons shortly to be expounded, that the women writers invariably represented the consensus, rather than the criticism of it; to assume that their gender made them part of the consensus in a way that prevented them from partaking in the criticism. The presence of these women and their works is acknowledged in literary theory and history as an impediment and obstacle, that which the essential American literature had to criticize as its chief task.

[11]Lionel Trilling, *The Liberal Imagination* (New York: Anchor, 1950), 7–9.

So, in his lively and influential book of 1960, *Love and Death in the American Novel,*
Leslie Fiedler describes women authors as creators of the "flagrantly bad best-seller"
against which "our best fictionists"—all male—have had to struggle for "their integrity
and their livelihoods."[12] And, in a 1978 reader's introduction to an edition of Charles
Brockden Brown's *Wieland,* Sydney J. Krause and S. W. Reid write as follows:

> What it meant for Brown personally, and belles lettres in America historically, that he
> should have decided to write professionally is a story unto itself. Americans simply had no
> great appetite for serious literature in the early decades of the Republic—certainly nothing
> of the sort with which they devoured . . . the ubiquitous melodramas of beset woman-
> hood, "tales of truth," like Susanna Rowson's *Charlotte Temple* and Hannah Foster's *The Co-
> quette.*[13]

There you see what has happened to the woman writer. She has entered literature history
as the enemy. The phrase "tales of truth" is put in quotes by the critics, as though to cast
doubt on the very notion that a "melodrama of beset womanhood" could be either true or
important. At the same time, ironically, they are proposing for our serious consideration,
as a candidate for intellectually engaging literature, a highly melodramatic novel with an
improbable plot, inconsistent characterizations, and excesses of style that have posed
tremendous problems for all students of Charles Brockden Brown. But, by this strategy it
becomes possible to begin major American fiction historically with male rather than female authors. The certainty here that stories about women could not contain the essence
of American culture means that the matter of American experience is inherently male.
And this makes it highly unlikely that American women would write fiction encompassing such experience. I would suggest that the theoretical model of a story which may become the vehicle of cultural essence is: "a melodrama of beset manhood." This melodrama
is presented in a fiction which, as we'll later see, can be taken as representative of the author's literary experience, his struggle for integrity and livelihood against flagrantly bad
best-sellers written by women. Personally beset in a way that epitomizes the tensions
of our culture, the male author produces his melodramatic testimony to our culture's
essence—so the theory goes.

Remember that the search for cultural essence demands a relatively uncircumstantial
kind of fiction, one which concentrates on national universals (if I may be pardoned the
paradox). This search has identified a sort of nonrealistic narrative, a romance, a story free
to catch an essential, idealized American character, to intensify his essence and convey his
experience in a way that ignores details of an actual social milieu. This nonrealistic or an-
tisocial aspect of American fiction is noted—as a fault—by Trilling in a 1947 essay,
"Manners, Morals, and the Novel." Curiously, Trilling here attacks the same group of
writers he had rescued from Parrington in "Reality in America." But, never doubting that
his selection represents "the" American authors, he goes ahead with the task that really interests him—criticizing the culture through its representative authors. He writes:

> The novel in America diverges from its classic [i.e., British] intention which . . . is the
> investigation of the problem of reality beginning in the social field. The fact is that Ameri-
> can writers of genius have not turned their minds to society. Poe and Melville were quite
> apart from it: the reality they sought was only tangential to society. Hawthorne was acute

[12]Leslie Fiedler, *Love and Death in the American Novel* (New York: Criterion Books, 1960), 93.

[13]Charles Brockden Brown, *Wieland,* ed. Sydney J. Krause and S. W. Reid (Kent, Ohio: Kent State
Univ. Press, 1978), xii.

when he insisted that he did not write novels but romances—he thus expressed his awareness of the lack of social texture in his work. . . . In America in the nineteenth century, Henry James was alone in knowing that to scale the moral and aesthetic heights in the novel one had to use the ladder of social observation.[14]

Within a few years after publication of Trilling's essay, a group of Americanists took its rather disapproving description of American novelists and found in this nonrealism or romanticism the essentially American quality they had been seeking. The idea of essential Americanness then developed in such influential works of criticism as *Virgin Land* by Henry Nash Smith (1950), *Symbolism and American Literature* by Charles Feidelson (1953), *The American Adam* by R. W. B. Lewis (1955), *The American Novel and its Tradition* by Richard Chase (1957), and *Form and Fable in American Fiction* by Daniel G. Hoffman (1961). These works, and others like them, were of sufficiently high critical quality, and sufficiently like each other, to compel assent to the picture of American literature that they presented. They used sophisticated New Critical close-reading techniques to identify a myth of America which had nothing to do with the classical fictionist's task of chronicling probable people in recognizable social situations.

The myth narrates a confrontation of the American individual, the pure American self divorced from specific social circumstances, with the promise offered by the idea of America. This promise is the deeply romantic one that in this new land, untrammeled by history and social accident, a person will be able to achieve complete self-definition. Behind this promise is the assurance that individuals come before society, that they exist in some meaningful sense prior to, and apart from, societies in which they happen to find themselves. The myth also holds that, as something artificial and secondary to human nature, society exerts an unmitigatedly destructive pressure on individuality. To depict it at any length would be a waste of artistic time; and there is only one way to relate it to the individual—as an adversary.

One may believe all this and yet look in vain for a way to tell a believable story that could free the protagonist from society or offer the promise of such freedom, because nowhere on earth do individuals live apart from social groups. But in America, given the original reality of large tracts of wilderness, the idea seems less a fantasy, more possible in reality or at least more believable in literary treatment. Thus it is that the essential quality of America comes to reside in its unsettled wilderness and the opportunities that such a wilderness offers to the individual as the medium on which he may ascribe, unhindered, his own destiny and his own nature.

As the nineteenth century wore on, and settlements spread across the wilderness, the struggle of the individual against society became more and more central to the myth; where, let's say, Thoreau could leave in Chapter 1 of *Walden,* Huckleberry Finn has still not made his break by the end of Chapter XLII (the conclusion) of the book that bears his name. Yet, one finds a struggle against society as early as the earliest Leatherstocking tale (*The Pioneers,* 1823). In a sense, this supposed promise of America has always been known to be delusory. Certainly by the twentieth century the myth has been transmuted into an avowedly hopeless quest for unencumbered space (*On the Road*), or the evocation of flight for its own sake (*Rabbit, Run* and *Henderson the Rain King*), or as pathetic acknowledgment of loss—e.g., the close of *The Great Gatsby* where the narrator Nick Carraway summons up "the old island here that flowered once for Dutch sailors' eyes—a fresh, green breast of the

---

[14]*The Liberal Imagination,* 206.

new world . . . the last and greatest of all human dreams" where man is "face to face for the last time in history with something commensurate to his capacity for wonder."

We are all very familiar with this myth of America in its various fashionings and owing to the selective vision that has presented this myth to us as the whole story, many of us are unaware of how much besides it has been created by literary Americans. Keeping our eyes on this myth, we need to ask whether anything about it puts it outside women's reach. In one sense, and on one level, the answer is no. The subject of this myth is supposed to stand for human nature, and if men and women alike share a common human nature, then all can respond to its values, its promises, and its frustrations. And in fact as a teacher I find women students responsive to the myth insofar as its protagonist is concerned. It is true, of course, that in order to represent some kind of believable flight into the wilderness, one must select a protagonist with a certain believable mobility, and mobility has until recently been a male prerogative in our society. Nevertheless, relatively few men are actually mobile to the extent demanded by the story, and hence the story is really not much more vicarious, in this regard, for women than for men. The problem is thus not to be located in the protagonist or his gender per se; the problem is with the other participants in his story—the entrammelling society and the promising landscape. For both of these are depicted in unmistakably feminine terms, and this gives a sexual character to the protagonist's story which does, indeed, limit its applicability to women. And this sexual definition has melodramatic, misogynist implications.

In these stories, the encroaching, constricting, destroying society is represented with particular urgency in the figure of one or more women. There are several possible reasons why this might be so. It seems to be a fact of life that we all—women and men alike—experience social conventions and responsibilities and obligations first in the persons of women, since women are entrusted by society with the task of rearing young children. Not until he reaches mid-adolescence does the male connect up with other males whose primary task is socialization; but at about this time—if he is heterosexual—his lovers and spouses become the agents of a permanent socialization and domestication. Thus, although women are not the source of social power, they are experienced as such. And although not all women are engaged in socializing the young, the young do not encounter women who are not. So from the point of view of the young man; the only kind of women who exist are entrappers and domesticators.

For heterosexual man, these socializing women are also the locus of powerful attraction. First, because everybody has social and conventional instincts; second, because his deepest emotional attachments are to women. This attraction gives urgency and depth to the protagonist's rejection of society. To do it, he must project onto the woman those attractions that he feels, and cast her in the melodramatic role of temptress, antagonist, obstacle—a character whose mission in life seems to be to ensnare him and deflect him from life's important purposes of self-discovery and self-assertion. (A Puritan would have said: from communion with Divinity.) As Richard Chase writes in *The American Novel and its Tradition*, "The myth requires celibacy." It is partly against his own sexual urges that the male must struggle, and so he perceives the socializing and domesticating woman as a doubly powerful threat; for this reason, Chase goes on to state, neither Cooper nor "any other American novelist until the age of James and Edith Wharton" could imagine "a fully developed woman of sexual age."[15] Yet in making this statement, Chase is talking about his myth rather than Cooper's. (One should add that, for a homosexual male, the demands of society

---

[15] Richard Chase, *The American Novel and its Tradition* (New York: Anchor, 1957), 55, 64.

that he link himself for life to a woman make for a particularly misogynist version of this aspect of the American myth, for the hero is propelled not by a rejected attraction, but by true revulsion.) Both heterosexual and homosexual versions of the myth cooperate with the hero's perceptions and validate the notion of woman as threat.

Such a portrayal of women is likely to be uncongenial, if not basically incomprehensible, to a woman. It is not likely that women will write books in which women play this part; and it is by no means the case that most novels by American men reproduce such a scheme. Even major male authors prominent in the canon have other ways of depicting women; e.g., Cooper's *Pathfinder* and *The Pioneers,* Hemingway's *For Whom the Bell Tolls,* Fitzgerald's *The Beautiful and The Damned.* The novels of Henry James and William Dean Howells pose a continual challenge to the masculinist bias of American critical theory. And in one work—*The Scarlet Letter*—a "fully developed woman of sexual age" who is the novel's protagonist has been admitted into the canon, but only by virtue of strenuous critical revisions of the text that remove Hester Prynne from the center of the novel and make her subordinate to Arthur Dimmesdale.

So Leslie Fiedler, in *Love and Death in the American Novel,* writes this of *The Scarlett Letter:*

> It is certainly true, in terms of the plot, that Chillingworth drives the minister toward confession and penance, while Hester would have lured him to evasion and flight. But this means, for all of Hawthorne's equivocations, that the eternal feminine does not draw us on toward grace, rather that the woman promises only madness and damnation. . . . [Hester] is the female temptress of Puritan mythology, but also, though sullied, the secular madonna of sentimental Protestantism (236).

In the rhetorical "us" Fiedler presumes that all readers are men, that the novel is an act of communications among and about males. His characterization of Hester as one or another myth or image makes it impossible for the novel to be in any way about Hester as a human being. Giving the novel so highly specific a gender reference, Fiedler makes it inaccessible to women and limits its reference to men in comparison to the issues that Hawthorne was treating in the story. Not the least of these issues was, precisely, the human reference of a woman's tale.

Amusingly, then, since he has produced this warped reading, Fiedler goes on to condemn the novel for its sexual immaturity. *The Scarlet Letter* is integrated into Fiedler's general exposure of the inadequacies of the American male—inadequacies which, as his treatment of Hester shows, he holds women responsible for. The melodrama here is not Hawthorne's, but Fiedler's—the American critic's melodrama of beset manhood. Of course, women authors as major writers are notably and inevitably absent from Fiedler's chronicle.

In fact many books by women—including such major authors as Edith Wharton, Ellen Glasgow, and Willa Cather—project a version of the particular myth we are speaking of but cast the main character as a woman. When a woman takes the central role, it follows naturally that the socializer and domesticator will be a man. This is the situation in *The Scarlet Letter.* Hester is beset by the male reigning oligarchy and by Dimmesdale, who passively tempts her and is responsible for fathering her child. Thereafter, Hester (as the myth requires) elects celibacy, as do many heroines in versions of this myth by women: Than in Cather's *The Song of the Lark,* Dorinda in Glasgow's *Barren Ground,* Anna Leath in Wharton's *The Reef.* But what is written in the criticism about these celibate women? They are said to be untrue to the imperatives of their gender, which require marriage, childbearing, domesticity. Instead of being read as a woman's version of the myth, such novels are read as stories of the frustration of female nature. Stories of female frustration are not perceived as commenting on, or containing, the essence of our culture, and so we don't find them in the canon.

So the role of entrapper and impediment in the melodrama of beset manhood is reserved for women. Also, the role of the beckoning wilderness, the attractive landscape, is given a deeply feminine quality. Landscape is deeply imbued with female qualities, as society is; but where society is menacing and destructive, landscape is compliant and supportive. It has the attributes simultaneously of a virginal bride and a nonthreatening mother; its female qualities are articulated with respect to a male angle of vision: what can nature do for me, asks the hero, what can it give me?

Of course, nature has been feminine and maternal from time immemorial, and Henry Nash Smith's *Virgin Land* picks up a timeless archetype in its title. The basic nature of the image leads one to forget about its potential for imbuing any story in which it is used with sexual meanings, and the gender implications of a female landscape have only recently begun to be studied. Recently, Annette Kolodny has studied the traditional canon from this approach.[16] She theorizes that the hero, fleeing a society that has been imagined as feminine, then imposes on nature some ideas of women which, no longer subject to the correcting influence of real-life experience, become more and more fantastic. The fantasies are infantile, concerned with power, mastery, and total gratification: the all-nurturing mother, the all-passive bride. Whether one accepts all the Freudian or Jungian implications of her argument, one cannot deny the way in which heroes of American myth turn to nature as sweetheart and nurture, anticipating the satisfaction of all desires through her and including among these the desires for mastery and power. A familiar passage that captures these ideas is one already quoted: Carraway's evocation of the "fresh green breast" of the new world. The fresh greenness is the virginity that offers itself to the sailors, but the breast promises maternal solace and delight. *The Great Gatsby* contains our two images of women: while Carraway evokes the impossible dream of a maternal landscape, he blames a nonmaternal woman, the socialite Daisy, for her failure to satisfy Gatsby's desires. The true adversary, of course, is Tom Buchanan, but he is hidden, as it were, behind Daisy's skirts.

I have said that women are not likely to cast themselves as antagonists in a man's story; they are even less likely, I suggest, to cast themselves as virgin land. The lack of fit between their own experience and the fictional role assigned to them is even greater in the second instance than in the first. If women portray themselves as brides or mothers it will not be in terms of the mythic landscape. If a woman puts a female construction on nature—as she certainly must from time to time, given the archetypal female resonance of the image—she is likely to write of it as more active, or to stress its destruction or violation. On the other hand, she might adjust the heroic myth to her own psyche by making nature out to be male—as, for example, Willa Cather seems to do in *O Pioneers!* But a violated landscape or a male nature does not fit the essential American pattern as critics have defined it, and hence these literary images occur in an obscurity that criticism cannot see. Thus, one has an almost classic example of the "double bind." When the woman writer creates a story that conforms to the expected myth, it is not recognized for what it is because of a superfluous sexual specialization in the myth as it is entertained in the critics' minds. (Needless to say, many male novelists also entertain this version of the myth, and do not find the masculinist bias with which they imbue it to be superfluous. It is possible that some of these novelists, especially those who write in an era in which literary

16Annette Kolodny, *The Lay of the Land* (Chapel Hill: Univ. of North Carolina Press, 1975).

criticism is a powerful influence, have formed their ideas from their reading in criticism.) But if she does not conform to the myth, she is understood to be writing minor or trivial literature.

Two remaining points can be treated much more briefly. The description of the artist and of the act of writing which emerges when the critic uses the basic American story as his starting point contains many attributes of the basic story itself. This description raises the exclusion of women to a more abstract, theoretical—and perhaps more pernicious— level. Fundamentally, the idea is that the artist writing a story of this essential American kind is engaging in a task very much like the one performed by his mythic hero. In effect, the artist writing his narrative is imitating the mythic encounter of hero and possibility in the safe confines of his story; or, reversing the temporal order, one might see that mythic encounter of hero and possibility as a projection of the artist's situation.

Although this idea is greatly in vogue at the moment, it has a history. Here, for example, is Richard Chase representing the activity of writing in metaphors of discovery and exploration, as though the writer were a hero in the landscape: "The American novel has usually seemed content to explore . . . the remarkable and in some ways unexampled territories of life in the New World and to reflect its anomalies and dilemmas. It has . . . wanted . . . to discover a new place and a new state of mind."[17] Richard Poirier takes the idea further:

> The most interesting American books are an image of the creation of America itself. . . . They carry the metaphoric burden of a great dream of freedom—of the expansion of national consciousness into the vast spaces of a continent and the absorption of those spaces into ourselves. . . . The classic American writers try through style temporarily to free the hero (and the reader) from systems, to free them from the pressures of time, biology, economics, and from the social forces which are ultimately the undoing of American heroes and quite often of their creators. . . . The strangeness of American fiction has . . . to do . . . with the environment [the novelist] tries to create for his hero, usually his surrogate.[18]

The implicit union of creator and protagonist is made specific and overt at the end of Poirier's passage here. The ideas of Poirier and Chase, and others like them, are summed up in an anthology called *Theories of American Literature,* edited by Donald M. Kartiganer and Malcolm A. Griffith.[19] The editors write, "It is as if with each new work our writers feel they must invent again the complete world of a literary form." (Yet, the true subject is not what the writers feel, but what the critics think they feel.) "Such a condition of nearly absolute freedom to create has appeared to our authors both as possibility and liability, an utter openness suggesting limitless opportunity for the imagination, or an enormous vacancy in which they create from nothing. For some it has meant an opportunity to play Adam, to assume the role of an original namer of experience" (4–5). One can see in this passage the transference of the American myth from the Adamic hero *in* the story, to the Adamic creator *of* the story, and the reinterpretation of the American myth as a metaphor for the American artist's situation.

This myth of artistic creation, assimilating the act of writing novels to the Adamic myth, imposes on artistic creation all the gender-based restrictions that we have already

---

[17]Chase, *American Novel,* 5.

[18]Poirier, *A World Elsewhere,* 3, 5, 9.

[19]Donald M. Kartiganer and Malcolm A. Griffith, eds., *Theories of American Literature* (New York: Macmillan, 1962).

examined in that myth. The key to identifying an "Adamic writer" is the formal appearance, or, more precisely the *informal* appearance, of his novel. The unconventionality is interpreted as a direct representation of the open-ended experience of exploring and taming the wilderness, as well as a rejection of "society" as it is incorporated in conventional literary forms. There is no place for a woman author in this scheme. Her roles in the drama of creation are those allotted to her in a male melodrama: either she is to be silent, like nature: or she is the creator of conventional works, the spokesperson of society. What she might do as an innovator in her own right is not to be perceived.

In recent years, some refinements of critical theory coming from the Yale and Johns Hopkins and Columbia schools have added a new variant to the idea of creation as a male province. I quote from a 1979 book entitled *Home as Found* by Eric Sundquist. The author takes the idea that in writing a novel the artist is really writing a narrative about himself and proposes this addition:

> Writing a narrative about myself may represent an extremity of Oedipal usurpation or identification, a bizarre act of self fathering. . . . American authors have been particularly obsessed with *fathering* a tradition of their own, with becoming their "own sires." . . . The struggle . . . is central to the crisis of representation, and hence of style, that allows American authors to find in their own fantasies those of a nation and to make of those fantasies a compelling and instructive literature.[20]

These remarks derive clearly from the work of such critics as Harold Bloom, as any reader of recent critical theory will note. The point for our purpose is the facile translation of the verb "to author" into the verb "to father," with the profound gender-restrictions of that translation unacknowledged. According to this formulation, insofar as the author writes about a character who is his surrogate—which, apparently, he always does—he is trying to become his own father.

We can scarcely deny that men think a good deal about, and are profoundly affected by, relations with their fathers. The theme of fathers and sons is perennial in world literature. Somewhat more spaciously, we recognize that intergenerational conflict, usually perceived from the point of view of the young, is a recurrent literary theme, especially in egalitarian cultures. Certainly, this idea involves the question of authority, and "authority" is a notion related to that of "the author." And there is some gender-specific significance involved since authority in most cultures that we know tends to be invested in adult males. But the theory has built from these useful and true observations to a restriction of literary creation to a sort of therapeutic act that can only be performed by men. If literature is the attempt to *father* oneself by the author, then every act of writing by a woman is both perverse and absurd. And, of course, it is bound to fail.

Since this particular theory of the act of writing is drawn from psychological assumptions that are not specific to American literature, it may be argued that there is no need to confine it to American authors. In fact, Harold Bloom's *Anxiety of Influence,* defining literature as a struggle between fathers and sons, or the struggle of sons to escape from their fathers, is about British literature. And so is Edward Said's book *Beginnings,* which chronicles the history of the nineteenth-century British novel as exemplification of what he calls "filiation." His discussion omits Jane Austen, George Eliot, all three Brontë sisters, Mrs. Gaskell, Mrs. Humphrey Ward—not a sign of a woman author is found in his treatment of Victorian fiction. The result is a revisionist approach to British fiction that recasts it in

---

[20]Eric Sundquist, *Home as Found* (Baltimore: Johns Hopkins Univ. Press, 1979), xviii–xix.

the accepted image of the American myth. Ironically, just at the time that feminist critics are discovering more and more important women, the critical theorists have seized upon a theory that allows the women less and less presence. This observation points up just how significantly the critic is engaged in the act of *creating* literature.

Ironically, then, one concludes that in pushing the theory of American fiction to this extreme, critics have "deconstructed" it by creating a tool with no particular American reference. In pursuit of the uniquely American, they have arrived at a place where Americanness has vanished into the depths of what is alleged to be the universal male psyche. The theory of American fiction has boiled down to the phrase in my title: a melodrama of beset manhood. What a reduction this is of the enormous variety of fiction written in this country, by both women and men! And, ironically, nothing could be further removed from Trilling's idea of the artist as embodiment of a culture. As in the working out of all theories, its weakest link has found it out and broken the chain.

William Boelhower
....
A Modest Ethnic Proposal

> For now we see through a glass, darkly; but then face to face: now I know in part; but then shall I know even as also I am known.
>
> *1 Corinthians 13, 12*

The issue of ethnicity in the United States inevitably surfaces at the national level whenever the ideology of the American Dream or of Americanism *tout court* malfunctions or hyperfunctions or simply comes in for such routine scrutiny as the presidential elections. In between times, almost everywhere in America it remains the great unknown local fact. Given the continuing success of the founding political experiment, during which the Enlightenment words of constitutional guarantee were forever fixed and sealed, the issue itself remains somewhat of a scandal—for mere repetition of the alchemical formula *E PLURIBUS UNUM* would not really convert the base metals of a pluralistic society into a finely beaten national gold. Yet this is the impossible possibility, the asylum foundation, on which Enlightenment and even contemporary America is built. It is necessary to know that by definition the American belongs preeminently to the genus *citoyen* (he is above all a political animal), while ethnicity is his specific difference. Only the genus legitimizes his global circulation within national boundaries. Cultural differences within them remain territorially local. Thus, during a recent television debate involving democratic candidates for the presidency, Jewish-American journalist Marvin Kalb attacked Jesse Jackson with these words: "What we can't understand is if you are a black who happened to be born in America or an American who was born black." Obviously aware of the ideological teeth treacherously hidden in Kalb's trap, Jackson simply danced through it like an ethnic

Pan by repeating the quintessential American paradox: "I'm an American born inside a black." Black American, Italian American, Jewish American, Spanish American, Chinese American, Vietnamese American, Native American—where should one put the accent? On the adjective or the noun, or are both to be read as nouns? The predictive predicament of American behavioral expression is as complex as it is perennial.

On his visit to Ellis Island in 1904, Henry James, certainly one of the most acute framers of what he called "the great 'ethnic' question," left the scene with a metaphysical *feritas,* saying that he had "eaten of the tree of knowledge, and the taste will be for ever in his mouth" (1968: 120, 85). What caused "the new chill in his heart" was knowledge that he had "to share the sanctity of his American consciousness, the intimacy of his American patriotism, with the inconceivable alien" (85). It is worth hearing James out in full, for in 1980 alone more than 1.25 million foreigners took up residence in the United States, thus matching the levels reached in the first decade of this century and corroborating the novelist's voiced presentiment of the same period: "The after-sense of that acute experience, however, I myself found, was by no means to be brushed away: I felt it grow and grow, on the contrary, wherever I turned: other impressions might come and go, but this affirmed claim of the alien, however immeasurably alien, to share in one's supreme relation was everywhere the fixed element, the reminder not to be dodged" (85). As any student of the American Revolution knows, one's "supreme relation" is with one's country and beyond it no people with pretensions to nationhood will ever go. If the updated image that the age demanded "of its accelerated grimace" (Pound, "Hugh Selwyn Mauberley") became the melting pot, the basic scandal Kalb would hint at remained, almost *verbatim,* the same. James asks, "Which is the American, by these scant measures?—which is *not* the alien, over a large part of the country at least, and where does one put a finger on the dividing line, or, for that matter, 'spot' and identify any particular phase of the conversion, any one of its successive moments" (124)?

TWO PARADIGMS, ONE PROBLEM

Since Oscar Handlin's book *The Uprooted* (1953), it is common knowledge that immigration, far from being a peripheral matter, is the very history of America. In the words of David Potter, "Unlike most nationality groups in the world today, the people of the United States are not ethnically rooted in the land where they live" (1975: 229). This situation has led to a permanent "identity crisis" which the coiner of that term, Erik Erikson, attributed to "the experience of emigration, immigration, and Americanization" (Gleason 1981: 31). Until the instauration of a new multi-ethnic paradigm in the 1960s (Boelhower 1982: 219–30)—and none the less problematical than the preceding monocultural matrix—a super-identity was projected as the solution to ethnic anarchy. It now seems evident that the two extremities of the yardstick used to determine cultural citizenship, namely assimilation and pluralism, correspond to the unilinearity of the two paradigmatic ideologies, and on this basis it is easy to agree with those who claim that the fault lines of conflict in America are invariably ethnic (Birnbaum 1983: 45; Rothschild 1981, Ital. tr., 8, 41). Yet, the basic question regarding the real nature of ethnicity is equally shared by both paradigms and both intend the ethnic factor as a *distinctio,* as an absolute principle of exclusion and inclusion. In fact, advocates of the multi-ethnic paradigm now often repeat the essentialist errors of their monocultural predecessors in attempting to trace out a blueprint of clear and distinct and ultimately reified ethnic categories. According to the monocultural or assimilationist paradigm, one begins by looking through a glass darkly; but thanks to the melting pot process, everybody in America will eventually see face to face—as Americans. This, after all, is the soteriological backbone of the American idea. According to the multicultural or pluralist paradigm, only by exalting ethnic face-work will United Statesers be able to strip away the rigid American mask and see face to face.

But what Kalb did not understand and James did is that neither the concept of "American" nor that of "ethnic" is separately definable, for neither is an immediately given or individual entity in itself. On the contrary, what stands out as a suitable definition to the question "what is an American" is not the answer but the question itself. Those who really expect an answer, and they are the majority since both paradigms are desperately trying to see face to face (whether it be with one's political and juridical neighbor or with one's immigrant grandparents), deserve no better answer than the one a person received when he asked Louis Armstrong for a definition of jazz: "Honey, if you don't know what it is I can't tell you." Americans and ethnics in America are doomed to see through a glass darkly, doomed to the vicious circle of their own question and answer format. In *The American Scene,* however, James offers a simple but revolutionary bypass to the progressive "now . . . but then" fable of Paul the Apostle's First Letter to the Corinthians by abandoning the sacred rage of theory for simple method, by abandoning problem-solving for a hermeneutical problematics, in short, by accepting as positive the inevitability of the circle. The new scripture, which will serve as a working hypothesis for all I have to say in these pages, goes as follows:

> He had been, on the Jersey shore, walking with a couple of friends through the grounds of a large new rural residence, where groups of diggers and ditchers were working, on those lines of breathless haste which seem always, in the United States, of the essence of any question. . . . To pause before them, for interest in their labour, was, and would have been everywhere, instinctive; but what came home to me on the spot was that whatever more would have been anywhere else involved had here inevitably to lapse.
>
> What lapsed, on the spot, was the element of communication with the workers, as I may call it for want of a better name; that element which, in a European country would have operated from side to side, as the play of mutual recognition, founded on old familiarities and heredities, and involving, for the moment, some impalpable exchange. The men, in the case I speak of, were Italians, of superlatively southern type, and any impalpable exchange struck me as absent from the air to positive intensity, to mere unthinkability. It was as if contact were out of the question and the sterility of the passage between us recorded with due dryness, in our staring silence. (1968: 118–9).

It should be remembered that by 1904 James had written such major-phase novels as *The Ambassadors, The Wings of the Dove,* and *The Golden Bowl.* Each work was a wholly new start, a wholly new attempt, to study shifting points of view and complex relations. Indeed, if there is a single impetus behind the Jamesian corpus, then it is surely the very drama, the very process, of seeing. It is this relentless practice of "flying in the face of presumptions" (James 1968b: 90) that he brought to the ethnic question and that causes him to raise his habitually musing brow in the above passage. Here the reader is faced with a *locus classicus* of ethnic interactional behavior, but more importantly with an approach that can be read as a modest proposal for an ethnic semiotics. Almost immediately James discards the realm of the *a priori* by admitting the vanity of generalization (the "whatever more . . . had here inevitably to lapse"), as if to anticipate Wittgenstein's last proposition in his *Tractatus logico-philosophicus:* about that which one cannot speak, one must keep silent. In this case, silence concerns the very "element of communication" the absence of which can be read in the very tentativeness and jerkiness of James's syntax.

AN ETHNIC KÍNESIS

If the play of the eyes is crucial in the above passage, there seem to be no preestablished rules for ordering the actual game of the face-work (Goffman 1967: 5–45). When "on the spot," the "old familiarities" must be abandoned; there is no aprioristic legitimizing frame for the Jamesian *hic et nunc*. One can even argue that the failure to set up an *adaequatio* between seeing and thing seen marks an implicit abandonment of theory, of the possibility of constructing broad metaphysical-like paradigms. In effect, James calls his own objectivity into question by making contact itself the syntactic subject of the passage. Focalization is "between us" and on "our staring silence." At second glance, it is not at all clear here who is doing the looking or who is staring down whom. Most likely it is the Italian "ditchers" who save face, for James does suggest earlier that "the alien was . . . truly in possession" (117). At any rate, the question is now irrelevant because what the passage underlines above all else is the fact that this ethnic *topos* is a conjunctural context, which means that both parties are decentered onlookers, both on the margins. At the center is not an entity or a content or a definable subject, but a dynamic relation, a qualifying energy, in short an ethnic *kínesis* (Sini 1982). Presumably, in the very transaction of gazing there are also two different codifications of the same reality (understood here as the product of an organizing activity). Otherwise there would be no crisis of interpretation or no need to learn how to analyze the American scene from more than one perspective.

As a matter of fact, from the unilateral and decontextualized vantage point of the monocultural paradigm, the American's gaze is obvious, natural, and universal. If the supporters of the multi-ethnic paradigm tend to fictionalize such a stance (since the proliferation and defense of many points of view are essentially deconstructive), they often do so at the expense of cancelling or separating out the dominant paradigm with equally univocal passion. In this way they run the risk of setting up a rival myth by assuming the formal paradigm attributes of their melting-pot predecessors.

James, on the other hand, weaves between both paradigms by dislocating the fixed point of view, by making the relation rather than the immobile subject central. In this way what both paradigms exclude (i.e., the interpretative dynamics of the other), James reinstates, thereby opening up a fluid process of ethnic semiosis. Simply put, there is no American scene outside an interpretation of it, and in the light of an ethnic semiotics, I might add, a costructuring of interpretations. That James actually does suggest such a working hypothesis is confirmed by the strategy of questions he then maneuvers onto the page. Taking up both paradigm programs, he converts them into merely provisional points of view by formulating them as questions without answers. There is nothing conclusive in James's handling of them or no attempt to formulate a definitive strategy out of them, even though he shows awareness of the already codified status of the categories he must inevitably use. Both paradigm interpretations are for him mere shifting points of view, since both necessarily imply a relativizing "for whom."

It is also intuitively natural for James to take up the assimilationist perspective first, it being the dominant and more institutionalized order of discourse. Before following him, though, we might note that James first attends to the action, the energy, of the ethnic gaze and only then tries to come to an intellectual understanding of the great ethnic issue. For the method I wish to outline here, this means that the context is all; that no theoretical ordering can ever fly free of the tenuous ground of its own making. Any passage from *descriptio* to *prescriptio* can only have the pragmatic status of an interpretation, which in turn is intrinsically tied down to the moment of ethnic contact.

THE SENSE OF THE CAULDRON

Bound to this drama of seeing and this hermeneutical circle, James submits himself to the first of what will finally prove to be an open series of musings and questions: "The sense of the elements in the cauldron—the cauldron of the 'American' character—becomes thus about as vivid a thing as you can at all quietly manage, and the question [the great "ethnic question"] settles into a form which makes the intelligible answer further and further recede" (1968: 120–1). Thus does James engage the central category of the monocultural (Americanizing) paradigm, which by 1904 had become a categorical imperative. But he refuses to offer the reader the comfort of a simple repetition or restatement of its essential solution. Instead, he chooses to upset the paradigm's lexicon by using the pincers of quotation marks around the key words ("American" and "ethnic") and in this way both defamiliarizes them and suggests that their conventional status is historical rather than ahistorical. His troping strategy then focuses attention on his own "sense of dispossession" (86), but by setting up an I-you pronominal contract with his reader he makes his ensuing identity crisis a contagious public disease.

To make sure that his reader is infected, he asks the inevitable question—"Who am I?"—in its broadest social terms. Indeed, by rephrasing his personally felt alienation in the words of the perennial, but for him ineffable, question of American identity, he implicitly undermines the very foundations of the E PLURIBUS UNUM seal. This is the way he draws open the curtains on the ethnic semiotic abyss: "What meaning, in the presence of such impressions, can continue to attach to such a term as the 'American' character?—what type, as the result of such a prodigious amalgam, such a hotch-potch of racial ingredients, is to be conceived as shaping itself" (121)? Were he now to provide the rehearsed answer of the assimilationist ideology, he would close the curtains on the abyss and reconfirm the ruling paradigm of the day. By not doing so, he makes the question itself a scandal, one whose answer is unspeakable. Since it is the constructing context of the alien that binds him to the question, it must be entertained within that very context or else risk being falsified. As a consequence, the basic difference of the ethnic gaze will have been falsely sublated or simply ignored. If James chooses to live the question, to let the question wander dialogically within its relational frame, it is because the answer can only be echoed back as the ethnic question. The very question that wants an answer (the melting pot) is an intrinsic part of the difference that originated the question in the first place. But let us see how James himself sets up this endless semiosis:

> It is more than a comfort to him, truly, in all the conditions, this accepted vision of the too-defiant scale of numerosity and quantity—the effect of which is so to multiply the possibilities, so to open, by the million, contingent doors, and windows: he rests in it at last as an absolute luxury. . . . He doesn't know, he can't say, before the facts, and he doesn't even want to know or to say; the facts themselves loom, before the understanding, in too large a mass for a mere mouthful: it is as if the syllables were too numerous to make a legible word. The illegible word, accordingly, the great inscrutable answer to questions, hangs in the vast American sky, to his imagination, as something fantastic and abracadabrant, belonging to no known language. . . . (121–22)

THE NEW LOOK, THE LOST WORD

In this way James anticipates yet another of Wittgenstein's propositions from the *Tractatus* 5.6: The limits of one's language signify the limits of one's world. There is no American *verbum* that can predict and control the play of interpretations springing from the silent dynamics of the ethnic gaze. The fact, the energy, of multicultural contact precedes monocultural comprehension, and the language that is already forged must defer to ethnic kinesis. But this renunciation of theory for a weak strategy of "contingent doors and windows" (see also James's notion of the house of fiction) is positive cause for further ethnic contact, which is "an absolute luxury"—here to be taken in its etymological sense of excess, extravagance, and superabundance. In place of the rage for a reductive clarity, therefore, he opts for the multiplication of possibilities. Seeing face to face, after all, would mean the end of interpretation and the beginning of the reign of definition. Indeed, if on the one hand James's "inscrutable answer" belongs to "no known language," on the other, the energy of ethnic/American contact seems to generate the language of identity in the form of an endless production of questions. In the United States, need one be reminded, the great question is ethnic. That is, the semantics of American identity must be built out of the syntax of ethnic materials. The costructuring relationship is all embracing: so we are now back to an American born inside the body of a black, the word incarnate, the political idea given a local habitation and a name.

But in dislocating his point of view to the Italian "ditchers" and to "the rich Rutgers Street perspective" (133), James, as his reader might now expect, is in no hurry to exalt what in the late 1960s would become the multi-ethnic paradigm. In short, one will find in James's shift no recentering strategy. On the contrary, he reinforces the mobile perspective by keeping on the move and manages next to address the problem of "the unconverted residuum" (124), "the launched condition" (125) of the alien, in an electric car. In this kinetic context he notes, "The carful, again and again, is a foreign carful; a row of faces, up and down, testifying, without exception, to alienism, unmistakable, alienism undisguised and unashamed" (125).

This observation is not, as it may seem, a nativist restatement of the Bostonian point of view. As a matter of fact, James is shocked by their *new* look, by the consecrating varnish from the "huge white-washing brush," of Americanism and is ultimately led to ask, "If there are several lights in which the great assimilative organism itself may be looked at, does it not still perhaps loom largest as an agent for revealing to the citizen-to-be the error in question" (127)? James is speaking on behalf of cultural diversity and within the realm of the plural where the "residuum" is conjugated as it once was by Ahab's cabin boy, Pip: I see, you see, he sees. Of course, the real issue is more serious: "It has taken long ages of history, in the other world, to produce them, and you ask yourself, with independent curiosity, if they may really be thus extinguished in an hour," James notes, adding, "And if they are not extinguished, into what pathless tracts of the native atmosphere do they virtually, do they provisionally, and so all undiscoverably, melt? Do they burrow underground, to await their day again?—or in what strange secret places are they held in deposit and in trust" (129)?

What is remarkable here and in the earlier passage is the fact that James accomplishes his balancing act of steering between the two major paradigms of assimilation and pluralism by means of the simple strategy of converting the objectivizing confidence of the declarative mode into the subjectivizing hermeneutics of interrogation. His working method seems quite apparent: first statement is bracketed and undercut by the conditional "if" and then its finite sense of closure is burst open by a presumably inexhaustible volley of questions. But the key to this method, its revolutionary aspect, does not lie in a simple act of interrogation or in nibbling away at a central ideological kernel from a mobile position on the margins; rather it lies in deferring the calm language of statement (with its metaphysical and reifying tendencies) to the dynamic realm of semiotic instability.

THE GREAT MYTH OF NATIONALISM

In 1904, but also in 1782 with Crèvecoeur's *Letters from an American Farmer*, most statesmen fervidly believed (as they do today) in the great myth of nationalism and in the inevitable fulfillment of its program (Rothschild: 41–49; Smith 1981, Ital. tr., 14–26). According to this myth, the conquest of nationhood was to lead to, if not be based on, an ethnically homogeneous population. It was presumed that ethnicity would be a neutral factor at the macrosocial level. According to the program, laissez-faire capitalism, with its rationalized bureaucratic state and role specialization, with its glorification of constant change and market mobility, was to produce such a level of political and economic freedom that the ethnic factor would be modernized out of existence. It was the universal liberal belief that such primordial ties as religion, language, and race would disappear; and in its more contemporary version, that technology, consumerism, and the mass media would unify, would cancel, all internal differences. Progress would know no barriers. There would be a single, standardized mass society and Walt Whitman's democratic man *en masse* at the helm. All this we now know simply did not come about. Only the imperialism of an incredibly entrenched world view could have taken for granted that the American, the Western man par excellence, would become a merely political and economic subject, that culture would be unilaterally based on these components alone.

It did not take an ethnic revival (largely the invention of the same paradigm logic described above) to mark the systematic dimensions of the lie. As Anthony Smith has noted in his book *The Ethnic Revival*, not only is it impossible to speak coherently of the United States (or, for that matter, the great majority of modern nations) as a single national culture but also the very designation of "nation state" as a concept of cultural purity is erroneous and illegitimate (Ital., tr., 1984: 19, 26). Furthermore, it is historiographically dilettantish to consider the ethnic question a passing or, even worse, a recent phenomenon, since ethnic consciousness itself is the very product, and not a deviation, of economic development and advanced capitalist society. As a rule, modernization tends to increase differences rather than eliminate them, while capitalism by its very nature generates ethnic protest. These observations will receive sharper focus in the next chapter, which will deal with ethnogenesis in colonial America and in particular in the United States of the nineteenth century.

At any rate, because of his inquisitive way of approaching things, James was not deceived by what he called the "scientific force" (1968: 128) of the colossal machinery (120) of the melting pot, for if we pick him up where we last left him, we find him musing. "Isn't it conceivable that, for something like a final efflorescence, the business of slow comminglings and makings-over at last ended, they may rise again to the surface, affirming their vitality and value and playing their part" (129)? The melting pot for James is not unlike Melville's sea—often glassy smooth on top but underneath seething with unclassifiable variety. He writes, "The cauldron, for the great stew, has such circumference and such depth that we can only deal here with ultimate syntheses, ultimate combinations and possibilities" (130). By speaking from within the plural, the deferring theory to the fishy, elusive detail at the bottom of the pot and to the single fleeting glance of an Italian ditcher, James is able to contact the local, where the American residuum betrays an irreducible ethnic energy; where ethnic *kínesis* reveals itself in the very act of its concealment.

THE INEFFABLE ETHNIC DIFFERENCE

The national category of the global cannot control its own internal colonies. Who can predict when the ethnic difference will surface, and where, and why, and how? Was the gap between James and the Italian workers social? Perhaps he was dressed in a cool linen shirt and carried a walking stick; perhaps from the ditch they noticed only the polish of his shoes or the fine English fabric of his trousers. And they, it is very likely they still wore their old-world peasant garb. Maybe, though, the gap was economic, a difference in wages, food, residence. Or was it political? In 1904 Italians were often stereotyped as anarchists, socialists or radicals. Were they nurturing some hidden revolutionary scheme? No, more likely the ethnic stare was racial or religious or linguistic (James speaking Italian and they Sicilian) or perhaps only a matter of customary reserve.

The point, I think, is clear: there is almost no way to identify any single ethnic factor. Nor did James care to. All of the above factors can be ethnic and ethnic contact can invoke them all. Well-ordered taxonomies, James seems to imply, pertain to a one-sided paradigm strategy that favors definition and theoretical elaboration, as if a set of rigidly constructed categories could, through description, control the energy of the ethnic sign. James, however, offers a corrective working hypothesis that dwells on the *production* of ethnic semiotic activity, on that unchartable non-space where a sign becomes ethnic. Here lies all the difference and it will be the concern of my third chapter to develop his hints into a local model of ethnic semiosis. The need for such a model can be shown easily enough by repeating Thomas Sowell's recent remark, "In short, ethnic identity has been a complex and elusive phenomenon" (1981: 294). Almost everybody who has ever embarked on the taxonomic quest would agree.

Rothschild lists race, consanguinity, religion, language, customs and practices, regionalism, and political experience as ethnic components (92–99), only to conclude that the identity and boundaries of ethnic groups are very flexible and multiple (132). Smith defines an ethnic group in this way: a social group whose members share a sense of common origins, claim a shared and distinct historical past and destiny, possess one or more distinguishing cultural attributes and have a sense of collective unity and solidarity (114). In keeping with Rothschild and Sowell, however, he too admits that an accurate definition of ethnicity escapes him (29).

Perhaps one of the most important examples of the hopelessness of the encyclopedic approach to ethnicity is the *Harvard Encyclopedia of American Ethnic Groups,* where the descriptive urge is quite exhaustive. There sixteen control features are listed for group entries (1981: viii): origins, migration, arrival, settlement, economic life, social structure, social organization, family and kinship, behavior and personal/individual characteristics, culture, religion, education, politics, intergroup relations, group maintenance, individual ethnic commitment. Nonetheless, the editors are also quick to admit that any definition of ethnicity must remain "flexible and pragmatic." "The fluid and situational nature of ethnicity makes precise estimates of the numbers of 'ethnic' and 'nonethnic' Americans impossible," they confess (vii).

Indeed, a single ethnic contact, like James's, or even a single ethnic sign seems to be able to bring the whole descriptive house down. In short, no encyclopedia can pretend to control ethnic sign production. Between inventory and event one finds the same chasm that separated James's working hypothesis from the false presumptions of the melting pot paradigm. In cauldron terms, the difference is between the smooth surface and the boiling stew beneath.

THE REALM OF CONTACT, THE LOCAL PLACE

But as a rival paradigm the multi-ethnic ideology is on no more solid grounds when it tries to develop a theory of ethnicity in substantive rather than relational terms. Berndt Ostendorf is quite right in arguing that ethnicity is not "an absolute cultural or social essence (whether genetic, psychological, cultural, or social is here beside the point)" (1983: 152). In effect, it is misguided even to speak of a multi-ethnic paradigm if by that one means to claim for it a status and tactics similar to the so-called monocultural paradigm. Of course, with the help of James, I hope I have made it clear that the identity crisis of Americans can only be handled as ethnic discourse, since everybody in America is willy-nilly an ethnic subject. The question "What is an American?" is also an ethnic question for obvious genealogical reasons. I do not mean to say that both paradigms have not served in crucial ideological battles. The point is another. Neither model of interpretation can claim for itself an univocally self-referential foundation. Context and not content must ultimately serve as the epistemological touchstone. Calling on Gregory Bateson, it might even be better to speak of an inclusive "transcontextuality" or contextual structure whereby to act as one of two terms (assimilation and Americanization versus pluralism and ethnification) of a structure of interaction means immediately to summon the other term (1972, Ital. tr., 1976: 295, 298–9).

While attempts to purify research activity by ordering one's investigations in a single direction do ban ambiguity and methodological anarchy from paradigm analyses, in the same stroke they also detach ethnic cultures and discourse from the central issues of the dominant culture. In contact situations, on the contrary, the two domains are indissolubly interwoven, since both are condemned to share the same semiotic space. The only way for the ethnic individual to get "outside" of American culture is by burrowing ever more deeply "inside" it, which is basically a movement from the global to the local. Inevitably, therefore, both insiders and outsiders must also confront the same spatio-temporal context; that is, both must confront the common problematic of *habitare*, which I will treat in subsequent chapters. There will, however, only be a valid multi-ethnic paradigm when Americans really decide to discover the authenticity of place within their national space, when Americans really decide to face the problem of *habitare*—which is one with the concept of identity crisis—within their political boundaries. But here we have come back to the genealogical dilemma that underlies both the monocultural and multi-ethnic paradigms and disseminates cultural instability at their very centers.

MAINSTREAM AND ETHNIC LITERATURE:
UNEASY BEDFELLOWS

Mainstream and ethnic literature has also been deeply affected by paradigm decontextualization. Indeed, the long established practice of compartmentalizing American literature into mainstream and ethnic cannot but lead to the belief that they are separable if not separate canons. There was, in fact, a highly entrenched critical tradition based on a consensus matrix that succeeded in establishing a rather untouchable and, I might add, apparently non-ethnic pantheon. In the genre of autobiography, for example, one would most likely find the names of Franklin, Thoreau, and Adams, but not those of Louis Adamic, Constantine Panunzio, and Mary Antin. On the other hand, a contemporary course on ethnic literature might include the last three texts but not the first three. In this light it does appear that many multi-ethnic advocates have played into the hands of the dominant paradigm's strategy of reductionism. They might argue, of course, that by separating ethnic literature from the mainstream canon, it will finally get its due attention. Yes and no. No, because for the dominant critical matrix ethnic literature in such a framework will remain poor, minor, ephemeral, local, aesthetically inferior, and thus easily dismissible. In fact, this ghettoized version of ethnic literature may even lead to this extreme underestimation of its peculiar identity by Berndt Ostendorf: "Its victory as literature spells its defeat as ethnic culture" (150).

The non-dialogical stance, in effect, is too neat and theoretically assailable. Sooner or later multi-ethnic critics, like their mainstream counterparts, will have to play the rather academic game of literary purity: this is ethnic, this is not. And it can only end up in a bloody tactics of massacre in which a kind of mystic Solomon's sword is used to cast judgment over texts by amputating not only one text from another but one part of a text from another. According to this logic, it is presumed that the sole area where true ethnic signs are produced and circulate is in ethnic literature. But if one sets up such an absolute category, one is then forced to follow the one-way path of the encyclopedia and establish a set of contents as the dominant aesthetic norm. As the Jamesian example has shown, though, there is no parthenogenesis of ethnic codes. One ethnic novel or a particular ethnic encyclopedia does not account for the production of another. In truth, there is no unilateral aesthetic starting point for the multi-ethnic critic; he must learn to be contented with James's tentative *va-et-vient* between the two epistemes.

Moreover, this situation is far from being desperate. Why not, for example, consider the ethnic novel (and I am too sceptical to believe that such an animal really exists) as a novel with a difference or with a play of differences. In other words, it can be ordered by such various narratological programs as the detective story, the pastoral novel, the utopia, the proletarian novel, and so forth, but what distinguishes it from mainstream samples of these literary typologies is the fact that it circulates ethnic signs with a greater or lesser degree of frequency and intensity. The very "ethnicity" of ethnic and, for that matter, mainstream fiction then becomes pangeneric and transcultural.

By avoiding totalizing concepts like the ethnic novel, by transforming issues of substance into a strategy of pragmatics, one can indeed include in his reading list for a course on ethnic fiction such texts as Mark Twain's *Adventures of Huckleberry Finn,* William Faulkner's *Light in August,* and Willa Cather's *My Antonia* along with Ralph Ellison's *Invisible Man,* Henry Roth's *Call It Sleep,* and Mario Puzo's *The Fortunate Pilgrim.* Not only does such a list show how ubiquitous the ethnic sign is in American literature but also how hopelessly American ethnic fiction is. Through such a confrontation one can also avoid reducing the polysemic richness of texts to a mere genre check-up, a practice which has not served ethnic literary discourse well. As I will show in a later chapter, there is a highly codified immigrant narrative regime (Boelhower 1981: 3–13) that functions as a kind of epicenter for ethnic discourse, but it is exactly through a comparison with this text type that one learns how chamelion-like ethnic literary forms are.

THE SINGLE ETHNIC SIGN

It is by giving full critical attention to the highly local ethnic sign (a name like James Gatz, for instance, or Queequeg's tattoos or an involuntary Talmudic gesture by Abraham Cahan's David Levinsky) that one can hope to verify Werner Sollors's remark, "American literature as a whole can be read as the ancestral footstep or coded hieroglyph in the present" (1981: 649). In terms of my monograph, this means that the ethnic sign and the empirical traces of ethnic discourse are so capillary, so pervasive, so inseparable from the mainstream literary corpus that any effort to relieve American literature of its ethnic corpuscles by means of critical blood-letting could only result in its bleeding to death. If this is true, then heuristic tools must also be found which are capable of radiographing how the ethnic subject imposes or positions itself at all levels of the various cultural systems to which it belongs, either as presence or absence. Naturally, such tools should also allow one to go beyond the vague concept of ethnic fiction or it will remain impossible to understand how the ethnic sign is produced. In the end one must return to the local horizon of James's ethnic stare in order to build the foundations of a model of ethnic semiosis with a range that covers both the minimal aleatory trace and the highly institutionalized genre. Ethnic fluency depends on such a broad potential of semiotic reconnaissance.

Where monocultural and genre interpretations flatten the ethnic sign to summary equivalences, for example by canceling the ethnic reading of Upton Sinclair's *The Jungle* in favor of a merely proletarian version, our local model of semiosis shows how a weak ethnic discourse, even by its progressive evaporation, is actually capable of calling into question the totalizing criterion of a genre program. This same ethnic deconstructive energy is also at work in the so-called pastoral trilogies of William Carlos Williams and Sophus Keith Winther, to cite another example of how an entrenched narrative continuum can be resegmented ethnically or, if you will, against the common American grain. The point is, without such a local ethnic semiotics, ethnically embedded signs would often be dissolved in signifying solutions that are more stringent and systematic than they are. At the same time, it is precisely the aleatory and marginal status of the ethnic sign, its virtual uncontrollability and ubiquity, that makes its presence a constant source of disturbance in so-called dominant cultural texts.

Given its normally subaltern status, the ethnic sign's appearance in various fictional genres is often too fluid and unstable to be easily detected and evaluated. If we go back to James's ethnic gaze, we can understand why no encyclopedic set of cultural contents and descriptions, no extensional operation, could explain how ethnicity actually works as a weak or even strong intentional mechanism. After all, James did not see face to face, but through a glass darkly. The sign gaze did not establish a series of semantic correspondences but offered instead an inferencing context. The gaze, the sign, is above all an interpretative relation, a putting into relation. Only for the above-mentioned paradigm ideologies does meaning precede context. By choosing the context, James put himself in a position to see how ethnic semiosis can disrupt the very authority of paradigm logic. Not having the latter's authority to dictate its own terms, the ethnic context modestly implies a different interpretative posture, an altogether different way of looking at the terms themselves. Moreover, the scandal that James revealed some sixty years ahead of time could only have been made possible within the relational structure of the ethnic sign itself. What the Jamesian gaze really uncovered was not the sociological information produced, but the different structural processes behind its production. His choice of the context over the melting pot paradigm was radically innovative for his day and offered *in nuce* a model for rereading all of American literature with an eye to the single ethnic sign.

A sign is only ethnic if it is produced or interpreted as such by an intending subject. Beginning with it, one can catch a glimpse of an entire ethnic world, for ethnic semiosis, as Umberto Eco helps to explain, carries with it a set of instructions for an interpretative program (1984: 5, 118–20). In other words the semiotic process involves not so much a particular group of things as it does their being grouped in a certain way. It is, in short, a position of reading. In this light the very notion of an ethnic encyclopedia as a rigid inventory of classified data is recast as a complex chain of ethnic sign relations. But this will be taken up more fully in the third chapter. Here I simply want to note that it is the specific type of cognitive gaze that alone generates a cognitive map equivalent to an ethnic world. Consequently, we must begin and end with its relational energy. The only objection that I have to the construction of ethnic encyclopedias such as the very fine *Harvard* volume is that they are so easily used to reinforce the decontextualized and static practices of the monocultural and multi-ethnic paradigms. Indeed, I am almost tempted to conclude that the ethnic sign and its importance have been neglected largely because of such reified inventories. What we really need in order to strengthen ethnic-reader competence is a working hypothesis like James's; that is, a model of participation which will permit us to see the laws of ethnic semiotic production.

For James, the occasion of ethnic contact began with an initial stare and opened up to a horizonless inferencing field. It was this hermeneutical context with its dialogical foundation that allowed him to identify the fundamental structure of cultural differences making up the very spatio-temporal boundaries of dwelling in the United States. On this foundation I will try to build a specific model of ethnic semiotics capable of identifying ethnic *kínesis*. The task will involve establishing rules for determining the major or minor necessity of ethnic implication—in short, rules of institutionality or a grammar of an ethnic system of signs (Eco 1984: 51, xi). But beyond this model, which basically involves a discourse of origins, is the problem of the origins of ethnic discourse. In Eco's words, "The science of signs is the science of how the subject is historically constructed" (1984: 54). In order to explain the fact that American literature is irremediably ethnic, no matter what form the latter might take (latent or manifest, passive or aggressive, involuntary or voluntary), I must approach it genetically. The next chapter, therefore, will be on ethnogenesis or the making of American identity.

Jane Tompkins

"But Is It Any Good?":
The Institutionalization of
Literary Value

People often object, when presented with the arguments I have made above, that while one may affirm the power or centrality of a novel on the grounds that it intersects with widely-held beliefs and grapples with pressing social problems, that affirmation does not prove anything one way or another about the literary value of the text, and does nothing to guarantee its status as a work of art. This objection seems particularly trenchant in the present context because while it grants the validity of my argument on one level and even suggests that the point is obvious—*of course* best-sellers reflect the concerns of the passing moment—it denies the relevance of the argument to literary criticism. For criticism, the objection goes, concerns itself with the specifically *literary* features of American writing. And what distinguishes a work *as literature* is the way it separates itself from transitory issues of the kind I have been discussing—revolution (Brockden Brown), consolidation (Cooper), revival (Warner), and abolition (Stowe). The fact that a work engages such issues, in this view, is an index not of its greatness, but of its limitation; the more directly it engages purely local and temporal concerns, the less literary it will be, not only because it is captive to the fluctuations of history, but also because in its attempt to mold public opinion it is closer to propaganda than to art, and hence furnishes material for the historian rather than the literary critic.

The objection, as I have phrased it, is never put in exactly this way, but usually takes the form of a question like: but are these works really any *good?* or, what about the *literary* value of *Uncle Tom's Cabin?* or, do you really want to defend Warner's *language?* These questions imply that the standards of judgment to which they refer are not themselves challengeable, but are taken for granted among qualified readers. "You and I know what a good novel is," the objection implies, "and we both know that these novels fall outside that category." But the notion of good literature that the question invokes is precisely what we are arguing about. That tacit sense of what is "good" cannot be used to determine the value of these novels because literary value *is* the point at issue. At this juncture, people will frequently attempt to settle the question empirically by pointing to one or another indisputably "great" work, such as *Moby-Dick* or *The Scarlet Letter,* and asking whether *The Wide, Wide World* is as good as *that.*

But the issue cannot be settled by invoking apparently unquestionable examples of literary excellence such as these as a basis of comparison, because these texts already represent one position in the debate they are being called upon to decide. That is, their value, their identity, and their constituent features have been made available for description by the very modes of perception and evaluation that I am challenging. It is not from any neutral space that we have learned to see the epistemological subtleties of Melville or Hawthorne's psychological acuity. Those characteristics have been made available by critical strategies that have not always been respectable, but had to be explained, illustrated, and argued for (as I am arguing now) against other critical assumptions embodied in other masterpieces that seemed just as invincible, just as unquestionably excellent as these now do. Such strategies do not remain stable and do not emerge in isolation, but are forged in the context of revolutions, revivals, periods of consolidation or reform—in short, in the context of all those historical circumstances by which literary values are supposed to re-main unaffected. Even in the last sixty years, the literary canon has undergone more than one major shift as the circumstances within which critics evolved their standards of judg-ment changed.

The evidence for this assertion becomes dramatically available when one examines the history of literary anthologies. Between the time that Fred Pattee made selections for *Century Readings for a Course in American Literature* (1919) and the time that Perry Miller and his coeditors decided whom to include in *Major Writers of America* (1962), the notion of who counted as a major writer and even the concept of the "major writer" had altered dra-matically. Whereas Pattee's single volume, compiled at the close of World War I, con-tained hundreds of writers, Miller's much larger two-volume work, published at the close of the Cold War, contained only twenty-eight. Three years earlier, Gordon Ray's *Masters of American Literature* had reduced the number to eighteen; the Macmillan anthology, pub-lished in the same year as Miller's, had pared the number to twelve; and in 1963, a Nor-ton anthology edited by Norman Foerster and Robert Falk had reduced it to only eight. "In choosing Emerson, Thoreau, Hawthorne, Poe, Melville, Whitman, Mark Twain, James, Emily Dickinson, Frost, Eliot, and Faulkner," the Macmillan editors write, "we can imagine little dispute." But if they had looked back at the literary anthologies pub-lished since Pattee's, they might have been less sure about the absence of debate. Howard Mumford Jones and Ernest Leisy, in the preface to *Major American Writers* (1935), state categorically that "there can be no question that Franklin, Cooper, Irving, Bryant, Emer-son, Hawthorne, Longfellow, Whittier, Lincoln, Poe, Thoreau, Lowell, Melville, Whit-man, and Mark Twain constitute the heart of any course in American literary history."

The contradiction that emerges when one places these statements side by side springs from a contradiction internal to the project of anthology-making as these editors conceive it. The difference between the two lists of "central" authors stems from the fact that the editors are active shapers of the canon, whose differing aims and assumptions determine what will seem central and what peripheral. This fact emerges clearly in the prefaces, where the editors anxiously justify their choices, defend them against other possible selec-tions, and apologize for significant omissions. But the editors' beliefs about the nature of literary value—i.e., that it is "inherent in the works themselves," timeless, and univer-sal—prevent them from recognizing their own role in determining which are the truly great works. In describing their own activity, therefore, they speak as if they themselves had played virtually no part in deciding which authors deserved to be included, but were simply codifying choices about which there could be "no question." This mode of self-characterization is most explicitly illustrated by Perry Miller, who pictures the authors in his anthology as forcing themselves upon him and his coeditors. We were free, he says, from the obligation to cleave to a "'party-line,'" but adds, "this is not to say that the American *writers* represented in the pages which follow left their editors alone. Quite the contrary. In fact, *Major Writers of America* may best be taken as a varied testimony to the force that the literature continues to exert over and against time. Such attraction at such a distance is what signalizes a major writer. But if it is the literature that governs a critic's choices, and not the critic himself, or a "line" imposed upon him, then it is hard to ex-plain the drastic alterations that took place in literary anthologies between 1919 and 1962. It is not just a question of disagreement over exactly which authors are to be con-sidered major; the whole character of the anthologies changes in the interval.

Indeed, if we take Pattee and Miller as representative, we can see that in addition to a sharp narrowing in the range and number of authors, there has been a virtual rewriting of literary history, as entire periods, genres, and modes of classification disappear. Between

1919 and 1962 more than a dozen authors have dropped away in the Colonial period alone, while in the Revolutionary period, only one out of seven makes it through; the Revolutionary songs and ballads are missing entirely. The Federalist period disappears altogether and so does most of the first half of the nineteenth century. Gone are the *fin-de-siècle* poets—John Trumbull, Timothy Dwight, Joel Barlow—and with them the lyricists of the early century—Richard Henry Dana, Edward Coate Pinckney, Richard Henry Wilde, and John Howard Payne. None of the songwriters survive—George Pope Morris, Samuel Woodworth, Thomas Dunn English, Phoebe Cary, Stephen Foster. The selections from D. G. Mitchell's *Reveries of a Bachelor* disappear, along with the orations of John C. Calhoun and Daniel Webster. The historians of the mid-nineteenth century, W. H. Prescott, John Lothrop Motley, and Francis Parkman vanish, as do the southern writers (Simms, Timrod, Paul Hamilton Hayne) and the antislavery writers—Whittier and Stowe. Gone are Abraham Lincoln and all the songs and ballads of the Civil War. Out of six western humorists, only Twain survives; of the "transition poets"—Bayard Taylor, Edmund Clarence Stedman, Thomas Bailey Aldrich, Sidney Lanier, Thomas Buchanan Read, George Henry Boker, Richard Henry Stoddard, and Celia Leighton Thaxter—not one. Of the late nineteenth-century nature writers, not one. Out of a dozen poets of the same period, only Crane and Dickinson. The local colorists—Bret Harte, General Lewis Wallace, Edward Eggleston, John Hay, Joaquin Miller, Helen Hunt Jackson, Henry Grady, Hamlin Garland, George Washington Cable, Joel Chandler Harris, Sarah Orne Jewett, Mary Wilkins Freeman, Mary Noialles Murfree, Charles Dudley Warner—cede their places to Henry James, Henry Adams, and Theodore Dreiser. The critics are wiped out in toto, along with Edward Everett Hale, Ambrose Bierce, Henry Cuyler Bunner, and Frank Stockton. The "feminine novelists" of the twentieth century whom Pattee added to his 1932 edition—Willa Cather and Edith Wharton—give way to Faulkner, Fitzgerald, and Hemingway, and, with the exception of Frost, all of the twentieth-century poets—Robinson, Lindsay, Masters, Sandburg, Lowell, Sterling, and Millay—disappear.

The emphases have also changed. In 1919 Emma Lazarus is represented by four poems and Emily Dickinson by six. Henry James and Constance Fenimore Woolson are allotted two stories apiece; Bret Harte is represented by five selections, Mark Twain by one. Pattee includes just as many Civil War songs as poems by Walt Whitman, and in his introduction mentions "Poe or Lowell or Whitman or Burroughs" in a single breath, implying that they are all of similar stature; but hardly anyone knows who Burroughs is anymore (he wrote eighteen volumes of essays on nature in the late nineteenth century), and today Lowell is not considered the equal of Whitman and Poe.

I have listed these excisions and revisions at length because they show in a detailed and striking manner that "literature" is not a stable entity, but a category whose outlines and contents are variable. The anthologies of the 1930s, midway between Pattee and Miller, show unmistakably that this variability is a function of the political and social circumstances within which anthologists work. The thirties' anthologies include items that had not appeared in such collections before and have seldom appeared there since—cowboy songs, Negro spirituals, railroad songs, southwestern yarns, and, in translation, the songs and prayers of Native Americans. They include letters, extracts from journals, passages from travel literature, and a large number of political speeches—Woodrow Wilson's "Address to Newly Naturalized Citizens," Lee's "Farewell to the Army of Northern Virginia." There are essays by Margaret Fuller and Sophia Ripley from *The Dial,* excerpts from Henry George's *Progress and Poverty* and *Social Problems,* William James' "What Pragmatism Means," and John Fiske's "Darwinism Verified." There are descriptions of America written by European writers, and a great deal of writing about, as well as by, Abraham

Lincoln. One anthology, prepared by teachers from New York City, even turns the last forty pages into a sort of "melting pot" selection from the literatures of Europe and the Orient—passages from the Egyptian Book of the Dead; the sayings of Confucius and Gautama Buddha; an excerpt from Lady Murasaki; Greek, Hebrew, and Latin poetry; and translations from the literatures of Germany, Scandinavia, France, Spain, Italy, and Russia.

In their introductions, the editors of these anthologies seem to be trying to reformulate their notions of what an anthology should represent, and of what literature itself should do. They say that "ethical as well as aesthetic ideals have been kept in mind in making this volume." They say they want to combine "selections which embody reflections of the political and social history of the age with those which embody their authors' best literary art." They speak of presenting a "variety of reactions" to "our great political experiment—democracy," by including writers "of recognized importance often overlooked by anthologists." In all of their remarks, the editors evince a need to show the "connection" between "our literature and American life and thought," as if somehow literature had been delinquent in its responsibility to society. In short, the social and political consciousness of the thirties changes anthologists' sense of their aims as literary critics.

That same sense changes again in the fifties and early sixties. *Major Writers of America, Masters of American Literature,* and Macmillan's *Twelve American Writers,* coming at the end of the McCarthy era, the Cold War, and the heyday of New Criticism, are a response to the conservative temper of the post-war years, just as the collections of the thirties are to the Depression. Miller is not concerned to demonstrate literature's relation to social change, "democracy," or "American life"; on the contrary, he insists that "we must vindicate the study of literature primarily because the matter is *literature* and only secondarily because it is American." He concerns himself not with the social relevance of literature, but with evaluation, or, as he puts it, making clear "which are the few peaks and which the many low-lying hills." Miller's agenda, as I will demonstrate in a moment, belongs to the Eisenhower years, just as the thirties anthologies did to the New Deal. The different conceptions of literature these two kinds of anthologies represent—one seeing literature as a "voice of the people," emphasizing its relation to historical events, the other preoccupied with questions of aesthetic excellence and the formal integrity of individual works—show up in the split that develops within the anthology-making tradition. From about 1950 forward, three different types of anthologies are discernible: the "major masters" type represented by Perry Miller, Pochman and Allen, Gordon Ray, and Gibson and Arms; the "rich variety" type represented by Leon Howard, and Edwin Cady; with texts like the new Norton and the 1980 Macmillan falling somewhere in between.

Yet even though anthologists characterize their projects differently, and although the contents of their volumes vary drastically, the one element that, ironically, remains unchanged throughout them all is the anthologists' claim that their *main* criterion of selection has been literary excellence. But, as has by now become abundantly clear, while the *term* "literary excellence" or "literary value" remains constant over time, its *meaning*—what literary excellence turns out to be in each case—does not. Contrary to what Miller believed, great literature does not exert its force over and against time, but changes with the changing currents of social and political life.

Still, someone might object that Miller's theory, whatever its abstract merits, justifies itself on practical grounds. Surely the authors represented in his anthology *are* the major writers of America, give or take a few names, while the works the anthology excludes are minor works at best. Most educated people today, if asked to say which was better, a poem by Stedman or a poem by Dickinson, would choose the latter without hesitation. And this fact would seem to bear out the rightness of Miller's intuitions about which writers ought to be considered great. But our conviction that Miller's choice was correct does not prove anything about the intrinsic superiority of the texts he chose; it proves only that we were introduced to American literature through the medium of anthologies similar to his. The general agreement about which writers are great and which are minor that exists at any particular moment in the culture creates the impression that these judgments are obvious and self-evident. But their obviousness is not a natural fact; it is constantly being produced and maintained by cultural activity: by literary anthologies, by course syllabi, book reviews, magazine articles, book club selections, radio and television programs, and even such apparently peripheral phenomena as the issuing of commemorative stamps in honor of Hawthorne and Dickinson, or literary bus tours of New England stopping at Salem and Amherst. The choice between Stedman and Dickinson, Stowe and Hawthorne, is never made in a vacuum, but from within a particular perspective that determines in advance which literary works will seem "good."

In saying that judgments of literary value are always perspectival, and not objective or disinterested, I do not wish to be understood as claiming that there is no such thing as value or that value judgments cannot or should not be made. We are always making choices, and hence value judgments, about which books to read, teach, write about, recommend, or have on our shelves. The point is not that these discriminations are baseless; the point is that the grounds on which we make them are not absolute and unchanging but contingent and variable. As Barbara Smith has recently argued, our tastes, emphases, preferences, and priorities, literary or otherwise, do not exist in isolation, but emerge from within a dynamic system of values which determines what, at a given moment, will be considered best. Thus, for example, when the anthology editors of the late fifties and early sixties decided to limit their selection of American writers to a handful, they did so within a framework of critical beliefs that were themselves embedded in a larger cultural context. The notion that fullness and depth of representation are preferable to variety was already implicit in the New Critical insistence on studying "wholes" rather than "parts"; and that insistence, in turn, was implicit in the premium that formalism placed on making judgments about the aesthetic as opposed to the historical significance of works of art. Moreover, the formalist doctrines that stood behind the exclusivity of these anthologies did not take shape in isolation either, but were themselves implicated in a web of political, legislative, demographic, and institutional circumstances, and of disciplinary rivalries, that affected the way critics articulated and carried out their aims.

The New Critics' emphasis on the formal properties of literary discourse was part of a struggle that literary academicians had been waging for some time to establish literary language as a special mode of knowledge, so that criticism could compete on an equal basis with other disciplines, and particularly with the natural sciences, for institutional support. That struggle, whose nature had been determined by the growing prestige of science in the twentieth century, was intensified in the fifties by the arms race and especially by the launching of Sputnik, which added impetus to the rivalry between the sciences and the humanities and urgency to the claims that critics made for the primacy of form in understanding "how poems mean." At the same time, the emphasis on formal properties accommodated another feature of the academic scene in the 1950s, namely, the tripling of the college population, brought about by the GI Bill, postwar affluence, and an increasing demand for people with advanced degrees. The theory of literature that posited a unique interrelation of form and content justified close reading as an analytic technique that lent itself successfully to teaching literature on a mass scale. These connections between the contents of literary anthologies and historical phenomena such as the Depression, the GI Bill, and the arms race, show that *literary* judgments of value do not depend on literary considerations alone, since the notion of what is literary is defined by and nested within changing historical conditions of the kind I have outlined here. Thus, the emphasis on "major" writers did not come about in response to a sudden perception of the greatness of a few literary geniuses; it emerged from a series of interconnected circumstances that moved the theory, teaching, and criticism of literature in a certain direction.

But in arguing that criteria of literary judgment depend upon an array of fluctuating historical conditions, I do not mean to imply that "historical conditions" are a root cause from which everything else can be derived or that literature and criticism are always finally interpretable in the light of "brute facts" that exist independently of our systems of valuation. I do not wish to exempt descriptions of "historical context" from the variability and contingency to which I have said literary values are subject. "Historical conditions" are not external to the systems of valuation that they modify, but are themselves articulated within them. Thus, for example, the economic conditions of the Depression that called attention to working class, immigrant, and minority experience, and altered the contents of literary anthologies accordingly, could have been seen and described as they were only from within a value system that already insisted on the importance of the common man and took seriously the sufferings of ordinary people. The democratic tradition of values enabled certain "events" or "conditions" to be noticed and to assume a shape and significance such that they assumed priority in people's thinking and provided a basis for deciding what kind of experience a selection of American writing ought to represent. American literature itself, as represented in literary anthologies, affects the way people understand their lives and hence becomes responsible for defining historical conditions. Thus, if literary value judgments respond to changing historical conditions, the reverse is also true.

You will recall that the entire argument thus far has been a response to the question "but is it any good?" which implies that the works I have discussed are not really literary and are therefore not worth discussing. My tactic has been to show that the assumptions behind this question—namely, that literary values are fixed, independent, and demonstrably present in certain masterworks—are mistaken, and I have used the evidence of the literary anthologies to challenge these notions one by one. But at this point someone might observe that despite changes in the contents of the anthologies, there are some authors and some works that do persist from one decade to the next and that therefore, although the perimeters of the canon may vary, its core remains unchanged, a testimony to the enduring merits of a few great masterpieces. To this objection I would reply that the evidence of the anthologies demonstrates not only that works of art are not selected according to any unalterable standard, but that their very essence is always changing in accordance with the systems of description and evaluation that are in force. Even when the "same" text keeps turning up in collection after collection, it is not really the same text at all.

Let us take as an example Hawthorne's short story "The Maypole of Merrymount," which appears in the 1932 edition of *Century Readings in American Literature* along with "Sights from a Steeple," "The White Old Maid," "David Swan," and "The Old Manse." The other selections Pattee has chosen signal immediately that, although its title may be the same, this is not the tale Hershel Parker has included in the 1979 Norton anthology. For the context in which "The Maypole of Merrymount" appears in the Norton anthology is entirely different. I will come to that context in a moment; but first, let us look at how the tale is framed in 1932.

Pattee's introduction places all the emphasis on Hawthorne's personality and habits and has very little to say about the tales themselves. His biographical sketch depicts Hawthorne as "shy and solitary," "writing, dreaming, wandering about the city at night," a writer whose Puritanism was a "pale night flower" that bloomed amidst the "old decay and ruin" of a town whose moldering docks conveyed a sense of "glory departed." The romanticism of this portrait stands in sharp contrast to Pattee's dry, taxonomic approach to Hawthorne's work. Pattee tells us he has chosen these pieces because they illustrate five of the eight "types" into which he has divided Hawthorne's shorter writings. Thus for Pattee's readers, Hawthorne's story emerges as an object to be identified and catalogued within a highly articulated system of classification. For not only is the tale one of four types within a subgroup (tales) within the classification "shorter writings," which is contrasted to another classification, "major romances," under the rubric "Hawthorne"; the author himself is identified as the member of a group, "The Concord Group" (made up of Hawthorne, Emerson, and Thoreau), which is one of six such groups—"The Mid-Century Historians" (Prescott, Motley, and Parkman), "The Cambridge Scholars" (Longfellow, Holmes, and Lowell), "Melville and Dana" in a category of their own, "The Southern Group" (Poe, Simms, and Hayne), and "The Anti-Slavery Movement" (Whittier, Stowe, Lincoln, and songs and ballads of the Civil War)—all of which constitute the category "The Mid-Nineteenth Century" that in its turn is one of the six historical periods into which Pattee divides all of American literature. This classificatory scheme, with its geographical and chronological bias, reproduces itself inevitably in the anthologist's only comment on "The Maypole of Merrymount," namely, that it is a "New England legend." Given his taxonomic approach to literary texts, there is little else that it could be.

This approach to Hawthorne reverses itself dramatically when one turns to the 1979 Norton anthology. Here it is the biography that is matter-of-fact; Hershel Parker's introduction gives us the "healthy" Hawthorne of Randall Stewart's revisionist biography, the Hawthorne who loved "tramping," drinking, smoking, and cardplaying, who socialized, flirted, and traveled "as far as Detroit." Parker doesn't get excited until he starts talking about the tales, and then the fascination with morbidity and introversion that had animated Pattee's discourse on the "pale night flower" reappears. The tales Parker reprints along with "The Maypole"—"My Kinsman, Major Molineux," "Young Goodman Brown," "Rappaccini's Daughter," "Wakefield," "The Minister's Black Veil,"—are all, according to him, concerned with the "futility," "difficulty," and "impossibility" of dealing with the problems of "sin," "guilt," and "isolation." These are the somber Freudian texts that mid-twentieth-century critics have created, texts that "muse obsessively over a small range of psychological themes," are full of "curiosity about the recesses of . . . men's . . . hearts," tales by "a master of psychological insight," whose "power of psychological burrowing" was nevertheless a source of "ambivalence" because of its invasive and prurient nature. Thus, when the reader comes to "The Maypole of Merrymount" in the context provided by the Norton anthology, the tale is no longer a "New England legend"; it is a probe into the depths of the human heart. Parker's reading of the tale as "a conflict between lighthearted and somber attitudes towards life" springs directly from an interpretive framework that sees literary texts as vehicles of "psychological insight," just as Pattee's definition sprang from an interpretive framework that classified texts according to historical, geographical, and generic categories.

The context within which "The Maypole of Merrymount" appears in each case frames the story so differently that the story itself changes. Neither its meaning nor its value remains constant from 1932 to 1979 because the strategies through which editors and their readers construct literary texts have changed in the intervening years. We may feel that the Norton editor is right, and that Hawthorne really was the "master of psychological insight" he is represented as here. But that is because our sense of Hawthorne's art, like Parker's, has been influenced by books such as Frederick Crews' *The Sins of the Fathers,* and by an entire tradition of describing and interpreting human behavior that arose after psychoanalysis took root in the United States.

It is worth dwelling a moment longer on this example because it illustrates something important about the influence criticism has on the canon and what it represents. Crews' reading of Hawthorne reinforced the psychological perspective on his work and helped to determine *which* of Hawthorne's tales would be read by hundreds of thousands of Norton readers, and also *the way* those tales would be interpreted. The critical strategy that guides Crews' reading in effect constructs a new Hawthorne, who becomes for a time *the* Hawthorne—the only one that many students will ever know. As Crews' book is to "Hawthorne," so other broad-gauge and highly influential critical works are to "American literature." Books like R. W. B. Lewis' *The American Adam* and Richard Chase's *The American Novel and its Tradition* have become responsible for the way we understand entire genres and whole periods of literary history, determining which authors are important, which texts are read, what vocabulary critics use to discuss them, and so on. These authors, texts, and issues are now regarded as permanent features of the literary landscape, and seem, like Perry Miller's "mountain peaks," to have been there always.

It is important to recognize that criticism creates American literature in its own image because American literature gives the American people a conception of themselves and of their history. As a spectacular example of this phenomenon, consider F. O. Matthiessen's *American Renaissance,* of which perhaps the most important sentences are these:

> The half-decade of 1850–55 saw the appearance of *Representative Men* (1850), *The Scarlet Letter* (1850), *The House of the Seven Gables* (1851), *Moby-Dick* (1851), *Pierre* (1852), *Walden* (1854), and *Leaves of Grass* (1855). You might search all the rest of American literature without being able to collect a group of books equal to these in imaginative vitality.

With this list Matthiessen determined the books that students would read and critics would write about for decades to come. More important, he influenced our assumptions about what kind of person can be a literary genius, what kinds of subjects great literature can discuss, our notions about who can be a hero and who cannot, notions of what constitutes heroic behavior, significant activity, central issues. Matthiessen, who believed that criticism should "be for the good and enlightenment of all the people, and not for the pampering of a class," believed that the books he had chosen were truly representative of the American people, for these works, more than any others, called "the whole soul of man into activity."

But from the perspective that has ruled this study, Matthiessen's list is exclusive and class-bound in the extreme. If you look at it carefully, you will see that in certain fundamental ways the list does not represent what most men and women were thinking about between 1850 and 1855, but embodies the views of a very small, socially, culturally, geographically, sexually, and radically restricted elite. None of the works that Matthiessen names is by an orthodox Christian, although that is what most Americans in the 1850s were, and although religious issues pervaded the cultural discourse of the period. None deals explicitly with the issues of abolition and temperance which preoccupied the country in this period, and gave rise to such popular works as *Uncle Tom's Cabin* and T. S. Arthur's *Ten Nights in a Barroom*. None of the works on the list achieved great popular success, although this six-year period saw the emergence of the first American best-sellers. The list includes no works by women, although women at that time dominated the literary marketplace. The list includes no works by males not of Anglo-Saxon origin, and indeed, no works by writers living south of New York, north of Boston, or west of Stockbridge, Massachusetts. From the point of view that has governed the foregoing chapters, these exclusions are a more important indicator of the representativeness of literary works than their power to engage "the whole soul of man."

What I want to stress is that the present study and Matthiessen's are competing attempts to constitute American literature. This book makes a case for the value of certain novels that Matthiessen's modernist critical principles had set at a discount. Instead of seeing such novels as mere entertainment, or as works of art interpretable apart from their context, which derive their value from "imaginative vitality" and address themselves to transhistorical entities such as the "soul of man," I see them as doing a certain kind of cultural work within a specific historical situation, and value them for that reason. I see their plots and characters as providing society with a means of thinking about itself, defining certain aspects of a social reality which the authors and their readers shared, dramatizing its conflicts, and recommending solutions. It is the notion of literary texts as doing work, expressing and shaping the social context that produced them, that I wish to substitute finally for the critical perspective that sees them as attempts to achieve a timeless, universal ideal of truth and formal coherence. The American Renaissance, as we now know it, provides people with an image of themselves and of their history, with conceptions of justice and of human nature, attitudes towards race, class, sex; and nationality. The literary canon, as codified by a cultural elite, has power to influence the way the country thinks across a broad range of issues. The struggle now being waged in the professoriate over which writers deserve canonical status is not just a struggle over the relative merits of literary geniuses; it is a struggle among contending factions for the right to be represented in the picture America draws of itself.

Henry Louis Gates, Jr.

Writing, "Race," and the Difference It Makes

The truth is that, with the fading of the Renaissance ideal through progressive stages of specialism, leading to intellectual emptiness, we are left with a potentially suicidal movement among "leaders of the profession," while, at the same time, the profession sprawls, without its old center, in helpless disarray.

One quickly cited example is the professional organization, the Modern Language Association. . . . A glance at its thick program for its last meeting shows a massive increase and fragmentation into more than 500 categories! I cite a few examples: . . . "The Trickster Figure in Chicano and Black Literature." . . . Naturally, the progressive trivialization of topics has made these meetings a laughingstock in the national press.

W. Jackson Bate

. . . language, for the individual consciousness, lies on the borderline between oneself and the other. The word in language is half someone else's. It becomes "one's own" only when the speaker populates it with his own intention, his own accent, when he appropriates the word, adapting it to his own semantic and expressive intention. Prior to this moment of appropriation, the word does not exist in a neutral and impersonal language (it is not, after all, out of a dictionary that the speaker gets his words!), but rather it exists in other people's mouths, in other people's contexts, serving other people's intentions: it is from there that one must take the word, and make it "one's own."

Mikhail Bakhtin

They cannot represent themselves; they must be represented.

Marx

"Writing 'Race,' and the Difference it Makes" by Henry Louis Gates, Jr. first appeared in *Critical Inquiry* 12:1, p. 1–20. Copyright 1985.

I

Of what import is "race" as a meaningful category in the study of literature and the shaping of critical theory? If we attempt to answer this question by examining the history of Western literature and its criticism, our initial response would ostensibly be "nothing," or at the very least, "nothing explicitly." Indeed, until the past decade or so, even the most subtle and sensitive literary critics would most probably have argued that, except for aberrant moments in the history of criticism, "race" has been brought to bear upon the study of literature in no apparent way. The Western literary tradition, after all, and the canonical texts that comprise this splendid tradition, has been defined since Eliot as a more-or-less closed set of works that somehow speak to, or respond to, the "human condition" and to each other in formal patterns of repetition and revision. And while judgment is subject to the moment and indeed does reflect temporal-specific presuppositions, certain works seem to transcend value judgments of the moment, speaking irresistibly to the "human condition." The question of the place of texts written by "the Other" (be that odd metaphor defined as African, Arabic, Chinese, Latin American, female, or Yiddish authors) in the proper study of "literature," "Western literature," or "comparative literature" has, until recently, remained an unasked question, suspended or silenced by a discourse in which the "canonical" and the "noncanonical" stand as the ultimate opposition. "Race," in much of the thinking about the proper study of literature in this century, has been an invisible quality, present implicitly at best.

This was not always the case, of course. By the middle of the nineteenth century, "national spirit" and "historical period" had become widely accepted metaphors within theories of the nature and function of literature which argued that the principal value in a "great" work of literary art resided in the extent to which these categories were *reflected* in that work of art. Montesquieu's *Esprit des lois* had made a culture's formal social institution the repository of its "guiding spirit," while Vico's *Principii d'una scienza nuova* had read literature against a complex pattern of historical cycles. The two Schlegels managed rather deftly to bring to bear upon the interpretation of literature "both national spirit and historical period," as Walter Jackson Bate has shown. But it was Taine who made the implicit explicit by postulating "race, moment, and *milieu*" as positivistic criteria through which any work could be read, and which, by definition, any work reflected. Taine's *History of English Literature* is the great foundation upon which subsequent nineteenth-century notions of "national literatures" would be constructed.

What Taine called "race" was the source of all structures of feeling. To "track the root of man," he wrote, "is to consider the race itself, . . . the structure of his character and mind, his general processes of thought and feeling, . . . the irregularity and revolutions of his conception, which arrest in him the birth of fair dispositions and harmonious forms, the disdain of appearances, the desire for truth, the attachment for bare and abstract ideas, which develop in him conscience, at the expense of all else." In "race," Taine concluded, was predetermined "a particularity inseparable from all the motions of his intellect and his heart. Here lie the grand causes, for they are the universal and permanent causes, . . . indestructible, and finally infallibly supreme." "Poetries," as Taine put it, and all other forms of social expression, "are in fact only the imprints stamped by their seal."

"Race," for Taine was "the first and richest source of these master faculties from which historical events take their rise"; it was a "community of blood and intellect which to this day binds its off-shoots together." Lest we misunderstand the *naturally* determining role of "race," Taine concluded that it "is no simple spring but a kind of lake, a deep reservoir wherein other springs have, for a multitude of centuries, discharged their several streams."

Taine's originality lay not in these ideas about the nature and role of race, but in their almost "scientific" application to the history of literature. These ideas about race were received from the Enlightenment, if not from the Renaissance. By midpoint in the nineteenth century, ideas of irresistible racial differences were commonly held: when Abraham Lincoln invited a small group of black leaders to the White House in 1862 to share with them his ideas about returning all blacks in America to Africa, his argument turned upon these "natural" differences. "You and we are different races," he said. "We have between us a broader difference than exists between any other two races." Since this sense of difference was never to be bridged, Lincoln concluded, the slaves and the ex-slaves should be returned to their own. The growth of canonical "national" literatures was coterminous with the shared assumption among intellectuals that "race" was a "thing," an ineffaceable quantity, which irresistibly determined the shape and contour of thought and feelings as surely as it did the shape and contour of human anatomy.

How did the great movement away from "race, moment, and *milieu*" and toward the language of the text in the 1920s and 1930s in the Practical Criticism movement at Cambridge and the New Criticism movement at Yale affect this category of "race" in the reading of literature? Race, along with all sorts of other unseemly or untoward notions about the composition of the literary work of art, was bracketed or suspended. Race, within these theories of literature to which we are all heir, was rendered *implicit* in the elevation of ideas of canonical *cultural* texts that comprise the Western tradition in Eliot's simultaneous order, with a simultaneous existence. History, *milieu,* and even moment were brought to bear upon the interpretation of literature through philology and etymology: the dictionary—in the Anglo-American tradition, the *Oxford English Dictionary*—was the castle in which Taine's criteria took refuge. Once the concept of value became encased in the belief in a canon of texts whose authors purportedly shared a "common culture" inherited from *both* the Greco-Roman and the Judeo-Christian traditions, no one need speak of matters of "race" since "the race" of these authors was "the same." One not heir to these traditions was, by definition, of another "race." This logic was impenetrable.

Despite their beliefs in the unassailable primacy of language in the estimation of a work of literature, however, both I. A. Richards and Allen Tate, in separate prefaces to books of poems by black authors, paused to wonder aloud about the black faces of the authors, and the import this had upon the reading of their texts. The often claimed "racism" of the Southern Agrarians, while an easily identifiable target, was only an explicit manifestation of presuppositions that formed a large segment of the foundation upon which formalism was built. The citizens of the republic of literature, in other words, were all white, and mostly male. Difference, if difference obtained at all, was a difference obliterated by the "simultaneity" of Eliot's "tradition." Eliot's fiction of tradition, for the writer of a culture of color, was the literary equivalent of the "grandfather clause." So, in response to Robert Penn Warren's statement in "Pondy Woods"—"Nigger, your breed ain't metaphysical"—Sterling A. Brown wrote, "Cracker, your breed ain't exegetical." The Signifyin(g) pun deconstructed the "racialism" inherent in these claims of tradition.

II

"Race" as a meaningful criterion within the biological sciences has long been recognized to be a fiction. When we speak of the "white race" or the "black race," the "Jewish race" or the "Aryan race," we speak in misnomers, biologically, and in metaphors, more generally.

Nevertheless, our conversations are replete with usages of *race* which have their sources in the dubious pseudo-science of the eighteenth and nineteenth centuries. One need only flip through the pages of the *New York Times* to find headlines such as "Brown University President Sees School Racial Problems," or "Sensing Racism, Thousands March in Paris." In a lead editorial of its March 29, 1985, number, "The Lost White Tribe," the *Times* notes that while "racism is not unique to South Africa," we must condemn that society because "Betraying the religious tenets underlying Western culture, it has made race the touchstone of political rights." Eliot's "dissociation of sensibility," caused in large part by the "fraternal" atrocities of the World War I, and then by the inexplicable and insane murder of European Jews two decades later, the *Times* editorial echoes. (For millions of people who originated outside Europe, however, this dissociation of sensibility had its origins in colonialism and human slavery.) *Race,* in these usages, pretends to be an objective term of classification, when in fact it is a trope.

The sense of difference defined in popular usages of the term *race* has been used both to describe and *inscribe* differences of language, belief system, artistic tradition, "gene pool," and all sorts of supposedly "natural" attributes such as rhythm, athletic ability, cerebration, usury, and fidelity. The relation between "racial character" and these sorts of "characteristics" has been inscribed through tropes of race, lending to even supposedly "innocent" descriptions of cultural tendencies and differences the sanction of God, biology, or the natural order. "Race consciousness," Zora Neale Hurston wrote, "is a deadly explosive on the tongues of men." I even heard a member of the House of Lords in 1973 describe the differences between Irish Protestants and Catholics in terms of their "distinct and clearly definable differences of race."

"You mean to say that you can tell them apart?" I asked incredulously.

"Of course," responded the lord. "Any Englishman can."

Race has become a trope of ultimate, irreducible difference between cultures, linguistic groups, or practitioners of specific belief systems, who more often than not have fundamentally opposed economic interests. Race is the ultimate trope of difference because it is so very arbitrary in its application. The sanction of biology contained in sexual difference, simply put, does not and can never obtain when one is speaking of "racial difference." Yet, we carelessly use language in such a way as to *will* this sense of *natural* difference into our formulations. To do so is to engage in a pernicious act of language, one which exacerbates the complex problem of cultural or "ethnic" difference, rather than assuages or redresses it. This is especially the case at a time when racism has become fashionable, once again. That, literally every day, scores of people are killed in the name of differences ascribed to "race" only makes even more imperative this gesture to "deconstruct," if you will, the ideas of difference inscribed in the trope of race, to take discourse itself as our common subject to be explicated to reveal the latent relations of power and knowledge inherent in popular and academic usages of "race." When twenty-five thousand people feel compelled to gather on the Rue de Rivoli in support of the antiracist "Ne touche pas à mon pote" movement, when thousands of people willingly accept arrest to protest apartheid, when Iran and Iraq feel justified in murdering the other's citizens because of their "race," when Beirut stands as a museum of shards and pieces reflecting degrees of horror impossible to comprehend, the gesture that we make here seems local and tiny.

There is a curious dialectic between formal language use and the inscription of metaphorical "racial" differences. At times, as Nancy Stepan expertly shows in *The Idea of Race in Science,* these metaphors have sought a universal and transcendent sanction in biological science. Western writers in French, Spanish, German, Portuguese, and English have sought to make literal these rhetorical figures of "race," to make them natural, absolute, essential. In doing so, they have *inscribed* these differences as fixed and finite categories which they merely report or draw upon for authority. But it takes little reflection to recognize that these pseudoscientific categories are themselves figures of thought. Who has seen a black or red person, a white, yellow, or brown? These terms are arbitrary constructs, not reports of reality. But language is not only the medium of this often pernicious tendency, it is its *sign.* Language use signifies the difference between cultures and their possession of power, spelling the difference between subordinate and superordinate, between bondsman and lord. Its call into use is simultaneous with the shaping of an economic order in which the cultures of color have been dominated in several important senses by Western Judeo-Christian, Greco-Hellenic cultures and their traditions. To use contemporary theories of criticism to explicate these modes of inscription is to demystify large and obscure ideological relations and indeed theory itself. It would be useful here to consider a signal example of the black tradition's confinement and delimitation by the commodity of writing. For literacy, as I hope to demonstrate, could be the most pervasive emblem of capitalist commodity functions.

III

Where better to test this thesis than in the example of the black tradition's first poet in English, the African slave girl Phillis Wheatley. Let us imagine a scene:

One bright morning in the spring of 1772, a young African girl walked demurely into the courthouse at Boston, to undergo an oral examination, the results of which would determine the direction of her life and work. Perhaps she was shocked upon entering the appointed room. For there, gathered in a semicircle, sat eighteen of Boston's most notable citizens. Among them was John Erving, a prominent Boston merchant; the Reverend Charles Chauncey, pastor of the Tenth Congregational Church and a son of Cotton Mather; and John Hancock, who would later gain fame for his signature on the Declaration of Independence. At the center of this group would have sat His Excellency, Thomas Hutchinson, governor of the colony, with Andrew Oliver, his lieutenant governor, close by his side.

Why had this august group been assembled? Why had it seen fit to summon this young African girl, scarcely eighteen years old, before it? This group of "the most respectable characters in *Boston,*" as it would later define itself, had assembled to question the African adolescent closely on the slender sheaf of poems that the young woman claimed to have written by herself. We can only speculate on the nature of the questions posed to the fledgling poet. Perhaps they asked her to explain for all to hear exactly who were the Greek and Latin gods and poets alluded to so frequently in her work. Or perhaps they asked her to conjugate a verb in Latin, or even to translate randomly selected passages from the Latin, which she and her master, John Wheatley, claimed that she "had made some progress in." Or perhaps they asked her to recite from memory key passages from the texts of Milton and Pope, the two poets by whom the African claimed to be most directly influenced. We do not know.

We do know, however, that the African poet's responses were more than sufficient to prompt the eighteen august gentlemen to compose, sign, and publish a two-paragraph "Attestation," an open letter "To the Publick" that prefaces Phillis Wheatley's book, and which reads in part:

> We whose Names are underwritten, do assure the World, that the poems specified in the
> following Page, were (as we veribly believe) written by Phillis, a young Negro Girl, who was

but a few Years since, brought an uncultivated Barbarian from *Africa,* and has ever since been, and now is, under the Disadvantage of serving as a Slave in a Family in this Town. She has been examined by some of the best judges, and is thought qualified to write them.

So important was this document in securing a publisher for Phillis's poems that it forms the signal element in the prefatory matter printed in the opening pages of her *Poems on Various Subjects, Religious and Moral,* published at London in 1773.

Without the published "Attestation," Wheatley's publisher claimed, few would believe that an African could possibly have written poetry all by herself. As the eighteen put the matter clearly in their letter, "Numbers would be ready to suspect they were not really the Writings of Phillis." Phillis's master, John Wheatley, and Phillis had attempted to publish a similar volume in 1770 at Boston, but Boston publishers had been incredulous. Three years later, "Attestation" in hand, Phillis and her mistress's son, Nathaniel Wheatley, sailed for England, where they completed arrangements for the publication of a volume of her poems, with the aid of the Countess of Huntington and the Earl of Dartmouth.

This curious anecdote, surely one of the oldest oral examinations on record, is only a tiny part of a larger, and even more curious, episode in the eighteenth century's Enlightenment. At least since 1600, Europeans had wondered aloud whether or not the African "species of men," as they most commonly put it, *could* ever create formal literature, could ever master the "arts and sciences." If they could, the argument ran, then the African variety of humanity and the European variety were fundamentally related. If not, then it seemed clear that the African was destined by nature to be a slave.

Determined to discover the answer to this crucial quandary, several Europeans and Americans undertook experiments in which young African slaves were tutored and trained along with white children. Phillis Wheatley was merely one result of such an experiment. Francis Williams, a Jamaican who took the B.A. at the University of Cambridge before 1730; Jacobus Capitein, who earned several degrees in Holland; Wilheim Amo, who took the doctorate degree in philosophy at Halle; and Ignatius Sancho, who became a friend of Sterne's and who published a volume of letters in 1782—these were just a few of the black subjects of such "experiments." The published writings of these black men and one woman, who wrote in Latin, Dutch, German, and English, were seized upon both by pro- and antislavery proponents as proof that their arguments were sound.

So widespread was the debate over "the nature of the African" between 1730 and 1830 that not until the Harlem Renaissance would the work of black writers be as extensively reviewed as it was in the eighteenth century. Phillis Wheatley's list of reviewers includes Voltaire, Thomas Jefferson, George Washington, Samuel Rush, and James Beatty, to name only a few. Francis William's work was analyzed by no less than David Hume and Immanuel Kant. Hegel, writing in the *Philosophy of History* in 1813, used the writings of these Africans as the sign of their innate inferiority. The list of commentators is extensive, amounting to a "Who's Who" of the French, English, and American Enlightenment.

Why was the *creative writing* of the African of such importance to the eighteenth century's debate over slavery? I can briefly outline one thesis: After Descartes, *reason* was privileged, or valorized, among all other human characteristics. Writing, especially, after the printing press became so widespread, was taken to be the *visible* sign of reason. Blacks were "reasonable," and hence "men," if—and only if—they demonstrated mastery of the "arts and sciences," the eighteenth century's formula for writing. So, while the Enlightenment is famous for establishing its existence upon the human ability to reason, it simultaneously used the absence and presence of "reason" to delimit and circumscribe the very humanity of the cultures and people of color which Europeans had been "discovering" since the Renaissance. The urge toward the systematization of all human knowledge, by which we characterize the Enlightenment, led directly to the relegation of black people to a lower rung on the Great Chain of Being, an eighteenth-century construct that arranged all of creation on a vertical scale from animals and plants and insects through humans to the angels and God himself.

By 1750, the chain had become individualized; the human scale slid from "the lowliest Hottentot" (black south Africans) to "glorious Milton and Newton." If blacks could write and publish imaginative literature, then they could, in effect, take a few Giant Steps up the Chain of Being, in a pernicious game of "Mother, May I?" As the Reverend James W. C. Pennington, an ex-slave who wrote a slave narrative and who was a prominent black abolitionist, summarized this curious idea in his prefatory note "To the Reader" that authorized Ann Plato's 1841 book of essays, biographies, and poems: "The history of the arts and sciences is the history of individuals, of individual nations." Only by publishing books such as Plato's, he argued, could blacks demonstrate "the fallacy of that stupid theory, *that nature has done nothing but fit us for slaves, and that art cannot unfit us for slavery!*"

IV

The relation between what, for lack of a better term, I shall call the "nonwhite" writer and the French, Portuguese, Spanish, and English languages and literatures manifests itself in at least two ways of interest to theorists of literature and literary history. I am thinking here of what in psychoanalytic criticism is sometimes called "the other," and more especially of this "other" as the subject and object in literature. What I mean by citing these two overworked terms is precisely this: how blacks are figures in literature, and also how blacks *figure*, as it were, literature of their own making.

These two poles of a received opposition have been formed, at least since the early seventeenth century, by an extraordinary *subdiscourse* of the European philosophies of aesthetic theory and language. The two subjects, often in marginal ways, have addressed directly the supposed relation among "race," defined variously as language use and "place in nature." Human beings wrote books. Beautiful books were reflections of sublime genius. Sublime genus was the province of the European.

Blacks, and other people of color, could not "write." "Writing," these writers argued, stood alone among the fine arts as the most salient repository of "genius," the visible sign of reason itself. In this subordinate role, however, "writing," although secondary to "reason," was nevertheless the *medium* of reason's expression. They *knew* reason by its writing, by its representations. This representation could assume the spoken or the written form. And while several superb scholars gave priority to the *spoken* as the privileged of the pair, in their writings about blacks, at least, Europeans privileged *writing* as the principal measure of Africans' "humanity," their "capacity for progress," their very place in "the great chain of being."

This system of signs is arbitrary. Key words, such as *capacity*, which became a metaphor for cranial size, reflect the predominance of "scientific" discourse in metaphysics. That "reason," moreover, could be seen to be "natural" was the key third term of a homology which, in practice, was put to pernicious uses. The transformation of writing from an activity of mind into a commodity not only reflects larger mercantile relations between Africa and Europe but is also the subject I wish to explore here. Let me retrace, in brief, the history of this idea, of the relationship of the absence of "writing" and the absence of "humanity" in European letters of 1600.

We must understand this correlation of use and *presence* in language if we are to begin to learn how to read, for example, the slave's narrative within what Geoffrey H. Hartman calls its "text-milieu." The slave narratives, taken together, represent the attempt of blacks to *write themselves into being*. What a curious idea: Through the mastery of formal Western languages, the presupposition went, a black person could posit a full and sufficient self, as an act of self-creation through the medium of language. Accused of having no collective history by Hegel, blacks effectively responded by publishing hundreds of individual histories which functioned as the part standing for the whole. As Ralph Ellison defined this relation, "We tell ourselves our individual stories so as to become aware of our *general* story."

Writing as the visible sign of Reason, at least since the Renaissance in Europe, had been consistently invoked in Western aesthetic theory in the discussion of the enslavement and status of the black. The origin of this received association of political salvation and artistic genius can be traced at least to the seventeenth century. What we arrive at by extracting a rather black and slender thread from among the philosophical discourses of the Enlightenment is a reading of another side of the philosophy of enlightenment, indeed its nether side. Writing in *The New Organon* in 1620, Sir Francis Bacon, confronted with the problem of classifying the people of color which a seafaring Renaissance Europe had "discovered," turned to the arts as the ultimate measure of a race's place in nature. "Again," he wrote, "let a man only consider what a difference there is between the life of men in the most civilized province of Europe, and in the wildest and most barbarous districts of New India; he will feel it be great enough to justify the saying that 'man is a god to man,' not only in regard to aid and benefit, but also by comparison of condition. And this difference comes not from soil, not from climate, not from race, but from the arts." Eleven years later, Peter Heyln, in his *Little Description of the Great World,* used Bacon's formulation to relegate the blacks to a subhuman status: Black Africans, he wrote, lacked completely "the use of Reason which is peculiar unto man; [they are] of little Wit; and destitute of all arts and sciences; prone to luxury, and for the greatest part Idolators." All subsequent commentaries on the matter were elaborations upon Heylyn's position.

By 1680, Heylyn's key words, *reason* and *wit,* had been reduced to "reading and writing," as Morgan Godwyn's summary of received opinion attests:

> [A] disingenuous and unmanly *Position* had been formed; and privately (and as it were *in the dark*) handed to and again, which is this, That the Negro's though in their figure they carry some resemblances of manhood, yet are indeed no men. . . . the consideration of the shape and figure of our Negro's Bodies, their Limbs and members; their Voice and Countenance, in all things according with other mens; together with their *Risibility* and *Discourse* (man's Peculiar Faculties) should be sufficient Conviction. How should they otherwise be capable of *Trades,* and other no less manly imployments; as also of *Reading and Writing,* or show so much Discretion in management of Business; . . . but wherein (we know) that many of our own People are *deficient,* were they not truly Men?

Such a direct correlation of political rights and literacy helps us to understand both the transformation of writing into a commodity and the sheer burden of received opinion that motivated the black slave to seek his or her text. As well, it defined the "frame" against which each black text would be read. The following 1740 South Carolina Statute was concerned to make it impossible for black literacy mastery even to occur:

And whereas the having of slaves taught to write, or suffering them to be employed in writing, may be attending with great inconveniences;

Be it enacted, that all and every person and persons whatsoever, who shall hereafter teach, or cause any slave or slaves to be taught to write, or shall use or employ any slave as a scribe in any manner of writing whatsoever, hereafter taught to write; every such person or persons shall, for every offense, forfeith the sum of one hundred pounds current money.

Learning to read and to write, then, was not only difficult, it was a violation of a law. That Frederick Douglass, Thomas Smallwood, William Wells Brown, Moses Grandy, James Pennington, and John Thompson, among numerous others, all rendered statements about the direct relation between freedom and discourse not only as central scenes of instruction but also as repeated fundamental structures of their very rhetorical strategies only emphasizes the dialectical relation of black texts to a "context," defined here as *"other,"* racist texts, against which the slave's narrative, by definition, was forced to react.

By 1705, a Dutch explorer, William Bosman, had encased Peter Heylyn's bias into a myth which the Africans he had "discovered" had purportedly related to him. It is curious insofar as it justifies human slavery. According to Bosman, the blacks "tell us that in the beginning God created Black as well as White men; thereby giving the Blacks the first Election, who chose Gold, and left the Knowledge of Letters to the White. God granted their request, but being incensed at their Avarice, resolved that the Whites should ever be their masters, and they obliged to wait on them as their slaves." Bosman's fabrication, of course, was a myth of origins designed to sanction through mythology a political order created by Europeans. It was David Hume, writing at midpoint in the eighteenth century, who gave to Bosman's myth the sanction of Enlightenment philosophical reasoning.

In a major essay, "Of National Characters" (1748), Hume discussed the "characteristics" of the world's major division of human beings. In a footnote added to his original text in 1753 (the margins of his discourse), Hume posited with all of the authority of philosophy the fundamental identity of complexion, character, and intellectual capacity. "I am apt to suspect the negroes," he wrote,

and in general all the other species of men (for there are four or five different kinds) to be naturally inferior to the whites. There never was a civilized nation of any other complexion that white, nor even any individual eminent either in action or speculation. No ingenious manufacturers amongst them, *not arts, no sciences.* . . . Such a uniform and constant difference could not happen, in so many countries and ages, if *nature* had not made our original distinction betwixt these breeds of men. Not to mention our colonies, there are Negroe slaves dispersed all over Europe, of which none ever discovered any symptoms of ingenuity; . . . In Jamaica, indeed they talk of one negroe as a man of parts and learning [Francis Williams, the Cambridge-educated poet who wrote verse in Latin]; but 'tis likely he is admired for very slender accomplishments, like a parrot who speaks a few words plainly.

Hume's opinion on the subject, as we might expect, became prescriptive.

Writing in 1764, in his *Observations on the Feelings of the Beautiful and the Sublime,* Immanuel Kant elaborated upon Hume's essay in a fourth section entitled "Of National Characteristics, as far as They Depend upon the Distinct Feeling of the Beautiful and the Sublime." Kant first claimed that "So fundamental is the difference between [the black and white] races of man, and it appears to be as great in regard to mental capacities as in color." Kant, moreover, was one of the earliest major European philosophers to conflate "color" with "intelligence," a determining relation he posited with dictatorial surety. The excerpt bears citation:

. . . Father Labat reports that a Negro carpenter, whom he reproached for haughty treatment toward his wives, answered: "You whites are indeed fools, for first you make great concessions to your wives, and afterward you complain when they drive you mad." And it might be that there were something in this which perhaps deserved to be considered; but in short, this fellow was *quite black* from head to foot, a clear proof that what he said was stupid. (emphasis added)

The correlation of "blackness" and "stupidity" Kant posited as if self-evident.

Writing in "Query XIV" of *Notes on the State of Virginia,* Thomas Jefferson maintained that "Never yet could I find that a black had uttered a thought above the level of plain narration, never see even an elementary trait of painting or sculpture." Of Wheatley, the first black person to publish a book of poetry in England, Jefferson the critic wrote, "Misery is often the parent of the most affecting touches in poetry. Among the blacks is misery enough, God knows, but not poetry. . . . The compositions published under her name are below the dignity of criticism."

In that same year (1785), Kant, basing his observations on the absence of published writing among blacks, noted as if simply obvious that "Americans [Indians] and blacks are lower in their mental capacities than all other races." Again, Hegel, echoing Hume and Kant, noted the absence of history among black people and derided them for failing to develop indigenous African scripts, or even to master the art of writing in modern languages.

Hegel's strictures on the African about the absence of "history" presume a crucial role of *memory*—a collective, cultural memory—in the estimation of civilization. Metaphors of the "childlike" nature of the slaves, of the masked, puppetlike "personality" of the black, all share this assumption about the absence of memory. Mary Langdon, in her 1855 novel *Ida May: A Story of Things Actual and Possible,* wrote that "but then they *are* mere children. . . . You seldom hear them say much about anything that's past, if they only get enough to eat and drink at the present moment." Without writing, there could exist no *repeatable* sign of the workings of reason, of mind. Without memory or mind, there could exist no history. Without history, there could exist no "humanity," as defined consistently from Vico to Hegel. As William Gilmore Simms argued at the middle of the nineteenth century:

[If one can establish] that the negro intellect is fully equal to that of the white race . . . you not only take away the best argument for keeping him in subjection, but you take away the possibility of doing so. *Prima facie,* however, the fact that he *is* a slave, is conclusive against the argument for his freedom, as it is against his equality of claim in respect of intellect. . . . Whenever the negro shall be fully fit for freedom, he will make himself free, and no power on earth can prevent him.

V

Ironically, Anglo-African writing arose as a response to allegations of its absence. Black people responded to these profoundly serious allegations about their "nature" as directly as they could: they wrote books, poetry, autobiographical narratives. Political and philosophical discourse were the predominant forms of writing. Among these, autobiographical "deliverance" narratives were the most common, and the most accomplished. Accused of lacking a formal and collective history, blacks published individual histories which, taken together, were intended to narrate, in segments, the larger yet fragmented history of blacks in Africa, now dispersed throughout a cold New World. The narrated, descriptive "eye" was put into service as a literary form to posit both the individual "I" of the black author and the collective "I" of the race. Text created author, and black authors, it was hoped, would create, or re-create, the image of the race in European discourse. The very *face* of the race, representations of the features of which are common in all sorts of writings about blacks at this time, was contingent upon the recording of the black *voice*. Voice presupposes a face but also seems to have been thought to determine the contours of the black face.

The recording of an "authentic" black voice, a voice of deliverance from the deafening discursive silence which an enlightened Europe cited as proof of the absence of the African's humanity, was the millennial instrument of transformation through which the African would become the European, the slave become the ex-slave, the brute animal become the human being. So central was this idea to the birth of the black literary tradition in the eighteenth century that five of the earliest slave narratives draw upon the figure of the voice in the text as crucial "scenes of instruction" in the development of the slave on the road to freedom. James Gronniosaw in 1770, John Marrant in 1785, Ottobah Cugoano in 1787, Olaudah Equiano in 1789, and John Jea in 1815—all drew upon the trope of the talking book. Gronniosaw's usage bears citing here especially because it repeats Kant's correlation of physical—and, as it were, metaphysical—characteristics:

> My master used to read prayers in public to the ship's crew every Sabbath day; and when I first saw him read, I was never so surprised in my life, as when I saw the book talk to my master, for I thought it did, as I observed him to look upon it, and move his lips. I wished it would do so with me. As soon as my master had done reading, I followed him to the place where he put the book, being mightily delighted with it, and when nobody saw me, I opened it, and put my ear down close upon it, in great hope that it would say something to me; but I was very sorry, and greatly disappointed, when I found that it would not speak. This thought immediately presented itself to me, that every body and every thing despised me because I was black.

Even for this black author, his own mask of black humanity was a negation, a sign of absence. Gronniosaw accepted his role as a nonspeaking would-be subject and the absence of his common humanity with the European.

That the figure of the talking book recurs in these five black eighteenth-century texts says much about the degree of presupposition and intertextuality in early black letters, more than we heretofore thought. Equally important, however, this figure itself underscores the received correlation between silence and blackness which we have been tracing, as well as the urgent need to make the text speak, the process by which the slave marked his distance from the master. The voice in the text was truly a millennial voice for the African person of letters in the eighteenth century, for it was that very voice of deliverance and of redemption which would signify a new order for the black.

These narrators, linked by revision of a trope into the very first black chain of signifiers, implicitly signify upon another "chain," the metaphorical Great Chain of Being. Blacks were most commonly represented on the chain either as the "lowest" of the human races, or as first cousin to the ape. Since writing, according to Hume, was the ultimate sign of difference between animal and human, these writers implicitly were Signifyin(g) upon the figure of the chain itself, simply by publishing autobiographies that were indictments of the received order of Western culture, of which slavery, to them, by definition stood as the most salient sign. The writings of Gronniosaw, Marrant, Equiano, Cugoano, and Jea served as a critique of the sign of the Chain of Being and the black person's figurative "place" on the chain. This chain of black signifiers, regardless of their intent or desire, made the first political gesture in the Anglo-African literary tradition "simply" by the act of writing, a collective act that gave birth to the black literary tradition and defined it as the "other's chain," the chain of black being as black people themselves would have it. Making the book speak, then, constituted a motivated, and political, engagement with and condemnation of Europe's fundamental figure of domination, the Great Chain of Being.

The trope of the talking book is not a trope of the presence of voice at all, but of its absence. To speak of a "silent voice" is to speak in an oxymoron. There is no such thing as a silent voice. Furthermore, as Juliet Mitchell has put the matter, there is something untenable about the attempt to represent what is not there, to represent that which is *missing* or absent. Given that this is what these five black authors sought to do, we are justified in wondering aloud if the sort of subjectivity that they sought could be realized through a process that was so very ironic from the outset. Indeed, how can the black subject posit a full and sufficient self in a language in which blackness is a sign of absence? Can writing, the very "difference" it makes and marks, mask the blackness of the black face that addresses the text of Western letters, in a voice that "speaks English" in an idiom that contains the irreducible element of cultural difference that shall always separate the white voice from the black? Black people, we know, have not been "liberated" from racism by their writings, and they accepted a false premise by assuming that racism would be destroyed once white racists became convinced that we were human, too. Writing stood as a complex "certificate of humanity," as Paulin J. Hountondji put it. Black writing, and especially the literature of the slave, served not to obliterate the difference of "race," as a would-be white man such as Gronniosaw so ardently desired; rather, the inscription of the black voice in Western literatures has preserved those very cultural differences to be imitated and revised in a separate Western literary tradition, a tradition of black difference.

Blacks, as we have seen, tried to write themselves out of slavery, a slavery even more profound than mere physical bondage. Accepting the challenge of the great white Western tradition, black writers wrote as if their lives depended upon it—and, in a curious sense, their lives did, the "life" of "the race" in Western discourse. But if blacks accepted this challenge, we also accepted its premises, premises in which perhaps lay concealed a trap. What trap might this be? Let us recall the curious case of M. Edmond Laforest.

In 1915, Edmond Laforest, a prominent member of the Haitian literary movement called La Ronde, made of his death a symbolic, if ironic, statement of the curious relation of the "non-Western" writer to the act of writing in a modern language. M. Laforest, with an inimitable, if fatal, flair for the grand gesture, stood upon a bridge, calmly tied a Larousse dictionary around his neck, then proceeded to leap to his death by drowning. While other black writers, before and after M. Laforest, have suffocated as artists beneath the weight of various modern languages, Laforest chose to make his death an emblem of this relation of indenture.

It is the challenge of the black tradition to critique this relation of indenture, an indenture that obtains for our writers and for our critics. We must master, as Derrida wrote, "how to speak the other's language without renouncing (our) own." When we attempt to appropriate, by inversion, *race* as a term for an essence, as did the Negritude movement, for example ("We feel, therefore we are," as Senghor argued of the African), we yield too much, such as the basis of a shared humanity. Such gestures, as Anthony Appiah has observed, are futile, and dangerous because of their further inscription of new and bizarre stereotypes. [How] do we meet Derrida's challenge in the discourse of criticism? The Western critical tradition has a canon, just as does the Western literary tradition. Whereas I once thought it our most important gesture to *master* the canon of criticism, to *imitate* and *apply* it, I now believe that we must turn to the black tradition itself to arrive at theories of criticism indigenous to our literatures. Alice Walker's revision of a parable of white interpretation written in 1836 by Rebecca Cox Jackson, a Shaker eldress and black visionary, makes this point most tellingly. Jackson, who like John Jea claimed to have been taught to read by the Lord, wrote in her autobiography that she dreamed that a "white man" came to her house to teach her how to *interpret* and "understand" the word of God, now that God had taught her to read:

> A white man took me by my right hand and led me on the north side of the room, where sat a square table. On it lay a book open. And he said to me, "Thou shall be instructed in this book, from Genesis to Revelations." And then he took me on the west side, where stood a table. And it looked like the first. And said, "Yea, thou shall be instructed from the beginning of creation to the end of time." And then he took me on the east side of the room also, where stood a table and book like the two first, and said, "I will instruct thee—yea, thou shall be instructed from the beginning of all things to the end of all things. Yea, thou shall be well instructed, I will instruct."
>
>   . . .
>
> And then I awoke, and I saw him as plain as I did in my dream. And after that he taught me daily. And when I would be reading and come to a hard word, I would see him standing by my side and he would teach me the word right. And often, when I would be in meditation and looking into things which was hard to understand, I would find him by me, teaching and giving me understanding. And oh, his labor and care which he had with me often caused me to weep bitterly, when I would see my great ignorance and the great trouble he had to make me understand eternal things. For I was so buried in the depth of the tradition of my forefathers, that it did seem as if I never could be dug up.

In response to Jackson's relation of interpretive indenture to a "white man," Alice Walker, writing in *The Color Purple,* records and exchange between Celie and Shug about turning away from "the old white man," which soon turns into a conversation about the elimination of "man" as a mediator between a woman and "everything":

> . . . You have to git man off your eyeball, before you can see anything a'tall.
>   Man corrupt everything, say Shug. He on your box of grits, in your head, and all over the radio. He try to make you think he everywhere. Soon as you think he everywhere, you think he God. But he ain't. Whenever you trying to pray, and man plot himself on the other end of it, tell him to git lost, say Shug.

Celie and Shug's omnipresent "man," of course, echoes the black tradition's epithet for the white power structure, "the man."

For non-Western, so-called noncanonical critics, getting the "man off your eyeball" means using the most sophisticated critical theories and methods generated by the Western tradition to reappropriate and to define our own "colonial" discourses. We must use these theories and methods insofar as these are relevant and applicable to the study of our own literatures. The danger in doing so, however, is best put, again by Anthony Appiah in his definition of what he calls the "Naipaul fallacy": "It is not necessary to show that African literature is fundamentally the same as European literature in order to show that it can be treated with the same tools. . . . Nor should we endorse a more sinister line . . . : the post-colonial legacy which requires us to show that African literature is worthy of study precisely (but only) because it is fundamentally the same as European literature." We *must* not, Appiah concludes, "ask the reader to understand Africa by embedding it in European culture."

We must, of course, analyze the ways in which writing relates to "race," how attitudes toward racial differences generate and structure literary texts by us *and* about us; we must determine how critical methods can effectively disclose the traces of racial difference in literature; but we must also understand how certain forms of difference and the *languages* we employ to define those supposed "differences" not only reinforce each other but tend to create and maintain each other. Similarly, and as importantly, we must analyze the language of contemporary criticism itself, recognizing that hermeneutical systems, especially, are not "universal," "color-blind," or "apolitical," or "neutral." Whereas some critics wonder aloud, as Appiah notes, about such matters as whether or not "a structuralist poetics is inapplicable in Africa because structuralism is European," the concern of the "Third World" critic should properly be to understand the ideological subtext which any critical theory reflects and embodies, and what relation this subtext bears to the production of meaning. No critical theory—be that Marxism, feminism, poststructuralism, Nkrumah's consciencism, or whatever—escapes the specificity of value and ideology, no matter how mediated these may be. To attempt to appropriate our own discourses using Western critical theory "uncritically" is to substitute one mode of neocolonialism for another. To begin to do this in my own tradition, theorists have turned to the black vernacular tradition—to paraphrase Rebecca Cox Jackson, to dig into the depths of the tradition of our foreparents—to isolate the signifying black difference through which to theorize about the so-called Discourse of the Other.

Eve Kosofsky Sedgwick

The Beast in the Closet: James and the Writing of Homosexual Panic

I. HISTORICIZING MALE HOMOSEXUAL PANIC

At the age of twenty-five, D.H. Lawrence was excited about the work of James M. Barrie. He felt it helped him understand himself and explain himself. "*Do* read Barrie's *Sentimental Tommy* and *Tommy and Grizel*," he wrote Jessie Chambers. "They'll help you understand how it is with me. I'm in exactly the same predicament."[1]

Fourteen years later, though, Lawrence placed Barrie among a group of writers whom he considered appropriate objects of authorial violence. "What's the good of being hopeless, so long as one has a hob-nailed boot to kick [them] with? *Down with the Poor in Spirit!* A war! But the Subtlest, most intimate warfare. Smashing the face of what one *knows* is rotten."[2]

Eve Kosofsky Sedgwick, "The Beast in the Closet: James and the Writing of Homosexual Panic," from *Sex, Science, and the 19th Century Novel*, pp. 148–186. Copyright 1986, The English Institute. Reprinted by permission of the Johns Hopkins University Press.

It was not only in the intimate warfares of one writer that the years 1910 to 1924 marked changes. But Lawrence's lurch toward a brutal, virilizing disavowal of his early identification with Barrie's sexually irresolute characters reflects two rather different trajectories: first, of course, changes in the historical and intellectual context within which British literature could be read; but second, a haltingly crystallized literalization, as *between* men, of what had been in Barrie's influential novels portrayed as exactly "the Subtlest, most intimate warfare" *within* a man. Barrie's novel sequence was also interested, as Lawrence was not, in the mutilating effects of this masculine civil war on women.

I argue that the Barrie to whom Lawrence reacted with such volatility and finally with such virulence was writing out of a post-Romantic tradition of fictional meditations on the subject specifically of male homosexual panic. The writers whose work I adduce here include—besides Barrie—Thackeray, George Du Maurier, and James: an odd mix of big and little names. The cheapnesses and compromises of this tradition will, however, turn out to be as important as its freshest angularities, since one of the functions of a tradition is to create a path-of-least-resistance (or at the last resort, a pathology-of-least-resistance) for the expression of previously inchoate material.

An additional problem: This tradition was an infusing rather than a generically distinct one in British letters, and it is thus difficult to discriminate it with confidence or to circumscribe it within the larger stream of nineteenth-century fictional writing. But the tradition is worth tracing partly on that very account, as well: the difficult questions of generic and thematic embodiment resonate so piercingly with another set of difficult questions, those precisely of sexual definition and embodiment. The supposed oppositions that characteristically structure this writing—the respectable "versus" the bohemian, the cynical "versus" the sentimental, the provincial "versus" the cosmopolitan, the anesthetized "versus" the sexual—seem to be, among other things, recastings and explorations of another pseudo-opposition that had come by the middle of the nineteenth century to be cripplingly knotted into the guts of British men and, through them, into the lives of women. The name of this pseudo-opposition, when it came to have a name, was homosexual "versus" heterosexual.

Recent sexual historiography by, for instance, Alan Bray in his *Homosexuality in Renaissance England* suggests that until about the time of the Restoration, homophobia in England, while intense, was for the most part highly theologized, was anathematic in tone and structure, and had little cognitive bite as a way for people to perceive and experience their own and their neighbors' actual activities.[3] Homosexuality "was not conceived as part of the created order at all," Bray writes, but as "part of its dissolution. And as such it was not a sexuality in its own right, but existed as a potential for confusion and disorder in one undivided sexuality."[4] If sodomy was the most characteristic expression of antinature or the anti-Christ itself, it was nevertheless, or perhaps for that very reason, not an explanation that sprang easily to mind for those sounds from the bed next to one's own— or even for the pleasures of one's own bed. Before the end of the eighteenth century, however, Bray shows, with the beginnings of a crystallized male homosexual role and male homosexual culture, a much sharper-eyed and acutely psychologized secular homophobia was current.

I have argued (in *Between Men: English Literature and Male Homosocial Desire*) that this development was important not only for the persecutory regulation of a nascent minority population of distinctly homosexual men but also for the regulation of the male homosocial bonds that structure *all* culture—at any rate, all public or heterosexual culture.[5] This argument follows Lévi-Strauss in defining culture itself, like marriage, in terms of a "total relationship of exchange . . . not established between a man and a woman, but between two groups of men, [in which] the woman figures only as one of the objects in the exchange, not as one of the partners";[6] or follows Heidi Hartmann in defining patriarchy itself as "*relations between men,* which have a material base, and which, though hierarchical, establish or create interdependence and solidarity among men that enable them to dominate women."[7] To this extent, it makes sense that a newly active concept—a secular, psychologized homophobia—that seemed to offer a new proscriptive or descriptive purchase on the whole continuum of male homosocial bonds, would be a pivotal and embattled concept indeed.

Bray describes the earliest legal persecutions of the post-Restoration gay male subculture, centered in gathering places called "molly houses," as being random and, in his word, "pogrom"-like in structure.[8] I would emphasize the specifically terroristic or exemplary workings of this structure: because a given homosexual man could not know whether or not to expect to be an object of legal violence, the legal enforcement had a disproportionately wide effect. At the same time, however, an opening was made for a subtler strategy in response, a kind of ideological pincers-movement that would extend manyfold the impact of this theatrical enforcement. As *Between Men* argues, under this strategy (or, perhaps better put, in this space of strategic potential).

> not only must homosexual men be unable to ascertain whether they are to be the objects of "random" homophobic violence, but no man must be able to ascertain that he is not (that his bonds are not) homosexual. In this way, a relatively small exertion of physical and legal compulsion potentially rules great reaches of behavior and filiation.
>
> So-called "homosexual panic" is the most private, psychologized form in which many . . . western men experience their vulnerability to the social pressure of homophobic blackmail.[9]

Thus, at least since the eighteenth century in England and America, the continuum of male homosocial bonds has been brutally structured by a secularized and psychologized homophobia, which has excluded certain shiftingly and more or less arbitrarily defined segments of the continuum from participating in the overarching male entitlement—in the complex web of male power over the production, reproduction, and exchange of goods, persons, and meanings. I argue that the historically shifting, and precisely the arbitrary and self-contradictory, nature of the way *homosexuality* (along with its predecessor terms) has been defined in relation to the rest of the male homosocial spectrum has been an exceedingly potent and embattled locus of power over the entire range of male bonds, and perhaps especially over those that define themselves, not *as* homosexual, but *as against* the homosexual. Because the paths of male entitlement, especially in the nineteenth century, required certain intense male bonds that were not readily distinguishable from the most reprobated bonds, an endemic and ineradicable state of what I am calling male homosexual panic became the normal condition of the male heterosexual entitlement.

Some consequences and corollaries of this approach to male relationships should perhaps be made more explicit. To begin with, as I suggested earlier, the approach is not founded on an essential differentiation between "basically homosexual" and "basically heterosexual" men, aside from the historically small group of consciously and self-acceptingly homosexual men, who are no longer susceptible to homosexual panic as I define it here. If such compulsory relationships as male friendship, mentorship, admiring identification, bureaucratic subordination, and heterosexual rivalry all involve forms of investment that force men into the arbitrarily mapped, self-contradictory, and anathema-riddled quicksands of the middle distance of male homosocial desire, then it appears that men enter into adult masculine entitlement only through acceding to the permanent threat that the small space they have cleared for themselves on this terrain may always, just as arbitrarily and with just as much justification, be punitively and retroactively foreclosed.

The result of men's accession to this double bind is, first, the acute *manipulability,* through the fear of one's own "homosexuality," of acculturated men; and second, a reservoir of potential for *violence* caused by the self-ignorance that this regime constitutively enforces. The historical emphasis on homophobic enforcement in the armed services in, for instance, England and the United States supports this analysis. In these institutions, where both men's manipulability and their potential for violence are at the highest possible premium, the *pre*scription of the most intimate male bonding and the *pro*scription of (the remarkably cognate) "homosexuality" are both stronger than in civilian society—are, in fact, close to absolute.

My specification of widespread, endemic male homosexual panic as a post-Romantic phenomenon rather than as coeval with the beginnings, under homophobic pressure, of a distinctive male homosexual culture a century or so earlier, has to do with (what I read as) the centrality of the paranoid Gothic[10] as the literary genre in which homophobia found its most apt and ramified embodiment. Homophobia found in the paranoid Gothic a genre of its own, not because the genre provided a platform for expounding an already-formed homophobic ideology—of course, it did no such thing—but through a more active, polylogic engagement of "private" with "public" discourses, as in the wildly dichotomous play around solipsism and intersubjectivity of a male paranoid plot like that of *Frankenstein.* The transmutability of the intrapsychic with the intersubjective in these plots where one man's mind could be read by that of the feared and desired other; the urgency and violence with which these plots reformed large, straggly, economically miscellaneous families such as the Frankensteins in the ideologically hypostatized image of the tight Oedipal family; and then the extra efflorescence of violence with which the remaining female term in these triangular families was elided, leaving, as in *Frankenstein,* a residue of two potent male figures locked in an epistemologically indissoluble clench of will and desire—through these means, the paranoid Gothic powerfully signified, at the very moment of crystallization of the modern, capitalism-marked Oedipal family, the inextricability from that formation of a strangling double bind in male homosocial constitution. Put another way, the usefulness of Freud's formulation, in the case of Dr. Schreber, that paranoia in men results from the repression of their homosexual desire,[11] has nothing to do with a classification of the paranoid Gothic in terms of "latent" or "overt" "homosexual" "types," but everything to do with the foregrounding, under the specific, foundational historic conditions of the early Gothic, of intense male homosocial desire as at once the most compulsory and the most prohibited of social bonds.

To inscribe that vulgar classification supposedly derived from Freud on what was arguably the founding moment of the world view and social constitution that he codified would hardly be enlightening. Still, the newly formulated and stressed "universal" imperative/prohibition attached to male homosocial desire, even given that its claim for universality already excluded (the female) half of the population, nevertheless required, of course, further embodiment and specification in new taxonomies of personality and character. These taxonomies would mediate between the supposedly classless, "personal" entities of the ideological fictions and the particular, class-specified, economically inscribed lives that they influenced; and at the same time, the plethoric and apparently comprehensive pluralism of the taxonomies occluded, through the illusion of choice, the overarching existence of the double bind that structured them all.

Recent gay male historiography, influenced by Foucault, has been especially good at unpacking and interpreting those parts of the nineteenth-century systems of classification that clustered most closely around what current taxonomies construe as "the homosexual." The "sodomite," the "invert," the "homosexual," the "heterosexual" himself, all are objects of historically and institutionally explicable construction.[12] In the discussion of male homosexual *panic*, however—the treacherous middle stretch of the modern homosocial continuum, and the terrain from whose wasting rigors *only* the homosexual-identified man is at all exempt—a different and less distinctly sexualized range of categories needs to be opened up. Again, however, it bears repeating that the object of doing that is not to arrive at a more accurate or up-to-date assignment of "diagnostic" categories, but to better understand the broad field of forces within which masculinity—and thus, *at least* for men, humanity itself—could (can) at a particular moment construct itself.

I want to suggest here that with Thackeray and other early and mid-Victorians, a character classification of "the bachelor" came into currency, a type that for some men both narrowed the venue, and at the same time startingly desexualized the question, of male sexual choice.[13] Later in the century, when a medical and social-science model of "the homosexual man" had institutionalized this classification for a few men, the broader issue of endemic male homosexual panic was again up for grabs in a way that was newly redetached from character taxonomy and was more apt to be described narratively, as a decisive moment of choice in the developmental labyrinth of the generic individual (male). As the unmarried gothic hero had once been, the bachelor became once again the representative man: James wrote in his 1881 *Notebook*, "I take [London] as an artist and as a bachelor; as one who has the passion of observation and whose business is the study of human life."[14] In the work of writers like Du Maurier, Barrie, and James, among others, male homosexual panic was acted out as a sometimes agonized sexual anesthesia that was damaging to both its male subjects and its female nonobjects. The paranoid Gothic itself, a generic structure that seemed to have been domesticated in the development of the bachelor taxonomy, returned in some of these works as a formally intrusive and incongruous, but strikingly persistent, literary element.[15]

II. MEET MR. BATCHELOR

"Batchelor, my elderly Tiresias, are you turned into a lovely young lady par hasard?"
"Get along, you absurd Trumperian professor!" say I.

                                                                    Thackeray[16]

In Victorian fiction, it is perhaps the figure of the urban bachelor, especially as popularized by Thackeray, who personifies the most deflationary tonal contrast to the eschatological harrowings and epistemological doublings of the paranoid Gothic. Where the Gothic hero had been solipsistic, the bachelor hero is selfish. Where the Gothic hero had raged, the bachelor hero bitches. Where the Gothic hero had been suicidally inclined, the bachelor hero is a hypochondriac. The Gothic hero ranges from euphoria to despondency—the bachelor hero, from the eupeptic to the dyspeptic.

Structurally, moreover, whereas the Gothic hero had personified the concerns and tones of an entire genre, the bachelor is a distinctly circumscribed and often a marginalized figure in the books he inhabits. Sometimes, like Archie Clavering, Major Pendennis, and Jos Sedley, he is simply a minor character; but even when he is putatively the main character, like Surtee's hero "Soapey" Sponge, he more often functions as a clotheshorse or comic place-marker in a discursive plot.[17] The bachelor hero can only be mock-heroic: not merely diminished and parodic himself, he symbolizes the diminution and undermining of certain heroic and totalizing possibilities of generic embodiment. The novel of which the absurd Jos Sedley is not the hero is a novel *without* a hero.

It makes sense, I think, to see the development of this odd character the bachelor, and his dissolutive relation to romantic genre, as, among other things, a move toward the re-cuperation as character taxonomy of the endemic double blind of male-homosexual panic that had been acted out in the paranoid Gothic as plot and structure. This recuperation is perhaps best described as, in several senses, a domestication. Most obviously, in the in-creasingly stressed nineteenth-century bourgeois dichotomy between domestic female space and extrafamilial, political and economic male space, the bachelor is at least partly feminized by his attention to and interest in domestic concerns. (At the same time, though, his intimacy with clubland and bohemia gives him a special passport to the world of men, as well.) Then, too, the disruptive and self-ignorant potential for violence in the Gothic hero is replaced in the bachelor hero by physical timidity and, often, by a high valuation on introspection and by (at least partial) self-knowledge. Finally, the bachelor is housebroken by the severing of his connections with a discourse of genital sexuality.

The first-person narrators of much of Thackeray's later fiction are good examples of the urban bachelor in his major key. Even though the Pendennis who narrates *The Newcomes* and *Philip* is supposedly married, his voice, personality, and tastes are strikingly similar to those of the archetypal Thackeray bachelor, the narrator of his novella *Lovel the Widower* (1859)—a man called, by no coincidence at all, Mr. Batchelor. (Of course, Thackeray's own ambiguous marital status—married, but to an inveterately sanitarium-bound, psy-chotically depressed woman—facilitated this slippage in the narrators whom Thackeray seemed to model on himself.) Mr. Batchelor is, as James says of Olive Chancellor, unmar-ried by every implication of his being. He is compulsively garrulous about marital prospects, his own (past and present) among others, but always in a tone that points, in one way or another, to the absurdity of the thought. For instance, his hyperbolic treat-ment of an early romantic disappointment is used both to mock and undermine the im-portance to him of that incident, and at the same time, by invidious comparison, to dis-credit in advance the seriousness of any later involvement:

> Some people have the small-pox twice; *I do not.* In my case, if a heart is broke, it's broke: if a flower is withered, it's withered. If I choose to put my grief in a ridiculous light, why not? why do you suppose I am going to make a tragedy of such an old, used-up, battered, stale, vulgar, trivial every-day subject as a jilt who plays with a man's passion, and laughs at him, and leaves him? Tragedy indeed! Oh, yes! poison—black-edged note-paper—Waterloo Bridge—one more unfortunate, and so forth! No: if she goes, let her go! —*si celeres quatit pen-nas,* I puff the what-d'ye-call-it away! (Ch. 2)

The plot of *Lovel*—slight enough—is an odd local station on the subway from *Liber Amoris* to Proust, Mr. Batchelor, when he lived in lodgings, had had a slightly tender friendship with his landlady's daughter Bessy, who at that time helped support her family by dancing in a music hall. A few years later, he gets her installed as governess in the home of his friend Lovel, the widower. Several men in the vicinity are rivals for Bessy's affections: the local doc-tor, the shrewd autodidact butler, and, halfheartedly, Batchelor himself. When a visiting bounder attacks Bessy's reputation and her person, Batchelor, who is eavesdropping on the scene, fatally hesitates in coming to her defense, suddenly full of doubts about her sexual pu-rity ("Fiends and anguish! he had known her before" [Ch. 5]) and his own eagerness for mar-riage. Finally it is the audodidact butler who rescues her, and Lovel himself who marries her.

If the treatment of the romantic possibilities that are supposedly at the heart of *Lovel* has a tendency to dematerialize them almost before they present themselves, the treatment of certain other physical pleasures is given an immediacy that seems correspondingly heightened. In fact, the substantiality of physical pleasure is explicitly linked to the state of bachelorhood.

> To lie on that comfortable, cool bachelor's bed. . . . Once at Shrublands I heard steps pacing overhead at night, and the feeble but continued wail of an infant. I wakened from my sleep, was sulky, but turned and slept again. Biddlecombe the barrister I knew was the occupant of the upper chamber. He came down the next morning looking wretchedly yellow about the cheeks, and livid round the eyes. His teething infant had kept him on the march all night. . . . He munched a shred of toast, and was off by the omnibus to chambers. I chipped a second egg; I may have tried one or two other nice little things on the table (Strasbourg pâté I know I never can resist, and am convinced it is perfectly wholesome). I could see my own sweet face in the mirror opposite, and my gills were as rosy as any broiled salmon. (Ch. 3)

Unlike its sacramental, community-building function in Dickens, food in Thackeray— even good food—is most apt to signify the bitterness of dependency or inequality. The exchange value of food and drink, its expensiveness or cheapness relative to the status and expectations of those who partake, the ostentation or stinginess with which it is doled out, or the meanness with which it is cadged, mark out for it a shifty and invidious path through each of Thackeray's books, including this one. The rounded Pickwickian self-complacency of the rosy-gilled bachelor at breakfast is, then, all the more striking by contrast. In Thackeray's bitchy art where, as in James's, the volatility of the perspective regularly corrodes both the object and the subject of perception, there are moments when the bachelor hero, exactly through his celibacy and selfishness, can seem the only human particle atomized enough to plump through unscathed.

Sometimes unscathed; never unscathing. Of course one of the main pleasures of reading this part of Thackeray's oeuvre is precisely its feline gratuitousness of aggression. At odd moments we are apt to find kitty's unsheathed claws a millimeter from our own eyes. "Nothing, dear friend, escapes your penetration: if a joke is made in your company, you are down upon it instanter, and your smile rewards the wag who amuses you: so you knew at once. . . . " (Ch. 1). When one bachelor consults another bachelor about a third bachelor, nothing is left but ears and whiskers.

> During my visit to London, I had chanced to meet my friend Captain Fitzb——dle, who belongs to a dozen clubs, and knows something of every man in London. "Know anything of Clarence Baker?" "Of course I do," says Fitz; "and if you want any *renseignement* my dear fellow, I have the honor to inform you that a blacker little sheep does not trot the London *pavé* . . . know anything of Clarence Baker! My dear fellow, enough to make your hair turn white, unless (as I sometimes fondly imagine) nature has already performed that process, when of course I can't pretend to act upon mere hair-dye." (The whiskers of the individual who addressed me, innocent, stared me in the face as he spoke, and were dyed of the most unblushing purple.) . . . ". . . . From the garrison towns where he has been quartered, he has carried away not only the hearts of the milliners, but their gloves, haberdashery, and perfumery." (Ch. 4)

If, as I am suggesting, Thackeray's bachelors created or reinscribed as a personality type one possible path of response to the strangulation of homosexual panic, their basic strategy is easy enough to trace: a preference of atomized male individualism to the nuclear family (and a corresponding demonization of women, especially of mothers); a garrulous and visible refusal of anything that could be interpreted as genital sexuality, toward objects male or female; a corresponding emphasis on the pleasures of the other senses; and a well-defended social facility that freights with a good deal of magnetism its proneness to parody and to unpredictable sadism.

I must say that this does not strike me as a portrait of an exclusively Victorian human type. To refuse sexual choice, in a society when sexual choice for men is both compulsory and always self-contradictory, seems, at least for educated men, still often to involve invoking the precedent of this nineteenth-century persona—not Mr. Batchelor himself perhaps, but generically, the self-centered and at the same time self-marginalizing bachelor he represents. Nevertheless, this persona *is* highly specified as a figure of the nineteenth-century metropolis. He has close ties with the *flâneurs* of Poe, Baudelaire, Wilde, Benjamin. What is most importantly specified in his pivotal class position between the respectable bourgeoisie and bohemia—a bohemia that, again, Thackeray in the Pendennis novels half invented for English literature and half merely housetrained.

Literally, it was Thackeray who introduced both the word and the concept of bohemia to England from Paris.[18] As a sort of reserve labor force and a semiporous, limited space for vocational sorting and social rising and falling, bohemia could seemingly be entered from any social level; but, at least in these literary versions, it served best the cultural needs, the fantasy needs, and the needs for positive and negative self-definition of an anxious and conflicted bourgeoisie. Except to homosexual men, the idea of "bohemia" seems before the 1880s not to have had a distinctively gay coloration. In these bachelor novels the simple absence of an enforcing family structure was allowed to perform its enchantment in a more generalized way; and the most passionate male comradeship subsisted in an apparently loose relation to the erotic uses of a common pool of women. It might be more accurate, however, to see the flux of bohemia as the *temporal* space where the young, male bourgeois literary subject was required to navigate his way through his "homosexual panic"—seen here as a *developmental* stage—toward the more repressive, self-ignorant, and apparently consolidated status of the mature bourgeois *paterfamilias*.

Among Thackeray's progeny in the exploration of bourgeois bachelors in bohemia, the most self-conscious and important are Du Maurier, Barrie, and—in a book like *The Ambassadors*—James. The filiations of this tradition are multiple and heterogeneous. For instance, Du Maurier offered James the plot of *Trilby* years before he wrote the novel himself.[19] Or again, Little Bilham in *The Ambassadors* seems closely related to Little Billee, the hero of *Trilby,* a small girlish-looking Left Bank art student. Little Billee shares a studio with two older, bigger, more virile English artists, whom he loves deeply—a bond that seems to give erotic point to Du Maurier's use of the Thackeray naval ballad from which Du Maurier, in turn, had taken Little Billee's name.

> There was gorging Jack and guzzling Jimmy,
> And the youngest he was little Billee.
> Now when they got as far as the Equator
> They's nothing left but one split pea.
>
> Says gorging Jack to guzzling Jimmy,
> "I am extremely hungaree."
> To gorging Jack says guzzling Jimmy,
> "We've nothing left, us must eat we."
>
> Says gorging Jack to guzzling Jimmy,
> "With one another we shouldn't agree!
> There's little Bill, he's young and tender,
> We're old and tough, so let's eat he.

"Oh! Billy, we're going to kill and eat you,
So undo the button of your chemie. . . ."[20]

As one moves past Thackeray toward the turn of the century, toward the ever greater visibility across class lines of a medicalized discourse of—and newly punitive assaults on—male homosexuality, however, the comfortably frigid campiness of Thackeray's bachelors gives way to something that sounds more inescapably like panic. Mr. Batchelor had played at falling in love with women, but felt no urgency about proving that he actually could. For the bachelor heroes of *Trilby* and *Tommy and Grizel,* though, even that renunciatory high ground of male sexlessness has been strewn with psychic landmines.

In fact, the most consistent keynote of this late literature is exactly the explicitly thematized sexual anesthesia of its heroes. In each of these fictions, moreover, the hero's agonistic and denied sexual anesthesia is treated as being *at the same time* an aspect of a particular, idiosyncratic personality type *and also* an expression of a great Universal. Little Billee, for instance, the hero of *Trilby,* attributes his sudden inability to desire a woman to "a pimple" inside his "bump of" "fondness"—"for that's what's the matter with me—a pimple—just a little clot of blood at the root of a nerve, and no bigger than a pin's point!"[21] In the same long monologue, however, he again attributes his lack of desire, not to the pimple, but on a far different scale to his status as Post-Darwinian Man, unable any longer to believe in God. "Sentimental" Tommy, similarly, the hero of Barrie's eponymous novel and also of *Tommy and Grizel,* is treated throughout each of these astonishingly acute and self-hating novels both as a man with a crippling moral and psychological defect and as the very type of the great creative artist.

III. READING JAMES STRAIGHT

James's "The Beast in the Jungle" (1902) is one of the bachelor fictions of this period that seems to make a strong implicit claim of "universal" applicability through heterosexual symmetries, but that is most movingly subject to a change of Gestalt and of visible saliencies as soon as an assumed heterosexual male norm is at all interrogated. Like *Tommy and Grizel,* the story is of a man and a woman who have a decade-long intimacy. In both stories, the woman desires the man but the man fails to desire the woman. In fact—in each story—the man simply fails to desire at all. Sentimental Tommy desperately desires to feel desire; confusingly counterfeits a desire for Grizel; and, with all the best intentions, finally drives her mad. John Marcher, in James's story, does not even know that desire is absent from his life, nor that May Bartram desires him, until after she has died from his obtuseness.

To judge from the biographies of Barrie and James, each author seems to have made erotic choices that were complicated enough, shifting enough in the gender of their objects, and, at least for long periods, kept distant enough from *éclaircissement* or physical expression, to make each an emboldening figure for a literary discussion of male homosexual panic.[22] Barrie had an almost unconsummated marriage, an unconsummated passion for a married woman (George Du Maurier's daughter!), and a lifelong uncategorizable passion for her family of sons. James had—well, exactly that which we now all know that we know not. Oddly, however, it is simpler to read the psychological plot of *Tommy and Grizel*—the horribly thorough and conscientious ravages on a woman of a man's compulsion to pretend he desires her—into the cryptic and tragic story of James's involvement with Constance Fenimore Woolson, than to read it directly into any incident of Barrie's life. It is hard to read Leon Edel's account of James's sustained (or repeated) and intense, but peculiarly furtive,[23] intimacies with this deaf, intelligent American woman author who clearly loved him, without coming to a grinding sense that James felt he had with her above all something, sexually, to prove. And it is hard to read about what seems to have been her suicide without wondering whether the expense of James's heterosexual self-probation—an expense, one envisions if one has Barrie in mind, of sudden "generous" "yielding" impulses in him and equally sudden revulsions—was not charged most intimately to this secreted-away companion of so many of his travels and residencies. If this is true, the working-out of his denied homosexual panic must have been only the more grueling for the woman in proportion to James's outrageous gift and his moral magnetism.

If something like the doubly destructive interaction I am sketching here did in fact occur between James and Constance Fenimore Woolson, then its structure has been resolutely reproduced by virtually all the critical discussion of James's writing. James's mistake here, biographically, seems to have been in moving blindly from a sense of the good, the desirability, of love and sexuality, to the automatic imposition on himself of a specifically *hetero*sexual compulsion. (I say "imposition on himself," but of course he did not invent the heterosexual specificity of this compulsion—he merely failed, at this point in his life, to resist it actively.) The easy assumption (by James, the society, and the critics) that sexuality and heterosexuality are always exactly translatable into one another is, obviously, homophobic. Importantly, too, it is deeply heterophobic: it denies the very possibility of *difference* in desires, in objects. One is no longer surprised, of course, at the repressive blankness on these issues of most literary criticism; but for James, in whose life the pattern of homosexual desire was brave enough and resilient enough to be at last biographically inobliterable, one might have hoped that in criticism of his work the possible differences of different erotic paths would not be so ravenously subsumed under a compulsorily—and hence, never a truly "hetero"—heterosexual model. With strikingly few exceptions, however, the criticism has actively repelled any inquiry into the asymmetries of gendered desire.

It is possible that critics have been motivated in this active incuriosity by a desire to protect James from homophobic misreadings in a perennially repressive sexual climate. It is possible that they fear that, because of the asymmetrically marked structure of heterosexual discourse, *any* discussion of homosexual desires or literary content will marginalize him (or them?) as, simply, *homosexual*. It is possible that they desire to protect him from what they imagine as anachronistically "gay" readings, based on a late twentieth-century vision of men's desire for men that is more stabilized and culturally compact than James's own. It is possible that they read James himself as, in his work, positively refusing or evaporating this element of his eros, translating lived homosexual desires, where he had them, into written heterosexual ones so thoroughly and so successfully that the difference *makes* no difference, the transmutation leaves no residue. Or it is possible that, believing—as I do—that James often, though not always, attempted such a disguise or transmutation, but reliably left a residue both of material that he did not attempt to transmute and of material that could be transmuted only rather violently and messily, some critics are reluctant to undertake the "attack" on James's candor or artistic unity that could be the next step of that argument. Any of these critical motives would be understandable, but their net effect is the usual repressive one of elision and subsumption of supposedly embarrassing material. In dealing with the multiple valences of sexuality, critics' choices should not be limited to crudities of disruption or silences of orthodox enforcement.

Even Leon Edel, who traced out *both* James's history with Constance Fenimore Woolson *and* some of the narrative of his erotic desires for men, connects "The Beast in the Jungle" to the history of Woolson,[24] but connects neither of these to the specificity of James's—or of any—sexuality. The result of this hammeringly tendentious blur in virtually all the James criticism is, for the interpretation of "The Beast in the Jungle," seemingly in the interests of showing it as universally applicable (e.g., about "the artist"), to assume without any space for doubt that the moral point of the story is not only that May Bartram desired John Marcher but that John Marcher *should have desired* May Bartram.

Tommy and Grizel is clear-sighted on what is essentially the same point. "*Should have desired,*" that novel graphically shows, not only is nonsensical as a moral judgment but is the very mechanism that enforces and perpetuates the mutilating charade of heterosexual exploitation. (James's compulsive use of Woolson, for instance.) Grizel's tragedy is not that the man she desires fails to desire her—which would be sad, but, the book makes clear, endurable—but that he pretends to desire her, and intermittently even convinces himself that he desires her, when he does not.

Impressively, too, the clarity with which *Tommy and Grizel* conveys this process and its ravages seem *not* to be dependent on a given, naive, or monolithic idea of what it would mean for a man to "really" desire someone. On that issue the novel seems to remain agnostic—leaving open the possibility that there is some rather different quantity that is "real" male desire, or alternatively that it is only more and less intermittent infestations of the same murderous syndrome that fuel any male eros at all. That the worst violence of heterosexuality comes with the male *compulsion to desire* women and its attendant deceptions of self and other, however, Barrie says quite decisively.

Tommy and Grizel is an extraordinary, and an unjustly forgotten, novel. What has dated it and keeps it from being a great novel, in spite of the acuteness with which it treats male desire, is the—one can hardly help saying Victorian—mawkish opportunism with which it figures the desire of women. Permissibly, the novel's real imaginative and psychological energies focus entirely on the hero. Impermissibly—and here the structure of the novel itself exactly reproduces the depredations of its hero—there is a moralized pretense at an equal focus on a rounded, autonomous, imaginatively and psychologically invested female protagonist, who however—far from being novelistically "desired" in herself—is really, transparently, created in the precise negative image of the hero, created to be the single creature in the world who is most perfectly fashioned to be caused the most exquisite pain and intimate destruction by him and him only. The fit is excruciatingly seamless. Grizel is the daughter of a mad prostitute, whose legacies to her—aside from vitality, intelligence, imagination—have been a strong sensuality and a terror (which the novel highly valorizes) of having that sensuality stirred. It was acute of Barrie to see that this is the exact woman—were such a woman possible—who, appearing strong and autonomous, would be most unresistingly annihilable precisely by Tommy's two-phase rhythm of sexual come-on followed by repressive frigidity, and his emotional geology of pliant sweetness fundamented by unyielding compulsion. But the prurient exactitude of the female fit, as of a creature bred for sexual sacrifice without resistance or leftovers, drains the authority of the novel to make an uncomplicit judgment on Tommy's representative value.

Read in this context, "The Beast in the Jungle" looks—from the point of view of female desire—potentially revolutionary. Whoever May Bartram is and whatever she wants (I discuss this more later), clearly at least the story has the Jamesian negative virtue of not pretending to present her rounded and whole. She is an imposing character, but—*and*—a bracketed one. James's bravura in manipulating point of view lets him dissociate himself critically from John Marcher's selfishness—from the sense that there is *no possibility* of a subjectivity other than Marcher's own—but lets him leave himself in place of that selfishness finally an *askesis,* a particular humility of point of view as being *limited* to Marcher's. Of May Bartram's history, of her emotional determinants, of her erotic structures, the reader learns very little; we are permitted, if we pay attention at all, to *know* that we have learned very little. Just as, in Proust, it is always open to any minor or grotesque character to turn out at any time to have a major artistic talent with which, however, the novel does not happen to busy itself, so "The Beast in the Jungle" seems to give the reader permission to imagine some female needs and desires and gratifications that are not structured exactly in the image of Marcher's or of the story's own laws.

It is only the last scene of the story—Marcher's last visit to May Bartram's grave—that conceals or denies the humility, the incompleteness of the story's presentation of her subjectivity. This is the scene in which Marcher's sudden realization that *she* has felt and expressed desire for *him* is, as it seems, answered in an intensely symmetrical, "conclusive" rhetorical clinch by the narrative/authorial prescription: "The escape would have been to love her; then, *then* he would have lived."[25] The paragraph that follows, the last in the story, has the same climactic, authoritative (even authoritarian) rhythm of supplying Answers in the form of symmetrical supplementarities. For this single, this conclusive, this formally privileged moment in the story—this resolution over the dead body of May Bartram—James and Marcher are presented as coming together, Marcher's revelation underwritten by James's rhetorical authority, and James's epistemological askesis gorged, for once, beyond recognition, by Marcher's compulsive, ego-projective certainties. In the absence of May Bartram, the two men, author/narrator and hero, are reunited at last in the confident, shared, masculine knowledge of what she Really Wanted and what she Really Needed. And what she Really Wanted and Really Needed show, of course, an uncanny closeness to what Marcher Really (should have) Wanted and Needed, himself.

Imagine "The Beast in the Jungle" without this enforcing symmetry. Imagine (remember) the story with May Bartram alive.[26] Imagine a possible alterity. And the name of alterity is not *always* "woman." What if Marcher himself had other desires?

IV. THE LAW OF THE JUNGLE

Names . . . *Assingham—Padwick—Lutch—Marfle—Bross—Crapp—Didcock—Wichells—Putchin—Brind—Coxeter—Coxster* . . . *Dickwinter* . . . *Jakes* . . . *Marcher—*
                                                                    James, Notebook, 1901

There has so far seemed no reason, or little reason, why what I have been calling "male homosexual panic" could not just as descriptively have been called "male heterosexual panic"—or, simply, "male sexual panic." Although I began with a structural and historicizing narrative that emphasized the pre- and proscriptively defining importance of men's bonds with men, potentially including genital bonds, the books I have discussed have not, for the most part, seemed to center emotionally or thematically on such bonds. In fact, it is, explicitly, a male panic in the face of *hetero*sexuality that many of these books most describe. It is all very well to insist, as I have done, that homosexual panic is necessarily a problem only, but endemically, of nonhomosexual-identified men; nevertheless the lack in these books of an embodied male-homosexual thematics, however inevitable, has had a dissolutive effect on the structure and texture of such an argument. Part, although only part, of the reason for that lack was historical: it was only close to the end of the nineteenth century that a cross-class homosexual role and a consistent, ideologically full thematic discourse of male homosexuality became entirely visible, in developments that were publicly dramatized in—though far from confined to—the Wilde trials.

In "The Beast in the Jungle," written at the threshold of the new century, the possibility of an embodied male-homosexual thematics has, I would like to argue, a precisely liminal presence. It is present as a—as a very particular, historicized—thematics of absence, and specifically of the absence of speech. The first (in some ways the only) thing we learn about John Marcher is that he has a "secret" (358), a destiny, a something unknown in his future. "You said," May Bartram reminds him, "you had from your earliest time, as the deepest thing within you, the sense of being kept for something rare and strange, possibly prodigious and terrible, that was sooner or later to happen" (359). I would argue that to the extent that Marcher's secret has *a* content, that content is homosexual.

Of course the extent to which Marcher's secret has anything that could be called a content is, not only dubious, but in the climactic last scene actively denied. "He had been the man of his time, *the* man, to whom nothing on earth was to have happened" (401). The denial that the secret has a content—the assertion that its contents is precisely a lack—is a stylish and "satisfyingly" Jamesian formal gesture. The apparent gap of meaning that it points to is, however, far from being a genuinely empty one; it is no sooner asserted than filled to a plentitude with the most orthodox of ethical enforcements. To point rhetorically to the emptiness of the secret, "the nothing that is," is, in fact, oddly, *the same gesture* as the attribution to it of a compulsory content about heterosexuality—of the content specifically, "He should [have] desired[d] her."

> *She* was what he had missed. . . . The fate he had been marked for he had met with a vengeance—he had emptied the cup to the lees; he had been the man of his time, *the* man, to whom nothing on earth was to have happened. That was the rare stroke—that was his visitation. . . . This the companion of his vigil had at a given moment made out, and she had then offered him the chance to baffle his doom. One's doom, however, was never baffled, and on the day she told him his own had come down she had seen him but stupidly stare at the escape she offered him.
>
> The escape would have been to love her; then, *then* he would have lived. (401).

The "empty" meaning of Marcher's unspeakable doom is thus necessarily, specifically heterosexual; it refers to the perfectly specific absence of a prescribed heterosexual desire. If critics, eager to help James moralize this ending, persist in claiming to be able to translate freely and without residue from that (absent) heterosexual desire to an abstraction of all possibilities of human love, there are, I think, good reasons for trying to slow them down. The totalizing, insidiously symmetrical view that the "nothing" that is Marcher's unspeakable fate is necessarily a mirror image of the "everything" he could and should have had is, specifically, in an *oblique* relation to a very different history of meanings for assertions of the erotic negative.

The "full" meaning of that unspeakable fate, on the other hand, comes from the centuries-long historical chain of substantive uses of space-clearing negatives to void and at the same time to underline the possibility of male homosexual genitality. The rhetorical name for this figure is *preterition*. Unspeakable, Unmentionable, *nefandam libidinem,* "that sin which should be neither named nor committed,"[27] the "detestable and abominable sin, amongst Christians not to be named,"

> Whose vice in special, if I would declare,
> It were enough for to perturb the air,

"things fearful to name," "the obscene sound of the unbeseeming words,"

> A sin so odious that the fame of it
> Will fright the damned in the darksome pit,[28]

"the Love that dare not speak its name,"[29]—such *were* the speakable nonmedical terms, in Christian tradition, of the homosexual possibility for men. The marginality of these terms' semantic and ontological status as substantive nouns reflected and shaped the exiguousness—but also, the potentially enabling secrecy—of that "possibility." And the newly specifying, reifying medical and penal public discourse of the male homosexual role, in the years around the Wilde trials, far from retiring or obsolescing these preteritive names, seems instead to have packed them more firmly and distinctively with homosexual meaning.[30]

John Marcher's "secret" (358), "his singularity" (366), "the thing she knew, which grew to be at last, with the consecration of the years, never mentioned between them save as 'the real truth' about him" (366), "the abyss" (375), "his queer consciousness" (378), "the great vagueness" (379), "the secret of the gods" (379), "what ignominy or what monstrosity" (379), "dreadful things . . . I couldn't name" (381): the ways in which the story refers to Marcher's secret fate have the same quasi-nominative, quasi-obliterative structure.

There are, as well, some "fuller," though still highly equivocal, lexical pointers to a homosexual meaning: "The rest of the world of course thought him *queer*, but she, she only, knew how, and above all why, queer; which was precisely what enabled her to dispose the concealing veil in the right folds. She took his *gaity* from him—since it had to pass with them for gaiety—as she took everything else. . . . She traced his unhappy *perversion* through reaches of its course into which he could scarce follow it" (367; emphasis added). Still, it is mostly in the reifying grammar of periphrasis and preterition—"such a cataclysm" (360), "the great affair" (360), "the catastrophe" (361), "his predicament" (364), "their real truth" (368), "his inevitable topic" (371), "all that they had thought, first and last" (372), "horrors" (382), something "more monstrous than all the monstrosities we've named" (383), "all the loss and all the shame that are thinkable" (384)—that a homosexual meaning becomes, to the degree that it does become, legible. "I don't focus it. I can't name it. I only know I'm exposed" (372).

I am convinced, however, that part of the point of the story is that the reifying effect of periphrasis and preterition on this particular meaning is, if anything, *more* damaging than (though not separable from) its obliterative effect. To have succeeded—which was not to be taken for granted—in cracking the centuries-old code by which the-articulated-denial-of-articulability always had the possibility of meaning two things, of meaning either (heterosexual) "nothing" or "homosexual meaning," would also always have been to assume one's place in a discourse in which there was *a* homosexual meaning, in which all homosexual meaning meant a single thing. To crack a code and enjoy the reassuring exhilarations of knowingness is to buy into the specific formula, "We Know What That Means." (I assume it is this mechanism that makes even critics who know about the male-erotic pathways of James's personal desires appear to be so untroubled about leaving them out of accounts of his writing.[31] As if this form of desire were the most calculable, the simplest to add or subtract or allow for in moving between life and art!) But if, as I suggested in Section 1, men's accession to heterosexual entitlement has, for these modern centuries, always been on the ground of a cultivated and compulsory denial of the *un*know-ability, of the arbitrariness and self-contradictoriness, of homosexual/heterosexual definition, then

the fearful or triumphant interpretive formula "We Know What That Means" seems to
take on an odd centrality. First, it is a lie. But second, it is the particular lie that animates
and perpetuates the mechanism of homophobic male self-ignorance and violence and manipulability.

It is worth, then, trying to discriminate the possible plurality of meanings behind the
unspeakables of "The Beast in the Jungle." To point, as I argue that the narrative itself
points and as we have so far pointed, simply to *a* possibility of "homosexual meaning," is
to say worse than nothing—it is to pretend to say one thing. But even on the surface of
the story, the secret, "*the* thing," "the thing she knew," is discriminated, first of all discriminated temporally. There are at least two secrets: Marcher feels that he knows, but has
never told anyone but May Bartram (secret number one) that he is reserved for some very
particular, uniquely rending fate in the future, whose nature is (secret number two) unknown to himself. Over the temporal extent of the story, both the balance, between the
two characters, of cognitive mastery over the secrets' meanings, and the temporal placement, between future and past, of the second secret, shift; it is possible, in addition, that
the actual content (if any) of the secrets changes with these temporal and cognitive
changes, if time and intersubjectivity are of the essence of the secrets.

Let me baldly, then, spell out my hypothesis of what a series of "full"—that is, homo-
sexually tinged—meanings for the Unspeakable might look like for this story, differing
both over time and according to character.

For John Marcher, let us hypothesize, the future secret—the secret of his hidden fate—
importantly includes, though it is not necessarily limited to, the possibility of something
homosexual. *For Marcher,* the presence or possibility of a homosexual meaning attached to
the inner, the future secret, has exactly the reifying, totalizing, and blinding effect we described earlier in regard to the phenomenon of the Unspeakable. Whatever (Marcher feels)
may be to be discovered along those lines, it is, in the view of his panic, *one* thing, and the
worst thing, "the superstition of the Beast" (394). His readiness to organize the whole
course of his life around the preparation for it—the defense against it—remakes his life
monolithically in the image of *its* monolith of, in his view, the inseparability of homosexual desire, yielding, discovery, scandal, shame, annihilation. Finally, he has "but one desire
left": that *it* be "decently proportional to the posture he had kept, all his life, in the
threatened presence of it" (379).

This is how it happens that the outer secret, the secret of having a secret, functions, in
Marcher's life, precisely as *the closet*. It is not a closet in which there is a homosexual man,
for Marcher is not a homosexual man. Instead, however, it is the closet of, simply, the homosexual secret—the closet of imagining *a* homosexual secret. Yet it is unmistakable that
Marcher lives as one who is *in the closet*. His angle on daily existence and intercourse is that
of the closeted person,

> the secret of the difference between the forms he went through—those of his little office
> under government, those of caring for his modest patrimony, for his library, for his garden in
> the country, for the people in London whose invitations he accepted and repaid—and the de-
> tachment that reigned beneath them and that made of all behaviour, all that could in the
> least be called behaviour, a long act of dissimulation. What it had come to was that he wore
> a mask painted with the social simper, out of the eye-holes of which there looked eyes of an
> expression not in the least matching the other features. This the stupid world, even after
> years, had never more than half-discovered. (367–78)

Whatever the content of the inner secret, too, it is one whose protection requires, for
him, a playacting of heterosexuality that is conscious of being only window dressing.

"You help me," he tells May Bartram, "to pass for a man like another" (375). And "what saves us, you know," she explains, "is that we answer so completely to so usual an appearance: that of the man and woman whose friendship has become such a daily habit—or almost—as to be at last indispensable" (368–69). Oddly, they not only appear to be but are such a man and woman. The element of deceiving the world, of window dressing, comes into their relationship *only* because of the compulsion he feels to invest it with the legitimating stamp of visible, institutionalized genitality: "The real form it should have taken on the basis that stood out large was the form of their marrying. But the devil in this was that the very basis itself put marrying out of the question. His conviction, his apprehension, his obsession, in short, wasn't a privilege he could invite a woman to share; and that consequence of it was precisely what was the matter with him" (365).

Because of the terrified stultification of his fantasy about the inner or future secret, Marcher has, until the story's very last scene, an essentially static relation to and sense of both these secrets. Even the discovery that the outer secret is already shared with someone else, and the admission of May Bartram to the community it creates, "the dim day constituted by their discretions and privacies" (363), does nothing to his closet but furnish it—camouflage it to the eyes of outsiders, and soften its inner cushioning for his own comfort. In fact, the admission of May Bartram importantly *consolidates and fortifies* the closet for John Marcher.

In my hypothesis, however, May Bartram's view of Marcher's secrets is different from his and more fluid. I want to suggest that—while it is true that she feels desire for him—her involvement with him occurs originally on the ground of her understanding that he is imprisoned by homosexual panic; and her interest in his closet is not at all in helping him fortify it but in helping him dissolve it.

In this reading, May Bartram from the first sees, correctly, that the possibility of Marcher's achieving a genuine ability to attend to a woman—sexually or in any other way—depends as an absolute precondition on the dispersion of his totalizing, basilisk fascination with and terror of homosexual possibility. It is only through his coming out of the closet—whether as *a homosexual man,* or as a man with a less exclusively defined sexuality that nevertheless admits the possibility of desires for other men—that Marcher could even begin to perceive the attention of a woman as anything other than a terrifying demand or a devaluing complicity. The truth of this is already evident at the beginning of the story, in the surmises with which Marcher first meets May Bartram's allusion to something (he cannot remember what) he said to her years before: "The great thing was that he saw in this no vulgar reminder of any 'sweet' speech. The vanity of women had long memories, but she was making no claim on him of a compliment or a mistake. With another woman, a totally different one, he might have feared the recall possibly even of some imbecile 'offer'" (356). The alternative to this, however, in his eyes, is a different kind of "sweetness," that of a willingly shared confinement: "her knowledge . . . began, even if rather strangely, to taste sweet to him" (358). "Somehow the whole question was a new luxury to him—that is from the moment she was in possession. If she didn't take the sarcastic view she clearly took the sympathetic, and that was what he had had, in all the long time, from no one whomsoever. What he felt was that he couldn't at present have begun to tell her, and yet could profit perhaps exquisitely by the accident of having done so of old" (358). So begins the imprisonment of May Bartram in John Marcher's closet—an imprisonment that, the story makes explicit, is founded on his inability to perceive or value her as a person beyond her complicity in his view of his own predicament.

The conventional view of the story, emphasizing May Bartram's interest in liberating, unmediatedly, Marcher's heterosexual possibilities, would see her as unsuccessful in doing so until too late—until the true revelation that comes, however, only after her death. If what needs to be liberated is in the first place Marcher's potential for homosexual desire, however, the trajectory of the story must be seen as far bleaker. I hypothesize that what May Bartram would have liked for Marcher, the narrative she wished to nurture for him, would have been a progress from a vexed and gaping self-ignorance around his homosexual possibilities to a self-knowledge of them that would have freed him to find and enjoy a sexuality of whatever sort emerged. What she sees happen to Marcher, instead, is the "progress" that the culture more insistently enforces: the progress from a vexed and gaping self-ignorance around his homosexual possibilities, to a completed and rationalized and wholly concealed and accepted one. The moment of Marcher's full incorporation of his erotic self-ignorance is the moment at which the imperatives of the culture cease to enforce him, and he becomes instead the enforcer of the culture.

Section 4 of the story marks the moment at which May Bartram realizes that, far from helping dissolve Marcher's closet, she has instead and irremediably been permitting him to reinforce it. It is in this section and the next, too, that it becomes explicit in the story that Marcher's fate, what was to have happened to him and did happen, involves a change in him from being the suffering object of a Law or judgment (of a doom in the original sense of the word) to being the embodiment of that Law.

If the transition I am describing is, in certain respects, familiarly Oedpial, the structuring metaphor behind its description here seems to be oddly alimentative. The question that haunts Marcher in these sections is whether what he has thought of as the secret of his future may not be, after all, in the past; and the question of passing, of who is passing through what or what is passing through whom, of what residue remains to *be* passed, is the form in which he compulsively poses his riddle. Is the beast eating him, or is he eating the beast? "It hasn't passed you by," May Bartram tells him. "It has done its office. It has made you its own" (389). "It's past. It's behind, she finally tells him, to which he replies, "*Nothing*, for me, is past; nothing *will* pass till I pass myself, which I pray my stars may be as soon as possible. Say, however, . . . that I've eaten my cake, as you contend, to the last crumb—how can the thing I've never felt at all be the thing I was marked out to feel?" (391). What May Bartram sees, that Marcher does not, is that the process of incorporating—of embodying—the Law of masculine self-ignorance, is the one that has the least in the world to do with feeling.[32] To gape at and, rebelliously, be forced to swallow the Law is to feel; but to have it finally stick to one's ribs, become however incongruously a part of one's own organism, is then to perfect at the same moment a new hard-won insentience of it and an assumption of (or subsumption by) an identification with it. May Bartram answers Marcher's question, "You take your 'feelings' for granted. You were to suffer your fate. That was not necessarily to know it" (391). Marcher's fate is to cease to suffer fate, and, instead, to become it. May Bartram's fate, with the "slow fine shudder" that climaxes her ultimate appeal to Marcher, is herself to swallow this huge, bitter bolus with which *she* can have *no* deep identification, and to die of it—of what is, to her, knowledge, not power. "So on her lips would the law itself have sounded" (389). Or, tasted.

To end a reading of May Bartram with her death, to end with her silenced forever in that ultimate closet, "her" tomb that represents (to Marcher) *his fate,* would be to do to her feminine desire the same thing I have already argued that James M. Barrie, unforgivably, did to Grizel's. That is to say, it leaves us in danger of figuring May Bartram, or more generally the woman in heterosexuality, as only the exact, heroic supplement to the murderous enforcements of male homophobic/homosocial self-ignorance. "The Fox," Emily Dickinson wrote, "fits the Hound."[33] It would be only too easy to describe May Bartram as the fox that most irreducibly fits this particular hound. She seems the woman (don't we all know them?) who has not only the most delicate nose for but the most potent attraction toward men who are at crises of homosexual panic . . . —Though for that matter, won't most women admit that an arousing nimbus, an excessively refluent and dangerous maelstrom of eroticism, somehow attends men in general at such moments, even otherwise boring men?

If one is to avoid the Barrie-ism of describing May Bartram in terms that reduce her perfectly to the residue-less sacrifice John Marcher makes to his Beast, it might be by inquiring into the difference of the paths of her own desire. What does she want—not for him, but for herself—from their relationship? What does she actually get? To speak less equivocally from my own eros and experience, there is a particular relation to truth and authority that a mapping of male homosexual panic offers to a woman in the emotional vicinity. The fact that male heterosexual entitlement in (at least modern Anglo-American) culture depends on a perfected but always friable self-ignorance in men as to the significance of their desire for other men, means that it is always open to women to know something that it is much more dangerous for any nonhomosexual-identified man to know. The ground of May Bartram's and John Marcher's relationship from the first is that she has the advantage of him, cognitively: she remembers, as he does not, where and when and with whom they have met before, and most of all she remembers his "secret" from a decade ago while he forgets having told it to her. This differential of knowledge affords her a "slight irony," an "advantage" (353)—but one that he can at the same time use to his own profit as "the buried treasure of her knowledge," "this little hoard" (363). As their relationship continues, the sense of power and of a marked, rather free-floating irony about May Bartram becomes stronger and stronger, even in proportion to Marcher's accelerating progress toward self-ignorance and toward a blindly selfish expropriation of her emotional labor. Both the care and the creativity of her investment in him, the imaginative reach of her fostering his homosexual potential as a route back to his truer perception of herself, are forms of gender-political resilience in her as well as of love. They are forms of excitement, too, of real though insufficient power, and of pleasure.

In the last scene of the "The Beast in the Jungle," John Marcher becomes, in this reading, not the finally self-knowing man who is capable of heterosexual love, but the irredeemably self-ignorant man who embodies and enforces heterosexual compulsion. In this reading, that is to say, May Bartram's prophecy to Marcher that "You'll never know now" (390) is *a true one*.

Importantly for the homosexual plot, too, the final scene is also the only one in the entire story that reveals or tests the affective quality of Marcher's perception of another man. "The shock of the face" (399)—this is, in the last scene, the beginning of what Marcher ultimately considers "the most extraordinary thing that had happened to him" (400). At the beginning of Marcher's confrontation with this male figure at the cemetery, the erotic possibilities of the connection between the men appear to be all open. The man, whose "mute assault" Marcher feels "so deep down that he winced at the steady thrust," is mourning profoundly over "a grave apparently fresh," but (perhaps only to Marcher's closet-sharpened suspicions?) a slightest potential of Whitmanian cruisiness seems at first to tinge the air, as well.

> His pace was slow, so that—and all the more as there was a kind of hunger in his look—the two men were for a minute directly confronted. Marcher knew him at once for one of the deeply stricken . . . nothing lived but the deep ravage of the features he showed. He *showed*

> them—that was the point; he was moved, as he passed, by some impulse that was either a
> signal for sympathy or, more possibly, a challenge to an opposed sorrow. He might already
> have been aware of our friend. . . . What Marcher was at all events conscious of was in the
> first place that the image of scarred passion presented to him was conscious too—of some-
> thing that profaned the air; and in the second that, roused, startled, shocked, he was yet the
> next moment looking after it, as it went, with envy. (400–401)

The path traveled by Marcher's desire in this brief and cryptic non-encounter reenacts a
classic trajectory of male entitlement. Marcher begins with the possibility of *desire for* the
man, in response to the man's open "hunger" ("which," afterward, "still flared for him like a
smoky torch" [401]). Deflecting that desire under a fear of profanation, he then replaces it
with envy, with an *identification with* the man in that man's (baffled) desire for some other, female, dead object. "The stranger passed, but the raw glare of his grief remained, making our
friend wonder in pity what wrong, what wound it expressed, what injury not to be healed.
What had the man *had,* to make him by the loss of it so bleed and yet live?" (401).

What had the man *had?* The loss by which a man *so bleeds and yet lives* is, is it not, supposed to be the castratory one of the phallus figured as mother, the inevitability of whose
sacrifice ushers sons into the status of fathers and into the control (read both ways) of the
Law. What is strikingly open in the ending of "The Beast in the Jungle" is how central to
that process is man's desire for man—and the denial of that desire. The imperative that
there *be* a male figure to take this place is the clearer in that, at an earlier climactic moment, in a female "shock of the face," May Bartram has presented to Marcher her own face,
in a conscious revelation that was far more clearly of desire.

> It had become suddenly, from her movement and attitude, beautiful and vivid to him that
> she had something more to give him; her wasted face delicately shone with it—it glittered
> almost as with the white lustre of silver in her expression. She was right, incontestably, for
> what he saw in her face was the truth, and strangely, without consequence, while their talk of
> it as dreadful was still in the air, she appeared to present it as inordinately soft. This,
> prompting bewilderment, made him but gape the more gratefully for her revelation, so that
> they continued for some minutes silent, her face shining at him, her contact imponderably
> pressing, and his stare all kind but all expectant. The end, none the less, was that what he
> had expected failed to come to him. (386)

To the shock of the female face, Marcher is not phobic but simply numb. It is only by
turning his desire for the male face into an envious identification with male loss that
Marcher finally comes into *any* relation to a woman—and then it is a relation through one
dead woman (the other man's) to another dead woman of his own. That is to say, it is the
relation of *compulsory* heterosexuality.

When Lytton Strachey's claim to be a conscientious objector was being examined, he
was asked what he would do if a German were to try to rape his sister. "I should," he is
said to have replied, "try and interpose my own body."[34] Not the gay self-knowledge but
the heterosexual, self-ignorant acting out of just this fantasy ends "The Beast in the Jungle." To face the gaze of the Beast would have been, for Marcher, to dissolve it.[35] To face
the "kind of hunger in the look" of the grieving man—to explore at all into the sharper
lambencies of that encounter—would have been to dissolve the closet. Marcher, instead,
to the very end, turns his back—re-creating a double scenario of homosexual compulsion
and heterosexual compulsion. "He saw the Jungle of his life and saw the lurking Beast;
then, while he looked, perceived it, as by a stir of the air, rise, huge and hideous, for the
leap that was to settle him. His eyes darkened—it was close; and, instinctively turning, in
his hallucination, to avoid it, he flung himself, face down, on the tomb" (402).

NOTES

This essay has profited—though not as fully as I wish I had been able to make it do—from especially helpful readings by Maud Ellmann, Neil Hertz, H. A. Sedgwick, D. A. Miller, and Ruth Bernard Yeazell.

1. Lawrence to Jessie Chambers, Aug. 1910, *The Collected Letters of D.H. Lawrence,* ed. Harry T. Moore (London: W. H. Heinemann, 1962), 1: 63.

2. Lawrence to Rolf Gardiner, Aug. 9, 1924, in ibid. 2: 801.

3. Alan Bray, *Homosexuality in Renaissance England* (London: Gay Men's Press, 1982), chs. 1–3. Note the especially striking example on pp. 68–69, 76–77.

4. Ibid., p. 25.

5. Eve Kosofsky Sedgwick, *Between Men: English Literature and Male Homosocial Desire* (New York: Columbia University Press, 1985), pp. 83–96.

6. Claude Lévi-Strauss, *The Elementary Structures of Kinship* (Boston: Beacon Press, 1969), p. 115; also quoted and well discussed in Gayle Rubin, "The Traffic in Women: Notes Toward a Political Economy of Sex," in *Toward an Anthropology of Women,* ed. Rayna Reiter (New York: Monthly Review Press, 1975), pp. 157–210.

7. Heidi Hartmann, "The Unhappy Marriage of Marxism and Feminism: Towards a More Progressive Union," in *Women and Revolution: A Discussion of the Unhappy Marriage of Marxism and Feminism,* ed. Lydia Sargent (Boston: South End Press, 1981), p. 14; emphasis added.

8. Bray, *Homosexuality,* ch. 4.

9. Sedgwick, *Between Men,* pp. 88–89.

10. By "paranoid Gothic" I mean Romantic novels in which a male hero is in a close, usually murderous relation to another male figure, in some respects his "double," to whom he seems to be mentally transparent. Examples of the paranoid Gothic include, besides *Frankenstein,* Ann Radcliffe's *The Italian,* William Godwin's *Caleb Williams,* and James Hogg's *Confessions of a Justified Sinner.* This tradition is discussed more fully in my *Between Men,* chs. 5 and 6.

11. Sigmund Freud, "Psycho-Analytic Notes of an Autobiographical Account of a Case of Paranoia (Dementia Paranoides), in *The Standard Edition of the Complete Psychological Works of Sigmund Freud,* trans. and ed. James Strachey et al. (London: Hogarth Press, 1953–73). 12: 143–77.

12. On this see, along with Bray, *Homosexuality,* such works as John Boswell, *Christianity, Social Tolerance, and Homosexuality: Gay People in Western Europe from the Beginning of the Christian Era to the Fourteenth Century* (Chicago: University of Chicago Press, 1980); Jonathan Katz, *A Gay/Lesbian Almanac* (New York: Thomas Y. Crowell Co., 1982); Jeffrey Weeks, *Coming Out: Homosexual Politics in Britain from the Nineteenth Century to the Present* (London: Quartet Books, 1977); and Weeks, *Sex, Politics, and Society: The Regulation of Sexuality since 1800* (London: Longman & Co., 1981).

13. For more on bachelors see Frederic Jameson, *Wyndham Lewis: Fables of Aggression* (Berkeley and Los Angeles: University of California Press, 1979), ch. 2; also, cited in Jameson, Jean Borie, *Le Célibataire français* (Paris: Le Sagittaire, 1976); and Edward Said, *Beginnings* (New York: Basic Books, 1975), pp. 137–52.

14. F. O. Matthiessen and Kenneth B. Murdock, eds., *The Notebooks of Henry James* (New York: Oxford University Press, 1947), p. 28.

15. Bachelor literature in which the paranoid Gothic—or more broadly, the supernatural—makes a reappearance includes, besides Du Maurier's *Trilby,* George Eliot's *The Lifted Veil,* Robert Louis Stevenson's *Dr. Jekyll and Mr. Hyde,* numerous Kipling stories such as "In the Same Boat," and numerous James stories such as "The Jolly Corner."

16. *Lovel the Widower,* in *Works of Thackeray* (New York: National Library, n.d.), 1: ch. 1. Subsequent references to this novel are to this edition and are cited parenthetically in the text by chapter number.

17. In, respectively, Trollope's *The Claverings* and Thackeray's *Pendennis* and *Vanity Fair;* "Soapey" Sponge is in R. S. Surtee's *Mr. Sponge's Sporting Tour.*

18. Richard Miller, *Bohemia: The Protoculture Then and Now* (Chicago: Nelson-Hall Co., 1977), p. 58.

19. *Notebooks of James,* Matthiessen and Murdock, eds., pp. 97–98.

20. "Ballads," *Works of Thackeray* 6: 337.

21. George Du Maurier, *Trilby* (New York: Harper & Bros., 1922), p. 271.

22. The effect of emboldenment should be to some extent mistrusted—not, I think, because the attribu-
    tion to these particular figures of a knowledge of male homosexual panic is likely to be wrong, but
    because it is so much easier to be so emboldened about men who are arguably homosexual in (if such
    a thing exists) "basic" sexual orientation; while what I am arguing is that panic is proportioned not
    to the homosexual but to the nonhomosexual-identified elements of these men's characters. Thus, if
    Barrie and James are obvious authors with whom to *begin* an analysis of male homosexual panic, the
    analysis I am offering here must be inadequate to the degree that it does not work just as well—even
    better—for Joyce, Milton, Faulkner, Lawrence, Yeats.

23. Leon Edel, *Henry James: The Middle Years: 1882–1895,* vol. 3 of *The Life of Henry James* (New York:
    J. B. Lippincott, Co., 1962; repr., Avon Books, 1978), makes clear that these contacts—coincid-
    ing visits to some cities and shared trips to others (e.g., 3: 94), "a special rendezvous" in Geneva
    (3: 217), a period of actually living in the same house (3: 215–17)—were conducted with a con-
    sistent and most uncharacteristic extreme of secrecy. (James seems also to have taken extraordinary
    pains to destroy every vestige of his correspondence with Woolson.) Edel cannot, nevertheless,
    imagine the relationship except as "a continuing 'virtuous' attachment": "That this pleasant and
    méticuleuse old maid may have nourished fantasies of a closer tie does not seem to have occurred to
    him at this time. If it had, we might assume he would have speedily put distance between him-
    self and her" (3: 217). Edel's hypothesis does nothing, of course, to explain the secrecy of these and
    other meetings.

24. Edel, *Life of James,* vol. 4, *The Master: 1910–1916,* pp. 132–40.

25. "The Beast in the Jungle," in *The Complete Tales of Henry James,* ed. Leon Edel (London: Rupert Hart-
    Davis, 1964), 11: 401. All subsequent references to this work are to this edition and are cited paren-
    thetically in the text by page number.

26. Interestingly, in the 1895 germ of (what seems substantially to be) "The Beast in the Jungle," in
    James's *Notebooks,* p. 184, the woman outlives the man. "It's *the woman's sense of what might [have been]
    in him* that arrives at the intensity. . . . *She is his Dead Self: he is alive in her and dead in himself*—that
    is something like the little formula I seem to *entrevoir.* He himself, the man, must, *in* the tale, also
    materially die—die in the flesh as he has died long ago in the spirit, the *right* one. Then it is that his
    lost treasure revives most—no longer *contrarié* by his material existence, existence in his false self,
    his wrong one."

27. Quoted in Boswell, *Christianity,* p. 349 (from a legal document dated 533) and p. 380 (from a 1227
    letter from Pope Honorious III).

28. Quoted in Bray, *Homosexuality*—the first two from p. 61 (from Edward Coke's *Institutes* and Sir
    David Lindsay's *Works*), the next two from p. 62 (from William Bradford's *Plimouth Plantation* and
    Guillaume Du Bartas's *Divine Weeks*), and the last from p. 22, also from Du Bartas.

29. Lord Alfred Douglas, "Two Loves," from *The Chameleon,* quoted in Byron, R. S. Fone, *Hidden Her-
    itage: History and the Gay Imagination* (New York: Irvington Publishers, 1981), p. 196.

30. For a striking anecdotal example of the mechanism of this, see Beverley Nichols, *Father Figure* (New
    York: Simon & Schuster, 1972), pp. 92–99.

31. Exceptions that I know of include Georges-Michel Sarotte's discussions of James in *Like a Brother,
    Like a Lover: Male Homosexuality in the American Novel and Theater from Herman Melville to James Bald-
    win,* trans. Richard Miller (New York: Doubleday & Co./Anchor, 1978); Richard Hall, "Henry
    James: Interpreting an Obsessive Memory," *Journal of Homosexuality* 8, no. 3/4 (Spring/Summer
    1983): 83–97; and Robert K. Martin, "The 'High Felicity' of Comradeship: A New Reading of
    Roderick Hudson," *American Literary Realism* 11 (Spring 1978): 100–108.

32. A fascinating passage in James's *Notebooks,* p. 318, written in 1905 in California, shows how a
    greater self-knowledge in James, and a greater acceptance and *specificity* of homosexual desire, trans-

forms this half-conscious enforcing rhetoric of anality, numbness, and silence into a much richer, pregnant address to James's male muse, an invocation of fisting-as-*écriture*:

I sit here, after long weeks, at any rate, in front of my arrears, with an inward accumulation of material of which I feel the wealth, and as to which I can only invoke my familiar demon of patience, who always comes, doesn't he?, when I call. He is here with me in front of this cool green Pacific—he sits close and I feel his soft breath, which cools and steadies and inspires, on my cheek. Everything sinks in: nothing is lost; everything abides and fertilizes and renews its golden promise, making me think with closed eyes of deep and grateful longing when, in the full summer days of L[amb] H[ouse], my long dusty adventure over, I shall be able to [plunge] my hand, my arm, in, deep and far, and up to the shoulder—into the heavy bag of remembrance— of suggestion—of imagination—of art—and fish out every little figure and felicity, every little fact and fancy that can be to my purpose. These things are all packed away, now, thicker than I can penetrate, deeper than I can fathom, and there let them rest for the present, in their sacred cool darkness, till I shall let in upon them the mild still light of dear old L[amb] H[ouse]—in which they will begin to gleam and glitter and take form like the gold and jewels of a mine.

33. *Collected Poems of Emily Dickinson*, ed. Thomas H. Johnson (Boston: Little, Brown & Co., 1960), p. 406.

34. Lytton Strachey, quoted in Michael Holroyd, *Lytton Strachery: A Critical Biography* (London: W. H. Heinemann, 1968), 2: 179.

35. Ruth Bernard Yeazell makes clear the oddity of having Marcher turn his back on the Beast that is supposed, at this late moment, to represent his self-recognition (in *Language and Knowledge in the Late Novels of Henry James* [Chicago: University of Chicago Press, 1976], pp. 37–38).

Hortense J. Spillers

Mama's Baby, Papa's Maybe: An American Grammar Book

Let's face it. I am a marked woman, but not everybody knows my name. "Peaches" and "Brown Sugar," "Sapphire" and "Earth Mother," "Aunty," "Granny," God's "Holy Fool," a "Miss Ebony First," or "Black Woman at the Podium": I describe a locus of confounded identities, a meeting ground of investments and privations in the national treasury of rhetorical wealth. My country needs me, and if I were not here, I would have to be invented.

W. E. B. DuBois predicted as early as 1903 that the twentieth century would be the century of the "color line." We could add to this spatiotemporal configuration another thematic of analogously terrible weight: if the "black woman" can be seen as a particular figuration of the split subject that psychoanalytic theory posits, then this century marks the site of "its" profoundest revelation. The problem before us is deceptively simple: the terms enclosed in quotation marks in the preceding paragraph isolate overdetermined nominative properties. Embedded in bizarre axiological ground, they demonstrate a sort of telegraphic coding; they are markers so loaded with mythical prepossession that there is

Spillers, Hortense, "Mama's Baby, Papa's Maybe: An American Grammar Book," *Diacritics* 17.2 (1987), pp. 65–81.

no easy way for the agents buried beneath them to come clean. In that regard, the names
by which I am called in the public place render an example of signifying property *plus*. In
order for me to speak a truer word concerning myself, I must strip down through layers of
attenuated meanings, made an excess in time, over time, assigned by a particular historical order, and there await whatever marvels of my own inventiveness. The personal pronouns are offered in the service of a collective function.

In certain human societies, a child's identity is determined through the line of the
Mother, but the United States, from at least one author's point of view, is not one of them:
"In essence, the Negro community has been forced into a matriarchal structure which, because it is so far out of line with the rest of American society, seriously retards the progress
of the group as a whole, and imposes a crushing burden on the Negro male and, in consequence, on a great many Negro women as well" [Moynihan 75; emphasis mine].

The notorious bastard, from Vico's banished Roman mothers of such sons, to Caliban,
to Heathcliff, and Joe Christmas, has no official female equivalent. Because the traditional
rites and laws of inheritance rarely pertain to the female child, bastard status signals to
those who need to know which son of the Father's is the legitimate heir and which one the
impostor. For that reason, property seems wholly the business of the male. A "she" cannot,
therefore, qualify for bastard, or "natural son" status, and that she cannot provides further
insight into the coils and recoils of patriarchal wealth and fortune. According to Daniel
Patrick Moynihan's celebrated "Report" of the late sixties, the "Negro Family" has no Father to speak of—his Name, his Law, his Symbolic function mark the impressive missing
agencies in the essential life of the black community, the "Report" maintains, and it is,
surprisingly, the fault of the Daughter, or the female line. This stunning reversal of the
castration thematic, displacing the Name and the Law of the Father to the territory of the
Mother and Daughter, becomes an aspect of the African-American female's misnaming.
We attempt to undo this misnaming in order to reclaim the relationship between Fathers
and Daughters within this social matrix for a quite different structure of cultural fictions.
For Daughters and Fathers are here made to manifest the very same *rhetorical* symptoms of
absence and denial, to embody the double and contrastive agencies of a *prescribed* in-
ternecine degradation. "Sapphire" enacts her "Old Man" in drag, just as her "Old Man"
becomes "Sapphire" in outrageous caricature.

In other words, in the historic outline of dominance, the respective subject-positions of
"female" and "male" adhere to no symbolic integrity. At a time when current critical discourses appear to compel us more and more decidedly toward gender "undecidability," it
would appear reactionary, if not dumb, to insist on the integrity of female/male gender.
But undressing these conflations of meaning, as they appear under the rule of dominance,
would restore, as figurative possibility, not only Power to the Female (for Maternity), but
also Power to the Male (for Paternity). We would gain, in short, the *potential* for gender
differentiation as it might express itself along a range of stress points, including human
biology in its intersection with the project of culture.

Though among the most readily available "whipping boys" of fairly recent public discourse concerning African-Americans and national policy, "The Moynihan Report" is by
no means unprecedented in its conclusions; it belongs, rather, to a class of symbolic paradigms that 1) inscribe "ethnicity" as a scene of negation and 2) confirm the human body
as a metonymic figure for an entire repertoire of human and social arrangements. In that
regard, the "Report" pursues a behavioral rule of public documentary. Under the Moynihan rule, "ethnicity" itself identifies a total objectification of human and cultural motives—the "white" family, by implication, and the "Nero Family," by outright assertion,
in a constant opposition of binary meanings. Apparently spontaneous, these "actants" are

wholly generated, with neither past nor future, as tribal currents moving out of time. Moynihan's "Families" are pure present and always tense. "Ethnicity" in this case freezes in meaning, takes on consistency, assumes the look and the affects of the Eternal. We could say, then, that in its powerful stillness, "ethnicity," from the point of view of the "Report," embodies nothing more than a mode of memorial time, as Roland Barthes outlines the dynamics of myth [see "Myth Today" 109–59; esp. 122–23]. As a signifier that has no movement in the field of signification, the use of "ethnicity" for the living becomes purely appreciative, although one would be unwise not to concede its dangerous and fatal effects.

"Ethnicity" perceived as mythical time enables a writer to perform a variety of conceptual moves all at once. Under its hegemony, the human body becomes a defenseless target for rape and veneration, and the body, in its material and abstract phase, a resource for metaphor. For example, Moynihan's "tangle of pathology" provides the descriptive strategy for the work's fourth chapter, which suggests that "underachievement" in black males of the lower classes is primarily the fault of black females, who achieve out of all proportion, both to their numbers in the community and to the paradigmatic example before the nation: "Ours is a society which presumes male leadership in private and public affairs. . . . A subculture, such as that of the Negro American, in which this is not the pattern, is placed at a distinct disadvantage" [75]. Between charts and diagrams, we are asked to consider the impact of qualitative measure on the black male's performance on standardized examinations, matriculation in schools of higher and professional training, etc. Even though Moynihan sounds a critique on his own argument here, he quickly withdraws from its possibilities, suggesting that black males should reign because that is the way the majority culture carries things out: "It is clearly a disadvantage for a minority group to be operating under one principle, while the great majority of the population . . . . is operating on another" [75]. Those persons living according to the perceived "matriarchal" pattern are, therefore, caught in a state of social "pathology."

Even though Daughters have their own agenda with reference to this order of Fathers (imagining for the moment that Moynihan's fiction—and others like it—does not represent an adequate one and that there *is,* once we dis-cover him, a Father here), my contention that these social and cultural subjects make doubles, unstable in their respective identities, in effect transports us to a common historical ground, the socio-political order of the New World. That order, with its human sequence written in blood, *represents* for its African and indigenous peoples a scene of *actual* mutilation, dismemberment, and exile. First of all, their New-World, diasporic plight marked a *theft of the body*—a willful and violent (and unimaginable from this distance) severing of the captive body from its motive will, its active desire. Under these conditions, we lose at least *gender* difference *in the outcome,* and the female body and the male body become a territory of cultural and political maneuver, not at all gender-related, gender-specific. But this body, at least from the point of view of the captive community, focuses a private and particular space, at which point of convergence biological, sexual, social, cultural, linguistic, ritualistic, and psychological fortunes join. This profound intimacy of interlocking detail is disrupted, however, by externally imposed meanings and uses: 1) the captive body becomes the source of an irresistible, destructive sensuality; 2) at the same time—in stunning contradiction—the captive body reduces to a thing, becoming *being for* the captor; 3) in this absence *from* a subject position, the captured sexualities provide a physical and biological expression of "otherness"; 4) as a category of "otherness," the captive body translates into a potential for pornotroping and embodies sheer physical powerlessness that slides into a more general "powerlessness" resonating through various centers of human and social meaning.

But I would make a distinction in this case between "body" and "flesh" and impose that distinction as the central one between captive and liberated subject-positions. In that sense, before the "body" there is the "flesh," that zero degree of social conceptualization that does not escape concealment under the brush of discourse, or the reflexes of iconography. Even though the European hegemonies stole bodies—some of them female—out of West African communities in concert with the African "middleman," we regard this human and social irreparability as high crimes against the *flesh*, as the person of African females and African males registered the wounding. If we think of the "flesh" as a primary narrative, then we mean its seared, divided, ripped-apartness, riveted to the ship's hole, fallen, or "escaped" overboard.

One of the most poignant aspects of William Goodell's contemporaneous study of the North American slave codes gives precise expression to the tortures and instruments of captivity. Reporting an instance of Jonathan Edwards's observations on the tortures of enslavement, Goodell narrates: "The smack of the whip is all day long in the ears of those who are on the plantation, or in the vicinity; and it is used with such dexterity and severity as not only to lacerate the skin, but to tear out small portions of the flesh at almost every stake" [221]. The anatomical specifications of rupture, of altered human tissue, take on the objective description of laboratory prose—even beaten out, arms, backs, skulls branded, a left jaw, a right ankle, punctured; teeth missing, as the calculated work of iron, whips, chains, knives, the canine patrol, the bullet.

These undecipherable markings on the captive body render a kind of hieroglyphics of the flesh whose severe disjunctures come to be hidden to the cultural seeing by skin color. We might well ask if this phenomenon of marking and branding actually "transfers" from one generation to another, finding its various *symbolic substitutions* in an efficacy of meanings that repeat the initiating moments? As Elaine Scarry describes the mechanisms of torture [Scarry 27–59], these lacerations, woundings, fissures, tears, scars, openings, ruptures, lesions, rendings, punctures of the flesh create the distance between what I would designate a cultural *vestibularity* and the *culture*, whose state apparatus, including judges, attorneys, "owners," "soul drivers," "overseers," and "men of God," apparently colludes with a protocol of "search and destroy." This body whose flesh carries the female and the male to the frontiers of survival bears in person the marks of a cultural text whose inside has been turned outside.

The flesh is the concentration of "ethnicity" that contemporary critical discourses neither acknowledge nor discourse away. It is this "flesh and blood" entity, in the vestibule (or "pre-view") of a colonized North America, that is essentially ejected from "The Female Body in Western Culture" [see Suleiman, ed.], but it makes good theory, or commemorative "herstory" to want to "forget," or to have failed to realize, that the African female subject, under these historic conditions, is not only the target of rape—in one sense, an interiorized violation of body and mind—but also the topic of specifically externalized acts of torture and prostration that we imagine as the peculiar province of *male* brutality and torture inflicted by other males. A female body strung from a tree limb, or bleeding from the breast on any given day of field work because the "overseer," standing the length of a whip, has popped her flesh open, adds a lexical and living dimension to the narratives of women in culture and society [Davis 9]. This materialized scene of unprotected female flesh—of female flesh "ungendered"—offers a praxis and a theory, a text for living and for dying, and a method for reading both through their diverse mediations.

Among the myriad uses to which the enslaved community was put, Goodell identifies its value for medical research: "Assortments of diseased, *damaged,* and disabled Negroes, deemed incurable and otherwise worthless are *bought up,* it seems . . . by medical institutions, to be experimented and operated upon, for purposes of 'medical education' and the interest of medical science" [86–87; Goodell's emphasis]. From the *Charleston Mercury* for October 12, 1838, Goodell notes this advertisement:

> 'To planters and others.—Wanted, fifty Negroes, any person, having sick Negroes, considered incurable by their respective physicians, and wishing to dispose of them, Dr. S. will pay *cash* for Negroes affected with scrofula, or king's evil, confirmed hypochondriasm, apoplexy, diseases of the liver, kidneys, spleen, stomach and intestines, bladder and its appendages, diarrhea, dysentery, etc. The highest cash *price will be paid,* on application as above.' at No. 110 Church Street, Charleston. [87; Goodell's emphasis]

This profitable 'atomizing' of the captive body provides another angle on the divided flesh; we lose any hint or suggestion of a dimension of ethics, of relatedness between human personality and its anatomical features, between one human personality and another, between human personality and cultural institutions. To that extent, the procedures adopted for the captive flesh demarcate a total objectification, as the entire captive community becomes a living laboratory.

The captive body, then, brings into focus a gathering of social realities as well as a metaphor for *value* so thoroughly interwoven in their literal and figurative emphases that distinctions between them are virtually useless. Even though the captive flesh/body has been "liberated," and no one need pretend that even the quotation marks do not *matter,* dominant symbolic activity, the ruling episteme that releases the dynamics of naming and valuation, remains grounded in the originating metaphors of captivity and mutilation so that it is as if neither time nor history, nor historiography and its topics, shows movement, as the human subject is "murdered" over and over again by the passions of a bloodless and anonymous archaism, showing itself in endless disguise. Faulkner's young Chick Mallison in *The Mansion* calls "it" by other names—"the ancient subterrene atavistic fear . . ." [227]. And I would call it the Great Long National Shame. But people do not talk like that anymore—it is "embarrassing," just as the retrieval of mutilated female bodies will likely be "backward" for some people. Neither the shameface of the embarrassed, nor the not-looking-back of the self-assured is of much interest to us, and will not help at all if rigor is our dream. We might concede, at the very least, that sticks and bricks *might* break our bones, but words will most certainly *kill* us.

The symbolic order that I wish to trace in this writing, calling it an "American grammar," begins at the "beginning," which is really a rupture and a radically different kind of cultural continuation. The massive demographic shifts, the violent formation of a modern African consciousness, that take place on the subsaharan Continent during the initiative strikes which open the Atlantic Slave Trade in the fifteenth century of our Christ, interrupted hundreds of years of black African culture. We write and think, then, about an outcome of aspects of African-American life in the United States under the pressure of those events. I might as well add that the familiarity of this narrative does nothing to appease the hunger of recorded memory, nor does the persistence of the repeated rob these well-known, oft-told events of their power, even now, to startle. In a very real sense, every writing as revision makes the "discovery" all over again.

2

The narratives by African peoples and their descendants, though not as numerous from those early centuries of the "execrable trade" as the researcher would wish, suggest, in their rare occurrence, that the visual shock waves touched off when African and European "met" reverberated on both sides of the encounter. The narrative of the "Life of Olaudah Equiano, or Gustavus Vassa, the African. Written by Himself," first published in London in 1789, makes it quite clear that the first Europeans Equiano observed on what is now Nigerian soil were as unreal for him as he and others must have been for the European captors. The cruelty of "these white men with horrible looks, red faces, and long hair," of these "spirits," as the narrator would have it, occupies several pages of Equiano's attention, alongside a first-hand account of Nigerian interior life [27 ff.]. We are justified in regarding the outcome of Equiano's experience in the same light as he himself might have—as a "fall," as a veritable descent into the loss of communicative force.

If, as Todorov points out, the Mayan and Aztec peoples "lost control of communication" [61] in light of Spanish intervention, we could observe, similarly, that Vassa falls among men whose language is not only strange to him, but whose habits and practices strike him as "astonishing":

[The sea, the slave ship] filled me with astonishment, which was soon converted into terror, when I was carried on board. I was immediately handled, and tossed up to see if I were sound, by some of the crew; and I was now persuaded that I had gotten into a world of bad spirits, and that they were going to kill me. Their complexions, too, differing so much from ours, their long hair, and the language they spoke (which was different from any I had ever heard), united to confirm me in this belief. [*Equiano 27*]

The captivating party does not only "earn" the right to dispose of the captive body as it sees fit, but gains, consequently, the right to name and "name" it; Equiano, for instance, identifies at least three different names that he is given in numerous passages between his Benin homeland and the Virginia colony, the latter and England—"Michael," "Jacob," "Gustavus Vassa" [35; 36].

The nicknames by which African-American women have been called, or regarded, or imagined on the New World scene—the opening lines of this essay provide examples— demonstrate the powers of distortion that the dominant community seizes as its unlawful prerogative. Moynihan's "Negro Family," then, borrows its narrative energies from the grid of associations, from the semantic and iconic folds buried deep in the collective past, that come to surround and signify the captive person. Though there is no absolute point of chronological imitation, we might repeat certain familiar impression points that lend shape to the business of dehumanized naming. Expecting to find direct and amplified reference to African women during the opening years of the Trade, the observer is disappointed time and again that this cultural subject is concealed beneath the mighty debris of the itemized account, between the lines of the massive logs of commercial enterprise that overrun the sense of clarity we believed we had gained concerning this collective humiliation. Elizabeth Donnan's enormous, four-volume documentation becomes a case in point.

Turning directly to this source, we discover what we had not expected to find—that this aspect of the search is rendered problematic and that observations of a field of manners and its related sociometries are an outgrowth of the industry of the "exterior other" [Todorov 3], called "anthropology" later on. The European males who laded and captained these galleys and who policed and corralled these human beings, in hundreds of vessels from Liverpool to Elmina, to Jamaica; from the Cayenne Islands, to the ports at Charleston and Salem, and for three centuries of human life, were not curious about this "cargo" that bled, packed like so many live sardines among the immovable objects. Such inveterate obscene blindness might be denied, point blank, as a possibility for anyone, except that we know it happened.

Donnan's first volume covers three centuries of European "discovery" and "conquest," beginning 50 years before pious Cristobal, Christum Ferens, the bearer of Christ, laid claim to what he thought was the "Indies." From Gomes Eannes de Azurara's "Chronicle of the Discovery and Conquest of Guinea, 1441–1448" [Donnan 1: 18–41], we learn that the Portuguese probably gain the dubious distinction of having introduced black Africans to the European market of servitude. We are also reminded that "Geography" is not a divine gift. Quite to the contrary, its boundaries were shifted during the European "Age of Conquest" in giddy desperation, according to the dictates of conquering armies, the edicts of prelates, the peculiar myopia of the medieval Christian mind. Looking for the "Nile River," for example, according to the fifteenth-century Portuguese notion, is someone's joke. For all that the pre-Columbian "explorers" knew about the sciences of navigation and geography, we are surprised that more parties of them did not end up "discovering" Europe. Perhaps, from a certain angle, that is precisely all that they found—an alternative reading of ego. The Portuguese, having little idea where the Nile ran, at least understood right away that there were men and women darker-skinned than themselves, but they were not specifically knowledgeable, or ingenious, about the various families and groupings represented by them. De Azurara records encounters with "Moors," "Mooresses," "Mulattoes," and people "black as Ethiops" [1:28], but it seems that the "Land of Guinea," or of "Black Men," or of "The Negroes" [1:35] was located anywhere southeast of Cape Verde, the Canaries, and the River Senegal, looking at an eighteenth-century European version of the subsaharan Continent along the West African coast [1:frontispiece].

Three genetic distinctions are available to the Portuguese eye, all along the riffs of melanin in the skin: in a field of captives, some of the observed are "white enough, fair to look upon, and well-proportioned." Others are less "white like mulattoes," and still others "black as Ethiops, and so ugly, both in features and in body, as almost to appear (to those who saw them) the images of a lower hemisphere" [1:28]. By implication, this "third man," standing for the most aberrant phenotype to the observing eye, embodies the linguistic community most unknown to the European. Arabic translators among the Europeans could at least "talk" to the "Moors" and instruct them to ransom themselves, or else. . . .

Typically, there is in this grammar of description the perspective of "declension," not of simultaneity, and its point of initiation is solipistic—it begins with a narrative self, in an apparently unity of feeling, and unlike Equiano, who also saw "ugly" when he looked out, this collective self uncovers the means by which to subjugate the "foreign code of conscience," whose most easily remarkable and irremediable difference is perceived in skin color. By the time of De Azurara's mid-fifteenth century narrative and a century and a half before Shakespeare's "old black ram" of an Othello "tups" that "white ewe" of a Desdemona, the magic of skin color is already installed as a decisive factor in human dealings.

In De Azurara's narrative, we observe males looking at other males, as "female" is subsumed here under the general category of estrangement. Few places in these excerpts carve out a distinct female space, though there are moments of portrayal that perceive female captives in the implications of socio-cultural function. When the field of captives (referred to above) is divided among the spoilers, no heed is paid to relations, as fathers are separated from sons, husbands from wives, brothers from sisters and brothers, mothers from children—male and female. It seems clear that the political program of European Christianity promotes this hierarchical view among *males,* although it remains puzzling to us exactly how this version of Christianity transforms the "pagan" also into the "ugly." It appears that human beings came up with degrees of "fair" and then the "hideous," in its overtones of bestiality, as the opposite of "fair," all by themselves, without stage direction, even though there is the curious and blazing exception of Nietzsche's Socrates, who was Athens's ugliest and wisest and best citizen. The intimate choreography that the Portuguese narrator sets going between the "faithless" and the "ugly" transforms a partnership of dancers into a single figure. Once the "faithless," indiscriminate of the three stops of Portuguese skin color, are transported to Europe, they become an *altered* human factor:

> And so their lot was now quite contrary to what it had been, since before they had lived in perdition of soul and body; of their souls, in that they were yet pagans, without the clearness and the light of the Holy Faith; and of their bodies, in that they lived like beasts, without any custom of reasonable beings—for they, had no knowledge of bread and wine, and they were without covering of clothes, or the lodgment of houses; and worse than all, through the great ignorance that was in them, in that they had no understanding of good, but only knew how to live in bestial sloth. [*1:30*]

The altered human factor renders an alterity of European ego, an invention, or "discovery" as decisive in the full range of its social implications as the birth of a newborn. According to the semantic alignments of the excerpted passage, personhood, for this European observer, locates an immediately outward and superficial determination, gauged by quite arbitrarily opposed and *specular* categories: that these "pagans" did not have "bread" and "wine" did not mean that they were feastless, as Equiano observes about the Benin diet, c. 1745, in the province of Essaka:

> Our manner of living is entirely plain; for as yet the natives are unacquainted with those refinements in cookery which debauch the taste; bullocks, goats, and poultry supply the greatest part of their food. (These constitute likewise the principal wealth of the country, and the chief articles of its commerce.) The flesh is usually stewed in a pan; to make it savory we sometimes use pepper, and other spices, and we have salt made of wood ashes. Our vegetables are mostly plaintains, eadas, yams, beans and Indian corn. The head of the family usually eats alone; his wives and slaves have also their separate tables. . . . [*Equiano 8*]

Just as fufu serves the Ghanaian diet today as a starch-and-bread-substitute, palm wine (an item by the same name in the eighteenth-century palate of the Benin community) need not be Heitz Cellars Martha's Vineyard and vice-versa in order for a guest, say, to imagine that she has enjoyed. That African housing arrangements of the fifteenth century did not resemble those familiar to De Azurara's narrator need not have meant that the African communities he encountered were without dwellings. Again, Equiano's narrative suggests that by the middle of the eighteenth century, at least, African living patterns were not only quite distinct in their sociometrical implications, but that also their architectonics accurately reflected the climate and availability of resources in the local circumstance: "These houses never exceed one story in height; they are always built of wood, or stakes driven into the ground, crossed with wattles, and neatly plastered within and without" [9]. Hierarchical impulse in *both* De Azurara's Equiano's narratives translates all *perceived* difference as a fundamental degradation or transcendence, but at least in Equiano's case, cultural practices are not observed in any intimate connection with skin color. For all intents and purposes, the politics of melanin, not isolated in its strange powers from the imperatives of a mercantile and competitive economics of European nation-states, will make of "transcendence" and "degradation" the basis of a historic violence that will rewrite the histories of modern Europe and black Africa. These mutually exclusive nominative elements come to rest on the same governing semantics—the ahistorical, or symptoms of the "sacred."

By August 1518, the Spanish king, Francisco de Los Covos, under the aegis of a powerful negation, could order "4000 negro slaves both male and female, provided they be

Christians" to be taken to the Caribbean, "the islands and the mainland of the ocean sea already discovered or to be discovered" [Donnan 1:42]. Though the notorious "Middle Passage" appears to the investigator as a vast background without boundaries in time and space, we see it related to Donnan's accounts to the opening up of the entire Western hemisphere for the specific purposes of enslavement and colonization. De Azurara's narrative belongs, then, to a discourse of appropriation whose strategies will prove fatal to communities along the coastline of West Africa, stretching, according to Olaudah Equiano, "3400 miles, from Senegal to Angola, and [will include] a variety of kingdoms" [Equiano 5].

The conditions of "Middle Passage" are among the most incredible narratives available to the student, as it remains not easily imaginable. Late in the chronicles of the Atlantic Slave Trade, Britain's Parliament entertained discussions concerning possible "regulations" for slave vessels. A Captain Perry visited the Liverpool port, and among the ships that he inspected was "The Brookes," probably the most well-known image of the slave galley with its representative *personae* etched into the drawing like so many cartoon figures. Elizabeth Donnan's second volume carries the "Brookes Plan," along with an elaborate delineation of its dimensions from the investigative reporting of Perry himself: "Let it now be supposed . . . further, that every man slave is to be allowed six feet by one foot four inches for room, every woman five feet ten by one foot four, every boy five feet by one foot two, and every girl four feet six by one foot . . ." [2:592, n]. The owner of "The Brookes," James Jones, had recommended that "five females be reckoned as four males, and three boys or girls as equal to two grown persons" [2:592].

These scaled inequalities complement the commanding terms of the dehumanizing, ungendering, and defacing project of African persons that De Azurara's narrator might have recognized. It has been pointed out to me that these measurements do reveal the application of the gender rule to the material conditions of passage, but I would suggest that "gendering" takes place within the confines of the domestic, an essential metaphor that then spreads its tentacles for male and female subject over a wider ground of human and social purposes. Domesticity appears to gain its power by way of a common origin of cultural fictions that are grounded in the specificity of proper names, more exactly, a patronymic, which, in turn, situates those persons it "covers" in a particular place. Contrarily, the cargo of a ship might not be regarded as elements of the domestic, even though the vessel that carries it is sometimes romantically (ironically?) personified as "she." The human cargo of a slave vessel—in the fundamental effacement and remission of African family and proper names—offers a counter-narrative to notions of the domestic.

Those African persons in "Middle Passage" were literally suspended in the "oceanic," if we think of the latter in its Freudian orientation as an analogy for undifferentiated identity: removed from the indigenous land and culture, and not-yet "American" either, these captive persons, without names that their captors would recognize, were in movement across the Atlantic, but they were also *nowhere* at all. Inasmuch as, on any given day, we might imagine, the captive personality did not know where s/he was, we could say that they were the culturally "unmade," thrown in the midst of a figurative darkness that "exposed" their destinies to an unknown course. Often enough for the captains of these galleys, navigational science of the day was not sufficient to guarantee the intended destination. We might say that the slave ship, its crew, and its human-as-cargo stand for a wild and unclaimed richness of *possibility* that is not interrupted, not "counted"/"accounted," or differentiated, until its movement gains the land thousands of miles away from the point of departure. Under these conditions, one is neither female, nor male, as both subjects are taken into "account" as *quantities*. The female in "Middle Passage," as the apparently smaller physical mass, occupies "less room" in a directly translatable money economy. But she is, nevertheless, quantifiable by the same rules of accounting as her male counterpart.

It is not only difficult for the student to find "female" in "Middle Passage," but also, as Herbert S. Klein observes, "African women did not enter the Atlantic slave trade in anything like the numbers of African men. At all ages, men outnumbered women on the slave ships bound for America from Africa" [Klein 29]. Though this observation does not change the reality of African women's captivity and servitude in New World communities, it does provide a perspective from which to contemplate the *internal* African slave trade, which, according to Africanists, remained a predominantly *female* market. Klein nevertheless affirms that those females forced into the trade were segregated "from men for policing purposes" ["African Women" 35]. He claims that both "were allotted the same space between decks . . . and both were fed the same food" [35]. It is not altogether clear from Klein's observations *for whom* the "police" kept vigil. It is certainly known from evidence presented in Donnan's third volume ("New England and the Middle Colonies") that insurrection was both frequent and feared in passage, and we have not yet found a great deal of evidence to support a thesis that female captives participated in insurrectionary activity [see White 63–64]. Because it was the rule, however—not the exception—that the African female, in both indigenous African cultures and in what becomes her "home," performed tasks of hard physical labor—so much so that the quintessential "slave" is *not* a male, but a female—we wonder at the seeming docility of the subject, granting her a "feminization" that enslavement kept at bay. Indeed, across the spate of discourse that I examined for this writing, the acts of enslavement and responses to it comprise a more or less agonistic engagement of confrontational hostilities among males. The visual and historical evidence betrays the dominant discourse on the matter as incomplete, but *counter*-evidence is inadequate as well: the sexual violation of captive females and their own express rage against their oppressors did not constitute events that captains and their crews rushed to record in letters to their sponsoring companies, or sons on board in letters home to their New England mamas.

One suspects that there are several ways to snare a mockingbird, so that insurrection might have involved, from time to time, rather more subtle means than mutiny on the "Felicity," for instance. At any rate, we get very little notion in the written record of the life of women, children, and infants in "Middle Passages," and no idea of the fate of the pregnant female captive and the unborn, which startling thematic Bell Hooks addresses in the opening chapter of her pathfinding work [see Hooks 15–49]. From Hooks's lead, however, we might guess that the "reproduction of mothering" in this historic instance carries few of the benefits of a *patriarchilized* female gender, which, from one point of view, is the *only* female gender there is.

The relative silence of the record on this point constitutes a portion of the disquieting lacunae that feminist investigation seeks to fill. Such silence is the nickname of distortion, of the unknown human factor that a revised public discourse would both undo *and* reveal. This cultural subject is inscribed historically as anonymity/anomie in various public documents of European-American mal(e)venture, from Portuguese De Azurara in the middle of the fifteenth century, to South Carolina's Henry Laurens in the eighteenth.

What confuses and enriches the picture is precisely the sameness of anonymous portrayal that adheres tenaciously across the division of gender. In the vertical columns of accounts and ledgers that comprise Donnan's work, the terms "Negroes" and "Slaves" denote a common status. For instance, entries in one account, from September 1700 through September 1702, are specifically descriptive of the names of ships and the private traders in Barbados who will receive the stipulated goods, but "No. Negroes" and "Sum sold for per head" are so exactly arithmetical that it is as if these additions and multiplications belong to the other side of an equation [Donnan 2:25]. One is struck by the detail and precision that characterize these accounts, as a narrative, or story, is always implied by a man or woman's *name:* "Wm. Webster," "John Dunn," "Thos. Brownbill," "Robt. Knowles." But the "other" side of the page, as it were, equally precise, throws no *face* in view. It seems that nothing breaks the uniformity in this guise. If in no other way, the destruction of the African name, of kin, of linguistic, and ritual connections is so obvious in the vital stats sheet that we tend to overlook it. Quite naturally, the trader is not interested, in any *sematic* sense, in this "baggage" that he must deliver, but that he is not is all the more reason to search out the metaphorical implications of *naming* as one of the key sources of a bitter Americanizing for African persons.

The loss of the indigenous name/land provides a metaphor of displacement for other human and cultural features and relations, including the displacement of the genitalia, the female's and the male's desire that engenders future. The fact that the enslaved persons' access to the use of his/her own body is not entirely clear in this historic period throws in crisis all aspects of the blood relations, as captors apparently felt no obligation to acknowledge them. Actually trying to understand how the confusions of consanguinity worked becomes the project, because the outcome goes far to explain the rule of gender and its application to the African female in captivity.

3

Even though the essays in Claire C. Robertson's and Martin A. Klein's *Women and Slavery in Africa* have specifically to do with aspects of the internal African slave trade, some of their observations shed light on the captivities of the Diaspora. At least these observations have the benefit of altering the kind of questions we might ask of these silent chapters. For example, Robertson's essay, which opens the volume, discusses the term "slavery" in a wide variety of relationships. The enslaved person as *property* identifies the most familiar element of a most startling proposition. But to overlap *kinlessness* on the requirements of property might enlarge our view of the conditions of enslavement. Looking specifically at documents from the West African societies of Songhay and Dahomey, Claude Meillassoux elaborates several features of the property/kinless constellation that are highly suggestive for our own quite different purposes.

Meillassoux argues that "slavery creates an economic and social agent whose virtue lies in being outside the kinship system" ["Female Slavery," Robertson and Klein 50]. Because the Atlantic trade involved heterogeneous social and ethnic formations in an explicit power relationship, we certainly cannot mean "kinship system" in precisely the same way that Meillassoux observes at work within the intricate calculus of descent among West African societies. However, the idea becomes useful as a point of contemplation when we try to sharpen our own sense of the African female's reproductive uses within the diasporic enterprise of enslavement and the genetic reproduction of the enslaved. In effect, under conditions of captivity, the offspring of the female does not "belong" to the Mother, nor is s/he "related" to the "owner," though the latter "possesses" it, and in the African-American instance, often fathered it, *and,* as often, without whatever benefit of patrimony. In the social outline that Meillassoux is pursuing, the offspring of the enslaved, "being unrelated both to their begetters and to their owners . . . . find themselves in the situation of being orphans" [50].

In the context of the United States, we could not say that the enslaved offspring was "orphaned," but the child does become, under the press of a patronymic, patrifocal, patri-lineal, and patriarchal order, the man/woman on the boundary, whose human and familial status, by the very nature of the case, had yet to be defined. I would call this enforced state of breach another instance of vestibular cultural formation where "kinship" loses meaning, *since it can be invaded at any given and arbitrary moment by the property relations.* I certainly do not mean to say that African peoples in the New World did not maintain the powerful ties of sympathy that bind blood-relations in a network of feeling, of continuity. It is pre-cisely that relationship—not customarily recognized by the code of slavery—that histori-ans have long identified as the inviolable "Black Family" and further suggest that this structure remains one of the supreme social achievements of African-Americans under conditions of enslavement [see John Blassingame 79 ff.].

Indeed, the *revised* "Black Family" of enslavement has engendered an older tradition of historiographical and sociological writings than we usually think. Ironically enough, E. Franklin Frazier's *Negro Family in the United States* likely provides the closest *contempo-rary* narrative of conceptualization for the "Moynihan Report." Originally published in 1939, Frazier's work underwent two redactions in 1948 and 1966. Even though Frazier's outlook on this familial configuration remains basically sanguine, I would support Angela Davis's skeptical reading of Frazier's "Black Matriarchate" [Davis 14]. *"Except where the master's will was concerned,"* Frazier contends, this matriarchal figure "developed a spirit of independence and a keen sense of her personal rights" [1966: 47; emphasis mine]. The "exception" in this instance tends to be overwhelming, as the African-American female's "dominance" and "strength" come to be interpreted by later generations—both black and white, oddly enough—as a "pathology," as an instrument of castration. Frazier's larger point, we might suppose, is that African-Americans developed such resourcefulness under conditions of captivity that "family" must be conceded as one of their redoubtable social attainments. This line of interpretation is pursued by Blassingame and Eugene Genovese [*Roll, Jordan, Roll* 70–75], among other U.S. historians, and indeed assumes a centrality of focus in our own thinking about the impact and outcome of captivity.

It seems clear, however, that "Family," as we practice and understand it "in the West"—the *vertical* transfer of a bloodline, of a patronymic, of titles and entitlements, of real estate and the prerogatives of "cold cash," from *fathers* to *sons* and in the supposedly free exchange of affectional ties between a male and a female of *his* choice—becomes the mythically revered privilege of a free and freed community. In that sense, African peoples in the historic Diaspora had nothing to prove, *if* the point had been that they were not ca-pable of "family" (read "civilization"), since it is stunningly evident, in Equiano's narra-tive, for instance, that Africans were not only capable of the concept and the practice of "family," including "slaves," but in modes of elaboration and naming that were at least as complex as those of the "nuclear family" "in the West."

Whether or not we decide that the support systems that African-Americans derived under conditions of captivity should be called "family," or something else, strikes me as supremely impertinent. The point remains that captive persons were *forced* into patterns of *dispersal,* beginning with the Trade itself, into the *horizontal* relatedness of language groups, discourse formations, bloodlines, names, and properties by the legal arrangements of enslavement. It is true that the most "well-meaning" of "masters" (and there must have been some) *could not, did not* alter the *ideological* and hegemonic mandates of dominance. It must be conceded that African-Americans, under the press of a hostile and compulsory patriarchal order, bound and determined to destroy them, or to preserve them only in the service and at the behest of the "master" class, exercised a degree of courage and will to survive that startles the imagination even now. Although it makes good revisionist history to read this tale *liberally,* it is probably truer than we know at this distance (and truer than contemporary social practice in the community would suggest on occasion) that the captive person developed, time and again, certain ethical and sentimental features that tied her and him, *across* the landscape to others, often sold from hand to hand, of the same and different blood in a common fabric of memory and inspiration.

We might choose to call this connectedness "family," or "support structure," but that is a rather different case from the moves of a dominant symbolic order, pledged to maintain the supremacy of race. It is that order that forces "family" to modify itself when it does not mean family of the "master," or dominant enclave. It is this rhetorical and symbolic move that declares primacy over any other human and social claim, and in that political order of things, "kin," just as gender formation, has no decisive legal or social efficacy.

We return frequently to Frederick Douglass's careful elaborations of the arrangements of captivity, and we are astonished each reading by two dispersed, yet poignantly related, familial enactments that suggest a connection between "kinship" and "property." Douglass tells us early in the opening chapter of the 1843 *Narrative* that he was separated in infancy from his mother: "For what this separation is [sic] done, I do not know, unless it be to hinder the development of the child's affection toward its mother, and to blunt and destroy the natural affection of the mother for the child. This is the inevitable result" [22].

Perhaps one of the assertions that Meillassoux advances concerning indigenous African formations of enslavement might be turned as a question, against the perspective of Douglass's witness: is the genetic reproduction of the slave and the recognition of the rights of the slave to his or her offspring a check on the *profitability* of slavery? And how so, if so? We see vaguely the route to framing a response, especially to the question's second half and perhaps to the first: the enslaved must not be permitted to perceive that he or she has any human rights that matter. Certainly if "kinship" were possible, the property relations would be undermined, since the offspring would then "belong" to a mother and a father. In the system that Douglass articulates, genetic reproduction becomes, then, not an elaboration of the life-principle in its cultural overlap, but an extension of the boundaries of proliferating properties. Meillassoux goes so far as to argue that "slavery exists where the slave class is reproduced through institutional apparatus: war and market" [50]. Since, in the United States, the market of slavery identified the chief institutional means for maintaining a class of enforced servile labor, it seems that the biological reproduction of the enslaved was not alone sufficient to reinforce the estate of slavery. If, as Meillassoux contends, "feminity loses its sacredness in slavery" [64], then so does "motherhood" as female blood-rite/right. To that extent, the captive female body locates precisely a moment of converging political and social vectors that mark the flesh as a prime commodity of exchange. While this proposition is open to further exploration, suffice it to say now that this open exchange of female bodies in the raw offers a kind of Ur-text to the dynamics of signification and representation that the gendered female would unravel.

For Douglass, the loss of his mother eventuates in alienation from his brother and sisters, who live in the same house with him: "The early separation of us from our mother had well nigh blotted the fact of our relationship from our memories" [45]. What could this mean? The *physical* proximity of the siblings survives the mother's death. They grasp their connection in the physical sense, but Douglass appears to mean a *psychological* bonding whose success mandates the *mother's* presence. Could we say, then, that the feeling of kinship is *not* inevitable? That it describes a relationship that appears "natural," but must be "cultivated" under actual material conditions? If the child's humanity is mirrored initially in the eyes of its mother, or the maternal function, then we might be able to guess that the social subject grasps the whole dynamic or resemblance and kinship by way of the same source.

There is an amazing thematic synonymity on this point between aspects of Douglass's *Narrative* and Malcolm El-Hajj Malik El Shabazz's *Autobiography of Malcolm X* [21 ff.]. Through the loss of the mother, in the latter contemporary instance, to the institution of "insanity" and the state—a full century after Douglass's writing and under social conditions that might be designated a post-emancipation neo-enslavement—Malcolm and his siblings, robbed of their activist father in a kkk-like ambush, are not only widely dispersed across a makeshift social terrain, but also show symptoms of estrangement and "disremembering" that require many years to heal, and even then, only by way of Malcolm's prison ordeal turned, eventually, into a redemptive occurrence.

The destructive loss of the natural mother, whose biological/genetic relationship to the child remains unique and unambiguous, opens the enslaved young to social ambiguity and chaos: the ambiguity of his/her fatherhood and to a structure of other relational elements, now threatened, that would declare the young's connection to a genetic and historic future by way of their own siblings. That the father in Douglass's case was most likely the "master," not by any means special to Douglass, involves a hideous paradox. Fatherhood, at best a supreme cultural courtesy, attenuates here on the one hand into a monstrous accumulation of power on the other. One has been "made" and "bought" by disparate currencies, linking back to a common origin of exchange and domination. The denied genetic link becomes the chief strategy of an undenied ownership, as if the interrogation into the father's identity—the blank space where his proper name will fit—were answered by the fact, *de jure* of a material possession. "And this is done," Douglass asserts, "too obviously to administer to the [masters] own lusts, and make a gratification of their wicked desires profitable as well as pleasurable" [23].

Whether or not the captive female and/or her sexual oppressor derived "pleasure" from their seductions and couplings is not a question we can politely ask. Whether or not "pleasure" is possible at all under conditions that I would aver as non-freedom for both or either of the parties has not been settled. Indeed, we could go so far as to entertain the very real possibility that "sexuality," as a term of implied relationship and desire, is dubiously appropriate, manageable, or accurate to *any* of the familial arrangements under a system of enslavement, from the master's family to the captive enclave. Under these arrangements, the customary lexis of sexuality, including "reproduction," "motherhood," "pleasure," and "desire" are thrown into unrelieved crisis.

If the testimony of Linda Brent/Harriet Jacobs is to be believed, the official mistresses of slavery's "masters" constitute a privileged class of the tormented, if such contradiction can be entertained [Brent 29–35]. Linda Brent/Harriet Jacobs recounts in the course of her narrative scenes from a "psychodrama," opposing herself and "Mrs. Flint," in what we have come to consider the classic alignment between captive woman and free. Suspecting that her husband, Dr. Flint, has sexual designs on the young Linda (and the doctor is nearly humorously incompetent at it, according to the story line), Mrs. Flint assumes the role of a perambulatory nightmare who visits the captive woman in the spirit of a veiled seduction. Mrs. Flint imitates the incubus who "rides" its victim in order to exact confession, expiation, and anything else that the immaterial power might want. [Gayle Jones's *Corregidora* [1975] weaves a contemporary fictional situation around the historic motif of entangled female sexualities.) This narrative scene from Brent's work, dictated to Lydia Maria Child, provides an instance of a repeated sequence, purportedly based on "real" life. But the scene in question appears to so commingle its signals with the fictive, with casebook narratives from psychoanalysis, that we are certain that the narrator has her hands on an explosive moment of New-World/U.S. history that feminist investigation is beginning to unravel. The narrator recalls:

> Sometimes I woke up, and found her bending over me. At other times she whispered in my ear, as though it were her husband who was speaking to me, and listened to hear what I would answer. If she startled me, on such occasion, she would glide stealthily away; and the next morning she would tell me I had been talking in my sleep, and ask who I was talking to. At last, I began to be fearful for my life. . . . [Brent 33]

The "jealous mistress" here (but "jealous" for whom?) forms an analogy with the "master" to the extent that male dominative modes give the male the material means to fully act out what the female might only *wish*. The mistress in the case of Brent's narrative becomes a metaphor for his madness that arises in the ecstasy of unchecked power. Mrs. Flint enacts a male alibi and prosthetic motion that is mobilized at *night,* at the material place of the dream work. In both male and female instances, the subject attempts to *inculcate* his or her will into the vulnerable, supine body. Though this is barely hinted on the surface of the text, we might say that Brent, between the lines of her narrative, demarcates a sexuality that is neuter-bound, inasmuch as it represents an open vulnerability to a gigantic sexualized repertoire that may be alternately expressed as male/female. Since the gendered female *exists* for the male, we might suggest that the ungendered female—in an amazing stroke of pansexual potential—might be invaded/raided by another *woman* or man.

If *Incidents in the Life of a Slave Girl* were a novel, and not the memoirs of an escaped female captive, then we might say that "Mrs. Flint" is also the narrator's projection, her creation, so that for all her pious and correct umbrage toward the outrage of her captivity, some aspect of Linda Brent is released in a manifold repetition crisis that the doctor's wife comes to stand in for. In the case of both an imagined fiction and the narrative we have from Brent/Jacobs/Child, published only four years before the official proclamations of Freedom, we could say that African-American women's community and Anglo-American women's community, under certain shared cultural conditions, were the twin actants on a common psychic landscape, were subject to the same fabric of dread and humiliation. Neither could claim her body and its various productions—for quite different reasons, albeit—as her own, and in the case of the doctor's wife, *she* appears not to have wanted *her* body at all, but to desire to enter someone else's, specifically, Linda Brent's, in an apparently classic instance of sexual "jealousy" and appropriation. In fact, from one point of view, we cannot unravel one female's narrative from the other's, cannot decipher one without tripping over the other. In that sense, these "threads cable-strong" of an incestuous, interracial genealogy uncover slavery in the United States as one of the richest displays of the psychoanalytic dimensions of culture before the science of European psychoanalysis takes hold.

4

But just as we duly regard similarities between life conditions of American women—captive and free—we must observe those undeniable contrasts and differences so decisive that the African-American female's historic claim to the territory of womanhood and "femininity" still tends to rest too solidly on the subtle and shifting calibrations of a liberal ideology. Valerie Smith's reading of the tale of Linda Brent as a tale of "garreting" enables our notion that female gender for captive women's community is the tale writ between the lines and in the not-quite spaces of an American domesticity. It is this tale that we try to make clearer, or, keeping with the metaphor, "bring on line."

If the point is that the historic conditions of African-American women might be read as an unprecedented occasion in the national context, then gender and the arrangements of gender are both crucial and evasive. Holding, however, to a specialized reading of female gender as an *outcome* of a certain political, socio-cultural empowerment within the context of the United States, we would regard dispossession as the *loss* of gender, or one of the chief elements in an altered reading of gender: "Women are considered of no value, *unless* they continually increase their owner's stock. They were put on par with animals" [Brent 49; emphasis mine]. Linda Brent's witness appears to contradict the point I would make, but I am suggesting that even though the enslaved female reproduced other enslaved persons, we do not read "birth" in this instance as a reproduction of mothering precisely because the female, like the male, has been robbed of the parental right, the parental function. One treads dangerous ground in suggesting an equation between female gender and mothering; in fact, feminist inquiry/praxis and the actual day-to-day living of numberless American women—black and white—have gone far to break the enthrallment of a female subject-position to the theoretical and actual situation of maternity. Our task here would be lightened considerably if we could simply slide over the powerful "No," the significant *exception*. In the historic formation to which I point, however, motherhood and female gendering/ungendering appear so intimately aligned that they *seem* to speak the same language. At least it is plausible to say that motherhood, while it does not exhaust the problematics of female gender, offers one prominent line of approach to it. I would go farther: Because African-American women experienced uncertainty regarding their infants' lives in the historic situation, gendering, in its coeval reference to African-American women, *insinuates* an implicit and unresolved puzzle both within current feminist discourse *and* within those discursive communities that investigate the entire problematics of culture. Are we mistaken to suspect that history—at least in this instance—repeats itself yet again?

Every feature of social and human differentiation disappears in public discourses regarding the African-American person, as we encounter, in the juridical codes of slavery, personality reified. William Goodell's study not only demonstrates the rhetorical and moral passions of the abolitionist project, but also lends insight into the corpus of law that underwrites enslavement. If "slave" is perceived as the essence of stillness (an early version of "ethnicity"), or of an undynamic human state, fixed in time and space, then the law articulates this impossibility as its inherent feature: "Slaves shall be deemed, sold, taken, reputed and adjudged in law to be *chattels personal,* in the hands of their owners and possessors, and their executors, administrators, and assigns, to all intents, constructions, and purposes whatsoever" [23; Goodell emphasis].

Even though we tend to parody and simplify matters to behave as if the various civil codes of the slave-holding United States were monolithically informed, unified, and executed in their application, or that the "code" itself is spontaneously generated in an undivided historic moment, we read it nevertheless as exactly this—the *peak points,* the salient and characteristic features of a human and social procedure that evolves over a natural historical sequence and represents, consequently, the narrative *shorthand* of a transaction that is riddled, *in practice,* with contradictions, accident, and surprise. We could suppose that the legal encodations of enslavement stand for the statistically average case, that the legal code provides the *topics* of a project increasingly threatened and self-conscious. It is, perhaps, not by chance that the laws regarding slavery appear to crystallize in the precise moment when agitation against the arrangement becomes articulate in certain European and

New-World communities. In that regard, the slave codes that Goodell describes are themselves an instance of the counter and isolated text that seeks to silence the contradictions and antitheses engendered by it. For example, aspects of Article 461 of the South Carolina Civil Code call attention to just the sort of uneasy oxymoronic character that the "peculiar institution" attempts to sustain in transforming *personality* into *property.*

1. The "slave" is movable by nature, but "immovable by the operation of law" [Goodell 24]. As I read this, law itself is compelled to a point of saturation, or a reverse zero degree, beyond which it cannot move in the behalf of the enslaved or the free. We recall, too, that the "master," under these perversions of judicial power, is impelled to treat the enslaved as property, and not as person. These laws stand for the kind of social formulation that armed forces will help excise from a living context in the campaigns of civil war. They also embody the untenable human relationship that Henry David Thoreau believed occasioned acts of "civil disobedience," the moral philosophy to which Martin Luther King, Jr. would subscribe in the latter half of the twentieth century.

2. Slaves shall be *reputed* and *considered* real estate, "subject to be mortgaged, according to the rules prescribed by law" [Goodell 24]. I emphasize "reputed" and "considered" as predicate adjectives that invite attention because they denote a *contrivance,* not an intransitive "is," or the transfer of nominative property from one syntactic point to another by way of a weakened copulative. The status of the "reputed" can change, as it will significantly before the nineteenth century closes. The mood here—the "shall be"—is pointedly subjunctive, or the situation devoutly to be wished. The slave-holding class is forced, in time, to think and do something else is the narrative of violence that enslavement itself has been preparing for a couple of centuries.

Louisiana's and South Carolina's written codes offer a paradigm for praxis in those instances where a *written* text is missing. In that case, the "chattel principle has . . . been affirmed and maintained by the courts, and involved in legislative acts" [Goodell 25]. In Maryland, a legislative enactment of 1798 shows so forceful a synonymity of motives between branches of comparable governance that a line between "judicial" and "legislative" functions is useless to draw: "In case the personal property of a ward shall consist of specific articles, such as slaves, working beasts, animals of any kind, stock, furniture, plates, books, and so forth, the Court if it shall deem it advantageous to the ward, may at any time, pass an order for the sale thereof" [56]. This inanimate and corporate ownership— the voting district of a ward—is here spoken for, or might be, as a single slave-holding male in determinations concerning property.

The eye pauses, however, not so much at the provisions of this enactment as at the details of its delineation. Everywhere in the descriptive document, we are stunned by the simultaneity of disparate items in a grammatical series: "Slave" appears in the same context with beasts of burden, *all* and *any* animal(s), various livestock, and a virtually endless profusion of domestic content from the culinary item to the book. Unlike the taxonomy of Borges's "Certain Chinese encyclopedia," whose contemplation opens Foucault's *Order of Things,* these items from a certain American encyclopedia do not sustain discrete and localized "powers of contagion," nor has the ground of their concatenation been desiccated beneath them. That imposed uniformity comprises the shock, that somehow this mix of named things, live and inanimate, collapsed by contiguity to the same text of "realism," carries a disturbingly prominent item of misplacement. To that extent, the project of liberation for African-Americans has found urgency in two passionate motivations that are twinned—1) to break apart, to rupture violently the laws of American behavior that make such *syntax* possible; 2) to introduce a new semantic field/fold more appropriate to his/her

own historic movement. I regard this twin compulsion as distinct, though related, moments of the very same narrative process that might appear as a concentration or a dispersal. The narratives of Linda Brent, Frederick Douglass, and Malcolm El-Hajj Malik El-
Shabazz (aspects of which are examined in this essay) each represent both narrative
ambitions as they occur under the auspices of "author."

Relatedly, we might interpret the whole career of African-Americans, a decisive factor
in national political life since the mid-seventeenth century, in light of the *intervening, in-
truding* tale, or the tale—like Brent's "garret" space—"between the lines," which are already inscribed, as a *metaphor* of social and cultural management. According to this reading, gender, or sex-role assignation, or the clear differentiation of sexual stuff, sustained
elsewhere in the culture, does not emerge for the African-American female in this historic
instance, except indirectly, except as a way to reenforce through the process of birthing,
"the reproduction of the relations of production" that involves "the reproduction of the
values and behavior patterns necessary to maintain" the system of hierarchy in its various
aspects of gender, class, and race or ethnicity" [Margaret Strobel, "Slavery and Reproductive Labor in Mombasa," Robertson and Klein 121]. Following Strobel's lead, I would
suggest that the foregoing identifies one of the three categories of reproductive labor that
African-American females carry out under the regime of captivity. But this replication of
ideology is never simple in the case of female subject-positions, and it appears to acquire a
thickened layer of motives in the case of African-American females.

If we can account for an originary narrative and judicial principle that might have engendered a "Moynihan Report," many years into the twentieth century, we cannot do
much better than look at Goodell's reading of the *partus sequitur ventrem:* the condition of
the slave mother is "forever entailed on all her remotest posterity." This maxim of civil
law, in Goodell's view, the "genuine and degrading principle of slavery, inasmuch as it
places the slave upon a level with brute animals, prevails universally in the slave-holding
states" [Goodell 27]. But what is the "condition" of the mother? Is it the "condition" of
enslavement the writer means, or does he mean the "mark" and the "knowledge" of the
mother upon the child that here translates into the culturally forbidden and impure? In an
elision of terms, "mother" and "enslavement" are indistinct categories of the illegitimate
inasmuch as each of these synonymous elements defines, in effect, a cultural situation that
is *father-lacking.* Goodell, who does not only report this maxim of law as an aspect of his
own factuality, but also regards it, as does Douglass, as a fundamental degradation, supposes descent and identity through the female line as comparable to a brute animality.
Knowing already that there are human communities that align social reproductive procedure according to the line of the mother, and Goodell himself might have known it some
years later, we can only conclude that the provisions of patriarchy, here exacerbated by the
preponderant powers of an enslaving class, declare Mother Right, by definition, a negating feature of human community.

Even though we are not even talking about *any* of the matriarchal features of social pro-
duction/reproduction—matrifocality, matrilinearity, matriarchy—when we speak of the
enslaved person, we perceive that the dominant culture, in a fatal misunderstanding, assigns a matriarchist value where it does not belong; actually *misnames* the power of the female regarding the enslaved community. Such naming is false because the female could
not, in fact, claim her child, and false, once again, because "motherhood" is not perceived
in the prevailing social climate as a legitimate procedure of cultural inheritance.

The African-American male has been touched, therefore, by the *mother, handed* by her
in ways that he cannot escape, and in ways that the white American male is allowed to
temporize by a fatherly reprieve. This human and historic development—the text that has

been inscribed on the benighted heart of the continent—takes us to the center of an inexorable difference in the depths of American women's community: the African-American woman, the mother, the daughter, becomes historically the powerful and shadowy evocation of a cultural synthesis long evaporated—the law of the Mother—only and precisely because legal enslavement removed the African-American male not so much from sight as from *mimetic* view as a partner in the prevailing social fiction of the Father's name, the Father's law.

Therefore, the female, in this order of things, breaks in upon the imagination with a forcefulness that marks both a denial and an "illegitimacy." Because of this peculiar American denial, the black American male embodies the *only* American community of males which has had the specific occasion to learn *who* the female is within itself, the infant child who bears the life against the could-be fateful gamble, against the odds of pulverization and murder, including her own. It is the heritage of the *mother* that the African-American male must regain as an aspect of his own personhood—the power of "yes" to the "female" within.

This different cultural text actually reconfigures, in historically ordained discourse, certain *representational* potentialities for African-Americans: 1) motherhood as female bloodrite is outraged, is denied, at the *very same time* that it becomes the founding term of a human and social enactment; 2) a dual fatherhood is set in motion, comprised of the African father's *banished* name and body and the captor father's mocking presence. In this play of paradox, only the female stands *in the flesh*, both mother and mother-dispossessed. This problematizing of gender places her, in my view, *out* of the traditional symbolics of female gender, and it is our task to make a place for this different social subject. In doing so, we are less interested in joining the ranks of gendered femaleness than gaining the *insurgent* ground as female social subject. Actually *claiming* the monstrosity (of a female with the potential to "name"), which her culture imposes in blindness, "Sapphire" might rewrite after all a radically different text for a female empowerment.

WORKS CITED

Barthes, Roland. *Mythologies*. Trans. Annette Lavers. New York: Hill and Wang, 1972.

Blassingame, John. *The Slave Community: Plantation Life in the Antebellum South*. New York: Oxford UP, 1972.

Brent, Linda. *Incidents in the Life of a Slave Girl*. Ed. L. Maria Child. Introduced by Walter Teller. Rpt. New York: Harvest/HBJ Book, 1973.

Davis, Angela Y. *Women, Race, and Class*. New York: Random House, 1981.

De Azurara, Gomes Eannes. *The Chronicle of the Discovery and Conquest of Guinea*. Trans. C. Raymond Beazley and Edgar Prestage. London: Hakluyt Society, 1896, 1897, in Elizabeth Donnan, *Documents Illustrative of the History of the Slave Trade to America*. Washington, D.C.: Carnegie Institution of Washington, 1932, 1:18–41.

Donnan, Elizabeth. *Documents Illustrative of the History of the Slave Trade to America;* 4 vols. Washington, D.C.: The Carnegie Institution of Washington, 1932.

Douglass, Frederick. *Narrative of the Life of Frederick Douglass An American Slave, Written by Himself*. Rpt. New York: Signet Books, 1968.

El-Shabazz, Malcolm El-Hajj Malik. *Autobiography of Malcolm X*. With Alex Haley. Introduced by M. S. Handler. New York: Grove Press, 1966.

Equiano, Olaudah. "The Life of Olaudah Equiano, or Gustavus Vassa, The African, Written by Himself," in *Great Slave Narratives*. Introduced and selected by Arna Bontemps. Boston: Beacon Press, 1969. 1–192.

Faulkner, William. *The Mansion*. New York: Vintage Books, 1965.

Frazier, E. Franklin. *The Negro Family in the United States*. Rev. with foreword by Nathan Glazer. Chicago: The U of Chicago P, 1966.

Genovese, Eugene. *Roll, Jordan, Roll: The World the Slaves Made*. New York: Pantheon Books, 1974.

Goodell, William. *The American Slave Code in Theory and Practice Shown By Its Statutes, Judicial Decisions, and Illustrative Facts;* 3rd ed. New York: American and Foreign Anti-Slavery Society, 1853.

Hooks, Bell. *Ain't I a Woman: Black Women and Feminism*. Boston: South End Press, 1981.

Klein, Herbert S. "African Women in the Atlantic Slave Trade." Robertson and Klein 29–39.

Meillassoux, Claude. "Female Slavery." Robertson and Klein 49–67.

Moynihan, Daniel P. "The Moynihan Report" [*The Negro Family: The Case for National Action*. Washington, D.C.: U.S. Department of Labor, 1965]. *The Moynihan Report and the Politics of Controversy: A Transaction Social Science and Public Policy Report*. Ed. Lee Rainwater and William L. Yancy. Cambridge: MIT Press, 1967. 47–94.

Robertson, Claire C., and Martin A. Klein, eds. *Women and Slavery in Africa*. Madison: U of Wisconsin P, 1983.

Scarry, Elaine. *The Body in Pain: The Making and Unmaking of the World*. New York: Oxford UP, 1985.

Smith, Valerie. "Loopholes of Retreat: Architecture and Ideology in Harriet Jacobs' *Incidents in the Life of a Slave Girl*." Paper presented at the 1985 American Studies Association Meeting, San Diego. Cited in Henry Louis Gates, Jr. "What's Love Got to Do With It?" *New Literary History* 18.2 (Winter 1987): 360.

Strobel, Margaret. "Slavery and Reproductive Labor in Mombasa." Robertson and Klein 111–30.

Suleiman, Susan Rubin, ed. *The Female Body in Western Culture*. Cambridge: Harvard UP, 1986.

Rodorov, Tzvetan. *The Conquest of America: The Question of the Other*. Trans. Richard Howard. New York: Harper Colophon Books, 1984.

White, Deborah Grey. *Ar'n't I A Woman? Female Slaves in the Plantation South*. New York: Norton, 1985.

Sacvan Bercovitch

Hawthorne's A-Morality of Compromise

Midway through the novel, in the course of a subtle and devastating critique of Hester's radicalism, Hawthorne remarks that "the scarlet letter had not done its office."[1] Hester still has to learn the folly of her wild "freedom of speculation" (259)—has yet to recognize that her love requires, more than a consecration of its own, the consecration of history and community. When in the Conclusion she returns to New England, Hester reveals what has been implicit all along, that the office of the A is socialization. She neither reaffirms her adulterous love nor disavows it; or rather, she does both by incorporating it into the vision of an age of love to come. It is an act of compromise—bridging memory and hope; self and society; nature and institutions; past, present, and future—that reconciles the novel's various antinomies:

"Hawthorne's A-Morality of Compromise" by Sacvan Berkovitch. Copyright 1988. Originally appeared in *Representations* 24, pp. 1–27. Reprinted by permission of the author.

Women, more especially . . . came to Hester's cottage, demanding why they were so wretched, and what the remedy! Hester comforted and counseled them, as best she might. She assured them, too, of her firm belief, that, at some brighter period, when the world should have grown ripe for it, in Heaven's own time, a new truth would be revealed, in order to establish the whole relation between man and women on a surer ground of mutual happiness. Earlier in life, Hester had vainly imagined that she herself might be the destined prophetess, but had long since recognized the impossibility that any mission of divine and mysterious truth should be confided to a woman stained with sin, bowed down with shame, or even burdened with a life-long sorrow. The angel and apostle of the coming revelation must be a woman, indeed, but lofty, pure, and beautiful; and wise, moreover, not through dusky grief, but the ethereal medium of joy. (344–45)

The entire novel tends toward this moment of reconciliation, but the basis for reconciliation, the source of Hester's re-vision, remains entirely unexplained. The problem is not that she returns, which Hawthorne does account for, in his way ("There was a more real life for Hester Prynne, here, in New England"; 344). Nor is it that she resumes the A; we might anticipate that return to beginnings, by the principles of narrative closure. What remains problematic, what Hawthorne compels us to explain for ourselves (as well as on Hester's behalf), is her dramatic change of purpose and belief. Throughout her "seven years of outlaw and ignominy," Hester had considered her A a "scorching stigma" and herself "the people's victim and life-long bond-slave" (331, 291, 313–14). Now she takes up the letter—"of her own free will, for not the sternest magistrate of that iron period would have imposed it" (344)—and reconstitutes herself a counselor of patience and faith. This is not some formulaic Victorian ending. We accept it as inevitable, as readers did from the start, because Hawthorne has prepared us for it. All his strategies of ambiguity and irony *require* Hester's conversion to the letter. And since the magistrates themselves do not impose the A; since the community has long since come to regard Hester as an "angel or apostle" in her own right; since, moreover, we never learn the process of her conversion to the A (while her development through the novel tends in exactly the opposite direction); since, in short, neither author nor characters help us, we must meet the requirement ourselves.

"The scarlet letter had not done its office," and when it has, Hester is transformed unaccountedly into an agent of social cohesion and continuity. Much the same might be said, earlier, about Dimmesdale's metamorphosis, from secret rebel into prophet of New Israel. Hawthorne specifies the state of despair in which the minister agrees to leave, details the disordered fantasies that follow, and yet leaves it to us to explain his change of mind and heart. In this case, however, the explanation is inherent in the Puritan vision. "The minister," Hawthorne tells us, "had never gone through an experience calculated to lead him beyond the scope of generally received laws; although, in a single instance, he had so fearfully transgressed one of the most sacred of them. But this had been a sin of passion, not of principle, nor even purpose" (290). When, accordingly, he resolves to flee with Hester, he does so only because he believes he is "irrevocably doomed" (291), and we infer upon his return that he has made peace at last with the familiar Puritan paradox, has finally come to terms with the ambiguities of mercy and justice he had forgotten in the forest. The reasons for Hester's reversal are far more complex. It takes the whole story to work them through. It is the office of *The Scarlet Letter* to teach us why this tragic-romantic heroine, who had made being compromised a source of uncompromising resistance, *must* now make compromise the work of culture. In an earlier essay, I discussed that cultural work in terms of Hawthorne's aesthetic techniques.[2] In this essay, I turn the text inside out, as it were, in order to focus directly on ideological context. My purpose is to explain our complicity in Hester's return by exploring the historical ground and substance of her heroism of compromise.

The most direct connection between text and context is the community to which Hester returns. I refer to the Puritan myth endorsed by mid-nineteenth-century America. For like the letter they impose, Hawthorne's settlers are a cultural artifact—a very sophisticated one, to be sure, and cunningly embroidered with his personal concerns, broad learning, and elaborate ironies, but woven nonetheless out of the same cultural cloth that produced the legend of the Puritan "founders" (158). It is no accident that Dimmesdale's sermon on the future marks the transition of government from John Winthrop to John Endicott. The unspoken link between the two governors is nothing less than the national tradition that connects Hester to Hawthorne. It represents what by 1850 was the widely celebrated continuity from the New England Way to the American Way—from Winthrop, the *ur*-father, to Endicott, the *ur*-patriot, whose rending of "the Red Cross from New England's banner" (Hawthorne writes elsewhere) was "the first omen of that deliverance which our fathers consummated" in 1776.[3]

These mythic Puritans have had a long life in the national consciousness.[4] At mid century they served above all to provide a crucial contrast between Puritanism in Old and New England. According to general belief, one that was shared by Whigs and Democrats alike—by New York's cultural pundit, Evert Duyckinck (a founder of the Young America Movement and Hawthorne's major advocate in the literary world); by Henry Wadsworth Longfellow (Hawthorne's life-long friend and his first important reviewer); by the epic historian of the era, George Bancroft (who helped Hawthorne secure his appointment as surveyor at the Salem Customs House); and by the manifest destinarian John Louis O'Sullivan (Hawthorne's publisher and godfather to his first child, Una)—there were two Puritan revolutions in the early 1600's. One was the Puritan exodus to the New World. It was a revolution for liberty that offered a model of progress by harnessing the energies of radicalism to the process of settlement, expansion, and consolidation. The Old World counterpart was the Puritan revolution (1642–49) that failed—a revolution prefigured (in Hawthorne's view) by the "mobocracies" of the past, and itself a prefiguration of the failed continental upheavals of the next two centuries, including those perpetrated by "the terrorists of France" of 1789, 1830, and 1848 (165).

Hawthorne suggests the reasons for failure in an essay on Cromwell. When Oliver was a child, he writes, a "huge ape, which was kept in the family, snatched up little Noll in his fore-paws, and clambered with him to the roof of the house. . . . The event was afterwards considered an omen that Noll would reach a very elevated station in the world."[5] It is a parable for the embittered young radical whose clambering "enthusiasm of thought" (260) Hawthorne details midway through *The Scarlet Letter* (shortly after his reference to the "terrorists of France"):

> [This] was an age in which the human intellect, newly emancipated, had taken a more active and a wider range than for many centuries before. Men of the sword had overthrown nobles and kings. Men bolder than these had overthrown and rearranged—not actually, but within the sphere of theory, which was their most real abode—the whole system of ancient prejudice, wherewith was linked much of ancient principle. Hester Prynne imbibed this spirit. She assumed a freedom of speculation, then common enough on the other side of the Atlantic, but which our forefathers, had they known of it, would have held to be a deadlier crime than that stigmatised by the scarlet letter. In her lonesome cottage by the sea-shore, thoughts visited her, such as dared to enter no other dwelling in New England; shadowy guests . . . perilous as demons. (259).

The key word is *forefathers*. It carries the entire force of the ideological contrast I mentioned, between upheaval in the Old World and progress in the New. And it applies as such directly to what Hawthorne recalled in 1852 as the era of "The Compromise."[6] His return to Puritan New England in *The Scarlet Letter* joins two historical time frames: first, the fictional time frame, 1642–49, with its implied contrast between Cromwell's revolt and the American Puritan venture in "Utopia" (158); and second, the authorial time frame, 1848–52, with its ominous explosion of conflict at home and abroad.[7]

The "red year Forty-Eight," as Melville termed it, brought "the portent and the fact of war,/And terror that into hate subsides." He was referring to the series of revolutions from which Europe's kings "fled like the gods" (although by 1852 "even as the gods/ . . . return they made; and sate/And fortified their strong abodes"). But he might have been referring as well to what New England conservatives considered an ominous tendency toward confrontation following the victory of the Whigs. Polk's presidency, 1844–48, was a highpoint of Jacksonian chauvinism: Mexico had been defeated; the Oregon Territory appropriated (along with Nevada, New Mexico, Colorado, and parts of Utah); gold discovered in California; and Florida, Texas, Iowa, and Wisconsin admitted to the Union. Then in 1848 the unexpected defeat of Young Hickory called attention to long-festering internal divisions. We can see in retrospect how both tendencies, toward expansion and toward conflict, expressed the same process of ideological consolidation. But for a good many of the disempowered Democrats the tendency toward conflict evoked what newspapers called the "terrors of a European conflagration." It is no accident that Hawthorne connected the revolutions abroad with his loss of tenure at the Salem Customs House. As recent scholarship has demonstrated, he links both sets of events in the alternative title he offers for the novel, "The Posthumous Papers of a Decapitated Surveyor" (156), and the political innuendos here are expanded throughout "The Custom-House" introduction and the novel at large in recurrent imagery of the 1848–49 revolutions, including allusions to scaffold and guillotine.[8]

Eighteen-forty-eight, then, opens the novel's authorial time frame. Historians have called it the Year of the Red Scare: Chartist agitation in England, the First Paris Commune, *The Communist Manifesto,* and widespread revolt in Belgium, Germany, Poland, Austria, Italy, Czechoslovakia, Hungary. After a brief period of euphoria—when it seemed events were proving that "our country leads the world"—public opinion turned decisively against the radicals. Those who did the turning expressed disillusionment in many ways, but common to all was the contrast between Europe's class warfare and the war for American independence. By Fall 1848, Evert Duyckinck reported that New Yorkers associated the "agitation" with "recollections of Robespierre"; shortly after, George Bancroft wrote that it had Boston "frightened out of its wits"; in Paris, Emerson wondered whether the revolution was worth the trees it had cost to build the barricades; by early 1849 American conservatives concluded that "republics cannot grow on the soil of Europe." Worse still, they had already observed the incipient effect in America itself of European conflict—"Communism, Socialism, Pillage, Murder, Anarchy, and the Guillotine vs. Law and Order, Family and Property." George Bancroft, who at first tried to calm his frightened Boston friends—who in fact hoped (as he wrote to Secretary of State James Buchanan) that "the echo of American Democracy . . . from France, and Austria, and Prussia and all Old Germany . . . [would] stir up the hearts of the American people to new achievements"—came increasingly to concede that events were tending in just the opposite direction: geographically, from the Old World to the New, and morally, from liberty to license.[9]

License took many forms, as these antebellum Jeremiahs detailed its invasion of America. Hawthorne may be said to condense their complaints in his overview of Hester's nihilism, just before her forest meeting with Dimmesdale:

> She had wandered, without rule or guidance, in a moral wilderness . . . [and] looked from her estranged point of view at human institutions, and whatever priests or legislators had established; criticizing all with hardly more reverence than the Indian would feel for the clerical band, the judicial robe, the fireside . . . or the church. . . . The scarlet letter was her passport into *regions where other women dared not tread*. Shame, Despair, Solitude! These had been her teachers,—stern and wild ones,—and they had made her strong, but taught her much amiss. (290; my italics)

The regions to which Hawthorne refers had long been open territory to European radicals: "terrorists of France" as well as England (from Puritan Ranters to the Chartists of 1848). Even there, however, women had characteristically restrained themselves, because (Hawthorne explains) they intuited that to indulge such "tendency to speculation"—to venture into that "moral wilderness" beyond "Law and Order, Family and Property"—would be to alter their very "natures"; it would drain them of the "ethereal essence, wherein [woman] has her truest life" (260). This explanation is at once essentialist and political. It directly precedes his reminder that "the scarlet letter had not done its office," and there is every reason to assume that he was deliberately evoking what social commentators had just designated the first major symptom of the "red plague of European revolutions . . . on these shores." I refer to the Women's Rights Convention at Seneca Falls in 1848. Reports of "the female 'Reds' of Europe" had already "appalled the American public," and public spokesmen from pulpit, press, and political platform rushed to make the connection:

> This is the age of revolutions. To whatever part of the world the attention is directed, the political and social fabric is crumbling to pieces; and changes which far exceed the wildest dreams of the enthusiastic Utopians of the last generation, are now pursued with ardor and perseverance. The principal agent, however, that has hitherto taken part in these movements has been the rougher sex . . . and though it is asserted that no inconsiderable assistance was contributed by the gentler sex to the late sanguinary carnage at Paris, we are disposed to believe that such a revolting imputation proceeds from base calumniators, and is a libel upon woman.
>
> By the intelligence, however, which we have lately received, the work of revolution is no longer confined to the Old World, nor to the masculine gender. The flag of independence has been hoisted, for the second time, on this side of the Atlantic; and a solemn league and covenant has just been entered into by a Convention of women at Seneca Falls.
>
> [These women] seem to be really in earnest in their aim at revolution, and . . . evince entire confidence that "the day of their deliverance is at hand."[10]

Surely, Hawthorne means us to bear the strains of this American *Marseillaise* in Hester's "stern and wild" irreverence. And surely, too, his overall critique of her radicalism—from her bitter sense of herself as "martyr" (191) to her selfconscious manipulation of the townspeople (259–60) and her rising scorn for all "human institutions," "whatever priests or legislators had established" (290)—registers the reaction against the rising European "carnage" and its "revolting" influence "on this side of the Atlantic." That reaction included all five major writers of F. O. Matthiessen's *American Renaissance,* in spite of their common devotion to "the possibilities of democracy." Significantly, the most radically American among them was also clearest about ideological parameters. What made "European revolution" unfit for America, according to Emerson—what made it antithetical to "true democracy"—was the threat it posed to the tenets of free enterprise. It was not so much the violence that troubled him (though he lamented that "in France, 'fraternity' [and] 'equality' . . . are names for assassination"), nor was it the burdens of political engagement (though he noted in April 1848, concerning talk of "a Chartist revolution on Monday next, and an Irish revolution the following week," that the scholar's "kingdom is at once over & under these perturbed regions"). Emerson's complaints struck through what he considered "these political masks" to the "metaphysical evils" beyond them:

> This tin trumpet of a French Phalanstery [sounds] and the newsboys throw up their caps & cry, Egotism is exploded; now for Communism! But all that is valuable in the Phalanstery comes of individualism. . . . For the matter of Socialism, there are no oracles. The oracle is dumb. When we would pronounce anything truly of man, we retreat instantly on the individual.
>
> We are authorized to say much on the destinies of one, nothing on those of many. In the question of Socialism . . . one has only this guidance. You shall not so arrange property as to remove the motive to industry. If you refuse rent & interest, you make all men idle & immoral. As to the poor, a vast proportion have made themselves so, and in any new arrangement will only prove a burden on the state. . . .
>
> When men feel & say, "Those men occupy my place," the revolution is near. But I never feel that any men occupy my place; but that the reason I do not have what I wish, is, that I want the faculty which entitles. All spiritual or real power makes its own place. Revolutions of violence then are scrambles merely.[11]

Even Walt Whitman, Barnburner delegate, Chartist sympathizer, and Free Soiler, joined in elaborating this symbolic opposition between European and American revolution. In 1847 he had gone so far as to defend the French republican Reign of Terror, but when after 1849 the attack on property and individualism became an American issue, he steadily "recoiled." All that remains in *Leaves of Grass* of the Spirit of '48 (when "Like lightning Europe le'pt forth") is

> a Shape,
> Vague as the night, draped interminably, head front and form,
>   in scarlet folds.
> Whose face and eyes none may see,
> Out of its robes only this . . . the red robes, lifted by the arm,
> One finger crook'd pointed high over the top, like the head
>   of a snake appears.

Whitman consoled the "Foil'd European Revolutionaire" by recalling "that defeat [too] is great,/And that death and dismay are great"; and the moral he drew for "comederos" at home and abroad was "Educate, Educate,—it is the only true remedy for mobs, wild communistic theories, and red-republican ravings."[12]

Of all of Hawthorne's acquaintances only one, Margaret Fuller, continued to give her full support to the revolutionaries, and it has been argued persuasively that she figures not only in his story of ill-fated Zenobia but, together with her allegedly illegitimate child (the gossip of Brahmin New England in 1849), in his portrait of the tormented radical, Hester Prynne. If so, it might be regarded as a Hawthornesque irony that Fuller returned from Europe "possessed," as she put it, "of a great history"—convinced of the importance of "social struggle" as against the "consolations of prophecy," "fiction," and "the past"— and that she drowned within sight of the lifeboats grounded on the American shore.[13]

That was in 1850, which I take to be the centerpiece of the novel's authorial time frame. It was the year of the Compromise Resolutions, including the Fugitive Slave Act, and of

The Scarlet Letter. Eighteen-fifty-two marks the close of this period, with the return of Hawthorne's political fortune through the election to the presidency of his friend Franklin Pierce. Hawthorne did his share by writing the official campaign biography, in which he extols Pierce as "the statesman of practical sagacity—who loves his country *as it is,* and evolves good from things *as they exist"*—and he defends Pierce's support of the Fugitive Slave Act by comparing the abolitionists to Europe's "Red Republicans." The indirection of his comparison suggests a political balancing act, somewhat like the Compromise Bill itself: Hawthorne did not want to alienate those of Pierce's Young America supporters who persisted in identifying European insurrection with the claims of American expansionism. (Besides, Louis Kossuth was then touring the United States, and although Hawthorne himself felt "as enthusiastic [about him] as a lump of frozen mud," he had to acknowledge the "popularity" of the Hungarian revolutionary leader). Still, the comparatist implications in the Pierce biography are unmistakable. Hawthorne charges that (like the "terrorists of France") the abolitionists are hell bent on chaos: they would tear "to pieces the Constitution" and sever "into distracted fragments that common country which Providence brought into one nation, through a continued miracle of almost two hundred years, from the first settlement of the American wilderness until the Revolution."[14]

As critics are coming increasingly to recognize, the Civil War provides the latent context of the American Renaissance. *Moby-Dick, The Narrative of Frederick Douglass,* and *Uncle Tom's Cabin* (as well as Cooper's apocalyptic novel of 1849, *The Crater*) all deal more or less directly with loomings of national cataclysm. The visions of transcendent unity in *Walden, Leaves of Grass,* and *Eureka* all depend on a utopianism—utopian nostalgia in Thoreau's case, utopian futurism in Whitman's, dystopian metaphysics in Poe's—which circumvents or submerges the actual divisions of the time. Considered together with the popular sentimental and gothic novels of the period, these works provide a multivocal narrative of American liberal ideology during a crucial period of its formation. The special position of *The Scarlet Letter* in this narrative may be inferred from its centrist strategy: it employs sentimental themes and gothic techniques in order to mediate between utopian and dystopian resolutions, and its return to cultural origins speaks to the threat of cataclysm while evading the prospects of conflict.

No doubt the overall tendency is toward evasion. Indeed, we might almost read Hester's counsel (after the letter has done its office) as a preview of Hawthorne's answer to the abolitionists. Slavery, he explains in the Pierce biography, is "one of those evils which divine Providence does not leave to be remedied by human contrivances, but which, in its own good time, by some means impossible to be anticipated, but of the simplest and easiest operation, when all its uses shall have been fulfilled, it causes to vanish like a dream."[15] Only the security of commonplace could allow for this daring inversion in logic, whereby slavery is represented, symbolically, as part of the "continued miracle" of America's progress. Like the scarlet letter, Hawthorne's argument has the power of a long-preserved cultural artifact.

But of course the two artifacts are different in kind. The argument in the biography reflects a certain tactic of the culture; its power derives from a system of ideas connecting racism and progress. The power of the scarlet letter derives from its capacities for mediation. It reveals the variety of tactics available to the culture at a certain historical moment. And as I have noted, antebellum culture was particularly volatile—in the sense not of transition but of consolidation: volatility redirected into channels of social growth. It was a culture feeding on change, nourished by technological innovation, territorial expansion, shifts of power centers, and waves of immigration; and, as a symptom of its increasing confidence, accommodating itself to new conditions by moving toward a resolution by violence of its major internal conflict. To call Hawthorne's racism a cultural tactic is not to excuse it but to distinguish the biography from the novel. Considered as part of an intra-cultural debate, Hawthorne's response to the Fugitive Slave Act differs dramatically from that of abolitionists like Emerson and Stowe. But if we step outside that context the difference reflects something else entirely: a series of no longer avoidable contradictions within a system whose values and biases (including racism and American exceptionalism) they all shared. *The Life of Pierce* advances what turned out to be an inadequate mode of re-solving a social crisis. *The Scarlet Letter* expresses a particular culture's mode of resolving crisis. It is not that the novel transcends propaganda. It is that its imaginative forms re-veal the complexity of beliefs implicit but submerged in any single-minded doctrine we commonly associate with propaganda. The biography presents a certain choice; the novel represents a metaphysics of choosing. It advocates not a particular course of action but a world view within which that course of action makes sense and takes effect.

We might call the novel thick propaganda. Its range of possibilities includes virtually every form of resolution generated by the antebellum North. To repeat the logic of Hes-ter's vision (insofar as it prefigures the Pierce biography), injustice is to be removed by some "divine operation" that however has not yet done its office. This representation of contradiction as an ambiguity in the process of resolving itself is not substantially differ-ent from the Liberian solution proposed by Harriet Beecher Stowe and enacted in the happy ending to *Uncle Tom's Cabin* by her mulatto hero, George Harris. Nor is it different in substance from the expansionist argument that to repeal the Fugitive Slave Act would revitalize the national errand—in John Greenleaf Whittier's words, would inspire the "children of the Puritans," North and South, to cross "the prairie as of old/The pilgrims crossed the sea" and thereby ("Upbearing like the Ark of old,/The Bible in our van") has-ten "Freedom's holy Pentacost." Nor again is Hawthorne's solution different in substance from that proposed a decade later by those who believed *they* were the divine operation, providence incarnate, moving irresistibly toward the Armageddon of the Republic. In his debates with Douglas, Lincoln effectually reversed Hawthorne's argument—it was the anti-abolitionists, he charged, who were fragmenting the Union and subverting the fa-thers' legacy—and in his Second Inaugural Address of 1865, reviewing the causes of the Civil War, he described "American slavery" as "one of those offenses which, in the provi-dence of God, must needs come, but which, having continued through His appointed time, He now wills to remove."[16]

The difference between Lincoln's counsel for reconciliation and Hester's for patience is the turn of a certain circular symbolic logic. The Northern rhetoric of the Civil War rep-resents negation as affirmation—the destined union made manifest in violence. Haw-thorne's rhetoric builds on affirmation by negation—manifest inaction justified by na-tional destiny. From this perspective, it is worth recalling the enormous force of the negative imperative in *The Scarlet Letter*. Negation is far more than a form of moral, politi-cal, and aesthetic control. It is the very ground of Hawthorne's strategy of process as gradualism: the antidialectic through which he absorbs the radical energies of history into the polar oppositions of symbolic interpretation. "The scarlet letter had not done its of-fice": negation leads us forward toward that deeper significance which Hawthorne promises at the start—that comprehensive "deep meaning . . . most worthy of interpre-tation" (145–46)—precisely by evoking the fear of process run amuck, pluralism frag-menting into diversity, disharmony, discontinuity, chaos.

That is the overt purpose of Hawthorne's imperative. But the effect goes further than that. Hawthorne's mode of negation may almost be said to be taken on a counterdynamic of its own, as though in equal and opposite reaction to the fear of uncontrolled process.

Negation gathers such momentum in the course of the novel that it threatens the very process it is designed to guide. *Not* doing its office nearly comes to define the function of the symbol. When after "seven miserable years" Hester at last finds the strength to discard the A, it takes all of Hawthorne's resources (providence, Pearl, Dimmesdale, nature itself) to have her restore it against her will. And even so the restoration serves at first to highlight the letter's negative effects. As she awaits her moment of flight with Dimmesdale, Hester stands alone in the marketplace with a "frozen calmness," her face a death mask, *and because of that* with all the radical vitality for which we have come to admire her:

> After sustaining the gaze of the multitude through seven miserable years as a necessity, a penance, and something which it was a stern religion to endure, she now, for one last time more, encountered it freely and voluntarily, in order to convert what had so long been agony into a kind of triumph. "Look your last on the scarlet-letter and its wearer!"—the people's victim and life-long bond-slave, as they fancied her, might say to them. "Yet a little while, and she will be beyond your reach! A few hours longer, and the deep, mysterious ocean will quench and hide for ever the symbol which ye have caused to burn upon her bosom!" (313–14)

That is why Hawthorne must not only bring her back but force her to resume the A "freely and voluntarily," "of her own free will."[17] It is as though under pressure of her resistance the letter were slipping out of his grasp, losing its efficacy as an agent of reconciliation. In terms of what I have called the novel's latent context, the impending Civil War, the antinomies in this passage ("people" and "victim," "freely" and "bond-slave") assume an explosive force, an almost irrepressible tendency toward confrontation, that endangers both symbolic process and narrative closure. That tendency may be seen as the political after effect of the rhetoric of liberty, in which "slavery" served ambiguously to denote all forms of bondage, "private or public, civil or political." More directly, it is the rhetorical counterpart to what Edmund Morgan, describing the tensions in antebellum politics, termed "American freedom/American slavery."[18] It is a testament to Hawthorne's sensitivity to those rhetorical-political tensions that he allowed the danger to surface, that indeed he played it out almost to the point of no return. It is a testament to the resilience of the ideology it drew upon that nonetheless he could resume process, and as it were rescue the symbol from the ocean's depths, by simple, sweepingly, *assuming* an interpretative consensus.

For the silence surrounding Hester's final conversion to the letter is clearly deliberate on Hawthorne's part. It mystifies Hester's choice by forcing us to represent it through the act of interpretation. Having given us ample directives about how to understand the ways in which the letter had not done its office, Hawthorne now depends on us to recognize— freely and voluntarily, for his method depends on his seeming *not* to impose meaning (as in his remark that "the scarlet letter had not done its office")—the need for Hester's return. In effect, he invites us to participate in a free enterprise democracy of symbol making. Its cultural model is the ambiguity universalized in the Declaration of Independence: "*We* hold these truths to be *self*-evident." The silent problematic of "we" may be inferred from Pip's revelation of the plural meanings of the doubloon—"I look, you look, he looks, we look, ye look, they look"—especially if we remember, as Pip seems not to, that the grammatical declension makes a social hierarchy, *descending* from the captain's *I* to the shipstokers' *they*. The silenced problematic of "self-evident" may be inferred from the voluntaristic terms of Ahab's covenant: "I do not order ye; ye will it."[19]

Hawthorne, too, may be said to elicit these problematics, but unlike Melville he does so in order to guide us toward accommodation. When, in the most carefully prepared-for reversal in classic American literature, Hester herself imposes the symbol, she signals her recognition that what had seemed a basic problem—basic enough to have made her want to overturn society—is really a question of point of view; and Hawthorne so veils this epiphany that our multiple perspectives enact the same ideology of liberal consensus that his novel celebrates and represents.

It is an oblique mode of celebration, and all the more persuasive for its obliquity. Pierre Macherey argues that gaps and silences in narrative structure—the sorts of indirection in which Hawthorne specializes—demarcate the limits of ideology. According to Macherey, they are symptoms of fissures in the culture, the contradictions that the system can neither absorb nor wholly exclude. His theory seems especially pertinent to classic American literature, which abounds in strategies of process through hiatus, and to Hawthorne's work in particular. It is pertinent first of all because it conspicuously does *not* apply to the narrative gap that precedes Hester's return. Hawthorne makes that silence reverberate with all the voices of cultural authority. He transforms the gap into an ideological bridge (spanning two centuries of "continued miracle") between character, author, and reader. When midway through the novel we accept Hawthorne's judgment that the scarlet letter had not done its office, we acquiesce to the narrative, in a willing suspension of disbelief; but when at the end we ourselves require the letter to be imposed, inventing reasons (all of them necessarily incomplete) or synthesizing the partial views of others, we invest our very will to suspend disbelief in a joint stock company of pluralist interpretation. It is an ideological leap of faith for which the entire novel has been our preparation. Hawthorne's strategy of indirection allows us, like Hester, both to have our dissent and do the work of society too. And when we thus interpret away her repentance—or rather (as Charles Fiedelson put it in what remains the best New Critical reading of the novel), her penitence "yet to be" that, "will always be unfinished" because it involves "a perennial conversion of the stuff of sin and sorrow into positive freedom—the creativity, individuality and sympathetic community of men"—then *The Scarlet Letter* has done its office.[20]

What I would suggest is the ideological *power* of gaps and silences. In general, I refer to the special genius of liberal symbology in staging interpretation as a means of coopting dissent. In particular, I refer to the strategies by which the same visionary appeal that makes "America" into an ideological battleground also restricts the battle to the ground of American ideology. "From gap to gain is very American," as Norman Mailer remarks in *The Armies of the Night* (1968). In the mid nineteenth century, that very American notion found its main expression in the rhetoric of expansion, opportunity speculation, and enterprise—the symbiosis between verbal and territorial appropriation inherent in the appeal to "open country," "virgin land," "empty continent," "unmapped future," the interior "white on the chart" of the self, the I that *becomes all* by *being nothing*. In 1846, the year after John O'Sullivan popularized the phrase "manifest destiny" (in an editorial entitled "The Nation of Futurity"), the explorer/pioneer/politician William Gilpin elaborated that "divine task" in terms that may be said to foreshadow the prophecies of Dimmesdale and Hester. It was "the *untransacted* destiny of the American people," wrote Gilpin in a widely quoted passage, "to subdue the continent . . . to set free the enslaved . . . and through our errand of love . . . . to unite the world in one social family."[21]

These ambiguities served different offices in 1850, as they did again in the late 1960s.[22] In *The Scarlet Letter* and as *The Scarlet Letter,* their office is the transvaluation of the conflicts of compromise into the rhetoric of consensus. From 1848 to 1852 that rhetoric had two broad ideological aims: one, pragmatic and immediate, the tactics of concession; the other, visionary or teleological, the myth of continuing revolution. The two aims were intertwined. Continuing revolution posited the gradual ascent from Puritanism to the Revolution and the nation's continuing ascent thereafter, in accordance with the principles established by the Revolution. The tacticians of concession invoked that myth as a providential injunction against the prospect of civil war. According to "the great triumvirate" (John C. Calhoun, Henry Clay, and Daniel Webster), Compromise was at once the ideal of union and the essence of democratic pluralism. It embodied the reciprocities between private rights and civic responsibility under liberal law, as required by contract society, guaranteed by the Constitution, and consecrated by the Declaration.[23]

It is pertinent that at mid century the word *compromise* did not carry the pejorative meanings it does today ("a concession to something derogatory"; "to expose or discredit or mischief"; "to make a shameful or disreputable concession"). For the legislative majority who voted for Compromise at mid century, the term meant above all (according to Noah Webster's *Standard American Dictionary*) "to bind by mutual agreement," where the principles of binding had the doubled force of contract and of covenant: "an amicable agreement between parties in controversy to settle their differences, by mutual concessions"; "a mutual promise"; "an engagement to refer matters in dispute to the decision of arbitrators"; "to adjust and settle"; "to pledge by some act or declaration"; "see Promise." The weak point lay in the vagueness of "promise," especially under the *diverse* pressures to concede: pledge, arbitration, declaration, agreement. By the close of the Jacksonian period, vagueness had taken the form of ambiguity. In 1848, Chauncey A. Goodrich's "Revised and Enlarged" edition of Webster's *Standard Dictionary* officially announced that to compromise might mean "to put to hazard."[24] Apparently, the increasing dysfunctions of "mutual agreements" from Massachusetts to Kansas—and from the Missouri Compromise of 1820 (which established slavery in Missouri while prohibiting it in the Nebraska Territory) to the various mid-century compromises over the Southwest Territories—were affecting the course of "American English." If so, it is crucial to Hawthorne's achievement that the apotheosis of compromise came at the moment when the term was undergoing a decisive change.

Between 1848 and 1852, the ambiguity that the term *hazard* had brought into play endowed the primary meaning of *compromise* with the power of what Freud called the antithetical sense of primal words. "Compromise: *consent* reached by *mutual concession*"—all the volatile doubleness that had been explicit in the Revolutionary in the key word *independent* (isolated, cut off, mature, self-determined), and implicit in the ubiquitous Jacksonian *self* prefix (self-made, self-reliant, self-serving, self-centered), exploded in antebellum America in the struggle between the party for union and the party against concession. Both parties laid claim to "consent," of course, as the touchstone of liberal consensus. They divided mainly on pragmatics—the scope of consent, the nature of consensus—but it was pragmatism charged with prophetic import. Daniel Webster's concession to the South, according to Emerson, "was the darkest passage in [our] history," a "disastrous defection (on the miserable cry of Union)" from "the principles of culture and progress." For his part, Webster accused his opponents of a "fractiousness" that would "obliterate for ever all hopes of the republic." He was thinking mainly of Northern abolitionists and Southern secessionists, but he did not miss the opportunity to evoke the recent European "act[s] of folly." Against all these "enemies to culture and progress," he urged "union through compromise," so that—with "the eyes of all Christendom upon us," with the "whole world . . . looking towards us with extreme anxiety"—Americans could at last make visible, like a city set upon a hill, the "certain destiny . . . that belongs to us."[25]

From the revolutions of 1848 through the election of Franklin Pierce, this rhetoric of compromise occupied the center of a debate whose extremes were proslavery constitutionalism and proconstitutional abolitionism. I refer here only to the debate within the dominant culture, but it is astonishing how few voices challenged that "consensus," in what elsewhere (to recall Hawthorne's phrases) was a time of "radical speculation," "an age in which the human intellect, newly emancipated, had taken a more active and wider range than for many centuries before." As for Hawthorne, he scarcely wavered in his centrist convictions. In the Pierce biography, he recalled "The Compromise" as a triumphant "test" of "the reverence of the people for the constitution, and their attachment to the Union"; and as late as 1858 he said of a statue of Webster, "symbolizing him as the preserver of the Union," that "I never saw such . . . massive strength . . . [and] deep, pervading energy. . . . He looks really like a pillar of the state . . . very grand, very Webster . . . he is in the act of meeting a great crisis, and yet with the warmth of a great heart glowing through it."[26] But by then the crisis of industrial capitalism was calling for new sources of strength. After 1852, with Webster's death and the struggle for the Free States, the central cultural symbols shifted steadily to embrace the armies of the North, wielding God's terrible swift sword to cut the gordian knot of "consent"/"concession."

Not the ends but the means had changed. Compromise, "to bind by mutual agreement," had failed to provide either the mechanism for bonding or the metaphors for agreement, and with due alacrity the leaders of the dominant culture had moved to preserve the union against the *threat* of ambiguity. Some four months before Hawthorne's encomium to Webster, Lincoln set out the new rhetoric of consent in a Senate campaign speech that appropriated the Southern imagery of fragmentation for the Yankee cause: "I do not expect the house to *fall*—but I *do* expect it will cease to be divided. It will become *all* one thing, or *all* the other." A year later, Emerson displayed the recuperative powers of that revision in his tribute to John Brown. Far from being a threat to consensus, "the hero of Harper's Ferry," Emerson declared, was the "representative of the American Republic. . . . He joins that perfect Puritan faith which brought his fifth ancestor to Plymouth rock, with his grandfather's ardor in the Revolution. He believes in two articles—two instruments shall I say?—the Golden Rule and the Declaration of Independence."

Instruments was the better word. In 1866, as though to commemorate the triumphant reincorporation of the myth, Webster's *Standard American Dictionary*—now "*Thoroughly* Revised, [and] *Greatly* Enlarged and Improved" by Noah Porter and Chauncey Goodrich—officially retired (as archaic) the once primary meaning of *compromise:* "to bind by mutual agreement, *obs.*"[27]

It is a nice irony of our literary history that Hawthorne's absolutist Concord neighbors, Emerson and Thoreau, managed to span the spectrum of response, whereas sceptical, many-faceted Hawthorne remained ideologically fixated, like some Ahab of compromise. I do not think we can say that his incapacity to accept the change ruined his career, as it did Pierce's and Webster's. But to some extent at least it drained him of crucial intellectual and moral resources. On some level, it accounts for the increasing tendency of his fiction to expose (rather than reconcile) ideological contradictions. For the fact is that of all his novels it is only about *The Scarlet Letter* that we can say, as Henry James did *in praise of Hawthorne's art,* that "the reader must look for his local and national qualities between the lines of his writing and in the *indirect* testimony of his tone, his accent, his temper, of his very omissions and suppressions." Consider the difference in this respect between Hester's return on the one hand and on the other Holgrave's conversion, Coverdale's confession, or (most pointedly) the homecoming of Hilda, that other wandering daughter of the Puritans. In his European letters and journals, Hawthorne often hints at the cause of his failing strategies of omission. He is most explicit in the preface to his last book, *Our Old Home,* which appropriately he dedicated to his old friend, Franklin Pierce:

> The Present, the Immediate, the Actual, has proved too potent for me. It takes away not only my scanty faculty, but even my desire for imaginative composition, and leaves me sadly content to scatter a thousand peaceful fantasies upon the hurricane that is sweeping us all along with it, possibly, into a Limbo where our nation and its polity may be as literally the fragments of a shattered dream as my unwritten Romance.[28]

This was 1863, at the height of the war, and it is not hard to understand Hawthorne's bewilderment and dismay. In 1860 he had returned to an America where (he professed to believe) there was "no shadow, no antiquity, no mystery, no picturesque and gloomy wrong, nor anything but a commonplace prosperity, in broad and simple daylight." Two years later he confessed in an essay "Chiefly About War-Matters": "The general heart-quake of the country long ago knocked at my cottage-door, and compelled me, reluctantly, to suspend the contemplation of certain fantasies." We might well see in this image (as in that limbo of shattered dreams) an unconscious inversion of Hester's return. But we should also keep in mind the hurricanes of the actual that a decade earlier had *not* disturbed Hawthorne's fantasies: Southern slavery; Indian genocide; the Mexican War (through which General Pierce became a national hero); expansionist demands by men like Pierce for war against Cuba and Latin America; pervasive ethnic and religious discrimination; child labor in Northern mill towns; the grievances listed by the Seneca Falls Convention; the manifold abuses documented in the petitions circulated by New England's abolitionist sewing circles.[29]

Hawthorne was aware in 1850 of these present and pressing evils. Some of them had earlier found their way into his short stories; some are actually recorded in the Pierce biography; others may be said to underlie the discontents that Hester, in her sewing circle of one, embroiders into her scarlet letter; still others are implicit in her confrontation with the immigrant "bond-servant" at Governor Bellingham's mansion, "a free-born Englishman, but now a seven years' slave" (206); and others again may be discerned in the "sorrows and perplexities" that the townspeople bring to Hester, after her return, "demanding why they were so wretched, and what the remedy!" No American writer felt more detached from party politics than Hawthorne did; few were more engaged in the affairs of political office; and none was so deeply learned in American political history. There is no paradox in this. Hawthorne sought to rise above politics not by escaping history but by representing it symbolically. To that end (in "The Custom-House" introduction) he exposes the miasma of mid-nineteenth-century patronage and (in the novel proper) the excesses of partisanship. The hiatus between introduction and story is the ideological link between Hawthorne and Hester. Her reconciliation at the end is the link in turn between the novel and the biography: first, in the image that Hester may be said to project of Hawthorne's return to the patronage system; then, in the biographical image of Pierce as the great reconciler; and finally in Hawthorne's implied contrast between process in the New World and upheaval in the Old. Revolutionary Europe in this view was political in the narrowly sectarian, exclusivist meaning of ideology. The United States transcended ideology, so defined, for the same reason that the concept of America transcended politics: because as "America" it stood for transpartisan, pluralistic development through compromise.

That liberal ideology fills the silence between Hester's cold defiance at the election-day ceremony and her final consolation for dissidents. Far from wanting to mute sorrow and perplexity, Hawthorne emphatically gives voice to the wretched, to a degree his contemporaries sometimes considered morbid. But he does so to elicit our acquiescence to what he believed was "the remedy," working uncoerced, in its own time and ways. I refer to the myth of continuing revolution, which Hawthorne made a main theme of his work—most bluntly in the Pierce biography, most elaborately in his short stories, and most subtly and complexly in *The Scarlet Letter*. The central act of the national drama that underlies the novel—the event that best explains Hawthorne's prophetic gloss on the midnight revelation of the A (midway through the novel), and that most firmly links this (at the end) both to Dimmesdale's prophecy and to Hester's—is the American Revolution. Indeed, it is not too much to say that, together with adultery, the Revolution is the novel's fundamental *donné*. Adultery is pre-text, and issues in the wrong kind of revolt; the Revolution is post-script, and vindicates the role of process in an unadulterated world.

The vindication is prospective as well as retrospective. It applies no less to the adulterated world of the Customs House than to Puritan New England. The conspicuous absence from the novel of the word *adultery* facilitates a process of interpretation through which a problem in social accountability is deepened (Hawthorne would have us believe) into a process of symbolic perspective. So, too, in the case of the absent word *compromise*: it serves by "*indirect* testimony" to recast fears of concession into faith in consensus. And so, too, with the American Revolution. Only here Hawthorne does break the silence, briefly, in the introduction. "The British army in its flight from Boston," he writes, had discarded as worthless the "packet" containing the letter; and the "ancient yellow parchment," tied up in "faded red tape," had "remained ever since unopened" (143–45). Seventeen-seventy-six thus serves to confirm the letter's venerable antiquity ("Prior to the Revolution"), its rare value as a native artifact (the British had "carried off" most "earlier documents"), and its aesthetic-historical significance—from Hester to Surveyor Pue (whose given name, Jonathan, casts him on the American side, against the Royalist John Bull) to Hawthorne, and from the Puritan forefathers through their latter-day heir to us (144–45):

> I, the present writer, as their representative, hereby take their shame upon myself for their sakes, and pray that any curse incurred by them [for their acts of persecution] may be now and henceforth removed. (127)

For all its irony, the anecdote is crucial to the letter's design. It transforms the accidents of conflict into a historical chain of providences in which the Revolution is the pivotal link. As an emblem of what the British left behind, the A sanctifies the Puritan legacy, foreshadows the pattern of Hester's flight, justifies the wisdom of her return, and validates the spirit, if not the letter, of her prophecy. It amounts to a figural endorsement of Hawthorne's strategy of reconciliation.

But the same figural logic points in another, opposite direction. I said earlier that the myth of continuing revolution was the visionary side of the rhetoric of compromise. Symbolically, however, the Revolution carried in it a wholly different model of consensus: not union through compromise but regeneration through violence. That variant model was equally rooted in the culture. It may be traced from the Puritans' Wars of the Lord (correlative of their gradual, forever "preparatory" errand into the wilderness) through the libertarian summons to "civil war" and nationhood. "We had been in the steady way of maturation," declared Samuel Sherwood in the most popular sermon of 1776, when suddenly "floods poured from the mouth of the serpent, which at length have brought on a civil war"; and several months earlier, in the most popular pamphlet of the year, Tom Paine contrasted independence (as "growth" and "maturation") with "the least inclination toward a compromise." "Reconciliation," he concluded, "is *now* a fallacious dream." This model of unity through confrontation is inscribed in representative works like Timothy Dwight's epic of the Revolution, *The Conquest of Canaan*, in cultural keywords like *manifest destiny*, and in large-scale social actions like the extermination of the Indians. The "savages," went the argument, were by definition an "extinct race"—if not now, then "in

Heaven's own time"; the issue was not agency but destiny, working itself out either by natural or by human means. Andrew Jackson mobilized the human means; Emerson opted for nature. It was "the great charity of God to the human race," he explained, to prepare for "new individuals and races" by "extinguishing" old ones, and charity should be allowed to take its own course.[30]

In the antebellum North, with the Indian problem fundamentally settled, the debate shifted to the question of slavery. It is characteristic of the flexibility of the American symbology—its special capacities to recast violence as gradualism (and vice versa)—that the metaphysicians of Indian killing should have become leading advocates of Compromise. They wanted nature and providence to usher in what Webster called "the certain destiny that awaits us." Their adversaries took "the great charity of God" into their own hands. Probably the most revealing opposition statement is Emerson's. Delivered in 1854, four years after the Fugitive Slave Act, when the negative connotations of *compromise* ("derogatory," "shameful," "disreputable") were beginning to eclipse the "promise" of "mutual concession," Emerson's attack on Webster is the ideological counterpart to Hawthorne's ambiguities of reconciliation:

> Slavery is disheartening; but Nature is not so helpless but it can rid itself at last of every wrong. But the spasms of Nature are centuries and ages, and will tax the faith of short-lived men. Slowly, slowly the Avenger comes, but comes surely. The proverbs of the nations affirms these delays, but affirm the arrival. They say, "God may consent, but not forever." The delay of the Divine Justice—this was the meaning and soul of the Greek Tragedy. . . .
>
>   These delays, you see them now in the . . . torpor [that] exists here . . . on the subject of domestic slavery. . . . Yes, that is the stern edict of Providence, that liberty shall be no hasty fruit, but that event on event, population on population, age on age, shall cast itself into the opposite scale, and not until liberty has slowly accumulated weight enough to countervail and preponderate against all this, can the sufficient recoil come. . . .
>
>   Whilst the inconsistency of slavery with the principles on which the world is built guarantees its downfall, I own that the patience it requires is almost too sublime for mortals, and seems to demand of us more than mere hoping. And when one sees how fast the rot spreads . . . we demand of superior men that they be superior in this—that the mind and the virtue shall give their verdict in their day, and accelerate so far the progress of civilization. . . . But be that sooner or later, I hope we have . . . come to a belief that there is a divine Providence in the world, which will not save us but through our own cooperation.[31]

These winding negations, *whilsts,* and *buts* invert Hawthorne's strategy of inaction, but the inversion begins with and returns to a common ideology. Hawthorne translates radical potential into social integration; Emerson, into cultural renewal. His summons to avenge, like Hawthorne's to patience, mobilizes all the universals on the side of Northern ideology. "Nature," "Divine Justice," "liberty," "the mind," "virtue," "the progress of civilization"—the very "principles on which the world is built" serve to consecrate the Yankee *our*.

This sort of troping is most pronounced in the later Emerson. But it may be traced throughout his writings: in "The American Scholar," for example, which compensates for the Depression of 1837 by prophesying "America" as a millennial "nation of men . . . inspired by the Divine Soul"; and in *Representative Men,* published in 1850, the year of the Compromise, which resolves anxieties about American newness in declaring that "Nature has a high end in the production of individuals, namely *ascension*"; and again, in "The Fortune of the Republic," which makes civil war the occasion for celebrating "a nation of individuals," America, *now* (1863, 1866, 1870, 1874) representing "the sentiment and the future of mankind."[32]

I do not mean by this to deny the radicalism inherent in Emerson's great essays from 1836 through 1850. My point is not the weakness of his later vision but the persistent power of cultural symbology. Characteristically, the Emersonian mode (even in "The Fortune of the Republic") is subversive of fixed meaning. And characteristically it defines itself (especially in the early essays, such as "The American Scholar") through the *state* of transition—a quality of mind reflecting a community-in-process. In short, it is a mode of subversion that is by definition *confined to resistance*. On principle, it can never take sides, except provisionally, can never find "repose" in any commitment, not even to itself. And Hester's return shows how this may entail *as a prerequisite* our acceptance of society as it is and things as they exist.

In this perspective, Emersonian potential may be seen as a form of liminality that flowered under the pressures of massive social change in the Jacksonian period. It expresses the antistructures of free-enterprise capitalism in an "open," "empty," and apparently endlessly malleable New World. *The Scarlet Letter* expresses the conservative thrust of that ritual mode—the integrative, consolidating function of liminality—and the contrast is all the more striking if we consider the formalist differences between Emerson the essayist and Hawthorne the novelist. I have in mind recent theories of genre, from Mikhail Bakhtin to Paul Ricoeur and Hans Blumenberg. More than any other form of "artistic modernity," writes Blumenberg, the novel "legitimates the aesthetic qualities of *novitas* . . . removes the dubiousness from what is new, and so *terra incognita,* or the *munda novus,* becomes possible."[33] Like Macherey's theory, Blumenberg's conspicuously does *not* apply to *The Scarlet Letter.* Hawthorne's novel functions precisely to reign in what "becomes possible." Its office (aesthetically, as *novitas*) is to enclose "the new world" within culture, *as* culture. Hester's letter may be a tragic symbol of memory, the *memento mori* of her radical fantasies in the forest; but more largely *and constrictingly,* it is the symbol of Emersonian hope—hope in prophecy, as being more subversive than argument; hope in vision, as being a more effective agent of progress than action; hope in the individual, as being both ends and means of change; and hope in the future, as the boundless prospect of liberal/liminal things to come.

This is essentially the "spirit as of prophecy" for which Dimmesdale remains, and to which Hester returns—Dimmesdale, "to foretell a high and glorious destiny for the newly gathered people of the Lord" (332–33); Hester, to herald "the destined prophetess . . . angel and apostle of the coming revelation." And that rhetoric is authorized by essentially the same sense of destiny that Julia Ward Howe endorsed, when (speaking as "angel or apostle" of the Union) she announced: "Mine eyes have seen the glory of the coming of the Lord."[34]

Hawthorne did not intend the ambiguity this implies, one that makes Hester's vision a foreshadowing of "The Battle Hymn of the Republic." Let us say that his rhetoric of violence was intended by the symbology he inherited. In any case, it forms a minor but persistent theme of the novel. The reference to the Revolution makes it integral to the meanings of the A that it is a trophy of war, and that particular meaning is extended through the imagery that connects the introduction to the story proper: for example, the instability inherent in a politics of self-interest, "where brethren of the same household must diverge from one another"; or the prospect of economic and political "warfare," waged in the "fierce and bitter spirit of malice and revenge," "poisoned with ill-will," and leaving the defeated, after "seething turmoil," "at the mercy of a hostile administration" (154–56).

These contrapuntal ambiguities add another level of complexity *and control* to Hawthorne's design. They give a great density to his strategy of multiple choice, and lend a deeper resonance to the pervasive force of negation, which verges on the dialectical only to veer in precisely the opposite direction. From all these angles, they find the right symbolic focus in the national eagle, icon of the Revolution, as Hawthorne describes it in the introduction. An "enormous specimen of the American eagle," he writes, hovered above the Customs House door,

> with outspread wings, a shield before her breast, and a bunch of intermingled thunderbolts and barbed arrows in each claw. With the customary infirmity of temper that characterizes this unhappy fowl, she appears, by the fierceness of her beak and eye and the general truculency of her attitude, to threaten mischief to the inoffensive community; and especially to warn all citizens, careful of their safety, against intruding on the premises. . . . Nevertheless, vixenly as she looks, many people are seeking, at this very moment, to shelter themselves under the wing of the federal eagle. . . . .But she has no great tenderness, even in her best of moods, and, sooner or later,—oftener sooner than late,—is apt to fling off her nestlings with a scratch of her claw, a dab of her beak, or a rankling wound from her barbed arrows. (122–23)

The eagle and the A: for all the oppositions between them, they are symbols made out of the same cultural materials. Both are ambiguous artifacts of authority; both are social emblems transformed by private vision in such a way as simultaneously to assert the self and to accommodate community; and in both cases the act of accommodation recasts the untoward events of history—the "ulcerated wound" of Hester's penance (191), the wounds that Hawthorne received in 1849 from the claw of Whig party functionaries—in terms of art as cultural work. It is the myth of Philoctetes, historicized. And it is appropriate that the two symbols, so historicized, should find common ground in the Salem Customs House—"Uncle Sam's brick edifice" (128), entry to the republic of 1849, as the Puritans were (for Hawthorne) the entry to national history. The extraordinary cunning and force of Hawthorne's vision here attests to the symbolic resources of what by 1850 was becoming the single most cohesive ideology of the modern world.

I have been arguing that text and context are reciprocal: that to understand *The Scarlet Letter* in its own terms is not only to see the ideological dimensions of its art but to bring into view the aesthetic richness of mid-nineteenth-century American liberalism. My purpose in this respect has been to explore (rather than expose) Hawthorne's morality of compromise, and more largely the culture's powers of mystification. Still, ideological analysis assumes a priori that those powers are limited by history; and since the limitations constitute the adversarial *donné* of this essay—much as adultery serves as the novel's *donné*—I would like in closing to take account of these, however briefly and sketchy. To that end, I return to the ground on which I began, Hawthorne's insistent directives for interpretation. They are a form of special pleading, I would suggest, which betrays an underlying cultural-authorial anxiety. Hawthorne's winding ironies and ambiguities—like the subtle links between the eagle and the A—are meant to keep our interpretations under control, but the windings themselves make for what he privately called "a h—l-f—d story." The repressed letters may be taken as the first sign of a strain in his method. The second was Sophia's splitting headache, after he read the last chapter aloud to her. When she recovered, she wrote to her sister Mary: "I don't know what you will think of the Romance. It is most powerful and contains a moral as terrific & stunning as a thunderbolt. It shows that the Law cannot be broken."[35]

Sophia was not just thinking of the Seventh Commandment. She was reacting, as Nathaniel was, to the enormous cultural pressures brought to bear upon the Conclusion:

"The scarlet letter had not done its office": the entire novel asks us to interpret this in the affirmative, and by the end *compels* us to, as a grim necessity. It is as though Hawthorne had to overcompensate for the enormous radical potential inherent in his characters and symbols; had to find some moral absolute—some equivalent in the liberal imagination for the *Thou Shalt Nots* delivered from Mount Sinai—powerful enough to recall all those unleashed energies of will, eros, and language back into the culture from which they arose and, in his view, to which they belonged. He found the solution in the act of ideological mimesis that his novel endorses and enacts. It was to represent the continuities of national history—both progressively, by our assent to the almost absent Revolution that connects the novel's twin time frames, and conservatively, by our rejection of the radical politics that Hester disavows *in absentia*—to set forth the dynamics of antebellum liberalism, so interpreted, as the iron link between culture, nature, and the self, "the Law [that] cannot be broken."

It is to Sophia's credit that she found the "moral as terrific and stunning as a thunderbolt." And it is to Hawthorne's credit that he not only made full use of the morality of compromise but had the integrity to indicate, if not the full costs involved, then at least some signs whereby those costs might be inferred: the coercive force, for example, of containments by consensus, including the containment of the hell-fired artist in liberal democracy, which forms an illicit bond between the secret Hawthorne and the hidden Hester. As a symbol for this and other traces of dialectics in the novel—silences that (again to Hawthorne's credit) do not quite succeed in silencing conflict—I should like to appropriate the "angry eagle" of "The Custom-House" for my own purposes, relocating her from "The Custom-House" of 1849 to the "War-Matters" of 1862. In the later essay, Hawthorne sought to reconcile himself to the consensus of another "iron age," and instinctively he returned once again to the myth of national origins:

> There is an historical circumstance, known to few, that connects the children of the Puritans with those Africans of Virginia in a very singular way. They are our brethren, as being lineal descendants of the Mayflower, the fated womb which in its first labor brought forth a brood of Pilgrims on Plymouth Rock, and, in a subsequent one, spawned slaves upon the Southern soil,—a monstrous birth, but one with which we have an instinctive sense of kindred, and so are stirred by an irresistible impulse to attend their rescue even at the cost of blood and ruin. The character of our sacred ship, I fear, may suffer a little by this revelation; but we must let her white progeny offset her dark one,—and two such portents never sprang from an identical source before.[36]

Hawthorne's *Mayflower* has all the major imaginative ingredients of the dominant culture: the legend of the Puritan theocracy, womb of American democracy; the ambiguities of good and evil, agency of compromise; and the ironies of regeneration through violence, rationale for civil war. But it is a symbol overdetermined by history. Its "deeper meanings" point insistently to the *contradictions* of process, the *irresolutions* of closure, the *precariousness* of the gap or silence that links "rescue" to "blood and ruin"—precarious because the historical details *resist* symbolic reciprocity. The return of the *Mayflower* is a parable of social conflict following upon cultural myth. It reverberates with ambiguities at cross-purposes with each other—for example, the recurrent American nightmare of miscegenation; the long literary procession of mutually destructive dark-white kin (from *Clotel* through *Clarel* and *Pudd'nhead Wilson* to *Absalom, Absalom!*); the biblical types of the elect and the damned (Seth and Ham, Jacob and Esau) through which the South defended its peculiar institution; and the racist use of the image of Christian sacrifice through which the North sanctified first the Union Cause and then the Martyrdom of Lincoln.

Considered together with the "unhappy fowl," this "sacred ship" blackened by "revelation" is itself a monstrous birth, a Frankenstein's monster of the culture: history returning in the guise of figures designed to control it—the most familiar of symbols that now streams forth disjunctions, mocks the compromise of morality, and directs us to the contradictions repressed by the novel's twin contexts, 1642–49 and 1848–52.

Let me conclude with that image, and underscore its uncanny quality by recalling the image that Hester projects upon her return. First, then, Hawthorne's *Mayflower*-eagle, mother of nationhood and vixen of contradictions; second, Hester come home, the dissenter as agent and socialization, a self-professed sinner self-transformed into a herald of progress. Two figures of symbolic ambiguity; two models of historical irony; two examples of the relation between rhetoric and social action; two intersections between power and imagination—they are opposites, and uncannily alike, like the object and its reflection in a *camera obscura,* or like two sides of the same symbolic coin, representing the American liberal ideology.

NOTES

A shorter version of this paper was delivered as a talk at the University of California at Berkeley. I want to thank Mitchell Breitweiser, Walter Benn Michaels, Carolyn Porter, and Eric Sundquist for their generous response. Some of the research for this essay was done at the American Antiquarian Society. My thanks to the Society and to the National Endowment for the Humanities for their support.

1. Nathaniel Hawthorne, *The Scarlet Letter,* in *Novels,* ed. Millicent Bell, The Library of America (New York, 1983), 261. All quotations are from this edition.

2. Sacvan Bercovitch, "The A-Politics of Ambiguity in *The Scarlet Letter,*" *New Literary History* 19 (1988): 629–54.

3. Nathaniel Hawthorne, "Endicott and the Red Cross," in *Tales and Sketches,* ed. Roy Harvey Pearce, The Library of America (New York, 1982), 548.

4. To note only the ideological uses of the myth that may be inferred from *The Scarlet Letter:* the Puritans provided a native heroic age to displace Old World traditions; a common point of origin for a diversity of immigrant groups; a sacred mission to mask the motives of imperialism; a language of prophecy antedating nationhood, through which separation from England could be declared a fulfillment of promise as well as a "new beginning"; an indigenous "national past" within which the (civil) war of independence could be recast as a united struggle against tyranny; and a cultural meta-identity ("utopians," "visionaries," "pilgrims," "forefathers") by which to meld and remold the raw facts of credal, social, and ethnic difference. The main repository of myth in this respect was George Bancroft's *History of the United States;* applications may be traced throughout the literature: in historical novels of the time, in political orations of virtually all parties, and in sermons of virtually all denominations. A convenient mid-nineteenth-century summary is Horace Bushnell's "The Fathers of New England" (1849), alternately titled "The Founders Great in Their Unconscious."

5. Nathaniel Hawthorne, "Oliver Cromwell," in *True Stories from History and Biography,* ed. William Charvat et al., vol. 6 of The Centenary Edition (Columbus, Ohio, 1972), 252. See also Hawthorne's comments on the Cromwell Revolution in *The French and Italian Notebooks,* ed. Thomas Woodson, vol. 14 of The Centenary Edition (Columbus, Ohio, 1980), 9–10, 47–48; and compare these to his comments in this volume on the French Revolution (13–15, 38–39); to George Bancroft's contrast between Cromwell and George Washington in the 1850 revision of his *History of the United States,* 10 vols. (Boston, 1852), 2:23–27; and to Julian Hawthorne's recollections of his father's views of the American Revolution in *Memoirs,* ed. Edith G. Hawthorne (New York, 1938), 19. In *Exile and the Narrative Imagination* (New Haven, 1986), 29ff., Michael Seidel, analyzing *Robinson Crusoe,* offers a striking corollary to Hawthorne's use of historical analogues.

6. Nathaniel Hawthorne, *Life of Franklin Pierce* (Boston, 1852), 109–10. The most incisive use of the biography in this regard is Jonathan Arac, "The Politics of *The Scarlet Letter*," in *Ideology and Classic American Literature*, ed. Sacvan Bercovitch and Myra Jehlen (Cambridge, 1986), 247–66. I am much indebted to Arac's essay.

7. Hawthorne makes the connection explicit in the famous introductory passage where he "tries on" the "rag of scarlet cloth" (145). It is pertinent to my argument that this act of identification also serves to link Hester's "art . . . of needle-work" (188) to his own role as writer. As though to underscore the latter meaning, Hawthorne takes the occasion of his "*Preface* to the Second Edition" (30 March 1850) to record the "violent" response in "the respectable community immediately around him" to "The Custom House" introduction—the "public disapprobation [which] would weigh very heavily on him, were he conscious of deserving it," and "the atrocities of which he has been adjudged guilty" (119). The very vehemence of his language calls attention to the connections implied in the introduction between the office of his novel and that of Hester's A. I refer not only to Hawthorne's complaint about the Puritans' view of art but, more important, to the relation between the public humiliation that forces Hester to undertake the burden of the A and the political scandal that forced Hawthorne out of office in 1849 and thereby prepared the way for *The Scarlet Letter*. Authorial identification thus opens into a commentary on art as cultural work. Hawthorne tells us of Hester's needlework (with a laconic air reminiscent of his allusions in the introduction to his own situation as a writer) that her "art . . . sufficed, even in a land that afforded comparatively little scope for its exercise, to supply food for her thriving infant, and herself" (188). It provides her, too, with "a part to perform in the world" (190), one that is virtually shamanlike in its "unearthly" effects of healing, its "inexhaustible . . power to do, and power to sympathize" (257). After seven years, the A comes to impart to its "wearer a kind of sacredness" (258), and by the end Hester's very marginality is a mainstay of social order. So it is also in Hawthorne's case. When he places the letter on his breast, he transforms himself—as writer, as victim of party politics, as a marginal member of society, and as a son of the Puritans—into a symbol of cultural cohesion and continuity.

8. Herman Melville, *Clarel: A Poem and Pilgrimage in the Holy Land*, ed. Walter E. Bezanson (New York, 1960), 281, 157; Larry J. Reynolds, "*The Scarlet Letter* and Revolutions Abroad," *American Literature* 77 (1983): 44–67. Reynolds has expanded his research into a valuable book-length study, *Revolutions Abroad and the American Renaissance*, forthcoming.

9. Evert Duyckinck, quoted in Reynolds, "*Scarlet Letter*," 49; George Bancroft, quoted in Elizabeth Brett White, *American Opinion of France* (New York, 1927), 121; Ralph Waldo Emerson, *Journals*, ed. Edward Waldo Emerson, 10 vols. (Boston, 1910–14), 7:452; *New York Courier and Inquirer*, 14 July 1848, 1; George Bancroft, *Life and Letters*, ed. Mark A. De Wolfe Howe, 2 vols. (New York, 1908), 2:31, 33.

10. *New York Herald* and *Rochester Democrat*, reprinted in *History of Woman Suffrage*, ed. Elizabeth Cady Stanton, Susan B. Anthony, and Matilda Joslyn Gage, 6 vols. (New York, 1969), 1:805, 804.

11. F. O. Matthiessen, *American Renaissance: Art and Expression in the Age of Emerson and Whitman* (New York, 1941), 14: Ralph Waldo Emerson, *Complete Works*, ed. Edward Waldo Emerson, 12 vols. (Boston, 1903–4), 5:82; Emerson, *Journals and Miscellaneous Notebooks*, ed. Merton M. Sealts, Jr., 16 vols. (Cambridge, Mass., 1973), 10:154, 310, 312, 318.

12. Walt Whitman, "Europe, the 72nd and 73rd Years of These States," in *Complete Poetry and Collected Prose*, ed. Justin Kaplan, The Library of America (New York, 1982), 133; Whitman, quoted in Reynolds, *Revolutions Abroad*.

13. Ann Douglas, *The Feminization of American Culture* (New York, 1977), 259 (quoting Fuller); see also Francis E. Kearns, "Margaret Fuller as a Model for Hester Prynne," *Jahrbuch für Amerikastudien* 10 (1965): 191–97; and Belle Gale Chevigny, "To the Edges of Ideology; Margaret Fuller's Centrifugal Evolution," *American Quarterly* 38 (1986): 173–201.

14. Nathaniel Hawthorne, quoted in Reynolds, *Revolutions Abroad* (on Kossuth); and Hawthorne, *Life of Pierce*, 111–12.

15. Hawthorne, *Life of Pierce*, 113–14.

16. John Greenleaf Whittier, "The Kansas Emigrants," in *Complete Poetical Works* (Boston, 1894), 317; Abraham Lincoln, "Second Inaugural Address," in *Collected Works,* vol. 8, ed. Roy P. Basler (New Brunswick, N.J., 1953), 333.

17. Hawthorne's reference at this point to the Puritans' "iron" judgments is meant to remind us that *what is* is not only something *from* which society has evolved but something to which it *will* evolve. It is the climax of a long series of similar directives for interpretation, and he conveys it with appropriately intricate irony. At the moment that Hester comes to terms with Puritan judgment, we confront the full harshness of Puritan authority to allusion to the novel's most negative image of "that iron period," the "convex mirror" of Governor Bellingham's breastplate—the iron breastplate in which (many years before) Hester had seen "the scarlet letter . . . represented in [such] exaggerated and gigantic proportions [that] . . . she seemed absolutely hidden behind it" (208). Precisely at the point, then, where Hester registers her conversion to the A, we are asked to recall the distortions and concealments of Puritan exegesis at its most grotesque, so that we can better grasp the relation between compromise, continuity, and progress.

18. Bernard Bailyn, *The Ideological Origins of the American Revolution* (Cambridge, Mass., 1967), 232–33; Edmund Morgan, *American Freedom/American Slavery: The Ordeal of Colonial Virginia* (New York, 1975), passim.

19. Herman Melville, *Moby-Dick; or, The Whale,* in *Redburn, White-Jacket, Moby-Dick,* ed. G. Thomas Tanselle, The Library of America (New York, 1983), 1258, 969. See Paul Royster's brilliant "Melville's Economy of Language," in Bercovitch and Jehlen, *Ideology and Classic American Literature,* 313–36.

20. Pierre Macherey, *A Theory of Literary Production,* trans. Geoffrey Wall (London, 1978); Charles Feidelson, *"The Scarlet Letter,"* in *Hawthorne Centenary Essays,* ed. Roy Harvey Pearce (Columbus, Ohio, 1964), 62–63.

21. Norman Mailer, *The Armies of the Night: The Novel as History, History as the Novel* (New York, 1968), 44; Henry David Thoreau, *Walden; or, Life in the Woods,* in *A Week on the Concord and Merrimack Rivers, Walden, The Maine Woods, Cape Cod,* ed. Robert F. Sayre, The Library of America (New York, 1985), 577; Ralph Waldo Emerson, *Nature,* in *Essays and Lectures,* ed. Joel Porte, The Library of America (New York, 1983), 10; William Gilpin, quoted in Thomas L. Karnes, *William Gilpin, Western Nationalist* (Austin, Tex., 1970), 136. These vacancies of time and space were constructed so that the facts they displaced could be filled by ideology. Their function was not just to white out the actual process of emptying a continent. It was to make the territory anew—negatively as "wilderness," positively as "Nature"—in order to shape the mind of its invaders in the image of that ideological newness. The West was the scene of imperial rhetoric throughout the Americas, from the Canadian Bush Country to the Spanish American El Dorado; but only in the United States did the dominant culture find a rhetoric commensurate with territorial prospects: a symbology of wonder that could reconstitute the new inhabitants (and successive waves of immigrants after them) as a *tabula rasa* to be imprinted with images of "America" ("Adamic," "innocent") and typed forth as "representative Americans." The correspondences here between nature, the mind, spiritual rebirth, and national mission build directly on the language of errand. They create an alchemical *nihilum ex verbo,* a perpetual gap between words and facts through which words are transmuted into prophetic evidence and facts refined into symbols in process, like the scarlet letter.

22. One is utopian-pastoral, as in James Fennimore Cooper's *Deerslayer* (1841): the hero who does *not* return, and whose claim to office, accordingly, lies in his capacity to channel our protest into nostalgia. Another is dystopian-apocalyptic: the hero who *forces* the facts toward fulfillment, although what they signify is doom—the errand into self-obliteration that finds its classic expression in Melville's literary development, from *Mardi* (1848–49) through *Pierre* (1851–52). A third instance may be found in Emerson's major essays. Emersonian troping is nothing less than a transvaluation of the entire process of westwarding into an interior process of vision that re-presents America as potential. In effect, Emerson marshals the rhetoric of progress against imperialism; self-possession against pos-

sessive individualism; transition against upward mobility; marginality against the facts of the frontier; speculation against the marketplace; and summarily "America" against the United States. This is adversarial rhetoric but also an example par excellence of cultural counterdependence.

23. See Merrill D. Peterson, *The Great Triumvirate: Webster, Clay, and Calhoun* (Oxford, 1987), passim.

24. Noah Webster, *American Dictionary of the English Language* (New York, 1828); *American Dictionary* (New York, 1832); and *American Dictionary . . . Revised and Enlarged,* ed. Chauncey A. Goodrich (Springfield, Mass., 1848).

25. Ralph Waldo Emerson, "The Fugitive Slave Law," in *Complete Works,* 11:216; Daniel Webster, *On the Subject of Slavery* (Boston, 1850), 28–29; and Webster, *On the Compromise Bill* (Washington, D.C., 1850), 19.

26. Hawthorne, *Life of Pierce,* 110; and *French and Italian Notebooks,* September 1858, 433. On the parallels between Webster's view and Hawthorne's, see Frank Preston Stearns, *The Life and Genius of Nathanial Hawthorne* (Philadelphia, 1906), 261; and on the parallels between Webster's views and John Louis O'Sullivan's, see Albert K. Weinberg, *Manifest Destiny: A Study of Nationalist Expansionism in American History* (Baltimore, 1935), 66 and passim.

27. Abraham Lincoln, "A House Divided," in *Collected Works,* 2:461; Ralph Waldo Emerson, "John Brown," in *Complete Works,* 11:251–52 ("Boston Speech"); Noah Webster, *American Dictionary . . . Improved,* ed. Chauncey A. Goodrich and Noah Porter (Springfield, Mass., 1866).

28. Henry James, *Hawthorne,* in *Essays on Literature: American Writers, English Writers,* ed. Leon Edel, The Library of America (New York, 1984), 412; Nathaniel Hawthorne, *Our Old Home,* ed. William Charvat et al., vol. 5 of The Centenary Edition (Columbus, Ohio, 1970), 4.

29. Nathaniel Hawthorne, preface to *The Marble Faun,* in *Novels,* 854; "Chiefly About War-Matters," *Atlantic Monthly* 10 (1862): 43.

30. Samuel Sherwood, *The Church's Flight into the Wilderness* (Boston, 1776), 31; Thomas Paine, *Common Sense,* ed. Nelson F. Adkins (New York, 1953), 25–27; Andrew Jackson, "Second Annual Message" (6 December 1830), in *Antebellum American Culture: An Interpretive Anthology,* ed. David Brion Davis (Lexington, Ky., 1979), 241; Ralph Waldo Emerson, "The Method of Nature," in *Essays and Lectures,* 124.

31. Ralph Waldo Emmerson, "The Fugitive Slave Law," in *Complete Works,* 11:224–30.

32. Ralph Waldo Emerson, "The American Scholar," in *Essays and Lectures,* 71; Emerson, *Representative Men,* in *Essays and Lectures,* 616; Emerson, "The Fortune of the Republic," in *Complete Works,* 11:541.

33. Hans Blumenberg, "The Concepts of Reality and the Possibility of the Novel," in *New Perspectives in German Literary Criticism,* ed. Richard Amacher and Victor Lange (Princeton, N.J., 1979), 32.

34. Julia Ward Howe, "Battle Hym of the Republic," in *Parnassus,* ed. Ralph Waldo Emerson (Boston, 1875), 230. In "Una Hawthorne, Little Pearl, and the Cultural Construction of Gender," *PMLA* 103 (1988): 285–97. J. Walter Herbert draws an interesting comparison between Hester's prophecy and Hawthorne's culture's creed of domesticity. An equally pertinent comparison for my purpose is the "statute of liberty" sculpted by Hiram Powers, upon whom (in part) Hawthorne modeled Kenyon, the artist-hero of *The Marble Faun.* Powers began work on the statue in Florence in 1848; by 1852 he was lamenting the misfortune of creating the "goddess of Liberty in this land of . . . anarchy"—"but," he added, "as she is not likely to remain here very long it is to be hoped that she will not carry the infection [of European revolution] . . . with her to *America, where . . . her doctrine is received as gospel."* Powers called the statue *America,* and Hawthorne, who urged Pierce to purchase it for the Capitol, approved (it "embodies the ideas of youth, freedom, progress"), adding privately that the sculptor was not only "a great artist" but "very American"; *French and Italian Notebooks;* 436–37. Quotations from Powers are from Jean F. Yellin, "Caps and Chains: Hiram Powers' Statue of 'Liberty,' " *American Quarterly* 38 (1986): 798–826.

35. See Horatio Bridge, *Personal Recollections of Nathaniel Hawthorne* (New York, 1893), 112.

36. Hawthorne, "Chiefly About War-Matters," 66. On Hawthorne's deliberate distortion of the Customs House eagle, see Hugh J. Dawson, *"The Scarlet Letter's* Angry Eagle and the Salem Customs House," *Essex Institute Historical Collections* 120 (1986): 30–34.

Toni Morrison

Unspeakable Things Unspoken: The Afro-American Presence in American Literature

I

I planned to call this paper "Canon Fodder," because the terms put me in mind of a kind of trained muscular response that appears to be on display in some areas of the recent canon debate. But I changed my mind (so many have used the phrase) and hope to make clear the appropriateness of the title I settled on.

My purpose here is to observe the panoply of this most recent and most anxious series of questions concerning what should or does constitute a literary canon in order to suggest ways of addressing the Afro-American presence in American Literature that require neither slaughter nor reification—views that may spring the whole literature of an entire nation from the solitude into which it has been locked. There is something called American literature that, according to conventional wisdom, is certainly not Chicano literature, or Afro-American literature, or Asian-American, or Native American, or . . . . It is somehow separate from them and they from it, and in spite of the efforts of recent literary histories, restructured curricula and anthologies, this separate confinement, be it breached or endorsed, is the subject of a large part of these debates. Although the terms used, like the vocabulary of earlier canon debates, refer to literary and/or humanistic value, aesthetic criteria, value-free or socially anchored readings, the contemporary battle plain is most often understood to be the claims of others against the whitemale origins and definitions of those values; whether those definitions reflect an eternal, universal and transcending paradigm or whether they constitute a disguise for a temporal, political and culturally specific program.

Part of the history of this particular debate is located in the successful assault that the feminist scholarship of men and women (black and white) made and continues to make on traditional literary discourse. The male part of the whitemale equation is already deeply engaged, and no one believes the body of literature and its criticism will ever again be what it was in 1965: the protected preserve of the thoughts and works and analytical strategies of whitemen.

It is, however, the "white" part of the question that this paper focuses on, and it is to my great relief that such terms as "white" and "race" can enter serious discussion of literature. Although still a swift and swiftly obeyed call to arms, their use is no longer forbidden.[1] It may appear churlish to doubt the sincerity, or question the proclaimed well-intentioned self-lessness of a 900-year-old academy struggling through decades of chaos to "maintain standards." Yet of what use is it to go on about "quality" being the only criterion for greatness knowing that the definition of quality is itself the subject of much rage and is seldom universally agreed upon by everyone at all times? Is it to appropriate the term for reasons of state; to be in the position to distribute greatness or withhold it? Or to actively pursue the ways and places in which quality surfaces and stuns us into silence or into language worthy enough to describe it? What is possible is to try to recognize, identify and applaud the fight for and triumph of quality when it is revealed to us and to let go the notion that only the dominant culture or gender can make those judgments, identify that quality or produce it.

Those who claim the superiority of Western culture are entitled to that claim only when Western civilization is measured thoroughly against other civilizations and not found wanting, and when Western civilization owns up to its own sources in the cultures that preceded it.

A large part of the satisfaction I have always received from reading Greek tragedy, for example, is in its similarity to Afro-American communal structures (the function of song and chorus, the heroic struggle between the claims of community and individual hubris) and African religion and philosophy. In other words, that is part of the reason it has quality for me—I feel intellectually at home there. But that could hardly be so for those unfamiliar with my "home," and hardly a requisite for the pleasure they take. The point is, the form (Greek tragedy) makes available these varieties of provocative love because *it* is masterly—not because the civilization that is its referent was flawless or superior to all others.

One has the feeling that nights are becoming sleepless in some quarters, and it seems to me obvious that the recoil of traditional "humanists" and some post-modern theorists to this particular aspect of the debate, the "race" aspect, is as severe as it is because the claims for attention come from that segment of scholarly and artistic labor in which the mention of "race" is either inevitable or elaborately, painstakingly masked; and if all of the ramifications that the term demands are taken seriously, the bases of Western civilization will require re-thinking. Thus, in spite of its implicit and explicit acknowledgement, "race" is still a virtually unspeakable thing, as can be seen in the apologies, notes of "special use" and circumscribed definitions that accompany it[2]—not least of which is my own deference in surrounding it with quotation marks. Suddenly (for our purposes, suddenly) "race" does not exist. For three hundred years black Americans insisted that "race" was no usefully distinguishing factor in human relationships. During those same three centuries every academic discipline, including theology, history, and natural science, insisted "race" was *the* determining factor in human development. When blacks discovered they had shaped or become a culturally formed race, and that it had specific and revered difference, suddenly they were told there *is* no such thing as "race," biological or cultural, that matters and that genuinely intellectual exchange cannot accommodate it.[3] In trying to come to some terms about "race" and writing, I am tempted to throw my hands up. It always seemed to me that the people who invented the hierarchy of "race" when it was convenient for them ought not to be the ones to explain it away, now that it does not suit their purposes for it to exist. But there is culture and both gender and "race" inform and are informed by it. Afro-American culture exists and though it is clear (and becoming clearer) how it has responded to Western culture, the instances where and means by which it has shaped Western culture are poorly recognized or understood.

I want to address ways in which the presence of Afro-American literature and the awareness of its culture both resuscitate the study of literature in the United States and raise that study's standards. In pursuit of that goal, it will suit my purposes to contextualize the route canon debates have taken in Western literary criticism.

I do not believe this current anxiety can be attributed solely to the routine, even cyclical arguments within literary communities reflecting unpredictable yet inevitable shifts in taste, relevance or perception. Shifts in which an enthusiasm for and official endorsement of William Dean Howells, for example, withered; or in which the legalization of Mark Twain in critical court rose and fell like the fathoming of a sounding line (for which he may or may not have named himself); or even the slow, delayed but steady swell of attention and devotion on which Emily Dickinson soared to what is now, surely, a permanent crest of respect. No. Those were discoveries, reappraisals of individual artists. Serious but not destabilizing. Such accommodations were simple because the questions they posed were simple: Are there one hundred sterling examples of high literary art in American literature and no more? One hundred and six? If one or two fall into disrepute, is there space, then, for one or two others in the vestibule, waiting like girls for bells chimed by future husbands who alone can promise them security, legitimacy—and in whose hands alone rests the gift of critical longevity? Interesting questions, but, as I say, not endangering.

Nor is this detachable academic sleeplessness the consequence of a much more radical shift, such as the mid-nineteenth century one heralding the authenticity of American literature itself. Or an even earlier upheaval—receding now into the distant past—in which theology and thereby Latin, was displaced for the equally rigorous study of the classics and Greek to be followed by what was considered a strangely arrogant and upstart proposal: that English literature was a suitable course of study for an aristocratic education, and not simply morally instructive fodder designed for the working classes. (The Chaucer Society was founded in 1848, four hundred years after Chaucer died.) No. This exchange seems unusual somehow, keener. It has a more strenuously argued (and felt) defense and a more vigorously insistent attack. And both defenses and attacks have spilled out of the academy into the popular press. Why? Resistance to displacement within or expansion of a canon is not, after all, surprising or unwarranted. That's what canonization is for. (And the question of whether there should be a canon or not seems disingenuous to me—there always is one whether there should be or not—for it is in the interests of the professional critical community to have one.) Certainly a sharp alertness as to *why* a work is or is not worthy of study is the legitimate occupation of the critic, the pedagogue and the artist. What is astonishing in the contemporary debate is not the resistance to displacement of works or to the expansion of genre within it, but the virulent passion that accompanies this resistance and, more importantly, the quality of its defense weaponry. The guns are very big; the trigger-fingers quick. But I am convinced the mechanism of the defenders of the flame is faulty. Not only may the hands of the gun-slinging cowboy-scholars be blown off, not only may the target be missed, but the subject of the conflagration (the sacred texts) is sacrificed, disfigured in the battle. This canon fodder may kill the canon. And I, at least, do not intend to live without Aeschylus or William Shakespeare, or James or Twain or Hawthorne, or Melville, etc., etc., etc. There must be some way to enhance canon readings without enshrining them.

When Milan Kundera, in *The Art of the Novel,* identified the historical territory of the novel by saying "The novel is Europe's creation" and that "The only context for grasping a novel's worth is the history of the European novel," the *New Yorker* reviewer stiffened. Kundera's "personal 'idea of the novel,'" he wrote, "is so profoundly Eurocentric that it's likely to seem exotic, even perverse, to American readers. . . . *The Art of the Novel* gives off the occasional (but pungent) whiff of cultural arrogance, and we may feel that Kundera's discourse . . . reveals an aspect of his character that we'd rather not have known about. . . . In order to become the artist he now is, the Czech novelist had to discover himself a second time, as a European. But what if that second, grander possibility hadn't been there to be discovered? What if Broch, Kafka, Musil—all that reading—had never been a part of his education, or had entered it only as exotic, alien presence? Kundera's polemical fervor in *The Art of the Novel* annoys us, as American readers, because we feel defensive, excluded from the transcendent 'idea of the novel' that for him seems simply to have been there for the taking. (If only he had cited, in his redeeming version of the novel's history, a few more heroes from the New World's culture.) Our novelists don't discover cultural values within themselves; they invent them."[4]

Kundera's views, obliterating American writers (with the exception of William Faulkner) from his own canon, are relegated to a "smugness" that Terrence Rafferty disassociates from Kundera's imaginative work and applies to the "sublime confidence" of his critical prose. The confidence of an exile who has the sentimental education of, and the choice to become, a European.

I was refreshed by Rafferty's comments. With the substitution of certain phrases, his observations and the justifiable umbrage he takes can be appropriated entirely by Afro-American writers regarding their own exclusion from the "transcendent 'idea of the novel.'"

For the present turbulence seems not to be about the flexibility of a canon, its range among and between Western countries, but about its miscegenation. The word is informative here and I do mean its use. A powerful ingredient in this debate concerns the incursion of third-world or so-called minority literature into a Eurocentric stronghold. When the topic of third world culture is raised, unlike the topic of Scandinavian culture, for example, a possible threat to and implicit criticism of the reigning equilibrium is seen to be raised as well. From the seventeenth century to the twentieth, the arguments resisting that incursion have marched in predictable sequence: 1) there is no Afro-American (or third world) art. 2) it exists but is inferior. 3) it exists and is superior when it measures up to the "universal" criteria of Western art. 4) it is not so much "art" as ore—rich ore—that requires a Western or Eurocentric smith to refine it from its "natural" state into an aesthetically complex form.

A few comments on a larger, older, but no less telling academic struggle—an extremely successful one—may be helpful here. It is telling because it sheds light on certain aspects of this current debate and may locate its sources. I made reference above to the radical upheaval in canon-building that took place at the inauguration of classical studies and Greek. This canonical re-routing from scholasticism to humanism, was not merely radical, it must have been (may I say it?) savage. And it took some seventy years to accomplish. Seventy years to eliminate Egypt as the cradle of civilization *and* its model and replace it with Greece. The triumph of that process was that Greece lost its own origins and became itself original. A number of scholars in various disciplines (history, anthropology, ethnobotany, etc.) have put forward their research into cross-cultural and inter-cultural transmissions with varying degrees of success in the reception of their work. I am reminded of the curious publishing history of Ivan van Sertima's work, *They Came Before Columbus,* which researches the African presence in Ancient America. I am reminded of Edward Said's *Orientalism,* and especially the work of Martin Bernal, a linguist, trained in Chinese history, who has defined himself as an interloper in the field of classical civilization but who has offered, in *Black Athena,* a stunning investigation of the field. According to Bernal, there are two "models" of Greek history: one views Greece as Aryan or European (the Aryan Model); the other sees it as Levantine—absorbed by Egyptian and Semitic culture (the Ancient Model). "If I am right," writes Professor Bernal, "in urging the overthrow of the Aryan Model and its replacement by the Revised Ancient one, it will be necessary not only to rethink the fundamental bases of 'Western Civilization' but also to recognize the penetration of racism and 'continental chauvinism' into all our historiography, or philosophy of writing history. The Ancient Model had no major 'internal' deficiencies or weaknesses in explanatory power. It was overthrown for external reasons. For eighteenth and nineteenth century Romantics and racists it was simply intolerable for Greece, which was seen not merely as the epitome of Europe but also as its pure childhood, to have been the result of the mixture of native Europeans and *colonizing* Africans and Semites. Therefore the Ancient Model had to be overthrown and replaced by something more acceptable."[5]

It is difficult not to be persuaded by the weight of documentation Martin Bernal brings to his task and his rather dazzling analytical insights. What struck me in his analysis were the *process* of the fabrication of Ancient Greece and the *motives* for the fabrication. The latter (motive) involved the concept of purity, of progress. The former (process) required mis-reading, pre-determined selectivity of authentic sources, and—silence. From the Christian theological appropriation of Israel (the Levant), to the early nineteenth-century work of the prodigious Karl Müller, work that effectively dismissed the Greeks' own record of their influences and origins as their "Egyptomania," their tendency to be "wonderstruck" by Egyptian culture, a tendency "manifested in the 'delusion' that Egyptians and other non-European 'barbarians' had possessed superior cultures, from which the Greeks had borrowed massively,"[6] on through the Romantic response to the Enlightenment, and the decline into disfavor of the Phoenicians, "the essential force behind the rejection of the tradition of massive Phoenician influence on early Greece was the rise of racial—as opposed to religious—anti-semitism. This was because the Phoenicians were correctly perceived to have been culturally very close to the Jews."[7]

I have quoted at perhaps too great a length from Bernal's text because *motive,* so seldom an element brought to bear on the history of history, is located, delineated and confronted in Bernal's research, and has helped my own thinking about the process and motives of scholarly attention to and an appraisal of Afro-American presence in the literature of the United States.

Canon building is Empire building. Canon defense is national defense. Canon debate, whatever the terrain, nature and range (of criticism, of history, of the history of knowledge, of the definition of language, the universality of aesthetic principles, the sociology of art, the humanistic imagination), is the clash of cultures. And *all* of the interests are vested.

In such a melee as this one—a provocative, healthy, explosive melee—extraordinarily profound work is being done. Some of the controversy, however, has degenerated into *ad hominem* and unwarranted speculation on the personal habits of artists, specious and silly arguments about politics (the destabilizing forces are dismissed as merely political; the status quo sees itself as not—as though the term "*a*political" were only its prefix and not the most obviously political stance imaginable since one of the functions of political ideology is to pass itself off as immutable, natural and "innocent"), and covert expressions of critical inquiry designed to neutralize and disguise the political interests of the discourse. Yet much of the research and analysis has rendered speakable what was formerly unspoken and has made humanistic studies, once again, the place where one has to go to find out what's going on. Cultures, whether silenced or monologistic, whether repressed or repressing, seek meaning in the language and images available to them.

Silences are being broken, lost things have been found and at least two generations of scholars are disentangling received knowledge from the apparatus of control, most notably those who are engaged in investigations of French and British Colonialist Literature, American slave narratives, and the delineation of the Afro-American literary tradition.

Now that Afro-American artistic presence has been "discovered" actually to exist, now that serious scholarship has moved from silencing the witnesses and erasing their meaningful place in and contribution to American culture, it is no longer acceptable merely to imagine us and imagine for us. We have always been imagining ourselves. We are not Isak Dinesen's "aspects of nature," nor Conrad's unspeaking. We are the subjects of our own narrative, witnesses to and participants in our own experience, and, in no way coincidentally, in the experience of those with whom we have come in contact. We are not, in fact, "other." We are choices. And to read imaginative literature by and about us is to choose to examine centers of the self and to have the opportunity to compare these centers with the "raceless" one with which we are, all of us, most familiar.

II

Recent approaches to the reading of Afro-American literature have come some distance; have addressed those arguments, mentioned earlier, (which are not arguments, but attitudes) that have, since the seventeenth century, effectively silenced the autonomy of that literature. As for the charge that "there is no Afro-American art," contemporary critical analysis of the literature and the recent surge of reprints and re-discoveries have buried it, and are pressing on to expand the traditional canon to include classic Afro-American works where generically and chronologically appropriate, and to devise strategies for reading and thinking about these texts.

As to the second silencing charge, "Afro-American art exists, but is inferior," again, close readings and careful research into the culture out of which the art is born have addressed and still address the labels that once passed for stringent analysis but can no more: that it is imitative, excessive, sensational, mimetic (merely), and unintellectual, though very often "moving," "passionate," "naturalistic," "realistic" or sociologically "revealing." These labels may be construed as compliments or pejoratives and if valid, and shown as such, so much the better. More often than not, however, they are the lazy, easy brand-name applications when the hard work of analysis is deemed too hard, or when the critic does not have access to the scope the work demands. Strategies designed to counter this lazy labeling include the application of recent literary theories to Afro-American literature so that non-canonical texts can be incorporated into existing and forming critical discourse.

The third charge, that "Afro-American art exists, but is superior only when it measures up to the 'universal' criteria of Western art," produces the most seductive form of analysis, for both writer and critic, because comparisons are a major form of knowledge and flattery. The risks, nevertheless, are twofold: 1) the gathering of a culture's difference into the skirts of the Queen is a neutralization designed and constituted to elevate and maintain hegemony. 2) circumscribing and limiting the literature to a mere reaction to or denial of the Queen, judging the work solely in terms of its referents to Eurocentric criteria, or its sociological accuracy, political correctness or its pretense of having no politics at all, cripple the literature and infantilize the serious work of imaginative writing. This response-oriented concept of Afro-American literature contains the seeds of the next (fourth) charge: that when Afro-American art is worthy, it is because it is "raw" and "rich," like ore, and like ore needs refining by Western intelligences. Finding or imposing Western influences in/on Afro-American literature has value, but when its sole purpose is to *place* value only where that influence is located it is pernicious.

My unease stems from the possible, probable, consequences these approaches may have upon the work itself. They can lead to an incipient orphanization of the work in order to issue its adoption papers. They can confine the discourse to the advocacy of diversification within the canon and/or a kind of benign co-existence near or within reach of the already sacred texts. Either of these two positions can quickly become another kind of silencing if permitted to ignore the indigenous created qualities of the writing. So many questions surface and irritate. What have these critiques made of the work's own canvas? Its paint, its frame, its framelessness, its spaces? Another list of approved subjects? Of approved treatments? More self-censoring, more exclusion of the specificity of the culture, the gender, the language? Is there perhaps an alternative utility in these studies? To advance power or locate its fissures? To oppose elitist interests in order to enthrone egalitarian effacement? Or is it merely to rank and grade the readable product as distinct from the writerable production? Can this criticism reveal ways in which the author combats and confronts received prejudices and even creates *other terms* in which to rethink one's attachment to or intolerance of the material of these works? What is important in all of this is that the critic not be engaged in laying claim on behalf of the text to his or her own dominance and power. Nor to exchange his or her professional anxieties for the imagined turbulence of the text. "The text should become a problem of passion, not a pretext for it."

There are at least three focuses that seem to me to be neither reactionary nor simple pluralism, nor the even simpler methods by which the study of Afro-American literature remains the helpful doorman into the halls of sociology. Each of them, however, requires wakefulness.

One is the development of a theory of literature that truly accommodates Afro-American literature: one that is based on its culture, its history, and the artistic strategies the works employ to negotiate the world it inhabits.

Another is the examination and re-interpretation of the American canon, the founding nineteenth-century works, for the "unspeakable things unspoken"; for the ways in which the presence of Afro-Americans had shaped the choices, the language, the structure—the meaning of so much American literature. A search, in other words, for the ghost in the machine.

A third is the examination of contemporary and/or non-canonical literature for this presence, regardless of its category as mainstream, minority, or what you will. I am always amazed by the resonances, the structural gear-shifts, and the *uses* to which Afro-American narrative, persona and idiom are put in contemporary "white" literature. And in Afro-American literature itself the question of difference, of essence, is critical. What makes a work "Black"? The most valuable point of entry into the question of cultural (or racial) distinction, the one most fraught, is its language—its unpoliced, seditious, confrontational, manipulative, inventive, disruptive, masked and unmasking language. Such a penetration will entail the most careful study, one in which the impact of Afro-American presence on modernity becomes clear and is no longer a well-kept secret.

I would like to touch, for just a moment, on focuses two and three.

We can agree, I think, that invisible things are not necessarily "not-there"; that a void may be empty, but is not a vacuum. In addition, certain absences are so stressed, so ornate, so planned, they call attention to themselves; arrest us with intentionality and purpose, like neighborhoods that are defined by the population held away from them. Looking at the scope of American literature, I can't help thinking that the question should never have been "Why am I, an Afro-American, absent from it?" It is not a particularly interesting query anyway. The spectacularly interesting question is "What intellectual feats had to be performed by the author or his critic to erase me from a society seething with my presence, and what effect has that performance had on the work?" What are the strategies of escape from knowledge? Of willful oblivion? I am not recommending an inquiry into the obvious impulse that overtakes a soldier sitting in a World War I trench to think of salmon fishing. That kind of pointed "turning from," deliberate escapism or transcendence may be life-saving in a circumstance of immediate duress. The exploration I am suggesting is, how does one sit in the audience observing, watching the performance of Young America, say, in the nineteenth century, say, and reconstruct the play, its director, its plot and its cast in such a manner that its very point never surfaces? Not why. How? Ten years after Tocqueville's prediction in 1840 that "'Finding no stuff for the ideal in what is real and true, poets would flee to imaginary regions . . .' in 1850 at the height of slavery and burgeoning abolitionism, American writers chose romance."⁸ Where, I wonder, in these romances is the shadow of the presence from which the text has fled? Where does it heighten, where does it dislocate, where does it necessitate novelistic invention; what does it release; what does it hobble?

The device (or arsenal) that serves the purpose of flight can be Romanticism versus verisimilitude; new criticism versus shabbily disguised and questionably sanctioned "moral uplift"; the "complex series of evasion," that is sometimes believed to be the essence of modernism; the perception of the evolution of art; the cultivation of irony, parody; the nostalgia for "literary language"; the rhetorically unconstrained textuality versus socially anchored textuality, and the undoing of textuality altogether. These critical strategies can (but need not) be put into service to reconstruct the historical world to suit specific cultural and political purposes. Many of these strategies have produced powerfully creative work. Whatever *uses* to which Romanticism is put, however suspicious its origins, it has produced an incontestably wonderful body of work. In other instances these strategies have succeeded in paralyzing both the work and its criticism. In still others they have led to a virtual infantilization of the writer's intellect, his sensibility, his craft. They have reduced the meditations on theory into a "power struggle among sects" reading unauthored and unauthorable material, rather than an outcome of reading *with* the author the text both construct.

In other words, the critical process has made wonderful work of some wonderful work, and recently the means of access to the old debates have altered. The problem now is putting the question. Is the nineteenth century flight from blackness, for example, successful in mainstream American literature? Beautiful? Artistically problematic? Is the text sabotaged by its proclamations of "universality"? Are there ghosts in the machine? Active but unsummoned presences that can distort the workings of the machine and can also *make* it work? These kinds of questions have been consistently put by critics of Colonial Literature vis-à-vis Africa and India and other third world countries. American literature would benefit from similar critiques. I am made melancholy when I consider that the act of defending the Eurocentric Western posture in literature as not only "universal" but also "race-free" may have resulted in lobotomizing that literature, and in diminishing both the art and the artist. Like the surgical removal of legs so that the body can remain enthroned, immobile, static—under house arrest, so to speak. It may be, of course, that contemporary writers deliberately exclude from their conscious writerly world the subjective appraisal of groups perceived as "other," and whitemale writers frequently abjure and deny the excitement of framing or locating their literature in the political world. Nineteenth-century writers, however, would never have given it a thought. Mainstream writers in Young America understood their competition to be national, cultural, but only in relationship to the Old World, certainly not vis-à-vis an ancient race (whether Native American or African) that was stripped of articulateness and intellectual thought, rendered, in D. H. Lawrence's term, "uncreate." For these early American writers, how could there be competition with nations or peoples who were presumed unable to handle or uninterested in handling the written word? One could write about them, but there was never the danger of their "writing back." Just as one could speak to them without fear of their "talking back." One could even observe them, hold them in prolonged gaze, without encountering the risk of being observed, viewed, or judged in return. And if, on occasion, they were themselves viewed and judged, it was out of political necessity and, for the purposes of art, could not matter. Or so thought Young America. It could never have occurred to Edgar Allan Poe in 1848 that I, for example, might read *The Gold Bug* and watch his efforts to render my grandfather's speech to something as close to braying as possible, an effort so intense you can see the perspiration—and the stupidity—when Jupiter says, "I knows," and Mr. Poe spells the verb "nose."*

Yet in spite or because of this monologism there is a great, ornamental, prescribed absence in early American literature and, I submit, it is instructive. It only seems that the canon of American literature is "naturally" or "inevitably" "white." In fact it is studiously so. In fact these absences of vital presences in Young American literature may be the insistent fruit of the scholarship rather than the text. Perhaps some of these writers, although under current house arrest, have much more to say than has been realized. Perhaps some were not so much transcending politics, or escaping blackness, as they were transforming it into intelligible, accessible, yet artistic modes of discourse. To ignore this possibility by never questioning the strategies of transformation is to disenfranchise the writer, diminish the text and render the bulk of the literature aesthetically and historically incoherent—an exorbitant price for cultural (white-male) purity, and, I believe, a spendthrift one. The reexamination of founding literature of the United States for the unspeakable unspoken may reveal those texts to have deeper and other meanings, deeper and other power, deeper and other significances.

One such writer, in particular, it has been almost impossible to keep under lock and key is Herman Melville.

Among several astute scholars, Michael Rogin has done one of the most exhaustive studies of how deeply Melville's social thought is woven into his writing. He calls our attention to the connection Melville made between American slavery and American freedom, how heightened the one rendered the other. And he has provided evidence of the impact on the work of Melville's family, milieu, and, most importantly, the raging, all-encompassing conflict of the time: slavery. He has reminded us that it was Melville's father-in-law who had, as judge, decided the case that made the Fugitive Slave Law law, and that "other evidence in *Moby Dick* also suggests the impact of Shaw's ruling on the climax of Melville's tale. Melville conceived the final confrontation between Ahab and the white whale some time in the first half of 1851. He may well have written his last chapters only after returning from a trip to New York in June. [Judge Shaw's decision was handed down in April, 1851]. When New York anti-slavery leaders William Seward and John van Buren wrote public letters protesting the *Sims* ruling, the New York *Herald* responded. Its attack on "The Anti-Slavery Agitators" began: "Did you ever see a whale? Did you ever see a mighty whale struggling?" . . .⁹

Rogin also traces the chronology of the whale from its "birth in a state of nature" to its

---

*Author's Note: Older America is not always distinguishable from its infancy. We may pardon Edgar Allan Poe in 1848 but it should have occurred to Kenneth Lynn in 1986 that some young Native American might read his Hemingway biography and see herself described as "squaw" by this respected scholar, and that some young men might shudder reading the words "buck" and "half-breed" so casually included in his scholarly speculations.

final end as commodity.[10] Central to his argument is that Melville in *Moby Dick* was being allegorically and insistently political in his choice of the whale. But within his chronology, one singular whale transcends all others, goes beyond nature, adventure, politics and commodity to an abstraction. What is this abstraction? This "wicked idea"? Interpretation has been varied. It has been viewed as an allegory of the state in which Ahab is Calhoun, or Daniel Webster; an allegory of capitalism and corruption, God and man, the individual and fate, and most commonly, the single allegorical meaning of the white whale is understood to be brute, indifferent Nature, and Ahab the madman who challenges that Nature.

But let us consider, again, the principal actor, Ahab, created by an author who calls himself Typee, signed himself Tawney, identified himself as Ishmael, and who had written several books before *Moby Dick* criticizing missionary forays into various paradises.

Ahab loses sight of the commercial value of his ship's voyage, its point, and pursues an idea in order to destroy it. His intention, revenge, "an audacious, immitigable and supernatural revenge," develops stature—maturity—when we realize that he is not a man mourning his lost leg or a scar on his face. However intense and dislocating his fever and recovery had been after his encounter with the white whale, however satisfactorily "male" this vengeance is read, the vanity of it is almost adolescent. But if the whale is more than blind, indifferent Nature unsubduable by masculine aggression, if it is as much its adjective as it is its noun, we can consider the possibility that Melville's "truth" was his recognition of the moment in America when whiteness became ideology. And if the white whale is the ideology of race, what Ahab has lost to it is personal dismemberment and family and society and his own place as a human in the world. The trauma of racism is, for the racist and the victim, the severe fragmentation of the self, and has always seemed to me a cause (not a symptom) of psychosis—strangely of no interest to psychiatry. Ahab, then, is navigating between an idea of civilization that he renounces and an idea of savagery he must annihilate, because the two cannot co-exist. The former is based on the latter. What is terrible in its complexity is that the idea of savagery is not the missionary one: it is white racial ideology that is savage and if, indeed, a white, nineteenth-century, American male took on not abolition, not the amelioration of racist institutions or their laws, but the very concept of whiteness as an inhuman idea, he would be very alone, very desperate, and very doomed. Madness would be the only appropriate description of such audacity, and "he heaves me," the most succinct and appropriate description of that obsession.

I would not like to be understood to argue that Melville was engaged in some simple and simple-minded black/white didacticism, or that he was satanizing white people. Nothing like that. What I am suggesting is that he was overwhelmed by the philosophical and metaphysical inconsistencies of an extraordinary and unprecedented idea that had its fullest manifestation in his own time in his own country, and that that idea was the successful assertion of whiteness as ideology.

On the *Pequod* the multiracial, mainly foreign, proletariat is at work to produce a commodity, but it is diverted and converted from that labor to Ahab's more significant intellectual quest. We leave whale as commerce and confront whale as metaphor. With that interpretation in place, two of the most famous chapters of the book become luminous in a completely new way. One is Chapter 9, The Sermon. In Father Mapple's thrilling rendition of Jonah's trials, emphasis is given to the purpose of Jonah's salvation. He is saved from the fish's belly for one single purpose, "To preach the Truth to the face of Falsehood! That was it!" Only then the reward "Delight"—which strongly calls to mind Ahab's lonely necessity. "Delight is to him . . . who against the proud gods and commodores of this earth, ever stand forth his own inexorable self. . . . Delight is to him whose strong arms yet support him, when the ship of this base treacherous world has gone down beneath him. Delight is to him who gives no quarter in the truth and kills, burns, and destroys all *sin* though he pluck it out from under the robes of Senators and Judges. Delight—top-gallant delight is to him who acknowledges no law or lord, but the Lord his God, and is only a *patriot to heaven"* [italics mine]. No one, I think, has denied that the sermon is designed to be prophetic, but it seems unremarked what the nature of the sin is—the sin that must be destroyed, regardless. Nature? A sin? The terms do not apply. Capitalism? Perhaps. Capitalism fed greed, lent itself inexorably to corruption, but probably was not in and of itself sinful to Melville. Sin suggests a moral outrage within the bounds of man to repair. The concept of racial superiority would fit seamlessly. It is difficult to read those words ("destruction of sin," "patriot to heaven") and not hear in them the description of a different Ahab. Not an adolescent male in adult clothing, a maniacal egocentric, or the "exotic plant" that V. S. Parrington thought Melville was. Not even a morally fine liberal voice adjusting, balancing, compromising with racial institutions. But another Ahab: the only white male American heroic enough to try to slay the monster that was devouring the world as he knew it.

Another chapter that seems freshly lit by this reading is Chapter 42, The Whiteness of the Whale. Melville points to the do-or-die significance of his effort to say something unsayable in this chapter. "I almost despair," he writes, "of putting it in a comprehensive form. It was the whiteness of the whale that above all things appalled me. But how can I hope to explain myself here; and yet in some dim, random way, explain myself I must, *else all these chapters might be naught"* [italics mine]. The language of this chapter ranges between benevolent, beautiful images of whiteness and whiteness as sinister and shocking. After dissecting the ineffable, he concludes: "Therefore . . . symbolize whatever grand or gracious he will by whiteness, no man can deny that in its profoundest *idealized significance* it calls up a peculiar apparition to the soul." I stress "idealized significance" to emphasize and make clear (if such clarity needs stating) that Melville is not exploring white *people,* but whiteness idealized. Then, after informing the reader of his "hope to light upon some chance clue to conduct us to the hidden course we seek," he tries to nail it. To provide the key to the "hidden course." His struggle to do so is gigantic. He cannot. Nor can we. But in nonfigurative language, he identifies the imaginative tools needed to solve the problem: "subtlety appeals to subtlety, and without imagination no man can follow another into these halls." And his final observation reverberates with personal trauma. "This visible [colored] world seems formed in love, the invisible [white] spheres were formed in fright." The necessity for whiteness as privileged "natural" state, the invention of it, was indeed formed in fright.

"Slavery," writes Rogin, "confirmed Melville's isolation, decisively established in *Moby Dick,* from the dominant consciousness of his time." I differ on this point and submit that Melville's hostility and repugnance for slavery would have found company. There were many white Americans of his acquaintance who felt repelled by slavery, wrote journalism about it, spoke about it, legislated on it and were active in abolishing it. His attitude to slavery alone would not have condemned him to the almost autistic separation visited upon him. And if he felt convinced that blacks were worthy of being treated like whites, or that capitalism was dangerous—he had company or could have found it. But to question the very notion of white progress, the very idea of racial superiority, of whiteness as privileged place in the evolutionary ladder of humankind, and to meditate on the fraudulent, self-destroying philosophy of that superiority, to "pluck it out from under the robes of Senators and Judges," to drag the "judge himself to the bar,"—that was dangerous, solitary, radical work. Especially then. Especially now. To be "only a patriot to heaven" is no mean aspiration in Young America for a writer—or the captain of a whaling ship.

A complex, heaving, disorderly, profound text is *Moby Dick,* and among its several meanings it seems to me this "unspeakable" one has remained the "hidden course," the "truth in the Face of Falsehood." To this day no novelist has so wrestled with its subject. To this day literary analyses of canonical texts have shied away from that perspective: the informing and determining Afro-American presence in traditional American literature. The chapters I have made reference to are only a fraction of the instances where the text surrenders such insights, and points a helpful finger toward the ways in which the ghost drives the machine.

Melville is not the only author whose works double their fascination and their power when scoured for this presence and the writerly strategies taken to address or deny it. Edgar Allan Poe will sustain such a reading. So will Nathaniel Hawthorne and Mark Twain; and in the twentieth century, Willa Cather, Ernest Hemingway, F. Scott Fitzgerald, and William Faulkner, to name a few. Canonical American literature is begging for such attention.

It seems to me a more than fruitful project to produce some cogent analysis showing instances where early American literature identifies itself, risks itself, to assert its antithesis to blackness. How its linguistic gestures prove the intimate relationship to what is being nulled by implying a full descriptive apparatus (identity) to a presence-that-is-assumed-not-to-exist. Afro-American critical inquiry can do this work.

I mentioned earlier that finding or imposing Western influences in/on Afro-American literature had value provided the valued process does not become self-anointing. There is an adjacent project to be undertaken—the third focus in my list: the examination of contemporary literature (both the sacred and the profane) for the impact Afro-American presence has had on the structure of the work, the linguistic practice, and fictional enterprise in which it is engaged. Like focus two, this critical process must also eschew the pernicious goal of equating the fact of that presence with the achievement of the work. A work does not get better because it is responsive to another culture; nor does it become automatically flawed because of that responsiveness. The point is to clarify, not to enlist. And it does not "go without saying" that a work written by an Afro-American is automatically subsumed by an enforcing Afro-American presence. There is a clear flight from blackness in a great deal of Afro-American literature. In others there is the duel with blackness, and in some cases, as they say, "You'd never know."

III

It is on this area, the impact of Afro-American culture on contemporary American literature, that I now wish to comment. I have already said that works by Afro-Americans can respond to this presence (just as non-black works do) in a number of ways. The question of what constitutes the art of a black writer, for whom that modifier is more search than fact, has some urgency. In other words, other than melanin and subject matter, what, in fact, may make me a black writer? Other than my own ethnicity—what is going on in my work that makes me believe it is demonstrably inseparable from a cultural specificity that is Afro-American?

Please forgive the use of my own work in these observations. I use it not because it provides the best example, but because I know it best, know what I did and why, and know how central these queries are to me. Writing is, *after* all, an act of language, its practice. But *first* of all it is an effort of the will to discover.

Let me suggest some of the ways in which I activate language and ways in which that language activates me. I will limit this perusal by calling attention only to the first sentences of the books I've written, and hope that in exploring the choices I made, prior points are illuminated.

The Bluest Eye begins "Quiet as it's kept, there were no marigolds in the fall of 1941." That sentence, like the ones that open each succeeding book, is simple, uncomplicated. Of all the sentences that begin all the books, only two of them have dependent clauses; the other three are simple sentences and two are stripped down to virtually subject, verb, modifier. Nothing fancy here. No words need looking up; they are ordinary, everyday words. Yet I hoped the simplicity was not simple-minded, but devious, even loaded. And that the process of selecting each word, for itself and its relationship to the others in the sentence, along with the rejection of others for their echoes, for what is determined and what is not determined, what is almost there and what must be gleaned, would not theatricalize itself, would not erect a proscenium—at least not a noticeable one. So important to me was this unstaging, that in this first novel I summarized the whole of the book on the first page. (In the first edition, it was printed in its entirety on the jacket).

The opening phrase of this sentence, "Quiet as it's kept," had several attractions for me. First, it was a familiar phrase familiar to me as a child listening to adults; to black women conversing with one another; telling a story, an anecdote, gossip about some one or event within the circle, the family, the neighborhood. The words are conspiratorial. "Shh, don't tell anyone else," and "No one is allowed to know this." It is a secret between us and a secret that is being kept from us. The conspiracy is both held and withheld, exposed and sustained. In some sense it was precisely what the act of writing the book was: the public exposure of a private confidence. In order fully to comprehend the duality of that position, one needs to think of the immediate political climate in which the writing took place, 1965–1969, during great social upheaval in the life of black people. The publication (as opposed to the writing) involved the exposure; the writing was the disclosure of secrets, secrets "we" shared and those withheld from us by ourselves and by the world outside the community.

"Quiet as it's kept," is also a figure of speech that is written, in this instance, but clearly chosen for how speakerly it is, how it speaks and bespeaks a particular world and its ambience. Further, in addition to its "black fence" connotation, its suggestion of illicit gossip, of thrilling revelation, there is also, in the "whisper," the assumption (on the part of the reader) that the teller is on the inside, knows something others do not, and is going to be generous with this privileged information. The intimacy I was aiming for, the intimacy between the reader and the page, could start up immediately because the secret is being shared, at best, and eavesdropped upon, at the least. Sudden familiarity or instant intimacy seemed crucial to me then, writing my first novel. I did not want the reader to have time to wonder "What do I have to do, to give up, in order to read this? What defense do I need, what distance maintain?" Because I know (and the reader does not—he or she has to wait for the second sentence) that this is a terrible story about things one would rather not know anything about.

What, then, is the Big Secret about to be shared? The thing we (reader and I) are "in" on? A botanical aberration. Pollution, perhaps. A skip, perhaps, in the natural order of things: a September, an autumn, a fall without marigolds. Bright common, strong and sturdy marigolds. When? In 1941, and since that is a momentous year (the beginning of

World War II for the United States), the "fall" of 1941, just before the declaration of war, has a "closet" innuendo. In the temperate zone where there is a season known as "fall" during which one expects marigolds to be at their peak, in the months before the beginning of U.S. participation in World War II, something grim is about to be divulged. The next sentence will make it clear that the sayer, the one who knows, is a child speaking, mimicking the adult black women on the porch or in the back yard. The opening phrase is an effort to be grown-up about this shocking information. The point of view of a child alters the priority an adult would assign the information. "We thought it was because Pecola was having her father's baby that the marigolds did not grow" foregrounds the flowers, backgrounds illicit, traumatic, incomprehensible sex coming to its dreaded fruition. This foregrounding of "trivial" information and backgrounding of shocking knowledge secures the point of view but gives the reader pause about whether the voice of children can be trusted at all or is more trustworthy than an adult's. The reader is thereby protected from a confrontation too soon with the painful details, while simultaneously provoked into a desire to know them. The novelty, I thought, would be in having this story of female violation revealed from the vantage point of the victims or could-be victims of rape—the persons no one inquired of (certainly not in 1965)—the girls themselves. And since the victim does not have the vocabulary to understand the violence or its context, gullible, vulnerable girl friends, looking back as the knowing adults they pretended to be in the beginning, would have to do that for her, and would have to fill those silences with their own reflective lives. Thus, the opening provides the stroke that announces something more than a secret shared, but a silence broken, a void filled, an unspeakable thing spoken at last. And they draw the connection between a minor destabilization in seasonal flora with the insignificant destruction of a black girl. Of course "minor" and "insignificant" represent the outside world's view—for the girls both phenomena are earthshaking depositories of information they spend that whole year of childhood (and afterwards) trying to fathom, and cannot. If they have any success, it will be in transferring the problem of fathoming to the presumably adult reader, to the inner circle of listeners. At the least they have distributed the weight of these problematical questions to a larger constituency, and justified the public exposure of a privacy. If the conspiracy that the opening words announce is entered into by the reader, then the book can be seen to open with its close: a speculation on the disruption of "nature," as being a social disruption with tragic individual consequences in which the reader, as part of the population of the text, is implicated.

However a problem, unsolved, lies in the central chamber of the novel. The shattered world I built (to complement what is happening to Pecola), its pieces held together by seasons in childtime and commenting at every turn on the incompatible and barren white-family primer, does not in its present form handle effectively the silence at its center. The void that is Pecola's "unbeing." It should have had a shape—like the emptiness left by a boom or a cry. It required a sophistication unavailable to me, and some deft manipulation of the voices around her. She is not *seen* by herself until she hallucinates a self. And the fact of her hallucination becomes a point of outside-the-book conversation, but does not work in the reading process.

Also, although I was pressing for a female expressiveness (a challenge that re-surfaced in *Sula*), it eluded me for the most part, and I had to content myself with female personae because I was not able to secure throughout the work the feminine subtext that is present in the opening sentence (the women gossiping, eager and aghast in "Quiet as it's kept"). The shambles this struggle became is most evident in the section on Pauline Breedlove where I resorted to two voices, hers and the urging narrator's, both of which are extremely unsatis-

factory to me. It is interesting to me now that where I thought I would have the most difficulty subverting the language to a feminine mode, I had the least: connecting Cholly's
"rape" by the whitemen to his own of his daughter. This most masculine act of aggression
becomes femininized in my language, "passive," and, I think, more accurately repellent
when deprived of the male "glamor of shame" rape is (or once was) routinely given.

The points I have tried to illustrate are that my choices of language (speakerly, aural,
colloquial), my reliance for full comprehension on codes embedded in black culture, my
effort to effect immediate co-conspiracy and intimacy (without any distancing, explanatory fabric), as well as my (failed) attempt to shape a silence while breaking it are attempts
(many unsatisfactory) to transfigure the complexity and wealth of Afro-American culture
into a language worthy of the culture.

In *Sula,* it's necessary to concentrate on *two* first sentences because what survives in print is
not the one I had intended to be the first. Originally the book opened with "Except for
World War II nothing ever interfered with National Suicide Day." With some encouragement, I recognized that it was a false beginning. *"In medias res"* with a vengeance, because
there was no *res* to be in the middle of—no implied world in which to locate the specificity and the resonances in the sentence. More to the point, I knew I was writing a second
novel, and that it too would be about people in a black community not just foregrounded
but totally dominant; and that it was about black women—also foregrounded and dominant. In 1988, certainly, I would not need (or feel the need for) the sentence—the short
section—that now opens *Sula.* The threshold between the reader and the black-topic text
need not be the safe, welcoming lobby I persuaded myself it needed at that time. My preference was the demolition of the lobby altogether. As can be seen from *The Bluest Eye,* and
in every other book I have written, only *Sula* has this "entrance." The others refuse the
"presentation"; refuse the seductive safe harbor; the line of demarcation between the sacred and the obscene, public and private, them and us. Refuse, in effect, to cater to the diminished expectations of the reader, or his or her alarm heightened by the emotional luggage one carries into the black-topic text. (I should remind you that *Sula* was begun in
1969, while my first book was in proof, in a period of extraordinary political activity.)

Since I had become convinced that the effectiveness of the original beginning was only
in my head, the job at hand became how to construct an alternate beginning that would
not force the work to genuflect and would complement the outlaw quality in it. The problem presented itself this way: to fashion a door. Instead of having the text open wide
the moment the cover is opened (or, as in *The Bluest Eye,* to have the book stand exposed
before the cover is even touched, much less opened, by placing the complete "plot" on
the first page—and finally on the cover of the first edition), here I was to posit a door,
turn its knob and beckon for some four or five pages. I had determined not to mention
any characters in those pages, there would be no people in the lobby—but I did, rather
heavy-handedly in my view, end the welcome aboard with the mention of Shadrack and
Sula. It was a craven (to me, still) surrender to a worn-out technique of novel writing: the
overt announcement to the reader whom to pay attention to. Yet the bulk of the opening
I finally wrote is about the community, a view of it, and the view is not from within (this
is a door, after all) but from the point of view of a stranger—the "valley man" who might
happen to be there on some errand, but who obviously does not live there and to and for
whom all this is mightily strange, even exotic. You can see why I despise much of this beginning. Yet I tried to place in the opening sentence the signature terms of loss: "There
used to be a neighborhood here; not any more." That may not be the world's worst sentence, but it doesn't "play," as they say in the theater.

My new first sentence became "In that place, where they tore the nightshade and blackberry patches from their roots to make room for the Medallion City Golf Course, there was once a neighborhood." Instead of my original plan, here I am introducing an outside-the-circle reader into the circle. I am translating the anonymous into the specific, a "place" into a "neighborhood," and letting a stranger in through whose eyes it can be viewed. In between "place" and "neighborhood" I now have to squeeze the specificity and the *difference;* the nostalgia, the history, and the nostalgia for the history; the violence done to it and the consequences of that violence. (It took three months, those four pages, a whole summer of nights.) The nostalgia is sounded by "once"; the history and a longing for it is implied in the connotation of "neighborhood." The violence lurks in having something torn out by its roots—it will not, cannot grow again. Its consequences are that what has been destroyed is considered weeds, refuse necessarily removed in urban "development" by the unspecified but no less known "they" who do not, cannot, afford to differentiate what is displaced, and would not care that this is "refuse" of a certain kind. Both plants have darkness in them: "black" and "night." One is unusual (nightshade) and has two darkness words: "night" and "shade." The other (blackberry) is common. A familiar plant and an exotic one. A harmless one and a dangerous one. One produces a nourishing berry; one delivers toxic ones. But they both thrived there together, *in that place when it was a neighborhood.* Both are gone now, and the description that follows is of the other specific things, in this black community, destroyed in the wake of the golf course. Golf course conveys what it is not, in this context: not houses, or factories, or even a public park, and certainly not residents. It is a manicured place where the likelihood of the former residents showing up is almost nil.

I want to get back to those berries for a moment (to explain, perhaps, the length of time it took for the language of that section to arrive). I always thought of Sula as quintessentially black, metaphysically black, if you will, which is not melanin and certainly not unquestioning fidelity to the tribe. She is new world black and new world woman extracting choice from choicelessness, responding inventively to found things. Improvisational. Daring, disruptive, imaginative, modern, out-of-the-house, outlawed, unpolicing, uncontained and uncontainable. And dangerously female. In her final conversation with Nel she refers to herself as a special kind of black person woman, one with choices. Like a redwood, she says. (With all due respect to the dream landscape of Freud, trees have always seemed feminine to me.) In any case, my perception of Sula's double-dose of *chosen* blackness and *biological* blackness is in the presence of those two words of darkness in "nightshade" as well as in the uncommon quality of the vine itself. One variety is called "enchanter," and the other "bittersweet" because the berries taste bitter at first and then sweet. Also nightshade was thought to counteract witchcraft. All of this seemed a wonderful constellation of signs for Sula. And "blackberry patch" seemed equally appropriate for Nel: nourishing, never needing to be tended or cultivated, once rooted and bearing. Reliably sweet but thorn-bound. Her process of becoming, heralded by the explosive dissolving of her fragilely-held-together ball of string and fur (when the thorns of her self-protection are removed by Eva), puts her back in touch with the complex, contradictory, evasive, independent, liquid modernity Sula insisted upon. A modernity which overturns pre-war definitions, ushers in the Jazz Age (an age *defined* by Afro-American art and culture), and requires new kinds of intelligences to define oneself.

The stage-setting of the first four pages is embarrassing to me now, but the pains I have taken to explain it may be helpful in identifying the strategies one can be forced to resort to in trying to accommodate the mere fact of writing about, for and out of black culture while accommodating and responding to mainstream "white" culture. The "valley man's" guidance into the territory was my compromise. Perhaps it "worked," but it was not the work I wanted to do.

Had I begun with Shadrack, I would have ignored the smiling welcome and put the reader into immediate confrontation with his wound and his scar. The difference my preferred (original) beginning would have made would be calling greater attention to the traumatic displacement this most wasteful capitalist war had on black people in particular, and throwing into relief the creative, if outlawed, determination to survive it whole. Sula as (feminine) solubility and Shadrack's (male) fixative are two extreme ways of dealing with displacement—a prevalent theme in the narrative of black people. In the final opening I replicated the demiurge of discriminatory, prosecutorial racial oppression in the loss to commercial "progress" of the village, but the references to the community's stability and creativeness (music, dancing, craft, religion, irony, wit all referred to in the "valley man's" presence) refract and subsume their pain while they are in the thick of it. It is a softer embrace than Shadrack's organized, public madness—his disruptive remembering presence which helps (for a while) to cement the community, until Sula challenges them.

"The North Carolina Mutual Life Insurance agent promised to fly from Mercy to the other side of Lake Superior at 3:00."

This declarative sentence is designed to mock a journalistic style; with a minor alteration it could be the opening of an item in a small-town newspaper. It has the tone of an everyday event of minimal local interest. Yet I wanted it to contain (as does the scene that takes place when the agent fulfills his promise) the information that *Song of Solomon* both centers on and radiates from.

The name of the insurance company is real, a well known black-owned company dependent on black clients, and in its corporate name are "life" and "mutual;" *agent* being the necessary ingredient of what enables the relationship between them. The sentence also moves from North Carolina to Lake Superior—geographical locations, but with a sly implication that the move from North Carolina (the south) to Lake Superior (the north) might not actually involve progress to some "superior state"—which, of course it does not. The two other significant words are "fly," upon which the novel centers and "Mercy," the name of the place from which he is to fly. Both constitute the heartbeat of the narrative. Where is the insurance man flying to? The other side of Lake Superior is Canada, of course, the historic terminus of the escape route for black people looking for asylum. "Mercy," the other significant term, is the grace note; the earnest though, with one exception, unspoken wish of the narrative's population. Some grant it; some never find it; one, at least, makes it the text and cry of her extemporaneous sermon upon the death of her granddaughter. It touches, turns and returns to Guitar at the end of the book—he who is least deserving of it—and moves him to make it his own final gift. It is what one wishes for Hagar; what is unavailable to and unsought by Macon Dead, senior; what his wife learns to demand from him, and what can never come from the white world as is signified by the inversion of the name of the hospital from Mercy to "no-Mercy." It is only available from within. The center of the narrative is flight; the springboard is mercy.

But the sentence turns, as all sentences do, on the verb: promised. The insurance agent does not declare, announce, or threaten his act. He promises, as though a contract is being executed—faithfully—between himself and others. Promises broken, or kept; the difficulty of ferreting out loyalties and ties that bind or bruise wend their way throughout the action and the shifting relationships. So the agent's flight, like that of the Solomon in the title, although toward asylum (Canada, or freedom, or home, or the company of the welcoming dead), and although it carries the possibility of failure and the certainty of danger, is toward change, an alternative way, a cessation of things-as-they-are. It should not be understood as a simple desperate act, the end of a fruitless life, a life without gesture, without examination, but as obedience to a deeper contract with his people. It is his commitment to them, regardless of whether, in all its details, they understand it. There is, however, in their response to his action, a tenderness, some contrition, and mounting respect ("They didn't know he had it in him.") and an awareness that the gesture enclosed rather than repudiated themselves. The note he leaves asks for forgiveness. It is tacked on his door as a mild invitation to whomever might pass by, but it is not an advertisement. It is an almost Christian declaration of love as well as humility of one who was not able to do more.

There are several other flights in the work and they are motivationally different. Solomon's the most magical, the most theatrical and, for Milkman, the most satisfying. It is also the most problematic—to those he left behind. Milkman's flight binds these two elements of loyalty (Mr. Smith's) and abandon and self-interest (Solomon's) into a third thing: a merging of fealty and risk that suggests the "agency" for "mutual" "life," which he offers at the end and which is echoed in the hills behind him, and is the marriage of surrender and domination, acceptance and rule, commitment to a group *through* ultimate isolation. Guitar recognizes this marriage and recalls enough of how lost he himself is to put his weapon down.

The journalistic style at the beginning, its rhythm of a familiar, hand-me-down dignity is pulled along by an accretion of detail displayed in a meandering unremarkableness. Simple words, uncomplex sentence structures, persistent understatement, highly aural syntax—but the ordinariness of the language, its colloquial, vernacular, humorous and, upon occasion, parabolic quality sabotage expectations and mask judgments when it can no longer defer them. The composition of red, white and blue in the opening scene provides the national canvas/flag upon which the narrative works and against which the lives of these black people must be seen, but which must not overwhelm the enterprise the novel is engaged in. It is a composition of color that heralds Milkman's birth, protects his youth, hides its purpose and through which he must burst (through blue Buicks, red tulips in his waking dream, and his sisters' white stockings, ribbons and gloves) before discovering that the gold of his search is really Pilate's yellow orange and the glittering metal of the box in her ear.

These spaces, which I am filling in, and can fill in because they were planned, can conceivably be filled in with other significances. That is planned as well. The point is that into these spaces should fall the ruminations of the reader and his or her invented or recollected or misunderstood knowingness. The reader as narrator asks the questions the community asks, and both reader and "voice" stand among the crowd, within it, with privileged intimacy and contact, but without any more privileged information than the crowd has. That egilatarianism which places us all (reader, the novel's population, the narrator's voice) on the same footing reflected for me the force of flight and mercy, and the precious, imaginative yet realistic gaze of black people who (at one time, anyway) did not mythologize what or whom it mythologized. The "song" itself contains this unblinking evaluation of the miraculous and heroic flight of the legendary Solomon, an unblinking gaze which is lurking in the tender but amused choral-community response to the agent's flight. Sotto (but not completely) is my own giggle (in Afro-American terms) of the proto-myth of the journey to manhood. Whenever characters are cloaked in Western fable, they are in deep trouble; but the African myth is also contaminated. Unprogressive, unreconstructed, self-born Pilate is unimpressed by Solomon's flight and knocks Milkman down when, made new by his appropriation of his own family's fable, he returns to educate her with it. Upon hearing all he has to say, her only interest is filial. "Papa? . . . I've been carryin' Papa?" And her longing to hear the song, finally, is a longing for balm to die by, not a submissive obedience to history—anybody's.

The opening sentence of *Tar Baby*, "He believed he was safe," is the second version of itself. The first, "He thought he was safe," was discarded because "thought" did not contain the doubt I wanted to plant in the reader's mind about whether or not he really was—safe. "Thought" came to me at once because it was the verb my parents and grandparents used when describing what they had dreamed the night before. Not "I dreamt," or "It seemed" or even "I saw or did" this or that—but "I thought." It gave the dream narrative distance (a dream is not "real") and power (the control implied in *thinking* rather than *dreaming*). But to use "thought" seemed to undercut the faith of the character and the distrust I wanted to suggest to the reader. "Believe" was chosen to do the work properly. And the person who does the believing is, in a way, about to enter a dream world, and convinces himself, eventually, that he is in control of it. He believed; was convinced. And although the word suggests his conviction, it does not reassure the reader. If I had wanted the reader to trust this person's point of view I would have written "He was safe." Or, "Finally, he was safe." The unease about this view of safety is important because safety itself is the desire of each person in the novel. Locating it, creating it, losing it.

You may recall that I was interested in working out the mystery of a piece of lore, a folk tale, which is also about safety and danger and the skills needed to secure the one and recognize and avoid the other. I was not, of course, interested in re-telling the tale; I suppose that is an idea to pursue, but it is certainly not interesting enough to engage me for four years. I have said, elsewhere, that the exploration of the Tar Baby tale was like stroking a pet to see what the anatomy was like but not to disturb or distort its mystery. Folk lore may have begun as allegory for natural or social phenomena; it may have been employed as a retreat from contemporary issues in art, but folk lore can also contain myths that re-activate themselves endlessly through providers—the people who repeat, reshape, reconstitute and reinterpret them. The Tar Baby tale seemed to me to be about masks. Not masks as covering what is to be hidden, but how masks come to life, take life over, exercise the tensions between itself and what it covers. For Son, the most effective mask is none. For the others the construction is careful and delicately borne, but the masks they make have a life of their own and collide with those they come in contact with. The texture of the novel seemed to want leanness, architecture that was worn and ancient like a piece of mask sculpture: exaggerated, breathing, just athwart the representational life it displaced. Thus, the first and last sentences had to match, as the exterior planes match the interior, concave ones inside the mask. Therefore "He believed he was safe" would be the twin of "Lickety split, lickety split, lickety lickety split." This close is 1) the last sentence of the folk tale. 2) the action of the character. 3) the indeterminate ending that follows from the untrustworthy beginning. 4) the complimentary meter of its twin sister [u u / u u / with u u u / u u u/], and 5) the wide and marvelous space between the contradiction of those two images: from a dream of safety to the sound of running feet. The whole mediated world in between. This masked and unmasked; enchanted, disenchanted; wounded and wounding world is played out on and by the varieties of interpretation (Western and Afro-American) the Tar Baby myth has been (and continues to be) subjected to. Winging one's way through the vise and expulsion of history becomes possible in creative encounters with that history. Nothing, in those encounters, is safe, or should be. Safety is the foetus of power as well as protection from it, as the uses to which masks and myths are put in Afro-American culture remind us.

"124 was spiteful. Full of a baby's venom."

Beginning *Beloved* with numerals rather than spelled out numbers, it was my intention to give the house an identity separate from the street or even the city; to name it the way "Sweet Home" was named; the way plantations were named, but not with nouns or "proper" names—with numbers instead because numbers have no adjectives, no posture of coziness or grandeur or the haughty yearning of arrivistes and estate builders for the parallel beautifications of the nation they left behind, laying claim to instant history and legend. Numbers here constitute an address, a thrilling enough prospect for slaves who had owned nothing, least of all an address. And although the numbers, unlike words, can have no modifiers, I give these an adjective—spiteful (There are three others). The address is therefore personalized, but personalized by its own activity, not the pasted on desire for personality.

Also there is something about numerals that makes them spoken, heard, in this context, because one expects words to read in a book, not numbers to say, or hear. And the sound of the novel, sometimes cacaphonous, sometimes harmonious, must be an inner ear sound or a sound just beyond hearing, infusing the text with a musical emphasis that words can do sometimes even better than music can. Thus the second sentence is not one: it is a phrase that properly, grammatically, belongs as a dependent clause with the first. Had I done that, however, (124 was spiteful, comma, full of a baby's venom, or 124 was full of a baby's venom) I could not have had the accent on *full* [/ u u / u / u pause / u u u u / u}.

Whatever the risks of confronting the reader with what must be immediately incomprehensible in that simple, declarative authoritative sentence, the risk of unsettling him or her, I determined to take. Because the *in medias res* opening that I am so committed to is here excessively demanding. It is abrupt, and should appear so. No native informant here. The reader is snatched, yanked, thrown into an environment completely foreign, and I want it as the first stroke of the shared experience that might be possible between the reader and the novel's population. Snatched just as the slaves were from one place to another, from any place to another, without preparation and without defense. No lobby, no door, no entrance—a gangplank, perhaps (but a very short one). And the house into which this snatching—this kidnapping—propels one, changes from spiteful to loud to quiet, as the sounds in the body of the ship itself may have changed. A few words have to be read before it is clear that 124 refers to a house (in most of the early drafts "The women *in the house* knew it" was simply "The women knew it." "House" was not mentioned for seventeen lines), and a few more have to be read to discover why it is spiteful, or rather the source of the spite. By then it is clear, if not at once, that something is beyond control, but is not beyond understanding since it is not beyond accommodation by both the "women" and the "children." The fully realized presence of the haunting is both a major incumbent of the narrative and sleight of hand. One of its purposes is to keep the reader preoccupied with the nature of the incredible spirit world while being supplied a controlled diet of the incredible political world.

The subliminal, the underground life of a novel is the area most likely to link arms with the reader and facilitate making it one's own. Because one must, to get from the first sentence to the next, and the next and the next. The friendly observation post I was content to build and man in *Sula* (with the stranger in the midst), or the down-home journalism of *Song of Solomon* or the calculated mistrust of the point of view in *Tar Baby* would not serve here. Here I wanted the compelling confusion of being there as they (the characters) are; suddenly, without comfort or succor from the "author," with only imagination, intelligence, and necessity available for the journey. The painterly language of *Song of Solomon*

was not useful to me in *Beloved*. There is practically no color whatsoever in its pages, and
when there is, it is so stark and remarked upon, it is virtually raw. Color seen for the first
time, without its history. No built architecture as in *Tar Baby,* no play with Western
chronology as in *Sula;* no exchange between book life and "real" life discourse—with
printed text units rubbing up against seasonal black childtime units as in *The Bluest Eye*.
No compound of houses, no neighborhood, no sculpture, no paint, no time, especially no
time because memory, pre-historic memory, has no time. There is just a little music, each
other and the urgency of what is at stake. Which is all they had. For that work, the work
of language is to get out of the way.

I hope you understand that in this explication of how I practice language is a search for
and deliberate posture of vulnerability to those aspects of Afro-American culture that can
inform and position my work. I sometimes know when the work works, when *nommo* has
effectively summoned, by reading and listening to those who have entered the text. I learn
nothing from those who resist it, except, of course, the sometimes fascinating display of
their struggle. My expectations of and my gratitude to the critics who enter, are great. To
those who talk about how as well as what; who identify the workings as well as the work;
for whom the study of Afro-American literature is neither a crash course in neighborliness
and tolerance, nor an infant to be carried, instructed or chastised or even whipped like a
child, but the serious study of art forms that have much work to do, but are already legiti-
matized by their own cultural sources and predecessors—in or out of the canon—I owe
much.

For an author, regarding canons, it is very simple: in fifty, a hundred or more years his
or her work may be relished for its beauty or its insight or its power; or it may be condemned for its vacuousness and pretension—and junked. Or in fifty or a hundred years
the critic (as canon builder) may be applauded for his or her intelligent scholarship and
powers of critical inquiry. Or laughed at for ignorance and shabbily disguised assertions of
power—and junked. It's possible that the reputations of both will thrive, or that both will
decay. In any case, as far as the future is concerned, when one writes, as critic or as author,
all necks are on the line.

NOTES

1. See *"Race," Writing, and Difference,* ed. Henry Louis Gates (University of Chicago Press, 1988).
2. Among many examples, *They Came Before Columbus, The African Presence in Ancient America* by Ivan
   van Sertima (New York: Random House, 1976), pp. xvi–xvii.
3. Tzvetan Todorov, "'Race,' Writing, and Culture," translated by Loulou Mack, in Gates, *op cit,*
   pp. 370–380.
4. Terrence Rafferty, "Articles of Faith," *The New Yorker,* 16 May 1988, pp. 110–118.
5. Martin Bernal, *Black Athena: The Afroasiatic Roots of Classical Civilization, volume 1: The Fabrication of
   Ancient Greece 1785–1985* (Rutgers University Press, 1987), p. 2.
6. *Ibid.,* p. 310.
7. *Ibid.,* p. 337.
8. See Michael Paul Rogin, *Subversive Genealogy: The Politics and Art of Herman Melville* (University of
   California Press, 1985), p. 15.
9. Ibid., pp. 107 and 142.
10. *Ibid.,* p. 112.

Walter Benn Michaels

The Vanishing American

When Tom Outland discovers that his friend Roddy Blake has sold their collection of Indian "relics," he makes him an outraged speech that Roddy ruefully describes as a "Fourth of July talk" (245). The burden of the speech is that Roddy has failed to understand "the kind of value" the relics have to Tom; the Fourth of July part involves the accusation that Roddy, "like Dreyfus," has sold his "country's secrets" to a German. "They belonged to this country, to the State, and to all the people," Tom says, and "You've gone and sold them to a country that's got plenty of relics of its own" (245). Although Roddy thinks his mistake has been to sell Tom's "private property," insofar as the relics are a public "trust," he is more a traitor than a thief. And insofar as the relics belong to the "State" only because they belonged to the Indians whom Tom describes as his and Roddy's "ancestors," Roddy's lack of patriotism is really a lack of (what Tom calls) "filial piety" (251). Roddy has thought of their "find" as "no different than anything else a fellow might run on to: a gold mine or a pocket of turquoise," but Tom has come to think of it as a collection of family heirlooms, the "pots and pans that belonged to my poor grandmothers a thousand years ago" (243). In selling the relics, then, Roddy has betrayed his country by betraying his family, all the boys, "like you and me," Tom says, "that have no other ancestors to inherit from" (242). And Tom himself spends the rest of that summer on the mesa in an orgy of "filial piety" (251), reading the *Aeneid* and "tidying up" the ancestral "ruins," imagining himself as the pious Aeneas rather than as the unpatriotic Dreyfus.

This experience is not available to Roddy Blake, who can't read Latin and who persists in thinking that Dreyfus was framed; indeed, Tom's whole speech is, Roddy says, "away out of" his "depth." And Roddy is surely right to call attention at least to its peculiarity. The equation of "relics" with state "secrets" is odd, as is the more general preoccupation with ancestors. But the contrast to Dreyfus and the fact that *The Professor's House* was written mainly in 1924, the year in which postwar nativism climaxed in the passage of the Johnson Immigration Act, may help to dispel at least some of the oddity. The Johnson Act did not only limit the number of immigrants to 150,000 a year (as opposed to the approximately one million a year of the period immediately preceding the War): it did so (through the Reed Amendment) by linking the "annual quota of each nationality" to the "number of inhabitants of the United States having that national origin" (qtd. in Hutchinson 192), thus requiring a "racial analysis" of the current American population and making everyone's ancestry an essential element in the future determination of eligibility for American citizenship. Giving a *real* "Fourth of July talk" to the National Education Association in 1924, Calvin Coolidge cited the Johnson Act as one of his administration's chief accomplishments in the effort, as he put it, to help "America . . . remain American" (28); from this perspective, the fact that Tom's patriotism takes the form of an interest in his ancestors recapitulates the newly official interest in everybody's ancestors.

But Tom's preoccupation with his ancestors is, in any event, less surprising than his claim that the ancestors in question are *his*. This is surprising not only because Tom is "a kind of stray" who has "no family" (185) and not only because whatever family he once had obviously wasn't Indian, but also because the Indians themselves belong to a "race" that Cather insists has "died off" (119). Her cliff dwellers embody absolutely the myth of the Indians as a "vanishing race" and Tom's claimed descent from them is not only false

but on her and his own terms impossible; since the cliff dwellers were "utterly exterminated" (221), *no one* is descended from them. But just as the Johnson Immigration Act
helps make sense of Tom's preoccupation with ancestors by insisting on a new connection
between one's racial descent and one's qualifications for American citizenship, so another
text of 1924, the Indian Citizenship Act, helps make sense of his desire to claim descent
from Indians.

Throughout the nineteenth and early twentieth centuries, Indians had been anomalies
with respect to American citizenship, regarded first as citizens of their tribes and then,
with the passage of the Dawes Act of 1887, as potential citizens of the US. Indian potential for citizenship was identified with the ability to adopt "the habits of civilized life"
(Prucha, *Documents* 174) and Indian policy was increasingly directed at "the absorption of
the Indians into our national life, not as Indians, but as American citizens" (Morgan 177).
Thus a series of government initiatives, from the Lacey Act of 1907 (authorizing the Secretary of the Interior to grant individual Indians individual control of their "pro rata
share" [Prucha, *Documents* 210] of tribal funds), through the Sells "Declaration" of 1917
(authorizing a series of measures designed to "speedily achieve" the "ultimate absorption
of the Indian race into the body politic of the Nation" [214–15]), to the Citizenship for
World War I Veterans Act of 1919 (authorizing citizenship for every veteran who "desires" it [215]) encouraged the normalization of the Indians' status as citizens. And the
Citizenship Act of 1924, declaring "all non-citizen Indians born within the territorial
limits of the United States . . . to be citizens of the United States" (218) represented
the triumphant end of this progress. Where the Johnson Act identified the racial groups
which were to be prevented, if possible, from becoming American, the Citizenship Act
celebrated that racial group which had succeeded. Better, in Cather's terms, to be the
imaginary Indian Tom Outland than the real Jew Louie Marsellus, better (in Scott Mc-
Gregor's words) "Outland" than "outlandish" (43).[1]

In fact, however, the Citizenship Act of 1924 did not mark anything like the successful
culmination of the policy of assimilation; in fact, the policy of assimilation failed: as the
Indian hero of Zane Grey's *The Rainbow Trail* (1915) puts it, "the white man's ways and
his life and his God are not the Indian's. They never can be" (41).[2] Instead of being absorbed into the body politic, Indians were increasingly relegated to "a peripheral role in
society" (Hoxie 236). And from this perspective, the Citizenship Act could seem at best a
futile gesture, at worst a cynical acknowledgment of the ultimate irrelevance of citizenship to the Indians' predicament.

But the discrepancy between the status envisioned for them by the Citizenship Act and
the actual social status of the Indians should not be understood to exhaust its meaning.
The perceived impossibility of assimilating large numbers of Eastern European immigrants had led to the erection in the Johnson Act of barriers to citizenship; the actual failure to assimilate the Indians led through the Citizenship Act to citizenship. Undoubtedly,
as Robert F. Berkhofer points out, the Congress was more afraid of "millions of Southern
and Eastern Europeans" than of "a few hundred thousand pacified Indians" (177). In any
event, however, the sense in which these two Acts were opposed—one designed to exclude, the other to include—is less striking than the sense in which they were complementary: they were both designed to keep people from *becoming* citizens. The Johnson Act
guaranteed that aliens not become citizens by putting a halt to mass immigration; the
Citizenship Act guaranteed that Indians not become citizens by declaring that they already were citizens. Both Acts, that is, participated in a recasting of American citizenship,
transforming it from a condition that could be achieved through one's own actions (immi-
grating, becoming "civilized," getting "naturalized") to an identity that could better be

understood as inherited.[3] "America," as Charles W. Gould had described it in a racist tract of 1922, was "A Family Matter" and the only way to keep the family strong was to "utterly reject . . . . foreigners" (4). American traditions, Gould wrote, "cannot be taught, they must come to us with the mother's milk . . . and grow with our nerves and thews and sinews until they become part and parcel of our very being" (163). "Repeal our naturalization laws," Gould urged his readers, "secure our children and our children's children in their legitimate birthright" (165).

At least part of what it means, then, for Tom to claim descent from Indians is to claim exemption from the perils of assimilation and naturalization, perils that Cather insists upon by contrasting him with the man who would be his "brother" when he should be his "rival" (166), Louie Marsellus. For *The Professor's House* is also, as the title of Book One ("The Family") suggests, a family matter and one of its central concerns is with exactly who can and who can't belong to the Professor's family. Tom can: even before his engagement to the Professor's daughter, Rosie, he was "like an older brother" (132); marrying him would have been marrying someone who was already "almost a member of the family" (173). Louie can't: the Professor is amazed by and somewhat contemptuous of his wife's (atavistic, as if she were still committed to the melting pot) willingness "to adopt anyone so foreign into the family circle" (78). And the Professor's other daughter, Kitty, to whom Rosie has been "a kind of ideal" (86), is "done with her sister . . . all at once" (89) upon the announcement of her engagement to Louie. Married to a "stranger," Rosie is lost from the family; the family's regret is that, if it hadn't been for Marsellus, "we might have kept Rosie . . . in the family, for ourselves" (87).

The idea of keeping the family intact by saving sisters from marriage to—or, at least, intercourse with—strangers is a central concern of the American novel in the '20s, one that finds figurative expression in texts like *The Great Gatsby* (1925) and *The Sun Also Rises* (1926) and literal expression in *The Sound and the Fury* (1929). In Hemingway and Fitzgerald, the families from which Robert Cohn and Jimmy Gatz are to be excluded require a blood supplement to count as real families—"afición" in Hemingway, a more subtle mixture of class and race in Fitzgerald.[4] But in Faulkner the St. Peters are evenly matched by the Compsons. Of course, Kitty St. Peter has no sexual interest in Rosie but then Quentin Compson doesn't have much sexual interest in Caddy either. What he wants is to "isolate her out of the loud world" (220); by saying that he has committed incest to make it so that "it would have been so and then the others wouldn't be so and then the world would roar away." Incest is, from this standpoint, nothing but one of *The Sound and the Fury*'s strategies (along with suicide, castration, and contraception) for avoiding assimilation. Quentin's attempt to keep Caddy from Dalton Ames, like Jason's attempt to keep Quentin from the man in the red tie, are efforts to save the family from strangers; "blood is blood," Jason says, "and you can't get around it" (303). The man with the red tie is one of the show people who have "brought nothing to the town" (243), who, like the Jews, Jason says, "produce nothing" (237–38). Jason has known "some jews that were fine citizens" and he has "nothing against jews as an individual"; "It's just the race" (237). Jews, even New York Jews, are "foreigners" (citizens of somewhere else); Jason is "an American."

But if *The Sound and the Fury*, like *The Professor's House*, is hostile to assimilation, it is, unlike *The Professor's House* or *The Great Gatsby* or *The Sun Also Rises*, skeptical about the stranger's desire to be assimilated. All four of these novels commit themselves to the construction of citizenship as identity (as a function of what you are rather than what you do) but the three earlier ones do so in the context of the foreigner's presumed eagerness to alter his. Neither Dalton Ames nor the man in the red tie (not even, despite his telling

Quentin, "I belong to the family now" [136], Herbert Head) manifests the desire expressed in different ways by Jimmy Gatz, Robert Cohn, and Louie Marsellus to belong to the families that Nick Carraway and Daisy Buchanan, Jake Barnes and Brett Ashley, Tom Outland and Rosamond St. Peter can be imagined as belonging to. By the late '20s, the invention of cultural pluralism (an invention that is taking place in these texts of the early '20s) made the mark of the alien his indifference—even hostility—to assimilation. Quentin calls the Italian girl he picks up "sister" but he is Dalton Ames to her real brother Julio, "You steela my seester," Julio says, "I killa heem" (174); in *The Sound and the Fury,* Italians can be Compsons too. But in Hemingway, Fitzgerald, and Cather, the only thing strangers want is to join the family. What is to be feared most is the foreigner's desire to become American.

This itself, of course, represented a significant change from the prewar commitment to "Americanization," which encouraged both immigration and the immigrants' desire to join what Teddy Roosevelt called "the American race." But it represents at the same time a continuation of the exclusionism that characteristically accompanied the welcoming discourse of the melting pot: Italians, Jews, Poles, and Irish were regarded by Progressive Era America as eligible for citizenship; Asians and blacks were not. Indeed, the very possibility of American citizenship was a function of the event that, according to Progressive racists, had created the American state by creating the conditions of white racial purity, the Civil War. The "Nation" that could not "exist half slave and half free," says Abraham Lincoln in Thomas Dixon's *The Clansman,* "cannot now exist half white and half black" (47). The significance of the Civil War, according to Dixon, was that it replaced class and sectional differences between whites with racial differences between whites and blacks. Hence, while encouraging the immigration of whites (he was an advocate of the melting pot), Dixon advocated also the "colonisation" (repatriation) of blacks, characterizing them (in terms that anticipated those of the '20s) as an "alien" "race," "whose assimilation is neither possible nor desirable." The Civil War had made what Dixon called the "ideal Union" possible by eliminating the racial obstacle to political identity; because (under Jim Crow) no black person could become an American citizen, any white person could. For whites, joining the American race required nothing more or less than learning to identify oneself as an American, rather than as a Southerner or Northerner, an Italian or a Jew.

Citizenship is imagined here as something that can be (except for blacks) and must be (even for whites) achieved, a matter of ideology rather than birthplace. Cather's early short story, "The Namesake" (1907), makes this point by imagining its hero, a sculptor distinguished above all by his relation to America ("He seemed, almost more than any other one living man, to mean all of it—from ocean to ocean" [167].) as both an immigrant and an expatriate. Born in Italy, living in France, his only American experience is a two-year visit to his aunt's house in the suburbs of Pittsburgh, and even here, he "never" feels "at home" (175); the one thing American that inspires in him a "sense of kinship" is a portrait of the namesake, his uncle, "killed in one of the big battles of Sixty-four" (171). And it is this attraction to the uncle that results in his Americanization.

From interrogating the local veterans about the circumstances of his uncle's death, he progresses to reading books about the Civil War and searching the house for the dead hero's memorabilia. The culmination of all this is an exceptionally intense Memorial Day on which, sent by his aunt to fetch the flag from the attic, he discovers an old trunk containing, among other things, a copy of the *Aeneid* with his "own name" written on the front flyleaf and written again, along with a drawing and inscription, on the back flyleaf. The drawing is of "the Federal flag" (178) and the inscription—"Oh, say, can you see by the dawn's early light/What so proudly we hailed at the twilight's last gleaming"—is from "The Star Spangled Banner," which would not officially become, until nine years after Cather's writing (by executive order of Dixon's graduate school classmate, President Wilson), the national anthem, but which here, unofficially, makes the immigrant-expatriate feel, "for the first time . . . the pull of race and blood and kindred" (179). After which he goes back to Paris and starts producing the "monuments" to "the heroes of the Civil War" and the sculptures on American topics ("his *Scout,* his *Pioneer,* his *Gold Seekers*" [170]) that make his artistic career.

In Dixon, the Civil War makes American national identity possible; in Cather, Civil War literature performs the same function. "The Namesake" is essentially a story about assimilation, about a "citizenship" which, although it is linked to "race and blood and kindred," is more a matter of "experience" than of heredity.[5] Where Dixon's heroes become Americans (instead of Northerners or Southerners) by fighting in the War, Cather's hero becomes American (instead of French or Italian) by reading about his uncle fighting in it. The fact that his "citizenship" is, as he himself puts it, "somewhat belated" (170), marks the sense in which he can be said to have acquired rather than inherited it, or rather it marks the transformation of an inheritance into an achievement. This is precisely what, according to Dixon, the Civil War was all about, the transformation of the founding fathers' legacy into their grandchildren's political creation; that's why *The Birth of a Nation* (made, of course, from Dixon's *The Clansman*) was called *The Birth of a Nation*.[6] Cather, by invoking "The Star Spangled Banner" on behalf of the Civil War dead, helps to transform the almost Revolutionary song of 1812 into the national anthem of 1916.

For Dixon, racism was crucial to the reinvention of the American state; only by freeing themselves from slavery, destroying their familial bonds to blacks and intermarrying with their racial kinsmen from across the Mason-Dixon line, could whites become Americans. But antiblack racism plays no role in "The Namesake"; my point in comparing Cather to Dixon is only to suggest that her concern in "The Namesake" with the question of American identity involves the characteristic Progressive understanding of that identity as essentially political, reenabled by the Civil War as the refounding of the American nation. By the mid-'20s however, by the time, that is, of *The Great Gatsby, The Sun Also Rises,* and *The Professor's House,* although the question of American identity remained an urgent one, it had come to seem less obviously political. In the July Fourth address to the NEA in which he cited the Johnson Act as his administration's major contribution toward enabling "America" to "remain American," Coolidge went on to remark that "acts of legislation" were in themselves of little importance. Real progress toward "increased National freedom" (22) depended not on the "interposition of the government" but on "the genius of the people themselves" (13), and it was this genius that a liberal education, he told his audience of liberal educators, was designed to cultivate. One element in this education would, of course, be what he had called in another speech to teachers, "critical inquiry" into the nature of our "institutions" with an eye toward "a better understanding of the American form of government" (33). But this course of study, a staple of Progressive assimilationism and of the effort toward Americanization that we have seen embodied in "The Namesake," could not be adequate to a conception of identity that went beyond "legislation" to the "genius" of the people. What was required, he told yet another educational audience, was more "intense" study of "the heritage of civilization" (68); "We do not need more government," he said, "we need more culture" (74).

Thus, although it was Coolidge who said that what was good for business was good for America, in his frequent speeches on education, he took a somewhat different line, distinguishing between the "material advantage" and the "cultural advantage of learning" (15) and reminding his listeners that "vocational and trade schools" could be at best a supplement to a "liberal education" (63). Like Cather's Professor, who resists in his university the "new commercialism" and who defends "purely cultural studies" (140), Coolidge compared the "commercial" unfavorably to the "ideal" (69); "It is not the skill of a Fagin that is sought," he wrote, "but, rather, the wisdom of a Madame Curie" (60–61). The "teachings of history" (37), for example, he thought essential to an understanding of why different nations "cling to their customs" and of why reforms that "might produce good results in one country [say, in the wake of the 'Red scare' of 1919–20, Soviet Russia] would be found to be not workable in another" (37–38); it was thus "especially . . . desirable" to obtain "more accurate knowledge of the causes and events which brought about the settlement of our own land and which went into the formation of its institutions" (38). Where the racist writers of the Progressive Era had appealed to the founding authority of the Civil War, racist writers of the '20s—like Lothrop Stoddard in *The Rising Tide of Color against White World-Supremacy* (1920) and in *Re-forging America* (1927)— looked, like Coolidge, beyond the Civil War and beyond even the Revolution to what Stoddard called "the racial and cultural foundations of the early colonial period." Fitzgerald makes fun of Stoddard in *The Great Gatsby:* "*The Rise of the Colored Empires* by this man Goddard" (13) is one of the "deep books with long words in them" that Tom cites as "scientific" evidence that "Civilization's going to pieces." But the famous last scene of *The Great Gatsby*—with its transformation of Nick's eyes into the "Dutch sailors' eyes" seeing once again the "vanished trees" of the "fresh, green breast of the new world" (182)—is as true to Coolidge's exhortation to "search out and think the thoughts of those who established our institutions" as even Stoddard could have wished. And Professor St. Peter's *Spanish Adventures in North America* is an exercise in "purely cultural studies" designed precisely to provide the "more accurate knowledge of the causes and events which brought about the settlement of our own land and which went into the formation of its institutions" that Coolidge and Stoddard hoped would help America "remain American."

But in *The Professor's House,* not even the Spanish explorers count as the originators of American culture; the episode in the "history" of his "country" (222) that concerns Tom Outland goes back to "before Columbus landed" (119). In this respect, Cather participates in a more general discussion of what was perceived to be a crisis in contemporary American culture, a discussion that, as it began to raise questions about the nature of culture itself, tended increasingly to focus on the American Indian. Indians were the exemplary instance of a society that could be understood as having a culture: thus Edward Sapir, writing on "Culture, Genuine and Spurious" in the *American Journal of Sociology* (1924), characterized Indian salmon-spearing as a "culturally higher type of activity" (316) than the labor of a "telephone girl" or "mill hand" because it worked in "naturally with all the rest of the Indian's activities instead of standing out as a desert patch of merely economic effort in the whole of life." For Sapir, the life of "the average participant in the civilization of a typical American Indian tribe" provided a model of "genuine culture," the experience of society as a "significant whole" (318), and of an individuality that avoids modern fragmentation because it both grows "organically" out of culture and contributes constructively to it: "A healthy national culture is never a passively accepted heritage from the past, but implies the creative participation of the members of the community," Sapir wrote, echoing Coolidge's insistence that, although "We did not acquire our position through our own individual efforts. We were born into it," "it is only by intense application that the individual comes into the . . . possession of the heritage of civilization" (68). "It was possession," Tom says, when he begins "for the first time" to study "methodically" and "intelligently" (251) that summer on the mesa, and when he starts to see things that summer, also for "the first time," "as a whole" (250).

And the Indian is also understood as the exemplary instance of what it means no longer to have a culture. The "fragmentary existence" of the modern Indian—the "integrity of his tribe" destroyed and the "old cultural values" dead—leaves him, Sapir wrote, "with an uneasy sense of the loss of some vague and great good, some state of mind that he would be hard put to define but which gave him courage and joy . . ." (318). The "happiness unalloyed" that Tom experiences on the Blue Mesa is thus the recovery of Indian culture, which is to say, of the very idea of culture. Feeling toward the cliff-dwellers the "filial piety" he is reading about in Virgil, he experiences "for the first time" what Sapir called "genuine" culture, the culture the Indians had had but lost, the culture that modern Americans were looking for, the culture that, according to Coolidge, would take the place of "government."

The transformation of the *Aeneid* from a poem about political identity—inscribed, in "The Namesake," with a "drawing" of the "federal flag"—into a poem about cultural identity—inscribed, in Tom's imagination, with the "picture" of the cliff-dwellers' tower, "rising strong, with calmness and courage" (253)—marks in Cather the emergence of culture not only as an aspect of American identity but as one of its determinants. That, after all, was what the classics were for. "Modern civilization dates from Greece and Rome" (47), Coolidge said in an address before the annual meeting of the American Classical League at the University of Pennsylvania in 1921. As Greece and Rome had been "the inheritors of a civilization which had gone before" (47), we were now their "inheritors." Hence, in the effort to form a cultural in addition to a political identity, it was study of the classics rather than the Constitution that would promote (as had the Johnson Act) the modern American's desire "to be supremely American" (56). The answer to the question, "What are the fundamental things that young Americans should be taught?" was "Greek and Latin literature" (44–45).

Coolidge's word for cultural identity was "character" and his interest in education was a consequence of his view that the "first great duty" of education was "the formation of character, which is the result of heredity and training" (51–52). What the Johnson Act (keeping out, among others, the descendants of the Greeks and Romans) would contribute to the heredity side of American character formation, a classical education (studying the literature of the ancestors whose descendants the Johnson Act was excluding) would contribute to the training side. Indeed, insofar as Greek and Latin civilization was itself our inheritance (the civilization ours was descended from), our training could be understood not only to supplement but to double our heredity. More striking still, since we had no biological relation to Greece or Rome (and since the point of the Johnson Act was to make sure that we would continue to have no biological relation to them) our training could be understood not only as doubling but as constituting our heredity; it is only our education in our origins that guarantees that those origins will indeed be ours. "Culture is the product of a continuing effort," Coolidge told the classicists, "The education of the race is never accomplished" (49). The education of the race can never be accomplished because it is only education that makes the race. Our descent from the Greeks and Romans in Coolidge parallels Tom Outland's descent from the Indians in Cather, and the classical education Tom gets among the cliff dwellers exemplifies the "instruction in the classics" that Coolidge hoped would one day "be the portion of every American" (57). In Coolidge and Cather both, identity is a function of inheritance, but what gets inherited is not just a biology—it's a culture.

Sapir called this "social inheritance" and he was careful to distinguish it from the Stoddard-like assumption that "the so-called 'genius' of a people is ultimately reducible to certain hereditary traits of a biological and psychological nature" (311). Insisting that "what is assumed to be an innate racial characteristic" usually turns out to be "the resultant of purely historical causes," Sapir deploys the idea of a culture against the idea of a race. But the advantage of culture here is not purely destructive, that is, Sapir is not concerned to deny the existence of those "distinctive modes of thinking or types of reaction" from which the idea of "a national genius" is abstracted and which writers like Gould and Stoddard identified as racial characteristics. On the contrary, he is concerned to relocate the national genius, replacing biologically inherited traits with "established and all but instinctive forms" (312). Culture does for the anthropologist what biology did for the racist.[7]

In fact, it does more. Replacing biology with culture, as Sapir understands it, involves something more than attributing the transmission of national identity to "more or less consciously imitative processes" instead of "purely hereditary qualities" (309). For if culture were nothing but imitative processes, then it would be nothing more than social environment, whatever beliefs and practices the individual happened to be raised in. And if culture were nothing more than social environment, then the Indian, for example, could never have the experience, so powerfully described by Sapir, of having "slipped out of the warm embrace of a culture into the cold air of a fragmentary existence" (318). Social environment in this respect is too much like genetic inheritance: everyone always has one. But a culture is something that (unlike the genes you happen to have and the things you happen to do) can be lost. Which is why, although it must be inherited, it can never just be inherited: it is "never a passively accepted heritage from the past, but implies the creative participation of the members of the community." If, then, as an inheritance, culture is unlike the citizenship of the melting pot because it cannot simply be achieved, it is also unlike race and environment in that it cannot simply be inherited. The distinctive mark of culture is that it must be both achieved and inherited.

This is why the American Indian—conceived at the same time as biologically unrelated to and as an ancestor of boys like Tom Outland (who is a "stray" and has "no family" but whose cliff-dweller "grandmothers" owned the "pots and pans" that Roddy sells to the Germans)—plays so crucial a role in the developing idea of cultural identity. The "utterly exterminated" tribe of *The Professor's House* and the tribe "without culture" that exterminated them represent, because the one biologically disappeared and the other culturally never existed, the possibility of an identity that insofar as it is neither simply biological nor simply environmental, can be properly cultural. Neither by blood as such nor through education as such can Tom come into "possession" of himself, but only through a process of what is essentially acculturation, a process imaginable only as a kind of education which is simultaneously a kind of blood affiliation. If Tom had really been related to Indians or if he'd grown up speaking Latin around the house, this process would have been impossible. So although Coolidge had protested that Latin and Greek weren't really "dead languages," in fact, it was only because they *were* dead that they could assume the status of cultural standards. If the Italian immigrants disembarking at Ellis Island had spoken Latin, Coolidge wouldn't have urged the schools to teach it any more than Cather would have had Tom read it: a truly "living" language could not be an object of "purely cultural study." And if the Indians had not been perceived as vanishing, they could not have become the exemplary instance of what it meant to have a culture. "The sun of the Indian's day is setting" (137), an old chief tells Nophaie, the hero of Zane Grey's *The Vanishing American*. It is because the Indian's sun was perceived as setting that he could become, I want to argue, a kind of paradigm for increasingly powerful American notions of ethnic identity, for the idea of an ethnicity that could be threatened or defended, repudiated or reclaimed.[8]

Grey's Nophaie is a Navajo, raised among whites and now returned to his tribe; with "an Indian body and white man's mind" (94), he represents a synergetic combination of the means by which the vanishing Indian was supposed to vanish: cultural assimilation and biological obliteration. Raised among whites, he loves a white woman and because he cannot marry her and will not (loving a member of an "alien" "race" [14]) marry a woman of his own race, he sees that he is "the last of his family and he would never have a child" (114). In the version published by Harper & Brothers in 1925, this turns out to be literally true: offended by the prospect of an Indian man marrying a white woman (the reverse was more acceptable), Harper & Brothers had required Grey to make changes in the original serial (published in the *Ladies' Home Journal* in 1922) that resulted in Nophaie dying unwed under what Grey's son Loren calls "quite mysterious and really illogical circumstances" (vii). But even in the uncensored version, where Nophaie ends up marrying white Marian after all, the spirit of his prediction, his representation of himself as "the last of his family," comes true. For, in marrying Marian, he tells her, "I shall be absorbed by you—by your love—by your children. . . ." Imagining their children as her children (and himself as her), Nophaie treats assimilation exactly as if it were a form of instead of an alternative to biological extinction, and approves it—"It is well" (342). Whether responding to racist demands or rejecting them, Grey made sure that the Indian vanished.

But Grey's title is not (the title of Curtis's famous photograph) "The Vanishing Race" or "The Vanishing Indian"; it is *The Vanishing American*. And if, from the standpoint of assimilationism, this makes a certain sense—since it was in ceasing to be an Indian that the Indian would become an American—it makes even more sense from the standpoint of the hostility to assimilation that we have seen at work in Cather and that finds an important expression also in Grey. For *The Vanishing American*'s villains are the missionaries who preach to the Indians that by adopting "the white man's way, his clothes, his work, his talk, his life, and his God" they will become "white in heart" (183). In Indians like Nophaie, whose "soul" has "as much right to its inheritance of ideals and faith as any white man's" (103–04), these teachings produce a "spiritual catastrophe." But the War, which dealt in fact a major blow to the project of assimilating the immigrant—"The war virtually swept from the American consciousness the old belief in unrestricted immigration" (Higham 301)—deals a major blow in *The Vanishing American* to the project of assimilating the Indian. That is, like the Indian Citizenship Act, it renders the project of assimilation impossible because unnecessary. For the War reveals the missionaries as themselves *less American* than the Indians. Grey's missionaries are "all German" (213); "their forefathers," as an old Navajo chief puts it, "belonged to that wicked people who practice war. They are not American. They are not friends of the Indian" (227–28). And the Indian, by contrast and "by every right and law and heritage," is "the first and best blood of America." Offered the opportunity to enlist, Nophaie immediately volunteers, "I will go," he says, "I am an American" (224).[9]

The neat trick here of representing the Germans as the ancestral enemies of the Indians (and it is a German who buys the Indian relics that by rights, Tom Outland thinks, should be in the Smithsonian—it is not just, as Indiana Jones puts it, that "they belong to a museum," they belong in an American museum) pales by comparison to the truly astonishing rearrangement of ancestry that the War makes possible. Attempting to persuade his fellow tribesmen to enlist, Nophaie gives what Grey calls "a trenchant statement of his own stand": "Nophaie will go to war. He will fight for the English, who are forefathers of Americans. Nophaie and all the Nopahs are the first of Americans. He will fight for them" (229). If the Indians are the first Americans and the Americans are descended from the English, then the English become the "forefathers" of the Indians and the Indians going off to fight for them are fighting as Americans for their ancestors and against the ancestors of the un-American missionaries. Or to put this from the standpoint not of the Indians *about* whom Grey was writing but of the white Americans *for* whom he was writing, if the Indians are the "first Americans," then the Americans now going off to war are descended from them; the Indians, whose forefathers are the English, are themselves the forefathers of the Americans. Volunteering to fight and so proving themselves as American as the white man, they make it possible for the white man to become their descendent and so to become as American as the Indian.

The readers of *The Vanishing American* are thus understood to bear the same relation to the Indians that Tom Outland does. And when Nophaie vanishes at *The Vanishing American*'s end, he is only following in the footsteps of the cliff dwellers whose disappearance as a people made possible their arrival as a culture. In *The Professor's House,* one's ancestors cannot be the members of one's family; this is why the defense of the family against "strangers" like Louie Marsellus is bound to fail—the essence of the family is its inability to maintain the integrity to which the theorists of racial purity were committed. Rosamond is the chief site of this failure; the "peculiar kind of hurt" a man "can get from his daughter" (155) is the destruction of his family: "When a man had lovely children in his house . . . why couldn't he keep them?" the Professor wonders, "Was there no way but Medea's?" (126). Marrying them to their brother (Tom) might have been a way; imagining a family without women altogether might be another: the "happy family" (198) on the Blue Mesa (Tom, Roddy, and Henry) is one such model of America as "a family matter," as is Louie's vision of the Professor's books as his "sons," his "splendid Spanish adventurer sons" (165).[10] But Tom calls such "substitutions" "sad" and they are, in any case, ineffective: he is himself betrayed by Roddy (as the Professor is by Rosie) and Louie gets himself "related to" the books just as he got himself related to Tom, "by marriage."

Thus the only way to save the family is indeed to destroy it, Medea's way, by killing your children or, the Professor's way, by imagining you never had any. For while his family is in Europe (and while his daughter is participating in the production of "a young Marsellus" [273]), the Professor is becoming "the Kansas boy" he once was, who "had never married, never been a father" (265). And "this Kansas boy" is not only much younger than the Professor but much older, he is "a primitive" "nearing the end of his life." Going back to what he calls a "beginning" that is simultaneously an ending, the Professor embodies an "extinction" that guarantees the purity Tom experiences on the Blue Mesa. In Washington, looking for help with what he's found, Tom is sent first to the Indian Commissioner and then, after being informed that the Commission's business is "with living Indians, not dead ones" (226), to the Smithsonian, where they also—albeit for different reasons—turn out not to "care much about dead and gone Indians" (235). Tom, however, has no interest in living Indians; he mentions them only once to compare the men's "contemptible" habit of helping to shop for their wives' clothes to the practice of the pathetic bureaucrat Bixby; and the paradigm of a man who shops with women is, of course, Louie, who chooses all his wife's clothes; when the Professor receives the "cruellest" hurt "that flesh is heir to" (155) from his daughter, it is on a "shopping expedition" (281) with her to Chicago, an expedition that marks not only the fact that he has lost Rosamond to Louie but also that, in losing her to Louie, he has, like Rosamond herself, "become Louie" (86). So in *The Professor's House,* the only good Indians are dead ones; and it is to avoid becoming a living Indian (or a Washington bureaucrat, or a Jew) that the Professor imagines himself not only dead but (like the cliff dwellers) extinct.

Cultural purity thus emerges as an ideal of miraculous preservation, like the Cliff City; a high-tech racial purity that can survive the cruel hurts that flesh is heir to and even transform those hurts into the technology of survival: becoming extinct, the Indians become the "first Americans," the "forefathers" of Tom Outland. Or to put the point more precisely, culture becomes a way of insisting that citizenship is a function of identity without reducing identity to nothing but biology. The assimilationism of the early years of the twentieth century, racist though it was, had understood citizenship as the consequence of certain transforming actions; excluding blacks, it conferred eligibility on all whites and appealed to the political authority of the Civil War as the founding moment of the American state. The racism of the '20s (one might, with a nod to Paul de Man, call it vulgar racism) replaced the political state with the biological family, the overwhelming difference between blacks and whites with intrawhite distinctions like those among Nordics, Alpines, and Mediterraneans, and the Civil War with the arrival on American shores of the first Nordics. Its antiassimilationism consisted not only in its attempt to limit the numbers of those who could actually become citizens but also in its understanding of citizenship as "a family matter"; "blood is blood," as Faulkner says, and a fellow citizen is someone of the same blood. *The Professor's House* clearly participates in this form of antiassimiliationism, repulsing at every opportunity the stranger's attempt to join the family. But *The Professor's House* also stages a critique of Gould's and Grant's and Stoddard's vulgar racism: the technology by which the family perpetuates itself is represented as destroying its purity and so the ideal of citizenship becomes participation in a family that, already dead, exists instead as a culture: the Greeks, the Romans, the cliff dwellers.

"Modern American books," complained D. H. Lawrence, are "empty of any feeling," especially by contrast to "the old American books," in which Lawrence found a feeling that seemed to him, writing in 1923, still "new." *Studies in Classic American Literature* claims the status of "classic" for Melville. Hawthorne, and the rest by attempting to add them to a canon that should be understood as already including, Coolidge-style, not only the Greeks and Romans (Lawrence in fact begins with Lucretius and Apuleius), but also the Indians who, as is well known, play a crucial symbolic role in his account of American literature. He identifies Indians with "blood-knowledge" instead of "mind-knowledge," preferring, in what is perhaps the book's most famous formulation, "red-skins" to "palefaces." But Lawrence's involvement with Indians was more than symbolic: Mabel Dodge had invited him to Taos in the hope of getting him to write a book that would help save the Indians, and for the first two months of his stay Lawrence lived next door to John Collier, the single most important figure in what his biographer has called the "assault" on the Indian Bureau's policy of assimilation. The possibility of the American classic thus emerges out of the antiassimilationism that was excluding aliens and rescuing Indians. The Americanization of Lawrentian ideas about race took place in the context of a nativism that was culminating in the discovery of the Native American.[11]

But where Collier thought of saving what he called "the Indian culture system" (Kelly 326) as a matter of saving the Indians, Lawrence embodied even more clearly than Cather the desire to keep Indian culture alive by killing the Indians off. What Lawrence calls the "Spirit of Place," the "living homeland" that, in words almost identical to Sapir's descriptions of the vanished Indian culture, is available only to the members of a "living, organic, *believing* community" (6), will be available to white Americans, he argues, only when the Indians have disappeared. The "Spirit of Place" can't exert its "full influence upon a newcomer until the old inhabitant is dead or absorbed" (35). So it is only after "the last nuclei of Red life break up in America" that white men will encounter "the demon of the continent." Only the extermination of the Indian will make possible the emergence of Indian culture as "classic" American culture.

Sapir had emblematized in the living Indian the "sense" of "loss" (318); Tom, reading

Virgil among the dead Indians, wakes up "every morning," feeling "that I had found everything, instead of having lost everything" (251). As I have argued and as Lawrence makes clear, what Tom has found is what the Indians have lost, their culture; he has come into "possession" of his identity as an American. But in imagining a culture that can be lost and found, Cather was participating in the construction of a technology that went beyond creating Americans. Indeed, from the perspective of such a culture, Tom and Cather's Indians are only stalking horses for the emerging ethnics of the '20s. They are defined in opposition to Louie Marsellus, but the Indians will be his ancestors too, "outlandish" will take its place alongside "Outland." Hoxie makes a version of this point in his final chapter, "The Irony of Assimilation," when he says that "The assimilation effort, a campaign to draw Native Americans into a homogeneous society, helped create its antithesis—a plural society" (243) and goes on to remark that "Other groups traveled this path to cultural survival"; blacks, Jews, and Catholics "forged a potent political interest group amid the nativist hysteria of the 1920's. Rejection and exclusion . . . bred self-consciousness, resourcefulness, and aggressive pride" (246). But Hoxie writes here as if cultural pluralism were simply a reaction against nativism; I have been arguing that the commitment to cultural identity is a form of nativism—it shares with nativism the claim that all politics are identity politics. The cliff dwellers provide for Cather a paradigm of the American but they provide, more generally, a paradigm of cultural identity itself; the rejection, on their behalf, of Louie's efforts to assimilate will become, in time, Louie's assertion of his own Jewishness.

Such assertions have themselves often emerged in the form of vulgar racism, and Werner Sollors, in his extremely important *Beyond Ethnicity: Consent and Descent in American Culture,* has made devastating fun of the willingness of "consent-conscious Americans" to "perceive ethnic distinctions—differentiations which they seemingly base exclusively on descent, no matter how far removed and how artificially selected and constructed—as powerful and as crucial" (13). It would be a mistake, however, to see the commitment to descent (to, in Cather's terms, the family) as undone by the revelation of its artificial (i.e., cultural) competent. On the contrary, the very idea of cultural identity requires both the extension and the critique of descent-based, biological identity.

For if political citizenship is essentially a matter of what you do, and familial citizenship is essentially a matter of what you are, the elegance of cultural citizenship consists in its refusal to choose between these options. Thus it must be simultaneously racist and compatible with a certain critique of racism. It is racist in that, refusing to identity "our" culture (whoever "we" are) with whatever it is we do and believe, it imagines instead that our culture is the culture of our ancestors, so that we can be understood, for example, to participate more fully in our culture when we find out about and imitate the social or religious practices of our great-grandparents. Their genetic makeup is (at least partially) ours through biology; their culture is ours only through the biologization of that culture. But culture involves also the critique of biology, for if culture were simply biological, we could never fail fully to participate in it; if our "heritage" were genetically encoded, we would always be in full possession of it.

Hence the extraordinary power of culture as a concept: it is manufactured out of an insistence upon the discrepancy between social and biological criteria of identity but it is at the same time hostile to any attempt to require a choice between the two sets of criteria. On the contrary, the essence of culture is that it cannot be reduced to either the social or the biological; culture's project—the project embedded in the very idea of culture—is to reconcile them.[12] And such a project is as available to Jews about whom there is "nothing Semitic" (43) but their noses as it is to Tom Outland who doesn't exactly look Indian. If, then, *The Professor's House* provides a model of cultural Americanism, it does so only by providing a model of culture that can by no means be limited to native Americans. And it may be this model of culture that has turned out to be—for better or for worse—the great cultural contribution of the classic American literature of the '20s.

Notes

I want to thank Lady Falls Brown and Patrick Shaw for encouraging me to think about Cather by inviting me to the Santa Fe Cather Conference (August 1989) where a version of this essay was first delivered as a talk, and I want to thank Michael Fried for suggesting to me, after reading "The Souls of White Folk," that *The Professor's House* would be a text I would find interesting.

1. Critics of *The Professor's House* tend either to ignore or play down the question of anti-Semitism, attaching it (when they bring it up at all) to Cather's ambivalence about Isabelle McClung's Jewish husband (Edel 212–15) or to her general hostility to the American "preoccupation with material wealth" (Stouck 100–09). This seems to me a mistake but not exactly one I mean to correct here, since my own interest is less in anti-Semitism as such than in the role played by anti-Semitism (as by love of the classics and admiration for dead Indians) in the reconstruction of American citizenship.

2. In *The Rainbow Trail,* the Indian is called Nas Ta Bega and he is based on a Paiute named Nasja Begay who, with John Wetherill, guided Grey to the giant natural arch, *Nonnezoshe* and through Monument Valley in 1913. It was Wetherill's brothers, Richard and Al, who in December 1888 had discovered the Anasazi ruin that they called Cliff Palace and that became Cather's Cliff City.

3. For an important discussion of the differences between "consensual membership" and "birthright citizenship" (4), see Schuck and Smith 9–41.

4. For a discussion of family, race, and culture in Hemingway and Fitzgerald, see Michaels 193–206.

5. Sharon O'Brien convincingly describes "The Namesake" as an "autobiographical" account of Cather's developing commitment to an "art" with its "source in American soil, American history, and American lives" (329). The question, however, is what is meant by "American."

6. Indeed for Griffith, as Michael Rogin points out in a brilliant essay on race, nationality, and aesthetics both in *The Birth of a Nation* and in Progressivism more generally, the movie itself could be understood to succeed the Klan and Wilsonian Progressivism in a series of "linked attributions of national paternity" (192).

7. Thus in "Franz Boas and the Culture Concept," George W. Stocking writes that Boas's "problem as a critic of racial thought was in a sense to define 'the genius of a people' in other terms than racial heredity. His answer, ultimately, was the anthropological idea of culture" (214). Stocking thinks of racial identity and cultural identity as fundamentally opposed; in my own view, as the following pages will make clear, the idea of cultural identity proved for many to be a way of renovating rather than repudiating racial identity.

8. Actually the number of Indians had increased from 237,196 in 1900 to 244,437 in 1920, and would rise to 357,499 by 1950 (Prucha, *Documents* 57).

9. As a way of guaranteeing their un-American status, Grey makes the missionaries "Bolshevists" (157) as well as Germans, proleptically (from the standpoint of the time when the story takes place) retrofitting (from the standpoint of the time when the story was written) the wartime enemy as the postwar enemy alien.

10. Eve Kosofsky Sedgwick's acute description of the relation between Roddy and Tom as a "gorgeous homosocial romance" (68) becomes all the more convincing in the light of the benefit to racial purity of a nonreproductive sexuality. The happy homosexual finally appears here as the eugenically utopian alternative to the unhappy heterosexual one, a machine (even if, as it turns out, a rather fragile one) for turning race to culture.

11. Which is not to say that American Indian policy proceeded smoothly along antiassimilationist lines. For one thing, Collier's tenure as Commissioner of Indian Affairs was followed by a period of "termi-

nation," devoted in part to rolling back Collier's reforms. And, for another, the reforms themselves (particularly with respect to the reorganization of tribal government) were sometimes viewed by the Indians as "crass instances of continuing government paternalism" (Prucha, *Documents* 66).

12. From this perspective, one might also describe "The Namesake" as at least pointing the way beyond a national to a cultural identity since, even though it insists on the primacy of "experience" in becoming American, the experience insisted upon turns out to be that of discovering that one already is American.

Works Cited

Berkhofer, Robert F. *The White Man's Indian.* New York: Knopf, 1978.

Cather, Willa. "The Namesake." *24 Stories.* Ed. Sharon O'Brien. New York: Meridian, 1987.

———, *The Professor's House.* 1925. New York: Vintage, 1973.

Coolidge, Calvin. *America's Need For Education.* Boston: Houghton, 1925.

Dixon, Thomas, Jr. *The Clansman: An Historical Romance of the Ku Klux Klan.* Lexington: U of Kentucky P, 1970.

Edel, Leon. "A Cave of One's Own." *Critical Essays on Willa Cather.* Ed. John J. Murphy. Boston: G. K. Hall, 1984. 200–17.

Faulkner, William. *The Sound and the Fury.* 1929. New York: Vintage, 1954.

Fitzgerald, F. Scott. *The Great Gatsby.* New York: Scribner's, 1925.

Gould, Charles W. *America, A Family Matter.* New York: Scribner's, 1922.

Grey, Zane. *The Rainbow Trail.* 1915. New York: Pocket, 1961.

———. *The Vanishing American.* 1922. New York: Pocket, 1982.

Higham, John. *Strangers in the Land: Patterns of American Nativism, 1860–1925.* 1955. New Brunswick: Rutgers UP, 1988.

Hutchinson, E. P. *Legislative History of American Immigration Policy, 1798–1965.* Philadelphia: U of Pennsylvania P, 1981.

Hoxie, Frederick E. *A Final Promise: The Campaign to Assimilate the Indians, 1880–1920.* 1984. Cambridge: Cambridge UP, 1989.

Kelly, Lawrence C. *The Assault on Assimilation: John Collier and the Origins of Indian Policy Reform.* Albuquerque: U of New Mexico P, 1983.

Lawrence, D. H. *Studies in Classic American Literature.* 1923. New York: Viking, 1964.

Michaels, Walter Benn. "The Souls of White Folk." *Literature and the Body.* Ed. Elaine Scarry. Baltimore: John Hopkins UP, 1988. 183–209.

Morgan, Thomas J. "Annual Report of the Commissioner of Indian Affairs, October, 1889." Prucha, *Documents.*

O'Brien, Sharon. *Willa Cather: The Emerging Voice.* New York: Oxford UP, 1987.

Prucha, Francis P., ed. *Documents of United States Indian Policy.* Lincoln: U of Nebraska P, 1975.

———. *The Indians in American Society.* Berkeley: U of California P, 1985.

Rogin, Michael, *Ronald Reagan, the Movie and Other Episodes in Political Demonology.* Berkeley: U of California P, 1987.

Sapir, Edward. "Culture, Genuine and Spurious." *Selected Writings in Language, Culture, and Personality.* Ed. David G. Mandelbaum. 1949. Berkeley: U of California P, 1985. 308–31.

Schuck, Peter H., and Rogers M. Smith, *Citizenship Without Consent: Illegal Aliens in the American Polity.* New Haven: Yale UP, 1985.

Sedgwick, Eve Kosofsky. "Across Gender, Across Sexuality: Willa Cather and Others." *South Atlantic Quarterly* 88 (1989): 53–72.

Sollors, Werner. *Beyond Ethnicity: Consent and Descent in American Culture.* New York: Oxford UP, 1986.

Stouck, David. *Willa Cather's Imagination.* Lincoln: U of Nebraska P, 1975.

Stocking, George W., Jr. *Race, Culture, and Evolution: Essays in the History of Anthropology.* Chicago: U of Chicago P, 1982.

Stoddard, Lothrop. *Re-Forging America.* New York: Scribner's, 1927.

———. *The Rising Tide of Color Against White World-Supremacy.* New York: Scribner's, 1920.

Fredric Jameson

The Cultural Logic of Late Capitalism

II

The disappearance of the individual subject, along with its formal consequence, the increasing unavailability of the personal style, engender the well-nigh universal practice today of what may be called pastiche. This concept, which we owe to Thomas Mann (in *Doktor Faustus*), who owed it in turn to Adorno's great work on the two paths of advanced musical experimentation (Schoenberg's innovative planification and Stravinsky's irrational eclecticism), is to be sharply distinguished from the more readily received idea of parody.

To be sure, parody found a fertile area in the idiosyncrasies of the moderns and their "inimitable" styles: the Faulknerian long sentence, for example, with its breathless gerundives; Lawrentian nature imagery punctuated by testy colloquialism; Wallace Stevens's inveterate hypostasis of nonsubstantive parts of speech ("the intricate evasions of as"); the fateful (but finally predictable) swoops in Mahler from high orchestral pathos into village accordion sentiment; Heidegger's meditative-solemn practice of the false etymology as a mode of "proof" . . . All these strike one as somehow characteristic, insofar as they ostentatiously deviate from a norm which then reasserts itself, in a not necessarily unfriendly way, by a systematic mimicry of their willful eccentricities.

Yet in the dialectical leap from quantity to quality, the explosion of modern literature into a host of distinct private styles and mannerisms has been followed by a linguistic fragmentation of social life itself to the point where the norm itself is eclipsed: reduced to a neutral and reified media speech (far enough from the Utopian aspirations of the inventors of Esperanto or Basic English), which itself then becomes but one more idiolect among many. Modernist styles thereby become postmodernist codes. And that the stupendous proliferation of social codes today into professional and disciplinary jargons (but also into the badges of affirmation of ethnic, gender, race, religious, and class-factional adhesion) is also a political phenomenon, the problem of micropolitics sufficiently demonstrates. If the idea of a ruling class were once the dominant (or hegemonic) ideology of bourgeois society, the advanced capitalist countries today are now a field of stylistic and discursive heterogeneity without a norm. Faceless masters continue to inflect the economic strategies which constrain our existences, but they no longer need to impose their speech (or are henceforth unable to); and the postliteracy of the late capitalist world reflects not only the absence of any great collective project but also the unavailability of the older national language itself.

In this situation parody finds itself without a vocation; it has lived, and that strange new thing pastiche slowly comes to take its place. Pastiche is, like parody, the imitation of a peculiar or unique, idiosyncratic style, the wearing of a linguistic mask, speech in a dead language. But it is a neutral practice of such mimicry, without any of parody's ulterior motives, amputated of the satiric impulse, devoid of laughter and of any conviction that alongside the abnormal tongue you have momentarily borrowed, some healthy linguistic normality still exists. Pastiche is thus blank parody, a statue with blind eyeballs: it is to parody what that other interesting and historically original modern thing, the practice of a kind of blank irony, is to what Wayne Booth calls the "stable ironies" of the eighteenth century.

Fredric Jameson, "The Cultural Logic of Late Capitalism," in *Postmodernism: or, The Cultural Logic of Late Capitalism*. Durham, N.C.: Duke University Press, 1991. Reprinted with permission.

It would therefore begin to seem that Adorno's prophetic diagnosis has been realized, albeit in a negative way: not Schönberg (the sterility of whose achieved system he already glimpsed) but Stravinsky is the true precursor of postmodern cultural production. For with the collapse of the high-modernist ideology of style—what is as unique and unmistakable as your own fingerprints, as incomparable as your own body (the very source, for an early Roland Barthes, of stylistic invention and innovation)—the producers of culture have nowhere to turn but to the past: the imitation of dead styles, speech through all the masks and voices stored up in the imaginary museum of a now global culture.

This situation evidently determines what the architecture historians call "historicism," namely, the random cannibalization of all the styles of the past, the play of random stylistic allusion, and in general what Henri Lefebvre has called the increasing primacy of the "neo." This omnipresence of pastiche is not incompatible with a certain humor, however, nor is it innocent of all passion: it is at the least compatible with addiction—with a whole historically original consumers' appetite for a world transformed into sheer images of itself and for pseudo-events and "spectacles" (the term of the situationists). It is for such objects that we may reserve Plato's conception of the "simulacrum," the identical copy for which no original has ever existed. Appropriately enough, the culture of the simulacrum comes to life in a society where exchange value has been generalized to the point at which the very memory of use value is effaced, a society of which Guy Debord has observed, in an extraordinary phrase, that in it "the image has become the final form of commodity reification" (*The Society of the Spectacle*).

The new spatial logic of the simulacrum can now be expected to have a momentous effect on what used to be historical time. The past is thereby itself modified: what was once, in the historical novel as Lukács defines it, the organic genealogy of the bourgeois collective project—what is still, for the redemptive historiography of an E. P. Thompson or of American "oral history," for the resurrection of the dead of anonymous and silenced generations, the retrospective dimension indispensable to any vital reorientation of our collective future—has meanwhile itself become a vast collection of images, a multitudinous photographic simulacrum. Duy Debord's powerful slogan is now even more apt for the "prehistory" of a society bereft of all historicity, one whose own putative past is little more than a set of dusty spectacles. In faithful conformity to poststructuralist linguistic theory, the past as "referent" finds itself gradually bracketed, and then effaced altogether, leaving us with nothing but texts.

Yet it should not be thought that this process is accompanied by indifference: on the contrary, the remarkable current intensification of an addiction to the photographic image is itself a tangible symptom of an omnipresent, omnivorous, and well-nigh libidinal historicism. As I have already observed, the architects are this (exceedingly polysemous) word for the complacent eclecticism of postmodern architecture, which randomly and without principle but with gusto cannibalizes all the architectural styles of that past and combines them in overstimulating ensembles. Nostalgia does not strike one as an altogether satisfactory word for such fascination (particularly when one thinks of the pain of a properly modernist nostalgia with a past beyond all but aesthetic retrieval), yet it directs our attention to what is a culturally far more generalized manifestation of the process in commercial art and taste, namely the so-called nostalgia film (or what the French call *la mode rétro*).

Nostalgia films restructure the whole issue of pastiche and project it onto a collective and social level, where the desperate attempt to appropriate a missing past is now refracted through the iron law of fashion change and the emergent ideology of the generation. The inaugural film of this new aesthetic discourse, George Lucas's *American Graffiti*

(1973), set out to recapture, as so many films have attempted since, the henceforth mesmerizing lost reality of the Eisenhower era; and one tends to feel, that for Americans at least, the 1950s remain the privileged lost object of desire—not merely the stability and prosperity of a pax Americana but also the first naïve innocence of the countercultural impulses of early rock and roll and youth gangs (Coppola's *Rumble Fish* will then be the contemporary dirge that laments their passing, itself, however, still contradictorily filmed in genuine nostalgia film style). With this initial breakthrough, other generational periods open up for aesthetic colonization: as witness the stylistic recuperation of the American and the Italian 1930s, in Polanski's *Chinatown* and Bertolucci's *Il Conformista,* respectively. More interesting, and more problematical, are the ultimate attempts, through this new discourse, to lay siege either to our own present and immediate past or to a more distant history that escapes individual existential memory.

Faced with these ultimate objects—our social, historical, and existential present, and the past as "referent"—the incompatibility of a postmodernist "nostalgia" art language with genuine historicity becomes dramatically apparent. The contradiction propels this mode, however, into complex and interesting new formal inventiveness; it being understood that the nostalgia film was never a matter of some old-fashioned "representation" of historical content, but instead approached the "past" through stylistic connotation, conveying "pastness" by the glossy qualities of the image, and "1930s–ness" or "1950s–ness" by the attributes of fashion (in that following the prescription of the Barthes of *Mythologies,* who saw connotation as the purveying of imaginary and stereotypical idealities: "Sinité," for example, as some Disney-EPCOT "concept" of China).

The insensible colonization of the present by the nostalgia mode can be observed in Lawrence Kasdan's elegant film *Body Heat,* a distant "affluent society" remake of James M. Cain's *Double Indemnity,* set in a contemporary Florida small town a few hours' drive from Miami. The word *remake* is, however, anachronistic to the degree to which our awareness of the preexistence of other versions (previous films of the novel as well as the novel itself) is now a constitutive and essential part of the film's structure: we are now, in other words, in "intertextuality' as a deliberate, built-in feature of the aesthetic effect and as the operator of a new connotation of "pastness" and pseudohistorical depth, in which the history of aesthetic styles displaces "real" history.

Yet from the outset a whole battery of aesthetic signs begin to distance the officially contemporary image from us in time: the art deco scripting of the credits, for example, serves at once to program the spectator to the appropriate "nostalgia" mode of reception (art deco quotation has much the same function in contemporary architecture, as in Toronto's remarkable Eaton Centre). Meanwhile, a somewhat different play of connotations is activated by complex (but purely formal) allusions to the institution of the star system itself. The protagonist, William Hurt, is one of a new generation of film "stars" whose status is markedly distinct from that of the preceding generation of male superstars, such as Steve McQueen or Jack Nicholson (or even, more distantly, Brando), let alone of earlier moments in the evolution of the institution of the star. The immediately preceding generation projected their various roles through and by way of their well-known off-screen personalities, which often connoted rebellion and nonconformism. The latest generation of starring actors continues to assure the conventional functions of stardom (most notably sexuality) but in the utter absence of "personality" in the older sense, and with something of the anonymity of character acting (which in actors like Hurt reaches virtuoso proportions, yet of a very different kind than the virtuosity of the older Brando or Olivier). This "death of the subject" in the institution of the star now, however, opens up the possibility of a play of historical allusions to much older roles—in this case to those associated with Clark Gable—so that the very style of the acting can now also serve as a "connotator" of the past.

Finally, the setting has been strategically framed, with great ingenuity, to eschew most of the signals that normally convey the contemporaneity of the United States in its multinational era: the small-town setting allows the camera to elude the high-rise landscape of the 1970s and 1980s (even though a key episode in the narrative involves the fatal destruction of older buildings by land speculators), while the object world of the present day—artifacts and appliances, whose styling would at once serve to date the image—is elaborately edited out. Everything in the film, therefore, conspires to blur its official contemporaneity and make it possible for the viewer to receive the narrative as though it were set in some eternal thirties, beyond real historical time. This approach to the present by way of the art language of the simulacrum, or of the pastiche of the stereotypical past, endows present reality and the openness of present history with the spell and distance of a glossy mirage. Yet this mesmerizing new aesthetic mode itself emerged as an elaborated symptom of the waning of our historicity, of our lived possibility of experiencing history in some active way. It cannot therefore be said to produce this strange occultation of the present by its own formal power, but rather merely to demonstrate, through these inner contradictions, the enormity of a situation in which we seem increasingly incapable of fashioning representations of our own current experience.

As for "real history" itself—the traditional object, however it may be defined, of what used to be the historical novel—it will be more revealing now to turn back to that older form and medium and to read its postmodern fate in the work of one of the few serious and innovative leftist novelists at work in the United States today, whose books are nourished with history in the more traditional sense and seem, so far, to stake out successive generational moments in the "epic" of American history, between which they alternate. E. L. Doctorow's *Ragtime* gives itself officially as a panorama of the first two decades of the century (like *World's Fair*); his most recent novel, *Billy Bathgate,* like *Loon Lake* addresses the thirties and the Great Depression, while *The Book of Daniel* holds up before us, in painful juxtaposition, the two great moments of the Old Left and the New Left, of thirties and forties communism and the radicalism of the 1960s (even his early western may be said to fit into this scheme and to designate in a less articulated and formally self-conscious way the end of the frontier of the late nineteenth century).

The *Book of Daniel* is not the only one of these five major historical novels to establish an explicit narrative link between the reader's and the writer's present and the older historical reality that is the subject of the work; the astonishing last page of *Loon Lake,* which I will not disclose, also does this in a very different way; it is a matter of some interest to note that the first version of *Ragtime* positions us explicitly in our own present, in the novelist's house in New Rochelle, New York, which at once becomes the scene of its own (imaginary) past in the 1900s. This detail has been suppressed from the published text, symbolically cutting its moorings and freeing the novel to float in some new world of past historical time whose relationship to us is problematical indeed. The authenticity of the gesture, however, may be measured by the evident existential fact of life that there no longer does seem to be any organic relationship between the American history we learn from schoolbooks and the lived experience of the current multinational, highrise, stagflated city of the newspapers and of our own everyday life.

A crisis in historicity, however, inscribes itself symptomatically in several other curious formal features within this text. Its official subject is the transition from a pre-World War I radical and working-class politics (the great strikes) to the technological invention and new commodity production of the 1920s (the rise of Hollywood and of the image as commodity): the interpolated version of Kleist's *Michael Kohlhaas,* the strange, tragic episode of the black protagonist's revolt, may be thought of as a moment related to this process. That *Ragtime* has political content and even something like a political "meaning" seems in any case obvious and has been expertly articulated by Lynda Hutcheon in terms of

> its three paralleled families: the Anglo-American establishment one and the marginal immi-grant European and American black ones. The novel's action disperses the center of the first and moves the margins into the multiple "centers" of the narrative, in a formal allegory of the social demographics of urban America. In addition, there is an extended critique of American democratic ideals through the presentation of class conflict rooted in capitalist property and moneyed power. The black Coalhouse, the white Houdini, the immigrant Tateh are all working class, and because of this—not in spite of it—all can therefore work to create new aesthetic forms (ragtime, vaudeville, movies).

But this does everything but the essential, lending the novel an admirable thematic co-herence few readers can have experienced in parsing the lines of a verbal object held too close to the eyes to fall into these perspectives. Hutcheon is, of course, absolutely right, and this is what the novel would have meant had it not been a postmodern artifact. For one thing, the objects of representation, ostensibly narrative characters, are incommensu-rable and, as it were, of incomparable substances, like oil and water—Houdini being a *his-torical* figure, Tateh a *fictional* one, and Coalhouse an *intertextual* one—something very dif-ficult for an interpretive comparison of this kind to register. Meanwhile, the theme attributed to the novel also demands a somewhat different kind of scrutiny, since it can be rephrased into a classic version of the Left's "experience of defeat" in the twentieth cen-tury, namely, the proposition that the depolitization of the workers' movement is attribut-able to the media or culture generally (what she here calls "new aesthetic forms"). This is, indeed, in my opinion, something like the elegiac backdrop, if not the meaning, of *Rag-time,* and perhaps of Doctorow's work in general; but then we need another way of describ-ing the novel as something like an unconscious expression and associative exploration of this left doxa, this historical opinion or quasi-vision in the mind's eye of "objective spirit." What such a description would want to register is the paradox that a seemingly realistic novel like *Ragtime* is in reality a nonrepresentational work that combines fantasy signifiers from a variety of ideologemes in a kind of hologram.

My point, however, is not some hypothesis as to the thematic coherence of this decen-tered narrative but rather just the opposite, namely, the way in which the kind of reading this novel imposes makes it virtually impossible for us to reach and thematize those offi-cial "subjects" which float above the text but cannot be integrated into our reading of the sentences. In that sense, the novel not only resists interpretation, it is organized systemat-ically and formally to short-circuit an older type of social and historical interpretation which it perpetually holds out and withdraws. When we remember that the theoretical critique and repudiation of interpretation as such is a fundamental component of post-structuralist theory, it is difficult not to conclude that Doctorow has somehow deliberately built this very tension, this very contradiction, into the flow of his sentences.

The book is crowded with real historical figures—from Teddy Roosevelt to Emma Goldman, from Harry K. Thaw and Stanford White to J. Pierpont Morgan and Henry Ford, not to mention the more central role of Houdini—who interact with a fictive family, simply designated as Father, Mother, Older Brother, and so forth. All historical novels, beginning with those of Sir Walter Scott himself, no doubt in one way or another involve a mobilization of previous historical knowledge generally acquired through the schoolbook history manuals devised for whatever legitimizing purpose by this or that national tradition—thereafter instituting a narrative dialectic between what we already "know" about The Pretender, say, and what he is then seen to be concretely in the pages of the novel. But Doctorow's procedure seems much more extreme than this; and I would argue that the designation of both types of characters—historical names and capitalized family roles—operates powerfully and systematically to reify all these characters and to make it impossible for us to receive their representation without the prior interception of already acquired knowledge or doxa—something which lends the text an extraordinary sense of déjà vu and a peculiar familiarity one is tempted to associate with Freud's "return of the repressed" in "The Uncanny" rather than with any solid historiographic formation on the reader's past.

Meanwhile, the sentences in which all this is happening have their own specificity, allowing us more concretely to distinguish the moderns' elaboration of a personal style from this new kind of linguistic innovation, which is no longer personal at all but has its family kinship rather with what Barthes long ago called "white writing." In this particular novel, Doctorow has imposed upon himself a rigorous principle of selection in which only simple declarative sentences (predominantly mobilized by the verb "to be") are received. The effect is, however, not really one of the condescending simplification and symbolic carefulness of children's literature, but rather something more disturbing, the sense of some profound subterranean violence done to American English, which cannot, however, be detected empirically in any of the perfectly grammatical sentences with which this work is formed. Yet other more visible technical "innovations" may supply a clue to what is happening in the language of *Ragtime*: it is, for example, well known that the source of many of the characteristic effects of Camus's novel *The Stranger* can be traced back to that author's willful decision to substitute, throughout, the French tense of the *passé composé* for the other past tenses more normally employed in narration in that language. I suggest that it is as if something of that sort were at work here: *as though* Doctorow had set out systematically to produce the effect or the equivalent, in his language, of a verbal past tense we do not possess in English, namely, the French preterite (or *passé simple*), whose "perfective" movement, as Émile Benveniste taught us, serves to separate events from the present of enunciation and to transform the stream of time and action into so many finished, complete, and isolated punctual event objects which find themselves sundered from any present situation (even that of the act of story telling or enunciation).

E. L. Doctorow is the epic poet of the disappearance of the American radical past, of the suppression of older traditions and moments of the American radical tradition: no one with left sympathies can read these splendid novels without a poignant distress that is an authentic way of confronting our own current political dilemmas in the present. What is culturally interesting, however, is that he has had to convey this great theme formally (since the waning of the content is very precisely his subject) and, more than that, has had to elaborate his work by way of that very cultural logic of the postmodern which is itself the mark and symptom of his dilemma. *Loon Lake* much more obviously deploys the strategies of the pastiche (most notably in its reinvention of Dos Passos); but *Ragtime* remains the most peculiar and stunning monument to the aesthetic situation engendered by the disappearance of the historical referent. This historical novel can no longer set out to represent the historical past; it can only "represent" our ideas and stereotypes about that past (which thereby at once becomes "pop history"). Cultural production is thereby driven back inside a mental space which is no longer that of the old monadic subject but rather that of some degraded collective "objective spirit": it can no longer gaze directly on some putative real world, at some reconstruction of a past history which was once itself a present; rather, as in

Plato's cave, it must trace our mental images of that past upon its confining walls. If there is any realism left here, it is a "realism" that is meant to derive from the shock of grasping that confinement and of slowly becoming aware of a new and original historical situation in which we are condemned to seek History by way of our own pop images and simulacra of that history, which itself remains forever out of reach. . . .

VI

The conception of postmodernism outlined here is a historical rather than a merely stylistic one. I cannot stress too greatly the radical distinction between a view for which the postmodern is one (optional) style among many others available and one which seeks to grasp it as the cultural dominant of the logic of late capitalism: the two approaches in fact generate two very different ways of conceptualizing the phenomenon as a whole: on the one hand, moral judgments (about which it is indifferent whether they are positive or negative), and, on the other, a genuinely dialectical attempt to think our present of time in History.

Of some positive moral evaluation of postmodernism little needs to be said: the complacent (yet delirious) camp-following celebration of this aesthetic new world (including its social and economic dimension, greeted with equal enthusiasms under the slogan of "postindustrial society") is surely unacceptable, although it may be somewhat less obvious that current fantasies about the salvational nature of high technology, from chips to robots—fantasies entertained not only by both left and right governments in distress but also by many intellectuals—are also essentially of a piece with more vulgar apologias for postmodernism.

But in that case it is only consequent to reject moralizing condemnations of the postmodern and of its essential triviality when juxtaposed against the Utopian "high seriousness" of the great modernisms: judgments one finds both on the Left and on the radical Right. And no doubt the logic of the simulacrum, with its transformation of older realities into television images, does more than merely replicate the logic of late capitalism; it reinforces and intensifies it. Meanwhile, for political groups which seek actively to intervene in history and to modify its otherwise passive momentum (whether with a view toward channeling it into a socialist transformation of society or diverting it into the regressive reestablishment of some simpler fantasy past), there cannot but be much that is deplorable and reprehensible in a cultural form of image addiction which, by transforming the past into visual mirages, stereotypes, or texts, effectively abolishes any practical sense of the future and of the collective project, thereby abandoning the thinking of future change to fantasies of sheer catastrophe and inexplicable cataclysm, from visions of "terrorism" on the social level to those of cancer on the personal. Yet if postmodernism is a historical phenomenon, then the attempt to conceptualize it in terms of moral or moralizing judgments must finally be identified as a category mistake. All of which becomes more obvious when we interrogate the position of the cultural critic and moralist; the latter, along with all the rest of us, is now so deeply immersed in post-modernist space, so deeply suffused and infected by its new cultural categories, that the luxury of the old-fashioned ideological critique, the indignant moral denunciation of the other, becomes unavailable.

The distinction I am proposing here knows one canonical form in Hegel's differentiation of the thinking of individual morality or moralizing (*Moralität*) from that whole very different realm of collective social values and practices (*Sittlichkeit*). But it finds its definitive form in Marx's demonstration of the materialist dialectic, most notably in those classic pages of the *Manifesto* which teach the hard lesson of some more genuinely dialectical way to think historical development and change. The topic of the lesson is, of course, the historical development of capitalism itself and the deployment of a specific bourgeois culture. In a well-known passage Marx powerfully urges us to do the impossible, namely, to think this development positively *and* negatively all at once; to achieve, in other words, a type of thinking that would be capable of grasping the demonstrably baleful features of capitalism along with its extraordinary and liberating dynamism simultaneously within a single thought, and without attenuating any of the force of either judgment. We are somehow to lift our minds to a point at which it is possible to understand that capitalism is at one and the same time the best thing that has ever happened to the human race, and the worst. The lapse from this austere dialectical imperative into the more comfortable stance of the taking of moral positions is inveterate and all too human: still, the urgency of the subject demands that we make at least some effort to think the cultural evolution of late capitalism dialectically, as catastrophe and progress all together.

Such an effort suggests two immediate questions, with which we will conclude these reflections. Can we in fact identify some "moment of truth" within the more evident "moments of falsehood" of postmodern culture? And, even if we can do so, is there not something ultimately paralyzing in the dialectical view of historical development proposed above; does it not tend to demobilize us and to surrender us to passivity and helplessness by systematically obliterating possibilities of action under the impenetrable fog of historical inevitability? It is appropriate to discuss these two (related) issues in terms of current possibilities for some effective contemporary cultural politics and for the construction of a genuine political culture.

To focus the problem in this way is, of course, immediately to raise the more genuine issue of the fate of culture generally, and of the function of culture specifically, as one social level or instance, in the postmodern era. Everything in the previous discussion suggests that what we have been calling postmodernism is inseparable from, and unthinkable without the hypothesis of, some fundamental mutation of the sphere of culture in the world of late capitalism, which includes a momentous modification of its social function. Older discussions of the space, function, or sphere of culture (mostly notably Herbert Marcuse's classic essay "The Affirmative Character of Culture") have insisted on what a different language would called the "semiautonomy" of the cultural realm: its ghostly, yet Utopian, existence, for good or ill, above the practical world of the existent, whose mirror image it throws back in forms which vary from the legitimations of flattering resemblance to the contestatory indictments of critical satire or Utopian pain.

What we must now ask ourselves is whether it is not precisely this semiautonomy of the cultural sphere which has been destroyed by the logic of late capitalism. Yet to argue that culture is today no longer endowed with the relative autonomy it once enjoyed as one level among others in earlier moments of capitalism (let alone in precapitalist societies) is not necessarily to imply its disappearance or extinction. Quite the contrary; we must go on to affirm that the dissolution of an autonomous sphere of culture is rather to be imagined in terms of an explosion: a prodigious expansion of culture throughout the social realm, to the point at which everything in our social life—from economic value and state power to practices and to the very structure of the psyche itself—can be said to have become "cultural" in some original and yet untheorized sense. This proposition is, however, substantively quite consistent with the previous diagnosis of a society of the image or the simulacrum and a transformation of the "real" into so many pseudoevents.

It also suggests that some of our most cherished and time-honored radical conceptions about the nature of cultural politics may thereby find themselves outmoded. However distinct those conceptions—which range from slogans of negativity, opposition, and subversion to critique and reflexivity—may have been, they all shared a single, fundamentally spatial, presupposition, which may be resumed in the equally time-honored formula of "critical distance." No theory of cultural politics current on the Left today has been able to do without one notion or another of a certain minimal aesthetic distance, of the possibility of the positioning of the cultural act outside the massive Being of capital, from which to assault this last. What the burden of our preceding demonstration suggests, however, is that distance in general (including "critical distance" in particular) has very precisely been abolished in the new space of postmodernism. We are submerged in its henceforth filled and suffused volumes to the point where our now postmodern bodies are bereft of spatial coordinates and practically (let alone theoretically) incapable of distantiation; meanwhile, it has already been observed how the prodigious new expansion of multinational capital ends up penetrating and colonizing those very precapitalist enclaves (Nature and the Unconscious) which offered extraterritorial and Archimedean footholds for critical effectivity. The shorthand language of co-optation is for this reason omnipresent on the left, but would now seem to offer a most inadequate theoretical basis for understanding a situation in which we all, in one way or another, dimly feel that not only punctual and local countercultural forms of cultural resistance and guerrilla warfare but also even overtly political interventions like those of *The Clash* are all somehow secretly disarmed and reabsorbed by a system of which they themselves might well be considered a part, since they can achieve no distance from it.

What we must now affirm is that it is precisely this whole extraordinarily demoralizing and depressing original new global space which is the "moment of truth" of postmodernism. What has been called the postmodernist "sublime" is only the moment in which this content has become most explicit, has moved the closest to the surface of consciousness as a coherent new type of space in its own right—even though a certain figural concealment or disguise is still at work here, most notably in the high-tech thematics in which the new spatial content is still dramatized and articulated. Yet the earlier features of the postmodern which were enumerated above can all now be seen as themselves partial (yet constitutive) aspects of the same general spatial object.

The argument for a certain authenticity in these otherwise patently ideological productions depends on the prior proposition that what we have been calling postmodern (or multinational) space is not merely a cultural ideology or fantasy but has genuine historical (and socioeconomic) reality as a third great original expansion of capitalism around the globe (after the earlier expansions of the national market and the older imperialist system, which each had their own cultural specificity and generated new types of space appropriate to their dynamics). The distorted and unreflexive attempts of newer cultural production to explore and to express this new space must then also, in their own fashion, be considered as so many approaches to the representation of (a new) reality (to use a more antiquated language). As paradoxical as the terms may seem, they may thus, following a classic interpretive option, be read as peculiar new forms of realism (or at least of the mimesis of reality), while at the same time they can equally well be analyzed as so many attempts to distract and divert us from that reality or to disguise its contradictions and resolve them in the guise of various formal mystifications.

As for that reality itself, however—the as yet untheorized original space of some new "world system" of multinational or late capitalism, a space whose negative or baleful aspects are only too obvious—the dialectic requires us to hold equally to a positive or "progressive" evaluation of its emergence, as Marx did for the world market as the horizon of national economies, or as Lenin did for the older imperialist global network. For neither Marx nor Lenin was socialism a matter of returning to smaller (and thereby less repressive and comprehensive) systems of social organization; rather, the dimensions attained by capital in their own times were grasped as the promise, the framework, and the precondition for the achievement of some new and more comprehensive socialism. Is this not the case with the yet more global and totalizing space of the new world system, which demands the intervention and elaboration of an internationalism of a radically new type? The disastrous realignment of socialist revolution with the older nationalisms (not only in Southeast Asia), whose results have necessarily aroused much serious recent left reflection, can be adduced in support of this position.

But if all this is so, then at least one possible form of a new radical cultural politics becomes evident, with a final aesthetic proviso that must quickly be noted. Left cultural producers and theorists—particularly those formed by bourgeois cultural traditions issuing from romanticism and valorizing spontaneous, instinctive, or unconscious forms of "genius," but also for very obvious historical reasons such as Zhdanovism and the sorry consequences of political and party interventions in the arts—have often by reaction allowed themselves to be unduly intimidated by the repudiation, in bourgeois aesthetics and most notably in high modernism, of one of the age-old functions of art—the pedagogical and the didactic. The teaching function of art was, however, always stressed in classical times (even though it there mainly took the form of moral lessons), while the prodigious and still imperfectly understood work of Brecht reaffirms, in a new and formally innovative and original way, for the moment of modernism proper, a complex new conception of the relationship between culture and pedagogy. The cultural model I will propose similarly foregrounds the cognitive and pedagogical dimensions of political art and culture, dimensions stressed in very different ways by both Lukács and Brecht (for the distinct moments of realism and modernism, respectively).

We cannot, however, return to aesthetic practices elaborated on the basis of historical situations and dilemmas which are no longer ours. Meanwhile, the conception of space that has been developed here suggests that a model of political culture appropriate to our own situation will necessarily have to raise spatial issues as its fundamental organizing concern. I will therefore provisionally define the aesthetic of this new (and hypothetical) cultural form as an aesthetic of *cognitive mapping*.

In a classic work, *The Image of the City*, Kevin Lynch taught us that the alienated city is above all a space in which people are unable to map (in their minds) either their own positions or the urban totality in which they find themselves: grids such as those of Jersey City, in which none of the traditional markers (monuments, nodes, natural boundaries, built perspectives) obtain, are the most obvious examples. Disalienation in the traditional city, then, involves the practical reconquest of a sense of place and the construction or reconstruction of an articulated ensemble which can be retained in memory and which the individual subject can map and remap along the moments of mobile, alternative trajectories. Lynch's own work is limited by the deliberate restriction of his topic to the problems of city form as such; yet it becomes extraordinarily suggestive when projected outward onto some of the larger national and global spaces we have touched on here. Nor should it be too hastily assumed that his model—while it clearly raises very central issues of representation as such—is in any way easily vitiated by the conventional poststructural critiques of the "ideology of representation" or mimesis. The cognitive map is not exactly mimetic in that older sense; indeed, the theoretical issues it poses allow us to renew the analysis of representation on a higher and much more complex level.

There is, for one thing, a most interesting convergence between the empirical problems studied by Lynch in terms of city space and the great Althusserian (and Lacanian) re-definition of ideology as "the representation of the subject's *Imaginary* relationship to his or her *Real* conditions of existence." Surely this is exactly what the cognitive map is called upon to do in the narrower framework of daily life in the physical city: to enable a situational representation on the part of the individual subject to that vaster and properly unrepresentable totality which is the ensemble of society's structures as a whole.

Yet Lynch's work also suggests a further line of development insofar as cartography itself constitutes its key mediatory instance. A return to the history of this science (which is also an art) shows us that Lynch's model does not yet, in fact, really correspond to what will become map-making. Lynch's subjects are rather clearly involved in precartographic operations whose results traditionally are described as itineraries rather than as maps: diagrams organized around the still subject-centered or existential journey of the traveler, along which various significant key features are marked—oases, mountain ranges, rivers, monuments, and the like. The most highly developed form of such diagrams is the nautical itinerary, the sea chart, or *portulans,* where coastal features are noted for the use of Mediterranean navigators who rarely venture out into the open sea.

Yet the compass at once introduces a new dimension into sea charts, a dimension that will utterly transform the problematic of the itinerary and allow us to pose the problem of a genuine cognitive mapping in a far more complex way. For the new instruments—compass, sextant, and theodolite—correspond not merely to new geographic and navigational problems (the difficult matter of determining longitude, particularly on the curving surface of the planet, as opposed to the simpler matter of latitude, which European navigators can still empirically determine by ocular inspection of the African coast); they also introduce a whole new coordinate: the relationship to the totality, particularly as it is mediated by the stars and by new operations like that of triangulation. At this point, cognitive mapping in the broader sense comes to require the coordination of existential data (the empirical position of the subject) with unlived, abstract conceptions of the geographic totality.

Finally, with the first globe (1490) and the invention of the Mercator projection at about the same time, yet a third dimension of cartography emerges, which at once involves what we would today call the nature of representational codes, the intrinsic structures of the various media, the intervention, into more naïve mimetic conceptions of mapping, of the whole new fundamental question of the languages of representation itself, in particular the unresolvable (well-nigh Heisenbergian) dilemma of the transfer of curved space to flat charts. At this point it becomes clear that there can be no true maps (at the same time it also becomes clear that there can be scientific progress, or better still, a dialectical advance, in the various historical moments of mapmaking).

Transcoding all this now into the very different problematic of the Althusserian definition of ideology, one would want to make two points. The first is that the Althusserian concept now allows us to rethink these specialized geographical and cartographic issues in terms of social space—in terms, for example, of social class and national or international context, in terms of the ways in which we all necessarily *also* cognitively map our individual social relationship to local, national, and international class realities. Yet to reformulate the problem in this way is also to come starkly up against those very difficulties in mapping which are posed to heightened and original ways by that very global space of the postmodernist or multinational moment which has been under discussion here. These are not merely theoretical issues; they have urgent practical political consequences, as is evident from the conventional feelings of First World subjects that existentially (or "empirically") they really do inhabit a "postindustrial society" from which traditional production has disappeared and in which social classes of the classical type no longer exist—a conviction which has immediate effects on political praxis.

The second point is that a return to the Lacanian underpinnings of Althusser's theory can afford some useful and suggestive methodological enrichments. Althusser's formulation remobilizes an older and henceforth classical Marxian distinction between science and ideology that is not without value for us even today. The existential—the positioning of the individual subject, the experience of daily life, the monadic "point of view" on the world to which we are necessarily, as biological subjects, restricted—is in Althusser's formula implicitly opposed to the realm of abstract knowledge, a realm which, as Lacan reminds us, is never positioned in or actualized by any concrete subject but rather by that structural void called *le sujet supposé savoir* (the subject supposed to know), a subject-place of knowledge. What is affirmed is not that we cannot know the world and its totality in some abstract or "scientific" way. Marxian "science" provides just such a way of knowing and conceptualizing the world abstractly, in the sense in which, for example, Mandel's great book offers a rich and elaborated *knowledge* of that global world system, of which it has never been said here that it was unknowable but merely that it was unrepresentable, which is a very different matter. The Althusserian formula, in other words, designates a gap, a rift, between existential experience and scientific knowledge. Ideology has then the function of somehow inventing a way of articulating those two distinct dimensions with each other. What a historicist view of this definition would want to add is that such coordination, the production of functioning and living ideologies, is distinct in different historical situations, and, above all, that there may be historical situations in which it is not possible at all—and this would seem to be our situation in the current crisis.

But the Lacanian system is threefold, and not dualistic. To the Marxian-Althusserian opposition of ideology and science correspond only two of Lacan's tripartite functions: the Imaginary and the Real, respectively. Our digression on cartography, however, with its final revelation of a properly representational dialectic of the codes and capacities of individual languages or media, reminds us that what has until now been omitted was the dimension of the Lacanian Symbolic itself.

An aesthetic of cognitive mapping—a pedagogical political culture which seeks to endow the individual subject with some new heightened sense of its place in the global system—will necessarily have to respect this now enormously complex representational dialectic and invent radically new forms in order to do it justice. This is not then, clearly, a call for a return to some older kind of machinery, some older and more transparent national space, or some more traditional and reassuring perspectival or mimetic enclave: the new political art (if it is possible at all) will have to hold to the truth of postmodernism, that is to say, to its fundamental object—the world space of multinational capital—at the same time at which it achieves a breakthrough to some as yet unimaginable new mode of representing this last, in which we may again begin to grasp our positioning as individual and collective subjects and regain a capacity to act and struggle which is at present neutralized by our spatial as well as our social confusion. The political form of postmodernism, if there ever is any, will have as its vocation the invention and projection of a global cognitive mapping, on a social as well as a spatial scale.

Gloria Anzaldúa

How to Tame a Wild Tongue

"We're going to have to control your tongue," the dentist says, pulling out all the metal from my mouth. Silver bits plot and tinkle into the basin. My mouth is a motherlode.

The dentist is cleaning out my roots. I get a whiff of the stench when I gasp. "I can't cap that tooth yet, you're still draining," he says.

"We're going to have to do something about your tongue," I hear the anger rising in his voice. My tongue keeps pushing out the wads of cotton, pushing back the drills, the long thin needles. "I've never seen anything as strong or as stubborn," he says. And I think, how do you tame a wild tongue, train it to be quiet, how do you bridle and saddle it? How do you make it lie down?

> "Who is to say that robbing a people of its language is less violent than war?"
>
> *Ray Gwyn Smith*

I remember being caught speaking Spanish at recess—that was good for three licks on the knuckles with a sharp ruler. I remember being sent to the corner of the classroom for "talking back" to the Anglo teacher when all I was trying to do was tell her how to pronounce my name. "If you want to be American, speak 'American.' If you don't like it, go back to Mexico where you belong."

"I want you to speak English. *Pa' hallar buen trabajo tienes que saber hablar el inglés bien. Qué vale toda in educación si todavía hablas inglés con un* 'accent,'" my mother would say, mortified that I spoke English like a Mexican. At Pan American University, I, and all Chicano students were required to take two speech classes. Their purpose: to get rid of our accents.

Attacks on one's form of expression with the intent to censor are a violation of the First Amendment. *El Anglo con cara de inocente nos arrancó la lengua.* Wild tongues can't be tamed, they can only be cut out.

OVERCOMING THE TRADITION OF SILENCE

> Ahogadas, escupimos el oscuro.
> Peleando con nuestra propia sombra
> el silencio nos sepulta.

En boca cerrada no entran moscas. "Flies don't enter a closed mouth" is a saying I kept hearing when I was a child. *Ser habladora* was to be a gossip and a liar, to talk too much. *Muchachitas bien criadas,* well-bred girls don't answer back. *Es una falta de respeto* to talk back to one's mother or father. I remember one of the sins I'd recite to the priest in the confession box the few times I went to confession: talking back to my mother, *hablar pa' 'tras, repelar. Hocicona, repelona, chismosa,* having a big mouth, questioning, carrying tales are all signs of being *mal criada.* In my culture they are all words that are derogatory if applied to women—I've never heard them applied to men.

The first time I heard two women, a Puerto Rican and a Cuban, say the word *"nosotras,"* I was shocked. I had not known the word existed. Chicanas use *nosotros* whether we're male

From *Borderlands/La Frontera: The New Mestiza.* Copyright 1987 by Gloria Anzaldúa. Reprinted with permission from Aunt Lute Books.

or female. We are robbed of our female being by the masculine plural. Language is a male discourse.

> And our tongues have become
> dry the wilderness has
> dried out our tongues   and
> we have forgotten speech.
>
> *Irena Klepfisz*

Even our own people, other Spanish speakers *nos quieren poner candados en la boca*. They would hold us back with their bag of *reglas de academia*.

OYÉ COMO LADRA: EL LENGUAJE DE LA FRONTERA

> Quien tiene boca se equivoca.
> *Mexican saying*

"*Pocho,* cultural traitor, you're speaking the oppressor's language by speaking English, you're ruining the Spanish language," I have been accused by various Latinos and Latinas. Chicano Spanish is considered by the purist and by most Latinos deficient, a mutilation of Spanish.

But Chicano Spanish is a border tongue which developed naturally. Change, *evolución, enriquecimiento de palabras nuevas por invención o adopción* have created variants of Chicano Spanish, *un nuevo lenguaje Un lenguaje que corresponde a un modo de vivir.* Chicano Spanish is not incorrect, it is a living language.

For a people who are neither Spanish nor live in a country in which Spanish is the first language; for a people who live in a country in which English is the reigning tongue but who are not Anglo; for a people who cannot entirely identity with either standard (formal, Castillian) Spanish nor standard English, what recourse is left to them but to create their own language? A language which they can connect their identity to, one capable of communicating the realities and values true to themselves—a language with terms that are neither *español ni inglés,* but both. We speak a patois, a forked tongue, a variation of two languages.

Chicano Spanish sprange out of the Chicanos' need to identify ourselves as a distinct people. We needed a language with which we could communicate with ourselves, a secret language. For some of us, language is a homeland closer than the Southwest—for many Chicanos today live in the Midwest and the East. And because we are a complex, heterogeneous people, we speak many languages. Some of the languages we speak are:

1. Standard English

2. Working class and slang English

3. Standard Spanish

4. Standard Mexican Spanish

5. North Mexican Spanish dialect

6. Chicano Spanish (Texas, New Mexico, Arizona and California have regional variations)

7. Tex-Mex

8. *Pachuco* (called *caló*)

My "home" tongues are the languages I speak with my sister and brothers, with my friends. They are the last five listed, with 6 and 7 being closest to my heart. From school, the media and job situations, I've picked up standard and working class English. From Mamagrande Locha and from reading Spanish and Mexican literature, I've picked up Standard Spanish and Standard Mexican Spanish. From *los recién llegados,* Mexican immigrants, and *braceros,* I learned the North Mexican dialect. With Mexicans I'll try to speak either Standard Mexican Spanish or the North Mexican dialect. From my parents and Chicanos living in the Valley, I picked up Chicano Texas Spanish, and I speak it with my mom, younger brother (who married a Mexican and who rarely mixes Spanish with English), aunts and older relatives.

With Chicanas from *Nueva México* or *Arizona* I will speak Chicano Spanish a little, but often they don't understand what I'm saying. With most California Chicanas I speak entirely in English (unless I forget). When I first moved to San Francisco, I'd rattle off something in Spanish, unintentionally embarrassing them. Often it is only with another Chicano *tejana* that I can talk freely.

Words distorted by English are known as angelicisms or *pochismos.* The *pocho* is an anglicized Mexican or American of Mexican origin who speaks Spanish with an accent characteristic of North Americans and who distorts and reconstructs the language according to the influence of English. Tex-Mex, or Spanglish, comes most naturally to me. I may switch back and forth from English to Spanish in the same sentence or in the same word. With my sister and my brother Nune and with Chicano *tejano* contemporaries I speak in Tex-Mex.

From kids and people my own age I picked up *Pachuco. Pachuco* (the language of the zoot suiters) is a language of rebellion, both against Standard Spanish and Standard English. It is a secret language. Adults of the culture and outsiders cannot understand it. It is made up of slang words from both English and Spanish. *Ruca* means girl or woman, *vato* means guy or dude, *chale* means no, *simón* means yes, *churro* is sure, talk is *periquiar, pigionear* means petting, *que gacho* means how nerdy, *ponte águila* means watch out, death is called *la pelona.* Through lack of practice and not having others who can speak it, I've lost most of the *Pachuco* tongue.

CHICANO SPANISH

Chicanos, after 250 years of Spanish/Anglo colonization, have developed significant differences in the Spanish we speak. We collapse two adjacent vowels into a single syllable and sometimes shift the stress in certain words such as *maíz/maiz, cohete/cuete.* We leave out certain consonants when they appear between vowels: *lado/lao, mojado/mojao.* Chicanos from South Texas pronounce *f* as *j* as in *jue* (*fue*). Chicanos use "archaisms," words that are no longer in the Spanish language, words that have been evolved out. We say *semos, truje, haiga, ansina,* and *naiden.* We retain the "archaic" *j,* as in *jalar,* that derives from an earlier *h,* (the French *halar* or the Germanic *halon* which was lost to standard Spanish in the 16th century), but which is still found in several regional dialects such as the one spoken in South Texas. (Due to geography, Chicanos from the Valley of South Texas were cut off linguistically from other Spanish speakers. We tend to use words that the Spaniards brought over from Medieval Spain. The majority of the Spanish colonizers in Mexico and the Southwest came from Extremadura—Hernán Cortés was one of them—and Andalucía.

Andalucians pronounce *ll* like a *y,* and their *d*'s tend to be absorbed by adjacent vowels: *tirado* becomes *tirao.* They brought *el lenguaje popular, dialectos y regionalismos.*)

Chicanos and other Spanish speakers also shift *ll* to *y* and *z* to *s.* We leave out initial syllables, saying *tar* for *estar, toy* for *estoy, hora* for *ahora* (*cubanos* and *puertorriqueños* also leave out initial letters of some words). We also leave out the final syllable such as *pa* for *para.* The intervocalic *y,* the *ll* as in *tortilla, ella, botella,* gets replaced by *tortia* or *tortiya, ea, botea.* We add an additional syllable at the beginning of certain words: *atocar* for *tocar, agastar* for *gastar.* Sometimes we'll say *lavaste las vacijas,* other times *lavates* (substituting the *ates* verb endings for the *aste*).

We use angelicisms, words borrowed from English: *bola* from ball, *carpeta* from carpet, *máchina de lavar* (instead of *lavadora*) from washing machine. Tex-Mex argot, created by adding a Spanish sound at the beginning or end of an English word such as *cookiar* for *cook, watchar* for watch, *parkiar* for park, and *rapiar* for rape, is the result of the pressures in Spanish speakers to adapt to English.

We don't use the word *vosotros/as* or its accompanying verb form. We don't say *claro* (to mean yes), *imagínate,* or *me emociona,* unless we picked up Spanish from Latinas, out of a book, or in a classroom. Other Spanish-speaking groups are going through the same, or similar, development in their Spanish.

LINGUISTIC TERRORISM

> *Deslenguadas. Somos los del español deficiente.* We are your linguistic nightmare, your linguistic aberration, your linguistic *mestisaje,* the subject of your *burla.* Because we speak with tongues of fire we are culturally crucified. Racially, culturally and linguistically *somos huérfanos*—we speak an orphan tongue.

Chicanas who grew up speaking Chicano Spanish have internalized the belief that we speak poor Spanish. It is illegitimate, a bastard language. And because we internalize how our language has been used against us by the dominant culture, we use our language differences against each other.

Chicana feminists often skirt around each other with suspicion and hesitation. For the longest time I couldn't figure it out. Then it dawned on me. To be close to another Chicana is like looking into the mirror. We are afraid of what we'll see there. *Pena.* Shame. Low estimation of self. In childhood we are told that our language is wrong. Repeated attacks on our native tongue diminish our sense of self. The attacks continue throughout our lives.

Chicanas feel uncomfortable talking in Spanish to Latinas, afraid of their censure. Their language is not outlawed in their countries. They had a whole lifetime of being immersed in their native tongue; generations, centuries in which Spanish was a first language, taught in school, heard on radio and TV, and read in the newspaper.

If a person, Chicana or Latina, has a low estimation of my native tongue, she also has a low estimation of me. Often with *mexicanas y latinas* we'll speak English as a neutral language. Even among Chicanas we tend to speak English at parties or conferences. Yet, at the same time, we're afraid the other will think we're *agringadas* because we don't speak Chicano Spanish. We oppress each other trying to out-Chicano each other, vying to be the "real" Chicanas, to speak like Chicanos. There is no one Chicano language just as there is no one Chicano experience. A monolingual Chicana whose first language is English or Spanish is just as much a Chicana as one who speaks several variants of Spanish. A Chicana from Michigan or Chicago or Detroit is just as much a Chicana as one from the Southwest. Chicano Spanish is as diverse linguistically as it is regionally.

By the end of this century, Spanish speakers will comprise the biggest minority group in the U.S., a country where students in high schools and colleges are encouraged to take French classes because French is considered more "cultured." But for a language to remain alive it must be used. By the end of this century English, and not Spanish, will be the mother tongue of most Chicanos and Latinos.

So, if you want to really hurt me, talk badly about my language. Ethnic identity is twin skin to linguistic identity—I am my language. Until I can take pride in my language, I cannot take pride in myself. Until I can accept as legitimate Chicano Texas Spanish, Tex-Mex and all the other languages I speak, I cannot accept the legitimacy of myself. Until I am free to write bilingually and to switch codes without having always to translate, while I still have to speak English or Spanish when I would rather speak Spanglish, and as long as I have to accommodate the English speakers rather than having them accommodate me, my tongue will be illegitimate.

I will no longer be made to feel ashamed of existing. I will have my voice: Indian, Spanish, white. I will have my serpent's tongue—my woman's voice, my sexual voice, my poet's voice. I will overcome the tradition of silence.

> My fingers
> move sly against your palm
> Like women everywhere, we speak in code. . . .
> *Melanie Kaye/Kantrowitz*

"VISTAS," CORRIDOS, Y COMIDA: MY NATIVE TONGUE

In the 1960s, I read my first Chicano novel. It was *City of Night* by John Rechy, a gay Texan, son of a Scottish father and a Mexican mother. For days I walked around in stunned amazement that a Chicano could write and could get published. When I read *I Am Joaquín* I was surprised to see a bilingual book by a Chicano in print. When I saw poetry written in Tex-Mex for the first time, a feeling of pure joy flashed through me. I felt like we really existed as a people. In 1971, when I started teaching High School English to Chicano students, I tried to supplement the required texts with works by Chicanos, only to be reprimanded and forbidden to do so by the principal. He claimed that I was supposed to teach "American" and English literature. At the risk of being fired, I swore my students to secrecy and slipped in Chicano short stories, poems, a play. In graduate school, while working toward a Ph.D., I had to "argue" with one advisor after the other, semester after semester, before I was allowed to make Chicano literature an area of focus.

Even before I read books by Chicanos or Mexicans, it was the Mexican movies I saw at the drive-in—the Thursday night special of $1.00 a carload—that gave me a sense of belonging. *"Vámonos a las vistas,"* my mother would call out and we'd all—grandmother, brothers, sister and cousins—squeeze into the car. We'd wolf down cheese and bologna white bread sandwiches while watching Pedro Infante in melodramatic tear-jerkers like *Nosotros los pobres,* the first "real" Mexican movie (that was not an imitation of European movies). I remember seeing *Cuando los hijos se van* and surmising that all Mexican movies played up the love a mother has for her children and what ungrateful sons and daughters suffer when they are not devoted to their mothers. I remember the singing-type "westerns" of Jorge Negrete and Miquel Aceves Mejía. When watching Mexican movies, I felt a sense of homecoming as well as alienation. People who were to amount to something didn't go to Mexican movies, or *bailes* or tune their radios to *bolero, rancherita,* and *corrido* music.

The whole time I was growing up, there was *norteño* music sometimes called North Mexican border music, or Tex-Mex music, or Chicano music, or *cantina* (bar) music. I grew up listening to *conjuntos,* three- or four-piece bands made up of folk musicians playing guitar, *bajo sexto,* drums and button accordion, which Chicanos had borrowed from the German immigrants who had come to Central Texas and Mexico to farm and build breweries. In the Rio Grande Valley, Steve Jordan and Little Joe Hernández were popular, and Flaco Jiménez was the accordion king. The rhythms of Tex-Mex music are those of the polka, also adapted from the Germans, who in turn had borrowed the polka from the Czechs and Bohemians.

I remember the hot, sultry evenings when *corridos*—songs of love and death on the Texas-Mexican borderlands—reverberated out of cheap amplifiers from the local *cantinas* and wafted in through my bedroom window.

Corridos first became widely used along the South Texas/Mexican border during the early conflict between Chicanos and Anglos. The *corridos* are usually about Mexican heroes who do valiant deeds against the Anglo oppressors. Pancho Villa's song, *"La cucaracha,"* is the most famous one. *Corridos* of John F. Kennedy and his death are still very popular in the Valley. Older Chicanos remember Lydia Mendoza, one of the great border *corrido* singers who was called *la Gloria de Tejas.* Her *"El tango negro,"* sung during the Great Depression, made her a singer of the people. The everpresent *corridos* narrated one hundred years of border history, bringing news of events as well as entertaining. These folk musicians and folk songs are our chief cultural mythmakers, and they made our hard lives seem bearable.

I grew up feeling ambivalent about our music. Country-western and rock-and-roll had more status. In the 50s and 60s, for the slightly educated and *agringado* Chicanos, there existed a sense of shame at being caught listening to our music. Yet I couldn't stop my feet from thumping to the music, could not stop humming the words, nor hide from myself the exhilaration I felt when I heard it.

There are more subtle ways that we internalize identification, especially in the forms of images and emotions. For me food and certain smells are tied to my identity, to my homeland. Woodsmoke curling up to an immense blue sky; woodsmoke perfuming my grandmother's clothes, her skin. The stench of cow manure and the yellow patches on the ground; the crack of a .22 rifle and the reek of cordite. Homemade white cheese sizzling in a pan, melting inside a folded *tortilla.* My sister Hilda's hot, spicy *menudo, chile colorado* making it deep red, pieces of *panza* and hominy floating on top. My brother Carito barbequing *fajitas* in the backyard. Even now and 3,000 miles away, I can see my mother spicing the ground beef, pork and venison with *chile.* My mouth salivates at the thought of the hot steaming *tamales* I would be eating if I were home.

SI LE PREGUNTAS A MI MAMÁ, "¿QUÉ ERES?"

> Identity is the essential core of who we are as individuals, the conscious experience of the self inside.
>
> *Kaufman*

Nosotros los Chicanos straddle the borderlands. On one side of us, we are constantly exposed to the Spanish of the Mexicans, on the other side we hear the Anglos' incessant clamoring so that we forget our language. Among ourselves we don't say *nosotros los ameri-canos, o nosotros los españoles, o nosotros los hispanos.* We say *nosotros los mexicanos* (by *mexicanos* we do not mean citizens of Mexico; we do not mean a national identity, but a racial one). We distinguish between *mexicanos del otro lado* and *mexicanos de este lado.* Deep in our hearts we believe that being Mexican has nothing to do with which country one lives in. Being Mexican is a state of soul—not one of mind, not one of citizenship. Neither eagle nor serpent, but both. And like the ocean, neither animal respects borders.

> Dime con quien andas y te diré quien eres.
> (Tell me who your friends are and I'll tell you who you are.)
> *Mexican saying*

Si le preguntas a mi mamá, "¿Qué eres?" te dirá, "Soy mexicana." My brothers and sisters say the same. I sometimes will answer *"soy mexicana"* and at others will say *"soy Chicana" o "soy tejana."* But I identified as *"Raza"* before I ever identified as *"mexicana"* or "Chicana."

As a culture, we call ourselves Spanish when referring to ourselves as a linguistic group and when copping out. It is then that we forget our predominant Indian genes. We are 70–80% Indian. We call ourselves Hispanic or Spanish-American or Latin American or Latin when linking ourselves to other Spanish-speaking peoples of the Western hemisphere and when copping out. We call ourselves Mexican-American to signify we are neither Mexican nor American, but more the noun "American" than the adjective "Mexican" (and when copping out).

Chicanos and other people of color suffer economically for not acculturating. This voluntary (yet forced) alienation makes for psychological conflict, a kind of dual identity—we don't identify with the Anglo-American cultural values and we don't totally identity with the Mexican cultural values. We are a synergy of two cultures with various degrees of Mexicanness or Angloness. I have so internalized the borderland conflict that sometimes I feel like one cancels out the other and we are zero, nothing, no one. *A veces no soy nada ni nadie. Pero hasta cuando no lo soy, lo soy.*

When not copping out, when we know we are more than nothing, we call ourselves Mexican, referring to race and ancestry; *mestizo* when affirming both our Indian and Spanish (but we hardly ever own our Black ancestory); Chicano when referring to a politically aware people born and/or raised in the U.S.; *Raza* when referring to Chicanos; *tejanos* when we are Chicanos from Texas.

Chicanos did not know we were a people until 1965 when Ceasar Chavez and the farmworkers united and *I Am Joaquín* was published and *la Raza Unida* party was formed in Texas. With that recognition, we became a distinct people. Something momentous happened to the Chicano soul—we became aware of our reality and acquired a name and a language (Chicano Spanish) that reflected that reality. Now that we had a name, some of the fragmented pieces began to fall together—who we were, what we were, how we had evolved. We began to get glimpses of what we might eventually become.

Yet the struggle of identities continues, the struggle of borders is our reality still. One day the inner struggle will cease and a true integration take place. In the meantime, *tenémos que hacer la lucha. ¿Quién está protegiendo los ranchos de mi gente? ¿Quién está tratando de cerrar la fisura entre la india y el blanco en nuestra sangre? El Chicano, si, el Chicano que anda como un ladrón en su propia casa.*

Los Chicanos, how patient we seem, how very patient. There is the quiet of the Indian about us. We know how to survive. When other races have given up their tongue, we've kept ours. We know what it is to live under the hammer blow of the dominant *norteamericano* culture. But more than we count the blows, we count the days the weeks the years the centuries the eons until the white laws and commerce and customs will rot in the deserts they've created, lie bleached. *Humildes* yet proud, *quietos* yet wild, *nosotros los mexicanos-Chicanos* will walk by the crumbling ashes as we go about our business. Stubborn, persevering, impenetrable as stone, yet possessing a malleability that renders us unbreakable, we, the *mestizas* and *mestizos,* will remain.

Lawrence Buell

American Literary Emergence as a Postcolonial Phenomenon

1

As the first colony to win independence, America has a history that Americans have liked to offer as a prototype for other new nations, yet which by the same token might profitably be studied by Americans themselves in light of later cases. In the field of American literary history, however, such a retrospective rereading has rarely been tried. This essay attempts precisely that: to imagine the extent to which the emergence of a flourishing national literature during the so-called Renaissance period of the mid-nineteenth century can be brought into focus through the lens of more recent post-colonial literatures. This is a project I have come to as an Americanist by training who has since turned to studying Anglophone writing on a more global scale. Although this body of writing and the critical commentary that has arisen to frame it interest me mainly for their own sake, as an Americanist I have also found that they have caused me to rethink what I thought I already knew.

If my approach seems strange, as I hope it will, the reasons should be clear. Some formidable barriers inhibit Americanists from analogizing between this country's literary emergence and even that of Canada or Australia, let alone West India or West Africa— barriers both of ignorance and of principle. Most Americanists know little about these other literatures, nor am I much beyond my novitiate. As to the barrier of principle, even mildly liberal academics will suspect the possible hypocrisy of an exercise in imagining America of the expansionist years as a postcolonial rather than proto-imperial power, as if to mystify modern America's increasingly interventionist role in world affairs. All the more so is my study subject to such suspicions given the ease with which it is possible to slide from thinking about America as the first new nation to thinking about America as the model for other new nations. And all the *more* so if the analogizing also risks, as mine will, blurring the distinction between the European settler as colonial and the indigene as colonial. I shall return to these issues at the end of my essay but shall bracket them for now.

"American Literary Emergence as a Postcolonial Phenomenon" by Lawrence Buell. First appeared in *American Literary History*. Reprinted by permission of Oxford University Press.

A more discipline-specific barrier is that American literary study has tended to focus so overwhelmingly on American texts as to reduce the internationalist (usually European) quotient within its field of vision. This foreshortening of vision can happen as easily to scholars of cosmopolitan erudition as to Americanists who in fact know little more than American literary history. In Harold Bloom's theory of American poetic succession, for example, no foreign power disrupts the symposium once Emerson enters it; British and American literary histories are kept rigorously distinct, though presumably Bloom is quite aware that until well into the twentieth century the "strong" American poets read Anglo-European masters more attentively than they read each other. Of course, American literary scholarship always has and probably always will recognize the legitimacy of monographs on Emerson and Carlyle, Fuller and Goethe, and so forth, but such influence studies implicitly occupy a minor niche in the larger scheme of things, the equivalent of the prefatory section on the zeitgeist or background influences in a large-scale thematic study.

Up to a point, there is certainly nothing strange or amiss about focusing the study of American letters on America. Studies of all national literary histories commit the same reductionism. A problem more particular to American literary studies arises, however, when the restriction of focus to the national field is regulated in terms of notions of American cultural distinctiveness used to sort authors and texts in or out according to a criterion of emerging indigenousness that fails to take account of such factors as the interpenetration of the "indigenous" and the "foreign," the extent to which the former is constructed by the latter, and consequently the extent to which the sorting of individual authors in or out of the American canon by this criterion (Hawthorne in, Longfellow out) is arbitrary and quixotic. But precisely this has been the tendency since the establishment of American literature as a scholarly subfield in the 1920s, which also (by no coincidence) marked the point at which literary historiography began to be practiced in the climate of major thesis books about the coherence of the American literary tradition, for example, in the pioneering work of D. H. Lawrence, William Carlos Williams, Lewis Mumford, and Vernon L. Parrington. One of the reasons F. O. Matthiessen's *American Renaissance* continues to endure as a landmark study is that it was the last major precontemporary book on the era to be informed by a profound appreciation for Anglo-American intertexts: how his five figures saturated themselves in the rhetorics of Shakespeare, Milton, metaphysical poetry and prose, neoclassicism, and Romanticism. Since Matthiessen, however, the study of American literary emergence has revolved around assumptions about the coherence of the American canon formed in the image of such myths of American distinctiveness as Puritan inheritance or Adamic innocence, generic patterns like the jeremiad or the captivity or the romance considered as national artifacts, as well as particular lineal succession stories like from Edwards to Emerson, Emerson to Whitman, Whitman to Stevens, and so on. Through these devices the unity, the density, and (of course) the respectability of the specialization gets consolidated. These are indeed important reference points; the problem lies not so much in the scholarship that has established them as in its unintended consequence of prompting ever-more-intensive refinements of the map of American letters.

Thus we find ourselves practicing de facto a kind of cisatlantic hermeticism. This starts with our experience as students in American literature courses, when we are socialized (for instance) into forgetting that except for Thoreau's debt to Emerson no American Renaissance writer can confidently be said to have formed his or her style chiefly from native influences, nor with the exception of Melville's essay on Hawthorne is there a clear case on record of one canonical American Renaissance writer insisting that another ranks with the great world authors. We form the habit of picturing Hawthorne as leading to Melville rather than to, say, George Eliot, even though nothing in the Melville canon follows a Hawthornian pretext more faithfully than *Adam Bede* follows *The Scarlet Letter* (see Mills 52–71). We then find ourselves perpetuating the same aesthetic order in American Renaissance courses.

Today, we are better able than in the recent past to combat such parochialisms. Feminist and African-Americanist critiques of the American canon as it crystallized between the 1920s and the 1960s have begun to inspire a pervasive reflexivity about all our instruments of classification, including our conception of literary genealogy, and have in some instances prodded us into thinking transatlantically, as with Henry Louis Gates's exposition of the permutations of Eshu in *The Signifying Monkey* or the image of a Euro-American community of nineteenth-century women writers implicit in feminist criticism of Emily Dickinson since Gilbert and Gubar's *The Madwoman in the Attic*.[1] A small but growing number of Americanists have even taken Anglo-American or Euro-American literary interrelations as their main subject: for example, Jonathan Arac (*Commissioned Spirits*), Leon Chai (*The Romantic Foundations of the American Renaissance*), Nicolaus Mills (*American and English Fiction in the Nineteenth Century*), Larry Reynolds (*European Revolutions and the American Literary Renaissance*), Robert Weisbuch (*Atlantic Double-Cross*), and William Spengemann (*A Mirror for Americanists*), not to mention monographs on single figures like George Dekker's *James Fenimore Cooper: The American Scott* and Jeffrey Rubin-Dorsky's study of Irving, *Adrift in the Old World*.[2]

This work, however, has not yet seriously affected the way Americanists conduct business as usual. The pedagogy and criticism if not the personal conviction of literary Americanists still for the most part give the appearance of being driven, as Spengemann puts it, by "the idea that an appreciation of American writing depends upon our keeping it separate from the rest of the world" (141). Spengemann seems to believe this holds for all eras of American literary historiography. Maybe so; but I confine myself here to the period of literary emergence, not only because I know it best but also because the compartmentalizing seems more customary than in the study of, say, literary modernism or the early colonial period. We continue to think much more about how Hawthorne might have read Puritan literature than about how he might have read Scott, more about how Whitman's prosodic experimentalism might have been encouraged by Emerson or Poe than by Keats or Tennyson. We know much more about how American writers of woman's fiction relate to each other than how they related to Dickens or other popular British sentimentalists of either sex. The average article or monograph therefore projects a vision of nineteenth-century American literary history far more autotelic than that of the writers themselves except in their wildest cultural nationalist dreams. This is probably not so much because American literary scholarship continues to be passionately attached to the idea of American distinctiveness at this late date, as because the familiar procedure of grouping American writers together is so ingrained. The effect is to perpetuate at the level of literary commentary the utopian fantasy of American literary autonomy cherished during the early national period, and to abet, in consequence, an American exceptionalist mentality that may without our fully realizing it reinforce in us—or in those who listen unwarily to us—an insularity of perspective that is hazardously inaccurate. It is striking, for example, that for all its critical sophistication, the New Historicist critique of the ideological duplicity of classic American Renaissance texts (their ostensible radicalism versus their actual centrism) has not seriously challenged the assumption that these texts can be adequately understood as an internally coherent and nationally distinctive series.

My own approach to resisting Americanist centripetalism, for which I hold myself as accountable as anyone, will be to reexamine the notion of American literary emergence itself. I do not intend to argue that the American Renaissance never happened, but rather that its achievement, and by extention the "native" literary traditions it helped to create or sustain, cannot be understood without taking into account the degree to which those traditions arose out of "a culture in which the ruled were constantly tempted to fight their rulers within the psychological limits set by the latter," to appropriate Ashis Nandy's diagnosis of the intellectual climate of colonial India (3). To transpose from the colonial to the postcolonial stage of the first half of the American nineteenth century, we need only substitute cultural authority for political/military authority as the object of resistance. Although the 13 American colonies never experienced anything like the political/military domination colonial India did, the extent of cultural colonization by the mother country, from epistemology or aesthetics to dietetics, was on the whole much more comprehensive—and partly because of the selfsame comparative benignity of the imperial regime.

2

For most students of the American Renaissance, the phenomenon of American writers' cultural dependence has come increasingly to look like a side issue and, after about 1830, a virtual nonissue. Especially since the intensification of Puritan legacy studies, the seeds of an indigenous culture have come to seem so early planted and so deeply rooted as to assure its full flowering eventually if not immediately, so as to make America's continuing imbrication in old-world culture seem uninterestingly epiphenomenal. This mentality has conduced to the view that postcolonial dependency was merely a virus that infected the juvenilia of the great canonical writers of the antebellum era. I daresay many of us who teach nineteenth-century American literature have set up our courses by using British reviewer Sydney Smith ("In the four quarters of the globe, who reads an American book?") as a straw man for our syllabi to refute rather than as an ever-present anxiety and constituent shaping force.

If so, consider the case of Henry T. Tuckerman, whose *American and Her Commentators* (1964), a self-consciously monumental and monumentally self-conscious synopsis of the history of transatlantic views of America, is still a useful sourcebook. Tuckerman asserts that Smith's dictum is "irrelevant and impertinent to-day" (286): "In history, poetry, science, criticism, biography, political and ethical discussions, the records of travels, of taste, and of romance, universally recognized and standard exemplars, of American origin, now illustrate the genius and culture of the nation" (285–86); but his project refutes him, preoccupied as it is with expounding upon how America has been anatomized as literary object rather than reborn as literary force. The idea of America's emerging culture elicits Tuckerman's patriotism, but what commands his awe is the conviction that "never was there a populous land whose inhabitants were so uniformly judged *en masse*" (444). Tuckerman's argument that Americans are no longer mere culture consumers is quixotic and halfhearted. "The statistics of the book trade and the facts of individual culture prove that the master minds of British literature more directly and universally train and nurture the American than the English mind," argues Tuckerman ingeniously (287–88). This glosses over the statistics themselves (as late as 1876, the ratio of American book imports to exports stood at 10 to 1) and the consumer mentality that Tuckerman gamely tries to make the best of: namely that from the "distance that leads enchantment" as well as the diffusion of general education, "Shakespeare and Milton, Bacon and Wordsworth, Byron and Scott have been and are more generally known, appreciated, and loved, and have entered more deeply into the average intellectual life, on this than on the other side of the Atlantic" (288). In short, American cultural autonomy is proven by the fact that more copies of the English classics are bought and avidly read in America than in Britain. Tuckerman's book is itself a kind of vade mecum for the discriminating book importer.

Tuckerman does not draw a connection between how British classics "enchant" American readers and his efforts throughout his assiduous compendium to resist the enchantment of foreign travelers' representations of America. Yet his book, by its mere existence, dramatizes that the authority of European letters was felt to extend itself to the form of an extensive discourse of America that the American writer had to reckon with. Although scholars have been studying this body of travelers' reports for more than half a century, and some of its most distinguished examples are well known (notably Alexis de Tocqueville's *Democracy in America*), the significance of this "occidentalist" writing emerges more fully in light of recent studies of colonial discourse.[3] During what is now called our literary renaissance, America remained for many foreign commentators (especially the British), albeit diminishingly, the unvoiced "other"—with the predictable connotations of exoticism, barbarism, and unstructuredness. This notwithstanding America's legislative innovations and growing economic potency, notwithstanding that no racial barrier separated most travelers from the dominant American racial group, and notwithstanding that European travelers were very well aware that *these* natives had the will and the technology to answer them back publicly in a European language. Indeed, American sensitiveness to foreign opinion was proverbial, and several travelers commented that this severely diminished the frankness with which they could write or speak. Still, it is clear that many nineteenth-century Americans considered themselves to be treated as a minor power by foreign visitors, like the politician who complained to British geologist Charles Lyell that "you class us with the South American republics; your embassadors [sic] to us come from Brazil and Mexico to Washington, and consider it a step in their advancement to go from the United States to . . . some second-rate German court" (1: 226).

For this there was much evidence. Foreign visitors denied America refinement (the want of which was, for Frances Trollope in *Domestic Manners of the Americans,* the greatest American defect). Nineteenth-century travelers on the notorious American practice of tobacco chewing and spitting, for instance, sound like V.S. Naipaul on Indian shitting.[4] European travelers acknowledged American skill at practical calculation (deprecating it as part of the apparatus of American materialism) but tended to depict Americans as more irrational than rational, as an unphilosophical culture whatever its legislative genius, as hasty and slapdash nation builders. They regularly denied America a voice in a culturally substantial sense à la mode Sydney Smith. ("If the national mind of America be judged of by its legislation, it is of a very high order. . . . If the American nation be judged by its literature, it may be pronounced to have no mind at all" (Martineau 2: 200–01].) They even denied the Americans language in the spirit of Rudyard Kipling's remark that "the American has no language," only "dialect, slang, provincialism, accent, and so forth" (24).[5]

It was common for foreign travelers to frame their accounts as narratives of disillusionment, to stress that they started with hopeful, even utopian, expectations of finding a model nation-in-the-making only to discover a cultural backwater. Dickens is a notable case in point, since his *American Notes* avoids stating his disillusionment overtly but proceeds to narrativize it more dramatically than most, as if this were a spontaneous deposition. Starting exuberantly with a stimulating visit to Boston, Dickens gradually sours amid New York slums, Washington rowdiness, and an arduous trip to the interior that reaches a positively Conradian moment during a steamboat voyage down the Ohio River.

Dickens luridly evokes the dreary solitude ("For miles, and miles, and miles . . . unbroken by any human footstep"), the sudden ugly rent in the forest for a primitive cabin and straggling field ("full of great unsightly stumps, like earthy butchers'-blocks"), and the malevolent tangle of fallen trees in the current ("their bleached arms start out . . . and seen to try to grasp the boat, and drag it under water") (*American Notes* 159–60). This is merely the travel-book version, the equivalent of Conrad's Congo diaries. For purposes of Martin Chuzzlewit's ill-fated venture to "Eden," the *Heart of Darkness* equivalent, the phantasmagoria is heightened:

> On they toiled through great solitudes, where the trees upon the banks grew thick and close; and floated in the stream; and held up shrivelled arms from out the river's depths; and slid down from the margin of the land, half growing, half decaying, in the miry water. On through the weary day and melancholy night: beneath the burning sun, and in the mist and vapour of the evening: on, until return appeared impossible, and restoration to their home a miserable dream. (375)

Both Dickens and Tocqueville, in their separate ways, reckoned America a country of the future; but Tocqueville's estimate (that America represented the vanguard of the inevitable democratization of modern society that was afoot, willy-nilly, in Europe also) was less typical than Dickens's estimate of America as a crudely vigorous young country still a long way from maturity. Not surprisingly, Tuckerman lauded Tocqueville and deplored Dickens's "superficial and sneering" manner (130–31, 221). Yet Tocqueville himself exhibits perhaps the single most condescending occidentalist gesture, also a hallmark of Orientalism: the overbearing confidence with which occidental traits are generalized. "Americans of all ages, all conditions, and dispositions constantly form associations"; "the Americans are much more addicted to the use of general ideas than the English and entertain a much greater relish for them"; "the love of wealth is . . . to be traced, as either a principal or an accessory motive, at the bottom of all that the Americans do" (2: 114, 15, 240). Tocqueville's many shrewd hits should not blind us to the arrogance of this rhetoric of the imperial generalization. One wonders, as when reading Foucault, whether Tocqueville felt a need to make magisterialism compensate for his theory of individual powerlessness at the level of his sociohistorical vision. The imperial generalization, in any case, is a time-honored device for formulating natives, as Albert Memmi and others have pointed out.[6]

3

The Americans encapsulated in nineteenth-century European travelers' reports were thus by no means wholly like Africans or Asians: they were, after all, mostly Anglo-Saxon, as well as being energetic entrepreneurs of burgeoning economic and military potency, impressive for their efforts at general education if not for their high culture. But as a civilization, America was still comparatively barbarous, the frontier hinterland its dominant reality and its gentry (as Francis Grund stressed in *Aristocracy in America*) pathetic cardboard Europhiles. A thriving oral culture existed, but with exceptions most travelers could count on the fingers of one hand, literary culture did not, and the most visible approximation to a literary class were American journalists, a disreputable lot. Though an American businessman would not have found this composite portrait especially daunting, an aspiring writer would have felt almost as marginalized by it qua writer as Caliban contemplated by Prospero.

With this as our backdrop, we can better understand the terms under which Whitman sought to give voice to American poetry in *Leaves of Grass*. The 1855 Preface starts with the magisterial image of America as the calm witness to the corpse of European tradition being "slowly borne from the eating and sleeping rooms of the house" (709). Because Whitman craftily adopts a pose of impassivity here, and because we are taught to classify this document firmly within the success story of American literary independence, it takes an effort of will to realize that what he has actually done is to make grotesque a trope from the traditional repertoire of Eurocentrism, the *translatio studii*—the transfer of art and learning from the Old World to the New—a trope that had been invoked to underwrite colonization efforts and subsequently the hegemony of the late colonial gentry. It is a figure Whitman uses not just once but repeatedly, for example, in the 1871 "Song of the Exposition," which noisily summons the Muse to "migrate from Greece and Ionia," to "Placard 'Removed' and 'To Let' on the rocks of your snowy Parnassus," and envisions her wafting her way amid the "thud of machinery and shrill steam-whistle undismay'd," "Bluff'd not . . . by drain-pipe, gasometers, artificial fertilizers. / Smiling and pleas'd with palpable intent to stay. / . . . install'd amid the kitchen ware!" (196, 198). The calculated tackiness that subverts old-world decorums while nominally observing them seems more pointed if we see it as akin to, for example, modern West Indian inversions of the Prospero-Caliban trope, as in George Lamming's autobiographical essays *The Pleasures of Exile* and Aimé Cesaire's dramatic redaction *A Tempest,* or (analogously) the Crusoe-Friday inversion in Derek Walcott's play *Pantomine*. For what Whitman has done in these passages I have cited is in effect to Calibanize *translatio studii,* to render it hairy and gross and thereby to reveal America's ongoing struggle to extricate its forms of thought from old-world categories, meaning not just rhetorical figures but also social figurations like the Americans-as-barbarians stereotype. To see this, however, one needs to know what the prototypes of struggle have been. Even if we know something about the history of *translatio studii,* we Americanists tend not to think this far, because we think of *translatio studii* as a motif that America left behind soon after the turn of the nineteenth century; and we have lately grown accustomed to thinking of Caliban as a figure elevated to hero status by third-world, particularly Caribbean, intellectuals, over against a Eurocentrism that includes America as well as the earlier imperial powers. Yet as the most articulate West Indian proponent of Caliban as "our symbol" sheepishly admits, Caliban appears to have been associated with Yankeedom before Latin Americans thought to canonize him (Fernández Retamar 10). Whitman himself, in fact, was likened in one British review to "Caliban flinging down his logs, and setting himself to write a poem"—the reviewer's proof text being the "barbaric yawp" passage (qtd. in Murphy 60). Whitman proceeded to select this among other excerpts to append as promotional material for the 1856 edition of *Leaves of Grass*.

As the Caliban analogy suggests, Whitman's rewriting of *translatio studii* anticipates one of the major modern postcolonial strategies. Indeed, *Leaves of Grass* as a whole makes the same move on a much vaster scale, with its bending and breaking of epic tradition (McWilliams 218–37). This rewriting process reflects a resistance-deference syndrome that artists and scholars alike have found it hard to talk about without hypocrisy. Whitman by turns sought to eradicate old-world myth and to reinstate it ("Old Brahm I, and I Saturnius am" [443]). The critic for whom the narrative of national differentiation is primary is tempted to identify the former posture as more "authentic" or "progressive" than the latter, when in fact it was the creative irritant of their interaction that produced their unique result, an interaction in which the "imperial" epic model figures as part of the empowerment as well as an object of resistance.

Another case that will help to clinch this point is James Fenimore Cooper's Leatherstocking. No vernacular hero has been more influential in all of American literary history, with the possible exception of Huckleberry Finn, for whom Natty Bumppo probably helped to prepare the way. Yet Bumppo was not, strictly speaking, an indigenous figure, though he can be traced to "real-life" frontiersman prototypes, so much as the result of a rewriting of the trope of the general protagonist cum vernacular comic sidekick in Scott's Waverley novels (e.g., Henry Morton and Cuddie Headrigg in *Old Mortality*), a characterological pattern that indeed dates from the very beginnings of the "modern" novel (in *Don Quixote*). Cooper's inversion of this pattern was of landmark significance, providing American literature's first compelling model of the common unlettered person as hero. Yet this breakthrough did not come easily to Cooper; he seems to have discovered his desire to upend the Scottian hierarchy only during the process of composing *The Pioneers,* which begins squarely focused upon the Oliver Edwards-Judge Temple melodrama and only gradually discovers that Bumppo is a much more interesting character than either. Even at that, Cooper continues to require a Waverley figure as a concomitant and to labor over the proper mimetic level at which to peg Bumppo, whose speech, as Richard Bridgman remarks, "wobbles from one realm of usage to another," from racy slang to grand-manner cliché (67). As if to hold his incipient populism in check, Cooper sees to it that Bumppo retains his vassal status through the first four Leatherstocking tales; only after Cooper has reinvented him at his most decorous, in *The Deerslayer,* does Bumppo finally cease playing the factotum.

The imperfectness of Cooper's break from Scott might be seen as a mark of the "colonized mind." Natty's genteel charges, like Oliver Edwards and Duncan Uncas Middleton of *The Prairie,* are indeed pathetic residues of Cooper's classism, as is the savagist machinery that motors Chingachgook, Bumppo's Indian companion. But why expect a clean break in the first place, and why indeed should one even long to find one when the hierarchicatized genteel hero/folk companion pattern proved to be so productive of innovation? Cooper's achievement looks more substantial when considered as a hard-won new-world adjustment of a transcontinental intertext than either as a homespun invention compromised by the pollution of foreign mannerisms, or (see Green 129–50) as another avatar of old-world conquest narrative.[7]

A third exhibit to set beside Whitman and Cooper is Emerson's "The American Scholar," "our intellectual declaration of independence," as twentieth-century American scholars (following Oliver Wendell Holmes) still like to call it. Its exordium contains Emerson's most famous literary nationalist aperçu: "Our day of dependence, our long apprenticeship to the learning of other lands, draws to a close" (52). But when we examine the two specific signs of this, deferred until the end of the discourse, we find them presented as European-instigated trends only now on the verge of coming to fruition in the New World: the valorization of the humble and the familiar ("This idea has inspired the genius of Goldsmith, Burns, Cowper, and, in a newer time, of Goethe, Wordsworth, and Carlyle" [68]) and the renewed respect accorded the individual person—which Emerson makes a point of emphasizing has not yet trickled over to America ("We have listened too long to the courtly muses of Europe. The spirit of the American freeman is already suspected to be timid, imitative, tame" [69]). Emerson seeks, paradoxically, to shame his nation into celebrating common life and self-sufficiency by reminding his countrymen that they are living in "the age of Revolution" (67). Unlike Tocqueville, Emerson makes no claim that America is already in the vanguard of this international movement, although nothing would have been easier given the nature of the occasion than for him to do so; it is as if he has chosen to create his national history in the image of his own belated intellectual emergence, for which Coleridge helped much more than any American thinker to provide the scaffolding. Perhaps this helps explain why the whole literary nationalist theme, as "The American Scholar" handles it, is so comparatively muted and so belated. The bulk of the discourse is taken up with expounding the scholar's triad of resources—nature, books, and action—which in principle can be seen as a distinctly "new-world" recipe (the argument being to devalue classical education, indeed formal study in general, and to aggrandize direct noncosmopolitan experience and pragmatic application) yet which does not explicitly define this regimen as a cultural nationalist program. One further lesson that might be drawn from this silence, a lesson that much of Whitman's poetry teaches also, is that the whole issue of cultural distinctiveness versus internationalism is not equally pressing throughout a writer's canon, or even throughout the space of an individual work. Perhaps because he was addressing one of the most Anglophile audiences in America, but more likely because he himself was too cosmopolitan (and too honest) to restrict the scholar solely to American influences or to exerting a solely American influence, Emerson kept his cultural nationalist rhetoric to a minimum: a few mandatory flourishes at start and close. Self-reliance clearly interested Emerson far more than national self-sufficiency.

Altogether, "The American Scholar" and Whitman's 1855 Preface might be taken as the two poles between which the literary nationalism of American Renaissance high culture tends to oscillate: on the one hand, Emerson's vision of cultural emergence catalyzed by auspicious international tendencies that emergence might be expected to develop further; on the other hand, Whitman's vision of a scandalously different American voice whose international precedents have been repressed, although by no means deleted, out of self-mystification and dramatic effect. In either case, "Europe" plays a weighty, conflict-producing role, measured by citation or elision, as the case may be.

4

Intimately related to the question of the models underlying-literary practice is the question of the audience to which writing is implicitly directed. This has been a major subject of debate in the study of so-called newer English literatures, which appear, in some interpretations, to represent national culture with international audiences in mind. For a sense of what is at stake, consider this short passage toward the start of Chinua Achebe's *Things Fall Apart,* the first third-world novel accepted into the Anglophone canon. "Okoye said the next half a dozen sentences in proverbs. Among the Ibo the art of conversation is regarded very highly, and proverbs are the palm-oil with which words are eaten" (10). Such expository rhetoric, common in African Anglophone writing, immediately raises such questions as: For whom is this passage written? Do Ibos need to hear it? Do even Yoruba and Hausa readers need to hear it? Is Achebe mainly addressing a Euro-American audience, then? (Achebe denies this but also declares that "my audience is not limited to Nigeria. Anybody who is interested in the ideas I am expounding is my audience" [Egejuru 17].)[8] The rhetoric of this passage, anyhow, carefully negotiates the insider-outsider dualism by explicating ethnic custom with anthropological lucidity while casting the explanation in Ibo form, as a proverb.

A comparable instance from classic American literature might be this passage from an early chapter in Herman Melville's *White-Jacket:* "Owing to certain vague, republican scruples, about creating great officers of the navy, America has thus far had no admirals;

though, as her ships of war increase, they may become indispensable. This will assuredly be the case should she ever have occasion to employ large fleets; when she must adopt something like the English plan . . ." (20).

Americanists do not usually read American Renaissance texts as if the implied reader were other than American; yet on reflection we know that is nonsense: actually, American writers keenly desired to be read abroad. Melville himself voyaged to England in order to market *White-Jacket* and sometimes made (or consented to) substantive revisions in the interest of British readers. Indeed, the very first words of Melville's first book (the preface to *Typee*) were got up with British readership in mind, and that narrative is strategically sprinkled with familiarizing English place references (Chettenham, Stonehenge, Westminster Abbey, etc. [96, 154, 161]).[9] In the passage from *White-Jacket,* the expository elaborateness and the obliquity with which it edges toward the narrator's outspoken anti-authoritarianism become more understandable if we take them as studiously devious in anticipation of being read by both patriotic insiders and Tory outsiders, whether literal foreigners or Yankee Anglophiles. We know from Melville's letters and criticism that he was acutely aware of the problem of negotiating between ideologically disparate readerships, but no one thinks much about the possibility that his doctrine that the great writer communicates to his ideal reader through double meanings which philistine readers are intended to miss might have been brought into focus partly by his position as a postcolonial writer.

The textual consequences of anticipating transcontinental readership are admittedly harder to establish than the impact of foreign literary influences. Open-and-shut cases like the diplomatically vacillating chapter on European travelers' accounts of America in Irving's *The Sketch Book* are rare. Direct evidence is usually limited to textual variants for which the responsibility is unclear (Did the author devise? advise? consent? reluctantly agree to delegate?), or to ex cathedra statements (like Cooper's to a British publisher that *The Prairie* "contains nothing to offend an English reader" [I: 166]) which do not in themselves prove that the work would have been written differently had the author designed it for an American readership alone. What we can assert more positively is this. First, that some of the most provincially embedded American Renaissance texts bear at least passing direct witness to anticipating foreign readers, like Thoreau's *Walden,* which (in keeping with its first "publication" before the Concord lyceum) begins by addressing fellow townspeople but ends by musing as to whether "John or Jonathan will realize all this" (333). And second, that the hypothesis of Americans imagining foreign as well as native opinion, whatever their conscious expectation of literal readership, makes luminous some otherwise puzzling moments in American Renaissance literature. One such moment is Whitman's abrupt reconception of his persona between 1855 and 1856 as coextensive not simply with America but with the world (e.g., in "Salut au Monde!"). Another is the oddly extended sequence in *Moby-Dick* reporting the gam between the *Pequod* and the *Samuel Enderby,* and its aftermath (chs. 100–01).

James Snead remarks that Achebe's novels "provide an unexpectedly tricky reading experience for their western audience, using wily narrative stratagems to undermine national and racial illusions," such as "the almost casual manner in which they present African norms" to international readers: glossary apparatus that seems deliberately incomplete, interjection of reminders of the Western reader's outsidership in the course of a cozily familiar-seeming, European-style realist narrative (241). For example, the guidebook dimension of the passage quoted above creates a deceptive degree of transparency for the Western reader, inasmuch as its "we have a saying" formula is a common introductory formula in Ibo proverbial statement not remarked upon as such; the passage, then, maintains a certain covertness despite, indeed because of, its forthrightness. Melville uses narrative geniality and cross-culturalism somewhat similarly in the sequence under view so as to sustain the young-America-style jauntiness with which *Moby-Dick* customarily treats old-world cultures, but without the kind of bluntness used against "the Yarman," for instance (Melville, *Moby-Dick* 351–60).

The gam with the *Samuel Enderby* reworks a cross-cultural comparison repeatedly made by British travelers to America: that Americans were grim workaholic zealots with no time for small talk. The chapter is obviously framed with national stereotypes in mind. Melville initially sketches the encounter between Ahab and Captain Boomer, or rather the interruptive byplay between Boomer and the ship's surgeon, so as to make the Englishmen seem like patronizing boobies. Yet is is Ahab's truculence that finally comes off as more disturbing and that makes English joviality (itself an American stereotype) seem healthy by comparison. The last emotion to be expressed is the good-humored British captain's honest astonishment. In the ensuing chapter ("The Decanter") Ishmael aligns himself with that same spirit of comic banter (long since identified as an Ishmaelite trait) and pays a mock-heroic homage to the whole firm of Enderby, which in fact turns out to have dispatched the first ships ever to hunt the sperm whale in the Pacific, the waters the *Pequod* is about to enter. Ishmael then proceeds, in what first looks like a complete digression, to report a later, more convivial and rousing gam with the *Samuel Enderby* in which he partook, a drunken feast "at midnight somewhere off the Patagonian coast" (444).

Ishmael's reinstitution of good fellowship with his English counterparts "atones" ex post facto for Ahab's bad manners and "validates" the English captain's good-humored bewilderment at Ahab's stormy departure. Yet through this dexterous maneuver, Melville is given license to laugh at the cliché version of British thickheadedness not once but twice—first apropos Ahab's tragedy, then apropos the farce of sailorly roistering—thereby propitiating American cultural nationalism without offending British readers. It is testimony both to Melville's witness and to his deference that the vigorous in-house censorship upon which his British publishers insisted, of religiously and culturally offensive matter in the manuscript of *The Whale* (resulting in the deletion of chapter 25 on British coronation procedures, for instance), left chapters 100–01 untouched (Melville, *Moby-Dick* 681–83).[10]

5

The marks of postcolonialism in American Renaissance writing are far more numerous than a short article can hope to discuss. Here is a brief checklist of some of the most salient.

1. *The semi-Americanization of the English language.* What language shall we speak? American settlers did not face this question in its most radical form, as put by Ngugi wa Thiong'o in *Decolonizing the Mind,* which argues that African literature should be written in the indigenous languages. But the weaker version of the argument (namely how to creolize and neologize American English so that it spoke a voice of the culture distinct from the standardizing mother tongue) does certainly link Cooper and Emerson and Whitman and Twain with Amos Tutuola, Gabriel Okara, and Raja Rao, whose work sheds light on such subissues as the inextricability of "naturalness" and "artifice" in Whitman's diction and the inextricability of idealization and caricature in Cooper's vernacular heroes like Natty Bumppo, Bill Ashcroft, Gareth Griffiths, and Helen Tiffin remark that postcolonial

literatures are "always written out of the tension between the abrogation of the received English which speaks from the center, and the act of appropriation which brings it under the influence of a vernacular tongue" (39). That is a duality crucial to American literary emergence as well. In the early national period, we see it especially in texts that counterpoint characters who speak dialect (who are always comic) with characters who speak Standard English, for example, Colonel Manly versus his servant Jonathan in Royall Tyler's *The Contrast* and Captain Ferrago versus his servant Teague O'Reagan in Hugh Henry Brackenridge's *Modern Chivalry*. At this stage, the vernacluar is still clearly a national embarrassment to be indulged only obliquely, through satire. "Vulgarity," as Bridgman puts it, "had to be fenced in with quotation marks" (7). This is the American equivalent of, say, the colloquial dramatic monologues of Indo-Anglian poet Nissim Ezekiel:

> I am standing for peace and non-violence
> Why world is fighting fighting
> Why all people of world
> Are not following Mahatma Gandhi
> I am simply not understanding. (22)

By the time of Thoreau and Whitman, the American inventiveness with language, through individual neologizing and provincial variant usages, that Tocqueville (and others) considered one of the most "deplorable" consequences of democratization had become positive aesthetic values (Tocqueville 2: 71). Thus without any hint of parody, in section 5 of "Song of Myself," Whitman could allow the sublime vision following from the persona's possession by his soul to come to rest on "the mossy scabs of the worm-fence" (33)—the latter an American coinage never used in poetry before, referring to a characteristic motif of American agricultural construction that foreign visitors often singled out as particularly wasteful and ugly (Mesick 161–62). The "mossy scabs" metaphor makes it absolutely clear, if further proof be needed, that Whitman seeks to fashion the sublime from the positively vulgar. Not that he was prepared to forgo literary English. His position—almost quintessentially postcolonial in this respect—was to justify an Americanization of English expression as the poetic way of the future on the ground that English itself was remarkable for its engraftment of other linguistic strains (Warren 5–69).

2. *The issue of cultural hybridization.* Another recurring motif in American Renaissance texts is their fondness for cross-cultural collages: Whitman's composite persona; Thoreau's balancing between the claims of post-Puritan, Greco-Roman, Native American, and Oriental mythographies in *A Week* and *Walden;* Melville's multimythic elaboration of the whale symbol in tandem with the *Pequod* as a global village; Cooper's heteroglossic tapestry of six or seven different nationalities in *The Pioneers*. David Simpson argues, respecting Cooper, that Templeton's polyglot character, each resident speaking his or her own peculiar dialect (except for the Temple family, of course), registers the social fissures of still-experimental nationhood (149–201); and I think we might further understand this phenomenon by thinking of it in reference to (for example) composite national-symbol characters like Salman Rushdie's Saleem Sinai (in *Midnight's Children*) and G. V. Desani's Mr. Hatterr, or the syncretisim of Wole Soyinka's interweave between Yoruba and Greek mythology. What Lewis Nkosi says of modern African Anglophone poetry's quest to define its path applies beautifully to the world of Cooper's *Pioneers:* "[T]he first requirement . . . was precisely to articulate the socio-cultural conditions in which the modern African writer had to function, the heterogeneity of cultural experiences among which the poet had to pick his or her way" (151).[11]

3. *The expectation that artists be responsible agents for achieving national liberation,* which in turn bespeaks a nonspecialized conception of art and an ambivalence toward aestheticism that threatens to produce schizophrenia. Soyinka calls attention to the pressure upon the postcolonial African writer to "postpone that unique reflection on experience and events which is what makes a writer—and constitute himself into a part of that machinery that will actually shape events" (16). Emerson wrestles with a very similar looking public/private dilemma in "The American Scholar" and later attempts at political interventions like the first Fugitive Slave Law address. Anozie's statement that "[t]here seemed to exist a genetic struggle between a romantic pursuit of art for its own sake and a constantly intensive awareness of the social relevance of art" could apply equally well to Soyinka and Emerson, though in fact it refers to Nigerian poet Christopher Okigbo (175), the closest approximation to a "pure aesthete" among the major figures of the illustrious first contemporary generation of Nigeria's Anglophone literati but later killed as a soldier in the Biafran war.

4. *The problem of confronting neocolonialism,* the disillusionment of revolutionary hopes, which threatens to turn the artist against the audience that was prepared to celebrate him or her as symptomatic of cultural emergence. Postcolonial Africa, for instance, has inspired an oppositional literature that both helps to explain American Renaissance oppositionalism as a predictable postrevolutionary symptom and to define its limits. Thoreau as individualistic civil disobedient both is and is not the counterpart of Ngugi's revolutionary socialism.

5. *The problem of "alien genres":* Eurocentric genres that carry authority but seem not to be imitable without sacrifice of cultural authenticity. There is a striking semicorrespondence here between the critique of the protagonist-centered realist novel by third-world intellectuals and complaints by nineteenth-century American fictionists from Cooper to Hawthorne to James that the novel was not transplantable to American soil. Conversely, some genres have seemed not only transplantable with great ease but precisely tailored for American and other new-world contexts. A prime example is my next and last rubric, which I should like to unfold at somewhat greater length than the others.

6. *New-world pastoral.* "Pastoralism" in the broadest sense of a recurring fascination with physical nature as subject, symbol, and theater in which to act out rituals of maturity and purification has long been seen as a distinctive American preoccupation, but without it being grasped how this can be generalized. Mutatis mutandis the same can be said of Canadian and Australian writing, although their versions of nature are (and for more complicated reasons than just geography) less benign than ours; and a version of the same can be said of third-world writing as well, despite manifest differences between white-settler pastoral and nonwhite indigene pastoral. Here the obvious analogue is negritude, as well as other forms of cultural nationalism that hold up a precolonial ideal order as a salvific badge of distinctiveness. Retrospective pastoralization of ancient tribal structures occurs in the American Renaissance as well: particularly in the more sentimental treatments of Puritan heritage and the old plantation order, not to mention the even more vicarious sort of nostalgia represented by Anglo-American savagist fantasies like Longfellow's *Song of Hiawatha.* Perhaps this explains why Thoreau became simultaneously addicted to nature and to New England antiquities. *Walden* and *The Scarlet Letter* are predictably complements in their mutual preoccupation with cultural origins.

But to stay with pastoral at the level of physical nature, what Americanists tend to miss, and what recent postcolonial critiques have been helpful in pointing out (e.g., Amuta 49), is the extent to which the conception of naturism as a mark of cultural independence needs to be countered by the conception of naturism as a neocolonial residue. Thomas Jefferson's *Notes on the State of Virginia,* which contains the classical statement of the American pastoral ideal, shows this clearly. Jefferson recommends that the new country follow the agrarian way in the explicit awareness that that will mean dependence on European manufactures. The preservation of national virtue, which he associates with rurality, he considers worth the cost. Some, even today, would argue that it is. But my point here is the lacuna in Jefferson's earlier thinking: his belief that moral self-sufficiency can coexist with economic dependence. Some years later, as Leo Marx shows in *The Machine in the Garden* (139), Jefferson changed his mind about America industrializing. What Marx does *not* diagnose is the status of Jefferson's original position as the intellectual artifact of a late-colonial intellectual. Marx shows, of course, that the conception of America as a pastoral utopia originates in Europe, but he ceases to think of European antecedence as important once pastoral thinking becomes naturalized in America by the mid-eighteenth century, and this in turn keeps him from beginning to approach figures like Jefferson and Thoreau in the light of being driven against their conscious intent by an ideological mechanism set in place to appropriate the New World in the interest of the Old—the antithesis of the state both men saw themselves as promoting.

Nothing could have been more natural than for the American Romantics to valorize physical nature as a central literary subject (whether benign, as in Transcendentalism, or ominous, as in *Moby-Dick* or the forest sequence in *The Scarlet Letter*), for this was an obvious way of turning what had often been deemed a cultural disadvantage into a cultural asset. But this same move, which capitalized upon an aesthetic value of international Romanticism as well as an established old-world image of the New World, was not without its risks. A text that illustrates these is the well-known sonnet addressed by William Cullen Bryant in farewell to his friend the painter Thomas Cole, bound for Europe.

> Thine eyes shall see the light of distant skies:
> > Yet, Cole! thy heart shall bear to Europe's strand
> > A living image of thy native land,
> Such as on thy own glorious canvass lies;
> Lone lakes—savannahs where the bison roves—
> > Rocks rich with summer garlands—solemn streams—
> > Skies, where the desert eagle wheels and screams—
> Spring bloom and autumn blaze of boundless groves.
> Fair scenes shall greet thee where thou goest—fair,
> > But different—every where the trace of men,
> > Paths, homes, graves, ruins, from the lowest glen
> To where life shrinks from the fierce Alpine air.
> > Gaze on them, till the tears shall dim thy sight,
> > But keep that earlier, wilder image bright!

Bryant's valedictory tribute affirms a nationalist vision of America as nature's nation (lakes, savannahs, rocks, skies), over against a European scene that everywhere bears "the trace of men." Bryant rightly credits Cole's American landscape paintings with having registered this sense of the American difference. Like Whitman, Bryant revises *translatio studii,* charging Cole to bear an American aesthetic gospel to Europe, but the poem's cautionary ending betrays a postcolonial anxiety as to whether Cole will keep the faith. That very significant and well-warranted anxiety is, however, a telling moment, the only moment that the poem begins to acknowledge the extent to which Bryant and Cole have in fact always already been affected by the European gravitational field whether consciously or not. Cole, like other self-consciously American landscape painters of his day, had been deeply influenced by the tropes of European Romantic landscape (and in his case also history) painting (Novak 226–73). As for Bryant, although his poem is replete with distinctively American references (such as bison, eagle, and the fall colors that regularly amazed European travelers), what strikes a modern reader much more strongly is its bondage to old-world language and form: "savannahs" as a cosmopolitan synonym for "prairies"; the placement of the eagle in a generic, symbolic "desert"; "Alpine" as a surrogate for the sublimity of American mountains; and above all, Bryant's unconsciously ironic choice of sonnet—a hypercivilized form if ever there was one—as the vehicle for enjoining his gospel of the "wilder image." In short, the authentic insider's view of America Bryant/Cole have to offer Europe as new-world cultural evangelists is at most a slightly nuanced version of the view that their position as Euro-American settlers has prepared them for.

In an excellent recent study of American landscape representation in the Revolutionary era, Robert Lawson-Peebles discusses this effect under the heading of "the hallucination of the displaced terrain."[12] Lawson-Peebles points out that cultural nationalist visions of a pastoralized America pulled "towards Europe and away from the facts of the American continent. Even the writers who attended closely to those facts shaped them so that they answered European criticisms, and in doing so they collaborated in a dream-world" (57). Bryant is a clear case in point: it is almost as if "the American Wordsworth" had set out with the intention of playing back to Coleridge an image of America just slightly (but not alarmingly) more feral than Coleridge had entertained 30 years before in *his* sonnet on "Pantisocracy," which envisions a rural valley purified of nightmare and neurosis, where "Virtue" dances "to the moonlight roundelay" and "the rising Sun" darts "new rays of pleasuance trembling to the heart" (68–69).

In stressing the postcolonial basis of American pastoral visions like Bryant's, I do not mean to discredit them; on the contrary, I am convinced they potentially have great power even today as mimetic and ideological instruments. No doubt, for example, the American pastoral tradition helps account for the high degree of public environmental concern that now obtains in America, despite notorious slippages between doctrine and daily practice, between law and implementation. But in order to understand the potentially formidable continuing power of pastoral as a cultural instrument, we need also to understand the element of mimetic desire that has historically driven the pastoralizing impulse.

In Naipaul's autobiographical narrative, *The Enigma of Arrival,* he remembers how

> as a child in Trinidad I had projected everything I read onto the Trinidad landscape, the Trinidad countryside, the Port of Spain streets. (Even Dickens and London I incorporated into the streets of Port of Spain. Were the characters English, white people, or were they transformed into people I knew? A question like that is a little like asking whether one dreams in color or in black and white. But I think I transfered the Dickens characters to people I knew. Though with a half or a quarter of my mind I knew that Dickens was all English, yet my Dickens cast, the cast in my head, was multiracial.) (169–70)

The resemblance to Thoreau's projective creation of Walden is quite close. During the first summer's Walden journal, Thoreau sustains his high excitement by repeatedly imagining his experience in epic and pastoral terms, ancient Greece connotating for him, as for other Romantics, the morning of Western culture: the pastoral moment of the race. This carries over into the book itself, especially the "Visitors" and the "Reading" chapters. In the encounter with the woodchopper, particularly, Thoreau plays the kind of game Naipaul describes: loving and believing in the magnification that he halfway allows himself to realize is a game. This awareness is manifested elsewhere too in "The Ponds" chapter in his reference to his locale as "my lake country." His first descriptive encapsulation of the pond environment stresses that "for the first week, whenever I looked out on the pond it impressed me like a tarn high up on the side of a mountain" (86): Walden as Alpine lake. In order for Thoreau's spirit to accompany his body to the literal spot, or rather in order for the Thoreauvian persona to re-present the pond in a serious work of American literature, he must approach this bit of Yankee real estate as the image of some more resonantly romantic elsewhere.

For both Naipaul and Thoreau, the game of animating the provincial quotidian with imagery from the repertoire of metropolitan culture is of course class-specific (the elegant recreation of the cultivated person for whom Euroculture is the touchstone for local knowledge), but in either case this type of consciousness entails not simply a limitation of vision but an access of vision also, vision indeed of two types (both of the ordinary object, now seem luminously, and of oneself, of one's own imagination's tricks and needs). Their visions should not, then, be seen as nothing more than false consciousness. But they invite that interpretation (in Thoreau's case, for example) if we begin from the premise that his pastoralizing ought to be read as American Adamism deployed against Euroculture, rather than simply a development within the latter camp.

6

The case of Thoreau, whose art is patently more homegrown than Bryant's, raises the question of when, if at all, the postcolonial moment in American literary history ended or at what point "postcolonialism" ceases to become a meaningful category of analysis. To settle the point with respect to this, the first postcolonial literature, might be especially helpful in orienting discussion of later instances as well as the American one. The beginning of an answer is to recognize that no clear answer can be given. On the one hand, "postcolonial" is from the start an objectionably reductive term since it coerces us to look at everything within the indigenous cultural field as old-world driven. On the other hand, American culture can be said to remain at least vestigially postcolonial as long as Americans are impressed by the sound of an educated British accent—or (to take a more pertinent example) as long as D. H. Lawrence's *Studies in Classic American Literature* remains an iconic text for American literary studies. American scholarship has, ironically, absorbed Lawrence's wilderness-romance-oriented paradigm of American literature as obsessed with rebellion against civilized structures while largely deleting the Lawrentian premise that gave rise to it, that is, the vision of America as a postcolonial society caught in a state of cultural adolescence because still caught in the same escapist impulse that originated in the desire to flee from the motherland.[13] This diagnosis reflects, of course, the uses to which Lawrence himself put aboriginal America (Cowan 1–12, 124–28)—Lawrence being a Coleridgean dreamer who really acted out his dreams.

It could be argued that once "civilization" becomes imaginatively localized within America instead of placed across the Atlantic as in Bryant's sonnet, then American pastoral becomes for all practical purposes fully Americanized—although of course this happened for different writers at different times, and for some nineteenth-century American writers, like Henry James, it never happened at all. Another criterion might be the rise in the nineteenth century of what is now called American imperialism. One might argue that by the time Mark Twain, in *The Connecticut Yankee,* could imagine an American state of military and political superiority to an archaized Britain (reversing the British traveler's report of a generation earlier), or when Melville could imagine a Yankee entrepreneurialism roughly homologous to a decadent Spanish imperialism in "Benito Cereno," the American postcolonial moment was over, or at least evanescent. This, however, raises another fundamental question as to the link between American postcolonialism and American imperialism. Such a link there seems indeed to be. Captain Frederick Marryat, who as naval officer and as author of juvenile fiction helped to underwrite British expansionism, was told during his visit to America that Britain need not exult over its continuing superiority as an imperial power because America would soon pick up some colonies for itself (*A Diary in America*).

In the literary sphere, Cooper and Whitman are interesting text cases. The anxious patriotic hubris is that generated the Whitmanesque "I" can never rest until it circles the globe in massive retaliatory overcompensation. Cooper played the postcolonial to the extent that he deferred to Scott's plot forms, but he played the imperialist to the extent that his own narratives reflected and perpetuated the romance of American expansionism. It begins to appear, then, that the old-world tropes whose ingestion by the new-world citizen marks his or her cultural subordination can in turn become reactivated, whether on the frontier within one's own borders or on the frontiers beyond (e.g., bwana Hemingway in East Africa), to reproduce new versions of cultural subordination. This, again, is not the whole or inevitable consequence of postcolonialsm, only the most disturbing, but it is by the same token the most dramatic reminder of the quixotism of positing a firm boundary between a postcolonial era and what follows it.

NOTES

Preliminary versions of this essay were delivered as lectures of Texas A & M University, Columbia University, Brown University, and the American Antiquarian Society. I am most grateful for comments and suggestions received on all four occasions.

1. Gilbert and Gubar may be credited with establishing "I think I was enchanted" (593)—a reflection upon the influence of Elizabeth Barrett Browning—as central to the Dickinson canon (647–48; Gilbert 33–37). An interesting test case of the larger consequences of this placement of Dickinson among a Euro-American sisterhood, as opposed to the Edwards-Emerson tradition, is the shifting interpretation of "He fumbles at your soul" (315). Before 1980, the generally preferred approach—still sometimes espoused (e.g., Phillips 179–80)—was to read the "He" as bullying preacher or perhaps deity (Duchac 149–51). Feminist revisionism ensured the currency of a more specifically gendered reading of the "He" as "the pure energy of the *idea* of the masculine" (Dobson 81). The two readings can of course be conflated (e.g., Rich 56–57), but in practice a critical emphasis on gender tends to run counter to a "New England mind"-oriented reading. This may also be the place to comment on my almost total concentration in the balance of this essay, seemingly ironic in light of my honorific citation of feminist and African-American revisionism, upon white male writers. My choice reflects these two hypotheses: that the main symptom of "colonization" in antebellum African-American discourse arises from the pressure on black writers to write in "white" genres and rhetorical forms, and, secondly, that women writers of the period were less troubled about extricating themselves from the shadow cast by Europe than were their male counterparts, partially though not exclusively for the reason advanced by Gilbert and Gubar (i.e., that premodern women writers were not mutually competitive, anxious for rather than repressed by their female precursors). These concerns, which require further research, I intend to pursue on another occasion.
2. I have profited from all of these works. Spengemann presents the most outspoken theoretical/historical argument for considering Anglo-American writing as part of English literature generally. Arac, Chai, Reynolds, and Mills provide more specific, less polemical case studies: Arac, of literature as social prophecy in the nineteenth century; Chai, of tendencies in international Romanticism; Reynolds, of American responses to 1848. Mills undertakes specific book-to-book comparisons of

American and English authors. All these writers focus on intertextual and intercultural influences or connections with minimal attention to American cultural dependence as a (post)colonial event. Weisbuch comes closest to my approach in a series of somewhat Bloomian studies of American writers reacting against British precursors, set in the context of a defensive-antagonistic model of Anglo-American literary relations. This leads to results that are very illuminating and provocative, although I think the variability of American attitudes toward European culture (including extreme deference and total insouciance, as well as rivalry and antagonism, sometimes all of these commingling in the same person or text) needs to be taken more greatly into account. In addition to the studies of broad scope just mentioned, a growing number of significant monographs on individual authors address issues of postcolonialism without necessarily conceptualizing them as such: e.g., Rubin-Dorsky and Dekker.

3. My term "occidentalism" designedly echoes Said's use of "Orientalism." Some differences between the two discourses are noted below. My lowercase "o" registers another: "occidentalism" is my neologism, not a term of European usage, much less of the long-established field of academic research Said's *Orientalism* was written to critique. (The academic field of American studies is of course the obverse of Orientalism in having been constituted in the US and still largely dominated by American scholars.) Yet Said's larger argument, that Europeans formulated a condescending discourse of the "other" region as a fascinating but inferior civilization, also applies to antebellum travel narratives, and even more exactly to American perceptions of how they were viewed by these. "Orientalism," writes Said, "is premised upon exteriority, that is, on the fact that the Orientalist, poet or scholar, makes the Orient speak, describes the Orient, renders its mysteries plain for and to the West. . . . What he says and writes, by virtue of the fact that it is said or written, is meant to indicate that the Orientalist is outside the Orient, both as an existential and as a moral fact" (20–21). This is largely true for what I am calling "occidentalism" as well. In focusing on America as the object of "occidentalist" discourse, it should, of course, not be forgotten that (Euro-)Americans were at the same time themselves "Orientalists"; see, for example, Baird 3–80.

4. Naipaul: "Indians defecate everywhere. They defecate, mostly, beside the railroad tracks. But they also defecate on the beaches; they defecate on the river banks; they defecate on the streets; they never look for cover" (*Area* 74). Dickens: "In the courts of law, the judge has his spittoon, the crier his, the witness his, and the prisoner his; while the jurymen and spectators are provided for, as so many men who in the course of nature must desire to spit incessantly" (*American Notes* 112–13). In this way both writers, with nervous/sardonic intensity, put the former colony under the sign of filth.

5. The pervasiveness of these and other motifs of commentary are conveniently summarized by Tuckerman; Mesick; and Berger.

6. See Memmi: "Another sign of the colonized's depersonalization is what one might call the mark of the plural. The colonized is never characterized in an individual manner; he is entitled only to drown in any anonymous collectivity ('They are this.' 'They are all the same.')" (85). Of course it would be rash to say that Tocqueville and other generalizers thought they acutely knew America thoroughly, to the core. On the contrary, America often seemed mysterious to them; its inchoate ungraspability inspired a range of vertiginous sensations in the observer, both painful and pleasurable. Indeed, American mysteriousness and the will to explicate it through clarifying generalization were opposite sides of the same coin: see Tocqueville on "that strange melancholy which often haunts the inhabitants of democratic countries in the midst of their abundance" (2: 147). Additional light is shed on this fusion of opposites by Conrad's study of British travelers from Frances Trollope to Christopher Isherwood. Conrad shows that they resolutely created America in the image of their own fantasies, but that the fantasies often sprang from their own baffled malaise (e.g., 7–15).

7. Green oversimplifies in diagnosing the Leatherstocking saga as "the next great stage," after the Daniel Boone myth, "of the WASP adventure tale and adventure hero" (133), but he is right to place Cooper in the context of the history of the imperial adventure tale. The limitation of Green's approach to Cooper is that he does not apply to Cooper his good insight concerning Scott's ambivalence toward the absorption of Scotland into Great Britain: "If anyone could have written the serious

novel of adventure, it probably would have been a Scotsman, because of the mode of Scots participation in the Empire—the disengagement (compared to England) despite the deep involvement" (121). Cooper manifests, it seems to me, even deeper reservations abut the march of civilization than Scott; indeed, this note of reservation seems to me to be one of the motifs Cooper took over from Scott and extended.

8. Egejuru is not justified in concluding from this and other statements that "the African writer is very much controlled by an external audience whose existence he consciously tries to erase" (36), but it is clear that the writers she interviewed were somewhat hard-pressed to reconcile their Africanist commitments with the fact of being published and (often) more widely read abroad. Part of their dilemma must be political, part the result of the impossibility of bringing unconscious motives to full consciousness. Nineteenth-century American writers faced a similar if less intense set of pressures.

9. My thanks to Eric Haralson for first calling my attention to signs of dual audience consciousness in *Typee*.

10. Though they seldom raise the issue as a subject of direct remark, American writers of the Renaissance period must have been acutely aware of being vulnerable to both European and nativist scrutiny and criticism whenever they penned a scene that suggested a value judgment one way or another on national traits. In *Martin Chuzzlewit,* Dickens registers both sensitivities at once in his caricature of the egregious Mrs. Hominy, the American "literary" person who builds her reputation by purveying jingoistic cliché. Mrs. Hominy is the Tocquevillean democratic writer, the "independent" American constrained to speak in the voice of the majority; Dickens's narrator is the cosmopolitan Britisher recoiling against American boorishness. Postcolonial writers in other cultures have experienced similar pressures. Rajan wittily remarks on an Indian counterpart to Mrs. Hominy: "Countries which are newly independent can attach undue importance to the image of themselves which their literatures present, thus degrading the writer into a public relations officer. "You have been unfair to the South Indian mother-in-law," a critic told me indignantly at a railway station. It was well that I restrained my inclination to laugh. He was deadly serious and not unrepresentative in his seriousness" (81).

11. Nkosi proceeds to quote from Abioseh Nicol's "African Easter," which begins with a nursery rhyme ("Ding, dong bell") and juxtaposes this with "matin bells," the cry of the muezzin and "pagan drums" (qtd. in 151–52). An intercultural salad considerably more diverse than Cooper's Templeton.

12. Lawson-Peebles borrows this term from art critic Harold Rosenberg (23).

13. Leslie Fiedler and Wright Morris have both written rather severely about American pastoralism as a form of cultural immaturity, in *Love and Death in the American Novel* and *The Territory Ahead,* respectively (Fielder in particular being indebted to Lawrence), but formulating their position as a critique of social pathology without regard to America's postcolonial history.

Works Cited

Achebe, Chinua. *Things Fall Apart.* 1958. Greenwich, CT: Fawcett, 1959.

Amuta, Chidi. *The Theory of African Literature.* London: Zed, 1989.

Anozie, Sunday. *Christopher Okigbo: Creative Rhetoric.* London: Evans, 1972.

Ashcroft, Bill, Gareth Griffiths, and Helen Tiffin. *The Empire Writes Back: Theory and Practice in Post-Colonial Literatures.* London: Routledge, 1989.

Baird, James. *Ishmael: A Study of the Symbolic Mode in Primitivism.* New York: Harper, 1956.

Berger, Max. *The British Traveler in America, 1785–1835.* New York: Columbia, UP, 1922.

Bridgman, Richard. *The Colloquial Style in America.* New York: Oxford UP, 1966.

Bryant, William Cullen. "Sonnet—to an American Painter Departing for Europe." *The Norton Anthology of American Literature.* Ed. Nina Baym, et al. 3rd ed. Vol. 1. New York: Norton, 1989, 893 94. 2 vols.

Coleridge, Samuel Taylor. *The Poems of Samuel Taylor Coleridge.* Ed. Ernest Hartley Coleridge. London: Oxford UP, 1931.

Conrad, Peter. *Imagining America*. New York: Oxford UP, 1980.

Cooper, James Fenimore. *Letters and Journals*. Ed. James Franklin Beard, 6 vols. Cambridge: Belknap-Harvard UP, 1960–68.

Cowan, James C. *D. H. Lawrence's American Journey*. Cleveland: P of Case Western Reserve U, 1970.

Dickens, Charles. *American Notes and Pictures from Italy*. London: Oxford UP, 1957.

———. *Martin Chuzzlewit*. London: Oxford UP, 1966.

Dobson, Joanne A. "'Oh, Susie, it is dangerous': Emily Dickinson and the Archetype." *Feminist Critics Read Emily Dickinson*. Ed. Suzanne Juhasz. Bloomington: Indiana UP, 1983. 80–97.

Duchac, Joseph. *The Poems of Emily Dickinson: An Annotated Guide to Commentary Published in English*. Reference Publication in Literature. Boston: Hall, 1979.

Egejuni, Phanuel. *Towards African Literary Independence: A Dialogue with Contemporary African Writers*. Contributions in Afro-American and African Studies 53. Westport, CT: Greenwood, 1980.

Emerson, Ralph Waldo, *The Collected Works of Ralph Waldo Emerson*. Ed. Robert E. Spiller and Alfred R. Ferguson. Vol. 1. Cambridge: Belknap-Harvard UP, 1971. 4 vols. 1971–87.

Ezekiel, Nissim. *Latter-Day Psalms*. Delhi: Oxford UP: 1982.

Fernández Retamar, Roberto. *Caliban and Other Essays*. Trans. Edward Baker. Minneapolis: U of Minnesota P, 1989.

Gilbert, Sandra M. "The Wayward Nun beneath the Hill: Emily Dickinson and the Mysteries of Womanhood." *Feminist Critics Read Emily Dickinson*. Ed. Suzanne Juhasz. Bloomington: Indiana UP, 1983. 22–24.

Gilbert, Sandra M. and Susan Gubar. *The Madwoman in the Attic: The Woman Writer and the Nineteenth-Century Literary Imagination*. New Haven: Yale UP, 1979.

Green, Martin. *Dreams of Adventure, Deeds of Empire*. New York: Basic, 1979.

Kipling, Rudyard. *American Notes*. New York: Arcadia, 1950.

Lawrence, D. H. *Studies in Classic American Literature*. 1923. Garden City, NY: Doubleday, 1951.

Lawson-Peebles, Robert. *Landscape and Written Expression in Revolutionary America: The World Turned Upside Down*. Cambridge: Cambridge UP, 1988.

Lyell, Charles. *A Second Visit to the United States of North America*. 3 vols. New York, 1849.

McWilliams, John P., Jr. *The American Epic: Transforming a Genre: 1770–1860*. Cambridge Studies in American Literature and Culture. Cambridge: Cambridge UP, 1989.

Martineau, Harriet. *Society in America*. 2 vols. New York, 1837.

Marx, Leo. *The Machine in the Garden: Technology and the Pastoral Ideal in America*. New York: Oxford UP, 1964.

Melville, Herman. *Moby-Dick*. Ed. Harrison Hayford, Hershel Parker, and G. Thomas Tanselle. Evanston: Northwestern UP; Chicago: Newberry Library, 1988.

———. *Typee*. Ed. Harrison Hayford, Hershel Parker, and G. Thomas Tanselle. Evanston: Northwestern UP; Chicago: Newberry Library, 1968.

———. *White Jacket*. Ed. Harrison Hayford, Hershel Parker, and G. Thomas Tanselle. Evanston: Northwestern UP; Chicago: Newberry Library, 1970.

Memmi, Albert. *The Colonizer and the Colonized*. Trans. Howard Greenfield. Boston: Beacon, 1965.

Mesick, Jane Louise. *The English Traveler in America, 1836–1860*. New York: Columbia UP, 1922.

Mills, Nicholaus. *American and English Fiction in the Nineteenth Century: An Antigenre Critique and Comparison*. Bloomington: Indiana UP, 1974.

Murphy, Francis, ed. *Walt Whitman: A Critical Analogy*. Baltimore: Penguin, 1970.

Naipaul, V. S. *An Area of Darkness*. New York: Vintage, 1964.

———. *The Enigma of Arrival: A Novel in Five Sections*. New York: Viking, 1987.

Nandy, Ashis. *The Intimate Enemy: Loss and Recovery of Self Under Colonialism*. Delhi: Oxford UP, 1983.

Ngugi wa Thiong'o. *Decolonizing the Mind: The Politics of Language in African Literature*. London: Currey, 1986.

Nkosi, Lewis. *Tasks and Masks: Themes and Styles of African Literature*. Essex: Longman, 1981.

Novak, Barbara. *Nature and Culture: American Landscape and Painting, 1825–1875*. New York: Oxford UP, 1980.

Phillips, Elizabeth. *Emily Dickinson: Personnae and Performance*. University Park: Pennsylvania State UP, 1988.

Rajan, Ballachandra. "The Indian Virtue." *Journal of Commonwealth Literature* 1 (1965): 79–85.

Rich, Adrienne. "Vesuvius at Home: The Power of Emily Dickinson." *Parnassus* 5 (1976): 49–74.

Said, Edward W. *Orientalism*. New York: Vintage, 1978.

Simpson, David. *The Politics of American English, 1776–1850*. New York: Oxford UP, 1986.

Snead, James. "European Pedigrees/African Contagions: Nationality, Narrative, and Commonality in Tutuola, Achebe, and Reed." *Nation and Narration*. Ed. Homi K. Bhabha. London: Routledge, 1990. 231–49.

Soyinka, Wole. *Art, Dialogue and Outrage: Essays on Literature and Culture*. Ed. Biodun Jcyifo. Ibadan, Nigeria: New Horn, 1988.

Spengemann, William C. *A Mirror for Americanists: Reflections on the Idea of American Literature*. Hanover, NH: UP of New England, 1989.

Thoreau, Henry David. *Walden*. Ed. J. Lyndon Shanley. Princeton: Princeton UP, 1973.

Tocqueville, Alexis de. *Democracy in America*. Trans. Henry Reeve. Ed. Phillips Bradley. 2 vols. New York: Vintage, 1945.

Tuckerman, Henry T. *America and Her Commentators*. New York, 1864.

Warren, James Perrin. *Walt Whitman's Language Experiment*. University Park: Pennsylvania State UP, 1990.

Whitman, Walt. *Leaves of Grass*. Ed. Harold W. Blodgett and Sculley Bradley. Comprehensive Reader's Ed. New York: New York UP, 1965.